Historic Documents
of 2006

Historic Documents

of 2006

Includes Cumulative Index, 2002–2006

A Division of Congressional Quarterly Inc.
Washington, D.C.

CQ Press
1255 22nd Street, NW, Suite 400
Washington, DC 20037

Phone: 202-729-1900; toll-free, 1-866-4CQ-PRESS (1-866-427-7737)

Web: www.cqpress.com

Cover design: McGaughy Design, Centerville, Virginia
Cover photos: AP/Wide World Photos
Composition: Aptara, Inc.

⊗ The paper used in this publication exceeds the requirements of the American National Standard for Information Sciences—Permanence of Paper for Printed Library Materials, ANSI Z39.48-1992.

Printed and bound in the United States of America

11   10   09   08   07   1   2   3   4   5

Historic Documents of 2006
Editors: Martha Gottron, John Felton, Bruce Maxwell
Production and Associate Editor: Kerry V. Kern
Indexer: Victoria Agee

The Library of Congress cataloged the first issue of this title as follows:
Historic documents. 1972–
Washington. Congressional Quarterly Inc.

1. United States—Politics and government—1945– —Yearbooks.
2. World politics—1945– —Yearbooks. I. Congressional Quarterly Inc.
E839.5H57   917.3'03'9205   72-97888

ISSN 0892-080X
ISBN 978-0-87289-374-0

Contents

January

February

March

April

July

August

September

October

November

Thematic Table of Contents

List of Document Sources

Non-U.S. Governments

U.S. Nongovernmental Organizations

White House and the President

Preface

Escalating violence in Iraq and Afghanistan, political scandal in Washington, national debate on immigration, and a dramatic power shift in Congress are just a few of the topics of national and international interest chosen for discussion in *Historic Documents of 2006*. This edition marks the thirty-fifth volume of a CQ Press project that began with *Historic Documents of 1972*. This series allows students, librarians, journalists, scholars, and others to research and understand the most important issues and events of each year through primary source documents. Some of the more lengthy documents written for specialized audiences have been excerpted to highlight the most important sections. The official statements, news conferences, speeches, special studies, and court decisions presented here should be of lasting public and academic interest.

Historic Documents of 2006 opens with an "Overview of 2006," which puts key events and issues in political, historical, and social contexts. The balance of the book is organized chronologically, with each article comprising an introduction entitled "The Document in Context" and one or more related documents on a specific event, issue, or topic. When relevant, the introductions provide context and an account of further developments during the year. A thematic table of contents (page xiv) and a list of documents organized by source (page xviii) follow the standard table of contents and assist readers in locating events and documents.

As events, issues, and consequences become more complex and far-reaching, these introductions and documents yield important information and deepen understanding about the world's increasing interconnectedness. As memories of current events fade, these selections will continue to further understanding of the events and issues that have shaped the lives of people around the world.

How to Use This Book

Each of the seventy-three articles in this edition consists of two parts: a comprehensive introduction followed by one or more primary source documents. The articles are arranged in chronological order by month. There are several ways to find events and documents of interest:

By date: If the approximate date of an event or document is known, browse through the titles for that month in the table of contents. Alternatively, browse the monthly tables of contents that appear at the beginning of each month's articles.

By theme: To find a particular topic or subject area, browse the thematic table of contents.

By document type or source: To find a particular type of document or document source, such as the White House or Congress, review the list of document sources.

By index: Using the five-year index, locate references to specific events or documents as well as entries on the same or related subjects. The index in this volume covers the years 2002–2006. A separate volume, *Historic Documents Cumulative Index, 1972–2005,* may also be useful.

Each article begins with an introduction entitled "The Document in Context." This feature provides historical context for the documents that follow. Documents are reproduced with the spelling, capitalization, and punctuation of the original or official copy. Ellipsis points indicate textual omissions, and brackets are used for editorial insertions within documents for text clarification. Full citations to the official print and online sources appear at the end of each document. If a document is not available on the Internet, this too is noted. For further reading on a particular topic, consult the "Other Documents of Interest" box at the end of each article. These boxes provide cross-references for related articles in this edition of *Historic Documents.* Cross-references to material in previous editions of *Historic Documents* can be found in the "Document in Context" section. References to articles from past volumes include the year and page number for easy retrieval.

Overview of 2006

It was not supposed to be like this. By 2006, according to the pronouncements of the George W. Bush administration three years earlier, Iraq was to have been a democratic, peaceful, and prosperous country, and good measures of these three virtues were to have been sown in much of the rest of the Middle East. The ousting of Iraqi leader Saddam Hussein was to have been a major achievement in the U.S. "global war on terror" to discourage attacks against U.S. interests and allies in the Middle East and elsewhere.

Events on the ground, however, raised considerable doubt about the possibility of lasting peace and stability in Iraq. In February 2006 the country advanced toward civil war, as sectarian killings became as widespread as the suicide bombings that already had plunged much of the country into chaos despite the presence of some 130,000 U.S. troops. For Iraqis, 2006 was the deadliest year yet since the U.S. invasion in 2003, with the United Nations reporting that more than 34,000 civilians had been "violently killed" over the course of the year. The new Iraqi leaders elected by voters in 2005 did little to unite the country, as they appeared more interested in protecting their own sectarian interests than those of the nation as a whole.

Thus, rather than brandishing Iraq as a foreign policy triumph, President Bush was on the defensive for most of the year, as support for U.S. involvement in Iraq plummeted almost as far domestically as it already had internationally. Voters sent a resounding antiwar message to Washington in November, removing Republicans from power in Congress. Even some Republicans who had distanced themselves from Bush and the war were defeated in favor of Democrats who pledged to try to bring U.S. troops home.

The news elsewhere around the world was not much more encouraging. In the Middle East, the war in Iraq was merely the worst of a series of unpleasant events. Israel and the Shiite organization Hezbollah fought a brief but bloody war in Lebanon from mid-July to mid-August in which Hezbollah won a moral victory and the new Israeli leaders appeared to mishandle the confrontation. Palestinians held a genuinely free election in January and put the Islamist group Hamas in power; this was a victory for the democratic principles the Bush administration had advocated but certainly not for U.S. policy. If anyone emerged in a stronger position in the Middle East during 2006, it was Iran's Islamist leaders, who appeared to be weathering international pressure against their presumed ambitions to build a nuclear weapons and were increasingly seen as a more credible force in the region than the United States. U.S. objectives also were endangered in Afghanistan. In 2006 Washington and its European allies realized that the government they supported in Kabul was fading quickly in the face of a resurgence by the Taliban, whose government had been ousted by the United States five years earlier.

In the United States, the economy remained strong, at least according to the technical indexes economists like to use. Even so, millions of working-class Americans felt uneasy about their futures—and their children's futures. Americans were still getting used to the idea that within the not-too-distant future, China would likely replace the United States as the country with the world's biggest economy. Although this did not yet have much practical day-to-day effect, it did compound the sense many people had—accurately or not—that more good-paying jobs were flowing out of the United States than were being created.

A Downward Spiral in Iraq

Some of the goals the United States had established for Iraq were reached in 2006. Notably, Iraqis formed a new government in elections declared generally fair by the international community. Taking place in the midst of violent conflict, the elections, in December 2005, and the subsequent drawn-out process of elected politicians negotiating a new government were extraordinary achievements.

The results, however, were not nearly as inspiring as the process. Iraqis created a government that closely reflected the country's deep divisions along sectarian lines and in which politicians were unable or unwilling to act decisively as national leaders. Despite heading a country in crisis, Iraq's new leaders appeared to lack all sense of urgency. U.S. officials tried persuasion, and even occasional outright threats, to get the new government to act. At the top of Washington's to-do list were such items as cracking down on the sectarian militias that were killing Iraqis by the dozens each day and passing legislation making Iraq's oil wealth a national resource, rather than one subject to sectarian control. Put in office by the voters, Iraq's new leaders had a legitimacy that could not be denied, so Bush administration officials found themselves uncertain of how hard and how fast to push.

As politicians and officials pondered in the Green Zone—the U.S.-protected oasis of relative calm in the center of Baghdad—the rest of the capital and much of the rest of Iraq had grown more violent, not less. Shortly after the United States ousted Saddam Hussein in April 2003, an insurgency of Sunni militants—along with remnants of Hussein's former regime—began carrying out thousands of bombings and other attacks against the U.S. military, the new Iraqi security forces, and, increasingly, Iraqi civilians. These attacks reached a dangerous new level on February 22, 2006, when a bomb destroyed one of the holiest Shiite shrines—the golden-domed Askariya mosque in Samarra, just north of Baghdad and said to be the burial place of two revered Shiite saints. Shiite militias retaliated, the Sunni bombers retaliated against them, and the cycle of violence deepened. One of the most insidious results was stepped-up ethnic cleansing, particularly in Baghdad: Shiite and Sunni fighters forced members of the opposing sect out of neighborhoods, and many areas where Shiites and Sunnis once had lived together were transformed into single-sect enclaves where bitterness replaced any sense of hope.

The UN Assistance Mission for Iraq compiled statistics showing that 34,452 civilians had been killed in Iraq during 2006, and another 36,685 had been injured. These were regarded by many as minimal figures, given the chaos in much of the country. The bottom line was that 2006 set a new record for violence in Iraq since the U.S. invasion.

The number of U.S. service personnel killed in Iraq declined slightly in 2006, to 821 from 846 in 2005. That put the total number of U.S. dead since the invasion at 3,001. Thousands more had been wounded, some of them with devastating injuries.

On trial in Baghdad, Saddam Hussein was found responsible for the deaths in 1982 of 148 Shiite boys and men in the town of Dujail, north of Baghdad. Hussein was sentenced to hang, although his trial continued for the murder of tens of thousands of Kurds in the late 1980s. The Iraqi government rushed to carry out the death sentence before year's end. Film of Hussein being taunted by Shiite guards as he was about to be executed, and then photographs of his actual hanging, brought widespread criticism of Iraq's leaders.

The Political Weight of Iraq in Washington

The daily drumbeat of violence, compounded by the continuing toll on U.S. personnel, undercut domestic support for Bush's policies in Iraq. By the middle of 2006 opinion polls showed that a strong majority of Americans had concluded that the president's promise of eventual victory was unrealistic and that invading Iraq had been a mistake. Americans were unsure what to do about Iraq, however. Most wanted to pull the troops out sooner rather than later, but they did not want to do so precipitously.

The growing public unease about Iraq led Congress to propose the appointment of an independent commission to study the matter. The commission that took on the task consisted of some of the most respected figures from Washington's recent past. Its cochairs were former secretary of state James A. Baker III and former House member Lee H. Hamilton, who also had cochaired the commission that examined the September 11, 2001, attacks against the United States. As this commission, called the Iraq Study Group, held hearings and debated ideas, members of Congress in both parties began looking to it as a political lifeline—something they could point to when anxious voters asked about Iraq. The Iraq Study Group deliberately withheld its report until after the November 7 elections, hoping to keep its recommendations from becoming political fodder.

Voters took thirty seats from the Republicans in the House and six in the Senate, giving the Democrats control of both chambers of Congress for the first time in a dozen years. Iraq was the dominant reason for the Republican defeat, although other issues played a role, particularly in some individual congressional districts. Bush moved quickly to accommodate himself to the new political reality. The day after the elections, he accepted the resignation of Secretary of Defense Donald H. Rumsfeld, the war's most prominent architect, and replaced him with former CIA director Robert Gates, a member of the Iraq Study Group.

Less than a month later, the Iraq Study Group issued a report that in one blunt sentence swept away the cheery optimism characteristic of statements from the White House and Pentagon: "The situation in Iraq is grave and deteriorating." Even the experienced men and women on the commission could not offer a set of proposals they felt comfortable claiming would produce victory in Iraq. Instead, they settled on a middle-ground approach that emphasized increased U.S. training of Iraqi security personnel and more pressure on the Iraqi government to crack down on sectarian militias. By far their most controversial recommendation was that the United States sit down with leaders from around the Middle East—including Iran and Syria—to discuss mutual interests in ending the chaos in Iraq.

After politely thanking the commission members and saying he would consider their ideas, Bush made it clear that he viewed them as unworkable. Instead, at year's end, the president was reviewing options for a short-term "surge"—in other words, sending another 20,000 or more U.S. troops to join the 130,000 already in Iraq, with a new emphasis on restoring order in Baghdad. This decision, running counter to the message the voters had sent in November, seemed certain to escalate political anxieties in Washington as it escalated the U.S. presence in Iraq.

Elsewhere in the Middle East

The Bush administration faced several other important challenges in the Middle East in 2006. In three important areas, the administration sustained significant setbacks likely to make U.S. policymaking more difficult in coming years, not to mention for people in the region.

The first setback came as a consequence of something the Bush administration had advocated: free elections in the Arab world. In an election that was widely credited as being honest and fair, Palestinians in January chose the Islamist faction Hamas to lead their government. Hamas won just 45 percent of the vote but took a much higher share of seats in parliament because the Fatah faction, which had clear U.S. backing, had failed to prevent its own candidates from splitting the vote in some districts. More important, Palestinians were frustrated by the incompetence and corruption of the Fatah leadership and accepted Hamas's pledge to be the party of "change and renewal." Faced with a Palestinian government headed by men the United States long had called terrorists, the Bush administration joined with its European allies and Israel in a hard-line approach; there would be no international aid for the struggling Palestinian economy unless the new leaders renounced violence, recognized Israel, and accepted peace agreements that former Palestinian leader Yasir Arafat had signed with Israel. When Hamas refused to meet these conditions, most international aid for the Palestinian government was suspended, and the Palestinian territories descended further into violent chaos and economic collapse.

Israel went through its own political transition, this one the result of a massive stroke that incapacitated Prime Minister Ariel Sharon on January 4. That put power in the hands of Sharon's unpopular and untested deputy, Ehud Olmert, who managed to squeeze out a narrow victory in previously scheduled elections in late March. Olmert headed a center-left coalition government that had a popular mandate to eliminate some of the Jewish settlements from the West Bank. This withdrawal would complete a process of "disengagement" from the Palestinians that Sharon had begun in 2005 by closing down Jewish settlements and withdrawing militarily from the Gaza Strip.

Two events preempted Olmert's movement toward disengagement. In late June, Palestinian guerrillas captured an Israeli soldier and took him into the Gaza Strip. The Israeli government responded with a large military assault on Gaza that caused great destruction but failed to win freedom for the soldier.

As this campaign was under way, Hezbollah fighters crossed into Israel from Lebanon and captured two soldiers. Israel responded with a massive military assault, starting with hundreds of bombing raids in Lebanon and continuing with a ground invasion. Hezbollah launched its own attacks against Israel, firing hundreds of short-range and medium-range missiles, some of them reaching as far as Haifa (twenty-five miles south of the border). Lebanon's army stayed out of the fight, which the Lebanese government said killed about 1,200 residents (most of them civilians) and Israel said killed 39 of its civilians and 120 soldiers.

This battle between Israel and Hezbollah lasted just over a month and caused enormous physical damage throughout Lebanon, including parts of Beirut; there was lesser but still substantial damage in northern Israel. It also shook up the political balance of power in this part of the Middle East. Hezbollah proclaimed a "divine victory," having withstood a prolonged assault from the most powerful army in the region. This view was widely shared in the Middle East, where Hezbollah's leader, Hassan Nasrallah, suddenly became one of the region's most popular figures. Many Israelis also agreed that their country either had lost the war or, at best, had failed to win it. Olmert and his Labor Party coalition partner Amir Peretz (serving as defense minister) plummeted in opinion polls. By year's end, Israelis' self-confidence had evaporated as politicians bickered over the future. In Lebanon, Hezbollah pressed its advantage against the U.S.-backed government that had stood by, helpless, as Hezbollah and Israel fought it out.

This brief war caused additional damage to Washington's already sagging reputation in much of the Arab world. For about two weeks, the Bush administration blocked moves toward a cease-fire, giving Israel additional time to attack Hezbollah. This was widely seen as prolonging the war on Israel's behalf—confirming the view of many Arabs of unquestioning U.S. support of the Jewish state.

Regardless of the validity of Hezbollah's declaration of victory, it served the interests of that group's primary patron: Iran. According to U.S. intelligence services, the Islamist mullahs in Iran had provided most, if not all, of the missiles that Hezbollah had fired into Israel, along with the cash that Hezbollah used to finance schools, health clinics, and other social services that the Lebanese government could not afford. When Hezbollah emerged bloodied but undefeated after its battle against the Israeli army, Iran emerged with an enhanced reputation for influence well beyond its borders. Moreover, Iran appeared to be successfully withstanding a concerted diplomatic effort by the United States and its European allies against Iran's nuclear ambitions. Negotiations on that issue dragged on for a third year before finally reaching the UN Security Council. There, China and Russia blocked U.S. proposals for tough international sanctions to force Iran to back down. Instead, the council in December adopted mild sanctions against Iran's nuclear agencies, a step unlikely to have much effect.

Afghanistan Teetering

Another historic flashpoint—Afghanistan—appeared to be at a dangerous juncture in 2006. The United States in October 2001 ousted the Islamist Taliban regime but then turned its attention to Iraq. Under UN supervision, Afghanistan held a presidential election in 2004 and then a parliamentary election in 2005, but the government, headed by Hamid Karzai, was weak and divided along the country's many ethnic and tribal lines.

The Taliban, who had been dispersed but not destroyed in 2001, spent the intervening years regrouping—reportedly with at least implicit support from neighboring Pakistan—and came roaring back with a series of offensives early in 2006. The relatively small U.S.

and NATO military forces that had been protecting Karzai's government countered with stepped-up operations in the country's most dangerous southern and eastern regions. Even so, the Karzai government had lost much of its support because it had been unable to provide much in the way of security or economic opportunity. In fact, the only major source of jobs and money was the flourishing opium trade. At year's end, Karzai's Western backers appeared to be in a race with time to shore up the government and roll back the Taliban resurgence.

Bush's Vulnerability on Domestic Issues

The Bush administration's struggle to salvage the situations in Iraq and Afghanistan posed serious troubles for the president and the Republican Party in the months leading up to the midterm elections in November 2006. They were not, however, the only problems facing the GOP. At home, the administration had been hurt by its inept handling of the relief and recovery operations following Hurricane Katrina in 2005 that devastated New Orleans and left much of the rest of the Gulf Coast in shambles. Reports by Republican-led Senate and House investigating committees issued early in 2006 detailed just how incompetent the federal government's handling of the disaster had been. They also raised troubling questions about the government's ability to cope with a terrorist attack on American soil. The cancellation in February of a deal approved by the administration to allow a Dubai-owned company to manage six large American ports also eroded the administration's credibility with respect to homeland security. Although the company would not have been responsible for port security, Democrat and Republican legislators said the deal presented an unacceptable security risk.

As damaging to the president and his party, however, was a series of scandals involving Republican legislators, including former House majority leader Tom DeLay, that allowed Democrats to portray the GOP as the party of corruption. DeLay had temporarily stepped down as majority leader in 2005 after he was indicted in Texas on money laundering charges related to campaign financing contributions. DeLay also had close ties to Republican lobbyist Jack Abramoff, who pleaded guilty to federal corruption charges in early January 2006. DeLay, a fiercely partisan conservative Republican who had managed his caucus with an iron fist, announced a few days later that he would not seek reinstatement as majority leader, and in April he said he would resign his House seat. A second Republican legislator, Bob Ney of Ohio, also resigned his House seat, just days before the November election, after pleading guilty to corruption charges related to the Abramoff scandal. In March, former GOP lawmaker Randy "Duke" Cunningham was sentenced to eight years and four months in prison on charges of bribery and tax evasion. Cunningham had resigned his California House seat in December 2005 after being indicted. Continuing investigations resulting from the Cunningham case and the Abramoff scandal touched on Republican lawmakers, lobbyists, and administration officials throughout the year, making it difficult for the party to overcome Democratic allegations that it had fostered a "culture of corruption" in Washington.

From a political standpoint, however, one of the most damaging incidents may have been the resignation of Rep. Mark Foley, R-Fla., in late September amid allegations that he had made inappropriate advances to teenage male House pages and that the GOP

House leadership may have known about his conduct but did nothing about it. Democrats and even some Republicans called on House Speaker J. Dennis Hastert to resign. Hastert denied knowing anything about Foley's conduct until the day Foley resigned. The Speaker was cleared of any wrongdoing by a House ethics committee investigation in December, but by that time the Republicans had already lost control of the House, and Hastert had announced that he would not seek a leadership position in the new Congress.

Republican disarray in the House and election-year jockeying for position meant that Congress accomplished relatively little in 2006. After five years of debate, legislators passed a measure lifting the restrictions President Bush had placed on funding federal stem cell research in 2001. That forced Bush to issue the first veto of his presidency, which the House easily sustained. Conservatives in the House also blocked passage of Bush's top domestic priority—a bill that would have overhauled the nation's immigration policy and put some of the estimated 12 million illegal immigrants in the country on the path to citizenship. Conservatives said the policy amounted to amnesty for people who had broken the law. Instead, Congress agreed to a measure to build security fencing along stretches of the U.S.-Mexican border.

Social conservatives were dismayed when the Food and Drug Administration backed down from a long-running dispute and allowed the sale of the "morning-after" emergency contraception pill without prescription to women over the age of seventeen. Many conservatives were disappointed when voters in South Dakota rejected that state's strict ban on abortion. They took heart in January, however, when the Senate confirmed Judge Samuel A. Alito Jr. to fill the seat on the Supreme Court left vacant by the retirement of Justice Sandra Day O'Connor. Although Alito would not discuss his views on abortion at his confirmation hearing, it was widely believed that he might vote to weaken if not overturn the 1973 ruling that made abortion legal in the United States.

Alito was in the minority when the Supreme Court struck down as unconstitutional the system of special military tribunals Bush had authorized to try terrorist suspects detained in the naval prison at Guantanamo Bay, Cuba. The Court ruled not only that Bush lacked the authority to establish the tribunals, but that they also violated standards of U.S. military justice and obligations under the Geneva Conventions for the humane treatment of war prisoners. The ruling was a victory for human rights organizations and others concerned by allegations of abuse and torture of detainees at Guantanamo as well as other military bases and CIA secret prisons overseas. The administration had not yet confirmed the existence of such prisons and had denied that detainees were tortured. As part of a drive to persuade Congress to overturn the Supreme Court ruling and authorize the special tribunals, Bush in early September announced that fourteen "high-value" terrorist suspects had been moved to Guantanamo from secret prisons overseas, where they had been subjected to what Bush described as "tough" but "legal" interrogation procedures. One of the fourteen was Khalid Sheikh Mohammad, the alleged "mastermind" of the September 11, 2001, al Qaeda attacks.

Congress gave Bush a major victory when it agreed to authorize the commissions largely along the lines he had requested. The rules Congress approved would allow the government to hold enemy combatants indefinitely, without charge or means of challenging their detention in U.S. civilian courts. The measure also allowed the administration to continue its secret interrogations of detainees and protected CIA operatives and others from lawsuits by them alleging that they had been tortured.

Americans may well have thought that such measures were the only thing standing between them and destruction at the hands of terrorists, but they were apparently growing increasingly cynical about the war in Iraq and the scandals in Washington. On November 7, voters turned over control of the House and Senate to Democrats for the first time since 1994. House Democrats quickly elected Nancy Pelosi of California as Speaker in the 110th Congress. Pelosi became the first woman to hold the position, the highest political office ever held by a woman in the United States.

Pelosi and her fellow Democrats had a long list of items that they pledged to enact within their first hours and days in Congress. Democrats also pledged numerous oversight hearings into various actions by the Bush administration. Regardless, it seemed certain at year's end that the main item on Washington's agenda in 2007 would be the same as it had been in 2006—bringing the war in Iraq to a satisfactory conclusion.

John Felton and Martha Gottron

January

2006 HISTORIC DOCUMENTS

Johnson-Sirleaf on Her Inauguration as President of Liberia

January 16, 2006

Liberia in 2006 took its first steps down what was certain to be a long road of recovery from two decades of political instability and murderous civil war. A dynamic new president—the first woman ever elected to head an African government—took office on January 16, and she seemed determined to pull Liberia out of its misery. Ellen Johnson-Sirleaf, a Harvard-trained economist who had worked at the United Nations and the World Bank and had also served time in Liberian prisons during the country's political crises, was certain to need every ounce of the courage and determination that led her countrymen to call her the "Iron Lady."

Founded by former American slaves in the mid-nineteenth century, Liberia once had been one of the most prosperous countries in West Africa. Starting in 1980, however, a series of coups led to civil wars that killed an estimated 200,000 people, displaced about one-half of the population of 3 million, and ruined nearly every aspect of the country. The man responsible for much of the bloodshed, President Charles Taylor, fled into exile in Nigeria in 2003 under international pressure. An interim government, backed by a large UN peacekeeping force, took power and set the stage for elections in 2005. *(Background, Historic Documents of 2005, p. 800)*

Johnson-Sirleaf in Office

Johnson-Sirleaf won a comfortable victory in the second round of elections in late 2005, defeating soccer star George Weah, who had aimed his appeal at young males who had been combatants in the country's civil wars. Weah at first protested that the election had been stolen from him, and for a few weeks it appeared that his supporters might turn violent, but he ultimately accepted Johnson-Sirleaf's election.

The inauguration for Johnson-Sirleaf, a sixty-seven-year-old grandmother, took place on the grounds of the bullet-scarred Capitol building, with Liberia summoning up all the extravagance it could. Thousands of volunteers had repainted downtown buildings and cleared tons of trash from the streets, and white plastic chairs were set on the Capitol's rain-soaked lawn for visiting dignitaries, including First Lady Laura Bush and Secretary of State Condoleezza Rice from the United States and presidents Thabo Mbeki from South Africa and Olusegun Obasanjo from Nigeria. Weah, the defeated presidential contender, sat in the front row, apparently symbolizing his acceptance of the election results.

In her inaugural address, Johnson-Sirleaf acknowledged the enormous obstacles that she and Liberia faced but expressed confidence that the country could meet its challenges. "We are a good and friendly people, braced for hope even as we wipe away the tears of past suffering and despair," she said. "Our challenge, therefore, is to transform adversity into opportunity, to renew the promises upon which our nation was founded: freedom, equality, unity, and individual progress." Given the country's recent history of governments that preyed on, rather than served, the citizens, Johnson-Sirleaf also promised "transparency, open government, and participatory democracy for all our citizens." She acknowledged the long-time scourge of corruption in Liberia and pledged that it "will be the major public enemy."

Following through on her anticorruption pledge, Johnson-Sirleaf in February fired key officials of the finance ministry, which had been accused of misappropriating millions of dollars, and ordered top officials of the former interim government not to leave the country while a financial audit was under way. The new government also established a Truth and Reconciliation Commission to investigate human rights violations during the civil war. Johnson-Sirleaf asked the commission to make "clear and workable recommendations" on how the country could "make restitution for the past." The commission began hearings in October and was expected to complete its work by 2008.

Johnson-Sirleaf spent a week in the United States in mid-March, meeting with Bush administration officials and the UN Security Council and addressing a joint meeting of Congress. The latter appearance was a particular triumph for an African leader who had spent years in the United States; members of Congress gave her an exceptionally warm welcome and followed with a pledge of $50 million in development aid.

United Nations Peacekeeping

The United Nations since 2003 had stationed about 16,000 peacekeeping troops and police officers in Liberia—many of them from other African countries. Johnson-Sirleaf asked the Security Council in February to keep that mission in place until the country had been stabilized. She had support in that request from Alan Doss, the special representative for Liberia of UN Secretary General Kofi Annan, who told the Security Council on March 24 that the next two years would be "critical" for Liberia. "Experience has taught us that an incomplete effort in consolidating the peace is often a prelude to renewed conflict," Doss said.

Annan visited Liberia on July 4 and pledged continued UN support for the country. He said it was "imperative" that the international community "stay with Liberia in the long term." At his request, the Security Council in September voted to extend the UN peacekeeping mission in Liberia until September 2007.

Dealing with Charles Taylor

Although he had been out of power, and out of the country, for three years, Charles Taylor remained a dominant figure in Liberia. A United Nations tribunal in Sierra Leone had indicted Taylor on eleven war crimes charges stemming from his support for antigovernment rebels in that country's murderous civil war, which ended in 2002. Taylor had been under house arrest in Nigeria since he fled Liberia in 2003, essentially living under the protection of Nigerian president Obasanjo, who had promised not to turn him over to the Sierra Leone tribunal unless the new Liberian government asked him to do so. Even during his exile in Nigeria, there were persistent reports that Taylor was attempting to interfere in Liberia and elsewhere in West Africa by funneling money to rebel groups.

On March 17, Johnson-Sirleaf formally asked Obasanjo to extradite Taylor to Sierra Leone where he could be tried by the UN court. Ten days later, the Nigerian government reported that Taylor had mysteriously disappeared from the villa where he was being held in the southern town of Calabar. On the morning of March 29, a customs official at a border outpost in northern Nigeria recognized Taylor, and arrested him as he tried to escape into neighboring Cameroon. The Nigerian government then flew Taylor to Liberia and turned him over to UN peacekeepers, who then flew him to Sierra Leone and handed him over to the UN tribunal. The dramatic capture of Taylor occurred on the same day that Obasanjo was scheduled to meet in Washington with President George W. Bush; until Taylor was captured, U.S. officials had considered canceling the meeting to put pressure on Obasanjo to make sure Taylor did not escape. After the two leaders met, Obasanjo said he felt "vindicated" by the turn of events and denied rumors that his government had schemed to allow Taylor to escape.

Taylor appeared before the UN court on April 3 and pleaded not guilty to the war crimes charges against him. Taylor also said he refused to recognize the jurisdiction of the court, which he said was attempting to "divide and rule the people of Liberia and Sierra Leone." In a sign that the mere presence of Taylor was considered potentially destabilizing to Sierra Leone and the entire region, the UN Security Council on June 16 adopted a resolution that authorized moving his case to the courtrooms—but not the jurisdiction—of the new International Criminal Court in The Hague, Netherlands. The Dutch government assented, but only on the condition that Taylor not serve his sentence there if convicted. The British government agreed to allow Taylor to serve any prison time there. A trial was expected to begin by mid-2007 and last up to two years.

Rebuilding Liberia

The two decades of political instability and civil war in Liberia had left the country a wreck in every sense. From Monrovia to the most remote villages, the country's infrastructure was destroyed, public services were nonexistent, the vast majority of adults were unemployed, and few children attended school. International donors pledged money for specific projects; for example, the European Union committed $70 million to restore electricity to Monrovia, and the United States funded the rebuilding of a new army, with training provided by the private contractor, DynCorp. Some donors, however, were reluctant to commit large resources until it became clear that peace had returned to Liberia and that the new government would be more honest than the previous, blatantly corrupt ones.

Symbolically important steps came in late July when parts of Monrovia received running water for the first time in years and electrical generators enabled the government to turn on street lights in a suburb of the capital that had been without electricity since 1991. Both of these achievements were courtesy of the government of Ghana, which provided the necessary equipment and technicians. Businesses and the few relatively well-to-do residents of the capital had relied on generators in the meantime, while the poor simply did without electricity of any kind. Monrovia also had lacked running water.

Economically, one of the most important questions facing Liberia involved sanctions that the UN Security Council had imposed in 2002 to deprive Taylor of hard currency. The most important sanctions were bans on international trade in diamonds and timber from Liberia—two of the commodities that Taylor had used to fund his wars at home and in Sierra Leone and other countries in the region. The sanctions also included an arms embargo against Liberia and a ban on travel by Liberian officials and rebel leaders associated with Taylor.

Johnson-Sirleaf appealed to the UN to lift the sanctions on diamonds and lumber. The Security Council responded on June 20 by lifting the sanctions against Liberia's timber exports but retained sanctions on diamond exports for another six months, saying the government needed more time to set up a "certificate of origin" program so buyers would know that Liberian diamonds were legitimate. The council also modified the arms embargo so the new Liberian army and police forces could receive weapons.

The Security Council reaffirmed its diamond ban on two occasions late in the year, on October 20 and December 21. In both cases, the council said it wanted to lift that ban "as soon as possible" but expressed increasing frustration that the Liberian government had not followed through on pledges to protect its diamond exports. A panel of experts, appointed by the council, had reported on December 19 that Liberia had not yet met the requirements of an international program called the Kimberley Process that was intended to prevent international trade in so-called blood diamonds from conflict zones.

On August 25 the United Nations Development Programme issued a comprehensive report on development needs in Liberia. The report included an extensive list of services that needed to be restored before the country could begin functioning at anywhere near its prewar level. One notable obstacle, the report said, was a shortage in trained and motivated public servants to put the country back together again. Johnson-Sirleaf also had drawn attention to this problem, calling on Liberians, like herself, who had emigrated to the United States and other countries to return home, where their skills were urgently needed.

These appeals had some impact. News reports cited several cases of business executives, accountants, economists, and others who trickled back to Liberia, inspired by Johnson-Sirleaf's own example and her appeal. Also returning were most of the refugees who had fled the country during the war years, most of them to other countries in West Africa. The United Nations High Commissioner for Refugees reported in February that about 200,000 refugees had returned to Liberia since Taylor fled in 2003, and the agency hoped to repatriate another 100,000 in 2006. The UN mission in Liberia also reported that about 300,000 internally displaced people—those who had fled their homes during the war but remained in the country—had returned to their homes in recent years. Most of these refugees and displaced people were poor farm families with few skills and no money. Upon their return, they were given UN assistance, including food, clothing, other humanitarian supplies, and cash for immediate needs.

Following are excerpts from a speech by Ellen Johnson-Sirleaf upon her inauguration as president of Liberia on January 16, 2006, following the end of a long and destructive civil war.

DOCUMENT

"Inaugural Speech of President Ellen Johnson-Sirleaf"

... Before I begin this address, which signifies the high-noon of this historic occasion, I ask that we bow our heads for a moment of silent prayer in memory of the thousands of our compatriots who have died as a result of the many conflicts.

Thank you! ...

Vice President [Joseph] Boakai and I have just participated in the time-honored constitutional ritual of oath-taking as we embark upon our responsibilities to lead this Republic. This ritual is symbolically and politically significant and substantive. It reflects the enduring character of the democratic tradition of the peaceful and orderly transfer of political power and authority. It also confirms the culmination of a commitment to our nation's collective search for a purposeful and responsive national leadership.

We applaud the resilience of our people who, weighed down and dehumanized by poverty and rendered immobile by the shackles of fourteen years of civil war, went courageously to the polls, to vote—not once but twice, to elect Vice President Joseph Boakai and me to serve them. We express to you, our people, our deep sense of appreciation and gratitude for the opportunity to serve you and our common Republic. We pledge to live up to your expectations of creating a government that is attentive and responsive to your needs, concerns, and the development and progress of our country.

We know that your vote was a vote for change; a vote for peace, security and stability; a vote for individual and national prosperity; a vote for healing and leadership. We have heard you loudly, and we humbly accept your vote of confidence and your mandate.

This occasion, held under the cloudy skies, marks a celebration of change and a dedication to an agenda for a socio-economic and political reordering; indeed, a national renewal.

Today, we wholeheartedly embrace this change. We recognize that this change is not change for change sake, but a fundamental break with the past, thereby requiring that we take bold and decisive steps to address the problems that for decades have stunted our progress, undermined national unity, and kept old and new cleavages in ferment.

As we embrace this new commitment to change, it is befitting that, for the first time, the inauguration is being held on the Capitol Grounds, one of the three seats of Government. We pledge anew our commitment to transparency, open government, and participatory democracy for all of our citizens. ...

Fellow Liberians, Ladies and Gentlemen:

No one who has lived in or visited this country in the past fifteen years will deny the physical destruction and the moral decadence that the civil war has left in its wake here in Monrovia and in other cities, towns, and villages across the nation. We have all suffered. The individual sense of deprivation is immense. It is therefore understandable that our people will have high expectations and will demand aggressive solutions to the socio-economic and societal difficulties that we face.

Our record shows that we are a strong and resilient people, able to survive; able to rise from the ashes of civil strife and to start anew; able to forge a new beginning, forgiving if not forgetting the past. We are a good and friendly people, braced for hope even as we wipe away the tears of past suffering and despair. Our challenge, therefore, is to transform adversity into opportunity, to renew the promises upon which our nation was founded: freedom, equality, unity and individual progress.

In the history of our nation, in the history of every nation, each generation, each Administration is summoned to define its nation's purpose and character. Now, it is our time to state clearly and unequivocally who we are, as Liberians, as your leaders—and where we plan to take this country in the next six years.

Political Renewal

First, let me declare in our pursuit of political renewal, that the political campaign is over. It is time for us, regardless of our political affiliations and persuasions, to come together to heal and rebuild our nation. For my part, as President of the Republic of Liberia, my Government extends a hand of friendship and solidarity to the leadership and members of all political parties, many of them sitting right in front of me, which participated in our recent presidential and legislative elections. I call upon those who have been long in the struggle—and those who recently earned their stripes—to play important roles in the rebuilding of our nation.

Committed to advance the spirit of inclusion, I assure all Liberians and our international partners and friends that our Government will recognize and support a strong democratic and loyal opposition in Liberia. This is important because we believe that our democratic culture and our nation are best served when the opposition is strong and actively engaged in the process of nation building.

Moreover, we call upon our colleagues of all political persuasions now in the Diaspora to return home and join us in meeting this exciting challenge of national renewal.

We make a similar appeal to the thousands of our citizens who continue to live in refugee camps throughout the sub-region and beyond. We recognize and sympathize with your plight and will explore with our development partners ways and means to facilitate your early return home as a national imperative for our renewal and development.

To those who are still internally displaced, we pledge to work with our partners to get you back to your communities to enable you to start the process of rebuilding your lives.

We must have a new understanding. Your job, as citizens, is to work for your family and your country. Your country's only job is to work for you. That is the compact that I offer you today. . . .

Economic Renewal

In a similar quest for economic renewal, we start on the premise that we are a wealthy people. Our nation is blessed with an endowment, rich in natural and human resources.

Yet, our economy has collapsed due to several civil conflicts and economic mismanagement by successive governments. The task of reconstructing our devastated economy is awesome, for which there will be no quick fix.

Yet, we have the potential to promote a healthy economy in which Liberians and international investors can prosper. We can create an investment climate that gives confidence to Liberian and foreign investors. We can promote those activities that add value in the exploitation of our natural resources. We can recognize and give support to our small farmers and marketers who, through their own efforts over the years, have provided buoyancy and self-sufficiency in economic activity. We can revisit our land tenure system to promote more ownership and free holding for communities.

This will call for a transformation of our economic vision into economic goals that are consistent with our national endowment and regional and global dynamics. We will ensure that allocation of our own resources reflect those priorities formulated on the basis of sequential measures of structural change that need to provide this transformation. And we will call upon our development partners to likewise recognize that although they have made significant investment to bring peace to our country, this peace can only be consolidated and sustained if we bring development to our people.

With this in mind, we are working with our partners to identify key objectives and deliverables in the first one hundred and fifty days of our Administration, which coincides with the remaining budgetary period of the former government. We must meet our commitment to restore some measure of electricity to our capital city. We must put Liberians back to work again. We must put our economic and financial house in order. Most of all, we must revive our mindset of courage, hard work, honesty, and a can do spirit.

Our strategy is to achieve quick and visible progress that reaches significant number of our people, to gain momentum, consolidate support, and establish the foundation for sustained economic development.

For the long term, more will be required from us and our partners. We will formulate a multi-year economic reconstruction plan tied to a Poverty Reduction Strategy Program that relieves our country from a staggering US$3.5 billion debt and paves the way for acceleration in our national effort to make progress in the achievement of the Millennium Development Goals. We will also tackle the HIV/Aids problem, thereby enduring that this threat to our human capital and growth and prosperity is addressed.

Governance

We know that our desire for an environment for private sector-driven sustainable growth and development cannot be achieved without the political will and a civil service that is efficient, effective and honest. The workforce in our ministries and agencies is seriously bloated. Our Administration will therefore embark on a process of rationalizing our agencies of government to make them lean, efficient, and responsive to public service delivery. This will require the creation of a meritocracy that places premium on qualification, professionalism, and performance. . . .

Corruption

Fellow Liberians, we know that if we are to achieve our economic and income distribution goals, we must take on forcibly and effectively the debilitating cancer of corruption. Throughout the campaign, I assured our people that, if elected, we would wage war against corruption regardless of where it exists, or by whom it is practiced.

Today, I renew this pledge. Corruption, under my Administration, will be the major public enemy. We will confront it. We will fight it. Any member of my Administration who sees this affirmation as mere posturing or yet another attempt by another Liberian leader to play to the gallery on this grave issue should think twice.

In this respect, I will lead by example. I will expect and demand that everyone serving in my Administration leads by example. The first testament of how my Administration will tackle public service corruption will be that everyone appointed to high positions of public trust, such as in the Cabinet and heads of public corporations, will be required to declare their assets. I will be the first to comply, and I will call upon the Honorable Speaker and President Pro-Temps to say that they comply.

My Administration will also accord high priority to the formulation and passage into law of a National Code of Conduct, to which all public servants will be subjected.

My Fellow Liberians: If we are to achieve our development and anti-corruption goals, we must welcome and embrace the Governance and Economic Management Program [GEMAP], which the National Transitional Government of Liberia, working with our international partners, has formulated to deal with the serious economic and financial management deficiencies in our country.

We accept and enforce the terms of GEMAP, recognizing the important assistance which it is expected to provide during the early years of our Government. More importantly, we will ensure competence and integrity in the management of our own resources and insist on an integrated capacity building dimension initiative so as to render GEMAP non-applicable in a reasonable period of time.

Foreign Policy

...To our sister Republics West, East, and North of our borders, we make this pledge: under my Administration, no inch of Liberian soil will be used to conspire to perpetrate aggression against your countries. In making this commitment, we will work for a new regional security that is based upon economic partnership aimed at enhancing the prospects for regional cooperation and integration.

My Fellow Citizens:

Let me assure you that my Presidency shall remain committed to serve all Liberians without fear or favor. I am President for all of the people of the country. I therefore want to assure all of our people that neither I, nor any person serving my Administration will pursue any vendetta. There will be no vindictiveness. There will be no policies of political, social, and economic exclusion. We will be inclusive and tolerant, ever sensitive to the anxieties, fears, hopes, and aspirations of all of our people irrespective of ethnic, political, religious affiliation, and social status.

By their votes, the Liberian people have sent a clear message! They want peace; they want to move on with their lives. My charge as President is to work to assure the wishes of our people. We will therefore encourage our citizens to utilize our system of due process for settling differences. We will make sure that we work together as a people, knowing, however, that we will forcefully and decisively respond to any acts of lawlessness, threats to our hard earned peace, or destabilizing actions that could return us to conflict.

As we savor the new dawn of hope and expectation, I pledge to bring the Government closer to the people. The days of the imperial Presidency, of a domineering and threatening Chief Executive are over. This was my campaign promise, which I intend to keep.

And now, before I close, I would like to talk to the women—the women of Liberia, the women of Africa, and the women of the world. Until a few decades ago, Liberian women endured the injustice of being treated as second-class citizens. During the years of our civil war, they bore the brunt of inhumanity and terror. They were conscripted into war, gang raped at will, forced into domestic slavery. Yet, it is the women who labored and advocated for peace throughout our region.

It is therefore not surprising that during the period of our elections, Liberian women were galvanized—and demonstrated unmatched passion, enthusiasm, and support for my candidacy. They stood with me; they defended me; they worked with me; they prayed for me. The same can be said for the women throughout Africa. I want to here and now, gratefully acknowledge the powerful voice of women of all walks of life.

My Administration shall thus endeavor to give Liberian women prominence in all affairs of our country. My Administration shall empower Liberian women in all areas of our national life. We will support and increase the writ of laws that restore their dignity and deal drastically with crimes that dehumanize them. We will enforce without fear or favor the law against rape recently passed by the National Transitional Legislature. We shall encourage families to educate all children, particularly the girl child. We will also try to provide economic programs that enable Liberian women—particularly our market women—to assume their proper place in our economic process.

My Fellow Liberians:

We are moving forward. The best days are coming. The future belongs to us because we have taken charge of it. We have the resources, and we have the resourcefulness. We now have the right Government. And we have good friends, good brothers and sisters who will work with us. Our people are already building our roads, cleaning up our environment, creating jobs, rebuilding schools, bringing back water and electricity.

We are a good people; we are a kind people. We are a forgiving people—and we are a God-fearing people.

So, let us begin anew, moving forward into a future that is filled with promise, filled with hope!

"In Union Strong, Success is Sure! We cannot—fail. We must not—fail. We will not—fail."

God bless you all—and save the Republic.

I thank you.

Source: Republic of Liberia. The Embassy of Liberia in Washington, D.C. "Inaugural Speech of President Ellen Johnson-Sirleaf." Monrovia, Liberia. January 16, 2006. www.embassyofliberia.org/news/ Inaugural%20Speech.htm (accessed November 10, 2006).

Other Historic Documents of Interest

Chile elects first female president, p. 110

Election in Democratic Republic of the Congo, p. 414

Mexican presidential election, p. 695

Relations between Africa and China, p. 629

UN resolution on Darfur, p. 497

Middle East Quartet and Hamas on the New Palestinian Government

January 30 and March 20, 2006

■■■■■■■■■■ **THE DOCUMENT IN CONTEXT** ■■■■■■■■■

Hopes that arose during 2005 about the future of the Palestinian territories were dashed a year later. In 2005 Israel withdrew from the Gaza Strip, which it had occupied for nearly four decades, giving the Palestinians more control than ever before over a part of their own territory, and a successful presidential election appeared to herald a new era of democratic legitimacy for Palestinian leaders. But another round of elections in January 2006 put the radical Islamist party known as Hamas in charge of the Palestinian government, leading to a series of violent clashes between Palestinian political factions and resulting in international sanctions that plunged the local economy into a deep depression. Moreover, Israel responded forcefully to the kidnapping by Palestinian militants of an Israeli soldier in late June. A brief Israeli invasion of Gaza and subsequent attacks against Palestinian militants resulted in the deaths of more than 400 Palestinians during the last half of the year and deepened the economic crisis there and in the West Bank.

By year's end, the United States was financing military aid to security forces loyal to the politically moderate Palestinian president, Mahmoud Abbas, who was locked in a political struggle for power with Hamas. In turn, Abbas was threatening to call new elections, in hopes of pressuring Hamas leaders into allowing a "national unity" government that would be acceptable to the West and to Israel. The prospects for a peaceful resolution of the latest crisis to befall the Palestinians appeared dim, at best.

Historic Victory by Hamas

The Palestinians had won a measure of self-governance in the mid-1990s as the result of a series of peace agreements between Israel and then-Palestinian leader Yasir Arafat. In 1996 Arafat and his political party, known as Fatah, won the first-ever Palestinian elections and established a new government, the Palestinian Authority, which had limited control over most of the Gaza Strip and the major cities in the West Bank. Arafat died in November 2004 and was succeeded by Abbas, his long-time aide, who went on to win election in his own right as the Palestinian president in January 2005. Abbas also set in motion a series of elections—for municipal councils in 2005 and then for the national Legislative Council in 2006—that were intended to bring new legitimacy to the Palestinian government and to force Hamas to moderate by luring it into the political process.

Hamas emerged in the Palestinian territories in 1988; its name meant "zeal" and also was the acronym for the Islamic Resistance Movement. Hamas was an outgrowth of the local branch of the Muslim Brotherhood, a religious organization founded in Egypt during the 1920s that was banned in much of the Middle East. The Israeli government at first encouraged Hamas as a counter to Arafat and his Palestine Liberation Organization (PLO). Israel's attitude quickly changed, however, when Hamas became an active participant in the first Palestinian uprising—known as the intifada—which ran from late 1987 to 1993. The Israeli government withdrew its official recognition of Hamas and banned it as an organization, but Hamas expanded its influence by funding schools, health clinics, and other charities; these activities reportedly were financed in part by Iran. Hamas carried out its first suicide bombing against an Israeli target in 1994, one year after Israel and Arafat had signed a historic peace agreement. *(Israeli-Palestinian peace accord, Historic Documents of 1993, p. 747)*

During the 1990s and up until early 2005, Hamas continued its dual roles as a social service agency and a more radical alternative to Arafat's various bases of power, which included the PLO and (starting in 1996) the Palestinian Authority. Hamas sponsored numerous suicide bombings and other terrorist attacks against Israel even during the years of relative peace in the late 1990s. It stepped up those attacks when a second intifada began in September 2000, after the failure of U.S.-sponsored peace negotiations at Camp David. *(Second intifada, Historic Documents of 2000, p. 494)*

After winning the presidential election in January 2005, Abbas launched an electoral process that led eventually to the Hamas victory a year later. The first step of this process was the holding of elections for municipal councils in both Gaza Strip and the West Bank. Breaking with its past refusal to participate in politics (because that would recognize the legitimacy of the Palestinian Authority), Hamas fielded candidates in the local elections and scored surprising upsets—even in West Bank constituencies considered Fatah strongholds. Hamas took another significant step in February 2005, signing a cease-fire agreement, negotiated by Abbas with Egyptian help, calling for a halt in suicide bombings and other terrorist attacks against Israel. Hamas generally adhered to that agreement, although Israeli officials accused it of cooperating with other groups, such as Islamic Jihad, that had also signed the cease-fire but later abandoned it. *(Abbas elected president of Palestinian Authority, Historic Documents of 2005, p. 27)*

The ultimate step in the electoral process unleashed by Abbas was the holding of elections for the Palestinian legislature. Spurred by its victories at the local level, Hamas decided late in 2005 to participate. The election campaign began on January 3, 2006, with the various parties holding parades and rallies throughout Gaza and the West Bank. At the outset it was clear that Hamas gained a significant tactical advantage by fielding a single slate of candidates in local districts. Fatah, in contrast, offered in many districts two or even three candidates for voters to choose from, thus splitting the Fatah vote. Moreover, Hamas used the slogan "change and reform" to present itself as a break with the past, particularly from the corruption and incompetence of the Palestinian Authority under Arafat's leadership. Hamas thus attracted many voters who might not have embraced all elements of the movement's Islamist platform but were fed up with Fatah's failures.

The election took place in the context of ongoing chaos in the Gaza Strip, which had been under Palestinian control since Israel closed Jewish settlements and military installations there in the late summer of 2005. Abbas and other leaders had hoped the Palestinians would use the Israeli withdrawal to demonstrate a responsible stewardship of Gaza; instead, Fatah and Hamas factions battled for power and the region erupted with gun battles, kidnappings, and widespread fighting. By the time of the

January elections, most of Gaza was a zone of unending violence, cut off from the rest of the world by Israeli control of its borders and the seacoast. Its economy barely functioned. Israel had been thrown into its own political turmoil when Prime Minister Ariel Sharon suffered a massive stroke on January 4, 2006, and was succeeded by his deputy, Ehud Olmert. (Israeli withdrawal from Gaza, Historic Documents of 2005, p. 529)

The election on January 25 generally was orderly and peaceful, with international observer groups reporting that the voting was well managed and fair. The results were far from ordinary, however. Overall, Hamas candidates received only 45 percent of the 1.1 million votes, but as a result of the complex electoral system (and Fatah's fielding of multiple candidates in single districts) Hamas captured a strong majority of 74 of the 132 seats in the Legislative Council. Fatah candidates, by contrast, won only 45 seats. Several long-time Fatah leaders were defeated, among them Jibril Rajoub, who had been Arafat's security chief. The results appeared to surprise Hamas officials, who during the campaign had expressed a desire to win a significant number of seats as a means of pressuring Fatah but had acknowledged quietly they were unprepared to run the Palestinian government. Mahmoud Zahar, the leader of Hamas in Gaza, immediately outlined an ambitious program, saying he and his colleagues "are going to change every aspect, as regards the economy, industry, agriculture, as regards social aid, health, administration, education."

Jubilant Hamas supporters celebrated by hoisting the movement's distinctive green banners throughout Gaza and the West Bank, while Fatah officials and followers bickered about what to do next. Abbas gave a televised speech after the results were announced welcoming Hamas into the government but asserting that he would not abandon his position of attempting to negotiate a long-term peace agreement with Israel. "I am committed to implementing the program on which you elected me a year ago," he said.

International Reaction

Hamas leaders were not the only ones caught off guard by their victory. Foreign governments—many of which considered Hamas a terrorist organization—were shocked, and Israelis were appalled. Olmert, Israel's acting prime minister, met with his cabinet after the election results were announced and then issued a tough statement saying Israel "will not negotiate with a Palestinian administration if even part of it is an armed terrorist organization calling for the destruction of Israel." The next day, President George W. Bush said the United States would shun Hamas unless it abandoned its anti-Israel positions. "If your platform is the destruction of Israel, it means you're not a partner in peace, and we're interested in peace," he said. The Hamas victory came as a blow to Bush's policy of promoting democracy in the Middle East; Washington had pressed Israel to cooperate with the Palestinian election, apparently in hopes that Abbas's more moderate Fatah faction would emerge victorious.

The next few days saw officials from the United States and other countries scrambling to come up with a united position. The foremost question on the table concerned the fate of at least $1 billion in annual international aid to the Palestinian Authority, which for years had become the essential glue holding the Palestinian economy together. The key decision-making event was a meeting in London on January 30 of representatives of the diplomatic ensemble known as the "Quartet"—the European Union, Russia, the United Nations, and the United States. At this meeting, Secretary of State Condoleezza

Rice, UN Secretary General Kofi Annan, and other senior diplomats agreed not to cut off international aid to the Palestinians immediately but instead to establish tough standards for providing aid once Hamas took control of the Palestinian government. In a statement, the Quartet representatives said it was "inevitable" that donors would judge future aid to the Palestinian government according to its commitment to the principles of "nonviolence, recognition of Israel, and acceptance of previous agreements and obligations, including the Road Map." The last two phrases referred to a series of peace agreements signed by Arafat in the mid-1990s and to a phased peace plan, issued by the Quartet in 2003, titled "A Performance-Based Roadmap to a Permanent Two-State Solution to the Israeli-Palestinian Conflict." By early 2006 the peace agreements were largely in a state of suspension, and the road map never had been put into effect even though both Israel and the Palestinian Authority had accepted it, with reservations. *(Road map background, Historic Documents of 2003, p. 191)*

The Quartet's 2006 statement thus established a series of conditions for Palestinian aid that European countries and the United States would adhere to for the rest of the year. The main effect, once Hamas took office, was to suspend most international aid to the Palestinian Authority, the largest single employer in the Gaza Strip and West Bank with nearly 140,000 civil servants and security officers. Even so, the conditions allowed the granting of "humanitarian" aid (such as food and medicine) that did not pass through the Palestinian government; this included aid provided by the United Nations to Palestinians classified as refugees. Israel went further than the Quartet allies, however, announcing in mid-February that it would withhold payment to the Palestinian Authority of about $50 million in tax and customs revenue that it collected each month on behalf of the Palestinians; those taxes were the main source of domestic revenue for the Palestinian government. The Israeli move repeatedly led the Palestinian government—both before and after Hamas assumed power—to delay or cut back salaries to government employees, thus deepening an existing economic crisis in the territories.

On February 14, the *New York Times* reported that the United States, in conjunction with Israel, had settled on an ambitious plan to "destabilize" the new Hamas government once it took power. The point of this plan, the newspaper said, was to starve the Hamas government of money, thus forcing it to fail and leading to new elections that might be won by reformist Fatah leaders. Bush administration officials denounced the *Times* report as inaccurate, but subsequent developments during the year left no doubt that the Bush administration was, in fact, hoping to use the withholding of aid and other forms of pressure to force a collapse of the Hamas government.

Hamas Takes Control

The newly elected Palestinian legislature was not scheduled to take office for several weeks after the election—a period dominated by jockeying for power between Abbas's defeated Fatah faction and the victorious leaders of Hamas. On February 13, for example, the outgoing Fatah-dominated parliament passed measures giving additional powers to Abbas, including that of appointing a new "constitutional court" to review all legislation once Hamas took power. This period also saw Hamas officials struggling to adjust to the reality of power and responsibility; in the past, they could say or do whatever they wanted, but now their every word and action were taken seriously by world leaders as well as by ordinary Palestinians. Within a few days, Hamas leaders began moderating their rhetoric, including statements acknowledging that previous

Palestinian agreements with Israel were "a reality" and that extending the previous year's cease-fire would serve Palestinian, as well as Israeli, interests. Even so, top Hamas officials said there were limits to the changes they could make; among other things, they said Hamas would not formally recognize Israel or totally abandon the option of using violence against Israel if circumstances warranted.

Members of the new Palestinian legislature formally took their seats on February 18. Because of Israeli restrictions on travel by Hamas members, the opening legislative session—and all subsequent ones—took place simultaneously in two different places, one in Gaza City and the other in the West Bank city of Ramallah, with a video link between them. By that time Hamas officials had settled on Ismail Haniyeh, a senior Hamas representative in the Gaza Strip, as the prime minister, but most cabinet posts remained unfilled. In a speech to the opening session, Abbas said he remained committed to negotiations "as the sole practical, pragmatic, and strategic choice through which we reap the fruit of our struggle and sacrifices over the long decades." Abbas also denounced the "chaos" in the Palestinian territories and called on armed groups to recognize the legitimacy of "one arm" of security, that of the government rather than partisan militias.

In the weeks leading up to the installation of the new government, a major question was whether Fatah would take Hamas up on an offer to form a coalition government. Recognizing their inexperience in governing—and hoping the presence of Fatah leaders would help secure international aid—Hamas officials had offered to share some cabinet posts with experienced Fatah executives. Negotiations on a potential coalition dragged on for weeks and finally collapsed on March 16, when Hamas said it had failed to secure any cooperation from Fatah. The new Hamas government formally took power on March 30, with Haniyeh (who was considered relatively moderate) serving as prime minister and Mahmoud Zahar (a more radical Hamas leader in Gaza) serving as foreign minister. It later became clear, however, that the ultimate decision-making power in Hamas rested with Khaled Mashaal, the group's "exile" leader who lived in Damascus and reportedly controlled the flow of money to Hamas from Iran.

During the interim, Hamas on March 20 published its platform containing the essential points that party candidates had campaigned on during the election. In general, the platform was more moderate in tone than standard Hamas positions in previous years; for example, it did not use such terms as "the Zionist enemy" to refer to Israel and it made no mention of eliminating Israel from the face of the earth. The platform did call for ending Israeli "occupation" of the lands Israel had captured in the June 1967 war (including East Jerusalem and the West Bank), and it called for the right of Palestinian refugees to return to the homes they had lost in the 1948 and 1967 wars; these were standard Palestinian demands and did not represent a radical new policy. The platform also called for "reconsidering" the peace agreements that Arafat had signed with Israel but did not renounce those agreements altogether.

The main challenge facing the new government was a financial one: Haniyeh announced on April 5 that the Palestinian government had "an entirely empty treasury" and had been unable to issue paychecks that were due on April 1 to teachers, policemen, and other civil service workers. Israel was continuing to block the tax revenues normally used to pay those salaries. On April 7, the United States and the European Union formally announced that they had suspended all aid that went to the Palestinian Authority but would increase aid for food and other humanitarian supplies, to be provided through the United Nations and other independent agencies. Saudi Arabia and several of its oil-rich Persian Gulf neighbors promised tens of millions of dollars to keep the Palestinian government afloat, but the United States used its control of key elements of the international banking system to prevent the transfer of money to the Palestinian treasury. In desperation, Palestinian officials, including Haniyeh and Zahar, began smuggling large amounts of cash from Arab governments through the Rafah border crossing between the Gaza Strip and Egypt.

Israel Invades Gaza

Turmoil in the Palestinian territories was bad enough as a result of the economic crisis stemming from the cut-off of international aid and the political crisis resulting from disagreements between Abbas and the new Hamas-led government. A new, equally dangerous situation arose in late June that led to an Israeli military invasion of parts of the Gaza Strip.

This situation began on June 25 when eight Palestinian militants—some of them members of Hamas—used an underground tunnel to cross into Israel from the Gaza Strip. There, they attacked an Israeli military post, killing two soldiers, wounding three others, and capturing a fourth solider, Corporal Gilad Shalit. Two of the Palestinians were killed in an ensuing gun battle, but the others escaped back into Gaza, with Shalit in their custody.

Israel responded with an escalating series of moves, first by sending tanks just across the border into northern Gaza, then by launching air strikes against the Palestinian Interior Ministry and other Hamas targets and detaining more than sixty Hamas officials (including legislators) in the West Bank. On July 6, Israel mounted a full-scale invasion of northern Gaza, an invasion that later was extended into the southern part of the tiny territory. The government offered two reasons for these attacks: forcing Hamas to give up Corporal Shalit and pressuring Hamas to curtail the launching (primarily by other Palestinian militant groups) of homemade rockets, called Qassams, across the border into Israel. The Qassams caused little damage and only rarely killed or wounded Israelis, but they terrified Israelis living near Gaza and routinely provoked massive Israeli retaliation.

In the course of its military operations Israel destroyed the main electrical generating station in Gaza, thus depriving much of the area of electricity. Israel withdrew most of its ground forces from Gaza late in July, after the outbreak of another war between Israel and the Hezbollah militia in Lebanon, but it kept up the pressure on Hamas with repeated air strikes and more limited ground operations in Gaza all through the rest of the year.

By year's end, the Israeli military and police had killed 660 Palestinians (including 405 in Gaza during the second half of the year), according to the Israeli human rights group, B'Tselem. Of those killed, 141 (or about 21 percent) were minors. The largest one-day death toll came on November 8, when 28 Palestinians were killed by Israeli military action. Sixteen of those were civilian members of a single extended family (most of them women and children) in the northern Gaza town of Beit Hanoun; they were killed by an Israeli artillery strike as they slept in their apartment—the result, the military later said, of shells going off course. By contrast, B'Tselem said, Palestinians killed 23 Israelis during the year, including 17 civilians and 6 security personnel. Eleven of the Israeli civilians died in the only deadly Palestinian suicide bombing of the year, an April 17 attack on a fast-food stand in Tel Aviv.

Since the outbreak of the Palestinian intifada in September 2000, according to B'Tselem figures, 4,005 Palestinians and 701 Israelis had been killed in violence between the two sides; of these totals, 1,920 Palestinians and 385 Israelis were civilians who were not involved in any hostile action against the other side. The Israeli military routinely gave much lower figures for the deaths of Palestinian civilians and counted as "terrorists" nearly all Palestinians who died at the scene of violent incidents.

Despite the military pressure, Corporal Shalit reportedly remained in Palestinian hands, and several attempts to negotiate an exchange involving him and Palestinians jailed in Israeli prisons came to naught. At year's end, UN officials said Gaza had fallen into a humanitarian catastrophe, with most of the territory's 1.4 million citizens living in "deep poverty"—in other words, unable to meet daily subsistence needs without regular outside aid.

Clashes between Hamas and Fatah

The takeover of the Palestinian government by Hamas, followed by the Israeli invasion of Gaza in late June, escalated the violence that had plagued Gaza and the West Bank since well before Arafat died in 2004. With increasing frequency, gunmen loyal to one faction or another would attack leaders of opposing factions, public buildings associated with opposing factions, or even ordinary people suspected of siding with perceived enemies. This violence was further complicated by the fact that Arafat had created about one dozen security services within the Palestinian Authority, some that came under the control of the new Hamas government and others that remained loyal to Abbas and the Fatah party.

Among flash-points for violence were numerous protests by members of Fatah-dominated security services because of the government's failure to issue paychecks. Starting in mid-June, policemen and other civil servants massed outside government buildings demanding to be paid; often these protests resulted in gun battles in which people were killed or wounded. Clashes between Fatah and Hamas forces soared after a December 11 shooting in which three sons, aged three to nine, of a senior Palestinian security officer were killed. Over the course of the year, according to the B'Tselem human rights group, 55 Palestinians were killed by other Palestinians, most of them in partisan clashes. At year's end, Palestinians across the political spectrum expressed worries about the violence emerging into a full-scale civil war in Gaza and possibly in the West Bank as well.

Attempts at Political Compromise

While Fatah and Hamas fighters were battling each other in the streets, political leaders made numerous attempts during the year to reach a political compromise that would ease the international pressure and allow the resumption of direct aid to the Palestinian Authority. The first of these compromise attempts came from a seemingly unlikely source: militants serving time in Israeli prisons. In mid-May, senior Fatah and Hamas leaders in Hadarim Prison, near the Israeli city of Netanya, developed a proposal that implied recognition of Israel and called for creation of a Palestinian state "in all the lands occupied in 1967"—in other words, in the Gaza Strip, East Jerusalem, and the West Bank. This proposal became the basis for several subsequent negotiations between Abbas and Hamas leaders over the direction of the Palestinian government.

At several points the two sides announced they had reached agreement, but each time the agreement fell apart over fundamental issues, notably Abbas's demand that Hamas recognize Israel and renounce violence. A key stumbling block appeared to be

Mashaal, the Hamas leader in exile in Syria, who intervened to thwart all the agreements that Haniyeh and other "internal" Hamas leaders reached during the year with Abbas.

Frustrated by the stalemate, Abbas on December 16 said he would call early presidential and legislative elections in 2007. "Let's return to the people to have their say, and let them be the judge," he said. Abbas did not set a date for the elections, however, and he implied he would back down if Hamas finally agreed to creation of a national unity government. Hamas officials insisted the call for early elections was illegal, and by year's end the dramatic move by Abbas had failed to break the deadlock.

In an effort to boost Abbas, Olmert met with him on December 23—their only substantive encounter of the year—and agreed to release $100 million of the Palestinian tax money Israel had been withholding for most of the year. Olmert also said Israel would ease or remove about forty checkpoints used by the army to control travel by Palestinians in the West Bank. Over the years the Israeli army had installed several hundred checkpoints in the West Bank for the stated purpose of preventing terrorists from entering Israel; the barriers and other Israeli military restrictions also made it difficult, and in many cases impossible, for ordinary Palestinians to travel from their homes to work and school.

In an even more direct step to bolster Abbas, the U.S. government said it would provide $26 million in aid to Palestinian security forces loyal to him. On December 28, the Israeli newspaper *Haaretz* quoted Israeli officials as saying that Egypt had shipped 2,000 rifles, 20,000 ammunition clips, and 2 million bullets to Palestinian security forces loyal to Abbas; *Haaretz* said the shipments had been approved by Israel and the United States.

Following are two documents: first, the text of a statement released on January 30, 2006, by representatives of the "Quartet" (the European Union, Russia, the United Nations, and the United States) listing the conditions under which aid would be given to the newly elected Palestinian Authority government; second, the English-language text of a report released on March 20, 2006, by the Palestinian Authority's State Information Service outlining the main points of the agenda of the new Hamas-led government.

▬▬▬▬▬▬ DOCUMENT ▬▬▬▬▬▬

"Quartet Statement on the Situation in the Middle East"

Representatives of the Quartet—United Nations Secretary-General Kofi Annan, Russian Foreign Minister Sergei Lavrov, Austrian Foreign Minister Ursula Plassnik, United States Secretary of State Condoleezza Rice, High Representative for European Common Foreign and Security Policy Javier Solana, and European Commissioner for External Relations Benita Ferrero-Waldner—met today in London to discuss the situation in the Middle East.

The Quartet congratulated the Palestinian people on an electoral process that was free, fair and secure. The Quartet believes that the Palestinian people have the right to expect that a new Government will address their aspirations for peace and Statehood, and it welcomed President Abbas' affirmation that the Palestinian Authority is committed to the Road Map, previous agreements and obligations between the parties, and a negotiated two-State solution to the Israeli-Palestinian conflict. It is the view of the Quartet that all members of a future Palestinian Government must be committed to non-violence, recognition of Israel, and acceptance of previous agreements and obligations, including the Road Map. We urge both parties to respect their existing agreements, including on movement and access.

The Quartet received updates from Quartet Special Envoy James Wolfensohn and United States Security Coordinator Lieutenant General Keith Dayton at today's meeting. We also had the good fortune of hearing from former President Carter, who helped supervise elections a few days ago. The Quartet called on the Palestinian Authority to ensure law and order, prevent terrorist attacks and dismantle the infrastructure of terror. The Quartet acknowledged the positive role of the Palestinian Authority security forces in helping maintain order during the recent elections. It expressed its view that progress on further consolidation, accountability and reform remains an important task.

Mindful of the needs of the Palestinian people, the Quartet discussed the issue of assistance to the Palestinian Authority. First, the Quartet expressed its concern over the fiscal situation of the Palestinian Authority, and urged measures to facilitate the work of the caretaker Government to stabilize public finances, taking into consideration established fiscal accountability and reform benchmarks. Second, the Quartet concluded that it was inevitable that future assistance to any new Government would be reviewed by donors against that Government's commitment to the principles of non-violence, recognition of Israel, and acceptance of previous agreements and obligations, including the Road Map. The Quartet calls upon the newly elected Palestinian Legislative Council (PLC) to support the formation of a Government committed to these principles, as well as the rule of law, tolerance, reform and sound fiscal management.

Both parties are reminded of their obligations under the Road Map to avoid unilateral actions which prejudice final status issues. The Quartet reiterated its view that settlement expansion must stop, reiterated its concern regarding the route of the barrier, and noted Acting Prime Minister [Ehud] Olmert's recent statements that Israel will continue the process of removing unauthorized outposts.

The Quartet expressed its concern for the health of [Israeli] Prime Minister [Ariel] Sharon and its hope for his rapid recovery.

Finally, the Quartet reiterated its commitment to the principles outlined in the Road Map and previous statements, and reaffirmed its commitment to a just, comprehensive and lasting settlement to the Arab-Israeli conflict, based upon United Nations Security Council resolutions 242 and 338. The Quartet will remain seized of the matter and will engage key regional actors.

Source: U.S. Department of State. "Quartet Statement on the Situation in the Middle East." January 30, 2006. www.state.gov/r/pa/prs/ps/2006/60068.htm (accessed February 9, 2007).

██████████████ **DOCUMENT** ██████████████

"Program of the Hamas Government"

1. Removing Occupation and building the Independent Palestinian state with whole sovereignty with Jerusalem its capital.
2. Keeping on the Palestinian refugees' right of return to their homes and their properties as the individuals and a public right could not be abandoned.
3. Working on releasing all the prisoners, facing the occupation's procedures on earth, especially; Judaizing Jerusalem, annexing the valleys, expanding settlements, tearing down the West Bank, apartheid separation wall and the practices resulted, facing the collective sanctions, rejecting blackmailing and rapping the Authority' merits.
4. Resistance with all its forms is a legal right for the Palestinian people to end the occupation and regaining the people's national rights that legally could not be abandoned.
5. Holding comprehensive reforms for the internal situation, building the people and society's institutions on democratic basics that guarantee justice, equality and partnership, practicing political variety, acting the jurisdiction of law, separating between authorities, enabling that the judiciary is independent as well as protecting it, guaranteeing the private and public freedoms.
6. Building our different national institutions on national and professional bases far away from appropriation and factionalism.
7. The government confirmed adherence to implement Cairo understandings and talks held on March 2005 between the Palestinian national and Islamic factions over the issue of PLO and its institutions.
8. Dealing with all previous agreements assigned between PNA [Palestinian National Authority] and Israelis, the government has the right for reconsidering depending on respecting the international law, and applying its texts in respecting Palestinian people's rights and interests.

Among other points of the agenda, the government will deal with the international resolutions that save and protect the Palestinian people and their interests.

Cooperating with the international community in order to remove the Israeli occupation from the 1967-occupied territories including east Jerusalem, as a proposal to accomplish stability and calm in the region, particularly, in this period.

Source: Palestinian National Authority. State Information Service. International Press Center. "Program of the Hamas Government." March 20, 2006. www.ipc.gov.ps/ipc_new/english/details.asp?name=14573 (accessed January 10, 2007).

Other Historic Documents of Interest

Israeli politics, p. 193
UN resolution on Iran, p. 791

War between Israel and Hezbollah,
p. 454

State of the Union Address and Democratic Response

January 31, 2006

■■■■■■■■ **THE DOCUMENT IN CONTEXT** ■■■■■■■■

What a difference a year makes. At his State of the Union address in 2005, President George W. Bush exuded confidence. He had just won reelection, Iraqis had just turned out in massive numbers to elect an interim government—a first important step in creating a democracy in that war-weary country, and the president was ready to put forward an ambitious domestic legislative agenda whose centerpiece was the privatization of the Social Security system. Bush was ready to make good on his postelection promise to spend the political capital he claimed to have earned during the election campaign.

A year later, having spent much of his political capital with little to show for it, a more diffident president outlined a much more modest legislative agenda for 2006. When the president delivered his 2006 State of the Union address to a joint session of Congress on January 31, there was no apparent end to the Iraq conflict in sight, congressional Republicans were beset by ethics problems, and massive budget deficits narrowed the government's latitude for undertaking any new spending. Bush's popularity ratings were near their all-time lows, and Democrats were beginning to think they might have a chance to take control of the House and perhaps even the Senate.

Bush offered his usual vigorous defense of his Iraq and antiterrorism policies and focused his domestic agenda on issues of greatest interest to voters, including high energy costs. But many of his proposals were initiatives that he had been seeking for years, such as making the tax cuts of his first term permanent. His own party had already rejected key elements of other proposals, such as his plan for overhauling immigration policy. In a departure from previous policy, Bush offered support for alternative fuels as a means of curbing America's dependence on Middle Eastern oil. And to keep America competitive, he called for more funding for basic scientific research and for placing more math and science teachers in the schools.

In the end, however, Bush's speech did little to allay the country's nervousness or divert its attention from the war overseas and economic troubles at home. Democrats continued to assail Bush and the Republicans for getting bogged down in what was looking more and more like a civil war in Iraq, for a "middle-class squeeze" in the economy, and for failures of management epitomized by the administration's woefully inadequate response to Hurricane Katrina. Democrats also played up ethical lapses by congressional Republicans that dogged the party throughout the year. When the votes from the November 8 midterm elections were counted, Democrats had won a solid majority in the House and a one-seat majority in the Senate. Responding finally to his critics, Bush fired Defense Secretary Donald Rumsfeld and announced that he would undertake a thorough review of his options in Iraq.

Iraq and the War on Terrorism

In his remarks on Iraq, Bush insisted that his administration had "a clear plan for victory." He said the United States was "helping Iraqis build an inclusive government, so that old resentments would be eased," was continuing reconstruction efforts to help Iraqis build a modern economy, and was continuing to train Iraqi soldiers to fight their own battles. "Fellow citizens," he declared, "we are in this fight to win, and we are winning." Despite this rhetoric, violence escalated in Iraq all through the year, particularly after the bombing in February of a mosque set off increased fighting between Sunni and Shiite Muslims. Bush moderated his rhetoric later in the year, for example by dropping what had been frequent pledges to "stay the course" in Iraq.

In his speech, Bush warned Iran to abandon its program to develop nuclear weapons and said Iran's sponsorship of terrorists in Lebanon and the Palestinian territories "must come to an end." Bush also had a warning for the leaders of Hamas, the Islamist party that had won in Palestinian elections earlier in January and was set to take control of the Palestinian Authority in March. "Hamas must recognize Israel, disarm, reject terrorism, and work for lasting peace," the president said. These were the conditions that the United States and the European Union laid down for the provision of aid to the Hamas-led government—conditions that Hamas refused to meet.

On one of the most controversial issues of the day, Bush strongly defended his order, revealed in mid-December, authorizing secret surveillance of telephone calls and e-mails made by the people in the United States, including U.S. citizens, without obtaining court warrants. "If there are people inside our country who are talking with Al Qaida, we want to know about it," the president said, "because we will not sit back and wait to be hit again." Bush said the program was "essential to the security" of the United States and had helped prevent terrorist attacks, although he did not specify where or how. Despite widespread criticisms that Bush had overstepped his authority, the president insisted that he had the power, under both the Constitution and statute, to issue the order, that other presidents had exercised the same authority, and that federal courts had approved its use. Although both chambers of Congress considered new rules to govern a warrantless electronic surveillance program, those efforts stalled in the Senate. *(Warrantless wiretaps, Historic Documents of 2005, p. 958)*

Congress did renew several key expiring provisions of the Patriot Act, the antiterrorism law that gave domestic law enforcement agencies wide powers to track down terrorist suspects, including access to a wide array of business records and the power to seek "roving wiretaps." In the wake of a Supreme Court decision throwing out the administration's plan for military tribunals for accused terrorists imprisoned at Guantanamo Bay, Cuba, Congress also agreed to new rules for their trials and treatment. *(Patriot Act background, Historic Documents of 2003, p. 607)*

Domestic Agenda

Even though Bush's legislative agenda was relatively modest, Congress gave scant attention to much of it. His call for permanently extending the tax cuts enacted in 2001 and 2003 were never seriously considered, although a GOP plan to couple a boost in the minimum wage with a measure to permanently reduce the federal estate tax fell victim to a filibuster in the Senate. In the face of overwhelming opposition among the public and in Congress, Bush did not revive his plan to privatize Social Security but instead proposed that a bipartisan commission study the sustainability of the country's three major entitlement programs—Social Security, Medicare, and

Medicaid. The commission had not been appointed by the end of the year. *(Social Security privatization proposal, Historic Documents of 2005, p. 111)*

Bush did win an expansion of health savings accounts, long one of his top domestic priorities. Created in 2003, the accounts allowed consumers to put aside tax-free income to spend on health costs and insurance deductibles. Congress included the expansion in the tax and trade measure passed at the end of the session. But legislators took no action on Bush's perennial calls to help small businesses afford health insurance by making it easier for them to band together across state lines to increase their purchasing power. Nor did they act on another perennial request to overhaul the medical malpractice system. Bush also made no mention in his speech of the Medicare prescription drug coverage Congress enacted in 2003. The program was once expected to be a pillar of the GOP's midterm reelection campaign, but its cost and complexity had made it unpopular among many of the seniors it was meant to help. *(Prescription drug measure, Historic Documents of 2003, p. 1119)*

Declaring that America was "addicted to oil," Bush called for a 22 percent increase in research funding for alternative sources of energy such as wind and solar power, for developing better batteries for hybrid and electric cars, and for developing ethanol made from wood chips and other plant materials in addition to corn. Bush said the goal was to replace three-fourths of America's oil imports from the Middle East by 2025. Despite a flurry of proposals and months of debate sparked by high oil and gasoline prices, the only significant energy legislation enacted in 2006 was a measure to allow new offshore drilling in the Gulf of Mexico. The president's proposals to boost American competitiveness by funding more basic research and hiring more math and science teachers received little attention in Congress.

One issue Bush highlighted, an overhaul of immigration policy, did receive considerable congressional attention. As he had in the past, the president called for a guest worker program. But rank-and-file House Republicans and some Democrats were more concerned that the estimated 12 million illegal immigrants living in the United States presented a security risk. Although the Senate passed a broad overhaul measure with the backing of legislators from both parties, House Republicans refused to back the president's request for a guest worker program and instead insisted on legislation criminalizing illegal immigrants and anyone who helped them. With the overhaul legislation all but dead, House Republicans pushed through a measure to build a security fence along the entire U.S. border with Mexico. That bill passed just two weeks before the mid-term election, but funding to build the fence had yet to be appropriated.

Bush made only passing reference to two other topics of substantial interest. On ethics problems that had ensnared several GOP legislators, including House Majority Leader Tom DeLay who gave up his post after being indicted on money-laundering charges, Bush said only that he supported the reform efforts of legislators in both parties. On recovery from Hurricanes Katrina and Rita, Bush spoke only of ongoing programs, but offered no new money or initiatives to help Gulf Coast residents displaced by the storms put their lives back together.

Democratic Response

In the formal Democratic response to the president's speech, Virginia governor Timothy M. Kaine said the Bush administration's "poor choices and bad management" had failed the American people and argued that both parties needed to refocus their efforts on service to their constituents. "If we want to replace the division that's been gripping our nation's capital, we need a change," Kaine said, speaking from the governor's mansion in Richmond. "Democrats are leading that reform effort, working to restore honesty and openness to our government, working to replace a culture of partisanship and cronyism with an ethic of service and results." Kaine, who was elected governor of Virginia in 2005, was chosen to showcase the Democrats' ability to win elections in conservative states.

Kaine's formal response, comments by other Democratic leaders, and a television advertisement created specifically for the State of the Union address all sought to paint the president and his party as beholden to special interests and the rich. The ad, paid for by the Democratic Congressional Campaign Committee, suggested that Bush's proposals on Social Security, health care, and energy were heavily influenced by industry interests and asked, "What special interest will the Republican Congress rubber-stamp this time."

Democrats shied away from any discussion of Iraq in their remarks before the president's speech, but Kaine sought to assert the Democratic Party's support for the war on terrorism while criticizing the president's rationale for invading Iraq, his failure to ensure that troops there had the best body armor and the best intelligence information, and his plans to reduce military and veterans benefits. "The president called again tonight for our commitment to win the war on terror and to support our troops," Kaine said. "Every American embraces those goals. We can—and we must— defeat those who attack and kill innocent people." But, he added, "our commitment to winning the war on terror compels us to ask this question: Are the president's policies the best way to win this war?" That was the question Democrats clearly wanted voters to think about as they decided whom to support in the midterm elections.

Following are the texts of the State of the Union address, delivered January 31, 2006, by President George W. Bush at a joint session of Congress and a response, delivered immediately afterward, by Timothy M. Kaine, the Democratic governor of Virginia, who was speaking from the governor's mansion in Richmond.

DOCUMENT

"Address on the State of the Union"

Thank you all. Mr. Speaker [Dennis Hastert], Vice President [Dick] Cheney, Members of Congress, members of the Supreme Court and diplomatic corps, distinguished guests, and fellow citizens: Today our Nation lost a beloved, graceful, courageous woman who called America to its founding ideals and carried on a noble dream. Tonight we are comforted by the hope of a glad reunion with the husband who was taken so long ago, and we are grateful for the good life of Coretta Scott King.

Every time I'm invited to this rostrum, I'm humbled by the privilege and mindful of the history we've seen together. We have gathered under this Capitol dome in moments of national mourning and national achievement. We have served America through one of the most consequential periods of our history, and it has been my honor to serve with you.

In a system of two parties, two chambers, and two elected branches, there will always be differences and debate. But even tough debates can be conducted in a civil tone, and our differences cannot be allowed to harden into anger. To confront the great issues before us, we must act in a spirit of goodwill and respect for one another—and I will do my part. Tonight the state of our Union is strong, and together we will make it stronger.

In this decisive year, you and I will make choices that determine both the future and the character of our country. We will choose to act confidently in pursuing the enemies of freedom, or retreat from our duties in the hope of an easier life. We will choose to build our prosperity by leading the world economy, or shut ourselves off from trade and opportunity. In a complex and challenging time, the road of isolationism and protectionism may seem broad and inviting, yet it ends in danger and decline. The only way to protect our people, the only way to secure the peace, the only way to control our destiny is by our leadership. So the United States of America will continue to lead.

Abroad, our Nation is committed to an historic, long-term goal: We seek the end of tyranny in our world. Some dismiss that goal as misguided idealism. In reality, the future security of America depends on it. On September the 11th, 2001, we found that problems originating in a failed and oppressive state 7,000 miles away could bring murder and destruction to our country. Dictatorships shelter terrorists, and feed resentment and radicalism, and seek weapons of mass destruction. Democracies replace resentment with hope, respect the rights of their citizens and their neighbors, and join the fight against terror. Every step toward freedom in the world makes our country safer, so we will act boldly in freedom's cause.

Far from being a hopeless dream, the advance of freedom is the great story of our time. In 1945, there were about two dozen lonely democracies in the world. Today, there are 122. And we're writing a new chapter in the story of self-government—with women lining up to vote in Afghanistan, and millions of Iraqis marking their liberty with purple ink, and men and women from Lebanon to Egypt debating the rights of individuals and the necessity of freedom. At the start of 2006, more than half the people of our world live in democratic nations. And we do not forget the other half—in places like Syria and Burma, Zimbabwe, North Korea, and Iran—because the demands of justice and the peace of this world require their freedom as well.

No one can deny the success of freedom, but some men rage and fight against it. And one of the main sources of reaction and opposition is radical Islam—the perversion by a few of a noble faith into an ideology of terror and death. Terrorists like [Osama] bin Laden are serious about mass murder, and all of us must take their declared intentions seriously. They seek to impose a heartless system of totalitarian control throughout the Middle East and arm themselves with weapons of mass murder.

Their aim is to seize power in Iraq and use it as a safe haven to launch attacks against America and the world. Lacking the military strength to challenge us directly, the terrorists have chosen the weapon of fear. When they murder children at a school in Beslan or blow up commuters in London or behead a bound captive, the terrorists hope these horrors will break our will, allowing the violent to inherit the Earth. But they have miscalculated: We love our freedom, and we will fight to keep it.

In a time of testing, we cannot find security by abandoning our commitments and retreating within our borders. If we were to leave these vicious attackers alone, they would not leave us alone. They would simply move the battlefield to our own shores. There is no peace in retreat, and there is no honor in retreat. By allowing radical Islam to work its will, by leaving an assaulted world to fend for itself, we would signal to all that we no longer believe in our own ideals or even in our own courage. But our enemies and our friends can be certain: The United States will not retreat from the world, and we will never surrender to evil.

America rejects the false comfort of isolationism. We are the nation that saved liberty in Europe and liberated death camps and helped raise up democracies and faced down an evil empire. Once again, we accept the call of history to deliver the oppressed and move this world toward peace. We remain on the offensive against terror networks. We have killed or captured many of their leaders—and for the others, their day will come.

We remain on the offensive in Afghanistan, where a fine President and a National Assembly are fighting terror while building the institutions of a new democracy. We're on the offensive in Iraq with a clear plan for victory.

First, we're helping Iraqis build an inclusive government, so that old resentments will be eased and the insurgency will be marginalized. Second, we're continuing reconstruction efforts and helping the Iraqi Government to fight corruption and build a modern economy, so all Iraqis can experience the benefits of freedom. And third, we're striking terrorist targets while we train Iraqi forces that are increasingly capable of defeating the enemy. Iraqis are showing their courage every day, and we are proud to be their allies in the cause of freedom.

Our work in Iraq is difficult because our enemy is brutal. But that brutality has not stopped the dramatic progress of a new democracy. In less than 3 years, the nation has gone from dictatorship to liberation, to sovereignty, to a Constitution, to national elections. At the same time, our coalition has been relentless in shutting off terrorist infiltration, clearing out insurgent strongholds, and turning over territory to Iraqi security forces. I am confident in our plan for victory; I am confident in the will of the Iraqi people; I am confident in the skill and spirit of our military. Fellow citizens, we are in this fight to win, and we are winning.

The road of victory is the road that will take our troops home. As we make progress on the ground and Iraqi forces increasingly take the lead, we should be able to further decrease our troop levels. But those decisions will be made by our military commanders, not by politicians in Washington, DC.

Our coalition has learned from our experience in Iraq. We've adjusted our military tactics and changed our approach to reconstruction. Along the way, we have benefitted from responsible criticism and counsel offered by Members of Congress of both parties. In the coming year, I will continue to reach out and seek your good advice. Yet there is a difference between responsible criticism that aims for success and defeatism that refuses to acknowledge anything but failure. Hindsight alone is not wisdom, and second-guessing is not a strategy.

With so much in the balance, those of us in public office have a duty to speak with candor. A sudden withdrawal of our forces from Iraq would abandon our Iraqi allies to death and prison, would put men like bin Laden and [Abu Musab al-] Zarqawi in charge of a strategic country, and show that a pledge from America means little. Members of Congress, however we feel about the decisions and debates of the past, our Nation has only one option: We must keep our word, defeat our enemies, and stand behind the American military in this vital mission.

Our men and women in uniform are making sacrifices and showing a sense of duty stronger than all fear. They know what it's like to fight house to house in a maze of streets, to wear heavy gear in the desert heat, to see a comrade killed by a roadside bomb. And those who know the costs also know the stakes. Marine Staff Sergeant Dan Clay was killed last month fighting in Fallujah. He left behind a letter to his family, but his words could just as well be addressed to every American. Here is what Dan wrote: "I know what honor is—it has been an honor to protect and serve all of you. I faced death with the secure knowledge that you would not have to. Never falter. Don't hesitate to honor and support those of us who have the honor of protecting that which is worth protecting."

Staff Sergeant Dan Clay's wife, Lisa, and his mom and dad, Sara Jo and Bud, are with us this evening. Welcome.

Our Nation is grateful to the fallen, who live in the memory of our country. We're grateful to all who volunteer to wear our Nation's uniform. And as we honor our brave troops, let us never forget the sacrifices of America's military families.

Our offensive against terror involves more than military action. Ultimately, the only way to defeat the terrorists is to defeat their dark vision of hatred and fear by offering the hopeful alternative of political freedom and peaceful change. So the United States of America supports democratic reform across the broader Middle East. Elections are vital, but they are only the beginning. Raising up a democracy requires the rule of law and protection of minorities and strong, accountable institutions that last longer than a single vote.

The great people of Egypt have voted in a multiparty Presidential election, and now their Government should open paths of peaceful opposition that will reduce the appeal of radicalism. The Palestinian people have voted in elections, and now the leaders of Hamas must recognize Israel, disarm, reject terrorism, and work for lasting peace. Saudi Arabia has taken the first steps of reform; now it can offer its people a better future by pressing forward with those efforts. Democracies in the Middle East will not look like our own because they will reflect the traditions of their own citizens. Yet liberty is the future of every nation in the Middle East because liberty is the right and hope of all humanity.

The same is true of Iran, a nation now held hostage by a small clerical elite that is isolating and repressing its people. The regime in that country sponsors terrorists in the Palestinian territories and in Lebanon, and that must come to an end. The Iranian Government is defying the world with its nuclear ambitions, and the nations of the world must not permit the Iranian regime to gain nuclear weapons. America will continue to rally the world to confront these threats.

Tonight let me speak directly to the citizens of Iran: America respects you, and we respect your country. We respect your right to choose your own future and win your own freedom. And our Nation hopes one day to be the closest of friends with a free and democratic Iran.

To overcome dangers in our world, we must also take the offensive by encouraging economic progress and fighting disease and spreading hope in hopeless lands. Isolationism would not only tie our hands in fighting enemies, it would keep us from helping our friends in desperate need. We show compassion abroad because Americans believe in the God-given dignity and worth of a villager with HIV/AIDS or an infant with malaria or a refugee fleeing genocide or a young girl sold into slavery. We also show compassion abroad because regions overwhelmed by poverty, corruption, and despair are sources of terrorism and organized crime and human trafficking and the drug trade.

In recent years, you and I have taken unprecedented action to fight AIDS and malaria, expand the education of girls, and reward developing nations that are moving forward with economic and political reform. For people everywhere, the United States is a partner for a better life. Shortchanging these efforts would increase the suffering and chaos of our world, undercut our long-term security, and dull the conscience of our country. I urge Members of Congress to serve the interests of America by showing the compassion of America.

Our country must also remain on the offensive against terrorism here at home. The enemy has not lost the desire or capability to attack us. Fortunately, this Nation has superb professionals in law enforcement, intelligence, the military, and homeland security. These men and women are dedicating their lives, protecting us all, and they deserve our support and our thanks. They also deserve the same tools they already use to fight drug trafficking and organized crime, so I ask you to reauthorize the Patriot Act.

It is said that prior to the attacks of September the 11th, our Government failed to connect the dots of the conspiracy. We now know that two of the hijackers in the United States placed telephone calls to Al Qaida operatives overseas. But we did not know about their plans until it was too late. So to prevent another attack—based on authority given to me by the Constitution and by statute—I have authorized a terrorist surveillance program to aggressively pursue the international communications of suspected Al Qaida operatives and affiliates to and from America. Previous Presidents have used the same constitutional authority I have, and Federal courts have approved the use of that authority. Appropriate Members of Congress have been kept informed. The terrorist surveillance program has helped prevent terrorist attacks. It remains essential to the security of America. If there are people inside our country who are talking with Al Qaida, we want to know about it, because we will not sit back and wait to be hit again.

In all these areas—from the disruption of terror networks, to victory in Iraq, to the spread of freedom and hope in troubled regions—we need the support of our friends and allies. To draw that support, we must always be clear in our principles and willing to act. The only alternative to American leadership is a dramatically more dangerous and anxious world. Yet we also choose to lead because it is a privilege to serve the values that gave us birth. American leaders—from [Franklin D.] Roosevelt to [Harry] Truman to [John F.] Kennedy to [Ronald] Reagan—rejected isolation and retreat, because they knew that America is always more secure when freedom is on the march.

Our own generation is in a long war against a determined enemy, a war that will be fought by Presidents of both parties, who will need steady bipartisan support from the Congress. And tonight I ask for yours. Together, let us protect our country, support the men and women who defend us, and lead this world toward freedom.

Here at home, America also has a great opportunity: We will build the prosperity of our country by strengthening our economic leadership in the world.

Our economy is healthy and vigorous and growing faster than other major industrialized nations. In the last 2 1/2 years, America has created 4.6 million new jobs—more than Japan and the European Union combined. Even in the face of higher energy prices and natural disasters, the American people have turned in an economic performance that is the envy of the world.

The American economy is preeminent, but we cannot afford to be complacent. In a dynamic world economy, we are seeing new competitors like China and India, and this creates uncertainty, which makes it easier to feed people's fears. So we're seeing some old temptations return. Protectionists want to escape competition, pretending that we can keep our high standard of living while walling off our economy. Others say that the government needs to take a larger role in directing the economy, centralizing more power in Washington and increasing taxes. We hear claims that immigrants are somehow bad for the economy—even though this economy could not function without them. All these are forms of economic retreat, and they lead in the same direction, toward a stagnant and second-rate economy.

Tonight I will set out a better path: An agenda for a nation that competes with confidence; an agenda that will raise standards of living and generate new jobs. Americans should not fear our economic future because we intend to shape it.

Keeping America competitive begins with keeping our economy growing. And our economy grows when Americans have more of their own money to spend, save, and invest. In the last 5 years, the tax relief you passed has left $880 billion in the hands of American workers, investors, small businesses, and families. And they have used it to help produce more than 4 years of uninterrupted economic growth. Yet the tax relief is set to expire in the next few years. If we do nothing, American families will face a massive tax increase they do not expect and will not welcome. Because America needs more than a temporary expansion, we need more than temporary tax relief. I urge the Congress to act responsibly and make the tax cuts permanent.

Keeping America competitive requires us to be good stewards of tax dollars. Every year of my Presidency, we've reduced the growth of nonsecurity discretionary spending, and last year you passed bills that cut this spending. This year my budget will cut it again, and reduce or eliminate more than 140 programs that are performing poorly or not fulfilling essential priorities. By passing these reforms, we will save the American taxpayer another $14 billion next year and stay on track to cut the deficit in half by 2009.

I am pleased that Members of Congress are working on earmark reform, because the Federal budget has too many special interest projects. And we can tackle this problem together, if you pass the line-item veto.

We must also confront the larger challenge of mandatory spending, or entitlements. This year, the first of about 78 million baby boomers turn 60, including two of my Dad's favorite people—me and President [Bill] Clinton. This milestone is more than a personal crisis—it is a national challenge. The retirement of the baby boom generation will put unprecedented strains on the Federal Government. By 2030, spending for Social Security, Medicare, and Medicaid alone will be almost 60 percent of the entire Federal budget. And that will present future Congresses with impossible choices—staggering tax increases, immense deficits, or deep cuts in every category of spending. Congress did not act last year on my proposal to save Social Security, yet the rising cost of entitlements is a problem that is not going away. And every year we fail to act, the situation gets worse.

So tonight I ask you to join me in creating a commission to examine the full impact of baby boom retirements on Social Security, Medicare, and Medicaid. This commission should include Members of Congress of both parties, and offer bipartisan solutions. We need to put aside partisan politics and work together and get this problem solved.

Keeping America competitive requires us to open more markets for all that Americans make and grow. One out of every five factory jobs in America is related to global trade, and we want people everywhere to buy American. With open markets and a level playing field, no one can outproduce or outcompete the American worker.

Keeping America competitive requires an immigration system that upholds our laws, reflects our values, and serves the interests of our economy. Our Nation needs orderly and secure borders. To meet this goal, we must have stronger immigration enforcement and border protection. And we must have a rational, humane guest worker program that rejects amnesty, allows temporary jobs for people who seek them legally, and reduces smuggling and crime at the border.

Keeping America competitive requires affordable health care. Our Government has a responsibility to provide health care for the poor and the elderly, and we are meeting that responsibility. For all Americans, we must confront the rising cost of care, strengthen the doctor-patient relationship, and help people afford the insurance coverage they need.

We will make wider use of electronic records and other health information technology, to help control costs and reduce dangerous medical errors. We will strengthen health savings accounts, making sure individuals and small-business employees can buy insurance with the same advantages that people working for big businesses now get. We will do more to make this coverage portable, so workers can switch jobs without having to worry about losing their health insurance. And because lawsuits are driving many good doctors out of practice, leaving women in nearly 1,500 American counties without a single ob-gyn, I ask the Congress to pass medical liability reform this year.

Keeping America competitive requires affordable energy. And here we have a serious problem: America is addicted to oil, which is often imported from unstable parts of the world. The best way to break this addiction is through technology. Since 2001, we have spent nearly $10 billion to develop cleaner, cheaper, and more reliable alternative energy sources. And we are on the threshold of incredible advances.

So tonight I announce the Advanced Energy Initiative—a 22-percent increase in clean-energy research—at the Department of Energy, to push for breakthroughs in two vital areas. To change how we power our homes and offices, we will invest more in zero-emission coal-fired plants, revolutionary solar and wind technologies, and clean, safe nuclear energy.

We must also change how we power our automobiles. We will increase our research in better batteries for hybrid and electric cars and in pollution-free cars that run on hydrogen. We'll also fund additional research in cutting-edge methods of producing ethanol, not just from corn but from wood chips and stalks or switch grass. Our goal is to make this new kind of ethanol practical and competitive within 6 years.

Breakthroughs on this and other new technologies will help us reach another great goal: To replace more than 75 percent of our oil imports from the Middle East by 2025. By applying the talent and technology of America, this country can dramatically improve our environment, move beyond a petroleum-based economy, and make our dependence on Middle Eastern oil a thing of the past.

And to keep America competitive, one commitment is necessary above all: We must continue to lead the world in human talent and creativity. Our greatest advantage in the world has always been our educated, hard-working, ambitious people. And we're going to keep that edge. Tonight I announce an American Competitiveness Initiative, to encourage innovation throughout our economy and to give our Nation's children a firm grounding in math and science.

First, I propose to double the Federal commitment to the most critical basic research programs in the physical sciences over the next 10 years. This funding will support the work of America's most creative minds as they explore promising areas such as nanotechnology, supercomputing, and alternative energy sources.

Second, I propose to make permanent the research and development tax credit to encourage bolder private-sector initiatives in technology. With more research in both the public and private sectors, we will improve our quality of life and ensure that America will lead the world in opportunity and innovation for decades to come.

Third, we need to encourage children to take more math and science, and to make sure those courses are rigorous enough to compete with other nations. We've made a good start in the early grades with the No Child Left Behind Act, which is raising standards and lifting test scores across our country. Tonight I propose to train 70,000 high school teachers to lead advanced-placement courses in math and science, bring 30,000 math and science professionals to teach in classrooms, and give early help to students who struggle with math, so they have a better chance at good, high-wage jobs. If we ensure that America's children succeed in life, they will ensure that America succeeds in the world.

Preparing our Nation to compete in the world is a goal that all of us can share. I urge you to support the American Competitiveness Initiative, and together we will show the world what the American people can achieve.

America is a great force for freedom and prosperity. Yet our greatness is not measured in power or luxuries but by who we are and how we treat one another. So we strive to be a compassionate, decent, hopeful society.

In recent years, America has become a more hopeful nation. Violent crime rates have fallen to their lowest levels since the 1970s. Welfare cases have dropped by more than half over the past decade. Drug use among youth is down 19 percent since 2001. There are fewer abortions in America than at any point in the last three decades, and the number of children born to teenage mothers has been falling for a dozen years in a row.

These gains are evidence of a quiet transformation, a revolution of conscience, in which a rising generation is finding that a life of personal responsibility is a life of fulfillment. Government has played a role. Wise policies, such as welfare reform and drug education and support for abstinence and adoption have made a difference in the character of our country. And everyone here tonight, Democrat and Republican, has a right to be proud of this record.

Yet many Americans, especially parents, still have deep concerns about the direction of our culture and the health of our most basic institutions. They're concerned about unethical conduct by public officials and discouraged by activist courts that try to redefine marriage. They worry about children in our society who need direction and love, and about fellow citizens still displaced by natural disaster, and about suffering caused by treatable diseases.

As we look at these challenges, we must never give in to the belief that America is in decline or that our culture is doomed to unravel. The American people know better than that. We have proven the pessimists wrong before, and we will do it again.

A hopeful society depends on courts that deliver equal justice under the law. The Supreme Court now has two superb new members on its bench, Chief Justice John Roberts and Justice Sam Alito. I thank the Senate for confirming both of them. I will continue to nominate men and women who understand that judges must be servants of the law and not legislate from the bench.

Today marks the official retirement of a very special American. For 24 years of faithful service to our Nation, the United States is grateful to Justice Sandra Day O'Connor.

A hopeful society has institutions of science and medicine that do not cut ethical corners and that recognize the matchless value of every life. Tonight I ask you to pass legislation to prohibit the most egregious abuses of medical research: Human cloning in all its forms; creating or implanting embryos for experiments; creating human-animal hybrids; and buying, selling, or patenting human embryos. Human life is a gift from our Creator, and that gift should never be discarded, devalued, or put up for sale.

A hopeful society expects elected officials to uphold the public trust. Honorable people in both parties are working on reforms to strengthen the ethical standards of Washington. I support your efforts. Each of us has made a pledge to be worthy of public responsibility, and that is a pledge we must never forget, never dismiss, and never betray.

As we renew the promise of our institutions, let us also show the character of America in our compassion and care for one another.

A hopeful society gives special attention to children who lack direction and love. Through the Helping America's Youth Initiative, we are encouraging caring adults to get involved in the life of a child. And this good work is being led by our First Lady, Laura Bush. This year we will add resources to encourage young people to stay in school, so more of America's youth can raise their sights and achieve their dreams.

A hopeful society comes to the aid of fellow citizens in times of suffering and emergency, and stays at it until they're back on their feet. So far the Federal Government has committed $85 billion to the people of the gulf coast and New Orleans. We're removing debris and repairing highways and rebuilding stronger levees. We're providing business loans and housing assistance. Yet as we meet these immediate needs, we must also address deeper challenges that existed before the storm arrived.

In New Orleans and in other places, many of our fellow citizens have felt excluded from the promise of our country. The answer is not only temporary relief but schools that teach every child and job skills that bring upward mobility and more opportunities to own a home and start a business. As we recover from a disaster, let us also work for the day when all Americans are protected by justice, equal in hope, and rich in opportunity.

A hopeful society acts boldly to fight diseases like HIV/AIDS, which can be prevented and treated and defeated. More than a million Americans live with HIV, and half of all AIDS cases occur among African Americans. I ask Congress to reform and reauthorize the Ryan White Act and provide new funding to States, so we end the waiting lists for AIDS medicines in America. We will also lead a nationwide effort, working closely with African American churches and faith-based groups, to deliver rapid HIV tests to millions, end the stigma of AIDS, and come closer to the day when there are no new infections in America.

Fellow citizens, we've been called to leadership in a period of consequence. We've entered a great ideological conflict we did nothing to invite. We see great changes in science and commerce that will influence all our lives. Sometimes it can seem that history is turning in a wide arc toward an unknown shore. Yet the destination of history is determined by human action, and every great movement of history comes to a point of choosing.

Lincoln could have accepted peace at the cost of disunity and continued slavery. Martin Luther King could have stopped at Birmingham or at Selma and achieved only half a victory over segregation. The United States could have accepted the permanent division of Europe and been complicit in the oppression of others. Today, having come far in our own historical journey, we must decide: Will we turn back or finish well?

Before history is written down in books, it is written in courage. Like Americans before us, we will show that courage, and we will finish well. We will lead freedom's advance. We will compete and excel in the global economy. We will renew the defining moral commitments of this land. And so we move forward—optimistic about our country, faithful to its cause, and confident of the victories to come.

May God bless America.

Source: U.S. Executive Office of the President. "Address before a Joint Session of the Congress on the State of the Union." January 31, 2006. *Weekly Compilation of Presidential Documents* 42, no. 5 (February 6, 2006): 145–152. Washington, D.C.: National Archives and Records Administration. www.gpoaccess.gov/wcomp/v42no05.html (accessed October 31, 2006).

▬▬▬▬▬ DOCUMENT ▬▬▬▬▬

"Virginia Governor's Response to the State of the Union"

My fellow Americans, good evening.

I'm Tim Kaine, the governor of the commonwealth of Virginia. And it's an honor tonight to give the Democratic response to President Bush on behalf of my commonwealth, my fellow Democratic governors and the Democratic Party.

I worked as a missionary when I was a young man and I learned to measure my life by the difference I can make in someone else's life.

Coretta Scott King embodied that value. And tonight, as a nation, we mourn her passing.

Our faith and values teach us that there's no higher calling than serving others.

Our federal government should serve the American people. But that mission is frustrated by this administration's poor choices and bad management.

Families in the Gulf Coast see that as they wait to rebuild their lives. Americans who lose their jobs see that as they look to rebuild their careers. And our soldiers in Iraq see that as they try to rebuild a nation. As Americans, we do great things when we work together. Some of our leaders in Washington seem to have forgotten that.

I want to offer some good news tonight: There is a better way.

In Virginia—and other states—we're moving ahead by focusing on service, competent management and results. It's all about bringing people together to find common-sense solutions to our common problems.

That's how we in Virginia earned the ranking of America's "Best Managed State."

You know, no matter what political philosophy you hold or what state you call home, you have a right to expect that your government can deliver results.

When there's a crime or a fire, you expect that police and firefighters have the tools to respond. When there's a natural disaster, you expect a well-managed response. When you send your children to school, you expect them to be prepared for success. And, you have a right to expect government to be fiscally responsible, pay the bills and live within its means. Tonight we heard the president again call to make his tax policies permanent, despite his administration's failure to manage our staggering national debt.

Over the past five years, we've gone from huge surpluses to massive deficits.

Now, no parent makes their child pay the mortgage bill.

Why should we allow this administration to pass down the bill for its reckless spending to our children and grandchildren?

There's a better way.

Two years ago in Virginia, Democrats and Republicans worked together to reform our budget.

By focusing on results, we were able to keep the budget balanced, preserve our strong credit rating and protect the essential services that families rely on: education, health care, law enforcement.

States all across this country are doing this right now, as the federal government falls further and further into debt.

Think about what's occurring in education.

The administration's No Child Left Behind Act is wreaking havoc on local school districts. Despite the insistence of Democrats in Congress that the program should be funded as promised, the administration has opposed full funding and is refusing to let states try innovative alternatives.

Now the Republican leadership in Washington is actually cutting billions of dollars from the student loan programs that serve working families, helping to get their children through college.

There's a better way.

Last year, governors from across the country worked together in a bipartisan fashion to reform the senior year of high school to make it serve our students better.

Many states are working to make high-quality pre-kindergarten accessible to every family.

Congressional Democrats have a plan to educate 100,000 new engineers, scientists and mathematicians in the next four years. And in Virginia, Democrats and Republicans alike worked together to make record investments in education.

The results: more accredited schools, better student test scores.

Look at what's happening in health care. Skyrocketing costs are hurting small businesses and pushing millions of working Americans into the ranks of the uninsured.

The White House has made efforts to cut Medicaid funds for our most vulnerable citizens. Our seniors were promised that the new federal Medicare drug plan would make it easier and cheaper to obtain their medication.

Instead, many have fallen victim to the program's poor planning. They find getting their medicine to be more complex, more expensive and less reliable.

There's a better way.

Health care reforms have to focus on making the system serve consumers better. Many states, following the lead of Illinois, have set up simple ways to help seniors purchase safe,

American-made prescription drugs from other countries at a fraction of the price they would pay here.

And the administration actually fought against that Democratic effort.

In Virginia, we've worked to provide health insurance coverage for nearly 140,000 children who weren't covered four years ago. And Republicans and Democrats alike have come together to fight the administration's efforts to slash Medicaid and push more costs onto the states.

The president called again tonight for our commitment to win the war on terror and to support our troops. Every American embraces those goals. We can—we must—defeat those who attack and kill innocent people.

While the images of the World Trade Center are seared in the minds of all Americans, so too are the memories of those who died on sacred ground here in Virginia in the attack on the Pentagon.

Our commitment to winning the war on terror compels us to ask this question: Are the president's policies the best way to win this war?

We now know that the American people were given inaccurate information about reasons for invading Iraq. We now know that our troops in Iraq were not given the best body armor or the best intelligence.

We now know the administration wants to cut tens of thousands of troops from the Army Reserves and the National Guard at the very time that we're facing new and dangerous threats.

And we now know that the administration wants to further reduce military and veterans' benefits.

There's a better way.

Working together, we have to give our troops the tools they need to win the war on terror. And we can do it without sacrificing the liberty that we've sent our troops abroad to defend.

Our support has to begin here at home.

That's why we in Virginia—Democrats and Republicans—have reformed and enhanced our Department of Veterans Services to help our veterans and their family members access the federal benefits that they've earned. And we're working to provide state re-enlistment bonuses to honor those Virginians who stay in service to commonwealth and country.

When it comes to energy, Americans are using more than ever, paying more for it, and are more dependent on the Middle East than ever before.

There's a better way.

Last summer, I joined Democrats in Washington and in other states and called on oil companies to share in our sacrifice and return some of their record-breaking excess profits.

Democrats at both the state and national levels are leading the way on energy reforms, calling for greater public investments for alternative, advanced energy technologies. These investments will promote energy independence, boost the nation's economy, create jobs and strengthen national security.

The failure of the federal government to implement and enforce a rational immigration policy has resulted in a confusing patchwork of state and local efforts. Of course, we should welcome those who seek to lawfully join and contribute to our American family—and we must.

But at the same time, we have to ensure that our homeland defense efforts begin with consistent federal action to protect our borders.

The administration is falling behind in other critical areas: preserving the environment, keeping our workplaces safe, protecting family farms, keeping jobs in America.

Our communities are then left to deal with the challenges and the consequences of these federal failures without a reliable partner.

But we managed to find a better way.

The better way is to focus on service. It's about measuring what we do in terms of real results for real people.

It's not about partisanship or political spin. It's about protecting the rights endowed by our creator, fulfilling the principle of equality set out in our Declaration of Independence, and ensuring that the light of liberty shines on every American. If we want to replace the division that's been gripping our nation's capital, we need a change.

Democrats are leading that reform effort, working to restore honesty and openness to our government, working to replace a culture of partisanship and cronyism with an ethic of service and results.

Our greatest need is for America to heal its partisan wounds and become one people. You know, those are words Thomas Jefferson expressed after he was elected president. And they ring as true today as they did in 1800.

Tonight we pray, earnestly and humbly, for that healing and for the day when service returns again as the better way to a new national politics. We ask all Americans to join us in that effort because, together, America can do better.

Thank you for listening, and God bless the United States of America.

Source: Democratic National Committee. "Virginia Governor Tim Kaine's Response to the State of the Union." January 31, 2006. www.democrats.org/a/2006/02/virginia_govern_1.php (accessed October 31, 2006).

Other Historic Documents of Interest

February

President Bush and Judge Alito on Joining the Supreme Court

February 1, 2006

■■■■■■■■■■■■■ **THE DOCUMENT IN CONTEXT** ■■■■■■■■■■

Samuel A. Alito Jr., a federal appeals court judge with a solid conservative reputation, was formally sworn in as an associate justice of the United States Supreme Court on February 1, 2006, taking the seat vacated by Justice Sandra Day O'Connor. In recent years O'Connor often had been the deciding vote on the Court on many divisive issues, including abortion, the death penalty, and presidential powers. Alito's seating was considered a major victory for conservatives who had held President George W. Bush to his promise to name justices to the Court in the mold of its two most conservative members, Antonin Scalia and Clarence Thomas. These three justices, together with the new chief justice, John G. Roberts Jr., were expected to form a staunch conservative core, balanced by a core of the four more liberal justices (Stephen Breyer, Ruth Bader Ginsburg, David Souter, and John Paul Stevens). That left Justice Anthony M. Kennedy, a conservative who occasionally sided with the liberal bloc on some issues, as the most likely justice to assume the centrist role held by O'Connor.

In his first months in office, Alito did not disappoint his supporters. In important cases involving presidential authority during wartime, search and seizure, and the application of the death penalty, Alito sided with the conservatives. The shape of the new Court was likely to emerge in the 2006–2007 term, when the Court was scheduled to decide cases on abortion, affirmative action, and global warming.

Bush's Third Nominee

Alito was actually Bush's third nominee to fill O'Connor's seat. After she announced her retirement on July 1, 2005, the president nominated Roberts as her replacement. But when Chief Justice William H. Rehnquist died of thyroid cancer on September 3, 2005, Bush nominated Roberts as chief justice. A highly respected attorney sitting on the U.S. Court of Appeals for the District of Columbia, Roberts was a conservative jurist in Rehnquist's mold and easily won confirmation in time for the opening of the 2005–2006 term.

Bush's second choice to fill O'Connor's seat was White House counsel Harriet Miers. She was forced to withdraw her nomination three weeks later in the face of strong opposition from Bush's conservative political base who questioned her commitment to their positions on abortion and other key issues. Bush then turned to Alito, who had been a judge on the U.S. Court of Appeals for the Third Circuit in Philadelphia since 1990 and had worked in the Justice Department during the Reagan administration. *(Roberts, Miers nominations, Historic Documents of 2005, p. 558)*

Alito was born in 1950 to Italian-American parents in Trenton, New Jersey. He attended Princeton University and Yale Law School during the tumultuous years of the 1960s and early 1970s. Classmates described him as consistent, studious, and a proponent of orderly change, but one who generally kept his views to himself. One of his college professors wrote that "the logic and precision that Mr. Alito uses in both oral and written presentations is almost palpable. None of it is aggressive, indeed sometimes it is self-effacing."

Upon graduation from Yale, Alito clerked for Appeals Court Judge Leonard I. Garth in Newark, N.J., and then worked in the appellate section of the U.S. attorney's office in Newark. Alito moved to Washington in August 1981 to work in the solicitor general's office in the Reagan administration, and in 1985 he became a deputy assistant attorney general in the Office of Legal Counsel at the Department of Justice. President George H. W. Bush named Alito to the federal appeals court in 1990.

Conservatives were delighted with Alito's nomination to the Supreme Court for the same reason that many liberals were appalled—his record both in the Justice Department and on the bench indicated that he was likely to move the Supreme Court to the right. Liberals were particularly concerned about his views on abortion and individual and civil rights; they also said he was too quick to support government and big business over individuals and the elected branches of government over the judiciary.

Confirmation Hearings

Precisely because of his conservative record and because he would be replacing the more centrist O'Connor, Alito was expected to face tough scrutiny both from the public and during his Senate confirmation hearings. But attempts to rally significant opposition to the nomination fell flat.

Immediately after Bush announced Alito's nomination on October 31, 2005, both supporters and opponents kicked their public campaigns aimed at influencing Senate votes into high gear. Democrats particularly had hoped that by drawing attention to what they saw as Alito's extremist views, they could raise the same levels of public opposition that helped them defeat the nomination of Robert H. Bork in 1987 and nearly defeat the nomination of Clarence Thomas in 1991. But according to opinion polling, the campaigns for and against Alito barely registered with the public. Most polls showed Republicans favoring Alito's confirmation, with Democrats and those identifying themselves as liberals about evenly split. "A groundswell of opposition hasn't arisen," Andrew Kohut, director of the Pew Research Center for People and the Press, told the *Washington Post* before the confirmation hearings began on January 9. *(Bork nomination, Historic Documents of 1987, p. 717; Thomas nomination, Historic Documents of 1991, p. 551)*

Senate Democrats on the Judiciary Committee fared little better during the confirmation hearings. During four days of questioning, senators were unable to shake the nominee, who answered questions deftly and patiently. Asked, for example, about a 1985 application for a job at the Justice Department in which he wrote that the Constitution did not protect the right to an abortion, Alito acknowledged that the statement was "a true expression of my views at the time." But he added that he had been acting as an attorney then and that, as a judge, he would "approach the question with an open mind" if confirmed. He said precedent deserved great respect, but added that following precedent was "not an inexorable command"—the same wording Rehnquist once used to argue in favor of overturning *Roe v. Wade,* the 1973 case that upheld a woman's constitutional right to an abortion.

On the issue of the day—the recent revelations that the president had authorized the warrantless surveillance of Americans' phone calls and e-mails under certain conditions—Alito affirmed that no one, "no matter how high or powerful," was "above the law." But he skirted the question whether Bush had exceeded his authority when he issued the surveillance order. Such issues, he said, "are obviously very difficult and important and complicated questions that are quite likely to arise in litigation perhaps in my own court or before the Supreme Court." He did say that he endorsed O'Connor's statement in the case of *Hamdi v. Rumsfeld* in 2004 that "a state of war is not a blank check for the president when it comes to the rights of citizens." When asked about another statement in the 1985 job application in which he appeared to endorse "the supremacy of the elected branches of government," Alito disavowed it. "It's an inapt phrase and I certainly didn't mean that literally at the time, and I wouldn't say that today. The branches of the government are equal."

Seeking to raise questions about Alito's ethics, Democratic senators also asked Alito about his failure to recuse himself in an appeals court case involving a mutual fund in which he had invested money. Alito told the senators that the case had slipped through the court's screening process for conflicts of interest. Once the plaintiff challenged the potential conflict, Alito said, he stepped aside as a judge and the case was reheard by other judges on the appeals court. He added that he wished he had never heard the case in the first place.

Alito also denied having any memory of joining a group, Concerned Alumni of Princeton, although he had listed the organization as one of his conservative bona fides in his 1985 job application. That group had opposed the admission of women and minorities to the school, and liberals had hoped to use Alito's membership as evidence of his hostility to those groups. Alito told the committee that the "important thing" was that he did not share the views the group was purported to represent. "They're not my views now; they never were my views. They represent things that I deplored. I have always deplored any form of racial discrimination or bigotry. I was never opposed to the admission of women at Princeton."

Frustrated Democrats accused Alito of not revealing enough of his beliefs in his answers. "A response is not an answer," Sen. Charles E. Schumer, D-N.Y., said at one point. "You've responded to more than 300 questions, but in all due respect you haven't answered enough of them." Although Alito was deft at avoiding direct answers, reporters and others covering the hearings noted that Democratic senators were often inept in their questioning, frequently failing to follow up on their own questions or taking most of their allotted time in talking themselves rather than probing the nominee. In the end the committee approved Alito's nomination on a 10–8 party-line vote.

When the nomination came to the Senate floor on January 30, Massachusetts Democrats Edward M. Kennedy and John Kerry mounted a quixotic bid to filibuster the nomination, but in its first roll call of the year, the Senate easily agreed to invoke cloture. The vote was 72–25—twelve more votes than needed to cut off debate. Nineteen Democrats, many of whom opposed Alito's confirmation, nonetheless voted to cut off debate. Alito was confirmed the following day, January 31. The vote was 58–42, the second closest vote for a confirmed nominee, after that for Thomas, in modern times. Alito was sworn in at a private ceremony later that day and made his first public appearance as a justice of the Supreme Court at the president's State of the Union address that evening. On February 1, Alito was sworn in again at a public ceremony in the White House. In his brief remarks, Alito pledged to "do everything in my power to live up to the trust that has been placed in me."

Early Record on the Court

Because he joined the Court in the middle of its 2005–2006 term, Alito did not participate in every decision issued between his swearing-in and the end of the term. But in at least two cases the new justice appeared to have reversed O'Connor's likely vote and the outcome of the case. Both cases had been argued before O'Connor left the Court upon Alito's confirmation, and both were then reargued, indicating that O'Connor's was the deciding vote and that Alito's view of the issue differed from hers. In the case of *Hudson v. Michigan,* Alito joined with Roberts, Scalia, Thomas, and Kennedy to hold that evidence obtained when police entered a house without following the established "knock and announce" procedure did not have to be suppressed. The liberal bloc on the court argued that the ruling effectively gutted any meaningful protection from unlawful search and seizures. In the case of *Kansas v. Marsh,* Alito again voted with the four other conservatives to uphold a Kansas law that required the imposition of the death sentence when a jury gave equal weight to mitigating and aggravating evidence. The Kansas Supreme Court had found the law unconstitutional, saying that it created an impermissible presumption in favor of death and thus violated the Eighth Amendment ban on cruel and unusual punishment.

Alito also confirmed his conservative views on presidential powers in the case of *Hamdan v. Rumsfeld,* in which the Court, by a 5–4 vote, ruled that the military tribunal system President Bush had set up to try alleged enemy combatants imprisoned at Guantanamo Bay, Cuba, violated U.S. and international law. Although Alito had said during his confirmation hearings that he did not believe in "the supremacy" of the elected branches of government, he joined a dissent by Thomas saying that the judiciary had a "duty to respect the Executive's judgment in matters of military operations and foreign affairs." He also joined a separate dissent by Scalia endorsing the use of presidential "signing statements"—the declarations presidents make when signing a bill into law, thus setting out their interpretation of the executive branch's duties under the new statute. Since his days in the Justice Department, Alito had been a strong proponent of the use of signing statements to create a record that federal courts could weigh along with the legislative record in interpreting the intentions underlying a particular statute.

Following is the text of remarks made by President George W. Bush and Justice Samuel A. Alito Jr. on the occasion of Alito's formal swearing-in as an associate justice of the United States Supreme Court at the White House on February 1, 2006.

▬▬▬▬▬▬ DOCUMENT ▬▬▬▬▬▬

"Swearing-in Ceremony for Associate Justice Samuel Alito"

President George W. Bush: Good afternoon. Laura and I welcome you to the White House. Mr. Chief Justice [John Roberts], thank you for coming. Members of the Supreme Court, thank you all for being here. Members of the Senate, honored you're here. Ladies and gentlemen, appreciate you joining us on this historic occasion. . . .

Yesterday the United States Senate confirmed Sam Alito as the 110th Justice of the Supreme Court of the United States. Last night [at the State of the Union Address] he looked pretty good in that black robe sitting there.

It's a proud day for Judge Alito and his entire family. We extend a special welcome to Martha, who has been at his side for more than 20 years. And with us, you can see his son, Phil, and daughter, Laura. If they're anything like our daughters, they're probably telling their dad how to behave and how to testify.

I appreciate Rosemary [Alito's sister] being with us today, and we're thinking of Sam's mom, Rose, who turned 91 in December. And of course, as we think of Rose, we think of her husband, Sam's late father. He came to our country as an immigrant from Italy in 1914. Sam Alito, Sr. instilled in his son a deep commitment to serving his fellow Americans. And I'm sure he's looking down with pride as Sam takes his place on the highest court of the United States of America.

Sam Alito is replacing an extraordinary Justice, Sandra Day O'Connor. Justice O'Connor has been an admired member of the Supreme Court for 24 years. She has served our nation with decency and spirit and great devotion, and I thank her on behalf of all the American people. . . .

Judge Alito becomes Justice Alito. As he becomes Justice Alito, our nation completes a process that was ordained by our founders in Philadelphia more than 200 years ago. Under the Constitution, the President nominates, and by and with the consent—advice and consent of the Senate, appoints the justices of the Supreme Court. This process has been carried out many times since the beginning of our democracy. And each new appointment represents a renewal of the promise of our country and our constitutional order.

Our founders thought carefully about the role they wanted judges to play in the American republic. They decided on a court system that would be independent from political or public pressure, with judges who serve for life. America expects members of our judiciary to be prudent in exercising judicial power, and firm in defending judicial independence. So every member of the Supreme Court takes an oath to uphold the Constitution and administer justice faithfully and impartially. This is a solemn responsibility.

And the man we honor today has demonstrated his devotion to our courts and law through years of service to our country. Sam Alito has distinguished himself as a member of our military, a federal prosecutor, assistant to the Solicitor General, U.S. Attorney in New Jersey, and for the last 15 years, a highly respected judge on the Third Circuit Court of Appeals.

Sam Alito is known for his steady demeanor, careful judgment and complete integrity. Throughout his career he has treated others with respect. In return he has earned the admiration of his colleagues on the bench, the lawyers who have come before it, and, of course, a very devoted group of proud law clerks.

During the confirmation process, the American people saw a man of character and legal brilliance. Like our fellow citizens, I was impressed by the dignity Sam—by the dignity Sam Alito and his family displayed during the Senate hearings, and by the thoughtful scholarship and reverence of the Constitution that have always defined his approach to the law.

A Supreme Court justice must meet the highest standard of legal excellence, while serving with humility and fidelity to our founding promise of equal justice under the law. These are qualities Americans want in a Supreme Court justice. These are qualities Americans see in Sam Alito. He will make a superb justice of the Supreme Court, and I know this son of New Jersey will make all Americans proud.

Sam, I thank you for agreeing to serve our country again, and for accepting this new call to duty.

Now I ask the Chief Justice of the United States, John Roberts, to please step forward and administer the oath.

[The oath of office is administered.]

Justice Samuel A. Alito: I'm really overwhelmed by this occasion, and I thank you all for that applause, and thank you for coming.

And thank you very much, Mr. President. Thank you for nominating me, and for all of the time and attention and personal support and encouragement that you have given to me and to my family at every step of this process, from the nomination all the way through the confirmation. My family and I are deeply—.

I am very thankful for all the people who helped me get through the past three months. And I really wish that I could name them all, but we would be here all afternoon if I did that. . . .

As I said, I feel bad that I can't mention everybody's name. But I hope they all know how much I appreciate everything that they've done for me.

I want to express my gratitude to members of the Senate. I will always be very grateful to Chairman Specter for ensuring that—for the very fair and expert way in which the proceedings before the Senate Judiciary Committee were conducted, and to all of the members of the Judiciary Committee who ensured that the record of the hearing contained all the information that was necessary for a fair assessment of my nomination.

I also—I'm very grateful to Senator [Bill] Frist and to Senator [Mitch] McConnell for all of their efforts, and for all the members of the Senate who supported me and gave fair and conscientious consideration to my nomination. Thank you very much.

Many people helped me at various stages of my legal career, and I hope they all know how much I appreciate what they've done for me. And again, I'd love to mention everybody, but I won't do that. But I hope they know how much it means to me that so many of them are here today, and all the things that they've done for me.

This is a very happy occasion for me, but I am sorry to be leaving some wonderful colleagues on the United States Court of Appeal for the Third Circuit. But I'm comforted by the fact that we will always be close friends. And I was very touched yesterday by the extremely gracious and warm reception that I received from my new colleagues.

During my 15 years on the Court of Appeals my law clerks were absolutely indispensable. And I can't begin to tell them how much I appreciate all the things that they did for me over the last three months.

My family, as usual, has been incredible. They mean everything to me, and I hope they know how much I love them and how much their support has meant to me.

And finally, I want to express my thanks from the bottom of my heart to the many people—friends and neighbors and colleagues and many other people who have gone out of their way since the day of my nomination to extend words of support and encouragement to me. So many people have written me letters; so many people from all walks of life have stopped me on the street to tell me that they were praying for me and for members of my family. And the prayers of so many diverse people around the country have been a really palpable and a powerful force. And I'm very grateful to all of them.

I don't think that anyone can become a justice of the Supreme Court of the United States without feeling a tremendous weight of responsibility and a tremendous sense of humility. And of course, it's particularly humbling to try to succeed Justice O'Connor, to whom the country owes such a great debt of gratitude for her tremendous service.

I will not go on too long. I will just conclude by saying that the many letters that I've received over the past three months have reminded me how much the people of the United States revere our Constitution and our form of government, and how much they look to the Supreme Court of the United States to protect our form of government and our freedoms. That is an awesome responsibility. And in light of that, I think it's only—only very simple and very sincere words are appropriate in closing. And so I simply pledge that I will do everything in my power to live up to the trust that has been placed in me.

Thank you very much.

Source: U.S. Executive Office of the President. Office of the Press Secretary. "President Attends Swearing-in Ceremony for Associate Justice Samuel Alito." February 1, 2006. www.whitehouse.gov/news/releases/2006/02/20060201-4.html (accessed November 16, 2006).

Other Historic Documents of Interest

London Conference "Compact" on Afghanistan

February 1, 2006

■■■■■■■■■ **THE DOCUMENT IN CONTEXT** ■■■■■■■■■

The international community stepped up its efforts to bolster the struggling government of Afghanistan in 2006, first by promising billions of dollars in additional aid and then by boosting a NATO-led military force that was attempting to quell a resurgence of the Taliban—the extreme Islamist group that ruled the country before the United States military invaded in October 2001. Both aspects of this international effort encountered serious trouble, and by year's end Afghanistan appeared to be once again teetering on the brink of chaos.

U.S. military leaders in Afghanistan said the Taliban and other insurgent groups were taking advantage of the country's weak governing institutions, which controlled little more than the capital of Kabul. Strengthening the pro-Western government was the only long-term solution, officials said, but on many days it was difficult to see much progress. *(Background, Historic Documents of 2005, p. 970)*

The Political Situation

Weeks after the U.S. invasion that ousted the Taliban from power in 2001, the United Nations convened a conference in Bonn, Germany, of Afghan leaders. That conference led to the appointment of Hamid Karzai, a leader of Afghanistan's largest ethnic group, the Pashtuns, to head an interim government. Karzai in 2004 won election to a five-year term as president of a new permanent government, and in 2005 Afghans went to the polls again to select a new parliament, which convened for the first time that December.

Much of 2006 was consumed by political struggles in Kabul, as Karzai and the new parliament each attempted to define their powers in the new world of collective, democratic decision making. Karzai, who had governed alone for nearly three years but whose authority had been limited primarily to Kabul, appeared by 2006 to be a frequently indecisive leader who tolerated corrupt or incompetent aides and was eager to appease political opponents in hopes of preventing challenges to his authority. A skilled diplomat with many years of experience on the world stage, Karzai retained strong support from the U.S. and European governments, but aid workers and other foreigners responsible for carrying out the policies of backing his government were becoming increasingly disenchanted by 2006—as were many of Karzai's constituents. Sixty members of parliament signed a petition in August complaining about the appointment of corrupt officials; news reports said such complaints were increasingly common, even at the local level, where people complained of having to pay bribes to get any service from government officials, including judges and policemen.

For its part, the new parliament was dominated by former warlords and tribal leaders who appeared to be more interested in serving narrow ethnic or regional interests than those of the country as a whole. The parliament ratified most of Karzai's proposals that were submitted to it in 2006, but legislators rejected five of the president's cabinet appointments and his initial nominee to head the supreme court, in the latter case on grounds of excessive corruption. Many governments at the provincial and local levels either were nonexistent, corrupt, or led by men who were afraid to alienate sources of power, including the Taliban.

In an unblinking report to the Security Council on September 11, UN Secretary General Kofi Annan noted several "worrying trends" about the parliament, including corruption and the refusal of several members to break their ties with armed militias and criminal networks. Warlords and other "traditional power brokers" also threatened legislators with impunity, Annan said.

An even tougher assessment of the government's failures came in a November 2 report by the International Crisis Group, a Brussels-based policy institute that since 2002 had warned of failings by Karzai's government and its international sponsors. "Today, people are pulling back from a government that is failing them, if not preying on them," the report said, noting that even some people who previously had supported the government were now thoroughly disillusioned by it.

A few voices within Afghanistan spoke out against the corruption and apparent impunity of warlords and narcotics traffickers. One of the most outspoken was Malali Joya, a female member of parliament from the province of Farah who denounced some of her fellow legislators in a speech on May 7—provoking a brief melee within the parliament chambers. Joya repeated her charges the next day, saying: "They may kill me, they may slash my neck. I will never stop my words against the criminals, against the drug dealers."

The London "Compact"

During the first four years after Karzai took office as Afghanistan's interim leader, the United States and other international donors provided about $9 billion to build governing institutions and to reconstruct a country that had been largely destroyed by nearly three decades of war; of the total, about $4 billion came from the United States and the rest from Great Britain, Japan, other countries, and international institutions such as the World Bank.

The aid was used to construct hundreds of new schools and health clinics, rebuild the country's most vital roads, support the new government, and make a start toward meeting the many needs of a modern society. Even so, most reports said that by 2006 the vast majority of Afghanistan's more than 30 million residents were only marginally better off than before the U.S. invasion. Shoppers in Kabul could now buy fine French perfumes (if they had the money), but life for the impoverished rural majority remained much the same.

As a follow-up to the earlier international promises on Afghanistan's behalf, the British government and the United Nations sponsored a conference in London on January 31 and February 1 to ratify a new "compact" between Karzai's government and the international community. The compact was drafted jointly by representatives from Afghanistan and sixty countries and institutions such as the United Nations and the World Bank. Officials at the London meeting did not formally vote on the compact, but their presence generally was assumed to signify the support of the countries and institutions they represented. The UN Security Council endorsed the compact two weeks later, saying in Resolution 1659 that it provided "the framework for the partnership between the Afghan government and the international community."

In a speech to the London conference on January 31, Karzai thanked donor countries and institutions for their "generous support," which he said had enabled 6 million children to attend schools, had made creation of his new government possible, and had begun the process of building other national institutions such as the army and police. In a reminder that the September 11, 2001, terrorist attacks had been planned by the al Qaeda network from its headquarters in Afghanistan, Karzai also said other countries had a self-interest in what happened in his country: "Ladies and gentlemen, a stable, peaceful and prosperous Afghanistan is not a blessing for the Afghans alone; it is for all of us," he said. *(Background, Historic Documents of 2001, pp. 614, 627)*

The compact laid out what it called three essential "pillars" supporting Afghanistan's future: security, governance (including rule of law and human rights), and economic and social development. In contrast to many international documents that made sweeping promises but had little to back them up, the core of the Afghan compact was an annex setting out detailed "benchmarks and timelines" under which Karzai's government pledged to take specific steps (for example, ratifying a UN anticorruption treaty); in turn, donor nations and institutions promised financial and technical support to help the government carry out those steps. The London conference also issued, although not as part of the compact, a list of $10.5 billion in "preliminary" aid pledges for a five-year program called the Interim Afghanistan National Development Strategy. The United States commitment was $4 billion, followed by $1.2 billion from the World Bank, $1 billion from the Asian Development Bank, and $885 million from Great Britain.

Despite the specific promises in the compact, it was just a matter of weeks before the deadlines began slipping. The first delay came in March when all deadlines were pushed back by three months. The stated purpose was to put the deadlines in compliance with Afghanistan's use of a solar calendar, under which the year started with the beginning of spring in late March; most observers, however, said the shift simply was an attempt to give Karzai's government more time to carry out its promises.

Compliance with the compact was to be monitored by a committee of officials from Afghanistan, the United Nations, and other organizations, called the Joint Coordination and Monitoring Board. That group issued its first assessment of the compact in November, saying there had been only "limited progress" on most of the promised steps but that at least seven benchmarks would be reached by March 2007. Some experts said the most important of these benchmarks was creation of a system to ensure that the officials Karzai appointed to high-level posts were qualified and not tainted by corruption. Karzai established such a system just before the September 30 deadline.

A rare bit of good news for the economy came on September 10, when Karzai presided over the opening of a Coca-Cola bottling plant in Kabul. The plant, which was to employ 600 people, was the first major new factory in Afghanistan in many years.

Narcotics Production

Afghanistan's many problems were made worse by the country's narcotics trade, which remained the most successful element of the economy, generating an estimated $3 billion annually. Afghanistan for years had been the world's foremost source of opium poppies, which were used to make heroin. The Taliban had cracked down on the cultivation of poppies during their years in power, but after they were ousted farmers rushed thousands of acres back into production and staunchly resisted U.S.-funded eradication programs.

Officials said the cultivation of poppies, and the subsequent production of opium, fell in 2005, only to rise again in 2006. According to U.S. figures, in 2005 cultivation dropped by 48 percent from the previous year, but because of "favorable climate conditions" the production of opium fell only 10 percent. The trend was sharply upward in 2006 when, according to United Nations figures released in September, poppy cultivation increased by 59 percent over 2005 and production of opium surged by nearly 50 percent, from 4,100 tons to 6,100 tons.

A joint report by the World Bank and the UN's Office on Drugs and Crime, issued on November 28, painted a pessimistic picture of international efforts to stem Afghanistan's narcotics trade, which was aided by a convergence of interest between the Taliban and narcotics traffickers, often in league with corrupt government officials. The report noted that narcotics traffickers sought protection not only from the Taliban but also from "high-level" government officials. Without mentioning names of individuals, the report cited a "complex pyramid of protection and patronage, effectively providing state protection to criminal trafficking activities."

U.S.-funded eradication campaigns had adversely affected poor farmers, the report said, while in many cases opium production merely moved from one province to another. Antonio Maria Costa, executive director of the UN's antinarcotics agency, said eradication programs would not be successful until the Afghan government "sacked" corrupt officials and prosecuted everyone involved in the narcotics trade. A similar report, released in early December by the inspectors general of the U.S. Defense and State departments, said Afghanistan's narcotics industry was controlled by twenty-five to thirty key traffickers, most in southern Afghanistan, "working closely with sponsors in top government and political positions."

Karzai and Musharraf on Border Problems

The year's upsurge in violence by the Taliban led almost inevitably to heightened tensions between the governments of Afghanistan and Pakistan. Both had become heavily dependent on the United States since 2001 but were divided by historical forces even stronger than the British-drawn Durand Line that served as their mutual border.

The most recent divisions between the two countries dated back just two decades. In the 1980s Pakistan had been the main base from which the United States, Saudi Arabia, and other countries had supplied weapons to the Islamist guerilla warriors known as the *mujahidin* and warlords who were battling the Soviet Union's occupation of Afghanistan. Pakistan also played a central role in the bloody civil war among Afghanistan's various factions during the decade after the Soviets left in 1989. The Taliban eventually emerged as the victor in this conflict, thanks in large part to aid from Pakistan's military intelligence services.

Pakistan continued to be the main patron of the Taliban right up until the United States invaded Afghanistan in October 2001. After that invasion, Pakistan's military president, Pervez Musharraf, pledged to support the U.S. effort to implant a stable new government in Afghanistan, but in subsequent years his government appeared to do little to restrain Taliban leaders and fighters who had taken up residence in Pakistan.

Early in 2006 Karzai's government began producing evidence supporting its claim that Pakistan was doing nothing to stop Taliban attacks across the borders. One piece of evidence supporting the Afghan claim was a series of taped interviews of three Pakistanis who were arrested by Afghan authorities in January; they described how they and others had been recruited inside Pakistan to carry out attacks in Afghanistan.

At a meeting in February Karzai gave Musharraf a list of Taliban and al Qaeda leaders he said were hiding in Pakistan. In particular, Karzai reportedly said that former Taliban leader Mullah Mohammed Omar and several of his senior associates were living in Quetta, the capital of Pakistan's Baluchistan province, about 120 miles south of Kandahar.

The two sides traded more charges about Pakistan's involvement in the violence, but on September 7 Musharraf traveled to Kabul and acknowledged, for the first time, that al Qaeda and Taliban fighters "are crossing from the Pakistan side and causing bomb blasts in Afghanistan." Even so, he insisted his government did not support these attacks and, in fact, was rounding up members of both militant groups.

Musharraf's appearance in Kabul came just two days after his government signed an agreement with tribal elders in North Waziristan, a lawless region of Pakistan abutting Afghanistan's eastern border. That agreement essentially gave a free hand to al Qaeda and Taliban fighters operating in the area, so long as they promised not to attack Afghanistan—a promise that Pakistan had no real way of enforcing. U.S. officials later said a surge in Taliban attacks could be attributed, at least in part, to the freedom of movement the Pakistan agreement gave them. The *New York Times* on December 11 quoted diplomats and intelligence officials as saying the agreement had made North Waziristan "virtually a Taliban ministate."

Karzai and Musharraf met again on September 27, this time on relatively neutral territory: at a White House dinner presided over by President George W. Bush. In the run-up to that session, Karzai again accused Musharraf of failing to crack down on the Taliban, and Musharraf compared Karzai to "an ostrich" who failed to deal with problems at home. Despite this spat, the leaders emerged from their private discussion with Bush insisting it had generated "positive" action. However, U.S. officials later acknowledged that Bush had been unable to get concrete pledges from Musharraf to crack down on Afghan insurgents on his side of the border.

Karzai kept up the verbal pressure on his neighbor, telling reporters on December 12 that Pakistan, as well as Afghanistan, would "run into hell" if the Taliban were not defeated. "The state of Pakistan was supporting the Taliban [before 2001], so we presume if there is still any Taliban, that they are still being supported by a state element," he said. This last phrase appeared to refer to Pakistan's military intelligence service, which had long been a source of official support for the Taliban.

Following are excerpts from the Afghanistan Compact, presented on February 1, 2006, to the London Conference on Afghanistan, which was attended by representatives from Afghanistan and sixty donor nations and international organizations. The compact set out specific steps to be taken by the Afghan government to improve security, governance, and economic and social development, along with pledges of assistance by the international community.

DOCUMENT

"The Afghanistan Compact"

The Islamic Republic of Afghanistan and the international community:

Determined to strengthen their partnership to improve the lives of Afghan people, and to contribute to national, regional, and global peace and security;

Affirming their shared commitment to continue, in the spirit of the Bonn, Tokyo and Berlin conferences, to work toward a stable and prosperous Afghanistan, with good governance and human rights protection for all under the rule of law, and to maintain and strengthen that commitment over the term of this Compact and beyond;

Recognising the courage and determination of Afghans who, by defying violent extremism and hardship, have laid the foundations for a democratic, peaceful, pluralistic and prosperous state based on the principles of Islam;

Noting the full implementation of the Bonn Agreement through the adoption of a new constitution in January 2004, and the holding of presidential elections in October 2004 and National Assembly and Provincial Council elections in September 2005, which have enabled Afghanistan to regain its rightful place in the international community;

Mindful that Afghanistan's transition to peace and stability is not yet assured, and that strong international engagement will continue to be required to address remaining challenges;

Resolved to overcome the legacy of conflict in Afghanistan by setting conditions for sustainable economic growth and development; strengthening state institutions and civil society; removing remaining terrorist threats; meeting the challenge of counter-narcotics; rebuilding capacity and infrastructure; reducing poverty; and meeting basic human needs;

Have agreed to this Afghanistan Compact.

Purpose

The Afghan Government has articulated its overarching goals for the well-being of its people in the *Afghanistan Millennium Development Goals Country Report 2005—Vision 2020.* Consistent with those goals, this Compact identifies three critical and interdependent areas or pillars of activity for the five years from the adoption of this Compact:

1. Security;
2. Governance, Rule of Law and Human Rights; and
3. Economic and Social Development.

A further vital and cross-cutting area of work is eliminating the narcotics industry, which remains a formidable threat to the people and state of Afghanistan, the region and beyond.

The Afghan Government hereby commits itself to realising this shared vision of the future; the international community, in turn, commits itself to provide resources and support to realise that vision. Annex I of this Compact sets out detailed outcomes, benchmarks and timelines for delivery, consistent with the high-level goals set by the Afghanistan National Development Strategy (ANDS). The Government and international community also commit themselves to improve the effectiveness and accountability of international assistance as set forth in Annex II.

Principles of Cooperation

As the Afghan Government and the international community embark on the implementation of this Compact, they will:

1. Respect the pluralistic culture, values and history of Afghanistan, based on Islam;
2. Work on the basis of partnership between the Afghan Government, with its sovereign responsibilities, and the international community, with a central and impartial coordinating role for the United Nations;
3. Engage further the deep-seated traditions of participation and aspiration to ownership of the Afghan people;
4. Pursue fiscal, institutional and environmental sustainability;
5. Build lasting Afghan capacity and effective state and civil society institutions, with particular emphasis on building up human capacities of men and women alike;
6. Ensure balanced and fair allocation of domestic and international resources in order to offer all parts of the country tangible prospects of well-being;
7. Recognise in all policies and programmes that men and women have equal rights and responsibilities;
8. Promote regional cooperation; and
9. Combat corruption and ensure public transparency and accountability.

Security

Genuine security remains a fundamental prerequisite for achieving stability and development in Afghanistan. Security cannot be provided by military means alone. It requires good governance, justice and the rule of law, reinforced by reconstruction and development. With the support of the international community, the Afghan Government will consolidate peace by disbanding all illegal armed groups. The Afghan Government and the international community will create a secure environment by strengthening Afghan institutions to meet the security needs of the country in a fiscally sustainable manner.

To that end, the NATO-led International Security Assistance Force (ISAF), the US-led Operation Enduring Freedom (OEF) and partner nations involved in security sector reform will continue to provide strong support to the Afghan Government in establishing and sustaining security and stability in Afghanistan, subject to participating states' national approval procedures. They will continue to strengthen and develop the capacity of the national security forces to ensure that they become fully functional. All OEF counter-terrorism operations will be conducted in close coordination with the Afghan Government and ISAF. ISAF will continue to expand its presence throughout Afghanistan, including through Provincial Reconstruction Teams (PRTs), and will continue to promote stability and support security sector reforms in its areas of operation.

Full respect for Afghanistan's sovereignty and strengthening dialogue and cooperation between Afghanistan and its neighbours constitute an essential guarantee of stability in Afghanistan and the region. The international community will support concrete confidence-building measures to this end.

Governance, Rule of Law and Human Rights

Democratic governance and the protection of human rights constitute the cornerstone of sustainable political progress in Afghanistan. The Afghan Government will rapidly expand its capacity to provide basic services to the population throughout the country. It will recruit competent and credible professionals to public service on the basis of merit; establish a more effective, accountable and transparent administration at all levels of Government; and implement measurable improvements in fighting corruption, upholding justice and the rule of law and promoting respect for the human rights of all Afghans.

The Afghan Government will give priority to the coordinated establishment in each province of functional institutions—including civil administration, police, prisons and judiciary. These institutions will have appropriate legal frameworks and appointment procedures; trained staff; and adequate remuneration, infrastructure and auditing capacity. The Government will establish a fiscally and institutionally sustainable administration for future elections under the supervision of the Afghanistan Independent Electoral Commission.

Reforming the justice system will be a priority for the Afghan Government and the international community. The aim will be to ensure equal, fair and transparent access to justice for all based upon written codes with fair trials and enforceable verdicts. Measures will include: completing legislative reforms for the public as well as the private sector; building the capacity of judicial institutions and personnel; promoting human rights and legal awareness; and rehabilitating judicial infrastructure.

The Afghan Government and the international community reaffirm their commitment to the protection and promotion of rights provided for in the Afghan constitution and under applicable international law, including the international human rights covenants and other instruments to which Afghanistan is party. With a view to rebuilding trust among those whose lives were shattered by war, reinforcing a shared sense of citizenship and a culture of tolerance, pluralism and observance of the rule of law, the Afghan Government with the support of the international community will implement the Action Plan on Peace, Justice and Reconciliation.

Economic and Social Development

The Afghan Government with the support of the international community will pursue high rates of sustainable economic growth with the aim of reducing hunger, poverty and unemployment. It will promote the role and potential of the private sector, alongside those of the public and non-profit sectors; curb the narcotics industry; ensure macroeconomic stability; restore and promote the development of the country's human, social and physical capital, thereby establishing a sound basis for a new generation of leaders and professionals; strengthen civil society; and complete the reintegration of returnees, internally displaced persons and ex-combatants.

Public investments will be structured around the six sectors of the pillar on economic and social development of the Afghanistan National Development Strategy:

1. Infrastructure and natural resources;
2. Education;
3. Health;
4. Agriculture and rural development;

5. Social protection; and
6. Economic governance and private sector development.

In each of these areas, the objective will be to achieve measurable results towards the goal of equitable economic growth that reduces poverty, expands employment and enterprise creation, enhances opportunities in the region and improves the well-being of all Afghans.

Counter-Narcotics—A Cross-Cutting Priority

Meeting the threat that the narcotics industry poses to national, regional and international security as well as the development and governance of the country and the well-being of Afghans will be a priority for the Government and the international community. The aim will be to achieve a sustained and significant reduction in the production and trafficking of narcotics with a view to complete elimination. Essential elements include improved interdiction, law enforcement and judicial capacity building; enhanced cooperation among Afghanistan, neighbouring countries and the international community on disrupting the drugs trade; wider provision of economic alternatives for farmers and labourers in the context of comprehensive rural development; and building national and provincial counter-narcotics institutions. It will also be crucial to enforce a zero-tolerance policy towards official corruption; to pursue eradication as appropriate; to reinforce the message that producing or trading opiates is both immoral and a violation of Islamic law; and to reduce the demand for the illicit use of opiates.

Coordination and Monitoring

The Afghan Government and the international community are establishing a Joint Co-ordination and Monitoring Board for the implementation of the political commitments that comprise this Compact. As detailed in Annex III, this Board will be co-chaired by the Afghan Government and the United Nations and will be supported by a small secretariat. It will ensure greater coherence of efforts by the Afghan Government and international community to implement the Compact and provide regular and timely public reports on its execution.

Annex I: Benchmarks and Timelines

The Afghan Government, with the support of the international community, is committed to achieving the following benchmarks in accordance with the timelines specified.

Security

International Security Forces
Through end–2010, with the support of and in close coordination with the Afghan Government, the NATO-led International Security Assistance Force (ISAF), Operation Enduring Freedom (OEF) and their respective Provincial Reconstruction Teams (PRTs) will

promote security and stability in all regions of Afghanistan, including by strengthening Afghan capabilities.

Afghan National Army

By end–2010: A nationally respected, professional, ethnically balanced Afghan National Army will be fully established that is democratically accountable, organized, trained and equipped to meet the security needs of the country and increasingly funded from Government revenue, commensurate with the nation's economic capacity; the international community will continue to support Afghanistan in expanding the ANA towards the ceiling of 70,000 personnel articulated in the Bonn talks; and the pace of expansion is to be adjusted on the basis of periodic joint quality assessments by the Afghan Government and the international community against agreed criteria which take into account prevailing conditions.

Afghan National and Border Police

By end–2010, a fully constituted, professional, functional and ethnically balanced Afghan National Police and Afghan Border Police with a combined force of up to 62,000 will be able to meet the security needs of the country effectively and will be increasingly fiscally sustainable.

Disbandment of Illegal Armed Groups

All illegal armed groups will be disbanded by end–2007 in all provinces.

Counter-Narcotics

By end–2010, the Government will strengthen its law enforcement capacity at both central and provincial levels, resulting in a substantial annual increase in the amount of drugs seized or destroyed and processing facilities dismantled, and in effective measures, including targeted eradication as appropriate, that contribute to the elimination of poppy cultivation.

By end–2010, the Government and neighbouring and regional governments will work together to increase coordination and mutual sharing of intelligence, with the goal of an increase in the seizure and destruction of drugs being smuggled across Afghanistan's borders and effective action against drug traffickers.

Mine Action and Ammunition

By end–2010, in line with Afghanistan's Millennium Development Goals (MDGs) and Afghanistan's Ottawa Convention obligations, the land area contaminated by mines and unexploded ordnance will be reduced by 70%; all stockpiled anti-personnel mines will be located and destroyed by end–2007; and by end–2010, all unsafe, unserviceable and surplus ammunition will be destroyed.

Governance, Rule of Law and Human Rights

Public Administrative Reform

By end–2010: Government machinery (including the number of ministries) will be restructured and rationalised to ensure a fiscally sustainable public administration; the civil service commission will be strengthened; and civil service functions will be reformed to reflect core functions and responsibilities.

A clear and transparent national appointments mechanism will be established within 6 months, applied within 12 months and fully implemented within 24 months for all senior level appointments to the central government and the judiciary, as well as for provincial governors, chiefs of police, district administrators and provincial heads of security.

By end–2006 a review of the number of administrative units and their boundaries will be undertaken with the aim of contributing to fiscal sustainability.

By end–2010, in furtherance of the work of the civil service commission, merit-based appointments, vetting procedures and performance-based reviews will be undertaken for civil service positions at all levels of government, including central government, the judiciary and police, and requisite support will be provided to build the capacity of the civil service to function effectively. Annual performance-based reviews will be undertaken for all senior staff (grade 2 and above) starting by end–2007.

Anti-Corruption

The UN Convention against Corruption will be ratified by end–2006, national legislation adapted accordingly by end–2007 and a monitoring mechanism to oversee implementation will be in place by end–2008.

The Census and Statistics

The census enumeration will be completed by end–2008 and the complete results published.

Reliable statistical baselines will be established for all quantitative benchmarks by mid-2007 and statistical capacity built to track progress against them.

National Assembly

The National Assembly will be provided with technical and administrative support by mid-2006 to fulfil effectively its constitutionally mandated roles.

Elections

The Afghanistan Independent Electoral Commission will have the high integrity, capacity and resources to undertake elections in an increasingly fiscally sustainable manner by end–2008, with the Government of Afghanistan contributing to the extent possible to the cost of future elections from its own resources. A permanent civil and voter registry with a single national identity document will be established by end–2009.

Gender

By end–2010: the National Action Plan for Women in Afghanistan will be fully implemented; and, in line with Afghanistan's MDGs, female participation in all Afghan governance institutions, including elected and appointed bodies and the civil service, will be strengthened.

Rule of Law

By end–2010, the legal framework required under the constitution, including civil, criminal and commercial law, will be put in place, distributed to all judicial and legislative institutions and made available to the public.

By end–2010, functioning institutions of justice will be fully operational in each province of Afghanistan, and the average time to resolve contract disputes will be reduced as much as possible.

A review and reform of oversight procedures relating to corruption, lack of due process and miscarriage of justice will be initiated by end–2006 and fully implemented by end–2010; by end–2010, reforms will strengthen the professionalism, credibility and integrity of key institutions of the justice system (the Ministry of Justice, the Judiciary, the Attorney-General's office, the Ministry of Interior and the National Directorate of Security).

By end–2010, justice infrastructure will be rehabilitated; and prisons will have separate facilities for women and juveniles.

Land Registration

A process for registration of land in all administrative units and the registration of titles will be started for all major urban areas by end–2006 and all other areas by end–2008. A fair system for settlement of land disputes will be in place by end–2007. Registration for rural land will be under way by end–2007.

Counter-Narcotics

By end–2010, the Government will increase the number of arrests and prosecutions of traffickers and corrupt officials and will improve its information base concerning those involved in the drugs trade, with a view to enhancing the selection system for national and sub-national public appointments, as part of the appointments mechanism mentioned earlier in this annex.

Human Rights

By end–2010: The Government's capacity to comply with and report on its human rights treaty obligations will be strengthened; Government security and law enforcement agencies will adopt corrective measures including codes of conduct and procedures aimed at preventing arbitrary arrest and detention, torture, extortion and illegal expropriation of property with a view to the elimination of these practices; the exercise of freedom of expression, including freedom of media, will be strengthened; human rights awareness will be included in education curricula and promoted among legislators, judicial personnel and other Government agencies, communities and the public; human rights monitoring will be carried out by the Government and independently by the Afghan Independent Human Rights Commission (AIHRC), and the UN will track the effectiveness of measures aimed at the protection of human rights; the AIHRC will be supported in the fulfilment of its objectives with regard to monitoring, investigation, protection and promotion of human rights.

The implementation of the Action Plan on Peace, Justice and Reconciliation will be completed by end–2008.

Source: United Kingdom. Foreign and Commonwealth Office. Building on Success: The London Conference on Afghanistan. "The Afghanistan Compact." February 1, 2006. www.fco.gov.uk/servlet/Front?pagename=OpenMarket/Xcelerate/ShowPage&c=Page&cid=1134650705195 (accessed February 15, 2007).

Other Historic Documents of Interest

Statements on Executive Power and NSA Surveillance Authority

February 6, 2006

■■■■■■■■ **THE DOCUMENT IN CONTEXT** ■■■■■■■■

Heated debate involving several intelligence-gathering programs of the Bush administration and such issues as privacy rights, freedom of the press, the constitutional separation of powers among the branches of government, and fighting terrorism during an age of rapid technological change gathered force during the year. Newspaper reports in late 2005 and early 2006 detailed how the administration had cast a broad net for information about international terrorists, in some cases utilizing programs that were kept secret from Congress.

Administration officials angrily denounced the newspaper reports, and some Republicans on Capitol Hill joined in those denunciations. President George W. Bush, Vice President Dick Cheney, and other officials said the administration's efforts to combat terrorism had been damaged by the public debate, but they said they could offer no details because of the sensitive nature of those efforts. Congress demanded the information that had been withheld from it, but neither Congress nor the courts took definite action during the year to impose new restrictions on what the administration had been doing. At year's end it appeared that the intelligence gathering was still continuing. Democrats said they intended to raise new questions about the administration's antiterrorism powers after they took control of Congress in January 2007.

One question that was discussed only rarely concerned the effectiveness of the administration's antiterrorism programs. Administration officials insisted that all of its surveillance programs had produced useful information in its war against terrorism. Officials generally refused to publicize any specific cases, however, and a handful of news reports during the year raised questions about the actual value of the programs. On January 16, for example, the *New York Times* said FBI agents had expressed frustration that surveillance of thousands of telephone calls had produced a "flood" of leads that, almost without exception, produced "dead ends or innocent Americans."

NSA Warrantless Surveillance

There never was any secret that the Bush administration was using all of its legal powers to go after alleged international terrorists, such as the al Qaeda network that had planned the September 11, 2001, terrorist attacks against the United States. Bush and other officials said repeatedly, in the wake of those attacks, that they would fight terrorists both with military and nonmilitary force, including legal prosecution. What was not clear publicly, until the revelations started late in 2005, were the specifics of some of the administration's actions. *(Terrorism background, Historic Documents of 2001, p. 614)*

The first, and by far the most controversial, revelation was a *New York Times* report on December 16, 2005, saying that the administration had been monitoring thousands of telephone conversations and e-mail messages between people in the United States and people overseas who were believed to be connected to terrorist groups. This monitoring was conducted by the top-secret National Security Agency (NSA), the *Times* said, and had not been authorized by court warrants, even by a special court created by Congress in 1978 for the express purpose of approving secret wiretaps in sensitive cases. President Bush acknowledged that he had ordered the warrantless surveillance, which he defended as necessary to catch terrorists, and he denounced the newspaper's report as damaging to national security. *(Background, Historic Documents of 2005, p. 957)*

The *Times* report set off a legal and political furor that lasted for several months during 2006, only to quiet down after the administration provided details of its surveillance program to the House and Senate intelligence committees. Previously, the administration had given only limited information to a handful of congressional leaders under circumstances that some members said prevented them from understanding the full scope of the surveillance.

Much of the controversy concerned whether President Bush had overstepped his authority by ordering the surveillance without seeking warrants from a special court established under the Foreign Intelligence Surveillance Act (PL 96–511, known as FISA). Consisting of federal judges appointed by the chief justice of the United States, that court's sole function was to review, in secret, the administration's requests for warrants to monitor telephone calls of people who were suspected of posing national security threats to the United States. The court rarely turned down such requests. The Bush administration said its surveillance of terrorism suspects did not need to be reviewed by that court because the president had the constitutional power, as commander-in-chief of the armed forces, to order the surveillance. Administration officials also said Congress had given Bush broad authority in September 2001 when it passed a joint resolution authorizing him to take "necessary" action to combat terrorism; Bush had used that authority the following month to order the invasion of Afghanistan, but it was not known at the time that he also considered the resolution as giving him much broader powers.

Bush's assertion of powers generated a fierce legal debate early in 2006, when numerous legal experts, including lawyers for the Congressional Research Service at the Library of Congress, raised questions about whether Bush had overstepped his authority. These experts said the September 2001 resolution, and the congressional debate about it, clearly concerned the pending invasion of Afghanistan and not the use of electronic surveillance of domestic telephone conversations in the United States. Bush defended the program on numerous occasions, saying it was aimed at suspected terrorists and their accomplices, not at innocent Americans, and that he had the constitutional authority to order it. "I'm mindful of your civil liberties, and so I had all kinds of lawyers review the process," he told an audience at Kansas State University on January 13. "We briefed members of the United States Congress" about the program, he said.

Bush's assertions were greeted with skepticism by many members of Congress, both on legal grounds and because few members had been given any detailed information about the surveillance program. Among the most skeptical was Arlen Specter,

R-Pa., who chaired the Senate Judiciary Committee. Specter was a staunch advocate of the Senate's privileges.

Specter's committee held the first full-scale public hearing on the matter on February 6, when Attorney General Alberto R. Gonzales defended the NSA surveillance as "lawful in all respects." Gonzales insisted that Congress had implicitly authorized the surveillance when it authorized the war in Afghanistan, and he said the NSA program fell within the "long tradition" of surveillance of enemies in wartime.

The committee's ranking Democrat, Patrick J. Leahy of Vermont, said the president had chosen to conduct the wiretapping "illegally," had never sought congressional approval of it, and was thwarting congressional efforts to learn the details. Several committee Republicans also expressed skepticism about Gonzales's legal rationales. Lindsey Graham, R-S.C., said the administration's assertion—that by authorizing military action in Afghanistan, Congress also was implicitly authorizing the warrantless surveillance—would make it more difficult for future presidents to get such sweeping military authorizations from Congress. "When I voted for it, I never envisioned that I was giving this president or any other president the ability to go around FISA carte blanche," Graham told Gonzales.

Over the next several months, much of the debate about the matter on Capitol Hill concerned whether the administration had adequately notified Congress about the NSA surveillance program. Bush insisted he had "fully briefed" Congress, and White House officials produced records purporting to show thirty occasions on which one or more senior leaders had been given information about it. Those briefed included the top leaders of the House and Senate, plus the chairmen and ranking minority members of the two intelligence committees. Most members who spoke about the matter said they had not been given enough information to judge the program on its merits.

Despite the complaints, administration officials continued for several weeks to rebuff most congressional requests for information—a stance that angered even some Republicans who normally gave the administration nearly complete support. That stance changed in May when the White House realized that Bush's nominee to head the CIA—former NSA director Gen. Michael V. Hayden—would bear the brunt of questioning unless more members were brought into the loop. On May 17 senior officials gave briefings about the surveillance program, in closed-door sessions, to all members of the two intelligence committees. Hayden defended the surveillance program in his testimony the following day, and the Senate confirmed him as CIA director on May 26.

The administration also gradually changed its position on whether Congress should pass legislation authorizing the NSA surveillance program retroactively. In his February 6 testimony to the Senate Judiciary Committee, and in other statements early in the year, Gonzales insisted Congress did not need to authorize the surveillance because the president already had all the authority he needed. Members of Congress in both parties, however, increasingly called for legislation putting the surveillance on firm legal ground and imposing some limits on it.

In early March White House officials negotiated a compromise with some Republican members of the Senate Judiciary Committee, led by Mike DeWine of Ohio, that authorized the eavesdropping program in essentially the same form as ordered by Bush, but with requirements that congressional leaders be kept informed about it. Committee chairman Specter later engaged in his own negotiations with the White House that led to a competing proposal giving the president expanded authority for the surveillance. Specter's committee in September approved three bills taking separate approaches, but the full Senate did not act on any of them.

The House took its own action on September 29, passing a bill (HR 5825) by Heather A. Wilson, R-N.M., authorizing the warrantless wiretaps for fixed, renewable periods but with a requirement that the president notify the congressional intelligence committees and the FISA court. This bill was passed on a largely party-line vote of 232–191 after Republican leaders turned back attempts by Democrats and some Republicans to place tighter restrictions on the administration's use of surveillance. The White House endorsed Wilson's bill just before the House acted, even though administration officials had tried to get her to embrace DeWine's milder bill still pending in the Senate.

After Democrats captured control of both chambers of Congress in the November midterm elections, Bush pressed for action on the pending legislation during a lame-duck session in late November and early December. Democrats, however, used their new political clout to block action and said they would conduct new hearings on Bush's antiterrorism programs early in 2007.

Legal Action

In addition to political concerns, one of the reasons for the administration's sudden willingness to negotiate legislation with Congress was the prospect of legal action in the courts. The American Civil Liberties Union (ACLU) and other organizations filed suits in several different courts around the country alleging that the NSA surveillance program violated the 1978 FISA law and the constitution. The administration sought to stifle these suits by filing motions alleging that court consideration of them would endanger national security by forcing the disclosure of "state secrets." Officials also concluded that congressional authorization of the surveillance, even with modest restrictions, would lead judges to dismiss the suits.

The ACLU won the first round in its suit, filed in U.S. district court in Detroit. On August 17, Judge Anna Diggs Taylor ruled that the NSA surveillance violated privacy and free-speech rights as well as the 1978 FISA law. Judge Taylor ordered an end to the surveillance but set aside that order while the government appealed her ruling, which came in the case *ACLU v. National Security Agency.* Bush denounced the ruling and argued that the ACLU and others who supported it "simply do not understand the nature of the world in which we live." A three-judge panel of the Sixth Circuit Court of Appeals was scheduled to hear the government's appeal early in 2007.

Also pending at year's end was a criminal investigation by the Justice Department into the original leaking of information that led to the *New York Times* report disclosing the NSA surveillance program. The *Times* reported on February 11 that federal agents had interviewed numerous law enforcement and national security officials about the leak, but no results of the investigation were made public as of the end of the year.

Searches of Telephone Records

A separate, but related, controversy arose midyear as the result of a report by *USA Today* on May 10 that the NSA was secretly collecting "tens of millions" of domestic telephone records from three major carriers: AT&T, BellSouth, and Verizon. The report said the program collected information "about the calls of ordinary Americans, most of whom aren't suspected of any crime." The NSA was not listening to or recording conversations, the newspaper said, but since late 2001 had collected information on "billions" of calls and telephone numbers to locate patterns (which experts called "social networks") that might point to terrorist activity. The newspaper said only one major regional telephone company, Qwest, had refused to give the NSA access to its customers' calling records because of concerns about the legality of the NSA request. BellSouth and Verizon later denied that the NSA had asked them for customer information.

Responding to the *USA Today* report, Bush said: "We're not mining or trolling through the personal lives of millions of innocent Americans. Our efforts are focused on links to al Qaeda and their known affiliates." The president's assurances failed to satisfy members of Congress in both parties, who said they had not been told about this program. The administration later briefed them.

In a follow-up report, and an accompanying editor's note, on June 30, *USA Today* quoted members of Congress as confirming some elements of its original story but casting doubt on other aspects, notably the participation of BellSouth and Verizon. This report said BellSouth apparently did not directly hand over its telephone records, although the records of its customers who used AT&T as their long-distance carrier might have been collected by the government. The nature of Verizon's participation was less clear, the newspaper reported. The company in January had acquired the long-distance carrier MCI, which had provided call records to the government, the newspaper said. In a statement, Verizon refused to confirm or deny that MCI had been involved.

Telecommunications regulators in Connecticut, Maine, Missouri, and New Jersey began examining whether Verizon had violated state privacy protection laws. The Justice Department in August and September filed suits to try to block those inquiries, which were still pending at year's end.

Other attempts by administration critics to block the administration's telephone data-mining program met various fates, generally because the Justice Department responded aggressively with assertions that court action would force disclosure of "state secrets." A district court judge in Chicago accepted the administration argument on July 25 in rejecting a suit filed against AT&T by author Studs Terkel and several others. However, a judge in San Francisco in July rebuffed the administration when it tried to block a class-action lawsuit against AT&T filed by the Electronic Frontier Foundation, a privacy rights group. That suit was based, in part, on documents provided by a former AT&T technician, Mark Klein, describing equipment that had been installed in 2003 at a company office in San Francisco that was capable of monitoring millions of e-mail messages, telephone calls placed over the Internet, and other Internet traffic. The judge's ruling in that case was on appeal before the Ninth Circuit Court of Appeals at year's end.

Searches of Bank Accounts

Yet another revelation of the extent of the Bush administration's use of extraordinary law enforcement tools came with a June 23 report by the *New York Times.* This report said the CIA and Treasury Department had gained access to financial records of people suspected of having ties to al Qaeda. The administration accomplished this by accessing records of international transactions passing through a banking consortium in Brussels known as the Society for Worldwide Interbank Financial Telecommunication (or SWIFT). The report said the administration obtained the records by using "broad administrative subpoenas for millions of records" rather than by seeking court-approved warrants or subpoenas for individual transactions—as was customary in criminal investigations. The *Times* report quoted a senior Treasury official as saying the searches were subject to several "safeguards," including the use of an outside auditing firm to verify that the searches were based on intelligence leads about terrorist suspects. The report also cited what officials claimed were successes as a result of the searches, notably the use of financial data leading to the capture in 2003 of an al Qaeda leader, Riduan Isamuddin (known as Hambali), who was said to have planned the 2002 bombing of a resort on the Indonesian island of Bali. *(Bali bombing, Historic Documents of 2002, p. 702)*

Vice President Cheney and other administration officials reacted angrily to the *Times* report, saying it undermined their efforts to track and stifle financing for terrorist groups. "What I find most disturbing about these stories is the fact that some of the news media take it upon themselves to disclose vital national security programs, thereby making it more difficult for us to prevent future attacks against the American people. That offends me," he said. Peter King, R-N.Y., who chaired the House Homeland Security Committee, denounced the newspaper's report as "treasonous."

The *Times* defended its report, and executive editor Bill Keller published a letter noting that the administration itself had "trumpeted" its work to track international financing of terrorists. Keller's letter did not satisfy administration supporters, however. By a largely party-line vote, the Republican-controlled House of Representatives on June 29 adopted a resolution (H Res 895) condemning the *Times* report. Even so, members of both parties expressed frustration that the administration had not told anyone in Congress about the program that tracked international banking records. "Many people in Congress who should have been briefed by the administration were not," Rep. Sue Kelly, R-N.Y., told a senior Treasury Department official at a July 11 hearing. "What else is it that we don't know?"

SWIFT, the international bank consortium, came under widespread criticism in Europe for its cooperation with the Bush administration. Belgium's privacy commission on September 28 said the organization should not have given banking records to the United States without obtaining stronger assurances about how the information would be used. Belgian prime minister Guy Verhofstadt noted that SWIFT was in "a conflicting position between American and European law," the latter of which had "stronger guarantees of privacy protection." A similar ruling came on November 22 when a European Union (EU) panel said SWIFT had violated EU regulations by turning the bank records over to the United States.

Extending the Patriot Act

The *New York Times* report in December 2005 revealing the NSA surveillance program derailed plans by congressional leaders to extend sixteen provisions of antiterrorism legislation, called the USA Patriot Act (PL 107–56) that were due to expire at the end of that year. Congress passed two short-term extensions that kept negotiations going through February 2006. In the meantime, Sen. John E. Sununu, R-N.H., negotiated several small changes to satisfy some complaints by civil liberties advocates about the broad reach of the act. The Senate approved those provisions, along with an extension of the Patriot Act (in S 2271—PL 109–178) on March 1, and the House cleared the bill for the president on March 7. The bill made fourteen of the sixteen provisions permanent but placed four-year sunsets on the two most contentious ones: giving the FBI authority to seize a business records with court approval and the power to seek "roving wiretaps" that followed an individual no matter which telephone he used.

One new provision in the Patriot Act extension required the administration to make public some information about its use of so-called national security letters to compel businesses to give the government detailed information about their customers—even without a warrant. The letters said the information was necessary to protect the national security, and recipients had no legal recourse to resist. On April 28 the Justice Department said that the FBI in 2005 had sought information on 3,501 American citizens, and legal residents in the United States, by using the national security letters. The information was sought in 9,254 letters sent to banks, credit card issuers, and telephone and Internet providers; no warrants were sought or issued.

The *Washington Post*, which in November 2005 had published an extensive report on the administration's use of the security letters, said the figures released on April 28 covered only requests for detailed information, such as bank account transactions, and did not include thousands of additional requests for limited information, such as the name and address of a bank customer.

Following are excerpts from two prepared statements given at a February 6, 2006, hearing of the Senate Judiciary Committee on the subject of "Wartime Executive Power and the NSA's Surveillance Authority." The first statement is by Sen. Patrick J. Leahy of Vermont, the ranking Democrat on the committee; the second is by Attorney General Alberto R. Gonzales.

◼◼◼◼◼◼◼ DOCUMENT ◼◼◼◼◼◼◼

"Wartime Executive Power and the NSA's Surveillance Authority"

Statement of Senator Patrick Leahy, Ranking Member, Senate Judiciary Committee

. . . There is much that we do not know about the President's secret spying programs. I hope that we will begin to get some real answers from the Administration today—not simply more self-serving characterizations. Let's start with what we do know.

Point One—The President's secret wiretapping program is not authorized by the Foreign Intelligence Surveillance Act ["FISA"].

That law expressly states that it provides the "exclusive" source of authority for wiretapping for intelligence purposes. Wiretapping that is not authorized under that statute is a federal crime. That is what the law says, and that is what the law means. This law was enacted to define how domestic surveillance for intelligence purposes may be conducted while protecting the fundamental liberties of Americans. Two or more generations of Americans are too young to know this from their experience, but there's a reason we have the FISA law. It was enacted after decades of abuses by the Executive, including the wiretapping of

Dr. Martin Luther King Jr. and other political opponents of earlier government officials, and the White House "horrors" of the Nixon years, during which another President asserted that whatever he did was legal because he was the President.

The law has been updated five times since September 11, 2001, in order to keep pace with intelligence needs and technological developments. It provides broad and flexible authority. On July 31, 2002, the Justice Department testified that this law "is a highly flexible statute that has proven effective" and noted: "When you are trying to prevent terrorist acts, that is really what FISA was intended to do and it was written with that in mind."

The Bush Administration now concedes that this President knowingly created a program involving thousands of wiretaps of Americans in the United States over the period of the last four to five years without complying with FISA. Legal scholars and former Government officials have been almost unanimous in stating the obvious: This is against the law.

Point Two—The Authorization for the Use of Military Force that Democratic and Republican lawmakers joined together to pass in the days immediately after the September 11 attacks did not give the President the authority to go around the FISA law to wiretap Americans illegally.

That resolution authorized the military action of sending military troops into Afghanistan to kill or capture Osama bin Laden and those acting with him—in the words of the statute, "to use the United States Armed Forces against those responsible for the recent attacks launched against the United States."

It did not authorize domestic surveillance of United States citizens without a warrant from a judge. Nothing in the Authorization for the Use of Military Force was intended secretly to undermine the liberties and rights of Americans. Rather, it was to defend our liberties and rights that Congress authorized the President to use our Armed Forces against those responsible for the 9/11 attacks.

Let me be clear: It is only Republican Senators who are talking about "special rights for terrorists." I have no interest in that. I wish the Bush Administration had done a better job with the vast powers Congress has given it to destroy al Qaeda and kill or capture Osama bin Laden. But it has not.

My concern is for peaceful Quakers who are being spied upon and other law-abiding Americans and babies and nuns who are placed on terrorist watch lists.

Point Three—The President never came to Congress and never sought additional legal authority to engage in the type of domestic surveillance in which the NSA has been secretly engaged for the last several years.

After September 11, 2001, I helped lead a bipartisan effort to provide tools and legal authorities to improve our capabilities to prevent terrorist attacks. We enacted amendments to FISA in the USA PATRIOT ACT in October 2001 and four additional times subsequently. Ironically, when a Republican Senator proposed a legal change to the standard needed for a FISA warrant, the Bush Administration did not support that effort but raised questions about its constitutionality and testified that it was not needed. This Administration told the Senate that FISA was working just fine and that it did not seek additional adjustments. Attorney General Gonzales has said that the Administration did not ask for legislation authorizing warrantless wiretapping of Americans and did not think such legislation would pass.

Not only did the Bush Administration not seek broader legal authority, it kept the very existence of its domestic wiretapping program without warrants completely secret from 527 of the 535 Members of Congress, including Members on this Committee and on the Intelligence Committee, and placed limits and restrictions on what the eight Members who were told anything could know or say.

The Administration had not suggested to Congress and the American people that FISA was inadequate, outmoded or irrelevant until it was caught violating the statute with a secret program of wiretapping Americans without warrants. Indeed, in 2004, two years after he authorized the secret warrantless wiretapping program, the President told the American people:

> *"Anytime you hear the United States government talking about wiretap, a wiretap requires a court order." He continued: "Nothing has changed. . . . When we're talking about chasing down terrorists, we're talking about getting a court order before we do so." In light of what we now know, that statement was, at best, misleading.*

The Rule of Law

I have many questions for the Attorney General. But first, I have a message to give him and the President. It is a message that should be unanimous, from every Member of Congress regardless of party and ideology. Under our Constitution, Congress is the co-equal branch of Government that makes the laws. If you believe we need new laws, you can come to us and tell us. If Congress agrees, we will amend the law. If you do not even attempt to persuade Congress to amend the law, you must abide by the law as written. That is as true for this President as it is for any other American. That is the rule of law, on which our Nation was founded, and on which it endures and prospers.

Prepared Statement of Hon. Alberto R. Gonzales, Attorney General of the United States

. . . It has become more clear in the days, weeks, and years since September 11th that our enemy in this war is no ordinary terrorist organization. Al Qaeda demonstrated on September 11th that it could execute a highly sophisticated operation, one that required al Qaeda operatives to live in our midst for years, to transfer money into the country, to arrange training, and to communicate with planners overseas. And it has promised similar attacks in the future. . . .

In confronting this new and deadly enemy, President Bush promised that "[w]e will direct every resource at our command—every means of diplomacy, every tool of intelligence, every tool of law enforcement, every financial influence, and every weapon of war—to the disruption of and to the defeat of the global terror network." President Bush Address to a Joint Session of Congress (Sept. 20, 2001). The terrorist surveillance program described by the President is one such tool and one indispensable aspect of this defense of our Nation.

The terrorist surveillance program targets communications where one party to the communication is outside the U.S. and the government has "reasonable grounds to believe" that at least one party to the communication is a member or agent of al Qaeda, or an affiliated terrorist organization. This program is reviewed and reauthorized by the President approximately every 45 days. The Congressional leadership, including the leaders of the Intelligence Committees of both Houses of Congress, has been briefed about this program more than a dozen times since 2001. The program provides the United States with the early warning system we so desperately needed on September 10th.

The terrorist surveillance program remains highly classified, as it should be. We must protect this tool, which has proven so important to protecting America. An open discussion of the operational details of this program would put the lives of Americans at risk. The need to protect national security also means that I must confine my discussion of the legal analysis to those activities confirmed publicly by the President; I cannot and will not address operational aspects of the program or other purported activities described in press reports. These press accounts are in almost every case, in one way or another, misinformed, confused, or wrong.

Congress and the American people are interested in two fundamental questions: is this program necessary and is it lawful. The answer to both questions is yes.

The question of necessity rightly falls to our Nation's military leaders, because the terrorist surveillance program is an essential element of our military campaign against al Qaeda. I therefore address it only briefly. The attacks of September 11th placed the Nation in a state of armed conflict. In this armed conflict, our military employs a wide variety of tools and weapons to defeat the enemy. General Michael Hayden, Principal Deputy Director of National Intelligence and former Director of the NSA, recently explained why a terrorist surveillance program that allows us quickly to collect important information about our enemy is so vital and necessary to the War on Terror.

The conflict against al Qaeda is, in fundamental respects, a war of information. We cannot build walls thick enough, fences high enough, or systems strong enough to keep our enemies out of our open and welcoming country. Instead, as the bipartisan 9/11 and WMD [weapons of mass destruction] Commissions have urged, we must understand better who the enemy is and what he is doing. We have to collect the right dots before we can "connect the dots." The terrorist surveillance program allows us to collect more information regarding al Qaeda's plans, and, critically, it allows us to locate al Qaeda operatives, especially those already in the United States and poised to attack. We cannot defend the Nation without such information, as we painfully learned on September 11th.

As Attorney General, I am primarily concerned with the legal basis for these necessary military activities. The Attorney General of the United States is the chief legal adviser for the President and the Executive Branch. Accordingly, the Department of Justice has thoroughly examined this program and concluded that the President is acting within his power in authorizing it. The Department of Justice is not alone in concluding that the program is lawful. Career lawyers at NSA and its Inspector General office have been intimately involved in the oversight of the program. The lawyers have found the program to be lawful and reviewed its conduct. The Inspector Genera's office has exercised vigorous reviews of the program to provide assurance that it is carried out within the terms of the President's authorization.

The terrorist surveillance program is firmly grounded in the President's constitutional authorities. The Constitution charges the President with the primary responsibility for protecting the safety of all Americans, and the Constitution gives the President the authority necessary to fulfill this solemn duty. See, e.g., *The Prize Cases*, 67 U.S. (2 Black) 635, 668

(1863). It has long been recognized that the President's constitutional powers include the authority to conduct warrantless surveillance aimed at detecting and preventing armed attacks on the United States. Presidents have repeatedly relied on their inherent power to gather foreign intelligence for reasons both diplomatic and military, and the federal courts have consistently upheld this longstanding practice. . . .

If this authority is available in ordinary times, it is even more vital in the present circumstances of our armed conflict with al Qaeda. The President authorized the terrorist surveillance program in response to the deadliest foreign attack on American soil, and it is designed solely to prevent the next al Qaeda attack. After all, the goal of our enemy is to blend in with our civilian population in order to plan and carry out future attacks within America. We cannot forget that the September 11th hijackers were in our country, living in our communities.

The President's authority to take military action—including the use of communications intelligence targeted at the enemy—does not come merely from his constitutional powers. It comes directly from Congress as well. Just a few days after the attacks of September 11th, Congress enacted a joint resolution to support and authorize the military response to the attacks on American soil. Authorization for Use of Military Force, Pub. L. No. 107–40, 115 Stat. 224 (Sept. 18, 2001) ("AUMF"). In the AUMF, Congress did two important things. First, it expressly recognized the President's "authority under the Constitution to take action to deter and prevent acts of international terrorism against the United States." Second, it supplemented that authority by authorizing the President to "use all necessary and appropriate force against those nations, organizations, or persons he determines planned, authorized, committed, or aided the terrorist attacks" in order to prevent further attacks on the United States. . . .

Some have suggested that the AUMF did not authorize intelligence collection inside the United States. That contention cannot be squared with the reality of the September 11th attacks on our soil, launched from within the country, and carried out by sleeper agents who had lived amongst us. Given this background, Congress certainly intended to support the President's use of force to repel an unfolding attack within the United States. Congress also must be understood to have authorized the traditional means by which the military detects and responds to such attacks. Nor can this contention be squared with the language of the AUMF itself, which calls on the President to protect Americans both "at *home* and abroad," to take action to prevent further terrorist attacks "against the United States," and directs him to determine who was responsible for the attacks. Such a contention is also contrary to the long history of wartime surveillance, which has often involved the interception of enemy communications into and out of the United States.

Against this backdrop, the NSA's focused terrorist surveillance program falls squarely within the broad authorization of the AUMF even though, as some have argued, the AUMF does not expressly mention surveillance. The AUMF also does not mention detention of enemy combatants. But we know from the Supreme Court's decision in *Hamdi* that such detention is authorized even for U.S. citizens. Justice O'Connor reasoned: "Because detention to prevent a combatant's return to the battlefield is a fundamental incident of waging war, in permitting the use of 'necessary and appropriate force,' Congress has clearly and unmistakably authorized detention in the narrow circumstances considered here." . . .

Many people ask why the President elected not to use FISA's procedures for securing court orders for the terrorist surveillance program. We have to remember that what is at issue is a wartime intelligence program designed to protect our Nation from another attack in the middle of an armed conflict. It is an "early warning system" with only one purpose: to detect and prevent the next attack on the United States from foreign agents hiding in our midst. It is imperative for national security that we can detect reliably, immediately, and without delay whenever communications associated with al Qaeda enter or leave the United States. That may be the only way to alert us to the presence of an al Qaeda agent in our country and to the existence of an unfolding plot. . . .

No one takes lightly the concerns that have been raised about the interception of domestic communications inside the United States. But this terrorist surveillance program involves intercepting the *international* communications of persons reasonably believed to be members or agents of al Qaeda or affiliated terrorist organizations. This surveillance is narrowly focused and fully consistent with the traditional forms of enemy surveillance found to be necessary in all previous armed conflicts. The need for the program is reviewed at the highest levels of government approximately every 45 days to ensure that the al Qaeda threat to the national security of this Nation continues to exist. Moreover, although the Fourth Amendment does not require application of a probable cause standard in this context, the "reasonable grounds to believe" standard employed in this program is the traditional Fourth Amendment probable cause standard. As the Supreme Court has stated, "The substance of all the definitions of probable cause is a *reasonable ground for belief of guilt.*" . . .

This Administration has chosen to act now to prevent the next attack with every lawful tool at its disposal, rather than wait until it is too late. It is hard to imagine a President who would not elect to use these tools in defense of the American people—in fact, it would be irresponsible to do otherwise. The terrorist surveillance program is both necessary and lawful. Accordingly, as the President has explained, he intends to continue to exercise this authority as long as al Qaeda poses such a grave threat to the national security. If we conduct this reasonable surveillance—while taking special care to preserve civil liberties as we have—we can all continue to enjoy our rights and freedoms for generations to come. . . .

Source: U.S. Congress. Senate. Committee on the Judiciary. "Wartime Executive Power and the National Security Agency's Surveillance Authority." 109th Cong., 2nd sess., February 6, 2006. S. Hrg. 109–500, serial J–109–59. Washington, D.C.: U.S. Government Printing Office. http://purl.access.gpo.gov/GPO/LPS74664 (accessed February 11, 2007).

House Report on the Government Response to Hurricane Katrina

February 15, 2006

■■■■■■■■■■ **THE DOCUMENT IN CONTEXT** ■■■■■■■■■■

Lengthy investigations by congressional committees, the White House, and other federal agencies all confirmed what most Americans already knew—that the government response to the Gulf Coast devastation of Hurricane Katrina in 2005 was disastrous. Although the reports differed in their emphases, they all cited a lack of leadership and preparation, failures of communication and coordination, and bureaucratic squabbling that, in the words of the House investigating committee, "cost lives, prolonged suffering, and left all Americans justifiably concerned our government is no better prepared to protect its people than it was" before the terrorist attacks of September 11, 2001.

Meanwhile, New Orleans and the other Gulf Coast areas destroyed by Katrina's high winds, storm surges, and flooding were still trying to recover. It was an often discouraging task, one snarled in confusions, disagreements, and bureaucratic red tape. While some neighborhoods appeared to be getting back on their feet, others were still struggling just to get rid of storm debris. Complaints that insurance companies were refusing to cover some storm damage were widespread. Thousands of people displaced from their homes were still living in temporary housing, while thousands of others had decided to make a new home elsewhere. The one spot of good news was that the 2006 hurricane season was much calmer than expected. Forecasters had predicted a more active storm season than usual, but once again Mother Nature fooled them—only five hurricanes formed in the Atlantic during the year, and none of them made landfall in the United States.

A Tale of Two Disasters: One Natural, One Manmade

Hurricane Katrina slammed into the Gulf Coast on the morning of August 29, 2005, killing more than 1,300 people, dislocating about 1.5 million people, and destroying homes and other buildings in coastal Louisiana, Mississippi, and Alabama. Most of New Orleans was flooded when the levee system protecting the city broke in several key sites. Despite ample warning beforehand, the city, which lay below sea level, had not been evacuated before the storm hit. When the flooding began tens of thousands of people took refuge in the Superdome athletic arena and the city convention center, where they endured days without adequate food, water, or sanitation before finally being evacuated. *(Background, Historic Documents of 2005, p. 539)*

Louisiana and city officials, notably Governor Kathleen Babineaux Blanco and Mayor C. Ray Nagin, came in for heavy criticism, particularly for not ordering people to evacuate sooner, for failing to have an effective plan to evacuate residents lacking transportation, and for generally losing control of the situation once the storm hit. But most criticism was directed at the White House and the Department of Homeland Security (DHS) for the slow and often incompetent federal response both to immediate rescue efforts and to the longer-term relief and recovery programs that followed. Top officials, including President George W. Bush and DHS secretary Michael Chertoff, seemed ill-informed and disengaged in the hours and days following the storm. Bush, in particular, did not appear to appreciate the magnitude of the storm, the human suffering it was causing, or the political damage he could suffer from failing to respond appropriately. Michael D. Brown, the head of the Federal Emergency Management Agency (FEMA), had little experience in relief and rescue operations and often appeared more interested in bureaucratic infighting and finger-pointing than in getting relief to storm victims. A week after Bush praised him for "doing a heck of a job," Brown was fired. *(Government response to Katrina, Historic Documents of 2005, p. 566)*

In the meantime, news reporting had painted a vivid if disheartening picture of FEMA as an agency demoralized when it was incorporated into the Department of Homeland Security in 2003 and stripped of much of its responsibility for overseeing relief efforts. Brown did little to help the situation, according to reports, by refusing to cooperate with his superiors in the DHS on defining FEMA's mission and role within the department. By the time Katrina hit about a dozen of FEMA's top operations officers had left the troubled agency, putting disaster planning largely in the hands of inexperienced personnel. Chertoff was criticized for focusing too much of the department's energies and resources on the threat of another terrorist attack at the expense of being prepared for a natural disaster. Given the department's poor preparations for dealing with a storm that had been predicted for several days, commentators raised pointed questions about how the government would cope with a terrorist attack that would come with little or no warning.

A Flood of Investigations

Those questions and more were addressed by two congressional committees, the White House, and the Government Accountability Office (GAO, the investigative arm of Congress), all of whom issued reports in the first half of 2006. Virtually all the reports cited a failure of leadership and a lack of communication and coordination as the main problems affecting the federal response.

The first congressional committee to report was the House Select Bipartisan Committee to Investigate the Preparation for and Response to Hurricane Katrina. Chaired by Rep. Thomas M. Davis, R-Va., the committee was bipartisan in name only. Just two Democrats, both from Louisiana, agreed to participate in the committee's work and then only informally. House Democratic leaders shunned the committee, charging that its investigation would simply whitewash the administration's shortcomings, and called for creation of an independent investigatory commission similar to the one that investigated the September 11 attacks. *(Commission investigation on terrorist attacks, Historic Documents of 2004, p. 450)*

But in an unusually forthright and blunt report, issued on February 15 after a four-month investigation, the committee said that governments, particularly the federal government, had failed because they either had not learned from past experience or did not implement lessons thought to have been learned. "If 9/11 was a failure of imagination," the committee wrote, "then Katrina was a failure of initiative. It was a failure of leadership"—a failure, the committee added, that "should disturb all Americans." The House committee said a "blinding lack of situational awareness and disjointed decision making" in the White House and the Department of Homeland Security "needlessly compounded and prolonged Katrina's horror."

Chertoff and Brown came in for especially heavy criticism. The committee said Chertoff was late in declaring Katrina an "incident of national significance"—a designation that was supposed to trigger an increased level of response. The committee also questioned why Chertoff had put Brown in charge of managing the federal government's response to the storm, considering Brown's inexperience in dealing with disasters and his demonstrated reluctance to accept FEMA's reduced role in DHS's disaster planning. The report also said that it was not a lack of information but rather the failure of the president's Homeland Security Council "to resolve conflicts in information" that caused confusion at the top levels of the federal government about what was happening during and after the storm, especially in New Orleans. The council had been created specifically to monitor the government's response to crisis, and its failure, the committee said, showed that the government was still "woefully incapable" of managing information in a disaster.

In an addendum to its February 15 report, the House Select Committee took former FEMA director Brown to task for circumventing his superiors at DHS and communicating directly with the White House. By disregarding the chain of command established under the federal government's National Recovery Plan for dealing with disasters, Brown denied "the nation the opportunity to determine" whether key elements of that plan worked as anticipated, the committee said.

The White House weighed in with its own findings on February 24. The 228-page report by Frances Frago Townsend, the White House homeland security adviser, did not single out any individual for blame. Instead, Townsend acknowledged that the government's system for coping with catastrophic disasters was structurally flawed, and she outlined 125 recommendations for fixing the problems. Among the recommendations: greater reliance on the military for support during the emergency, development of a more comprehensive national communications system for first responders, and creation of a one-stop process for federal assistance for disaster victims.

Similar themes were sounded by the GAO and by FEMA itself. In testimony before the Senate Committee on Homeland Security and Governmental Affairs on March 8, Comptroller General David M. Walker, the head of the GAO, said the lessons of Katrina were similar to those learned from other catastrophic disasters, namely, the "critical importance" of preparing and training for disasters, clearly defining and communicating leadership roles, clarifying response procedures, and strengthening the government's capabilities for responding to disaster.

The last of the major reports to appear, "Hurricane Katrina: A Nation Still Unprepared," came from the Senate Committee on Homeland Security and Governmental Affairs. The committee held twenty-two hearings, interviewed more than 320 people, and read through more than 830,000 pages of documents before releasing its final report to key senators on April 27 and to the public on May 3. By and large, the committee echoed the findings of its House counterpart and other investigations, but it also recommended changes in the way the Department of Homeland Security was organized, including reversing some of the structural changes that Chertoff had ordered in 2005 and that Congress imposed when it created the agency in 2003. Among its dozens of recommendations, the Senate committee called for the creation of a National Operations Center to communicate with and coordinate various government agencies before, during, and after a disaster; the formation of regional strike teams; and the provision of enough resources and funding to ensure that the disaster response was effective. A principal recommendation was to scrap FEMA and create a National Preparedness and Response Authority within DHS, giving it responsibility to both prepare for and respond to disasters. "We have concluded that FEMA is in shambles and beyond repair, and that it should be abolished," committee chairman Susan Collins, R-Maine, said in a written statement.

FEMA Overhaul

Several prominent lawmakers, including Representative Davis who headed the special House committee, had called for taking FEMA out of DHS and making it an independent agency. But in the end Congress opted to follow many of the Senate committee's recommendations when it cleared legislation restructuring FEMA while keeping it within the Department of Homeland Security. The overhaul, which was enacted as part of the Fiscal Year 2007 Homeland Security Appropriations Bill (PL 109–295), gave FEMA responsibility for preparing for disasters and responding to them. The measure authorized a system of FEMA regional offices with strike teams to respond quickly to disasters, created a National Advisory Council to allow state and local first-responders to advise FEMA, and authorized 10 percent funding increases for the agency for the next three years.

The FEMA director was given more power to advise the president on disasters. The overhaul also required that the FEMA director have five years of executive experience and an emergency management background—a provision aimed at avoiding the appointment of another FEMA administrator like Brown who had strong political credentials but little emergency management experience. President Bush took exception to that provision, contending in an October signing statement that he was not obligated to follow that requirement in appointing an administrator. The current head of FEMA, R. David Paulison, who was named in September 2005 to replace Brown, had extensive experience managing emergency relief operations.

Allegations of Fraud and Waste

Investigations by GAO and others during 2006 also found an exceptionally high incidence of fraud and waste connected with the government's disaster relief and rebuilding efforts. A GAO audit released in June estimated that the government might have been defrauded of as much as $1.4 billion of the $6.3 billion it distributed in immediate disaster relief, which included emergency housing and rental assistance as well as debit cards worth $2,000. According to the report the scale of fraud was limited only by the imagination of the defrauder; relief funds were used to pay for football tickets, pornographic videos, and in one case a weeklong Caribbean vacation. More than $5 million was paid to people who listed cemeteries or post office boxes as the addresses of damaged property. Tens of thousands of people gave false names or addresses to receive the debit cards, while others used duplicate or fake Social Security numbers for identification. Several state and federal government employees were also found to have engaged in fraudulent schemes

The GAO report faulted FEMA for failing to perform routine identity checks. FEMA officials defended their actions, saying the agency's top priority was getting emergency aid to storm victims as quickly as possible. Agency officials said FEMA was taking steps to correct the problems, including installing a system that would prevent more than one payment from going to the same Social Security number.

Other investigations faulted FEMA and other government agencies for wasting taxpayer money on overpriced, no-bid contracts and on ill-considered relief efforts, such as the purchase of about 10,000 mobile homes at a cost of $860 million that were sitting unused at an airfield in Arkansas. In May 2006 prosecutors and inspectors general from five federal agencies warned that some of the biggest opportunities for fraud were yet to come because the government was just beginning to dispense contracts for large rebuilding efforts.

On April 25, Hector V. Barretto, the head of the Small Business Administration—another agency that had been sharply criticized for its inept handling of the hurricane disaster—announced his resignation. According to the *New York Times*, in the three months following Hurricane Katrina the agency had processed only 30 percent of the 276,000 applications it had received for disaster loans to homeowners and small companies, and the agency had rejected more than 80 percent of the applications it had processed. Barretto said he had not been asked to resign, and his tenure at the agency was praised by Rep. Donald Manzullo, R-Ill., chairman of the House Small Business Committee. The GAO, however, told Congress that the agency had been unprepared to handle such a major disaster and was largely in a "reactive state."

New Orleans Recovery

In New Orleans recovery moved in fits and starts. There were some signs, symbolic and tangible, that the city was coming back to life. A smaller-than-usual but nonetheless exuberant crowd turned out for the annual Mardi Gras celebration on February 28. C. Ray Nagin was reelected as mayor, narrowly defeating the state's lieutenant governor, Mitch Landrieu, in a runoff election held May 21. Displaced New Orleanians, many of them poor and black and perhaps unlikely ever to return, cast absentee ballots or voted at satellite polling places scattered around the state.

Just before the election, Nagin published a new evacuation plan that involved using buses and trains to transport people out of the city and that would not use the Superdome or city convention center as shelters of last resort. The Superdome reopened September 25, with a victory by the New Orleans Saints football team over the Atlanta Falcons. The Army Corps of Engineers completed repairs and improvements to the city's flood protection system at the end of May, meeting its deadline for being ready for the start of the next hurricane season on June 1. Despite efforts to strengthen the levees, most experts, including the corps, said the embankments could still be vulnerable to another storm as big as Katrina. President Bush made a symbolic visit on the first anniversary of the storm, where he took "full responsibility" for the inept federal response and promised again that "we will do what it takes to help you recover."

Despite those assurances, many of the federal programs were still faltering. For example, FEMA's management of its temporary rental assistance program for storm evacuees was sharply attacked by a federal judge in Washington, D.C. Judge Richard J. Leon of the Federal District Court for the District of Columbia on November 29 ruled the agency had violated evacuees' constitutional rights by cutting off rental assistance payments without notice, explanation, or avenue of appeal. A federally funded program called the "Road Home" was also encountering management problems. Designed to give Louisiana residents up to $150,000 each to rebuild or sell homes severely damaged by the storm, the $9 billion grant program was expected to help about 200,000 homeowners or apartment dwellers in the state. But according to the *New York Times,* by early November only 1,721 applicants had been told how much grant money they would receive and only 22 had actually received the grants.

The inability to agree on a comprehensive, coordinated plan for rebuilding the city also slowed progress—and caused widespread frustration. With the mayoral election behind them, Nagin and other city officials were finally able to agree in July on a process for developing a rebuilding plan; that plan was still being worked on at the end of the year.

City services were also coming back on line only slowly. By year's end, less than half of the city's public schools had reopened, according to the Brookings Institution. More than one-third of the city's hospitals were still closed for repairs, public transportation was running at about half strength, and gas and electricity services were still not fully operative. In addition, crime was rising to alarming levels.

All these factors, along with the lack of job opportunities, a shortage of livable and affordable housing, and uncertainty about the future, combined to keep many residents from returning home. A year after the storm, the city's population had dropped by nearly 60 percent, and the racial composition of the city had shifted to be about half white and half black. Before the storm, two-thirds of the city's residents were African American. Lack of housing was thought to be a main reason why so few blacks had returned to the city. Many blacks had lived in rental housing, much of which was destroyed in the storm, producing a shortage of rentals and thus a spike in rental prices, which many former poor residents were unable to afford. Moreover, city officials said they were planning to restore only a small proportion of the city's public housing units. One of the most vocal outcries came in December, when the federal Department of Housing and Urban Development announced that that it had decided to tear down four public housing complexes, with a total of 3,500 apartments. Residents charged that the move was deliberately intended to keep poor blacks from moving back into the city.

Other Fallout from Katrina and Rita

Several other developments occurred during the year that were directly related to the hurricanes. The American Red Cross announced that it was undertaking a radical overhaul of its organizational structure. Among other things, it would explicitly delegate day-to-day operations to its professional management and focus its board of governors on long-range strategic oversight. Friction between the board and management had been a major factor hampering the charity's relief efforts after hurricanes Katrina and Rita. The Red Cross had been widely criticized for being unprepared, for responding too slowly in some low-income communities, and for being reluctant to work with other charities and nonprofits. The organization was also embarrassed by revelations that some of its workers were involved in schemes to defraud the charity. After an internal investigation the Red Cross acknowledged that it had relied too heavily on overwhelmed and inexperienced volunteers and that it needed to create a more flexible bureaucratic structure and implement an effective system for preventing fraud.

Another development was the increasing reluctance of insurance companies to write home insurance policies in disaster-prone areas, forcing homeowners to turn to state-run plans that tended to be subsidized by taxpayers. Several insurance companies warned that a combination of climate change and population growth in vulnerable coastal areas could lead to an insurance catastrophe the next time a major disaster struck.

Controversy continued to swirl around proposals by the Army Corps of Engineers to repair and protect the Gulf Coast from future hurricanes. Although the corps had until the end of 2007 to present a long-range plan to Congress, several geologists were already sharply questioning some of the elements the corps was considering, among them the restoration of barrier islands and beachfront neighborhoods that had already been leveled twice—once in 1969 by Hurricane Camille and again in 2005 by Katrina. The scientists warned that such projects would cost billions but remain vulnerable to devastation in future storms. The corps was also criticized for failing to close immediately a seventy-six-mile long shipping channel, known as the "hurricane highway" by locals who said it funneled water from storm surges into the city. In a preliminary report sent to Congress on December 15, the corps denied that the channel had contributed to the flooding in New Orleans's Ninth Ward but still urged Congress to close the channel.

Following is the text of the executive summary and conclusion from "A Failure of Initiative," the final report of the House Select Bipartisan Committee to Investigate the Preparation for and Response to Hurricane Katrina, issued on February 15, 2006.

DOCUMENT

"A Failure of Initiative"

Executive Summary of Findings

The Select Committee identified failures at all levels of government that significantly undermined and detracted from the heroic efforts of first responders, private individuals and organizations, faith-based groups, and others.

The institutional and individual failures we have identified became all the more clear when compared to the heroic efforts of those who acted decisively. Those who didn't flinch, who took matters into their own hands when bureaucratic inertia was causing death, injury, and suffering. Those whose exceptional initiative saved time and money and lives.

We salute the exceptions to the rule, or, more accurately, the exceptions that proved the rule. People like Mike Ford, the owner of three nursing homes who wisely chose to evacuate his patients in Plaquemines Parish before Katrina hit, due in large part to his close and long-standing working relationship with Jesse St. Amant, Director of the Plaquemines Office of Emergency Preparedness.

People like Dr. Gregory Henderson, a pathologist who showed that not all looting represented lawlessness when, with the aid of New Orleans police officers, he raided pharmacies for needed medication and supplies and set up ad hoc clinics in downtown hotels before moving on to the Convention Center.

But these acts of leadership were too few and far between. And no one heard about or learned from them until it was too late.

The preparation for and response to Hurricane Katrina show we are still an analog government in a digital age. We must recognize that we are woefully incapable of storing, moving, and accessing information—especially in times of crisis.

Many of the problems we have identified can be categorized as "information gaps"—or at least problems with information-related implications, or failures to act decisively because information was sketchy at best. Better information would have been an optimal weapon against Katrina. Information sent to the right people at the right place at the right time. Information moved within agencies, across departments, and between jurisdictions of government as well. Seamlessly. Securely. Efficiently.

Unfortunately, no government does these things well, especially big governments.

The federal government is the largest purchaser of information technology in the world, by far. One would think we could share information by now. But Katrina again proved we cannot.

We reflect on the 9/11 Commission's finding that "the most important failure was one of imagination." The Select Committee believes Katrina was primarily a failure of initiative. But there is, of course, a nexus between the two. Both imagination and initiative—in other words, *leadership*—require good information. And a coordinated process for sharing it. And a willingness to use information—however imperfect or incomplete—to fuel action.

With Katrina, the reasons reliable information did not reach more people more quickly are many, and these reasons provide the foundation for our findings.

In essence, we found that while a national emergency management system that relies on state and local governments to identify needs and request resources is adequate for most disasters, a catastrophic disaster like Katrina can and did overwhelm most aspects of the system for an initial period of time. No one anticipated the degree and scope of the destruction the storm would cause, even though many could and should have.

The failure of local, state, and federal governments to respond more effectively to Katrina—which had been predicted in theory for many years, and forecast with startling accuracy for five days—demonstrates that whatever improvements have been made to our capacity to respond to natural or man-made disasters, four and half years after 9/11, we are still not fully prepared. Local first responders were largely overwhelmed and unable to perform their duties, and the National Response Plan did not adequately provide a way for federal assets to quickly supplement or, if necessary, supplant first responders.

The failure of initiative was also a failure of agility. Response plans at all levels of government lacked flexibility and adaptability. Inflexible procedures often delayed the response. Officials at all levels seemed to be waiting for the disaster that fit their plans, rather than planning and building scalable capacities to meet whatever Mother Nature threw at them. We again encountered the risk-averse culture that pervades big government, and again recognized the need for organizations as agile and responsive as the 21st century world in which we live.

One-size-fits-all plans proved impervious to clear warnings of extraordinary peril. Category 5 needs elicited a Category 1 response. Ours was a response that could not adequately accept civilian and international generosity, and one for which the Congress, through inadequate oversight and accounting of state and local use of federal funds, must accept some blame.

In crafting our findings, we did not guide the facts. We let the facts guide us. The

Select Committee's report elaborates on the following findings, which are summarized in part here, in the order in which they appear:

The accuracy and timeliness of National Weather Service and National Hurricane Center forecasts prevented further loss of life

The Hurricane Pam exercise reflected recognition by all levels of government of the dangers of a category 4 or 5 hurricane striking New Orleans

- Implementation of lessons learned from Hurricane Pam was incomplete.

Levees protecting New Orleans were not built for the most severe hurricanes

- Responsibilities for levee operations and maintenance were diffuse.
- The lack of a warning system for breaches and other factors delayed repairs to the levees.
- The ultimate cause of the levee failures is under investigation, and results to be determined.

The failure of complete evacuations led to preventable deaths, great suffering, and further delays in relief

- Evacuations of general populations went relatively well in all three states.
- Despite adequate warning 56 hours before landfall, Governor [Kathleen Babineaux] Blanco and Mayor [Ray] Nagin delayed ordering a mandatory evacuation in New Orleans until 19 hours before landfall.
- The failure to order timely mandatory evacuations, Mayor Nagin's decision to shelter but not evacuate the remaining population, and decisions of individuals led to an incomplete evacuation.
- The incomplete pre-landfall evacuation led to deaths, thousands of dangerous rescues, and horrible conditions for those who remained.
- Federal, state, and local officials' failure to anticipate the post-landfall conditions delayed post-landfall evacuation and support.

Critical elements of the National Response Plan were executed late, ineffectively, or not at all

- It does not appear the President received adequate advice and counsel from a senior disaster professional.
- Given the well-known consequences of a major hurricane striking New Orleans, the Secretary should have designated an Incident of National Significance no later than Saturday, two days prior to landfall, when the National Weather Service predicted New Orleans would be struck by a Category 4 or 5 hurricane and President Bush declared a federal emergency.
- The Secretary should have convened the Interagency Incident Management Group on Saturday, two days prior to landfall, or earlier to analyze Katrina's potential consequences and anticipate what the federal response would need to accomplish.
- The Secretary should have designated the Principal Federal Official [PFO] on Saturday, two days prior to landfall, from the roster of PFOs who had successfully completed the required training, unlike then-FEMA [Federal Emergency Management Agency] Director Michael Brown. Considerable confusion was caused by the Secretary's PFO decisions.
- A proactive federal response, or push system, is not a new concept, but it is rarely utilized.
- The Secretary should have invoked the Catastrophic Incident Annex to direct the federal response posture to fully switch from a reactive to proactive mode of operations.
- Absent the Secretary's invocation of the Catastrophic Incident Annex, the federal response evolved into a push system over several days.

- The Homeland Security Operations Center failed to provide valuable situational information to the White House and key operational officials during the disaster.
- The White House failed to de-conflict varying damage assessments and discounted information that ultimately proved accurate.
- Federal agencies, including DHS, had varying degrees of unfamiliarity with their roles and responsibilities under the National Response Plan and National Incident Management System.
- Once activated, the Emergency Management Assistance Compact [EMAC] enabled an unprecedented level of mutual aid assistance to reach the disaster area in a timely and effective manner.
- Earlier presidential involvement might have resulted in a more effective response.

DHS and the states were not prepared for this catastrophic event

- While a majority of state and local preparedness grants are required to have a terrorism purpose, this does not preclude a dual use application.
- Despite extensive preparedness initiatives, DHS was not prepared to respond to the catastrophic effects of Hurricane Katrina.
- DHS and FEMA lacked adequate trained and experienced staff for the Katrina response.
- The readiness of FEMA's national emergency response teams was inadequate and reduced the effectiveness of the federal response.

Massive communications damage and a failure to adequately plan for alternatives impaired response efforts, command and control, and situational awareness

- Massive inoperability had the biggest effect on communications, limiting command and control, situational awareness, and federal, state, and local officials' ability to address unsubstantiated media reports.
- Some local and state responders prepared for communications losses but still experienced problems, while others were caught unprepared.
- The National Communication System met many of the challenges posed by Hurricane Katrina, enabling critical communication during the response, but gaps in the system did result in delayed response and inadequate delivery of relief supplies.

Command and control was impaired at all levels, delaying relief

- Lack of communications and situational awareness paralyzed command and control.
- A lack of personnel, training, and funding also weakened command and control.
- Ineffective command and control delayed many relief efforts.

The military played an invaluable role, but coordination was lacking

- The National Response Plan's Catastrophic Incident Annex as written would have delayed the active duty military response, even if it had been implemented.
- DOD/DHS coordination was not effective during Hurricane Katrina.
- DOD, FEMA, and the state of Louisiana had difficulty coordinating with each other, which slowed the response.
- National Guard and DOD response operations were comprehensive, but perceived as slow.
- The Coast Guard's response saved many lives, but coordination with other responders could improve.
- The Army Corps of Engineers provided critical resources to Katrina victims, but pre-landfall contracts were not adequate.

- DOD has not yet incorporated or implemented lessons learned from joint exercises in military assistance to civil authorities that would have allowed for a more effective response to Katrina.
- The lack of integration of National Guard and active duty forces hampered the military response.
- Northern Command does not have adequate insight into state response capabilities or adequate interface with governors, which contributed to a lack of mutual understanding and trust during the Katrina response.
- Even DOD lacked situational awareness of post-landfall conditions, which contributed to a slower response.
- DOD lacked an information sharing protocol that would have enhanced joint situational awareness and communications between all military components.
- Joint Task Force Katrina command staff lacked joint training, which contributed to the lack of coordination between active duty components.
- Joint Task Force Katrina, the National Guard, Louisiana, and Mississippi lacked needed communications equipment and the interoperability required for seamless on-the-ground coordination.
- EMAC processing, pre-arranged state compacts, and Guard equipment packages need improvement.
- Equipment, personnel, and training shortfalls affected the National Guard response.
- Search and rescue operations were a tremendous success, but coordination and integration between the military services, the National Guard, the Coast Guard, and other rescue organizations was lacking.

The collapse of local law enforcement and lack of effective public communications led to civil unrest and further delayed relief

- A variety of conditions led to lawlessness and violence in hurricane stricken areas.
- The New Orleans Police Department was ill-prepared for continuity of operations and lost almost all effectiveness.
- The lack of a government public communications strategy and media hype of violence exacerbated public concerns and further delayed relief.
- EMAC and military assistance were critical for restoring law and order.
- Federal law enforcement agencies were also critical to restoring law and order and coordinating activities.

Medical care and evacuations suffered from a lack of advance preparations, inadequate communications, and difficulties coordinating efforts

- Deployment of medical personnel was reactive, not proactive.
- Poor planning and pre-positioning of medical supplies and equipment led to delays and shortages.
- New Orleans was unprepared to provide evacuations and medical care for its special needs population and dialysis patients, and Louisiana officials lacked a common definition of "special needs."
- Most hospital and Veterans Affairs Medical Center emergency plans did not offer concrete guidance about if or when evacuations should take place.
- New Orleans hospitals, Veterans Affairs Medical Center, and medical first responders were not adequately prepared for a full evacuation of medical facilities.
- The government did not effectively coordinate private air transport capabilities for the evacuation of medical patients.

- Hospital and Veterans Affairs Medical Center emergency plans did not adequately prepare for communication needs.
- Following Hurricane Katrina, New Orleans Veterans Affairs Medical Center and hospitals' inability to communicate impeded their ability to ask for help.
- Medical responders did not have adequate communications equipment or operability.
- Evacuation decisions for New Orleans nursing homes were subjective and, in one case, led to preventable deaths.
- Lack of electronic patient medical records contributed to difficulties and delays in medical treatment of evacuees.
- Top officials at the Department at Health and Human Services and the National Disaster Medical System do not share a common understanding of who controls the National Disaster Medical System under Emergency Support Function-8.
- Lack of coordination led to delays in recovering dead bodies.
- Deployment confusion, uncertainty about mission assignments, and government red tape delayed medical care.

Long-standing weaknesses and the magnitude of the disaster overwhelmed FEMA's ability to provide emergency shelter and temporary housing

- Relocation plans did not adequately provide for shelter. Housing plans were haphazard and inadequate.
- State and local governments made inappropriate selections of shelters of last resort. The lack of a regional database of shelters contributed to an inefficient and ineffective evacuation and sheltering process.
- There was inappropriate delay in getting people out of shelters and into temporary housing— delays that officials should have foreseen due to manufacturing limitations.
- FEMA failed to take advantage of the Department of Housing and Urban Development's expertise in large-scale housing challenges.

FEMA logistics and contracting systems did not support a targeted, massive, and sustained provision of commodities

- FEMA management lacked situational awareness of existing requirements and of resources in the supply chain. An overwhelmed logistics system made it challenging to get supplies, equipment, and personnel where and when needed.
- Procedures for requesting federal assistance raised numerous concerns.
- The failure at all levels to enter into advance contracts led to chaos and the potential for waste and fraud as acquisitions were made in haste.
- Before Katrina, FEMA suffered from a lack of sufficiently trained procurement professionals. DHS procurement continues to be decentralized and lacking a uniform approach, and its procurement office was understaffed given the volume and dollar value of work.
- Ambiguous statutory guidance regarding local contractor participation led to ongoing disputes over procuring debris removal and other services.
- Attracting emergency contractors and corporate support could prove challenging given the scrutiny that companies have endured.

Contributions by charitable organizations assisted many in need, but the American Red Cross and others faced challenges due to the size of the mission, inadequate logistics capacity, and a disorganized shelter process. . . .

Conclusion

The preparation for and response to Hurricane Katrina should disturb all Americans. While the Select Committee believes all people involved, at all levels of government, were trying their best to save lives and ease suffering, their best just wasn't good enough.

In this report we have tried to tell the story of the inadequate preparation and response. We cover a lot of territory—from evacuations to medical care, communications to contracting. We hope our findings will prompt the changes needed to make all levels of government better prepared and better able to respond the next time.

The resolution that created the Select Committee charged us with compiling findings, not recommendations. But in reality that's a distinction without a difference. Moving from our findings to legislative, organizational, and policy changes need not be a long or difficult journey.

We are left scratching our heads at the range of inefficiency and ineffectivness that characterized government behavior right before and after this storm. But passivity did the most damage. The failure of initiative cost lives, prolonged suffering, and left all Americans justifiably concerned our government is no better prepared to protect its people than it was before 9/11, even if we are.

How can we set up a system to protect against passivity? Why do we repeatedly seem out of synch during disasters? Why do we continually seem to be one disaster behind?

We have not found every fact nor contemplated all successes and failures. What we have done over four months is intensely focus on a three-week period, uncovering a multitude of problems. We have learned more than enough to instruct those who will now have to craft and execute changes for the future.

We leave it to readers to determine whether we have done a fair and thorough job, and whether we identified and supported findings in a way that will foster change. Some predicted we would place disproportionate blame on one person or another, or that we would give some others a pass. We hope it is clear we have done neither. We have not sought to assign individual blame, though it is clear in our report that some were not up to the challenge that was Katrina. Rather, we have tried to tell the story of government's preparation for and response to a massive storm, and identify lessons learned.

Our interaction with the White House illustrates this point. Some insist the White House's failure to provide, for example, e-mails to and from the White House Chief of Staff means we have insufficient information to determine why government failed. That view exalts political curiosity over the practical realities of a serious investigation.

While our dealings with the White House proved frustrating and difficult, we ended up with more than enough information to determine what went wrong there, to form a picture of a White House that, like many entities, was overcome by the fog of war. There is a big difference between having enough information to find institutional fault, which we do, and having information to assign individual blame, which, in the case of the White House, in large part we do not.

It's the former that's important if the goal is to be better prepared the next time. This was not about some individual's failure of initiative. It was about organizational and societal failures of initiative. There was more than enough failure to go around:

- Tardy and ineffective execution of the National Response Plan.
- An under-trained and under-staffed Federal Emergency Management Agency.

- A Catastrophic Incident Annex that was never invoked, and doubt that it would have done the job anyway.
- A perplexing inability to learn from Hurricane Pam and other exercises.
- Levees not built to withstand the most severe hurricanes.
- An incomplete evacuation that led to deaths and tremendous suffering.
- A complete breakdown in communications that paralyzed command and control and made situational awareness murky at best.
- The failure of state and local officials to maintain law and order.
- Haphazard and incomplete emergency shelter and housing plans.
- An overwhelmed FEMA logistics and contracting system that could not support the effective provision of urgently needed supplies.

The Select Committee encountered shortcomings and challenges even among those response elements that went relatively well and saved many lives. The military performed an invaluable role once forces were deployed, but encountered coordination problems with FEMA, the National Guard, and state officials. State-to-state emergency aid compacts were critical in restoring law and order and accelerating relief supplies, but too many people remain unfamiliar with the process. Contributions from charitable groups were enormously helpful, but they too were overwhelmed by the size of the storm.

Many of our findings are mixed in nature. Evacuations of general populations, for example, went relatively well in all three states. But declarations of mandatory evacuations in metropolitan New Orleans came late or not at all, and that, coupled with the decision to shelter but not evacuate the remaining population prolonged suffering. We saw heroic examples of medical care and patient needs being met under dire circumstances. But too often the deployment of medical personnel was reactive, not proactive.

The Select Committee acknowledges it was often torn between sympathy and incredulity, compassion and criticism. On the one hand, we understood Katrina was so big and so devastating that death and chaos were inevitable. We understood that top federal, state, and local officials overlooked some steps and some needs in the hours and days after landfall because they were focused on saving lives. But on the other hand, a dispassionate review made it clear that even an extraordinary lack of situational awareness could not excuse many of the shortcomings and organizational inaction evident in the documents and communications the Select Committee reviewed.

Leadership requires decisions to be made even when based on flawed and incomplete information. Too often during the immediate response to Katrina, sparse or conflicting information was used as an excuse for inaction rather than an imperative to step in and fill an obvious vacuum. Information passed through the maze of departmental operations centers and ironically named "coordinating" committees, losing timeliness and relevance as it was massaged and interpreted for internal audiences.

As a result, leaders became detached from the changing minute-to-minute realities of Katrina. Information translated into pre-cast bureaucratic jargon put more than geographic distance between Washington and the Gulf coast. Summaries and situation reports describing the gross totals of relief supplies directed to affected areas did not say when or how or to whom those desperately needed supplies would be delivered. And apparently no one asked.

Communications aren't a problem when you're only talking to yourself.

The Select Committee believes too many leaders failed to lead. Top aides failed as well, primarily in misprioritizing their bosses' attention and action. Critical time was wasted on issues of no importance to disaster response, such as winning the blame game, waging a public relations battle, or debating the advantages of wardrobe choices.

We have spared our readers a rehashing of unflattering e-mails involving Michael Brown and Governor Blanco and others, as they have been given more than enough attention by the media. We will pause only briefly here to urge future responders to make people, not politics, their priority.

We further urge public officials confronting the next Katrina to remember disaster response must be based on knowledge, not rumors. Government at all levels lost credibility due to inaccurate or unsubstantiated public statements made by officials regarding law and order, levee breaches, and overall response efforts.

The media must share some of the blame here. The Select Committee agrees the media can and should help serve as the public's "first informer" after disasters. In the 21st century, Americans depend on timely and accurate reporting, especially during times of crisis. But it's clear accurate reporting was among Katrina's many victims. If anyone rioted, it was the media. Many stories of rape, murder, and general lawlessness were at best unsubstantiated, at worst simply false. And that's too bad, because this storm needed no exaggeration.

As discussed in our report, widely-distributed uncorroborated rumors caused resources to be deployed, and important time and energy wasted, chasing down the imaginary. Already traumatized people in the Superdome and elsewhere, listening to their transistor radios, were further panicked.

"The sensational accounts delayed rescue and evacuation efforts already hampered by poor planning and a lack of coordination among local, state, and federal agencies. People rushing to the Gulf coast to fly rescue helicopters or to distribute food, water and other aid steeled themselves for battle. In communities near and far, the seeds were planted that the victims of Katrina should be kept away, or at least handled with extreme caution," the *Washington Post* reported on October 5.

Lt. Gen. H. Steven Blum told the Select Committee on October 27, "We focused assets and resources based on situational awareness provided to us by the media, frankly. And the media failed in their responsibility to get it right. . . . we sent forces and capabilities to places that didn't need to go there in numbers that were far in excess of what was required, because they kept running the same B roll over and over. . . . and the impression to us that were watching it was that the condition did not change. But the conditions were continually changing."

E-mails obtained by the Select Committee reinforce the conclusion that top military officials were relying on news reports for information—information used to plan and deploy resources.

The Select Committee does not mean to suggest the media is solely responsible for responders' lack of situational awareness, or the destruction of communications infrastructure that thrust television into the role of first informer for the military as well as the general public. Nor is the media solely responsible for reporting comments from sources they believed to be credible—especially top officials.

The Select Committee does, however, believe such circumstances make accurate reporting, especially in the period immediately after the storm, all the more important. Skepticism and fact-checking are easier when the sea is calm, but more vital when it is not.

As with so many other failures related to Katrina, what's most vexing is that emergency managers should have known such problems would arise among the chaos. Dr. Kathleen Tierney, head of the University of Colorado- Boulder Natural Hazards Center, told Select Committee staff that misleading or completely false media reports should have been among the most foreseeable elements of Katrina. "It's a well-documented element of disaster response," she said. "What you do has to be based on knowledge, not rumor, and you're going to be faced with a lot of rumors."

Benigno Aguirre, sociology professor at the University of Delaware Disaster Research Center, told the *Philadelphia Inquirer*, "It's discouraging for those who spend their lives studying disaster behavior that journalists so often get it wrong."

Former FEMA Director Michael Brown told the Select Committee one of his biggest failures was failing to properly utilize the media as first informer. "I failed initially to set up a series of regular briefings to the media about what FEMA was doing throughout the Gulf coast region," Brown said at the Select Committee's September 27 hearing. "Instead, I became tied to the news shows, going on the news shows early in the morning and late at night, and that was just a mistake. We should have been feeding that information to the press . . . in the manner and time that we wanted to, instead of letting the press drive us."

Finally, a word about public communications. Both the message and the messengers were ineffective before and after Katrina. Messages to the public were uncoordinated and often confusing, leaving important questions unanswered. Federal, state, and local officials did not have a unified strategy for communicating with the public.

Risk communication is a well-researched field of study. There are accepted core principles for successfully communicating risks to the public. Information about threats should be consistent, accurate, clear, and provided repeatedly through multiple methods. It should be timely. It should be specific about the potential threat. It needs to get to people regardless of their level of access to information.

The Select Committee heard loud and clear from Gulf coast residents that the dangers of the coming hurricane could have been presented in a more effective manner, an issue which also carried racial and socioeconomic implications. If people don't hear a message from someone they trust, they will be skeptical.

Doreen Keeler, a New Orleans resident who evacuated before Mayor Nagin called for a mandatory evacuation, told the Select Committee local officials should have called for mandatory evacuations earlier, noting how difficult it was to convince the elderly residents of New Orleans to leave. "If a mandatory evacuation would have been called earlier," she said, "it would have been easier to move seniors out of the area and many lives would have been saved. It took me almost 24 hours to get my in-laws to leave. Others tell the same story. The severity of the storm was not stressed by elected officials."

The relevant "elected officials," we are sure, would contest that. In fact they did, in testimony before the Select Committee. But it's the public perception of what was stressed that's important here. The failure of initiative was also a failure of empathy, a myopia to the need to reach more people on their own terms.

Four and half years after 9/11, Americans deserve more than the state of nature after disaster strikes. With this report we have tried to identify where and why chaos ensued, so that even a storm the size of Katrina can be met with more order, more urgency, more coordination, and more initiative.

Source: U.S. Congress. House. Select Bipartisan Committee to Investigate the Preparation for and Response to Hurricane Katrina. "A Failure of Initiative: The Final Report of the Select Bipartisan Committee to Investigate the Preparation for and Response to Hurricane Katrina." February 15, 2006. Washington, D.C.: U.S. Government Printing Office. http://purl.access.gpo.gov/GPO/LPS68393 (accessed January 27, 2007).

Other Historic Documents of Interest

Midterm elections, p. 645   State of the Union, p. 23
Presidential signing statements,
   p. 447

March

President Bush and Prime Minister Singh on U.S.-Indian Relations

March 2, 2006

■■■■■■■ **THE DOCUMENT IN CONTEXT** ■■■■■■■

More than three decades after it exploded its first nuclear weapon, India in 2006 took a major step toward becoming a formal member of the world's most exclusive club—that of nations with the internationally recognized right to have nuclear weapons. Under a landmark agreement negotiated with the United States, India earned the right to buy nuclear fuel and technology on the open market even as it continued producing material to expand its nuclear weapons arsenal.

President George W. Bush pushed for the nuclear agreement with India and lobbied Congress and other countries to endorse it, as part of his plan to improve relations between the United States and India. Bush said he saw vast opportunities for commerce with a country with a rapidly expanding economy, one that in a few years would overtake China as the world's most populous nation. Administration officials also clearly viewed India as a potential counterweight to China—the country that many people believed might one day replace the United States as the world's foremost superpower.

Bush's embrace of India as a nuclear partner raised many questions about the future prospects of a decades-long international effort to contain the spread of nuclear weapons. Critics worried, in particular, that the agreement with India would raise new hurdles to negotiations that were under way to control the nuclear weapons ambitions of Iran and North Korea. Also of concern was the impact on India's neighbor and archrival Pakistan, which also had built its own nuclear weapons. *(India-Pakistan weapons race, Historic Documents of 1998, p. 326; U.S.-India agreement, Historic Documents of 2005, p. 462)*

March 2 Agreement

President Bush and Indian prime minister Manmohan Singh had first signaled their plans for a nuclear cooperation agreement during a meeting at the White House on July 18, 2005. In a historic announcement at that meeting, the two leaders said they planned to negotiate an agreement under which the United States could sell fuel and technology to India for its civilian nuclear power industry. Such sales were prohibited under U.S. law—the Nuclear Non-Proliferation Act of 1978 (PL 95–242)—because India had built nuclear weapons and had not signed a 1970 United Nations accord—the Treaty on the Non-Proliferation of Nuclear Weapons, commonly known as the Nuclear Non-Proliferation Treaty (NPT)—that tried to halt the spread of nuclear weapons. The United States also was one of forty-five members of the Nuclear Supplies Group, an association of countries that sold nuclear technology on the open market and had developed regulations barring such sales to India and other countries that did not abide by the NPT.

During the rest of 2005, and into early 2006, U.S. and Indian officials negotiated the details of the general agreement Bush and Singh had announced at the White House. During the course of these negotiations, State Department officials assured Congress that the final agreement would have "credible, transparent, and defensible" provisions to ensure that India would not build more nuclear weapons using the supplies it purchased from the United States.

The pace of negotiations picked up early in 2006 in advance of a long-planned visit to India by Bush, the first during his presidency. Officials on both sides hoped to be able to announce a formal agreement on the nuclear issue during that visit. As had been the case during earlier negotiations, the central issue was a U.S. demand that India strictly separate the civilian and military components of its nuclear industry so that anything provided by the United States would be put to civilian use and not diverted into weapons. According to subsequent reports, negotiations on these matters stalled right before Bush's arrival in New Delhi, with Indian negotiators refusing to accept key U.S. demands for dividing the civilian and military components. Bush himself reportedly broke the impasse by accepting India's position.

Bush and Singh announced their agreement in a news conference at the prime minister's official residence, Hyderabad House, on March 2. Each hailed the agreement as "historic," and Bush said his actions were guided by the need to respond to changes in the world. "I am trying to think differently, not to stay stuck in the past, and recognize that by thinking differently, particularly on nuclear power, we can achieve some important objectives."

From New Delhi, Bush flew to Islamabad, the capital of Pakistan. There, President Pervez Musharraf reportedly asked Bush for a similar U.S. agreement to aid his country's nuclear program—a request Bush said he rejected. "I explained that Pakistan and India are different countries with different needs and different histories," Bush told reporters after the meeting. "So as we proceed forward, our strategy will take in effect those well-known differences."

Key Elements of the March 2 Agreement

The U.S.-India nuclear agreement was important for India because of the promise for fuel and new technology for its nuclear power plants at a time when demand for electricity was booming, along with the country's economy. Nuclear power provided less than 3 percent of India's electricity in 2006, but officials expressed hope that figure could rise to about 25 percent by the middle of the twenty-first century. India's own supply of uranium—the basic material needed to run nuclear reactors—was dwindling rapidly, and under current international restrictions India was unable to buy uranium on the open market. The prime immediate advantage of the deal for the United States was that it opened the potentially large Indian market for sales of uranium, other supplies, and even entire nuclear power plants by the long-troubled U.S. nuclear industry. U.S. officials said India planned to buy eight 1,000-megawatt reactors to provide electrical power in coming years.

The central issues in the agreement involved:

Testing. India promised to refrain from further tests of nuclear weapons, but only so long as other nations (meaning Pakistan) also refrained from testing. India had not signed the Comprehensive Test Ban Treaty, which would have obligated it to halt tests, but the Bush administration was not in a position to demand Indian adherence to the treaty, which the Senate had rejected in 1998 and 1999 because of Republican objections. *(Test ban treaty, Historic Documents of 1999, p. 600)*

Separating civilian from military facilities. This was the crux of the negotiations. India agreed to classify fourteen of its twenty-two nuclear reactors as civilian and to make them subject to restrictions on their use (called "safeguards") and to regular inspections by the International Atomic Energy Agency (IAEA) by 2014. Any new civilian-use reactors built by India also would be subject to these safeguards and inspections. The IAEA safeguards would remain in place on India's civilian nuclear facilities permanently, according to Nicholas Burns, the undersecretary of state for political affairs, who negotiated the agreement for the United States. However, India retained the right to produce nuclear weapons fuel at the other eight reactors, which were designated as having military uses. Among these were two "fast-breeder" reactors capable of producing weapons-grade plutonium. India refused to promise to end production of weapons-grade fuel or to place any new military reactors under inspections.

Export controls. India promised it would not export nuclear supplies or technology to other countries without approval from the original sources of that material. Bush administration officials said India—unlike its neighbor Pakistan—had never been accused of selling nuclear materials on the black market.

Reaction

In India, the deal won praise from the business community and among those who had long sought better relations with the United States. However, it came under fierce criticism from leftist politicians—including some in Singh's coalition—who feared that Washington's only interest in India was as a balance against China. Large-scale demonstrations against Bush's visit were mounted in New Delhi, Calcutta, and Mumbai (Bombay). Several protesters carried banners denouncing Bush's alleged attempt to include India in an American "empire" replacing the British empire, which long had India as its center.

U.S. experts on weapons proliferation also had differing reactions. Some said the deal, in its totality, served the global interest in containing the number of countries with nuclear weapons; others argued that specific provisions undermined that interest. Among those holding the latter view was Robert J. Einhorn, who had been a senior State Department official in the Clinton administration and was working at the Center for Strategic and International Studies, a Washington foreign policy think tank. Along with others, he expressed concern that the deal allowed India to continue, and even expand, its production of weapons-grade material at the eight reactors designated for military use. Einhorn and other critics said they were particularly concerned that, by selling uranium to India for its civilian plants, the United States simply would allow India to use its own uranium for weapons. "One has to assume that the administration was so interested in concluding a deal that it was prepared to cave into the demands of the Indian nuclear establishment," Einhorn told the *New York Times*.

Politicians and weapons policy experts also had conflicting views on whether the deal would set back international efforts to contain nuclear weapons programs in Iran and North Korea, and whether it would speed up the nuclear arms race between India and Pakistan. Einhorn and other critics said that the administration, by giving India special privileges despite its three-decade-long refusal to accept the NPT, was signaling to Iran and North Korea that they, too, could continue their weapons programs and expect rewards some time in the future. Administration officials rejected this argument, insisting that India had been a "responsible" nuclear power, but that neither Iran nor North Korea were likely to fall into that category.

One of the most influential voices supporting the agreement was that of Mohammed ElBaradei, the director general of the IAEA. ElBaradei had been critical of the Bush administration's claims in 2002–2003 about Iraq's presumed weapons of mass destruction, and the administration had sought to oust him from office. But he supported the U.S.-India negotiations and said in a statement that the March 2 agreement would "bring India closer as an important partner in the nonproliferation regime" by helping it obtain nuclear supplies on the open market.

Congressional Action

The nuclear deal with India put Congress in a box. On the one hand, there was broad bipartisan support for improving relations with India after decades of distrust, and members of Congress responded positively to business leaders who saw the potential for vastly expanded commerce with India. Moreover, most members who had been active in nuclear nonproliferation issues acknowledged the validity of the administration's argument that getting India's cooperation on those matters was an important achievement. Lawmakers expressed worries about the potentially negative impact of rejecting the deal, or even trying to impose significant conditions on it. Even so, there was broad skepticism in Congress about some of the specific provisions of the agreement—notably the lack of control on India's military reactors—and concern about the potential impact on negotiations with India and North Korea.

To carry out the agreement with India, the administration needed to get Congress to revise several specific provisions of U.S. law that barred sales of nuclear supplies to India because it had built nuclear weapons by illicitly using equipment and material provided by the United States and Canada. Bush, Undersecretary Burns from the State Department, and other officials lobbied members of Congress on the issue for months after the March 2 agreement. For its part, the Indian government hired several well-connected Washington lobbyists to push for the legislation.

The first action came in late June when the House International Relations and Senate Foreign Relations committees approved legislation (HR 5682 and S 3709, respectively) amending U.S. law, and thereby approving the March 2 agreement. Both versions included provisions requiring the president to assert to Congress that India had, in fact, fully separated its civilian and military nuclear programs. Such provisions brought a complaint from Singh that Congress was attempting to rewrite the agreement he and Bush had reached in March.

The House of Representatives endorsed the legislation on July 26, by a vote of 359–68. The India nuclear legislation languished in the Senate and was still pending at the time Congress took its break for the midterm elections. The Senate finally acted on November 17, rejecting several attempts that would have derailed the agreement and endorsing the India legislation by an unexpectedly wide 85–12 vote. Among those supporting the measure was Sen. Richard G. Lugar, R-Ind., who chaired the Foreign Relations Committee and who long had been one of the staunchest congressional advocates of controlling nuclear weapons proliferation.

House and Senate leaders quickly took their slightly differing bills to a conference committee, and the final version cleared the House on December 8 and the Senate on December 9. Bush signed the measure into law (PL 109–401) on December 18. "After thirty years outside the system, India will now operate its civilian nuclear energy program under internationally accepted guidelines and the world is going to be safer as a result," he said. Some critics remained unimpressed, however. Rep. Edward Markey, D-Mass., who chaired a bipartisan caucus on weapons proliferation issues, said the agreement "may well become the death warrant to the international nuclear nonproliferation regime." Singh also faced critics in India, who said the United States was attempting to impose unacceptable conditions on India's nuclear programs. "The primary [U.S.] objective is to cap, roll back, and ultimately eliminate its [India's] nuclear weapons capability," said L.K. Advani, leader of the opposition Bharatiya Janata Party.

Even with congressional action, the U.S.-India nuclear agreement still faced several procedural hurdles. The two countries needed to complete a formal nuclear cooperation agreement (known as a "123 agreement" after the relevant provision of U.S. law), which was subject to approval by both the Senate and in the Indian parliament. India also needed to negotiate an agreement for inspections of its civilian nuclear facilities by the IAEA. Also, the administration needed to convince fellow member nations in the Nuclear Suppliers Group to lift restrictions on nuclear sales to India. Administration officials said they had been sounding out other group members on the issue for months and expected no difficulty in getting approval, even though the process could take another year or more to complete.

Following are excerpts from a news conference, held in New Delhi on March 2, 2006, by India's prime minister, Manmohan Singh, and President George W. Bush, announcing the signing of an agreement under which the United States would allow sales of nuclear materials, equipment, and supplies to India for its civilian nuclear power industry.

■■■■■■■■ DOCUMENT ■■■■■■■■

"Remarks Following Discussions with Prime Minister Singh of India"

Prime Minister Singh: Mr. President, ladies and gentlemen of the press: President Bush and I have completed very cordial and productive discussions this morning. We reviewed the status of our cooperation, including the agenda that was set on July 18, 2005. The joint statement that will be shared with all of you today contains a number of announcements and initiatives that underline the significant progress in our relationship.

Many of the areas that our cooperation now covers are essential to India's national development. They include energy, agriculture, science and technology, trade and investment, high technology, health, and a clean environment. This is a highly ambitious agenda, one that is befitting our growing strategic partnership. When implemented, they will make a real difference to the lives of our people.

The President and I had an opportunity to review the global situation in our talks. As you're all aware, India and the United States are working together increasingly on global issues. This is not just good for our two countries but also benefits the international community, as we can complement each others' capabilities and share responsibilities. President Bush is admired for his strong position on terrorism. And I was particularly pleased that we agreed on the need to root out terrorism, of which India has been a major victim.

I'm particularly pleased that we have reached an understanding on the implementation of our agreement on civil nuclear cooperation of July 18, 2005. I have conveyed to the President that India has finalized the identification of civilian facilities to which we had committed. I was also happy to hear from the President that he now intended to approach the U.S. Congress to amend U.S. laws and the Nuclear Supplier Group to adjust its guideline. We will discuss with the International Atomic Energy Agency [IAEA] in regard to fashioning an appropriate India-specific safeguards agreement. You will appreciate I cannot say more now, while our Parliament is in session.

Before concluding, I would like to express my warm appreciation for the personal interest shown and the leadership role that President Bush has played in the transformation of our ties. I have met the President a number of times, and on each occasion, I have admired his vision, his resolve, and his commitment to strengthening our bilateral relations. Our discussion today make me confident that there are no limits to the Indo-U.S. partnerships.

May I invite you, Mr. President, now to make your remarks.

President Bush: Mr. Prime Minister, thank you very much. It's a joy to be here. Laura and I are really thankful for your hospitality, and I appreciate the lengthy and constructive dialog we just had on a wide range of issues. I particularly thank the CEOs from both the United States and India who have worked hard to help develop a way forward to make sure our relationship is constructive and long-lasting.

India and America have built a strategic partnership based upon common values. Our two democracies respect religious pluralism and the rule of law. We seek to foster economic development through trade and advancing the entrepreneurial spirit in both countries.

We're working as partners to make the world safer. India and America both suffered from terrorist attacks on our home soil. Terrorists attacked New Delhi. We're sharing information to protect each other. We have a common desire to enhance the security of our peoples. We're cooperating on the military front. We worked as partners in responding to the tsunami. I was struck, and so were the American people, that the Indian Air Force delivered Hurricane Katrina aid to an Air Force base in Little Rock, Arkansas. And for that, Mr. Prime Minister, thank you. . . .

As the Prime Minister mentioned, we concluded an historic agreement today on nuclear power. It's not an easy job for the Prime Minister to achieve this agreement, I understand. It's not easy for the American President to achieve this agreement. But it's a necessary agreement. It's one that will help both our peoples.

Again, I applaud you for your courage and your leadership. I'm looking forward to working with our United States Congress to change decades of law that will enable us to move forward in this important initiative.

Also, we talked about the Advanced Energy Initiative that I'm proposing in my own country. Listen, the whole purpose of the Advanced Energy Initiative is to end our dependence on oil, and as we develop technologies that will enable us to do so, we look forward to working with India so we can achieve the same objectives. Dependency upon fossil fuels causes, particularly during times of shortage, causes prices to rise in both our countries.

And it's in our interests that we share technologies to move away from the era of fossil fuels.

India and Pakistan have an historic opportunity to work toward lasting peace. Prime Minister Singh and President [Pervez] Musharraf [of Pakistan] have shown themselves to be leaders of courage and vision. And I encourage them to continue making progress on all issues, including Kashmir.

India and America are partners in addressing other global issues like HIV/AIDS and pandemic flu. In other words, this partnership of ours is substantive, and it's important, and it's strategic. And I thank the Prime Minister for working with me to advance this relationship in such a way that we can define our previous meetings and today's meeting as historic in nature. I'm confident that the relationship between India and the United States is good for the United States of America. I hope it's good for the people of India, and I know it's going to be good for laying the foundations of peace in this world of ours.

So, Mr. Prime Minister, thank you very much for having me.

Prime Minister Singh: It's a great honor, Mr. President, to have you.

Civilian Nuclear Power Program in India/United Nations Security Council Membership

Question: Thank you, Mr. Prime Minister. Thank you, Mr. President. Sir, since you have said that India-U.S. nuclear cooperation agreement is on, what we would like to know from you that how are you going to ensure that India's concerns and Indian scientific community's concerns regarding nonstop supply of fuel, and also protecting India's three-phased nuclear research program?

And excuse me, sir, Mr. President, I have a question for you too, sir. Sir, you know, everybody is saying that India and the United States are natural allies. And you have also said many times that our strategic partnership is based on common values, shared values. Sir, then why the largest democracy of the world is reluctant or not forthcoming to support—the oldest democracy of the world is not supporting the largest democracy of the world to have a permanent membership of the United Nations Security Council? This is an issue India would like to hear from you more, sir. Thank you. Thank you, Prime Minister.

Prime Minister Singh: You have asked me about the nuclear agreement. As I mentioned, we have reached a mutually satisfactory understanding with regard to carrying forward the process that was outlined in the July 18 statement which I and President Bush signed.

An important step forward is the preparation of a separation plan, a separation plan which separates the civilian nuclear program from the military program. That phase has been successfully completed. Now it is for the United States to go to the Congress for necessary amendments in U.S. laws. Also, the U.S. will approach the members of the Nuclear Supplier Groups, and thereafter we'll also have to go to the International Atomic Energy Agency for India-specific safeguards.

So we have made very satisfactory progress. And I thank the President for his initiative. But for his leadership this day would probably have not come so soon.

President Bush: Thank you for your question on the U.N. Security Council. I'm not surprised you asked it. As a matter of fact, I gave an interview to a person from the India media in Washington, DC, prior to my trip, and that was one of the questions asked.

My answer hasn't changed, by the way, which is this: One, we support United Nations Security Council reform, and we're interested in different ways to reform the United Nations Security Council. My concern all along, however, is that if we only stick to the United Nations Security Council reform, we miss an opportunity to reform the United Nations overall. And so our position is, let's make sure reform overall moves forward as we think about the best way to reform the Security Council.

The United Nations is a very important international body. It's one that does, however, require better accountability and—accountability on how we spend money and accountability on getting results. One such area, for example, is the Human Rights Commission. The Human Rights Commission needs to be reformed in a way that actually is able to achieve significant results on behalf of the world.

And so we're open minded, and we're listening. But what we don't want to do is have a Security Council reform measure that causes the other reforms not to go forward.

War on Terror/India-U.S. Relations

Question: President Bush, two questions for you. First—

President Bush: Only two? That's good.

Question: First, on the nuclear deal, how do you plan to sell the agreement to a very powerful nonproliferation lobby in Washington which has opposed the deal? And second, on the issue of terrorism, in the context of today's bomb blasts in Karachi, how do you propose to work with India on terrorism, considering India considers that the epicenter of terrorism is in Pakistan?

President Bush: Well, one way we work together on terrorism is to make sure our intelligence services share information. The way you defeat terrorists is you—in the short term—is you anticipate and react to their motives and their actions through good intelligence.

We're involved in a different kind of war. This is a war where people hide and plot and plan and then, all of a sudden, emerge and kill. And so it requires a different response. And part of the response is to commit our intelligence services to sharing information. We spent some time talking about that issue today.

As well, I will send—bring the same message to President Musharraf, that we will continue to work with the President to share information to bring terrorists to justice. Terrorism is not prevalent only in this part of the world. It's prevalent in the Middle East as well. In the long run, terrorism will be defeated by giving people hope and opportunity as opposed to systems of government which breed resentment and provide—and as a result of that resentment, provide opportunity for these killers to recruit.

In terms of convincing the Congress, the first thing I will say to our Congress is that our relationship is changing to the better. You know, sometimes it's hard to get rid of history, and short-term history shows that the United States and India were divided. We didn't have much of a relationship. And as a result, there are laws on the books that reflect that. Now the relationship is changing dramatically. People in the United States have got to understand that trade with India is in our interests, that diplomatic relations with India is in our interests, that cultural exchanges with India are in our interest.

One of the things that helps make that case, of course, is the—there's a lot of Indian Americans making important contributions to our country. And we welcome those contributions. I think there needs to be more student exchanges between our countries. I think we ought to expand H1B visas for Indian scientists and engineers and physicists and people in our country.

In other words, what I'm trying to explain to you is that it's a changing relationship, and part of that change is going to be how to deal with the nuclear issue. Now, proliferation is certainly a concern and a part of our discussions, and we've got a good faith gesture by the Indian Government that I'll be able to take to the Congress. But the other thing that our Congress has got to understand, that it's in our economic interests that India have a civilian nuclear power industry to help take the pressure off of the global demand for energy.

Obviously, nuclear power is a renewable source of energy, and the less demand there is for nonrenewable sources of energy like fossil fuels, the better off it is for the American people. Increasing demand for oil from America, from India and China, relative to a supply that's not keeping up with demand, causes our fuel prices to go up. And so to the extent that we can reduce demand for fossil fuels, it will help the American consumer.

And so there are several ways for me to make the case, which I'm kind of laying out for you now, so that—but this is what I'll be telling our Congress.

Civilian Nuclear Power Program in India

Question: Mr. President, Mr. Prime Minister, following up on this just a touch, what kind of message, sir, does it send to the world that India, which has been testing as late as 1998, nuclear testing, and is not—has not signed the Nuclear Nonproliferation Treaty [NPT]—is this a reward for bad behavior, as some critics suggest? And what kind of message does it send to other countries that are in the process of developing nuclear technology? Why should they sign the NPT if India is getting a deal without doing so, sir?

President Bush: What this agreement says is, things change, times change, that leadership can make a difference, and telling the world—sending the world a different message from that which is—what used to exist in people's minds.

I—listen, I've always said this was going to be a difficult deal for the Prime Minister to sell to his Parliament, but he showed great courage and leadership. And it's difficult for the American President to sell to our Congress, because some people just don't want to change and change with the times. I understand that. But this agreement is in our interests, and therefore, Jim, I'm confident we can sell this to our Congress as in the interest of the United States and, at the same time, make it clear that there's a way forward for other nations to participate in a—in civilian nuclear power in such a way as to address nonproliferation concerns.

India has charted a way forward. You heard the Prime Minister talk about going to the IAEA. That group exists to help safeguard the world from proliferation.

Listen, I proposed reprocessing agreements—that stands in stark contrast to current nuclear theology that we shouldn't reprocess for proliferation concerns. I don't see how you can advocate nuclear power, in order to take the pressure off of our own economy, for example, without advocating technological development of reprocessing, because reprocessing will not only—reprocessing is going to help with the environmental concerns with nuclear power. It will make there—to put it bluntly, there will be less material to dispose.

And so I'm trying to think differently, not to stay stuck in the past, and recognize that by thinking differently, particularly on nuclear power, we can achieve some important objectives, one of which is less reliance on fossil fuels; second is to work with our partners to help both our economies grow; and thirdly is to be strong on dealing with the proliferation issues.

Well, Mr. Prime Minister, it's been a joy.

Prime Minister Singh: Thank you very much, Mr. President. We have made history today, and I thank you.

President Bush: Thank you, sir. Thank you.

Source: U.S. Executive Office of the President. "Remarks Following Discussions with Prime Minister Manmohan Singh of India and an Exchange with Reporters in New Delhi." March 2, 2006. *Weekly Compilation of Presidential Documents* 42, no. 9 (March 6, 2006): 375–380. Washington, D.C.: National Archives and Records Administration. www.gpoaccess.gov/wcomp/v42no09.html (accessed February 8, 2007).

Other Historic Documents of Interest

North Korean nuclear weapons issue, p. 606   *UN resolution on Iran, p. 781*

Former Congressman Cunningham Sentenced to Federal Prison Term

March 3, 2006

████████ **THE DOCUMENT IN CONTEXT** ████████

The sentencing of a former Republican lawmaker and the continuing investigation of a Democratic legislator, both on separate charges of bribery, contributed to the "culture of corruption" that sullied the halls of Congress in 2006. Former Republican representative Randy "Duke" Cunningham of California was sentenced to eight years and four months in prison on March 3, 2006, for accepting bribes from defense contractors in exchange for legislative favors. "It is my hope that Congressman Cunningham will spend his incarceration thinking long and hard about how he broke the trust of the voters that elected him and those on Capitol Hill who served with him," House Speaker J. Dennis Hastert, R-Ill., said in a statement after the sentencing.

To the dismay of the Speaker and other Republican House members, Cunningham's sentencing did not end the case. The Justice Department was continuing to look into the activities of Cunningham and his coconspirators in a probe that some feared might involve additional House members.

In a separate case, Democratic representative William J. Jefferson of Louisiana was elected to a ninth term in office in November, despite a continuing Justice Department investigation of allegations that he, too, had solicited bribes. Jefferson steadfastly maintained his innocence.

Both of these inquiries were separate from and often overshadowed by inquiries surrounding Republican lobbyist Jack Abramoff, whose influence-peddling schemes led to the resignations of House Majority Leader Tom DeLay of Texas and another Republican lawmaker, Bob Ney of Ohio. A fourth Republican House member, Mark Foley, resigned in September after it was revealed that he had made inappropriate advances to underage male congressional pages.

The Cunningham Case

Cunningham appeared in U.S. District Court in San Diego on March 3, where he was sentenced to eight years and four months in prison and ordered to forfeit cash and property worth more than $4 million. Cunningham had pleaded guilty in November 2005 to one count of bribery and one count of tax evasion. Cunningham was the first U.S. legislator to be sent to prison since Ohio representative James A. Traficant Jr. (1985–2002), a Democrat, was sentenced in 2002 to eight years in prison and fined $150,000 on ten counts of bribery, racketeering, and tax evasion. Cunningham, an eight-term House member, had resigned his seat on December 1, 2005. "No one can serve the public and his own greed at the same time. Mr. Cunningham failed his office, his colleagues, and his nation," said the U.S. attorney in San Diego, Carol C. Lam, in a Department of Justice press release announcing the sentence.

Cunningham, one of the first graduates of the navy's Strike Fighter Tactics Course—more commonly known as "top gun" training, had been a highly decorated pilot during the Vietnam War and went on to become a top gun instructor. His experiences are thought to have been the inspiration for the movie *Top Gun.* Cunningham was elected to the House of Representatives in 1991 and became an influential voice on defense and intelligence matters during his time in Congress.

In his November plea bargain with federal prosecutors, Cunningham admitted accepting at least $2.4 million in cash, as well as rugs, antiques, furniture, yacht club fees, boat repairs, moving costs, and vacation expenses, in exchange for using his seat on the House Appropriations Committee to obtain earmarks—that is, designated federal spending directed toward specific companies or organizations—on behalf of defense contractors. The bribes included the profit he received through the sale of his Del Mar, California, home to a defense contractor at an inflated price. Cunningham used those proceeds to move into a $2.5 million mansion in the exclusive San Diego community of Rancho Santa Fe. As part of his plea agreement, Cunningham agreed to pay $1.8 million in back taxes, penalties, and interest owed, and to forfeit another $1.8 million from the sale of the Rancho Santa Fe mansion and antiques that he had gained illegally .

That contractor, Mitchell Wade, pleaded guilty on February 24 to bribery (including giving $1 million to Cunningham in bribes), corruption, and election fraud charges and was said to be cooperating with federal prosecutors. Still under investigation was another Cunningham coconspirator, Brent R. Wilkes, a defense contractor whose companies had received some $100 million in contracts, and Kyle "Dusty" Foggo, who resigned from the CIA, where he ran the agency's day-to-day operations.

In addition, prosecutor Lam's office issued a request in March for a large number of documents from three House committees and for interviews with nine aides from two committees on which Cunningham had served, the House Intelligence Committee and the House Appropriations Committee. According to news reports, the investigation had been broadened to include several members of the appropriations committee, including its chairman, Jerry Lewis, R-Calif., who denied any wrongdoing.

On May 17, the House ethics committee, formally known as the Committee on Standards of Official Conduct, said it would begin its own investigation. Doc Hastings, R-Wash., the committee's chairman, and Howard L. Berman, D-Calif., the ranking Democrat, said they opened the case because "there have been continuing reports regarding [Cunningham's] conduct, the conduct of his alleged coconspirators and others that, if true, raise serious issues concerning possible violations of the House Rules and Standards." The committee's preliminary inquiry was not completed by the end of the year and was carried over into the new Congress, which would have to decide whether to pursue a formal investigation.

Three weeks before the midterm elections, the ranking Democrat on the House Intelligence Committee, Jane Harman of California, released the executive summary of a classified report prepared by a special investigator hired by the committee to examine Cunningham's conduct while a member of the committee. The investigator concluded that Cunningham had steered more than $70 million in classified federal spending to Wade and Wilkes by taking advantage of the secrecy surrounding the contracts and by bullying committee staff members as well as officials at the Department of Defense.

The release of the report, which had been completed in May, drew almost as much outrage as its contents. Harman said she acted because she had been trying for months, with no success, to have the committee produce an unclassified version of the report. She said the public had a right to see what the inquiry had concluded. Committee chairman Peter Hoekstra of Michigan said Harman's release of the classified document was "disturbing and beyond the pale."

Jefferson Investigation

The Democrats' accusations that the Republicans were swept up in a culture of corruption in Congress lost some of their punch amid ongoing revelations of wrongdoing by one of their own. Rep. William J. Jefferson, a Democrat from New Orleans, had been a target of a federal corruption probe since March 2005 in a case involving his attempt to facilitate a deal between iGate, a Kentucky-based telecommunications company, and Nigerian officials to market Internet and other communications technology in Africa. The investigation had included FBI raids on Jefferson's homes in Washington and New Orleans in the summer of 2005.

No charges had been brought against Jefferson as of the end of 2006, and the lawmaker steadfastly asserted his innocence. Nonetheless, details of the case against Jefferson that emerged after two men entered plea bargains in connection with the case appeared damning. One of the men, Brent Pfeffer, was a former aide to Jefferson. The other, Vernon L. Jackson, was the former chairman and chief executive officer of iGate. According to Justice Department court papers, Jefferson worked on Jackson's behalf to orchestrate a deal with a Nigerian company that would hire iGate to provide Internet technology throughout Africa. In exchange, the documents said, Jackson paid more than $400,000, in monthly payments, into a fake company created under the name of Jefferson's wife. The documents further described Jefferson soliciting a percentage of sales and a million shares of iGate stock from Jackson to help facilitate the deal.

The scandal heated up in May when the House ethics committee voted May 17 to launch an investigation of Jefferson. Then, on May 20, FBI agents searched Jefferson's congressional office, spending several hours there. On Sunday the contents of the search warrant and other documents in the case were made public. In one set of documents the FBI said it had videotapes of Jefferson receiving a briefcase containing $100,000 in marked $100 bills from an FBI informant and of agents finding $90,000 of that money hidden in Jefferson's home freezer. The FBI alleged that Jefferson intended to use the money to bribe a Nigerian vice president, Atiku Abubakar, in exchange for his help in securing contracts in Nigeria. Abubakar, who was running for president of Nigeria, denied the charges, as did Jefferson.

The heavily publicized case against Jefferson and the array of embarrassing evidence against him forced House Democrats to ask Jefferson to step down voluntarily from his seat on the powerful Ways and Means Committee while the investigation continued. When he refused, House Democrats voted to remove him. "Our House Democratic Caucus is determined to uphold a high ethical standard," said House Minority Leader Nancy Pelosi, D-Calif. "We said it and now we're doing it." Despite the ongoing investigation, Jefferson ran for and won a ninth term in a December 9 runoff election.

Republicans and Democrats alike were initially outraged by the FBI search of Jefferson's office, the first such search in the country's history. Lawmakers, including Jefferson, said the search was an abuse of the separation of powers and demanded that the FBI return the documents it had removed from the office. The Justice

Department held firm, however, saying the search was conducted under a search warrant signed by a judge and only after Jefferson had refused to comply with a subpoena. President George W. Bush stepped in and asked the solicitor general to take control of the seized papers and computer hard drives and floppy disks, while the lawmakers' challenge was heard. On July 10, U.S. District Court Judge Thomas F. Hogan rejected Jefferson's demand that the material be returned to him. Hogan acknowledged that the case was "unprecedented," but he said that a prohibition on all searches of legislators' offices "would have the effect of converting every congressional office into a taxpayer-subsidized sanctuary for crime." House leaders promised to try to work out procedures for future searches with the Justice Department. Jefferson's attorney immediately filed an appeal of Hogan's decision; that case had not been resolved as of the end of the year.

Other Ethics Probes and Scandals

Several other legislators also faced questions during 2006 about their conduct. Among them were the following:

- Rep. Curt Weldon, R-Pa., was under investigation by the Justice Department and the House ethics committee for allegations that he used his office to help his daughter's lobbying firm. Weldon denied any wrongdoing. The ethics committee dropped its inquiry after Weldon lost his bid for reelection in November, but the Justice Department probe was continuing.
- Another Republican from Pennsylvania, Don Sherwood, lost his bid for reelection after he was accused of physically abusing his former mistress of five years, Cynthia Ore, and then giving her a $5.5 million settlement that was conditioned on her not discussing the settlement until after the election. Sherwood admitted the affair but denied that he had ever been abusive. The legislator, who ran on a family-values platform, had been considered a shoo-in until Ore sued him in June 2005.
- Alan B. Mollohan, D-W.Va., stepped down from his seat as the ranking Democrat on the House ethics committee on April 21 after being accused of steering earmarks toward nonprofit groups with which he was associated and from whom he benefited financially. Earmarks had grown increasingly popular in Congress in recent years and had come under increasing criticism as a conduit for influence peddling. Mollohan said the charges were "spurious" and politically motivated, but said he felt compelled to step down from his ethics post because fighting the charges would "require my time and attention." A week later the FBI notified three nonprofit organizations with which Mollohan was associated of forthcoming subpoenas for financial and other records. The case was still under investigation at the end of the year. Mollohan won reelection in November.
- Senate Minority Leader Harry Reid, D-Nev., on October 11 offered to amend his financial disclosure statements to clarify his situation in a land deal where his family reportedly made a profit of $700,000. In 2001 Reid transferred ownership of some residential property he had bought for $400,000 on the outskirts of Las Vegas to a holding company in which he was part owner. The land was rezoned and then sold for $1.6 million for development as a shopping center. Reid, whose share of the sale was $1.1 million, never reported on his Senate financial disclosure forms that he had transferred the land to the holding company. Aides to Reid told the Associated Press that the senator had not disclosed the original transfer because he considered it a "technical transfer."

Ethics experts thought Reid's failure to disclose the transaction was at least a technical violation of Senate ethics rules. "Whether you make a profit or a loss, you've got to put that transaction down so the public, voters, can see exactly what kind of money is moving to or from a member of Congress," said Kent Cooper, who oversaw government disclosure reports for two decades for the Federal Election Commission. "It is especially disconcerting when you have a member of the leadership, of either party, not putting in the effort to make sure this is a complete and accurate report." Stanley Brand, the former Democratic chief counsel of the House, agreed. "It's like everything else we've seen in the last two years. If it is not enforced, people think it's not enforced and they get lax and sloppy," he said.

Following is the text of a press release, dated March 3, 2006, from Carol C. Lam, U.S. attorney for the Southern District of California, announcing that Randy "Duke" Cunningham, a former member of the U.S. House of Representatives from San Diego, had been sentenced to eight years and four months in federal prison on two counts of bribery and tax evasion.

DOCUMENT

"Former Congressman Cunningham Sentenced to Eight Years in Prison"

United States Attorney Carol C. Lam announced that today former Congressman Randall "Duke" Cunningham was sentenced in United States District Court in San Diego by the Honorable Larry A. Burns to serve 100 months in custody, followed by 3 years' supervised release, based on his convictions for conspiring to commit Bribery, Honest Services Fraud, and Tax Evasion, and for a substantive count of Tax Evasion involving more than $1 million of unreported income. Cunningham also was ordered to pay $1,804,031.50 in restitution for back taxes, penalties and interest owed to the government. In addition, the Court ordered Cunningham to forfeit an additional $1,851,508 in U.S. currency, based upon cash payments he received during the conspiracy. Finally, Mr. Cunningham has forfeited his entire interest in the following property: Cunningham's Rancho Santa Fe residence and more than a dozen pieces of antiques, furniture, and Persian-style rugs. The Court ordered Cunningham immediately into custody to begin serving his sentence.

According to Assistant U.S. Attorneys Sanjay Bhandari, Jason A. Forge and Phillip L.B. Halpern, who prosecuted the case, Cunningham pled guilty on November 28, 2005, to a two-count Information. In pleading guilty, Mr. Cunningham, who was elected to represent the 50th Congressional District in San Diego for eight terms, admitted that he received at least $2.4 million in bribes. These bribes were paid to Cunningham by several coconspirators through a variety of methods, including checks totaling over $1 million, cash, rugs, antiques, furniture, yacht club fees, boat repairs, moving costs, and vacation expenses. The bribery, fraud, and tax evasion conspiracy described in the Information included: the purchase of Cunningham's home in Del Mar, California, at an artificially inflated price by a defense contractor; the subsequent payoff of the mortgage on Cunningham's new, multi-million dollar home in Rancho Santa Fe by another defense contractor; a $200,000 down payment by a third coconspirator to enable Cunningham to purchase a condominium in Arlington, Virginia; the payment of the capital gains tax by the purchaser of Cunningham's Del Mar home; the purchase and maintenance by a defense contractor of a yacht (the "Duke-Stir") and a Rolls Royce for Cunningham; as well as payments by a defense contractor for a graduation party for Cunningham's daughter, jewelry, home furnishings, and travel and hotel expenses. Cunningham failed to disclose any of the benefits on his Financial Disclosure Statements to the U.S. House of Representatives or on his federal tax return. Cunningham further admitted that in return for these bribes he used his public office and took other official action to influence the appropriations of funds and the execution of government contracts in ways that would benefit two of the coconspirators, who were the majority owners of defense contracting companies.

United States Attorney Lam said, "No one can serve the public and his own greed at the same time. Mr. Cunningham failed his office, his colleagues, and his nation."

FBI Special Agent-in-Charge Daniel R. Dzwilewski commented, "Today brings to a close a sad chapter regarding the corrupt actions of a member of the U.S. Congress. Through this on-going investigation and others, the FBI will continue its efforts to combat corruption at all levels of government."

Kenneth J. Hines, IRS Criminal Investigation Special Agent-in-Charge for San Diego stated, "Today's sentencing demonstrates that power is thought to be associated with wealth and that wealth is sometimes obtained through greed and not earned. IRS Criminal Investigation will aggressively follow the money trail and pursue those elected officials who disregard their oath of office. The message is clear—Congress belongs to the people and can't be bought."

Rick Gwin, Defense Criminal Investigative Service (DCIS), Western Field Office, stated, "This is one of the most blatant examples of corruption I have seen. Moreover, it's an elected official's betrayal of the trust of his constituents, the American people, and our soldiers, sailors, airmen and Marines. Let me make one thing very clear—the safety and welfare of our warfighters, the young men and women who must go in harm's way, are not for sale. They deserve only the best, and I can assure you that the special agents and prosecutors who worked so hard on this case are going to continue to make every effort to ensure that the procurement process our warfighters rely upon to provide them the best tools essential to their survival is not compromised by greed."

This case is the result of an investigation by Special Agents of the Federal Bureau of Investigation (FBI), Internal Revenue Service—Criminal Investigation Division (IRS-CI), and Defense Criminal Investigative Service (DCIS), with the assistance of prosecutors and federal agents in Washington, D.C., Eastern District of Virginia, and the Eastern District of New York.

Defendant

Randall Harold Cunningham

Summary of Charges and Maximum Penalties
Count 1

Conspiracy to commit Bribery, Honest Services Fraud, and Tax Evasion, in violation of Title 18, United States Code, Section 371, which is punishable by 5 years in prison and/or a $250,000 fine.

Count 2

Tax Evasion, in violation of Title 26, United States Code, Section 7201, which is punishable by 5 years in prison and/or a $100,000 fine.

Investigating Agencies

Federal Bureau of Investigation
Internal Revenue Service—Criminal Investigation Division
Defense Criminal Investigative Service

Source: U.S. Department of Justice. Office of the United States Attorney for the Southern District of California. "Former Congressman Cunningham Sentenced to More Than Eight Years in Prison." Press release, March 3, 2006. www.usdoj.gov/usao/cas/press/cas60303-1.pdf (accessed March 10, 2007).

Other Historic Documents of Interest

Bachelet on Her Inauguration as President of Chile

March 11, 2006

■■■■■■■ **THE DOCUMENT IN CONTEXT** ■■■■■■■

Chile in 2006 began one new era, with the election and inauguration of its first female president, Michelle Bachelet, and closed out another era, with the death of former dictator Augusto Pinochet. The contrasts between Bachelet and Pinochet could not have been greater—illustrating the dramatic changes in Chile since Pinochet reluctantly gave up power in 1990.

Bachelet represented the Concertación de Partidos por la Democracia (Coalition of Parties for Democracy), the partnership of four center-left parties that had governed Chile since the first post-Pinochet elections in 1990. Under the Concertación's politically balanced policies of free trade, increased social programs, and fiscal conservatism, Chile maintained one of the most vibrant economies in Latin America—enabling it to weather financial storms during the 1990s that severely battered many of its neighbors. Chile also evolved into a genuine democracy, setting aside the violence and political repression that had tarnished Pinochet's rule, particularly in the early years after his 1973 military coup that ousted an elected socialist president. Bachelet's predecessor and political mentor, Ricardo Lagos, who barely won election in 2000, went on to a highly successful presidency and left office as Chile's most popular politician.

Bachelet's election appeared to confirm a trend of center-left, or even far-left, candidates winning high office in Latin America. A leftist candidate, Evo Morales, won the presidency in Bolivia in 2005, and elections during 2006 also produced victories for left-of-center presidents in Brazil (where Luiz Inácio Lula da Silva won a second term), in Nicaragua (where former Sandinista president Daniel Ortega returned to office after nearly twenty years), and in Venezuela (where the far-left Hugo Chavez won his third term). *(Morales election, Historic Documents of 2005, p. 769)*

Bachelet Emerges a Winner

A former pediatrician, Bachelet had a remarkable personal history. In 1975, when she was a twenty-two-year-old medical student, she and her mother were imprisoned by Pinochet's regime at a notorious detention center outside Santiago. Her father, air force general Alberto Bachelet, had been imprisoned earlier for opposing the 1973 coup; he was tortured and died in prison in 1974 of a heart attack. Bachelet and her mother, Angela Jeria, were released after several weeks in prison, both having reportedly been subjected to repeated abuses. They went into exile, first to Australia and then to East Germany. She married a fellow Chilean exile in East Germany, and the couple had two children but separated several years after she returned to Chile in 1979. After completing medical school, Bachelet worked at clinics, but in 1996 she enrolled at the national war college. She worked briefly for the defense ministry before Lagos appointed her as health minister in 2000. Because of her military education, she was shifted to the defense ministry two years later.

Bachelet acknowledged that Chile's conservative military leaders would not approve of her background: "I was a woman, separated, a socialist, an agnostic all possible sins together."

As the candidate of Lagos's Socialist Party, Bachelet secured 46 percent of the vote in the first round of presidential elections on December 11, 2005—short of the absolute majority needed to win. The second-place finisher was Sebastián Piñera of the center-right National Renewal Party, with 26 percent. A former senator, Piñera was one of Chile's wealthiest men—he called himself a self-made billionaire—but he advocated moderate economic and social policies and distanced himself from the Pinochet era. Piñera also portrayed himself as a more traditional candidate for Chileans, who tended to be conservative on religious and social matters. He described himself as a religious family man, and he often appeared publicly with his wife and four children. Some of Piñera's aides and supporters, although not the candidate himself, often compared his more traditional lifestyle with Bachelet's divorce and self-proclaimed agnosticism.

Bachelet and Piñera went into a second-round runoff on January 15 with opinion polls showing Bachelet having a narrow lead. Political analysts said her compelling life story and warm personality gave voters positive reasons to support her. The polls proved correct: Bachelet emerged with 53.5 percent of the vote. The December 2005 elections had given Bachelet's coalition a majority in both chambers of Congress for the first time since it took power in 1990—thus enhancing Bachelet's political power. However, she was to serve a single four-year term, rather than the six years of previous presidents, under constitutional changes enacted in August 2005. Those changes also eliminated nine Senate seats that had been reserved for unelected members, as well as the senator-for-life positions held by retired officials, such as Pinochet.

Bachelet became the third woman to be elected president of a Latin American country, following Violeta Chamorro of Nicaragua (first elected in 1990) and Mireya Moscoso of Panama (elected in 1999). Chamorro and Moscoso were elected in large part because of their locally famous husbands, but Bachelet had no such advantage.

Bachelet took office on March 11 at a ceremony attended by numerous Latin leaders, including Morales and Chavez. The U.S. government was represented by Secretary of State Condoleezza Rice.

Bachelet gave her first speech from the balcony of the presidential palace where Chile's first socialist president, Salvador Allende, was driven from power by Pinochet's coup in 1973. Bachelet emphasized inclusion at all levels of Chilean society, saying the time "when we were divided against ourselves" had passed for good. "Today, there is something different in the air. We have been able to build a new society, where the noble desire for a better future for all Chileans unites us. Everyone has a place in that future, with an inclusive homeland, where no diversity is left out and no one feels like their destiny is left hanging in the breeze."

Sagging Popularity

In her campaign Bachelet had promised to implement three dozen policy changes during her first one hundred days in office, including pension reform, establishment of a public security ministry, and subsidies for child care and preschool studies for children of poor families. She also promised equal rights for women, saying that half the cabinet positions would go to women. That promise was one of the first she kept, naming a cabinet in February that was split evenly between ten men and ten women. Women were named to head up the economy and defense ministries. This move pleased many women but angered some conservatives, who said it meant lowering standards just to achieve artificial gender equality,

Bachelet moved quickly to implement other campaign promises, including offering a one-time $35 grant to more than 1 million low-income families, financing scholarships for poor students, and building new hospitals and nursery schools. The new president's support for social programs proved controversial early in June, however, when she appeared to give into the weeks-long protests of more than 500,000 high school and college students demanding greater support for education. She declared the student demands "fully legitimate" and promised to try to meet them; after some commentators complained that she was too soft and accommodating, Bachelet appeared to reverse course and said she could make only limited concessions. The students eventually called off their protests after Bachelet stuck to her harder line. Even so, her handling of the student protests caused a sharp plunge in Bachelet's popular standing and led her in July to replace three top cabinet ministers, just four months after they assumed office.

While the student protests were under way, Bachelet visited Washington, where she was warmly received by President George W. Bush and other political leaders. Bush said he was particularly impressed by her "life story," but he made no mention of active U.S. support for the 1973 military coup in Chile that was a significant component of that story, as well as of broader Chilean history.

More controversy came in September when the government began distributing free morning-after birth control pills to girls as young as fourteen. This step was part of a broader campaign on sexual health and fertility, but it ignited a firestorm of criticism from the Roman Catholic Church and conservative politicians.

Pinochet: More Disgrace, then Death

Just as the election of Bachelet opened a new period in Chile's history, another event later in the year appeared to close a painful period of the recent past. Augusto Pinochet died on December 10 at the age of ninety-one, after suffering complications from surgery to repair damage from an acute heart attack. Pinochet continued to be a center of controversy in death, as he long had been in life. Supporters bitterly denounced numerous efforts to hold him legally accountable for the human rights abuses—notably the documented deaths of nearly 3,200 regime opponents and others—committed during his seventeen years in power. Bachelet and most other top government officials and political leaders refused to attend his funeral—where they almost certainly would not have been welcome anyway.

Pinochet's fall from power began in 1988 when Chileans voted to reject a proposal allowing him to continue as president indefinitely. He stepped down two years later after the first genuine elections in nearly two decades resulted in a victory by Patricio Aylwin, who represented the center-left Concertación alliance. Even so, Pinochet remained as head of the armed forces until 1998, when he was given an honorary post as senator-for-life. Among other things, the latter position protected him from legal jeopardy arising from human rights and other crimes committed during his presidency; this was in addition to an amnesty law that his government had adopted in 1978.

Despite his legal protections at home, Pinochet faced prosecution overseas beginning in October 1998, when a Spanish investigating judge, Baltazar Garzon, issued an international warrant charging him with the murder of Spanish citizens. Pinochet was in London at the time and was held by British authorities until January 2000, when he was declared medically unfit to stand trial and allowed to return to Chile. Shortly after his return, human rights charges were filed against him in Chile, but courts dismissed them because of his failing health; he had been diagnosed as suffering from a mild case of dementia as a result of several strokes. However, Pinochet was indicted in 2004 on tax evasion charges after a U.S. Senate investigation showed he had built up a multimillion-dollar fortune in overseas bank accounts.

The Chilean Supreme Court on September 8, 2006, upheld a lower court ruling stripping Pinochet of the immunity he had enjoyed as a former president. Six weeks later, on October 30, Pinochet was indicted, and placed under house arrest, on charges arising from torture at a secret prison—the same one where Bachelet had been held.

Pinochet's final months were marked by another indignity. In July the former chief of his secret police said Pinochet had built much of his personal fortune by trafficking in drugs and guns. Gen. Manuel Contreras, who himself was imprisoned, provided no proof of these charges, which Pinochet's lawyers denied—but the allegation further sullied the former dictator's reputation.

Following is the text of the March 11, 2006, inaugural address to the nation by Michelle Bachelet, shortly after she was sworn in as the first female president of Chile.

DOCUMENT

"President Calls on Chileans to Work for Well-Being of Country"

Thank you, women and men of Chile.

Thank you for your applause, thank you for the smiles that you confer upon me so much, and thank you for the hugs. I feel truly privileged to receive so much affection from you.

I want to address my words to all Chilean women and men, without exclusions.

There have been times in our history when we were divided amongst ourselves. We looked at each other with distrust, suspicion and disdain.

Over the past 16 years of democracy, we have worked hard together to smooth over the sharp edges of a divided society, a society that separated "us" from "them." Now is the time that we all feel part of a larger "us."

Today, there is something different in the air. We have been able to build a new society, where the noble desire for a better future for all Chileans unites us. Everyone has a place in that future, with an inclusive homeland, where no diversity is left out and no one feels like their destiny is left dangling in the breeze.

We have prepared ourselves for this great challenge. The 21st century will bring new tasks for us, some of which are unknown to us at this moment. Aside from the technological revolution unfolding before our eyes, I think that there is another revolution afoot in the way we relate to each other, the way we interact within our communities, and our manner of combating individualism, indifference and hopelessness. The time has come for us to look one another in the eye, without resentments or suspicion.

The past is what it is: the past. We will never forget it. As President Lagos said, "There is no tomorrow without yesterday," and we do not want to repeat the errors of the past. We want a more prosperous, just, egalitarian and participative future.

We know that we are not going to solve all our problems in four years—that was never part of the discourse of my campaign. But we are going to take a great step forward.

This will be a government of citizens, from the most neglected to the most entrepreneurial, an infinite range of colors, perceptions and faces that imbue our society with so much richness. These citizens, you, have in me a President that will also speak the language of the truth.

Difficulties will arise, without a doubt; every government experiences them. "Campaigns," a great thinker once said, "happen in poetry, but governments happen in prose."

However, the relationship between you and us, and I, will not be affected by any such difficulties, because I want to establish a dialogue based on frankness and participation. It will be a great pact between the citizens and those who govern.

You know that I follow through with my commitments. I will say what I think, and I will do what I say. I give you my word!

In our quest to move towards a Chile that is better every day for every one of our citizens, I want to gather the efforts of citizens and the Congress, which is the expression of the legitimacy of our laws. With all of them, we will work towards a shared ideal: the good of Chileans, and justice throughout our country. And to do this, I am asking for the support of all women and men in Congress.

We will focus our efforts on our children, like the children who greeted me when I entered La Moneda [the president palace] through Citizens' Plaza. That way, all our children will be able to learn and develop equally from the time they are born, and we can eliminate all traces of inequality in our country.

We will focus our efforts on our beloved elders, our senior citizens, to compensate them for what they contributed to our country.

We will focus our efforts on everyone who is looking for work. But, as I said during the campaign, I don't mean just any kind of job; I am talking about decent and respectable jobs. The workers of our country deserve it.

We will support our talented young people, who want to go to college or technical institutes, who want to be entrepreneurs and forge their own destinies. They are our future—our present and our future—and we are going to strongly support them.

We will focus our efforts on women, because women deserve it.

We will stand with the indigenous peoples of our country.

We will focus our efforts on those who are disabled.

The government should be at the service of those who endure the bitterness of feeling defenseless, as well as those who want to move ahead.

No citizens will be forgotten in Chile. That is my commitment. We will be actively present in all regions of the country. There will be no town or village overlooked.

That was why my first public event, on the way from Valparaíso to Santiago, was to go to Casablanca, because I want all of us to feel part of Chile, and I want all regions to feel relevant and have an important role to play.

And if it doesn't happen that way, men and women of Chile, you can feel free to remind me.

You know that I never asked for power. I am willing to serve. You have granted me the position that I am taking today, and I feel the weight of the responsibility involved.

All Chileans, all Chileans, will be on my mind and in my heart at all times, like everyone who stood along the roads as I came into Santiago. Thank you to all of you for the tremendous love and support. I insist that I am clear on the responsibilities involved in carrying the hopes, needs and affection of so many people on my shoulders. I am going to work very hard to respond to these hopes and expectations.

I know the realities of my country very well; I have traveled up and down Chile many times. You have opened your hearts, as well as the doors of your homes, to me. I know about precariousness and inequality. I also know about invaluable successes, like our Nobel Prizes, the artists and creators that have forged our culture, the achievements of our athletes, the work and qualifications of our professionals and our workers, the force of our land.

I think about so many that have been able to stand up and work hard in the face of adversity.

All of them, up and down our long country, will form the backbone of my administration.

My friends:

This is a very solemn moment for the country. I ask you to turn your heads and look at the statues of the illustrious citizens adorning this plaza. This is the Republic, my friends. There in the front is Diego Portales, the symbol of a small, growing Republic, modest at the time, but thriving, orderly and able to resolve disputes with the law rather than by taking up arms.

Jorge Alessandri, Salvador Allende and Eduardo Frei Montalva [former presidents] also stand in this plaza. I pay tribute to them, as they symbolize our modern homeland, the country of the 20th century, vocations for democracy and eras of development and social progress.

I personify a whole history, which had dark and bitter moments, but I knew how to recover. Today, we Chileans live better and more free than before. We have had three successful administrations. I feel proud to continue along a path that has borne so many fruits.

I salute and send my affection for President Patricio Aylwin and President Eduardo Frei Ruiz-Tagle.

The Chile we are building today stands upon the foundations that they built in the past.

At this time, I not only want to express admiration and fondness, but also my special gratitude for a great President of the Republic of Chile, Ricardo Lagos Escobar.

What great pride we all felt today when we saw him walk out of this Palace this morning to the ovations of the people. Yes, my friends, clap loudly, because Ricardo Lagos Escobar deserves it. When we applaud this great President, who did his work so well, we are applauding for the entire Republic!

Finally, there is one more tribute that I cannot leave out. One March 12th, 32 years ago, at the age of 50, my father, Alberto Bachelet Martínez, died. In the future I will be there with him, but I know that he is here with me, as I said the night I won the election.

In memory of my father, General Bachelet, I would like to salute the Chilean military, who are an important part of our history. Today they are part of the heritage of all Chileans.

My friends:

We will continue working to make our country more developed, with more justice and better opportunities.

The world is watching us. The world is closely observing what is happening in this small country in the south of the world that was able to restore freedom and rights—with effort and pain, yes—but it built a solid democracy. It brought about reconciliation and it is progressing. It has been able to pull millions out of poverty, in the name of freedom and dignity.

May the famous visitors here visiting us know that this small country wants to take a great step forward in history, towards prosperity for its children, but also towards a new way of seeing and practicing politics. It has forged more inclusive, participatory, more open and more transparent politics, for, by and with all citizens.

My fellow Chileans:

I know full well that there are many needs that remain unmet. I know that every family has aspirations and hopes. I want to channel my experience, my sensibilities and my efforts into the beautiful task of leading this country towards a better destiny. That is what I want for Chile, and I know that together, we can achieve it.

Today, Chile has a new government, led by a woman, which is the expression of a new era. Now is the time for happiness, for men as well, for young people and children, for seniors, and, of course, women.

Now is the time for everyone, in this, my dear homeland, the homeland of all Chilean women and men.

Thank you very much, my friends, because I want Chile to belong to everyone. I want Chile to be the great country that we all want it to be. We are going to work hard for that, to make our homeland a more just, humane, charitable and egalitarian place. That is the dream of everyone here right now; that is the dream that runs through our entire country, from Africa to Antarctica.

I and everyone in my administration, throughout the country, will work to make that dream a reality, without rest. Four years is a short time, so we are going to work at full throttle. Together, we will make Chile a much better place.

So, my friends, we will continue working, because we want all children, men and women to have a better present and future.

Now let us celebrate, because we are going to continue making progress with our country, so that great avenues can open up to all women and men.

"Viva Chile!"

Source: Republic of Chile. Chilean Government. "President Bachelet Calls on Chileans to Work for the Well-Being of the Country." March 11, 2006. www.chileangovernment.cl/index.php?option=com_content&task=view&id=704&Itemid=5 (accessed October 31, 2006).

Other Historic Documents of Interest

Government Accountability Office on Border Security Problems

March 28, 2006

Nearly five years after the Bush administration pledged to take all available steps to keep terrorist threats away from American borders, several incidents in 2006 demonstrated how much work remained to be done. In February bipartisan congressional opposition forced the cancellation of a deal, approved by the administration, to allow a company based in the United Arab Emirates (UAE) to manage six large U.S. ports. Although the company would not have been responsible for port security, Democrats and Republicans alike said the deal presented an unacceptable security risk.

Just as the furor over that incident began to die down, the Government Accountability Office (GAO) revealed in March that undercover agents had crossed into the United States from two points in Canada and Mexico, transporting enough radioactive material to make two "dirty" bombs. Although customs agents detected the radioactive material, they never questioned the phony government permits the GAO agents carried. In August the GAO reported that its undercover agents successfully entered the United States from Canada and Mexico nine times using fake driver's licenses and other phony documentation. In two instances the agents gained admittance without showing any documentation at all.

Frustrated with what it saw as the Bush administration's slow pace in providing comprehensive port security, Congress easily passed a measure in 2006 to beef up inspection and detection systems at ports both in the United States and abroad. But there was more than a little politics in the port security debate, with Democrats judging that the issue could embarrass President George W. Bush on the one issue on which he had seemed invulnerable—the fight against terrorism. Seeking to open a wedge there, Democrats were already attacking the president for failing to follow through on the security recommendations made by the independent, bipartisan 9/11 Commission. They pledged to make implementation of those recommendations a top priority if they won control of Congress in the midterm elections. *(9/11 Commission on implementing recommendations, Historic Documents of 2005. p. 893)*

Background

Ever since the terrorist attacks of September 11, 2001, securing the country against another attack—and being prepared to cope with a national emergency—had been the signature theme of Bush's presidency. Keeping terrorists at bay was the driving force behind the war in Afghanistan, a primary rationale for going to war in Iraq, and the explanation the administration gave for electronically eavesdropping on Americans without a warrant. The administration claimed these and other actions had been successful in thwarting several terrorist attacks on the United States.

But many critics said the administration and the Republican-led Congress had yet to take some important security measures, such as inspecting all or even most cargo containers, doing background checks on truckers and other commercial transportation workers, or coordinating several lists of terror suspects maintained by various federal agencies. Nor, they worried, had the government been successful in tightening up its border controls. Determined terrorists could exploit any one of these security gaps, they said. Critics also pointed to the administration's dismal response to Hurricane Katrina, the storm that struck the Gulf Coast in August 2005, killing more than 1,300 people and devastating much of New Orleans. Committees in both the House and Senate judged that the Bush administration had failed miserably in planning for and providing emergency aid to the millions of people displaced by the storm and concluded that the performance would have been no better in the event of a terrorist attack.

Port Operations Sale

The congressional investigations of the government's response to Katrina were just wrapping up as the proposed takeover of operations at six American ports by DP World was coming to public attention. The company, which was owned by the government of Dubai, acquired the operations of cargo container terminals in Baltimore, Miami, Newark, New Orleans, and Philadelphia and a passenger terminal in New York through the purchase of a British-owned company, Peninsular & Oriental Steam Navigation Co., which had been managing the ports. The deal had been approved by the Committee on Foreign Investment in the United States, a group representing six cabinet departments and six other U.S. agencies, whose mandate was to review foreign investments that could have national security implications.

But on February 16 a bipartisan group of Senate and House members, many of them from the New York metropolitan area, raised concerns about the purchase. Although the UAE was considered a U.S. ally, the country—a confederation of seven emirates, including Dubai)—had been home to two of the September 11 hijackers and was thought to be a transfer point for nuclear weapons components shipped to Iran, Libya, and North Korea. The UAE was also one of three countries that had recognized al Qaeda's protectors, the Taliban, as the legitimate government of Afghanistan.

Within days the port deal was a leading subject on web blogs and TV talk shows. The fact that DP World would have no role in security at the U.S. ports (which was the responsibility of the Coast Guard and the customs agency) did not seem to calm the furor. By February 21 even Republican leaders in Congress were beginning to question the deal publicly. President Bush vigorously defended the sale, calling the UAE a "committed ally in the war on terror" and accusing those leading the opposition to the deal as being politically motivated. He also said he was "concerned about a broader message this issue could send to our friends and allies around the world, particularly in the Middle East," and he threatened to veto any legislation that would kill the deal.

But when the public uproar refused to die down, the White House and DP World agreed to a forty-five day review period. That move did not appease the deal's critics, however, and, faced with the certainty that both the House and Senate would vote against the deal, DP World announced on March 9 that it would sell operations for the six ports to a U.S. entity. President Bush and his allies in Congress, including senators John McCain, R-Ariz., and John W. Warner, R-Va., said the incident had jeopardized U.S. relations in the Middle East. Gen. John Abizaid, commander of U.S. Central

Command, which oversaw military operations in Iraq, said he was "very dismayed by the emotional responses some people have put on the table here in the United States that really comes down to Arab and Muslim bashing that was totally unnecessary."

Port Security Legislation

Spurred by the port security concerns, Congress quickly passed legislation, the Security and Accountability for Every (SAFE) Port Act of 2006 (HR 4954—PL 109–447), authorizing $2 billion over five years for local port security grants, $443 million for a cargo container security initiative, and $213 million for a program known as the Customs-Trade Partnership against Terrorism. The partnership was a voluntary program to provide incentives, such as fewer customs inspections, to shippers that took a variety of security precautions, including voluntary submission of manifest data, the use of a container security device to deter tampering with cargo, and self-assessment of the security of the shipper's supply chain. The cargo container initiative established pilot programs to evaluate the feasibility of scanning all foreign cargo for nuclear and radiological material before being shipped into a U.S. port. Ironically, the UAE was the first Middle Eastern country to sign up for the program, which allowed U.S. inspectors in foreign ports to identify suspicious cargo and ask that it be inspected locally before being shipped to the United States. Currently only about 6 percent of the 9 million cargo containers that entered the United States every year were subjected to a thorough physical inspection.

The SAFE Port Act also required the twenty-two largest U.S. ports to install radiation-detection technology by the end of 2007; those ports handled 98 percent of all incoming cargo. The bill authorized funding for the development of advanced inspection technology so that containers could be searched for dangerous materials without having to be opened. It set timetables and procedures for expediting the nationwide rollout of the Transportation Worker Identification Credential, a standardized biometric ID card for transportation workers, including truckers who delivered and picked up cargo containers at the nation's ports. Plans to require all transportation workers to carry the special identification, which would be issued only after the worker had passed a background check, had been repeatedly delayed, in part because of opposition to the required criminal background checks.

"We'll do everything we can to prevent an attack, but if the terrorists succeed in launching an attack, we'll be ready to respond," President Bush said October 13 as he signed the bill into law. "We're going to protect our ports, we're going to defend this homeland, and we're going to win the war on terror." In May the White House had issued a policy statement opposing the port security grants as an "unnecessary" duplication of grant programs already in place.

GAO's "Dirty Bomb" Sting

Demonstrating the relative ease with which determined terrorists could bring nuclear weapons into the United States, officials from the GAO revealed on March 28 that undercover agents had brought enough cesium-137 through border checkpoints in Washington and Texas to made two "dirty bombs." Dirty bombs were composed of a conventional explosive combined with radiological material designed not so much to kill as to contaminate an area with harmful radioactive material and thus force it to be closed down. Cesium-37 in very small quantities was used in a number of industrial and scientific devices.

The undercover agents made no attempt to hide the fact that they were carrying the radioactive material, but they used the Internet to counterfeit Nuclear Regulatory Commission licenses authorizing the licensee to buy and transfer the material. At both checkpoints, radiation detectors alerted customs and border protection agents to the presence of the cesium-137, but the agents never questioned the authenticity of the documentation. Calling that failure a "significant gap" in security procedures, GAO officials said that "unless nuclear smugglers in possession of faked license documents raised suspicions in some other way, [customs] officers could follow agency guidelines yet unwittingly allow them to enter the country with their illegal nuclear cargo." A spokesperson for the Nuclear Regulatory Commission disputed that the undercover agents had bought and smuggled in enough cesium-137 to create a dirty bomb, but he promised the commission would work with the customs agency to develop a system for quickly verifying the authenticity of the commission's licenses.

In a second report released March 28, "Combating Nuclear Smuggling," the GAO found numerous problems in the Homeland Security Department's plan to scan cargo containers for radioactive materials before they left foreign ports bound for the United States. The problems included foreign corruption, poor maintenance, and technical difficulties. Still, a customs agency spokesman said U.S. customs officers had scanned more than 80 million containers since 2000 without finding any illegal material.

Questions about the capability of radiation-detection technology, however, undermined those reassurances. Existing monitors could detect the presence of radiological materials but could not always distinguish dangerous materials such as highly enriched uranium (used in making nuclear weapons) from harmless radiological material that appeared in such things as kitty litter and some ceramic tile. In July the Department of Homeland Security announced that it had awarded contracts worth $1.2 billion to three companies to develop and purchase new, more accurate monitors over the next five years. However, in its fiscal 2007 appropriations, Congress restricted funding for full procurement until the department could certify that the effectiveness of the radiation monitors had been significantly improved.

On October 17 the GAO released a cost-benefit analysis, "Combating Nuclear Smuggling," that reinforced the congressional concern. According to the GAO, test results showed that the nuclear-detection devices the Department of Homeland Security was planning to buy were unreliable. The agency said that the next-generation devices currently could not meet the department's own standard of detecting enriched uranium 95 percent of the time. Moreover, when the uranium was shielded, GAO investigators found, the detection rates ranged from 17 percent to 53 percent. A spokesman for Homeland Security said the department was continuing to test the devices and would not "put devices in the field unless they meet" the 95 percent reliability standard.

In another undercover operation, the GAO demonstrated how easy it was for its agents to use counterfeit identification to walk or drive across the border. On nine separate occasions in early 2006, agents used phony driver's licenses and other identification to cross into the country. In two cases, the customs agents never even looked at the identification. It was the fourth time since 2002 that GAO agents had entered the country with illegal documents; in only one instance was an agent denied entry. "These GAO investigators could have been known criminals, wanted fugitives, or even terrorists. But they were just waved into the country," said Sen. Charles E. Grassley, R-Iowa, on August 2. Grassley had requested the study. "Frankly, it's hard to believe that there has been so little progress in plugging this gaping security hole." The GAO warned that plans to require travelers to the United States to have a passport or other secure identification would be successful only if border agents were trained to recognize counterfeit documents. *(Background on GAO border crossings, Historic Documents of 2003, p. 218)*

Following are excerpts from "Border Security: Investigators Successfully Transported Radioactive Sources across Our Nation's Borders at Selected Locations," a report presented on March 28, 2006, to Sen. Norm Coleman, R-Minn., chairman of the Senate Permanent Subcommittee on Investigations, by officials of the Government Accountability Office detailing how undercover agents brought radiological material into the United States using counterfeited documents that were not questioned by customs agents.

DOCUMENT

"Border Security"

... This report responds to your request that we investigate potential security weaknesses related to the installation of radiation detection equipment at U.S. ports of entry. Based on discussions with your staff, we focused our efforts on testing whether the radiation portal monitors installed at the U.S. ports of entry would detect radioactive material transported in vehicles attempting to enter the United States. We also agreed to provide our observations regarding the procedures that Department of Homeland Security U.S. Customs and Border Protection (CBP) inspectors followed when the radiation portal monitors detected such material....

Scope and Methodology

We selected two land ports of entry that had radiation portal monitors installed: one at the U.S.-Canadian border and one at the U.S.-Mexican border. Radiation portal monitors are large pieces of stationary equipment that CBP uses as part of its overall strategy to thwart radiological terrorism by detecting the presence of radioactive materials by screening people, vehicles, and cargo as they pass through ports of entry. In order to safely plan and execute our undercover operation, several of our investigators attended training at the National Institute of Standards and Technology (NIST) in Gaithersburg, Maryland. Our investigators received training on the safe handling, storage, and transport of radioactive materials.

When considering the type of radioactive sources to use in our undercover operation, we decided to use one of the most common radioisotopes used in industry for its strong radioactivity. After consulting with an outside expert, we used an amount of radioactive sources that we determined was sufficient to manufacture a dirty bomb.

As part of our investigation, we purchased a small quantity of the radioactive sources from a commercial source by posing as an employee of a fictitious company. This was to demonstrate that anyone can purchase small quantities of radioactive sources for stockpiling because suppliers are not required to exercise any due diligence in determining whether the buyer has a legitimate use for the radioactive sources and suppliers are not required to ask the buyer to produce a Nuclear Regulatory Commission (NRC) document when making purchases in small quantities. We then deployed two teams of investigators to the field to make simultaneous border crossings at the northern and southern borders in an attempt to transport radioactive sources into the United States.

While making our simultaneous crossings, we focused our investigation on whether the radiation portal monitors would detect the radioactive sources we carried and whether CBP inspectors exercised due diligence to determine the authenticity of paperwork presented by individuals attempting to transport radioactive sources across our borders. Although we offer observations on the procedures that CBP inspectors followed for our two border crossings, we did not evaluate the adequacy of the design or effectiveness of those procedures. Our investigation also tested whether an NRC document could be counterfeited using data easily accessible and available to the public. We conducted our investigation from July 2005 through December 2005 in accordance with quality standards for investigations as set forth by the President's Council on Integrity and Efficiency....

Background

A dirty bomb, or a radiological dispersal device, combines a conventional explosive with radioactive material. In most cases, the conventional explosive would have more immediate lethality than the radioactive material. A dirty bomb would most likely result in small radiation exposures and would typically not contain enough radiation to kill people or cause severe illnesses. However, by scattering the radioactive material, the dirty bomb has the effect of contaminating an area. The extent of local contamination depends on several factors, including the size of the explosive, the amount and type of radioactive material used, and weather conditions. While there could be an increase in the cancer risk among those exposed to radiation from a dirty bomb, the more significant effect of a dirty bomb could be the closing of contaminated areas. The direct costs of cleanup and the indirect losses in trade and business in the contaminated areas could be large. Hence, dirty bombs are generally considered to be weapons of mass disruption instead of weapons of mass destruction.

Many radioactive materials are used in a variety of industrial, scientific, and medical applications. For instance, radioactive materials are used in smoke detectors and for cancer treatments. However, few of the materials are considered suitable for use in a dirty bomb. A Department of Energy and Nuclear Regulatory Commission Interagency Working Group identified radioactive materials of highest concern based on the potential dose impacts of the materials and the availability of such materials in sufficient quantities.

To address the threat of dirty bombs and other nuclear material, the federal government has programs in place that regulate the transportation of radioactive material and to prevent illegal transport of radioactive material across our nation's borders. CBP uses radiation detection equipment at ports of entry to prevent the illicit transport of radioactive material into the United States. The goal of CBP's inspection program is to "...thwart the operations of terrorist organizations by detecting, disrupting, and preventing the cross-border travel of terrorists, terrorist funding, and terrorist implements, including Weapons of Mass Destruction and their precursors." Deploying radiation detection equipment is part of CBP's strategy for thwarting radiological terrorism and CBP is using a range of such equipment to meet its goal of screening all cargo, vehicles, and individuals coming into the United States.

Most travelers enter the United States through the nation's 154 land border ports of entry. CBP inspectors at ports of entry are responsible for the primary inspection of travelers to determine their admissibility into the United States and to enforce laws related to preventing the entry of contraband, such as drugs and weapons of mass destruction.

Radiation Detection Devices

To help detect the presence of radiation and identify the type of radiation present, CBP generally relies on three types of radiation detection devices—radiation portal monitors, Personal Radiation Detectors (PRDs), and Radiation Isotope Identifier Devices (RIIDs). Radiation portal monitors have the ability to detect the presence of gamma radiation, which is emitted by all radioactive materials of greatest concern, and neutrons, which are emitted by only a limited number of materials, including plutonium. CBP uses PRDs that detect the presence of gamma radiation but not neutrons. CBP requires its inspectors to wear PRDs while on duty and ensure that the PRDs are activated. PRDs alert inspectors to the presence of harmful levels of radiation when they are conducting cargo and vehicle searches. PRDs can detect radioactive materials that could be used in a radiological dispersal device, also known as a dirty bomb. Another type of radiation detection equipment that CBP uses are RIIDs, which are handheld devices designed to determine the identity of the radioactive material, whether it is a radiological source used in medicine or industry, a naturally occurring source of radiation, or weapons-usable nuclear material.

Radiation Detection Alerts

For the purposes of this report, we focused only on the procedures for gamma radiation, the type of radiation used in our tests. To identify the type of radiation present, inspectors use a handheld RIID. If the radiation portal monitor and the RIID do not detect the presence of neutrons, inspectors follow gamma radiation procedures, which require that they first use their PRDs to determine the safe distance at which to conduct an inspection.

If, after reviewing documentation or obtaining advice from Laboratories and Scientific Services personnel, the CBP inspectors are satisfied that the radioactive source is properly documented or is consistent with innocent radiation sources, the vehicle and passengers can be released. If CBP inspectors are not satisfied that the source is documented or innocent, they must obtain guidance from the Laboratory and Scientific Services.

Documentation Was Produced to Support Undercover Investigation

As part of our undercover investigation, we produced counterfeit documents before sending our two teams of investigators out to the field. We found two NRC documents and a few examples of the documents by searching the Internet. [None of these documents were available on the NRC Web site.] We subsequently used commercial, off-the-shelf computer software to produce two counterfeit NRC documents authorizing the individual to receive, acquire, possess, and transfer radioactive sources.

To support our investigators' purported reason for having radioactive sources in their possession when making their simultaneous border crossings, a GAO graphic artist designed a logo for our fictitious company and produced a bill of lading using computer software.

With Ease, Investigators Purchased, Received, and Transported Radioactive Sources across Both Borders

Our two teams of investigators each transported an amount of radioactive sources sufficient to manufacture a dirty bomb when making their recent, simultaneous border crossings. In our earlier work, we had purchased radioactive sources, two containers to store and transport the material, and we had obtained a genuine NRC document.

For the purposes of our current undercover investigation, we purchased a small amount of radioactive sources and one container for storing and transporting the material from a commercial source over the telephone. One of our investigators, posing as an employee of a fictitious company, stated that the purpose of his purchase was to use the radioactive sources to calibrate personal radiation detectors. According to the NRC, suppliers are not required to determine whether the buyer has a legitimate use for the radioactive sources, nor are suppliers required to ask the buyer to produce an NRC document when making purchases in small quantities. The amount of radioactive sources our investigator sought to purchase did not require an NRC document. The company mailed the radioactive sources to an address in Washington, D.C. We could have purchased all of the radioactive sources used in our two undercover border crossings by making multiple purchases from different suppliers, using similarly convincing cover stories, using false identities, and had all of the radioactive sources conveniently shipped to our nation's capital.

We have pointed out the weaknesses in federal and state controls over the security of sealed sources in our prior work, noting that it is possible that these materials can be obtained for malicious intent. Sealed radioactive sources, radioactive material encapsulated in stainless steel or other metal, are used worldwide in medicine, industry, and research. We recommended in August 2003 that NRC modify its process of issuing specific licenses to ensure that sealed sources cannot be purchased before NRC's verification—through inspection or other means—that the materials will be used as intended. NRC has not implemented our licensing recommendation to date, more than 2 years later. However, NRC has recently established an interagency task force to evaluate the licensing, use, and security of radioactive materials. Further delays in implementing our licensing recommendation, given today's security environment, continues to leave NRC's licensing process vulnerable to compromise and inadequate in terms of precluding the smuggling of radioactive material across our nation's borders.

Two Teams of Investigators Conducted Simultaneous Crossings at the U.S.-Canadian Border and U.S.-Mexican Border

Northern Border Crossing

On December 14, 2005, our investigators placed two containers of radioactive sources into the trunk of their rental vehicle. Our investigators—acting in an undercover capacity— drove to an official port of entry between Canada and the United States. They also had in their possession a counterfeit bill of lading in the name of a fictitious company and a counterfeit NRC document.

At the primary checkpoint, our investigators were signaled to drive through the radiation portal monitors and to meet the CBP inspector at the booth for their primary inspection. As our investigators drove past the radiation portal monitors and approached the primary checkpoint booth, they observed the CBP inspector look down and reach to his right side of his booth. Our investigators assumed that the radiation portal monitors had activated and signaled the presence of radioactive sources. The CBP inspector asked our investigators for identification and asked them where they lived. One of our investigators on the two- man undercover team handed the CBP inspector both of their passports and told him that he lived in Maryland while the second investigator told the CBP inspector that he lived in Virginia.

The CBP inspector also asked our investigators to identify what they were transporting in their vehicle. One of our investigators told the CBP inspector that they were transporting specialized equipment back to the United States. A second CBP inspector, who had come over to assist the first inspector, asked what else our investigators were transporting. One of our investigators told the CBP inspectors that they were transporting radioactive sources for the specialized equipment. The CBP inspector in the primary checkpoint booth appeared to be writing down the information. Our investigators were then directed to park in a secondary inspection zone, while the CBP inspector conducted further inspections of the vehicle.

During the secondary inspection, our investigators told the CBP inspector that they had an NRC document and a bill of lading for the radioactive sources. The CBP inspector asked if he could make copies of our investigators' counterfeit bill of lading on letterhead stationery as well as their counterfeit NRC document. Although the CBP inspector took the documents to the copier, our investigators did not observe him retrieving any copies from the copier.

Our investigators watched the CBP inspector use a RIID, which he said is used to identify the source of radioactive material, to examine the investigators' vehicle. He used the RIID to identify the source of radiation emanating from the investigators' vehicle. He told our investigators that he had to perform additional inspections. After determining that the investigators were not transporting additional sources of radiation, the CBP inspector made copies of our investigators' drivers' licenses, returned their drivers' licenses to them, and our investigators were then allowed to enter the United States. At no time did the CBP inspector question the validity of the counterfeit bill of lading or the counterfeit NRC document.

Southern Border Crossing

On December 14, 2005, our investigators placed two containers of radioactive sources into the trunk of their vehicle. Our investigators drove to an official port of entry at the southern border. They also had in their possession a counterfeit bill of lading in the name of a fictitious company and a counterfeit NRC document.

At the primary checkpoint, our two-person undercover team was signaled to drive through the radiation portal monitors through the use of a traffic light signal and stopped at the primary checkpoint for their primary inspection. As our investigators drove past the portal monitors and approached the primary checkpoint, they observed that the CBP inspector remained in the primary checkpoint for several moments prior to approaching our investigators' vehicle. Our investigators assumed that the radiation portal monitors had activated and signaled the presence of radioactive sources.

The CBP inspector asked our investigators for identification and asked them if they were American citizens. Our investigators told the CBP inspector that they were both American citizens and handed him their state issued driver's licenses. The CBP inspector also asked our investigators about the purpose of their trip to Mexico and asked whether they were bringing anything into the United States from Mexico. Our investigators told the CBP inspector that they were returning from a business trip in Mexico and were not bringing anything into the United States from Mexico.

While our investigators remained inside their vehicle, the CBP inspector used what appeared to be a RIID to scan the outside of the vehicle. One of our investigators told him that they were transporting specialized equipment. The CBP inspector asked one of our investigators to open the trunk of the rental vehicle and to show him the specialized equipment. Our investigator told the CBP inspector that they were transporting radioactive sources in addition to the specialized equipment. The primary CBP inspector then directed our investigators to park in a secondary inspection zone for further inspection.

During the secondary inspection, the CBP inspector said he needed to verify the type of material our investigators were transporting, and another CBP inspector approached with what appeared to be a RIID to scan the cardboard boxes where the radioactive sources was placed. The instrumentation confirmed the presence of radioactive sources.

When asked again about the purpose of their visit to Mexico, one of our investigators told the CBP inspector that they had used the radioactive sources in a demonstration designed to secure additional business for their company. The CBP inspector asked for paperwork authorizing them to transport the equipment to Mexico. One of our investigators provided the counterfeit bill of lading on letterhead stationery, as well as their counterfeit NRC document. The CBP inspector took the paperwork provided by our investigators and walked into the CBP station. He returned several minutes later and returned the paperwork. At no time did the CBP inspector question the validity of the counterfeit bill of lading or the counterfeit NRC document.

Corrective Action Briefings

We conducted corrective action briefings with CBP officials and NRC officials shortly after completing our undercover operations. On December 21, 2005, we briefed CBP officials about the results of our border crossing tests. CBP officials agreed to work with the NRC and CBP's Laboratories and Scientific Services to come up with a way to verify the authenticity of NRC materials documents.

We conducted two corrective action briefings with NRC officials on January 12 and January 24, 2006, about the results of our border crossing tests. NRC officials disagreed with the amount of radioactive material we determined was needed to produce a dirty bomb, noting that NRC's "concern threshold" is significantly higher. We continue to believe that our purchase of radioactive sources and our ability to counterfeit an NRC document are matters that NRC should address. Further, we believe that the amount of radioactive sources that we were able to transport into the United States during our operation would be sufficient to produce two dirty bombs, which could be used as weapons of mass disruption. Finally, NRC officials told us that they are aware of the potential problems of counterfeiting documents and that they are working to resolve these issues. . . .

Gregory D. Kutz
Managing Director
Forensic Audits and Special Investigations

Keith A. Rhodes
Chief Technologist
Center for Technology and Engineering

Gene Aloise
Director
Natural Resources and Environment

Source: U.S. Congress. Government Accountability Office. "Border Security: Investigators Successfully Transported Radioactive Sources across Our Nation's Borders at Selected Locations." GAO-06-545R, March 28, 2006. http://purl.access.gpo.gov/GPO/LPS70498 (accessed January 28, 2007).

Government Accountability Office on Prescription Drug Safety

March 31, 2006

■■■■■■■ **THE DOCUMENT IN CONTEXT** ■■■■■■■

Two significant studies released in 2006 sharply criticized the performance of the Food and Drug Administration (FDA) in monitoring the safety of prescription drugs on the market. The Government Accountability Office (GAO) and the Institute of Medicine (IOM) both cited poor management, bureaucratic squabbling, lack of authority, and underfunding as factors preventing the FDA from ensuring that drugs newly brought to market were safe for use. Both reports recommended that Congress give the agency express authority to require drug manufacturers to do follow-up safety studies on drugs already on the market. The institute's report also recommended several other specific steps.

The reports were issued at the behest of Congress and the FDA after the pharmaceutical giant Merck pulled its best-selling painkiller Vioxx off pharmacy shelves in September 2004 after studies showed the drug caused an increased risk of heart attack and stroke. The abrupt move raised questions about Merck's slowness in responding to earlier warnings about the drug's safety. The withdrawal also focused attention on whether the FDA should have approved the drug in the first place and whether it was adequately monitoring drug safety once new drugs came on the market. A claim by one of the FDA's own researchers that the agency had tried to suppress his findings about the dangers of Vioxx further inflamed the controversy. Similar complaints had arisen earlier in 2004 in connection with reports linking antidepressant drugs to an increased risk of suicide among adolescents. Altogether drug makers had pulled ten drugs from the market since 2000 after deaths and other injuries called their safety into question. (*Antidepressants and suicide, Historic Documents of 2004, p. 746; Vioxx withdrawal, Historic Documents of 2004, p. 850*)

Background

Safety issues for drugs already on the market could arise for several reasons. The FDA was under intense pressure from drug manufacturers and patient advocacy groups to get potentially beneficial and life-saving drugs to the market as fast as possible. Critics of the drug industry and FDA's approval process also said it was too easy for drug companies to cover up a new drug's potential safety problems.

Moreover, the clinical drug trials required for FDA approval generally involved only a few hundred or a few thousand people who were followed for comparatively short periods of time. These trials could reveal common adverse side effects that could force the drug maker to stop the trial. Pfizer, for example, announced in December that it was discontinuing research on a drug to raise the levels of "good" cholesterol after a clinical trial involving 15,000 patients found an unacceptably high risk of death and heart problems. But rarer side effects were likely to appear only after hundreds of thousands or millions of people were taking the drugs. Some side effects did not appear until patients had taken the drug for extended periods of time.

Although the FDA often asked drug makers to study specific drugs for adverse side effects once they were on the market, the agency reported in March that nearly two-thirds of the requested studies had never been completed. Such studies were expensive to conduct, patients who had access to drugs that might cure or arrest their disease were unlikely to join a trial in which they might be given a placebo, and the FDA had never withdrawn a drug from the market because its manufacturer had failed to complete a postmarket study. The FDA did not have authority to order such studies, nor did it have sufficient funding to conduct large trial studies itself.

By the end of 2006 serious safety concerns had been raised about several popular drugs on the market. Among them were the antibiotic Ketek and some uses of the heart medication Plavix, both made by the French company Sanofi-Aventis; Eli Lilly's schizophrenia drug Zyprexia; and a class of popular medications to treat heartburn including Nexium, Prevacid, and Prilosec.

The GAO Study

The GAO investigation, which was dated March 31 but released to the public on April 24, found serious shortcomings in the FDA's organizational structure for dealing with drug safety. The investigation had been requested by two Republican lawmakers, Sen. Charles E. Grassley of Iowa and Rep. Joe L. Barton of Texas, following the Vioxx withdrawal. The GAO acknowledged that the FDA had subsequently undertaken several initiatives to improve its monitoring of drug safety. But, the GAO said, those steps were "unlikely to cover all the gaps." The report concluded that the agency still "lacks a clear and effective process" for making decisions and managing oversight of drug safety, nor did it have "criteria for determining what safety actions to take and when to take them."

The GAO report also said that the FDA's two drug offices had poor communications and that the role of the Office of Drug Safety (ODS) was unclear. The ODS oversaw postmarket safety issues but had no decision-making power. The office served more as a "consultant" to the much bigger Office of New Drugs (OND), which was responsible for approving all new drugs and had decision-making authority over safety matters once drugs were on the market. According to the GAO, the Office of New Drugs sometimes ignored studies and recommendations from the ODS and occasionally even barred ODS scientists from presenting their findings to FDA scientific advisory committees, adding that some Office of Drug Safety scientists referred to the OND as "the black hole" or "abyss."

The newly created Drug Safety Oversight Board, consisting primarily of FDA officials, might improve oversight of high-level decisions about drug safety, the GAO said, but it did little to address the need for systematic tracking of ongoing safety issues. Moreover, the oversight board's dispute resolution process might not be "sufficiently independent" to resolve internal disagreements over drug safety. The GAO also recommended that Congress consider expanding the FDA's authority to require drug companies to conduct postmarket studies to address safety concerns.

Institute of Medicine Study

The report by the Institute of Medicine, which the FDA had requested, was broader in scope than the GAO report and more assertive both in its findings and in its recommendations. The drug safety system was "impaired," it said, by "serious resource constraints that weaken the quality and quantity of the science that it brought to bear on drug safety; an organizational culture that is not optimally functional; and unclear and insufficient regulatory authorities, particularly with respect to enforcement." Contending that the FDA devoted too much attention to getting new drugs to market and not enough attention on ensuring their safety, the study said the FDA "needs a more nuanced set of tools to signal uncertainties, to reduce advertising that drives rapid uptake of new drugs, or to compel additional studies in the actual patient populations who take the drug after its approval."

The report, "The Future of Drug Safety: Promoting and Protecting the Health of the Public," was issued September 22 by the Committee on the Assessment of the United States Drug Safety System, a fifteen-member panel of experts convened by the IOM, which was an arm of the National Academies, chartered by Congress to advise it on health and science issues. The panel was chaired by Sheila P. Burke, deputy secretary and chief operating officer of the Smithsonian Institution. The FDA had agreed to pay $3 million for the study.

Among its specific recommendations, the panel suggested that each newly approved drug be labeled with a symbol, such as a black triangle, for two years to warn consumers that the benefits and risks of the drug were not yet fully studied or understood; it also urged that advertising of these new drugs be restricted during the two-year period. The panel said the FDA should review the safety of drugs at least every five years and that Congress should expand the FDA's enforcement tools, giving it express authority to impose fines, injunctions, and drug withdrawals when drug manufacturers did not comply with requests for additional safety studies. It also recommended that the FDA commissioner be appointed for a six-year term. Currently the commissioner served at the pleasure of the president, subject to Senate confirmation. Since 2001 the FDA had had three commissioners or acting commissioners. "Without stable leadership strongly and visibly committed to drug safety," the panelists wrote, "all other efforts to improve the effectiveness of the agency or position it effectively for the future will be seriously, if not fatally, compromised."

The panel also expressed concern about a controversial law passed in 1992 under which drug makers paid millions of dollars in fees in return for a speedy review of their new drug applications. The panel said that legislation, which was up for renewal in 2007, not only limited "the ability of reviewers to examine safety signals as thoroughly as they might like," but also raised "serious concerns" among some "that the regulator has been 'captured' by the industry it regulates."

Medication Errors

In a related development, on July 20 the Institute of Medicine released its findings that errors in medication were far more prevalent than previously thought. Based on studies of adverse drug effects, a study group for the institute estimated that medication errors injured at least 1.5 million Americans every year and that the actual number might be much higher. It was likely, the panel said, that at least 400,000 hospital patients sustained preventable injury attributable to medication error every year, at a cost of at least $3.5 billion. The report said the problem was so widespread that a patient could expect to endure one drug-related error for each day hospitalized. Other studies cited by the panel estimated that 800,000 drug-related injuries and deaths occurred in nursing homes and that 530,000 occurred among Medicare recipients in outpatient clinics. The panel did not estimate how many of these medication errors might result in death.

The errors occurred for a variety of reasons, the report said, including unexpected interactions among drugs, confusion caused by the similarity of drug names or by illegible handwritten prescriptions, hospital nurses mistakenly giving a patient a drug intended for another patient, pharmacists dispensing the wrong drug or the wrong dosage, and patients not taking the drugs as prescribed. "The incidence of medication errors was surprising even to us," J. Lyle Bootman, dean of the University of Arizona College of Pharmacy and a member of the study group, said July 20 when the report was released. "The solutions are complex and far-reaching and will present challenges."

Among the solutions were electronic prescribing and standardized bar coding of all medications. Currently six different bar-coding systems, each requiring a different "reader," were in use, making bar codes less useful as a safety tool than a single system, the report said. The report urged all health care providers to use electronic prescribing by 2010. On June 30, the FDA finalized its plans for clarifying and standardizing information on drug labels; the revision was expressly intended to reduce medication errors and make electronic prescribing easier, the FDA said.

The IOM study, *Preventing Medication Errors*, was the latest in a series from the prestigious advisory organization designed to call attention to the personal suffering and financial costs of all types of medical errors. The first publication, *To Err Is Human: Building a Safer Health System,* shocked the nation in 1999 when it reported that as many as 98,000 deaths were caused by medical error each year. Of those, about 7,000 were attributed to medication errors. *(1999 report, Historic Documents of 1999, p. 779)*

Following are excerpts from "Drug Safety: Improvement Needed in FDA's Postmarket Decision-making and Oversight Process," a report by the Government Accountability Office, dated March 31, 2006, and released to the public on April 24, 2006.

■■■■■■■ **DOCUMENT** ■■■■■■■

"Drug Safety: Improvement Needed in FDA's Oversight Process"

In 2004, several high-profile drug safety cases raised concerns about the Food and Drug Administration's (FDA) management of safety issues concerning drugs that have been approved for marketing. At congressional hearings in September 2004, FDA was criticized for taking too long to tell physicians and patients about studies linking the use of antidepressants among children to an increased risk of suicidal behavior. Similarly, at a congressional hearing in November 2004, it was alleged that FDA did not act quickly enough on evidence it obtained in 2001 about the cardiovascular risks of Vioxx, an anti-inflammatory drug. In these cases and others there were disagreements within FDA about how to address safety issues. There were also reports that some FDA scientists were discouraged by supervisors from raising questions about the safety of certain drugs.

Problems with FDA's postmarket drug safety program have been raised before. There have been numerous reviews by external and internal groups dating back over 30 years that have identified problems with the federal government's postmarket drug surveillance program and that have made recommendations for improvement. Following passage of the Prescription Drug User Fee Act of 1992 (PDUFA), additional concerns were raised about drug safety. Under PDUFA, drug companies ("sponsors") began paying fees to FDA, which used the funds to hire more drug application reviewers and make other changes in order to speed up the drug review process. As a result, FDA was able to review drug applications and approve new drugs for marketing more rapidly than before. However, the increased attention to timely drug approval decisions led to increased attention to monitoring of postmarket safety as well, which was reflected in the 2002 reauthorization of PDUFA. The 2002 act states that FDA should continue to strengthen and improve the review and monitoring of drug safety, and the PDUFA goals, incorporated by reference into the act, state that FDA will allocate almost $71 million over a 5-year period for postmarket drug safety. FDA subsequently increased its risk management activities, drafted guidance for industry to help drug companies assess and minimize drug risks, and used PDUFA revenues to upgrade its system for adverse event reporting and to acquire external sources of data. In late 2004 and 2005, in response to the safety issues raised in the case of Vioxx and other drugs, FDA announced plans to further strengthen its management of postmarket drug safety. These initiatives, some of which are in an early stage of implementation, include launching a new Web page to make public information on emerging drug safety issues while FDA evaluates them, finalizing the risk management guidance for industry, and making other organizational and policy process changes.

In light of the recent controversy about drug safety, you asked us to conduct a review of FDA's current organizational structure and decision- making process for postmarket drug safety. In this report we (1) describe FDA's organizational structure and process for postmarket drug safety decision making, (2) assess the effectiveness of the postmarket drug safety decision-making process, and (3) assess steps FDA is taking to improve postmarket drug safety decision making.

To describe FDA's organizational structure and process for postmarket drug safety decision making, we analyzed FDA's organizational charts and annual reports, the roles and responsibilities of staff working on drug safety, documents describing internal FDA policies and procedures, and other relevant FDA documents. Our review focused on two offices within FDA's Center for Drug Evaluation and Research (CDER) that are involved in postmarket drug safety activities: the Office of New Drugs (OND) and the Office of Drug Safety (ODS). We interviewed ODS, OND, and other CDER managers and staff about their roles, responsibilities, workloads, and the process for postmarket drug safety decision making. We also interviewed former FDA officials and drug safety experts from outside FDA. To assess the effectiveness of the postmarket drug safety decision-making process, we analyzed documents describing internal FDA policies and procedures and interviewed FDA officials. In order to obtain an in-depth understanding of FDA's policies and procedures, we conducted case studies of four drugs—Arava, Baycol, Bextra, and Propulsid—that help to illustrate the current decision-making process. Each of these drugs presented significant postmarket safety issues that FDA acted upon in recent years, and they reflect differences in the type of adverse event or potential safety problem associated with the drug, the safety actions taken, and the OND and ODS staff involved. For our case studies we reviewed relevant FDA documents and conducted interviews with OND and ODS staff and former FDA staff who were directly involved in the cases. We focused on (1) significant postmarket drug safety regulatory actions; (2) analyses that ODS conducted on the safety concerns; and (3) internal FDA meetings, especially those that involved ODS. We did not examine other elements of the postmarket drug safety decision-making process, such as internal OND meetings. In some cases there may be gaps in our description of events because there was no documentation available about that point in the process. We also did not evaluate the scientific validity of FDA's data, methodologies, or decisions in these or other cases. Our cases cannot be generalized to FDA's deliberations about postmarket drug safety issues for other drugs. Finally, to assess FDA's actions to improve postmarket drug safety decision making, we reviewed relevant FDA documents and interviewed FDA officials and outside drug safety experts. We conducted our review from December 2004 through March 2006 in accordance with generally accepted government auditing standards.

Results in Brief

Two organizationally distinct FDA offices, OND and ODS, are involved in postmarket drug safety activities. OND, which holds responsibility for approving drugs, is involved in safety activities throughout the life cycle of a drug, and it has the decision-making responsibility to take regulatory actions concerning the postmarket safety of drugs. OND staff include physicians, pharmacologists, toxicologists, and microbiologists who are focused on providing health care practitioners and patients with a range of drugs for treatment of a specific disease or condition. OND's work and its pace are driven by PDUFA goals that FDA make drug approvability decisions within certain time frames. OND works closely with ODS to make postmarket drug safety decisions. In contrast to OND's broad perspective, ODS's primary focus is on postmarket drug safety. ODS serves primarily as a consultant to OND and does not have independent decision-making responsibility. ODS has been reorganized several times over the years, and its Division of Drug Risk Evaluation (DDRE) is the primary unit responsible for postmarket safety surveillance. The Division's safety evaluators, who are generally pharmacists, review and analyze adverse event reports. Its epidemiologists, taking a population-based perspective, analyze adverse events in the context of drug utilization, and conduct postmarket drug safety research in collaboration with scientists outside of FDA. There has been high turnover of ODS directors in the past 10 years, with eight different directors of the office and its various predecessors. In our case studies we observed that the decision-making process for postmarket drug safety is complex, involving input from a variety of FDA staff and organizational units and information sources, but the central focus of the process is the iterative interaction between OND and ODS.

FDA lacks a clear and effective process for making decisions about, and providing management oversight of, postmarket drug safety issues. The process has been limited by a lack of clarity about how decisions are made and about organizational roles, insufficient oversight by management, and data constraints. We observed that there is a lack of criteria for determining what safety actions to take and when to take them. Certain parts of ODS's role in the process are unclear, including ODS's participation in scientific advisory committee meetings that are organized by OND to discuss specific drugs. While ODS staff have presented their analyses during some of these meetings, our case studies and others provide examples of the exclusion of ODS staff. Insufficient communication between ODS and OND's divisions has been an ongoing concern and has hindered the decision-making process. Specifically, ODS does not always know how OND has responded to ODS's safety analyses and recommendations. ODS management does not systematically track information about the recommendations its staff make and OND's response to them. This limits the ability of ODS management to provide effective oversight so that FDA can ensure that safety concerns are addressed and resolved in a timely manner. FDA faces data constraints that contribute to the difficulty in making postmarket safety decisions. For example, FDA relies on clinical trials, reports of adverse drug reactions, and studies following the use of drugs in ongoing medical care in order to evaluate safety concerns and support its decisions, but each type of data has weaknesses. FDA also lacks authority to require certain studies and has resource limitations for obtaining data.

Some of FDA's initiatives, such as the establishment of a Drug Safety Oversight Board (DSB), a draft policy on major postmarket drug safety decision making, and the identification of new data sources, may improve the postmarket drug safety decision-making process, but they will not address all the gaps we identified. FDA's newly created DSB may help provide oversight of important, high-level safety decisions; however, it does not address the lack of systematic tracking of safety issues and their resolution. Other initiatives such as FDA's draft policy on major postmarket decisions and regular meetings between OND divisions and ODS may help improve the clarity and effectiveness of the process, but they are incomplete, and do not clarify ODS's role in certain scientific advisory committee meetings. FDA's dispute resolution processes to help resolve organizational and individual disagreements over postmarket drug safety decisions have not been used and may not be viewed as sufficiently independent. FDA is taking steps to identify additional data sources, including data on Medicare beneficiaries using drugs covered by the new prescription drug benefit, but data constraints remain.

To help improve the decision-making process for postmarket drug safety, we suggest that the Congress consider expanding FDA's authority to require drug sponsors to conduct postmarket studies when additional data are needed. We are also making recommendations to the Commissioner of FDA to improve the process by establishing a mechanism for systematically tracking postmarket drug safety issues, revising and implementing FDA's draft policy on major postmarket drug safety decisions, improving CDER's dispute resolution process, and clarifying ODS's role in FDA's scientific advisory committee meetings.

In commenting on a draft of this report, FDA stated that the conclusions reached by GAO were reasonable and consistent with actions that it has already begun or planned. FDA did not comment on our recommendations.

Conclusions

Postmarket drug safety decision making at FDA is a complex process that sometimes results in disagreements, as observed in our case studies. Scientific disagreements may be expected in a large regulatory agency, especially given the different professional orientations of the key players, OND and ODS, and the inherent limitations of the available data. However, because of the potential public health consequences of FDA's decisions about postmarket drug safety issues, it is important to come to a decision quickly. In our review, we observed opportunities for improving the clarity and oversight of the process and strengthening the information used for decision making. FDA has recently made some important organizational and policy changes, but more could be done to improve management oversight of postmarket drug safety issues, to improve the dispute resolution process, and to strengthen the collaboration between OND and ODS. In order to address the serious limitations of the data, FDA will need to continue its efforts to develop useful observational studies and to access and use additional healthcare databases. However, even if FDA is successful in expanding its data sources for postmarket drug safety surveillance, it would still benefit from information from long-term clinical trials of certain drugs and the additional authority to require that these studies be carried out.

Matter for Congressional Consideration

To improve the decision-making process for postmarket drug safety, the Congress should consider expanding FDA's authority to require drug sponsors to conduct postmarket studies, such as clinical trials or observational studies, as needed, to collect additional data on drug safety concerns.

Recommendations for Executive Action

To improve the postmarket drug safety decision-making process, we recommend that the Commissioner of FDA take the following four actions:

- establish a mechanism for systematically tracking ODS's recommendations and subsequent safety actions;
- with input from the DSB and the Process Improvement Teams, revise and implement the draft policy on major postmarket drug safety decisions;
- improve CDER's dispute resolution process by revising the pilot program to increase its independence; and
- clarify ODS's role in FDA's scientific advisory committee meetings involving postmarket drug safety issues. . . .

Source: U.S. Congress. Government Accountability Office. "Drug Safety: Improvement Needed in FDA's Postmarket Decision-making and Oversight Process." GAO-06-402, March 31, 2006 (released April 24, 2006). http://purl.access.gpo.gov/GPO/LPS70603 (accessed January 25, 2007).

April

2006 HISTORIC DOCUMENTS

President Bush on Gasoline Prices and Oil Dependence

April 25, 2006

■■■■■ **THE DOCUMENT IN CONTEXT** ■■■■■

Energy prices reached new highs in 2006, pumped up by continuing high demand around the world, increased instability in the Middle East and other oil-producing areas, and fears of another damaging hurricane season in the United States. World oil prices reached a record high of $78 a barrel in July before falling back to finish the year at a little under $60 a barrel. Gasoline prices in the United States also soared, reaching or exceeding $3.00 a gallon for several months in the spring and summer before falling to around $2.25 late in the year.

As it had the year before, the American economy seemed to absorb the high energy prices. Overall, the economy grew at a respectable pace of 3.3 percent for the year, inflation remained stable, and corporate profits advanced. Consumers, however, felt the pinch of higher gasoline and fuel prices in their wallets and wasted no time in blaming big oil companies for price manipulation and demanding that politicians in Washington do something. Lawmakers responded with dozens of proposals, such as taxing windfall profits, offering a gas tax holiday or rebate, and increasing the fuel economy of cars, trucks, and sports utility vehicles (SUVs). Even President George W. Bush, a staunch ally of the oil industry, offered a slew of proposals for easing dependence on oil, including spending more money on alternatives to gasoline. But partisan politics in an election year where control of Congress was at stake, complicated by regional alignments on energy policy that crossed party lines, doomed all but one of the proposals—a measure to expand oil and gas production in the Gulf of Mexico. After Democrats won control of Congress in the November elections, they promised to forge ahead with their plans to roll back some tax preferences given to oil and gas producers and collecting some unpaid royalties on oil and gas leases in the Gulf of Mexico.

Prices Ratcheting Upward

World oil prices had climbed upward, steadily if erratically, since the United States invaded Iraq in March 2003, when a barrel of crude oil cost about $27. In 2004 prices crossed the psychological threshold of $50 a barrel to reach a high of $55, before settling back to about $45 a barrel at the end of the year. A year later, in June 2005, oil prices jumped over $60 a barrel for the first time and briefly surged above $70 a barrel after Hurricanes Katrina and Rita roared through the Gulf of Mexico in late August and mid-September, severely damaging production and refining capacity. Prices retreated into the mid-$60s range in October and then fell again, ending the year in the mid- to high-$50s range. *(Background, Historic Documents of 2005, p. 777)*

In addition to the short-term price hikes caused by the storms, the main drivers of the price increases were strong demand not only from the United States and other industrialized countries but also from fast-developing countries, such as China and India; instability in the world's main oil-producing regions, especially the Middle East, Nigeria, and Venezuela; a desire by some members of the Organization of Petroleum Exporting Countries (OPEC) to keep prices high; and the market speculation caused by so much uncertainty. All those factors and then some were at work to push prices to record levels in 2006.

In January prices surged to a four-month high, to about $68 a barrel, as a stand-off between Western countries and Iran over Iran's nuclear programs and escalating violence in Nigeria's oil-producing region raised fears of future shortages. Iran, which exported 2.5 million barrels a day, mostly to Asia, threatened to raise prices if the West intervened to stop its nuclear program. In Nigeria, tribal conflicts were slowing the country's production of about 2.25 million barrels a day. Prices moderated somewhat in February but then began to climb again as the situation in Nigeria deteriorated further and little headway was made in negotiations with Iran. Those concerns pushed oil above $75 a barrel for the first time on April 21.

At the same time, U.S. gasoline prices were rising, in part because of limited refining capacity and in part because of a switchover in gasoline additives from methyl tertiary-butyl ether (MTBE) to ethanol. Both additives helped gasoline burn more cleanly, but MTBE had been found to contaminate drinking water and was being phased out. By mid-April the average price for a gallon of unleaded regular gasoline was nearly $2.89, and in many areas the price was near or above $3.00.

Consumer fears that prices would go even higher over the summer were realized in late July after Hezbollah, the radical Shiite group in Lebanon, provoked a war with Israel that further destabilized the Middle East. World oil prices briefly rose above $78 a gallon in July, while U.S. gasoline prices reached an all-time high national average of $3.03 a gallon in mid-August. Oil prices began to fall back after August 11 when the United Nations Security Council imposed a cease-fire on the warring parties. By mid-September world oil prices were back to about $65 a barrel, eased not only by an end to the war in Lebanon but also by a relaxation of the tensions with Iran, a milder-than-expected hurricane season, and signs of a slowing U.S. economy, which would reduce demand. For the rest of the year oil prices hovered in the high $50s, down roughly $20 a barrel from their peaks in July, while gasoline prices dropped back to about $2.20 a gallon—roughly the same level as at the beginning of the year.

One new element of concern arose at the end of the year, when OPEC for the second time in three months agreed to cut back its production. The group of eleven oil-producing countries, primarily in the Middle East and Africa, supplied about 40 percent of the world's oil exports and had been producing at near-capacity for the last two years to meet increasing demand. But with demand slowing and oil prices falling, OPEC agreed in October to cut back production by 1 million barrels a day to 26.3 million barrels a day. That move hardly raised an eyebrow in the world trade markets, but that was not the case in December when OPEC decided to reduce its oil production by another 500,000 barrels a day, to 25.8 million, starting on February 1, 2007. OPEC's announcement on December 14 came after a month of rapidly declining inventories and steadily rising prices. "It's a very aggressive, assertive move," Edward Morse, the chief energy economist for Lehman Brothers told the *New York Times*. "Clearly, some OPEC members want to keep a $60 floor" on the price of a barrel of oil.

So far, the impact of the oil price hikes on the U.S. economy had been surprisingly mild, according to analysts. Unlike the oil crises of the 1970s and early 1980s, which sent the country into recession, this latest round of oil price hikes had only a modest effect on the economy so far. In July the bipartisan Congressional Budget Office (CBO) estimated that increased energy prices had a minimal impact on inflation and caused gross domestic product to be about 1 percent lower than it would have been if prices had not risen. The CBO attributed this mild response to several factors, including a more flexible economy and the strong belief that the Federal Reserve Board would take steps to control inflation. For many of the same reasons, the corporate world had also weathered the price hikes in reasonably good shape. One notable exception was the American auto industry, whose reliance on gas-guzzling trucks and SUVs and sluggishness in developing alternative-fuel vehicles was costing it dearly. The "Big Three"—General Motors, Ford, and Daimler Chrysler—were all going through major restructuring efforts at the end of the year.

Households were most affected by the energy price hike, the CBO said. Between 2003 and mid-2006, the average household's annual spending on energy rose by $1,700; a sharp drop in the household saving rate "helped dampen the negative effects" of higher energy prices over the short term, the CBO said. Higher energy prices were also likely to depress the U.S. standard of living "for many years," CBO warned, because consumers would "have to exchange more of their production for a barrel of oil" than would have been the case if oil prices had not changed.

Response in Washington to Higher Prices

Since entering the White House in 2001 President Bush and Vice President Dick Cheney, both former oil industry executives, had aggressively sought tax breaks, government subsidies, and reduced environmental regulations to encourage increased domestic production of oil and natural gas. Both men gave short shrift to development of alternative fuels and derided energy conservation as, in Cheney's words, a "personal virtue" but not "the basis for sound energy policy." That began to change after the 2005 hurricanes knocked out oil and gas production in much of the Gulf— for the first time in his presidency Bush on September 26, 2005, asked Americans to conserve energy. In his State of the Union on January 31, 2006, Bush acknowledged that the country was "addicted to oil" and offered a raft of proposals to break the habit. These included increased funding for research into alternative fuels and fuel-efficient vehicles and incentives to develop wind and solar power, "zero-emission" coal technology, and clean nuclear power.

Seeking to deflect voter anger over steadily rising gasoline prices, Bush on April 25 announced a series of steps that he hoped would ease energy prices in the short run, including holding off for a few months on making any more additions to the Strategic Petroleum Reserve, which he said was already large enough to cover any short-term disruptions in the oil supply. In a speech to the Renewable Fuels Association in Washington, D.C., Bush also called on Congress to repeal about $2 billion in what he called "unnecessary" tax breaks for energy companies contained in the Energy Policy Act enacted at the end of 2005, and he asked Congress to make all hybrid vehicles sold in 2006 eligible for federal tax credits.

Over the longer haul, Bush offered a plan for investing in alternative fuels to reduce the country's demand for oil and gasoline. That plan included expanding the use of ethanol made from corn while developing ethanol made from wood chips, switch grasses, and other natural materials; developing biodiesel fuel; and supporting hydrogen fuel cell technology. But in calling for a lessening of dependence on foreign oil, the president also pushed policies he had long advocated, including opening the Arctic National Wildlife Refuge (ANWR) to oil exploration and easing restrictions on clean air and water regulations to encourage construction of oil refineries and power plants.

Although virtually everyone admitted that there was little lawmakers could do to ease energy prices in the short term, Republicans and Democrats alike introduced dozens of proposals, largely intended to show their constituents they were doing something to address the problem. One proposal that met an early death was a plan offered by the Republican Senate leadership to mail $100 rebate checks to taxpayers to help defray the increased cost of gasoline. The plan was quickly dropped after consumers and commentators across the political spectrum ridiculed it as pandering to the voters before the election. Conservative talk show host Rush Limbaugh captured the general public sentiment, when he asked on his radio program: "What kind of insult is this? Instead of buying us off and treating us like we're a bunch of whores, just solve the problem."

Democrats also accused the Republicans of posturing for the voters while doing the bidding of the energy industry. Senate Minority Leader Harry M. Reid, D-Nev., repeatedly said that the administration and Republican-led Congress were "content to let the market and Big Oil crush consumers, squeezing every last coin out of their pockets." House Minority Leader Nancy Pelosi, D-Calif., chastised the administration for "reneging on promises to invest in alternative energy sources." In July she said the president's budget for fiscal 2007 proposed a 46 percent cut for renewable energy research from the level authorized in the 2005 Energy Policy Act and actually cut funding for energy efficiency and conservation programs. Democrats continued to press for a windfall profits tax and tighter fuel economy standards for cars and trucks, both of which were nonstarters among Republicans.

After dozens of proposals and months of debate, Congress enacted only one significant piece of energy legislation in 2006. The measure, which was attached to a tax and trade package (HR 6111—PL 109–432), cleared on the last day of the session. It opened 8.3 million acres in the Gulf of Mexico south of the Florida panhandle to oil and gas drilling. For the first time, Alabama, Louisiana, Mississippi, and Texas would receive a share (37.5 percent) of the revenue from new leases in the Gulf Coast. All four states, but particularly Louisiana, could use the additional revenue to help rebuild from the 2005 hurricanes. The bill also created drilling-free buffer zones to protect Florida's west coast beaches. The House had passed a much broader measure earlier in the year that would have allowed oil and gas drilling along most of the U.S. coastline but was forced to accept the Senate version of the bill when it became clear that Democrats would filibuster the broader measure.

The House also passed a largely symbolic measure to authorize energy development in the Arctic National Wildlife Refuge in northern Alaska. One of the last large pieces of totally unspoiled wilderness in the United States, the refuge sat above large oil reserves and environmentalists successfully fought off attempts by the petroleum industry to open the area to exploration for oil and gas production. In 2005 Republicans, who generally backed the exploration, made their strongest attempt in years to open the refuge, but that effort failed in the Senate, which did not take up the issue again in 2006. With Democrats taking control of Congress in 2007, it was widely thought that ANWR was safe from oil exploration for at least a few more years.

Going after Big Oil

The main target of consumer wrath continued to be the big oil companies that were reporting huge profits every quarter, while consumers saw more of their paychecks going to pay for gasoline and other fuels. The figures were indeed eye-popping. In 2006 ExxonMobil posted a net profit of $39.5 billion, a record among American companies that made it not only the largest oil company in the world, but also the largest company, surpassing Wal-mart. Together ExxonMobil, ConocoPhillips, and Chevron earned net income of $72.4 billion in 2006, up from $64 billion the previous year.

In a bit of political theater, the executives of five major oil companies were commanded to appear at a Senate hearing in November 2005 to justify their unprecedented profits. The companies' explanations—in essence, that their profits were in line with the average but that the numbers were huge because the scale of the industry was huge—offered little comfort to consumers. On March 14, most of the same executives were again hauled before a Senate committee, this time the Judiciary Committee, where they were again lectured about high prices and warned that Congress might impose restrictions on oil company mergers to prevent the industry from becoming any more concentrated and less competitive.

Another swipe at the oil industry fell flat, when an investigation by the Federal Trade Commission (FTC) into the gasoline price spikes after Hurricane Katrina found no evidence of price gouging. Consumers had long complained that oil companies and gas stations were using the hurricanes and instability in the Middle East as excuses to raise the price of gasoline illegally, and in the fall of 2005 Congress ordered the FTC to investigate. In its report, released on May 22, 2006, the FTC said the price spikes had not been illegally manipulated and could be explained in virtually every case by regional or local market trends. "The evidence collected in this investigation indicated that firms behaved competitively," the report said. The release of the FTC report undercut legislation passed by the House on May 4 that would have banned price gouging in petroleum markets; the Senate took no action on the measure. Only a week earlier, President Bush had signaled his approval of such a measure when he told the Renewable Fuels Association that he would not tolerate price manipulation and had directed a separate federal investigation of any illegal price gouging.

By year's end, the oil industry was engaged in another confrontation with Washington, this one over allegations that it had underpaid royalties on offshore leases for oil and gas drilling. An Interior Department error in more than 1,000 leases issued in 1998 and 1999 was expected to cost taxpayers more than $10 billion over the life of the leases, according to government estimates. While the department was able to renegotiate leases with a handful of companies, about fifty others refused, prompting Democrats and some Republicans to back legislation that would require companies to either renegotiate or pay a "conservation" fee as a condition for bidding on future leases. Democrats promised to push the legislation when they took over Congress in 2007.

In a related development, the Interior Department's inspector general, Earl E. Devaney, reported on December 6 that an eight-month investigation found the department's program for auditing royalty payments riddled with problems. Devaney said data were often inaccurate, that many companies and properties escaped audit altogether, and that the audits that were done often relied too heavily on statements by oil companies rather than actual records. Devaney's report prompted the Justice Department to initiate two criminal investigations of the Minerals Management Service, the agency in the Interior Department responsible for the royalty program. On December

14, Rep. Edward Markey, D-Mass., a longtime critic of the Bush Interior Department, said that the criminal investigations were "proof positive that the conflicts of interest between the Bush administration regulators and those they regulate in the oil and gas industry are costing the American taxpayers billions in royalty revenues." The investigations were expected to take several months to complete.

Following are excerpts from a speech by President George W. Bush, on April 25, 2006, to the Renewable Fuels Association in Washington, D.C., outlining his plan for reducing gasoline prices in the short term and cutting America's dependence on oil in the long term.

DOCUMENT

"Remarks to the Renewable Fuels Association"

Thank you all. . . .

For 25 years, the Renewable Fuels Association has been a tireless advocate for ethanol producers. Your advocacy is paying off. Renewable energy is one of the great stories of recent years, and it's going to be a bigger story in the years to come.

I like the idea of talking to people who are growing America's energy security. I like the idea of policy that combines agriculture and modern science with the energy needs of the American people. I'm here to talk to you about the contributions you are making, and I'm here to talk to you about the need for this country to get off our dependency of oil. . . .

We've got good news here at home on the economic front too. This economy of ours is growing, and the entrepreneurial spirit in America is strong. . . .

Yet amongst this hopeful—these hopeful signs, there's an area of serious concern, and that is high energy prices. And the prices that people are paying at the gas pumps reflect our addiction to oil. Addiction to oil is a matter of national security concerns. After all, today we get about 60 percent of our oil from foreign countries. That's up from 20 years ago where we got oil from—about 25 percent of our oil came from foreign countries. Now part of the problem is, is that some of the nations we rely on for oil have unstable governments or agendas that are hostile to the United States. These countries know we need their oil, and that reduces our influence, our ability to keep the peace in some areas. And so energy supply is a matter of national security. It's also a matter of economic security.

What people are seeing at their gasoline pumps reflects the global economy in which we live. See, when demand for oil goes up in China or India, two fast-growing economies, it affects the price of oil nation—worldwide. And when the price of crude oil goes up, because it's such an important part of the price of gasoline, the average citizen sees the price of gasoline go up at the pump.

Gasoline price increases are like a hidden tax on the working people. They're like a tax on our farmers. They're like a tax on small businesses. Energy prices are—energy experts predict gas prices are going to remain high throughout the summer, and that's going to be a continued strain on the American people.

And so the fundamental question is, what are we going to do? What can the Government do? One of the past responses by Government, particularly from the party of which I am not a member, has been to have—to propose price fixing or increase the taxes. Those plans haven't worked in the past. I think we need to follow suit on what we have been emphasizing, particularly through the energy bill, and that is to encourage conservation, to expand domestic production, and to develop alternative sources of energy like ethanol.

Signing the energy bill was one thing, and I want to thank the Members of Congress for getting a comprehensive energy bill to my desk, but there's a lot more to be done. First thing is to make sure that the American consumers are treated fairly at the gas pump. Americans understand, by and large, that the price of crude oil is going up and that the prices are going up, but what they don't want and will not accept is manipulation of the market. And neither will I.

The Federal Trade Commission is investigating whether price of gasoline has been unfairly manipulated in any way. I'm also directing the Department of Justice to work with the FTC and the Energy Department to conduct inquiries into illegal manipulation or cheating related to the current gasoline prices. The FTC and the Attorney General are contacting 50 State attorney generals to offer technical assistance, to urge them to investigate possible illegal price manipulation within their jurisdictions. In other words, this administration is not going to tolerate manipulation. We expect our consumers to be treated fairly.

To reduce gas prices, our energy companies have got a role to play. Listen, at record prices, these energy companies have got large cash flows, and they need to reinvest those cash flows into expanding refining capacity or researching alternative energy sources or developing new technologies or expanding production in environmentally friendly ways. That's what the American people expect. We expect there to be strong reinvestment to help us with our economic security needs and our national security needs.

Record oil prices and large cash flows also mean that Congress has got to understand that these energy companies don't need unnecessary tax breaks like the writeoffs of certain geological and geophysical expenditures or the use of taxpayers' money to subsidize energy companies' research into deep-water drilling. I'm looking forward to Congress to take about $2 billion of these tax breaks out of the budget over a 10-year period of time. Cash flows are up. Taxpayers don't need to be paying for certain of these expenses on behalf of the energy companies.

Second part of a good plan is—to confront high gasoline prices, is to promote greater fuel efficiency. And the easiest way to promote fuel efficiency is to encourage drivers to purchase highly efficient hybrid or clean diesel vehicles which, by the way, can run on alternative energy sources. Hybrid vehicles run on a combination of a traditional engine and an electric battery. The twin sources of power allow hybrid cars and trucks to travel about twice as far on a gallon of fuel as gasoline-only vehicles. When people are driving hybrids, they're conserving energy.

Clean diesel vehicles take advantage of advances in diesel technology to run on 30 percent less fuel than gasoline vehicles do. More than 200,000 hybrid and clean diesel vehicles were sold in the United States last year. It's the highest sales in history. Congress wisely, in the energy bill, expanded a tax credit for purchases of hybrids and clean diesel vehicles up to—as much as up to $3,400 per purchase. That made sense.

If we're trying to conserve energy, if we want to become less dependent on oil, let's provide incentives for consumers to use less energy. The problem is that these tax credits apply to only a limited number of hybrid and clean diesel vehicles for each manufacturer. If the automakers sell more than their limit, new purchasers are not eligible for the full tax credit. And so here's an idea that can—gets more of these vehicles on the road, and that is to have Congress make all hybrid and clean diesel vehicles sold this year eligible for Federal tax credits. We want to encourage people to make wise choices when it comes to the automobiles they drive.

Third part of the plan to confront high gas prices is to boost our supplies of crude oil and gasoline. It makes sense when—the supply-and-demand world, if prices are high, it means demand is greater than supply. One way to ease price is to increase supply. One immediate way we can signal to people we're serious about increasing supply is to stop making purchases or deposits to the Strategic Petroleum Reserve for a short period of time. I've directed the Department of Energy to defer filling the reserve this summer. Our strategic reserve is sufficiently large enough to guard against any major supply disruption over the next few months. So by deferring deposits until the fall, we'll leave a little more oil on the market. Every little bit helps.

We also need to ensure that there are not needless restrictions on our ability to get gasoline to the pump. Under Federal quality—air quality laws, some areas of the country are required to use fuel blend called reformulated gasoline. Now, as you well know, this year we're going—undergoing a rapid transition in the primary ingredient in reformulated gas—from MTBE [methyl tertiary-butyl ether] to ethanol. And I appreciate the role the ethanol producers are playing to meet this challenge. You're playing a vital role.

Yet State and local officials in some parts of our country worry about supply disruption for the short term. They worry about the sudden change from MTBE to ethanol—the ethanol producers won't be able to meet the demand. And that's causing the price of gasoline to go up some amount in their jurisdictions.

And some have contacted us to determine whether or not they can ask the EPA to waive local fuel requirements on a temporary basis. And I think it makes sense that they should be allowed to. So I'm directing EPA Administrator [Steve] Johnson to use all his available authority to grant waivers that would relieve critical fuel supply shortages. And I do that for the sake of our consumers. If Johnson finds that he needs more authority to relieve the problem, we're going to work with Congress to obtain the authority he needs.

Secondly, we also need to confront the larger problem of too many localized fuel blends, which are called boutique fuels. The number of boutique fuels has expanded rapidly over the years, and America now has an uncoordinated and overly complex set of fuel rules. And when you have a uncoordinated, overly complex set of fuel rules, it tends to cause the price to go up.

And so I'm asking Director—directing Administrator Johnson to bring the Governors together to form a task force on boutique fuels. And the mission of this task force will be to find ways to reduce the number of boutique fuels and to increase cooperation between States on gasoline supply decisions. I want to simplify the process for the sake of our consumers. And then I'm asking them to get these recommendations to my desk, and I look forward to working with the United States Congress to simplify the process.

Listen, we need to expand our refining capacity. One of the problems we face is that we've got tight supplies because we haven't expanded refining capacity. There hasn't been a new refinery built in 30 years. If you're worried about the price of gasoline at the pump, it makes sense to try to get more supply to the market. That will be beneficial for American consumers, to get more supply to the market.

Part of the reasons why we haven't expanded or built new refineries to the extent we need to is because the permitting process in this country is extremely complicated. Companies that want to upgrade their equipment or expand their existing refineries or build new ones often have to wade through long, bureaucratic delays and/or lawsuits. To make this gasoline supply more affordable and more secure, Congress needs to allow refiners to make modifications on their refineries without having to wait for years to get something—to get their idea approved. I mean, if we want more supply, let's reduce the paperwork and the regulations.

Congress also needs to simplify and speed up the permitting process for refinery construction and expansion. And so I'm going to work with Congress. It's important for Congress to cut through the red tape and guarantee refinery construction permits will be processed within a single year.

We also need to be mindful of the fact that we can find additional crude oil in our own country in environmentally friendly ways. The technology is such that we're capable of environmentally sensitive exploration. We got tight crude oil supplies, and it seems like it makes sense for us to use our new technologies to find more crude, particularly crude here at home.

One of the issues that you know, that has been confronting Congress is ANWR [Arctic National Wildlife Refuge]. And I fully recognize that the passage of ANWR will not increase the oil supply immediately. But it's also important to understand that if ANWR had been law a decade ago, America would be producing about a million additional barrels of oil a day, and that would increase our current level of domestic supply by 20 percent. We've got to be wise about energy policy here in America. We've got to make sure that we protect the environment, but we've also got to make sure that we find additional supplies of crude oil in order to take the pressure off the price of crude, which takes the pressure off the price of gasoline at the pump.

And all I've outlined here today are interim strategies—short-term and interim strategy. The truth of the matter is, the long-term strategy is to power our automobiles with something other than oil, something other than gasoline, which is derived from oil.

And we're making progress. In my State of the Union Address, I talked about the Advanced Energy Initiative. And this is an aggressive plan, a wise way of using taxpayers' money to get us off our addiction to oil. We have a unique opportunity to continue forward with this plan.

Technology is the way, really, to help us—to help change America for the better. Years of investment in fuels like ethanol have put us on the threshold of major breakthroughs. And those breakthroughs are becoming a reality for our consumers. I set a goal to replace oil from around the world. The best way and the fastest way to do so is to expand the use of ethanol.

The Advanced Energy Initiative is focused on three promising ways to reduce gasoline consumption. One is increasing the use of ethanol; another is improving hybrid vehicles;

and finally, one is developing hydrogen technology. All three go hand in hand; all three are an important part of a strategy to help us diversify away from hydrocarbons.

Ethanol is—has got the largest potential for immediate growth. Most people may not know this, but today, most of ethanol produced in America today is from corn. Most vehicles can use 10 percent ethanol—in their automobiles.

What's interesting that Americans don't realize, with a little bit of expenditure, we can convert a—kind of, the standard automobile to what's called a flex-fuel automobile. And that flex-fuel vehicle can use ethanol that is—or fuel that is 85 percent ethanol. It's amazing, isn't it? Without much cost, your automobile can be converted to be able to burn fuel with 85 percent ethanol, or a product made from corn grown right here in America.

Ethanol is a versatile fuel, and the benefits are—the benefits are easy to recognize when you think about it. One, the use of ethanol in our automobiles is good for the agricultural sector. I'm one of these people who believes when the agricultural sector is strong, America is strong. The way I like to put it, it would be a good thing when a President can sit there and say, "Gosh, we've got a lot of corn, and it means we're less dependent on foreign sources of oil."

Years back, they'd say, "Oh, gosh, we've got a lot of corn, worried about the price." Ethanol is good for our rural communities. It's good economic development for rural America. New bio-refinery construction creates jobs and local tax revenues. When the farmer—when the family farmer is doing well, it's good for the local merchants.

Ethanol is good for the environment. I keep emphasizing that we can be good stewards of our environment and, at the same time, continue with our economic expansion. And ethanol will help meet that strategy. You don't have to choose between good environment and good economics. You can have both by the use of technology. And ethanol is an example of what I'm talking about. And ethanol is good for drivers. Ethanol is home-grown. Ethanol will replace gasoline consumption. . . .

The ethanol industry is booming. It must be exciting to have worked for as long as you have on encouraging alternative sources of energy and then all of a sudden see the work come to fruition.

Last year, America used a record 4 billion gallons of ethanol. There are now 97 ethanol refineries in our country, and 9 of those are expanding. And 35 more are under construction. The ethanol industry is on the move, and America is better off for it.

Many of these refineries are in the Midwest, the Midwest because that is where the source of that—the feedstock for ethanol comes from. That happens to be corn. But what's really interesting is, there are new plants springing up in unexpected areas like the Central Valley of California or Arizona or, of course, in the sugar fields of Hawaii. After all, sugar is also an important—can be used for ethanol. As a matter of fact, it's a very efficient feedstock for ethanol.

Ethanol required our support. In other words, to get this new industry going, it required a little nudge from the Federal Government. Since I took office, we've extended the tax credit to 51 cents per gallon for suppliers. We've created a new 10-cent per gallon tax credit to provide extra help to small ethanol producers and farmers, provided $85 million of loans and grants for the ethanol business ventures.

In other words, this is a collaborative effort. The Federal Government has got a role to play to encourage new industries that will help this Nation diversify away from oil. And so we're strongly committed to corn-based ethanol produced in America. Yet there—you got to recognize there are limits to how much corn can be used for ethanol. After all, we got to eat some, and the animals have got to eat.

And so I am committed to furthering technological research to find other ways, other sources for ethanol. We're working on research—strong research to figure out cellulosic ethanol that can be made from wood chips or stalks or switch grass. These materials are sometimes waste products and are just simply thrown away. And doesn't it make sense for us—I think it does—to use taxpayers' money to determine whether or not we can use these new—these raw materials to make something out of nothing, so that we continue the advance of ethanol, so the market for ethanol expands throughout the United States.

We're spending—I proposed, and I'm working with these members of the Renewable Caucus—$150 million in next year's budget for research in advanced forms of ethanol. And that's a significant increase over previous levels. I think it makes sense. And surely the prices at the gas pump should say to the taxpayer, it makes sense for this Government to spend money on research and development to find alternative sources of energy.

I also support biodiesel fuel, which can substitute for regular diesel in cars, trucks, buses, and farm equipment. Last year, I went out to see a biodiesel refinery in Virginia that's making clean-burning fuel from soybean oil. And it was a really interesting process to watch. I don't know if you know this or not, but they're able to use waste products like recycled cooking grease to manufacture biodiesel. In other words, research and development has led to new alternative sources of energy like biodiesel. So that's one of the reasons why I signed into law the first ever Federal tax credit for biodiesel producers. In other words, we're interested in addressing our energy security needs on a variety of fronts. It makes sense for the United States to have a comprehensive strategy to help us diversify away from oil.

And so we also have got to understand that we got to research not only to find—to invest in ethanol and biodiesel, but part of a comprehensive strategy is to spend money on researching new battery technologies. And one of the really interesting opportunities available for the American consumer will be the ability to buy a plug-in hybrid vehicle that will be able to drive up to 40 miles on electricity. Seems to make sense to me, if we're trying to get us off gasoline, with crude oil as the main—as its main feedstock, then why wouldn't we explore ways to be able to have vehicles that use less gasoline? And one way to do so is to use electricity to power vehicles.

And we're pretty close to a breakthrough. We believe we're close to a technology that will make it possible to drive up to 40 miles on electricity alone. And then if you have to drive more than 40, then your gasoline kicks in.

But you can imagine what that will mean for a lot of drivers in big cities who, on a daily basis, they don't drive over 40 miles. And so therefore, a lot of drivers that are going back and forth from work in big cities won't be using gasoline. And that's going to help. We've got $31 million in our budget to speed up research and development into advanced battery technologies.

And finally, one other opportunity that is more long-run than ethanol or biodiesel or plug-in hybrid vehicles or encouraging people to buy the hybrids that are on the market today, is hydrogen—we're spending about $1.2 billion over 5 years to research the use of hydrogen to power vehicles. And it makes a lot of sense when you think about it, because hydrogen produces zero emissions. The only emission it produces is water. And when I was out there in California, I visited the California Fuel Cell Partnership and saw buses and cars and SUVs that are driving on the highways out there powered by hydrogen. And the research and development money that we have spent has lowered the cost of hydrogen fuel cells; it's helped make them lighter. In other words, there's an industry coming, and it's an industry that will enable consumers to drive to work, just like we're doing today, but not rely on foreign sources of oil.

What I'm describing to you today is a strategy that recognizes the realities of the world in which we live. Our dependency on oil has created economic security issues for us and national security issues for us. And therefore, this country must use our brainpower and entrepreneurial spirit to diversify away from the hydrocarbon economy. You all have known this a lot longer than most Americans. You've known that we've needed to have this strategy, and that's why you're on the forefront of incredible changes that are taking place in this country.

You know, there's no doubt in my mind that one of these days, instead of people driving up to a gas station, they're going to be going up to a fueling station. And they'll be able to have choices to choose from. Got a hydrogen-powered car, you'll be able to have that choice. If you want 85 percent, maybe someday 100 percent ethanol, that will be an option available too.

We owe it to the American people to be aggressive on price gouging now. We owe it to the American people to be promoting alternative ways to drive their car so as to make us less dependent on foreign sources of oil. We owe it to the American people to be aggressive in the use of technology so we can diversify away from the hydrocarbon society. And that's precisely what we're doing, and I'm glad to stand with you.

I appreciate your work for the United States of America. Thank you for letting me come by and talk to you, and may God bless you.

Source: U.S. Executive Office of the President. "Remarks to the Renewable Fuels Association." April 25, 2006. *Weekly Compilation of Presidential Documents* 42, no. 17 (May 1, 2006): 786–792. Washington, D.C.: National Archives and Records Administration. www.gpoaccess.gov/wcomp/v42no17.html (accessed December 12, 2006).

Other Historic Documents of Interest

Crisis in the auto industry, p. 293
Midterm elections, p. 645
State of the Union address, p. 23

UN resolution on Iran, p. 781
War between Israel and Hezbollah,
   p. 454

Federal Reserve Chief Bernanke on the Outlook for the U.S. Economy

April 27, 2006

■ THE DOCUMENT IN CONTEXT ■

Based strictly on the numbers, the U.S. economy performed reasonably well in 2006. Despite record high oil prices, a marked slowing in the housing market, and continued turmoil in the auto industry, the economy grew at an annual rate of 3.3 percent, inflation stayed within a healthy range, more than 2 million jobs were created, and unemployment remained low. Reflecting investor confidence, the stock market reached record highs, with the Dow Jones industrial average rising above 12,000 points for the first time in its history.

But many Americans appeared to feel that the benefits from the growing economy were passing them by. Overall American wages went up in 2006, but wage increases for many middle-class and low-income workers were barely keeping up with inflation or lagging behind, while high gas prices and rising interest rates, especially on adjustable home mortgages, absorbed a greater portion of their paychecks. Although new jobs were being created, manufacturing jobs continued to disappear or move overseas; most of the new jobs were either technology related, requiring skills that many workers did not have, or low-skill service jobs that paid low wages and few if any benefits.

As a factor in the November midterm elections, the economy was overshadowed by voter dissatisfaction with the war in Iraq and a series of corruption scandals in Congress. But there were clear indications that many voters were also unhappy with their slice of the economy. Exit polls found that about 30 percent of all voters said they were moving ahead financially, while 50 percent said they had just enough to maintain their standard of living , and 20 percent said they were falling behind. The Democrats' pledge to raise the minimum wage if they gained control of Congress may have had just as much or more resonance with the voters than the Republicans' call for continued tax cuts. In a *Newsweek* poll conducted in the two days following the November 7 election, 89 percent of those surveyed said they supported a hike in the minimum wage.

Overview of the U.S. Economic Situation

For the year, the economy grew at a rate of 3.3 percent. But the annual figure masked a downhill slide, from 5.6 percent in the first quarter to 2.6 percent in the second, 2.0 percent in the third, and 2.2 in the fourth. The declines were largely attributable to the slumping auto and housing industries. Already struggling to stay afloat, American automakers were hit hard by high gasoline prices that turned consumers away from the trucks and sport utility vehicles the "Big Three"—General Motors, Ford, and Daimler Chrysler—produced and toward smaller, more fuel-efficient cars sold primarily by Toyota, Honda, and other foreign automakers. The cooling of the overheated housing market, which had begun to slow in 2005, continued into 2006. December sales of existing homes were 7.9 percent lower than the previous December, while the pace of new housing starts had fallen by an estimated 18 percent, from slightly more than 2 million in December 2005 to 1.6 million a year later.

Unemployment was stable throughout the year, averaging 4.6 percent. Of the 2.3 million new jobs created, about 25 percent were in health care and food services. Overall, 72,000 manufacturing jobs were lost, many of them in the auto industry where thousands of workers took up Ford and General Motors on their buyout and early retirement offers. Job losses in residential construction were offset by increases in nonresidential and heavy construction. For the first time in several years, hourly wages grew faster than the rate of inflation; wages grew 4.2 percent for the year, while the consumer price index rose 3.4 percent. Those wage increases helped keep consumer spending chugging along as the main driver of economic growth. Whether the wage increases signaled the beginning of a sustained period of pay growth remained to be seen.

Inflation was a continuing concern throughout the year, pushed up by ballooning energy prices before moderating in tandem with a drop-off in those prices. For the year the consumer price index rose an estimated 3.4 percent, while the core inflation rate—the rate excluding food and energy prices—rose 2.6 percent. The personal consumption expenditure index, the index most closely watched by the Federal Reserve Board as it set interest rates, rose 2.8 percent for the year, with the core index at 2.3 percent. That range was acceptable to most economists, even though they preferred the inflation rate to be a little lower, somewhere around or under 2 percent.

In August the Federal Reserve Board, under its new chairman, Ben S. Bernanke, announced that it would hold its benchmark interest rate steady, at 5.25 percent. The announcement brought to a close a remarkable period that began in January 2001 when the Fed began to cut its federal funds rate on overnight loans to banks to stimulate an economy that was showing signs of slipping into recession. The Fed dropped the rate from 6.5 percent, where it had been for much of 2000, to 6.0 percent in January 2001 and then lowered it ten more times during 2001, to 1.75 percent, the lowest the federal funds rate had been in forty years. Facing a slow recovery, the Fed dropped the rate three more times, reaching 1.0 percent in June 2003. It remained at the level until June 2004, when renewed economic growth threatened to boost inflation to unacceptably high levels. Under Bernanke's predecessor, Alan Greenspan, the Fed embarked on a campaign of automatically raising interest rates by one-quarter of a point at each of its rate-setting meetings. On January 31, 2006, his last day in office, Greenspan announced the fourteenth rate hike, to 4.5 percent, and indicated that the rate increases might end soon.

But with the economy growing rapidly in the first quarter, the Fed raised the rate three more times, in March, May, and June, before announcing in August that it would take a break. By that time the economy was showing clear signs of slowing, and the Fed and other analysts worried that another rate hike could slow growth more than desired. Although the Fed made clear that it was prepared to raise rates again if inflation flared, it held the federal funds rate at 5.25 percent for the rest of the year. *(Background and Greenspan retirement, Historic Documents of 2005, p. 137)*

Bernanke, who had promised to bring more openness to policymaking at the Fed, got off to a rough start early in his chairmanship when several of his remarks about the Federal Reserve Board's intentions on inflation policy were misread by investors in the stock and bond markets. The most serious incident began on April 27, when Bernanke told the Joint Economic Committee (a bicameral congressional committee) that the Federal Open Market Committee, which set interest rates, could decide "at some point in the future" that it would "take no action at one or more meetings in the interest of allowing more time" to study incoming information on the economic situation. Many investors read that statement as meaning the Fed was preparing to end its interest rate hikes at its May or June policy meeting, and stocks began to climb as a result. A few days later stocks plunged after it was reported that Bernanke had said the market misinterpreted his April 27 remarks.

Other investors began to grow concerned that Bernanke was not as committed to fighting inflation as Greenspan had been. That fear was largely allayed when Bernanke, speaking to a group of bankers on June 5, declared recent increases in inflation measures to be "unwelcome developments" that the Fed would do its best to reverse. The stock markets fell again as many investors concluded that the Fed would continue to raise rates incrementally. Communications began to improve after the June policy-making meeting; the Federal Open Market Committee raised the federal funds rate one-quarter of a point, to 5.25 percent, but indicated it might not raise rates in August. For the rest of the year Bernanke generally had smooth sailing.

The Fed's pause in interest rate hikes helped propel the stock market to one of its best showings in recent years. The Dow Jones industrial average, a basket of thirty blue-chip stocks, closed above 12,000 for the first time in its history on October 19. It reached 12,529 in late December before closing for the year at 12,463. The year began with the Dow closing above 11,000 (on January 9) for the first time since June 2001, apparently propelled by speculation that the Fed's steady march to higher interest rates was nearing an end. Ten days later it dropped back below 11,000 on dismal corporate profits report and oil price hikes, only to recover by mid-February. For the next several months the industrial average advanced and retreated with changes in oil prices and other indicators and in reaction to Bernanke's remarks. But it began to pick up steam after the Fed's August 8 announcement that it was not raising interest rates for the first time in more than two years and, buoyed by a dramatic drop in world oil prices, continued to climb for the rest of the year. Overall the Dow Jones industrial average rose 16.3 percent for the year, the Standard &Poor's 500 index rose 13.6 percent, and the NASDAQ composite index rose 9.5 percent.

Continuing Wage Disparities

Strong job creation, rising wages, and low unemployment were all good news for the nation's workers, but there was still evidence of a wide income gap between rich and poor. Average wages were rising, but they were rising much faster for people at the highest income levels than for those at lower levels. According to one set of figures, based on data from the Labor Department, the average wage for upper-middle-income jobs rose 5.8 percent between 2003 and 2005, while low-wage jobs rose 3.4 percent— barely enough to keep pace with inflation. Another set of data showed that the top 1 percent of workers received 11.2 percent of all wages in 2004. These data did not take into account the very wealthy whose income came from investments rather than wages.

The Census Bureau reported in late August that median household income rose faster than inflation for the first time in six years, even while individual workers were earning less in 2005 than they had in 2004. The difference was that more family members were working to make ends meet and some families received money from investments and other nonwage sources of income. Young workers were particularly hard hit. According to a study by the Economic Policy Institute in Washington, entry-level wages fell by more than 4 percent from 2001 to 2005. Median income for families with one parent, age twenty-five to thirty-four, fell nearly 6 percent, to $48,405, between 2000 and 2005, after increasing 12 percent during the 1990s.

At the lowest end of the wealth spectrum were the 37 million Americans living below the poverty line, defined as $19,971 for a family of four. The overall poverty rate remained virtually unchanged from 2004 to 2005 at 12.6 percent. But according to the Center on Budget and Policy Priorities, the poor were getting poorer; 43 percent of the poor earned less than half of the poverty limit, the highest such percentage ever recorded by the Census Bureau.

Some of those living below the poverty line were earning the federal minimum wage of $5.15 an hour. For a full-time worker that amounted to about $10,700 a year, about the same as the poverty line for a single person and about half of the poverty line for a family of four. The approach of the midterm elections in November lent new momentum to a Democratic push to raise the federal minimum wage, which had not been changed since 1997, to $7.25 an hour. Although many moderate Republicans in the House pushed their leadership for a vote on the increase, the leadership decided to link an increase in the minimum wage to elimination of the estate tax, a long-sought goal of conservative Republicans. That measure passed the House, but Democrats, objecting to the estate tax provision, killed it in the Senate. House Minority Leader Nancy Pelosi made the minimum wage hike a prominent campaign theme and promised that in a Democratic-led House, she would bring the minimum wage raise to a vote on the House floor within her first one hundred hours as Speaker.

In addition to coping with higher gas and fuel prices, many families also were grappling with increases in their adjustable interest mortgages and rising health care costs. Interest rates were scheduled to rise on some $1 trillion worth of mortgages in 2007 and on another $1 trillion in 2008. "About 4 million to 5 million households will be negatively impacted," David Kotok, of Cumberland Advisers in Vineland, New Jersey, told the *Christian Science Monitor* in December. "This is mainly people in the lower and middle class, the Wal-Mart shopper, not the Tiffany shopper."

The continuing high cost of health insurance and the declining number of employers that picked up all or some of their workers' health care costs continued to raise the number of people without health insurance. Census Bureau data for 2005 showed that number grew from 45.3 million in 2004 to 46.6 million in 2005. The number of children without health care coverage had declined in recent years, but the Census data showed a reverse in that trend, with 11.2 percent of children uncovered in 2005, compared with 10.8 percent in 2004.

In anticipation of Labor Day, the Pew Research Center, a nonpartisan polling organization, released a new survey at the end of August showing that "the public thinks that workers were better off a generation ago than they are now on every key dimension of worker life—be it wages, benefits, retirement plans, on-the-job stress, the loyalty they are shown by employers or the need to regularly upgrade work skills." The survey found that 62 percent said there was less job security and 59 percent said Americans had to work harder to earn decent livings. Nearly one in seven respondents said there was more on-the-job stress than there had been a decade ago; about one in three said their job could be outsourced to someone working in another country.

Federal and Trade Deficits

In a bit of good news, the Bush administration announced October 11 that the federal budget deficit for the fiscal year that ended on September 30 was $247.7 billion—far smaller than earlier projections. In February the White House had said federal spending on the wars in Iraq and Afghanistan and on recovery from Hurricane Katrina could push the deficit up to $423 billion, which would have made it the highest on record (measured in dollars). The lower actual deficit left in place the old record of $413 billion, posted in 2004. The unexpected decline was attributed to a sharp and unforeseen rise in tax revenues from corporations and wealthy individuals. By mid-2006 corporate tax revenues, which had been steadily rising since 2003, jumped 27 percent, to $354 billion, the Congressional Budget Office (CBO) reported in August. Individual income tax receipts rose 12 percent overall, driven by higher salaries, bonuses, and nonwage income from stock market gains, according to the CBO.

On the campaign trail, President George W. Bush hailed the declining deficit and climbing tax revenues as solid evidence that his "pro-growth economic policies," including massive tax cuts in 2001 and 2003 on individual income and capital gains, were succeeding. "Tax relief fuels economic growth. And growth—when the economy grows, more tax revenues come to Washington. And that's what's happened," he said. Economists disputed that notion. "Federal revenue is lower today than it would have been without the tax cuts. There's really no dispute about that among economists," Alan D. Viard, a former economist in the Bush White House, told the *Washington Post*. Viard added that while it was possible that a tax cut could stimulate the economy enough to pay for itself, "There's no evidence that these tax cuts would come anywhere close to that."

Democrats had their own view of the lower-than-expected deficit. "Only a president with such a historically bad economic record would be this excited about a $248 billion deficit," said Rep. Carolyn Maloney, D-N.Y. "Under his watch . . . record surpluses turned into record deficits as far as the eye can see."

That long-term outlook was particularly frightening to many economists and analysts who warned that the rising federal costs of Medicare and Social Security caused by the aging of the baby boom generation were likely to result in unsustainably high federal deficits unless Congress and the president made painful political choices either to raise taxes or cut benefits or both. "The long-term outlook is such a deep well of sorrow that I can't get much happiness" out of the lower 2006 budget deficit, Douglas Holtz-Eakin, a former CBO director and a former White House economist, told the *New York Times*. (Background on long-term budget issues, Historic Documents of 2005, p. 121)

Despite the smaller deficit, Congress in March was forced to raise the federal debt ceiling—the limit on how much the government can legally borrow—by $781 billion to a total of $8.96 trillion. It was the fourth increase since President Bush took office in 2001; taken together the four increases amounted to more than $3 trillion. Congress had little choice but to act; the government would otherwise have had to default on its payment. Still Democrats and some Republicans took the opportunity to lament the rising debt limit. "The question is: Are we staying on this course to keep running up the debt, debt on top of debt, increasingly financed by foreigners, or are we going to change course?" asked Sen. Kent Conrad, the ranking Democrat on the Senate Budget Committee.

Meanwhile, the U.S. trade deficit rose to a new record for the fifth year in a row. For all of 2006, the United States imported $763.6 billion more than it exported. That compared with the $716.7 billion deficit registered in 2005. Although the 2006 trade deficit was the highest dollar figure ever recorded, the percentage increase, at 6.5 percent, was far smaller than the 17.3 percent recorded in 2005 and the 23.5 percent jump in 2004. The surge in oil prices was the major factor in the increase. America's bill for foreign oil reached a record $302.5 billion.

The U.S. trade deficit with China also set a new record—$232.5 billion—the largest deficit ever recorded with any one country. American manufacturers blamed the deficit with China on that country's persistent undervaluation of its currency, the yuan, against the dollar. The gap made Chinese imports into the United States cheaper, while American goods exported into China were more expensive. The Bush administration had been leaning for years on the Chinese to revalue the yuan, to little apparent effect.

Following is the text of testimony given on April 27, 2006, to the bicameral Joint Economic Committee on the outlook for the U.S. economy by Ben S. Bernanke, chairman of the Federal Reserve Board.

■■■■■■■■■■■■■■■■ DOCUMENT ■■■■■■■■■■■■■■■■

"Outlook for the U.S. Economy"

Mr. Chairman and members of the Committee, I am pleased to appear before the Joint Economic Committee to offer my views on the outlook for the U.S. economy and on some of the major economic challenges that the nation faces.

Partly because of last year's devastating hurricanes, and partly because of some temporary or special factors, economic activity decelerated noticeably late last year. The growth of the real gross domestic product (GDP) slowed from an average annual rate of nearly 4 percent over the first three quarters of 2005 to less than 2 percent in the fourth quarter. Since then, however, with some rebound in activity under way in the Gulf Coast region and continuing expansion in most other parts of the country, the national economy appears to have grown briskly. Among the key economic indicators, growth in nonfarm payroll employment picked up in November and December, and job gains averaged about 200,000 per month between January and March. Consumer spending and business investment, as inferred from data on motor vehicle sales, retail sales, and shipments of capital goods, are also on track to post sizable first-quarter increases. In light of these signs of strength, most private-sector forecasters, such as those included in the latest Blue Chip survey, estimate that real GDP grew between 4 and 5 percent at an annual rate in the first quarter.

If we smooth through the recent quarter-to-quarter variations, we see that the pace of economic growth has been strong for the past three years, averaging nearly 4 percent at an annual rate since the middle of 2003. Much of this growth can be attributed to a substantial expansion in the productive capacity of the U.S. economy, which in turn is largely the result of impressive gains in productivity—that is, in output per hour worked. However, a portion of the recent growth reflects the taking up of economic slack that had developed during the period of economic weakness earlier in the decade. Over the past year, for example, the unemployment rate has fallen nearly 1/2 percentage point, the number of people working part time for economic reasons has declined to its lowest level since August 2001, and the rate of capacity utilization in the industrial sector has moved up 1 1/2 percentage points. As the utilization rates of labor and capital approach their maximum sustainable levels, continued growth in output—if it is to be sustainable and non-inflationary—should be at a rate consistent with the growth in the productive capacity of the economy. Admittedly, determining the rates of capital and labor utilization consistent with stable long-term growth is fraught with difficulty, not least because they tend to vary with economic circumstances. Nevertheless, to allow the expansion to continue in a healthy fashion and to avoid the risk of higher inflation, policymakers must do their best to help to ensure that the aggregate demand for goods and services does not persistently exceed the economy's underlying productive capacity.

Based on the information in hand, it seems reasonable to expect that economic growth will moderate toward a more sustainable pace as the year progresses. In particular, one sector that is showing signs of softening is the residential housing market. Both new and existing home sales have dropped back, on net, from their peaks of last summer and early fall. And, while unusually mild weather gave a lift to new housing starts earlier this year, the reading for March points to a slowing in the pace of homebuilding as well. House prices, which have increased rapidly during the past several years, appear to be in the process of decelerating, which will imply slower additions to household wealth and, thereby, less impetus to consumer spending. At this point, the available data on the housing market, together with ongoing support for housing demand from factors such as strong job creation and still-low mortgage rates, suggest that this sector will most likely experience a gradual cooling rather than a sharp slowdown. However, significant uncertainty attends the outlook for housing, and the risk exists that a slowdown more pronounced than we currently expect could prove a drag on growth this year and next. The Federal Reserve will continue to monitor housing markets closely.

More broadly, the prospects for maintaining economic growth at a solid pace in the period ahead appear good, although growth rates may well vary quarter to quarter as the economy downshifts from the first-quarter spurt. Productivity growth, job creation, and capital spending are all strong, and continued expansion in the economies of our trading partners seems likely to boost our export sector. That said, energy prices remain a concern: The nominal price of crude oil has risen recently to new highs, and gasoline prices are also up sharply. Rising energy prices pose risks to both economic activity and inflation. If energy prices stabilize this year, even at a high level, their adverse effects on both growth and inflation should diminish somewhat over time. However, as the world has little spare oil production capacity, periodic spikes in oil prices remain a possibility.

The outlook for inflation is reasonably favorable but carries some risks. Increases in energy prices have pushed up overall consumer price inflation over the past year or so. However, inflation in core price indexes, which in the past has been a better indicator of longer-term inflation trends, has remained roughly stable over the past year. Among the factors restraining core inflation are ongoing gains in productivity, which have helped to hold unit labor costs in check, and strong domestic and international competition in product markets, which have restrained the ability of firms to pass cost increases on to consumers. The stability of core inflation is also enhanced by the fact that long-term inflation expectations—as measured by surveys and by comparing yields on nominal and indexed Treasury securities—appear to remain well-anchored. Of course, inflation expectations will remain low only so long as the Federal Reserve demonstrates its commitment to price stability. As to inflation risks, I have already noted that continuing growth in aggregate demand in excess of increases in the economy's underlying productive capacity would likely lead to increased inflationary pressures. In addition, although pass-through from energy and commodity price increases to core inflation has thus far been limited, the risk exists that strengthening demand for final products could allow firms to pass on a greater portion of their cost increases in the future.

With regard to monetary policy, the Federal Open Market Committee (FOMC) has raised the federal funds rate, in increments of 25 basis points, at each of its past fifteen meetings, bringing its current level to 4.75 percent. This sequence of rate increases was necessary to remove the unusual monetary accommodation put in place in response to the soft economic conditions earlier in this decade. Future policy actions will be increasingly dependent on the evolution of the economic outlook, as reflected in the incoming data. Specifically, policy will respond to arriving information that affects the Committee's assessment of the medium-term risks to its objectives of price stability and maximum sustainable employment. Focusing on the medium-term forecast horizon is necessary because of the lags with which monetary policy affects the economy.

In the statement issued after its March meeting, the FOMC noted that economic growth had rebounded strongly in the first quarter but appeared likely to moderate to a more sustainable pace. It further noted that a number of factors have contributed to the stability in core inflation. However, the Committee also viewed the possibility that core inflation might rise as a risk to the achievement of its mandated objectives, and it judged that some further policy firming may be needed to keep the risks to the attainment of both sustainable economic growth and price stability roughly in balance. In my view, data arriving since the meeting have not materially changed that assessment of the risks. To support continued healthy growth of the economy, vigilance in regard to inflation is essential.

The FOMC will continue to monitor the incoming data closely to assess the prospects for both growth and inflation. In particular, even if in the Committee's judgment the risks to its objectives are not entirely balanced, at some point in the future the Committee may decide to take no action at one or more meetings in the interest of allowing more time to receive information relevant to the outlook. Of course, a decision to take no action at a particular meeting does not preclude actions at subsequent meetings, and the Committee will not hesitate to act when it determines that doing so is needed to foster the achievement of the Federal Reserve's mandated objectives.

Although recent economic developments have been positive, the nation still faces some significant longer-term economic challenges. One such challenge is putting the federal budget on a trajectory that will be sustainable as our society ages. Under current law, federal spending for retirement and health programs will grow substantially in coming decades—both as a share of overall federal spending and relative to the size of the economy—especially if health costs continue to climb rapidly. Slower growth of the workforce may also reduce growth in economic activity and thus in tax revenues.

The broad dimensions of the problem are well-known. In fiscal year 2005, federal outlays for Social Security, Medicare, and Medicaid totaled about 8 percent of GDP. According to the projections of the Congressional Budget Office (CBO), by the year 2020 that share will increase by more than three percentage points of GDP, an amount about equal in size to the current federal deficit. By 2040, according to the CBO, the share of GDP devoted to those three programs (excluding contributions by the states) will double from current levels, to about 16 percent of GDP. Were these projections to materialize, the Congress would find itself in the position of having to eliminate essentially all other non-interest spending, raising federal taxes to levels well above their long-term average of about 18 percent of GDP, or choosing some combination of the two. Absent such actions, we would see widening and eventually unsustainable budget deficits, which would impede capital accumulation, slow economic growth, threaten financial stability, and put a heavy burden of debt on our children and grandchildren.

The resolution of the nation's long-run fiscal challenge will require hard choices. Fundamentally, the decision confronting the Congress and the American people is how large a share of the nation's economic resources should be devoted to federal government programs, including transfer programs like Social Security, Medicare, and Medicaid. In making that decision, the full range of benefits and costs associated with each program should be taken into account. Crucially, however, whatever size of government is chosen, tax rates will ultimately have to be set at a level sufficient to achieve a reasonable balance of spending and revenues in the long run. Members of the Congress who want to extend tax cuts and keep tax rates low must accept that low rates will be sustainable over time only if outlays can be held down sufficiently to avoid large deficits. Likewise, members who favor a more expansive role of the government must balance the benefits of government programs with the burden imposed by the additional taxes needed to pay for them, a burden that includes not only the resources transferred from the private sector but also the reductions in the efficiency and growth potential of the economy associated with higher tax rates.

Another important challenge is the large and widening deficit in the U.S. current account. This deficit has increased from a little more than $100 billion in 1995 to roughly $800 billion last year, or 6 1/2 percent of nominal GDP. The causes of this deficit are complex and include both domestic and international factors. Fundamentally, the current account deficit reflects the fact that capital investment in the United States, including residential construction, substantially exceeds U.S. national saving. The opposite situation exists abroad, in that the saving of our trading partners exceeds their own capital investment. The excess of domestic investment over domestic saving in the United States, which by definition is the same as the current account deficit, must be financed by net inflows of funds from investors abroad. To date, the United States has had little difficulty in financing its current account deficit, as foreign savers have found U.S. investments attractive and foreign official institutions have added to their stocks of dollar-denominated international reserves. However, the cumulative effect of years of current account deficits have caused the United States to switch from being an international creditor to an international debtor, with a net foreign debt position of more than $3 trillion, roughly 25 percent of a year's GDP. This trend cannot continue forever, as it would imply an ever-growing interest burden owed to foreign creditors. Moreover, as foreign holdings of U.S. assets increase, at some point foreigners may become less willing to add these assets to their portfolios. While it is likely that current account imbalances will be resolved gradually over time, there is a small risk of a sudden shift in sentiment that could lead to disruptive changes in the value of the dollar and in other asset prices.

Actions both here and abroad would contribute to a gradual reduction in the U.S. current account deficit and in its mirror image, the current account surpluses of our trading partners. To reduce its dependence on foreign capital, the United States should take action to increase its national saving rate. The most direct way to accomplish this objective would be by putting federal government finances on a more sustainable path. Our trading partners can help to mitigate the global imbalance by relying less on exports as a source of growth, and instead boosting domestic spending relative to their production. In this regard, some policymakers in developing Asia, including China, appear to have recognized the importance of giving domestic demand a greater role in their development strategies and are seeking to increase domestic spending through fiscal measures, financial reforms, and other initiatives. Such actions should be encouraged. For these countries, allowing greater flexibility in exchange rates would be an important additional step toward helping to restore greater balance both in global capital flows and in their own economies. Structural reforms to enhance growth in our industrial trading partners could also be helpful. Each of these actions would be in the long-term interests of the countries involved, regardless of their effects on external imbalances. On the other hand, raising barriers to trade or flows of capital is not a constructive approach for addressing the current account deficit because such barriers would have significant deleterious effects on both the U.S. and global economies.

In conclusion, Mr. Chairman, the economy has been performing well and the near-term prospects look good, although as always there are risks to the outlook. Monetary policy will continue to pursue its objectives of helping the economy to grow at a strong, sustainable pace while seeking to keep inflation firmly under control. And, while many of the fundamental factors that determine longer-term economic growth appear favorable, actions to move the federal budget toward a more sustainable position would do a great deal to help ensure the future prosperity of our country.

Source: U.S. Federal Reserve Board. "Outlook for the U.S. Economy." Testimony by Federal Reserve Board Chairman Ben S. Bernanke before the congressional Joint Economic Committee. April 27, 2006. www.federalreserve.gov/boarddocs/testimony/2006/20060427/default.htm (accessed March 8, 2007).

Report of the Special Inspector General on Iraq Reconstruction

April 30, 2006

███████████ **THE DOCUMENT IN CONTEXT** ███████

Three years after President George W. Bush promised Iraqis that the United States would spend billions of dollars to rebuild their country, the U.S. reconstruction effort by the end of 2006 had accomplished only a fraction of what Bush had pledged. By year's end the $21 billion in U.S. taxpayer money that had been appropriated by Congress for rebuilding Iraq had been spent or allocated for future spending, as was about $20 billion in Iraqi oil revenue that was turned over to Washington after the U.S. invasion in 2003.

The money repaired some aspects of Iraq's vital oil industry and built new electrical power facilities, water treatment plants, schools, and medical clinics. However, regular audits by U.S. inspectors and reports by other observers showed that the billions of dollars spent fell far short of meeting the expectation of Iraqis that the United States somehow would repair their country, which had been broken by years of war, economic sanctions, corruption, and the dictatorial rule of Saddam Hussein. Much of the money—by some estimates up to one-half—went not to rebuild Iraq but to train Iraqi security forces, build prisons, and provide security and overhead support for international contractors and administrators.

By some measures, many Iraqis were no better off in 2006 than they had been before the U.S. invasion that ousted Saddam from power in April 2003. Oil production, the underpinning of Iraq's economy, still was routinely lower than before the invasion; most of Iraq's 25 million people still had fewer hours of electricity each day and no better access to clean drinking water and sewer service than previously. The ongoing violence by the anti-U.S. insurgency and sectarian fighting between Shiite and Sunni Muslims made several sections of Iraq, notably Baghdad, too unsafe for people to venture far from their homes.

"What reconstruction?" Baghdad taxi driver Sattar Khalid Othman was quoted as saying in a November 12 *Washington Post* report. "Today we are drinking untreated water from a plant built decades ago that was never maintained. The electricity only visits us two hours a day. And now we are going backwards. We cook on the firewood we gather from the forests because of the gas shortage."

U.S. officials had begun scaling back expectations for rebuilding Iraq as early as 2004. By 2006 the State Department was drawing up "lessons learned" plans for similar postwar situations in the future; a key assumption was that it would be a mistake to promise massive rebuilding projects in a war-torn country until security had been restored. In 2006 U.S. officials also began putting pressure on other countries, notably

Iraq's oil-rich neighbors, to help pay for Iraq's reconstruction, using the argument that a collapsed Iraq would endanger the entire region. This pressure appeared to bear little fruit. *(Background, Historic Documents of 2003, p. 947; Historic Documents of 2004, p. 405; Historic Documents of 2005, p. 717)*

Overall Reconstruction

Following a request by President Bush in September 2003, Congress in 2003 and 2004 allocated $21 billion for reconstruction programs in Iraq. All of that money had been spent, or set aside for future spending, as of the end of fiscal year 2006 on September 30. Iraqi oil revenue that had been held in escrow during the 1990s by the United Nations and then turned over to Washington shortly after Saddam's ouster added about another $20 billion in spending in 2003–2004. Most of the oil money went to subsidize the early postinvasion editions of a new Iraqi government and to repair parts of the country's dilapidated oil industry, which had not been maintained for more than a decade.

From 2003 through 2005 the U.S. government supervised nearly every aspect of the reconstruction work, most of which was carried out by private contractors. During 2006, however, the Bush administration progressively turned responsibility over to the new Iraqi government, starting at the local and provincial levels. The Iraqi government was to be assisted by provincial reconstruction teams composed of diplomats, aid experts, and other officials from the United States and (in southern Iraq) Britain. Even so, U.S. officials said they were concerned about the lack of management expertise in Iraq's government and the high degree of corruption there.

Inspector General's Report

Under pressure from Congress, President Bush in 2004 appointed a special auditor to review the complex U.S. aid effort in Iraq. Stewart W. Bowen, a lawyer and former Republican Party official, took the job as special inspector general for Iraq reconstruction and demonstrated a doggedness that surprised many observers. Bowen and his on-the-ground team of auditors uncovered numerous cases in which aid projects had fallen short of expectations—and some examples of rebuilding efforts that worked. In 2005 Bowen created a bit of controversy when he drew attention to a "reconstruction gap" between what the United States had promised Iraqis and what had been delivered so far. Bowen also warned that even some successful projects were jeopardized by the inability of Iraqis to manage them once the United States left.

In reports during his first two years of work, Bowen focused attention on the rebuilding of Iraq's most essential services: the oil and gas industry, electricity generation, and water supply. Bowen's "April 2006 Quarterly Report," issued on April 30, was the first to review other aspects of reconstruction in Iraq, including education, health care, transportation, communications, private sector development, and promotion of democracy. In general, Bowen said his inspectors found numerous problems in these sectors, but "the overall picture conveys a sense of substantial progress" toward the rebuilding of Iraq. In each case, the report found that some projects had been completed, but the vast majority of projects were behind schedule or over budget because of security concerns, lack of oversight, and other problems.

Even some projects that were fully completed did not result in automatic improvements in the daily lives of Iraqis. One example cited in the report was the successful reconstruction of the country's 107 train stations; despite the rebuilding, only 4 percent of trains were running on a daily basis because of the lack of security. One of the most successful construction efforts was the building of a cellular telephone network, primarily through private investment, which provided service for about 5.3 million subscribers as of March 2006; that was more than five times the combined number of landline and cellular telephone subscribers before the U.S. invasion.

One area with specific problems highlighted in Bowen's report concerned a high-priority plan to build 150 primary health care centers around Iraq at a total cost of $243 million. As of March 2006, only six of the clinics had been completed, all in Baghdad. Fourteen others were to be completed under the government's original contract with Parsons Inc. (a large U.S. construction company), Bowen said, but serious construction flaws raised questions about their usability. Plans for the remaining 130 clinics were phased back or cancelled altogether.

Bowen criticized the Army Corps of Engineers, which managed the project, for placing unrealistic demands on the contractor and for failing to take even minimal steps to ensure that the clinics were being built properly and according to schedule. In particular, Bowen's inspectors found serious flaws with five clinics under construction in Kirkuk despite government progress reports claiming the clinics were nearing completion. Similar problems of delays and shoddy construction plagued other U.S. plans to build new hospitals or revitalize old ones in Iraq, Bowen said. The Army Corps disputed these findings, saying it had done the best it could given the lack of security. After Bowen issued his report, however, the Army Corps cancelled the contract with Parsons and turned some of the clinic projects over to Iraq firms.

Providing for security had driven up costs in nearly every area of reconstruction, Bowen reported. He estimated that about 25 percent of the overall aid budget was spent on security, thereby reducing the amount of money available for actual reconstruction. To pay for these costs, the administration shifted money from rebuilding projects; for example, nearly one-half of the $4.1 billion that had been allocated for water projects was shifted instead to security needs.

When his investigations found problems, Bowen rarely assigned blame to specific government agencies. A hard-hitting report to Congress on September 28, 2006, by the Government Accountability Office (GAO) was not so reticent, however. The report, "Rebuilding Iraq: Continued Progress Requires Overcoming Contract Management Challenges," identified what it called "systemic issues" in the Defense Department's oversight of Iraqi reconstruction. The Pentagon, according to the report, "made assumptions about funding and time frames that later proved to be unfounded. The failure to define realistic requirements has had a cascading effect on contracts and has made it difficult to take subsequent steps to get successful outcomes." Among numerous specific faults, the GAO criticized the Pentagon for issuing no-bid contracts to large U.S. construction firms. One such firm, the KBR subsidiary of Halliburton Corporation, faced widespread criticism for its exceptionally high overhead costs. Some Democrats also said they were suspicious about the Pentagon's awarding of contracts to Halliburton, which was headed during the 1990s by Vice President Dick Cheney.

Bowen's investigations uncovered several cases of direct fraud and corruption, some of them allegedly perpetrated by U.S. officials and contractors. One specific case was resolved in February 2006, with guilty pleas in U.S. federal court by a former Defense Department official in Iraq, Robert J. Stein Jr., and contractor Philip H. Bloom, who had defrauded the government of nearly $9 million for alleged work in the city of Hillah, south of Baghdad. Bloom agreed to repay the government $3.6 million, and he faced up to forty years in prison and a fine of $400,000. Stein admitted stealing

$2 million and accepting bribes for awarding contracts to Bloom; he faced up to thirty years in prison. On August 25, a U.S. Army Reserve officer, Lt. Col. Bruce D. Hopfengardner, who had been a special adviser to the U.S. occupation forces in Iraq, pleaded guilty to charges of wire fraud and conspiracy to commit money laundering; these charges were related to the frauds Bloom and Stein admitted perpetrating. The three men were to be sentenced in 2007.

Corruption in Iraq was a principal theme of Bowen's "July 2006 Quarterly and Semiannual Report," issued on July 31, covering the second quarter of 2006. Calling corruption "a virtual pandemic in Iraq," Bowen argued that it could jeopardize the stability of the new government unless steps were taken to control it.

Shutting Down the Inspections

Since taking office in January 2004, Bowen had issued quarterly reports, plus dozens of more detailed reviews of specific projects, that had been frank in assessing the failures of the reconstruction program, even while holding out the possibility that better results might come in the future. The reports deeply embarrassed the Bush administration, particularly the Defense Department, by highlighting the gap between what the United States had promised the Iraqi people in 2003 and what had been delivered. Bowen's reports also blamed U.S. officials—all appointed by the Pentagon—for failing to supervise the spending of millions of dollars of Iraqi oil money that the United States controlled after the invasions.

Bowen's frankness almost became his undoing. Late in the 2006 congressional session, Rep. Duncan Hunter, R-Calif., who chaired the House Armed Services Committee, inserted an amendment into the fiscal 2007 Defense Department Authorizations bill (PL 109–364) terminating Bowen's inspections on October 1, 2007. Although a few news reports noted the amendment at the time, many members of Congress apparently were not aware of the provision until the *New York Times* published a report about it on November 3. That report sparked bipartisan outrage, and Congress reversed itself during a lame-duck session in early December, clearing another measure (S 4046) extending Bowen's office well into 2008; Bush signed the measure into law (PL 109–440) on December 20.

State of the Economy

Despite the violence that hampered daily life in much of Iraq—particularly Baghdad and the predominantly Sunni Muslim areas in central Iraq—Iraq's overall economy grew in every year after the U.S. invasion in 2003. The main reason was an external one, however: the rapid rise in world oil prices starting in mid-2003. Oil production in Iraq still lagged behind pre-invasion levels—averaging 2.1 million barrels daily in 2005 and 2006, compared to about 2.6 million barrels in 2002—but the doubling of world oil prices more than made up for the difference.

Oil was by far the most important sector of the Iraqi economy, accounting for about 94 percent of the government's income, according to U.S. figures. Iraq's oil production had peaked at about 3.5 million barrels a day before the 1991 Persian Gulf War, and U.S. and Iraqi officials set a "near-term" target of reaching 3 million barrels. Oil industry experts said Iraq might not reach that goal for many years, however, because of the slow pace in repairing wells, pipelines, pumping stations, and other infrastructure that had deteriorated during the 1990s. Moreover, several investigations showed that at least

10 percent, and possibly as much as 20 percent, of Iraq's oil was stolen before reaching market. Another problem was that insurgents regularly attacked pipelines and other oil facilities, especially in northern Iraq, forcing supply interruptions and costly repairs. Endemic corruption posed still another challenge in all phases of Iraqi daily life, adding to the costs of doing business and diverting resources from productive enterprises.

Following are excerpts from the "April 30, 2006 Quarterly Report to Congress" of the Special Inspector General for Iraq Reconstruction, made public on April 30, 2006, which reviewed U.S.-funded programs to rebuild infrastructure in Iraq.

DOCUMENT

"April 30, 2006 Quarterly Report to Congress"

With 67% of the $21 billion in Iraq Relief and Reconstruction Funds (IRRF) now expended and only $2 billion left to obligate, the U.S. reconstruction program in Iraq is fully engaged in project execution and sustainment, contract close-out, and program transition. Effectively advancing the progress of reconstruction and development in Iraq at this critical juncture requires the U.S. government to work closely with the Iraqi government and international donors to sustain the substantial U.S. investment in Iraq's infrastructure. For this process to succeed, more investment is necessary. To that end, Congress is currently considering a new supplemental funding bill that will support work toward achieving and sustaining U.S. reconstruction goals. The increasing pace of transition in Iraq makes it all the more important that these funds become available soon.

A Year of Transition Update

In its January 2006 Report, the Special Inspector General for Iraq Reconstruction (SIGIR) observed that this is the Year of Transition in Iraq reconstruction. By the end of 2006, most programs and projects funded by the IRRF will be turned over to Iraqi authorities. With that prospect on the horizon, reconstruction planning and operations are increasingly becoming a joint enterprise, with U.S. and Iraqi officials coordinating on key initiatives.

Iraq's new government is re-staffing the 28 ministries responsible for managing government operations. For transition to succeed, Iraq must ensure that its ministries are ready to receive and capably manage completed projects. U.S. transition plans anticipate this structural development to occur within Iraq's government this year.

Insurgent activity continues to impede ongoing reconstruction projects and interrupt their transition to Iraqi control. But the attacks remain concentrated in a few areas, leaving daily life in much of the rest of Iraq—particularly the Kurdish north and some areas of the south—in a state of gradual recovery. Though recent reports indicate that attacks on infrastructure have abated, Iraq continues to suffer the ill effects of intermittent strikes on key energy nodes.

Critical Issue: Protecting Iraq's Infrastructure

In testimony before the Senate Foreign Relations Committee in early February 2006, the Inspector General noted his concern that attacks on Iraq's oil and gas and electrical infrastructures have limited progress in these key sectors. SIGIR subsequently announced and executed, during this reporting quarter, an audit of U.S. programs designed to improve the capacity of Iraqis to protect infrastructure—particularly the critical nodes in the oil and gas sector that have been most subject to attack since 2003. The Inspector General further addressed the matter with U.S. leadership in Baghdad during his eleventh trip to Iraq in February. Recognizing the importance of this issue, the U.S. Ambassador to Iraq has made infrastructure security an essential element of the Embassy Joint Blueprint for Success.

Through April 2006, the United States has invested more than $265 million to improve Iraq's capability to protect its oil and gas and electricity infrastructures. This investment is mission-critical because insurgent attacks and criminal sabotage diminish oil and gas production and reduce exports. SIGIR auditors reviewed $147 million of IRRF and Iraqi funds that supported Task Force Shield, a program established in September 2003 to build Iraq's capacity to protect its oil and gas and electrical infrastructure. Task Force Shield sought to cover 340 key installations, 7,000 kilometers of oil pipeline, and 14,000 kilometers of electrical transmission lines. The audit found that the program failed to adequately meet its goals. . . .

To address this critical issue, the Department of Defense (DoD) recently dispatched a team of experts to Iraq to assess the protection of oil and gas facilities. They examined the sector's infrastructure protection programs, seeking to identify current security challenges. The team is now drafting a strategy that will help the Iraqis more effectively protect their energy infrastructure.

Critical Issue: Closing the Reconstruction Gap

In its October 2005 Quarterly Report, SIGIR identified a "reconstruction gap," which acknowledges that—for a variety of reasons, security being the most salient—the U.S. relief and reconstruction program will accomplish less than originally planned. The shortfall in various sectors was caused by more than 250 reprogramming actions, delays driven by security and administrative problems, poorly managed cost-to-complete schedules, and shifting emphases in contracting and program management. Of note, another reprogramming of the IRRF occurred this quarter: $353 million was shifted from the electricity and health care construction sectors into non-construction programs.

The reconstruction gap, however, comprises more than simply the notion that fewer projects will be completed than expected; it also addresses the shortfall's impact on outputs and outcomes. Fewer projects completed axiomatically affects infrastructure outputs in Iraq—that is, fewer electrical projects means fewer megawatts on the grid, and fewer oil and gas projects means fewer barrels of oil produced per day. These constrictions have the cumulative effect of slowing improvement in the daily lives of Iraqis.

Ambassador Khalilzad's initiative to devolve more project decision-making to Iraqis at the local governorate level should help remediate the effects of the reconstruction gap. Iraqis are now exerting a formative influence over project choices. Their management of the process through the Provincial Reconstruction Development Councils, assisted by coalition-staffed Provincial Reconstruction Teams, is building local government capacity in Iraq. The aim of the Ambassador's initiative is to produce more immediate benefits for Iraqis in every governorate.

The success of the Ambassador's initiative depends, in part, on new funding. Thus, SIGIR strongly supports the President's FY 2006 supplemental and FY 2007 budget requests, which propose an additional $3.2 billion to help secure and sustain Iraq's critical infrastructure, to build the capacities of national and local governments, and to stimulate economic growth, increased employment, and private-sector development.

Critical Issue: Energizing the Oil and Gas Sector

Iraq has the second-largest oil and gas deposits in the world; revenue from this sector provides 94% of Iraq's national income. Several factors, however, have limited progress in the oil and gas sector: breakdowns in the sector's deteriorated infrastructure, delays in forming the new Iraqi government, uncertainties regarding the legal framework governing Iraq's petroleum industry, and attacks on the sector's critical nodes. The U.S. reconstruction plan allocated 9% of the IRRF for the rebuilding of Iraq's oil and gas infrastructure. Despite U.S. allocations of $1.7 billion and supplemental Iraqi expenditures, the sector has not returned to pre-war oil production levels. Consequently, Iraq's national income has yet to achieve its great potential, which will be necessary if the country is to fully shoulder its primary role in recovery and reconstruction.

Before the war, it was assumed that:

- Oil and gas revenues in post-war Iraq would pay for much of the reconstruction.
- Foreign private investment in the oil and gas sector would quickly flow into Iraq after the fall of Saddam.
- Post-war Iraq would be sufficiently secure to allow the development of oil and gas without hostile impediment.

To varying degrees, each of these assumptions has not been realized. Continuing attacks on the oil infrastructure have slowed production and cut revenue. Moreover, outside investors have been unwilling to commit capital to this sector until the insurgency abates and a permanent government takes power. Accordingly, the new Iraqi government, which is now forming, can provide necessary certainty by approving and implementing laws that govern foreign investment in the oil and gas sector.

SIGIR recommends that the United States and other donors develop strategies with the Iraqis that will increase oil and gas production and stimulate new capital infusion into the sector. These must include aggressive efforts to curb corruption, which reportedly plagues the oil and gas industry in Iraq. For example, the long-delayed installation of a metering system is essential. Succeeding in these various efforts is critical for Iraq to achieve its enormous economic potential.

Critical Issue: Bolstering Iraq's Anticorruption Efforts

Corruption is another form of insurgency in Iraq. This second insurgency can be defeated only through the development of democratic values and systems, especially the evolution of effective anticorruption institutions in Iraq. The primary players in this effort are the Commission on Public Integrity (CPI), the Board of Supreme Audit (BSA), and the 29 inspectors general (IGs) in the Iraqi ministries.

The Coalition Provisional Authority (CPA) [the U.S. occupation in Iraq in 2003 and early 2004] created the CPI and the IGs specifically to institutionalize anticorruption elements within the new Iraqi government. SIGIR worked at generating support for these institutions early on and continues to highlight the need to support them financially.

Iraq, the United States, and other donors should sustain and increase funding for these essential institutions. New funding will bolster their effectiveness, while raising general awareness of the new Iraqi government's commitment to fighting corruption. Foreign investment in Iraq may not appreciably increase until Iraq's anticorruption institutions meaningfully investigate and prosecute fraudulent government practices.

SIGIR previously reported that the Department of State (DoS) developed an initiative to strengthen anticorruption efforts in Iraq. Now, at the request of U.S. Embassy-Baghdad, SIGIR and the DoS Office of Inspector General have announced a coordinated survey of the $365 million supporting U.S. anticorruption programs in Iraq. The survey is intended to assess the initiatives and establish metrics to gauge progress.

Critical Issue: Encouraging More International Donor Participation

As IRRF funds draw down, the role of donor nations will become increasingly important. . . .

The next phase of Iraq's reconstruction will require a broader international effort. U.S. reconstruction officials should begin now to engage more directly and intensively with their international counterparts—the World Bank, in particular—to help ensure that donors implement pledges and develop, in close coordination with the Iraqis, the way forward for the next phase of reconstruction. Funding is now needed to stimulate the oil and gas sector, which has thus far underperformed for a variety of reasons. SIGIR notes the promising development of an integrated donor database to aid coordinating and deconflicting donor activities, but the system needs more comprehensive inputs from all donors before it can become an effective management tool. . . .

***

Source: Special Inspector General for Iraq Reconstruction. "April 30, 2006 Quarterly Report to Congress." April 30, 2006. www.sigir.mil/reports/quarterlyreports/Apr06/Default.aspx (accessed January 6, 2007).

Other Historic Documents of Interest

Execution of Saddam Hussein, p. 638   Security in Iraq, p. 702
Iranian president's comments to the   U.S. policy on Iraq, p. 725
    United States, p. 212   UN Resolution on Iran, p. 781

May

President Bush and Prime Minister Maliki on the Government of Iraq

May 1 and June 25, 2006

THE DOCUMENT IN CONTEXT

The second year of Iraq's experiment with democracy was not a happy one. A tenuous political process was overshadowed by unending violence, especially in Baghdad, and wracked at every stage by sectarian divisions that threatened to rip the country into pieces. Iraq had political leaders who were in place as the result of three separate elections in 2005, but key leaders appeared beholden to armed militias and the narrow interests of the sectarian parties that put them in office. These leaders also appeared to spend more time quarreling than deciding. And while they quarreled, Iraq disintegrated. The United States, with its approximately 140,000 troops, still provided most of what passed for security in Iraq. Even with that large military presence, Washington no longer was able to impose its will on Iraqi politicians who had gained power, and legitimacy, through the ballot box.

At year's end, President George W. Bush was pondering his latest attempt to develop a credible and effective policy for Iraq—a policy that would have to rely heavily on an Iraqi government that even his aides acknowledged was weak, indecisive, and fractured along sectarian lines. More than three years after he ordered an invasion of Iraq to oust the dictator Saddam Hussein, Bush could point proudly to the new democratic institutions there. He could not, however, boast that those institutions were stable, served national as opposed to narrow purposes, or had manifestly improved the lives of Iraq's 25 million citizens. The U.S. president also was just beginning to confront the reality that Iran was gaining increasing influence in Iraq, most likely at the expense of its old foe, the United States.

In a report to the United Nations Security Council on September 1, Secretary General Kofi Annan painted this grim picture: "As long as the people of Iraq do not have full confidence in the impartiality and accountability of the new government and its security forces, there is a danger of a vicious cycle in which rising levels of militia activities breed more fear and insecurity, which in turn will lead to a further increase in militia activities. This cycle must be broken." *(Background, Historic Documents of 2005, p. 941)*

Forming a New Government

The third of Iraq's three elections during 2005 had been for a new legislature, the 275-seat Council of Representatives, which would select a prime minister and his cabinet. This was to be the fifth governing body in Iraq since the U.S. invasion toppled

Saddam Hussein from power in April 2003; the first two were U.S. authorities run by the Defense Department, followed by two interim governments that served from late June 2004 until the formation of the "permanent" government in 2006.

The December 15, 2005, elections had resulted in a surprisingly strong victory for a coalition of Shiite Muslim parties, the United Iraqi Alliance, which won about 59 percent of the votes nationwide. Kurdish parties finished second with about 20 percent, and parties representing Sunni Muslims or secular groups won the rest. Some of the losers challenged the results, but the challenges were set aside after an investigation by a Western-led monitoring body, the International Mission for Iraqi Elections, reported on January 19 that the election "generally met international standards." Final results were announced on February 10, 2006. As was expected from the preliminary results, the United Iraqi Alliance won by far the largest block of seats, 128. A coalition of the two major Kurdish parties won 53 seats, and a coalition of Sunni parties (the Tawafoq Iraq Front) won 44 seats. The only major nonsectarian party, the Iraqi National List headed by former prime minister Ayad Allawi, finished with 25 seats. No major alliance won an absolute majority, but together the Shiite and Kurdish alliances (which had important interests in common) fell just short of the two-thirds majority needed for effective control of the 275-member chamber.

Announcement of the election results set in motion a fierce leadership contest within the Shiite alliance—a contest that produced one result only to spark yet more controversy leading to a different result. On February 12, Ibrahim al-Jaafari emerged as the narrow victor for prime minister, defeating Adel Abdul Mahdi by a 64–63 vote. Al-Jaafari, the leader of the Shiite religious party known as Dawa, also had served as prime minister of the transitional government elected one year earlier. His lackluster performance in that post was evident in the closeness of the vote. U.S. officials had preferred the more moderate Mahdi, saying he appeared more suited to leading a divided government faced with severe violence.

The challenge posed by Iraq's violence was illustrated yet again just ten days later, on February 22, when bombs destroyed one of Shiite Islam's holiest mosques, in Samarra. The bombing appeared to be a deliberate attempt by Sunni insurgents to provoke even more violence, and it succeeded. Shiite gangs and militias retaliated against Sunni communities, vastly escalating the degree of Iraq's sectarian bloodletting and making 2006 by far the deadliest since the U.S. invasion in 2003.

The parliament finally held its first meeting on March 16—four months after the election—but was unable to elect a speaker or other top officers because the various parties could not agree on the exact composition of what they said they wanted: a "national unity" government. The escalation of violence, and the still-sitting transitional government's inability to contain it, led to second thoughts in the Shiite alliance about retaining Jaafari as prime minister. Facing a potential defeat, Jaafari announced on April 20 that he would abide by whatever decision the United Iraqi Alliance made. The next day the alliance turned to another member of Jaafari's Dawa Party, Nouri al-Maliki, who had less visibility in Iraqi politics—and therefore fewer enemies who might want to block his rise to power. The full parliament then met on April 23 and approved Maliki's nomination as prime minister, along with the uncontested appointment of a senior Kurdish leader, Jalal Talabani, to the largely ceremonial role as president.

President Bush sent Secretary of State Condoleezza Rice and Defense Secretary Donald H. Rumsfeld to meet with the new Iraqi leaders. Rice and Rumsfeld reported back to Bush at the White House on May 1, and the president told reporters he was pleased by what he heard from his aides: "They said they [the new Iraqi leaders] were optimistic people, that they're full of energy, and they're very eager to succeed. And that's really important for the American people to know, that we've got partners in this effort who are dedicated to a unified Iraq and dedicated to putting a Government together that is one that will represent all the Iraqi people."

After taking office, Maliki took nearly a month to put together a thirty-six-member cabinet, which was approved by the parliament on May 20. Months later, Maliki reportedly acknowledged, in a speech to a closed session of parliament, that several cabinet members were incompetent and needed to be replaced. In that speech, he said some factions had waited until the last minute in May to present the names of nominees for cabinet posts, effectively preventing any serious review of their qualifications before parliament acted.

Two key cabinet posts—defense and interior—went unfilled for nearly three more weeks while the various factions sought them. Ultimately, Maliki's United Iraqi Alliance filled both jobs on June 8—completing the cabinet for a government elected nearly six months earlier. On that same day, U.S. forces scored what was seen at the time as a major triumph: the killing of Abu Musab al-Zarqawi, leader of the most violent Sunni insurgent group in Iraq, which called itself Al Qaeda in Mesopotamia.

Apparently seeking to capitalize on the momentum created by the appointment of the new government and the killing of Zarqawi, President Bush paid an unexpected visit to Baghdad on June 13. (It was only his second since the 2003 invasion.) After meeting with Maliki and members of his cabinet, Bush effusively praised the new government, noting that cabinet members came "from all parts of your country, representing the different religions, and the different histories and traditions." During the meeting, Bush later told reporters, "we discussed the security strategy. We discussed an economic strategy, a reconstruction strategy. And all of it makes sense to me." Maliki paid his own visit to Washington six weeks later and addressed a joint session of Congress on July 26. "Our nascent democracy faces numerous challenges and impediments, but our resolve is unbreakable and we will overcome them," he said.

A "Reconciliation" Process

After the prolonged bargaining over government portfolios, Maliki finally produced what was supposed to be a detailed prescription for ending the violence and bringing Iraq back together. His National Reconciliation Plan, unveiled on June 25, was a twenty-four-point initiative intended to provide an incentive for insurgents to stop the killing and for the government security forces to take control of the streets so the U.S. military could eventually leave Iraq. A key component of the plan was a limited amnesty for insurgents who renounced violence and had not been involved in attacks on Iraqis or foreign troops. Other components included reforms in the legal and judicial systems, increased government aid to the Sunni heartland areas where much of the violence took place, and the opening of a "dialogue" on changes demanded by the Sunnis to the constitution that voters approved the previous October. The plan also called for "disbanding" militias but offered no specifics for how that would be done.

"To those who want to rebuild our country, we present an olive branch," Maliki said in presenting the plan to the parliament. "And to those who insist on killing and terrorism, we present a fist with the power of law to protect our country and people."

The plan won quick endorsement from key leaders of all three major sects. In coming months, however, parliament adopted few of its major elements, and Maliki later issued revised plans that met no more success.

The proposed amnesty proved to be a sticking point. It was intended to encourage militant Sunnis, and even some renegade leaders from Saddam's disbanded Ba'ath Party, to lay down their arms and enter politics. Some of Maliki's Shiite allies opposed such an amnesty, and the United States—despite its rhetorical support for reconciliation—did not favor giving amnesty to Iraqis who had killed U.S. military personnel.

Meanwhile, the government made little progress on the matter that many Sunnis saw as the most urgent priority: revising the constitution, in particular its provisions that would allow Kurdish and Shiite regions considerable autonomy and control over the nation's oil wealth. Sunnis had participated in the December 2005 election on the condition that the constitution would be revised once the new government took power. Discussions about the constitution quickly became entwined with the government's plans for a new law setting out the powers of the various regions—the fundamental complaint Sunnis had about the new governmental structure. Many Sunnis feared that the Shiites and Kurds would effectively split off into regions controlling Iraq's oil, leaving them with little wealth.

Ultimately, in late September, the parliament narrowly adopted a law on the regions but, in a compromise, agreed to postpone its implementation for eighteen months while work proceeded on revising the constitution. This was one of the few cases in which the parliament successfully negotiated a procedural compromise on a highly contentious topic. The effect, however, was to postpone a political resolution even as sectarian divisions deepened, making an eventual agreement on the underlying issues potentially more difficult in the future.

Another explosive issue that also was postponed until an undefined date was the future of Kirkuk, the center of the oil-rich northern part of Iraq and a city claimed both by Kurds and Sunnis; thousands of the latter had been moved there by Saddam Hussein's government during the 1980s and 1990s. The constitution called for a committee to review the status of Kirkuk, and the parliament finally appointed the panel on October 11.

Even if the reconciliation process had succeeded in bringing together political leaders, it would have been undermined by daily events, notably the violence that was driving Iraqis ever further apart from one another. Since the middle of 2005 armed militias had engaged in what could only be described as ethnic cleansing, particularly in Baghdad. Armed Sunni gangs drove Shiites from some neighborhoods, while armed Shiites drove Sunnis from others—all in apparent attempts to create "pure" sectarian neighborhoods. One result was even greater suspicion and tension between the sects, imperiling the stated effort of politicians to bring Iraqis together. Even relatives of high political figures were not immune from the violence: two brothers and a sister of Vice President Tariq al-Hashemi, a Sunni, were killed in what appeared to be sectarian violence during 2006.

Ultimately, Maliki opted to use both the "fist" he had described to legislators and the reconciliation process. Maliki and U.S. military authorities announced in August an offensive in Baghdad, called "Operation Together Forward II," that featured stepped up military operations by both Iraqi and U.S. security forces, curfews, and other measures to stem the violence. This offensive was set for failure from the start, however, because Maliki's government provided only two of the six battalions it promised. Violence actually increased in Baghdad during the rest of the year.

Maliki and Sadr

From the perspective of Sunnis and some Kurds, U.S. diplomats and generals, and most other outside observers, the fundamental constraint facing Maliki was his heavy dependence on Moqtada al-Sadr, a junior Shiite cleric who controlled one of Iraq's largest and most violent militias. Sadr commanded the loyalty of several million impoverished Shiites, particularly in a vast Baghdad slum known as Sadr City, which was named after his father, a revered Shiite cleric who was killed by Saddam's government in 1999. Since 2003 Sadr also had built a large militia, called the Mahdi Army, whose black-clad fighters terrorized Sunni neighborhoods and acted as a protective force for Shiites. In 2005 Sadr decided to enter the political process, and politicians loyal to him won 30 seats in parliament. This was the largest single bloc of seats, and it gave Sadr enormous bargaining power. In the negotiations over formation of the government, Sadr won control of four cabinet ministries and was more responsible than anyone else for putting Maliki in office.

U.S. forces had clashed with Sadr in 2004, creating a mutual enmity that had not diminished two years later. American officials viewed Sadr and his militia as dangerous renegades who were backed by Iran and were responsible for much of the violence in Iraq. Moreover, U.S. officials accused Sadr's cabinet appointees of gross mismanagement, including outright looting of government resources.

Sadr's supporters, in turn, were angered by what they viewed as the U.S. failure to stop the numerous bombings of Shiite mosques and neighborhoods by Sunni insurgents. Many Shiites believed the United States was in league with the Sunnis to retake control of Iraq from them, perhaps because of the connection between Shiites in Iraq and Iran. As evidence for this conspiracy theory, some Shiites cited the fact that the U.S. ambassador to Iraq, Zalmay Khalilzad, was a Sunni Muslim born in Afghanistan.

By the middle of 2006 news accounts said key Iraqi generals were ready to disarm the militias loyal to Sadr and other leaders, but they were not given the go-ahead by the government. Even if Maliki had chosen to confront Sadr, it was uncertain whether a frontal attack on his militia would have succeeded; by most accounts the Mahdi army had split into numerous factions, some of which appeared to be beyond Sadr's direct control.

New U.S. Pressure for Action

Sadr and his militia appeared to be the core cause of increasing strains between Maliki and U.S. officials during the second half of the year. Several high-profile incidents illustrated a fundamental conflict: the United States wanted Maliki's government to crack down on the militias loyal to Sadr and other political leaders, while Maliki insisted such a crackdown was both politically and militarily impossible for his government. One early example was in August, when U.S. forces raided a headquarters of the Mahdi militia in Sadr City, prompting Maliki to go on national television criticizing the raid.

Maliki did take limited steps in response to U.S. pressure. On October 4 his government said it suspended an entire brigade of 700 policemen in Baghdad because of suspicions that its members had allowed or even engaged in killings by Shiite death squads. Later in the month, Interior Minister Jawad al-Bolani fired two senior police commanders because of involvement in sectarian killings; Bolani also said he fired another 3,000 interior ministry employees for security reasons.

However, tensions between U.S. officials and Maliki appeared to escalate in mid-October, when a series of incidents gave each side reason to question the actions of the other. In one notable example, U.S. troops on October 17 captured a senior aide to Sadr after evidence pointed to the aide's involvement in attacks on U.S. troops as well as on Sadr's Iraqi opponents. Maliki's government demanded that the man be released, and U.S. officials reluctantly complied.

This event took place at the same time that Bush and Maliki had a telephone conversation, during which Maliki asked if the United States was planning to replace him, according to White House spokesman Tony Snow. Maliki's concern apparently stemmed from numerous comments by U.S. officials that he had only about six months in which to take effective action or face failure. Because Maliki took office in May, a six-month period would run until about mid-November, thus explaining his concern in mid-October. In any event, Snow said Bush assured Maliki of his continued support.

Also in October, U.S. ambassador Khalilzad publicly laid out a "timeline" for a series of expected steps by the Iraqi government, including disbanding the militias, allowing for the rehabilitation of former members of Saddam's Ba'ath Party who had not commited crimes, and establishing a new system for the more equitable sharing of oil revenues among the regions. These steps were in keeping with Khalilzad's general stand of pushing the Shiites to respect the rights of the minority Sunnis—a stand that many Shiites resented as overt interference in favor of a minority that had been oppressive when it was in power. Maliki rejected the idea of timelines and said his government was acting as quickly as possible.

Perhaps the year's most obvious sign that the Bush administration and Maliki were not in sync—and possibly even working at cross-purposes—came in a November 28 report by the *New York Times,* which gave details of a classified memo to Bush written by his national security adviser after a meeting with Maliki a month earlier. In the memo, dated November 8, Stephen J. Hadley expressed serious doubts about whether Maliki was sincere when he insisted to U.S. officials that he wanted a unity government that would work on behalf of all Iraqis, not just Shiites. "We returned from Iraq convinced we need to determine if Prime Minister Maliki is both willing and able to rise above the sectarian agendas being promoted by others," the *Times* quoted the memo as saying. "Do we and Prime Minister Maliki share the same vision for Iraq? If so, is he able to curb those who seek Shia hegemony or the reassertion of Sunni power? The answers to these questions are key to determining whether we have the right strategy for Iraq."

In the memo, Hadley also said that in his meetings with Maliki, the Iraqi leader "impressed me as a leader who wanted to be strong but was having difficulty figuring out how to do so." This impression comported with the analysis of numerous other U.S. officials and Western experts who observed Maliki during the year.

Hadley's memo was one part of the Bush administration's reassessment of its strategy for Iraq, a reassessment that was prompted in large part by dwindling American public support for Bush's policy, as demonstrated in the November 2006 congressional elections. The president said early in December that he would give a major speech by year's end announcing the results of his reassessment; in an indication of the difficulties he was facing, Bush eventually postponed his speech until early January 2007. The centerpiece of his new policy was expected to be a short-term deployment of about 25,000 additional U.S. troops to Iraq to help bring the violence in Baghdad under control.

The *Times* report on the Hadley memo came at an embarrassing time—just one day before Bush was supposed to meet with Maliki and King Abdullah II for a two-day summit in Amman arranged by the Jordanian monarch. As Bush was arriving in Amman, Maliki abruptly cancelled the first meetings, creating the impression that he had snubbed the president because of the memo. The two men did meet the following day and insisted there were no serious differences in their approaches to the situation in Iraq.

While Maliki was in Amman, he came under political pressure at home from an unexpected source: his ally Moqtada al-Sadr. On November 30, Sadr said the four cabinet members and thirty parliament members from his party would "suspend" their participation in the government because of its dependence on the United States. Subsequent reports quoted Sadr's aides as saying he was pressuring Maliki not to give into U.S. demands for actions against Sadr's militia.

During the first half of December, it appeared that the Bush administration was pursuing a different aim, one that had been outlined by Hadley in his memo: promoting a coalition among Shiites, Sunnis, and Kurds that would sideline Sadr and his militia. As part of this effort, Vice President Dick Cheney visited Saudi Arabia and reportedly asked its leaders to pressure fellow Sunnis in Iraq to support Maliki's government. Bush also hosted key Iraqis at the White House, including Abdul Aziz al-Hakim (leader of an Iranian-backed Shiite party that often was at odds with Maliki) and Tariq al-Hashemi, the senior Sunni leader in Iraq's government.

The plans for a new coalition appeared to fall by the wayside, at least for the time being, on December 23 when Iraq's senior Shiite cleric, Grand Ayatollah Ali Sistani, expressed opposition. Aides said Sistani rejected any steps—such as excluding Sadr's party—that would weaken the United Iraqi Alliance, which had been assembled under Sistani's leadership.

Following are two documents: first, the text of a statement by President George W. Bush at the White House on May 1, 2006, following a meeting during which he heard a report from Secretary of State Condoleezza Rice and Defense Secretary Donald H. Rumsfeld on their meetings in Baghdad with the new leaders of the Iraqi government; second, the text of a statement on June 25, 2006, by the government of Iraqi prime minister Nouri al-Maliki on the National Reconciliation Plan he presented earlier in the day to the Council of Representatives (parliament).

DOCUMENT

"Remarks on Meeting with Secretary Rice and Secretary Rumsfeld"

I want to thank Secretary [of State Condoleezza] Rice and Secretary [of Defense Donald] Rumsfeld. And General [Peter] Pace [chairman of the Joint Chiefs of Staff], thank you for being here as well. Thank you for joining me this morning.

They came by the Oval Office to brief me on their recent trip to Iraq. First of all, I appreciate them both going over there to send my best wishes to the new Government and to Prime Minister-designate [Nouri Kamal al-] Maliki, as well as the new Speaker and the President. I had spoken to them on the phone, but I thought it was very important for both Secretaries to go firsthand, to be there with the leadership to say, we're supporting them. It's very important for these two senior officials to sit down with these new folks and say, "You have our support, and we want you to succeed."

And they brought back interesting impressions from the three new leaders. They said they were optimistic people, that they're full of energy, and they're very eager to succeed. And that's really important for the American people to know, that we've got partners in this effort who are dedicated to a unified Iraq and dedicated to putting a Government together that is one that will represent all the Iraqi people.

This new Government is going to represent a new start for the Iraqi people. It's a Government that understands they've got serious challenges ahead of them. And the three leaders spoke to Secretary Rice and Secretary Rumsfeld about their need to deploy the growing strength of the Iraqi security forces in such a way as to defeat the terrorists and the insurgents. And we will continue to support them in that effort that they talked about: the need to establish control over the militias and other unauthorized armed groups and enforce the rule of law. And we will support them in these efforts to achieve that important objective. They talked about the need to rebuild infrastructure and strengthen their economy, and we agree with that assessment.

And finally, they talked about the need to make sure that all Iraqis share in the benefits of this new democracy. A new Iraqi Government represents a strategic opportunity for America—and the whole world, for that matter. This Nation of ours and our coalition partners are going to work with the new leadership to strengthen our mutual efforts to achieve success, a victory in this war on terror. This is a—we believe this is a turning point for the Iraqi citizens, and it's a new chapter in our partnership.

The Secretaries began building this new partnership during their trip. In other words, the Iraqi leaders saw that we are committed to helping them succeed. They need to know that we stand with them. And the Iraqi people need to know that we stand with them, that we understand the strategic importance of a free Iraq in the Middle East, and that we understand the need to deny safe haven to the terrorists who have caused such turmoil and havoc inside of Iraq.

There's going to be more tough days ahead. These Secretaries know that. They're realistic people. They have brought an assessment of what they saw on the ground, and some of it's positive and, obviously, there's some difficult days ahead because there's still terrorists there who are willing to take innocent life in order to stop the progress of democracy. But this Government is more determined than ever to succeed, and we believe we've got partners to help the Iraqi people realize their dreams.

Last December, the Iraqi people voted to have a free government. I know it seems like a long time ago for the American people, but what we have begun to see now is the emergence of a unity government to represent the wishes of the Iraqi people. Last December, millions of people defied the terrorists and killers and said, "We want to be free; we want a unity government." And now what has happened is, after compromise and politics, the Iraqis have come together to form that Government. And our Secretaries went over there to tell them that we look forward to working with them as partners in peace.

So I want to thank you all for going. I appreciate your dedication to the cause of peace. Thank you.

Source: U.S. Executive Office of the President. "Remarks Following a Meeting with Secretary of State Condoleezza Rice and Secretary of Defense Donald H. Rumsfeld." May 1, 2006. *Weekly Compilation of Presidential Documents* 42, no. 18 (May 8, 2006): 829–830. Washington, D.C.: National Archives and Records Administration. www.gpoaccess.gov/wcomp/v42no18.html (accessed January 8, 2007).

▮▮▮▮▮ DOCUMENT ▮▮▮▮▮

"The Prime Minister Announces the National Reconciliation Project"

In The Name of God

The National Reconciliation and Dialogue project

In order to confirm the coherence between the Iraqi people, establishing the basis of national unity among their different components, to treat the remains of terrorism and administrative corruption, spreading the spirit of the loyal nationality to Iraq in order to build wide national front to confront challenges and to regain the pioneer position of Iraq regionally and internationally...for all that we release the initiative of national reconciliation and dialogue that depends on two basic elements:

1. The reliable procedure.
2. Principles and required policies.

First: Procedures

A. Forming national head committee (the head National Committee of National Reconciliation and Dialogue project) contains representatives from the three authorities, the state minister of the national dialogue and representatives from the parliamentary slates.

B. Forming sub-committees in the governorates by the head national committee, it takes over the tasks of the committee to expand the reconciliation horizontally.

C. Forming field committees to put horizontal cultural and media conceptions, follow up the process of reconciliation and evaluating it stages.

D. Held conferences for the different slices of life such as:
   1. Conference to the religious leaders to support the reconciliation process and announcing (Fatwa) to convince people.
   2. Conference to the heads of tribes issues covenant of honor to confront the state fighting and fighting terrorism.
   3. Conference to the effective political parties pledge to support the government, protect the political process and confront the terrorist challenge and corruption.
   4. Calling all the NGOs [nongovernmental organizations] to carry out activities, conferences, education campaigns to achieve the aims of reconciliation plan.

Second: The Principles and Policies Required

1. Adopting a political reasonable address by the political powers that take part in the political process, and by the government to bring back the alternating currents and to achieve media neutralism.

2. Adopting an honest national dialogue in dealing with all political visions and stances, which are opposite to those of the government in the political process.

3. Adopting the legal and constitutional legitimacy to solve the country's problems and to put an end to the assassination phenomenon.

4. The political powers, involved in the government should take a rejecting stance against the terrorists and Saddam's followers.

5. Issuing an amnesty to the prisoners who are not involved in crimes against humanity or terrorist acts and forming committees to set them free immediately. The insurgent who seeks to gain the amnesty opportunity has to denounce violence, support the national government and to obey the rule of law.

6. Preventing human rights violations, working on reforming the prisons and punishing those responsible for torture crimes and allowing the international organizations to visit the prisons.

7. Dealing with the MNF [multinational forces] to put mechanisms to prevent human rights violations and the civilians' abuses through military operations.

8. Finding solutions for the personnel of the dissolved departments, especially in relation to economic part and to take benefits of their expertise.

9. Reconsidering the Debaathification Board according to the Constitution, the judicial authorities and the Law to take a constitutional and vocational pattern.

10. Taking prompt procedures to improve the services, especially in the hot areas.

11. Activating the preparatory committees, emanated from the Cairo Conference for National Accord, in coordination with the UN and the Arab League and encouraging the Baghdad Peace Initiation.

12. The government should make a balanced Islamic-Arabic-Regional movement to make the other government be acquainted with what is going on in Iraq and gain their support to the National Accord Process, especially those enhancing terrorism or overlooking it.

13. Taking a serious and quick step towards establishing the armed forces which will take the responsibility of managing Iraq's security in preparation of withdrawal of the MNF.

14. Taking a serious and quick step towards establishing the armed forces in both Ministry of Defence and Ministry of Interior on professional and national bases for they will take the responsibility of managing Iraq's security instead of the MNF before they withdraw.

15. Activating the decisions that support victims of the former regime through compensations and making available all potentials to improve their living standards all over Iraq.

16. Removing all obstacles facing the Iraqi citizens or organizations to take part in building Iraq according to the Constitution if they did not commit any crime.

17. Giving compensations for those who have been suffering from terrorist acts, military operations or violence.

18. Activating the role of judiciary to punish the criminals, making it the only reference in dealing with crimes, former regime's top officials, terrorists and gangs of kidnapping and killing.

19. Making the armed forces independent on the influence of the competing political powers, disbanding the militias and illegal armed groups and treat them according to politics, economy and security.

20. Gathering the visions and stances towards the anti-Iraq terrorist and expiatory groups.

21. Starting a wide-scaled construction campaign all over Iraq to treat the unemployment phenomenon.
22. The elections led to the forming Parliament, constitution and a government of national unity as the only legal representative of the Iraqi peoples' will in dealing with sovereignty and the existence of MNF.
23. Make the deportees get back home. The government and the security systems are responsible for their return and safety to prevent the terrorists from harming them in addition to compensating them for all the damages they have and adopt a firm security plan that ensures protecting people and prevents them from being subject to blackmail.
24. Search and arrest operations happen according to judiciary orders before the raid or arrest. These orders should follow certain information, not vexatious one and should be in conformity with human rights. The military operations should also occur on the basis of official orders.

Source: Republic of Iraq. Iraqi Government. "The Prime Minister Announces the National Reconciliation Project before the Parliament." Press release. June 25, 2006. www.iraqigovernment.org/msalhaa.htm (accessed January 14, 2007).

Other Historic Documents of Interest

Execution of Saddam Hussein, p. 638   *Rumsfeld resignation, p. 662*
Iraq reconstruction, p. 161   *U.S. policy on Iraq, p. 725*
Security in Iraq, p. 702

Sentencing of Moussaoui for His Role in September 11 Attacks

May 4, 2006

■■■■■■■■■■ **THE DOCUMENT IN CONTEXT** ■■■■■■■■■■

Zacarias Moussaoui, often referred to as the twentieth hijacker, was spared the death penalty and instead was sentenced to life in prison without the possibility of parole for conspiring with al Qaeda to hijack airplanes and commit other acts of terrorism. "God curse America and save Osama bin Laden," an unrepentant Moussaoui shouted in the Alexandria, Virginia, courtroom as Federal District Judge Leonie M. Brinkema prepared to announce the sentence on May 4, 2006, bringing to an end a difficult and emotion-laden trial that had stretched over nearly four and a half years.

Moussaoui was the only person in the United States to be convicted for having a direct role in the September 11, 2001, terrorist attacks that killed nearly 3,000 people and touched off what President George W. Bush called a global war on terror, which was still raging more than five years later. The so-called mastermind of the terrorist plot, Kahlid Sheikh Mohammed, had been captured and held by CIA agents in a secret prison overseas, presumably in Pakistan, until September 2006, when he was brought to a U.S. prison in Guantanamo Bay, Cuba, where he was expected to stand trial in terrorism charges in 2007. Bin Laden, the leader of al Qaeda, had never been caught and was thought to be hiding in the mountainous regions of northwestern Pakistan. *(Terrorist attacks, Historic Documents of 2001, p. 614; war on terror launched, Historic Documents of 2001, p. 624)*

A few weeks after Moussaoui's sentencing, the first of the destroyed World Trade Center skyscrapers to be rebuilt since the attacks was opened for business, although occupancy remained low. The new building was on the site of the third building to collapse on September 11. Construction began in 2006 both on the memorial to the victims of the attacks and on the Freedom Tower, a 1,776-foot high building that would anchor the new World Trade Center. Construction was scheduled to be completed in 2011.

Meanwhile, the death toll from the attacks seemed likely to rise above the 2,749 deaths so far officially attributed to the attacks. In April a New Jersey coroner ruled that the death of thirty-four-year-old police detective was "directly related" to the September 11 tragedy. The detective had developed respiratory disease after spending nearly 500 hours helping with the cleanup after the towers collapsed. It was the first time that a death had been positively linked to the recovery work at the trade center.

Several studies monitoring the effects of the attacks on survivors painted bleak pictures of their health. One of the largest, conducted by researchers for Mount Sinai Medical Center in Manhattan and published in the September 2006 issue of *Environmental Health Perspectives,* reported that almost 70 percent of workers who helped with the cleanup at the World Trade Center had developed new respiratory problems or exacerbated old ones. "Many who worked at ground zero in the early days after the attacks have sustained serious and lasting health problems as a direct result of their exposure to the environment there," Dennis Charney, the dean for academic and scientific affairs at the Mount Sinai School of Medicine, said in a statement released with the report on September 5. "This study scientifically confirms high rates of respiratory problems in a large number of responders—including construction workers, law enforcement officers, utilities workers and public sector workers."

The Twentieth Hijacker?

Moussaoui, a thirty-seven-year-old French citizen of Moroccan descent, was arrested on August 17, 2001, on immigration charges after raising suspicions when he asked officials at a Minnesota flight school about learning to fly a Boeing 747, a jetliner used as a long-distance passenger plane by many commercial airlines. About three weeks later, nineteen Middle Eastern men hijacked four passenger planes and crashed two into the World Trade Center in New York, one into the Pentagon, and one into a field in Pennsylvania. Moussaoui was moved to New York and held as a material witness the same day. Three months later, Moussaoui was charged with six counts of conspiracy and moved to Alexandria, Virginia, for trial.

Delays, confusion, and frustration characterized Moussaoui's initial trial. Moussaoui, who represented himself for part of the trial, first refused to plead, then proclaimed his innocence, then tried to plead guilty but withdrew that plea when Judge Brinkema said she was not sure that he understood what he was doing. In 2003, after the government refused to let Moussaoui interview detained al Qaeda leaders, Brinkema prohibited the government from seeking the death penalty. In 2004 a federal appeals court reinstated the death penalty and said that Moussaoui could use government-prepared summaries from the detained al Qaeda leaders in his defense. Finally, in April 2005, Moussaoui told Brinkema he wanted to plead guilty and she deemed he was competent to do so. On April 22 he pleaded guilty to all six charges of conspiracy, including conspiracy to commit acts of terrorism and aircraft hijackings, conspiracy to use airplanes as weapons of mass destruction, and conspiracy to murder U.S. government employees. Moussaoui never admitted, however, that he was involved with the September 11 terrorists but maintained that he was in training for some future terrorist mission. Throughout this period, Moussaoui often disrupted the courtroom with inflammatory rants, cursing the United States, ridiculing the victims of the terrorist attacks and their relatives, and showing no remorse. He was repeatedly ejected from the courtroom, only to return with more rantings.

Phase 1: Death Eligibility

The sentencing trial was not much calmer. It took place in two parts. The first phase, which began on March 6, 2006, was to determine whether Moussaoui was eligible for the death penalty. Because Moussaoui had not admitted to involvement with the September 11 terrorists, government prosecutors had to prove a direct connection between him and the attacks to obtain the death penalty. In opening statements, the prosecution described Moussaoui as a man who "did his part as a loyal al Qaeda soldier" by refusing to tell authorities what he knew about the hijacking plot after he was arrested by the FBI in August 2001. Had Moussaoui told the FBI what he knew, the prosecution said, "the United States would have stopped the attacks. The FBI and other government agencies would have unraveled the plot. The FAA [Federal Aviation Administration] would have tightened security and stopped the hijackers from getting on the plane that day."

Moussaoui's defense team said he "wasn't part" of the September 11 plot "and was ignorant of its details." Seeking to put the government on trial, the defense argued that even if Moussaoui had known about the plot and had told FBI agents what he knew, the government would still have failed to act on the information. The defense's best evidence for this argument may have come from a government witness, Harry Samit, the FBI agent who arrested Moussaoui in August 2001. Samit testified that he had repeatedly tried and failed to get higher-ups in Washington to take seriously his concerns that Moussaoui might be plotting a terrorist action against an American target in the United States. Samit said he had later accused "the people in FBI headquarters" of "obstructionism, criminal negligence, and careerism" because they refused to seek search warrants for Moussaoui's computer and other belongings.

Samit's testimony on March 20 was the second time that the prosecution's case nearly derailed. A week earlier Brinkema had stopped the hearing after learning that an attorney for the Transportation Security Administration had improperly coached upcoming witnesses who were to testify about aviation security. Brinkema barred the prosecution from presenting the witnesses and any evidence about aviation security, a move that would have cut the heart out of the government's case. She also said she was considering eliminating the death penalty option. But, on March 17, she revised that ruling to allow the government to use witnesses who had not been coached, and the hearing went forward.

In one of his outbursts, and over the objections of his attorneys, Moussaoui took the stand on March 27 to say that he had been a part of the September 11 plot all along. Moussaoui said he was to have been part of a five-man crew that was supposed to fly a plane into the White House and that he had lied to FBI agents after his arrest "because I wanted my mission to go ahead." He said one "definite member" of his crew was to have been Richard Reid, the so-called shoe bomber. Reid had been arrested December 22, 2001, on a transatlantic flight after he tried to set off explosives hidden in his shoe; he was serving a life sentence in Colorado. Moussaoui also said he knew several of the September 11 hijackers, knowledge he had denied in the past.

The defense team tried to defuse Moussaoui's admissions by noting that "as an al Qaeda member, he believes it is okay to lie." They also presented evidence from interrogations of known terrorists to show that Moussaoui had not been selected as one of the hijackers and that, in the words of one of the terrorists, he was "not right in the head and having a bad character." Those arguments failed to persuade the jury, however, which on April 3 found Moussaoui eligible for the death penalty.

Second Phase: Sentencing

The second phase—to determine whether Moussaoui should be put to death or given life in prison, began on April 6. In some ways, this was perhaps the most difficult part of the entire four-year spectacle, not only for the jury and others in the court room, but also for the victims' relatives and survivors watching on closed-circuit television at eight locations in Massachusetts, New Jersey, New York, Pennsylvania, and Virginia. Testimony began with former New York City mayor Rudolph Giuliani describing the horror of watching people jumping to their deaths from the upper floors of the trade center and continued with the playing of the cockpit voice recording from the plane that crashed in Pennsylvania. That recording carried sounds of passengers pleading for mercy as their throats apparently were being cut, as well as of passengers apparently storming the cockpit in the seconds before it crashed. Survivors and victims' family members also testified, often in tears. Perhaps most difficult of all was Moussaoui's testimony; he belittled the family members, said it was his "pleasure" to accept a suicide mission from Osama bin Laden, and claimed his only regret was that more Americans did not die in the attacks.

Again the issue of Moussaoui's actual involvement in the plot was clouded when the prosecution acknowledged that the government had no evidence to corroborate his contention that Reid was to help him fly a plane into the White House on September 11. "To date, there is no information available that Richard Reid had preknowledge of the 9–11 attacks and was instructed by al Qaeda leadership to conduct an operation with Mr. Moussaoui," read a document prepared by FBI analysts and introduced into evidence by Moussaoui's attorneys.

The jury deliberated for seven days before telling Brinkema on May 3 that it could not reach a unanimous verdict in favor of the death penalty. According to later reporting by the *Washington Post,* a single juror (who remained anonymous) opposed the death penalty but refused to divulge his or her reasoning for that decision even to fellow members of the jury.

On May 4, Brinkema allowed Moussaoui one last rant before cutting him off and sentencing him to life in prison without the possibility of parole. After thanking both the prosecution and the defense for their efforts in what had clearly been an arduous legal proceeding, Brinkema turned one last time to Moussaoui: "As for you, Mr. Moussaoui, you came here to be a martyr and to die in a great big bang of glory, but to paraphrase the poet, T. S. Eliot, instead, you will die with a whimper. The rest of your life you will spend in prison. . . . . You will never again get a chance to speak, and that is an appropriate and fair ending."

Moussaoui was incarcerated in the federal government's super-maximum prison in Florence, Colorado.

Following are excerpts from the transcript of sentencing on May 4, 2006, in the matter of the United States of America vs. Zacarias Moussaoui, *held in the United States District Court for the Eastern District of Virginia, in which Judge Leonie M. Brinkema sentenced Zacarias Moussaoui to life in prison without the possibility of parole for conspiring to commit acts of terrorism against the United States.*

DOCUMENT

"Transcript of Sentencing before the Honorable Leonie M. Brinkema"

The Clerk: Criminal Case 2001–455, *United States of America v. Zacarias Moussaoui.* Counsel, please note their appearance for the record.

Mr. Spencer: Good morning, Your Honor. Rob Spencer, David Novak, and David Raskin for the United States. . . .

Mr. Zerkin: Good morning, Your Honor. Gerald Zerkin, Anne Chapman, Alan Yamamoto, Edward MacMahon, and Kenneth Troccoli for the defense.

The Court: Good morning. All right, counsel, as you know, this matter comes on for sentencing. Have each side had enough time to go over the presentence report? Yes?

Mr. Spencer: The government has, Your Honor. Thank you.

The Court: All right. Mr. Yamamoto?

Mr. Yamamoto: Mr. Moussaoui has, Your Honor.

The Court: All right. You've gone over it with him?

Mr. Yamamoto: I have not, Your Honor. I've given it to him. He did not want to go over it personally with me, but he's indicated to me that he has looked at it.

The Court: All right. Are you aware of any factual corrections, changes, additions, or deletions he wants made to the report?

Mr. Yamamoto: He's indicated to me that he felt that information should have been contained in the report about his request for—excuse me, about his apartment in France, about his traveling to Chechnya and what he did in Chechnya, and about his friend Djaffo in Britain. Other than that, he generally objects in total to the presentence report.

The Court: All right. Well, I find no rational basis to change any of the information in the presentence report. It appears to be completely accurate, and adding additional information along the lines that he wants would give—would add nothing to the report of any merit, and so I will deny the request to make any changes.

Now, as you know, the guidelines for this case, because I do not find that the defendant has accepted responsibility since he has expressed no remorse whatsoever for the actions in this case, therefore, the Court will use under the guidelines a total offense level of 58. His criminal history because of the nature of the convictions is a category VI.

Now, that means as to Count 1, the mandatory guideline sentence and statutory sentence would be life consecutive to any other sentence imposed, and the sentence required under the guidelines as to Counts 2, 3, 4, 5, and 6 is also life. There is no possibility for probation as to any of the counts of conviction.

As to supervised release, each count carries three to five years of supervised release. That's actually a legal fiction given the nature of the, of the sentence that must be imposed, but the law does require that a period of supervised release at least as a matter of formality be assigned to each conviction. The fine range for each of the six counts under the guidelines and statutes are 25,000 to 250,000 dollars.

Restitution is not an issue in this case. Special assessments of $100 are required as to each count of conviction, for a total of $600 in special assessments. And it's my understanding that the defense is not disputing that those are the appropriate guidelines for the six offenses for which the defendant has pled guilty. Correct?

Mr. Yamamoto: That's correct, Your Honor.

The Court: All right. I'll hear first from the United States as to any position you wish to take on sentencing. Mr. Spencer?

Mr. Spencer: Thank you, Your Honor. I have a very brief statement I'd like to make. Your Honor, thank you. Our focus today is solely on the victims of the September 11 attacks. Our focus is on the 2,972 who were killed that day and the many others who were injured but survived on that dark day, and our focus is on the families and friends left behind.

We're grateful that some of the victims were able to tell their stories in this courtroom during this trial. That was always one of our goals. And their stories of heroism, love, faith, pain, and despair touched everyone in this courtroom; everyone, that is, except that man, Zacarias Moussaoui, the defendant.

He listened without remorse and reveled in the pain and despair of those victims who testified, and it is impossible for the rest of us to fathom his hatred and his venom and his murderous intent.

And so our focus today remains where it has been throughout this case, and that's on the victims of the September 11 attacks. Our thoughts and prayers are with them, and they always will be. Thank you.

The Court: All right. And who is speaking on behalf of the defendant? Mr. Yamamoto, you or Mr. Zerkin? Mr. MacMahon?

Mr. Yamamoto: There's really not too much to say. I certainly echo Mr. Spencer's comments with respect to the victims and the victims' families. Our heart goes out to them and their loved ones, particularly those that came forward and testified here in court, gave us a snapshot of what they're going through in their lives, and I'm sure that is magnified by the number of other victims.

Mr. Moussaoui has not accepted responsibility, he's shown no remorse, but this system has shown that it doesn't matter, that the American justice system will still take into consideration the act and somebody's role in that act to determine a proper sentence.

We believe the sentence is a proper sentence, that he should spend the rest of his life incarcerated for his participation in this conspiracy. . . .

The Court: Are there any victims in the courtroom who would like to be heard before this proceeding is completed? . . .

Ms. Dillard: Judge, I've sat here daily, either here or been to closed caption, and I've listened to all the things, I've felt all the things that everyone else has felt.

I want you, Mr. Moussaoui, to know how you wrecked my life. You wrecked my career. You took the most important person in my life from me. I live alone. I think of that man every day, and with some of your help and some of the government's help, my husband should still be alive.

And though we sit here and we watch you twiddle at your beard, make faces, and feel no remorse, I hope that you sit in that jail without seeing the sky, without seeing the sun, without any contact with the world, and that your name never comes up in any newspaper again during the rest of my life and for history.

And I just want everybody else to know we appreciate what you did. We appreciate what you tried to do, and we appreciate what you had to do. But with you, I feel nothing but disgust. Thank you.

The Court: Thank you, Ms. Dillard. Are there any other victims or family members of victims who would like to testify? . . .

Mr. Scott: My name is Abraham Scott.

The Court: Yes, Mr. Scott.

Mr. Scott: I lost my wife, Janice Marie Scott, in the Pentagon that morning. We would have been married 24 years on the 27th of December, 2001. Her birthday, she would have been 46 on the 12th of October, 2001.

Moussaoui, I just want to say to you that I sit in this courtroom periodically, and I see the different remarks that you make about the victims, those 2,000-plus individuals, beautiful individuals that perished that day, but you and all of the rest of your colleagues will not deter this country from continuing to enjoy the freedom that it has for the past 2,000—200 years. I also look forward to bringing your colleague and whatever you call him, your God or whatever, Bin Laden, to justice in this courtroom, and he will, he will be here, trust me. And I just hope and pray that this country remains focused, not only remains focused, but gets focused in terms of getting this—getting the mission done, and that mission is to eventually capture your boss and bring him to justice. And I'm hoping, I'm hoping and praying that he will be put to death. You weren't put to death, but we're going to close this chapter and reopen a new chapter that hopefully will bring, bring your boss to justice. Thank you.

The Court: Thank you, sir. Good morning.

Ms. Dolan: Your Honor, good morning. My name is Lisa Dolan. I lost my husband, Captain Bob Dolan, at the Pentagon. First I'd like to say that my husband as a career naval officer spent his life making sure that our system of justice is what we've had here these last several months, and I'm proud of that. I also want to say to Mr. Moussaoui, and it's only one thing: There is still one final judgment day. Thank you.

The Court: Thank you, ma'am. Are there any other family members of victims who wish to be heard? (No response.)

The Court: In addition to the three people who've just spoke and to the 40 or 45 victims, family members of victims who testified during the trial, I want the record to reflect that these four volumes that are on the bench represent 408 victim impact statements from family members or other individuals representing among others 424 of those persons who died on September 11.

Each of those letters has been read by the Court and remains a permanent part of the record. They are not part of the public record, because they were done through the presentence process sent by the United States Attorney's Office to the Probation Office, but they are a part of the permanent record. They have been considered by the Court, and they represent additional input from victims into the final decisions for sentencing.

It is the normal practice in any criminal case to allow a defendant to speak before sentence is imposed. Mr. Moussaoui, do you have anything you want to say before sentence is imposed?

The Defendant: Yes, I do.

The Court: All right. Come into the witness box. Go ahead.

The Defendant: I've prepared something to say to you, but I would rather respond to the three victim family who just spoke.

The first one say that I destroy her life and she lost her husband. Maybe one day she can think how many people the CIA have destroyed their life. We say—you say that we are a hate organization. I say the CIA, it's a peace and love organization. The woman say that her husband were a naval officer. Of course, he was working for the development of peace and love in the world in his warship.

You have an amount of hypocrisy which is beyond any belief. Your humanity is a very selective humanity: Only you suffer, only you feel.

Mr. Spencer: Your Honor, I object. I think this is an appropriate time for Mr. Moussaoui to allocute regarding what sentence he receives. I do not think this is a time for him to make a political statement, and therefore, I object.

The Defendant: I'm just respond to what the victim family have been saying.

The Court: Mr. Moussaoui, as you know through the history of this case, I have permitted you to speak if the comments are appropriate to the proceeding. I agree with Mr. Spencer that you can't use this opportunity to make a political speech.

Your comments should be directed to the Court as to what appropriate sentence ought to be imposed on you at this time, anything you want the Court to take into consideration in making that decision.

The Defendant: You have branded me as a terrorist or whatever, criminal, or as David Novak say, a thug. You should look about yourself first. I fight for my belief, and I'm a *mujahid,* and you think that you own the world, and I would prove it that you are wrong.

I have nothing more to say because you don't want to hear the truth. It was a waste opportunity for this country to understand and to know why people like me, why people like Mohamed Atta and the rest have so much hatred for you. You don't want to hear about it. That's your rendition you hear. We will come back another day.

As long as you don't want to hear, you will feel, America. If you don't hear, you will feel. I have nothing more to say.

God curse America and save Usama Bin Laden. You'll never get him.

The Court: The Court will now pronounce the sentence, Mr. Moussaoui. As to Counts 2, 3, 4, 5, and 6, you are sentenced to life imprisonment without the possibility for release. As to Count 1, you are sentenced to a sentence of life imprisonment without the possibility for release, to run consecutive to the sentence imposed on the other five counts.

You are sentenced to five years of supervised release, to follow those life sentences. In essence, they will not go into effect, but you should know that for the record. You are required to pay a total of $600 in special assessments, that is, $100 per count of conviction. If you don't voluntarily pay that money, it will be taken from any resources you might have by the Federal Bureau of Prisons as part of the Prisoner Financial Responsibility Program.

If you were to ever be released—and again, that's an impossibility, but I have to say it for the record—you would be subject to deportation. That would be a necessary condition of your supervised release.

Although I believe it would be an act of futility, I am advising you that under our legal system, you do have a right to appeal the sentence. You do not have a right to appeal your convictions, as was explained to you when you pled guilty. You waived that right. If you want to appeal the sentence imposed on you, your notice of appeal must be filed within ten days. I will require your current defense counsel to file such a notice of appeal if one is requested. However, I am going to relieve your counsel of any further obligations to you, and if you do appeal, we will appoint substitute counsel for you.

Now, I am going to have a few comments that I am addressing to you as well as to the people in the courtroom and those who are watching this trial.

At the conclusion of yesterday's proceedings, I believe Mr. Moussaoui said words to the effect, "America, you lost; I won." Well, Mr. Moussaoui, if you look around this courtroom today, every person in this room when this proceeding is over will leave this courtroom, and they are free to go anyplace they want. They can go outside, and they can feel the sun, they can smell fresh air. They can hear the birds. They can eat what they want tonight. They can associate with whom they want.

But you when you leave this courtroom go back into custody. You will soon be out of Alexandria, and you will spend the rest of your life in a super-maximum security facility. In terms of winners and losers, it's quite clear who won yesterday and who lost yesterday.

The Defendant: That was my choice.

The Court: And—it was hardly your choice. The jury in this case rendered a decision after a trial that really has gone on about four-and-a-half years, and there have been a lot of criticism about whether this case should have been tried, whether it should have been tried in this courthouse in a civilian context or whether it should have been done in a military tribunal.

I have to tell you-all that I am satisfied that this day and yesterday represent great wins for the American people. It represents a great win for the American people because it once again shows that as a nation, we have rallied to a very significant challenge.

Nobody will probably ever truly know how incredibly complicated it was to put this prosecution together. These prosecutors and their investigators, who started working this case from September 11 of 2001, have spent untold hours slaving over minute details and, based on some of the evidence you-all saw in this courtroom today, some details of graphic and horrendous nature.

These prosecutors met with nearly every family member of a victim whom they could meet. Mr. Novak in particular spent years talking to victims.

Karen Spinks, who is an unknown member of this team because she's not an attorney, as the victim coordinator for the United States Attorney's Office, has worked for years with the families of victims. She worked tirelessly in helping to arrange support services for all of these family members. She and her colleagues worked at setting up the locations at the different courthouses where this trial was broadcast.

The kind of care which the prosecutors and the people in the United States Attorney's Office expended on, on the victims was extraordinary. The kind of detail that the investigators put—pulled together was truly extraordinary.

And a lot of the evidence in this case was classified, and both the prosecutors and the defense attorneys had to work around classification issues that were at one point, we all thought, insurmountable, and yet because we were dealing with extraordinarily professional attorneys for both sides, this evidence was able to be brought together in a format and presented openly in a public court of law. . . .

The defense team in this case rose, as I said yesterday and want to say again, to extraordinary challenges, starting with Frank Dunham, who was the Federal Public Defender at that time; Mr. Yamamoto; Mr. MacMahon; Mr. Zerkin; Mr. Troccoli; Ms. Chapman; and their incredible staff have had to do a nearly impossible job with an absolutely impossible defendant.

They've traveled around the world to interview witnesses, to try to uncover any bit of evidence that might assist them in defending their client, and they did so with incredible talent and perseverance, and with a client who is not popular and, therefore, subjecting them to potential public and media scorn, but they did their job, as our system would expect them to do. What was extraordinary about this case as well was the amount of evidence to which the parties were able to stipulate. If there ever was a difficult case, this was it, and yet the lawyers on both sides, as vigorously as they advocated for their positions, were able to come together and work out stipulations so that the evidence could be presented publicly and be evaluated in that respect. . . .

Lastly but not least, of course, are the victims and the witnesses who came into court and testified. It took great courage, and the fact that this defendant would sit here and smirk at you and make comments was outrageous, but all of you were courageous citizens in coming to court.

And lastly, in terms of courageous citizens, are those 17 people who sat in this jury box for weeks and then the 12 who finally decided this case.

Our legal system would collapse if we did not have citizens who were willing to put aside their normal routines and spend days in a courtroom, sometimes exposed to some terrible sights and sounds, which these jurors certainly were in this case, and then being called upon to judge another human being in a rational, dispassionate way, which again is what this jury did. This trial and this verdict are clear evidence of the enduring strength of this nation and its core values, which do not focus on hatred, bigotry, and irrationality. Rather, we believe that all persons are created equal and that when they appear in one of our courts of law, they will be treated as equals, regardless of their background or their political beliefs. So every American, that is, those who wanted to see this defendant executed and those who did not, should feel at this point satisfied that the system worked and this defendant received a fair trial and the American people were well represented by their institutions.

As for you, Mr. Moussaoui, you came here to be a martyr and to die in a great big bang of glory, but to paraphrase the poet, T. S. Eliot, instead, you will die with a whimper. The rest of your life you will spend in prison.

The Defendant: (Inaudible.)

The Court: You will never again get a chance to speak, and that is an appropriate and fair ending.

This case is now concluded. We'll recess court.

Source: U.S. United States District Court for the Eastern District of Virginia, Alexandria Division. *United States of America* vs. *Zacarias Moussaoui.* Criminal No. 1:01cr455. "Transcript of Sentencing before the Honorable Leonie M. Brinkema, United States District Judge." May 4, 2006. This document was not available on the Internet.

Other Historic Documents of Interest

Execution of Saddam Hussein, p. 638
National intelligence estimate on
terrorism, p. 574
Secret CIA prisons, p. 511

Supreme Court on the death penalty,
p. 337
Supreme Court on Guantanamo
tribunals, p. 374

Interim Prime Minister Olmert on the New Israeli Government

May 4, 2006

THE DOCUMENT IN CONTEXT

Israel faced a series of shocks during 2006, starting with the incapacitation of its prime minister and finishing with a war in Lebanon that was widely considered at least a tactical victory for one of Israel's bitterest enemies, the radical Shiite group Hezbollah. In between these events, Israelis watched in horror as another Islamist group, Hamas, won Palestinian legislative elections and took control of the Palestinian government. Israel also held its own election in 2006, but with ambiguous results, and the country's new leadership appeared to stumble from one crisis to another. By year's end, polls showed that many Israelis were fed up with their government, and political leaders were engaging in bickering that was exceptionally nasty, even by the usual standards of Israel's bare-knuckle politics.

Sharon Suffers a Stroke

The year's first shock for Israel came on January 4 when Prime Minister Ariel Sharon suffered a massive stroke and was hospitalized, in a coma. Doctors operated, but Sharon remained unconscious and in critical condition. Sharon, age seventy-seven, had suffered what doctors called a mild stroke just two weeks earlier and had been scheduled to undergo a surgical procedure on January 5 to repair a hole in his heart that, doctors believed, had contributed to his earlier stroke. He was still in a coma at the end of the year.

Sharon had been a towering figure for much of the time since Israel's founding in 1948, first as an extraordinarily aggressive army commander and later as a right-wing politician in a succession of governments before winning the top elected job in February 2001. Sharon had astounded his countrymen in December 2003 when he began advocating that Israel withdraw from civilian settlements and military posts in the Gaza Strip. This stance reversed his long-standing insistence on holding onto every inch of land that Israel had occupied since defeating its Arab neighbors in the June 1967 war. In 2004 and 2005, Sharon pushed legislation through his cabinet and the Knesset (parliament) requiring an end to Israel's occupation of Gaza, and in August 2005 his government used armed force to remove Jewish settlers from Gaza—many of whom had moved there years before as the result of his earlier policies. *(Background, Historic Documents of 2005, p. 529)*

Sharon justified his about-face on a simple demographic fact: if Israel retained control of Gaza, which had 1.3 million Palestinian Arab residents, within a few years the Jewish state would end up ruling over more Arabs than Jews, thus undermining its legitimacy as a democracy. For the same reason, Sharon began talking later in 2005 about consolidating Israel's Jewish settlements in the far-larger West Bank and turning the rest of that territory over to the Palestinians. This had been the conventional position for Israeli politicians of the left for more than a decade, but it represented another drastic shift for Sharon. Even so, he offered no details, leaving friend and foe alike to wonder exactly what he had in mind.

To solidify his political position in the wake of the controversial Gaza withdrawal, Sharon also announced in November 2005 that he was leaving his long-time political home, the right-wing Likud Party. He formed a new party, called Kadima (*forward* in Hebrew), to contest legislative elections scheduled for March 2006. Sharon gathered powerful support for his new party, including from his longtime political rival (but close personal friend) Shimon Peres, another giant of Israeli politics who had just lost his position as head of the left-leaning Labor Party.

Sharon's stroke on January 4, 2006, endangered his life, ended his political career, and threw Israeli politics into even more turmoil than was normal. Power passed quickly to Deputy Prime Minister Ehud Olmert, who had come to prominence in the 1980s as mayor of Jerusalem and had served more recently as Sharon's chief deputy. In that post, Olmert often floated potentially controversial ideas on his boss's behalf; he had been the first to advocate the Gaza withdrawal, for example. Unlike Sharon, however, Olmert did not have an extensive military background, and his perceived arrogance (coupled with numerous allegations of corruption) had made him a relatively unpopular figure. As acting prime minister, Olmert refused to sit in Sharon's chair for cabinet meetings, and it was only after several weeks that he appeared to speak his own mind.

There was to be no respite for Olmert after he assumed office. On January 25, the first Palestinian legislative elections in nearly ten years resulted in a stunning victory for Hamas, the Islamist group that had sponsored dozens of suicide bomb attacks against Israel since 1994. The Hamas victory, which appeared to come as a surprise even to Hamas leaders, ended any near-term prospect for resumption of peace negotiations between Israel and the Palestinians. It also put enormous political pressure on Olmert to appear tough in advance of Israel's own elections, scheduled for two months later, on March 28. Olmert and his foreign minister (and political rival) Tzipi Livni passed their first test by getting the diplomatic ensemble known as the Quartet (the European Union, Russia, the United Nations, and the United States) to adopt, on January 30, a hard-line position denying aid to or relations with Hamas unless it recognized Israel, renounced violence, and accepted previous Palestinian peace agreements with Israel.

Olmert's "Convergence" Plan

The Hamas victory complicated what apparently had been Sharon's plan, subsequently advanced by Olmert, to follow the Gaza withdrawal of 2005 with a bolder program of consolidating Israel's position in the West Bank. In essence, the idea was to complete work on a giant fence around the West Bank, which was intended to keep Palestinian suicide bombers from attacking Israel, and then to close down Jewish settlements in remote locations in the West Bank, with residents of those settlements to be relocated either to Israel proper or to the large group of settlements (known as "settlement blocks") that were closer to Israel.

Olmert put his own imprint on the West Bank plan in a series of speeches and news media interviews in the months before the election. The first of these was a speech on January 24, in which he endorsed creation of "a modern, democratic Palestinian state" and acknowledged the necessity of handing part of the West Bank over to the Palestinians. "We will not be able to continue ruling over the territories in which the majority of the Palestinian population lives," he said.

With the Hamas victory in elections the very next day, it no longer was clear that Israel's withdrawal from parts of the West Bank could be negotiated with the Palestinians. In fact, Olmert said on January 29 that "Israel won't hold any contacts with the Palestinians" unless Hamas changed its long-standing anti-Israel positions. Olmert held open the prospect of continued contacts with the moderate Palestinian president, Mahmoud Abbas, who remained in office but with reduced political clout.

Despite the Hamas victory, Olmert decided to move ahead with a West Bank consolidation plan, saying in a February 7 television interview that Israel should keep its major settlements there but give up the rest to the Palestinians, who would be kept separate from Israel by the security barrier (which Palestinians called a "wall").

Olmert offered more details in interviews published on March 9 by the *Jerusalem Post* and *Haaretz*, the two Israeli newspapers that were most widely read by opinion leaders in both Israel and internationally. In those interviews, Olmert said he intended to establish permanent borders for Israel, including new borders between Israel and the West Bank portion of a Palestinian state, by 2010. Most of the border, he said, would run along or near the route of the security barrier—a route that in some places cut deeply into the West Bank to enclose major Jewish settlements. The overriding goal of his plan, Olmert told the *Jerusalem Post*, was to create borders "whereby we will be completely separate from the majority of the Palestinian population and preserve a large and stable Jewish majority in Israel." In the weeks before the Israeli election, Olmert and his aides began using the term *convergence* to describe his plan for the West Bank; this was intended to soften the implications of the word *disengagement*, which Sharon had used to describe the withdrawal from Gaza in 2005.

Olmert's most controversial statement—at least outside Israel—was that he intended to build a long-stalled expansion (called the E-1 block) of Maale Adumim, a large West Bank settlement that essentially was a Jewish suburb of Jerusalem. Echoing concerns of Palestinians, the United States long had opposed building the E-1 block, which entailed about 3,500 homes, because it would cut off Palestinians living in East Jerusalem from the West Bank, thus reducing the viability of a Palestinian state.

Ambiguous Election Results

Polls taken just before Sharon's stroke showed his new Kadima Party likely to score what, in contemporary Israeli terms, would have been a major victory in the March 28 elections—gaining at least one-third of 120 seats in the Knesset, with the former main parties, Labor and Likud, trailing far behind. In recent decades no Israeli party had won an outright majority in the Knesset, so governments were formed by coalitions of disparate parties that banded together solely for the purpose of gaining power.

When the election campaign began officially on March 7, Kadima under Olmert was still far ahead of its rivals in the polls, but its support was heading downward rapidly. Several special-interest parties appeared to be gaining ground, among them a party representing pensioners and a relatively new party, Yisrael Beiteinu (Israel Is Our Home), that appealed to the estimated 1 million Russian Jews who had flocked to Israel in recent years. The latter party was founded by a far-right figure named Avigdor Lieberman, who advocated redrawing Israel's borders to exclude many of the country's 1 million Arab citizens.

Israelis were accustomed to ambiguous results from their elections, but the results of the voting on March 28 were even less clear than usual. The final results gave Olmert's Kadima Party only 29 seats, about one-third fewer than had been expected before Sharon fell ill. The Labor Party—which for decades had been the home of many of Israel's founding leaders—fell to its lowest point ever with just 19 seats. Sharon's former ruling party, the Likud, dropped to fourth place with 11 seats, one seat behind the Shas Party, which appealed to Sephardic Jews (those who came to Israel from North Africa and elsewhere in the Middle East). Many former Likud voters apparently defected to Lieberman's Yisrael Beiteinu Party, which also won 11 seats. Perhaps the biggest loser in the election was Likud leader Benjamin Netanyahu, a far-right politician who had served as prime minister in the mid-1990s and had been angling to return to power ever since. The poor showing of Likud reflected, at least in part, public disgust with Netanyahu's flagrantly self-serving maneuvering.

These results suggested that the only possible governing coalition would be among the so-called centrist parties, Kadima and Labor, which would be forced to turn to some of the special-interest parties for the remaining votes needed to achieve a majority in the 120-seat Knesset. Israel's president, Moshe Katsav, on April 6 formally assigned Olmert the task of forming a new government, setting off a scramble for cabinet posts among the parties likely to be in a coalition. Five days later, the cabinet officially declared Sharon to be permanently incapacitated; doctors had declared there was no hope for his recovery, although his life was no longer in immediate danger. Olmert assumed the title of interim prime minister.

The year's only fatal suicide bombing inside Israel took place on April 17, when a Palestinian bomber detonated a bag of explosives at a fast-food restaurant in a working-class neighborhood of Tel Aviv; eleven Israelis died and several dozen others were wounded, the highest casualty toll in such a bombing in nearly two years. Another suicide bomber had attacked the same restaurant on January 19; only the bomber died, but twenty Israelis were wounded in that attack. The radical Palestinian group Islamic Jihad took responsibility for both of these bombings, but the Israeli government held the new Hamas-led Palestinian government responsible because it refused to condemn the attacks.

Olmert finally assembled the coalition necessary to form a new government on April 30. The coalition included his Kadima Party (29 seats), the Labor Party (19 seats), the Shas Party (12 seats), and the Pensioners' Party (7 seats). Altogether, this alliance had 67 seats, more than enough for a majority in the Knesset. The new leader of the Labor Party, Amir Peretz, would serve as defense minister. To get support from the two smaller parties, Olmert had to promise increased spending on social programs.

Olmert presented his new government to the Knesset on May 4, exactly four months after Sharon fell ill. In addition to Olmert and Peretz, the major cabinet figures were Foreign Minister Livni, who also served as vice prime minister; former Labor Party leader Shimon Peres, who became deputy prime minister and minister for regional development; and Shaul Mofaz, the former defense minister who was shifted to the transport ministry to make room for Peretz. Of these appointments, the most controversial by far was that of Peretz, who had little military experience.

In his opening speech to the new Knesset, Olmert promised to carry out the plan for the West Bank, which had been the major theme of his campaign. While saying he still believed in Israel's "eternal right to the entire land of Israel" (which most Israelis believed included all of Gaza and the West Bank), Olmert said he had concluded that a compromise was necessary. "Even if the Jewish eye cries, and even if our hearts are broken, we must preserve the essence" of Israel, he said. "We must preserve a stable and solid Jewish majority in our state." Closing some—but certainly not all—Jewish settlements in the West Bank would be difficult, especially for the settlers, he said, "but I am convinced, with all my heart, that it is necessary and that we must do it with dialogue, internal reconciliation and broad consensus."

Despite this call for compromise, Olmert offered no specific details of his West Bank plan, and he pledged to engage in "continuous dialogue with the wonderful settlers" before carrying it out. Olmert also reached out to Palestinian President Abbas, saying Israel wanted to negotiate with Palestinians who were committed to peace. But in a reference to the new Hamas leadership, he said: "A Palestinian government led by terrorist factions will not be a partner for negotiation, and we will not have any practical or day-to-day relations" with it.

One small, but internationally controversial, detail of Olmert's West Bank plan emerged on June 2 when news reports said Israel was beginning construction of a new settlement, called Maskiot, in the Jordan River valley, deep inside the West Bank. This was to be the first entirely new West Bank settlement built in about ten years by the Israeli government, which had repeatedly pledged to the United States that it would not build any new ones, even as it expanded existing settlements. Initial plans called for Maskiot to house only about twenty families, but its creation was significant because it appeared to demonstrate Olmert's determination to hold on to much of the Jordan valley as a buffer against Israel's Arab neighbors.

Wars on Two Fronts

Within two months of taking office, Olmert's new government faced two major challenges that threw all previous plans up in the air and exposed the inherent weaknesses of that government. The first challenge came on June 25 when a group of eight Palestinian militants—some of them from Hamas—sneaked across the border from Gaza into Israel and attacked an army post. Two soldiers and three Palestinians were killed in the ensuing gun battle, but the remaining Palestinians escaped back into Gaza, taking with them a captured Israeli soldier, Corporal Gilad Shalit. Olmert demanded the return of Shalit, and early in July he sent the army into Gaza—causing massive physical damage to Palestinian property, killing more than 400 Palestinians by year's end, but failing to recover the captured soldier.

The second, more serious, challenge to Olmert's new government came on July 12 when Hezbollah, the Lebanese Shiite militia, launched its own attack on Israel. Hezbollah launched short-range Katyusha rockets across the border into Israel, and a small force of Hezbollah fighters crossed the border, killed three Israeli soldiers, and captured two Israeli army reserve soldiers, who were taken back across the border into Lebanon. In a subsequent skirmish, five more Israeli soldiers and an unknown number of Hezbollah fighters were killed.

Israel responded first with large-scale bombing and artillery strikes against Hezbollah positions in southern Lebanon. These attacks forced an estimated 400,000 people from their homes but failed to win the freedom of the two captured soldiers. Hezbollah responded by firing short-range and even medium-range rockets into Israel, some of them reaching as far as the coastal city of Haifa, twenty-five miles south of the border. These rockets killed thirty-nine Israeli civilians and forced thousands of Israelis into bomb shelters. Israel launched a major ground invasion into Lebanon on August 2 and reached as far as the Litani River (about twenty-five miles north of the border) before a United Nations-mandated cease-fire brought the war to an inconclusive end on August 14.

This brief war caused enormous damage in Lebanon, which was still recovering from decades of civil war, but for Israel it failed to achieve the return of the captured soldiers or to destroy Hezbollah's military capability. Hezbollah leader Hassan Nasrallah declared his group had achieved a "divine victory" against Israel. Many observers, even in Israel, agreed that Hezbollah had scored at least something of a success by surviving the Israeli onslaught, even if several hundred of its fighters had died.

Fallout from the Lebanon War

The Lebanon war had two immediate results in Israel. First, it shelved Olmert's West Bank convergence plan. Having withdrawn from southern Lebanon in 2000 after nearly two decades, and then from the Gaza Strip in 2005 after nearly four decades—only to experience attacks from both places in 2006—Israelis suddenly were in no mood for another withdrawal unless it was accompanied by an ironclad security guarantee.

The second consequence of the summer's war in Lebanon was an outbreak of exceptionally bitter political infighting in Israel. Even as the war was under way, critics across the political spectrum accused Olmert and Defense Minister Peretz of mismanaging it, in particular by relying too heavily on air power to destroy Hezbollah rocket launchers and other military positions. The infighting was especially severe in the Labor Party, where rivals of Peretz accused him of incompetence and undermining the party's position. Another target of criticism was Gen. Dan Halutz, the chief of staff of the Israeli Defense Forces. Halutz was the first air force general to hold that position, and critics said he failed to appreciate the limits of air power in attacking what was essentially a guerrilla group.

To bolster his coalition, Olmert decided in October on the risky move of asking for support from Lieberman and his Yisrael Beiteinu Party, which had 11 seats in the Knesset. Labor Party leaders at first balked at this inclusion of a far-right party in the coalition but ultimately accepted it. Lieberman joined the cabinet with the title of deputy prime minister responsible for "strategic threats" against Israel—specifically the threat of a nuclear-armed Iran. With Lieberman's party, Olmert now had 78 votes in the Knesset, enough to keep him in power even if one of the smaller coalition partners (Shas or the Pensioners' Party) bolted. Lieberman's new position apparently did not prevent him from voicing controversial views. He repeated his calls for many of Israel's Arabs to be "transferred" out of Israel, and on November 18 he called for the assassination of Hamas leaders and the abandonment of efforts to negotiate peace with the Palestinians.

Yet another jolt to Israel's political system came late in the year when prosecutors indicated that they intended to file sexual assault charges against President Katsav. Police began investigating Katsav early in the year when a former employee alleged that Katsav forced her to have sex with him; several other women also alleged that Katsav made unwanted sexual advances. Although Katsav's post was a largely honorary one, it still held great symbolic importance in Israel, and the prospect of a president being charged with sex crimes was an unsettling one for Israelis. There also were reports during the year that Israeli police were investigating some of Olmert's activities, including a questionable real estate deal.

At year's end, Olmert's government remained in office but polls showed that, in a new election, Israeli would take a sudden lurch back to the right. Olmert also was facing a potential leadership challenge from within his own party; Foreign Minister Livni, who had escaped criticism after the Lebanon war, began casting herself more openly as an alternative leader. Polls showed that Olmert and Labor leader Peretz had lost most of their support within their own parties, suggesting yet another period of political turbulence in Israel.

Following are excerpts from a speech by Interim Prime Minister Ehud Olmert on March 4, 2006, in which he presented his new cabinet to the Israeli Knesset (parliament).

DOCUMENT

"Address by PM on Presenting the New Government to the Knesset"

... From its birth, the State of Israel advocated two founding bases—the Jewish base and the democratic base: the supreme value of a "Jewish state", at the same time with the uncompromising demand that the democratic state of Israel will provide "complete social and political equality to all its citizens, regardless of religion, race or gender." These two bases embody the core values of the renewed Jewish sovereignty in the land of Israel. If you take one and disconnect if from the state, it is as if you cut off its lifeline.

Therefore, those wishing to look directly into our past, see the reality of our lives and look to the future, must do so with both eyes open—the Jewish eye and the democratic eye. Only then, with both eyes open, do the colors of Israeli society come together into one clear, vivid and meaningful picture.

I, like many others, also dreamed and yearned that we would be able to keep the entire land of Israel, and that the day would never come when we would have to relinquish parts of our land. Only those who have the land of Israel burning in their souls know the pain of relinquishing and parting with the land of our forefathers. I personally continue to advocate the idea of the entire land of Israel as a heart's desire. I believe with all my heart in the people of Israel's eternal historic right to the entire land of Israel. However, dreams and recognition of this right do not constitute a political program. Even if the Jewish eye cries, and even if our hearts are broken, we must preserve the essence. We must preserve a stable and solid Jewish majority in our State.

Therefore, we must focus on the area in which a Jewish majority is secured and ensured. The disengagement from the Gaza Strip and Northern Samaria was an essential first step in this direction, but the main part is still ahead. The continued dispersed settlement throughout Judea and Samaria creates an inseparable mixture of populations which will endanger the existence of the State of Israel as a Jewish state. It is those who believe, as I do, in [early twentieth-century Zionist leader Ze'ev] Jabotinsky's teachings and in full civil equality between Jews and Arabs, who must understand that partition of the land for the purpose of guaranteeing a Jewish majority is the lifeline of Zionism. I know how hard it is, especially for the settlers and those faithful to Eretz Yisrael ["the land of Israel"], but I am convinced, with all my heart, that it is necessary and that we must do it with dialogue, internal reconciliation and broad consensus.

This does not mean that the settlement enterprise was entirely in vain. On the contrary. The achievements of the settlement movement in its major centers will forever be an inseparable part of the sovereign State of Israel, with Jerusalem as our united capital. Let us come together around this consensus and turn it into a uniting political and moral fact.

The strength of this nation is in its unity. I will not help those wishing to cause a rift among the sectors of our nation. It is my intention to take all future steps through continuous dialogue with the wonderful settlers in Judea and Samaria. We are brothers and we will remain brothers.

From this podium, I again address the elected President of the Palestinian Authority, Mr. Mahmoud Abbas. The Government of Israel under my leadership prefers negotiations with a Palestinian Authority committed to the principles of the Roadmap, which fights terror, dismantles terrorist organizations, abides by the rules of democracy and upholds, practically and thoroughly, all agreements which have thus far been signed with the State of Israel. Negotiation with such an Authority is the most stable and desired basis for the political process, which can lead to an agreement which will bring peace. This is what we desire.

The guidelines of this Government propose this. The parliamentary majority which will back the Government policy is committed to this process. These conditions cannot be blurred. We will not, under any circumstances, relinquish these demands as a basis for negotiation.

The Palestinian Authority must make fundamental changes in its patterns of behavior, its reactions and its commitments to the principles which are the basis for any future negotiations.

A Palestinian Government led by terrorist factions will not be a partner for negotiation, and we will not have any practical or day-to-day relations.

The State of Israel is prepared to wait for this necessary change in the Palestinian Authority. We will closely follow the conduct of the Authority. We will continue to strike at terror and terrorists. We will not hesitate to reach terrorists, their dispatchers and operators anywhere—I repeat—anywhere, but we will give the Authority an opportunity to prove that it is aware of its responsibilities and willing to change.

That said, we will not wait forever. The State of Israel does not want, nor can it suspend the fateful decisions regarding its future—until the Palestinian Authority succeeds in implementing the commitments it undertook in the past. If we reach the conclusion that the Authority is dawdling and is not planning to engage in serious, substantial and fair negotiation—we will act in other ways.

We will also act without an agreement with the Palestinians to create an understanding which will, first and foremost, be founded on a correct definition of the desired borders for the State of Israel.

These borders must be defensible, and ensure a solid Jewish majority. The Security Fence will be adjusted to the borders formulated east and west. The operational range of the security forces will not be limited, and will be in accordance with the security reality with which we have to deal.

The State of Israel will invest its resources in areas which will be an organic part of it. The borders of Israel, which will be defined in the coming years will be significantly different from the areas controlled by the State of Israel today.

This is the Government's plan, it is the basis for its existence, it is the commitment made to the Israeli electorate whose trust we asked for—and received.

The agreement to which we aspire to shape the Middle East is based on consensus, broad consensus first and foremost within ourselves, and thereafter with our friends around the world.

No political process, certainly not one as fundamentally decisive and comprehensive as the one for which we are preparing, can be realized without the understanding of many officials in the international community. We have no intention of acting alone. We will consult, discuss, talk, and I am certain that we will reach understandings which will create a broad base of international backing for these steps, first and foremost with our ally and close friend, the United States led by President George Bush, and also with our friends in Europe.

Israel strives to improve the understandings and agreements with the countries of Europe. Today's European leaders better understand the complexity of the situation in the Middle East. They understand that there are no simple solutions, certainly given the upswing in fundamentalist religious fanaticism in various countries in the Middle East, and the ascendancy of the pro-Iranian Hamas to the Palestinian Authority. We will deepen dialogue with Europe and strive to include its leaders in the dialogue process with the United States.

I aspire to deepen the ties with Arab countries. Egypt and Jordan, countries with which we have peaceful relations, have leaders who are inspirational. President [Hosni] Mubarak [of Egypt] and King Abdullah the Second [of Jordan] are welcome, credible and responsible partners—for those goals which I defined. I will do all that I can so that our relations with Egypt and the Jordanian Kingdom will continue to strengthen, and serve as a basis for diplomatic and open relations with additional Arab countries.

The threat emanating from Iran is casting a heavy pall over the entire region and is endangering world peace. The pursuit by this rogue and terror-sponsoring regime of nuclear weapons is currently the most dangerous global development, and the international community must do its utmost to stop it. The statements by the President of Iran should not be taken lightly—he means what he says. The State of Israel, which is targeted for destruction by the evil leaders of Tehran, is not helpless. However, only a decisive and uncompromising international stand against Iran's goals can eliminate this threat to world peace....

[The remainder of the speech dealt with domestic issues.]

Source: State of Israel. Prime Minister's Office. "Address by Interim PM on Presenting the New Government to the Knesset." Translation. May 4, 2006. www.pmo.gov.il/PMOEng/Communication/PMSpeaks/speechkness040506.htm (accessed January 18, 2007).

Other Historic Documents of Interest

Palestinian elections, p. 13
United Nations on human rights,
   p. 765

UN resolution on Iran, p. 781
War between Israel and Hezbollah,
   p. 454

Vice President and Russian Foreign Minister on U.S.-Russian Relations

May 4 and 5, 2006

The Bush administration in May 2006 launched its harshest attack yet against the Russian government for its restrictions on political freedoms and its pressure on neighboring countries that were seeking closer ties with the West. Speaking in Latvia, which had been a satellite of the Soviet Union, Vice President Dick Cheney on May 4 decried the authoritarian streak of Russian president Vladimir Putin. Cheney's remarks set off a furious international debate about whether the United States was about to take a harder line against Russia, but that did not appear to be the case. In fact, the two countries six months later reached an agreement under which Russia would be able to join the World Trade Organization; this would be an important landmark in the country's economic transition from communism to a blend of free markets and government domination of key industries, notably oil and gas.

It was the Kremlin's domination of Russian political space that received much of the attention in 2006. In recent years Putin's government had eliminated independent television news reporting, made it nearly impossible for opposition political parties to compete effectively, consolidated the Kremlin's control of provincial governments, and appeared to threaten the independence of nongovernmental organizations, including those funded by Western governments. Putin and his aides said these actions merely were a manifestation of Russia's own version of democracy, but criticism by Cheney and others illustrated deepening concern outside Russia about a return to authoritarianism in Moscow.

Meanwhile, the Russian economy continued to boom, courtesy of the strong world energy markets. Russia was a major supplier of oil and one of the most important sources of natural gas for Europe. With oil prices holding at $60 a barrel or more, the Russian economy was growing at a pace of about 6 percent a year. That was enough to enrich a small urban class and an even smaller wealthy elite, but it gave only a marginal boost to the vast majority of Russia's working poor. *(Background, Historic Documents of 2005, p. 299)*

Cheney's Speech, Russia's Response

During 2005 President George W. Bush had gently chided Putin on several occasions for acting in ways Bush said endangered democracy. Putin rejected the criticism, but the two leaders still appeared to enjoy a good personal, as well as working, relationship.

By early 2006, it was clear that Putin was fed up with criticisms from the West, not just from the Bush administration but also from a broad range of human rights groups, academic specialists on Russia, and political figures. In his annual news conference on January 31, Putin was characteristically blunt in response to Western criticism of Russia, much of which he said came from "devoted Sovietologists who do not understand what is happening in our country, do not understand the changing world. They deserve a very brief response: 'To hell with you.'"

At the same time, according to news reports, the Bush administration was engaged in an internal debate about what approach to take toward Russia. Some officials reportedly advocated a tough line, complete with harsh denunciations of Putin's restrictions on the news media and political opponents and possibly even a symbolic rebuke, such as having President Bush refuse to attend the annual Group of Eight (G-8) summit, scheduled to be held in Russia for the first time ever, in St. Petersburg in July. This step was advocated by Sen. John McCain, R-Ariz., who planned to run for the presidency in 2008.

Other administration officials reportedly said a hard line toward Moscow could backfire in unpredictable and possibly dangerous ways; they called for keeping up pressure on Putin but in a diplomatic manner. Secretary of State Condoleezza Rice apparently was in this latter group. In her previous academic career, she had specialized in Russia. Appearing on the CBS News program *Face the Nation* on February 12, Rice said: "We are very concerned, particularly about some of the elements of democratization that seem to be going in the wrong direction." Even so, Rice appeared to reject a hard-line approach and said the two countries still had "very good relations," noting that contemporary Russia "is not the Soviet Union."

Rice did not say so, but an important consideration in the administration debate was the need to get Russian cooperation on several important matters pending before the United Nations Security Council. Among these were international efforts to halt nuclear weapons programs in Iran and North Korea and pressure on the Sudanese government to stop violence against civilians in the western region of Darfur. Russia was one of five Security Council members with veto power, and it had been a reluctant partner of U.S. policy in these and other matters.

A gloomy assessment of U.S.-Russian relations came in the report of a bipartisan task force commission by the Council on Foreign Relations, one of the country's premier foreign policy think tanks. Chaired by former senator and Democratic vice presidential candidate John Edwards, and former House member and Republican vice presidential candidate Jack Kemp, the March 6 report said relations between the two countries "are clearly headed in the wrong direction." The United States should adopt a policy of "selective cooperation" with the Kremlin and "selective opposition" to Russian policies, rather than a blanket approval of whatever Putin did, the task force said.

It was in this context that Vice President Cheney stepped before the microphones at a conference of eastern European officials in Vilnius, Latvia, on May 4 and lobbed verbal grenades in the direction of Russia, just across the border. While stating that Russia was not "fated to become an enemy," Cheney unleashed criticism of current Russian policy that clearly suggested he and others in the Bush administration believed the Kremlin was headed in that direction.

On Russian domestic affairs, Cheney said that "opponents of reform are seeking to reverse the gains of the last decade. In many areas of civil society—from religion and the news media, to advocacy groups and political parties—the government has unfairly and improperly restricted the rights of her people." Cheney also challenged some of the Kremlin's recent actions in dealing with its neighbors, including a brief shut-off of natural gas supplies to Ukraine at the end of 2005 (affecting several other countries in the region because key pipelines ran through Ukraine) and Russian support for separatist movements in Georgia and Moldova. "No legitimate interest is served when oil and gas become tools of intimidation or blackmail, either by supply manipulation or attempts to monopolize transportation," Cheney said. "And no one can justify actions that undermine the territorial integrity of a neighbor, or interfere with democratic movements."

Cheney had a receptive audience for this kind of talk. The three Baltic nations of Estonia, Latvia, and Lithuania had been forced into the Soviet Union in the World War II era and had been the first Soviet republics to declare independence after the Berlin Wall fell in 1989. All three had joined the European Union and NATO in 2004 and were looking westward for their futures—but were still nervous about Moscow. *(NATO membership, Historic Documents of 2004, p. 135; EU membership, Historic Documents of 2004, p. 197)*

Cheney's words, delivered in his typically gruff style, were by far the toughest yet to come from a senior U.S. official, and they generated a predictable response from the Kremlin. Several pro-Kremlin members of the Russian parliament heatedly denounced Cheney's speech as anti-Russian, and one of Moscow's leading newspapers called the speech "the beginning of a second cold war."

The official response came the next day from Foreign Minister Sergey Lavrov, who diplomatically suggested that Cheney had been misinformed by his aides about recent events in Russia. Referring, for example, to Cheney's statement that Russia was reversing the gains of the last decade, Lavrov said: "I think there is no need to explain to the Russian people in detail what kind of gains those where, when the country actually found itself on the brink of disintegration. What the Russian leadership is now doing is to ensure that Russia is preserved as a unified, integral, strong state in the interests of its citizens."

From the perspective of many in Russia—even some of Putin's critics—this last statement was the heart of the matter. Nearly fifteen years after the collapse of the Soviet Union, Russia was still in transition economically and politically, and many of its leaders and people still had not accepted Russia's diminished role in the world. Russians across the political spectrum had felt threatened by the expansion of the U.S.-led NATO alliance right up to their country's borders. They were worried by talk of expanding NATO again by incorporating Georgia and even Ukraine—the latter country having been, next to Russia, the biggest and most important component of the Soviet Union. "The idea of admitting Ukraine into NATO is hammering the final nail into the coffin of Russia as an independent great power," Sergei Rogov, director of the Institute of the United States and Canada told the *Washington Post* in April. "Unfortunately, it's almost a consensus in Russia that the West is trying to isolate Russia."

Russians also were uneasy about the Bush administration's plans to put components of a missile defense system in eastern Europe—a system that had only one conceivable purpose, to protect the new U.S. allies in eastern Europe from Russia. This concern was enhanced by an article in the March–April issue of the influential *Foreign Affairs* journal noting that Russia had become "vulnerable to a U.S. disarming attack."

One of the clearest conflicts between Moscow and Washington came in their respective responses to March 19 elections in Belarus, the small country perched uncomfortably between Russia and Poland. There, President Alexander G. Lukashenko claimed to have won a third presidential term with 83 percent of the vote, after having suppressed the only opposition party with any credibility. The Bush administration, along with most European countries, denounced the election as a sham, but Moscow congratulated Lukashenko on his democratic victory. Belarus and Russia had been talking about an association or union of some sort—talk that many in the West saw as Moscow's grab to resurrect a part of the Soviet Union but that officials in the two countries viewed as recognizing their mutual interests in the face of threats from the West.

An irony of Cheney's comments about Russian democracy was that he followed his speech in Latvia with a quick trip to Kazakhstan, where he praised that country's leader, Nursultan Nazarbayev. Of all the fifteen former Soviet republics, Kazakhstan in 2006 was one of the least democratic, Nazarbayev having won another term in office in an election the previous December that Western observers denounced as fraudulent. Kazakhstan also had seen a string of assassinations, including the killing in February of a top opposition politicians. Cheney made no mention of Kazakhstan's domestic politics, concentrating instead on the rapidly expanding production of the country's Caspian Sea oil fields, some developed by U.S. companies.

Putin himself drew attention to what his aides were calling Cheney's double standard. In his annual state of the nation address to parliament on May 10, Putin noted the Bush administration's close relations with Kazakhstan and Azerbaijan, another oil-rich dictatorship whose president had met with Bush at the White House in late April. "Where is all that pathos of the need to fight for human rights and democracy when it concerns the needs to realize their own interests?" Putin asked rhetorically of U.S. leaders.

Putin and His G-8 Leadership

In the wake of Cheney's speech, there was more than the usual speculation about the year's Group of Eight summit in St. Petersburg, notably how Bush and Putin would interact. Putin himself worked to play down the matter, saying for example in a June 2 speech to Western media executives that he was "satisfied with the level of quality" of relations with the United States.

Bush said he, too, believed U.S.-Russian relations were on an even keel. Just two weeks before the G-8 meeting, however, he also sent a pointed message to Putin by holding an exceptionally friendly meeting at the White House with Georgian president Mikhail Saakashvili and promised to aid his quest for membership in NATO. The United States had encouraged the so-called Rose Revolution in 2003 that brought Saakashvili to power and had since supported him in his struggle with separatist leaders in the regions of Abkhazia and South Ossetia, who were backed by Russia. *(Georgia transition, Historic Documents of 2003, p. 1039; Historic Documents of 2004, p. 73)*

By the time the G-8 summit began on July 15, it appeared that both U.S. and Russian officials had decided to cool the rhetoric so that the latest meeting between Bush and Putin could be as cordial as possible. On Russian soil, Bush offered no direct criticism of Russian domestic politics or international policy. Putin reciprocated, except for a dig at U.S. policy in Iraq, saying: "We certainly wouldn't want to have the kind of democracy that exists in Iraq." U.S. and Russian officials had hoped to finalize a long-stalled agreement providing for Russia to enter the World Trade Organization, but that did not happen in time for the summit, and the agreement was delayed until November.

Restrictions on Private Groups

Putin in January signed into law a series of restrictions on operations by private organizations that he said were being used by foreign governments as fronts for espionage against Russia. The new law gave the Federal Security Bureau—the Russian version of the FBI—the power to close down foreign groups thought to be working against Russian interests. The restrictions appeared to be aimed particularly at advocacy groups that received financing from the United States and European countries to promote democracy, human rights, and independent news media.

Two weeks after Putin signed that law, the government on January 23 said it had caught four British diplomats using secret communications devices to spy on Russia. These same diplomats, the government said, had funneled money to private groups in Russia, including the Eurasia Foundation (a U.S.-based group that openly aided nonprofit groups and independent news media in Russia) and the Moscow Helsinki Group, a human rights group often critical of Russian government policy.

Killing of Politkovskaya

At least one event a year over the past few years had seemed to symbolize the return of authoritarianism in Russia, including the closing of the last independent television station in 2003, the jailing of oil tycoon Mikhail Khodorkovsky in 2004, and Putin's decision in 2005 to dispense with the election of regional governors. For many in Russia and the outside world, the symbolic event of 2006 was the killing of one of the country's best-known and most passionate journalists. Anna Politkovskaya, an investigative journalist who had documented government abuses in Chechnya and fiercely criticized what she called the Kremlin's authoritarianism, was found dead in her Moscow apartment on October 7, the apparent victim of an assassination.

Government officials blamed Politkovskya's death on criminal gangs, but Putin's political opponents said the Kremlin had unleashed "dark forces" in society that led to her death and those of more than a dozen other journalists in recent years. "This state killed Anna Politkovskaya," opposition figure Grigory A. Yavlinsky said after the slain journalist's funeral on October 12. Putin called the murder a "loathsome brutality" but dismissed Politkovskya's influence as "extremely insignificant in scale." On October 12 an independent Moscow newspaper, *Novaya Gazeta*, published the final article Politkovskya had been writing at the time of her death: allegations that government security agents has tortured Chechens accused of collaborating with separatist guerrillas in Chechnya.

In Moscow on October 21 for talks with Russian officials, Secretary of State Rice made a point of meeting with the editors of *Novaya Gazeta*, including Politkovskya's son, Ilya. "There is still an independent print press," Rice said. "Unfortunately, there is not much left of independent television in Russia." All three of the national television channels were under the effective control of the government.

On November 23, a former Soviet secret agent living in London, Alexander V. Litvinenko, died in a London hospital—reportedly the victim of radiation poisoning. Litvinenko, who had become a fierce critic of Putin's government, had told associates that he was investigating the death of Politkovskaya. A written statement released after Litvienko's death, and attributed to him, accused Putin of having ordered him killed. Russian officials vigorously denied having anything to do with Litvinenko's death. British police treated Litvienko's death as murder and sent investigators to Moscow; the investigation was still in progress at year's end.

Chechnya

Seven years after it began, the second of Russia's two wars to regain control of the province of Chechnya appeared to have succeeded in 2006. Russian agents killed, or contributed to the deaths of, the two top leaders of Islamist groups that had sought independence from Moscow, rebuilding was under way, and the Kremlin installed its latest candidate for leadership of Chechnya. Russia had twice intervened to keep Chechnya in its orbit: the first effort, from 1994 to 1996, failed and resulted in a brief, de facto independence; the second started in 1999 when Putin sent in the Russian army to bring Chechnya back into the fold. *(Background, Historic Documents of 2005, p. 304)*

For Moscow, the year's best news came in early summer when both current Chechen independence leaders were killed. The first death came on June 17, when security forces killed Abdul Khalim Saidullayev, a little-known rebel who was chosen in 2005 to succeed the previous rebel leader, Aslan Maskhadov, after the military killed him. Immediately after Saidullayev's death, the Chechen rebels named Shamil Basayez as their leader. Basayez long had headed Russia's "most wanted list" because of the numerous terrorist attacks for which he had claimed responsibility, notably the September 2004 siege of a school in Beslan, southern Russia, that resulted in the deaths of 331 people, more than half of them children. Basayev's turn came on July 10, when security agents tracked him down in the region of Ingushetia, bordering Chechnya; he died in a massive explosion. *(Beslan siege, Historic Documents of 2004, p. 564)*

Earlier in the year, the Kremlin installed its latest leader in Chechnya. On February 28, Chechen prime minister Sergei Abramov stepped down and was replaced by Ramzan Kadyrov, who had been head of the region's secret police. This appointment was widely seen as an interim one to Kadyrov's eventual succession to the Chechen presidency. Kadyrov was the son of Akmad Kadyrov, who had been assassinated in 2004 after being installed by the Kremlin in 2003 as president of Chechnya in an effort to show that the war was over.

By 2006 Russia finally had begun extensive reconstruction work to repair the widespread damage to Chechnya, much of it caused by Russian bombers during the war. Much of Grozny, the capital, had been reduced to rubble but was now getting new houses, commercial buildings, public services, and even a giant mosque. The rebuilding was the clearest sign yet that the Kremlin really was confident it had won the war.

Following are two documents: first, excerpts from a speech by Vice President Dick Cheney, on May 4, 2006, to the Vilnius Conference, held in Vilnius, Latvia, in which he raised questions about Russian government policies; second, a reaction to Cheney's speech by Russian foreign minister Sergey Lavrov, released to the electronic media in Moscow on May 5, 2006.

━━━━━━━━━━ **DOCUMENT** ━━━━━━━━━━

"Vice President's Remarks at the 2006 Vilnius Conference"

... The spread of democracy is an unfolding of history; it is a benefit to all, and a threat to none. The best neighbor a country can have is a democracy—stable, peaceful, and open to relations of commerce and cooperation instead of suspicion and fear. The nations of the West have produced the most prosperous, tolerant system ever known. And because that system embraces the hopes and dreams of all humanity, it has changed our world for the better. We can and should build upon that successful record. The system that has brought such great hope to the shores of the Baltic can bring the same hope to the far shores of the Black Sea, and beyond. What is true in Vilnius is also true in Tbilisi [capital of Georgia] and Kiev [capital of Ukraine], and true in Minsk [capital of Belarus], and true in Moscow.

All of us are committed to democratic progress in Belarus. That nation has suffered in major wars and experienced terrible losses, and now its people are denied basic freedoms by the last dictatorship in Europe. With us today are democracy advocates from Belarus. We welcome you to this conference. I had also expected to meet today with the opposition leader, Alyaksander Milinkevich—but he was recently put in jail by the regime in Minsk. The regime should end this injustice and free Mr. Milinkevich, along with the other democracy advocates held in captivity. The world knows what is happening in Belarus. Peaceful demonstrators have been beaten, dissidents have vanished, and a climate of fear prevails under a government that subverts free elections and bans your own country's flag. There is no place in a Europe whole and free for a regime of this kind. The people of Belarus deserve better. You have the right to determine your destiny. And your great nation has a future in the community of democracies.

America and all of Europe also want to see Russia in the category of healthy, vibrant democracies. Yet in Russia today, opponents of reform are seeking to reverse the gains of the last decade. In many areas of civil society—from religion and the news media, to advocacy groups and political parties—the government has unfairly and improperly restricted the rights of her people. Other actions by the Russian government have been counterproductive, and could begin to affect relations with other countries. No legitimate interest is served when oil and gas become tools of intimidation or blackmail, either by supply manipulation or attempts to monopolize transportation. And no one can justify actions that undermine the territorial integrity of a neighbor, or interfere with democratic movements.

Russia has a choice to make. And there is no question that a return to democratic reform in Russia will generate further success for its people and greater respect among fellow nations. Democratization in Russia helped to end the Cold War, and the Russian people have made heroic progress in overcoming the miseries of the 20th century. They deserve now to live out their peaceful aspirations under a government that upholds freedom at home, and builds good relations abroad.

None of us believes that Russia is fated to become an enemy. A Russia that increasingly shares the values of this community can be a strategic partner and a trusted friend as we work toward common goals. In that spirit, the leading industrialized nations will engage Russia at the Group of Eight Summit in St. Petersburg this summer. We will make the case, clearly and confidently, that Russia has nothing to fear and everything to gain from having strong, stable democracies on its borders, and that by aligning with the West, Russia joins all of us on a course to prosperity and greatness. The vision we affirm today is of a community of sovereign democracies that transcend old grievances, that honor the many links of culture and history among us, that trade in freedom, respect each other as great nations, and strive together for a century of peace.

Our cooperation is vital, because democracies have great duties in today's world. The challenges of a new era require concerted action by nations and peoples who believe liberty is worth defending. For the sake of our security, we must act decisively against known dangers. And to secure freedom and peace for generations to come, we must be true to the democratic dreams of others, and remember our brothers and sisters who have kept their hopes in exile.

The end of the Cold War did not usher in an era of quiet and tranquility. A new enemy of freedom has emerged—and it is focused, resourceful, and rapacious. This enemy perverts a religious faith to serve a dark political objective—to establish, by violence and intimidation, a totalitarian empire that denies all political and religious freedom. To that end, the terrorists do not seek to build large standing armies. Instead, they want to demoralize free nations with dramatic acts of murder, and to gain weapons of mass destruction so they can hold power by threat or blackmail. We need not have any illusions about their ambitions, because the terrorists have stated them clearly. They have killed many thousands in many countries. They would, if able, kill hundreds of thousands more—and still not be finished.

This is not an enemy that can be ignored or appeased. And every retreat by civilized nations is an invitation to further violence against us. Men who despise freedom will attack freedom in any part of the world—and so responsible nations have a duty to stay on the offensive, together, to remove this threat. We are working to prevent attacks before they occur, by tracking down the terrorists wherever they dwell. We are working to deny weapons of mass destruction to outlaw states and their terrorist allies. We are working to prevent any nation from becoming a staging ground for future terrorist violence. And we are working to deny the terrorists future recruits, by replacing hatred and resentment with democracy and hope across the broader Middle East.

Our commitment to this cause is being tested today in Afghanistan and in Iraq. The task is difficult, but the progress has been steady, and the nations of our coalition have performed superbly. All 26 members of NATO have contributed assistance to operations in Iraq and Afghanistan. And some of the most steadfast allies in the cause are nations that have recently won their own freedom. From a Lithuanian Provincial Reconstruction team in Afghanistan; to Latvian military training teams in Iraq; to Estonian infantrymen; to Georgian security forces; to Polish and Romanian army units—countries that have known tyranny themselves have a clear understanding of what is at stake. And they have generously taken up the cause of democracy in other lands.

Because our coalition has stood by our commitment to the Afghan and Iraqi people, some 50 million men, women, and children who lived under dictators now live in freedom.

Afghanistan is a rising democracy, with the first fully elected government in its 5,000-year history. Iraq has the most progressive constitution and the strongest democratic mandate in the entire Arab world. And despite threats from assassins and car bombers, Iraqis came forward by the millions to cast their votes and to proclaim their rights as citizens of a free country.

Many days of challenge are still ahead in the war on terror, and much more will be asked of us as we help the peoples of a troubled region to consolidate their own democratic gains. And yet, as President Bush has said, the fight we have entered is "the current expression of an ancient struggle—between those who put their faith in dictators, and those who put their faith in the people." We have seen that fundamental clash of ideas played out in the history of Europe and the experience of Europe can be a source of confidence to us all.

We have learned, ladies and gentlemen, that the desire of human beings to be free is the most potent force on this Earth. Tyrants may, for a time, deny the hopes of others, violate the rights of others, and even take the lives of others. Yet they have no power to inspire hope or to raise the sights of a nation. The ideals that you and I believe in—liberty, and equality, and justice under law—speak to the best in mankind. We have seen these ideals lift up whole countries and secure generations of peace. And we will see that promise renewed in our own time, in places near and far. So let us persevere in freedom's cause—united, confident, and unafraid.

Thank you.

Source: U.S. Office of the Vice President. "Vice President's Remarks at the 2006 Vilnius Conference." May 4, 2006, Vilnius, Lithuania. www.whitehouse.gov/news/releases/2006/05/20060504-1.html (accessed March 11, 2007).

DOCUMENT

"Commentary Regarding U.S. Vice President Cheney's Remarks"

I think that a person who holds such a high government post should have the full amount of objective information, but everything indicates he was let down by his assistants or advisers. Thus, for example, we read that opponents of reform in Russia "are seeking to reverse the gains of the last decade." I think there is no need to explain to the Russian people in detail what kind of gains those were, when the country had actually found itself on the brink of disintegration. What the Russian leadership is doing now is to ensure that Russia is preserved as a unified, integral, strong state in the interests of its citizens.

Or take the statement that no legitimate interest is served when oil and gas become tools of intimidation or blackmail. We have heard such remarks from the lips of politicians lower in rank, but the US Vice President surely has to have the information that over the last forty years our country, either the USSR or the Russian Federation, has never breached any contract for the supply of oil and gas abroad. It is obvious that this information somehow failed to be conveyed to the Vice President likewise.

As to the charges that Russia's government has taken actions that "undermine the territorial integrity of a neighbor," what is there to say? In the early 90s it was at the cost of Russian peacekeepers' lives that the bloodshed was halted both in Georgia and in Moldova, thus saving the territorial integrity of these states. Not to remember that is, I would say, sacrilegious.

Where I can agree with Mr. Cheney is that he would like to see the world as a community of sovereign democracies. Russia wants to be and is becoming a sovereign, strong and stable democracy and expects that as such it will be perceived in the world arena as an equal partner without whose involvement not one global problem can be solved today. I think that such remarks will not undermine the efforts which we together with the US, together with Europe and together with other leading countries have been making in order to build a just world without conflicts where all countries will be able to develop in the conditions of stability and democracy; for democracy is needed not only within a state, but also on the international scene. Let us not forget about this.

Source: Russian Republic. Ministry of Foreign Affairs. Information and Press Department. "Commentary by Minister of Foreign Affairs of the Russian Federation Sergey Lavrov to Russian Electronic Media Regarding U.S. Vice President Richard Cheney's Remarks in Vilnius." May 5, 2006, Moscow. Unofficial translation. www.mid.ru/brp_4.nsf/e78a48070f128a7b43256999005bcbb3/dfacf18a7c7103f8c3257166004d6cef? OpenDocument

Other Historic Documents of Interest

International trade issues, p. 424

North Korean nuclear weapons issue, p. 606

UN Resolution on Darfur, p. 497

UN resolution on Iran, p. 781

Letter from Iranian President Ahmadinejad to President Bush

May 7, 2006

THE DOCUMENT IN CONTEXT

Iran moved to the center stage of world affairs in 2006, emboldened in part by its leverage in neighboring Iraq, where the United States was facing an increasingly difficult struggle against insurgents and sectarian militias, and by its ability to pursue an apparent nuclear weapons program despite intense diplomacy against it. Many experts, both in Western countries and in the Middle East, suggested during the year that the Islamic Republic of Iran was determined to replace the United States as the dominant player in the region.

Iran's assertive new president, Mahmoud Ahmadinejad, certainly appeared intent on claiming that role for his country. Ahmadinejad repeatedly defied international attempts to block Iran's nuclear ambitions. He twice reached out to the United States in personal letters defending Iran and denouncing U.S. policy in the Middle East. He traveled around the world proclaiming Iran's leadership of an anti-U.S. coalition, and he sponsored an international conference intended to disprove that millions of European Jews died at the hands of Nazi Germany.

The success of Iran's grasp for influence was evident in more tangible ways, notably in Iraq and Lebanon. In Iraq, Iranian-backed Shiite leaders headed the new government, and Shiite militias, some with clear links to Iran, were fomenting much of the sectarian conflict that made 2006 by far the most violent year since the United States invaded three years earlier. Iran also was the prime sponsor of Hezbollah, the Shiite militia and political party in Lebanon that triggered a brief but intense war with Israel from mid-July to mid-August. By surviving an enormous Israeli military onslaught, Hezbollah emerged as the symbolic victor, even in the eyes of Sunni Muslim Arabs who previously had feared that group and its Iranian benefactors.

Despite its success in asserting itself regionally and even globally, the Iranian leadership faced serious challenges at home. Ahmadinejad burnished his personal popularity by making dozens of promises as he traveled around the country, but he was unable to revive a struggling economy, which depended on oil production that was beginning to dwindle. Iranians remained deeply divided about the course of the 1979 Islamic revolution, as demonstrated by elections in December that appeared to signal a modest comeback for reformers and a setback for Ahmadinejad and other hard-liners.

The Bush administration responded to Iran with a mixture of policies that sent conflicting messages. The administration endorsed, albeit reluctantly, European diplomacy with Iran on the nuclear issue, and President George W. Bush even agreed to allow U.S. participation in multilateral negotiations with Iran on that issue—but under conditions that Iran refused. Bush repeatedly refused to rule out a military attack against

Iran, and there was increasing speculation that Israel would use airpower to attack Iran's nuclear installations—with or without U.S. support.

Reaching out to the United States

The complex nature of relations between the United States and Iran—or the lack of such relations—came into focus in midyear. On May 8, the Iranian government announced that Ahmadinejad had sent President Bush an eighteen-page letter that outlined "new solutions" for the long history of antagonism between the two countries. The letter at first was kept private, but Iran quickly posted Farsi and English versions of it on government Web sites, complete with a photograph of Ahmadinejad writing on a piece of paper.

The letter was a rambling dialectic, posing questions and then answering them, on a broad range of subjects including religion, the histories of the West and the Middle East, and U.S.-Iranian relations. It repeated many of Iran's long-standing grievances against the United States and its closest Middle Eastern ally, Israel, but the letter contained little of the overtly hostile rhetoric Ahmadinejad used in many of his speeches. Despite the Iranian government's claim that the letter offered new ideas, there were no proposals for action. So far as was known publicly, the letter was the first direct effort by any senior Iranian leader to establish high-level contact with the United States since the resolution of the U.S.-Iran hostage crisis in January 1981. *(Hostage crisis, Historic Documents of 2001, p. 137)*

If the letter was a genuine attempt to spark a dialogue, it failed. Top administration officials dismissed the letter as a rhetorical exercise, with Bush himself saying it did not answer "the main question the world is asking, and that is, 'When will you get rid of your nuclear program?'" News reports, however, said most Middle East experts at the State Department, the Pentagon, and U.S. intelligence services took the letter more seriously as a sign that Ahmadinejad was hoping to spark some kind of direct dialogue with the United States.

Two weeks later, the *Washington Post* reported that Iranian officials had made numerous efforts to follow up on Ahmadinejad's letter; messages had been sent to the United States through such intermediaries as UN Secretary General Kofi Annan and the director general of the International Atomic Energy Agency, Mohammed ElBaradei. Some of these approaches reportedly came from Ali Larijani, the chairman of Iran's Supreme National Security Council, who was seen by some Western experts on Iran as leading a faction of pragmatic conservatives interested in improved relations with the West in general and the United States in particular. The *Post* report noted that even Iran's most conservative leaders, including the supreme leader, Ayatollah Ali Khamenei, apparently endorsed the recent outreach attempts.

On May 31, Secretary of State Condoleezza Rice announced a significant shift in administration policy, saying the United States would be willing to participate in long-stalled direct negotiations between European nations and Iran on the nuclear issue. However, she made this a conditional offer, saying Iran would first have to suspend its uranium enrichment programs that were at the heart of the negotiations. "The United States is willing to exert strong leadership to give diplomacy its very best chance to succeed," she said. Administration officials said Rice's offer was not a direct response to the Ahmadinejad letter and other initiatives from Iran. Instead, they said, the offer reflected the administration's fears that China, the Europeans, and Russia would not agree to a hard line against Iran's weapons program unless another effort was made to explore Iran's willingness to back down.

This was the second such policy reversal by the Bush administration in little over a year. In March 2005, the administration accepted the European argument that the U.S. policy of threatening Iran with UN sanctions was not sufficient and needed to be accompanied by incentives for Tehran to drop its weapons ambitions. As incentives, the administration agreed at that point to drop long-standing U.S. opposition to Iranian membership in the World Trade Organization (which monitored compliance with international trading rules) and to consider allowing Europeans to sell spare parts to Iran for its large fleet of U.S.-made civilian airplanes. Rice in 2005 also had authorized the U.S. ambassador to Iraq, Zalmay Khalilzad, to engage in talks with Iranian officials about the deteriorating situation in Iraq. The concessions in 2005 appeared to produce no positive results, however, and no talks were ever held between Khalilzad and the Iranians.

Ahmadinejad followed his letter to Bush with two other approaches during the year. The first came on August 29, when he called on Bush to engage in a televised "debate" on matters of interest to the two countries. Bush quickly dismissed the idea. Another approach came on November 28, when the Iranian government published what it said was a letter from Ahmadinejad "to the American people." In this letter, Ahmadinejad sought to align himself with what he called the vast majority of "noble Americans" who opposed Bush's policies that had caused "many wars and calamities" in the Middle East. Expounding on one of his favorite themes, Ahmadinejad said the Jewish elite had tricked Americans into supporting Bush and his policy of backing Israel. "What have the Zionists done for the American people that the U.S. administration considers itself obliged to blindly support these infamous aggressors?" he asked, in a reference to Israel. "Is it not because they have imposed themselves on a substantial portion of the banking, financial, cultural and media sectors?"

As with the previous letter addressed to Bush, administration officials dismissed the November 28 letter as misguided. "It reflects a profound lack of understanding of the United States," said Nicholas Burns, the undersecretary of state for political affairs. Several Western experts on Iranian politics agreed that Ahmadinejad misunderstood American public opinion, but they suggested the letter was intended as yet another signal of Iran's eagerness for direct contacts with the United States.

The Military Option

In Washington there appeared to be more interest in the question of whether the Bush administration was preparing for a drastically different approach to Iran—the use of military force to destroy Iran's presumed work on nuclear weapons. U.S. officials, from President Bush on down, repeatedly refused to take that option off the table, and some officials in Israel began saying the question was when, not whether, military action would be necessary to stop Iran from building nuclear weapons.

While U.S. officials saw the question in terms of thwarting Iran's alleged ambition to establish hegemony over the Middle East, Israelis saw the matter in existential terms: a nuclear-armed Iran would attempt either to blackmail or destroy Israel, which had its own nuclear weapons. If a nuclear war broke out, just one or two bombs could destroy much of Israel because it was a small country. Such a consideration had led Israel in 1981 to destroy a nuclear reactor under construction in Iraq. Israel suffered wide condemnation for that attack, but Iran was a stronger force in the Middle East of 2006 than Iraq had been a quarter-century earlier—thus raising the risks of a similar attack. *(Israeli attack on Iraq, Historic Documents of 1991, p. 506)*

Numerous news reports during the year said both the Bush administration and Israeli officials were reviewing plans for potential air strikes to eliminate the key Iranian nuclear facilities. Because Iran had built some of these facilities deep underground, destroying them was considered much more difficult than Israel's bombing of the above-ground Iraqi reactor in 1981; some military experts said hundreds of bombing runs over a period of weeks would be necessary, unless the United States or Israel resorted to the use of nuclear weapons—a step fraught with unimaginable peril, both regionally and globally. Some experts said the United States had no real intention of attacking Iran but was simply using the threat of an attack to force Iran to back down.

Bush on April 10 said reports of potential strikes against Iran were "wild speculation." He insisted, however, that his policy remained that "the Iranians should not have a nuclear weapon." In one of many Iranian responses during the rhetoric, Ayatollah Khamenei, warned on April 26 that his country would retaliate against a U.S. attack "by damaging the U.S. interests worldwide twice as much as the U.S. may inflict on Iran."

Seeking, and Getting, Regional Influence

As recently as 2003 it could be argued that the Islamic revolution in Iran had nearly run its course. The majority of Iran's young people apparently were fed up with the restrictions on daily life that had been imposed by conservative mullahs, and they demonstrated eagerness for change by electing a moderate cleric, Mohammad Khatami, to the presidency in 1997 and 2001. Iran's economy was in the middle of a long downhill slide, caused in part by mismanagement by the clerics and in part by a decline in the production of oil and gas, the country's principal natural resources. *(Khatami election, Historic Documents of 1997, p. 284)*

The conservative forces in Iran gained new energy, however, after winning parliamentary elections in 2004; that victory was made possible when the clerics disqualified many reformist candidates and most other reform candidates dropped out. The surprise victory of Ahmadinejad in the 2005 presidential elections appeared to cement the control of the government by hard-line forces determined to fulfill the Islamist vision of the 1979 revolution. Another key development was the U.S. invasion of Iraq in 2003. At first that invasion appeared to be a setback for Iran, as about 150,000 American troops were now right next door. By 2006, however, the United States appeared to be bogged down in Iraq with only limited prospects for success, Iraq's new leaders had close ties to Iran, and Washington had more to fear about Tehran's actions in Iraq than vice versa.

The July–August war between Israel and Hezbollah in Lebanon also appeared to enhance Iran's prestige and influence in the region, at least in the immediate aftermath. As Hezbollah's main financier and arms supplier, Iran shared in the glory that many in the region heaped on Hezbollah after it withstood a month-long Israeli assault. Hezbollah already had stature from its claim of having forced Israel to withdraw from southern Lebanon in 2000 after nearly two decades. The assertion in August 2006 by Hezbollah leader Hassan Nasrallah that his group had again scored a "divine victory" against Israel was taken at face value by Arabs all over the Middle East—most of them Sunnis who otherwise had little regard for a Shiite group such as Hezbollah or its benefactor: Persian, primarily Shiite Iran.

By late 2006, many analysts of Middle East affairs—both in the region and in the West—said Iran was in a strengthened position, despite the pressure put on it because of the nuclear issue, and was demanding international recognition of that fact. "What Iran wants is for the United States to accept Central Asia, Afghanistan, and the Persian Gulf as Iran's 'near abroad'—a zone of influence in which Iran's interests would determine ebbs and flows of politics unencumbered by American interference—and to recognize Iranian presence in Syria and Lebanon," Vali R. Nasr, an expert on Iranian affairs wrote in the December 12 issue of the *New Republic* magazine.

A Setback for Hard-Liners in Iran

Despite their apparent success in keeping the West off balance, Ahmadinejad and his conservative allies in December suffered what many analysts saw as a potentially significant political defeat. Two elections were held on December 15.

One was for the Assembly of Experts, a body of eighty-six ayatollahs whose main job was to select the country's senior ayatollah, who held the position of supreme leader. The current occupant of that post, Ali Khamenei, was believed to be in ill health, so it appeared possible that the assembly elected for an eight-year term in 2006 would eventually select his successor. This election appeared to represent a victory for moderate conservatives led by former president Akbar Hashemi Rafsanjani, who easily defeated a staunch conservative, Ayatollah Mohammed Taghi Mesbah-Yazdi, who was a mentor to President Ahmadinejad. Rafsanjani's allies reportedly won a strong majority of the assembly seats.

In the other elections on December 15, allies of Ahmadinejad were defeated in contests for seats on municipal councils around the country. In the most closely watched contest, the president's allies won only two of the fifteen seats on the Tehran city council, with a slight majority going to more moderate conservatives. Ahmadinejad had been mayor of Tehran before his election as president in 2005.

Taken together, these elections were widely seen as demonstrating broad dissatisfaction with Ahmadinejad's performance on domestic issues, notably the lagging economy and his failure to follow through on the many promises he had made to generate jobs.

Following is the text of a letter sent to President George W. Bush on May 7, 2006, by Mahmoud Ahmadinejad, the president of Iran.

▬▬▬▬▬ DOCUMENT ▬▬▬▬▬

"Letter from President of Iran to U.S. President George W. Bush"

In the Name of God, the Compassionate, the Merciful,

Mr. George Bush,
President of the United States of America,

For sometime now I have been thinking, how one can justify the undeniable contradictions that exist in the international arena—which are being constantly debated, especially in political forums and amongst university students. Many questions remain unanswered.

These have prompted me to discuss some of the contradictions and questions, in the hope that it might bring about an opportunity to redress them.

Can one be a follower of Jesus Christ (PBUH [peace be upon him]), the great Messenger of God, feel obliged to respect human rights, present liberalism as a civilization model, announce one's opposition to the proliferation of nuclear weapons and WMDs [weapons of mass destruction], make "War on Terror" his slogan, and finally, work towards the establishment of a unified international community—a community which Christ and the virtuous of the Earth will one day govern, but at the same time, have countries attacked. The lives, reputations and possessions of people destroyed and on the slight chance of the presence of a few criminals in a village, city, or convoy for example, the entire village, city or convoy are set ablaze.

Or because of the possibility of the existence of WMDs in one country, it is occupied, around one hundred thousand people killed, its water sources, agriculture and industry destroyed, close to 180,000 foreign troops put on the ground, sanctity of private homes of citizens broken, and the country pushed back perhaps fifty years. At what price? Hundreds of billions of dollars spent from the treasury of one country and certain other countries and tens of thousands of young men and women—as occupation troops—put in harms way, taken away from family and loved ones, their hands stained with the blood of others, subjected to so much psychological pressure that everyday some commit suicide and those returning home suffer depression, become sickly and grapple with all sorts of ailments; while some are killed and their bodies handed to their families.

On the pretext of the existence of WMDs, this great tragedy came to engulf both the peoples of the occupied and the occupying country. Later it was revealed that no WMDs existed to begin with.

Of course Saddam was a murderous dictator. But the war was not waged to topple him, the announced goal of the war was to find and destroy weapons of mass destruction. He was toppled along the way towards another goal; nevertheless the people of the region are happy about it. I point out that throughout the many years of the imposed war on Iran Saddam was supported by the West.

Mr. President,

You might know that I am a teacher. My students ask me how can these actions be reconciled with the values outlined at the beginning of this letter and duty to the tradition of Jesus Christ (PBUH), the Messenger of peace and forgiveness?

There are prisoners in Guantanamo Bay that have not been tried, have no legal representation, their families cannot see them and are obviously kept in a strange land outside their own country. There is no international monitoring of their conditions and fate. No one knows whether they are prisoners, POWs, accused or criminals.

European investigators have confirmed the existence of secret prisons in Europe too. I could not correlate the abduction of a person, and him or her being kept in secret prisons, with the provisions of any judicial system. For that matter, I fail to understand how such actions correspond to the values outlined in the beginning of this letter, i.e. the teachings of Jesus Christ (PBUH), human rights and liberal values.

Young people, university students, and ordinary people have many questions about the phenomenon of Israel. I am sure you are familiar with some of them.

Throughout history many countries have been occupied, but I think the establishment of a new country with a new people, is a new phenomenon that is exclusive to our times. Students are saying that sixty years ago such a country did not exist. They show old documents and globes and say try as we have, we have not been able to find a country named Israel. I tell them to study the history of WW [World War] I and II. One of my students told me that during WWII, which more than tens of millions of people perished in, news about the war, was quickly disseminated by the warring parties. Each touted their victories and the most recent battlefront defeat of the other party. After the war they claimed that six million Jews had been killed. Six million people that were surely related to at least two million families. Again let us assume that these events are true. Does that logically translate into the establishment of the state of Israel in the Middle East or support for such a state? How can this phenomenon be rationalized or explained?

Mr. President,

I am sure you know how—and at what cost—Israel was established:

- Many thousands were killed in the process.
- Millions of indigenous people were made refugees.
- Hundreds of thousands of hectares of farmland, olive plantations, towns and villages were destroyed.

This tragedy is not exclusive to the time of establishment; unfortunately it has been ongoing for sixty years now. A regime has been established which does not show mercy even to kids, destroys houses while the occupants are still in them, announces beforehand its list and plans to assassinate Palestinian figures, and keeps thousands of Palestinians in prison. Such a phenomenon is unique—or at the very least extremely rare—in recent memory.

Another big question asked by the people is "why is this regime being supported?" Is support for this regime in line with the teachings of Jesus Christ (PBUH) or Moses (PBUH) or liberal values? Or are we to understand that allowing the original inhabitants of these lands—inside and outside Palestine—whether they are Christian, Moslem or Jew, to determine their fate, runs contrary to principles of democracy, human rights and the teachings of prophets? If not, why is there so much opposition to a referendum?

The newly elected Palestinian administration recently took office. All independent observers have confirmed that this government represents the electorate. Unbelievingly, they have put the elected government under pressure and have advised it to recognize the Israeli regime, abandon the struggle and follow the programs of the previous government. If the current Palestinian government had run on the above platform, would the Palestinian people have voted for it? Again, can such position taken in opposition to the Palestinian government be reconciled with the values outlined earlier? The people are also asking "Why are all UNSC resolutions in condemnation of Israel vetoed?"

Mr. President,

As you are well aware, I live amongst the people and am in constant contact with them—many people from around the Middle East manage to contact me as well. They do not have faith in these dubious policies either. There is evidence that the people of the region are becoming increasingly angry with such policies.

It is not my intention to pose too many questions, but I need to refer to other points as well.

Why is it that any technological and scientific achievement reached in the Middle East region is translated into and portrayed as a threat to the Zionist regime? Is not scientific R&D [research and development] one of the basic rights of nations?

You are familiar with history. Aside from the Middle Ages, in what other point in history has scientific and technical progress been a crime? Can the possibility of scientific achievements being utilized for military purposes be reason enough to oppose science and technology altogether? If such a supposition is true, then all scientific disciplines, including physics, chemistry, mathematics, medicine, engineering, etc. must be opposed.

Lies were told in the Iraqi matter. What was the result? I have no doubt that telling lies is reprehensible in any culture, and you do not like to be lied to.

Mr. President,

Don't Latin Americans have the right to ask why their elected governments are being opposed and coup leaders supported? Or, Why must they constantly be threatened and live in fear?

The people of Africa are hardworking, creative and talented. They can play an important and valuable role in providing for the needs of humanity and contribute to its material and spiritual progress. Poverty and hardship in large parts of Africa are preventing this from happening. Don't they have the right to ask why their enormous wealth—including minerals—is being looted, despite the fact that they need it more than others?

Again, do such actions correspond to the teachings of Christ and the tenets of human rights?

The brave and faithful people of Iran too have many questions and grievances, including: the coup d'etat of 1953 and the subsequent toppling of the legal government of the day, opposition to the Islamic revolution, transformation of an Embassy into a headquarters supporting the activities of those opposing the Islamic Republic (many thousands of pages of documents corroborate this claim), support for Saddam in the war waged against Iran, the shooting down of the Iranian passenger plane, freezing the assets of the Iranian nation, increasing threats, anger and displeasure vis-á-vis the scientific and nuclear progress of the Iranian nation (just when all Iranians are jubilant and celebrating their country's progress), and many other grievances that I will not refer to in this letter.

Mr. President,

September Eleven was a horrendous incident. The killing of innocents is deplorable and appalling in any part of the world. Our government immediately declared its disgust with the perpetrators and offered its condolences to the bereaved and expressed its sympathies.

All governments have a duty to protect the lives, property and good standing of their citizens. Reportedly your government employs extensive security, protection and intelligence systems—and even hunts its opponents abroad. September eleven was not a simple operation. Could it be planned and executed without coordination with intelligence and security services—or their extensive infiltration? Of course this is just an educated guess. Why have the various aspects of the attacks been kept secret? Why are we not told who botched their responsibilities? And, why aren't those responsible and the guilty parties identified and put on trial?

All governments have a duty to provide security and peace of mind for their citizens. For some years now, the people of your country and neighbors of world trouble spots do not have peace of mind. After 9.11, instead of healing and tending to the emotional wounds of the survivors and the American people—who had been immensely traumatized by the attacks—some Western media only intensified the climate of fear and insecurity—some constantly talked about the possibility of new terror attacks and kept the people in fear. Is that service to the American people? Is it possible to calculate the damages incurred from fear and panic?

American citizens lived in constant fear of fresh attacks that could come at any moment and in any place. They felt insecure in the streets, in their place of work and at home. Who would be happy with this situation? Why was the media, instead of conveying a feeling of security and providing peace of mind, giving rise to a feeling of insecurity?

Some believe that the hype paved the way—and was the justification—for an attack on Afghanistan. Again I need to refer to the role of media.

In media charters, correct dissemination of information and honest reporting of a story are established tenets. I express my deep regret about the disregard shown by certain Western media for these principles. The main pretext for an attack on Iraq was the existence of WMDs. This was repeated incessantly—for the public to finally believe—and the ground set for an attack on Iraq.

Will the truth not be lost in a contrived and deceptive climate?

Again, if the truth is allowed to be lost, how can that be reconciled with the earlier mentioned values? Is the truth known to the Almighty lost as well?

Mr. President,

In countries around the world, citizens provide for the expenses of governments so that their governments in turn are able to serve them.

The question here is "what has the hundreds of billions of dollars, spent every year to pay for the Iraqi campaign, produced for the citizens?"

As Your Excellency is aware, in some states of your country, people are living in poverty. Many thousands are homeless and unemployment is a huge problem. Of course these problems exist—to a larger or lesser extent—in other countries as well. With these conditions in mind, can the gargantuan expenses of the campaign—paid from the public treasury—be explained and be consistent with the aforementioned principles?

What has been said, are some of the grievances of the people around the world, in our region and in your country. But my main contention—which I am hoping you will agree to some of it—is:

Those in power have a specific time in office and do not rule indefinitely, but their names will be recorded in history and will be constantly judged in the immediate and distant futures.

The people will scrutinize our presidencies.

Did we mange to bring peace, security and prosperity for the people or insecurity and unemployment?

Did we intend to establish justice or just supported especial interest groups, and by forcing many people to live in poverty and hardship, made a few people rich and powerful—thus trading the approval of the people and the Almighty with theirs'?

Did we defend the rights of the underprivileged or ignore them?

Did we defend the rights of all people around the world or imposed wars on them, interfered illegally in their affairs, established hellish prisons and incarcerated some of them?

Did we bring the world peace and security or raised the specter of intimidation and threats?

Did we tell the truth to our nation and others around the world or presented an inverted version of it?

Were we on the side of people or the occupiers and oppressors?

Did our administrations set out to promote rational behavior, logic, ethics, peace, fulfilling obligations, justice, service to the people, prosperity, progress and respect for human dignity or the force of guns, intimidation, insecurity, disregard for the people, delaying the progress and excellence of other nations, and trample on people's rights?

And finally, they will judge us on whether we remained true to our oath of office—to serve the people, which is our main task, and the traditions of the prophets—or not?

Mr. President,

How much longer can the world tolerate this situation?

Where will this trend lead the world to?

How long must the people of the world pay for the incorrect decisions of some rulers?

How much longer will the specter of insecurity—raised from the stockpiles of weapons of mass destruction—hunt the people of the world?

How much longer will the blood of the innocent men, women and children be spilled on the streets, and people's houses destroyed over their heads?

Are you pleased with the current condition of the world?

Do you think present policies can continue?

If billions of dollars spent on security, military campaigns and troop movement were instead spent on investment and assistance for poor countries, promotion of health, combating different diseases, education and improvement of mental and physical fitness, assistance to the victims of natural disasters, creation of employment opportunities and production, development projects and poverty alleviation, establishment of peace, mediation between disputing states, and extinguishing the flames of racial, ethnic and other conflicts, were would the world be today? Would not your government and people be justifiably proud?

Would not your administration's political and economic standing have been stronger? And I am most sorry to say, would there have been an ever increasing global hatred of the American government?

Mr. President,

It is not my intention to distress anyone.

If Prophet Abraham, Isaac, Jacob, Ishmael, Joseph, or Jesus Christ (PBUH) were with us today, how would they have judged such behavior? Will we be given a role to play in the promised world, where justice will become universal and Jesus Christ (PBUH) will be present? Will they even accept us?

My basic question is this: Is there no better way to interact with the rest of the world? Today there are hundreds of millions of Christians, hundreds of millions of Muslims and millions of people who follow the teachings of Moses (PBUH). All divine religions share and respect one word and that is "monotheism" or belief in a single God and no other in the world.

The Holy Koran stresses this common word and calls on all followers of divine religions and says:

> *[3.64] Say: O followers of the Book! Come to an equitable proposition between us and you that we shall not serve any but Allah and (that) we shall not associate aught with Him, and (that) some of us shall not take others for lords besides Allah; but if they turn back, then say: Bear witness that we are Muslims. (The Family of Imran.)*

Mr. President,

According to divine verses, we have all been called upon to worship one God and follow the teachings of divine Prophets.

"To worship a God which is above all powers in the world and can do all He pleases"

"The Lord which knows that which is hidden and visible, the past and the future, knows what goes on in the Hearts of His servants and records their deeds"

"The Lord who is the possessor of the heavens and the earth and all universe is His court"

"planning for the universe is done by His hands, and gives His servants the glad tidings of mercy and forgiveness of sins"

"He is the companion of the oppressed and the enemy of oppressors"

"He is the Compassionate, the Merciful"

"He is the recourse of the faithful and guides them towards the light from darkness"

"He is witness to the actions of His servants"

"He calls on servants to be faithful and do good deeds, and asks them to stay on the path of righteousness and remain steadfast"

"Calls on servants to heed His prophets and He is a witness to their deeds"

"A bad ending belongs only to those who have chosen the life of this world and disobey Him and oppress His servants" and

"A good end and eternal paradise belong to those servants who fear His majesty and do not follow their lascivious selves."

We believe a return to the teachings of the divine prophets is the only road leading to salvation. I have been told that Your Excellency follows the teachings of Jesus (PBUH) and believes in the divine promise of the rule of the righteous on Earth.

We also believe that Jesus Christ (PBUH) was one of the great prophets of the Almighty. He has been repeatedly praised in the Koran. Jesus (PBUH) has been quoted in Koran as well:

> *[19.36] And surely Allah is my Lord and your Lord, therefore serve Him; this is the right path. Marium.*

Service to and obedience of the Almighty is the credo of all divine messengers.

The God of all people in Europe, Asia, Africa, America, the Pacific and the rest of the world is one. He is the Almighty who wants to guide and give dignity to all His servants. He has given greatness to Humans.

We again read in the Holy Book:

> *"The Almighty God sent His prophets with miracles and clear signs to guide the people and show them divine signs and purify them from sins and pollutions. And He sent the Book and the balance so that the people display justice and avoid the rebellious."*

All of the above verses can be seen, one way or the other, in the Good Book as well.

Divine prophets have promised: The day will come when all humans will congregate before the court of the Almighty, so that their deeds are examined. The good will be directed towards Haven and evildoers will meet divine retribution. I trust both of us believe in such a day, but it will not be easy to calculate the actions of rulers, because we must be answerable to our nations and all others whose lives have been directly or indirectly affected by our actions.

All prophets, speak of peace and tranquility for man—based on monotheism, justice and respect for human dignity.

> Do you not think that if all of us come to believe in and abide by these principles, that is, monotheism, worship of God, justice, respect for the dignity of man, belief in the Last Day, we can overcome the present problems of the world—that are the result of disobedience to the Almighty and the teachings of prophets—and improve our performance?
>
> Do you not think that belief in these principles promotes and guarantees peace, friendship and justice?
>
> Do you not think that the aforementioned written or unwritten principles are universally respected?
>
> Will you not accept this invitation? That is, a genuine return to the teachings of prophets, to monotheism and justice, to preserve human dignity and obedience to the Almighty and His prophets?

Mr. President,

History tells us that repressive and cruel governments do not survive. God has entrusted the fate of men to them. The Almighty has not left the universe and humanity to their own devices.

Many things have happened contrary to the wishes and plans of governments. These tell us that there is a higher power at work and all events are determined by Him.

Can one deny the signs of change in the world today?

Is the situation of the world today comparable to that of ten years ago? Changes happen fast and come at a furious pace.

The people of the world are not happy with the status quo and pay little heed to the promises and comments made by a number of influential world leaders. Many people around the world feel insecure and oppose the spreading of insecurity and war and do not approve of and accept dubious policies.

The people are protesting the increasing gap between the haves and the have-nots and the rich and poor countries.

The people are disgusted with increasing corruption.

The people of many countries are angry about the attacks on their cultural foundations and the disintegration of families. They are equally dismayed with the fading of care and compassion. The people of the world have no faith in international organizations, because their rights are not advocated by these organizations.

Liberalism and Western style democracy have not been able to help realize the ideals of humanity. Today these two concepts have failed. Those with insight can already hear the sounds of the shattering and fall of the ideology and thoughts of the Liberal democratic systems.

We increasingly see that people around the world are flocking towards a main focal point—that is the Almighty God. Undoubtedly through faith in God and the teachings of the prophets, the people will conquer their problems. My question for you is: "Do you not want to join them?"

Mr. President,
    Whether we like it or not, the world is gravitating towards faith in the Almighty and justice and the will of God will prevail over all things.
    Vasalam Ala Man Ataba'al hoda.

Mahmood Ahmadi-Nejad
President of the Islamic Republic of Iran

Source: Islamic Republic of Iran. The Permanent Mission of the Islamic Republic of Iran to the UN. "Letter from Mahmood Ahmadi-Nejad, President of the Islamic Republic of Iran, to U.S. President George W. Bush." May 8, 2006. www.un.int/iran/pressaffairs/pressreleases/2006/articles/1.html (accessed March 5, 2007).

Other Historic Documents of Interest

War between Israel and Hezbollah,
    p. 454
North Korean nuclear weapons issue,
    p. 606

UN resolution on Iran, p. 781
U.S.-India agreement on nuclear trade,
    p. 93
U.S. policy on Iraq, p. 725

Secretary of State Rice on Restoring Diplomatic Relations with Libya

May 15, 2006

The United States and Libya resumed normal diplomatic relations in 2006 after more than a quarter-century of hostility and suspicion. The diplomatic move was one of the most dramatic indications, in three years of significant steps, that Libya and its eccentric leader, Muammar Qaddafi, were returning to the good graces of the West.

During most of the 1970s and 1980s the United States had considered Libya a "rogue" nation because of its support for radical terrorist groups and its persistent meddling in the affairs of neighboring countries. Qadaffi, who as a twenty-seven-year-old army captain led a military coup against Libya's king in 1969, was one of the world's most mercurial and durable leaders. After years of anti-Western (particularly anti-U.S.) rhetoric and action, Qadaffi suddenly reversed course in 2003. *(Background, Historic Documents of 2003, p. 1218; Historic Documents of 2004, p. 168)*

Renewing Relations

Until the restoration of relations in May 2006, Libya was one of a handful of countries in the world with which the United States did not have formal diplomatic relations. The others were Cuba, Iran, Myanmar (formerly Burma), and North Korea.

The downhill slide in U.S.-Libya relations began in 1972, when the Nixon administration withdrew the U.S. ambassador to protest Libyan support for what the State Department called "international terrorism and subversion against moderate Arab and African governments." In December 1979, after a mob chanting pro-Iran slogans attacked and set fire to the U.S. embassy in Tripoli, the Carter administration withdrew the remaining U.S. diplomatic personnel, formally suspended relations with Libya, and placed Libya on a list of countries that sponsored terrorism. The Reagan administration took the further step in May 1981 of ordering the Libyan embassy in Washington closed and expelling the diplomatic staff. The low point came between 1986 and 1988. In January 1986, President Ronald Reagan banned all trade with Libya and froze Libyan government assets in the United States in retaliation for Qaddafi's alleged harboring of a Palestinian terrorist group headed by Abu Nidal; the previous month gunmen thought to be from that group had attacked travelers at El Al airline ticket counters in Rome and Vienna, killing twenty. Then, in April 1986, a bomb exploded at a nightclub in Berlin, killing two U.S. servicemen and a Turkish woman and wounding about 200 others; U.S. intelligence agencies determined that the Libyan government had played a role in the bombing. Nine days later, on April 14, a large-scale U.S. air strike against Libyan military targets killed dozens of people, including Qaddafi's adopted infant daughter. *(Air strike against Libya, Historic Documents of 1986, p. 347)*

Qaddafi got his revenge two years later, according to Western intelligence officials, by ordering the bombing on December 21, 1988, of Pan Am Flight 103 over Lockerbie, Scotland, killing 259 people on board and 11 people on the ground. The United Nations Security Council imposed sanctions against Libya to force the government to hand over two officials who were believed by U.S. and British intelligence agencies to have been responsible for the bombing. The men eventually were turned over to British custody in 1999, and in 2001 one of them was found guilty but the other man was acquitted of involvement in the bombing. Libya agreed in August 2003 to pay $2.7 billion in compensation to the families of victims.

The most important step forward in the improvement of relations between Libya and the West occurred in December 2003, when Qaddafi suddenly agreed to end Libya's programs to develop biological, chemical, and nuclear weapons and to submit his country's weapons industry to international inspections. That step, which resulted from diplomatic negotiations among U.S., British, and Libyan officials, was followed by several others:

- February 2004: The United States reopened its informal diplomatic mission in Tripoli (known as an "interests section") at the Belgian embassy and invited Libya to reopen its interests section in Washington, D.C.
- April 2004: President George W. Bush lifted most U.S. economic sanctions against Libya.
- June 2004: The State Department upgraded its diplomatic presence in Tripoli to a "liaison office," one step below that of an embassy.
- September 2004: President Bush formally lifted trade embargo against Libya.
- September 2005: Bush waived export regulations so U.S. companies could participate in the destruction of Libya's chemical weapons programs.

The culmination of these actions came on May 15, 2006, when Secretary of State Condoleezza Rice announced the planned reopening of the U.S. embassy in Libya and removal of Libya from the list of state sponsors of terrorism. "Today marks the opening of a new era in U.S.-Libya relations that will benefit Americans and Libyans alike," Rice said in her statement. Rice also pointedly compared Libya's recent actions with those of Iran and North Korea, both of which had been accused by the United States of developing nuclear weapons. "We urge the leadership of Iran and North Korea to make similar strategic decisions that would benefit their citizens," she said.

C. David Welch, the assistant secretary of state for near eastern affairs, told reporters that the United States remained concerned about other aspects of Libya's behavior, notably its human rights record. Establishing diplomatic relations, he said, "will enable us to engage with the Libyans more effectively on all issues." Welch and other U.S. officials also said Libya had been cooperating with the United States in its war against terrorism, particularly since the September 2001 terrorist attacks in New York City and Washington, D.C.

Libya's foreign minister, Abdel-Rahman Shalqam, rejected U.S. implications that the restoration of relations was Washington's "reward" to Libya for its cooperation on terrorism and weapons destruction. "It is a result of mutual interests, agreements, and understandings," he told the Associated Press. "In politics there is no such thing as a reward, but there are interests."

Some American foreign policy experts said the success of diplomatic negotiations with Libya held out a lesson for the Bush administration, which had been reluctant to engage in similar, direct diplomacy with Iran and North Korea and instead emphasized sanctions and the threat of military force. "The lesson here is that while it's useful to have force as a backdrop, this is really a story of serious diplomacy's success," Bruce Jentleson, a State Department official during the Clinton administration, told the *Christian Science Monitor*.

Despite the restoration of relations, another controversy arose later in 2006 when Libya said it would not complete the payments it had promised to the families of the Pan Am bombing victims. Under its 2003 agreement, Libya had pledged to pay each family $10 million, but $2 million of that was contingent on the United States removing Libya from the list of terrorism-supporting countries by early 2004. Libya paid the first $8 million to each family but withheld the final $2 million because Washington had not lifted those sanctions in 2004. Victims' families raised the matter again in 2006 after the Bush administration restored diplomatic relations and lifted the sanctions, but Libya said it no longer was obliged to pay the final $2 million per family (a total of $540 million for the 270 families involved).

Libya's Weapons Programs

Following its dramatic renunciation in December 2003 of weapons of mass destruction, Libya took several important steps to assure the world that its weapons programs in fact would be abandoned. Libya allowed U.S. weapons experts to dismantle the equipment it used to manufacture highly enriched uranium for nuclear weapons, and more than thirty pounds of the weapons fuel was shipped to Russia. In August 2006 Libya ratified an Additional Protocol, an agreement that enabled the International Atomic Energy Agency to conduct broad-ranging inspections of the country's civilian nuclear energy and research facilities.

In 2004 Libya signed and ratified the United Nations Chemical Weapons Convention (barring the production and use of chemical weapons), destroyed more than 3,600 unfilled chemical weapons bombs, and accepted U.S. help in devising a plan for destruction of about 23 tons of material for the production of mustard gas. In addition, Libya gave the United States access to its limited facilities to produce biological weapons and promised to eliminate all of its ballistic missiles with a range of 180 miles or more.

Other Developments Concerning Libya

One of the most important results from the ending of Libya's isolation from the United States and most other Western countries was the revival of the country's oil industry. Libya was believed to possess the world's ninth-largest reserves of oil, but production had lagged since the 1970s, when Qadaffi began nationalizing the oil industry. The American oil companies that had continued working in Libya were forced to withdraw in 1986, when President Reagan banned all U.S. trade with the country.

After the improvement in relations in late 2003, oil companies from the United States and Europe began negotiating contracts with Libya. Those negotiations resulted in contracts signed in July 2005 by Occidental Petroleum and in December 2005 by a consortium known as Oasis and consisting of Amerada Hess, Marathon, and ConocoPhillips. By dropping Libya from the list of terrorism-supporting countries, the Bush administration made it easier for these countries to ship to Libya high-tech equipment needed to boost oil production there.

Still pending at the end of 2006 was another high-profile controversy: Libya's prosecution of a Palestinian doctor and five Bulgarian nurses on charges that they had infected Libyan children with the HIV virus that causes AIDS. The medical personnel were imprisoned in 1999 after Qadaffi accused them of infecting the children under orders from the Central Intelligence Agency and Israel's intelligence agency, Mossad. Officials from the United States and many other countries had called on Libya to release the medical personnel, saying the charges against them were unfounded. A Libyan court convicted the defendants in 2004, but that conviction was overturned in 2005. After a retrial in 2006, the defendants once again were found guilty, and a court on December 19 ordered them to be shot by a firing squad. That decision brought another international demand for release of the medical personnel, which Qadaffi rejected on December 30, saying he opposed "Western intervention and pressure in this affair." The case was still pending at year's end, although some officials in Libya suggested the personnel could be freed if Bulgaria and Western countries provided funding for Libya's dilapidated health care system.

One other matter that had gotten Libya into trouble internationally was an allegation by Saudi Arabia that Libyan intelligence agents had fomented a plot in 2003 to assassinate then-Crown Prince Abdullah. After he became king of Saudi Arabia in August 2005, Abdullah pardoned the Libyans, and the two countries announced that they had resolved the controversy over the assassination plot.

Following is the text of a statement by Secretary of State Condoleezza Rice, on May 15, 2006, announcing that the United States was restoring full diplomatic relations with Libya and removing Libya from a list of nations that sponsored terrorism.

◾◾◾ DOCUMENT ◾◾◾

"U.S. Diplomatic Relations with Libya"

I am pleased to announce that the United States is restoring full diplomatic relations with Libya. We will soon open an embassy in Tripoli. In addition, the United States intends to remove Libya from the list of designated state sponsors of terrorism. Libya will also be omitted from the annual certification of countries not cooperating fully with United States anti-terrorism efforts.

We are taking these actions in recognition of Libya's continued commitment to its renunciation of terrorism and the excellent cooperation Libya has provided to the United States and other members of the international community in response to common global threats faced by the civilized world since September 11, 2001.

Today's announcements are tangible results that flow from the historic decisions taken by Libya's leadership in 2003 to renounce terrorism and to abandon its weapons of mass destruction programs. As a direct result of those decisions we have witnessed the beginning of that country's re-emergence into the mainstream of the international community. Today marks the opening of a new era in U.S.-Libya relations that will benefit Americans and Libyans alike.

Just as 2003 marked a turning point for the Libyan people so too could 2006 mark turning points for the peoples of Iran and North Korea. Libya is an important model as nations around the world press for changes in behavior by the Iranian and North Korean regimes – changes that could be vital to international peace and security. We urge the leadership of Iran and North Korea to make similar strategic decisions that would benefit their citizens.

For Libya, today's announcements open the door to a broader bilateral relationship with the United States that will allow us to better discuss other issues of importance. Those issues include protection of universal human rights, promotion of freedom of speech and expression, and expansion of economic and political reform consistent with President Bush's freedom agenda.

Source: U.S. Department of State. Secretary of State Condoleezza Rice. "U.S. Diplomatic Relations with Libya." May 15, 2006. www.state.gov/secretary/rm/2006/66235.htm (accessed January 9, 2006).

Other Historic Documents of Interest

Energy dependence, p. 139
Iranian president's comments to the
  United States, p. 212

North Korean nuclear weapons issue,
  p. 606
U.S. policy on Iraq, p. 725

President Bush on Proposed Overhaul of U.S. Immigration Law

May 15, 2006

■■■■■■ THE DOCUMENT IN CONTEXT ■■■■■■

Mirroring deep divisions within American society, Congress was unable to reach agreement on comprehensive immigration reform aimed at slowing the flood of undocumented workers into the country while allowing some illegals already here to work their way toward citizenship. House Republicans, who had initially approved legislation that would have made anyone in the United States without a valid visa a felon, refused to accept what many of them called an amnesty bill. Instead, they set aside the overhaul approved by the Senate and passed legislation calling for a 700-mile fence to be built along part of the U.S. border with Mexico. With polls showing that a solid majority of the population wanted the government to do more to keep out illegal immigrants, the Senate agreed to the measure, and the president signed it into law just two weeks before the midterm elections.

The House action was a slap in the face to President George W. Bush, who had championed broad immigration reform. It was the second year in a row that congressional Republicans had bucked the president on an issue he had described as a key legislative priority. In 2005 the president suffered a stunning defeat when lack of support from the public, united opposition among Democrats, and lack of enthusiasm among lawmakers in his own party forced him to shelve his plan to partially privatize Social Security. (Social Security, Historic Documents of 2005, p. 111)

The emotional debate played out across the country. Immigrants and their supporters took to the streets in many cities to push for broad reforms, and anti-immigrant groups took to the airwaves to advocate harsher border controls, including deportation even for those illegal immigrants who had lived in the country for years. The debate put Bush and his fellow Republicans in a tight political box during a critical election year. Some GOP lawmakers feared they would be penalized at the polls if they supported anything that might be called amnesty for illegal aliens, while others worried they might lose support among Republican business leaders and farm producers who relied on the immigrants as a source of cheap labor. Political strategists also warned that the failure to enact comprehensive immigration reform would undermine the party's efforts to attract Hispanic voters. At least in the short term, that warning appeared to be true; in the midterm elections, Democrats saw their percentage of the Latino vote increase 14 percent over 2004.

Background

Before the terrorist attacks of September 11, 2001, Bush and many members of Congress had supported efforts to make it easier for foreigners, especially citizens of Mexico, to work in the United States. After the attacks, in which nineteen terrorists from the Middle East exploited immigration laws to stay in the country, the political mood swung dramatically against immigration reform. Despite efforts to tighten border security, the number of illegal immigrants in the country continued to grow. The U.S. Census Bureau estimated that there were more than 7 million illegal immigrants in the United States as of the 2000 census; by 2005 the estimated number had swelled to as many as 12 million. The Pew Hispanic Center estimated in March 2006 that 56 percent of the illegals were Mexican; 22 percent came from other Latin American countries, mainly Central America; 13 percent from East Asia; and 6 percent from Europe and Canada. Most entered the country legally and became illegal when they overstayed their visas. But it was the image of illegal immigrants sneaking furtively across the border from Mexico—an image reinforced on the nightly news—that most Americans carried when they thought of illegal immigrants.

According to the Pew Hispanic Center, an estimated 7.5 million illegal immigrants held jobs, accounting for about 5 percent of the total American workforce. Conventional wisdom held that these undocumented workers took jobs that Americans were unwilling to do—as janitors and hotel housekeepers, dishwashers and short-order cooks, yard workers and nannies, construction laborers and agricultural workers. But some economists and anti-immigration groups contended that illegal workers took jobs away from low-skilled American workers because the illegals were willing to work for low wages and under often poor job conditions. Others complained that illegal immigrants were a burden on society, placing strains on housing, schools, the health care system, law enforcement, and welfare services. Still others, particularly in border states, were concerned about drugs being smuggled into the country and a rise in crime and gang activity that they associated with illegal immigrants. One outcome of that concern was the rise of the Minuteman Project, a band of private citizens who took it upon themselves to patrol some areas on the Mexican border. Governors in border states and in states with large immigrant populations also complained that their governments were having to pay for services that rightly should have been the responsibility of the federal government.

Public opinion polls showed that a majority of Americans thought illegal immigration was a serious problem and that the government was not doing enough to stop it. Americans were more divided about how to deal with undocumented workers already in the country. Hispanic advocacy groups, many religious organizations, and some business groups supported proposals allowing illegal immigrants to become legal residents and eventually citizens. Although they differed on the details, that broad approach was supported by the president, most Democrats, and some moderate Republicans. A bloc of Republicans in the House, led by Tom Tancredo of Colorado, however, viewed such proposals as a form of amnesty for people who broke the law by coming into or staying in the country illegally. Backed by conservative and anti-immigration groups, Tancredo introduced legislation in July 2005 that would make illegal immigration a felony and would subject employers who hired them to jail terms.

Under pressure to act while knowing they did not have support for broader reform, House Republican leaders decided to focus on beefing up border security and discouraging illegal immigrants. The centerpiece of the bill the House passed in December 2005 was a mandatory employee verification system and tamper-proof identification cards for all workers. The bill, which passed on a vote of 239–182, provided that anyone caught in the United States without a visa could be charged with a felony, and it punished anyone—including humanitarian workers, doctors, and clergy—found aiding illegal immigrants. It also called for the installation of 700 miles of fencing along the border with Mexico and took steps to enlist the aid of local police in arresting illegal immigrants.

2006 Legislative Action

In the Senate, Republicans were divided between those who supported the legislation passed in the House and those who were more receptive to business groups, religious leaders, and immigrant rights advocates who deplored the House bill and argued for a broader reform. Together with President Bush and most Democrats, these latter Republicans wanted to combine some of the less harsh border security aspects of the House measure with an economic plan that included legalizing millions of illegal immigrants and opening new channels for guest workers—immigrants who could stay and work only for limited periods before returning home again. After weeks of debate, the Senate Judiciary Committee reported out a bipartisan measure that its detractors immediately denounced as a "blanket amnesty bill" that "let the American people down," in the words of Sen. Jeff Sessions, R-Ala.

Fearing that there was enough Republican opposition to kill the committee bill, two Republican senators, Chuck Hagel of Nebraska and Mel Martinez of Florida, brokered a compromise that limited "earned citizenship" to illegal immigrants who could demonstrate that they had been in the country for at least two years. The compromise was heralded by both parties as a "huge breakthrough." But almost as soon as it was announced on April 6, a dispute over parliamentary procedures between the Republican and Democratic Senate leaders forced the Senate to postpone action.

During the next few weeks, pressure for action continued to mount outside Washington. Talk radio and television programs devoted hours to the issue, and mass demonstrations in favor of broad reforms were staged in several major cities around the country.

The debate also marked the first time that the Hispanic community in the United States rallied to demand better treatment for immigrants, both legal and illegal. Hispanics and their supporters took to the streets of several major cities in March and April to protest the restrictive legislation passed by the House. The protests reached their peak on May 1, when hundreds of thousands of immigrants, both legal and illegal, walked off their jobs, skipped school, and stayed away from stores to demonstrate their power within the American economy.

When Congress returned from its spring recess in April, President Bush summoned a bipartisan group of senators to the White House on April 25 to try to break the impasse. The president had maintained a low profile on the issue early in the year, but on May 15 he made a prime-time television address from the Oval Office that sought to bridge the differences between the two sides in the debate. Bush supported allowing illegal immigrants who had been in the country for several years to apply for citizenship after meeting certain conditions, such as paying back taxes. But he also announced that he would send up to 6,000 National Guard troops to help patrol the Mexican border for at least a year and take other steps to ensure that people trying to sneak into the country were turned back at the border. Bush said there was no contradiction between taking actions to make the border secure and allowing those already in the country to work toward citizenship. "America can be a lawful society and a welcoming society at the same time," he said. He also urged Americans to discuss the issue in a "reasoned and respectful tone," adding: "We cannot build a unified country by inciting people to anger, or playing on anyone's fears or exploiting the issue of immigration for political gain."

The next day, the Senate began considering a wide range of amendments to the compromise bill in the sort of old-fashioned, free-wheeling debate that rarely occurred in modern times. For the next several days prominent Republicans such as John McCain of Arizona joined Democrats to vote down any amendments that would have threatened the compromise legislation, and the measure was passed, 62–36, on May 25.

The vote was a victory for the president but it turned out to be his last on the issue for the year. Labeling the Senate bill "amnesty" and the work of Democrats, House Republicans refused to convene a conference between the two chambers to negotiate the differences. Instead during the traditional August recess, they held two dozen field hearings around the country aimed at promoting the need for greater border security and highlighting what they considered to be the dangers of granting citizenship to illegal immigrants. When Congress returned to Washington in September, the House passed a measure authorizing the construction of 700 miles of fencing along portions of the southwestern border with Mexico, as well as a "virtual fence" of cameras, sensors, unmanned aerial vehicles, and other surveillance technology along the entire U.S.-Mexico border. The Senate cleared the bill on September 29, just before Congress recessed to campaign for the November elections, and Bush signed it into law (PL 109–37) on October 29.

As the year ended, critics were questioning the likely effectiveness and cost of the border fence. Latin America leaders and their citizens viewed the fence as another sign that the United States was not the friendly neighbor it claimed to be. Environmentalists noted that extensive border fencing could have serious ecological consequences, particularly in the fragile desert lands where most of them would be built. Some critics said Congress was unlikely to appropriate the estimated $2 billion it would take to build the fence, while others said it was unlikely the fence would be completed by the 2008 deadline included in the measure. As evidence, they pointed to a fourteen-mile fence that separated San Diego from Tijuana across the Mexican border. Begun in the mid-1990s, construction of some sections of the fence was delayed for years by legal wrangles and still had not been finished by the end of 2006. Meanwhile, the cost, originally estimated at $14 million, was now expected to total $74 million.

Following is the text of a nationally televised address President George W. Bush made from the Oval Office of the White House on May 15, 2006, endorsing comprehensive immigration reform, including providing stronger controls at the border and offering a path to citizenship to millions of illegal immigrants already in the country.

■ DOCUMENT ■

"Address to the Nation on Immigration Reform"

Good evening. I've asked for a few minutes of your time to discuss a matter of national importance, the reform of America's immigration system.

The issue of immigration stirs intense emotions, and in recent weeks, Americans have seen those emotions on display. On the streets of major cities, crowds have rallied in support of those in our country illegally. At our southern border, others have organized to stop illegal immigrants from coming in. Across the country, Americans are trying to reconcile these contrasting images. And in Washington, the debate over immigration reform has reached a time of decision. Tonight I will make it clear where I stand and where I want to lead our country on this vital issue.

We must begin by recognizing the problems with our immigration system. For decades, the United States has not been in complete control of its borders. As a result, many who want to work in our economy have been able to sneak across our border, and millions have stayed.

Once here, illegal immigrants live in the shadows of our society.

Many use forged documents to get jobs, and that makes it difficult for employers to verify that the workers they hire are legal. Illegal immigration puts pressure on public schools and hospitals; it strains State and local budgets and brings crime to our communities. These are real problems. Yet we must remember that the vast majority of illegal immigrants are decent people who work hard, support their families, practice their faith, and lead responsible lives. They are a part of American life, but they are beyond the reach and protection of American law.

We're a nation of laws, and we must enforce our laws. We're also a nation of immigrants, and we must uphold that tradition, which has strengthened our country in so many ways. These are not contradictory goals. America can be a lawful society and a welcoming society at the same time. We will fix the problems created by illegal immigration, and we will deliver a system that is secure, orderly, and fair. So I support comprehensive immigration reform that will accomplish five clear objectives.

First, the United States must secure its borders. This is a basic responsibility of a sovereign nation. It is also an urgent requirement of our national security. Our objective is straightforward: The border should be open to trade and lawful immigration, and shut to illegal immigrants as well as criminals, drug dealers, and terrorists.

I was a Governor of a State that has a 1,200-mile border with Mexico. So I know how difficult it is to enforce the border and how important it is. Since I became President, we've increased funding for border security by 66 percent and expanded the Border Patrol from about 9,000 to 12,000 agents. The men and women of our Border Patrol are doing a fine job in difficult circumstances, and over the past 5 years, they have apprehended and sent home about 6 million people entering America illegally.

Despite this progress, we do not yet have full control of the border, and I am determined to change that. Tonight I'm calling on Congress to provide funding for dramatic improvements in manpower and technology at the border. By the end of 2008, we'll increase the number of Border Patrol officers by an additional 6,000. When these new agents are deployed, we'll have more than doubled the size of the Border Patrol during my Presidency.

At the same time, we're launching the most technologically advanced border security initiative in American history. We will construct high-tech fences in urban corridors and build new patrol roads and barriers in rural areas. We'll employ motion sensors, infrared cameras, and unmanned aerial vehicles to prevent illegal crossings. America has the best technology in the world, and we will ensure that the Border Patrol has the technology they need to do their job and secure our border.

Training thousands of new Border Patrol agents and bringing the most advanced technology to the border will take time. Yet the need to secure our border is urgent. So I'm announcing several immediate steps to strengthen border enforcement during this period of transition.

One way to help during this transition is to use the National Guard. So in coordination with Governors, up to 6,000 Guard members will be deployed to our southern border. The Border Patrol will remain in the lead. The Guard will assist the Border Patrol by operating surveillance systems, analyzing intelligence, installing fences and vehicle barriers, building patrol roads, and providing training. Guard units will not be involved in direct law enforcement activities; that duty will be done by the Border Patrol. This initial commitment of Guard members would last for a period of one year. After that, the number of Guard forces will be reduced as new Border Patrol agents and new technologies come on line. It is important for Americans to know that we have enough Guard forces to win the war on terror, to respond to natural disasters, and to help secure our border.

The United States is not going to militarize the southern border. Mexico is our neighbor and our friend. We will continue to work cooperatively to improve security on both sides of the border, to confront common problems like drug trafficking and crime, and to reduce illegal immigration.

Another way to help during this period of transition is through State and local law enforcement in our border communities. So we'll increase Federal funding for State and local authorities assisting the Border Patrol on targeted enforcement missions. We will give State and local authorities the specialized training they need to help Federal officers apprehend and detain illegal immigrants. State and local law enforcement officials are an important part of our border security, and they need to be a part of our strategy to secure our borders.

The steps I've outlined will improve our ability to catch people entering our country illegally. At the same time, we must ensure that every illegal immigrant we catch crossing our southern border is returned home. More than 85 percent of the illegal immigrants we catch crossing the southern border are Mexicans, and most are sent back home within 24 hours. But when we catch illegal immigrants from another country, it is not as easy to send them back home. For many years, the Government did not have enough space in our detention facilities to hold them while the legal process unfolded. So most were released back into our society and asked to return for a court date. When the date arrived, the vast majority did not show up. This practice, called catch-and-release, is unacceptable, and we will end it.

We're taking several important steps to meet this goal. We've expanded the number of beds in our detention facilities, and we will continue to add more. We've expedited the legal process to cut the average deportation time. And we're making it clear to foreign governments that they must accept back their citizens who violate our immigration laws. As a result of these actions, we've ended catch-and-release for illegal immigrants from some countries. And I will ask Congress for additional funding and legal authority so we can end catch-and-release at the southern border once and for all. When people know that they'll be caught and sent home if they enter our country illegally, they will be less likely to try to sneak in.

Second, to secure our border, we must create a temporary-worker program. The reality is that there are many people on the other side of our border who will do anything to come to America to work and build a better life. They walk across miles of desert in the summer heat or hide in the back of 18-wheelers to reach our country. This creates enormous pressure on our border that walls and patrols alone will not stop. To secure the border effectively, we must reduce the numbers of people trying to sneak across.

Therefore, I support a temporary-worker program that would create a legal path for foreign workers to enter our country in an orderly way for a limited period of time. This program would match willing foreign workers with willing American employers for jobs Americans are not doing. Every worker who applies for the program would be required to pass criminal background checks. And temporary workers must return to their home country at the conclusion of their stay.

A temporary-worker program would meet the needs of our economy, and it would give honest immigrants a way to provide for their families while respecting the law. A temporary-worker program would reduce the appeal of human smugglers and make it less likely that people would risk their lives to cross the border. It would ease the financial burden on State and local governments by replacing illegal workers with lawful taxpayers. And above all, a temporary-worker program would add to our security by making certain we know who is in our country and why they are here.

Third, we need to hold employers to account for the workers they hire. It is against the law to hire someone who is in this country illegally. Yet businesses often cannot verify the legal status of their employees because of the widespread problem of document fraud. Therefore, comprehensive immigration reform must include a better system for verifying documents and work eligibility. A key part of that system should be a new identification card for every legal foreign worker. This card should use biometric technology, such as digital fingerprints, to make it tamper-proof. A tamper-proof card would help us enforce the law and leave employers with no excuse for violating it. And by making it harder for illegal immigrants to find work in our country, we would discourage people from crossing the border illegally in the first place.

Fourth, we must face the reality that millions of illegal immigrants are here already. They should not be given an automatic path to citizenship. This is amnesty, and I oppose it. Amnesty would be unfair to those who are here lawfully, and it would invite further waves of illegal immigration.

Some in this country argue that the solution is to deport every illegal immigrant, and that any proposal short of this amounts to amnesty. I disagree. It is neither wise nor realistic to round up millions of people, many with deep roots in the United States, and send them across the border. There is a rational middle ground between granting an automatic path to citizenship for every illegal immigrant and a program of mass deportation. That middle ground recognizes there are differences between an illegal immigrant who crossed the border recently and someone who has worked here for many years and has a home, a family, and an otherwise clean record.

I believe that illegal immigrants who have roots in our country and want to stay should have to pay a meaningful penalty for breaking the law: to pay their taxes; to learn English; and to work in a job for a number of years. People who meet these conditions should be able to apply for citizenship, but approval would not be automatic, and they will have to wait in line behind those who played by the rules and followed the law. What I've just described is not amnesty; it is a way for those who have broken the law to pay their debt to society and demonstrate the character that makes a good citizen.

Fifth, we must honor the great American tradition of the melting pot, which has made us one Nation out of many peoples. The success of our country depends upon helping newcomers assimilate into our society and embrace our common identity as Americans. Americans are bound together by our shared ideals: an appreciation of our history; respect for the flag we fly; and an ability to speak and write the English language. English is also the key to unlocking the opportunity of America. English allows newcomers to go from picking crops to opening a grocery; from cleaning offices to running offices; from a life of low-paying jobs to a diploma, a career, and a home of their own. When immigrants assimilate and advance in our society, they realize their dreams; they renew our spirit; and they add to the unity of America.

Tonight I want to speak directly to Members of the House and the Senate: An immigration reform bill needs to be comprehensive, because all elements of this problem must be addressed together, or none of them will be solved at all. The House has passed an immigration bill. The Senate should act by the end of this month so we can work out the differences between the two bills, and Congress can pass a comprehensive bill for me to sign into law.

America needs to conduct this debate on immigration in a reasoned and respectful tone. Feelings run deep on this issue, and as we work it out, all of us need to keep some things in mind. We cannot build a unified country by inciting people to anger or playing on anyone's fears or exploiting the issue of immigration for political gain. We must always remember that real lives will be affected by our debates and decisions, and that every human being has dignity and value, no matter what their citizenship papers say.

I know many of you listening tonight have a parent or a grandparent who came here from another country with dreams of a better life. You know what freedom meant to them, and you know that America is a more hopeful country because of their hard work and sacrifice. As President, I've had the opportunity to meet people of many backgrounds and hear what America means to them. On a visit to Bethesda Naval Hospital, Laura and I met a wounded marine named Guadalupe Denogean. Master Gunnery Sergeant Denogean came to the United States from Mexico when he was a boy. He spent his summers picking crops with his family, and then he volunteered for the United States Marine Corps as soon as he was able. During the liberation of Iraq, Master Gunnery Sergeant Denogean was seriously injured. And when asked if he had any requests, he made two: a promotion for the corporal who helped rescue him and the chance to become an American citizen. And when this brave marine raised his right hand and swore an oath to become a citizen of the country he had defended for more than 26 years, I was honored to stand at his side.

We will always be proud to welcome people like Guadalupe Denogean as fellow Americans. Our new immigrants are just what they've always been—people willing to risk everything for the dream of freedom. And America remains what she has always been—the great hope on the horizon, an open door to the future, a blessed and promised land. We honor the heritage of all who come here, no matter where they come from, because we trust in our country's genius for making us all Americans—one Nation under God.

Thank you, and good night.

Source: U.S. Executive Office of the President. "Address to the Nation on Immigration Reform." May 15, 2006. *Weekly Compilation of Presidential Documents* 42, no. 20 (May 22, 2006): 931–934. Washington, D.C.: National Archives and Records Administration. www.gpoaccess.gov/wcomp/v42no20.html (accessed February 11, 2007).

Other Historic Documents of Interest

Statements after the Convictions of Former Enron Chief Executives

May 25, 2006

■■■■■■■ **THE DOCUMENT IN CONTEXT** ■■■■■■■

An era of extraordinary corporate greed and malfeasance came to a symbolic end in May 2006 with the conviction on criminal charges of the two men who led Enron Corporation, the energy company that grew to enormous size on a foundation of deceit and collapsed at the end of 2001. Kenneth L. Lay, the company's founder, and Jeffrey K. Skilling, its one-time chief executive, were convicted on May 25 on multiple charges of fraud and conspiracy. Lay died of a heart attack less than six weeks later, and his conviction was later set aside under standard federal court rules. Skilling continued to protest his innocence as he entered federal prison in December.

The collapse of Enron's house of cards in December 2001 was perhaps the defining moment in an era of high profits, surging stock prices, and astronomical pay for senior executives—in some cases also of crass manipulation or even violation of standard business rules to keep the dollars flowing. In terms of its estimated value, much of which turned out to be false, Enron was the biggest of a series of companies that lied to investors and the public, then faced bankruptcy and criminal or civil charges against the responsible executives. Adelphia Communications, Fannie Mae, HealthSouth, and WorldCom were some of the other companies where top executives arrogantly skirted or violated the rules in a mad rush for quick money.

Lay and Skilling were among the most important executives convicted of criminal charges, but they were far from the best known. That distinction was held by Martha Stewart, who built a media empire by providing advice to homemakers. She was convicted in 2004 of charges related to insider trading and spent five months in prison. Among the several dozen other senior executives who were sentenced to prison in the early years of the twenty-first century were John Rigas, the founder the cable television company Adelphia, and Bernie Ebbers, the founder of WorldCom, a telecommunications firm. The scandals also tainted entire industries: the investment banking industry in 2002, the mutual fund industry in 2003, and the insurance industry in 2004. *(Corporate scandal background, Historic Documents of 2004, p. 415)*

Lay, Skilling Convictions

Enron declared bankruptcy in December 2001 after its stock value plummeted. Thousands of employees were let go, and the company ultimately was broken into pieces, some of which were sold to other companies while others simply disappeared. Subsequent investigations showed, and the trials of Lay, Skilling, and other executives proved, that much of Enron's business value was a sham. Officials got the company into supposedly profitable ventures, but the profits were illusory; to keep up appearances, and shore up stock prices, the company engaged in a wide variety of creative accounting schemes, some of which were highly unusual and others of which, the courts found, broke the law. The most creative, and deceptive, of these schemes were off-the-books partnerships that were set up to inflate earnings and/or hide debt.

The Justice Department in 2002 established a special task force of prosecutors to dig into the Enron mess. By early 2006 prosecutors had secured sixteen guilty pleas, including one from the former chief financial officer, Andrew S. Fastow, and one from its chief accountant, Richard A. Causey. The task force had a more mixed record on cases that went to a jury, however. The trial of two executives from Enron's broadband Internet unit at first ended in a hung jury; on retrial the verdict was one conviction and one acquittal. Another case resulted in the conviction of five Enron and Merrill Lynch & Co. officials, but the convictions of the Merrill Lynch executives were overturned in August 2006 by an appellate court.

The government's chief targets were Skilling, who was indicted in February 2004, and Lay, who was indicted on July 8, 2004. Lay had been Enron's public face, a man who moved easily in the social circles of Houston, the company's headquarters city, and counted the family of President George W. Bush among his friends. Lay stuck with Enron until the end, and he lost nearly all his personal fortune in the process. Skilling bailed out in August 2001, just before Enron's final descent. In advance of the trial, Lay went on an unusual public relations offensive, accusing prosecutors of engaging in a "wave of terror" to intimidate former employees to testify against him.

The jury trial in Houston began on January 30 and attracted enormous news media coverage. In the opening weeks, much of the testimony was from former Enron executives who described complex—and in some cases nearly impenetrable—maneuverings the company had undertaken to maintain the appearance of profitability. For example, Kenneth D. Rice, a close friend of Skilling's who headed Enron's Internet broadband business from mid-1999 to mid-2000, testified on February 14 that the business collapsed after the implosion of the high-tech industry early in 2000. With virtually no customers or revenue, but operating expenses of $100 million each quarter, Enron's broadband business resorted to gimmicks such as the off-the-books partnerships managed by Fastow to create the appearance that cash was coming in the door.

Many of the witnesses directly tied Lay and Skilling to the questionable or illegal activities that caused Enron's downfall. The star witness in this respect was Fastow, who testified under the terms of his own guilty plea. He said both Lay and Skilling were aware of, and approved, the deceptive transactions, notably the partnerships with such names as LJM1, RADR, and Chewco. Fastow testified that he used the LJM1 partnership to "buy" a Brazilian power plant from Enron for $20 million. The sole purpose of the transaction, which Fastow said Skilling requested, was to allow Enron to report $20 million in earnings, even though the money came from a sale of assets, not from operating revenue and therefore should not have been reported as earnings. Fastow also testified that Lay was aware in August 2001 that Enron was teetering on the brink of insolvency—even as Lay was continuing to assure investors and employees that the company was in solid shape.

For many observers, the highlights of the trial were the days of testimony by the defendants. Skilling took the stand on April 10. Guided by defense lawyer Daniel M. Petrocelli, Skilling explained the complexities of Enron's many businesses and insisted that none of the financial schemes described by previous witnesses—his former colleagues—had been illegal or even particularly wrong. Skilling spent eight days on the witness stand, much of the time facing withering cross-examination from chief prosecutor Sean M. Berkowitz, who scorned Skilling's contention that he did not participate in any illegal maneuvers to inflate Enron's earnings or hide losses.

Lay took the stand on April 24 and immediately launched into a spirited defense of his own actions and cast all the blame for Enron's collapse on "the deceit of Andy Fastow and probably not more than one or two other people." On April 27, prosecutor John C. Hueston apparently surprised Lay with the news that Lay's son Mark, who handled the family investments, engaged in the short-selling of Enron stock—the very practice Lay had blamed for the company's collapse. Short-selling involved taking a position in a stock on the bet that its price would fall, then earning a profit when that happened.

The Enron case went to the jurors on May 17 after fifteen weeks of testimony from fifty-six witnesses. The jury deliberated for more than five days and on May 25 returned guilty verdicts against Lay and Skilling. The jury found Lay guilty of all six counts against him: one count of conspiracy, two counts of wire fraud, and three counts of securities fraud. Judge Simeon T. Lake also found Lay guilty of one count of bank fraud and three counts of making false statements to banks; these charges had been tried concurrently with the jury trial. Skilling was convicted on nineteen counts, including twelve counts of securities fraud, one count of insider trading, one count of conspiracy, and five counts of making false statements to auditors. He was acquitted of nine counts of insider trading. Judge Lake required Lay to hand over his passport and post a $5 million bond pending sentencing, scheduled for the fall.

In brief news conferences after the verdicts were read, Lay and Skilling both reiterated their innocence. Asked by a reporter if he was willing to admit to himself that he had committed crimes, Skilling flatly said, "No." Petrocelli, his lawyer, promised a "full and vigorous" appeal. Lay said the verdicts surprised him and added, "I firmly believe I'm innocent of the charges against me, as I have said from day one." Chief prosecutor Berkowitz said the verdict sent a message to corporate executives: "You can't lie to shareholders. You can't put yourself in front of your employees' interests. No matter how rich and powerful you are, you have to play by the rules." In comments to reporters, members of the jury said they simply could not believe the statements by Lay and Skilling that they were unaware of Enron's financial problems until it was too late. Jurors also said they felt sorry for the thousands of Enron employees who lost their jobs when the company folded—employees who, the jurors said, were let down by the men at the top.

Lay died of a heart attack on July 5 while on vacation in Aspen, Colorado. He was sixty-four. Under standard federal court rules, his conviction was set aside, but the government on October 25 sued Lay's estate to retrieve at least $12 million. On October 23, Judge Lake sentenced Skilling to a total of more than twenty-four years in prison and ordered him to forfeit $45 million, effectively eliminating his personal assets; that money was to be turned over to investors and former employees. "His crimes have imposed on hundreds, if not thousands of victims a life sentence of poverty," Lake said at the sentencing hearing. When Lake asked Skilling if he had any remorse, Skilling responded: "In terms of remorse, your honor, I can't imagine more remorse. That being said, your honor, I am innocent of these charges. I am innocent of every one of these charges." Despite his continued protestations of innocence, Skilling began serving his prison term on December 13, when he entered a low-security prison in Waseca, Minnesota. A judge had denied his request to remain free on bond pending his appeal.

Moves to Roll Back Reforms

In addition to legal actions against corporate executives, the federal government reacted to the scandals at Enron and other companies by enacting new regulations
and laws. Some of these changes tightened accounting standards, while others imposed new obligations on companies—and their executives—to be truthful in their
financial statements to investors. By far the most important of the regulatory changes
were those enacted by Congress in July 2002 in landmark legislation known as the
Sarbanes-Oxley Act. Among other things, this law required corporate executives to
certify in writing that quarterly financial statements were accurate. *(Background, Historic Documents of 2002, p. 1033)*

Many business leaders accepted these new regulations as a necessary price for
restoring public confidence in the wake of the scandals. By 2006, however, the U.S.
Chamber of Commerce and other business groups lobbied Congress, the Securities
and Exchange Commission (SEC), and other agencies to ease some of the restrictions,
which they said were costly and made it difficult for American businesses to compete
with foreign companies. These attempts to amend the text of the Sarbanes-Oxley Act
were unsuccessful, as of the end of 2006, but business groups succeeded in getting
the government to ease some rules. On December 13, for example, the SEC proposed
loosening some of the restrictions it had imposed under Sarbanes-Oxley on small-to-
medium size businesses (those with market values of $75 million to $700 million). The
new rules would reduce requirements for testing internal financial controls and providing documentation to the SEC. Some investor groups complained that the changes
would reopen loopholes, but SEC officials insisted investors would still be protected.

Other Business Scandals

The Enron case was the biggest of the corporate scandals that had rocked Wall Street,
the business community, and the nation at large in the early years of the twenty-first
century—but it was far from the only one. Some of the other cases still working their
way through the courts and regulatory system in 2006 were:

- **American International Group:** On February 9, AIG reached a $1.64 billion settlement with
  federal and New York state insurance and securities regulators. One of the world's largest
  insurance providers, AIG acknowledged in the settlement that it had deceived investors
  and regulators, in some cases for as long as two decades. The company was founded by
  the hard-charging Maurice R. Greenberg, who was ousted as chief executive by the board
  of directors in March 2005 as the result of a lawsuit by the equally hard-charging New York
  attorney general Eliot Spitzer. The company agreed to put $1.4 billion into three funds to
  benefit investors, former customers, and states that had been cheated by its deceptions.
  The settlement also imposed $200 million in fines and penalties, with the proceeds to be
  shared by the federal and New York governments.
- **Fannie Mae:** An investigation of business practices at Fannie Mae, the country's biggest
  buyer of home mortgages, resulted in a report, made public on February 23, that cited
  numerous cases in which the company violated standard accounting and business practices simply to show stable or rising earnings. The report cited an "attitude of arrogance"
  by the company's former leaders, who had been ousted as the result of earlier findings of
  irregularities. Former New Hampshire Republican senator Warren Rudman headed a team
  of investigators and lawyers who prepared the report. Fannie Mae agreed on May 23 to pay
  the federal government $400 million in fines because of its business practices. The Office
  of Federal Housing Enterprise Oversight said the company's former senior managers had
  "manipulated accounting, reaped maximum, undeserved bonuses, and prevented the rest
  of the world from knowing." Fannie Mae on December 6 eliminated $6.3 billion in "profit"

from its past earning reports for the years 2001 through the first half of 2004. Finally, on December 18 Fannie Mae's regulator filed 101 civil charges against the company's three former top executives, including former chief executive officer Franklin D. Raines.

- **Adelphia Communications:** One son the company's founder, John Rigas, was sentenced on March 3 to ten months of home confinement after he pleaded guilty to a technical bookkeeping error. The federal judge in the case said Michael Rigas was "close to being a pawn" for his father and brother Timothy, who ran the ran the company into bankruptcy. John and Timothy Rigas were both sentenced to prison terms (fifteen and twenty years, respectively) after they wee convicted in 2005 of misusing company funds. At the end of 2006, both were free pending appeal.

- **Frank P. Quattrone:** A Wall Street banker who had come to symbolize the excesses of the "dot com" boom of the late 1990s, Quattrone escaped a prison term in 2006 when a federal appeals court threw out his conviction on an obstruction of justice charge. As a banker with Credit Suisse First Boston, Quattrone had fashioned the initial public offerings of several Internet start-up firms, including Amazon.com, and had been widely criticized for his excessive claims about these firms. After an investigation, the government charged him with obstructing justice because he had approved a colleague's e-mail message telling employees to "clean up" files before government investigators arrived. The first trial of Quattrone ended in a mistrial in 2004; Quattrone was convicted by a jury in a second trial in 2005. On March 20, a three-judge panel of the U.S. Court of Appeals for the Second Circuit threw out the conviction because of flawed instructions by the trial judge and prejudicial comments by the prosecutors. On August 22, Quattrone and the Justice Department reached a settlement under which the charge would be dropped in one year if Quattrone stayed out of trouble.

- **Computer Associates:** Two top executives of Computer Associates, a high-flying software firm, pleaded guilty on April 24 to charges of fraud and obstruction of justice in U.S. district court in Brooklyn. Sanjay Kumar, the company's former chief executive, and Stephen Richards, the former top salesman, each pleaded guilty to nine counts of securities fraud and obstruction of justice. The government said the charges grew out of a scheme by the two men, along with other former executives, to inflate the company's profits, and thus its share price. Kumar on November 2 was sentenced to twelve years in prison.

Following are excerpts from statements by lead prosecutors Sean M. Berkowitz and John C. Hueston and former Enron Corporation executives Jeffrey K. Skilling and Kenneth L. Lay at news conferences after Skilling and Lay were convicted on May 25, 2006, on multiple charges of fraud and conspiracy.

DOCUMENT

"Enron Task Force Holds News Conference Following Trial Verdict"

Sean M. Berkowitz, Enron Task Force: You can't lie to shareholders. You can't put yourself in front of your employees' interests. No matter how rich and powerful you are, you have to play by the rules.

I want to say a few words about the victims in this case, those who lost their security and their retirement. Nothing that happened today is going to bring that back for them. They're not going to get their retirement money or their security back. What we do hope is that today's verdict lets them know the government will not let corporate leaders violate their trust and get way with it.

Many victims have personally come up to all of us throughout the trial and thanked us. They don't need to do that. We're doing our job and we're proud to do our job.

I'm proud of everybody on this team, and we'll introduce all of the lawyers—Mr. Hueston, Ms. Ruemmler, Mr. Wilton (ph), Mr. Wise, Mr. Stricklin, Mr. Atkins (ph), and Mr. Stolber (ph), who can't be with us.

The FBI has conducted a five-year investigation that has ended with today's verdict. And no matter how complicated or sophisticated the fraud that you might think of perpetrating, know that people like this stand ready to investigate and to try the cases as necessary.

To those who would think in the future of fraudulently misrepresenting your company to the public, know that people like this are ready. People like this are ready, and you will be held accountable for your actions.

I want to thank you. And I want to turn it over to Mr. Hueston, who wants to say a few words.

John C. Hueston, Enron Task Force: In the last few months of 2001, Ken Lay had a chance to prevent the outcome that happened. To prevent an outcome that threw thousands of employees out of work, to prevent the loss of retirement funds, of pension plans, of billions of dollars of investors' monies. He had a golden opportunity to save Enron, but he made a fateful choice in late 2001, and he made that choice to put his own interests ahead of that of his shareholders and investors.

And he did that by choosing not tell the unvarnished truth, and he did it by choosing not ask the hard questions. Not to ask the easy questions, when they were put in his own hands to ask, choosing time and time again to put himself in front of the investors, causing a collapse that has devastated America.

This jury has spoken. CEOs cannot hide behind accountants, they can't hide behind lawyers, they can't hide behind claims of ignorance. That's especially when they've been paid tens of millions of dollar to be the faithful stewards of shareholders and investors.

This jury has spoken and they have brought justice. We are proud to be a part of that justice. . . .

Source: CQ.com. CQ Transcriptions. "Enron Task Force Holds News Conference Following Enron Trial Verdict." May 25, 2006 (accessed March 12, 2007). This document was not available on the Internet.

■ DOCUMENT ■

"Enron CEO Skilling Holds News Conference Following Trial Verdict"

Daniel Petrocelli, attorney for Jeffrey Skilling: On behalf of Mr. Skilling, I would like to thank everyone. This is a difficult process for everyone. And everyone's treated us with utmost courtesy and respect and cooperation.

We had a trial. It obviously did not come out the way we had hoped. It doesn't change our view of what happened at Enron, and it certainly doesn't change our view of Jeff Skilling's innocence.

The jury saw it differently. That was their right. And we will take it from here and continue to fight the good fight.

This is obviously a very, very difficult time for Mr. Skilling, his children, his family. There's a lot of thinking to do about the next steps that we take. But we're going to stand behind him. As I told him, we have just begin the fight.

So again, thank you, all. If you have any questions, I'll be happy to try to answer them, but I want to be brief.

Question: Jeff, do you think you can ever—do you think you will ever be able to admit to yourself that you may have committed crimes?

Jeffrey Skilling, former Enron CEO: No.

Question: Why not?

Skilling: Because I didn't. But I would just like to thank my—first of all, I would like to thank Dan for all his support and everything that he made happen. I would like to thank my family for sticking by me, particularly my kids, Kristen (ph), Jeffrey, and J.T. (ph). They're just great.

And I think we fought—we fought a good fight. And some things work, some things don't. So—but thank you, guys, because you really have been very polite, very pleasant. And I appreciate it.

Question: What plans do you have?

Petrocelli: We're going to sit down and take a look at everything. And I know there are a number of issues that we litigated hard and lost before the trial, and even during the trial. It's too early for me to try to comment on that, but we will have a full—we will have a full and vigorous appeal.

Question: Did you expect the jury to come back this rapidly? I mean, this was five days. I mean, you know, I realize you can't guess on that, but....

Petrocelli: You can never tell. Yesterday we got a note that they wanted exhibit lists, and we all speculated they were going to be in there a bit longer. So we were a little surprised today, but they gave it five full days, and they saw it their way.

Question: You had said that you wanted to fight—you would fight with every ounce of your body, everything—something along those lines earlier. Do you still feel that way? And If you do, will you tell us about it?

Skilling: I still feel that way. Absolutely feel that way.

Question: Can you expand on that a little bit?

Skilling: Not much to expand on. We're going to have to go back and I guess think this thing through. But, obviously, I'm disappointed. But, you know, that's the way the system works. . . .

Source: CQ.com. CQ Transcriptions. "Former Enron CEO Skilling Holds News Conference Following Announcement of Enron Trial Verdict." May 25, 2006 (accessed March12, 2007). This document was not available on the Internet.

DOCUMENT

"Enron CEO Lay Holds Media Availability Following Trial Verdict"

Kenneth Lay, former Enron CEO: Certainly, we're surprised. I think, probably more appropriately to say: We're shocked. Certainly, this was not the outcome we expected.

I firmly believe I'm innocent of the charges against me, as I have said from day one. I still firmly believe that as of this day.

But despite what happened today, I am still a very blessed man. I have on my left this beautiful lady that's my wife. I have a very warm and loving and Christian family that supports me, a lot of friends, including some out there in the audience right now.

And most of all, we believe that God in fact is in control. And indeed, he does work all things for good for those who love the Lord. And we love our Lord and ultimately, all of these things will work for good.

Thank you so much for all of your courtesies, all of your interest. And obviously, as time goes on, we'll have more things to say, but that's all I want to say today. Thank you.

Source: CQ.com. CQ Transcriptions. "Former Enron CEO Ken Lay Holds Media Availability Following Announcement of Verdict in Enron Case." May 25, 2006 (accessed March 8, 2007). This document was not available on the Internet.

June

International Diplomats on the Peace Process in Sri Lanka

June 1 and November 21, 2006

A cease-fire that in 2002 had appeared to herald the end of Sri Lanka's bloody civil war collapsed in all but name during 2006. The government and rebels on the island nation resumed the campaign of assassinations, bombings, kidnappings, large-scale sweeps of civilian areas, and even battles at sea that had killed an estimated 64,000 people between 1983 and the cease-fire in 2002.

United Nations officials said another 3,000 people died during renewed violence in 2006. Moreover, the fighting displaced an estimated 200,000 people from their homes and severely damaged Sri Lanka's economy, which was still struggling to recover from the death and destruction caused by the Indian Ocean tsunami of December 2004.

After the year's first upsurge of violence in April and early May, the head of the Sri Lanka Monitoring Mission, an international peace-monitoring operation, acknowledged that Sri Lanka was slipping back into war. "We don't have a peace agreement, we have a cease-fire agreement," Ulf Henricsson of Norway told the Reuters news service on May 13. "So, there is a war ongoing. It is a low intensity war." Later in the year, the intensity of the war increased dramatically.

On one side of Sri Lanka's war was the government, which was dominated by representatives of the island's majority population of about 15 million ethnic Sinhalese, most of whom were Buddhists. Battling for independence in the north and east of the island was a guerrilla group called the Liberation Tigers of Tamil Eelam (or LTTE, but most widely known as the Tamil Tigers). This group claimed to represent Sri Lanka's 3 million or more ethnic Tamils, most of whom were Hindi. Another 1.4 million Sri Lankans were Muslims, most of whom spoke Tamil and lived in the eastern section of the country.

The Tamil Tigers launched their war of independence in 1983 and gained control over a large section of the Tamil homeland, partly through sophisticated guerrilla tactics but also through the extensive use of suicide bombs, a terror attack the group developed and that later was adopted by Islamist groups in the Middle East. By late 2001 the war between the government and the Tamil Tigers was in stalemate. Diplomatic mediation by Norway produced a short-term cease-fire in December 2001 that was extended into a "permanent" cease-fire the following February. *(Background, Historic Documents of 2002, p. 92)*

Slow Collapse of the Peace Process

Despite continued mediation by Norwegian diplomats, the opposing sides in Sri Lanka failed after 2002 to take the required steps to transform the cease-fire into a permanent political settlement of their underlying differences. The two sides agreed in December 2002 to the general features of a settlement under which Sri Lanka would be transformed into a federal system that would give the Tamils the right of "internal self-determination" in their home areas. That agreement was never put into final form, however, and in April 2003 the Tamil Tigers withdrew from peace talks, saying the government was attempting to "marginalize" them.

Ironically, another hope for peace emerged from one of the world's worst natural disasters in modern times: the December 2004 earthquake-induced tsunami that swept over much of the Indian Ocean region, killing hundreds of thousands of people, including more than 30,000 in Sri Lanka. *(Tsunami background, Historic Documents of 2004, p. 990; Historic Documents of 2005, p. 991)*

Following the disaster the Sri Lankan government and the Tamil Tigers engaged in a remarkable degree of cooperation to meet the needs of survivors, and in June 2005 the two sides reached agreement on sharing about $3 billion in international relief aid among the country's ethnic groups. A key Sinhalese nationalist group pulled out of the government coalition in opposition to that agreement, however, and in August 2005 the country's foreign minister, Lakshman Kadirgamar, was assassinated. These acts increased tensions that contributed to a rise in violence later in 2005 and all through 2006.

Although it was a relatively small island (about the size of West Virginia) with only 20 million people, Sri Lanka was one of the most complex societies in South Asia, in terms of both ethnic makeup and politics. Some critics said the peace process of 2002 did not take these complexities into full account, for example by failing to address the concerns of the large Muslim minority.

In the years after 2002 it also became clear that not all representatives of the Sinhalese majority were committed to reaching an accommodation with the Tamils. The cease-fire was negotiated by then-prime minister Ranil Wickremesinghe, of the United National Front Party. However, there was no direct backing for the peace talks from the president at the time, Chandrika Kumaratunga, who had been wounded in an attempted assassination by the Tamil Tigers. When Wickremesinghe in 2004 offered peace proposals that she opposed, President Kumaratunga intervened and called new elections, which ousted Wickremesinghe's party from office and led to a new government less committed to the peace process. A Tamil boycott of subsequent elections in 2005 helped defeat Wickremesinghe's bid for the presidency and reinforced the position of hard-line Sinhalese political and military leaders.

Another development contributing to the collapse of the peace process was a split in the rebel movement. In 2004 a Tamil Tiger commander in the eastern region, Vinayagamoorthy Muralitharan (better known as Colonel Karuna), broke off from the LTTE. Two years later, Karuna's group appeared to be acting as an ally of the government, further complicating any attempt to end the war.

A New Surge of Fighting

The cease-fire collapsed as the result of several waves of violence from late 2005 through late 2006. The first was a surge of bombings and other attacks in December 2005 and January 2006, including the assassination of a noted pro-Tamil Tiger politician. Three events in April 2006 led to another round of violence. On April 7 a Tamil political leader was assassinated in Trincomalee, a multiethnic port city in the eastern part of the country. Five days later, an LTTE bombing in that city killed five people, and subsequent rioting fomented by local Sinhalese killed nearly twenty more. Then, on April 25, a female suicide bomber from the LTTE attacked the main army compound in Colombo, killing eleven people and seriously wounding hard-line army commander Gen. Sarath Fonseca. In response to this apparent attempt to kill Fonseca, the army launched air attacks against LTTE military positions, and on May 11 government forces and the rebels engaged in a large-scale naval battle off the northern Jaffna Peninsula.

Violence broke out again in August after the Tamil Tigers shut off an irrigation canal that provided water to Sinhalese farmers in the northeast. Several hundred people were killed in subsequent fighting between the army and the guerrillas. Tens of thousands fled their homes, in what the Scandinavian peace monitors called the worst fighting since the 2002 cease-fire. In the midst of this fighting, seventeen local workers for the French aid agency, Action contre le Faim (Action against Hunger) were murdered; each side blamed the other, but Swedish peace monitors said government forces were responsible. Also in August the guerrillas opened another front by attacking government forces on the northern Jaffna Peninsula. This fighting closed the main road in that Tamil-dominated area, creating a humanitarian crisis by blocking deliveries of food and other urgent supplies. Attacks and counterattacks by the two sides continued throughout the rest of the year, notably an army offensive on the Jaffna Peninsula in mid-October that killed more than 130 people and a LTTE suicide bombing of a naval installation on October 16 that killed more than 100 people. These attacks in October appeared to be aimed at influencing, and possibly side-tracking, peace talks in Geneva scheduled for later in the month.

In most of these attacks, civilians suffered the most and made up the large majority of the year's estimated 3,000 casualties. The Scandinavian peace monitors and other outside observers said both the government and the rebels commited grave human rights abuses with their large-scale attacks. One of many examples was the army's November 8 bombing of a camp for displaced people in the eastern region of Batticaloa, killing 47 people and wounding more than 100 others. Moreover, even during the height of the peace process the Tamil Tigers never abandoned their practice of forcibly recruiting teenage soldiers, some as young as twelve. The United Nations and international human rights groups long had condemned the LTTE for this practice and other serious human rights violations, but the guerrillas appeared to ignore such criticisms. Late in the year a UN human rights envoy and the U.S.-based group Human Rights Watch also accused the government of abducting children and turning them over to the dissident Karuna rebel group.

An international effort to cut off fundraising had a more serious impact on the guerrillas, who received much of their financial support from the several hundred thousand Tamil exiles elsewhere in Asia and in Europe and the United States. According to most estimates, the LTTE raised millions of dollars for its guerrilla campaign from the Tamil diaspora. Much of that support was cut off when Britain and the United States, followed by the European Union (EU), designated the LTTE as a "terrorist" organization.

Attempts to Restart Peace Talks

Norwegian mediators sponsored three rounds of peace talks between the government and the LTTE rebels during 2006, none of which produced any substantive agreement.

Pressure on both sides also came from other international actors, including the United States and other countries that had donated money to Sri Lanka in response to the 2004 tsunami.

Talks in Geneva on February 22–23 were the first between the government and the Tamil Tigers in nearly three years, but they failed to make any headway. Hoping to put pressure on both sides in advance of another round of peace talks scheduled to take place in Oslo, the U.S. government sent its chief diplomat for South Asia, Assistant Secretary of State Richard A. Boucher, to Sri Lanka in early June. In a speech on June 1 to the American Chamber of Commerce in Colombo, Boucher placed most of the blame for the recent upsurge of violence on the Tamil Tigers but also called on the government to follow through on its pledges to respect human rights and to set out a "vision" of how a lasting peace could be achieved.

Boucher's visit and other diplomatic efforts bore little fruit, however. Representatives from both sides spent the first week in June in Oslo for what were supposed to be talks about the role of the Scandinavian truce monitors. Delegates from the Tamil Tigers pulled out on June 8 before the talks even got under way, objecting to the composition of the government delegation. Norwegian mediator Erik Solheim said the failure of the sides even to meet "shows we are in the deepest crisis in the peace process." The rebels had demanded that representatives from Denmark, Finland, and Sweden be excluded from the Sri Lanka Monitoring Mission, which was monitoring the cease-fire, because those countries were members of the EU, which had listed the Tamil Tigers as a terrorist group.

The year's final peace session was a round of talks in Geneva on October 28–29. Each side stuck to its previous positions and refused to offer serious concessions to the other, although both sides claimed to want to keep the 2002 cease-fire in place. These talks ended without any agreement, and no further negotiations were scheduled as of the end of the year.

In response to the latest failure of the Geneva talks, diplomats from the EU, Japan, Norway, and the United States met in Washington on November 21 and condemned both the Tamil Tigers and the government for violent acts, particularly those that killed and endangered civilians. "Only by committing to sustained and substantive negotiations can the downward spiral of hostilities and human rights violations be reversed," the diplomats said in a statement. These diplomats represented the countries that had met in Tokyo in June 2003 and pledged $4.5 billion in aid for Sri Lanka's peace process.

Despite this international pressure, there was no further progress toward peace in the last weeks of the year. In fact, Tamil Tiger leader Velupillai Prabhakaran said in his annual speech on November 27 that the cease-fire was "defunct" and new negotiations would not be worthwhile.

Following are two documents concerning violence in Sri Lanka: first, excerpts from a speech on June 1, 2006, to the American Chamber of Commerce in Colombo, Sri Lanka, by Richard A. Boucher, the U.S. assistant secretary of state for South and Central Asia; second, a joint statement by representatives from Norway, the United States, the European Union, and Japan following their November 21, 2006, meeting in Washington, D.C., as co-chairs of the Tokyo Donors Conference Regarding Violence in Sri Lanka.

DOCUMENT

"Remarks to the American Chamber of Commerce, Colombo, Sri Lanka"

. . . It is encouraging how much progress Sri Lanka has made in recovering from the [December 2004] Tsunami, but there are still reasons to be seriously concerned about the country's future. There was hope that this same spirit could be applied to overcoming a man-made disaster—Sri Lanka's long and violent ethnic conflict. Tragically, that has not happened, and if anything, the political situation has only worsened. The atrocities range from Foreign Minister [Lakshman] Kadirgamar's assassination [in August 2005] to the recent attempt on the life of the army commander and the massacre of civilians in Kayts and Wilikenda.

The violent incidents and serious violations of the 2002 Ceasefire agreement have been too numerous to list, and listing them merely overlooks the fact that each one of these incidents involves lives lost, individuals whose smile and creativity are lost to their families and to your nation's future. The United States believes the Liberation Tigers of Tamil Eelam bear the major responsibility for the upsurge in violence and near-breakdown of the ceasefire agreement. They have committed scores of unprovoked attacks on civilians and military personnel, carried out assassinations and suicide operations, continue to recruit children and prevented Tamils from exercising their democratic rights in last year's election. For nine years we have had them on our official list of Foreign Terrorist Organizations; they truly deserve the label. In that regard, we welcome the European Union's decision to list the Tigers in Europe as a Foreign Terrorist Organization.

As we've said many times and will continue to say, the Tamil Tigers must renounce terror in word and deed, stop the violence, and recognize that the only solution to the conflict in Sri Lanka is a political one. They need to focus their vision on how to achieve their legitimate goals through a legitimate process of negotiation. If the Tigers give up terrorism, the United States will be able to consider dealing with them. The Tiger leadership has to understand that the entire world is united in its determination to combat terror, whether it emanates from the mountains of Afghanistan or the fields of the Wanni [interior sections of northern Sri Lanka]. As a friend of Sri Lanka, the United States will do whatever we can to help the sovereign Sri Lankan government in its struggle against this menace.

We are working with other governments to cut off financing of terrorist groups, including the Tigers. The United States has also brought to Colombo experts in money laundering to assist the government in tracking these streams. We're also sending dozens of Sri Lankans to the U.S. for training in anti-terrorism programs. Our donation of a Coast Guard cutter last year to the Sri Lankan navy was a tangible symbol of our commitment to stand firm with the government in its opposition to the Tamil Tigers. It is important to be clear that the purpose of our assistance is not to encourage a return to war, because we firmly believe that there is no military solution to Sri Lanka's ethnic conflict. Rather, our assistance is meant to help Sri Lankans deter a return to war.

The Government of Sri Lanka also has responsibilities it must live up to. We have high expectations of a democratic government: respect for human rights, outreach to all citizens, respect for the rights of minorities, clean government for all, and a true vision of peace. In Geneva this February, the government agreed to prevent groups operating in areas under its control from carrying out armed attacks, and yet three months later it seems as if some groups continue to operate freely in those areas, carrying out their own violent operations.

We think the government should uphold law and order in all areas under its control, and when incidents occur, they must be investigated thoroughly and impartially. Arrests should be made, and the culprits prosecuted. All Sri Lankans—Tamils, Muslims and Sinhalese—need to have confidence that the government will protect them, or they will turn to other groups for protection. This is the government's responsibility in any country. As a recently elected member of the new UN Human Rights Council, the Sri Lankan government must firmly commit to upholding human rights at home so that it can more forcefully advocate protection of these rights within the Council.

We also think the government should provide a positive vision to Tamils and Muslims of a future Sri Lanka where their legitimate grievances are addressed and their security assured. President [Mahinda] Rajapaksa has spoken of "maximum devolution." Previous negotiations have agreed on "internal self-determination" within a federal framework. However the idea is expressed, it could offer hope to many in the North and East that they will have control over their own lives and destinies within a single nation of Sri Lanka. A further elaboration of this idea could spur much needed debate on the contours of a settlement acceptable to the Sri Lankan people. Already there are steps the government can take to reach out to demonstrate the sincerity of this vision. For example, Tamils can be assured of their right to use their language and provided with equal opportunities in public and private sector employment.

Naturally, neither the United States nor the Co-Chairs [of the 2003 Tokyo donors conference on Sri Lanka] nor the international community can dictate what a political solution should look like. Ambassador Lunstead and I have just come from a Co-Chairs meeting in Tokyo, and I'm sure most of you have seen the statement we put out Tuesday. We all remain extremely concerned about the deteriorating situation here. We've been urging all parties to cease the violence and get back into talks as soon as possible. We remain fully supportive of Norway's facilitation of the peace process and the work of the Sri Lanka Monitoring Mission. Frankly, we think that the criticism we've seen of Norway in the media is wholly unfair and unhelpful in getting parties back to the table.

Governments are not the only entities who have a role to play in fostering peace—as Ambassador Lunstead has said many times, the business community also has a helpful role to play. Peace and prosperity go hand in hand, whether here in Sri Lanka or elsewhere around the world. In a way, AmCham [the American Chamber of Commerce] is already in the peace-making business, and it needs to maintain a strong voice in support of peace. You know that Sri Lanka has already lost business because of the uncertainty of the situation here.

You know that if Sri Lanka reverts to a full-scale war, the consequences for the business climate will be devastating. Investors—be they foreign or local—won't support projects that could collapse in the chaos and uncertainty of a war-torn country. Tourists will almost certainly stay away, and insurance rates on shipping could go up significantly. The government's outlays for the cost of war will drain much needed resources from other development enterprises. . . .

Source: U.S. Department of State. Bureau of South and Central Asian Affairs. "Remarks to the American Chamber of Commerce, Colombo, Sri Lanka, [by] Richard A. Boucher, Assistant Secretary for South and Central Asia." June 1, 2006. www.state.gov/p/sca/rls/rm/2006/67382.htm (accessed January 15, 2007).

DOCUMENT

"Joint Statement Regarding Violence in Sri Lanka"

The Co-Chairs of the Tokyo Donors Conference—Norway, the United States, the European Union, and Japan—met in Washington, D.C., on November 21.

The Co-Chairs view with alarm the rising level of violence in Sri Lanka that has led to significant loss of life and widespread human rights violations. The Co-Chairs condemn the continued and systematic ceasefire violations by Government of Sri Lanka and LTTE [Liberation Tigers of Tamil Eelam]. We call on both sides to seize the historic opportunity created by the 2002 Cease-Fire Agreement to resolve the country's conflict peacefully. Only by committing to sustained and substantive negotiations can the downward spiral of hostilities and human rights violations be reversed.

The Co-Chairs particularly condemn the LTTE for initiating hostilities from heavily populated areas and the Government of Sri Lanka for firing into such vulnerable areas and killing and wounding innocent civilians. The Co-Chairs call on both sides to respect international humanitarian law and set aside demilitarized zones to protect internally displaced persons.

The Co-Chairs recall the responsibility of both parties to guarantee the security of the Sri Lanka Monitoring Mission [SLMM] to fully exercise its mandate. The Co-Chairs were disturbed by the incident on November 8 when the Head of Mission of the SLMM came under fire. The Co-Chairs remind the parties of their responsibility to respect all rulings by the SLMM and to implement the Cease-fire Agreement fully, including re-opening the A-9 highway.

The Co-Chairs recognize that talks took place on October 28–29 in Geneva. However, we urge the Parties to the conflict to commit to a structured and sustained process of further negotiations without preconditions once a proposal is available, as indicated by the Government and welcomed by the LTTE delegation in Geneva.

The agreement between the Sri Lankan Freedom Party and the opposition United National Party should lead to a credible power-sharing proposal that can help form the basis for a viable negotiated settlement between the Parties. At the same time, the specific arrangements for the north and east should not be disturbed as they are fundamental to continuing the dialogue to achieve an agreement. The legitimate interests and aspirations of all communities, including the Tamil, Muslim and Sinhala communities must be accommodated as part of a political settlement.

The Co-Chairs welcome the Government of Sri Lanka's progress in establishing a Commission of Inquiry for Human Rights with international observers. They condemn the growing violations of human rights by all sides and the fear that pervades civil society, politics and the media. The Commission of Inquiry and the Government should work promptly to bring the perpetrators to justice and to address the climate of impunity.

Citizens are caught in this conflict and agencies are unable to reach them. We recognize the efforts by government to provide essential supplies themselves and welcome the establishment of the consultative committee on humanitarian assistance that is addressing several humanitarian access issues for international agencies.

The Co-Chairs urge both parties to depoliticize the issue of humanitarian access and for the immediate, permanent and unconditional opening of the sea and road routes for humanitarian convoys of essential supplies. As a first step towards this, the Co-Chairs welcome the readiness of the Government to send one convoy via the A-9 highway to Jaffna and to allow International Non-Governmental Organizations with a proven track record immediate access to uncleared areas [the Sri Lankan government's term for areas under control of the Tamil Tigers] to restart their relief work. The Co-Chairs call on the LTTE to cooperate with such initiatives.

The Co-Chairs, together with other members of the international community, express their strong support for Norway's ongoing efforts to facilitate the peace process and the Sri Lanka Monitoring Mission's role in monitoring the Cease-Fire Agreement.

Source: U.S. Department of State. Office of the Spokesman. "Joint Statement by Co-Chairs of the Tokyo Donors Conference Regarding Violence in Sri Lanka." November 21, 2006. www.state.gov/r/pa/prs/ps/2006/76478.htm (accessed January 15, 2007).

FDA and CDC on the Cervical Cancer Vaccine

June 8 and 29, 2006

In a significant development for women's health, the federal Food and Drug Administration (FDA) announced June 8, 2006, that it had approved the first vaccine against cervical cancer, the second most common cancer in women worldwide. The vaccine, called Gardasil, was made by Merck & Co. and had been found to be highly effective against the two strains of the human papillomavirus (HPV) that caused 70 percent of all cervical cancers. Because HPV was a sexually transmitted disease (STD), the vaccine was most effective in females who were not yet sexually active. Three weeks after the FDA announcement, the federal Centers for Disease Control and Prevention (CDC) recommended on June 29 that all eleven- and twelve-year old girls routinely be given the vaccine and that it be made available to most young women.

Vaccinating young girls against a STD raised some concerns among religious and conservative groups, who said the vaccine might lead to promiscuity if young women mistakenly thought it protected them from all STDs. Most groups endorsed the recommendation, however, although some said vaccination should not be mandatory. A greater concern for many people was the vaccine's cost. At $360 for the three-shot regimen, not counting the costs of administering it, the vaccine's price tag could make it out of reach for large numbers of poor women, especially those in developing countries where the great majority of new cases of cervical cancers occurred.

The Vaccine

Worldwide, cervical cancer was the second most prevalent cancer in women, with more than 470,000 new cases each year and an estimated 233,000 deaths. About 90 percent of cases occurred in developing countries, where poor women did not have access to the screening and treatment common in developed countries. In the United States, where Pap smear testing was widely available, cervical cancer was the eighth most common form of cancer in women. On average, there were 9,710 new cases a year and 3,700 deaths in the United States.

The major cause of the cancer was the human papillomavirus, which was also the most common sexually transmitted disease in the United States. The CDC estimated that about 6.2 million Americans become infected with HPV every year and that over half of all sexually active men and women become infected at some point in their lives. Most people's immune systems rid the body of HPV before any related health problems resulted. But HPV could cause cervical cancer, genital warts, and some other cancers in both men and women.

Gardasil protected against the two strains of HPV that caused about 70 percent of all cervical cancers as well as two other strains that caused about 90 percent of all genital warts. Studies showed no serious side effects from the vaccine. Because it did not protect against other HPV strains that caused cancer, the FDA and CDC recommended that women continue their routine Pap testing. The vaccine also did not protect women if they were already infected with one or both strains in the vaccine. Because the vaccine was most effective in females who had not yet had sex, the CDC Advisory Committee on Immunization Practices recommended that it be given to all eleven- and twelve-year-old girls. But the vaccine was also approved for use in girls as young as nine and in women up to age twenty-six.

Merck was conducting additional studies to determine how long the vaccine was effective and whether a booster shot might be needed. Merck said it had documented immunity for only five years but believed from its surveillance studies that the vaccine provided a "durable immune response." The giant pharmaceutical company was also testing whether Gardasil might be effective in older women and in boys. Health experts said it made sense to vaccinate boys before they could transmit HPV. GlaxoSmithKline was expected to have a competitor to Gardasil, called Cervarix, ready for approval within a year or so.

Cost Concerns

Initial responses to the vaccine were generally positive. A spokesman for Merck said in early November that the company was "seeing a fairly remarkable uptake of Gardasil." Merck reported that vaccine sales had already reached $70 million, which was more than analysts had originally projected. Still, some parents expressed reservations about the safety of the vaccine and about immunizing young girls against a sexually transmitted disease. "We haven't even talked about the birds and the bees yet," one mother of an eleven-year-old told the *Washington Post*. "She needs to be innocent a little bit longer." Religious and social conservative groups also generally supported use of the vaccine so long as it was not made mandatory and parental consent was required. Some groups also were concerned about how the vaccine was portrayed to young women. "Our primary concern is with the message that would be delivered to nine- to twelve-year-olds with the administration of the vaccines," a policy analyst for the Family Research Council said. "Care must be taken not to communicate that such an intervention makes all sex 'safe.'"

The big hurdle for widespread adoption of the vaccine was likely to be its price. At $120 a dose, the three-shot regimen, given over a period of six months, was likely to cost $400 to $500 once doctors' charges were added. Several insurance companies quickly said they would cover the costs of the vaccine. The CDC advisory panel also recommended that the vaccine be provided to girls up to age nineteen who qualified for the federal Vaccines for Children program, which provided free vaccinations to about 40–45 percent of all poor children. Merck announced in early November that it had reached an agreement to provide the vaccine at a reduced rate to state vaccination programs serving the poor and to make the vaccine available free to poor women between ages nineteen and twenty-six who were not otherwise able to afford it. At least one state, New Hampshire, announced that starting in January 2007 it would provide Gardasil free to all girls ages eleven through eighteen. Many other states said they were unlikely to follow suit because they were already having trouble paying for early childhood vaccines against such diseases as measles, chicken pox, and polio.

The cost factor was an even bigger problem in developing countries, where the World Health Organization was still struggling to ensure that children received a $3.50 vaccine immunizing them against the five major childhood diseases. "Eighty percent of the women who die of cervical cancer are generally poor and live in underserved areas. They will be the ones to benefit most from affordable prices and access to this vaccine," said Arletty Pinel, the head of the UN Population Fund's Reproductive Health Branch. Health experts, representatives from Merck and other pharmaceutical companies, and aid and philanthropic organizations met at the end of the year to try to figure out ways to make the vaccine available to poor women in developing countries at an affordable price.

Big Drop in Breast Cancer

In another piece of good news for women's health, the federal government reported that breast cancer rates fell a stunning 7 percent in 2003, equal to about 14,000 cases. For women with estrogen-positive tumors, which accounted for 70 percent of all breast cancers, the decline was a remarkable 15 percent. The decline came a year after millions of women stopped taking hormone pills in the wake of a major study linking the hormones to a heightened risk of life-threatening diseases, including heart attacks, strokes, and blood clots, and a slightly elevated risk of breast cancer. The estrogen-based hormones relieved many of the symptoms, such as hot flashes, that women experienced in menopause when their bodies stopped producing natural estrogen. Until the study showed otherwise, it was also widely believed that hormones protected women against heart disease. *(Risks of hormone replacement therapy, Historic Documents of 2002, p. 503)*

Although researchers cautioned that more studies needed to be done to confirm their findings, they speculated that when women stopped taking the estrogen-based hormones, minuscule tumors that were fueled by estrogen stopped growing or even regressed so that they were undetectable by a mammogram. Some tumors that might have developed in the presence of the pills may never have formed, researchers from the M.D. Anderson Cancer Center in Houston said at a breast cancer conference in San Antonio on December 14. Support for that hypothesis came from a separate analysis in California, where both the drop in hormone use and the decline in breast cancer rates was larger. Overall breast cancer rates in California fell 11 percent in 2003 (compared with 7 percent nationwide).

Another cancer milestone also occurred in 2003. For the first time in more than seventy years, the American Cancer Society reported in February that the number of deaths from all forms of cancer dropped slightly in 2003. In 2003, the last year for which data were available, there were 556,902 cancer deaths— 369 fewer than in 2002. Although the death rate from cancer had been slowly declining, the overall growth and aging of the population meant that the actual number of deaths kept rising. "The decrease from 2002 to 2003 means that the decline in death rates has become sufficiently large" to outpace population growth, said Michael Thun, head of the society's epidemiological research. "You would predict this is a trend that may have a few bumps but will continue," he added.

Following are the texts of two press releases. The first, issued by the Food and Drug Administration on June 8, 2006, announced the agency's approval of Gardasil, the first vaccine licensed to prevent cervical cancer. The second, issued on June 29, 2006, by the Centers for Disease Control and Prevention's Advisory Committee on Immunization Practices, recommended that Gardasil be routinely used to vaccinate eleven- and twelve-year-old girls.

▮▮▮▮▮▮ DOCUMENT ▮▮▮▮▮▮

"FDA Licenses New Vaccine for Prevention of Cervical Cancer"

The Food and Drug Administration (FDA) today announced the approval of Gardasil, the first vaccine developed to prevent cervical cancer, precancerous genital lesions and genital warts due to human papillomavirus (HPV) types 6, 11, 16 and 18. The vaccine is approved for use in females 9–26 years of age. Gardasil was evaluated and approved in six months under FDA's priority review process—a process for products with potential to provide significant health benefits.

"Today is an important day for public health and for women's health, and for our continued fight against serious life-threatening diseases like cervical cancer," said Alex Azar, Deputy Secretary, U.S. Department of Health and Human Services (HHS). "HHS is committed to advancing critical health measures such as the development of new and promising vaccines to protect and advance the health of all Americans."

HPV is the most common sexually-transmitted infection in the United States. The Centers for Disease Control and Prevention estimates that about 6.2 million Americans become infected with genital HPV each year and that over half of all sexually active men and women become infected at some time in their lives. On average, there are 9,710 new cases of cervical cancer and 3,700 deaths attributed to it in the United States each year. Worldwide, cervical cancer is the second most common cancer in women; and is estimated to cause over 470,000 new cases and 233,000 deaths each year.

For most women, the body's own defense system will clear the virus and infected women do not develop related health problems. However, some HPV types can cause abnormal cells on the lining of the cervix that years later can turn into cancer. Other HPV types can cause genital warts. The vaccine is effective against HPV types 16 and 18, which cause approximately 70 percent of cervical cancers and against HPV types 6 and 11, which cause approximately 90 percent of genital warts.

"This vaccine is a significant advance in the protection of women's health in that it strikes at the infections that are the root cause of many cervical cancers," said Andrew C. von Eschenbach, MD, Acting Commissioner of Food and Drugs. "The development of this vaccine is a product of extraordinary work by scientists as well as by FDA's review teams to help facilitate the development of very novel vaccines to address unmet medical needs. This work has resulted in the approval of a number of new products recently, including Gardasil, which address significant public health needs."

Gardasil is a recombinant vaccine (contains no live virus) that is given as three injections over a six-month period. Immunization with Gardasil is expected to prevent most cases of cervical cancer due to HPV types included in the vaccine. However, females are not protected if they have been infected with that HPV type(s) prior to vaccination, indicating the importance of immunization before potential exposure to the virus. Also, Gardasil does not protect against less common HPV types not included in the vaccine, thus routine and regular pap screening remain critically important to detect precancerous changes in the cervix to allow treatment before cervical cancer develops.

"This is the first vaccine licensed specifically to prevent cervical cancer. Its rapid approval underscores FDA's commitment to help make safe and effective vaccines available as quickly as possible. Not only have vaccines dramatically reduced the toll of diseases in infants and children, like polio and measles, but they are playing an increasing role protecting and improving the lives of adolescents and adults," said Jesse Goodman, MD, MPH, Director of FDA's Center for Biologics Evaluation and Research.

Four studies, one in the United States and three multinational, were conducted in 21,000 women to show how well Gardasil worked in women between the ages of 16 and 26 by giving them either the vaccine or placebo. The results showed that in women who had not already been infected, Gardasil was nearly 100 percent effective in preventing precancerous cervical lesions, precancerous vaginal and vulvar lesions, and genital warts caused by infection with the HPV types against which the vaccine is directed. While the study period was not long enough for cervical cancer to develop, the prevention of these cervical precancerous lesions is believed highly likely to result in the prevention of those cancers.

The studies also evaluated whether the vaccine can protect women already infected with some HPV types included in the vaccine from developing diseases related to those viruses. The results show that the vaccine is only effective when given prior to infection.

Two studies were also performed to measure the immune response to the vaccine among younger females aged 9–15 years. Their immune response was as good as that found in 16–26 year olds, indicating that the vaccine should have similar effectiveness when used in the 9–15 year age group.

The safety of the vaccine was evaluated in approximately 11,000 individuals. Most adverse experiences in study participants who received Gardasil included mild or moderate local reactions, such as pain or tenderness at the site of injection.

The manufacturer has agreed to conduct several studies following licensure, including additional studies to further evaluate general safety and long-term effectiveness. The manufacturer will also monitor the pregnancy outcomes of women who receive Gardasil while unknowingly pregnant. Also, the manufacturer has an ongoing study to evaluate the safety and effectiveness of Gardasil in males.

Gardasil is manufactured by Merck & Co., Inc., of Whitehouse Station, NJ.

Source: U.S. Department of Health and Human Services. Food and Drug Administration. "FDA Licenses New Vaccine for Prevention of Cervical Cancer and Other Diseases in Females Caused by Human Papillomavirus." Press release P06-77, June 8, 2006. www.fda.gov/bbs/topics/NEWS/2006/NEW01385.html (accessed November 28, 2006).

DOCUMENT

"Advisory Committee Recommends HPV Vaccination"

The Advisory Committee on Immunization Practices (ACIP) voted Thursday to recommend that a newly licensed vaccine designed to protect against human papillomavirus virus (HPV) be routinely given to girls when they are 11–12 years old. The ACIP recommendation also allows for vaccination of girls beginning at nine years old as well as vaccination of girls and women 13–26 years old. HPV is the leading cause of cervical cancer in women.

According to the ACIP's recommendation, three doses of the new vaccine should be routinely given to girls when they are 11 or 12 years old. The advisory committee, however, noted that the vaccination series can be started as early as nine years old at the discretion of the physician or health care provider. The recommendation also includes girls and women 13–26 years old because they will benefit from getting the vaccine. The vaccine should be administered before onset of sexual activity (i.e., before women are exposed to the viruses), but females who are sexually active should still be vaccinated.

"This vaccine represents an important medical breakthrough," said Dr. Anne Schuchat, director of CDC's National Center for Immunization and Respiratory Diseases. "As a result, these vaccine recommendations address a major health problem for women and represent a significant advance in women's health. It has been tested in thousands of women around the world and has been found to be safe and effective in providing protection against the two types of HPV that cause most cervical cancers."

Gardasil®, manufactured by Merck, is the first vaccine developed to prevent cervical cancer, precancerous genital lesions and genital warts due to HPV. HPV causes genital warts in men and women. The vaccine is highly effective against four types of the HPV virus, including two that cause about 70 percent of cervical cancer. Those who have not acquired HPV would get the full benefits of the vaccine. On average, there are 9,710 new cases and 3,700 deaths from cervical cancer in the United States each year.

HPV is the most common sexually transmitted infection in the United States. More than 20 million men and women in the United States are currently infected with HPV and there are 6.2 million new infections each year. HPV is most common in young women and men who are in their late teens and early 20s. By age 50, at least 80 percent of women will have acquired HPV infection.

"Although an effective vaccine is a major advance in the prevention of genital HPV and cervical cancer, it will not replace other prevention strategies, such as cervical cancer screening for women or protective sexual behaviors," said Dr. Schuchat. "Women should continue to get pap tests as a safeguard against cervical cancer."

The ACIP, consisting of 15 members appointed by the Secretary of the Department of Health and Human Services (HHS), advises the director of CDC and Secretary of HHS on control of vaccine-preventable disease and vaccine usage. Recommendations of the ACIP become CDC policy when they are accepted by the director of CDC and are published in CDC's Morbidity and Mortality Weekly Report (MMWR). There are no federal laws requiring the immunization of children. All school and daycare entry laws are state laws and vary from state to state.

Source: U.S. Department of Health and Human Services. Centers for Disease Control and Prevention. Office of Communication. Division of Media Relations. "CDC's Advisory Committee Recommends Human Papillomavirus Virus Vaccination." Press release, June 29, 2006. www.cdc.gov/od/oc/media/pressrel/r060629.htm (accessed November 28, 2006).

Other Historic Documents of Interest

Emergency contraceptive drug, p. 466

Food safety, p. 538

GAO on drug safety, p. 129

Secondhand smoke, p. 350

Stem cell legislation, p. 407

Former House Majority Leader on His Resignation from Congress

June 8, 2006

■■■■■■■■■■ **THE DOCUMENT IN CONTEXT** ■■■■■■■■■

The "culture of corruption" that Democrats and other critics said tainted Republican members of the House of Representatives claimed a major victim in 2006 when former House majority leader Tom DeLay, R-Texas, announced he was resigning from Congress. DeLay's close ties to lobbyist Jack Abramoff, who pleaded guilty to federal corruption charges in early January, and the majority leader's indictment in his home state on money laundering charges made him a powerful negative symbol for the Republican Party during an election year when control of the House was at stake. According to friends, DeLay apparently decided he did not want to be blamed if the Republicans lost their House majority in November. He was also thought to be in danger of losing his own House seat if he remained in the race.

DeLay's departure removed a specific and significant target from Democratic attacks but did little to stem the tide of revelations and allegations of unethical conduct that swirled around several members of Congress as well as members of the Bush administration—and kept the Abramoff scandal in front of voters throughout the year. One legislator, Rep. Bob Ney, R-Ohio, agreed in mid-September to plead guilty to corruption charges in connection with Abramoff after denying all year that he had done anything wrong. Pointing to Ney's plea, and the sudden resignation of Rep. Mark Foley, R-Fla., at the end of September for making inappropriate advances to underage male House pages, Democrats said it was time for a change. Voters apparently agreed, turning over control of both the House and Senate to Democrats in the November 7 election.

DeLay's Departure

DeLay, a fiercely partisan conservative Republican, was elected to the U.S. House in 1984, became the GOP majority whip after Republicans took control of the House in 1994, and was elevated to majority leader in 2002. Arguably the most influential member of either party in the House, DeLay's power derived from his abilities as an effective fundraiser for his fellow Republicans and—as his nickname "The Hammer" suggested—from his willingness to play hardball to get what he wanted. To leverage his power, and to help keep Republicans in the majority, DeLay started what was known as the K Street Project to pressure Washington lobbying firms to support GOP causes and candidates. By the time DeLay became majority leader, several loyal former aides were running or working in some of the most influential lobbying organizations in town—including Abramoff's—helping ensure that DeLay got the support he needed to push forward his political agenda in the House. *(Background, Historic Documents of 2005, p. 631)*

DeLay's hard-charging, win-at-all-costs style began to catch up with him in 2004, when the House ethics committee admonished him for three separate events. Then, in September 2005, a Texas grand jury indicted him on charges of conspiring to funnel illegal corporate campaign contributions to Republican candidates for the Texas state legislature. DeLay denied the charges, saying they were an effort to exact revenge for the leading role he had played in redrawing the Texas congressional map to dilute the voting strength of the state's Democrats. Nonetheless, the indictment forced DeLay to step down temporarily as House majority leader in September 2005.

DeLay and other legislators had been coping with the steady fallout from the Abramoff corruption scandal, which began in March 2005, when news reports raised questions about luxurious overseas trips and golf outings that DeLay and others had taken that appeared to have been paid for by Abramoff and other lobbyists in violation of House rules. By October the Justice Department had confirmed that it was taking a close look at DeLay in connection with its investigation of Abramoff's questionable lobbying activities. The scandal moved closer to DeLay on November 18, when his former aide Michael Scanlon, an Abramoff associate, pleaded guilty to criminal charges of participating in a broad conspiracy to provide "things of value" to lawmakers and other federal officials in return for their agreeing to perform official acts.

On January 3, 2006, Abramoff, whom DeLay had once described as one of "my closest and dearest friends," pleaded guilty in federal district court in Washington to three felony counts of conspiracy, mail fraud, and tax evasion, largely in connection with his lobbying activities for Native American tribes. Abramoff also agreed to cooperate with federal law enforcement officials in their influence-peddling investigations, apparently in the hopes of reducing his prison sentence. Four days later, on January 7, DeLay said he would step down permanently as majority leader. The announcement came as a group of House Republican moderates and conservatives began circulating a petition calling for a GOP caucus meeting that likely would have forced an election to replace him.

On March 31, Tony Rudy, a former deputy chief of staff to DeLay, pleaded guilty to a conspiracy charge in the Abramoff scandal. DeLay was not implicated in any wrongdoing in the Rudy court documents, but he was described by prosecutors as "Representative No. 2," who, at Rudy's urging, took official actions that helped some of Abramoff's clients. Rudy at the time was still working for DeLay but taking money and other considerations from Abramoff, for whom he later went to work.

Just three weeks earlier DeLay had easily won his primary election in Texas. But both internal polling and external advisers warned DeLay that he had only a 50–50 chance of winning the general election in a race against the Democratic nominee, former Rep. Nick Lampson, who had lost his congressional seat in 2004 after the controversial mid-decade redistricting. Faced with those odds, DeLay announced on April 4 that he would leave Congress sometime in early June and not stand for reelection. "The voters of the 22nd District of Texas deserve a campaign about the vital national issues that they care most about and that affect their lives every day and not a campaign focused solely as a referendum on me," DeLay told supporters in his hometown of Sugar Land. Delivering his farewell address in the House on June 8, DeLay was characteristically unapologetic. "Given the chance to do it all again, there's only one thing I'd change," he said. "I'd fight even harder."

By the end of the year, DeLay's trial in Texas was still pending. Voters had given his congressional seat to Lampson, and a Democrat won another one of the seats that DeLay had drawn to be a Republican redoubt. For his part, DeLay had begun a blog designed to build an Internet presence for conservatives and serve as a fund-raising tool. "My goal is to push the conservative cause and conservative thought," he told the *New York Times.* "We need to use all media available to us."

The Abramoff investigations were also still in progress. In June a jury found David Safavian, chief of procurement in the White House Office of Management and Budget, guilty of lying about his relationship with Abramoff and obstruction of justice. Susan B. Ralston, an aide to presidential adviser Karl Rove, resigned in October after it was revealed that she had served as a conduit between the White House and Abramoff. Ralston was not accused of having done anything illegal.

Ney Resignation

The first, and so far only, member of Congress to plead guilty to corruption in connection with Abramoff was Bob Ney of Ohio. First elected to the House in 1994, Ney was seen as an up-and-coming member of the Republican leadership before coming under scrutiny from the Justice Department in 2005 over free travel and other gifts he had received from Abramoff. Ney was pressured by House GOP leadership to give up his chairmanship of the House Administration Committee, the panel that oversaw lobbying disclosures and had jurisdiction over lobbying reform. Agreeing to step aside in January 2006, Ney insisted that he would be "vindicated completely" at the end of the inquiry, a position he maintained in May when a former chief of staff who had left to work for Abramoff pleaded guilty to trying to bribe Ney with illegal gifts. In August Ney gave up an increasingly problematic bid for a seventh term in the House.

Then, on September 15, Ney did an abrupt about-face and agreed to plead guilty to two federal courts of conspiracy and false statements, putting Republicans' ethics troubles back in the spotlight just seven weeks before the midterm election. Ney admitted that he had received gifts, including expensive meals and trips worth more than $170,000, from Abramoff and his associates during the previous five years in exchange for trying to shape legislation and inserting statements into the *Congressional Record* for the benefit of Abramoff's clients. He also admitted to making false statements to Congress by not reporting his gifts in his travel and financial disclosure reports. Ney blamed alcohol for his problems and checked into a treatment program, but he refused to resign from Congress. After entering a formal guilty plea on October 13, Ney said he would resign in the "next few weeks." But GOP leaders demanded his immediate resignation and threatened to expel him if he did not cooperate. "There is no place for him in this Congress. If he chooses not to resign his office, we will move to expel him immediately as our first order of business when Congress resumes its legislative work in November," the top Republican House leaders said in a joint statement. Ney finally offered his resignation on November 3. His seat was claimed four days later by Democrat Zack Space, who won in a landslide.

Ney was scheduled to be sentenced on January 19, 2007. The Justice Department had recommended that he serve twenty-seven months in prison. He faced a maximum fine of $500,000.

Lobbying Rules

Abramoff's guilty plea in January—amid revelations that legislators were skirting their own rules for interactions with corporate lobbyists—sent Democrats and Republicans in both the House and Senate scrambling to line up behind proposals for new rules of conduct. Action was all the more urgent for members who wanted to put the taint of corruption behind them well in advance of the midterm elections in November. As a result, a slew of proposals were issued, sometimes in dramatic fashion. Nearly all of them would have limited congressional junkets funded by private interests, set new prohibitions on gifts from lobbyists, strengthened disclosure and conflict-of-interest laws, and cracked down on former legislators lobbying on the House and Senate floors.

The Senate easily passed legislation on March 29 that would have tightened some Senate rules governing contacts with lobbyists and significantly stepped up disclosure rules. The measure was passed by a 90–8 vote just a few hours after Abramoff was sentenced to nearly six years in jail for his role in an unrelated casino deal. Two of the no votes came from Republican John McCain of Arizona and Democrat Barack Obama of Illinois, who said the measure lacked any enforcement mechanism for truly changing the culture in Washington.

In the House momentum for passing tough lobbying provisions evaporated quickly. Rank-and-file Republicans, in an angry closed-door session, pushed back against a leadership proposal. Members balked at provisions banning privately funded travel, lowering the limit on the value of gifts that could be accepted, and increasing disclosure rules for lobbyists. Some legislators began to say that rules changes were unnecessary. House leaders scaled back the travel ban proposal and opted for a more modest package that would have required lobbyists to disclose more of their activities, while increasing fines for failure to comply. Even with those changes, the measure barely passed; the vote on May 3 was 217–213. Opponents of the bill, which included most Democrats and several interest groups, including Public Citizen and the League of Women Voters, said the bill would do so little to clean up sleazy and illegal behavior that it would be better to just start over.

As it turned out, the two chambers never even went to conference to try to resolve their differences on the legislation, so both measures died. In September the House did take steps to crack down on the abuse of earmarks, adopting a resolution that required sponsors of earmarks to identify the pet projects they insert into appropriations bills. Failure to enact new lobby rules gave Democrats additional fuel in their campaign to brand Republicans as the party of corruption. After winning control of both the House and Senate in the November elections, the new Democratic majority promised to make ethics rules and lobbying legislation top priorities of the 110th Congress.

Following is the text of the last formal speech former House majority leader Tom DeLay, R-Texas, made, on June 8, 2006, to the House of Representatives before resigning his seat in Congress.

■ DOCUMENT ■

"Resignation as Member of Committee on Appropriations"

Mr. Speaker, political careers tend to end in one of three ways: defeat, death, or retirement. And despite the fervent and mostly noble exertions of my adversaries over the years, I rise today to bid farewell to this House under the happiest of the available options.

I wish to begin the end of my congressional career by publicly thanking for the last time as their Representative the people of the 22nd District of Texas. Everything I have ever been able to accomplish here I owe and dedicate to them. It has been an honor and a privilege to serve them here.

Mr. Speaker, the real Speaker, he is on his way, I want to tell the real Speaker it has been a real honor to serve with Denny Hastert, who is my good friend, my most trusted partner and colleague. I want to take just a moment to congratulate him myself on becoming the longest serving Republican Speaker in history.

What a blessing this place is, Mr. Speaker. What a castle of hope this building is, this institution is for the people of the world. It is one of those things in political life that you always know, but seldom notice. The schedules we are forced to keep during our days in Washington are not always hospitable to sitting back and reflecting on the historical significance of our surroundings.

In the weeks since I announced my retirement, however, I have found myself doing just that. I notice things like I have not in years. I notice the monuments on the Mall. I notice that in Washington's obelisk, the Father of Our Country is represented not as an object of glory, but as a dutiful sentry at attention, minding his post for eternity.

I notice that under Jefferson's dome, the statue of the man is relatively understated, while his etched words still thunder from the marble with the power to drive history.

I notice that Lincoln's chair, the man who sought above all peace and reconciliation, keeps one of his hands in a perpetual fist. I walk these halls with a keener perspective. I notice now the statues of old and great, and in some cases almost forgotten, heroes that line the halls of this building, that stand in Statuary Hall.

In these halls I have also noticed in recent weeks the number of tourists in the Capitol who speak no English. They are not from America, most of these visitors, and yet, in a certain sense, of course they are. They may speak Italian or Polish or Japanese, but the freedoms they enjoy, both here and in their own country, have been inspired, won and secured by the ideals and the courage and the compassion of the American people.

These pilgrims come from all over the world to the House of Representatives to sit up in these galleries, photograph the statues, and stare up at the rotunda, to bear witness to the awesome feat of human liberty we have achieved right here.

The dome above us, Mr. Speaker, is a light house, a star even, by which all of the people in the world, no matter how oppressed, how impoverished, how seemingly without hope can chart a course towards security, prosperity, and freedom.

It is worth considering, though I will admit it is considerably easier to consider after you have announced your retirement, whether the days we lead here, the debates we wage, the work we do is always worthy of the elevated ideals embodied in that dome.

I submit that we could do better, as could all people in all things at all times, but perhaps not in the way some might think. In preparing for today, I found that it is customary in speeches such as these to reminisce about the good old days of political harmony, and across-the-aisle camaraderie, and to lament the bitter divisive partisan rancor that supposedly now weakens our democracy.

Well, I cannot do that, because partisanship, Mr. Speaker, properly understood, is not a symptom of democracy's weakness, but of its health and its strength, especially from the perspective of a political conservative.

Liberalism, after all, whatever you may think of its merits, is a political philosophy and a proud one, with a great tradition in this country with a voracious appetite for growth. In any place, or any time, on any issue, what does liberalism ever seek, Mr. Speaker? More. More government. More taxation. More control over people's lives and decisions and wallets.

If conservatives do not stand up to liberalism, no one will. And for a long time around here, almost no one did. Indeed, the common lament over the recent rise in political partisanship is often nothing more than a veiled complaint instead about the recent rise of political conservatism.

I should add here that I do not begrudge liberals their nostalgia for the days of a timid, docile, and permanent Republican minority. If we Republicans had ever enjoyed that same luxury over the last 12 years, heck, I would be nostalgic too.

Had liberals not fought us tooth and nail over tax cuts and budget cuts and energy and Iraq and partial birth abortion, those of us on this side of the aisle can only imagine all of the additional things we could have accomplished.

But the fact of the matter is, Mr. Speaker, they did not agree with us. So to their credit, they stood up to us. They argued with us. And they did so honorably on behalf of more than 100 million people, just like we did against President Clinton and they did against President Reagan.

Now, it goes without saying, Mr. Speaker, that by my count, our friends on the other side of the aisle lost every one of those arguments over the last 22 years, but that is besides the point. The point is, we disagree. On first principles, Mr. Speaker, we disagree. And so we debate, often loudly and often in vain, to convince our opponents and the American people of our point of view.

We debate here on the House floor. We debate in committees. We debate on television, and on radio and on the Internet and in the newspapers; and then every 2 years we have a huge debate, and then in November, we see who won.

That is not rancor; that is democracy. You show me a Nation without partisanship, and I will show you a tyranny. For all its faults, it is partisanship based on core principles that clarifies our debates, that prevents one party from straying too far from the mainstream, and that constantly refreshes our politics with new ideas and new leaders. Indeed, whatever role partisanship may have played in my own retirement today, or in the unfriendliness heaped upon other leaders in other times, Republican or Democrat, however unjust, all we can say is that partisanship is the worst means of settling fundamental political differences, except for all of the others.

Now, politics demands compromise, and, Mr. Speaker, even the most partisan among us have to understand that. But we must never forget that compromise and bipartisanship are means, not ends, and are properly employed only in the service of higher principles. It is not the principled partisan, however obnoxious he may seem to his opponents who degrade our public debate, but the preening self-styled statesman who elevates compromise to a first principle.

For the true statesman, Mr. Speaker, we are not defined by what they compromise, but what they do not. Conservatives, especially less enamored of government's lust for growth, must remember that our principles must always drive our agenda and not the other way around. For us conservatives, there are two such principles that can never be honorably compromised: human freedom and human dignity. Now, our agenda over the last 12 years has been an outgrowth of these first principles. We lowered taxes to increase freedom. We reformed welfare programs that however well intentioned undermined the dignity of work and personal responsibility and perpetuated poverty.

We have opposed abortion, cloning, and euthanasia because such procedures fundamentally deny the unique dignity of the human person. And we have supported the spread of democracy and the ongoing war against terror, because those policies protect and affirm the inalienable human right of all men and women and children to live in freedom.

Conservatism is often unfairly accused of being insensitive and mean-spirited, sometimes unfortunately, even by other conservatives. As a result, conservatives often attempt to soften that stereotype by overfunding broken programs or glossing over ruinous policies. But conservatism is not about feeling people's pain; it is about curing it.

And the results since the first great conservative victory in the 1980s speak for themselves. Millions of new jobs, new homes, and new businesses created, thanks to conservative economic reforms. Millions of families intact and enriched by the move from welfare to work. Hundreds of millions of people around the world liberated by a conservative foreign policy victory over Soviet Communism, and more than 50 million Iraqis and Afghanis liberated from tyranny since September 11, 2001.

To all of the critics of the supposedly mean-spirited conservative policies that brought about these results, I say only this: compassionate is as compassionate does.

Now, when I say that word, Mr. Speaker, compassionate, my thoughts turn to one person, my wife, Christine. Twelve years ago, Christine became what is called a court-appointed special advocate for abused and neglected children. And soon thereafter we became foster parents ourselves to three such children.

Over the last 10 years, I have spent more time and energy on the plight and needs of abused, neglected children than on any other single issue. It is an issue that transcends politics, let alone partisanship, and one that will continue to command a disproportionate amount of my time as a private citizen.

I am concerned, however, about whether it will receive the attention it deserves here in Washington, D.C. And because this is the last time I may ever command the attention of the House and of the national media, I will make one more plea before I go.

The catastrophe of America's child welfare and foster care systems is a national outrage, a government failure, and a bipartisan embarrassment. Congresses, administrations, Governors and State legislatures of every party and ideological bent for almost 100 years have thrown abused and neglected children into a vicious cycle of violence, fear, and instability.

Children who have already been beaten and betrayed by the people that are supposed to love them the most are routinely tossed from one temporary placement to another, often 10 to 20 times during their most formative, vulnerable years.

The system we have created still includes perverse economic incentives that deny children permanent homes, and in some States still lacks meaningful child monitoring or even background checks for perspective foster parents. The courts charged with overseeing each case are overrun with unrelated duties. So the thankless, unexciting work of looking after foster kids is just set aside in favor of more glamorous cases on the docket.

Bureaucracies layered one on top of another consign these children to the perdition of government and foster care for years at a time and with little or no effort made to finding them permanent loving forever families.

Instead, every few months these children throw their despair and distrust into a black plastic trash bag along with their few belongings and head off to the next place, the next letdown. They are abused and neglected long before they ever reach our abusive and neglectful foster care system and once in, things often only get worse.

Children are dying, Mr. Speaker, inside and out, and it is our fault. There is legislation now waiting in the Senate to help expedite interstate placement of foster children, and within its narrow focus this bill will do some good on the margins of some cases. I am proud of what little I have been able to accomplish for these children over the years, but in truth, I have only moved molehills, not mountains.

So I leave you today not by asking that one take up this cause, but by asking that all of you do. That you listen to the stories of these children and the stories that they tell and study the broken system we have created for them and help them, for God's sake, help them.

I ask this of Republicans and Democrats alike, not in the name of bipartisanship but in the name of principle, which brings me back, Mr. Speaker, to those memorials and those statues.

The great Americans honored here in bronze and marble, the heroes of our history and the ghosts of these halls were not made great because of what they were but because of what they did. George Washington and Abraham Lincoln have almost nothing in common with Junipero Serra and Jack Swigert, except the choice they each made, to live, to fight and even to die in the service of freedom. We honor men with monuments not because of their greatness or even simply because of their service, but because of their refusal even in the face of danger or death to ever compromise the principles they served.

Washington's obelisk still stands watch because democracy will always need a sentry. Jefferson's words will still ring because liberty will always need a voice. And Lincoln's left hand still stays clenched because tyranny will always need an enemy. And we are still here, Mr. Speaker, as a House and as a Nation because the torch of freedom cannot carry itself.

Here on this floor, I have caught and thrown spears of every sort. Over the course of 22 years, I have probably worked with and against almost everyone in this Chamber at least once. I have scraped and clawed for every vote, every amendment for every word of every bill that I believed in my heart would protect human freedom and defend human dignity. I have done so at all times honorably and honestly, Mr. Speaker, with God as my witness and history as my judge. And if given the chance to do it all again, there is only one thing I would change. I would fight even harder.

This place has given me so many memories, so much life. For 22 years, I have served the best I knew how. In this House, I have found my life's calling and my soul's savior. Eight years ago, I witnessed evil in the murder of two Capitol Hill police officers, one just outside my office and another, a very dear friend on my protection detail, inside my office itself. And 5 years ago, I witnessed unparalleled courage as their surviving comrades stood at their posts inside this building during the frantic evacuation on 9/11. They are around us every day, the Capitol Police force.

I tell you, those police officers are Members' and staffs' own personal army of guardian angels. They are the bravest men and women serving under this dome, and I offer them now, one more time, my great respect and admiration because believe it or not, Mr. Speaker, this is a happy day for me, though admittedly perhaps not as happy as it is for some of our old friends on the other side of the aisle. But nothing, not this retirement, not tough losses or old wounds, can detract from the joy that I feel and the blessings I offer to this House and its Members.

I say good-bye today, Mr. Speaker, with few regrets, no doubt. And so with love and gratitude for friends and foe alike, patriots all, I yield back the floor of our beloved House. And I exit as always, stage right.

Source: U.S. House. "Resignation as Member of Committee on Appropriations." 109th Cong., 2nd sess. *Congressional Record,* H3548–H3550. June 8, 2006. http://frwebgate.access.gpo.gov/cgi-bin/getpage.cgi?position=all&page=h3548&dbname=2006_record (accessed April 5, 2007).

Government Accountability Office on Safeguarding Personal Data

June 8, 2006

■■■■■ THE DOCUMENT IN CONTEXT ■■■■■

For the second year in a row, serious breaches in the way government agencies, financial institutions, credit agencies, and other data brokers safeguarded private personal data left millions of Americans vulnerable to potential identify theft. Many of the incidents involved the theft or loss of laptop computers containing thousands of names, Social Security numbers, birth dates, and other information that thieves could use to drain bank accounts, obtain credit, or run up debt while sticking the victims with the bills.

The largest theft involved a laptop and external hard drive containing the names of millions of military veterans that was stolen from the home of a Veterans Affairs Department employee. But several other federal agencies, state governments, universities, and private companies also reported significant loss or theft of personal data in 2006. On December 18, Kevin Poulsen, a senior editor for *Wired News*, wrote in his blog that more than 100 million personal records had been breached since early 2005, although the number of people whose data had been misused appeared to be far lower.

Consumer and privacy advocacy groups were concerned not only about the actual loss of the data but also about the lack of safeguards. Another issue was whether and under what circumstances information holders like government agencies or financial institutions should notify individuals that their data had been exposed to potential misuse. Although several congressional committees considered legislation to tighten controls to ensure data privacy, jurisdictional disputes prevented any measures from advancing beyond the committee stage in 2006.

A number of states took action, however. By the end of the year more than twenty states had adopted "credit freeze" laws, which allowed consumers to stop banks and credit agencies from issuing new credit accounts in their names. At least thirty states had passed laws requiring that consumers be notified whenever their data were lost or stolen.

The differing state laws prompted several high-tech firms, including Microsoft Corp. and Hewlett-Packard, to announce that they would lobby Congress to pass data-privacy legislation in 2007. The companies said it was time to enact a single federal law that would standardize privacy rules across states and industries. Many consumer advocacy groups feared that a federal law would be weaker than many of the state laws.

ChoicePoint Settlement

Although identity theft had been a growing concern for some time, public attention to breaches of personal data was heightened in February 2005 when ChoicePoint Inc., a private company that sold consumer information, revealed that it had been tricked into turning over personal information on more than 145,000 people to thieves pretending to be legitimate businesses. The Federal Trade Commission (FTC) announced on January 26, 2006, that it had reached a $15 million settlement with ChoicePoint over the commission's allegations that the data broker's failure to protect the records violated consumer privacy rights as well as federal law.

The FTC complaint said the commercial mail drops and apartment numbers the fake companies used as business addresses were "obvious red flags" that Choice-Point should have caught. So too were the cell phone numbers given as business numbers and the multiple applications for data with different company names but the same fax number. "The No. 1 point of this case is that companies that maintain sensitive personal information must employ reasonable safeguards. That should be fundamental in this day and age," said Lydia B. Parnes, director of the FTC's Bureau of Consumer Protection, announcing the settlement. James Lee, the chief marketing officer at ChoicePoint, said the company supported the settlement as the right thing to do and as being in the "best interests of everyone." He said the company had already taken several steps to tighten its controls over the sale of personal data, including making site visits to any business wanting information above a certain level.

Of the $15 million settlement, $5 million was earmarked for consumer compensation. The FTC said that at least 800 consumers had been victimized as a result of the ChoicePoint data breach (although the company said only sixteen cases of identity theft had been confirmed at the time of the settlement). The other $10 million was a fine for violating the federal Fair Credit Reporting Act. Although it represented the largest civil penalty the FTC had ever imposed for such violations, some consumer advocates said it was not enough. "While ChoicePoint has made efforts to atone for its wrongdoing, a light penalty like this says to other wrongdoers that acts like this are just the cost of doing business," Sen. Charles E. Schumer, D-N.Y., told the *New York Times.*

Several other commercial data brokers, financial advisers, universities, and private entities disclosed the theft or loss of personal private data in 2006. Among those who lost data on stolen laptops or other computer equipment were Ameriprise Financial, an investment advisory service spun off from American Express in 2005 (230,000 financial records); Hotels.com (243,000 customer records); and American International Group, Inc., an insurance provider (930,000 records containing medical data). The University of California at Los Angeles, the University of Texas, Georgetown University, and Ohio University, among others, were all victims of hackers, who in some cases had been stealing the personal data of thousands of students, faculty members, other employees, and alumni, in some cases for more than a year before being detected.

Data Thefts from the Federal Government

The federal government was one of the largest sources of lost or stolen data in 2006. In many cases the thefts involved data about government employees, but in other cases they involved personal data of citizens. By far the largest known theft occurred when a laptop and external hard drive containing personal records of 26.5

million military veterans was stolen from the home of Veterans Affairs Department employee on May 3. The data included names, Social Security numbers, and birth dates. The FBI announced on June 29 that it had recovered the laptop and drive and that the contents did not appear to have been copied or misused. Law enforcement officials said the two teens later arrested in the incident appeared to have been engaged in a routine burglary rather than directly targeting the data on the laptop. In the intervening two months, however, the employee who took the laptop home and his immediate superior were put on administrative leave, and the deputy secretary of veterans affairs for policy was forced to resign. Secretary of Veterans Affairs Jim Nicholson and officials from the Justice Department and the FBI were furious that they had not been told about the theft until two weeks after it happened, and veterans were angered that they were not notified until May 22. The department offered free credit monitoring to affected veterans, but some veterans groups were so outraged over the way the department had handled the incident that they filed a class-action lawsuit demanding $1,000 in damages for each person whose data were stolen.

The incident also gave the Democrats an opportunity to chastise the Bush administration for what many said was incompetence in securing sensitive data. Sen. Jack Reed, D-R.I., for example, said the theft was another example of "incompetence at the highest level of the administration." Some went further, admonishing the administration for its cavalier attitude toward private information as evidenced not only by data thefts but also by its secret and warrantless surveillance of phone records and e-mails of thousands of American citizens.

Secretary Nicholson promised that the department would take immediate steps to secure personal data, but the department sustained further embarrassment when the secretary announced on August 7 that a subcontractor, Unisys Corp., had lost a desktop computer containing medical insurance records for as many as 38,000 veterans. The computer was later located at a Unisys office. On August 14 the department announced plans to install new encryption technology on all agency computers; encryption was scheduled to begin on August 18.

Among other incidents affecting government agencies:

- A hacker stole sensitive information on about 1,500 employees of the nuclear weapons unit of the Energy Department, but neither the employees nor top officials at the department were told about the theft until nine months later. The stolen information included names, Social Security numbers, birth dates, and security clearances, which some security experts suggested could open the employees to threats or blackmail.
- The Commerce Department disclosed that it had lost more than 1,100 laptop computers since 2001, including about 250 from the Census Bureau that likely contained sensitive material for about 6,200 American households. The department said that all the equipment contained safeguards that would prevent a breach of personal data.
- In August the Education Department said it would arrange for free credit monitoring for as many as 21,000 student loan borrowers after personal information on the borrowers was inadvertently posted on the department's Web site. There were no immediate reports that any of the data had been misused.
- In June the U.S. Navy said it was beginning a criminal investigation after finding that Social Security numbers and other personal information for 28,000 sailors and family members on a civilian Web site. Three weeks later, in July, the Navy Safety Center shut down its Web site after finding that personal records for every Navy and Marine Corps aviator or aircrew member who had flown for the Navy in the past twenty years had been posted on the public site for the past six months. The posting, which the Navy Safety Center said appeared to be the result of human error, included more than 100,000 Social Security numbers.

Tightening Government Oversight

Two massive government databases were of particular concern. In October the Government Accountability Office (GAO) said that it had found forty-seven "weaknesses" in the computer system that the Centers for Medicare and Medicaid Services (CMS) used to send and receive bills and exchange medical data with health care providers for millions of patients in the government health care programs. "As a result, sensitive, personally identifiable medical data traversing this network are vulnerable to unauthorized disclosure," the GAO investigators said. "And these weaknesses could lead to disruptions in CMS operations." CMS administrator Mark McClellan said the agency had already corrected about half the problems noted by the GAO and was taking action to fix the rest. He also noted that the GAO had "found no evidence that confidential or sensitive information had actually been compromised."

Privacy advocates were also concerned about the security of a Justice Department database that would eventually be used by state and local police officials to search millions of case files from the FBI, Drug Enforcement Administration, and other federal law enforcement agencies. Civil liberties and privacy rights groups said they were concerned that the system invited abuse because local police would have access to personal data on thousands of people who had never been arrested or charged with a crime; such case files, they said, often contained inaccurate information that was never verified or corrected. "Information that's collected in the law enforcement realm can find [its way] into other arenas and be abused very easily," Marc Rotenberg, executive director of the Electronic Privacy Information Center, told the *Washington Post.*

Testifying before the House Committee on Government Reform on June 8, David M. Walker, the U.S. Comptroller General, said the federal government needed to do a better job of protecting personal data and of notifying the public when security breaches occurred. Walker urged each federal agency to analyze how it collected, stored, shared, and managed personal data and to put a "robust" information security program in place. Walker said agencies should consider limiting both the collection of personal information and the amount of time it was retained, limiting access to the information and ensuring that agency personnel were trained in using and storing it properly, and encrypting all personal data stored on mobile devices such as laptops and external hard drives.

A presidential commission, made up of representatives from seventeen federal agencies, offered interim recommendations on September 19 that tracked some of Walker's proposals. The Identity Theft Task Force said the government should review its use of Social Security numbers as employee identification. The task force also called for a governmentwide review of its guidelines on whether and how to give notice to affected individuals in the event of a breach of government data. Created in May by President George W. Bush, the task force was headed by Attorney General Alberto R. Gonzalez and FTC chairman Deborah Platt Majoras.

Following are excerpts from "Privacy: Preventing and Responding to Improper Disclosures of Personal Information," testimony presented on June 8, 2006, to the House Committee on Government Reform by U.S. Comptroller General David M. Walker.

DOCUMENT

"Privacy: Preventing Improper Disclosures of Personal Information"

Mr. Chairman and Members of the Committee:

I appreciate the opportunity to be here today to discuss key challenges federal agencies face in safeguarding personally identifiable information in their custody and taking action when that information is compromised. As the federal government obtains and processes personal information about individuals in increasingly diverse ways, it remains critically important that this information be properly protected and the privacy rights of individuals respected. Recently, as you know, personal data on millions of veterans was stolen from the home of an employee of the Department of Veterans Affairs, who had not been authorized to have the data at home. Compromises such as this raise important questions about what steps agencies should take to prevent such compromises and how they should notify citizens when breaches do occur. . . .

Results in Brief

Agencies can take a number of actions to help guard against the possibility that databases of personally identifiable information are inadvertently compromised. Two key steps are (1) to develop a privacy impact assessment—an analysis of how personal information is collected, stored, shared, and managed in a federal information system—whenever information technology is used to process personal information and (2) to ensure that a robust information security program is in place, as required by the Federal Information Security Management Act of 2002 (FISMA). More specific practical measures aimed at preventing inadvertent data breaches include limiting the collection of personal information, limiting data retention, limiting access to personal information and training personnel accordingly, and considering using technological controls such as encryption when data need to be stored on mobile devices.

When data breaches do occur, notification to the individuals affected and/or the public has clear benefits, allowing people the opportunity to take steps to protect themselves against the dangers of identity theft. It is also consistent with agencies' responsibility to inform individuals about how their information is being accessed and used and promotes accountability for its protection. At the same time, concerns have been raised that notifying individuals of security incidents that do not pose serious risks could be counterproductive and costly. Care is needed in defining appropriate criteria if agencies are required to report security breaches to the public, including coordinating with law enforcement. Care is also needed to ensure that notices are useful and easy to understand so that they are effective in alerting individuals to actions they may want to take to minimize the risk of identity theft.

We have made recommendations previously to OMB [Office of Management and Budget] and agencies to ensure they are adequately addressing privacy issues, including through the conduct of privacy impact assessments. We have also recommended that OMB implement improvements in its annual FISMA reporting guidance to help improve oversight of agency information security programs. In addition, the Congress should consider setting specific reporting requirements for agencies as part of its consideration of security breach legislation. Further Congress should consider requiring OMB to provide guidance to agencies on how to develop and issue security breach notices to affected individuals.

Background

The recent theft of personally identifiable information on millions of veterans is only the latest of a series of such data breaches involving the loss or theft of information on magnetic tapes, computer hard drives, and other devices, as well as incidents in which individuals gained unauthorized access to large commercial databases of such information. Concerns about possible identity theft resulting from such breaches are widespread. The Federal Trade Commission (FTC) reported in 2005 that identity theft represented about 40 percent of all the consumer fraud complaints it received during each of the last 3 calendar years. Identity theft generally involves the fraudulent use of another person's identifying information—such as name, address, Social Security number, date of birth, or mother's maiden name—to establish credit, run up debt, or take over existing financial accounts. According to identity theft experts, individuals whose identities have been stolen can spend months or years and thousands of dollars clearing their names. Some individuals have lost job opportunities, been refused loans, or even been arrested for crimes they did not commit as a result of identity theft.

Several Key Laws Govern Agency Privacy Practices

Federal agencies are subject to security and privacy laws aimed in part at preventing security breaches, including breaches that could enable identity theft. The major requirements for the protection of personal privacy by federal agencies come from two laws, the Privacy Act of 1974 and the E-Government Act of 2002. FISMA also addresses the protection of personal information in the context of securing federal agency information and information systems.

The Privacy Act places limitations on agencies' collection, disclosure, and use of personal information maintained in systems of records. The act describes a "record" as any item, collection, or grouping of information about an individual that is maintained by an agency and contains his or her name or another personal identifier. It also defines "system of records" as a group of records under the control of any agency from which information is retrieved by the name of the individual or by an individual identifier. The Privacy Act requires that when agencies establish or make changes to a system of records, they must notify the public by a "system-of-records notice" that is, a notice in the *Federal Register* identifying, among other things, the type of data collected, the types of individuals about whom information is collected, the intended "routine" uses of data, and procedures that individuals can use to review and correct personal information. Among other provisions, the act also requires agencies to define and limit themselves to specific predefined purposes.

The Office of Management and Budget...which is responsible for providing guidance to agencies on how to implement the provisions of the Privacy Act and other federal privacy and security laws, recently issued a memorandum reminding agencies of their responsibilities under the Privacy Act, other laws, and policy to appropriately safeguard sensitive personally identifiable information and train employees on their responsibilities in this area. The memo called on agency senior privacy officials to conduct a review of policies and processes to make sure adequate safeguards are in place to prevent the intentional or negligent misuse of, or unauthorized access to, personally identifiable information.

The provisions of the Privacy Act are largely based on a set of principles for protecting the privacy and security of personal information, known as the Fair Information Practices, which were first proposed in 1973 by a U.S. government advisory committee; these principles were intended to address what the committee termed a poor level of protection afforded to privacy under contemporary law. Since that time, the Fair Information Practices have been widely adopted as a standard benchmark for evaluating the adequacy of privacy protections....

The E-Government Act of 2002 strives to enhance protection for personal information in government information systems by requiring that agencies conduct privacy impact assessments (PIA). A PIA is an analysis of how personal information is collected, stored, shared, and managed in a federal system. More specifically, according to OMB guidance, a PIA is to (1) ensure that handling conforms to applicable legal, regulatory, and policy requirements regarding privacy; (2) determine the risks and effects of collecting, maintaining, and disseminating information in identifiable form in an electronic information system; and (3) examine and evaluate protections and alternative processes for handling information to mitigate potential privacy risks. To the extent that PIAs are made publicly available, they provide explanations to the public about such things as the information that will be collected, why it is being collected, how it is to be used, and how the system and data will be maintained and protected.

FISMA also addresses the protection of personal information. FISMA defines federal requirements for securing information and information systems that support federal agency operations and assets; it requires agencies to develop agencywide information security programs that extend to contractors and other providers of federal data and systems. Under FISMA, information security means protecting information and information systems from unauthorized access, use, disclosure, disruption, modification, or destruction, including controls necessary to preserve authorized restrictions on access and disclosure to protect personal privacy, among other things. Your committee has issued annual report cards on federal government information security based on reports submitted by agencies as required by FISMA.

Interest in Data Breach Notification Legislation Has Increased

Federal laws to date have not required agencies to report security breaches to the public, although breach notification has played an important role in the context of security breaches in the private sector. For example, California state law requires businesses to notify consumers about security breaches that could directly affect them. Legal requirements, such as the California law, led ChoicePoint, a large information reseller, to notify its customers in mid-February 2005 of a security breach in which unauthorized persons gained access to personal information from its databases. Since the ChoicePoint notification, bills were introduced in at least 44 states and enacted in at least 29 that require some form of notification upon a security breach. . . .

Agencies Can Take Steps to Reduce the Likelihood That Personal Data Will Be Compromised

A number of actions can be taken to help guard against the possibility that personal information maintained by agencies is inadvertently compromised. . . . Key strategic approaches include the following:

Conduct privacy impact assessments (PIAs). It is important that agencies identify the specific instances in which they collect and maintain personal information and proactively assess the means they intend to use to protect this information. This can be done most effectively through the development of PIAs, which, as I previously mentioned, are required by the E-Government Act of 2002 when using information technology to process personal information. PIAs are important because they serve as a tool for agencies to fully consider privacy implications of planned systems and data collections before those systems and collections have been fully implemented, when it may be relatively easy to make critical adjustments.

In prior work we have found that agencies do not always prepare PIAs as they are required. For example, our review of selected data mining efforts at federal agencies determined that PIAs were not always being done in full compliance with OMB guidance. Similarly, as identified in our work on federal agency use of information resellers, few PIAs were being developed for systems or programs that made use of information reseller data because officials did not believe they were required. Complete assessments are an important tool for agencies to identify areas of noncompliance with federal privacy laws, evaluate risks arising from electronic collection and maintenance of information about individuals, and evaluate protections or alternative processes needed to mitigate the risks identified. Agencies that do not take all the steps required to protect the privacy of personal information risk the improper exposure or alteration of such information. We recommended that the agencies responsible for the data mining efforts we reviewed complete or revise PIAs as needed and make them available to the public. We also recommended that OMB revise its guidance to clarify the applicability of the E-Gov Act's PIA requirement to the use of personal information from resellers. OMB stated that it would discuss its guidance with agency senior officials for privacy to determine whether additional guidance concerning reseller data was needed.

Ensure that a robust security program is in place. FISMA requires each agency to develop, document, and implement an agencywide information security program to provide security for the information and information systems that support the operations and assets of the agency, including those provided or managed by another agency, contractor, or other source. Key elements of this program include:

- periodic assessments of the risk and magnitude of harm that could result from the unauthorized access, use, disclosure, disruption, modification, or destruction of information or information systems;

- risk-based policies and procedures that cost-effectively reduce risks to an acceptable level and ensure that security is addressed throughout the life cycle of each information system;
- security awareness training for agency personnel, including contractors and other users of information systems that support the operations and assets of the agency;
- periodic testing and evaluation of the effectiveness of information security policies, procedures, and practices;
- a process for planning, implementing, evaluating, and documenting remedial action to address any deficiencies through plans of action and milestones; and:
- procedures for detecting, reporting, and responding to security incidents.

In prior reviews we have repeatedly identified weaknesses in almost all areas of information security controls at major federal agencies, and we have identified information security as a high risk area across the federal government since 1997. In July 2005, we reported that pervasive weaknesses in the 24 major agencies' information security policies and practices threatened the integrity, confidentiality, and availability of federal information and information systems. These weaknesses existed primarily because agencies had not yet fully implemented strong information security management programs, as needed to fully meet FISMA requirements. We recommended that OMB implement improvements in its annual FISMA reporting guidance to help improve oversight of agency information security programs. In March 2006, we reported that OMB had taken several actions to improve reporting and could further enhance the reliability and quality of reported information.

In the course of taking strategic approaches to protecting the privacy and security of personal information, agencies will likely consider a range of specific practical measures. Several that may be of particular value in preventing inadvertent data breaches include the following:

Limit collection of personal information. One item to be analyzed as part of a PIA is the extent to which an agency needs to collect personal information in order to meet the needs of a specific application. Limiting the collection of personal information, among other things, serves to limit the opportunity for that information to be compromised. For example, key identifying information—such as Social Security numbers—may not be needed for many agency applications that have databases of other personal information. Limiting the collection of personal information is also one of the fair information practices, which are fundamental to the Privacy Act and to good privacy practice in general.

Limit data retention. Closely related to limiting data collection is limiting retention. Retaining personal data longer than needed by an agency or statutorily required adds to the risk that the data will be compromised. In discussing data retention, California's Office of Privacy Protection recently reported an example in which a university experienced a security breach that exposed 15-year-old data, including Social Security numbers. The university subsequently reviewed its policies and decided to shorten the retention period for certain types of information. Federal agencies can make decisions up front about how long they plan to retain personal data as part of their PIAs, aiming to retain the data for as brief a period as necessary.

Limit access to personal information and train personnel accordingly. Only individuals with a need to access agency databases of personal information should have such access, and controls should be in place to monitor that access. Further, agencies can implement technological controls to prevent personal data from being readily transferred to unauthorized systems or media, such as laptop computers, discs, or other electronic storage devices. Security training, which is required for all federal employees under FISMA, can include training on the risks of exposing personal data to potential identity theft, thus helping to reduce the likelihood of data being exposed inadvertently.

Consider using technological controls such as encryption when data needs to be stored on mobile devices. In certain instances, agencies may find it necessary to enable employees to have access to personal data on mobile devices such as laptop computers. As discussed, this should be minimized. However, when absolutely necessary, the risk that such data could be exposed to unauthorized individuals can be reduced by using technological controls such as encryption, which significantly limits the ability of such individuals gaining access to the data. While encrypting data adds to the operational burden on authorized individuals, who must enter pass codes or use other authentication means to decrypt the data, it can provide reasonable assurance that stolen or lost computer equipment will not result in personal data being compromised, as occurred in the recent incident at the Department of Veterans Affairs. A decision about whether to use encryption would logically be made as an element of the PIA process and an agency's broader information security program.

While these suggestions do not amount to a complete prescription for protecting personal data, they are key elements of an agency's strategy for reducing the risks that could lead to identity theft.

Public Notification of Data Breaches Has Clear Benefits as Well as Challenges

I just discussed some preventive measures agencies can take to avoid a data breach. However, in the event an incident does occur, agencies must respond quickly in order to minimize the potential harm associated with identity theft. Applicable laws such as the Privacy Act currently do not require agencies to notify individuals of security breaches involving their personal information; however, doing so allows those affected the opportunity to take steps to protect themselves against the dangers of identity theft. For example, the California data breach notification law is credited with bringing to the public's notice large data breaches within the private sector, including at information resellers such as ChoicePoint and LexisNexis last year. Although we do not know how many instances of identity theft resulted from last year's data breaches, the Federal Trade Commission has previously reported that the overall cost of an incident of identity theft, as well as the harm to the victims, is significantly smaller if the misuse of the victim's personal information is discovered quickly. Arguably, the California law may have mitigated the risk of identity theft to affected individuals by keeping them informed about data breaches and thus enabling them to take steps such as contacting credit bureaus to have fraud alerts placed on their credit files, obtaining copies of their credit reports, scrutinizing their monthly financial account statements, and taking other steps to protect themselves. The chairman of the Federal Trade Commission has testified that the Commission believes that if a security breach creates a significant risk of identity theft or other related harm, affected consumers should be notified.

Breach notification is also important in that it can help an organization address key privacy rights of individuals. These rights ... have been widely adopted and are the basis of privacy laws and related policies in many countries, including the United States. In particular, the *openness* principle states that the public should be informed about privacy policies and practices, and individuals should have ready means of learning about the use of personal information. Breach notification is one way that organizations—either in the private sector or the government—can meet their responsibility for keeping the public informed of how their personal information is being used and who has access to it. Equally important is the *accountability* principle, which states that individuals controlling the collection or use of personal information should be accountable for taking steps to ensure the implementation of the other principles, such as use limitation and security safeguards. Public disclosure of data breaches is a key step in ensuring that organizations are held accountable for the protection of personal information.

Concerns Have Been Raised About the Criteria for Issuing Notices to the Public

Although the principle of notifying affected individuals (or the public) about data breaches has clear benefits, determining the specifics of when and how an agency should issue such notifications presents challenges, particularly in determining the specific criteria for incidents that merit notification. In congressional testimony, the Federal Trade Commission raised concerns about the threshold for which consumers should be notified of a breach, cautioning that too strict a standard could have several negative effects. First, notification of a breach when there is little or no risk of harm might create unnecessary concern and confusion. Second, a surfeit of notices, resulting from notification criteria that are too strict, could render all such notices less effective, because consumers could become numb to them and fail to act when risks are truly significant. Finally, the costs to both individuals and business are not insignificant and may be worth considering. The FTC points out that, in response to a security breach notification, a consumer may cancel credit cards, contact credit bureaus to place fraud alerts on credit files, or obtain a new driver's license number. These actions could be time-consuming for the individual and costly for the companies involved. Given these potential negative effects, care is clearly needed in defining appropriate criteria for required breach notifications.

While care needs to be taken to avoid requiring agencies to notify the public of trivial security incidents, concerns have also been raised about setting criteria that are too open-ended or that rely too heavily on the discretion of the affected organization. Some public advocacy groups have cautioned that notification criteria that are too weak would give companies an incentive not to disclose potentially harmful breaches. This concern could also apply to federal agencies. In congressional testimony last year, the executive director of the Center for Democracy and Technology argued that if an entity is not certain whether a breach warrants notification, it should be able to consult with the Federal Trade Commission. He went on to suggest that a two-tiered system may be desirable, with notice to the Federal Trade Commission of all breaches of personal data and notice to consumers where there is a potential risk of identity theft. The Center for Democracy and Technology's comments regarding the Federal Trade Commission were aimed at commercial entities such as information resellers. A different entity—such as OMB, which is responsible for overseeing security and privacy within the federal government—might be more appropriate to take on a parallel role with respect to federal agencies.

Effective Notices Should Provide Useful Information and Be Easy to Understand

Once a determination has been made that a public notice is to be issued, care must be taken to ensure that it does its job effectively. Designing useful, easy-to-understand notices has been cited as a challenge in other areas where privacy notices are required by law, such as in the financial industry—where businesses are required by the Gramm-Leach-Bliley Act to send notices to consumers about their privacy practices—and in the federal government, which is required by the Privacy Act to issue public notices in the *Federal Register* about its systems of records containing personal information. . . .

If an agency is to notify people of a data breach, it should do so in such a way that they understand the nature of the threat and what steps need to be taken to protect themselves against identity theft. In connection with its state law requiring security breach notifications, the California Office of Privacy Protection has published recommended practices for designing and issuing security breach notices. The office recommends that such notifications include, among other things,

- a general description of what happened;
- the type of personal information that was involved;
- what steps have been taken to prevent further unauthorized acquisition of personal information;
- the types of assistance to be provided to individuals, such as a toll-free contact telephone number for additional information and assistance;
- information on what individuals can do to protect themselves from identity theft, including contact information for the three credit reporting agencies; and:
- information on where individuals can obtain additional information on protection against identity theft, such as the Federal Trade Commission's Identity Theft Web site (www.consumer.gov/idtheft).

The California Office of Privacy Protection also recommends making notices clear, conspicuous, and helpful, by using clear, simple language and avoiding jargon and suggests avoiding using a standardized format to mitigate the risk that the public will become complacent about the process.

The Federal Trade Commission has issued guidance to businesses on notifying individuals of data breaches that reiterates several key elements of effective notification—describing clearly what is known about the data compromise, explaining what responses may be appropriate for the type of information taken, and providing information and contacts regarding identity theft in general. The Commission also suggests providing contact information for the law enforcement officer working on the case as well as encouraging individuals who discover that their information has been misused to file a complaint with the Commission.

Both the state of California and the Federal Trade Commission recommend consulting with cognizant law-enforcement officers about an incident before issuing notices to the public. In some cases, early notification or disclosure of certain facts about an incident could hamper a law enforcement investigation. For example, an otherwise unknowing thief could learn of the potential value of data stored on a laptop computer that was originally stolen purely for the value of the hardware. Thus it is recommended that organizations consult with law enforcement regarding the timing and content of notifications. However, law enforcement investigations should not necessarily result in lengthy delays in notification. California's guidance states that it should not be necessary for a law enforcement agency to complete an investigation before notification can be given....

In summary, agencies can take a number of actions to help guard against the possibility that databases of personally identifiable information are inadvertently compromised, among which developing PIAs and ensuring that a robust information security program is in place are key. More specific practical measures aimed at preventing inadvertent data breaches include limiting the collection of personal information, limiting data retention, limiting access to personal information and training personnel accordingly, and considering using technological controls such as encryption when data need to be stored on mobile devices. Nevertheless, data breaches can still occur at any time, and when they do, notification to the individuals affected and/or the public has clear benefits, allowing people the opportunity to take steps to protect themselves against the dangers of identity theft. Care is needed in defining appropriate criteria if agencies are to be required to report security breaches to the public. Further, care is also needed to ensure that notices are useful and easy-to-understand so that they are effective in alerting individuals to actions they may want to take to minimize the risk of identity theft.

As Congress considers legislation requiring agencies to notify individuals or the public about security breaches, it should ensure that specific criteria are defined for incidents that merit public notification. It may want to consider creating a two-tier reporting requirement, in which all security breaches are reported to OMB, and affected individuals are notified only of incidents involving significant risk. Further, Congress should consider requiring OMB to provide guidance to agencies on how to develop and issue security breach notices to affected individuals.

Mr. Chairman, this concludes my testimony today. I would happy to answer any questions you or other members of the committee may have.

Source: U.S. Congress. Government Accountability Office. "Privacy: Preventing and Responding to Improper Disclosures of Personal Information." Testimony by Comptroller General David M. Walker before the House Committee on Government Reform. GAO–06–833T, June 8, 2006. purl.access.gpo.gov/GPO/LPS73010 (accessed February 12, 2007).

International Survey on Public Attitudes toward the United States

June 13, 2006

████████ **THE DOCUMENT IN CONTEXT** ████████

Negative attitudes in the world toward the United States or its policies—especially the war in Iraq—increasingly encumbered U.S. foreign policy in 2006. Public opinion surveys and the statements of foreign governments showed a growing resistance in many places to the actions and policies of the Bush administration.

The Iraq War was by far the most controversial, as its growing unpopularity within the United States mirrored attitudes in most of the rest of the world, but other elements of the U.S. role internationally also were coming under challenge. Chief among these were Washington's policies toward Israel and the Palestinians and the perception that the United States was quick to lecture other countries but refused to abide by the lessons it tried to impose on others.

The administration of President George W. Bush had stepped up efforts to get its message across, particularly in the Middle East. One of Bush's closest aides, Karen Hughes, worked at the State Department to burnish the American image overseas, but she admitted in September it would be "the work of years and maybe decades" to overcome the current trend of anti-Americanism. *(Background, Historic Documents of 2005, p. 579)*

The Impact of the War and Abu Ghraib

After the collapse of the Soviet Union at the end of 1991, and all through the 1990s, global opinions of the United States generally were positive, according to reputable opinion surveys. Government officials, opinion leaders, and ordinary people in most countries believed the United States and the West "won" the cold war with the Soviet Union and that Washington was, at worst, a benign influence and, at best, a positive example. The United States also received an enormous sympathetic boost worldwide after the September 11, 2001, terrorist attacks in New York and Washington. Even some countries historically at odds with the United States, such as Iran and Syria, expressed sympathy and, in Iran's case, provided significant assistance to the U.S. military operation that ousted the Taliban regime in Afghanistan. *(September 11 background, Historic Documents of 2001, p. 614; Afghanistan invasion, Historic Documents of 2001, p. 686)*

Global attitudes quickly changed in the run-up to the U.S. invasion of Iraq in March 2003, however. While some key U.S. allies were supportive or even enthusiastic—notably British prime minister Tony Blair—most other countries either were grudging in their support or hostile to the invasion. Public attitudes were negative even in

Britain and some countries where leaders offered support to Bush. World attitudes toward the United States plummeted again in 2004 with the revelation that U.S. soldiers had humiliated Iraqi detainees at the Abu Ghraib prison near Baghdad. This incident compounded overwhelmingly negative views around the world about the seemingly endless detention of terrorism suspects at the U.S. naval base in Guantanamo Bay, Cuba, and news reports in 2005 that the CIA had tortured terrorism suspects at "secret prisons" in Europe.

Across much of the world, customary foes of the United States, and even some friends, said Washington preached human rights in other countries but did not hesitate to violate human rights when it felt the need. Such views were strongest in Muslim countries, where many people saw the invasion of Iraq, the war on terrorism, Abu Graib, and the Guantanamo imprisonments as establishing a pattern of anti-Muslim behavior by Washington. The Bush administration blamed the Abu Ghraib scandal on a small number of ill-supervised soldiers and insisted the detentions at Guantanamo Bay and similar actions were justified by the need to combat a particularly insidious brand of terrorism, but its justifications largely fell on deaf ears overseas. *(Abu Ghraib scandal, Historic Documents of 2004, p. 207)*

Survey of Global Opinions

Over the years 2002 through 2006 a series of surveys of global public opinion showed a decline in attitudes toward the United States in many—though not all—countries. One of the most extensive series of such surveys was conducted by the Pew Global Attitudes Project, a service of the nonpartisan Pew Research Center in Washington, D.C. Starting in 2002, the Pew project conducted annual opinion surveys in the United States and fourteen other countries, sampling views on major issues of the day, including attitudes toward the United States. As could be expected, opinions varied widely by country and by year. Attitudes toward the United States dropped substantially in several countries (particularly Muslim countries) in 2003 after the Iraq invasion but recovered slightly in some countries during 2004 and 2005, only to decline again in 2006.

"A year ago, anti-Americanism had showed some signs of abating, in part because of the positive feelings generated by U.S. aid for tsunami victims in Indonesia and elsewhere," the Pew Center's report said, referring to the massive tsunami that hit Indian Ocean countries at the end of 2004. "But favorable opinions of the United States have fallen in most of the fifteen countries surveyed" in early 2006. *(Tsunami background, Historic Documents of 2005, p. 990)*

In the 2006 survey, a majority of respondents in only four of the fourteen other countries besides the United States had a favorable opinion of the United States: Japan (63 percent), Nigeria (62 percent), India (56 percent), and Britain (56 percent). Attitudes toward the United States were distinctly unfavorable in the five Muslim-majority countries in the survey, with favorable responses of 30 percent each in Egypt and Indonesia, 27 percent in Pakistan, 15 percent in Jordan, and just 12 percent in Turkey. Turkey was a NATO ally of the United States, as were two European countries where only minorities had favorable views of the United States: Germany (37 percent) and Spain (27 percent). The percentages were marginally higher in three countries that were often at odds with U.S. foreign policy: China (47 percent), Russia (43 percent), and France (39 percent).

In general, the foreigners surveyed by Pew had an even dimmer view of President Bush than of the country he led. Bush received a positive majority in only two of the fourteen countries surveyed: India (56 percent) and Nigeria (52 percent). The relatively high figure in India might have resulted from the president's initiative to improve relations between the United States and India, starting with an agreement essentially acknowledging India as a nuclear power.

The Pew survey also showed that international support for the U.S. "global war on terror" had diminished sharply since 2002; only in India (65 percent) and Russia (52 percent) did absolute majorities still express support for the terrorism war; both of those countries had their own terrorism concerns (Kashmiri separatists, for India, and Chechen separatists, for Russia) and their leaders remained receptive to U.S. statements about the overriding importance of combating terrorism.

One of the most striking findings came from a question about whether the U.S. war to remove Saddam Hussein from power in Iraq had made the world safer or more dangerous. The United States was the only country where even a slim majority (51 percent) said the war had made the world safer. While 41 percent of respondents in both India and Nigeria thought the world safer, in most other countries strong majorities said the Iraq War had made the world more dangerous.

Other global opinion surveys during the year showed results that were similar to those in to the Pew survey. Particularly noteworthy was a survey, published by London's *Telegraph* newspaper on July 3, showing that a majority of Britons held a range of negative attitudes about the U.S. government and several perceived social characteristics of the American people, including their racial divisions and obsessions with money. Bush did not fare well in this survey: 34 percent rated him "pretty poor" as a leader and 43 rated him "terrible." A broader survey of Europeans, conducted by the German Marshall Fund of the United States and released on September 9, found that more than 75 percent of respondents disapproved of Bush's foreign policies and only about 35 percent said it was desirable for the United States to exert strong leadership in the world.

The standing of the United States in the Muslim world tumbled even further in mid-2006 as a result of the Bush administration's posture toward the brief but bloody war between Israel and the Hezbollah militia in Lebanon. The administration slowed down the international push for a Mideast cease-fire, allowing Israel to mount an invasion of southern Lebanon in pursuit of Hezbollah fighters and their missiles. This stance was widely viewed by Arabs and other Muslims as the latest manifestation of Washington's unquestioning support of Israel. Many Arabs, and more broadly, Muslims, also were angered by the Bush administration's rebuff of the new Hamas-led Palestinian government, which had come to power as a result of elections in January. Many in the Middle East said the administration was hypocritical, having pushed for democracy in the region but then refusing to accept the results when voters elected people with views unacceptable to Washington.

The current round of negative global attitudes toward the United States and its policies brought expressions of concern from many American politicians, academics, and newspaper editorialists. In general, these opinion leaders worried that international lack of support for the United States, or even outright hostility toward it, would undermine U.S. interests for years to come. They noted, for example, that the few countries that had sent troops to support the United States in Iraq in 2003 had since withdrawn nearly all of them—in most cases because of hostility to the Iraq War in those countries.

Others, however, said these attitudes represented just the latest wave of anti-Americanism stemming in part from global resentment of the United States as a superpower. Julia Sweig, an analyst at the Council on Foreign Relations, published a book in 2006 describing what she called the coming "anti-American century." In an interview on March 19, she said one reason for the intense worldwide focus on the United States was that "we remain the single superpower, and so all eyes are on us, and so what we do and what we don't do really matters."

Writing in the *Washington Post* on June 19, foreign policy specialist Robert Kagan recalled previous waves of anti-Americanism during the cold war and said the current trend "will ebb, just as in the past." Perceived legitimacy on the world stage was important for the United States, Kagan said, but "neither should we be paralyzed by the unavoidable resentments that our power creates. If we refrained from action out of fear that others around the world would be angry with us, then we would never act. And count on it: They'd blame us for that, too." Kagan was a senior associate at the Carnegie Endowment for International Peace in Washington, D.C., and had been a staunch advocate of Bush's muscular approach to Iraq and other matters.

Following are excerpts from "America's Image Slips, But Allies Share U.S. Concerns over Iran, Hamas," a report of the findings from the Pew Global Attitudes Survey, released on June 13, 2006. The survey was conducted among nearly 17,000 people in the United States and fourteen other nations from March 31 to May 14, 2006, by the Pew Global Attitudes Project, a service of the Pew Research Center in Washington, D.C.

▬▬▬▬▬ D O C U M E N T ▬▬▬▬▬

"America's Image Slips, But Allies Share Concerns over Iran, Hamas"

I. America's Image and U.S. Foreign Policy

With America's image declining in many parts of the world, favorability ratings for the United States continue to trail those of other major countries. In Europe, as well as predominantly Muslim countries, the U.S. is generally less popular than Germany, France, Japan, and China. However, the U.S. fares somewhat better in Asia; in fact, Indians rate the U.S. higher than Germany, France, or China and only slightly below Japan. However, America's favorability rating has dropped 15 points in India since last year.

Meanwhile, Japan and China, two neighboring Asian rivals with long histories of conflict, hold very negative opinions of one another. Slightly more than a quarter of Japanese (28%) have a positive opinion of China, and even fewer Chinese (21%) have a favorable view of Japan. On the other hand, traditional European rivals Germany and France rate one another quite positively; in fact, both rate the other country more favorably than their own.

In Western Europe, attitudes toward America remain considerably more negative than they were in 2002, prior to the Iraq war. However, in a reversal of recent patterns, this year young people in France and Germany are more likely to have a favorable opinion of the

U.S. than are their older counterparts. Over the last year, positive assessments of the U.S. have increased among French and German 18–34 year-olds, while declining among those age 35 and older.

Nigerians Split Over U.S.

In Nigeria, Christians and Muslims hold starkly different opinions of the U.S., and America's relatively high overall rating—62% favorable—masks deep divisions between the country's two main religious groups. Roughly nine-in-ten (89%) Nigerian Christians have a favorable view of the U.S., compared with only 32% of Nigerian Muslims.

This gap has grown slightly since 2003, when America's favorability was 85% among Christians and 38% among Muslims. Christians and Muslims have quite different views of other countries as well, but these two groups are especially polarized over the U.S., with Christians holding a more positive view of the U.S. than of other countries and Muslims having a more negative view of America than of other countries.

France's Image Slips

Turmoil in France over the last year—riots by immigrants and others last fall, as well as protests in February through April of this year over an attempt to change French labor law—appears to have taken a toll on France's image. In every country where trends are available—with one exception—the image of France has declined significantly since 2005, including double digit falls in Indonesia (from 68% to 52% favorable), Turkey (from 30% to 18%), and Great Britain (from 71% to 59%).

The lone exception is the U.S., where 52% now have a favorable impression of France, still below the pre-Iraq War level of 79% in February 2002, but up from 46% last year. France is considerably more popular now among Americans than in May 2003, when only 29% gave France a favorable grade.

Americans More Favorable

The improved attitudes in the U.S. toward France are part of a broader trend—the American public's feelings about other major countries are also more positive than in 2005. Germany, China, and Japan also receive more positive assessments from the American people.

A narrow majority of Americans (52%) now have a favorable opinion of China, up from 43% last year. And the already strong favorability rating for Germany has also improved, jumping from 60% in 2005 to 66% this year. Japan's rating has also grown from 63% to 66%; however, this is not a statistically significant change.

Views of the American People

Opinions of the American people have declined, in some cases substantially, since 2002. Nonetheless, publics around the world continue to have a more positive opinion of the American people than they do of the United States. In seven of the 14 foreign countries surveyed, at least half of respondents have a favorable impression of Americans; in contrast, four countries give the U.S. positive marks. Americans remain relatively popular in Britain, France, and Germany; however in Spain, the image of Americans has plummeted, dropping from 55% favorable last year to 37% this year. On this issue, the Spanish public is now more similar to Muslim countries than to its Western European neighbors.

Although Americans are still unpopular in the five predominantly Muslim countries, there have been slight, but significant, improvements in Jordan and Pakistan. These are balanced, however, by declines among Indonesians and Turks. In Turkey—a longstanding NATO ally—fewer than one-in-five (17%) have a favorable opinion of Americans.

Perceptions of the American people have grown more negative in Nigeria since 2003, however almost all of the decline has taken place among the country's Muslim population— in 2003 48% of Muslims had a favorable impression of Americans; three years later only 23% view Americans favorably. Meanwhile, Nigerian Christians continue to hold Americans in extraordinarily high regard (88% favorable in 2003, 86% favorable today).

Americans are relatively well-liked in the three Asian countries we surveyed, with 82% of Japanese giving the American people favorable marks, up from 73% in 2002. Americans remain popular in India (67% favorable), and in China the favorability rating for Americans has increased six points to 49%.

Bush Even Less Popular in Europe

While the past year has been a difficult one for President Bush domestically, his troubles are also reflected in international public opinion. Confidence in Bush to do the right thing in world affairs has dropped in seven of the 11 countries where trend data from 2005 is available. Opinion of Bush has continued to decline in European countries, while Muslims publics remain strongly opposed to the American president. At 3%, Turkey now registers the lowest level of confidence in President Bush. The country with the largest drop in confidence for Bush over the last year, however, is the U.S.; 62% had a lot or some confidence in Bush last year, compared to 50% this year.

Bush receives relatively low marks compared to the other European leaders tested on the survey—Great Britain's Tony Blair, France's Jacque Chirac, Germany's Angela Merkel, and Russia's Vladimir Putin—although there are some exceptions. For example, Bush is the highest rated leader in India and Nigeria. In the latter, Bush's popularity is overwhelmingly driven by the country's Christian population (82% a lot or some confidence among Christians, 19% among Muslims).

Tony Blair remains extremely popular among the American people, as two-in-three have confidence that he will do the right thing in world affairs. Despite being a left-of-center political figure in Britain, Blair is especially popular among Republicans (88% a lot or some confidence), although majorities of Democrats (55%) and independents (63%) also have confidence in the British prime minister. However, Americans place little trust in either Chirac or Putin. Meanwhile, despite two trips to the U.S. since her election as Germany's first female chancellor, a plurality (39%) of Americans declined to offer an opinion of Merkel. Among Germans, however, she is extremely popular—77% of Germans have confidence in her ability to handle international affairs.

Waning Support for the War on Terrorism

Nearly five years after the Sept. 11, 2001 attacks, international support for the U.S.-led war on terrorism continues to wane. Outside of the U.S. only two countries—India and Russia—register majority support for the war on terror, and it remains particularly unpopular in predominantly Muslim countries, although support has risen eight points since last year among Pakistanis, whose government is a key partner in efforts to combat Al Qaeda. Among several of America's traditional allies, support has fallen steeply since 2002, and it has virtually collapsed in two countries, Spain and Japan. In the former, the percentage who favor U.S. efforts against terrorism now stands at 19%, down from 63% in 2003, while among Japanese it has tumbled from 61% in 2002 to 26% today.

Ongoing Concerns about Iraq

As was true last year, publics from a variety of regions believe the war in Iraq has generated more instability in the world. In ten of fifteen countries, a majority say the war has made the world more dangerous. The French public is the most likely to believe this, followed by Jordan, Turkey, and Egypt. Meanwhile, the U.S. is the only country in which a majority—although a narrow one (51%)—believes the war has made the world a safer place, although pluralities in India and Nigeria also think the war has made the world safer.

International opinion on the future of Iraq is generally gloomy. Majorities in most countries surveyed believe that efforts to establish a stable democratic government in Iraq will ultimately fail. Pessimism is strongest in Spain, Turkey, Germany, Jordan, and Egypt—in all five countries, more than six-in-ten respondents believe efforts to establish democracy will definitely or probably fail.

However, a narrow majority in Great Britain, the country with the second largest military contingent in Iraq, believe these efforts will ultimately succeed. Even greater numbers of Indians and Nigerians believe democracy will be established in Iraq.

American public opinion also tends to be somewhat optimistic about the future of Iraq, with 54% saying efforts to establish a stable democratic government will be successful, up from 49% in March of this year, but down from 60% in July 2005. Views on this issue are driven at least in part by party affiliation—76% of Republicans believe the war will end in success, compared with only 39% of Democrats and 52% of independents.

Source: Pew Research Center. The Pew Global Attitudes Project. "America's Image Slips, But Allies Share U.S. Concerns over Iran, Hamas." June 13, 2006. http://pewglobal.org/reports/display.php?ReportID=252 (accessed March 16, 2007).

Other Historic Documents of Interest

Ford Executive on Problems Facing American Car Manufacturers

June 14, 2006

Burdened by stiff competition from foreign automakers, high gas prices, mounting employee benefit and pension costs, and the consequences of their own decisions, the "Big Three" American automakers—General Motors (GM), Ford Motor Company, and Chrysler—were in big trouble in 2006. GM, the largest auto manufacturer in the world since 1931, was on the verge of relinquishing that title to Toyota Motor Company of Japan, perhaps in 2007. Ford lost $12.7 billion in 2006, the biggest loss in its history. Chrysler, which ended 2005 in the black, fell into red ink midway through 2006. All three companies were struggling to find restructuring strategies that would put them back on a path to profitability.

The decline of the Big Three, long the symbol of American manufacturing might, was a concern not only to the companies' shareholders but also to their workers. Represented primarily by the powerful United Auto Workers (UAW) union, hourly workers in the auto and auto parts industry had long boasted some of the most generous wages and benefits of any blue-collar workers in U.S. manufacturing. But in the last two decades, the Big Three cut tens of thousands of jobs. Now, with several parts manufacturers already in bankruptcy and doubts about the viability of the three automakers, union workers were facing even more massive layoffs and benefit reductions. UAW president Ron Gettelfinger urged his membership to be prepared to make some significant wage and benefit concessions to help rescue the auto industry. "This isn't a cyclical downturn," he said June 12 at a UAW leadership convention in Las Vegas. "The kind of challenges we face aren't the kind that can be ridden out. They're structural challenges and they require new and farsighted solutions." Still, it was unclear how much in concessions the union was prepared to make. UAW contract negotiations with all three U.S. automakers were scheduled for 2007.

Insular Attitudes, Legacy Costs

Many of the problems facing the American car manufacturers in 2006 had been in the making for decades. Critics had long complained that the American companies had hurt themselves by making the cars they wanted to make, rather than making the cars American consumers wanted to buy. The "what's good for General Motors is good for America" attitude had worked in the past. But during the oil crises of the 1970s and the economic slowdown that followed, American buyers turned in droves to the more fuel-efficient, reliable Japanese cars that were just beginning to be imported into the United States. At about the same time, the American companies were grappling with meeting new government fuel-economy, clear air, and safety regulations. And the industry known for developing the assembly line and mass production also had to retool their factories toward the "lean production" patterns of their foreign rivals. All of these were matters that many critics said the American manufacturers had been slow to deal with. The combination of events gave Toyota and Honda a good foot in the door of the American market and threw the Big Three into their first serious financial crisis since the second World War.

As the general economy picked up in the mid-1990s, the domestic manufacturers increasingly left the small and luxury car markets to foreign makers and concentrated on building and selling popular and highly profitable pick-up trucks and sports utility vehicles (SUVs). By 2006 trucks, SUVs, and minivans had become the mainstay of the domestic auto industry, accounting for about 60 percent of GM sales, about 66 percent of Ford sales, and 75 percent of Chrysler sales. When spikes in world oil prices pushed gasoline prices above $2 a gallon in 2004 and above $3 a gallon for periods in 2005 and 2006, the American car makers once again had few smaller, more fuel-efficient cars to offer buyers. Instead the car makers offered large discounts on their gas-guzzling models, which greatly lowered their profitability.

In an unusually forthright statement, Mark Fields, president of the Ford Motor Company in the Americas, acknowledged that the company had made strategic mistakes that had hurt the profitability of the company. "Too often in the past, our philosophy was to move the metal—to build the vehicles we have the capacity to build and then price them—and often discount them—to get the customer to bite," Fields said June 14 in a speech to the U.S. Chamber of Commerce in Washington. "We allowed ourselves to get bogged down in the accumulated decisions and systems of the past, getting stuck in old ways of thinking, and producing products that were a reflection of that thinking. . . . Even when we had successes, like with our SUVs, we grew so dependent upon that success that we didn't look far enough beyond the horizon, tracking the trends, knowing our customers, and seeing the day when they might want something else."

Another long-standing problem facing the companies was the product of decades of generous pension and health benefits. The companies had been willing to guarantee generous benefits when they were competing primarily with each other. But those "legacy" costs mounted as auto workers aged and retired. They put the companies at a competitive disadvantage to foreign makers whose wage and benefit structures were lower. The collapse of the stock market and the slowdown of the economy in 2000, followed by years of slow recovery, left the U.S. companies with badly underfunded pension and health benefit funds for their current and retired workers. In May 2005 Standard & Poor's (S&P), the credit rating agency, marked Ford and General Motor's ratings down to "junk bond" status. At the time, S&P put Ford's unfunded pension liability at $12.3 billion and its unfunded health care liability at $32.4 billion. GM's pension funds were considered fully funded under current federal standards, but its unfunded health liability was put at $61 billion. Both companies said that health and pension costs accounted for about $1,800 of the cost of every car—considerably more than the steel used to make it. In 2005 the two companies negotiated a deal with the UAW that required auto workers to pick up more of the cost of their health care tab.

Competition: Seeking a Level Playing Field

In several speeches throughout 2006, top executives at all three companies acknowledged that they needed to make structural adjustments to correct for past mistakes in their own judgment and put them on a better competitive footing with foreign automakers in the U.S. market. But they also called upon Washington to help bolster their competitiveness. One request was for the Bush administration to push for more open markets overseas, particularly in South Korea. In his June 14 speech, for example, Ford's Fields noted that the administration was negotiating a bilateral trade agreement with South Korea and asked that it include "full and unimpeded access" for U.S.-made vehicles in the Korean market. Fields said that in 2000 fewer than 4,000 U.S.-made cars were allowed into South Korea, while more than 730,000 Korean cars were exported for sale to the United States.

The chief executives of the Big Three also said that exchange rate policy was hurting their bottom line. After a meeting with President George W. Bush on November 14, the auto executives generally praised the president for calling for free-but-fair trade. But they said they wanted the administration to do more about what they considered to be a systematic undervaluation of the Japanese yen against the dollar. Undervaluation of the yen "basically provides huge profits on the approximately 2.3 million vehicles that are being exported from Japan to the United States" every year, Alan Mulally, president and CEO of Ford Motor Co. explained to the *Washington Post*. That represented a "huge profit advantage," Mulally said, "which then can be used to reinvest in new technologies" and "puts us at a competitive disadvantage."

The chief executives also said they needed cooperation from the government if they were to build successful alternative fuel vehicles. Noting that the Big Three had already agreed to double production of "flexible fuel" vehicles by 2010, G. Richard Wagoner Jr., chairman and chief executive of General Motors, said they had "told the president if we could be assured of adequate availability of ethanol and adequate distribution capability, we would go significantly beyond that and produce up to 50 percent of our vehicles by the year 2012 that would be enabled to either use ethanol or biodiesel." The auto companies needed those assurances, Wagoner said, because drivers would not buy fuel flexible cars if they could not buy the alternative fuels at their local service stations. Of the 170,000 service stations in the United States, only about 700 sold the corn-based fuel E85 (a blend of 85 percent ethanol and 15 percent unleaded gasoline).

General Motors

GM lost $10.4 billion in 2005, its largest loss since 1992, when the company nearly went bankrupt and top management was ousted. In December 2005 the company announced a restructuring plan that included cutting 30,000 jobs and closing all or parts of twelve plants by 2008. It also pledged to cut its legacy costs by $7.5 billion a year. In the first few months of 2006 the company cut executive pay; sold a portion of its share of its finance unit, GMAC; and took several other steps to stabilize its operations. The big breakthrough, however, came in March, when GM, Delphi, and the UAW reached agreement on a worker buyout. Delphi, the auto parts company that was spun off from GM in 1999 and was still GM's largest supplier, had filed for bankruptcy in 2005. Under the agreement GM said it would offer up to $140,000 to any of its 113,000 hourly workers and to 13,000 of Delphi's hourly workers who decided to leave the company. In June GM announced that 47,600 workers—35,000 at GM and 12,600 at Delphi—had accepted the buyout package or early retirement.

Closely watching GM's turnaround efforts was billionaire Kirk Kerkorian, who started buying up GM shares in 2005 and soon held nearly 10 percent of the company, making him GM's largest and most influential shareholder. Kerkorian criticized

Wagoner and the rest of GM's management for not moving faster to solve GM's financial problems. His representative, Jerome B. York, who was named to GM's board of directors in February 2006, also kept pressure on the GM management team. Under intense prodding by Kerkorian and York, GM executives entered talks in July with Nissan and Renault about a possible alliance. But the three companies broke off talks on October 4. That development was seen as a victory for Wagoner, who had argued that the company was making progress on its own and did not need the support of other companies, and a loss for Kerkorian and York. Complaining that GM was too timid in addressing its problems, York resigned from GM's board on October 6, and Kerkorian began to sell his stock in the company. By December 1 Kerkorian had sold the last of his stock and was no longer an immediate threat to GM management.

GM finished the year with net income in the fourth quarter of $950 million, bringing its losses for the year to $2 billion. That was a substantial improvement over 2005, but the company was still facing nearly $50 billion in health care and other long-term liabilities and difficult negotiations in 2007 with the UAW and its other unions.

Ford

Of the Big Three, Ford Motor Co. posted the biggest loss of the year, $12.7 billion, the largest shortfall in its history. The company said about 75 percent of the loss was attributable to its restructuring effort in North America, announced in January. Called "The Way Forward," the plan anticipated layoffs of about 30,000 hourly workers—about one-quarter of its workforce—and closing as many as fourteen plants by 2012. Ford's goal was to become profitable in North America by 2008, company officials said.

But with sales continuing to sink, the company announced several more changes. In August, Ford announced that it would cut production by 168,000 vehicles, or 21 percent, in the fourth quarter. On September 5, company chairman William Clay Ford Jr., a great-grandson of company founder Henry Ford, turned over his role as chief executive officer to Alan Mulally. Earlier in the decade Mulally had helped turn around the fortunes of Boeing, the then-beleaguered airplane manufacturer. On September 15, Ford announced that it would cut 10,000 salaried jobs, close two more factories, and push its goal for reaching profitability to 2009. In a bit of good news, Ford announced on September 14 that it had reached agreement with the UAW to offer the company's 75,000 North American workers buyouts of up to $140,000 each. The agreement was similar to the one reached by GM and the UAW earlier in the year. Ford said in late November that 38,000 workers had already signed up for the buyout.

Chrysler

Chrysler avoided bankruptcy in 1979 when it won a controversial bailout from the federal government. The company recovered, repaid the government, and in 1998 merged with the German company Daimler Benz to become DaimlerChrysler. Its North American component, the Chrysler Group, remained headquartered in Detroit. Chrysler was the only one of the Big Three to begin the year with an operating profit, but with increases in the price of gasoline, steel, and other materials used in automaking, all three companies began to see sales fall off and costs creep up. In July, Chrysler's share of the U.S. market dropped to 10 percent, and the company was fifth behind GM, Toyota, Ford, and Honda.

By the end of the year, Chrysler was struggling with a large excess inventory, which the company built simply to keep its factories operating. It was also facing higher labor costs than its two American competitors because it had not yet been able to negotiate a deal with its unions, similar to the ones Ford and GM worked out in 2005, to have its workers pick up a greater share of their health care costs.

Chrysler was more reliant than the other two companies on trucks and SUVs. The company posted a $1.5 billion loss for the year, and rumors were flying that it was getting ready to lay off 10,000 workers and close some plants—and that the company might once again be on the market.

Following are excerpts from the text of a speech, delivered on June 14, 2006, by Mark Fields, president of the Ford Motor Company in the Americas, to the U.S. Chamber of Commerce in Washington, D.C., on the company's plans for returning to financial health.

■■■ DOCUMENT ■■■

"Remarks by Mark Fields, President, Ford Motor Company"

It's a pleasure to be here this morning at the United States Chamber of Commerce. Any corporate executive who has something to say—to consumers, to business colleagues, to the United States government—is lucky to get the chance to say it here.

The US Chamber was founded—at the request of a US President—because both corporate and government interests understood that the health of our society depends on the health of business in that society.

That's why societies have a profound interest in the health of their businesses—and the United States has a profound interest in the health of American business.

There is perhaps no business more iconic to America than the automobile industry. Kids sketch cars in their notebooks . . . musicians sing about them . . . everyone from Steve McQueen to Pixar have made movies about them. Automobiles move our families and are the backbone of our commerce. And nothing makes the heart race like seeing a Mustang GT tear down the road.

Our cars aren't just American icons. I'm here because a successful domestic automobile company is a national treasure.

And that imposes a unique responsibility on Ford as well as our partners in government.

Today, I want to talk with you about how Ford Motor Company is fulfilling our obligations, what our partners in government can do to help, and why it matters to America.

First, let me tell you how Ford is taking responsibility for its own future.

And that means first acknowledging that we've made mistakes in the past.

Perhaps, in the language of Washington, I should say, "Mistakes were made."

Too often in the past, our philosophy was to move the metal—to build the vehicles we had the capacity to build and then price them—and often discount them—to get the customer to bite.

We allowed ourselves to get bogged down in the accumulated decisions and systems of the past, getting stuck in old ways of thinking, and producing products that were a reflection of that thinking—vehicles that aimed to be all things to all people, but instead ended up being too little to too few.

Even when we had successes, like with our SUVs, we grew so dependent upon that success that we didn't look far enough beyond the horizon, tracking the trends, knowing our customers, and seeing the day when they might want something else.

Today, I'm proud to tell you, that's the Ford of the past—not the Ford of today.

True customer-focus means that our business decisions originate from our knowledge of what the customer wants, both today and tomorrow. "If you build it, they will buy it"—that's business as usual, and that's wrong. "If they will buy it, we will build it" is right—and we're going back to it.

Ford remains an iconic American brand, and we still enjoy economies of scale, loyal customers, great suppliers, committed dealers, productive workers, and visionary designers and engineers.

And, this is a bit of news that doesn't get reported enough: Even while we face a tough 2006 in North America, we continue to make money around the world. In fact, every one of our operations outside the United States—Asia, Europe, South America—was profitable last year and in the first quarter this year, with a solid foundation for growth in the long-term.

That said, it is our mission—and my intention—to return our North American automotive operations to profitability as well—and to do so no later than 2008.

To that end, we've launched a turnaround plan called The Way Forward. It was created by challenging some of the brightest minds in our business to question everything we did and then to draw up a blueprint for our success.

This plan has been characterized by some in the media as job cuts and plant closings. It does include those things, and they are painful to acknowledge and enact. But that's not the heart of the plan. We can't cut our way to growth. We have to innovate.

That means innovating under the hood . . . in design . . . in quality . . . in safety . . . in environmental impact . . . and in production. But innovation for its own sake won't work. We have to innovate for a purpose—and that purpose is building bold, relevant vehicles that people want to buy.

The United States is the most open and competitive automotive market in the world. By the end of the decade, there will be more than 300 models competing for customers' attention. If you miss the mark on what consumers want, they'll go somewhere else, fast.

That's the reality, and it's also a huge opportunity.

Because if you do hit that sweet spot—with vehicles that excite people and meet their needs—you can profit just as quickly, too.

Although it's still in its early days, we're already seeing The Way Forward at work.

Our new products—especially our fuel-efficient cars—are selling well. The Ford Fusion, Mercury Milan, and Lincoln Zephyr, all had their best months ever, and are gaining share at the expense of our Japanese competitors.

The new Ford Fusion in particular is our way of saying that the Honda Accord and Toyota Camry's reign at the top of the American sedan market are no longer unchallenged. And people are responding—Fusion buyers are younger than our average buyers, and 93% of them would recommend it to a friend.

We're also playing to our existing product strengths. The F-Series trucks are up in both sales and share this year—while Chevy, Nissan, and Toyota have all stagnated or lost share in that segment.

In addition, we're developing new strengths, with the new Ford Edge coming later this year poised to satisfy a growing demand for crossover vehicles, and with the Ford Escape and Mercury Mariner hybrids posting record sales of late.

Finally, we're looking beyond just the next quarter, or even the next year, but to the next generation of transportation. As we developed the hybrid engine that powers the Ford Escape and Mercury Mariner, our innovations led to more than 130 patents, with additional patents still pending. We're now applying those engineering insights to the hybrid hydrogen fuel cell powered vehicles we're currently testing.

And we're putting 250,000 flex-fuel E-85 vehicles on the road this year, while working on new alternatives, such as clean diesel and hydrogen internal combustion engines.

Our name is the Ford Motor Company. Nowhere does it say that we're the "Ford traditional gasoline-powered internal combustion Motor Company."

As a result of our new products, we've slowed our decline in market-share, our quality continues to improve, and we're on pace to convert three quarters of our North American assembly plants to flexible manufacturing by 2008—enabling us to switch between models and deliver more products faster based on changing demand.

We're also on schedule with plant idlings, we've completed our promised 10 percent reduction in salaried costs, we're making faster-than-expected progress on our hourly reductions, and our retiree health agreement is close to completion.

This is what Ford Motor Company can and must do to return to profitability in North America—and we're committed to it. But this is just part of the equation.

It's just as important that our partners in government work with us to ensure an even playing field as we compete with our automotive rivals from around the world.

In any export business, you hear the words "level playing field" quite a bit. In all my time in the auto industry, I'm not sure I've ever had the opportunity to play on one.

In my 17 years with Ford Motor Company, I've worked in auto markets around the world. Last September, I returned to the US after having spent the previous ten years abroad, including time in South America running Ford of Argentina, in Japan as CEO of Mazda, and in the United Kingdom as the head of Ford of Europe and President of Ford's Premier Automotive Group, which includes Volvo, Land Rover, Jaguar, and Aston Martin.

These experiences have given me a good perspective on how government can partner with—or stand in the way of—its manufacturing industries.

In Europe, manufacturing generally—and the automobile industry specifically—struggles to operate under a crushing burden of regulation imposed at the local, national, and European Union [EU] levels. By 2010, EU regulation already on the books—or those being speculated about—could add approximately 5,000 Euros—6,300 dollars—to the cost of vehicle we make in Europe.

How are companies responding to such regulatory and tax burdens? They're leaving. During my time in Europe, I witnessed a steady exodus of automotive jobs from every major automotive manufacturer, including ours.

During my time in Asia, I saw a different approach. Governments saw export industries as strategically important, vital to the national interest, and therefore deserving of crucial assistance from their government partners. So the government of Japan, whose automakers already enjoyed the competitive advantage of nationalized health care and pensions, also gave its automakers the further advantage of R&D [research and development] assistance and significant trade support, including a willingness to distort their currency—something I saw first hand.

It's not just Japan. Over the last two decades, the Korean government—as a matter of national policy—enacted a series of steps to close their market to imports while boosting its own automobile exports. The results are striking. Last year, less than 4,000 US-made vehicles were permitted to be sold in Korea—while Korean brands exported more than 730,000 vehicles to the United States.

These trade and economic policies, while offering some advantages to their national manufacturers and exporters, come at a cost. In Europe, it's a shrinking automotive manufacturing industry. In Japan, it's an economy that has stagnated due to excessive government intervention. In Korea, it's a lack of public faith among consumers due to the cozy—and even corrupt—relationship between government and industry.

There is a reason why governments around the world pay close attention to their domestic automobile industries. As an industry, automakers represent the single greatest engine of economic activity in the world. Automobile manufacturers drive raw materials development, financial systems, advanced materials and manufacturing development, safety innovations, and environmental controls.

In America, the domestic auto companies buy 60 percent of the country's rubber and nearly a third of its iron, aluminum, and steel. Domestic automakers also represent the largest source of corporate research in America. More than semiconductors, software or pharmaceuticals.

But when it comes to the economic benefits to American society, all cars are not created equal.

Foreign automakers own about 40 percent of the US market today, but they employ only about 20 percent of the workers—and purchase only 20 percent of the parts built here in the US.

Domestic manufacturers, on the other hand, build our cars with, on average, about 80 percent US content. For the record, Hyundai has about ten percent domestic content. VWs at 5 percent. Mitsubishi's at 36 percent. Toyota is about 47 percent.

If you don't see a big difference between 47 percent and 80 percent, you should. Parts makers employ nearly 3 times more Americans than automakers.

So, despite all their claims about being "American," most of the cars and trucks the foreign automakers sell in America aren't actually made in America. What's more, most of the design and engineering jobs are not located in America. And the profits from the sales of those foreign cars are largely not spent in America.

Now, we welcome foreign investment and new jobs. But, if this is going to be a fair fight, we have to understand America's business interests. If we think we can replace lost sales of domestic autos with rising sales of foreign imports or even domestically-built foreign cars, and suffer no significant economic loss, we are badly mistaken.

Taken together, GM, Ford, and Daimler-Chrysler directly employ about 350,000 autoworkers—eight out of ten workers in the industry. When you add in all the jobs they support—whether it's suppliers or accountants—that number jumps to 4.5 million US jobs, in communities across America. Put another way, for every assembly job that US automakers create here in the states, it creates between seven and 10 other jobs down the value stream. That's why it's in our national interest to seek a level playing field.

Just as the Japanese automotive industry is strategically important to the people of Japan, the health of the US auto industry is strategically important to the people of the US—even if you don't work for a US auto company or drive an American car.

So, what are we asking from our partners in government and industry? We are not asking for anybody to help us alone or help us uniquely. No bailouts. No handouts. But—having taken the steps to help ourselves—we think it's important that we all come together to address the external challenges that affect so many American businesses.

Let me just mention a couple of the areas where Ford's interest and our national interest intersect.

Energy

The first is energy. Ford is working to make our existing conventional engines more efficient and to invest in engines that run on new sources of energy, like battery power, ethanol, and other biofuels. Ford developed the first American hybrid—the Ford Escape Hybrid SUV. And, as I said earlier, we've made a significant investment in vehicles that run on E-85 ethanol, which support American agriculture, offers families a choice at the pump, and lessens our dependence on foreign oil.

Today, Ford has more than 1.6 million flex-fuel vehicles on the road, and we're committed to producing another quarter-million this year. We see renewable fuels as a vital part of our future, too, and that's why, along with GM and Daimler-Chrysler, we've endorsed the Energy Futures Coalition's goal of getting 25 percent of the country's transportation energy from renewable sources by 2025.

The problem is that, while our vehicles have the capability to use E-85, there aren't enough gas stations out there to supply it. There are 170,000 gas stations in the United States. But there are only about 700 E-85 gas pumps. If you have a flex fuel vehicle here in Washington, DC, there is not one station in The District where you can fill it up. In all of Virginia, there is only one. In Maryland, only four.

That's not enough. Right now, Ford is investing its own money, working with partners like VeraSun, the second largest ethanol producer in the country, to increase the number of E-85 ethanol pumps in America—a process that costs as little as $5,000 a pump. This is a place where businesses, such as the oil companies and the government, through incentives like tax credits can do much more than we ever could to increase retail distribution of E-85.

You know, there's a reason we're doing something about energy independence—it's what our President has called for, it's what the Congress has been working on, and, more importantly, it's good for America.

Health Care

It's no secret that the skyrocketing cost of health care is one of the greatest challenges any of us in business face. When costs are rising eight percent a year, it's a corporate competitiveness issue—and no business, big or small, can ignore it. This is especially true of Ford, when every car off the line has about $1,110 in worker and retiree health care costs built into it. That's more in health care than in steel, and that's $500 to $600 in costs our foreign competitors operating in the US don't have to carry.

Unfortunately, I don't have time to get into a discussion this morning, but I want you to know that we're working overtime in Detroit to get our health care costs in line. We've invested in health IT . . . we've steered our employees toward mail ordered maintenance drugs and generic versions when available . . . and we have innovative wellness and disease management programs. Taking on this issue is a little like boiling the ocean—and even big changes seem like we're just nibbling around the edges. It's going to take all of us—corporations, government, and the American people—to find a solution.

R&D

Another way to fuel greater competitiveness is to support the investments we're making in research and development. Research and development is the lifeblood of manufacturing, and currently, the automotive industry is the largest source of corporate R&D in the United States.

The Japanese auto manufacturers employ about 4,000 R&D jobs at 33 facilities nationwide. That's all well and good, but as a point of comparison, there are 65,000 people employed in auto R&D at 200 facilities in Michigan alone.

Ford alone spends about $7.5 billion a year on R&D. That's nearly as much as NASA and more than the Department of Agriculture, Interior, Labor, Justice, Commerce, Transportation, EPA, Education and Homeland Security combined.

We believe this is one of the best investments we can make. But we shouldn't have to make that investment alone. While the government of Japan directly supported the development of their first hybrid battery—one of the most complex and expensive components of a hybrid vehicle—we developed ours ourselves.

We don't need the full force of the federal government behind our efforts; all we are seeking is the certainty that allows us to make the investments we're already making. We're asking for a permanent research and development tax credit that we can count on through the highs and the lows of the business cycle.

But it's not just about developing new technologies; it's also about investing in the factories to put those new technologies to work.

Right now, the difficult truth is that it's a lot easier to build a brand new factory than to retrofit an old one. You are a hero to an entire state if you build a new plant. States and local governments subsidize new investments, in some cases as much as $160,000 per job. Governors get re-elected winning new plants.

But you don't get as much help, or credit, when you invest just as much money updating existing plants.

Ford, GM, and Daimler-Chrysler invested about $29 billion in America over the past three years. That's more than the 14 Japanese automakers doing business here have invested over the past 25 years.

Let me repeat that. We invested more in three years—despite dramatic economic hardships—than our competitors have invested here since 1980.

With the right incentives, we can develop new technology for advanced high-tech vehicles and components. That's why, like many of you, we're urging Congress to consider tax incentives to help American manufacturers do just that. This isn't just about what looks better on our balance sheet, but what is in our long-term national interest.

Trade

Similarly, we recognize that it is in America's national interest to remain the most open and competitive automotive market in the world. Even in the face of this increased competition, Ford is ready to defend our home turf against any foreign automaker. We're only asking for one thing: the opportunity to compete fairly on theirs.

Ford Motor Company does not support a protectionist trade policy—and we never have. In fact, our company has supported every free trade agreement negotiated by the United States since the US-Canada Auto Pact in 1965.

The qualifier to "free trade" is "fair trade." If foreign governments, like Japan and Korea, use non-tariff trade barriers to keep us out of their markets—well, there's nothing free or fair about that. Competing fairly means allowing the market to set the rates of currencies against one another—not governments.

Between 2000 and 2004, the Japanese government spent more than $400 billion to keep the yen weak. That artificial weakness is, in practice, a $3–7,000 per vehicle subsidy for exports.

We can compete with Toyota, or Honda, or Nissan—but we can't compete with the government of Japan.

Right now, the President and Congress are discussing a free trade agreement with Korea. As I said earlier, theirs is the most closed automotive market in the world—even as our market is wide open to Korean auto companies.

This potential trade agreement is an opportunity for the President and Congress to demand some reciprocity, including full and unimpeded access for US made vehicles to the Korean market. Anything less will not be worthy of our support. However, this potential trade agreement, if done right, is an opportunity to finally level the playing field.

This afternoon, I'm going to the Hill to talk to leaders of both parties about these and other issues, especially about how Ford is living up to its obligation to change.

Late in his life, Henry Ford was asked about the world changing nature of his achievements. His response was, "I don't do so much, I just go around lighting fires under other people."

It's clear that Henry Ford understood that you don't get anything done by yourself. You need partners.

Every business has an obligation to deliver quality products and services to their customers while respecting and protecting the wider interests of society. At the same time, our partners in government have an obligation to safeguard and enhance the ability of business to compete. In a town that loves to hate "special interests," I want to be clear that doing this is very much in the national interest.

When I first took the job of running Ford's North American operations, I wrote down several thoughts in a notebook. Looking through it recently, I came across one thought that has some currency for today: "What a turnaround feels like: uncomfortable and exhilarating all at the same time."

This is an exhilarating time to be at Ford. Sometimes finding the right balance, or charting a challenging new course forward, can be uncomfortable. But, with the right partnership between business and government—and smart decisions on our part—I know we can succeed.

Thank you very much.

Source: Ford Motor Company. "Remarks by Mark Fields, President of the Americas, Ford Motor Company, U.S. Chamber of Commerce." June 14, 2006. http://media.ford.com/print_doc.cfm?article_id=23632 (accessed December 11, 2006).

Other Historic Documents of Interest

Conviction of Enron executives, p. 239   *Outlook for the U.S. economy, p. 151*
International trade issues, p. 424   *State of the Union, p. 23*

Supreme Court on Police Searches

June 15, 2006

In a closely watched case, the Supreme Court ruled, 5–4, on June 15, 2006, that evidence collected as a result of an illegal search could be used against the defendant. The ruling called into question the continuing viability of both the "knock-and-announce" rule that police were supposed to use when conducting a search of a private home and the "exclusionary rule," which sought to discourage police from conducting illegal searches and seizures by prohibiting any evidence gathered in such searches from being used to prosecute the accused.

The ruling appeared to confirm the hopes of conservatives—and the fears of liberals—that the two justices appointed by President George W. Bush in 2005 would move the Supreme Court toward conservative views that typically favored the rights of the state over individuals. Chief Justice John G. Roberts Jr. and Justice Samuel A. Alito Jr. joined Justices Antonin Scalia, Clarence Thomas, and Anthony M. Kennedy in the judgment. Justices John Paul Stevens, David H. Souter, Ruth Bader Ginsburg, and Stephen G. Breyer dissented.

The case, *Hudson v. Michigan,* was argued twice, once in January when retiring Justice Sandra Day O'Connor was still on the bench and again in May after Alito had taken O'Connor's seat. It was widely assumed that Alito's vote had broken a 4–4 tie and that, had O'Connor remained on the bench, she would have joined the four liberal justices, making their viewpoint prevail.

An End to "Knock and Announce"?

The Fourth Amendment guaranteed the "right of the people to be secure in their persons, houses, papers, and effects, against unreasonable searches and seizures." The exclusionary rule, created by the Supreme Court in 1914 and applied to the states in 1961, sought to discourage overly aggressive or blatantly illegal police investigations by keeping improperly obtained evidence out of the courtroom. The exclusionary rule extended to coerced confessions as well as to illegal searches and seizures. The notion that police with a search warrant must first knock and announce their presence before entering was rooted in ancient English tradition and was first codified in 1917. In various rulings, the Court had held that the Fourth Amendment required use of the knock-and-announce rule but said there were exceptions when police had reason to believe the occupant of the house was potentially dangerous and might try to destroy the evidence. In 2003 the Court said police did not have to wait much more than fifteen or twenty seconds after knocking before forcing their way into a house.

The case of *Hudson v. Michigan* arose when police with a valid search warrant went to the Detroit home of Booker Hudson to search for drugs. They announced themselves and waited only three to five seconds before going inside, where they found Hudson in an armchair with a loaded gun and a large quantity of cocaine. Found guilty of drug possession, Hudson then sought to have his conviction overturned, arguing that police had violated his Fourth Amendment rights when they entered his house without knocking and that the cocaine they found and used to convict him should not have been admitted into evidence at his trial. A lower court agreed with Hudson, but that ruling was overturned by the Michigan Court of Appeals. The Supreme Court agreed.

Writing for the majority, Justice Antonin Scalia said the illegal entry into Hudson's home did not justify "the massive remedy of suppressing evidence of guilt." Had the police knocked and then waited fifteen or twenty seconds before entering the house, they still would have found Hudson's cocaine, he wrote. While the knock-and-announce rule was intended to protect life, property, and dignity, Scalia said, it "has never protected . . . one's interest in preventing the government from seeing or taking evidence described in a warrant." Moreover, he said it "is not easy to determine precisely what officers must do" to comply with the rule. "How many seconds' wait are too few?" he asked. Scalia predicted that a ruling in favor of Hudson would overwhelm the courts with "a constant flood of alleged" violations of the knock-and-announce rule.

Finally, Scalia said, there were other deterrents to discourage knock-and-announce violations that did not exist when the exclusionary rule was adopted in 1961, including the ability to bring civil rights suits against the government. Scalia also said police were now better trained and subject to more internal discipline, themselves deterrents to illegal actions. Given those developments, he said, a strict application of the exclusionary rule for knock-and-announce violations "would be forcing the public today to pay for the sins and inadequacies of a legal regime that existed almost half a century ago."

Although Justice Kennedy joined the majority in its judgment, he wrote a separate opinion to emphasize that the majority opinion should not be construed as suggesting that violations of the knock-and-announce rule were "trivial or beyond the law's concern." Kennedy also flatly stated that "the continued operation of the exclusionary rule, as settled and defined by our precedents, is not in doubt." That statement indicated that the four other majority justices might be willing to do away with the exclusionary rule altogether if they could find a fifth vote.

Writing for the four dissenters, Justice Breyer said the decision was "doubly troubling. It represents a significant departure from the Court's precedents. And it weakens, perhaps destroys, much of the practical value of the Constitution's knock-and-announce protection." Others agreed with the minority justices that police with search warrants were more likely to ignore the knock-and-announce rule as a result of the decision in *Hudson*. "The knock-and-announce rule is dead in the United States," David Moran, a Wayne State University professor who represented Hudson, told the Associated Press. "There are going to be a lot more doors knocked down. There are going to be a lot more people terrified and humiliated."

On June 19, four days after its ruling in *Hudson* the Court upheld a California law that allowed police to routinely search parolees. Under the law prisoners up for parole had to agree to the searches; if they did not agree, they were not released from prison. The vote was 6–3. Writing for the majority, Justice Thomas said California had a "special governmental interest" in controlling its large population of parolees. That interest, Thomas said, outweighed any expectation of privacy a parolee might have. In dissent, Justice Stevens said the law gave California police "a blanket grant of discretion untethered by procedural safeguards." The majority, he added, had "run roughshod" over previous rulings to sanction "an unprecedented curtailment of liberty." Souter and Breyer joined in Stevens's dissent.

Warrantless Searches

In a case involving a warrantless search, a narrow majority of the Court ruled against the police. Under long-standing Court rulings, a search warrant was unnecessary if the individual who owned or occupied the place being searched gave consent to the search. But the Court had not issued a clear ruling in cases where one occupant gave consent and the other refused. By a 5–3 vote, the Court ruled that police could not conduct a warrantless search where one spouse consented but the other objected.

The case, *Georgia v. Randolph,* involved a domestic dispute over child custody. When police arrived at the house in Americus, Georgia, to investigate, the wife invited the police in and told them where they could find her husband's cocaine. The husband, Scott Randolph, refused the police permission to search the house, but they went ahead anyway and found traces of what appeared to be cocaine. At that point, the police stopped the search until they had obtained a warrant. They then resumed the search and found more evidence of the drug, which was used to indict Randolph for drug possession.

The majority ruled that the search, over the clear objections of the husband, was unreasonable and therefore unconstitutional. "There is no common understanding that one co-tenant generally has a right or authority to prevail over the express wishes of another, whether the issue is the color of the curtains or invitations to outsiders," Justice David Souter wrote for the majority. In his first written dissent since joining the Court in September 2005, Chief Justice John G. Roberts Jr. said the majority's ruling gave no "practical guidance" to police or lower courts. He also warned that the ruling could work against victims of domestic abuse. "The majority's rule apparently forbids police from entering to assist with a domestic dispute if the abuser whose behavior prompted the request for police assistance objects," he wrote.

Calling that argument a "red herring," Souter said nothing in the ruling would prohibit police from entering a house, with or without a warrant, to protect someone who was in immediate danger, adding that no one claimed that Janet Randolph was in danger. Souter acknowledged the majority was "drawing a fine line; if a potential defendant with self-interest in objecting is in fact at the door and objects, the co-tenant's permission does not suffice for a reasonable search, whereas the potential objector, nearby but not invited to take part in the threshold colloquy loses out." Roberts foresaw the same circumstances in his dissent: "What the majority's rule protects is not so much privacy as the good luck of a co-owner who just happens to be present at the door when the police arrive."

Joining Souter in the majority were Stevens, Kennedy, Ginsburg, and Breyer. Scalia and Thomas dissented. Alito took no part in the case, which was argued before he was confirmed.

On May 22, a unanimous Court confirmed that police did not have to obtain a warrant before entering a private house to break up a fistfight. Police in Brigham City, Utah, had gone to the house in response to complaints about a loud party. When they arrived, they saw the fight through the windows. Although an officer opened a door to announce the arrival of the police, he was not heard over the noise in the house. At that point, the police "were free to enter; it would serve no purpose to require them to stand dumbly at the door awaiting a response while those within brawled on, oblivious to their presence," Chief Justice Roberts wrote. "The role of a police officer includes preventing violence and restoring order, not simply rendering first aid to casualties; an officer is not like a boxing (or hockey) referee, poised to stop a bout only if it becomes too one-sided." In a separate opinion, Justice Stevens called it "an odd flyspeck of a case" and said he did not understand why the courts had spent so much time on a matter involving comparatively minor offenses.

Following are excerpts from the majority opinion written by Justice Antonin Scalia, a concurring opinion written by Justice Anthony M. Kennedy, and the minority opinion written by Justice Stephen G. Breyer in the case of Hudson v. Michigan, *in which the Court ruled, 5–4, on June 15, 2006, that despite a violation of the knock-and-announce rule, evidence seized in an otherwise lawful search could be used in court against the defendant.*

DOCUMENT

Hudson v. Michigan

No. 04–1360

Booker T. Hudson, Jr., Petitioner
v.
Michigan

On writ of certiorari to
the Court of Appeals of Michigan

[June 15, 2006]

JUSTICE SCALIA delivered the opinion of the Court, except as to Part IV.

We decide whether violation of the "knock-and-announce" rule requires the suppression of all evidence found in the search.

I

Police obtained a warrant authorizing a search for drugs and firearms at the home of petitioner Booker Hudson. They discovered both. Large quantities of drugs were found, including cocaine rocks in Hudson's pocket. A loaded gun was lodged between the cushion and armrest of the chair in which he was sitting. Hudson was charged under Michigan law with unlawful drug and firearm possession.

This case is before us only because of the method of entry into the house. When the police arrived to execute the warrant, they announced their presence, but waited only a short time—perhaps "three to five seconds"—before turning the knob of the unlocked front door and entering Hudson's home. Hudson moved to suppress all the inculpatory evidence, arguing that the premature entry violated his Fourth Amendment rights.

The Michigan trial court granted his motion. On interlocutory review, the Michigan Court of Appeals reversed. . . . We granted certiorari.

II

The common-law principle that law enforcement officers must announce their presence and provide residents an opportunity to open the door is an ancient one.... Since 1917, when Congress passed the Espionage Act, this traditional protection has been part of federal statutory law.... We applied that statute in *Miller* v. *United States* (1958), and again in *Sabbath* v. *United States* (1968). Finally, in *Wilson* [v. *Arkansas* (1995)] we were asked whether the rule was also a command of the Fourth Amendment. Tracing its origins in our English legal heritage, we concluded that it was.

We recognized that the new constitutional rule we had announced is not easily applied. *Wilson* and cases following it have noted the many situations in which it is not necessary to knock and announce. It is not necessary when "circumstances presen[t] a threat of physical violence," or if there is "reason to believe that evidence would likely be destroyed if advance notice were given," or if knocking and announcing would be "futile."... We require only that police "have a reasonable suspicion ... under the particular circumstances" that one of these grounds for failing to knock and announce exists, and we have acknowledged that "[t]his showing is not high."

When the knock-and-announce rule does apply, it is not easy to determine precisely what officers must do. How many seconds' wait are too few? Our "reasonable wait time" standard ... is necessarily vague. [*United States* v.] *Bank* [(2003)] (a drug case, like this one) held that the proper measure was not how long it would take the resident to reach the door, but how long it would take to dispose of the suspected drugs—but that such a time (15 to 20 seconds in that case) would necessarily be extended when, for instance, the suspected contraband was not easily concealed. If our *ex post* evaluation is subject to such calculations, it is unsurprising that, *ex ante,* police officers about to encounter someone who may try to harm them will be uncertain how long to wait.

Happily, these issues do not confront us here. From the trial level onward, Michigan has conceded that the entry was a knock-and-announce violation. The issue here is remedy. *Wilson* specifically declined to decide whether the exclusionary rule is appropriate for violation of the knock-and-announce requirement. That question is squarely before us now.

III

A

In *Weeks* v. *United States* (1914), we adopted the federal exclusionary rule for evidence that was unlawfully seized from a home without a warrant in violation of the Fourth Amendment. We began applying the same rule to the States, through the Fourteenth Amendment, in *Mapp* v. *Ohio* (1961).

Suppression of evidence, however, has always been our last resort, not our first impulse. The exclusionary rule generates "substantial social costs" ... which sometimes include setting the guilty free and the dangerous at large. We have therefore been "cautio[us] against expanding" it ... and "have repeatedly emphasized that the rule's 'costly toll' upon truth-seeking and law enforcement objectives presents a high obstacle for those urging [its] application."... We have rejected "[i]ndiscriminate application" of the rule ... and have held it to be applicable only "where its remedial objectives are thought most efficaciously served" ... that is, "where its deterrence benefits outweigh its 'substantial social costs.'" ...

We did not always speak so guardedly. Expansive dicta in *Mapp*, for example, suggested wide scope for the exclusionary rule.... But we have long since rejected that approach. As explained in *Arizona* v. *Evans* (1995): "In [1971], the Court treated identification of a Fourth Amendment violation as synonymous with application of the exclusionary rule to evidence secured incident to that violation. Subsequent case law has rejected this reflexive application of the exclusionary rule."... We had said as much ... a decade earlier, when we explained that "[w]hether the exclusionary sanction is appropriately imposed in a particular case, ... is 'an issue separate from the question whether the Fourth Amendment rights of the party seeking to invoke the rule were violated by police conduct.'"...

In other words, exclusion may not be premised on the mere fact that a constitutional violation was a "but-for" cause of obtaining evidence. Our cases show that but-for causality is only a necessary, not a sufficient, condition for suppression. In this case, of course, the constitutional violation of an illegal *manner* of entry was *not* a but-for cause of obtaining the evidence. Whether that preliminary misstep had occurred *or not*, the police would have executed the warrant they had obtained, and would have discovered the gun and drugs inside the house. But even if the illegal entry here could be characterized as a but-for cause of discovering what was inside, we have "never held that evidence is 'fruit of the poisonous tree' simply because 'it would not have come to light but for the illegal actions of the police.'"... Rather, but-for cause, or "causation in the logical sense alone" ... can be too attenuated to justify exclusion.... Even in the early days of the exclusionary rule, we declined to

> "hold that all evidence is 'fruit of the poisonous tree' simply because it would not have come to light but for the illegal actions of the police. Rather, the more apt question in such a case is 'whether, granting establishment of the primary illegality, the evidence to which instant objection is made has been come at by exploitation of that illegality or instead by means sufficiently distinguishable to be purged of the primary taint.'"...

Attenuation can occur, of course, when the causal connection is remote.... Attenuation also occurs when, even given a direct causal connection, the interest protected by the constitutional guarantee that has been violated would not be served by suppression of the evidence obtained....

For this reason, cases excluding the fruits of unlawful warrantless searches ... say nothing about the appropriateness of exclusion to vindicate the interests protected by the knock-and-announce requirement. Until a valid warrant has issued, citizens are entitled to shield "their persons, houses, papers, and effects" ... from the government's scrutiny. Exclusion of the evidence obtained by a warrantless search vindicates that entitlement. The interests protected by the knock-and-announce requirement are quite different—and do not include the shielding of potential evidence from the government's eyes.

One of those interests is the protection of human life and limb, because an unannounced entry may provoke violence in supposed self-defense by the surprised resident. . . . Another interest is the protection of property. . . . The knock-and-announce rule gives individuals "the opportunity to comply with the law and to avoid the destruction of property occasioned by a forcible entry.". . . And thirdly, the knock-and-announce rule protects those elements of privacy and dignity that can be destroyed by a sudden entrance. . . . In other words, it assures the opportunity to collect oneself before answering the door.

What the knock-and-announce rule has never protected, however, is one's interest in preventing the government from seeing or taking evidence described in a warrant. Since the interests that *were* violated in this case have nothing to do with the seizure of the evidence, the exclusionary rule is inapplicable.

B

Quite apart from the requirement of unattenuated causation, the exclusionary rule has never been applied except "where its deterrence benefits outweigh its 'substantial social costs.'". . . The costs here are considerable. In addition to the grave adverse consequence that exclusion of relevant incriminating evidence always entails (viz., the risk of releasing dangerous criminals into society), imposing that massive remedy for a knock-and-announce violation would generate a constant flood of alleged failures to observe the rule. . . . The cost of entering this lottery would be small, but the jackpot enormous: suppression of all evidence, amounting in many cases to a get-out-of-jail-free card. Courts would experience as never before the reality that "[t]he exclusionary rule frequently requires extensive litigation to determine whether particular evidence must be excluded.". . . Unlike the warrant or *Miranda* requirements, compliance with which is readily determined (either there was or was not a warrant; either the *Miranda* warning was given, or it was not), what constituted a "reasonable wait time" in a particular case . . . (or, for that matter, how many seconds the police in fact waited) . . . is difficult for the trial court to determine and even more difficult for an appellate court to review.

Another consequence of the incongruent remedy Hudson proposes would be police officers' refraining from timely entry after knocking and announcing. As we have observed, the amount of time they must wait is necessarily uncertain. If the consequences of running afoul of the rule were so massive, officers would be inclined to wait longer than the law requires—producing preventable violence against officers in some cases, and the destruction of evidence in many others. . . .

Next to these "substantial social costs" we must consider the deterrence benefits, existence of which is a necessary condition for exclusion. . . . To begin with, the value of deterrence depends upon the strength of the incentive to commit the forbidden act. Viewed from this perspective, deterrence of knock-and-announce violations is not worth a lot. Violation of the warrant requirement sometimes produces incriminating evidence that could not otherwise be obtained. But ignoring knock-and-announce can realistically be expected to achieve absolutely nothing except the prevention of destruction of evidence and the avoidance of life-threatening resistance by occupants of the premises—dangers which, if there is even "reasonable suspicion" of their existence, *suspend the knock-and-announce requirement anyway.* Massive deterrence is hardly required.

It seems to us not even true, as Hudson contends, that without suppression there will be no deterrence of knock-and-announce violations at all. Of course even if this assertion were accurate, it would not necessarily justify suppression. Assuming (as the assertion must) that civil suit is not an effective deterrent, one can think of many forms of police misconduct that are similarly "undeterred." When, for example, a confessed suspect in the killing of a police officer, arrested (along with incriminating evidence) in a lawful warranted search, is subjected to physical abuse at the station house, would it seriously be suggested that the evidence must be excluded, since that is the only "effective deterrent"? And what, other than civil suit, is the "effective deterrent" of police violation of an already-confessed suspect's Sixth Amendment rights by denying him prompt access to counsel? Many would regard these violated rights as more significant than the right not to be intruded upon in one's nightclothes—and yet nothing but "ineffective" civil suit is available as a deterrent. And the police incentive for those violations is arguably greater than the incentive for disregarding the knock-and-announce rule.

We cannot assume that exclusion in this context is necessary deterrence simply because we found that it was necessary deterrence in different contexts and long ago. That would be forcing the public today to pay for the sins and inadequacies of a legal regime that existed almost half a century ago. . . .

Hudson complains that "it would be very hard to find a lawyer to take a case such as this." . . .

Hudson points out that few published decisions to date announce huge awards for knock-and-announce violations. But this is an unhelpful statistic. Even if we thought that only large damages would deter police misconduct (and that police somehow are deterred by "damages" . . .), we do not know how many claims have been settled, or indeed how many violations have occurred that produced anything more than nominal injury. It is clear, at least, that the lower courts are allowing colorable knock-and-announce suits to go forward, unimpeded by assertions of qualified immunity. . . . As far as we know, civil liability is an effective deterrent here, as we have assumed it is in other contexts. . . .

Another development over the past half-century that deters civil-rights violations is the increasing professionalism of police forces, including a new emphasis on internal police discipline. Even as long ago as 1980 we felt it proper to "assume" that unlawful police behavior would "be dealt with appropriately" by the authorities . . . , but we now have increasing evidence that police forces across the United States take the constitutional rights of citizens seriously. There have been "wide-ranging reforms in the education, training, and supervision of police officers." . . . Numerous sources are now available to teach officers and their supervisors what is required of them under this Court's cases, how to respect constitutional guarantees in various situations, and how to craft an effective regime for internal discipline. . . . Failure to teach and enforce constitutional requirements exposes municipalities to financial liability. . . . Moreover, modern police forces are staffed with professionals; it is not credible to assert that internal discipline, which can limit successful careers, will not have a deterrent effect. There is also evidence that the increasing use of various forms of citizen review can enhance police accountability.

In sum, the social costs of applying the exclusionary rule to knock-and-announce violations are considerable; the incentive to such violations is minimal to begin with, and the extant deterrences against them are substantial—incomparably greater than the factors deterring warrantless entries when *Mapp* was decided. Resort to the massive remedy of suppressing evidence of guilt is unjustified. . . .

For the foregoing reasons we affirm the judgment of the Michigan Court of Appeals.

It is so ordered.

JUSTICE KENNEDY, concurring in part and concurring in the judgment.

Two points should be underscored with respect to today's decision. First, the knock-and-announce requirement protects rights and expectations linked to ancient principles in our constitutional order. See *Wilson* v. *Arkansas,* 514 U. S. 927, 934 (1995). The Court's decision should not be interpreted as suggesting that violations of the requirement are trivial or beyond the law's concern. Second, the continued operation of the exclusionary rule, as settled and defined by our precedents, is not in doubt. Today's decision determines only that in the specific context of the knock-and-announce requirement, a violation is not sufficiently related to the later discovery of evidence to justify suppression.

As to the basic right in question, privacy and security in the home are central to the Fourth Amendment's guarantees as explained in our decisions and as understood since the beginnings of the Republic. This common understanding ensures respect for the law and allegiance to our institutions, and it is an instrument for transmitting our Constitution to later generations undiminished in meaning and force. It bears repeating that it is a serious matter if law enforcement officers violate the sanctity of the home by ignoring the requisites of lawful entry. Security must not be subject to erosion by indifference or contempt.

Our system, as the Court explains, has developed procedures for training police officers and imposing discipline for failures to act competently and lawfully. If those measures prove ineffective, they can be fortified with more detailed regulations or legislation. Supplementing these safeguards are civil remedies . . . that provide restitution for discrete harms. These remedies apply to all violations, including, of course, exceptional cases in which unannounced entries cause severe fright and humiliation.

Suppression is another matter. Under our precedents the causal link between a violation of the knock-and-announce requirement and a later search is too attenuated to allow suppression. . . . When, for example, a violation results from want of a 20-second pause but an ensuing, lawful search lasting five hours discloses evidence of criminality, the failure to wait at the door cannot properly be described as having caused the discovery of evidence.

Today's decision does not address any demonstrated pattern of knock-and-announce violations. If a widespread pattern of violations were shown, and particularly if those violations were committed against persons who lacked the means or voice to mount an effective protest, there would be reason for grave concern. Even then, however, the Court would have to acknowledge that extending the remedy of exclusion to all the evidence seized following a knock-and-announce violation would mean revising the requirement of causation that limits our discretion in applying the exclusionary rule. That type of extensional so would have significant practical implications, adding to the list of issues requiring resolution at the criminal trial questions such as whether police officers entered a home after waiting 10 seconds or 20.

In this case the relevant evidence was discovered not because of a failure to knock-and-announce, but because of a subsequent search pursuant to a lawful warrant. The Court in my view is correct to hold that suppression was not required. . . .

JUSTICE BREYER, with whom JUSTICE STEVENS, JUSTICE SOUTER, and JUSTICE GINSBURG join, dissenting.

In *Wilson* v. *Arkansas* (1995), a unanimous Court held that the Fourth Amendment normally requires law enforcement officers to knock and announce their presence before entering a dwelling. Today's opinion holds that evidence seized from a home following a violation of this requirement need not be suppressed.

As a result, the Court destroys the strongest legal incentive to comply with the Constitution's knock-and-announce requirement. And the Court does so without significant support in precedent. At least I can find no such support in the many Fourth Amendment cases the Court has decided in the near century since it first set forth the exclusionary principle. . . .

Today's opinion is thus doubly troubling. It represents a significant departure from the Court's precedents. And it weakens, perhaps destroys, much of the practical value of the Constitution's knock-and-announce protection.

[Section I omitted.]

II

Reading our knock-and-announce cases . . . in light of this foundational Fourth Amendment case law . . . it is clear that the exclusionary rule should apply. For one thing, elementary logic leads to that conclusion. We have held that a court must "conside[r]" whether officers complied with the knock-and-announce requirement "in assessing the reasonableness of a search or seizure." . . . The Fourth Amendment insists that an unreasonable search or seizure is, constitutionally speaking, an illegal search or seizure. And ever since *Weeks* (in respect to federal prosecutions) and *Mapp* (in respect to state prosecutions), "the use of evidence secured through an illegal search and seizure" is "barred" in criminal trials. . . .

For another thing, the driving legal purpose underlying the exclusionary rule, namely, the deterrence of unlawful government behavior, argues strongly for suppression. . . . [In three earlier cases, including *Mapp*], the Court based its holdings requiring suppression of unlawfully obtained evidence upon the recognition that admission of that evidence would seriously undermine the Fourth Amendment's promise. All three cases recognized that failure to apply the exclusionary rule would make that promise a hollow one . . . reducing it to "a form of words" . . . "of no value" to those whom it seeks to protect. . . . Indeed, this Court in *Mapp* held that the exclusionary rule applies to the States in large part due to its belief that alternative state mechanisms for enforcing the Fourth Amendment's guarantees had proved "worthless and futile."

Why is application of the exclusionary rule any the less necessary here? Without such a rule, as in *Mapp*, police know that they can ignore the Constitution's requirements without risking suppression of evidence discovered after an unreasonable entry. As in *Mapp*, some government officers will find it easier, or believe it less risky, to proceed with what they consider a necessary search immediately and without the requisite constitutional (say, warrant or knock-and-announce) compliance. . . .

Of course, the State or the Federal Government may provide alternative remedies for knock-and-announce violations. But that circumstance was true of *Mapp* as well. What reason is there to believe that those remedies (such as private damages actions...), which the Court found inadequate in *Mapp,* can adequately deter unconstitutional police behavior here?...

The cases reporting knock-and-announce violations are legion.... Yet the majority, like Michigan and the United States, has failed to cite a single reported case in which a plaintiff has collected more than nominal damages solely as a result of a knock-and-announce violation. Even Michigan concedes that, "in cases like the present one... damages may be virtually non-existent."... And Michigan's *amici* further concede that civil immunities prevent tort law from being an effective substitute for the exclusionary rule at this time....

... To argue that there may be few civil suits because violations may produce nothing "more than nominal injury" is to confirm, not to deny, the inability of civil suits to deter violations. And to argue without evidence (and despite myriad reported cases of violations, no reported case of civil damages, and Michigan's concession of their nonexistence) that civil suits may provide deterrence because claims *may* "have been settled" is, perhaps, to search in desperation for an argument. Rather, the majority, as it candidly admits, has simply "assumed" that, "[a]s far as [it] know[s], civil liability is an effective deterrent," a support-free assumption that *Mapp* and subsequent cases make clear does not embody the Court's normal approach to difficult questions of Fourth Amendment law....

... The Court has decided more than 300 Fourth Amendment cases since *Weeks.* The Court has found constitutional violations in nearly a third of them.... The nature of the constitutional violation varies. In most instances officers lacked a warrant; in others, officers possessed a warrant based on false affidavits; in still others, the officers executed the search in an unconstitutional manner. But in every case involving evidence seized during an illegal search of a home (federally since *Weeks,* nationally since *Mapp*), the Court, with the exceptions mentioned, has either explicitly or implicitly upheld (or required) the suppression of the evidence at trial.... In not one of those cases did the Court "questio[n], in the absence of a more efficacious sanction, the continued application of the [exclusionary] rule to suppress evidence from the State's case" in a criminal trial....

Neither can the majority justify its failure to respect the need for deterrence, as set forth consistently in the Court's prior case law, through its claim of "substantial social costs"—at least if it means that those "social costs" are somehow special here. The only costs it mentions are those that typically accompany *any* use of the Fourth Amendment's exclusionary principle: (1) that where the constable blunders, a guilty defendant may be set free (consider *Mapp* itself); (2) that defendants may assert claims where Fourth Amendment rights are uncertain (consider the Court's qualified immunity jurisprudence), and (3) that sometimes it is difficult to decide the merits of those uncertain claims. In fact, the "no-knock" warrants that are provided by many States, by diminishing uncertainty, may make application of the knock-and-announce principle less "cost[ly]" on the whole than application of comparable Fourth Amendment principles, such as determining whether a particular warrantless search was justified by exigency. The majority's "substantial social costs" argument is an argument against the Fourth Amendment's exclusionary principle itself. And it is an argument that this Court, until now, has consistently rejected.

[Section III omitted.]

IV

There is perhaps one additional argument implicit in the majority's approach. The majority says, for example, that the "cost" to a defendant of "entering this lottery," *i.e.,* of claiming a "knock-and-announce" violation, "would be small, but the jackpot enormous"—namely, a potential "get-out-of-jail-free card." It adds that the "social costs" of applying the exclusionary rule here are not worth the deterrence benefits. Leaving aside what I believe are invalid arguments based on precedent or the majority's own estimate that suppression is not necessary to deter constitutional violations, one is left with a simple unvarnished conclusion, namely, that in this kind of case, a knock-and-announce case, "[r]esort to the massive remedy of suppressing evidence of guilt is unjustified." Why is that judicial judgment, taken on its own, inappropriate? Could it not be argued that the knock-and-announce rule, a subsidiary Fourth Amendment rule, is simply not important enough to warrant a suppression remedy? Could the majority not simply claim that the suppression game is not worth the candle?

The answer, I believe, is "no." That "no" reflects history, a history that shows the knock-and-announce rule is important. . . . That "no" reflects precedent, precedent that shows there is no preexisting legal category of exceptions to the exclusionary rule into which the knock-and-announce cases might fit. That "no" reflects empirical fact, experience that provides confirmation of what common sense suggests: without suppression there is little to deter knock-and-announce violations.

There may be instances in the law where text or history or tradition leaves room for a judicial decision that rests upon little more than an unvarnished judicial instinct. But this is not one of them. Rather, our Fourth Amendment traditions place high value upon protecting privacy in the home. They emphasize the need to assure that its constitutional protections are effective, lest the Amendment 'sound the word of promise to the ear but break it to the hope.' They include an exclusionary principle, which since *Weeks* has formed the centerpiece of the criminal law's effort to ensure the practical reality of those promises. That is why the Court should assure itself that any departure from that principle is firmly grounded in logic, in history, in precedent, and in empirical fact. It has not done so. That is why, with respect, I dissent.

Source: U.S. Supreme Court of the United States. *Hudson v. Michigan* 547 U.S. — (2006), Docket 04-1360. June 15, 2006. www.supremecourtus.gov/opinions/05pdf/04-1360.pdf (accessed November 15, 2006).

President Bush on
Mine Safety Legislation

June 15, 2006

▮▮▮▮▮▮▮▮ THE DOCUMENT IN CONTEXT ▮▮▮▮▮▮▮▮

The deaths of nineteen underground coal miners in six separate accidents in the first four weeks of 2006 touched off a debate over mine safety that resulted in the first federal overhaul of mine safety regulations in nearly three decades. The deaths also focused widespread attention on new technologies and procedures that could be employed to make mines safer workplaces. Federal and state safety inspectors, union leaders, and others were looking particularly hard at the emergency oxygen tanks that miners were required to carry and that seemed to be more vulnerable to malfunction than previously realized.

Miners, their unions, and their supporters in Congress were also highly critical of the Mine Safety and Health Administration (MSHA), the agency within the Department of Labor that was charged with inspecting mines for safety violations, and also with the Bush administration, which had declined to go forward with several new safety regulations proposed by the Clinton administration just before it left office in 2001. Critics also complained about budget cuts, staff reductions, and lax enforcement at MSHA, and said that the Bush administration had installed former coal company officials more interested in profits than in safety in the top slots at the regulatory agency.

Altogether, forty-seven coal miners were killed in mine accidents in the United States in 2006, more than double the twenty-two who died in 2005 and the most since 1995, when forty-seven miners also died, according to MSHA. Some miners attributed the increase in the number of deaths to a rise in demand from electric utilities that nearly doubled the price of coal; mine operators wanting to cash in on the boomlet were not paying enough attention to safety, these miners said. Worldwide, it was estimated that at least 7,500 coal miners died every year. Most of the deaths occurred in China, which averaged about 6,000 deaths a year.

Despite the jump in U.S. mine deaths, coal mining was a far safer operation in 2006 than it had been a hundred years earlier when as many as 3,000 U.S. workers died every year in mine accidents. Mine fatalities began to drop dramatically after World War II, when coal companies shifted much of their operations from underground mining to far safer surface mining. New mining technologies, including automated mining machines, reduced the number of miners required in most underground mines, and more sophisticated safety measures and government regulation also helped reduce accidents, improve mine air quality, and save lives.

The Sago Accident

The first, and biggest, accident of the year occurred January 2 at the Sago mine near Buckhannon, West Virginia, where twelve miners died after a lightning strike touched off a methane explosion. Eight days later a miner was killed when a roof collapsed in a Kentucky mine. On January 19 two miners died in another fire in a West Virginia mine. Four more deaths occurred in three separate accidents in Kentucky, West Virginia, and Utah by February 1, bringing the number of deaths for one month close to the total for all of 2005.

The deaths at the Sago mine were all the more heartbreaking because the families had initially been told all but one of the thirteen men trapped underground had survived, only to learn a few hours later that all but one had died. The news touched off a near riot among families and friends waiting for word of the miners' fate at a nearby church. "People just lost it. They had the life stripped out of them," one witness said. "You couldn't imagine the anger," another said.

Public attention quickly fastened on two issues—the high number of safety citations MSHA had issued the mine in 2005, and the emergency and rescue procedures in place at the mine. More than an hour passed before state and federal safety officials were notified of the accident and more than another hour passed before a rescue team arrived on the scene. It then took more than forty hours for rescuers to reach the trapped men; all but one of the twelve who died had been killed by carbon monoxide gas.

The Sago mine had been operated by the International Coal Group under a management consultant contract since the middle of 2005; the group bought the mine in November 2005. During that year MSHA cited the mine for 208 safety violations, triple the 68 violations cited in 2004. Ninety-six of the violations were recorded as "serious and substantial," including collapsing mine roofs, electrical insulation problems, and inadequate ventilation plans. MSHA had fined the mine's owners a total of $24,374 in 2005, but critics were quick to point out that the amount was unlikely to act as much of a deterrent to a company whose reported net profit for the year was $110 million. "If fines are going to be that predictable and that small, it's much easier for the company to pay the fine than fix the problem," Sen. John D. Rockefeller IV, D-W.V., said at a March 2 Senate hearing.

At the urging of West Virginia governor Joe Manchin, legislators passed a new state mining safety law in a single day, January 23. The measure required mines in the state to store additional air supplies underground, to improve communications with and tracking of miners while they were underground, and to take steps to ensure a quick response in an emergency.

Federal Reaction

In Washington, MSHA quickly said it would issue emergency rules requiring, among other things, that mining companies immediately place more oxygen and breathing devices in mines, provide lifelines such as ropes with reflective materials so that miners could find their way through smoke to mine entrances, and notify authorities more quickly in the event of an accident. At least one of these rules had been among the safety regulations proposed by the Clinton administration but scrapped when Bush came into office in 2001. The temporary emergency rules took effect on March 9 and were made permanent in December. In January MSHA also began the process of seeking comment on several long-range safety measures, including whether rescue chambers should be required for coal mines and the potential for using robotics in mine rescue operations. MSHA asked Congress to raise the existing $60,000 cap on fines to $220,000 for flagrant violators but said it saw no need to amend existing federal mine safety law.

Given the public outcry and pressure from the families of the dead miners, Congress was almost certain to take some action. A letter written by Randal Mc-Cloy Jr., the only one of the men trapped in the Sago mine to survive the ordeal but who suffered brain damage, also added pressure. In the letter, which he wrote in April after leaving the hospital, McCloy said that not all the trapped miners had air packs and that some of the packs appeared to malfunction. In any event the packs had only an hour's supply of oxygen, not enough to last for the forty-one hours it took rescuers to reach the miners. McCloy also spoke of pounding on the roof of the mine chamber where they had sought refuge from poisonous gases in hopes that rescue workers aboveground would be able to use seismographic equipment to figure out where they were. "As my trapped co-workers lost consciousness one by one, the room grew still and I continued to sit and wait, unable to do much else," McCloy wrote.

In the wake of several more accidents, including one that killed five miners in Kentucky on May 20, the Senate approved a bipartisan measure, the Mine Improvement and New Emergency Response (MINER) Act of 2006 (S 2803—PL 109–236) on May 24. The legislation required mine operators to ensure that each miner had two hours of oxygen on hand, rather than the one required under existing law, and to provide for additional oxygen supplies to be stored underground. Mine operators were also required to report any life-threatening accident within fifteen minutes of finding out about it; violations of the notification requirement were subject to fines of as much as $60,000. The law also stipulated that trained rescue teams would have to be located within one hour of every underground coal mine. The Congressional Budget Office estimated that mine operators would need to spend $60 million or more for equipping and training 260 new rescue teams. Mine operators were also required to install, within three years, wireless communications equipment and tracking devices to locate miners in the event of an emergency. The law also called for the government to study whether rescue chambers should be required in underground coal mines. Such chambers were credited with saving the lives of seventy-two Canadian miners trapped in a potash mine earlier in the year.

The House cleared the bill by a vote of 381–37 on June 7. Final action had been delayed by Rep. George Miller of California, the senior Democrat on the House Education and Workforce Committee, who said the bill was not strong enough to prevent accidents of the type that occurred at the Sago mine. Miller demanded that the House consider amendments requiring faster installation of communications and tracking devices, specifying that mines contain forty-eight hours of oxygen for each miner, and requiring MSHA to randomly inspect breathing equipment at mines. He was thwarted, however, when the House passed the measure under suspension of the rules, which allowed no amendments.

President George W. Bush signed the bill into law on June 15, with McCloy in the audience. "We make this promise to American miners and their families," Bush said. "We'll do everything possible to prevent mine accidents and make sure you're able to return safely to your loved ones."

Stickler Nomination

Many Democrats and some Republicans, however, thought that the Bush administration could be doing far more than it was to protect miners. During consideration of the mine safety legislation, they complained that the Bush administration had filled the agency with former mine executives who were too cozy with the industry they were charged with regulating. The man who bore the brunt of that dissatisfaction during the year was Richard M. Stickler, President Bush's nominee to head MSHA. Stickler had worked for BethEnergy Mines in Pennsylvania for thirty years before heading the state's Bureau of Deep Mine Safety from 1997 to 2003. He was commended in 2002 for work he did on the scene when the Quecreek mine in Pennsylvania flooded and nine miners were nearly killed. Questions were later raised, however, about whether Stickler's agency should have identified the problems that led to the flooding before the accident happened and about Stickler's safety record when he was a mine supervisor. The United Mine Workers said that in some years Stickler's mines had twice as many accidents as the national average. "Mr. Stickler's history is long on coal production experience but short on ensuring worker safety," Sen. Edward M. Kennedy, D-Mass., said at a Senate confirmation hearing January 31.

Sen. Robert C. Byrd, D-W.V., put a "hold" on Stickler's nomination, which prevented the Senate from taking any action on it. The nomination was returned to the White House in August when Byrd and Kennedy refused to waive a rule keeping nominations open while Congress was in recess. Bush resubmitted the nomination in September. Byrd and Kennedy again returned the nomination to the White House when Congress recessed in October for the midterm elections, but this time Bush responded by giving Stickler a recess appointment. The confirmation was still stalemated at the end of the year.

Focus on Air Packs, Seals

Investigations of the Sago and other mine accidents during the year revealed that the seals used to wall off abandoned parts of mines were not strong enough to withstand the force of heavy explosions and that the air packs miners carried to provide emergency oxygen could become dysfunctional if exposed to excessive heat.

In July an investigation of the Sago mine concluded that the seals closing off the abandoned portion of the mine where the methane explosion occurred had been pulverized. Under federal regulation, such seals were required to withstand twenty pounds of pressure per square inch, but evidence showed that the Sago explosion had been much more powerful. MSHA officials said they would require new seals to be able to withstand fifty pounds of pressure per square inch. Even if seals of that strength had been in place in the Sago mine, it might not have been enough. Another report, issued by West Virginia's safety office in December, said ten seals in the mine had been subjected to at least ninety-five pounds of pressure per square inch.

That report, like earlier ones, also said that the emergency air packs, or "rescuers," had not performed as expected. Random inspections in both Kentucky and West Virginia in August uncovered air packs damaged by excessive heat, missing a heat damage indicator, or otherwise defective. On October 31 the West Virginia mine safety office warned that the heat packs were more susceptible to heat damage than preliminary tests had shown. Regulators said mine operators should take steps to protect air packs from heat generated by such things as hydraulic lines or heavy equipment and should get rid of any packs that might have been exposed to excessive heat. In

November state regulators cited the operator of the Sago mine for allowing miners, in September, to carry air packs whose heat indicators had gone into the danger zone. The company was contesting the citation.

Following are excerpts from the statement made by President George W. Bush at the White House on June 15, 2006, just before signing the Mine Improvement and New Emergency Response (MINER) Act of 2006 into law.

■■■■■ DOCUMENT ■■■■■

"Remarks on Signing the MINER Act"

Thanks for coming. Welcome to the White House, and thank you for witnessing this bill signing ceremony. In a few moments, I'm going to sign into law the most sweeping overhaul of Federal mine safety law in nearly three decades. The MINER Act of 2006 has strong support of mine workers and the mining industry, and it was overwhelmingly passed by the Congress. I want to thank the Members of the United States Congress who have joined us here for their hard work on this important measure.

I thank the Secretary of Labor, Elaine Chao, who has joined us. I appreciate the Governors from three important coal mining States, Joe Manchin [West Virginia], Ernie Fletcher [Kentucky], and Ed Rendell [Pennsylvania] for joining us here as well. I was struck by how the Governors handled the tragedies of the mine incidents. I thought they were able to convey a deep sense of compassion in an attempt to heal hearts. And I thank them for their courage. . . .

. . . I appreciate the leaders of the mining industry. I appreciate the workers who are here. Thanks for taking time in your day to come. I want to welcome the families of those—who mourn the loss of life. We share in your grief, and we honor the memories of your loved ones. I know it's hard. It's really hard for you. But we welcome you here, and we're honored you took time to be here.

I appreciate members of my administration who have joined us as well today. The hard work of American miners provides us with really important fuel. This economy is growing because of the work of our miners. Coal is an important part of our Nation's present and future.

Thanks to modern technology and equipment, we've come a long way from the days when a miner would take a canary into the coal mines. Passage—and since the passage of the Mine Safety and Health Act in '77—1977, America has seen significant decreases of injuries and fatal mining accidents.

Yet events in recent months have reminded us that mining is dangerous work. That's what we've seen. This year alone, accidents have taken the lives of 33 miners in our country. Just last month, five miners were killed in a mine explosion in Harlan County, Kentucky. And in January, Americans watched and prayed—a lot of Americans prayed with the people of West Virginia for the 13 miners that were trapped underground by the explosion in the Sago mine. Only one man came out, and he's with us today—Randal McCloy and his wife, Anna. And we welcome you all.

And we know—we know, and I hope you know that your fallen mining brothers are with us here today in spirit. They're with us today with their loved ones here—eyes wet with tears but proud of their accomplishments. We're glad you're here.

We honor the memory of all lost miners today; that's what we're doing signing this bill. We make this promise to American miners and their families: We'll do everything possible to prevent mine accidents and make sure you're able to return safely to your loved ones.

The bill I'm about to sign is an important part of the effort. The MINER Act will build on the Mine Safety and Health Administration's ongoing efforts to enhance mine safety training, to improve safety and communications technology for miners, and provide more emergency supplies of breathable air along escape routes.

This new legislation will require mine operators to report any life-threatening accident no later than 15 minutes after they know that one has occurred. And to ensure compliance with the law, the MINER Act will increase the maximum penalty for flagrant violations of mine safety regulations nearly fourfold.

To implement this new legislation, we need effective and experienced leadership at the Mine Safety and Health Administration. Last month, I named, or nominated Richard Stickler of the State of West Virginia to be the head of MSHA. He's got experience. He served for 6 years as the Director of Pennsylvania's Bureau of Deep Mine Safety. He was a miner, mine shift foreman, a superintendent, and a manager, and the Senate needs to confirm Richard Stickler to this key position.

America's miners work hard every day to support their families and support this country. It's hard work. You deserve the best training, the best equipment, and safeguards that we can provide to protect the lives. And this good legislation I'm signing today is an important part of honoring that commitment.

May God bless you all. May God bless our miners and their families, and may God continue to bless our country. And now it's my honor to sign the MINER Act into law.

Source: U.S. Executive Office of the President. "Remarks on Signing the MINER Act." June 15, 2006. *Weekly Compilation of Presidential Documents* 42, no. 24 (June 19, 2006): 1146–1147. Washington, D.C.: National Archives and Records Administration. www.gpoaccess.gov/wcomp/v42no24.html (accessed November 14, 2006).

Other Historic Documents of Interest

Energy dependence, p. 139

Food safety, p. 538

GAO on drug safety, p. 129

Katrina recovery, p. 73

Presidential signing statements, p. 447

Supreme Court on Federal Wetlands Regulation

June 19, 2006

Important challenges to federal air and water pollution control regulations moved into the courtroom in 2006. In June a thin majority of the Supreme Court appeared to side with developers when it ruled that regulators had gone too far in enforcing federal laws preserving wetlands, but the Court was unable to agree on guidelines for enforcement. In March environmental advocates won a major victory when a federal appeals court ruled that a different set of regulators had gone too far in easing rules that older power plants and industrial facilities had to follow to be in compliance with the federal Clean Air Act. In both cases, it seemed likely that further court action would be required before the issues were resolved.

Another set of regulations, involving emissions of soot and other fine particulate matter, pleased neither side and was being challenged in court. The industries subject to the regulations said they were too stringent, while scientists and environmental and health care advocates said they were not stringent enough to prevent asthmas and other respiratory diseases caused by soot.

Differing Definitions of Wetlands

Congress in 1972 passed the Clean Water Act, which was intended "to restore and maintain the chemical, physical, and biological integrity of the Nation's waters." To that end, the law barred the discharge of pollutants—including dirt, rocks, and other dredged and fill material—into navigable waters without a permit. Since the law was enacted, the Army Corps of Engineers had broadly interpreted it to require landowners to obtain permits before discharging pollutants not only into clearly navigable lakes, rivers, and ponds, but also into tributaries, including streambeds that might be dry for part of the year, and nearby wetlands. Wetlands were natural systems of bogs, marshes, and swamps that absorbed and filtered runoff from storms and provided important habitat for wildlife.

Developers, farmers, ranchers, and others had long complained that the government's interpretation of the Clean Water Act was so broad that it essentially gave the federal government regulatory control over virtually all water—including water on private property that was far away from any truly navigable water. Environmental advocates maintained that a broad interpretation was necessary to protect the purity of the nation's water. In two earlier decisions, the Supreme Court ruled that the government could regulate wetlands that were "adjacent" to navigable waters but could not regulate isolated pockets or ponds of water that had no "significant nexus" to navigable waters.

The ruling handed down on June 19 in the twin cases of *Rapanos v. United States* and *Carabell v. Army Corps of Engineers* concerned parcels of property in Michigan that had been designated as wetlands. Two of the Rapanos parcels were wetlands that drained into creeks that ran into two rivers that flowed into recognizably navigable waters. The Carabell property was a mile from Lake St. Clair and connected to it by a series of manmade ditches. Both property owners wanted permission to develop their property but were denied permits by the Army Corps of Engineers to fill their lands for building. Rapanos went ahead without a permit and was convicted and fined in 1995. The Michigan property owners and their supporters argued that the federal government was abridging their rights as property owners and ruining the value of their property. Ranged against them were the Bush administration, environmental organizations, and more than thirty state governments.

Five justices agreed that the federal regulators might have overreached in these two cases, but only four justices agreed on the limits of the federal regulation. Writing for the four, Justice Antonin Scalia said that regulation under the Clean Water Act should extend only to "relatively permanent bodies of water" and that "only those wetlands with a continuous surface connection to bodies that are 'waters of the United States' in their own right, so that there is no clear demarcation between the two, are 'adjacent' to such waters and covered by the act." Chief Justice John G. Roberts Jr. and Justices Clarence Thomas and Samuel A. Alito Jr. joined in Scalia's opinion.

In a separate opinion, Justice Anthony M. Kennedy concurred in that judgment, which sent the cases back to lower courts for further hearings. But he disagreed on the limits of regulation, arguing that the Clean Water Act extended to temporary channels of water so long as they "significantly affect the chemical, physical, and biological integrity of other covered waters more readily understood as 'navigable.'" Kennedy added that wetlands with only a "speculative or insubstantial" connection to navigable water would not be covered under the act. In the cases before the Court, Kennedy said, the evidence suggested "the possible existence of a significant nexus" between the properties and navigable wetlands that, if confirmed by the lower courts, would make them subject to regulation under the Clean Water Act.

The four dissenters were John Paul Stevens, David H. Souter, Ruth Bader Ginsburg, and Stephen G. Breyer, who saw no reason, in Stevens's words, to revise regulations "that have protected the quality of our waters for decades, that were implicitly approved by Congress, and that have been repeatedly enforced in case after case."

The likely impact of the decision was further litigation. "The practical effect" of the decision "is that some bright-line rules that have been applied for decades haven't been thrown out . . . but have had a significant cloud set over them by Justice Kennedy," Richard J. Lazarus, an environmental law professor at Georgetown University, told the *Washington Post*. Chief Justice Roberts agreed; in a concurring opinion, he lamented that "lower courts and regulated entities will now have to feel their way on a case-by-case basis."

Pollution Controls at Older Power Plants

A major controversy over federal air pollution policies centered on the 1970 Clean Air Act's "New Source Review" regulations, which required that certain older power plants, refineries, and factories that modified their facilities to make them more efficient or profitable also had to upgrade their pollution-control facilities. The regulations applied to about 800 coal-fired power plants and another 17,000 chemical plants, refineries, incinerators, and other industrial operations. Most utilities had escaped the law's requirements until several states and the Clinton administration's Environmental Protection Agency (EPA) began suing them in the late 1990s and winning judgments requiring upgrades of their emissions systems.

The Bush administration took office in 2001 promising to ease regulation of coal-fired power plants as part of a plan to increase energy production and to give some relief to companies facing huge settlements in cases put forth by the Clinton EPA. In 2002 and 2003 the Bush EPA announced revisions to relax New Source Review regulations that it said were too stringent and were preventing power plants and industrial factories from upgrading and expanding their facilities as well as their pollution controls. The revisions, the administration argued, would give power companies greater incentives to upgrade their emissions equipment. Environmental advocacy groups and governors of several states charged just the opposite, that the complex new rules would give the companies even greater leeway to pollute the air. Several suits challenging the new rules were filed, and in December 2003 the U.S. Court of Appeals for the District of Columbia, which handled most disputes dealing with government regulations, stayed the rules from taking effect.

In June 2004, a three-judge panel of the Court of Appeals ruled, in the case of *New York v. EPA,* that the Bush administration had the authority to issue revised New Source Review regulations, but held that several specific aspects of the revision violated the underlying Clean Air Act. *(Background, Historic Documents of 2005, p. 100)*

Still pending after that decision was a direct challenge to a revised regulation that states and environmentalists said would allow plants to modernize without updating their emissions control systems. Under the old rules, any modification other than routine maintenance triggered the need to also update pollution controls. The 2003 revision extended the definition of routine maintenance to include any modification whose cost amounted to less than 20 percent of the value of the facility. That threshold, the Bush EPA said, would allow plants to make repairs and minor upgrades without having to spend millions of dollars on state-of-the-art pollution controls. A coalition of states and environmental advocacy groups challenged the new rule, saying it would allow plants to increase their emissions of air pollutants.

On March 17, 2006, a three-judge panel of the Court of Appeals ruled unanimously in favor of the challengers, striking down the revision. Under the regulation, the panel wrote, "a law intended to limit increases in air pollution would allow sources operating below applicable emission limits to increase significantly the pollution they emit without government review." The panel said this amounted to "Humpty Dumpty" reasoning, which it declined to accept. The panel included two Clinton appointees, Judith W. Rogers and David Tatel, and Bush appointee Janice Rogers Brown. Brown was a conservative whose confirmation to the court had been blocked for several months by a Democratic filibuster in the Senate.

"Irish eyes are surely smiling—and we all will be breathing easier—with this green court ruling on St. Patrick's Day," John Walke, of the Natural Resources Defense Council, told the *Washington Post*. "This is about as thorough a rebuke [as] a court can give," he said. Eliot Spitzer, New York's attorney general and a candidate for governor who had been instrumental in bringing the challenge, hailed the decision as "an enormous victory over the concerted efforts by the Bush administration to dismantle the Clean Air Act."

On the other side was Scott Segal, director of the Electric Reliability Coordinating Council, a utility trade organization, who called it "a terrible decision." John Engler, president of the National Association of Manufacturers, said the ruling would "trigger an endless review process for power plants and other stationary sources of air emissions that merely want to repair or upgrade existing facilities." EPA's request for a rehearing of the case by the full appeals court was rejected on July 5.

In a related development, the U.S. Supreme Court heard arguments November 2 in a case challenging the standard under which the EPA measured a plant's pollution emissions. The case grew out of a ruling by a panel of the Fourth Circuit Court of Appeals in Richmond, Virginia, in June 2005. The court agreed with a challenge brought by Duke Energy, an electric utility operating in North and South Carolina, to the Clinton administration's interpretation of the New Source Review regulations, which said power plants that upgraded their facilities had to reduce their total annual emissions of air pollutants. Duke Energy argued that the Clinton administration was improperly imposing a new and more rigid standard and that the correct measurement was the hourly rate of pollution, not the total amount of pollution emitted. So long as the hourly rate did not rise, the plant would be in compliance, Duke Energy argued. The appeals court panel agreed, even though the utility acknowledged that its planned upgrades would result in more air pollution because its facilities would run for more hours. The advocacy group Environmental Defense appealed the ruling, and on May 16, 2006, the Supreme Court agreed to hear arguments.

Even before the appeals court decision was rendered, the Bush EPA had announced it would not bring any more suits against utilities and would change the Clinton administration revisions. After the appeals court ruled, the EPA in October 2005 issued a proposed rule to measure power plant emissions on an hourly basis rather than an annual basis. The administration also asked the Supreme Court not to intervene in the case. The Court's decision to hear the case despite that request was considered a surprise by many observers. But anyone who thought the Supreme Court might be preparing to rebuff the Bush administration and uphold the stricter Clinton administration interpretation might have had second thoughts after listening to the justices' questions during the November 2 arguments. "What I'm concerned about is companies can get whipsawed," Justice Scalia said at one point. A ruling was expected by the end of the Court's 2006–2007 term.

Controversial Rule on Soot

The EPA drew bitter criticisms from all sides of the spectrum when it issued new regulations on September 21 tightening only one of two emissions standards governing maximum public exposure to the fine particulate material that caused soot and dust. Generally invisible to the eye, the tiny particles were emitted primarily from diesel-powered vehicles, power plants, and factory smokestacks. When inhaled the particulates tended to penetrate deep into the lungs, exacerbating asthma and other respiratory conditions, especially in children and the elderly.

The new standard nearly cut in half the maximum daily public exposure allowable to 35 micrograms per cubic meter of air, from 65 micrograms. But the EPA declined to change the existing standard for average annual exposure (daily exposure averaged over a year); this long-range exposure level remained at 15 micrograms per cubic meter of air.

In leaving the annual exposure level unchanged, the EPA rejected the advice of its own Clean Air Scientific Advisory Council, which had recommended dropping the long-term exposure standard to 12 to 14 micrograms per cubic meter. The council was so disturbed by the EPA's refusal to take its advice when the agency issued draft standards in December 2005 that it went public with its objections and asked the EPA to reconsider. The council's position was backed by several prominent health and environmental organizations, including the American Medical Association, the American Lung Association, and Clean Air Watch. After EPA administrator Stephen L. Johnson announced the new regulation on September 21, the advisory council's chairman, Rogene Henderson, said, "We are, of course, very disappointed." The incident was one of several in which scientists had accused the Bush administration of ignoring or manipulating scientific evidence to suit its ideological agenda. *(Background, Historic Documents of 2004, p. 841)*

The new soot standard on daily exposure levels was no more popular with power plants and manufacturers who said it would cost them billions to implement. "EPA persists in overemphasizing studies that suggest a possible benefit to tightening the air quality standard while downplaying those suggesting that doing so may not provide the health benefits EPA is seeking to achieve," said Dan Reidinger, a spokesman for the Edison Electric Institute, an industry advocacy group. Reidinger added that the EPA had "jumped the gun by adopting a more stringent . . . standard before the existing standards have been given a chance to work." Although the existing standards were written in 1997, they did not take effect until 2004 because of opposition from industry groups who fought them unsuccessfully all the way to the U.S. Supreme Court.

EPA officials later acknowledged they made their decision on the standards before receiving the results of an analysis conducted by a twelve-member panel of scientists convened at the behest of the White House Office of Management and Budget and the National Academy of Sciences. In a report released October 6, the panel said that lowering the long-term average exposure by a single microgram could have saved up to 24,000 lives each year and saved between $4.3 billion and $51 billion in health care costs and other benefits at a cost of $1.9 billion to power plants, automakers, and other industries. The panel estimated that the EPA's decision to lower the daily exposure level could save as many as 13,000 lives and produce between $9 billion and $76 billion in social benefits annually at a cost of $5 billion. A dozen states, the District of Columbia, and a consortium of health and environmental groups called Earthjustice filed separate suits in December, challenging the EPA's refusal to follow the advice of its own experts.

Following are excerpts from the plurality opinion, written by Justice Antonin Scalia, and a concurring opinion, written by Justice Anthony M. Kennedy, in the cases of Rapanos v. United States *and* Carabell v. Army Corps of Engineers, *in which the Supreme Court on June 19, 2006, ruled on the definition of "wetlands" subject to regulation under the federal Clean Water Act.*

████ **DOCUMENT** ████

Rapanos v. United States

Nos. 04–1034 and 04–1384

John A. Rapanos, et ux., et al.,
    Petitioners 04–1034
        v.
    United States
    June Carabell et al.,
    Petitioners 04–1384
        v.
United States Army Corps
    of Engineers, et al.

On writs of certiorari to the United States
Court of Appeals for the Sixth Circuit

[June 19, 2006]

JUSTICE SCALIA announced the judgment of the Court, and delivered an opinion, in which THE CHIEF JUSTICE, JUSTICE THOMAS, and JUSTICE ALITO join.

In April 1989, petitioner John A. Rapanos backfilled wetlands on a parcel of land in Michigan that he owned and sought to develop. This parcel included 54 acres of land with sometimes-saturated soil conditions. The nearest body of navigable water was 11 to 20 miles away. . . . Regulators had informed Mr. Rapanos that his saturated fields were "waters of the United States" . . . that could not be filled without a permit. Twelve years of criminal and civil litigation ensued.

The burden of federal regulation on those who would deposit fill material in locations denominated "waters of the United States" is not trivial. In deciding whether to grant or deny a permit, the U. S. Army Corps of Engineers (Corps) exercises the discretion of an enlightened despot, relying on such factors as "economics," "aesthetics," "recreation," and "in general, the needs and welfare of the people.". . . The average applicant for an individual permit spends 788 days and $271,596 in completing the process, and the average applicant for a nationwide permit spends 313 days and $28,915—not counting costs of mitigation or design changes. . . .

The enforcement proceedings against Mr. Rapanos are a small part of the immense expansion of federal regulation of land use that has occurred under the Clean Water Act—without any change in the governing statute—during the past five Presidential administrations. In the last three decades, the Corps and the Environmental Protection Agency (EPA) have interpreted their jurisdiction over "the waters of the United States" to cover 270-to-300 million acres of swampy lands in the United States—including half of Alaska and an area the size of California in the lower 48 States. And that was just the beginning. The Corps has also asserted jurisdiction over virtually any parcel of land containing a channel or conduit—whether man-made or natural, broad or narrow, permanent or ephemeral—through which rainwater or drainage may occasionally or intermittently flow. On this view, the federally regulated "waters of the United States" include storm drains, roadside ditches, ripples of sand in the desert that may contain water once a year, and lands that are covered by floodwaters once every 100 years. Because they include the land containing storm sewers and desert washes, the statutory "waters of the United States" engulf entire cities and immense arid wastelands. In fact, the entire land area of the United States lies in some drainage basin, and an endless network of visible channels furrows the entire surface, containing water ephemerally wherever the rain falls. Any plot of land containing such a channel may potentially be regulated as a "water of the United States."

I

Congress passed the Clean Water Act (CWA or Act) in1972. The Act's stated objective is "to restore and maintain the chemical, physical, and biological integrity of the Nation's waters.". . . The Act also states that "[i]t is the policy of Congress to recognize, preserve, and protect the primary responsibilities and rights of States to prevent, reduce, and eliminate pollution, to plan the development and use (including restoration, preservation, and enhancement) of land and water resources, and to consult with the Administrator in the exercise of his authority under this chapter.". . .

One of the statute's principal provisions . . . provides that "the discharge of any pollutant by any person shall be unlawful." "The discharge of a pollutant" is defined broadly to include "any addition of any pollutant to navigable waters from any point source" . . . and "pollutant" is defined broadly to include not only traditional contaminants but also solids such as "dredged spoil . . . rock, sand, [and] cellar dirt.". . . And, most relevant here, the CWA defines "navigable waters" as "the waters of the United States, including the territorial seas.". . .

The Act also provides certain exceptions to its prohibition of "the discharge of any pollutant by any person.". . . Section 1342(a) authorizes the Administrator of the EPA to "issue a permit for the discharge of any pollutant . . . notwithstanding section 1311(a) of this title." Section 1344 authorizes the Secretary of the Army, acting through the Corps, to "issue permits . . . for the discharge of dredged or fill material into the navigable waters at specified disposal sites.". . . It is the discharge of "dredged or fill material"—which, unlike traditional water pollutants, are solids that do not readily wash downstream—that we consider today.

For a century prior to the CWA, we had interpreted the phrase "navigable waters of the United States" in the Act's predecessor statutes to refer to interstate waters that are "navigable in fact" or readily susceptible of being rendered so. . . . After passage of the CWA, the Corps initially adopted this traditional judicial definition for the Act's term "navigable waters.". . . After a District Court enjoined these regulations as too narrow . . . the Corps adopted a far broader definition. . . . The Corps' new regulations deliberately sought to extend the definition of "the waters of the United States" to the outer limits of Congress's commerce power. . . .

The Corps' current regulations interpret "the waters of the United States" to include, in addition to traditional interstate navigable waters . . . "[a]ll interstate waters including interstate wetlands" . . . "[a]ll other waters such as intrastate lakes, rivers, streams (including intermittent streams), mudflats, sandflats, wetlands, sloughs, prairie potholes, wet meadows, playa lakes, or natural ponds, the use, degradation or destruction of which could affect interstate or foreign commerce"... "[t]ributaries of [such] waters"... and "[w]etlands adjacent to [such] waters [and tributaries] (other than waters that are themselves wetlands)."... The regulation defines "adjacent" wetlands as those "bordering, contiguous [to], or neighboring" waters of the United States.... It specifically provides that "[w]etlands separated from other waters of the United States by man-made dikes or barriers, natural river berms, beach dunes and the like are 'adjacent wetlands.'"...

We first addressed the proper interpretation of [the] phrase "the waters of the United States" in *United States* v. *Riverside Bayview Homes, Inc.* ... (1985). That case concerned a wetland that "was adjacent to a body of navigable water," because "the area characterized by saturated soil conditions and wetland vegetation extended beyond the boundary of respondent's property to... a navigable waterway."... Noting that "the transition from water to solid ground is not necessarily or even typically an abrupt one," and that "the Corps must necessarily choose some point at which water ends and land begins"... we upheld the Corps' interpretation of "the waters of the United States" to include wetlands that "actually abut[ted] on" traditional navigable waters....

Following our decision in *Riverside Bayview*, the Corps adopted increasingly broad interpretations of its own regulations under the Act. For example, in 1986, to "clarify" the reach of its jurisdiction, the Corps announced the so-called "Migratory Bird Rule," which purported to extend its jurisdiction to any intrastate waters "[w]hich are or would be used as habitat" by migratory birds.... In addition, the Corps interpreted its own regulations to include "ephemeral streams" and "drainage ditches" as "tributaries" that are part of the "waters of the United States" ... provided that they have a perceptible "ordinary high water mark."... This interpretation extended "the waters of the United States" to virtually any land feature over which rainwater or drainage passes and leaves a visible mark—even if only "the presence of litter and debris."...

In *SWANCC [Solid Waste Agency of Northern Cook Cty.* v. *Army Corps of Engineers* (2001)], we considered the application of the Corps' "Migratory Bird Rule" to "an abandoned sand and gravel pit in northern Illinois."... Observing that "[i]t was the *significant nexus* between the wetlands and 'navigable waters' that informed our reading of the CWA in *Riverside Bayview*" (emphasis added), we held that *Riverside Bayview* did not establish "that the jurisdiction of the Corps extends to ponds that are not adjacent to open water."... On the contrary, we held that "nonnavigable, isolated, intrastate waters" ... which, unlike the wetlands at issue in *Riverside Bayview*, did not "actually abu[t] on a navigable waterway" ... were not included as "waters of the United States."

Following our decision in *SWANCC*, the Corps did not significantly revise its theory of federal jurisdiction.... Because *SWANCC* did not directly address tributaries, the Corps notified its field staff that they "should continue to assert jurisdiction over traditional navigable waters . . .and, generally speaking, their tributary systems (and adjacent wetlands)."... In addition, because *SWANCC* did not overrule *Riverside Bayview*, the Corps continues to assert jurisdiction over waters "'neighboring'" traditional navigable waters and their tributaries....

[Section II omitted.]

III

The Rapanos petitioners contend that the terms "navigable waters" and "waters of the United States" in the Act must be limited to the traditional definition . . . which required that the "waters" be navigable in fact, or susceptible of being rendered so. . . .

We need not decide the precise extent to which the qualifiers "navigable" and "of the United States" restrict the coverage of the Act. Whatever the scope of these qualifiers, the CWA authorizes federal jurisdiction only over "waters." . . . The only natural definition of the term "waters," our prior and subsequent judicial constructions of it, clear evidence from other provisions of the statute, and this Court's canons of construction all confirm that "the waters of the United States" . . . cannot bear the expansive meaning that the Corps would give it.

The Corps' expansive approach might be arguable if the [CWA] defined "navigable waters" as "water of the United States." But "the waters of the United States" is something else. The use of the definite article ("the") and the plural number ("waters") show plainly that [the CWA] does not refer to water in general. In this form, "the waters" refers more narrowly to water "[a]s found in streams and bodies forming geographical features such as oceans, rivers, [and] lakes," or "the flowing or moving masses, as of waves or floods, making up such streams or bodies." *Webster's New International Dictionary* (hereinafter *Webster's Second*). On this definition, "the waters of the United States" include only relatively permanent, standing or flowing bodies of water. The definition refers to water as found in "streams," "oceans," "rivers," "lakes," and "bodies" of water "forming geographical features." . . . All of these terms connote continuously present, fixed bodies of water, as opposed to ordinarily dry channels through which water occasionally or intermittently flows. Even the least substantial of the definition's terms, namely "streams," connotes a continuous flow of water in a permanent channel—especially when used in company with other terms such as "rivers," "lakes," and "oceans." None of these terms encompasses transitory puddles or ephemeral flows of water.

The restriction of "the waters of the United States" to exclude channels containing merely intermittent or ephemeral flow also accords with the commonsense understanding of the term. In applying the definition to "ephemeral streams," "wet meadows," storm sewers and culverts, "directional sheet flow during storm events," drain tiles, man-made drainage ditches, and dry arroyos in the middle of the desert, the Corps has stretched the term "waters of the United States" beyond parody. The plain language of the statute simply does not authorize this "Land Is Waters" approach to federal jurisdiction.

In addition, the Act's use of the traditional phrase "navigable waters" (the defined term) further confirms that it confers jurisdiction only over relatively *permanent* bodies of water. The Act adopted that traditional term from its predecessor statutes. . . . On the traditional understanding, "navigable waters" included only discrete *bodies* of water. . . .

Even if the phrase "the waters of the United States" were ambiguous as applied to intermittent flows, our own canons of construction would establish that the Corps' interpretation of the statute is impermissible. As we noted in *SWANCC*, the Government's expansive interpretation would "result in a significant impingement of the States' traditional and primary power over land and water use." . . . Regulation of land use, as through the issuance of the development permits sought by petitioners in both of these cases, is a quintessential state and local power. . . . The extensive federal jurisdiction urged by the Government would authorize the Corps to function as a *de facto* regulator of immense stretches of intrastate land—an authority the agency has shown its willingness to exercise with the scope of discretion that would befit a local zoning board. . . . We ordinarily expect a "clear and manifest" statement from Congress to authorize an unprecedented intrusion into traditional state authority. . . . The phrase "the waters of the United States" hardly qualifies.

Likewise, just as we noted in *SWANCC*, the Corps' interpretation stretches the outer limits of Congress's commerce power and raises difficult questions about the ultimate scope of that power. . . . Even if the term "the waters of the United States" were ambiguous as applied to channels that sometimes host ephemeral flows of water (which it is not), we would expect a clearer statement from Congress to authorize an agency theory of jurisdiction that presses the envelope of constitutional validity. . . .

In sum, on its only plausible interpretation, the phrase "the waters of the United States" includes only those relatively permanent, standing or continuously flowing bodies of water "forming geographic features" that are described in ordinary parlance as "streams[,] oceans, rivers, [and] lakes." . . . The phrase does not include channels through which water flows intermittently or ephemerally, or channels that periodically provide drainage for rainfall. The Corps' expansive interpretation of the "the waters of the United States" is thus not "based on a permissible construction of the statute." . . .

[Sections IV, V, VI, and VII omitted.]

VIII

Because the Sixth Circuit applied the wrong standard to determine if these wetlands are covered "waters of the United States," and because of the paucity of the record in both of these cases, the lower courts should determine, in the first instance, whether the ditches or drains near each wetland are "waters" in the ordinary sense of containing a relatively permanent flow; and (if they are) whether the wetlands in question are "adjacent" to these "waters" in the sense of possessing a continuous surface connection that creates the boundary-drawing problem we addressed in *Riverside Bayview*.

*   *   *

We vacate the judgments of the Sixth Circuit in both No. 04–1034 and No. 04–1384, and remand both cases for further proceedings.

It is so ordered.

JUSTICE KENNEDY, concurring in the judgment.

These consolidated cases require the Court to decide whether the term "navigable waters" in the Clean Water Act extends to wetlands that do not contain and are not adjacent to waters that are navigable in fact. In *Solid Waste Agency of Northern Cook Cty. v. Army Corps of Engineers* . . . the Court held, under the circumstances presented there, that to constitute "navigable waters" under the Act, a water or wetland must possess a "significant nexus" to waters that are or were navigable in fact or that could reasonably be so made. . . . In the instant cases neither the plurality opinion nor the dissent by JUSTICE STEVENS chooses to apply this test; and though the Court of Appeals recognized the test's applicability, it did not consider all the factors necessary to determine whether the lands in question had, or did not have, the requisite nexus. In my view the cases ought to be remanded to the Court of Appeals for proper consideration of the nexus requirement.

I [. . .]

A

...The statutory term to be interpreted and applied in the two instant cases is the term "navigable waters." The outcome turns on whether that phrase reasonably describes certain Michigan wetlands the Corps seeks to regulate. Under the Act "[t]he term 'navigable waters' means the waters of the United States, including the territorial seas.". . . In a regulation the Corps has construed the term "waters of the United States" to include not only waters susceptible to use in interstate commerce—the traditional understanding of the term "navigable waters of the United States" . . . but also tributaries of those waters and, of particular relevance here, wetlands adjacent to those waters or their tributaries. . . . The Corps views tributaries as within its jurisdiction if they carry a perceptible "ordinary high water mark. . . . An ordinary high-water mark is a "line on the shore established by the fluctuations of water and indicated by physical characteristics such as clear, natural line impressed on the bank, shelving, changes in the character of soil, destruction of terrestrial vegetation, the presence of litter and debris, or other appropriate means that consider the characteristics of the surrounding areas.". . .

Contrary to the plurality's description . . . wetlands are not simply moist patches of earth. They are defined as "those areas that are inundated or saturated by surface or ground water at a frequency and duration sufficient to support, and that under normal circumstances do support, a prevalence of vegetation typically adapted for life in saturated soil conditions. Wetlands generally include swamps, marshes, bogs, and similar areas.". . . The Corps' Wetlands Delineation Manual, including over 100 pages of technical guidance for Corps officers, interprets this definition of wetlands to require: (1) prevalence of plant species typically adapted to saturated soil conditions, determined in accordance with the United States Fish and Wildlife Service's National List of Plant Species that Occur in Wetlands; (2) hydric soil, meaning soil that is saturated, flooded, or ponded for sufficient time during the growing season to become anaerobic, or lacking in oxygen, in the upper part; and (3) wetland hydrology, a term generally requiring continuous inundation or saturation to the surface during at least five percent of the growing season in most years. . . .

II

Twice before the Court has construed the term "navigable waters" in the Clean Water Act. In *United States* v. *Riverside Bayview Homes, Inc.* . . . the Court upheld the Corps' jurisdiction over wetlands adjacent to navigable-in-fact waterways. . . . The property in *Riverside Bayview*, like the wetlands in the *Carabell* case now before the Court, was located roughly one mile from Lake St. Clair . . . though in that case, unlike *Carabell*, the lands at issue formed part of a wetland that directly abutted a navigable-in-fact creek. . . . In regulatory provisions that remain in effect, the Corps had concluded that wetlands perform important functions such as filtering and purifying water draining into adjacent water bodies . . . slowing the flow of runoff into lakes, rivers, and streams so as to prevent flooding and erosion . . . and providing critical habitat for aquatic animal species. . . . Recognizing that "[a]n agency's construction of a statute it is charged with enforcing is entitled to deference if it is reasonable and not in conflict with the expressed intent of Congress" . . . the Court held that "the Corps' ecological judgment about the relationship between waters and their adjacent wetlands provides an adequate basis for a legal judgment that adjacent wetlands may be defined as waters under the Act.". . . The Court reserved, however, the question of the Corps' authority to regulate wetlands other than those adjacent to open waters. . . .

In *SWANCC*, the Court considered the validity of the Corps' jurisdiction over ponds and mudflats that were isolated in the sense of being unconnected to other waters covered by the Act. . . . The property at issue was an abandoned sand and gravel pit mining operation where "remnant excavation trenches" had "evolve[ed] into a scattering of permanent and seasonal ponds.". . . Asserting jurisdiction pursuant to a regulation called the "Migratory Bird Rule," the Corps argued that these isolated ponds were "waters of the United States"(and thus "navigable waters" under the Act) because they were used as habitat by migratory birds. . . . The Court rejected this theory. "It was the significant nexus between wetlands and 'navigable waters,'" the Court held, "that informed our reading of the [Act] in *Riverside Bayview Homes*.". . . Because such a nexus was lacking with respect to isolated ponds, the Court held that the plain text of the statute did not permit the Corps' action. . . .

Riverside Bayview and *SWANCC* establish the framework for the inquiry in the cases now before the Court: Do the Corps' regulations, as applied to the wetlands in *Carabell* and the three wetlands parcels in *Rapanos*, constitute a reasonable interpretation of "navigable waters" as in *Riverside Bayview* or an invalid construction as in *SWANCC*? Taken together these cases establish that in some instances, as exemplified by *Riverside Bayview*, the connection between a nonnavigable water or wetland and a navigable water may be so close, or potentially so close, that the Corps may deem the water or wetland a "navigable water" under the Act. In other instances, as exemplified by *SWANCC*, there may be little or no connection. Absent a significant nexus, jurisdiction under the Act is lacking. Because neither the plurality nor the dissent addresses the nexus requirement, this separate opinion, in my respectful view, is necessary.

A

. . . The plurality's first requirement—permanent standing water or continuous flow, at least for a period of "some months" . . . makes little practical sense in a statute concerned with downstream water quality. The merest trickle, if continuous, would count as a "water" subject to federal regulation, while torrents thundering at irregular intervals through otherwise dry channels would not. Though the plurality seems to presume that such irregular flows are too insignificant to be of concern in a statute focused on "waters," that may not always be true. Areas in the western parts of the Nation provide some examples. The Los Angeles River, for instance, ordinarily carries only a trickle of water and often looks more like a dry roadway than a river. . . . Yet it periodically releases water—volumes so powerful and destructive that it has been encased in concrete and steel over a length of some 50 miles.... Though this particular waterway might satisfy the plurality's test, it is illustrative of what often-dry watercourses can become when rain waters flow....

To be sure, Congress could draw a line to exclude irregular waterways, but nothing in the statute suggests it has done so....

The plurality's second limitation—exclusion of wetlands lacking a continuous surface connection to other jurisdictional waters—is also unpersuasive. To begin with, the plurality is wrong to suggest that wetlands are "*indistinguishable*" from waters to which they bear a surface connection.... Even if the precise boundary may be imprecise, a bog or swamp is different from a river. The question is what circumstances permit a bog, swamp, or other nonnavigable wetland to constitute a "navigable water" under the Act.... *Riverside Bayview* addressed that question and its answer is inconsistent with the plurality's theory. There, in upholding the Corps' authority to regulate "wetlands adjacent to other bodies of water over which the Corps has jurisdiction," the Court deemed it irrelevant whether "the moisture creating the wetlands...find[s] its source in the adjacent bodies of water."... The Court further observed that adjacency could serve as a valid basis for regulation even as to "wetlands that are not significantly intertwined with the ecosystem of adjacent waterways."... "If it is reasonable," the Court explained, "for the Corps to conclude that in the majority of cases, adjacent wetlands have significant effects on water quality and the aquatic ecosystem, its definition can stand."...

In sum the plurality's opinion is inconsistent with the Act's text, structure, and purpose....

B

While the plurality reads nonexistent requirements into the Act, the dissent reads a central requirement out—namely, the requirement that the word "navigable" in "navigable waters" be given some importance. Although the Court has held that the statute's language invokes Congress' traditional authority over waters navigable in fact or susceptible of being made so ... the dissent would permit federal regulation whenever wetlands lie alongside a ditch or drain, however remote and insubstantial, that eventually may flow into traditional navigable waters. The deference owed to the Corps' interpretation of the statute does not extend so far.

Congress' choice of words creates difficulties, for the Act contemplates regulation of certain "navigable waters" that are not in fact navigable.... Nevertheless, the word "navigable" in the Act must be given some effect....

Consistent with *SWANCC* and *Riverside Bayview* and with the need to give the term "navigable" some meaning, the Corps' jurisdiction over wetlands depends upon the existence of a significant nexus between the wetlands in question and navigable waters in the traditional sense. The required nexus must be assessed in terms of the statute's goals and purposes. Congress enacted the law to "restore and maintain the chemical, physical, and biological integrity of the Nation's waters" ... and it pursued that objective by restricting dumping and filling in "navigable waters."... With respect to wetlands, the rationale for Clean Water Act regulation is, as the Corps has recognized, that wetlands can perform critical functions related to the integrity of other waters—functions such as pollutant trapping, flood control, and runoff storage.... Accordingly, wetlands possess the requisite nexus, and thus come within the statutory phrase "navigable waters," if the wetlands, either alone or in combination with similarly situated lands in the region, significantly affect the chemical, physical, and biological integrity of other covered waters more readily understood as "navigable." When, in contrast, wetlands' effects on water quality are speculative or insubstantial, they fall outside the zone fairly encompassed by the statutory term "navigable waters.". . .

III

In both the consolidated cases before the Court the record contains evidence suggesting the possible existence of a significant nexus according to the principles outlined above. Thus the end result in these cases and many others to be considered by the Corps may be the same as that suggested by the dissent, namely, that the Corps' assertion of jurisdiction is valid. Given, however, that neither the agency nor the reviewing courts properly considered the issue, a remand is appropriate, in my view, for application of the controlling legal standard. . . .

*   *   *

In these consolidated cases I would vacate the judgments of the Court of Appeals and remand for consideration whether the specific wetlands at issue possess a significant nexus with navigable waters.

Source: U.S. Supreme Court of the United States. *Rapanos v. United States.* 547 U.S. — (2006), Docket 04-1034. June 19, 2006. www.supremecourtus.gov/opinions/05pdf/04-1034.pdf (accessed March 13, 2007).

Supreme Court on the Death Penalty

June 26, 2006

■■■■ THE DOCUMENT IN CONTEXT ■■■■

Lethal injection, the most common form of execution in the United States, came under challenge on several fronts in 2006, even as the number of people sentenced to death continued to decline. In December executions were suspended, at least temporarily, in California, Florida, and Maryland because of concerns that the combination of drugs typically used in executions could cause excruciating pain if not administered properly. Earlier in the year, at least four other states stopped executions while special commissions reviewed the protocols in place for administering the lethal injections. The Supreme Court also weighed in on the matter, when it unanimously agreed that a Florida death row inmate had a civil right to a hearing to challenge the constitutionality of the three-drug combination that most states used in executions. But the Court refused to review any cases that directly challenged the constitutionality of lethal injections, leaving lower courts uncertain about the direction the Supreme Court would eventually take on this issue.

Perhaps in part because of the moratoriums, the number of executions in 2006 dropped to 53, the lowest number since 1996, when 45 inmates were executed. The number of death sentences was also declining. In December the Justice Department said there had been 128 death sentences in 2005, down about 60 percent from a high of 317 in 1996. The Death Penalty Information Center (DPIC), a group advocating an end to the death penalty, estimated there were no more than 114 death sentences in 2006. Several reasons were given for the decline in the number of death sentences, including a significant drop in violent crime, better legal representation for capital defendants, and an increasing number of states that offered life in prison without possibility of parole as an alternative to a death sentence.

DPIC and others also said that growing public uneasiness over possibly sentencing an innocent person to death was a factor. In recent years, the use of DNA testing and other sophisticated forensic technology had resulted in the freeing of many prisoners wrongfully convicted of capital and other crimes. Although it had not yet been shown that an innocent person had been executed, many parties to the debate thought that it was just a matter of time. According to DPIC, since 1976, when the death penalty was reinstated, 123 people had been freed from death row after significant questions were raised about their convictions—14 of them through DNA testing. "The fact is that they've gotten a lot of the wrong guys," Deborah Fleischaker, director of the American Bar Association's Death Penalty Moratorium Implementation Project, told the Associated Press in December. "There's no question that has . . . created a lot of doubt about how the death penalty is working."

Questions on the Court

It was also creating some degree of doubt among the nine Supreme Court justices. On June 12, the Court ruled 5–3 in the case of *House v. Bell* that a death row inmate in Tennessee could challenge the constitutionality of his murder conviction based on new evidence, including DNA testing, that raised serious questions about whether he was in fact guilty. Writing for the majority, Justice Anthony M. Kennedy said that when an inmate came to federal court with evidence of innocence, "the court's function is not to make an independent factual determination about what likely occurred, but rather to assess the likely impact of the evidence on reasonable jurors." In this case, Kennedy said, it was likely that no reasonable juror viewing the entire evidentiary record would find the inmate guilty beyond a reasonable doubt.

Two weeks later, in the case of *Kansas v. Marsh,* decided June 26 on a 5–4 vote, the Court upheld a state law requiring jurors to impose the death penalty where they found an equal balance between aggravating factors supporting a death sentence and mitigating factors supporting a life sentence. Writing for the majority, Justice Clarence Thomas said that the jury's finding of an equal balance between aggravating and mitigating factors did not indicate the jury was in doubt about the sentence, as the dissenting justices argued. The Kansas state jury instructions clearly informed the jury that "a determination that the evidence is in equipoise is a decision for . . . death," Thomas wrote.

Because it addressed a specific state sentencing law, the decision was not likely to have an effect outside Kansas. But the opinions were notable for the justices' public clash of views on the wider implications of the case. In a minority opinion signed by Justices John Paul Stevens, Ruth Bader Ginsburg, and Stephen G. Breyer, Justice David Souter called the decision "obtuse by any moral or social measure," particularly in view of the large number of individuals who had been removed from death row as a result of DNA testing and other evidence. A "new body of fact must be accounted for in deciding what, in practical terms, the Eighth Amendment guarantees should tolerate, for the period starting in 1989 has seen repeated exonerations of convicts under death sentences, in numbers never imagined before the development of DNA tests," Souter wrote. He added, however, that it was "far too soon for any generalization about the soundness of capital sentencing across the country."

In a concurring opinion directly rebutting Souter, Justice Antonin Scalia argued that there was no evidence that any innocent person had been executed in recent times, that the possibility of executing an innocent person had "been reduced to an insignificant minimum," and that far from showing that the system was a failure, DNA exonerations showed that legal safeguards were effective. Scalia then excoriated the minority for trying to impose its beliefs about capital punishment on the courts: "The American people have determined that the good to be derived from capital punish- ment . . . outweighs the risks. It is no proper part of the business of this Court, or of its Justices, to second-guess that judgment, much less to impugn it before the world, and less still to frustrate it by imposing judicially invented obstacles to its execution."

The case was also notable in that the Court's newest justice, Samuel A. Alito Jr., likely cast the deciding vote. Alito joined Thomas, Scalia, Kennedy, and Chief Justice John G. Roberts Jr. in the majority opinion. The case was argued twice, once while Sandra Day O'Connor was still on the bench and again after Alito took her place at the end of January. It was widely assumed that Alito's vote broke a 4–4 tie among the other eight justices.

Growing Questions about Lethal Injections

Since the Supreme Court reinstated the death penalty in 1976, all but one of the thirty-eight states that allowed capital punishment used lethal injection (the exception was Nebraska, which still used the electric chair). Most states used a combination of three drugs—first, an injection of sodium pentothal (also known as sodium thiopental) to deaden pain; then an injection of the paralytic pancuronium bromide (also called Pavulon); followed by a shot of potassium chloride, which induced cardiac arrest but was extremely painful in the absence of anesthesia. The combination was intended to avoid the "unnecessary and wanton infliction of pain" that the Supreme Court had said would amount to cruel and unusual punishment and thus be unconstitutional under the Eighth Amendment.

In recent years, however, reports began to circulate that the drugs did not always work as planned and that some inmates who had not been given a strong enough sedative appeared to suffer great pain and convulsions before dying. A Human Rights Watch report published in April 2006 said that prison officials in several states admitted medical professionals had not been involved in developing the procedures for administering the drugs and that prison personnel were often untrained in the procedures. The American Medical Association as well as the American Society of Anesthesiologists had advised doctors not to participate in executions.

Death row inmates were challenging the use of lethal injections in several states on a variety of fronts. In February Judge Jeremy Fogel of the federal district court in San Jose, California, stayed the execution of a convicted killer after two anesthesiologists refused for ethical reasons to participate in the execution. Fogel conducted a four-day hearing on the state's lethal injection protocol in September and on December 15 ruled that the procedure was unconstitutional. In a sharply critical report, Fogel said execution teams were poorly screened, badly trained, and inadequately supervised, and the chemicals sometimes were improperly prepared. Only hours earlier, Florida governor Jeb Bush announced a moratorium on executions in that state after a botched execution on December 13. The execution of Angel Nieves Diaz took thirty-four minutes, about twice as long as the normal procedure, and required two rounds of the lethal chemicals.

Both Judge Fogel and Governor Bush indicated that executions using lethal injections were likely to resume once new protocols were worked out. Bush convened a commission to investigate and make recommendations on implementation of lethal injections. Fogel, who said the system in California was broken but could be fixed, suggested one possibility was to execute convicts using a single large dose of anesthetic, the method most veterinarians used to euthanize animals. Fogel said that approach would "eliminate any constitutional concerns, subject only to the implementation of adequate verifiable procedures to ensure that the inmate actually receives a fatal dose of the anesthetic."

On December 19, Maryland's highest state court put executions there on hold while the state reviewed its protocol on lethal injection. Challenges to protocols were also pending in federal court in Maryland, as well as in Arkansas, Delaware, Missouri, and Ohio. In South Dakota, Gov. Mike Rounds halted all executions until the state legislature acted on a new procedure for implementing lethal injections.

Despite apparently contradictory rulings in lower federal courts, the Supreme Court had so far refused to intervene in any case directly challenging the constitutionality of lethal injections. In a narrow ruling on June 12, the Court unanimously agreed to open the procedural door for last-minute civil rights challenges not to a death sentence per se but rather to the way it would be conducted. The case involved Clarence Hill, who had been convicted of murdering a police officer in Florida and who was minutes away from being executed in January when the Supreme Court issued a stay. Hill argued that Florida's lethal injection procedure could cause him extreme pain and sought the right to challenge the procedure as a violation of his federal civil rights. Florida countered that the only proper challenge was under a petition for habeas corpus and that Hill had already exhausted his habeas corpus appeals. The Court sided with Hill and sent the case back to federal district court. However, both that court and the U.S. Appeals Court for the Eleventh Circuit ruled that Hill had waited too long to file his civil rights claim—he had done so just four days before he was to be executed—and was just trying to delay his death. By a 5–4 vote, the Supreme Court refused Hill's request for a second stay, and he was executed on September 20.

Following are excerpts from the majority opinion written by Justice Clarence Thomas, a concurring opinion written by Justice Antonin Scalia, and a dissenting opinion written by Justice David Souter, in the case of Kansas v. Marsh, *in which the Supreme Court on June 26, 2006, upheld, 5–4, the constitutionality of a Kansas law requiring the imposition of the death sentence in capital cases when juries find aggravating factors and mitigating circumstances to be in equal balance.*

DOCUMENT

Kansas v. Marsh

No. 04–1170

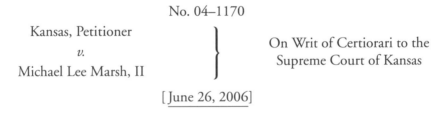

Kansas, Petitioner

v.

Michael Lee Marsh, II

On Writ of Certiorari to the
Supreme Court of Kansas

[June 26, 2006]

JUSTICE THOMAS delivered the opinion of the Court.

Kansas law provides that if a unanimous jury finds that aggravating circumstances are not outweighed by mitigating circumstances, the death penalty shall be imposed. We must decide whether this statute, which requires the imposition of the death penalty when the sentencing jury determines that aggravating evidence and mitigating evidence are in equipoise, violates the Constitution. We hold that it does not.

I

Respondent Michael Lee Marsh II broke into the home of Marry Ane Pusch and lay in wait for her to return. When Marry Ane entered her home with her 19-month-old daughter, M. P., Marsh repeatedly shot Marry Ane, stabbed her, and slashed her throat. The home was set on fire with the toddler inside, and M. P. burned to death. The jury convicted Marsh of the capital murder of M. P., the first-degree premeditated murder of Marry Ane, aggravated arson, and aggravated burglary. The jury found beyond a reasonable doubt the existence of three aggravating circumstances, and that those circumstances were not outweighed by any mitigating circumstances. On the basis of those findings, the jury sentenced Marsh to death for the capital murder of M. P. The jury also sentenced Marsh to life imprisonment without possibility of parole for 40 years for the first-degree murder of Marry Ane, and consecutive sentences of 51 months' imprisonment for aggravated arson and 34 months' imprisonment for aggravated burglary. . . .

[Remainder of Part I and Part II, on Supreme Court's jurisdiction in this case, has been omitted.]

III

This case is controlled by *Walton* v. *Arizona* (1990). . . . In that case, a jury had convicted Walton of a capital offense. At sentencing, the trial judge found the existence of two aggravating circumstances and that the mitigating circumstances did not call for leniency, and sentenced Walton to death. . . .

. . . Walton argued to this Court that the Arizona capital sentencing system created an unconstitutional presumption in favor of death because it "tells an Arizona sentencing judge who finds even a single aggravating factor, that death must be imposed, unless—as the Arizona Supreme Court put it in Petitioner's case—there are 'outweighing mitigating factors.'" . . . Rejecting Walton's argument . . . this Court stated:

> *"So long as a State's method of allocating the burdens of proof does not lessen the State's burden to prove every element of the offense charged, or in this case to prove the existence of aggravating circumstances, a defendant's constitutional rights are not violated by placing on him the burden of proving mitigating circumstances sufficiently substantial to call for leniency."*

This Court noted that, as a requirement of individualized sentencing, a jury must have the opportunity to consider all evidence relevant to mitigation, and that a state statute that permits a jury to consider any mitigating evidence comports with that requirement. . . . The Court also pointedly observed that while the Constitution requires that a sentencing jury have discretion, it does not mandate that discretion be unfettered; the States are free to determine the manner in which a jury may consider mitigating evidence. . . . So long as the sentencer is not precluded from considering relevant mitigating evidence, a capital sentencing statute cannot be said to impermissibly, much less automatically, impose death. . . . Indeed, *Walton* suggested that the only capital sentencing systems that would be impermissibly mandatory were those that would "automatically impose death upon conviction for certain types of murder." . . .

IV

A

Even if, as Marsh contends, *Walton* does not directly control, the general principles set forth in our death penalty jurisprudence would lead us to conclude that the Kansas capital sentencing system is constitutionally permissible. Together, our decisions in *Furman* v. *Georgia* (1972) and *Gregg* v. *Georgia* (1976) establish that a state capital sentencing system must: (1) rationally narrow the class of death-eligible defendants; and (2) permit a jury to render a reasoned, individualized sentencing determination based on a death-eligible defendant's record, personal characteristics, and the circumstances of his crime. . . . So long as a state system satisfies these requirements, our precedents establish that a State enjoys a range of discretion in imposing the death penalty, including the manner in which aggravating and mitigating circumstances are to be weighed. . . .

The use of mitigation evidence is a product of the requirement of individualized sentencing. . . .

In aggregate, our precedents confer upon defendants the right to present sentencers with information relevant to the sentencing decision and oblige sentencers to consider that information in determining the appropriate sentence. The thrust of our mitigation jurisprudence ends here. "[W]e have never held that a specific method for balancing mitigating and aggravating factors in a capital sentencing proceeding is constitutionally required." . . . Rather, this Court has held that the States enjoy "'a constitutionally permissible range of discretion in imposing the death penalty.'" . . .

B

The Kansas death penalty statute satisfies the constitutional mandates of *Furman* and its progeny because it rationally narrows the class of death-eligible defendants and permits a jury to consider any mitigating evidence relevant to its sentencing determination. It does not interfere, in a constitutionally significant way, with a jury's ability to give independent weight to evidence offered in mitigation.

Kansas' procedure narrows the universe of death-eligible defendants consistent with Eighth Amendment requirements. Under Kansas law, imposition of the death penalty is an *option* only after a defendant is convicted of capital murder, which requires that one or more specific elements beyond intentional premeditated murder be found. . . . Once convicted of capital murder, a defendant becomes *eligible* for the death penalty only if the State seeks a separate sentencing hearing . . . and proves beyond a reasonable doubt the existence of one or more statutorily enumerated aggravating circumstances. . . .

Consonant with the individualized sentencing requirement, a Kansas jury is permitted to consider *any* evidence relating to *any* mitigating circumstance in determining the appropriate sentence for a capital defendant, so long as that evidence is relevant. . . . Jurors are then apprised of, but not limited to, the factors that the defendant contends are mitigating. They are then instructed that "[e]ach juror must consider every mitigating factor that he or she individually finds to exist."

Kansas' weighing equation . . . merely channels a jury's discretion by providing it with criteria by which it may determine whether a sentence of life or death is appropriate. The system in Kansas provides the type of "'guided discretion'" . . . we have sanctioned. . . .

Contrary to Marsh's argument, [the Kansas law] does not create a general presumption in favor of the death penalty in the State of Kansas. Rather, the Kansas capital sentencing system is dominated by the presumption that life imprisonment is the appropriate sentence for a capital conviction. If the State fails to meet its burden to demonstrate the existence of an aggravating circumstance(s) beyond a reasonable doubt, a sentence of life imprisonment must be imposed. . . . If the State overcomes this hurdle, then it bears the additional burden of proving beyond a reasonable doubt that aggravating circumstances are not outweighed by mitigating circumstances. . . . Significantly, although the defendant appropriately bears the burden of proffering mitigating circumstances—a burden of production—he never bears the burden of demonstrating that mitigating circumstances outweigh aggravating circumstances. Instead, the State always has the burden of demonstrating that mitigating evidence does not outweigh aggravating evidence. Absent the State's ability to meet that burden, the default is life imprisonment. Moreover, if the jury is unable to reach a unanimous decision—in any respect—a sentence of life must be imposed. . . . This system does not create a presumption that death is the appropriate sentence for capital murder.

Nor is there any force behind Marsh's contention that an equipoise determination reflects juror confusion or inability to decide between life and death, or that a jury may use equipoise as a loophole to shirk its constitutional duty to render a reasoned, moral decision . . . regarding whether death is an appropriate sentence for a particular defendant. Such an argument rests on an implausible characterization of the Kansas statute—that a jury's determination that aggravators and mitigators are in equipoise is not a *decision*, much less a decision *for death*—and thus misses the mark. . . . Weighing is not an end; it is merely a means to reaching a decision. The decision the jury must reach is whether life or death is the appropriate punishment. The Kansas jury instructions clearly inform the jury that a determination that the evidence is in equipoise is a decision for—not a presumption in favor of—death. Kansas jurors, presumed to follow their instructions, are made aware that: a determination that mitigators outweigh aggravators is a decision that a life sentence is appropriate; a determination that aggravators outweigh mitigators *or* a determination that mitigators do not outweigh aggravators—including a finding that aggravators and mitigators are in balance—is a decision that death is the appropriate sentence; and an inability to reach a unanimous decision will result in a sentence of life imprisonment. So informed, far from the abdication of duty or the inability to select an appropriate sentence depicted by Marsh and JUSTICE SOUTER, a jury's conclusion that aggravating evidence and mitigating evidence are in equipoise is a *decision for death* and is indicative of the type of measured, normative process in which a jury is constitutionally tasked to engage when deciding the appropriate sentence for a capital defendant.

V

JUSTICE SOUTER argues (hereinafter the dissent) that the advent of DNA testing has resulted in the "exoneratio[n]" of "innocent" persons "in numbers never imagined before the development of DNA tests." Based upon this "new empirical demonstration of how 'death is different,'" the dissent concludes that Kansas' sentencing system permits the imposition of the death penalty in the absence of reasoned moral judgment.

But the availability of DNA testing, and the questions it might raise about the accuracy of guilt-phase determinations in capital cases, is simply irrelevant to the question before the Court today, namely, the constitutionality of Kansas' capital *sentencing* system. Accordingly, the accuracy of the dissent's factual claim that DNA testing has established the "innocence of numerous convicted persons under death sentences" and the incendiary debate it invokes—is beyond the scope of this opinion.

The dissent's general criticisms against the death penalty are ultimately a call for resolving all legal disputes in capital cases by adopting the outcome that makes the death penalty more difficult to impose. While such a bright-line rule may be easily applied, it has no basis in-law. Indeed, the logical consequence of the dissent's argument is that the death penalty can only be just in a system that does not permit error. Because the criminal justice system does not operate perfectly, abolition of the death penalty is the only answer to the moral dilemma the dissent poses. This Court, however, does not sit as a moral authority. Our precedents do not prohibit the States from authorizing the death penalty, even in our imperfect system. And those precedents do not empower this Court to chip away at the States' prerogatives to do soon the grounds the dissent invokes today.

*   *   *

We hold that the Kansas capital sentencing system, which directs imposition of the death penalty when a jury finds that aggravating and mitigating circumstances in equipoise, is constitutional. Accordingly, we reverse the judgment of the Kansas Supreme Court, and remand thecae for further proceedings not inconsistent with this opinion.

It is so ordered.

JUSTICE SCALIA, concurring.
   [Parts I and II omitted.]

III

Finally, I must say a few words (indeed, more than a few) in response to Part III of JUSTICE SOUTER's dissent....

There exists in some parts of the world sanctimonious criticism of America's death penalty, as somehow unworthy of a civilized society. (I say sanctimonious, because most of the countries to which these finger-waggers belong had the death penalty themselves until recently—and indeed, many of them would still have it if the democratic will prevailed.) It is a certainty that the opinion of a near-majority of the United States Supreme Court to the effect that our system condemns many innocent defendants to death will be trumpeted abroad as vindication of these criticisms. For that reason, I take the trouble to point out that the dissenting opinion has nothing substantial to support it.

It should be noted at the outset that the dissent does not discuss a single case—not one—in which it is clear that a person was executed for a crime he did not commit. If such an event had occurred in recent years, we would not have to hunt for it; the innocent's name would be shouted from the rooftops by the abolition lobby. The dissent makes much of the new-found capacity of DNA testing to establish innocence. But in every case of an executed defendant of which I am aware, that technology has *confirmed* guilt....

Remarkably avoiding any claim of erroneous executions, the dissent focuses on the large numbers of *non*-executed "exonerees" paraded by various professors. It speaks as though exoneration came about through the operation of some outside force to correct the mistakes of our legal system, rather than *as a consequence of the functioning of our legal system.* Reversal of an erroneous conviction on appeal or on habeas, or the pardoning of an innocent condemnee through executive clemency, demonstrates not the failure of the system but its success. Those devices are part and parcel of the multiple assurances that are applied before a death sentence is carried out.

Of course even in identifying exonerees, the dissent is willing to accept anybody's say-so. It engages in no critical review, but merely parrots articles or reports that support its attack on the American criminal justice system. The dissent places significant weight, for instance, on the Illinois Report (compiled by the appointees of an Illinois Governor who had declared a moratorium upon the death penalty and who eventually commuted all death sentences in the State . . . which it claims shows that "false verdicts" are "remarkable in number." The dissent claims that this Report identifies 13 inmates released from death row after they were determined to be innocent. To take one of these cases, discussed by the dissent as an example of a judgment "as close to innocence as any judgments courts normally render" . . . the defendant was twice convicted of murder. After his first trial, the Supreme Court of Illinois "reversed [his] conviction based upon certain evidentiary errors" and remanded his case for anew trial. The second jury convicted Smith again. The Supreme Court of Illinois again reversed the conviction because it found that the evidence was insufficient to establish guilt beyond a reasonable doubt. The court explained:

> "While a not guilty finding is sometimes equated with a finding of innocence, that conclusion is erroneous. Courts do not find people guilty or innocent. . . . A not guilty verdict expresses no view as to a defendant's innocence. Rather, [a reversal of conviction] indicates simply that the prosecution has failed to meet its burden of proof."

This case alone suffices to refute the dissent's claim that the Illinois Report distinguishes between "exoneration of a convict because of actual innocence, and reversal of a judgment because of legal error affecting conviction or sentence but not inconsistent with guilt in fact." The broader point, however, is that it is utterly impossible to regard "exoneration"—however casually defined—as a failure of the capital justice system, rather than as a vindication of its effectiveness in releasing not only defendants who are innocent, but those whose guilt has not been established beyond a reasonable doubt. . . .

The dissent's suggestion that capital defendants are *especially* liable to suffer from the lack of 100% perfection in our criminal justice system is implausible. Capital cases are given especially close scrutiny at every level, which is why in most cases many years elapse before the sentence is executed. And of course capital cases receive special attention in the application of executive clemency. Indeed, one of the arguments made by abolitionists is that the process of finally completing all the appeals and reexaminations of capital sentences is so lengthy, and thus so expensive for the State, that the game is not worth the candle. The proof of the pudding, of course, is that as far as anyone can determine (and many are looking), *none* of cases included in the .027% error rate for American verdicts involved a capital defendant erroneously executed.

Since 1976 there have been approximately a half million murders in the United States. In that time, 7,000 murderers have been sentenced to death; about 950 of them have been executed; and about 3,700 inmates are currently on death row. . . . As a consequence of the sensitivity of the criminal justice system to the due-process rights of defendants sentenced to death, almost two-thirds of all death sentences are overturned. "Virtually none" of these reversals, however, are attributable to a defendant's "'actual innocence.'" Most are based on legal errors that have little or nothing to do with guilt. The studies cited by the dissent demonstrate nothing more.

Like other human institutions, courts and juries are not perfect. One cannot have a system of criminal punishment without accepting the possibility that someone will be punished mistakenly. That is a truism, not a revelation. But with regard to the punishment of death in the current American system, that possibility has been reduced to an insignificant minimum. This explains why those ideologically driven to ferret out and proclaim a mistaken modern execution have not a single verifiable case to point to, whereas it is easy as pie to identify plainly guilty murderers who have been set free. The American people have determined that the good to be derived from capital punishment—in deterrence, and perhaps most of all in the meting out of condign justice for horrible crimes—outweighs the risk of error. It is no proper part of the business of this Court, or of its Justices, to second-guess that judgment, much less to impugn it before the world, and less still to frustrate it by imposing judicially invented obstacles to its execution.

JUSTICE SOUTER, with whom JUSTICE STEVENS, JUSTICE GINSBURG, and JUSTICE BREYER join, dissenting.

I

Kansas's capital sentencing statute provides that a defendant "shall be sentenced to death" if, by unanimous vote, "the jury finds beyond a reasonable doubt that one or more aggravating circumstances . . . exist and . . . that the existence of such aggravating circumstances is not outweighed by any mitigating circumstances which are found to exist." The Supreme Court of Kansas has read this provision to require imposition of the death penalty "[i]n the event of equipoise, [that is,] the jury's determination that the balance of any aggravating circumstances and any mitigating circumstances weighed equal." . . . Given this construction, the state court held the law unconstitutional on the ground that the Eighth Amendment requires that a "'tie g[o] to the defendant' when life or death is at issue." Because I agree with the Kansas judges that the Constitution forbids a mandatory death penalty in what they describe as "doubtful cases," when aggravating and mitigating factors are of equal weight, I respectfully dissent.

II

More than 30 years ago, this Court explained that the Eighth Amendment's guarantee against cruel and unusual punishment barred imposition of the death penalty under statutory schemes so inarticulate that sentencing discretion produced wanton and freakish results. . . . The Constitution was held to require, instead, a system structured to produce reliable . . . rational . . . and rationally reviewable . . . determinations of sentence.

Decades of back-and-forth between legislative experiment and judicial review have made it plain that the constitutional demand for rationality goes beyond the minimal requirement to replace unbounded discretion with a sentencing structure; a State has much leeway in devising such a structure and in selecting the terms for measuring relative culpability, but a system must meet an ultimate test of constitutional reliability in producing " 'a reasoned moral response to the defendant's background, character, and crime.' ". . . The Eighth Amendment, that is, demands both form and substance, both a system for decision and one geared to produce morally justifiable results.

The State thinks its scheme is beyond questioning, whether as to form or substance, for it sees the tie-breaker law as equivalent to the provisions examined in *Blystone* v. *Pennsylvania* (1990), and *Boyde* v. *California* (1990), where we approved statutes that required a death sentence upon a jury finding that aggravating circumstances outweighed mitigating ones. But the crucial fact in those systems was the predominance of the aggravators, and our recognition of the moral rationality of a mandatory capital sentence based on that finding is no authority for giving States free rein to select a different conclusion that will dictate death.

Instead, the constitutional demand for a reasoned moral response requires the state statute to satisfy two criteria that speak to the issue before us now, one governing the character of sentencing evidence, and one going to the substantive justification needed for a death sentence. As to the first, there is an obligation in each case to inform the jury's choice of sentence with evidence about the crime as actually committed and about the specific individual who committed it. . . . Since the sentencing choice is, by definition, the attribution of particular culpability to a criminal act and defendant . . . the sentencing decision must turn on the uniqueness of the individual defendant and on the details of the crime, to which any resulting choice of death must be "directly" related.

Second, there is the point to which the particulars of crime and criminal are relevant: within the category of capital crimes, the death penalty must be reserved for "the worst of the worst.". . . One object of the structured sentencing proceeding . . . is to eliminate the risk that a death sentence will be imposed in spite of facts calling for a lesser penalty . . . and the essence of the sentencing authority's responsibility is to determine whether the response to the crime and defendant "must be death.". . . Of course, in the moral world of those who reject capital punishment in principle, a death sentence can never be a moral imperative. The point, however, is that within our legal and moral system, which allows a place for the death penalty, "must be death" does not mean "may be death."

Since a valid capital sentence thus requires a choice based upon unique particulars identifying the crime and its perpetrator as heinous to the point of demanding death even within the class of potentially capital offenses, the State's provision for a tie breaker in favor of death fails on both counts. The dispositive fact under the tie breaker is not the details of the crime or the unique identity of the individual defendant. The determining fact is not directly linked to a particular crime or particular criminal at all; the law operates merely on a jury's finding of equipoise in the State's own selected considerations for and against death. Nor does the tie breaker identify the worst of the worst, or even purport to reflect any evidentiary showing that death must be the reasoned moral response; it does the opposite. The statute produces a death sentence exactly when a sentencing impasse demonstrates as a matter of law that the jury does not see the evidence as showing the worst sort of crime committed by the worst sort of criminal, in a combination heinous enough to demand death. It operates, that is, when a jury has applied the State's chosen standards of culpability and mitigation and reached nothing more than what the Supreme Court of Kansas calls a "tie.". . .

In Kansas, when a jury applies the State's own standards of relative culpability and cannot decide that a defendant is among the most culpable, the state law says that equivocal evidence is good enough and the defendant must die. A law that requires execution when the case for aggravation has failed to convince the sentencing jury is morally absurd, and the Court's holding that the Constitution tolerates this moral irrationality defies decades of precedent aimed at eliminating freakish capital sentencing in the United States.

That precedent, demanding reasoned moral judgment, developed in response to facts that could not be ignored, the kaleidoscope of life and death verdicts that made no sense in fact or morality in the random sentencing before *Furman* was decided in 1972.... Today, a new body of fact must be accounted for in deciding what, in practical terms, the Eighth Amendment guarantees should tolerate, for the period starting in 1989 has seen repeated exonerations of convicts under death sentences, in numbers never imagined before the development of DNA tests. We cannot face up to these facts and still hold that the guarantee of morally justifiable sentencing is hollow enough to allow maximizing death sentences, by requiring them when juries fail to find the worst degree of culpability: when, by a State's own standards and a State's own characterization, the case for death is "doubtful."

A few numbers from a growing literature will give a sense of the reality that must be addressed. When the Governor of Illinois imposed a moratorium on executions in 2000, 13 prisoners under death sentences had been released since 1977 after a number of them were shown to be innocent, as described in a report which used their examples to illustrate a theme common to all 13, of "relatively little solid evidence connecting the charged defendants to the crimes.".... During the same period, 12 condemned convicts had been executed. Subsequently the Governor determined that 4 more death row inmates were innocent.... Illinois had thus wrongly convicted and condemned even more capital defendants than it had executed, but it may well not have been otherwise unique; one recent study reports that between 1989 and 2003, 74 American prisoners condemned to death were exonerated... many of them cleared by DNA evidence.... Most of these wrongful convictions and sentences resulted from eyewitness misidentification, false confession, and (most frequently) perjury... and the total shows that among all prosecutions homicide cases suffer an unusually high incidence of false conviction, probably owing to the combined difficulty of investigating without help from the victim, intense pressure to get convictions in homicide cases, and the corresponding incentive for the guilty to frame the innocent.

We are thus in a period of new empirical argument about how "death is different.".... [N]ot only would these false verdicts defy correction after the fatal moment, the Illinois experience shows them to be remarkable in number, and they are probably disproportionately high in capital cases. While it is far too soon for any generalization about the soundness of capital sentencing across the country, the cautionary lesson of recent experience addresses the tie-breaking potential of the Kansas statute: the same risks of falsity that infect proof of guilt raise questions about sentences, when the circumstances of the crime are aggravating factors and bear on predictions of future dangerousness.

In the face of evidence of the hazards of capital prosecution, maintaining a sentencing system mandating death when the sentencer finds the evidence pro and con to be in equipoise is obtuse by any moral or social measure. And unless application of the Eighth Amendment no longer calls for reasoned moral judgment in substance as well as form, the Kansas law is unconstitutional.

Source: U.S. Supreme Court of the United States. *Kansas v. Marsh.* 548 U.S. — (2006), Docket 94-1170. June 26, 2006. www.supremecourtus.gov/opinions/05pdf/04-1170.pdf (accessed January 15, 2007).

Other Historic Documents of Interest

Surgeon General on the Dangers of Secondhand Smoke

June 27, 2006

■■■■■■■■■■ **THE DOCUMENT IN CONTEXT** ■■■■■■■■■■

The nation's top public health official on June 27, 2006, issued the strongest warning to date about the health consequences of exposure to tobacco smoke. Although he stopped short of endorsing a national ban on indoor smoking, U.S. Surgeon General Richard H. Carmona warned that there was no risk-free level of exposure to second-hand smoke. An estimated 126 million nonsmokers in the United States were at a substantially increased risk of developing heart disease and lung cancer because of exposure to secondhand smoke at home or in the workplace. "The health effects of secondhand smoke exposure are more pervasive than we previously thought," Carmona said in a televised news conference on June 27. "The scientific evidence is now indisputable: secondhand smoke is not a mere annoyance. It is a serious health hazard that can lead to disease and premature death in children and nonsmoking adults."

Carmona's warning came as what had been a steady decline in the number of American smokers appeared to stall. The federal Centers for Disease Control and Prevention (CDC) reported in October that the proportion of adults who smoked held steady at 20.9 percent in 2005, the same as in 2004. It was the first year since 1997 that the share of smokers had not dropped. Declines in teenage smoking also showed signs of stopping or perhaps even reversing, with slightly under one in every four high school students telling the CDC they had smoked within the last thirty days. Tobacco use was the leading preventable cause of death in the United States, causing more than 400,000 deaths a year. Worldwide an estimated 1.25 billion people smoked, and about 5 million died each year from tobacco-related cancers and cardiovascular and pulmonary diseases.

Several states and localities joined the growing number of places that banned smoking in most indoor public spaces. The smoke-filled local pub was on its way to being a thing of the past after Britain, Scotland, and Wales all imposed bans on smoking in enclosed public places. While applauding the smoking bans, health officials were increasingly worried about the spread of smokeless tobacco products, particularly among the young, about increased marketing of flavored and mild-tasting cigarettes that appealed to youth, and about the rise in popularity of alternatives to cigarettes, such as water pipes. "Tobacco can kill in any guise, regardless of whether you smoke it, chew it, or inhale it through a water pipe, and that is why all products containing tobacco need to be regulated immediately, in all forms," the director of the World Health Organization's Tobacco Free Initiative said in May.

Secondhand Smoke Report

Most scientists and health professionals had long warned that secondhand smoke, also known as passive or involuntary smoking, was potentially harmful to nonsmokers exposed to it. Secondhand smoke was composed of the smoke released from the burning end of a cigarette (known as *sidestream smoke*) and the smoke exhaled by the smoker (*mainstream smoke*), and it contained many of the same toxic chemicals that were found in the smoke inhaled by smokers.

The first surgeon general's report to raise concerns about the dangers of involuntary smoking was published in 1972, but it was not until 1986 that an entire report was devoted to the issue. That report concluded that exposure to secondhand smoke caused cancer in nonsmoking adults and compromised the respiratory health of children. It also concluded that separating smokers and nonsmokers within the same air space reduced but did not eliminate exposure to secondhand smoke. The 2006 report, "The Health Consequences of Involuntary Exposure to Tobacco Smoke," was the federal government's first thorough analysis of the scientific evidence on the health effects of secondhand smoke since the 1986 report. The evidence accumulated during the twenty years strongly reaffirmed the findings in the earlier report. The 2006 report came to six broad conclusions:

- Despite substantial progress in reducing smoking, millions of Americans—adults and children—were still exposed to secondhand smoke in their homes and workplaces. Levels of cotinine, the metabolized form of nicotine found in smoke, had fallen by 70 percent between 1988–1991 and 2001–2002, but 43 percent of all nonsmokers still had detectable levels of cotinine. Almost 60 percent of all children aged three to eleven were exposed to secondhand smoke, while about 30 percent of all indoor workers were exposed to smoke in their workplaces.
- Involuntary exposure to secondhand smoke caused disease and premature death in nonsmokers. The U.S. Environmental Protection Agency, the National Toxicology Program, and the International Agency for Research on Cancer had all designated secondhand smoke as a known cause of cancer in humans.
- Children exposed to secondhand smoke were at increased risk for sudden infant death syndrome (SIDS), acute respiratory infections, and ear problems; children who had asthma were at increased risk of more frequent and more severe attacks. Because their bodies were still developing, babies and very young children were especially vulnerable to health problems caused by secondhand smoke. Moreover, mothers exposed to secondhand smoke during pregnancy were more likely to have low birth weight babies, who were also more vulnerable to health problems. In his news conference, Carmona urged parents who smoked to try to quit and to smoke outdoors. "Make the home a smoke-free environment," he said.
- Exposure to secondhand smoke increased the risk of developing heart disease by 25–30 percent. The increased risk of developing lung cancer was put at 20–30 percent. In 2005 the CDC estimated that 3,000 nonsmokers died from lung cancer and 46,000 from heart disease because of exposure to secondhand smoke. As many as 430 babies may have died from SIDS as a result of their exposure.
- The scientific evidence indicated that there was no risk-free level of exposure to secondhand smoke. Even short exposures could cause changes in cardiovascular and respiratory systems that could lead to serious health problems.
- The only way to fully protect nonsmokers from these dangers was to eliminate smoking in indoor spaces. "Separating smokers from nonsmokers, cleaning the air, and ventilating buildings cannot eliminate exposure of nonsmokers to secondhand smoke," the report concluded.

Smoking Bans

"The good news," Carmona said, "is that, unlike some public health hazards, secondhand smoke exposure is easily prevented. Smoke-free indoor environments are proven, simple approaches that prevent exposure and harm." Concerns about the dangers of secondhand smoke had already led more than a dozen states and hundreds of cities and towns in the United States to ban smoking in public places, such as office buildings, bars, and restaurants. Arkansas, Hawaii, Louisiana, and New Jersey were among the states whose legislatures enacted indoor public smoking bans in 2006, while voters in Arizona, Nevada, and Ohio approved ballot initiatives in November calling for such bans. (A court in Nevada issued a stay to keep the new ban from being implemented in the Las Vegas area while its constitutionality was being challenged. Nevada had the highest rate of smoking-related deaths in the nation, according to the CDC.) In October Virginia governor Timothy M. Kaine ordered a ban on smoking in almost all state buildings and in state vehicles. The move was considered historic in the state that was home to Philip Morris, the world's largest cigarette manufacturer.

One of the toughest smoking bans was enacted in the city of Calabasas, California, near Los Angeles. It prohibited smoking in any public place, indoor or outdoor, where another person might be exposed to secondhand smoke. In related developments, the Westin and Marriott hotel chains announced that they would no longer allow smoking in their hotels.

Initiatives that would have substantially boosted the tax on cigarettes in California and Missouri failed at the ballot box in November, although voters approved lower tax increases in Arizona and South Dakota. Philip Morris and R. J. Reynolds reportedly spent nearly $100 million on campaigns to block the tax hikes as well as on alternatives to the smoking ban initiatives that passed in Arizona and Ohio.

Tobacco Companies in Court

U.S. tobacco companies won several important legal victories in 2006. In a landmark decision, Judge Gladys Kessler of the Federal District Court for the District of Columbia agreed with the federal government that the major American tobacco companies had conspired for decades to deceive the public about the dangers of smoking. But she rejected the government's request to force the companies to pay $10 billion to fund smoking cessation programs, saying that under a recent appeals court ruling, she did not have the authority to impose such large financial damages.

Kessler did, however, order the companies to stop labeling cigarettes as "low tar," "light," or "natural" or with any other "deceptive brand descriptors" that implied such cigarettes were less hazardous to smokers than regular cigarettes. The judge also ordered the companies to undertake a national advertising campaign on the dangers of smoking.

The companies immediately asked Kessler to allow them to continue marketing cigarettes without changing the labels, but Kessler said no. On October 31, however, a three-judge panel of the U.S. Circuit Court of Appeals for the District of Columbia reversed Kessler, allowing the companies to continue to label their cigarettes as "low-tar," "light," "ultra-light," and "mild" while Kessler's ruling was under appeal. The companies had argued that they would lose market share to companies not affected by Kessler's ruling if they were forced to stop selling light and low-tar cigarettes. It could take years before the issue was finally resolved.

A second legal attack on light cigarettes also was stalled by an appeals court. In September Judge Jack B. Weinstein of Federal District Court in Brooklyn ruled that people who smoked light cigarettes could band together in a class-action suit to press their claim that cigarette manufacturers had deliberately deceived them. Weinstein said there was "substantial evidence" that the tobacco companies knew their light cigarettes were at least as harmful as regular cigarettes. The cigarette companies claimed that their light and low-tar brands filtered out many of the harmful chemicals in regular cigarettes, but numerous studies showed that smokers of such brands were exposed to the same, if not higher, level of toxins as they received from the so-called full-flavored cigarettes.

Since 45 percent of all smokers currently smoked light cigarettes, the class-action suit could involve millions of smokers and billions of dollars. An attorney for the plaintiffs said damages could reach $200 billion. But that case too was put on hold when the Court of Appeals for the Second Circuit agreed to review Weinstein's decision to certify the class action.

The tobacco companies won at least two other decisions that overturned massive awards against them. In July the Florida Supreme Court upheld a lower court decision to throw out a $145 billion judgment granted in a personal injury class action against the cigarette makers. The Florida high court said the smokers' cases were "highly individualized" and did not "lend themselves to class-action treatment." On November 28, the U.S. Supreme Court refused, without comment, to review an Illinois Supreme Court decision overturning a $10.1 billion judgment against Philip Morris. The suit had been filed by smokers who said they were misled by the company's claims about the health risks associated with light cigarettes, but the state supreme court ruled that smokers could not sue under a state consumer protection law because the federal government had endorsed the "light" descriptions in earlier tobacco settlements.

The U.S. Supreme Court did hear arguments in October in a case involving a damage award of $79.5 million to the widow of a longtime smoker. Philip Morris, the defendant in the case, and several trade associations hoped the Court would take the occasion to set firm restrictions on the amount of punitive damages that could be awarded, but it was unclear whether the Court would rule on that precise issue. A decision in *Philip Morris USA v. Williams* was not handed down before the end of the year.

Following are excerpts from the introduction to "The Health Consequences of Involuntary Exposure to Tobacco Smoke," a report issued on June 27, 2006, in which U.S. Surgeon General Richard H. Carmona warned of the health risks associated with exposure to secondhand smoke.

▬ DOCUMENT ▬

"The Health Consequences of Exposure to Tobacco Smoke"

Introduction

The topic of passive or involuntary smoking was first addressed in the 1972 U.S. Surgeon General's report... only eight years after the first Surgeon General's report on the health consequences of active smoking. Surgeon General Dr. Jesse Steinfeld had raised concerns about this topic, leading to its inclusion in that report. According to the 1972 report, non-smokers inhale the mixture of sidestream smoke given off by a smoldering cigarette and mainstream smoke exhaled by a smoker, a mixture now referred to as "secondhand smoke" or "environmental tobacco smoke." Cited experimental studies showed that smoking in enclosed spaces could lead to high levels of cigarette smoke components in the air. For carbon monoxide (CO) specifically, levels in enclosed spaces could exceed levels then permitted in outdoor air. The studies supported a conclusion that "an atmosphere contaminated with tobacco smoke can contribute to the discomfort of many individuals." The possibility that CO emitted from cigarettes could harm persons with chronic heart or lung disease was also mentioned.

Secondhand tobacco smoke was then addressed in greater depth in Chapter 4 (Involuntary Smoking) of the 1975 Surgeon General's report, *The Health Consequences of Smoking*. The chapter noted that involuntary smoking takes place when nonsmokers inhale both sidestream and exhaled mainstream smoke and that this "smoking" is "involuntary" when "the exposure occurs as an unavoidable consequence of breathing in a smoke-filled environment." The report covered exposures and potential health consequences of involuntary smoking, and the researchers concluded that smoking on buses and airplanes was annoying to nonsmokers and that involuntary smoking had potentially adverse consequences for persons with heart and lung diseases. Two studies on nicotine concentrations in nonsmokers raised concerns about nicotine as a contributing factor to atherosclerotic cardiovascular disease in nonsmokers.

The 1979 Surgeon General's report, *Smoking and Health: A Report of the Surgeon General*, also contained a chapter entitled "Involuntary Smoking." The chapter stressed that "attention to involuntary smoking is of recent vintage, and only limited information regarding the health effects of such exposure upon the nonsmoker is available." The chapter concluded with recommendations for research including epidemiologic and clinical studies. The 1982 Surgeon General's report specifically addressed smoking and cancer. By 1982, there were three published epidemiologic studies on involuntary smoking and lung cancer, and the 1982 Surgeon General's report included a brief chapter on this topic. That chapter commented on the methodologic difficulties inherent in such studies, including exposure assessment, the lengthy interval during which exposures are likely to be relevant, and accounting for exposures to other carcinogens. Nonetheless, the report concluded that

"Although the currently available evidence is not sufficient to conclude that passive or involuntary smoking causes lung cancer in nonsmokers, the evidence does raise concern about a possible serious public health problem."

Involuntary smoking was also reviewed in the 1984 report, which focused on chronic obstructive pulmonary disease and smoking. Chapter 7 (Passive Smoking) of that report included a comprehensive review of the mounting information on smoking by parents and the effects on respiratory health of their children, data on irritation of the eye, and the more limited evidence on pulmonary effects of involuntary smoking on adults. The chapter began with a compilation of measurements of tobacco smoke components in various indoor environments. The extent of the data had increased substantially since 1972. By 1984, the data included measurements of more specific indicators such as acrolein and nicotine, and less specific indicators such as particulate matter (PM), nitrogen oxides, and CO. The report reviewed new evidence on exposures of nonsmokers using biomarkers, with substantial information on levels of cotinine, a major nicotine metabolite. The report anticipated future conclusions with regard to respiratory effects of parental smoking on child respiratory health.

Involuntary smoking was the topic for the entire 1986 Surgeon General's report, *The Health Consequences of Involuntary Smoking*. In its 359 pages, the report covered the full breadth of the topic, addressing toxicology and dosimetry of tobacco smoke; the relevant evidence on active smoking; patterns of exposure of nonsmokers to tobacco smoke; the epidemiologic evidence on involuntary smoking and disease risks for infants, children, and adults; and policies to control involuntary exposure to tobacco smoke. That report concluded that involuntary smoking caused lung cancer in lifetime nonsmoking adults and was associated with adverse effects on respiratory health in children. The report also stated that simply separating smokers and nonsmokers within the same airspace reduced but did not eliminate exposure to secondhand smoke. All of these findings are relevant to public health and public policy. The lung cancer conclusion was based on extensive information already available on the carcinogenicity of active smoking, the qualitative similarities between secondhand and mainstream smoke, the uptake of tobacco smoke components by nonsmokers, and the epidemiologic data on involuntary smoking. The three major conclusions of the report led Dr. C. Everett Koop, Surgeon General at the time, to comment in his preface that "the right of smokers to smoke ends where their behavior affects the health and well-being of others; furthermore, it is the smokers' responsibility to ensure that they do not expose nonsmokers to the potential [sic] harmful effects of tobacco smoke."

Two other reports published in 1986 also reached the conclusion that involuntary smoking increased the risk for lung cancer. The International Agency for Research on Cancer (IARC) of the World Health Organization concluded that "passive smoking gives rise to some risk of cancer." In its monograph on tobacco smoking, the agency supported this conclusion on the basis of the characteristics of sidestream and mainstream smoke, the absorption of tobacco smoke materials during an involuntary exposure, and the nature of dose-response relationships for carcinogenesis. In the same year, the National Research Council (NRC) also concluded that involuntary smoking increases the incidence of lung cancer in nonsmokers. In reaching this conclusion, the NRC report cited the biologic plausibility of the association between exposure to secondhand smoke and lung cancer and the supporting epidemiologic evidence. On the basis of a pooled analysis of the epidemiologic data adjusted for bias, the report concluded that the best estimate for the excess risk of lung cancer in nonsmokers married to smokers was 25 percent, compared with nonsmokers married to nonsmokers. With regard to the effects of involuntary smoking on children, the NRC report commented on the literature linking secondhand smoke exposures from parental smoking to increased risks for respiratory symptoms and infections and to a slightly diminished rate of lung growth.

Since 1986, the conclusions with regard to both the carcinogenicity of secondhand smoke and the adverse effects of parental smoking on the health of children have been echoed and expanded. In 1992, the U.S. Environmental Protection Agency (EPA) published its risk assessment of secondhand smoke as a carcinogen. The agency's evaluation drew on toxicologic information on secondhand smoke and the extensive literature on active smoking. A comprehensive meta-analysis of the 31 epidemiologic studies of secondhand smoke and lung cancer published up to that time was central to the decision to classify secondhand smoke as a group A carcinogen—namely, a known human carcinogen. Estimates of approximately 3,000 U.S. lung cancer deaths per year in nonsmokers were attributed to secondhand smoke. The report also covered other respiratory health effects in children and adults and concluded that involuntary smoking is causally associated with several adverse respiratory effects in children. There was also a quantitative risk assessment for the impact of involuntary smoking on childhood asthma and lower respiratory tract infections in young children.

In the decade since the 1992 EPA report, scientific panels continued to evaluate the mounting evidence linking involuntary smoking to adverse health effects. The most recent was the 2005 report of the California EPA [Cal/EPA]. Over time, research has repeatedly affirmed the conclusions of the 1986 Surgeon General's reports and studies have further identified causal associations of involuntary smoking with diseases and other health disorders. The epidemiologic evidence on involuntary smoking has markedly expanded since 1986, as have the data on exposure to tobacco smoke in the many environments where people spend time. An understanding of the mechanisms by which involuntary smoking causes disease has also deepened.

As part of the environmental health hazard assessment, Cal/EPA identified specific health effects causally associated with exposure to secondhand smoke. The agency estimated the annual excess deaths in the United States that are attributable to second-hand smoke exposure for specific disorders: sudden infant death syndrome (SIDS), cardiac-related illnesses (ischemic heart disease), and lung cancer. For the excess incidence of other health outcomes, either new estimates were provided or estimates from the 1997 health hazard assessment were used without any revisions. Overall, Cal/EPA estimated that about 50,000 excess deaths result annually from exposure to secondhand smoke. Estimated annual excess deaths for the total U.S. population are about 3,400 (a range of 3,423 to 8,866) from lung cancer, 46,000 (a range of 22,700 to 69,600) from cardiac-related illnesses, and 430 from SIDS. The agency also estimated that between 24,300 and 71,900 low birth weight or preterm deliveries, about 202,300 episodes of childhood asthma (new cases and exacerbations), between 150,000 and 300,000 cases of lower respiratory illness in children, and about 789,700 cases of middle ear infections in children occur each year in the United States as a result of exposure to secondhand smoke.

This new 2006 Surgeon General's report returns to the topic of involuntary smoking. The health effects of involuntary smoking have not received comprehensive coverage in this series of reports since 1986. Reports since then have touched on selected aspects of the topic: the 1994 report on tobacco use among young people, the 1998 report on tobacco use among U.S. racial and ethnic minorities, and the 2001 report on women and smoking. As involuntary smoking remains widespread in the United States and elsewhere, the preparation of this report was motivated by the persistence of involuntary smoking as a public health problem and the need to evaluate the substantial new evidence reported since 1986. This report substantially expands the list of topics that were included in the 1986 report. Additional topics include SIDS, developmental effects, and other reproductive effects; heart disease in adults; and cancer sites beyond the lung. For some associations of involuntary smoking with adverse health effects, only a few studies were reviewed in 1986 (e.g., ear disease in children); now, the relevant literature is substantial. Consequently, this report uses meta-analysis to quantitatively summarize evidence as appropriate. Following the approach used in the 2004 report . . . this 2006 report also systematically evaluates the evidence for causality, judging the extent of the evidence available and then making an inference as to the nature of the association.

[Sections on the organization and preparation of the report omitted.]

Definitions and Terminology

The inhalation of tobacco smoke by nonsmokers has been variably referred to as "passive smoking" or "involuntary smoking." Smokers, of course, also inhale secondhand smoke. Cigarette smoke contains both particles and gases generated by the combustion at high temperatures of tobacco, paper, and additives. The smoke inhaled by nonsmokers that contaminates indoor spaces and outdoor environments has often been referred to as "secondhand smoke" or "environmental tobacco smoke." This inhaled smoke is the mixture of sidestream smoke released by the smoldering cigarette and the mainstream smoke that is exhaled by a smoker. Sidestream smoke, generated at lower temperatures and under somewhat different combustion conditions than mainstream smoke, tends to have higher concentrations of many of the toxins found in cigarette smoke. However, it is rapidly diluted as it travels away from the burning cigarette.

Secondhand smoke is an inherently dynamic mixture that changes in characteristics and concentration with the time since it was formed and the distance it has traveled. The smoke particles change in size and composition as gaseous components are volatilized and moisture content changes; gaseous elements of secondhand smoke may be adsorbed onto materials, and particle concentrations drop with both dilution in the air or environment and impaction on surfaces, including the lungs or on the body. Because of its dynamic nature, a specific quantitative definition of secondhand smoke cannot be offered.

This report uses the term secondhand smoke in preference to environmental tobacco smoke, even though the latter may have been used more frequently in previous reports. The descriptor "secondhand" captures the involuntary nature of the exposure, while "environmental" does not. This report also refers to the inhalation of secondhand smoke as involuntary smoking, acknowledging that most nonsmokers do not want to inhale tobacco smoke. The exposure of the fetus to tobacco smoke, whether from active smoking by the mother or from her exposure to secondhand smoke, also constitutes involuntary smoking.

[Section on evidence evaluation omitted.]

Major Conclusions

This report returns to involuntary smoking, the topic of the 1986 Surgeon General's report. Since then, there have been many advances in the research on secondhand smoke, and substantial evidence has been reported over the ensuing 20 years. This report uses the revised language for causal conclusions that was implemented in the 2004 Surgeon General's report. Each chapter provides a comprehensive review of the evidence, a quantitative synthesis of the evidence if appropriate, and a rigorous assessment of sources of bias that may affect interpretations of the findings. The reviews in this report reaffirm and strengthen the findings of the 1986 report. With regard to the involuntary exposure of nonsmokers to tobacco smoke, the scientific evidence now supports the following major conclusions:

1. Secondhand smoke causes premature death and disease in children and in adults who do not smoke.
2. Children exposed to secondhand smoke are at an increased risk for sudden infant death syndrome (SIDS), acute respiratory infections, ear problems, and more severe asthma. Smoking by parents causes respiratory symptoms and slows lung growth in their children.
3. Exposure of adults to secondhand smoke has immediate adverse effects on the cardiovascular system and causes coronary heart disease and lung cancer.
4. The scientific evidence indicates that there is no risk-free level of exposure to secondhand smoke.
5. Many millions of Americans, both children and adults, are still exposed to secondhand smoke in their homes and workplaces despite substantial progress in tobacco control.
6. Eliminating smoking in indoor spaces fully protects nonsmokers from exposure to secondhand smoke. Separating smokers from nonsmokers, cleaning the air, and ventilating buildings cannot eliminate exposures of nonsmokers to secondhand smoke.

Chapter Conclusions
Chapter 2: Toxicology of Secondhand Smoke

Evidence of Carcinogenic Effects from Secondhand Smoke Exposure
1. More than 50 carcinogens have been identified in sidestream and secondhand smoke.
2. The evidence is sufficient to infer a causal relationship between exposure to secondhand smoke and its condensates and tumors in laboratory animals.
3. The evidence is sufficient to infer that exposure of nonsmokers to secondhand smoke causes a significant increase in urinary levels of metabolites of the tobacco-specific lung carcinogen 4-(methylnitrosamino)-1-(3-pyridyl)-1-butanone (NNK). The presence of these metabolites links exposure to secondhand smoke with an increased risk for lung cancer.
4. The mechanisms by which secondhand smoke causes lung cancer are probably similar to those observed in smokers. The overall risk of secondhand smoke exposure, compared with active smoking, is diminished by a substantially lower carcinogenic dose.

*Mechanisms of Respiratory Tract Injury and Disease Caused
by Secondhand Smoke Exposure*

5. The evidence indicates multiple mechanisms by which secondhand smoke exposure causes injury to the respiratory tract.
6. The evidence indicates mechanisms by which secondhand smoke exposure could increase the risk for sudden infant death syndrome.

Mechanisms of Secondhand Smoke Exposure and Heart Disease

7. The evidence is sufficient to infer that exposure to secondhand smoke has a prothrombotic effect.
8. The evidence is sufficient to infer that exposure to secondhand smoke causes endothelial cell dysfunctions.
9. The evidence is sufficient to infer that exposure to secondhand smoke causes atherosclerosis in animal models.

Chapter 3: Assessment of Exposure to Secondhand Smoke

Building Designs and Operations

1. Current heating, ventilating, and air conditioning systems alone cannot control exposure to secondhand smoke.
2. The operation of a heating, ventilating, and air conditioning system can distribute secondhand smoke throughout a building.

Exposure Models

3. Atmospheric concentration of nicotine is a sensitive and specific indicator for secondhand smoke.
4. Smoking increases indoor particle concentrations.
5. Models can be used to estimate concentrations of secondhand smoke.

Biomarkers of Exposure to Secondhand Smoke

6. Biomarkers suitable for assessing recent exposures to secondhand smoke are available.
7. At this time, cotinine, the primary proximate metabolite of nicotine, remains the biomarker of choice for assessing secondhand smoke exposure.
8. Individual biomarkers of exposure to second-hand smoke represent only one component of a complex mixture, and measurements of one marker may not wholly reflect an exposure to other components of concern as a result of involuntary smoking.

Chapter 4: Prevalence of Exposure to Secondhand Smoke

1. The evidence is sufficient to infer that large numbers of nonsmokers are still exposed to secondhand smoke.
2. Exposure of nonsmokers to secondhand smoke has declined in the United States since the 1986 Surgeon General's report, *The Health Consequences of Involuntary Smoking.*
3. The evidence indicates that the extent of secondhand smoke exposure varies across the country.
4. Homes and workplaces are the predominant locations for exposure to secondhand smoke.
5. Exposure to secondhand smoke tends to be greater for persons with lower incomes.
6. Exposure to secondhand smoke continues in restaurants, bars, casinos, gaming halls, and vehicles.

Chapter 5: Reproductive and Developmental Effects from Exposure to Secondhand Smoke

Fertility

1. The evidence is inadequate to infer the presence or absence of a causal relationship between maternal exposure to secondhand smoke and female fertility or fecundability. No data were found on paternal exposure to secondhand smoke and male fertility or fecundability.

Pregnancy (Spontaneous Abortion and Perinatal Death)

2. The evidence is inadequate to infer the presence or absence of a causal relationship between maternal exposure to secondhand smoke during pregnancy and spontaneous abortion.

Infant Deaths

3. The evidence is inadequate to infer the presence or absence of a causal relationship between exposure to secondhand smoke and neonatal mortality.

Sudden Infant Death Syndrome

4. The evidence is sufficient to infer a causal relationship between exposure to secondhand smoke and sudden infant death syndrome.

Preterm Delivery

5. The evidence is suggestive but not sufficient to infer a causal relationship between maternal exposure to secondhand smoke during pregnancy and preterm delivery.

Low Birth Weight

6. The evidence is sufficient to infer a causal relationship between maternal exposure to secondhand smoke during pregnancy and a small reduction in birth weight.

Congenital Malformations

7. The evidence is inadequate to infer the presence or absence of a causal relationship between exposure to secondhand smoke and congenital malformations.

Cognitive Development

8. The evidence is inadequate to infer the presence or absence of a causal relationship between exposure to secondhand smoke and cognitive functioning among children.

Behavioral Development

9. The evidence is inadequate to infer the presence or absence of a causal relationship between exposure to secondhand smoke and behavioral problems among children.

Height/Growth

10. The evidence is inadequate to infer the presence or absence of a causal relationship between exposure to secondhand smoke and children's height/growth.

Childhood Cancer

11. The evidence is suggestive but not sufficient to infer a causal relationship between prenatal and postnatal exposure to secondhand smoke and childhood cancer.
12. The evidence is inadequate to infer the presence or absence of a causal relationship between maternal exposure to secondhand smoke during pregnancy and childhood cancer.

13. The evidence is inadequate to infer the presence or absence of a causal relationship between exposure to secondhand smoke during infancy and childhood cancer.
14. The evidence is suggestive but not sufficient to infer a causal relationship between prenatal and postnatal exposure to secondhand smoke and childhood leukemias.
15. The evidence is suggestive but not sufficient to infer a causal relationship between prenatal and postnatal exposure to secondhand smoke and childhood lymphomas.
16. The evidence is suggestive but not sufficient to infer a causal relationship between prenatal and postnatal exposure to secondhand smoke and childhood brain tumors.
17. The evidence is inadequate to infer the presence or absence of a causal relationship between prenatal and postnatal exposure to secondhand smoke and other childhood cancer types.

Chapter 6: Respiratory Effects in Children from Exposure to Secondhand Smoke

Lower Respiratory Illnesses in Infancy and Early Childhood
1. The evidence is sufficient to infer a causal relationship between secondhand smoke exposure from parental smoking and lower respiratory illnesses in infants and children.
2. The increased risk for lower respiratory illnesses is greatest from smoking by the mother.

Middle Ear Disease and Adenotonsillectomy
3. The evidence is sufficient to infer a causal relationship between parental smoking and middle ear disease in children, including acute and recurrent otitis media and chronic middle ear effusion.
4. The evidence is suggestive but not sufficient to infer a causal relationship between parental smoking and the natural history of middle ear effusion.
5. The evidence is inadequate to infer the presence or absence of a causal relationship between parental smoking and an increase in the risk of adenoidectomy or tonsillectomy among children.

Respiratory Symptoms and Prevalent Asthma in School-Age Children
6. The evidence is sufficient to infer a causal relationship between parental smoking and cough, phlegm, wheeze, and breathlessness among children of school age.
7. The evidence is sufficient to infer a causal relationship between parental smoking and ever having asthma among children of school age.

Childhood Asthma Onset
8. The evidence is sufficient to infer a causal relationship between secondhand smoke exposure from parental smoking and the onset of wheeze illnesses in early childhood.
9. The evidence is suggestive but not sufficient to infer a causal relationship between secondhand smoke exposure from parental smoking and the onset of childhood asthma.

Atopy
10. The evidence is inadequate to infer the presence or absence of a causal relationship between parental smoking and the risk of immunoglobulin E-mediated allergy in their children.

Lung Growth and Pulmonary Function
11. The evidence is sufficient to infer a causal relationship between maternal smoking during pregnancy and persistent adverse effects on lung function across childhood.

12. The evidence is sufficient to infer a causal relationship between exposure to secondhand smoke after birth and a lower level of lung function during childhood.

Chapter 7: Cancer Among Adults from Exposure to Secondhand Smoke

Lung Cancer
1. The evidence is sufficient to infer a causal relationship between secondhand smoke exposure and lung cancer among lifetime nonsmokers. This conclusion extends to all secondhand smoke exposure, regardless of location.
2. The pooled evidence indicates a 20 to 30 percent increase in the risk of lung cancer from secondhand smoke exposure associated with living with a smoker.

Breast Cancer
3. The evidence is suggestive but not sufficient to infer a causal relationship between secondhand smoke and breast cancer.

Nasal Sinus Cavity and Nasopharyngeal Carcinoma
4. The evidence is suggestive but not sufficient to infer a causal relationship between secondhand smoke exposure and a risk of nasal sinus cancer among nonsmokers.
5. The evidence is inadequate to infer the presence or absence of a causal relationship between secondhand smoke exposure and a risk of nasopharyngeal carcinoma among nonsmokers.

Cervical Cancer
6. The evidence is inadequate to infer the presence or absence of a causal relationship between secondhand smoke exposure and the risk of cervical cancer among lifetime nonsmokers.

Chapter 8: Cardiovascular Diseases from Exposure to Secondhand Smoke
1. The evidence is sufficient to infer a causal relationship between exposure to secondhand smoke and increased risks of coronary heart disease morbidity and mortality among both men and women.
2. Pooled relative risks from meta-analyses indicate a 25 to 30 percent increase in the risk of coronary heart disease from exposure to secondhand smoke.
3. The evidence is suggestive but not sufficient to infer a causal relationship between exposure to secondhand smoke and an increased risk of stroke.
4. Studies of secondhand smoke and subclinical vascular disease, particularly carotid arterial wall thickening, are suggestive but not sufficient to infer a causal relationship between exposure to secondhand smoke and atherosclerosis.

Chapter 9: Respiratory Effects in Adults from Exposure to Secondhand Smoke

Odor and Irritation
1. The evidence is sufficient to infer a causal relationship between secondhand smoke exposure and odor annoyance.

2. The evidence is sufficient to infer a causal relationship between secondhand smoke exposure and nasal irritation.
3. The evidence is suggestive but not sufficient to conclude that persons with nasal allergies or a history of respiratory illnesses are more susceptible to developing nasal irritation from secondhand smoke exposure.

Respiratory Symptoms

4. The evidence is suggestive but not sufficient to infer a causal relationship between secondhand smoke exposure and acute respiratory symptoms including cough, wheeze, chest tightness, and difficulty breathing among persons with asthma.
5. The evidence is suggestive but not sufficient to infer a causal relationship between secondhand smoke exposure and acute respiratory symptoms including cough, wheeze, chest tightness, and difficulty breathing among healthy persons.
6. The evidence is suggestive but not sufficient to infer a causal relationship between secondhand smoke exposure and chronic respiratory symptoms.

Lung Function

7. The evidence is suggestive but not sufficient to infer a causal relationship between short-term secondhand smoke exposure and an acute decline in lung function in persons with asthma.
8. The evidence is inadequate to infer the presence or absence of a causal relationship between short-term secondhand smoke exposure and an acute decline in lung function in healthy persons.
9. The evidence is suggestive but not sufficient to infer a causal relationship between chronic secondhand smoke exposure and a small decrement in lung function in the general population.
10. The evidence is inadequate to infer the presence or absence of a causal relationship between chronic secondhand smoke exposure and an accelerated decline in lung function.

Asthma

11. The evidence is suggestive but not sufficient to infer a causal relationship between secondhand smoke exposure and adult-onset asthma.
12. The evidence is suggestive but not sufficient to infer a causal relationship between secondhand smoke exposure and a worsening of asthma control.

Chronic Obstructive Pulmonary Disease

13. The evidence is suggestive but not sufficient to infer a causal relationship between secondhand smoke exposure and risk for chronic obstructive pulmonary disease.
14. The evidence is inadequate to infer the presence or absence of a causal relationship between secondhand smoke exposure and morbidity in persons with chronic obstructive pulmonary disease.

Chapter 10. Control of Secondhand Smoke Exposure

1. Workplace smoking restrictions are effective in reducing secondhand smoke exposure.
2. Workplace smoking restrictions lead to less smoking among covered workers.
3. Establishing smoke-free workplaces is the only effective way to ensure that secondhand smoke exposure does not occur in the workplace.
4. The majority of workers in the United States are now covered by smoke-free policies.

5. The extent to which workplaces are covered by smoke-free policies varies among worker groups, across states, and by sociodemographic factors. Workplaces related to the entertainment and hospitality industries have notably high potential for secondhand smoke exposure.

6. Evidence from peer-reviewed studies shows that smoke-free policies and regulations do not have an adverse economic impact on the hospitality industry.

7. Evidence suggests that exposure to secondhand smoke varies by ethnicity and gender.

8. In the United States, the home is now becoming the predominant location for exposure of children and adults to secondhand smoke.

9. Total bans on indoor smoking in hospitals, restaurants, bars, and offices substantially reduce secondhand smoke exposure, up to several orders of magnitude with incomplete compliance, and with full compliance, exposures are eliminated.

10. Exposures of nonsmokers to secondhand smoke cannot be controlled by air cleaning or mechanical air exchange.

Source: U.S. Department of Health and Human Services. Centers for Disease Control and Prevention. Coordinating Center for Health Promotion. National Center for Chronic Disease Prevention and Health Promotion. Office on Smoking and Health. "The Health Consequences of Involuntary Exposure to Tobacco Smoke: A Report of the Surgeon General." June 27, 2006. www.surgeongeneral.gov/library/secondhandsmoke (accessed October 31, 2006).

Other Historic Documents of Interest

Cervical cancer vaccine, p. 257
Emergency contraceptive drug,
    p. 466

Food safety, p. 538
GAO on drug safety, p. 129
Stem cell legislation, p. 407

Montenegrin President Vujanovic on Independence from Serbia

June 28, 2006

■■■■■■ THE DOCUMENT IN CONTEXT ■■■■■

Some of the last elements of the former Yugoslavia came crashing down in 2006, fifteen years after that multiethnic state began to break apart. Former Yugoslav leader Slobodan Milosevic, whose vision of a Greater Serbia led to years of war that killed tens of thousands of people and destroyed most of his country, died in March of a heart attack in a United Nations prison—just as his long trial on war crimes charges was nearing an end. A little more than two months later, the only two remnants of Yugoslavia—Serbia and Montenegro—split apart when voters in the latter province decided they wanted to be independent of Belgrade.

At year's end it also was more likely than ever that Kosovo, another province that long had been an integral part of Serbia, would achieve de facto independence. United Nations–led negotiations appeared all but certain to give Albanian Muslims, who were the majority in Kosovo, near total responsibility for their own affairs, if only as an intermediate step toward actual independence.

Although the dissolution of the former Yugoslavia was complete, the region's problems remained just as interrelated as they had been since the onset of the Balkan wars in 1991–1992. The decision on Kosovo's future was expected to be particularly important because of its potential impact on yet another former element of Yugoslavia: Bosnia and Herzegovina. That country was still struggling with the nationalist demons that made it the center of the region's wars in the first half of the 1990s. By late 2006 some politicians were stoking nationalist sentiment in the Serb portion of Bosnia— threatening to push for independence there if the Kosovo Albanians succeeded in gaining independence from Serbia. *(Background, Historic Documents of 2005, p. 851)*

Despite the lingering effects of nationalism, political leaders in most parts of the former Yugoslavia by 2006 had set their sights on joining the European Union (EU). One former Yugoslav republic, Slovenia, already had achieved that goal, and EU leaders in Brussels were holding out prospective membership as an inducement for economic and political reforms in Bosnia, Croatia, Macedonia, Montenegro, and even Serbia. *(EU expansion background, Historic Documents of 2004, p. 197)*

Milosevic Death

More than any other person, Milosevic was at the center of the violence that consumed the former Yugoslavia. As the leader first of Serbia, then the national Yugoslav state, Milosevic whipped Serbian nationalism into a frenzy, thereby unleashing major wars in Bosnia, Croatia, and Kosovo that killed an estimated 250,000 people. In 1999 he became the first sitting head of state ever indicted on war crimes charges. Two years later his successors handed him over to a United Nations war crimes tribunal, which put him on trial in February 2002. Milosevic served as his own attorney, and he frequently used court sessions to engage in heated denunciations of European countries, the United States, the UN, and others he said were prejudiced against him and Serbia. After numerous interruptions, most because of Milosevic's failing health, the trial was nearing its conclusion when he was found dead in his cell on March 11. An autopsy showed that he died of a heart attack, at age sixty-four. The tribunal then ended the trial and set aside the charges against him.

Carla Del Ponte, the dogged Swiss prosecutor who pursued Milosevic and presented the case against him, expressed regret that the former leader would not face what she insisted would have been his certain conviction. "I also regret it for the victims, the thousands of victims, who have been waiting for justice," she said. Milosevic was buried in his hometown of Pozarevac, Serbia, on March 18 after a ceremony in his former capital, Belgrade, where fellow nationalists chanted his nickname, Slobo.

The death of Milosevic led to a brief flurry of criticism of the UN tribunal, notably the medical treatment it had provided him and the length of the proceedings against him. Family members insisted Milosevic should have been allowed to get treatment in Russia, as he had requested.

Milosevic died just five days after the UN tribunal announced that another major war crimes figure, Milan Babic, had committed suicide in prison. Babic, a leader of Serbs in Croatia, had been convicted in 2004 and sentenced to thirteen years in prison on charges that he attempted to force all non-Serbs out of the Krajina region of Croatia in 1991. Babic had testified against Milosevic in the early phases of that trial, in 2002.

The UN tribunal on September 27 convicted a former senior Bosnian Serb politician, Momcilo Krajisnik, on charges of having commited crimes against humanity during the war. He was sentenced to twenty-seven years in prison. However, the tribunal acquitted him of two charges of genocide, citing lack of evidence. Krajisnik was the highest-ranking Bosnian Serb official yet convicted by the UN court. He often was described as the senior aide to the wartime Bosnian Serb leader Radovan Karadzic, who also faced genocide charges but remained at large, presumably in Bosnia under the protection of his fellow Serbs. Also still at large was former commander of the Bosnian Serb army, Gen. Ratko Mladic. The UN tribunal said Mladic was living in Serbia under the protection of his former military colleagues. The EU made the handing over of Mladic a condition for Serbia's membership.

In a related development, the International Court of Justice (better known as the World Court) on February 27 began hearings in a case brought by Bosnia alleging the Serbian government was legally responsible for genocide and other war crimes. It was the first lawsuit ever filed by one country charging that another country committed genocide. The court was expected to make a decision early in 2007.

Montenegro Becomes Independent

Before it began its slide into chaos, Yugoslavia consisted of six provinces, or republics: Bosnia-Herzegovina, Croatia, Macedonia, Montenegro, Serbia, and Slovenia. All but Serbia and Montenegro peeled away during the wars of the 1990s, leaving Serbia and Montenegro as the last remnants of Yugoslavia. This was an unbalanced partnership, given that Serbia had a population of about 8 million and Montenegro only about

650,000. Even so, some local leaders in Montenegro advocated independence. In 2003 the two sides negotiated a new constitution, shedding the name Yugoslavia and replacing it with the unwieldy title Serbia and Montenegro. After three years, either party could seek independence from the other, but the constitution left the exact details vague. *(Background, Historic Documents of 2003, p. 44)*

By 2006 opinion polls showed a plurality of Montenegrins favoring independence from Serbia, but with about 25 percent of the population undecided. Ethnic Serbs, who made up about 33 percent of the total population, were the most strongly opposed to independence The province's political leaders had advocated independence even before the 2003 constitution and said they now would press for a referendum on the matter.

On May 21, the referendum day, 86 percent of Montenegro voters went to the polls and 55.5 percent said "yes" to independence. Jubilant leaders said the vote would unleash their tiny country from the shackles that had bound it to Serbia. "I expect fast economic development and an increase in living standards," President Filip Vujanovic said. "Montenegro was handicapped in its union with Serbia." Serbian officials reluctantly said they would accept the result.

Montenegro's parliament formally declared independence on June 3, saying the new country would be a "multiethnic, multicultural, and multireligious society"—a recognition that the country was divided along numerous sectarian lines. Wishing the new country well, Serbian president Boris Tadic insisted Serbia "will be the closest friend." The declaration restored the independence that Montenegro had enjoyed for four decades in the late nineteenth and early twentieth centuries. Serbia and Montenegro were joined in 1918 as part of the new state of Yugoslavia following the collapse of the Austro-Hungarian empire.

After its application was approved by the General Assembly, Montenegro became the 192nd member of the United Nations on June 28. In a speech to the assembly, Vujanovic said: "We are aware of many challenges that lie ahead, but after a long period of time, we shall be responsible for our own destiny, in line with the development capacities of our state."

The new country held its first parliamentary elections as an independent nation on September 10 and, as expected, returned to power the center-left government of Prime Minister Milo Djukanovic, who had spearheaded the drive for independence. Three weeks later, however, Djukanovic said he was stepping down for "personal reasons" and was succeeded by justice minister Zeljko Sturanovic.

As President Vujanovic had predicted after the referendum, Montenegro's economy boomed in the wake of independence. This was especially true of real estate prices along the country's picturesque Adriatic coast; prime vacation properties were snapped up by bargain hunters from Europe and Russia, tripling prices in just a few months.

Kosovo: Another Delay on Status

Kosovo's year of uncertainty began on a sad note, with the death on January 21 of Ibrahim Rugova, who had served as the region's president for more than five years. Rugova had been a pacifist whose nonviolent means to achieve independence for Kosovo's ethnic Albanian majority were swept aside in the bloody conflict that engulfed the province from late 1998 through the first half of 1999. Despite his disagreements with the more radical Kosovo Liberation Army, his moral authority made him Kosovo's natural leader after the war. His death from lung cancer deprived the Kosovar Albanians of experienced political leadership just as the hard diplomatic work of negotiating the region's future was about to begin. At a funeral service in Pristina on January 27, the EU's foreign policy chief, Javier Solana, called it "one of the cruel ironies of history that he left at the moment he was most needed." The Kosovo parliament on February 10 chose another moderate, Fatmir Sejdiu, to succeed Rugova. A law professor, Sejdiu headed the Democratic League of Kosovo, which had become the province's largest political party. *(Kosovo war, Historic Documents of 1999, p. 119)*

The first round of talks between leaders from Kosovo and Serbia began under UN supervision in Vienna on February 20. The talks were mediated by former Finnish president Martti Ahtisaari, who hoped to reach an agreement by year's end. Ahtisaari was among many European leaders who argued that Kosovo's limbo status—as an effective ward of the United Nations even while still officially a part of Serbia—needed to be ended so the people of Kosovo could get on with their lives.

Ahtisaari was attempting to bridge a wide divide, between Belgrade's insistence that Kosovo remain part of Serbia and the demand of Kosovo's ethnic Albanian majority for complete independence. This fundamental dispute was complicated by the presence, mostly in northern Kosovo, of about 100,000 ethnic Serbs, nearly all of whom wanted to remain part of Serbia.

Also complicating matters was the position of Russia, which as a permanent member of the UN Security Council had the ability to veto any settlement on Kosovo. Moscow in the past had sided with Serbia—a sister Slav state—in opposing Kosovo independence. By 2006 Russian president Vladimir Putin appeared to be using the Kosovo issue for his own purposes. Putin argued that independence for Kosovo might establish a precedent that could be followed by pro-Russian independence movements in two of Russia's neighbors, Georgia and Moldova. The question of Georgia was particularly incendiary, because U.S. and European leaders staunchly opposed allowing separatist regions favored by Moscow to split from the country.

After several months of midlevel talks, Ahtisaari on July 24 brought together the senior officials of Kosovo and Serbia for the first time—Kosovo's new president, Sejdiu, and President Tadic and Prime Minister Vojislav Kostunica from Serbia. Ahtisaari acknowledged afterward that the two sides remained far apart: "Belgrade would accept everything but independence, while Kosovo will accept nothing but the independence."

UN Secretary General Kofi Annan announced on October 7 that he was calling for "final status" talks to begin right away—in effect stepping up the pressure on the two sides to compromise or else leave it to the United Nations to put forward a final plan on its own. Even so, Ahtisaari said he did not yet see any signs that either side was ready to compromise.

Before the negotiations Annan proposed could begin, Serbia took a step clearly intended to lock its hard-line position in place. Serbian leaders drafted, and voters overwhelmingly approved in an October 27–28 referendum, a new constitution declaring Kosovo to be an "integral part of Serbia."

UN officials and Western diplomats said the Serbian vote would not dictate the ultimate decision on Kosovo's status, but they clearly were worried that an upsurge of Serbian nationalism could make reaching an agreement more difficult. On November 5 Annan suggested for the first time that the timetable for settling the status of Kosovo by year's end probably would slip. Five days later, Ahtisaari announced that he would present a plan for Kosovo's future after Serbian parliamentary elections scheduled for late January 2007. The delay brought a flurry of protests in Pristina by Kosovo nationalists demanding immediate independence.

Serbia

Of all the former Yugoslav republics, none seemed to be having more difficulty moving beyond the past than Serbia, which had been the driving force behind the violence of the 1990s. After Milosevic fell from power in 2000, politicians calling themselves "democrats" took over, but they were divided, particularly after the leading moderate figure, Prime Minister Zoran Djindjic, was assassinated in 2003, reportedly by a criminal gang with links to nationalist forces supporting Milosevic. *(Background, Historic Documents of 2003, p. 57)*

The European Union sought to use the lure of potential membership to persuade Serbian leaders to adopt economic and political reforms. The Milosevic era kept intruding, however, because the EU set as a minimal condition the handing over of General Mladic to the UN war crimes tribunal—something that Belgrade leaders were unwilling, or possibly unable, to do. The government arrested some of Mladic's associates and insisted it was trying to find him but been unable to do so. On May 3 the EU called off its negotiations with Serbia on potential membership because of the Mladic issue.

Bosnia

A U.S.-sponsored effort to negotiate a new political system for Bosnia collapsed in 2006, apparently ensuring that the cumbersome system that had been in place for a decade would continue for at least a few more years. Under that system, imposed by the Dayton peace agreement ending the 1992–1995 Bosnian war, Bosnia was divided along ethnic lines into two main components, one for Serbs (the Republika Srpska) and the other for Croats and Muslims (the Bosniak-Croat Federation), united by a weak national government. This system was made even more complex by the fact that Croats had created their own governing units parallel to the federation. In essence, most Bosnian Muslim leaders wanted a strong national government they would dominate as the majority population, most Croats were satisfied with a weak federal government that allowed them substantial autonomy, and Serb leaders were angling either for complete independence or some kind of direct affiliation with Serbia.

The United States in November 2005 had pushed leaders from across Bosnia's political spectrum to negotiate a new system providing for a stronger, unified government. The leaders began talking in December 2005 and held several sessions into the early part of 2006. On March 18 they agreed to a package of political reforms providing for a single president (with two vice presidents), a prime minister to run the government's day-to-day operations, and an expanded parliament with more national powers. The plan did not provide for the truly strong central government most outside experts had said Bosnia needed, but European leaders endorsed it as a major improvement, as did a slight majority of Bosnians, according to a public opinion poll in April. This agreement failed, however, on April 26 when it fell two votes short of the required two-thirds majority in the Bosnian parliament, despite intense lobbying by diplomats from the United States and other countries. Members of one Croat party voted against the plan because some of their demands had not been met, and moderate Muslim leaders feared Serbs would still be able to obstruct the work of the new government.

One of the reasons the constitutional reform plan failed was that 2006 was an election year in Bosnia, and some politicians in all three ethnic communities were reluctant to be seen as compromising with their opposite numbers. The elections, held on October 1, were remarkable only because they were the first since the end of the war that were run by the Bosnians themselves, not by the United Nations. Otherwise, the results once again fell along sectarian lines, with the parties that advocated the respective nationalist positions generally outpolling those that called for compromise.

The major change that did come to Bosnia during the year was the weakening of the international community's direct role in governing the country. Under a 1997 agreement modifying the Dayton treaty, the ultimate political power in Bosnia had been held by an official, called the high representative, who was appointed by a United Nations–authorized body called the Peace Implementation Council. The high representative had near dictatorial powers, including the right to fire Bosnian government officials or even overturn legislation passed by the parliament. If necessary, the high representative could use military force to ensure that his orders were carried out; he also controlled the international peacekeeping force in Bosnia, which was run by the NATO alliance until 2005, when the EU took over that responsibility.

British politician Paddy Ashdown held the high representative post for four years and used his powers extensively—even while acknowledging that his doing so made it difficult for Bosnian leaders to learn how to behave responsibly on their own. Ashdown had been especially tough on Bosnian Serb leaders, firing several of them from their posts because they refused to cooperate with the national government. In one of his last official acts, in January 2006, Ashdown confiscated funds from the Serbian Democratic Party because Serb leaders had failed to hand over Karadzic.

Ashdown left his post at the end of January and was replaced by a German political leader, Christian Schwarz-Schilling, who said he would be more reticent about exercising the powers of his office and instead would turn more responsibility over to the Bosnians themselves. Schwarz-Schilling told the UN Security Council on April 18 that the time had come to give Bosnians "ownership" of their government. Adopting his recommendation, the Peace Implementation Council on June 23 agreed to end the high representative's role as the ultimate arbiter in Bosnia, as of June 2007. Instead, Schwarz-Schilling and his successors simply would represent the European Union in Bosnia and offer advice but not give orders.

Following is the text of an address to the United Nations General Assembly on June 28, 2006, by Filip Vujanovic, president of the Republic of Montenegro, the newest member state of the United Nations.

DOCUMENT

"Montenegro Has Become United Nations Member State"

It gives me particular pleasure and honor to convey the gratitude of the Republic of Montenegro to the Member States of the General Assembly, which voted in favor of Montenegro's accession to the United Nations only five weeks after the decision of Montenegrin citizens to restore independence. I would also like to thank the Danish Foreign Minister Mr. Moller and other Security Council members for their recommendation that Montenegro should become a Member State of the world Organization. Of course, our special appreciation also goes the UN Secretary General Mr. Kofi Annan for his significant contribution to our fast inclusion in UN membership.

After eighty-eight years, Montenegro restored its independence on 21st May thus becoming the youngest country in the world. It restored the independence it had gained at the Berlin Congress back in 1878. Montenegro managed to restore its independence without a peace conference and in a democratic referendum in the process organized in compliance with the best democratic practice and international standards, as generally recognized by all international and local observers. As a result, and taking into account its high democratic maturity, Montenegro immediately received international recognition.

The referendum was held in close co-operation with the European Union and it was another significant step that we made towards our strategic priority related to European and Euro-Atlantic integrations, demonstrating that we have a democratic capacity required for further progress. Our membership in the UN represents a step forward in the overall development of Montenegro and another proof that we have been on the right track. We are aware of many challenges that lie ahead, but after a long period of time, we shall be responsible for our own destiny, in line with the development capacities of our state.

Ladies and Gentlemen,

For all of us in Montenegro, the United Nations have always represented an irreplace-able bond among different peoples and cultures, particularly at times of crises that the Balkans has experienced recently during the tragic war conflicts. Throughout that period, the role of the UN was of paramount importance for encouraging dialogue and compro-mise. Although Montenegro was not directly affected by the war, it was not saved from its consequences. As a result, the UN role in that period has been even more valued and respected. For this reason, as a new UN member state, Montenegro is ready to actively support the organization's efforts aimed at peacefully resolving the conflicts and making its contribution to the UN humanitarian efforts as well as peace building and peacekeeping missions.

I would like to remind of a significant, but perhaps not sufficiently known detail from Montenegrin history, which serves as a testimony of Montenegro's devotion to this high goal throughout its history. Namely, in January 1897, the Montenegrin Prince and later the Montenegrin King Nikola I Petrović Njegos, while sending Montenegrin soldiers to the island of Crete to join a peacekeeping mission of the then Great Powers to prevent the on-going conflict, proudly said: "Great European Powers paid me a great honor by inviting me to send troops composed of my Montenegrins to Crete and join the interna-tional army, because they believe that Montenegrins will discharge their duty as befitting them—honestly and heroically." I am sure that this principle, which is still alive, as well as Montenegro's commitment, regardless of its size, to contribute to peace will also be affirmed in future engagement of our country within the United Nations.

Based on the past experience, Montenegro has been deeply aware of the importance of establishing relations with other countries based on friendship and partnership, respecting their sovereignty and territorial integrity. In this regard, we attach special importance to good-neighborly relations and regional co-operation, ensuring economic and overall prosperity and stability.

We particularly want to further develop close co-operation with the Republic of Serbia, not only in the context of good-neighborly co-operation and commitment to European integrations, but in all spheres of common interest, reflecting our social and historical ties.

As a new UN member state Montenegro undertakes to respect all obligations under the UN Charter, including all UN documents signed and assumed in the framework of the State Union Serbia and Montenegro. Montenegro hereby confirms its dedication to observing the principles of international law as well as to respecting the International Court of Justice, which safeguards the said principles.

In the present context of challenges for global security, Montenegro wants to make its full contribution to the fight against terrorism, proliferation of weapons of mass destruction and fight against organized crime. To this end, Montenegro will particularly respect all UN Conventions defining measures to efficiently deal with these challenges.

As an ecological State, Montenegro has a special obligation to respect UN efforts aimed at promoting sustainable development at the global level, and it will actively continue to develop as a State enabling its citizens to enjoy overall progress on the basis of sustainability. In that respect, we find it particularly important that the first Eco Building in our region is to be built in Montenegro in co-operation with the UN, which will be used by various specialized UN agencies.

Taking into account UN efforts aimed at reducing the existing gap between the rich and poor, the developed and underdeveloped, the small and the big, Montenegro shall continue to work with dedication towards full implementation of the Millennium Development Goals, thus contributing to better living standards of its citizens and stability in general.

Montenegro will continue to shape its policy and develop in line with the principles enshrined in the UN Charter and the Universal Declaration on Human Rights, which serve as a basis for modern democracies. Furthermore, it will continue to implement and promote the policy that fully respects human rights and fundamental freedoms of all citizens regardless of their personal and other differences.

Montenegro has been very proud of its multiethnic and multi-religious harmony, which is one of its fundamental values that make Montenegro recognizable both in regional and a broader international context.

Ladies and Gentlemen,

Montenegro is aware of the opportunities offered by UN to small countries, which have a chance to preserve and protect their interests on an equal footing with other States and nations, able to promote their identity and specific qualities through UN Membership. In this respect, I am sure, and it has been proved in practice, that even a small country like Montenegro can contribute to the UN efficiency.

From the very beginning, the United Nations have been initiating positive changes and acted as an irreplaceable factor at the international scene, while the respect and promotion of its achievements and principles have been embraced by all modern and democratic States, including Montenegro. Despite the fact that there have always been and still are challenges ahead of the UN, I am confident that the United Nations have a clear and bright perspective and future. United by common goals of noble values that all of us are committed to, we can be sure of long-term stability, security and overall prosperity.

I am positive that Montenegro can make its contribution to this noble goal. Today, by becoming the 192nd Member State of the United Nations, Montenegro has assumed with pleasure and dignity such a challenge and responsibility, confident that it will justify equally the expectations and obligations.

Source: Republic of Montenegro. President of the Republic of Montenegro. "Montenegro Has Become United Nations Member State—Address of the President of the Republic." June 28, 2006. www.predsjednik.cg.yu/eng/?akcija=vijest&id=1143 (accessed February 20, 2007).

Other Historic Documents of Interest

*International attitudes toward
    the United States, p. 286*
International trade issues, p. 424

*United Nations on human rights,
    p. 765*
U.S.-Russian Relations, p. 202

Supreme Court on
Tribunals for Terrorism Suspects

June 29, 2006

In a battle over the reach of executive power, the Supreme Court ruled on June 29, 2006, in the case of *Hamdan v. Rumsfeld*, that the military commissions established by the Bush administration to try suspected terrorists did not conform to federal or military law and violated the Geneva Conventions. Congress struck back in September by authorizing new rules governing the treatment and trial of terrorism suspects detained at a U.S. prison in Guantanamo Bay, Cuba, that differed only in small degree from the rules the Supreme Court had struck down as unconstitutional just three months earlier. The rules, which would allow the government to hold those persons designated as "enemy combatants" indefinitely—without charge and with no means of appearing in a U.S. civilian court to challenge their detention, were sure to provoke a new round of constitutional challenges over the scope of the president's authority to prosecute the war on terror.

Passage of the Military Commissions Act of 2006 (PL 109–366) was a signal victory for President George W. Bush. Signing the measure into law on October 17, Bush hailed it as "one of the most important pieces of legislation in the war on terror" and praised Congress for allowing the CIA to continue its secret interrogations of detainees believed to be key terrorist operatives. Bush had acknowledged the existence of that program only in early September, when the administration decided to transfer to Guantanamo fourteen detainees held by the CIA in secret prisons overseas. One of the fourteen was Kahlid Sheikh Mohammed, said to be the mastermind of the September 11, 2001, terrorist attacks. Bush said the interrogation program had been one of the "most successful intelligence efforts in American history," but critics charged that the interrogations involved methods that would be considered torture under the international Geneva Conventions governing war crimes.

Mohammed was one of about two dozen detainees who were likely to stand trial before the special military commissions, perhaps as early as the middle of 2007. Left in limbo were another 430 detainees at Guantanamo, many of whom had been there since the prison opened in January 2002 and had yet to have their status reviewed or charges brought against them. Several thousand more detainees were being held at military prisons in Afghanistan and Iraq. Attorneys had filed habeas corpus petitions for many of the Guantanamo detainees in federal court, challenging the government's right to detain them. But the Military Commission Act withdrew the jurisdiction of federal courts to review such petitions, retroactive to September 11, 2001. Shortly after Bush signed the Military Commissions Act, the Justice Department asked that all pending habeas corpus petitions from detainees be dismissed as moot; a challenge to that ruling was pending before a three-judge panel of the Court of Appeals for the District of Columbia at the end of the year.

Beyond the legal issues, the detentions at Guantanamo and other places had become, internationally, one of the most controversial aspects of Bush's war against terrorism. Opinion surveys around the world routinely showed that the indefinite detention of terrorism suspects, as well as revelations of the abusive treatment some of them had endured, undermined support for the United States by ignoring the principles Bush claimed to be upholding. *(Background on detainee abuse, Historic Documents of 2005, p. 905)*

Background

The constitutional struggle over the legitimacy of the military tribunals began in November 2001, when President Bush signed an executive order creating special tribunals to handle the cases of enemy combatants captured during the war in Afghanistan and any subsequent actions in Bush's "global war on terror." The order, which was revised in 2002, set rules for trial that allowed convictions based on hearsay, classified information that would not be given to the defense, and evidence that had been extracted by torture. In the revised order, issued on February 7, 2002, Bush explicitly said that the Common Article 3 of the Geneva Conventions guaranteeing humane treatment and judicial protections for war prisoners would not apply to al Qaeda detainees.

The first Guantanamo detainee scheduled to be tried by a military commission was Salim Ahmed Hamdan, a Yemeni captured in Afghanistan in 2001 and sent to the Guantanamo prison in June 2002. The administration said Hamdan had worked as a bodyguard and driver for al Qaeda leader Osama bin Laden and charged him with conspiracy to commit terrorism. Hamdan's lawyers said he told them he worked for bin Laden simply to earn money and was not involved in al Qaeda's terrorist operations.

Pretrial proceedings in Hamdan's case began in November 2004 but were halted when James Robertson, a federal district judge in Washington, ruled that Hamdan was entitled to a habeas corpus hearing to determine if he had rights as a prisoner of war under the Geneva Conventions. A three-judge panel of the Circuit Court of Appeals for the District of Columbia reversed Robertson on June 15, 2005. The panel agreed with the Bush administration's argument that the Geneva Convention did not apply to people like Hamdan because they were not soldiers for foreign governments that had signed the conventions. *(Background, Historic Documents of 2005, p. 446)*

Jurisdictional Dispute Added

Hamdan's attorneys appealed to the Supreme Court, which agreed on November 7, 2005, to hear the appeal. At the end of that year, Congress adopted, and Bush signed, as part of the annual defense appropriations and authorization measures, language eliminating the jurisdiction of federal courts over habeas corpus claims by the foreign detainees at Guantanamo Bay. The language, offered by Sen. Lindsey Graham, R-S.C., allowed detainees limited access to the federal courts on other grounds but only after the commission trials were completed. Historically, habeas corpus was the procedure prisoners, such as Hamdan, used to challenge the legality of their detention in the first place. On January 12, 2006, the Bush administration asked the Supreme Court to dismiss Hamdan's appeal; citing the recently passed Graham language, the administration said the Court no longer had jurisdiction over the case. On February 21 the Court said it would not dismiss the case but would consider the jurisdictional issue as part of Hamdan's appeal.

Issuing its ruling on June 29, the Supreme Court rejected the argument that it did not have jurisdiction in the case, saying that Congress had not made the Graham language retroactive to already pending habeas corpus petitions. It then struck down the military commissions as an excessive use of executive power not authorized by Congress and as a violation of both U.S. and international law. The ruling was 5–3. Chief Justice John G. Roberts Jr. did not participate; before his confirmation to the Supreme Court, in September 2005, Roberts had served on the appeals court panel whose ruling upholding the commissions was the case under review. *(Roberts nomination as chief justice, Historic Documents of 2005, p. 558)*

The majority opinion, written by Justice John Paul Stevens, held that President Bush had exceeded his executive authority when he set up the military commissions. The administration had argued that Congress had given the president such power when it passed a resolution the week after the September 11, 2001, terrorist attacks authorizing him to "use all necessary and appropriate force" against those responsible for or supporting the attacks. Stevens said there was "nothing in the text or legislative history" of the resolution "even hinting that Congress intended to expand or alter" existing laws governing military trials.

The majority also said that the military commissions violated U.S. law because the administration had not shown the necessity for permitting trial procedures that were not allowed under regular courts martial. Those procedures would prohibit Hamdan from attending his own trial and would admit any evidence against Hamdan the government offered, including evidence that might have been extracted by torture. "It is not evident why the danger posed by international terrorism, considerable though it is, should require . . . any variance from the courts-martial rules," Stevens wrote.

Finally, the majority ruled that the Geneva Conventions, ratified in 1949, did apply to the war with Al Qaeda and that the Guantanamo detainees were protected by Common Article 3, contained in each of the four conventions, which required detainees to be tried in "a regularly constituted court affording all the judicial guarantees which are recognized as indispensable by civilized peoples." Since the administration had not demonstrated any "practical need" for the commission procedures to deviate from regular court martial procedures, the commissions could not be considered "regularly constituted" and thus were invalid, Stevens wrote.

"We have assumed, as we must, that the allegations made . . . against Hamdan are true. We have assumed . . . that Hamdan is a dangerous individual whose beliefs, if acted upon, would cause great harm and even death to innocent civilians, and who would act upon those beliefs if given the opportunity," Stevens wrote in conclusion. "But in undertaking to try Hamdan and subject him to criminal punishment, the Executive is bound to comply with the Rule of Law that prevails in this jurisdiction." Joining Stevens in the majority were Justices David H. Souter, Anthony M. Kennedy, Ruth Bader Ginsburg, and Stephen G. Breyer. Kennedy and Breyer also wrote concurring opinions.

Justices Antonin Scalia, Clarence Thomas, and Samuel A. Alito Jr. each wrote dissenting opinions. The three dissenters argued that under the 2005 legislation, the Court no longer had jurisdiction to hear a habeas corpus appeal, and they said, in

Thomas's words, that the majority's opinion on the merits of the case "openly flouts" the Court's "well-established duty to respect the Executive's judgment in matters of military operations and foreign affairs."

New Authorization for Military Commissions

After the Supreme Court opinion was announced, President Bush said his administration "would comply" with the Court's ruling. In what appeared to be a major reversal of policy, the Department of Defense on July 11 released a memo, dated July 7, from Deputy Defense Secretary Gordon R. England ordering that all detainees held by the army in the war on terror be treated in accordance with Common Article 3 of the Geneva Conventions. In addition to guaranteeing judicial protections, that article prohibited "humiliating and degrading treatment" of prisoners. On September 6 the Pentagon issued a revised Army Field Manual that barred the military from using several controversial interrogation techniques, including keeping detainees naked and forcing them to perform sexual acts; terrorizing them with dogs; and using beatings, electric shocks, and a technique known as "waterboarding" in which a prisoner was made to feel as it he was drowning.

On the same day, however, the administration formally proposed legislation authorizing the continuation of the special military commissions and making only modest changes in the rules under which they would operate. For example, hearsay evidence and coerced confessions would be permitted if a military judge deemed them probative and reliable. In addition to eliminating federal court jurisdiction over habeas corpus petitions, the proposed legislation also effectively withdrew the right of detainees to file claims in federal court under the Geneva Conventions.

In what seemed a contradiction to the interrogation policy laid out in the new Army Field Manual, the proposed legislation effectively allowed secret CIA interrogators to continue to use what Bush described as "tough" methods to pry information from "high-ranking terrorists." The measure also provided retroactive immunity to any government agents who might be charged with war crimes as a result of their interrogation methods.

Although news reports of abuses at these prisons had circulated since December 2002, it was the first time Bush had acknowledged their existence. Bush said that, for security reasons, he could not describe the specific methods used by CIA agents, but insisted they were "safe and lawful and necessary" to obtain information that would save American lives.

House and Senate Republican leaders quickly endorsed the proposed legislation, and despite Democratic opposition, it appeared likely to win speedy congressional approval. But in the Senate, objections from three Republican members with impeccable national security credentials—John W. Warner of Virginia, Lindsey Graham of South Carolina, and John McCain of Arizona—stalled the legislation. The three senators disagreed with several aspects of the president's bill but focused on its provisions allowing the United States to redefine its obligations under Common Article 3 of the Geneva Conventions dealing with the humane treatment of detainees. The administration claimed that authority was needed to "clarify" the interrogation techniques permissible under the article, but the three senators argued that any reinterpretation of the Geneva Conventions by the United States could encourage other countries to take similar actions, thus endangering any U.S. soldiers captured in war.

The White House undertook an intensive campaign to win Senate support for its legislation. Cabinet officials, Vice President Dick Cheney, CIA director Michael V. Hayden, and Bush himself repeatedly warned that the CIA would not be able to continue its interrogations if the proposal was not approved. "So Congress has got a decision to make," Bush said at a news conference on September 15. "Do you want the [interrogation] program to go forward or not?"

But, after several more days of standoff, it was the White House that made the decision, agreeing to drop its language redefining U.S. obligations under the Geneva Conventions. Instead the administration and the three dissident senators agreed to language that listed nine types of offense—including torture, rape, and hostage-taking—that would be considered grave breaches of Common Article 3 and could be prosecuted in U.S. federal court under the War Crimes Act. The offenses did not include Article 3's prohibition on "humiliating and degrading treatment," which the administration had said was so vague that it threatened the continuation of the CIA's interrogation program. The administration also agreed to remove language allowing detainees to be tried and convicted on the basis of classified material they were not allowed to see.

In return the administration won an expanded definition of unlawful enemy combatants that covered not only battlefield combatants but also those who had financed or otherwise "purposefully and materially supported hostilities against the United States" and its allies in the war on terrorism. The Senate passed the bill on September 28, by a vote of 65–34, after defeating several amendments, including one that would have stricken the habeas corpus restrictions from the bill. That amendment, offered by Sen. Arlen Specter, R-Pa., was rejected 48–51. The House cleared the bill on September 29 by a vote of 250–170.

The conflict over the legislation came just a few weeks before the November midterm elections, and Republicans, whose control of Congress appeared vulnerable, had hoped to use the bill as a part of a "security September" to dramatize GOP strength on national security issues. The other measure that would have been part of the "security" package was legislation establishing new rules to govern a warrantless electronic surveillance program set up by the president after the September 11, 2001, terrorist attacks. The secret program, which allowed the National Security Agency to monitor overseas telephone calls and e-mails from U.S. citizens without obtaining warrants, was revealed by the *New York Times* in December 2005.

Following are excerpts from the majority opinion, written by Justice John Paul Stevens and handed down on June 29, 2006, in the case of Hamdan v. Rumsfeld, *in which the Supreme Court, by a vote of 5–3, held that the special military commissions established by President George W. Bush to try terror suspects were unconstitutional.*

DOCUMENT

Hamdan v. Rumsfeld

No. 05–184

Salim Ahmed Hamdan, Petitioner
v.
Donald H. Rumsfeld, Secretary
of Defense, et al.

On writ of certiorari to the
United States Court of Appeals for
the District of Columbia circuit

[June 29, 2006]

JUSTICE STEVENS announced the judgment of the Court and delivered the opinion of the Court with respect to Parts I through IV, Parts VI through VI–D–iii, Part VI–D–v, and Part VII, and an opinion with respect to Parts V and VI–D–iv, in which JUSTICE SOUTER, JUSTICE GINSBURG, and JUSTICE BREYER join.

Petitioner Salim Ahmed Hamdan, a Yemeni national, is in custody at an American prison in Guantanamo Bay, Cuba. In November 2001, during hostilities between the United States and the Taliban (which then governed Afghanistan), Hamdan was captured by militia forces and turned over to the U. S. military. In June 2002, he was transported to Guantanamo Bay. Over a year later, the President deemed him eligible for trial by military commission for then-unspecified crimes. After another year had passed, Hamdan was charged with one count of conspiracy "to commit ... offenses triable by military commission."...

Hamdan filed petitions for writs of habeas corpus and mandamus to challenge the Executive Branch's intended means of prosecuting this charge. He concedes that a court-martial constituted in accordance with the Uniform Code of Military Justice (UCMJ) ... would have authority to try him. His objection is that the military commission the President has convened lacks such authority, for two principal reasons: First, neither congressional Act nor the common law of war supports trial by this commission for the crime of conspiracy—an offense that, Hamdan says, is not a violation of the law of war. Second, Hamdan contends, the procedures that the President has adopted to try him violate the most basic tenets of military and international law, including the principle that a defendant must be permitted to see and hear the evidence against him.

The District Court granted Hamdan's request for a writ of habeas corpus. ... The Court of Appeals for the District of Columbia Circuit reversed. ... Recognizing, as we did over a half-century ago, that trial by military commission is an extraordinary measure raising important questions about the balance of powers in our constitutional structure, *Ex parte Quirin* ... (1942), we granted certiorari. ...

For the reasons that follow, we conclude that the military commission convened to try Hamdan lacks power to proceed because its structure and procedures violate both the UCMJ and the Geneva Conventions. Four of us also conclude, see Part V, *infra*, that the offense with which Hamdan has been charged is not an "offens[e] that by . . . the law of war may be tried by military commissions."

[Section I omitted.]

II

On February 13, 2006, the Government filed a motion to dismiss the writ of certiorari. The ground cited for dismissal was the recently enacted Detainee Treatment Act of 2005 (DTA). . . . We postponed our ruling on that motion pending argument on the merits . . . and now deny it.

The DTA, which was signed into law on December 30, 2005, addresses a broad swath of subjects related to detainees. It places restrictions on the treatment and interrogation of detainees in U. S. custody, and it furnishes procedural protections for U. S. personnel accused of engaging in improper interrogation. . . .

The Government argues that §§1005(e)(1) and 1005(h) [of the DTA] had the immediate effect, upon enactment, of repealing federal jurisdiction not just over detainee habeas actions yet to be filed but also over any such actions then pending in any federal court—including this Court. Accordingly, it argues, we lack jurisdiction to review the Court of Appeals' decision below.

Hamdan objects to this theory on both constitutional and statutory grounds. Principal among his constitutional arguments is that the Government's preferred reading raises grave questions about Congress' authority to impinge upon this Court's appellate jurisdiction, particularly in habeas cases. Support for this argument is drawn from *Ex parte Yerger*. . . (1869), in which, having explained that "the denial to this court of appellate jurisdiction" to consider an original writ of habeas corpus would "greatly weaken the efficacy of the writ" . . . we held that Congress would not be presumed to have effected such denial absent an unmistakably clear statement to the contrary . . . Hamdan also suggests that, if the Government's reading is correct, Congress has unconstitutionally suspended the writ of habeas corpus.

We find it unnecessary to reach either of these arguments. Ordinary principles of statutory construction suffice to rebut the Government's theory—at least insofar as this case, which was pending at the time the DTA was enacted, is concerned.

The Government acknowledges that only paragraphs (2)and (3) of subsection (e) are expressly made applicable to pending cases . . . but argues that the omission of paragraph (1) from the scope of that express statement is of no moment. This is so, we are told, because Congress' failure to expressly reserve federal courts' jurisdiction over pending cases erects a presumption against jurisdiction, and that presumption is rebutted by neither the text nor the legislative history of the DTA.

The first part of this argument is not entirely without support in our precedents. . . . But the "presumption" that these cases have applied is more accurately viewed as the nonapplication of another presumption—viz., the presumption against retroactivity—in certain limited circumstances. If a statutory provision "would operate retroactively" as applied to cases pending at the time the provision was enacted, then "our traditional presumption teaches that it does not govern absent clear congressional intent favoring such a result.". . . We have explained, however, that, unlike other intervening changes in the law, a jurisdiction-conferring or jurisdiction-stripping statute usually "takes away no substantive right but simply changes the tribunal that is to hear the case.". . . If that is truly all the statute does, no retroactivity problem arises because the change in the law does not "impair rights a party possessed when he acted, increase a party's liability for past conduct, or impose new duties with respect to transactions already completed.". . . And if a new rule has no retroactive effect, the presumption against retroactivity will not prevent its application to a case that was already pending when the new rule was enacted.

That does not mean, however, that all jurisdiction-stripping provisions—or even all such provisions that truly lack retroactive effect—must apply to cases pending at the time of their enactment. "[N]ormal rules of construction," including a contextual reading of the statutory language, may dictate otherwise. . . . A familiar principle of statutory construction, relevant both in *Lindh* and here, is that a negative inference may be drawn from the exclusion of language from one statutory provision that is included in other provisions of the same statute. . . . The Court in *Lindh* [*v. Murphy* (1997)] relied on this reasoning to conclude that certain limitations on the availability of habeas relief imposed by AEDPA [Antiterrorism and Effective Death Penalty Act of 1996] applied only to cases filed after that statute's effective date. Congress' failure to identify the temporal reach of those limitations, which governed noncapital cases, stood in contrast to its express command in the same legislation that new rules governing habeas petitions in capital cases "apply to cases pending on or after the date of enactment.". . . That contrast, combined with the fact that the amendments at issue "affect[ed]substantive entitlement to relief" . . . warranted drawing a negative inference.

A like inference follows *a fortiori* from *Lindh* in this case. "If . . . Congress was reasonably concerned to ensure that [§§1005(e)(2) and (3)] be applied to pending cases, it should have been just as concerned about [§1005(e)(1)], unless it had the different intent that the latter [section]not be applied to the general run of pending cases.". . . If anything, the evidence of deliberate omission is stronger here than it was in *Lindh*. In *Lindh*, the provisions to be contrasted had been drafted separately but were later "joined together and . . . considered simultaneously when the language raising the implication was inserted.". . . We observed that Congress' tandem review and approval of the two sets of provisions strengthened the presumption that the relevant omission was deliberate. . . . Here, Congress not only considered the respective temporal reaches of paragraphs(1), (2), and (3) of subsection (e) together at every stage, but omitted paragraph (1) from its directive that paragraphs (2) and (3) apply to pending cases only after having rejected earlier proposed versions of the statute that would have included what is now paragraph (1) within the scope of that directive. . . . Congress' rejection of the very language that would have achieved the result the Government urges here weighs heavily against the Government's interpretation. . . .

[Remainder of section II and section III omitted.]

IV

. . . Whether . . . the President may constitutionally convene military commissions "without the sanction of Congress" in cases of "controlling necessity" is a question this Court has not answered definitively, and need not answer today. For we held in *Quirin* that Congress had, through Article of War 15, sanctioned the use of military commissions in such circumstances . . . Article 21 of the UCMJ, the language of which is substantially identical to the old Article 15 and was preserved by Congress after World War II, reads as follows:

> *"Jurisdiction of courts-martial not exclusive. "The provisions of this code conferring jurisdiction upon courts-martial shall not be construed as depriving military commissions, provost courts, or other military tribunals of concurrent jurisdiction in respect of offenders or offenses that by statute or by the law of war may be tried by such military commissions, provost courts, or other military tribunals.". . .*

We have no occasion to revisit *Quirin*'s controversial characterization of Article of War 15 as congressional authorization for military commissions. . . . Contrary to the Government's assertion, however, even *Quirin* did not view the authorization as a sweeping mandate for the President to "invoke military commissions when he deems them necessary."... Rather, the *Quirin* Court recognized that Congress had simply preserved what power, under the Constitution and the common law of war, the President had had before 1916 to convene military commissions—with the express condition that the President and those under his command comply with the law of war. . . .

The Government would have us . . . find in either the AUMF [Authorization for Use of Military Force, the joint resolution passed in 2001 authorizing use of all necessary and appropriate force to prevent further acts of terrorism against the United States] or the DTA specific, overriding authorization for the very commission that has been convened to try Hamdan. Neither of these congressional Acts, however, expands the President's authority to convene military commissions. First, while we assume that the AUMF activated the President's war powers . . . and that those powers include the authority to convene military commissions in appropriate circumstances . . . there is nothing in the text or legislative history of the AUMF even hinting that Congress intended to expand or alter the authorization set forth in Article 21 of the UCMJ. . . .

Likewise, the DTA cannot be read to authorize this commission. Although the DTA, unlike either Article 21 or the AUMF, was enacted after the President had convened Hamdan's commission, it contains no language authorizing that tribunal or any other at Guantanamo Bay. The DTA obviously "recognize[s]" the existence of the Guantanamo Bay commissions in the weakest sense . . . because it references some of the military orders governing them and creates limited judicial review of their "final decision[s],". . . But the statute also pointedly reserves judgment on whether "the Constitution and laws of the United States are applicable" in reviewing such decisions and whether, if they are, the "standards and procedures" used to try Hamdan and other detainees actually violate the "Constitution and laws.". . .

Together, the UCMJ, the AUMF, and the DTA at most acknowledge a general Presidential authority to convene military commissions in circumstances where justified under the "Constitution and laws," including the law of war. Absent a more specific congressional authorization, the task of this Court is . . . to decide whether Hamdan's military commission is so justified. It is to that inquiry we now turn.

[Section V omitted. This section found that the offense of conspiracy, with which Hamdan was charged, was not itself a war crime justifying trial by a military commission.]

VI

Whether or not the Government has charged Hamdan with an offense against the law of war cognizable by military commission, the commission lacks power to proceed. The UCMJ conditions the President's use of military commissions on compliance not only with the American common law of war, but also with the rest of the UCMJ itself, insofar as applicable, and with the "rules and precepts of the law of nations" ... including, *inter alia*, the four Geneva Conventions signed in 1949. . . . The procedures that the Government has decreed will govern Hamdan's trial by commission violate these laws.

[Section A omitted.]

B

Hamdan raises both general and particular objections to the procedures set forth in Commission Order No. 1. His general objection is that the procedures' admitted deviation from those governing courts-martial itself renders the commission illegal. Chief among his particular objections are that he may, under the Commission Order, be convicted based on evidence he has not seen or heard, and that any evidence admitted against him need not comply with the admissibility or relevance rules typically applicable in criminal trials and court-martial proceedings.

The Government objects to our consideration of any procedural challenge at this stage on the grounds that . . . Hamdan will be able to raise any such challenge following a "final decision" under the DTA, and . . . [that] "there is . . . no basis to presume, before the trial has even commenced, that the trial will not be conducted in good faith and according to law.". . . [N]either of [these contentions] is sound.

First, because Hamdan apparently is not subject to the death penalty (at least as matters now stand) and may receive a sentence shorter than 10 years' imprisonment, he has no automatic right to review of the commission's "final decision" before a federal court under the DTA. . . . Second, contrary to the Government's assertion, there is a "basis to presume" that the procedures employed during Hamdan's trial will violate the law: The procedures are described with particularity in Commission Order No. 1 [setting out the procedures guiding the operations of the military commissions], and implementation of some of them has already occurred. One of Hamdan's complaints is that he will be, and *indeed already has been*, excluded from his own trial. . . . Under these circumstances, review of the procedures in advance of a "final decision"—the timing of which is left entirely to the discretion of the President under the DTA—is appropriate. We turn, then, to consider the merits of Hamdan's procedural challenge.

C

In part because the difference between military commissions and courts-martial originally was a difference of jurisdiction alone, and in part to protect against abuse and ensure evenhandedness under the pressures of war, the procedures governing trials by military commission historically have been the same as those governing courts-martial. . . . As recently as the Korean and Vietnam wars, during which use of military commissions was contemplated but never made, the principle of procedural parity was espoused as a background assumption. . . .

The uniformity principle is not an inflexible one; it does not preclude all departures from the procedures dictated for use by courts-martial. But any departure must be tailored to the exigency that necessitates it. . . . That understanding is reflected in Article 36 of the UCMJ, which provides:

> "(a) The procedure, including modes of proof, in cases before courts-martial, courts of inquiry, military commissions, and other military tribunals may be prescribed by the President by regulations which shall, so far as he considers practicable, apply the principles of law and the rules of evidence generally recognized in the trial of criminal cases in the United States district courts, but which may not be contrary to or inconsistent with this chapter.
> "(b) All rules and regulations made under this article shall be uniform insofar as practicable and shall be reported to Congress.". . .

Article 36 places two restrictions on the President's power to promulgate rules of procedure for courts-martial and military commissions alike. First, no procedural rule he adopts may be "contrary to or inconsistent with" the UCMJ—however practical it may seem. Second, the rules adopted must be "uniform insofar as practicable." That is, the rules applied to military commissions must be the same as those applied to courts-martial unless such uniformity proves impracticable.

Hamdan argues that Commission Order No. 1 violates both of these restrictions; he maintains that the procedures described in the Commission Order are inconsistent with the UCMJ and that the Government has offered no explanation for their deviation from the procedures governing courts-martial, which are set forth in the *Manual for Courts-Martial.* . . . Among the inconsistencies Hamdan identifies is that between §6 of the Commission Order, which permits exclusion of the accused from proceedings and denial of his access to evidence in certain circumstances, and the UCMJ's requirement that "[a]ll . . . proceedings" other than votes and deliberations by courts-martial "shall be made a part of the record and shall be in the presence of the accused.". . . Hamdan also observes that the Commission Order dispenses with virtually all evidentiary rules applicable in courts-martial.

The Government has three responses. First, it argues, only 9 of the UCMJ's 158 Articles—the ones that expressly mention "military commissions"—actually apply to commissions, and Commission Order No. 1 sets forth no procedure that is "contrary to or inconsistent with" those 9 provisions. Second, the Government contends, military commissions would be of no use if the President were hamstrung by those provisions of the UCMJ that govern courts-martial. Finally, the President's determination [in his November 13, 2001, executive order] that "the danger to the safety of the United States and the nature of international terrorism" renders it impracticable "to apply in military commissions . . . the principles of law and rules of evidence generally recognized in the trial of criminal cases in the United States district courts" . . . is, in the Government's view, explanation enough for any deviation from court-martial procedures . . .

Hamdan has the better of this argument. Without reaching the question whether any provision of Commission Order No. 1 is strictly "contrary to or inconsistent with" other provisions of the UCMJ, we conclude that the "practicability" determination the President has made is insufficient to justify variances from the procedures governing courts-martial. Subsection (b) of Article 36 was added after World War II, and requires a different showing of impracticability from the one required by subsection(a). Subsection (a) requires that the rules the President promulgates for courts-martial, provost courts, and military commissions alike conform to those that govern procedures in *Article III courts,* "so far as *he considers* practicable.". . . Subsection (b), by contrast, demands that the rules applied in courts-martial, provost courts, and military commissions—whether or not they conform with the Federal Rules of Evidence—be "uniform *insofar as practicable.*". . . Under the latter provision, then, the rules set forth in the Manual for Courts-Martial must apply to military commissions unless impracticable.

The President here has determined, pursuant to subsection (a), that it is impracticable to apply the rules and principles of law that govern "the trial of criminal cases in the United States district courts" . . . to Hamdan's commission. We assume that complete deference is owed that determination. The President has not, however, made a similar official determination that it is impracticable to apply the rules for courts-martial. And even if subsection (b)'s requirements may be satisfied without such an official determination, the requirements of that subsection are not satisfied here.

Nothing in the record before us demonstrates that it would be impracticable to apply court-martial rules in this case. There is no suggestion, for example, of any logistical difficulty in securing properly sworn and authenticated evidence or in applying the usual principles of relevance and admissibility. Assuming *arguendo* that the reasons articulated in the President's Article 36(a) determination ought to be considered in evaluating the impracticability of applying court-martial rules, the only reason offered in support of that determination is the danger posed by international terrorism. Without for one moment underestimating that danger, it is not evident to us why it should require, in the case of Hamdan's trial, any variance from the rules that govern courts-martial.

The absence of any showing of impracticability is particularly disturbing when considered in light of the clear and admitted failure to apply one of the most fundamental protections afforded not just by the Manual for Courts-Martial but also by the UCMJ itself: the right to be present. . . . Whether or not that departure technically is "contrary to or inconsistent with" the terms of the UCMJ . . . the jettisoning of so basic a right cannot lightly be excused as "practicable."

Under the circumstances, then, the rules applicable in courts-martial must apply. Since it is undisputed that Commission Order No. 1 deviates in many significant respects from those rules, it necessarily violates Article 36(b).

The Government's objection that requiring compliance with the court-martial rules imposes an undue burden both ignores the plain meaning of Article 36(b) and misunderstands the purpose and the history of military commissions. The military commission was not born of a desire to dispense a more summary form of justice than is afforded by courts-martial; it developed, rather, as a tribunal of necessity to be employed when courts-martial lacked jurisdiction over either the accused or the subject matter. . . . Exigency lent the commission its legitimacy, but did not further justify the wholesale jettisoning of procedural protections. That history explains why the military commission's procedures typically have been the ones used by courts-martial. That the jurisdiction of the two tribunals today may sometimes overlap . . . does not detract from the force of this history; Article 21 did not transform the military commission from a tribunal of true exigency into a more convenient adjudicatory tool. Article 36, confirming as much, strikes a careful balance between uniform procedure and the need to accommodate exigencies that may sometimes arise in a theater of war. That Article not having been complied with here, the rules specified for Hamdan's trial are illegal.

D

The procedures adopted to try Hamdan also violate the Geneva Conventions. The Court of Appeals dismissed Hamdan's Geneva Convention challenge on three independent grounds: (1) the Geneva Conventions are not judicially enforceable; (2) Hamdan in any event is not entitled to their protections; and (3) even if he is entitled to their protections, [*Schlesinger v.*] *Councilman* [(1975)] abstention is appropriate.... As we explained in Part III, *supra*, the abstention rule applied in *Councilman* ... is not applicable here. And for the reasons that follow, we hold that neither of the other grounds the Court of Appeals gave for its decision is persuasive.

i

The Court of Appeals relied on *Johnson v. Eisentrager* ... (1950), to hold that Hamdan could not invoke the Geneva Conventions to challenge the Government's plan to prosecute him in accordance with Commission Order No. 1. *Eisentrager* involved a challenge by 21 German nationals to their 1945 convictions for war crimes by a military tribunal convened in Nanking, China, and to their subsequent imprisonment in occupied Germany. The petitioners argued, inter alia, that the 1929 Geneva Convention rendered illegal some of the procedures employed during their trials, which they said deviated impermissibly from the procedures used by courts-martial to try American soldiers.... We rejected that claim on the merits because the petitioners (unlike Hamdan here) had failed to identify any prejudicial disparity "between the Commission that tried [them] and those that would try an offending soldier of the American forces of like rank," and in any event could claim no protection, under the 1929 Convention, during trials for crimes that occurred before their confinement as prisoners of war....

Buried in a footnote of the opinion, however, is this curious statement suggesting that the Court lacked power even to consider the merits of the Geneva Convention argument:

> "*We are not holding that these prisoners have no right which the military authorities are bound to respect. The United States, by the Geneva Convention of July 27, 1929, 47 Stat. 2021, concluded with forty-six other countries, including the German Reich, an agreement upon the treatment to be accorded captives. These prisoners claim to be and are entitled to its protection. It is, however, the obvious scheme of the Agreement that responsibility for observance and enforcement of these rights is upon political and military authorities. Rights of alien enemies are vindicated under it only through protests and intervention of protecting powers as the rights of our citizens against foreign governments are vindicated only by Presidential intervention.*" ...

The Court of Appeals, on the strength of this footnote, held that "the 1949 Geneva Convention does not confer upon Hamdan a right to enforce its provisions in court." ...

Whatever else might be said about the *Eisentrager* footnote, it does not control this case. We may assume that "the obvious scheme" of the 1949 Conventions is identical in all relevant respects to that of the 1929 Convention, and even that that scheme would, absent some other provision of law, preclude Hamdan's invocation of the Convention's provisions as an independent source of law binding the Government's actions and furnishing petitioner with any enforceable right. For, regardless of the nature of the rights conferred on Hamdan . . . they are, as the Government does not dispute, part of the law of war. . . . And compliance with the law of war is the condition upon which the authority set forth in Article 21 is granted.

ii

For the Court of Appeals, acknowledgment of that condition was no bar to Hamdan's trial by commission. As an alternative to its holding that Hamdan could not invoke the Geneva Conventions at all, the Court of Appeals concluded that the Conventions did not in any event apply to the armed conflict during which Hamdan was captured. The court accepted the Executive's assertions that Hamdan was captured in connection with the United States' war with al Qaeda and that that war is distinct from the war with the Taliban in Afghanistan. It further reasoned that the war with al Qaeda evades the reach of the Geneva Conventions. . . . We . . . disagree with the latter conclusion.

The conflict with al Qaeda is not, according to the Government, a conflict to which the full protections afforded detainees under the 1949 Geneva Conventions apply because Article 2 of those Conventions (which appears in all four Conventions) renders the full protections applicable only to "all cases of declared war or of any other armed conflict which may arise between two or more of the High Contracting Parties." . . . Since Hamdan was captured and detained incident to the conflict with al Qaeda and not the conflict with the Taliban, and since al Qaeda, unlike Afghanistan, is not a "High Contracting Party"—i.e., a signatory of the Conventions, the protections of those Conventions are not, it is argued, applicable to Hamdan.

We need not decide the merits of this argument because there is at least one provision of the Geneva Conventions that applies here even if the relevant conflict is not one between signatories. Article 3, often referred to as Common Article 3 because, like Article 2, it appears in all four Geneva Conventions, provides that in a "conflict not of an international character occurring in the territory of one of the High Contracting Parties, each Party to the conflict shall be bound to apply, as a minimum," certain provisions protecting "[p]ersons taking no active part in the hostilities, including members of armed forces who have laid down their arms and those placed hors de combat by . . . detention." . . . One such provision prohibits "the passing of sentences and the carrying out of executions without previous judgment pronounced by a regularly constituted court affording all the judicial guarantees which are recognized as indispensable by civilized peoples." . . .

The Court of Appeals thought, and the Government asserts, that Common Article 3 does not apply to Hamdan because the conflict with al Qaeda, being "'international in scope,'" does not qualify as a "'conflict not of an international character.'" . . . That reasoning is erroneous. The term "conflict not of an international character" is used here in contradistinction to a conflict between nations. So much is demonstrated by the "fundamental logic [of] the Convention's provisions on its application." . . . Common Article 2 provides that "the present Convention shall apply to all cases of declared war or of any other armed conflict which may arise between two or more of the High Contracting Parties.". . . High Contracting Parties (signatories) also must abide by all terms of the Conventions vis-à-vis one another even if one party to the conflict is a nonsignatory "Power," and must so abide vis-à-vis the nonsignatory if "the latter accepts and applies" those terms. . . . Common Article 3, by contrast, affords some minimal protection, falling short of full protection under the Conventions, to individuals associated with neither a signatory nor even a nonsignatory "Power" who are involved in a conflict "in the territory of" a signatory. The latter kind of conflict is distinguishable from the conflict described in Common Article 2 chiefly because it does not involve a clash between nations (whether signatories or not). In context, then, the phrase "not of an international character" bears its literal meaning. . . .

iii

Common Article 3, then, is applicable here and, as indicated above, requires that Hamdan be tried by a "regularly constituted court affording all the judicial guarantees which are recognized as indispensable by civilized peoples.". . . While the term "regularly constituted court" is not specifically defined in either Common Article 3 or its accompanying commentary, other sources disclose its core meaning. The commentary accompanying a provision of the Fourth Geneva Convention, for example, defines "'regularly constituted'" tribunals to include "ordinary military courts" and "definitely exclud[e] all special tribunals.". . . And one of the Red Cross' own treatises defines "regularly constituted court" as used in Common Article 3 to mean "established and organized in accordance with the laws and procedures already in force in a country.". . .

The Government offers only a cursory defense of Hamdan's military commission in light of Common Article 3. . . . As JUSTICE KENNEDY explains, that defense fails because "[t]he regular military courts in our system are the courts-martial established by congressional statutes.". . . At a minimum, a military commission "can be 'regularly constituted' by the standards of our military justice system only if some practical need explains deviations from court-martial practice.". . . As we have explained . . . no such need has been demonstrated here.

iv

Inextricably intertwined with the question of regular constitution is the evaluation of the procedures governing the tribunal and whether they afford "all the judicial guarantees which are recognized as indispensable by civilized peoples.". . . Like the phrase "regularly constituted court," this phrase is not defined in the text of the Geneva Conventions. But it must be understood to incorporate at least the barest of those trial protections that have been recognized by customary international law. Many of these are described in Article 75 of Protocol I to the Geneva Conventions of 1949, adopted in 1977 (Protocol I). Although the United States declined to ratify Protocol I, its objections were not to Article 75 thereof. Indeed, it appears that the Government "regard[s] the provisions of Article 75 as an articulation of safeguards to which all persons in the hands of an enemy are entitled.". . . Among the rights set forth in Article 75 is the "right to be tried in [one's] presence.". . .

We agree with JUSTICE KENNEDY that the procedures adopted to try Hamdan deviate from those governing courts-martial in ways not justified by any "evident practical need" . . . and for that reason, at least, fail to afford the requisite guarantees . . . We add only that, as noted in Part VI–A, supra, various provisions of Commission Order No. 1 dispense with the principles, articulated in Article 75 and indisputably part of the customary international law, that an accused must, absent disruptive conduct or consent, be present for his trial and must be privy to the evidence against him. . . . That the Government has a compelling interest in denying Hamdan access to certain sensitive information is not doubted. . . . But, at least absent express statutory provision to the contrary, information used to convict a person of a crime must be disclosed to him.

v

Common Article 3 obviously tolerates a great degree of flexibility in trying individuals captured during armed conflict; its requirements are general ones, crafted to accommodate a wide variety of legal systems. But *requirements* they are nonetheless. The commission that the President has convened to try Hamdan does not meet those requirements.

VII

We have assumed, as we must, that the allegations made in the Government's charge against Hamdan are true. We have assumed, moreover, the truth of the message implicit in that charge—viz., that Hamdan is a dangerous individual whose beliefs, if acted upon, would cause great harm and even death to innocent civilians, and who would act upon those beliefs if given the opportunity. It bears emphasizing that Hamdan does not challenge, and we do not today address, the Government's power to detain him for the duration of active hostilities in order to prevent such harm. But in undertaking to try Hamdan and subject him to criminal punishment, the Executive is bound to comply with the Rule of Law that prevails in this jurisdiction.

The judgment of the Court of Appeals is reversed, and the case is remanded for further proceedings.

It is so ordered.

THE CHIEF JUSTICE took no part in the consideration or decision of this case.

Source: U.S. Supreme Court of the United States. Hamdan v. Rumsfeld. 548 U.S. — (2006), Docket 05–184. June 29, 2006. www.supremecourtus.gov/opinions/05pdf/05-184.pdf (accessed November 13, 2006).

July

New York Court of Appeals on Gay Marriage

July 6, 2006

■■■■■■ **THE DOCUMENT IN CONTEXT** ■■■■■■

Gay rights activists seeking the right to marry were thwarted at almost every turn in 2006. High courts in New Jersey, New York, and Washington state all declined to overturn state bars to same-sex marriage, saying that it was a matter for the state legislature to decide. Only the New Jersey legislature acted before the end of the year; it agreed to civil unions giving gay couples the legal rights and protections of marriage but refused them the act of marriage itself. The high court in Georgia rejected a challenge to the way the state's constitutional amendment had been presented to voters, who approved it in 2004.

Seven states adopted constitutional amendments banning gay marriages (and in some cases civil unions as well) following the November 2006 elections. However, House and Senate attempts to add a similar amendment to the federal Constitution failed, as expected. Republican legislators had pressed for the vote in an effort to appeal to conservative voters, but the issue did not appear to have the same resonance in 2006 that it did in 2004 when voters turning out to support gay marriage bans were a major, if not decisive, factor in the election of President George W. Bush. Commentators suggested that with more states adopting constitutional amendments banning the practice, voters were not as concerned as they once were about the issue. Some conservative voters may also have stayed home out of disgust after the abrupt resignation of Rep. Mark Foley, R-Fla., on September 29 and revelations that Republican House leaders had done nothing to stop his inappropriate advances to underage male congressional pages.

State Courts on Gay Marriage

Ever since the Supreme Judicial Court of Massachusetts ruled in 2003 that the state constitution required Massachusetts to recognize same-sex civil marriages, gay rights activists had been raising similar challenges in other states. In New York, forty-four gay couples had challenged that state's marriage law as denying their right to due process and equal protection of the law. Their argument closely tracked the reasoning put forth in the Massachusetts court case. But in a 4–2 decision announced on July 7, the New York Court of Appeals (the state's highest court) ruled that New York's marriage law was not unconstitutionally discriminatory. Unlike racism, which was patently discriminatory, the majority judges said, the "traditional definition of marriage" was "not merely a by-product of historical injustice." Instead, it was based on a rational determination that children fared best in traditional marriages. "Plaintiffs have not persuaded us that this long-accepted restriction is a wholly irrational one, based solely on ignorance and prejudice against homosexuals," Judge Robert S. Smith wrote. In a sharp dissent, the court's chief judge, Judith S. Kaye, wrote that the ban on same-sex marriage was equivalent to a ban on interracial marriage, which the U.S. Supreme Court struck down as discriminatory in 1967. "The long duration of a constitutional wrong cannot justify its perpetuation, no matter how strongly tradition or public sentiment might support it," she wrote. *(Massachusetts ruling, Historic Documents of 2003, p. 401)*

The majority also said it was not for the court "to say whether same-sex marriage is right or wrong." That was an issue for the state legislature to decide, the court added. George E. Pataki, New York's Republican governor who was retiring after three terms in office, had said he would veto any measure legalizing gay marriage in the state. Democrat Eliot Spitzer, who was running in the November election to succeed Pataki, had defended the existing law as the state's attorney general but said that he thought the law should be changed.

In Georgia the state supreme court was unanimous in upholding a ban on gay marriage that voters had strongly endorsed in a 2004 ballot initiative. A lower court judge had struck down the ban because it also barred the state from offering same-sex couples legal benefits and protections. The judge agreed with plaintiffs that the dual nature of the ballot initiative violated a state election law limiting ballot questions to a single subject. Supporters of gay rights argued that voters who approved of one part of the ballot question but not the other had no way to split their votes and either had to approve or disapprove both parts. The supreme court ruled, however, that the part on civil unions did not "address a different objective than that of the amendment as a whole" and therefore did not violate the election law.

The Georgia supreme court had expedited its ruling at the behest of Sonny Perdue, the state's first Republican governor in more than a century. Perdue, who was seeking election in November to a second term, had threatened to convene a special session of the legislature to enact a gay marriage ban if the court did not rule by August. Perdue praised the decision at a news conference on July 7 after the opinion was announced. "When we do a constitutional amendment, we are very respectful of the people's voice," he said. "Gay Georgians are free to work and to live their lives—they're just not free to marry in Georgia." (Like Spitzer in New York, Purdue won his election handily.)

The closest decision came in Washington, where the state supreme court on July 26 upheld a state law barring same-sex marriages by a 5–4 vote, with six different opinions. The ruling overturned decisions in two lower court cases striking down the 1998 law. As in the New York case, the majority said it was up to the state legislature to determine whether the state would permit same-sex marriages. "While same-sex marriage may be the law at a future time, it will be because the people declare it to be, not because five members of this court have dictated it," one justice wrote.

In New Jersey, the state supreme court ruled unanimously on October 26 that the legislature must grant same-sex couples all the same rights and protections of marriage enjoyed by opposite-sex couples, but four of the seven judges refused to accord these civil unions the status of marriage. "If the age-old definition of marriage is to be discarded," Justice Barry T. Albin wrote in the court's opinion, "such change must come from the crucible of the democratic process." Instructed to act within 180 days, the New Jersey legislature moved even faster, approving a civil union measure on December 14. Democratic governor Jon S. Corzine signed the measure into law on December 21, making New Jersey the third state, along with Vermont and Connecticut, to allow civil unions. Such unions gave same-sex couples all the legal benefits and responsibilities granted by the state to heterosexual couples, but the unions were not recognized by the federal government, so gay couples in civil unions could not, for example, collect Social Security benefits of their deceased partners. *(Vermont civil unions, Historic Documents of 2000, p. 158)*

The high courts in California, Connecticut, and Maryland were expected to issue opinions in 2007 on whether their state bars to same-sex marriage passed state constitutional muster. In Massachusetts, opponents of the court's 2003 ruling were seeking to place a constitutional amendment barring same-sex marriages on the ballot. Under state law the proposed amendment had to be approved by fifty lawmakers in two consecutive legislative sessions before it could be placed on the ballot. Although a majority of the state legislature favored same-sex marriages, at least fifty lawmakers thought the matter should be put before the voters. Supporters of same-six marriage managed to stall a vote in the legislature throughout 2006, but it was unclear how much longer the delaying tactics would work.

Meanwhile, voters in seven more states—Colorado, Idaho, South Carolina, South Dakota, Tennessee, Virginia, and Wisconsin—approved constitutional amendments banning same-sex marriages, bringing the number of states with such amendments to twenty-six. In Arizona, the only other state where an amendment was on the ballot, voters rejected the measure, in part because it also would have barred the legislature from granting civil unions. Nineteen states, including Arizona, had statutes barring same-sex marriages.

Constitutional Amendment

Congressional Republicans pushed the adoption of an amendment to the federal Constitution banning gay marriage, but it fell short in both chambers. The move seemed designed to rally conservative Republican voters in an election year; opinion polls indicated that these core supporters of the party might stay away from the ballot boxes in November because they were demoralized by the war in Iraq and were frustrated that the Republican-led Congress had been unable to enact more of the conservative agenda. In 2004 efforts to turn out conservatives to vote for state constitutional gay marriage bans, particularly in Ohio, were credited with helping Bush win the election. *(2004 presidential election results, Historic Documents of 2004, p. 773)*

As he had in the past, Bush supported the proposed constitutional amendment, but in a White House speech on June 5, the president couched his endorsement in terms of stopping "activist judges" from defining marriage as something other than a union between a man and a woman. Bush's support for the amendment had always seemed somewhat tepid, perhaps in part because it was opposed by Vice President Dick Cheney, whose daughter Mary was a lesbian. Mary Cheney and her longtime partner further dismayed many conservatives when they announced in December that Mary was expecting a baby. First Lady Laura Bush was also on record as saying she did not believe gay marriage should be used as a "campaign tool."

Senate debate on the amendment began June 5 and ended on June 7 when the Senate rejected a motion to end debate on the issue by a 49–48 vote. Sixty votes were required to invoke cloture. Despite the amendment's defeat in the Senate, House Republican leaders decided to go ahead with a vote as part of the GOP's American "values" initiative, designed to appeal to the party's conservative voters. Although 236 House members voted for the amendment, it still fell 46 votes short of the two-thirds vote needed to pass a constitutional amendment. With the Democratic takeover of the

House and Senate in the November elections, it appeared unlikely that a same-sex marriage amendment would reach the floor of either chamber during the next two years.

"Don't Ask, Don't Tell"

In other action on gay rights issues during 2006, the U.S. Supreme Court ruled that colleges and universities that accept federal funding must allow military recruiters on campus despite campus policies that opposed the Pentagon's "don't ask, don't tell" policy. That policy allowed gays and lesbians to serve in the armed forces so long as they did not reveal or act on their homosexuality; military personnel were also forbidden to ask troops about their sexual orientation. At issue in the case was a federal statute that required colleges opposed to the policy to give the same access to military recruiters that they gave civilian recruiters or to risk losing any federal funding they received for any program. A unanimous Court rejected plaintiffs' argument that the statute violated their First Amendment rights to free speech and association. The amendment "affects what . . . schools must do . . . not what they may or may not say," Chief Justice John G. Roberts Jr. wrote. "Schools remain free under the statute to express whatever views they may have on the military's congressionally mandated employment policy, all the while retaining eligibility for federal funds."

Activists had been trying to repeal the "don't ask, don't tell" policy ever since it went into effect in 1994 but to no avail. Defense Secretary Donald H. Rumsfeld made clear that the policy would not be changed under his watch. According to the Servicemembers Legal Defense Network, which represented service members affected by the policy, more than 10,000 service members had been discharged for homosexuality since 2004. In 2005, 726 service members were discharged for being gay, according to the group, up about 10 percent from 2004. Estimates put the cost of the policy at as much as $363.8 million in its first ten years for the costs of recruiting and training both the discharged troops and their replacements.

Gays and Religion

Several religious organizations continued to struggle with the place of homosexuals in the congregation and in the clergy. In November the United States Conference of Catholic Bishops voted to continue to support traditional Roman Catholic teachings that called on homosexuals to remain celibate. The bishops also reaffirmed their opposition to same-sex marriages and to adoptions by lesbian and gay couples. The vote came a year after the Vatican issued a statement barring gay men from entering seminary or taking holy orders; the statement called homosexual acts "intrinsically immoral" and "objectively disordered." *(Background, Historic Documents of 2005, p. 863)*

The U.S. Episcopal Church, a member of the worldwide Anglican Communion, tried to mend a rift with that body in June, when it voted to "exercise restraint by not consenting to the consecration of any candidate" for bishop who was openly gay. The American church had plunged its congregations as well as others throughout the world into turmoil in 2003 when it ordained V. Gene Robinson, an openly gay cleric, as the bishop of New Hampshire. While many American congregations supported Robinson's ordination, others were deeply troubled by it, and some were not appeased by the June vote. In December eight parishes in Virginia voted to break their ties with the Episcopal Church and join the convocation of Anglicans in North America, a group of churches that had allied themselves with Archbishop Peter Akinola of Nigeria, a leader of the movement within the Anglican Community to rid the church of homosexual influences.

The move by the Virginia parishes was seen as another step leading toward a possible schism in the Anglican Community. *(Background, Historic Documents of 2005, p. 865)*

Moving in an opposite if somewhat confusing direction, the Committee on Jewish Law and Standards, the body that interpreted religious law for Conservative Jews, adopted three conflicting policies in December that together appeared to allow individual congregations to make their own choice about whether to ordain gay rabbis. One of the policies upheld a long-standing prohibition on gay rabbis. Another upheld a ban on homosexual activity but permitted ordination of gays and blessings of same-sex unions, while the third policy reiterated a ban on gay sexual relations. The votes were seen as an effort to stop the loss of Conservative Jews either to the liberal Reform movement, which allowed gay rabbis, or to the traditional Orthodox movement, which forbid ordination of either gays or women.

Following are excerpts from the court opinion, written by Judge Robert S. Smith, and the dissenting opinion, written by Chief Judge Judith S. Kaye, in which the New York Court of Appeals ruled on July 6, 2006, that New York's ban on same-sex marriages did not violate the state constitution. The decision consolidated four cases: Seymour v. Holcomb, Kane v. Marsolais, Samuels v. New York State Dept. of Health, *and* Hernandez v. Robles.

■ DOCUMENT ■

Seymour v. Holcomb

R. S. SMITH, J.:

We hold that the New York Constitution does not compel recognition of marriages between members of the same sex. Whether such marriages should be recognized is a question to be addressed by the Legislature....

Discussion

I

All the parties to these cases now acknowledge, implicitly or explicitly, that the Domestic Relations Law limits marriage to opposite-sex couples....

New York's statutory law clearly limits marriage to opposite-sex couples. The more serious question is whether that limitation is consistent with the New York Constitution.

II

New York is one of many states in which supporters of same-sex marriage have asserted it as a state constitutional right.... Here, plaintiffs claim that, by limiting marriage to opposite-sex couples, the New York Domestic Relations Law violates two provisions of the State Constitution: the Due Process Clause....

We approach plaintiffs' claims by first considering, in section III below, whether the challenged limitation can be defended as a rational legislative decision. The answer to this question, as we show in section IV below, is critical at every stage of the due process and equal protection analysis.

III

It is undisputed that the benefits of marriage are many. The diligence of counsel has identified 316 such benefits in New York law, of which it is enough to summarize some of the most important: Married people receive significant tax advantages, rights in probate and intestacy proceedings, rights to support from their spouses both during the marriage and after it is dissolved, and rights to be treated as family members in obtaining insurance coverage and making health care decisions. Beyond this, they receive the symbolic benefit, or moral satisfaction, of seeing their relationships recognized by the State.

The critical question is whether a rational legislature could decide that these benefits should be given to members of opposite-sex couples, but not same-sex couples. The question is not, we emphasize, whether the Legislature must or should continue to limit marriage in this way; of course the Legislature may (subject to the effect of the Federal Defense of Marriage Act) extend marriage or some or all of its benefits to same-sex couples. We conclude, however, that there are at least two grounds that rationally support the limitation on marriage that the Legislature has enacted. Others have been advanced, but we will discuss only these two, both of which are derived from the undisputed assumption that marriage is important to the welfare of children.

First, the Legislature could rationally decide that, for the welfare of children, it is more important to promote stability, and to avoid instability, in opposite-sex than in same-sex relationships. Heterosexual intercourse has a natural tendency to lead to the birth of children; homosexual intercourse does not. Despite the advances of science, it remains true that the vast majority of children are born as a result of a sexual relationship between a man and a woman, and the Legislature could find that this will continue to be true. The Legislature could also find that such relationships are all too often casual or temporary. It could find that an important function of marriage is to create more stability and permanence in the relationships that cause children to be born. It thus could choose to offer an inducement—in the form of marriage and its attendant benefits—to opposite-sex couples who make a solemn, long-term commitment to each other.

The Legislature could find that this rationale for marriage does not apply with comparable force to same-sex couples. These couples can become parents by adoption, or by artificial insemination or other technological marvels, but they do not become parents as a result of accident or impulse. The Legislature could find that unstable relationships between people of the opposite sex present a greater danger that children will be born into or grow up in unstable homes than is the case with same-sex couples, and thus that promoting stability in opposite-sex relationships will help children more. This is one reason why the Legislature could rationally offer the benefits of marriage to opposite-sex couples only.

There is a second reason: The Legislature could rationally believe that it is better, other things being equal, for children to grow up with both a mother and a father. Intuition and experience suggest that a child benefits from having before his or her eyes, every day, living models of what both a man and a woman are like. It is obvious that there are exceptions to this general rule—some children who never know their fathers, or their mothers, do far better than some who grow up with parents of both sexes—but the Legislature could find that the general rule will usually hold.

Plaintiffs, and *amici* supporting them, argue that the proposition asserted is simply untrue: that a home with two parents of different sexes has no advantage, from the point of view of raising children, over a home with two parents of the same sex. Perhaps they are right, but the Legislature could rationally think otherwise.

To support their argument, plaintiffs and amici supporting them refer to social science literature reporting studies of same-sex parents and their children. Some opponents of same-sex marriage criticize these studies, but we need not consider the criticism, for the studies on their face do not establish beyond doubt that children fare equally well in same-sex and opposite-sex households. What they show, at most, is that rather limited observation has detected no marked differences. More definitive results could hardly be expected, for until recently few children have been raised in same-sex households, and there has not been enough time to study the long-term results of such child-rearing.

Plaintiffs seem to assume that they have demonstrated the irrationality of the view that opposite-sex marriages offer advantages to children by showing there is no scientific evidence to support it. Even assuming no such evidence exists, this reasoning is flawed. In the absence of conclusive scientific evidence, the Legislature could rationally proceed on the common-sense premise that children will do best with a mother and father in the home.... And a legislature proceeding on that premise could rationally decide to offer a special inducement, the legal recognition of marriage, to encourage the formation of opposite-sex households.

In sum, there are rational grounds on which the Legislature could choose to restrict marriage to couples of opposite sex. Plaintiffs have not persuaded us that this long-accepted restriction is a wholly irrational one, based solely on ignorance and prejudice against homosexuals. This is the question on which these cases turn. If we were convinced that the restriction plaintiffs attack were founded on nothing but prejudice—if we agreed with the plaintiffs that it is comparable to the restriction in *Loving v Virginia* [1967], a prohibition on interracial marriage that was plainly "designed to maintain White Supremacy"... we would hold it invalid, no matter how long its history. As the dissent points out, a long and shameful history of racism lay behind the kind of statute invalidated in *Loving*.

But the historical background of *Loving* is different from the history underlying this case. Racism has been recognized for centuries—at first by a few people, and later by many more—as a revolting moral evil. This country fought a civil war to eliminate racism's worst manifestation, slavery, and passed three constitutional amendments to eliminate that curse and its vestiges. *Loving* was part of the civil rights revolution of the 1950's and 1960's, the triumph of a cause for which many heroes and many ordinary people had struggled since our nation began.

It is true that there has been serious injustice in the treatment of homosexuals also, a wrong that has been widely recognized only in the relatively recent past, and one our Legislature tried to address when it enacted the Sexual Orientation Non-Discrimination Act four years ago.... But the traditional definition of marriage is not merely a byproduct of historical injustice. Its history is of a different kind.

The idea that same-sex marriage is even possible is a relatively new one. Until a few decades ago, it was an accepted truth for almost everyone who ever lived, in any society in which marriage existed, that there could be marriages only between participants of different sex. A court should not lightly conclude that everyone who held this belief was irrational, ignorant or bigoted. We do not so conclude.

IV

Our conclusion that there is a rational basis for limiting marriage to opposite-sex couples leads us to hold that that limitation is valid under the New York Due Process and Equal Protection Clauses, and that any expansion of the traditional definition of marriage should come from the Legislature.

This Court is the final authority as to the meaning of the New York Constitution. . . .

. . . But both New York and Federal decisions guide us in applying the Due Process and Equal Protection Clauses.

A. Due Process

In deciding the validity of legislation under the Due Process Clause, courts first inquire whether the legislation restricts the exercise of a fundamental right, one that is "deeply rooted in this Nation's history and tradition." . . . (In this case, whether the right in question is "fundamental" depends on how it is defined. The right to marry is unquestionably a fundamental right. . . . The right to marry someone of the same sex, however, is not "deeply rooted"; it has not even been asserted until relatively recent times. The issue then becomes whether the right to marry must be defined to include a right to same-sex marriage.

Recent Supreme Court decisions show that the definition of a fundamental right for due process purposes may be either too narrow or too broad. In *Lawrence v Texas* [2003], the Supreme Court criticized its own prior decision . . . defining the right at issue as the right of "homosexuals to engage in sodomy." The Lawrence court plainly thought the right should have been defined more broadly, as a right to privacy in intimate relationships. On the other hand, in *Washington v Glucksberg* [1997], the Court criticized a lower federal court for defining the right at issue too broadly as a "right to die"; the right at issue in *Glucksberg*, the Court said, was really the "right to commit suicide" and to have assistance in doing so.

The difference between *Lawrence* and *Glucksberg* is that in *Glucksberg* the relatively narrow definition of the right at issue was based on rational line-drawing. In *Lawrence*, by contrast, the court found the distinction between homosexual sodomy and intimate relations generally to be essentially arbitrary. Here, there are, as we have explained, rational grounds for limiting the definition of marriage to opposite-sex couples. This case is therefore, in the relevant way, like *Glucksberg* and not at all like *Lawrence*. Plaintiffs here do not, as the petitioners in *Lawrence* did, seek protection against State intrusion on intimate, private activity. They seek from the courts access to a State-conferred benefit that the Legislature has rationally limited to opposite-sex couples. We conclude that, by defining marriage as it has, the New York Legislature has not restricted the exercise of a fundamental right. . . .

Where no fundamental right is at issue, legislation is valid under the Due Process Clause if it is rationally related to legitimate government interests. . . . Again, our earlier discussion answers this question. Protecting the welfare of children is a legitimate governmental interest, and we have shown above that there is a rational relationship between that interest and the limitation of marriage to opposite-sex couples. That limitation therefore does not deprive plaintiffs of due process of law.

B. Equal Protection

Plaintiffs claim that the distinction made by the Domestic Relations Law between opposite-sex and same-sex couples deprives them of the equal protection of the laws. This claim raises, first, the issue of what level of scrutiny should be applied to the legislative classification. The plaintiffs argue for strict scrutiny, on the ground that the legislation affects their fundamental right to marry . . . a contention we rejected above. Alternatively, plaintiffs argue for so-called intermediate or heightened scrutiny on two grounds. They say that the legislation discriminates on the basis of sex, a kind of discrimination that has been held to trigger heightened scrutiny. . . . They also say that discrimination on the basis of sexual preference should trigger heightened scrutiny. . . . We reject both of these arguments, and hold that the restriction of marriage to opposite-sex couples is subject only to rational basis scrutiny.

By limiting marriage to opposite-sex couples, New York is not engaging in sex discrimination. The limitation does not put men and women in different classes, and give one class a benefit not given to the other. Women and men are treated alike—they are permitted to marry people of the opposite sex, but not people of their own sex. This is not the kind of sham equality that the Supreme Court confronted in *Loving;* the statute there, prohibiting black and white people from marrying each other, was in substance anti-black legislation. Plaintiffs do not argue here that the legislation they challenge is designed to subordinate either men to women or women to men as a class.

However, the legislation does confer advantages on the basis of sexual preference. Those who prefer relationships with people of the opposite sex and those who prefer relationships with people of the same sex are not treated alike, since only opposite-sex relationships may gain the status and benefits associated with marriage. This case thus presents the question of what level of scrutiny is to be applied to legislation that classifies people on this basis. . . .

We resolve this question in this case on the basis of the Supreme Court's observation that no more than rational basis scrutiny is generally appropriate "where individuals in the group affected by a law have distinguishing characteristics relevant to interests the State has the authority to implement." . . . A person's preference for the sort of sexual activity that cannot lead to the birth of children is relevant to the State's interest in fostering relationships that will serve children best. In this area, therefore, we conclude that rational basis scrutiny is appropriate.

Where rational basis scrutiny applies, "[t]he general rule is that legislation is presumed to be valid and will be sustained if the classification drawn by the statute is rationally related to a legitimate state interest." . . . Plaintiffs argue that a classification distinguishing between opposite-sex couples and same-sex couples cannot pass rational basis scrutiny, because if the relevant State interest is the protection of children, the category of those permitted to marry—opposite-sex couples—is both underinclusive and overinclusive. We disagree.

Plaintiffs argue that the category is underinclusive because, as we recognized above, same-sex couples, as well as opposite-sex couples, may have children. That is indeed a reason why the Legislature might rationally choose to extend marriage or its benefits to same-sex couples; but it could also, for the reasons we have explained, rationally make another choice, based on the different characteristics of opposite-sex and same-sex relationships. Our earlier discussion demonstrates that the definition of marriage to include only opposite-sex couples is not irrationally underinclusive.

In arguing that the definition is overinclusive, plaintiffs point out that many opposite-sex couples cannot have or do not want to have children. How can it be rational, they ask, to permit these couples, but not same-sex couples, to marry? The question is not a difficult one to answer. While same-sex couples and opposite-sex couples are easily distinguished, limiting marriage to opposite-sex couples likely to have children would require grossly intrusive inquiries, and arbitrary and unreliable line-drawing. A legislature that regarded marriage primarily or solely as an institution for the benefit of children could rationally find that an attempt to exclude childless opposite-sex couples from the institution would be a very bad idea.

. . . We conclude that permitting marriage by all opposite-sex couples does not create an irrationally over-narrow or overbroad classification. The distinction between opposite-sex and same-sex couples enacted by the Legislature does not violate the Equal Protection Clause.

V

We hold, in sum, that the Domestic Relations Law's limitation of marriage to opposite-sex couples is not unconstitutional. We emphasize once again that we are deciding only this constitutional question. It is not for us to say whether same-sex marriage is right or wrong. We have presented some (though not all) of the arguments against same-sex marriage because our duty to defer to the Legislature requires us to do so. We do not imply that there are no persuasive arguments on the other side—and we know, of course, that there are very powerful emotions on both sides of the question.

The dissenters assert confidently that "future generations" will agree with their view of this case. . . . We do not predict what people will think generations from now, but we believe the present generation should have a chance to decide the issue through its elected representatives. We therefore express our hope that the participants in the controversy over same-sex marriage will address their arguments to the Legislature; that the Legislature will listen and decide as wisely as it can; and that those unhappy with the result—as many undoubtedly will be—will respect it as people in a democratic state should respect choices democratically made.

Accordingly, the orders of the Appellate Division in each case should be affirmed without costs.

KAYE, CHIEF JUDGE (dissenting):

Plaintiffs (including petitioners) are 44 same-sex couples who wish to marry. They include a doctor, a police officer, a public school teacher, a nurse, an artist and a State legislator. Ranging in age from under 30 to 68, plaintiffs reflect a diversity of races, religions and ethnicities. They come from upstate and down, from rural, urban and suburban settings. Many have been together in committed relationships for decades, and many are raising children—from toddlers to teenagers. Many are active in their communities, serving on their local school board, for example, or their cooperative apartment building board. In short, plaintiffs represent a cross-section of New Yorkers who want only to live full lives, raise their children, better their communities and be good neighbors.

For most of us, leading a full life includes establishing a family. Indeed, most New Yorkers can look back on, or forward to, their wedding as among the most significant events of their lives. They, like plaintiffs, grew up hoping to find that one person with whom they would share their future, eager to express their mutual lifetime pledge through civil marriage. Solely because of their sexual orientation, however—that is, because of who they love—plaintiffs are denied the rights and responsibilities of civil marriage. This State has a proud tradition of affording equal rights to all New Yorkers. Sadly, the Court today retreats from that proud tradition.

I. Due Process

Under both the State and Federal Constitutions, the right to due process of law protects certain fundamental liberty interests, including the right to marry. Central to the right to marry is the right to marry the person of one's choice. . . . Again and again, the Supreme Court and this Court have made clear that the right to marry is fundamental. . . .

The Court concludes, however, that same-sex marriage is not deeply rooted in tradition, and thus cannot implicate any fundamental liberty. But fundamental rights, once recognized, cannot be denied to particular groups on the ground that these groups have historically been denied those rights. Indeed, in recasting plaintiffs' invocation of their fundamental right to marry as a request for recognition of a "new" right to same-sex marriage, the Court misapprehends the nature of the liberty interest at stake. In *Lawrence v Texas* . . . the Supreme Court warned against such error.

Lawrence overruled *Bowers v Hardwick* [1986], which had upheld a Georgia statute criminalizing sodomy. In so doing, the *Lawrence* Court criticized *Bowers* for framing the issue presented too narrowly. Declaring that "*Bowers* was not correct when it was decided, and it is not correct today" . . . *Lawrence* explained that *Bowers* purported to analyze—erroneously—whether the Constitution conferred a "fundamental right upon homosexuals to engage in sodomy." . . . This was, however, the wrong question. The fundamental right at issue, properly framed, was the right to engage in private consensual sexual conduct—a right that applied to both homosexuals and heterosexuals alike. In narrowing the claimed liberty interest to embody the very exclusion being challenged, *Bowers* "disclose[d] the Court's own failure to appreciate the extent of the liberty at stake." . . .

The same failure is evident here. An asserted liberty interest is not to be characterized so narrowly as to make inevitable the conclusion that the claimed right could not be fundamental because historically it has been denied to those who now seek to exercise it. . . .

Notably, the result in *Lawrence* was not affected by the fact, acknowledged by the Court, that there had been no long history of tolerance for homosexuality. Rather, in holding that "[p]ersons in a homosexual relationship may seek autonomy for the[] purpose [of making intimate and personal choices], just as heterosexual persons do" . . . *Lawrence* rejected the notion that fundamental rights it had already identified could be restricted based on traditional assumptions about who should be permitted their protection. As the Court noted, "times can blind us to certain truths and later generations can see that laws once thought necessary and proper in fact serve only to oppress. As the Constitution endures, persons in every generation can invoke its principles in their own search for greater freedom.". . .

Simply put, fundamental rights are fundamental rights. They are not defined in terms of who is entitled to exercise them.

Instead, the Supreme Court has repeatedly held that the fundamental right to marry must be afforded even to those who have previously been excluded from its scope—that is, to those whose *exclusion* from the right was "deeply rooted." Well into the twentieth century, the sheer weight of precedent accepting the constitutionality of bans on interracial marriage was deemed sufficient justification in and of itself to perpetuate these discriminatory laws . . . much as defendants now contend that same-sex couples should be prohibited from marrying because historically they always have been. . . .

Under our Constitution, discriminatory views about proper marriage partners can no more prevent same-sex couples from marrying than they could different-race couples. Nor can "deeply rooted" prejudices uphold the infringement of a fundamental right. . . .

It is no answer that same-sex couples can be excluded from marriage because "marriage," by definition, does not include them. . . .

The claim that marriage has always had a single and unalterable meaning is a plain distortion of history. In truth, the common understanding of "marriage" has changed dramatically over the centuries . . . Until well into the nineteenth century, for example, marriage was defined by the doctrine of coverture, according to which the wife's legal identity was merged into that of her husband, whose property she became. A married woman, by definition, could not own property and could not enter into contracts. Such was the very "meaning" of marriage. Only since the mid-twentieth century has the institution of marriage come to be understood as a relationship between two equal partners, founded upon shared intimacy and mutual financial and emotional support. . . .

That restrictions on same-sex marriage are prevalent cannot in itself justify their retention. After all, widespread public opposition to interracial marriage in the years before Loving could not sustain the anti-miscegenation laws. . . . The long duration of a constitutional wrong cannot justify its perpetuation, no matter how strongly tradition or public sentiment might support it.

II. Equal Protection

By virtue of their being denied entry into civil marriage, plaintiff couples are deprived of a number of statutory benefits and protections extended to married couples under New York law. Unlike married spouses, same-sex partners may be denied hospital visitation of their critically ill life partners. They must spend more of their joint income to obtain equivalent levels of health care coverage. They may, upon the death of their partners, find themselves at risk of losing the family home. The record is replete with examples of the hundreds of ways in which committed same-sex couples and their children are deprived of equal benefits under New York law. Same-sex families are, among other things, denied equal treatment with respect to intestacy, inheritance, tenancy by the entirety, taxes, insurance, health benefits, medical decisionmaking, workers' compensation, the right to sue for wrongful death, and spousal privilege. Each of these statutory inequities, as well as the discriminatory exclusion of same-sex couples from the benefits and protections of civil marriage as a whole, violates their constitutional right to equal protection of the laws. . . .

. . . Because, as already discussed, the legislative classification here infringes on the exercise of the fundamental right to marry, the classification cannot be upheld unless it is necessary to the achievement of a compelling state interest. . . .

Although the classification challenged here should be analyzed using heightened scrutiny, it does not satisfy even rational-basis review, which requires that the classification "rationally further a legitimate state interest.". . . Rational-basis review requires both the existence of a legitimate interest and that the classification rationally advance that interest. Although a number of interests have been proffered in support of the challenged classification at issue, none is rationally furthered by the exclusion of same-sex couples from marriage. Some fail even to meet the threshold test of legitimacy.

Properly analyzed, equal protection requires that it be the legislated *distinction* that furthers a legitimate state interest, not the discriminatory law itself. . . . In other words, it is not enough that the State have a legitimate interest in recognizing or supporting opposite-sex marriages. The relevant question here is whether there exists a rational basis for *excluding* same-sex couples from marriage, and, in fact, whether the State's interests in recognizing or supporting opposite-sex marriages are rationally *furthered* by the exclusion. . . .

Defendants primarily assert an interest in encouraging procreation within marriage. But while encouraging opposite-sex couples to marry before they have children is certainly a legitimate interest of the State, the *exclusion* of gay men and lesbians from marriage in no way furthers this interest. There are enough marriage licenses to go around for everyone.

Nor does this exclusion rationally further the State's legitimate interest in encouraging heterosexual married couples to procreate. Plainly, the ability or desire to procreate is not a prerequisite for marriage. The elderly are permitted to marry, and many same-sex couples do indeed have children. Thus, the statutory classification here—which prohibits only same-sex couples, and no one else, from marrying—is so grossly underinclusive and overinclusive as to make the asserted rationale in promoting procreation "impossible to credit.". . .

Of course, there are many ways in which the government could rationally promote procreation—for example, by giving tax breaks to couples who have children, subsidizing child care for those couples, or mandating generous family leave for parents. Any of these benefits—and many more—might convince people who would not otherwise have children to do so. But no one rationally decides to have children because gays and lesbians are excluded from marriage. . . .

Marriage is about much more than producing children, yet same-sex couples are excluded from the entire spectrum of protections that come with civil marriage—purportedly to encourage other people to procreate. Indeed, the protections that the State gives to couples who do marry—such as the right to own property as a unit or to make medical decisions for each other—are focused largely on the adult relationship, rather than on the couple's possible role as parents. Nor does the plurality even attempt to explain how offering only heterosexuals the right to visit a sick loved one in the hospital, for example, conceivably furthers the State's interest in encouraging opposite-sex couples to have children, or indeed how excluding same-sex couples from each of the specific legal benefits of civil marriage— even apart from the totality of marriage itself—does not independently violate plaintiffs' rights to equal protection of the laws. . . .

The State plainly has a legitimate interest in the welfare of children, but excluding same-sex couples from marriage in no way furthers this interest. In fact, it undermines it. Civil marriage provides tangible legal protections and economic benefits to married couples and their children, and tens of thousands of children are currently being raised by same-sex couples in New York. Depriving these children of the benefits and protections available to the children of opposite-sex couples is antithetical to their welfare, as defendants do not dispute. . . . The State's interest in a stable society is rationally advanced when families are established and remain intact irrespective of the gender of the spouses. . . .

III. The Legislature

The Court ultimately concludes that the issue of same-sex marriage should be addressed by the Legislature. If the Legislature were to amend the statutory scheme by making it gender neutral, obviously the instant controversy would disappear. But this Court cannot avoid its obligation to remedy constitutional violations in the hope that the Legislature might some day render the question presented academic. After all, by the time the Court decided Loving in 1967, many states had already repealed their anti-miscegenation laws. Despite this trend, however, the Supreme Court did not refrain from fulfilling its constitutional obligation.

The fact remains that although a number of bills to authorize same-sex marriage have been introduced in the Legislature over the past several years, none has ever made it out of committee. . . .

It is uniquely the function of the Judicial Branch to safeguard individual liberties guaranteed by the New York State Constitution, and to order redress for their violation. The Court's duty to protect constitutional rights is an imperative of the separation of powers, not its enemy.

I am confident that future generations will look back on today's decision as an unfortunate misstep.

Decided July 6, 2006

Source: State of New York. Court of Appeals. *Seymour v. Holcomb.* No. 86, No. 87, No. 88, and No. 89. July 6, 2006. www.courts.state.ny.us/ctapps/decisions/jul06/86-89opn06.pdf (accessed January 14, 2007).

Other Historic Documents of Interest

Foley resignation from Congress,
  p. 595
Midterm elections, p. 645

United Nations on human rights,
  p. 765

President Bush on Vetoing Stem Cell Legislation

July 19, 2006

■■■■■ **THE DOCUMENT IN CONTEXT** ■■■■■

President George W. Bush cast the first veto of his presidency on July 19, 2006, rejecting a measure that would have lifted restrictions that he had placed on human embryonic stem cell research five years earlier. The House sustained the veto later that day. Scientists said such research held great promise for finding treatments for a range of incurable illnesses and conditions, such as diabetes, Parkinson's disease, some cancers, and spinal cord injuries. Under an order Bush issued on August 9, 2001, federal funding of human embryonic stem cell research was restricted to cells derived from stem cell colonies, or lines, that existed before he imposed the restrictions. By 2006 only twenty-one of those colonies were viable, and many researchers complained that those lines were now largely contaminated or weakened.

Bush's veto spurred several states to proceed with plans to fund private stem cell research, which was not affected by the federal restrictions. Many of those efforts had been put on hold until the legislation's fate was known. The veto also guaranteed that the stem cell controversy would be a key campaign issue in several midterm election races and may have been a factor in the turnover of House and Senate control to the Democrats. The Democratic takeover also virtually ensured another move in Congress to lift the federal restrictions on stem cell research.

Legislation Vetoed

Embryonic stem cell research was highly controversial. The stem cells were usually derived from embryos left over from in vitro fertilization therapies. To obtain the stem cells, the embryos had to be destroyed—a procedure equated with abortion by many people who believed that life began with conception. Many pro-life advocacy groups and religious organizations, including the Roman Catholic Church, had pressed for a federal ban on human embryonic research for any purpose and were deeply disappointed in 2001 when Bush decided to allow even limited federal funding of the research. *(Funding limits, Historic Documents of 2001, p. 539)*

Expanding the number of embryonic stem cell lines available for federal funding became an issue in the 2004 presidential campaign, particularly for Republicans. Most public opinion polls showed that a solid majority of Americans supported the research, and expansion of federal funding had some influential advocates, including former first lady Nancy Reagan; President Ronald Reagan (1981–1989) died of Alzheimer's disease, one of the conditions that might some day be treated by stem cell therapy. *(Reagan's death, Historic Documents of 2004, p. 316)*

On May 24, 2005, fifty Republicans defied their leadership to vote for a measure (HR 810) authorizing federal funding of research on stem cells derived from surplus embryos that would otherwise be discarded by fertilization clinics. The vote was 238–194, well short of the two-thirds majority needed to override Bush's threatened veto. In the Senate, sponsors of the expanded research thought they had enough votes to pass a similar measure, but the Republican leadership refused to bring the bill to the floor. Then in July 2005 Senate Majority Leader Bill Frist, a heart transplant surgeon from Tennessee who had backed Bush's 2001 order, changed his mind and agreed to support the bill. It still took a year of negotiation before the measure came to the Senate floor, where it passed on July 18, 2006, by a vote of 63–37. *(2005 action, Historic Documents of 2005, p. 318)*

The Senate also passed two other measures that were intended to provide political cover for senators opposed to the House measure. One (S 2754) would have encouraged researchers to find ways to derive stem cells using techniques that did not knowingly harm the fetus. The other (S 3504) would ban facilities, called "fetal farms" by their opponents, that might create embryos strictly for research. No such facilities were known to exist. The House cleared the fetal farm bill later on July 18 without a single dissenting vote. The other bill, however, was brought up under suspension of the rules and did not muster the two-thirds vote required for passage.

President Bush signed the fetal farm bill on July 19 but vetoed the stem cell research measure. "This bill would support the taking of innocent human life in the hope of finding medical benefits for others," Bush said, speaking from the East Room of the White House, where he was surrounded by children produced from frozen embryos that their parents had adopted. "It crosses a moral boundary that our decent society needs to respect, so I vetoed it." The House sustained the veto later that day, by a vote of 235–193—51 votes short of the two-thirds needed. It was the only veto Bush issued in his first six years in office. The only two-term president never to have issued a single veto was Thomas Jefferson (1801–1809); Bush was the first president since John Quincy Adams to serve a full four-year term without vetoing a bill.

Midterm Elections

Bush's veto turned the topic into a campaign issue in several key Senate and House races, where Democrats were trying to wrest seats from incumbent Republicans. In two states the stem cell issue may have been decisive. In Maryland, Democratic representative Benjamin L. Cardin easily bested his Republican opponent, Michael S. Steele, in that state's Senate race with a campaign that focused on the war in Iraq and expanded stem cell research. In Missouri, where an initiative that would have limited the state legislature's ability to regulate stem cell research was also on the ballot, the Democratic Senate candidate, Claire McGaskill, a supporter of stem cell research, squeaked by Republican incumbent Jim Tennant, an opponent of the research, by 2 percentage points. The ballot referendum also passed by a 2 percentage-point margin. The victories helped Democrats take control of the U.S. Senate with a one-seat margin.

In the U.S. House, where Democrats also took control, the incoming Speaker of the House, Nancy Pelosi of California, pledged to make a bill overturning the federal limits on stem cell research one of the party's first priorities in the new Congress. Even if Congress passed such a bill, it remained to be seen whether a new Congress could override the veto that President Bush would likely issue.

State Funding of Stem Cell Research

Bush's veto also prompted several states to move forward on plans to fund their own embryonic stem cell research. Although federal funding was restricted, there were no limitations on funding for embryonic stem cell research from other sources. On July 20, the day after Bush's veto, California governor Arnold Schwarzenegger arranged for a $150 million state loan to the California Institute of Regenerative Medicine. Under an initiative approved by state voters in 2004, the institute had been authorized to administer $300 million a year in stem cell research funding. But challenges from taxpayer and religious groups had prevented the institute from issuing bonds and awarding research grants. On the same day, Democratic governor Rod R. Blagojevich of Illinois made another $5 million available for research grants in that state. In April the state had awarded $10 million in public health funds for the effort under an executive order signed by Blagojevich.

In early December Connecticut announced that it had awarded a total of $20 million to twenty-one research projects in that state. Connecticut was committed to spending $100 million over ten years for stem cell research. A week later, on December 14, the New Jersey legislature authorized the state to issue $270 million in bonds to begin construction of three stem cell research centers in the state. These states and others that were planning similar efforts all hoped to generate huge economic benefits if the research proved successful.

Many scientists also hoped the state research programs would help slow the migration of top American stem cell researchers to foreign countries that did not have such tight funding restrictions. A week after Bush's veto, the European Union (EU) agreed to continue funding human embryonic stem cell research, although it adopted new rules to prevent human cloning and stipulated that EU funding could not be used for research activities that destroyed embryos. Because of its liberal laws, Singapore could become the principal center for human embryonic stem cell research. It allowed stem cells to be derived from aborted fetuses or discarded embryos from fertilization treatments. The government was building a stem cell bank and was actively courting scientists from the United States and elsewhere to work in its research labs.

Aftermath of South Korean Scandal

Fallout from one of the most notorious scientific forgeries in modern time continued in 2006, when South Korean scientist Hwang Woo Suk was indicted on charges of fraud and embezzlement in May. Hwang had earlier admitted fabricating research purporting to show that his research team had found an efficient way to clone human embryonic stem cells. The initial announcement of Hwang's "success" in 2005 had set off a whirl of activity, with hundreds of scientists visiting Hwang's lab in South Korea and many planning collaborative research projects with him. Hwang's admission and subsequent announcements that his lab never cloned a single human embryo were deeply disappointing to those who had believed Hwang's "discovery" to be a significant advance in stem cell research. The admission was also a major embarrassment for the South Korean government, which had named Hwang a "supreme scientist" and given his lab millions of dollars in research grants, and for the journal *Science,* which had published Hwang's original articles claiming to have cloned human embryos. *(Background, Historic Documents of 2005, p. 320)*

Following are excerpts from the statement made by President George W. Bush in the East Room of the White House on July 19, 2006, when he vetoed legislation lifting restrictions on federal funding of human embryonic stem cell research.

DOCUMENT

"Remarks on Signing the Fetus Farming Prohibition Act"

Good afternoon. Congress has just passed and sent to my desk two bills concerning the use of stem cells in biomedical research. These bills illustrate both the promise and perils we face in the age of biotechnology. In this new era, our challenge is to harness the power of science to ease human suffering without sanctioning the practices that violate the dignity of human life.

In 2001, I spoke to the American people and set forth a new policy on stem cell research that struck a balance between the needs of science and the demands of conscience. When I took office, there was no Federal funding for human embryonic stem cell research. Under the policy I announced 5 years ago, my administration became the first to make Federal funds available for this research, yet only on embryonic stem cell lines derived from embryos that had already been destroyed. My administration has made available more than $90 million for research on these lines. This policy has allowed important research to go forward without using taxpayer funds to encourage the further deliberate destruction of human embryos.

One of the bills Congress has passed builds on the progress we have made over the last 5 years, so I signed it into law. Congress has also passed a second bill that attempts to overturn the balanced policy I set. This bill would support the taking of innocent human life in the hope of finding medical benefits for others. It crosses a moral boundary that our decent society needs to respect, so I vetoed it.

Like all Americans, I believe our Nation must vigorously pursue the tremendous possibility that science offers to cure disease and improve the lives of millions. We have opportunities to discover cures and treatments that were unthinkable generations ago. Some scientists believe that one source of these cures might be embryonic stem cell research. Embryonic stem cells have the ability to grow into specialized adult tissues, and this may give them the potential to replace damaged or defective cells or body parts and treat a variety of diseases.

Yet we must also remember that embryonic stem cells come from human embryos that are destroyed for their cells. Each of these human embryos is a unique human life with inherent dignity and matchless value. We see that value in the children who are with us today. [Several children surrounded the president as he delivered his speech.] Each of these children began his or her life as a frozen embryo that was created for in vitro fertilization but remained unused after the fertility treatments were complete. Each of these children was adopted while still an embryo and has been blessed with the chance to grow up in a loving family.

These boys and girls are not spare parts. They remind us of what is lost when embryos are destroyed in the name of research. They remind us that we all begin our lives as a small collection of cells. And they remind us that in our zeal for new treatments and cures, America must never abandon our fundamental morals.

Some people argue that finding new cures for disease requires the destruction of human embryos like the ones that these families adopted. I disagree. I believe that with the right techniques and the right policies, we can achieve scientific progress while living up to our ethical responsibilities. That's what I sought in 2001, when I set forth my administration's policy allowing Federal funding for research on embryonic stem cell lines where the life and death decision had already been made.

This balanced approach has worked. Under this policy, 21 human embryonic stem cell lines are currently in use in research that is eligible for Federal funding. Each of these lines can be replicated many times. And as a result, the National Institutes of Health have helped make more than 700 shipments to researchers since 2001. There is no ban on embryonic stem cell research. To the contrary, even critics of my policy concede that these federally funded lines are being used in research every day by scientists around the world. My policy has allowed us to explore the potential of embryonic stem cells, and it has allowed America to continue to lead the world in this area.

Since I announced my policy in 2001, advances in scientific research have also shown the great potential of stem cells that are derived without harming human embryos. My administration has expanded the funding of research into stem cells that can be drawn from children, adults, and the blood in umbilical cords, with no harm to the donor. And these stem cells are already being used in medical treatments. With us today are patients who have benefited from treatments with adult and umbilical-cord blood stem cells. And I want to thank you all for coming.

They are living proof that effective medical science can also be ethical. Researchers are now also investigating new techniques that could allow doctors and scientists to produce stem cells just as versatile as those derived from human embryos. One technique scientists are exploring would involve reprogramming an adult cell—for example, a skin cell to function like an embryonic stem cell. Science offers the hope that we may one day enjoy the potential benefits of embryonic stem cells without destroying human life.

We must continue to explore these hopeful alternatives and advance the cause of scientific research while staying true to the ideals of a decent and humane society. The bill I sign today upholds these humane ideals and draws an important ethical line to guide our research. The Fetus Farming Prohibition Act . . . prohibits one of the most egregious abuses in biomedical research, the trafficking in human fetuses that are created with the sole intent of aborting them to harvest their parts. Human beings are not a raw material to be exploited or a commodity to be bought or sold, and this bill will help ensure that we respect the fundamental ethical line.

I'm disappointed that Congress failed to pass another bill that would have promoted good research. This bill . . . would have authorized additional Federal funding for promising new research that could produce cells with the abilities of embryonic cells but without the destruction of human embryos. This is an important piece of legislation. This bill was unanimously approved by the Senate; it received 273 votes in the House of Representatives but was blocked by a minority in the House using procedural maneuvers. I'm disappointed that the House failed to authorize funding for this vital and ethical research.

It makes no sense to say that you're in favor of finding cures for terrible diseases as quickly as possible and then block a bill that would authorize funding for promising and ethical stem cell research. At a moment when ethical alternatives are becoming available, we cannot lose the opportunity to conduct research that would give hope to those suffering from terrible diseases and help move our Nation beyond the current controversies over embryonic stem cell research.

We must pursue this research. And so I direct the Secretary of Health and Human Services, Secretary [Mike] Leavitt, and the Director of the National Institutes of Health to use all the tools at their disposal to aid the search for stem cell techniques that advance promising medical science in an ethical and morally responsible way.

Unfortunately, Congress has sent me a bill that fails to meet this ethical test. This legislation would overturn the balanced policy on embryonic stem cell research that my administration has followed for the past 5 years. This bill would also undermine the principle that Congress itself has followed for more than a decade, when it has prohibited Federal funding for research that destroys human embryos.

If this bill would have become law, American taxpayers would, for the first time in our history, be compelled to fund the deliberate destruction of human embryos. And I'm not going to allow it.

I made it clear to the Congress that I will not allow our Nation to cross this moral line. I felt like crossing this line would be a mistake, and once crossed, we would find it almost impossible to turn back. Crossing the line would needlessly encourage a conflict between science and ethics that can only do damage to both and to our Nation as a whole. If we're to find the right ways to advance ethical medical research, we must also be willing, when necessary, to reject the wrong ways. So today, I'm keeping the promise I made to the American people by returning this bill to Congress with my veto.

As science brings us ever closer to unlocking the secrets of human biology, it also offers temptations to manipulate human life and violate human dignity. Our conscience and history as a nation demand that we resist this temptation. America was founded on the principle that we are all created equal and endowed by our Creator with the right to life. We can advance the cause of science while upholding this founding promise. We can harness the promise of technology without becoming slaves to technology. And we can ensure that science serves the cause of humanity instead of the other way around.

America pursues medical advances in the name of life, and we will achieve the great breakthroughs we all seek with reverence for the gift of life. I believe America's scientists have the ingenuity and skill to meet this challenge. And I look forward to working with Congress and the scientific community to achieve these great and noble goals in the years ahead.

Thank you all for coming, and may God bless.

Source: U.S. Executive Office of the President. "Remarks on Signing the Fetus Farming Prohibition Act and Returning without Approval to the House of Representatives the 'Stem Cell Research Enhancement Act of 2005." July 19, 2006. *Weekly Compilation of Presidential Documents* 42, no. 29 (July 24, 2006): 1362–1365. Washington, D.C.: National Archives and Records Administration. www.gpoaccess.gov/wcomp/v42no29.html (accessed December 1, 2006).

UNICEF on Children at Risk in the Democratic Republic of Congo

July 24, 2006

The Democratic Republic of Congo held its first-ever truly free elections in 2006, completing the long process of ending what had been the biggest and deadliest war anywhere in the world since World War II. Joseph Kabila, who for three years had been president of an interim government, won an internationally sponsored election as president, and a new national assembly represented all of the country's main political factions.

The end of the war and the elections offered hope for Congo's future, but it was difficult to look past the country's many crushing problems, starting with the immense human and physical devastation resulting from the war. Congo in 2006 had virtually no public services of any kind; an economy fueled by foreign aid, corruption, and theft of the country's vast natural resources; and a fragile peace enforced by the largest-ever United Nations peacekeeping force. The UN estimated that some 4 million of Congo's 60 million people had died during the civil war and that more than 1,000 people were still dying each day from disease and starvation directly related to the war.

The new government's ability to deal with these problems was in question. Although he scored a decisive win in the elections, Kabila headed a coalition of convenience that was unified in name only. The interim government he had headed since 2003 had proven to be nearly as corrupt as, and no more able to deliver basic services than, the dictatorships that had governed the country almost continuously since independence in 1960.

The election was just the latest stage in ending a conflict that raged from 1998 to 2002 and often was called "Africa's First World War" because it directly involved six other African nations. Rival factions in 2002 signed a peace agreement mediated by South Africa, and large-scale fighting stopped in most areas during 2003. Even so, battles among various militias and tribal groups in eastern Congo continued all through 2006. *(Background, Historic Documents of 2005, p. 1027)*

Another landmark event involving Congo took place on March 17 when the new International Criminal Court took into custody Thomas Lubanga, a former rebel leader in the eastern Ituri region who had been charged with crimes involving the use of children in the war. Lubanga had been captured early in 2005 after rebels from his Hema tribe were accused of killing nine Bangladeshi peacekeepers. He was the first person ever arrested on a warrant from the new court, which the UN established—over fierce opposition from the Bush administration—to deal with major war crimes cases. The court began initial, pretrial hearings in the Lubanga case on November 9. *(International Criminal Court background, Historic Documents of 2003, p. 99)*

Elections

The peace agreements ending Congo's war originally called for two elections in 2005: a referendum on a new constitution, to be followed by elections for president and parliament. That schedule slipped, however, and the only voting held in 2005 was on the constitution, which voters approved overwhelmingly.

The follow-up elections for president and parliament were then set for March 2006, but logistical difficulties forced two more postponements, first to June 18 and then to July 30. Even then, some politicians, joined by bishops of the Catholic Church, voiced suspicions about the fairness of the election process and called for further delay. Among them was the country's most prominent opposition politician, Etienne Tshisikedi, who boycotted the elections. These critics charged that the UN had rigged the elections in favor of Kabila, and as evidence they cited the printing of some 5 million "extra" ballots; UN officials said the additional ballots were needed to make sure all polling places had enough on hand, but Kabila's opponents insisted the ballots were being premarked for him.

The United Nations, which had managed elections in dozens of countries, said the Congolese election was its biggest such challenge ever because of the country's enormous size (equal to the entire United States east of the Mississippi) and near total lack of roads, electrical and telephone lines, and other infrastructure. The UN budgeted $430 million for the elections, much of it to issue 25.5 million voter identification cards, to print more than 60 million ballots (one-half for the presidential race and one-half for the parliamentary races), and to pay more than 300,000 electoral workers to staff 53,000 polling stations. Because Congo had only about 300 miles of paved roads, most election workers reached the polls by airplanes, helicopters, bicycles, and river boats—or by foot, in some cases after a week-long trek through the jungle.

The vast majority of potential voters were illiterate and had only the vaguest idea what the elections were all about, so voter education was one of the biggest tasks facing election organizers. That task was made even more complex by the crowded ballots; more than 9,500 candidates were contesting the 500 parliamentary seats and more than 10,000 candidates were running for provincial assemblies.

To provide security for the elections, the European Union sent about 2,000 soldiers to Congo, where they temporarily aided the 17,000 members of the UN's peacekeeping force, called the United Nations Mission in the Democratic Republic of Congo (MONUC, French acronym for the *Mission de l'Organisation des Nations Unies en République Démocratique du Congo*). Most of the additional troops came from France and Germany. The election campaign saw several outbreaks of violence, some of it involving the army, that appeared to be related to politics, but the level of violence was minor compared to the previous years of warfare.

In the weeks before the official start of the campaign on June 29, the level of political discourse deteriorated sharply. Some candidates accused others of terrible crimes, while some opposition candidates appealed to nationalist sentiment by claiming their opponents were not sufficiently *congolite*, or Congolese; this was primarily a reference to Kabila, who was raised in Tanzania.

Election day was relatively peaceful as millions of people stood in long lines to cast their votes. For most Congolese, this was their first vote of any kind since 1970, when longtime dictator Mobutu Sese Seko ran as the sole candidate. The only previous multiparty election was after independence in 1960, when the charismatic Patrice Lumumba was elected prime minister; he was assassinated a few months later, the apparent victim of the cold war rivalry between the United States and the Soviet Union for influence in Africa.

Many voters were enthusiastic, saying they were thrilled to be participating in the country's political life for the first time; they proudly showed their thumbs, purple from the indelible ink that proved they had voted. Others were skeptical that any good would come from the election. The UN said 70.5 percent of the 25 million registered voters went to the polls.

As could be expected in such a volatile environment, some candidates insisted they had won and others charged massive fraud, even before the votes were counted. One of the country's four vice presidents, Azarias Ruberwa, said the election commission had stuffed ballot boxes on Kabila's behalf. Ruberwa had headed one of the largest militias during the war and was said to still command the loyalty of thousands of armed fighters. Observers from several international groups that observed the election said they witnessed numerous logistical problems and incidents of potential tampering, such as the dumping of ballots, but it was unclear how extensive these problems were.

The elections commission on August 20 announced results showing that Kabila was leading in the presidential race with 45 percent of the vote, which was short of the majority needed to avoid a second-round runoff. His closest rival was Jean-Pierre Bemba, with 20 percent; Bemba was another of the former rebel leaders who had been a vice president since 2003 under the peace agreements ending the war. Even before these results were announced, armed men loyal to Kabila and Bemba began fighting in Kinshasha, the capital. The fighting escalated the next day when units from Kabila's presidential guard attacked Bemba's house, trapping the candidate and several foreign diplomats who were meeting with him, among them the American head of the UN mission, William Lacy Swing. UN peacekeepers had to intervene to rescue Bemba and the diplomats and enforce a cease-fire.

In parliamentary elections, loyalists in Kabila's Alliance of the Presidential Majority won nearly 60 percent of seats in the National Assembly. Parties supporting Bemba won most of the remaining seats.

The second round of elections was held on October 29, by which time some of the logistical difficulties of the first round had been overcome, but many voters still feared a return to violence. Although rioters destroyed the polling stations in two northeastern towns, the voting generally was peaceful around the country, and international observer missions deemed it fair. Voter turnout again was a strong 65 percent.

Final results, published on November 15, showed Kabila winning 58 percent of the vote. The results fell along regional lines, with Kabila carrying most of the eastern provinces, where he was seen as having ended the war, and Bemba winning strong majorities in the western and central provinces, including Kinshasa. Bemba at first challenged the result as fraudulent but eventually conceded defeat. He said he would lead parliamentary opposition if he was awarded one of the 108 Senate seats to be filled by provincial assemblies in January 2007.

Kabila, age thirty-five, was inaugurated as president on December 6. He said he would base his presidency on "the trilogy of good governance, democracy, and respect for human rights." On December 30 Kabila named as prime minister Antoine Gizenga, head of the United Lumambist Party. Gizenga, who at age eighty-one was one of the country's veteran politicians, had finished third in the first round of presidential voting but threw his support to Kabila in the runoff.

Attempting to Maintain Stability

As had been the case all through the war, the eastern provinces of Congo were the most volatile during the year. UN officials estimated that about 8,000 rebels from Rwanda and Uganda remained in eastern Congo, along with nearly that many members of various Congolese militias loyal to tribal groups and rebel leaders who had refused to lay down their arms. Most of the Rwandans and Ugandans were Hutus who fled to Congo (then called Zaire) after the 1994 Rwandan genocide, during which Hutu extremists massacred an estimated 800,000 Tutsis and moderate Hutus. The presence of these Hutus in the eastern provinces of Congo had been a driving force in the civil war there. *(Background, Historic Documents of 1999, p. 860)*

The worse fighting early in the year took place in southeastern Katanga province, where army forces loyal to Kabila battled with Mai-Mai rebels. That fighting, which began in late 2005, drove more than 200,000 people from their homes; thousands of people were subjected to atrocities by one side or the other, and in some cases by both sides, UN officials said. When heavy rains prevented aid trucks from entering the region in April, the United Nations World Food Programme resorted to food drops from airplanes to feed an estimated 13,000 of the most affected refugees. These were the UN's first airdrops of food anywhere in the world in recent years outside the Darfur region of Sudan.

During the last half of the year nearly 5,000 militia members surrendered in eastern Congo and joined a UN-sponsored disarmament and demobilization program. Among these were some of the forces loyal to a dissident warlord, Laurent Nkunda, who had refused to accept the peace process, and elements of the Mai-Mai tribal militia in Katanga. Despite these developments, fighting continued at year's end in some areas, notably North Kivu, which had been one of the most conflicted zones in the country.

Much of the responsibility for ensuring stability in Congo rested with the United Nations mission. All through the transition process, the UN mission had two main tasks: a political role in mediating disputes among Kabila and the various opposition leaders, and a military role in attempting to prevent localized conflicts from escalating into another major war.

In its early years, the UN mission was widely criticized, both in Congo and internationally, for taking a passive approach to violence. That changed after the murder of nine Bangladeshi peacekeepers in February 2005 suggested that some militias were determined to drive the peacekeepers out of the country. UN troops launched numerous attacks on rebels in response to those killings and seized several towns that had been held by rebel groups.

The mission's security function was expected to change over time into training of the Congolese army, but for the moment UN peacekeepers were still needed to ward off a return to violence. Recognizing that the situation remained fragile, the UN Security Council on December 22 extended for two more months the presence of 916 troops who had been added to the MONUC force for the elections. Officials said the UN mission's political role would diminish sharply as a result of the elections, with mission diplomats concentrating on helping the new government establish functioning ministries.

Humanitarian Issues

Despite the advent of peace in most of Congo in 2003, the country remained one of the world's biggest zones of humanitarian crisis. In addition to the estimated 4 million people who had died as a result of the war, another estimated 3.4 million people had been driven from their homes—many of them permanently. The United Nations also estimated that fully half the population—about 30 million people—did not have a steady supply of food.

The United Nations on February 13 launched what it called a Humanitarian Action Plan to help meet the emergency needs of the most vulnerable people in Congo. The plan carried a $681 million price tag and involved 330 projects dealing with the entire range of humanitarian issues. "We are talking about a country where 1,200 people die in silence every day from the lingering effects of war," UN Secretary General Kofi Annan said in explaining the breadth of the problem. The international response to the UN aid appeal was slow, however. By mid-May, the British charity Oxfam said only $94 million had been contributed.

The War's Impact on Children

As part of their campaign to get the world to pay more attention to the lingering consequences of the war in Congo, UN agencies during 2006 focused on the plight of millions of children who had been victimized by the war. On June 20, Annan sent a special report to the Security Council documenting abuses of children in the conflicted eastern provinces—abuses such as abduction, rape, and forced recruitment into armed forces—that Annan said were continuing long after the war technically had ended.

The United Nations Children's Fund (UNICEF) also highlighted the fate of Congo's children with a report, released on July 24, by British journalist Martin Bell, who served as a UNICEF ambassador for humanitarian emergencies. Reporting on a recent visit to Congo, Bell said children had suffered unimaginable trauma during the war and were still dying from consequences of the war at the estimated rate of 600 a day.

Bell focused particular attention on the tens of thousands of children who had been forced into service in the numerous armed groups. "Children are used not only as soldiers, but as porters, spies, and sexual slaves," he said, noting that an estimated 30 to 40 percent of the children forced into the militias were girls.

Later in the year, even after the elections, news organizations and human rights groups reported that some armed groups were still recruiting or holding children. In mid-October Amnesty International estimated that 11,000 of the estimated 30,000 children who had been forced into military service were still in the hands of rebel armies; many of them were girls whom fighters considered as their possessions, the organization said.

Following are excerpts from the report, "Child Alert: Democratic Republic of Congo," written by Martin Bell, a UNICEF ambassador for humanitarian emergencies, and published by UNICEF on July 24, 2006.

DOCUMENT

"Child Alert: Democratic Republic of Congo"

A Tsunami of Death Every Six Months

A human tragedy has unfolded in the Democratic Republic of the Congo (DRC) over the past eight years. The continuing conflict between the Congolese army and rebel militias—despite a nearly four-year-old peace agreement and a transitional government in place—has resulted in a death toll greater than in any conflict since World War II. Since 1998, nearly 4 million people have been killed by war or disease, or have simply disappeared without a trace. Put another way, every six months, the burden of death from conflict in the DRC is similar to the toll exacted by the 2004 Indian Ocean tsunami. The DRC is currently witnessing the world's deadliest humanitarian crisis since World War II.

Conflict-related deaths have exacerbated the national crude mortality rate. The International Rescue Committee has estimated that 1,200 people die each day in the DRC as a direct or indirect cause of the conflict. Over half of them are children.

As so often happens in conflicts, the casualties are disproportionately high among the young. Children bear the brunt of conflict, disease and death, not only as victims; they are also witnesses to, and sometimes forced participants in, atrocities and egregious crimes that can inflict lifelong physical and psychological harm. For many children growing up in DRC, particularly in the east, their childhoods have been, and are still being, stolen from them.

Part of the horror of this conflict is its scale. But the figures do not tell the full story. The conflict in DRC no longer makes waves or headlines. Perhaps because the war has gone on so long, or because the situation has at times seemed so hopeless, it is the war the world has largely forgotten.

Part of the reason for this may also be the lack of access to the conflict zones. Insecurity in the worst-affected areas in the east of the country has placed some of the victims beyond the reach of aid agencies. UNICEF and its partners are preparing to implement programmes that provide long-term development, in addition to emergency relief. But ongoing conflict has caused the displacement of millions of people, and without improvement in security, field offices in the eastern towns of Kalemie, Bunia and Goma, and mobile operations in Beni, as well as the southern town of Lubumbashi, are limited to helping people survive.

Peace is the missing link between a violent past and a more hopeful future. It is the prerequisite for investment in vital basic services that have been limited by conflict, such as free universal primary education, free basic health care for children under five, mosquito nets for pregnant women and children under five, rehabilitation of water sources, counselling and support for vulnerable women and children.

The road to peace can begin with free and fair elections. Elections are not a panacea for all a nation's woes, but they can go a long way to restoring order and stability. On 30 July

2006, for the first time in over 40 years, the Congolese people will have a real choice at the polls and a real chance to end what is often called the "First World War" of Africa.

The Burden of War

The burden of war has taken an enormous toll on Congolese children. Again, the figures speak for themselves: Each year, more children under five die in DRC than in China (a country with 23 times the population), and than in all the Latin American countries combined. Children are caught up in violence as victims: Sexual assaults on women and children have reached epidemic proportions; 25,000 *reported* cases of rape occurred in eastern DRC in 2005. They are caught up in war as refugees and internally displaced people: Constant migration robs them of schooling, health care and the chance for a normal life. And they are caught up in combat as soldiers and camp-followers.

Sexual Assaults on Women and Children

The victims of rape or other forms of sexual violence in DRC could easily be in the hundreds of thousands. The Heal Africa Hospital in Goma, run by the organization Doctors on Call for Service (DOCS), has provided care to more than 4,500 rape victims in the past three years alone. Sexual violence is consciously deployed as a weapon of war, by one group against another, to humiliate, intimidate and tear apart families and entire communities or even force them into an alliance. Gang rapes, mutilation, rape involving the insertion of objects into the victim's genitals and forced rape by one victim upon another are not uncommon in this largely ungoverned eastern part of the country.

The victims include those who are forced to witness these atrocities against their spouses, parents, children, relatives and friends.

Girls and women who become pregnant as a result of rape often become social pariahs, rejected by their families and their villages.

As a consequence of extreme sexual violence and difficult pregnancies for very young girls, an untold number of women suffer from vesicovaginal fistula, a debilitating condition resulting from trauma to the body that prevents women from controlling their bodily functions.

The number of people living with HIV is currently estimated at 1.1 million. For women and children whose lives are subjected to this extreme violence, HIV/AIDS is part of their daily reality: Many combatants involved in the war are HIV positive. The risk of transmission is higher when women, particularly young girls, are violently raped, because of internal injuries. Very young children and adolescent girls are frequently singled out for their youth and relative defencelessness or in the fallacious belief that having sex with them will cure AIDS.

Children Associated with Armed Groups or Forces

Exact numbers are hard to estimate, but DRC is thought to have the largest concentration of child soldiers in the world. At the height of the war, estimates suggested that as many as 30,000 children were fighting or living with armed forces or militia groups. Nine groups have been listed by the United Nations as parties to conflict that recruit or use children in armed conflict.

Children are forced into armed forces and groups by extreme poverty, abandonment, homelessness and the random hazards of war. Many are left with no choice but to join the militias who offer a modicum of protection and provisions. It is estimated that 30 to 40 per cent of children associated with armed forces and groups are girls. Many are held in captivity as sexual slaves for extended periods of time. Children are used not only as soldiers, but as porters, spies and sexual slaves.

Demobilization has been in operation since the peace agreement of 2003 and there have been signs of success. So far, 18,000 children have been released and reintegrated; however, a significant number still remains with armed groups resisting participation in the demobilization efforts. Reintegration of children in communities that were highly affected by the conflict and so have very limited prospects for children is proving to be a challenge. Faced with the choice of destitution at home or paid military service with the armed groups, the young former combatants will all too often re-enlist.

Violence Uproots Children's Lives

As of October 2005, at least 1.6 million people were internally displaced by conflict in DRC. Since then, the numbers have increased. At the close of 2005, it was estimated that 120,000 people were fleeing their homes every month. While the numbers are concentrated in the east, there are also displaced persons in the northern and western parts of the country. Violence and instability in the region have caused an estimated 400,000 refugees to flee DRC to Burundi, Rwanda and Sudan, among others. DRC itself is home to hundreds of thousands of refugees from neighbouring countries.

After fleeing their homes, refugees arrive by the thousands, often near the camps of the UN Mission to the DRC (MONUC) for security, with nothing but what they can carry. Refugee and internally displaced children are often separated from their families and become vulnerable to those who prey on them. The difficult living conditions are particularly hard on children, often causing poor nutrition and the spread of disease. It is a priority for aid agencies to establish safe spaces for children within camps so they may also continue their education. But when months in camps grow to years, as in eastern DRC, the disruption to the learning process has permanent consequences for children.

Growing Up without Access to Education or Health Care

DRC is one of the poorest countries in the world and the lack of education is chronic. The number of children out of primary school approaches 4.7 million children, including 2.5 million girls—almost half the total number of primary-school-age children. Even outside the areas of conflict, extreme poverty puts school out of reach for many because it is too expensive. Teachers are extremely underpaid or receive no pay at all.

The eight-year conflict has led, inevitably, to worsening poverty and deprivation in an already impoverished nation. According to the latest estimates, 71 per cent of the population have no access to adequate sanitation facilities and over half of the population lack access to improved drinking water sources.

As in other emergencies, children are the most vulnerable. About 1 out of every 3 children under the age of one is not vaccinated against measles. The chronic lack of basic health-care services heightens the risk of death from preventable causes. One such example is malaria, one of the biggest killers of children in DRC. Only 17 per cent of children under five with diarrhoea receive oral rehydration and continued feeding, one of the lowest rates in the world.

These conditions can have fatal consequences for children. DRC has among the worst child survival and nutrition rates in the world. Half a million children under five die each year, earning the DRC the grim distinction of being one of the top three deadliest places in the world in which to be born. An alarming 31 per cent of children under five are underweight.

Lost Childhood

DRC is a resource-rich country; gold, diamond, copper and cobalt are mined throughout the country. Too many children are forced to work in the dangerous and deplorable conditions that exist in these mines, more susceptible to illness and injury. Child labour is one of many reasons why so few children regularly attend school. In urban centres throughout DRC, children live on the streets, separated and sometimes abandoned by their families. They are routinely attacked by other street children and at times abused by the police. They are prime targets for armed forces and military groups looking for new recruits.

The Election: The Chance of a Lifetime

After so much suffering, DRC does not lack its champions and well-wishers. The United Nations is breaking records with its US $422 million support of the election scheduled for 30 July 2006. While this election represents an enormous challenge, there is reason to hope.

The election is historic because it is the country's first free vote in over 40 years.

The Congolese people *want* to vote. 25.6 million have already registered, over 77 per cent of the eligible population. Despite the war and the insecurity, 70 per cent turned out to vote in the referendum on 18-19 December 2005, approving a new constitution.

The election is critical. It is only a beginning, and will not by itself bring the conflict to an end. But it can be the catalyst for the emergence of a new DRC. Until now the lives of families and entire communities have been defined by conflict. Many children have grown up in the past eight years not knowing anything but war. The Congolese people must see results to encourage further peace and stability.

Children must be at the heart of the postelection agenda. Nothing else can have a greater effect in shaping the country's future.

A Call to Action

For the people of the Democratic Republic of the Congo, indifference is not an option. Most of the lives at stake are those of their children. UNICEF urges the international community to first fund measures to save the lives of displaced people and others affected by the conflicts and then to help them return to some sense of normalcy in the coming months.

As humanitarian aid workers continue the emergency response on the ground, it is critical that pressure be placed on the political factions in DRC to ensure that children are not manipulated and exploited as part of the election process. Leading up to the formation of a permanent government is the time to get children on the agenda.

The UN agencies in the DRC, including UNICEF, stand ready to help the new Congolese Government to rapidly emerge from the forthcoming elections so it may begin to develop the infrastructure and programmes needed to improve people's lives. That includes giving special priority to children by investing in the social services sector and committing to the demobilization of all remaining children associated with armed forces and groups.

The success of a newly elected government will depend on the international community to provide resources but also to be vigilant, long after the results of this election are announced.

Source: United Nations. United Nations Children's Fund (UNICEF). "Child Alert: Democratic Republic of Congo." July 24, 2006. www.unicef.org/childalert/drc (accessed February 25, 2007).

Other Historic Documents of Interest

Inauguration of Liberian president,
   p. 3
Peacekeeping operation in Somalia,
   p. 717

UN resolution on Darfur,
   p. 497
United Nations on human rights,
   p. 765

WTO Director General on the Suspension of Trade Talks

July 24, 2006

■■■■■■■■ **THE DOCUMENT IN CONTEXT** ■■■■■■■■

World trade talks intended to level the playing field between rich and poor countries collapsed at the end of July 2006 and had not resumed by the end of the year. The major stumbling block, as it had been since the talks began in 2001, was trade in agriculture, with the United States and the European Union (EU) each accusing the other of not going far enough to ease the tariffs and subsidies that protected domestic farmers, while most of the developing world remained unwilling to open their markets until the developed world acted.

The suspension of negotiations was a blow, perhaps mortal, to the ambitious "development agenda" underlying the trade talks, which were meant to lower trade barriers in ways that encouraged economic development in poor countries. In announcing the indefinite suspension of the talks on July 24, Pascal Lamy, the director general of the World Trade Organization (WTO), said the suspension could only hurt poor developing countries whose integration into global trade markets was their "best hope for growth and poverty alleviation." He also warned that outright failure could encourage a surge of protectionism that would hurt the global economy at a time when political instability was threatening many areas of the world. "Let me be clear: there are no winners and losers in this assembly," Lamy said. "Today there are only losers."

Farm Trade: A Perennial Stumbling Block

The trade talks were the latest in several rounds of international negotiations since the 1930s. These talks, known as the Doha Round, began at a meeting of trade ministers in Doha, Qatar, in November 2001, with the explicit aim of making it easier for developing countries to sell their products and services on world markets.

The central issue in these talks involved how and when the wealthy countries—principally the United States, Australia, Canada, and Europe—would abandon practices that hindered agricultural trade by the developing counties. These practices included export subsidies and price supports that gave financial benefits to farmers so their goods would be more competitive on world markets. The wealthy nations also imposed taxes, called tariffs, on imports of farm goods to protect their own farmers. Agriculture long had been the most controversial aspect of the trade talks because farmers retained substantial political clout in all the wealthy countries and were reluctant to give up any of their competitive advantages.

At negotiations in Hong Kong in December 2005, the United States and the EU offered the first major concession on agricultural trade. Under their plan, all farm export subsidies would be eliminated by 2013, but with an undefined "substantial" portion of the subsidies eliminated sooner. Negotiators hoped this concession would allow final agreement on a new world trade package by the end of 2006 so that the U.S. Congress could consider it by July 1, 2007. That date was important because it marked the expiration of the president's so-called fast track authority, which required Congress to vote on a trade deal in its entirety without amending it in ways that might be unacceptable to other countries. It was generally assumed that Congress would not extend this authority for President George W. Bush beyond that date—thus setting an effective deadline for concluding the trade negotiations. *(Background, Historic Documents of 2005, p. 409)*

No Agreement, Plenty of Recriminations

The year 2006 began with some optimism that the main parties to the dispute might be able to hammer out an agreement. "You see people coming together" to work out the disagreements, Rob Portman, the U.S. trade representative, told the *New York Times* on January 28. "If the Doha Round fails, we all have something to lose." But that optimism faded after meetings in London March 10–12 among negotiators from the so-called G-6—the European Union, United States, Brazil, India, Japan, and Australia—failed to break the deadlock. Hopes sunk further on April 18, when President Bush tapped Portman to head the White House Office of Management and Budget and made Portman's deputy, Susan C. Schwab, the chief U.S. trade negotiator. Although Schwab was widely respected for her trade knowledge and negotiating skills, the personnel shift was interpreted by many trade experts as a sign that the administration was not expecting a quick breakthrough in the Doha talks. "It's bad news as far as the Doha Round is concerned," said Sen. Charles E. Grassley, R-Iowa, chairman of the finance committee.

Talks in late April and early July again failed to make any progress on the main sticking points. The basic difficulty involved the concessions the United States was willing to make on domestic supports and those the EU was willing to make on tariffs. The United States, which spent about $19 billion a year to prop up the prices of corn, wheat, dairy products, and other major commodities, said it was willing to cut its farm subsidies by as much as 60 percent but only if other countries, including Europe and the big developing countries, cut their farm tariffs by an average of about two-thirds. Washington wanted to ensure that if American farmers were forced to give up most of their domestic subsidies, they would be able to offset those losses by having greater access to foreign markets.

Europe, however, was reluctant to make a substantial cut in its tariffs without commitments from emerging market countries, especially Brazil, India, and China, to reduce their tariffs on industrial goods. There was also some doubt that the EU trade representative, Peter Mandelson, could deliver on any promise to lower farm tariffs more than the 38 percent cut that was already on the table. As talks began at the WTO's Seventh Ministerial Conference in Geneva, Switzerland, on June 30, Mandelson said the EU was prepared to "significantly improve" its previous offers on tariffs, cutting them by 50 percent or so. Moments later, in a news conference, French trade minister Christine Lagarde refuted Mandelson's statement. "There is no room to maneuver in that direction," she said flatly. France, which arguably had the most powerful farm union in Europe, had long opposed concessions on tariffs. For their part, the developing countries said they were not willing to make any more concessions until the United States and Europe came up with better offers. "We're not here . . . to accept more market access," Zambia's trade minister, Dipak Patel, told the *Washington Post.* "We've had enough of that."

Despite the impasse, G-6 negotiators agreed to meet again at the end of July. For the next three weeks WTO director general Lamy worked intensely to try to salvage the negotiations. He attended the summit in St. Petersburg, Russia, of the Group of Eight (G-8) industrialized nations (Canada, France, Germany, Italy, Japan, Russia, the United Kingdom, and the United States), where he asked the leaders to give their trade representatives more negotiating flexibility. He met with trade envoys individually and privately, seeking to find out exactly what concessions they would be willing to make. On July 24, after yet another meeting with the G-6 trade ministers, Lamy announced that he was formally suspending the talks. "The gaps remain too wide," he said. The WTO General Council formally ratified the suspension on July 27.

The main parties to the failed talks lost no time blaming others for the collapse. "Unfortunately, the Americans were not able or willing to do their part. They preferred to stand still," Mandelson said. U.S. agriculture secretary Mike Johanns disagreed with that assessment. "We are ready to be flexible. There just was nothing there to grab onto to let us take that step," he said. To many developing countries and their advocates, the finger-pointing missed the point that the trade talks intended to spur economic growth in developing countries appeared to be "between intensive care and the crematorium," as India's trade minister Kamal Nath put it. Raymond C. Offenheiser, president of Oxfam America, lamented the loss of "the once-in-a-lifetime opportunity to bring about an international trading system that is not rigged for the rich and hurting the poor. . . . Five years of haggling and debate have ended in a sad display of political failure."

Although some trade experts continued to hold out hope that the trade talks might be restarted, those hopes faded when Democrats won control of Congress in the November midterm elections, making it all but certain that Congress would refuse to extend the president's fast-track authority when it expired in July 2007. Many parties to the Doha talks said they saw little hope of the talks reviving until after the 2008 presidential elections.

Meanwhile the United States, Europe, and other countries appeared to be stepping up their efforts to negotiate bilateral and regional trade agreements, which could lessen pressure for any international trade agreement. But protectionist sentiment was likely to be a major factor in the success of those agreements, as it was in the WTO talks. In the United States, for example, members of both political parties nearly scuttled a measure promoted by the Bush administration to provide normal trade relations with Vietnam. The measure was passed only at the end of the session and only after it was attached to an unrelated must-pass bill. One of the objections some lawmakers raised was the potential impact of the agreement on textile-producing areas in the United States.

Additionally, the EU and India announced in October that they hoped to complete a bilateral trade deal by early 2009, an ambitious schedule for negotiations whose ultimate goal was the elimination of regulations designed to protect domestic industries in both countries.

The collapse of the Doha Round also raised questions about the viability of the WTO itself, with some commentators suggesting that it was in danger of slipping into irrelevancy. Trade experts thought the failure of trade talks made it more likely that developing countries would pursue their grievances through litigation. Brazil, for example, was seeking permission from the WTO to impose punitive damages on U.S. imports because it said Washington had not done enough to reform its cotton subsidies, which the WTO had ruled illegal in 2005. Such disputes could eventually lead countries to defy WTO rules and rulings or they could be an impetus drawing WTO members back to the negotiating tables. One positive note was an agreement between the United States and Russia in November that helped clear the way for Russia's eventual entry into the WTO.

Following is the text of a statement on July 24, 2006, by Pascal Lamy, director general of the World Trade Organization, announcing at the seventh Ministerial Conference in Geneva, Switzerland, that he was recommending the formal suspension of the Doha Round of international trade negotiations.

■■■■■■■■■■■■■■■■■■ **DOCUMENT** ■■■■■■■■■■■■■■■■■■

"DG Lamy: Time Out Needed to Review Options and Positions"

Thanks a lot for coming here today at a very short notice but events have precipitated in the last hours and I feel it is essential that we lucidly look together at where we are and what remains of our goal of concluding the [Doha] Round by the end of the year. I cannot hide the sad truth: we are in dire straits.

On 1 July, the TNC [Trade Negotiations Committee] requested me to conduct intensive and wide-ranging consultations with the aim of facilitating the urgent establishment of modalities in agriculture and NAMA [Non-Agricultural Market Access]. I was also requested to report to you as soon as possible. As I stated at the time, my aim in these consultations would be to facilitate and catalyze agreement among Members, who continued to remain the main actors in the process.

Since then I have undertaken this consultative process as requested, starting with the members of the G6 and then progressively widening the circle of my contacts with individual delegations and with groups.

I also attended the outreach session at the G8 Summit in St. Petersburg, where a number of your Heads of State and Government were present. I was very frank with the Leaders, and told them that they needed to revise their instructions to you and give you more flexibility. My request for flexibilities was twofold: one, that they improve the numbers on the table and two, that they agree to adjust what they are ready to pay with what they can reasonably expect for that price. I also warned them that failing this, they risked the very situation in which we now find ourselves. During the meeting there were some encouraging signs of additional flexibility at that highest political level.

To follow up on these signals, the G6 Ministers held a meeting here yesterday, chaired by myself with the assistance of the Agriculture and NAMA Chairs. This was a lengthy and detailed meeting, but at its conclusion, it remained clear that the gaps remain too wide.

From the discussions over this weekend, it is clear that the main blockage is on the Agriculture legs of the triangle of issues the G6 has been trying to address. Despite some improvement on numbers which were informally floated and in particular on market access for developed countries, the gap in level of ambition between market access and domestic support remained too wide to bridge. This blockage was such that the discussion did not even move on to the third leg of the triangle—market access in NAMA.

The situation is now very serious. Without the modalities in Agriculture and NAMA, it is now clear that it will not be possible to finish the Round by the end of 2006. For one thing, the time necessary to prepare and finalize the schedules of concessions is just not there. Furthermore, while discussions among the G6 on a limited number of key issues have been a precondition to further progress, we need always to remember that the G6 does not negotiate for the rest of the membership. There are also many other issues than the so-called triangle which would remain to be addressed in order to reach agreement on full modalities. The timing has always been very tight, but the continuing blockage on a few key points means we have simply run out of time for the rest.

Faced with this persistent impasse, I believe that the only course of action I can recommend is to suspend the negotiations across the Round as a whole to enable the serious reflection by participants which is clearly necessary. Time-out to review the situation, examine available options and review positions.

In practical terms, this means that all work in all Negotiating Groups should now be suspended, and the same applies to the deadlines that various groups were facing.

It also means that the progress made to date on the various elements of the negotiating agenda is put on hold, pending the resumption of the negotiations when the negotiating environment is right. Significant progress has been made in all areas of the negotiations, and we must try together to reduce the risk that it unravels.

This is what I will suggest at the General Council meeting on Thursday. I do not intend to propose any new deadlines or a date for resumption of activity in the Negotiating Groups. This can only come when the conditions exist to permit renewed progress, and this means changes in entrenched positions. The ball is clearly in your court. I have discussed this suggestion with the Chairs of the Negotiating Groups just before this meeting and they agree with me that this is the best course of action at this moment.

In the meantime, I urge you all to use this period of reflection for precisely that—for serious and sober reflection on what is at stake here. We all know that this is the most ambitious of all the trade rounds over the past 50 years. In fact, what is already on the table today is potentially worth two to three times more than previous rounds, whether for developed or for developing countries.

As I told leaders in St Petersburg, failure of this Round would be a blow to the development prospects of the more vulnerable Members, for whom integration in international trade represents the best hope for growth and poverty alleviation. This is why it is called "the development round": it is intended to be a contribution to the Millennium Development Goals.

Failure, in my view, would also send out a strong negative signal for the future of the world economy and the danger of a resurgence of protectionism at a time when the pace of globalization is weighing heavily on the social and economic fabric of many countries and when geopolitical instability is on the rise. This is only too obvious if one looks today at the international situation out there, I mean, outside this room.

All your leaders and governments have repeatedly stressed their desire to conclude the Round, and it cannot be acceptable that this commitment is not acted upon. If the political will really exists, there must be a way. But it is not here today. And let me be clear: there are no winners and losers in this assembly. Today, there are only losers.

For my part, I will of course continue my contacts with participants at every level, and I will also remain available to all Members, as will the Negotiating Group Chairs, for any contacts you may wish to have with us. My priority as Director-General will continue to be to defend the integrity of the WTO system and to continue to assist the membership to reach agreement.

You can count on me to do everything I can to keep up the pressure for the political movement which would permit a resumption of the negotiations. However, it should remain clear that this must come from you, the Members. It is how you can achieve this movement that I urge you all to reflect upon during this time out.

Source: World Trade Organization. Trade Negotiations Committee. "DG Lamy: Time Out Needed to Review Options and Positions." July 24, 2006. www.wto.org/english/news_e/news06_e/tnc_dg_stat_24july06_e.htm (accessed December 4, 2006).

UN Secretary General Annan on the State of Affairs in Haiti

July 28, 2006

■■■■■■■■■ **THE DOCUMENT IN CONTEXT** ■■■■■■■■■

Voters in Haiti elected a new president and parliament in 2006, nearly two years after the previous, democratically elected president, Jean-Bertrand Aristide, was forced into exile as a result of a gang uprising and pressure by the United States. Elections in February returned to power Rene Preval, who once was a close ally of Aristide and the only elected president of Haiti who had completed a full five-year term in office. Preval took office on May 14 and pledged to address all the problems that made Haiti by far the poorest and most violence-prone country in the Western hemisphere.

Preval was certain to need sustained international support because Haiti could do little for itself. The United Nations stationed more than 8,300 peacekeeping troops and police officers in Haiti as part of a broad international effort to establish functioning governmental institutions and dampen chronic violence by the criminal gangs that terrorized the cities and countryside. Donor countries and international institutions had pledged $750 million in immediate aid to Haiti but often were slow in delivering on those promises.

The new government and its foreign backers made limited progress during the year on a daunting list of challenges. In a July 28 report to the UN Security Council on Haiti's initial postelection period, Secretary General Kofi Annan noted that the underlying causes of the February 2004 uprising against Aristide "still exist" and threatened the country's stability. These included the presence of armed gangs in urban slums (some run by former army officers), widespread unemployment, narcotics trafficking, and weak governmental institutions, including the police and criminal justice systems, Annan said. *(Background, Historic Documents of 2005, p. 329)*

Elections Finally Held

An interim government that took power after the ouster of Aristide promised to hold new elections but postponed the voting repeatedly during 2005 and once again at the beginning of 2006. Under the country's constitution, a new government was supposed to take office on February 7, 2006, which would have been the completion of Aristide's five-year term. When it became clear in late 2005 that the February 7 deadline would not be met, Haitian and international officials traded accusations over who was to blame, particularly for the slowness in distributing identity cards to more than 3.5 million potential voters. On January 7 the government set a new election date of February 7.

There was no shortage of candidates seeking office. Thirty-three candidates registered for the presidential contest, and forty-five political parties fielded more than 1,400 candidates for the 30 Senate and 90 Chamber of Deputies seats. An agronomist by profession, Preval was the leading presidential candidate from the outset. He had served as president from 1996 to 2001, filling in between the two terms to which Aristide was elected but did not complete because he was ousted from power. Although he had been closely associated with Aristide and his Fanmi Lavalas Party, Preval in 2005 had formed a new party called Lespwa ("hope") and claimed to be independent from the factionalism of the past. Since stepping down from the presidency in 2001, Preval had lived in his hometown of Marmelade in northern Haiti, where he ran agricultural development projects and provided community access to the Internet. He was expected to get most of his support from the country's most impoverished areas, including the vast, violence-plagued slum of Port-au-Prince known as Cite Soleil.

On February 7, more than 60 percent of registered voters went to the polls. The voting generally was peaceful, although there were a few incidents because of long lines and widespread confusion at polling stations. Two people reportedly died of exhaustion while waiting to vote, and two men (one of them a police officer) died in violence in one town. All of Haiti's previous experiences with elections had been marred by vote-rigging and charges of fraud, but many voters seemed confident that the election this time would be fair.

Initial results showed Preval well ahead with more than 60 percent of the vote, prompting charges of fraud from a competitor, industrialist Charles Henri Baker, who represented Haiti's small community of business leaders. The outlook changed suddenly on February 12, when the Provisional Electoral Council released new preliminary figures showing Preval's share had dropped below the 50 percent threshold needed to avoid a runoff election. More than 4 percent of all ballots were found to be blank, and more than 100,000 others were discarded because of irregularities. The number two candidate, Leslie Manigat, had just under 12 percent of the vote. Preval supporters reacted angrily to the news, staging large demonstrations in Port-au-Prince and other cities.

Preval urged calm but also said he likely would contest the results, which he said reflected "gross errors and probably gigantic fraud" in the electoral process. Worried that the protests by Preval's supporters would spiral into widespread violence, diplomats convened at the UN and in Haiti to discuss a proposal by Brazil—which commanded the UN peacekeeping force—to convince Manigat, Baker, and others to concede the election to Preval. While these talks were under way, boxes containing thousands of ballots—some marked for Preval and others left blank—were discovered in a dump north of Port-au-Prince.

After nearly three full days of protests by Preval supporters, the electoral council met late on February 15 and agreed on a compromise that cut short the counting of ballots. It was decided that the blank ballots would be allocated among the candidates in proportion to their share of the vote. This raised Preval's share of the total to 51.21 percent, enough to elect him without a runoff. Preval was declared the winner the next day, February 16.

Preval's supporters promptly switched their demonstrations from protests to joyful celebrations. Other candidates criticized the procedure and implied that Preval had stolen the election; Manigat, for one, called the result a "Machiavellian comedy of imposing a winner." Even so, the opponents did not file legal challenges or send their supporters into the streets. Diplomats involved in the compromise said it was necessary to avoid a prolonged election process that might have broken into violence and torn Haiti apart once again

Results for the parliamentary elections showed that only two candidates won enough votes to avoid a runoff, so another round of elections was scheduled for March. That voting was delayed until late April.

Among the dozens of pressing questions after the February elections was whether Preval would allow his former mentor, Aristide, to return to Haiti from his two-year exile in South Africa. Aristide told South African radio on February 21 that he planned to return home "as soon as possible." Preval immediately said Aristide, or any other Haitian, could return home. Aristide stayed in South Africa, however, reportedly because Preval later made it clear that he did not want him to return. It was widely assumed that Aristide's presence would undermine Preval's authority and might trigger renewed strife in Haiti.

Preval Takes Office

The latest electoral schedule called for the new president to take office on March 29—seven weeks behind the constitutional requirement—but even this plan fell victim to delay and was pushed back to mid-May, after the runoff in the parliamentary elections. In late March Preval traveled to the United States for meetings at the United Nations in New York and with the Organization of American States in Washington. In a speech to the Security Council and at a news conference on March 27, Preval appealed for increased international aid to Haiti, including the release of $1.2 billion he said had been pledged but not yet delivered.

The second round of parliamentary elections was held on April 21. This round featured none of the controversy that plagued the February 7 voting, but only about 20 percent of registered voters went to the polls. Preval's Lespwa Party captured the largest single block of seats in both chambers but did not secure a majority, thus ensuring that coalitions would be needed to form a government and pass legislation. Three seats went unfilled in this round; follow-up elections for them were held on December 3 as part of voting for more than 1,400 seats on municipal councils.

The newly elected parliament met for the first time on May 10, marking the first time any parliament had met since Aristide's ouster more than two years earlier. Preval finally took office on May 14 during a four-hour ceremony that featured large rallies where supporters chanted "Preval, Preval, we've been waiting for you." In a brief inaugural address, the soft-spoken president pleaded with his compatriots for calm and dialogue. "The answer is simple, the answer is clear: We have to build peace," he said. "If we don't talk to each other, we're going to fight each other." The day was marred only by a riot at the national prison about one-half mile from the parliament building. The United States was represented at the ceremony by Florida governor Jeb Bush, the younger brother of President George W. Bush.

Preval on June 6 appointed an eight-member cabinet, headed by Jacques-Edouard Alexis as prime minister and with members from seven parties represented in the parliament. The new government's chief priority was what it called a social pacification program, which emphasized creating jobs for many of the estimated two-thirds of adult Haitians who were unemployed—many of whom had never held a job. Alexis said a particular need was to provide jobs, roads, schools, and other services in rural areas to stem the flow of people into urban slums. By year's end aid from foreign countries and international institutions such as the UN and the World Bank had established programs to clean up and repair roads, bridges, canals, schools, and water-treatment systems; these programs were employing an average of 200,000 people a day.

The government took two potentially significant steps in August. First, on August 8, it outlined an extensive plan to reform the national police, beginning with a detailed review of current police officers and the launching in January 2007 of a large-scale training program. On August 29 the government appointed a seven-member commission to promote disarmament and dismantlement of urban gangs. As of mid-December, only two groups, with a total of 104 members, had entered a disarmament program, and UN officials said several of those gang members appeared to still be engaging in criminal activities.

On top of all its other problems, Haiti continued to suffer from natural disasters, the impact of which was heightened by the deforestation of nearly all the countryside. Hurricane Ernesto struck Haiti on August 27, killing four people and damaging or destroying more than 800 homes. Heavy rains in October and November destroyed hundreds more houses and severely damaged agricultural crops.

Renewed Violence

Haiti's many problems were compounded by violence that in recent years had become woven into the very fabric of national life. Much of the violence stemmed from the stresses in a society where unemployment was high and public services were all but nonexistent. The most dangerous violence was caused by dozens of armed gangs in the cities and even rural areas; some gangs simply reflected the frustrations of unemployed urban youth, but others were engaged in criminal activities, including narcotics trafficking and kidnappings for ransom.

Haiti had experienced a serious wave of kidnappings and shootings in December 2005, but the situation calmed down during much of the period before and after the elections early in 2006. A new wave of violence broke out the first week of July, when more than twenty people were killed in clashes between gangs in the Martissant neighborhood of Port-au-Prince. This was followed by a rash of kidnappings in the capital, during which more than thirty people were seized, three of them U.S. citizens. In September armed gangs in Port-au-Prince killed at least one dozen people, including a local human rights activist,, and on October 12 five people were executed, gangland style, in the capital. A report issued by the Roman Catholic Church in mid-November said at least 228 people had been killed in violent incidents from June through September.

The UN Mission

One of the many reasons for the violence in Haiti was the lack of a functioning security service. Aristide had disbanded the national army in 1995, creating a cadre of armed and angry former soldiers, many of whom formed the gangs and militias that eventually helped drive him from power in 2004. Haiti's national police counted some 4,000 members, but few had any training or equipment, and police units often were no matched for armed gangs. Much of the responsibility for providing security in Haiti fell instead to a Brazilian-led peacekeeping force, the United Nations Stabilization Mission in Haiti (MINUSTAH, French acronym for the *Mission des Nations Unies pour la stabilisation en Haïti*), which had been in place since mid-2004. As of late 2006, MINUSTAH had 6,662 military troops and officers and 1,742 police officers.

During its first year or so in Haiti, the UN force had come under wide criticism for failing to tackle the gangs. Some critics said the UN soldiers too often holed up in their command posts in urban slum areas and failed to patrol the streets; slum residents complained that the peacekeepers were trigger-happy and fired indiscriminately when attacked. The UN mission also experienced a number of personnel problems, which were highlighted by the suicide on January 7 of the Brazilian commander, Gen. Urano Teixeira DaMatta Bacellar, who was found dead in his Port-au-Prince hotel room.

After Preval took office, senior UN officials traveled to Haiti for discussions on the future role of MINUSTAH. In his report to the Security Council, Secretary General Annan said a high priority was helping the government establish rule of law and a governmental presence, particularly in the provinces, where the national government long had been weak. The Security Council on August 15 extended the mandate of MINUSTAH for six months.

MINUSTAH faced two large-scale, but generally nonviolent demonstrations in Port-au-Prince in mid-October. Annan later said these protests represented the common frustration of Haitians with the overall situation. Annan told the Security Council in July and December that a sizable UN force remained essential in Haiti for the immediate future and that cutbacks in the force would be possible only in proportion to Haiti's ability to manage by itself. The UN force stepped up its patrols of urban neighborhoods late in the year; one result was the killing by unidentified gunmen in Port-au-Prince of two soldiers from Jordan on November 11.

Foreign Aid

Because it had little in the way of a functioning economy, Haiti in recent years relied heavily on foreign aid, both in terms of grants and loans from foreign governments and international institutions, and from cash money (called remittances) sent back home by Haitians who had emigrated to the United States and other countries. About 54 percent of Haiti's population lived in extreme poverty, on below $1 a day; 78 percent existed on less than $2 a day.

During the last three years of Aristide's administration, foreign donors withheld more than $500 million in promised aid in hopes of pressuring him to keep a promise to hold new parliamentary elections. After Aristide was ousted, international donors in July 2004 pledged $1.3 billion in short-term aid. As of March 2006, about 90 percent of that had been disbursed to the Haitian government, but not all of it had been spent. One of the largest projects was the reconstruction of roads, which had deteriorated from decades of neglect. As of late 2006, about $210 million was being spent to rebuild roads, and another $280 million was planned for the coming two years. Despite these and other efforts, Annan said in his July report to the Security Council that the foreign aid so far had been "insufficient to produce a tangible improvement in the living situation of the Haitian people, to create jobs and ensure the delivery of basic services."

At a conference held in Port-au-Prince in July, international donors pledged another $750 million to fund economic recovery and other programs over the next year; this exceeded the $540 million sought by the Haitian government. At a follow-up conference in Madrid on November 30, Prime Minister Alexis noted that only 1 percent of the $750 million pledged in July had been delivered. Donor representatives said they were working to speed the delivery of aid, but they also called on Haiti's government to put more emphasis on battling corruption.

The U.S. Congress on December 11 cleared a omnibus trade and tax-cut package that included a provision eliminating tariffs on clothing manufactured in Haiti. The country's once-thriving apparel industry had fallen victim to the country's chronic instability as well as competition from China and other countries. President Bush signed that measure into law (PL 109–432) on December 20.

Following are excerpts from a July 28, 2006, report to the United Nations Security Council by Secretary General Kofi Annan on the situation in Haiti.

DOCUMENT

"The United Nations Stabilization Mission in Haiti"

II. Major Developments

A. Political Developments

2. During the reporting period, the most significant political event was the conduct of free and fair national elections, which led to the establishment of a broad-based Parliament and the formation of a multi-party Government, following extensive consultations. Those achievements, which took place in a fragile security environment, reflected the commitment of the Haitian people to a democratic electoral process, and the active and sustained support of MINUSTAH United Nations Stabilization Mission in Haiti] and the international community.

3. Despite the difficulties encountered, the elections were widely regarded as a success, enabling the Haitian population to exercise its vote freely and fairly. For the first time in recent history, the legitimacy of the elections was not contested. Forty-five political parties and 33 presidential candidates competed, and over 60 per cent of registered voters participated in the presidential and first-round legislative elections on 7 February 2006. Turnout in the second round of the legislative elections, which has traditionally enjoyed lower participation, still exceeded 1 million voters. . . .

VI. Observations and Recommendations

89. With the successful completion of the national elections, a new page in the history of Haiti has been turned. Today, the people of Haiti have a unique opportunity to break the cycle of violence and poverty and move towards a future of stable and peaceful development. In this, they will be guided by a new leadership which emerged from a free, fair and inclusive electoral process, conducted in safety and dignity. President Preval has shown a

commendable determination to reach out to all political and social forces in Haiti in a spirit of reconciliation and dialogue, leaving behind decades of tension and exclusion. The appointment of a broad-based Government under Prime Minister Alexis and the adoption by the Haitian authorities of an ambitious, yet balanced, policy agenda have laid the foundation for Haiti's recovery and renewal. The implementation of the reform agenda—the modernization of the State and wealth creation—could benefit from an enhanced partnership with the international community, including MINUSTAH and the United Nations country team. Ultimately, however, the Haitian authorities and the people will need to actively take ownership of that agenda in order to ensure its lasting success.

90. The needs of the country remain vast and the challenges immense. The security situation continues to be worrying and destabilizing, in particular the crime situation in the capital, as the sources of instability still exist and the national security capacity to address them remains inadequate. Illicit trafficking in weapons and drugs remains an obstacle to successfully fighting crime, impunity and corruption. The institutions of the State, including the Haitian National Police, the judicial system and the institutions of government, require extensive assistance in order to function appropriately at all levels. An inclusive country-wide dialogue with all political and social forces will need to be nurtured continuously in order to consolidate advances achieved so far. Poverty reduction and socio-economic development are important priorities, as are rapid and visible improvements in the daily lives of the Haitians.

91. At present, Haiti cannot address those challenges all by itself. International partners should therefore extend timely, adequate and coherent support to the new authorities in the above-mentioned areas. . . . MINUSTAH, as part of an international division of labour, stands ready to offer the Haitian authorities targeted assistance, based on its comparative advantages, in the following two areas: ensuring a secure and stable environment to allow the ongoing political process to continue and humanitarian and development work to be conducted in safety; and providing institutional support to rule of law reform and to institutions of governance, in particular at the regional and local levels. All these efforts will be underpinned by the human rights work of the Mission and a political role for my Special Representative, including through his good offices. In addition, MINUSTAH will provide support for the organization of the remaining elections, which should be held as soon as feasible. Enhanced MINUSTAH resources will be required to implement those activities. . . .

92. In particular, the MINUSTAH police need to be strengthened with SWAT-qualified personnel and equipment, as part of its formed police units, as well as with expert advisers in counter-kidnapping and anti-gang operations, as part of its police contingent, to better support the Haitian National Police. This qualitative strengthening is needed since gang violence and kidnappings have emerged as an overriding impediment to stabilization in Haiti. They block the sustainable implementation of institutional strengthening, poverty reduction and economic development programmes by the Haitian authorities and donors, and are a serious obstacle to normal economic activity and productive investment.

93. It is important to recognize that there are limitations to this mandate. While the Mission intends to maximize its crime prevention role, it will not be able to respond to criminality in an exhaustive manner. Neither will the MINUSTAH security presence at border crossings and selected ports and crossroads be sufficient to fully deter illicit activities, including the trans-shipment of drugs and weapons. I therefore call upon the international

community, in particular those with close relations to Haiti and its people, to come together in a unified fashion to complement the activities of MINUSTAH in areas where it does not have capacity or mandate and to work closely with MINUSTAH in those areas where it does. I would welcome in particular the involvement of regional partners, such as OAS [Organization of American States] and CARICOM [the Caribbean Community]. New opportunities may open up in this regard now that Haiti has found its place again among the countries of the Caribbean Community.

94. I also appeal to the Haitian authorities to take full advantage of the assistance offered by the international community and, drawing upon MINUSTAH support as required, to help further reforms by adopting key national policies, such as the Haitian National Police reform plan, key legislation related to the independence of the judiciary, a disarmament policy and priorities in the areas of dialogue and reconciliation. The Haitian authorities should make maximum use of the expertise and support available from MINUSTAH for the strengthening of the rule of law sector.

95. Now that an elected government and legislature are in place, the new authorities should be given adequate means to succeed, including for the organization of the outstanding elections. I therefore call on donors to provide urgent and generous support to the Haitian authorities, in particular in the context of the pledging conference held in Port-au-Prince on 25 July, especially to address those short-term socio-economic requirements that are indispensable for the continuing stability of the country given the high expectations of the people. At the same time, I would like to stress that pledges and disbursements are only a first step. Rapid implementation of development projects bringing visible relief to the Haitian people is essential. Job creation and delivery of basic services should be a key aim. The United Nations system stands ready to assist the Haitian authorities and donors to establish a monitoring and evaluation mechanism to facilitate the coordination of their efforts.

96. The United Nations reiterates its commitment to the Haitian authorities to assist with the implementation of national priorities. In order to enable MINUSTAH to do so effectively, I recommend that the Security Council approve the proposals regarding the mandate and resources of MINUSTAH set out in section 111 above and extend the Mission for a period of at least 12 months. This is the minimum time needed to establish a solid basis for rule of law reform, achieve some initial results and progress towards democratic governance, in particular at the local level. It would also send an important signal to the Haitian people of the enduring commitment of the international community. The Mission's military strength will need to be maintained at the current ceiling of 7,500 troops and the police strength augmented by 54 individual police officers for institutional support, which brings the total strength to 1,951. Furthermore, 16 seconded corrections officers are required to adequately discharge the responsibilities of MINUSTAH in the prison system.

97. The United Nations is grateful for the continuing engagement of troop- and police-contributing countries. Their engagement will need to be sustained and further augmented in the area of police with additional francophone officers possessing specific skills to support the reform of the National Police, as well as with specialized capacities to enhance the ability of MINUSTAH to deliver advice, training and operational support to the Haitian National Police in the fight against gang violence and kidnappings. The unwavering support of members of the Core Group, donors and regional organizations will remain equally important for MINUSTAH to succeed in its challenging mission.

98. Finally, I would like to extend my warm appreciation to Juan Gabriel Valdes, who served as my Special Representative until the end of May and whose remarkable political vision and inspiration were crucial to enabling credible and inclusive elections in Haiti. I would also like to welcome my new Special Representative, Edmond Mulet, and express my gratitude to him and to all MINUSTAH personnel for their dedication, perseverance and commitment to peace and security in Haiti, while carrying out their tasks in often dangerous and demanding circumstances.

Source: United Nations. Security Council. "Report of the Secretary-General on the United Nations Stabilization Mission in Haiti." S/2006/592, July 28, 2006. www.un.org/Docs/sc/sgrep06.htm (accessed February 20, 2007).

Other Historic Documents of Interest

President Castro on the Temporary Transfer of Power in Cuba

July 31, 2006

■■■■■■■■■■■■ **THE DOCUMENT IN CONTEXT** ■■■■■■■■■■■■

Cuban president Fidel Castro, the world's longest serving head of government and one of the world's most controversial and colorful leaders, stepped aside "provisionally" on July 31, 2006, after undergoing intestinal surgery. Castro, who turned eighty on August 13, yielded power to his younger brother, Raul Castro, who was seventy-five. Fidel Castro remained hospitalized, and Raul Castro apparently remained in power, through the rest of the year. While keeping Castro's precise condition a state secret, the Cuban government repeatedly denied rumors that he was suffering from cancer or some other terminal disease and insisted he would return to power soon.

Perhaps more than anyone else still alive in 2006, Castro personalized the cold war era, of which his revolution had been a notable event. With his brother and a band of leftist revolutionaries, Castro spent three years in the 1950s battling Cuba's authoritarian government, finally succeeding in January 1959 in driving president Fulgencio Batista from power. Castro established a "socialist republic" in Cuba and attempted to export his personalized brand of communism to other countries in Latin America and even in Africa. In the ensuing decades thousands of Cubans fled to the United States, especially Florida, where they became a major political force behind a policy of using economic sanctions to force Castro from power—a policy that still had not succeeded after four decades. *(Background, Historic Documents of 2004, p. 246)*

Shock in Cuba, Celebrations in Miami

The news of Castro's illness came on July 31, when the government published a "proclamation" in which Castro delegated the three main positions he had held in recent years—first secretary of the central committee of the Communist Party, commander-in-chief of the armed forces, and president of the Council of State and Government—to his brother. Castro also delegated to other aides his functions as "the main driving force" in Cuba's education, energy, and health programs.

News reports said Castro's announcement stunned Cubans, many of whom had never known a leader other than Castro. Several hundred people gathered in the center of Havana to demonstrate support for Castro, but most people seemed content to follow the news over state-run television and radio. Reporters quoted many Cubans as saying they expected Castro to recover, some of them citing the quality of the country's health system, which had been one of Castro's main achievements. The few antigovernment Cubans willing to speak to reporters said they feared yet another of the government's periodic crackdowns on dissidents.

Across the Florida Straits, Cuban exiles (and their descendants) in the Miami area were jubilant. Thousands of celebrating people crowded into the streets of Miami's "Little Havana" neighborhoods, honking car horns, dancing, and cheering "Cuba Libre!" ("Free Cuba!").

The following day, August 1, Cuban television aired a statement by Castro acknowledging that he was ill because of a "sharp intestinal crisis with sustained bleeding." Even so, the statement quoted Castro as saying he was "stable" and was feeling "perfectly fine."

The announcement of Castro's illness was all the more surprising because it came just five days after he delivered one of his trademark lengthy speeches to a crowd of cheering supporters. Castro spoke for more than two hours on July 26 at the annual Revolution Day ceremonies commemorating the guerrilla attack he led in 1953 against the army's Moncada barracks in the town of Santiago. That attack failed and Castro was briefly imprisoned, but three years later Castro and his band of leftist guerrillas launched a new war that brought them to power in 1959. Ever since, Castro had celebrated the July 26 anniversary of his assault on the Moncada barracks as the beginning of his revolution.

In his 2006 speech, Castro derided a proposal that had been endorsed two weeks earlier by President George W. Bush for an $80 million fund to help Cuban exiles plan what Bush called the "transition from the repressive control of the Castro regime to freedom and a genuine democracy." Castro said Cuba did not need U.S. help "to vaccinate and teach our people to read and write." In his July 31 proclamation, Castro said the "stress" of his July 26 appearances had contributed to his medical condition.

Most observers of the Cuban government said the transfer of power to Raul Castro was mostly symbolic. Raul Castro had been defense minister for years, had always served as his brother's chief deputy, and was widely expected to continue most major policies, even after Fidel Castro died. Raul Castro had suggested earlier in the year that he would head a collective leadership, rather than the one-man leadership of his brother; one indication of that change was Fidel Castro's designation of other aides to head the government's education, energy, and heath departments.

Some experts on Cuba also noted that the Castro brothers had built a strong cadre of supporters throughout the government and society generally—suggesting that the regime was not as fragile as communist governments in Eastern Europe and the Soviet Union, which collapsed in a two-year period starting in 1989. The collapse of the Soviet Union had a major impact on Cuba, which had long depended on handouts from Moscow to help it survive an economic embargo the United States imposed in stages since the early 1960s. Cuba endured economic hardship for much of the 1990s, only to find a savior in the person of Venezuelan president Hugo Chavez, who used his country's oil wealth to provide discounted energy supplies to Cuba. A rabble-rousing leftist, Chavez proclaimed himself as a protégé of Castro, and by 2006 Chavez had taken Castro's place as Washington's least favorite Latin American leader.

Castro's Slow Recovery

In the weeks and months after Castro's surprising announcement, the Cuban government had little to say about its leader's medical condition or recovery. Key aides emerged periodically to say Castro was doing well and to offer assurances that the government was in good hands and running efficiently, but they offered no specifics on Castro's medical condition. Some of these statements came in response to rumors that Castro was suffering from cancer or another terminal disease. Such rumors were fed by a statement issued in Castro's name on his eightieth birthday, in which he called on Cubans "to be optimistic, and at the same time to be ready to face any adverse news." The country, the statement said, "is marching on and will continue marching on perfectly well." One Havana newspaper also printed four pictures of a thin but alert Castro, one of which showed him holding a copy of the previous day's edition of the Communist Party newspaper, *Granma*.

Castro appeared on state television on October 28, saying he was "coming along just as planned." Looking frail, he again held up a copy of the current edition of *Granma*, apparently to prove that he was still alive. Castro did not show up for a long-planned parade on December 2 celebrating his birthday, but Raul addressed the crowd for a mere twenty minutes, offering the type of anti-U.S. rhetoric Fidel would have appreciated.

During the early months of Castro's illness, U.S. officials were careful to avoid any direct comment on the Cuban leader's health, saying they had no direct information. On December 14, however, John D. Negroponte, the director of national intelligence, told editors and reporters at the *Washington Post* that Castro appeared to be near death. "Everything we see indicates it will not be much longer . . . months, not years," the *Post* quoted Negroponte as saying. Three days later, Cuban officials told a group of U.S. House members, who were visiting Havana, that Castro did not have cancer or a terminal illness and would return to work. However, one of the lawmakers, Rep. William Delahunt, D-Mass., said he concluded from the remarks that Fidel would not resume his old role of running the government on a day-to-day basis but instead would set broad policy. Delahunt said he concluded that "the functioning of the government, that transition has occurred."

In yet another indication that Castro was still alive, a Spanish doctor, who said he examined him in mid-December, told a news conference in Madrid on December 26 that the Cuban leader did not have cancer and was recovering from his surgery. Castro's last message of the year came on December 30 when state-run radio stations carried a statement by Castro saying his recovery was "a long process but it's far from being a lost battle." He offered assurances that he was being kept informed of important events and had discussed them "with my closest colleagues when cooperation on vital matters is called for."

Havana and Washington: Watching Warily

For decades the unending hostility of the United States government was both a curse and a blessing for Fidel Castro: a curse because U.S. sanctions damaged the Cuban economy, and a blessing because Castro used the threat of a U.S. invasion to bolster public support for him and his government. In the wake of Castro's illness, there were no serious indications that either side was about to change its attitude or policies—but there were tentative suggestions that change might be possible once Castro passed from the scene.

One suggestion was a statement by Raul Castro in late August that he would support normalizing relations with the United States, but only if the government in Washington stopped interfering in Cuban politics. Another was a statement by the State Department's senior official on Latin America, Thomas Shannon, that the administration stood by a 2002 proposal to ease the embargo if Cuba took a series of steps, including releasing political prisoners, legalizing opposition parties, and creating a "pathway" to fully democratic elections.

On September 15, however, Raul Castro appeared to go out of his way to dampen speculation that Havana and Washington could be headed for some kind of reconciliation. In a fiery speech, reminiscent of many delivered by his brother, Raul Castro told delegates from "nonaligned" nations meeting in Havana that the United States had engaged in "unacceptable acts of aggression essentially motivated by insatiable appetite for strategic resources"—an apparent reference to the U.S. invasion of Iraq in 2003.

Following is the text of a proclamation issued by Cuban leader Fidel Castro on July 31, 2006, announcing that he had delegated his government responsibilities to his brother Raul and other officials while he recovered from surgery.

DOCUMENT

"Proclamation by the Commander in Chief to the People of Cuba"

As a result of the enormous effort entailed by my visit to the Argentinean city of Córdoba, my participation in the Mercosur meeting and in the closing ceremony of the People's Summit at the historic University of Córdoba, and my visit to the city of Altagracia, where Che spent his childhood, as well as the fact that immediately after this I attended the celebrations for the 53rd anniversary of the attacks on the Moncada and Carlos Manuel de Céspedes garrisons, which took place on the 26th of July 1953, held in the provinces of Granma and Holguín, and after days and nights of non-stop work with barely any sleep, my health, which has withstood every test, was put under extreme stress and submitted to the pressure.

This brought about an acute intestinal crisis with persistent bleeding which made it necessary for me to undergo complicated surgery. All the details concerning this health problem are contained in the x-rays, endoscopies and filmed material. This operation has forced me to take several weeks off, away from my responsibilities and duties.

Due to the fact that our country faces a threat from the Government of the United States in circumstances such as these, I have taken the following decisions:

1. I provisionally delegate my functions as First Secretary of the Central Committee of the Communist Party of Cuba to the Second Secretary, comrade Raúl Castro Ruz.
2. I provisionally delegate my functions as Commander-in-Chief of the heroic Revolutionary Armed Forces to the aforementioned comrade, Army General Raúl Castro Ruz.
3. I provisionally delegate my functions as President of the Council of State and Government of the Republic of Cuba to the First Vice-President Raúl Castro Ruz.
4. I provisionally delegate my functions as the main driving force behind the National and International Public Health Programme to the member of the Politburo and Minister of Public Health, comrade José Ramón Balaguer Cabrera.

5. I provisionally delegate my functions as the main driving force behind the National and International Education Programme to comrades José Ramón Machado Ventura and Esteban Lazo Hernández, members of the Politburo.

6. I provisionally delegate my functions as the main driving force behind the National Energy Revolution Programme being implemented in Cuba and abroad as part of a scheme of collaboration with other countries to comrade Carlos Lage Dávila, member of the Politburo and Secretary of the Executive Committee of the Council of Ministers.

The funds corresponding to these three programmes, namely Health, Education and Energy, should continue to be administered and given priority, as I myself have been doing, by comrades Carlos Lage Dávila, Secretary of the Executive Committee of the Council of Ministers, Francisco Soberón Valdés, Minister and President of the Central Bank of Cuba, and Felipe Pérez Roque, Minister of Foreign Relations, who have worked with me on this and who should form a commission to this end.

Our glorious Communist Party, with the support of grassroots organizations and the people as a whole is given the mission of assuming the task entrusted to it in this Proclamation.

The State and Cuban nation should give the Summit of the Non-Aligned Movement, to be held between the 11th and 16th of September, their devoted attention in order to ensure that it takes place on the envisaged dates and is a glittering success.

I ask that the celebrations for my 80th birthday, which thousands of people had so kindly planned for the 13th of August, be postponed until the 2nd of December of this year, which will mark the 50th anniversary of the Landing of the Granma.

It is my request that the Central Committee of the Party and the National Assembly of People's Power give their unwavering support to this Proclamation.

I have no doubt whatsoever that our people and our Revolution will fight to the very end to defend these ideas and measures, as well as any others that are necessary to safeguard this historic process.

Imperialism will never succeed in crushing Cuba.

The Battle of Ideas will go forth.

Long Live the Homeland!

Long Live the Revolution!

Long Live Socialism!

Ever Onward to Victory!

(Signed)

Fidel Castro Ruz
Commander-in-Chief
First Secretary of the Party and
President of the Councils of State and
Ministers of the Republic of Cuba

Source: Republic of Cuba. Cuban Permanent Mission in United Nations. "Proclamation by the Commander in Chief to the People of Cuba." July 31, 2006. www.cuba.cu/gobierno/discursos/2006/ing/f310706i.html (accessed January 10, 2007).

444   JULY

Other Historic Documents of Interest

August

American Bar Association on Presidential Signing Statements

August 8, 2006

President George W. Bush came under political challenge in 2006 for his aggressive use of an arcane practice known as presidential signing statements—statements a president issued at the same time he signed legislation into law. Such statements had been used since the early nineteenth century, largely to set out the president's interpretation of the meaning of any ambiguous provisions in the new law. But many legislators and lawyers said Bush's prolific use of the statements—and his frequent assertion that he reserved the right to disobey or ignore any provision of a statute that he believed was unconstitutional—was undermining the doctrine of separation of powers by allowing the president to determine which laws he would "faithfully execute" as chief executive and which he would not.

Although there was widespread concern about Bush's use of the statements, there was little agreement about what could or should be done to counter it. The American Bar Association (ABA) on August 8, 2006, adopted a set of recommendations urging the president to use his veto power if he believed all or part of a bill awaiting his signature was unconstitutional. In the first six years of his presidency, Bush had vetoed only one bill. In July Sen. Arlen Specter, R-Pa., chairman of the Senate Committee on the Judiciary, introduced legislation that would allow Congress to challenge Bush's use of the signing statement in court. Several other highly respected lawyers suggested that the problem was not the signing statements themselves and that there was little that either Congress or the courts could do unless and until Bush acted on the assertions of presidential authority he claimed in the signing statements. As of the end of 2006, no critic had shown that Bush had actually refused to enforce or comply with a law with which he disagreed.

Bush's use of signing statements was seen as part of his administration's broad effort to expand presidential powers, which Congress had curbed in the wake of the failed Vietnam War and the Watergate scandal. Bush and his vice president, Dick Cheney, were staunch advocates of the unitary executive theory, which held that all actions of the executive branch should emanate from the president. In addition to asserting broad powers as commander in chief to fight the war on terror, the Bush administration had exercised significant control over the making of rules and regulations and over the release of information about internal executive branch deliberations to Congress and the public. A notable example of the administration's refusal to disclose information came in its first year when Cheney refused to divulge anything about the activities of his national energy policy task force to the Government Accountability Office. *(Energy task force, Historic Documents of 2003, p. 1017)*

Signing Statements in History

Article I of the U.S. Constitution gave the president just two options when presented with a bill that both chambers of Congress had passed: if he approved the bill, the president could sign it into law; if he disapproved it, he could veto it and return it to Congress with an explanation of his objections. The measure would then become law only if Congress overrode the veto (or passed subsequent legislation dealing with the president's objections). Beginning with James Monroe (1817–1825), however, presidents from time to time issued statements setting out their understanding of the requirements of a particular law that they were signing. In some cases, these statements raised constitutional objections to the law or some of its provisions and asserted the president's authority to enforce the measure according to his interpretation of the law and his understanding of his presidential powers.

By the mid-twentieth century, presidents were using signing statements more regularly. President Harry S. Truman (1945–1953), for example, issued an average of about sixteen signing statements a year. It was under President Ronald Reagan (1981–1989), however, that the aggressive use of presidential signing statements began. In addition to preserving presidential powers, the Reagan administration sought to have the signing statements become part of the legislative history of a law that courts could take into account when they were making rulings regarding the law. This strategy was devised by, among others, Samuel A. Alito Jr., then a deputy assistant attorney general in the Office of Legal Counsel at the Department of Justice. Alito, who later served as a federal appeals court judge, was confirmed as an associate justice of the U.S. Supreme Court in January 2006. In a 1986 memorandum, Alito argued that "since the president's approval is just as important as that of the House or Senate, it seems to follow that the president's understanding of the bill should be just as important as that of Congress." To further that strategy Attorney General Edwin Meese III arranged for the signing statements to be included in the legislative histories published by West Publishing Company in its publication U.S. Code Congressional and Administration News.

According to a report by the Congressional Research Service (CRS), titled "Presidential Signing Statements: Constitutional and Institutional Implications" and dated September 20, 2006, President Reagan issued 276 signing statements during his eight years in office. Of these, 71 raised constitutional objections to provisions of legislation that he signed into law. Presidents George H. W. Bush (1989–1993) and Bill Clinton (1993–2001) made similar use of signing statements. Bush issued 214 statements during his four years in office, including 146 challenges on constitutional grounds. Clinton issued 391 signing statements, including 105 constitutional challenges during his eight years in office. As of mid-2006 George W. Bush had issued only 128 signing statements, but those statements challenged the constitutionality of more than 700 provisions of laws that he signed—a sharp increase over the three preceding presidents.

Bush's Use of Signing Statements

Until 2006 few of Bush's signing statements drew much notice. That changed after Bush signed a law on December 30, 2005, prohibiting U.S. interrogators from torturing or otherwise subjecting detained terrorism suspects to cruel, inhumane, and degrading treatment. Immediately after signing the law, Bush issued a signing statement saying the executive branch would construe the law "in a manner consistent with the constitutional authority of the President . . . as Commander in Chief" and the president's objective of "protecting the American people from further terrorist attacks." In effect, the president was reserving the right to waive the restrictions on torture if he thought it necessary to protect national security.

That signing statement might also have gone largely unnoticed but for veteran *Boston Globe* reporter Charlie Savage, whose January 4, 2006, story on the signing statement elicited objections to the president's action from the three Republican senators who drove the torture prohibition through Congress over the president's opposition. In a joint statement, John McCain of Arizona and John Warner of Virginia noted that Congress had explicitly refused to include a presidential waiver of the torture restrictions and vowed that the Senate Committee on Armed Services would exercise "strict oversight to monitor the administration's implementation of the new law." The third senator, Lindsey Graham of South Carolina, said he did "not believe that any political figure in the country has the ability to set aside any . . . law of armed conflict that we have adopted or treaties that we have ratified." *(Torture prohibition, Historic Documents of 2005, p. 905)*

Although Bush administration officials said the president intended to follow the law on torture, the fact that the president had apparently already permitted interrogation procedures that many critics said bordered on torture left many observers skeptical of the president's intentions. That skepticism was heightened in December 2005 when it was revealed that the president had authorized secret surveillance of telephone calls and e-mail messages made by people in the United States, including U.S. citizens, without obtaining court warrants as he was required to do under a 1978 law. Bush claimed that he had broad authority, under his constitutional powers as commander in chief of the armed forces, to take whatever action was necessary to protect the country from terrorist or other threats—a claim that many legislators and attorneys disputed. *(Warrantless domestic surveillance, Historic Documents of 2005, p. 958)*

A similar story unfolded regarding the reauthorization of the USA Patriot Act in March 2006. President Bush signed the measure into law on March 9, calling it "a piece of legislation that's vital to win the war on terror and to protect the American people." He also issued a signing statement setting out his belief that he could withhold information that Congress required on how the FBI was using its new authority under the act if he thought that disclosure would "impair foreign relations, national security, the deliberative process of the executive, or the performance of the executive's constitutional duties."

In a prepared statement issued on March 23, Sen. Patrick J. Leahy, D-Vt., the ranking minority member on judiciary committee, said Bush's signing statement was "nothing short of a radical effort to manipulate the constitutional separation of powers and evade accountability and responsibility for following the law. . . . The president's constitutional duty is to faithfully execute the laws as written by Congress, not cherry-pick the laws he decides he wants to follow. It is our duty to ensure, by means of congressional oversight, that he does so."

The statements regarding the torture ban and the Patriot Act were just two of many that dealt with national security issues. Although the Constitution granted Congress the power to raise and regulate armies, declare war, and write rules for dealing with those captured in war, Bush's signing statements in this area asserted that his constitutional power as commander in chief allowed him to ignore any congressional act that sought to regulate the military, the intelligence community, or any other facet of the country's national security apparatus. Bush had also issued signing statements stating that he was not obliged to comply with various congressional disclosure or reporting requirements, with "whistle-blower" job protections for federal employees, with congressional directives giving certain executive branch officials power to act independently of the president, or with restrictions on presidential appointments. Bush also appeared to defy the Supreme Court on affirmative action. While the Court allowed affirmative action programs so long as they did not impose quotas, Bush had objected in signing statements to fifteen provisions of laws seeking to ensure that minorities were represented in federal grants, contracts, and jobs. Bush said he would construe such provisions "in a manner consistent" with the Constitution's equal protection guarantee; some scholars said that statement could be interpreted as an argument that affirmative action amounted to reverse discrimination against whites.

Concerns, Curbs, and Cautions

Many legislators, presidential scholars, and attorneys expressed concerns about the breadth of the signing statements. "The administration has been very consistent," Philip J. Cooper, a presidential scholar at Portland State University, told *USA Today* in early June. "At every turn the White House has issued a reading as expansive as possible for its own authority, a reading as narrow as possible of congressional authority, and in some cases preempted the courts."

Others said the significance of the issue had been overblown. "Presidents have issued signing statements since the early days of the our country," White House spokeswoman Dana Perino said July 23. "President's Bush's signing statements are consistent with prior administrations' signing statements. He is exercising a legitimate power in a legitimate way." Jack Goldsmith, a Harvard Law School professor who headed the Justice Department's Office of Legal Counsel during Bush's first term, agreed. "Nothing in the world changes by the publication of a signing statement," he told Charlie Savage of the *Boston Globe*. "The statements merely serve as public notice about how the administration is interpreting the law. Criticism of this practice is surprising, since the usual complaint it that the administration is too secretive in its legal interpretations."

Cooper disagreed with Goldsmith's assessment, pointing out that executive branch officials were likely to follow Bush's interpretation of a law rather than Congress's when they implemented the law. "Years down the road, people will not understand why the policy doesn't look like the legislation," he told Savage.

Another concern was whether the original Reagan strategy for making signing statements part of the legislative record of any statute was working. The CRS report noted that the courts had not generally treated signing statements as a significant part of the legislative history. One recent exception, however, was a dissent by Justice Antonin Scalia in the case of *Hamdan v. Rumsfeld,* in which the Supreme Court ruled that the Detainee Treatment Act of 2005 barring lawsuits by detainees at Guantanamo Bay did not apply to lawsuits filed before the law was enacted. In his dissent, Scalia gave equal weight to the president's signing statement for that law, writing that the Court's majority "wholly ignores the president's signing statement, which explicitly set forth his understanding that the [Detainee Treatment Act] ousted jurisdiction over pending cases." Justices Alito and Clarence Thomas joined Scalia in signing the dissent, indicating that at least three justices agreed that signing statements should carry the same weight as the congressional debate on legislation.

Several opponents of signing statements argued that they amounted to an impermissible line-item veto for the president. They noted that Bush had vetoed only one bill—to expand federal funding for stem cell research—during his first six years in office. These opponents decried what they saw as the president's tactic of publicly compromising with Congress on controversial issues only to retract the compromise through subsequent signing statements. Perhaps the most prominent organization objecting to this practice was the American Bar Association. On August 8, the ABA adopted the recommendations of the eleven-member, bipartisan Task Force on Presidential Signing Statements and the Separation of Powers Doctrine, which had been set up in late June to study the issue. In a July 24 report, the task force said that the practice of claiming presidential authority to disregard or decline to enforce "all or part of a law he has signed, or to interpret such a law in a manner inconsistent with the clear intent of Congress" was "contrary to the rule of law and our constitutional system of separation of powers."

The task force argued that the Constitution required presidents either to sign or to veto bills, and that the Supreme Court, in the 1998 case of *Clinton v. New York,* had ruled that the line-item veto was unconstitutional even if authorized by Congress. "If our constitutional system of separation of powers is to operate as the framers intended, the President must accept the limitation imposed on his office by the Constitution itself. The use of presidential signing statements to have the last word as to which laws will be enforced and which will not is inconsistent with those limitations and poses a serious threat to the rule of law," the task force said.

The task force also recommended that Congress pass legislation requiring the president to submit all signing statements to Congress along with an explanation of the legal basis underpinning his intention to ignore the law as enacted by Congress. The task force further recommended that Congress pass legislation providing for judicial review of the constitutionality of signing statements. Senator Specter introduced legislation in July to do just that, but no further action was taken on the measure in 2006. Other proposals for curbing the use of signing statements included banning the use of any federal funds to produce, publish, or disseminate the statements and barring executive branch officials from taking the statements into account in implementing laws. As the CRS report noted, neither of these approaches appeared likely to "appreciably alter or confine" the Bush administration's use of signing statements.

Several prominent scholars and lawyers cautioned against curbs on signing statements. In an op-ed piece published in the *New York Times* on July 31, Walter Dellinger, a law professor at Duke University who served as head of the Justice Department's Office of Legal Counsel during the Clinton administration, said it would be "a mistake" to deny "to this and future presidents the essential authority, in appropriate and limited circumstances, to decline to execute unconstitutional laws." Dellinger also joined with several other Justice Department officials from the Clinton administration to oppose the ABA task force recommendations. Because Congress often packaged many different laws into a single bill, they argued it would be impractical to force the president to veto the entire bill simply to cure a couple of relatively minor constitutional problems. They speculated that if presidents were barred from using signing statements, they would still sign these omnibus bills and might still refuse to enforce specific provisions. Without signing statements, however, the public might never know that the president had declined to enforce a particular provision.

Laurence H. Tribe, a professor of constitutional law at Harvard, agreed with Dellinger that signing statements were not the "true source of the constitutional difficulty." In an August 9 op-ed piece in the *Boston Globe,* Tribe wrote that "challenging the signing statements themselves, or the general practice of using them, does not represent even a plausible way of contesting this president's manifestly unreviewable decision to sign rather than veto any particular law, however cynical that decision might be and however unconvincing his explanations are." The only way to test the constitutionality of the powers the president claimed in his signing statements, Tribe said, was in a court case arising "out of a decision to carry out the threat of nonenforcement made by his signing statement, and by someone with constitutional standing to press such a challenge against what amounts to an executive omission to act."

President Bush meanwhile appeared undaunted by the criticisms. On October 6 he signed legislation setting minimum job requirements for the director of the Federal Emergency Management Agency (FEMA), including experience in managing emergencies. Congress had set the requirements to avoid political appointments such as that of Michael D. Brown, the FEMA head whose performance during Hurricane Katrina was so widely criticized. Brown, an attorney, had no emergency management experience before taking the FEMA job. After signing the legislation, however, Bush also issued a signing statement saying he reserved the right to ignore those requirements. *(Brown performance, Historic Documents of 2005, p. 566)*

Following is the text of the recommendations on restricting the use of presidential signing statements adopted by the American Bar Association at its annual meeting on August 8, 2006.

DOCUMENT

"Recommendation"

RESOLVED, That the American Bar Association opposes, as contrary to the rule of law and our constitutional system of separation of powers, the misuse of presidential signing statements by claiming the authority or stating the intention to disregard or decline to enforce all or part of a law the President has signed, or to interpret such a law in a manner inconsistent with the clear intent of Congress;

FURTHER RESOLVED, That the American Bar Association urges the President, if he/she believes that any provision of a bill pending before Congress would be unconstitutional if enacted, to communicate such concerns to Congress prior to passage;

FURTHER RESOLVED, That the American Bar Association urges the President to confine any signing statements to his/her views regarding the meaning, purpose and significance of bills presented by Congress, and if he believes that all or part of a bill is unconstitutional, to veto the bill in accordance with Article 1, §7 of the Constitution of the United States, which directs him/her to approve or disapprove each bill in its entirety;

FURTHER RESOLVED, That the American Bar Association urges Congress to enact legislation requiring the President promptly to submit to Congress an official copy of all signing statements he/she issues, and in any instance in which he/she claims the authority, or states the intention, to disregard or decline to enforce all of part of a law he/she has signed, or to interpret such a law in a manner inconsistent with the clear intent of Congress, to submit to Congress a report setting forth in full the reasons and legal basis for the statement; and further requiring that all such submissions be available in a publicly accessible database; and

FURTHER RESOLVED, That the American Bar Association urges Congress to enact legislation enabling the President, Congress, or other entities or individuals, to seek judicial review, to the extent constitutionally permissible, in any instance in which the President claims the authority, or states the intention, to disregard or decline to enforce all or part of a law he/she has signed, or interprets such a law in a manner inconsistent with the clear intent of Congress, and urges Congress and the President to support a judicial resolution of the President's claim of interpretation.

Source: American Bar Association. House of Delegates. "Recommendation." August 8, 2006. www.abanet.org/leadership/2006/annual/dailyjournal/20060823144113.pdf (accessed March 20, 2007).

Other Historic Documents of Interest

Alito joins the Supreme Court, p. 41
Katrina recovery, p. 73
Secret CIA prisons, p. 511

Stem cell legislation, p. 407
*Supreme Court on Guantanamo
   tribunals, p. 374*

UN Security Council Resolution on War between Israel and Hezbollah

August 11, 2006

Just six years after ending its nearly two-decade occupation of southern Lebanon, Israel found itself involved in another war with that nation during the summer of 2006. At best, this war resulted in a draw, and it was widely seen in the Middle East—even by many Israelis—as a partial victory for Hezbollah, the radical Shiite group in Lebanon that had provoked the war.

Among its many consequences, the war put enormous pressure on Lebanon's pro-Western moderate government, which was trying to bolster the country's independent standing after decades of domination by Syria and partial occupation by Israel. The government had won elections in 2005 as the result of public outrage over a bombing that killed a popular former prime minister, Rafik Hariri. Many Lebanese blamed Syria for the bombing, and an ongoing United Nations investigation appeared to be pointing in that direction, as well. Even so, Lebanon was sharply divided between those who wanted a definitive break with Syria and others who, for various reasons, supported continued ties with Damascus. As part of this debate, Lebanon's government was paralyzed for much of the year over whether to request an international tribunal to try suspects in the Hariri bombing case, some of them senior Syrian officials. *(Background, Historic Documents of 2005, p. 686)*

Hezbollah's Raid and Israel's Response

Lebanon's latest descent into warfare and anarchy began in the morning of July 12, when Hezbollah launched several dozen short-range Katyusha rockets and mortars into Israel and Hezbollah guerrillas crossed the border and attacked two army vehicles patrolling the border. The guerrillas killed three soldiers and captured two reservists, taking them back across the border into Lebanon. During an Israeli army raid into Lebanese territory to rescue the soldiers, five more soldiers and an unknown number of Hezbollah fighters were killed. Hezbollah said it captured the two soldiers as a means of forcing Israel to release Palestinians being held in Israeli prisons. Israeli prime minister Ehud Olmert called the Hezbollah raid an "act of war" and promised "very painful and far-reaching action" against Lebanon unless the soldiers were returned immediately. Olmert said the Lebanese government was complicit in the raid because Hezbollah "is a part" of the government—a reference to Hezbollah members who held two cabinet seats. Israel already was engaged in a major military operation at the time in the northern Gaza Strip, attempting (without success) to force Palestinian guerrillas to release an Israeli soldier who had been captured in a similar raid on June 25.

Israel initially responded to the Hezbollah raid with a small-scale ground invasion of southern Lebanon and a much more ambitious attack by bombs and artillery. This aerial attack at first targeted known Hezbollah locations, such as guerrilla outposts, but it was quickly expanded into a much broader assault on bridges, roads, electrical lines, and other infrastructure. The next day, July 13, Israeli jets bombed runways at the Beirut airport, and the Israeli navy mounted a blockade of Lebanon's coastline—both steps, Israel said, were needed to cut off the international supply of weapons to Hezbollah. In turn, Hezbollah launched medium-range rockets into Israel, some hitting as far as the port city of Haifa, twenty-five miles south of the border. Civilians were the major casualties of this tit-for-tat escalation. Within a few days, more than 400,000 civilians fled their homes in southern Lebanon, and in northern Israel tens of thousands of people spent days in bomb shelters.

The big surprise in the early stages of the war was Hezbollah's rocket arsenal, which turned out to be much larger and more powerful than outsiders, especially Israel's vaunted intelligence services, had estimated. Before the war, Hezbollah had fired only short-range Katyusha rockets into Israel, few of which caused much damage. During this war, however, the group was able to launch hundreds of missiles deep into Israel territory, killing civilians and damaging buildings. Hezbollah also disabled an Israeli ship on July 14, reportedly using a sophisticated antiship missile obtained from Iran. Hezbollah's ability to withstand the Israeli assault also came as a surprise. In the early stages of the war, Israeli officials said they intended to "defeat" and "destroy" Hezbollah; after the first two weeks, however, the Israelis lowered their aims to punishing Hezbollah and creating conditions under which a strong international force could eliminate or minimize Hezbollah's armed presence in southern Lebanon.

When such wars broke out, it was standard practice for other countries to call for a cease-fire and mount diplomatic missions to pressure both sides to halt the fighting. This had been the case during a similar, though smaller-scale, war between Israel and Hezbollah in 1996. At that time, U.S. secretary of state Warren Christopher spent ten days shuttling between Middle Eastern capitals to broker a cease-fire. In the summer of 2006, many foreign leaders called for a cease-fire, UN Secretary General Kofi Annan demanded that both sides exercise restraint, and diplomats huddled at the United Nations and in other foreign capitals. In what was widely seen as an extraordinary step, the United States intervened to block an immediate move toward a cease-fire. Echoing statements from Israel, U.S. officials made it clear that Washington would not accept a UN Security Council resolution demanding a cease-fire until Hezbollah stopped its rocket attacks against Israel, agreed to disarm, and released the captured Israeli soldiers. "I have no interest in diplomacy for the sake of returning Lebanon and Israel to the status quo ante," Secretary of State Condoleeza Rice said on July 21 in dismissing calls for an immediate cease-fire. Rice and President George W. Bush both said a cease-fire would be effective only if it addressed the "root causes" of the conflict, which they defined as Hezbollah's military armaments and continued Syrian involvement in Lebanese politics. The Bush administration also rushed a delivery to Israel of a previously agreed upon shipment of precision-guided bombs. In an emotional speech on July 19 to foreign diplomats in Beirut, Prime Minister Fuad Siniora bitterly accused the world of standing by while his country "has been torn to shreds."

At this stage some UN officials and European leaders began accusing Israel of using "disproportionate" force against Lebanese civilian targets. Visiting Beirut on July 23, Jan Egeland, the UN's chief humanitarian aid coordinator, said he was shocked to see "block by block leveled to the ground" by Israeli air strikes. Hezbollah had provoked the war, he said, but "a disproportionate response by Israel is a violation of international humanitarian war." Israeli officials insisted they were attacking Hezbollah, not civilians, and Hezbollah was to blame for putting its rockets and military posts in civilian neighborhoods. Egeland later joined that condemnation of Hezbollah, accusing it of "cowardly blending" military positions "among women and children."

The criticisms of Israel's tactics reached a crescendo after July 30, when an Israeli air raid on the southern town of Qana destroyed an apartment building. Initial reports suggested 50 to 60 people were killed, but later investigations found just 28 bodies. Aside from the high toll, the bombing had immense symbolic significance in Lebanon because Qana was the site of a similar Israel attack in 1996, during which 100 people were killed and a similar number injured. Israel briefly curtailed its bombing raids at the request of Secretary of State Rice, who was in Israel at the time.

In the first phase of the war, through the end of July, Israel employed extensive air power over southern and central Lebanon. But the Israeli army used only limited ground combat forces to attack key Hezbollah strongholds near the border, notably the towns of Bint Jbail and Maroun al-Ras, which were the scene of fierce fighting in the last week of July.

Israel began changing tactics on August 1, launching the early part of a broader ground invasion deeper into Lebanon. This move was intended to push Hezbollah forces well north of the Litani River in hopes they could be forced to stay there by an international peacekeeping force once a cease-fire took effect. The Israeli air force also expanded its bombing attacks over much of Lebanon, including attacks in predominantly Christian areas north of Beirut and in the Bekaa Valley adjacent to Syria. In the latter case, Israel bombed the only road that remained open between Lebanon and the outside world; Israeli officials said Syria had been shipping missiles and other arms to Hezbollah using that road.

Even as Israel expanded its assault deeper in Lebanon, Hezbollah kept up its barrage of rocket fire into northern Israel. In early August, Hezbollah fired more than 100 rockets a day and on some days fired more than 200. The single deadliest Hezbollah attack was on August 6, when a Hezbollah rocket killed 12 Israeli soldiers. The Israeli military said it counted nearly 4,000 Hezbollah rocket attacks during the war; that total represented between one-fourth and one-third of the rocket arsenal Hezbollah claimed at various times.

By the time fighting ended on August 14, Israel counted 159 deaths during the month-long war, of whom 120 were soldiers and 39 were civilians, nearly all of the latter killed by Hezbollah rocket fire. Thirty-three of Israel's soldiers were killed in the final days of the war, after the UN Security Council had called for a cease-fire.

Various branches of the Lebanese government counted 1,100 to 1,200 dead during the war and said most of them were civilians. In the weeks after the war, Israel and Hezbollah engaged in a public relations battle over the number of Hezbollah fighters who had been killed: the Israeli military put the figure at more than 600, while the highest figure acknowledged by any senior Hezbollah official was 250.

The physical damage to Lebanon was enormous. The United Nations estimated that more than 900,000 Lebanese (one-fourth of the country's population) had been forced temporarily from their homes by the Israeli air and ground attacks; most of these displaced people had fled their homes in southern Lebanon, but tens of thousands of residents of the Beirut area also were displaced. An estimated 15,000 homes or apartments were totally or substantially destroyed, along with dozens of bridges, electrical installations, and many of the country's most important roads. Israeli also bombed several major oil and gas storage facilities, resulting in severe environmental damage that lasted for months. The UN's humanitarian office estimated in late August that the war had caused $3.6 billion in physical damage to Lebanon. Donors at an international aid conference in Stockholm pledged about $1.2 billion in aid on August 31.

Yet another long-term problem for Lebanon was the presence of thousands of unexploded cluster bombs Israel had dropped during the war. Many of the bombs, each smaller than a tin can, fell into civilian areas, where they were of particular danger to children. The United States, which had sold the bombs to Israel, later launched an investigation into the use of them in civilian areas.

The Security Council Resolution

The first serious diplomatic move toward ending the Israel-Lebanon conflict took place in Rome on July 26 when officials from Europe, the United States, and the UN gathered to discuss the prospects for a cease-fire to be enforced by some kind of international military presence. As in previous days, the United States blocked action toward an immediate cease-fire. "This is a region that has had too many broken cease-fires," Rice said. Once again, Lebanon's Siniora made an impassioned plea for international action to end the fighting. "Is the value of human life less in Lebanon than that of citizens elsewhere?" he asked the assembled diplomats. "Are we children of a lesser God? Is an Israeli teardrop worth more than a drop of Lebanese blood?" Siniora's powerful words brought calls for action from some delegates, but action was not yet forthcoming.

International outrage over the July 30 Qana bombing, along with Israeli's strong push into Lebanon with ground forces on August 1, finally stimulated serious diplomacy toward a cease-fire. Back in Washington from a brief visit to the region, Rice said that day that she hoped a cease-fire could come in "days, not weeks" and that it was "time to end the violence."

The main question at this point became one of how to mobilize and staff a new international peacekeeping force in southern Lebanon. Most diplomats agreed that such a force would need to be larger and more powerful than the small UN force—called the United Nations Interim Force in Lebanon (UNIFIL)—that had been in place since 1978. UNIFIL basically was a monitoring mission that lacked the manpower or authority to stop cross-border attacks, either by Hezbollah into Israel or Israeli into Lebanon. A related question was whether the Lebanese army could be strengthened enough so it could take control of the southern part of the country, something it had been unable to do since before a civil war broke out there in 1975.

Answering these questions took more than the few days that Rice had implied. The United States and France reached agreement on a draft UN resolution on August 5, but Lebanon objected to a provision allowing Israel to remain in the southern part of that country until the new international force was in place. It was not until August 11 that the UN Security Council was able to adopt, unanimously, Resolution 1701, which demanded a cease-fire, authorized a dramatic expansion of the UNIFIL force from 2,000 to 15,000 troops, pledged international aid so Lebanon's army could deploy an equivalent number of troops in the south, and called for the withdrawal of Israel's army. Secretary General Annan, serving his last months in office, praised the resolution but bemoaned the world's slowness in agreeing to it. "I am profoundly disappointed that the Council did not reach this point much, much earlier," he said. "I am convinced that my disappointment and sense of frustration are shared by hundreds of millions of people around the world."

The resolution's key language gave the expanded UNIFIL power to "insure that its area of operations is not utilized for hostile activities of any kind," which chiefly meant preventing Hezbollah from launching attacks into Israel. UNIFIL also was empowered "to resist attempts by forceful means to prevent it from discharging its duties"—a mandate that had been denied the previous UNIFIL. The UN force was to join Lebanon's army in patrolling the area of Lebanon north of the Israel border and south of the Litani River, a zone that averaged about fifteen miles in width. This zone was to be kept free of "all armed personnel, assets and weapons" other than those of the army and UNIFIL.

This last provision was an essential one for Israel, but Resolution 1701 did not specifically authorize UNIFIL to use force to disarm Hezbollah. Over the next several days diplomats issued varying interpretations of whether and how the UN force was to deal with any armed Hezbollah guerrillas it encountered. Once UNIFIL began deploying, its officers gave reporters a limited interpretation of their mission. Generally, UNIFIL commanders said the UN troops would help the Lebanese army regain control of the southern part of the country and prevent Hezbollah from launching rockets into Israel, but it would be up to the army to disarm Hezbollah. The army, however, was widely seen as incapable of carrying out such a task, partly because of Hezbollah's military strength and popular support and partly because many army soldiers also were Shiites sympathetic to Hezbollah.

The Lebanese army, which had stayed out of the fighting between Israel and Hezbollah, began moving south of the Litani River on August 17, three days after the cease-fire went into effect. After more than two weeks of confusion about which countries would be contributing to the new UN force, additional troops from Italy began arriving in the area on September 2. By year's end, UNIFL had more than 11,000 troops in the area, plus a small naval force patrolling the Lebanese coastline. Israel gradually withdrew from southern Lebanon as Lebanese army and UNIFIL troops arrived to take its place. The last Israeli contingent crossed back into Israel on October 1. Israel had lifted its air and sea blockades of Lebanon on September 7–8.

For the most part, Hezbollah fighters simply disappeared into the general population, apparently having stashed their weapons. Hezbollah civilian workers were more prominent, however; dozens of them appeared in Beirut and other locations and handed out wads of cash, reportedly averaging about $10,000 for each family that had lost a home. Apparently using money from its patron, Iran, Hezbollah also announced plans to rebuild entire neighborhoods, putting itself well ahead of the government, which was counting on formal foreign aid channels that would take months to deliver.

Who Won the War?

Many wars result in a clear victory by one party and a clear defeat of the other. The Israel-Hezbollah war in the summer of 2006 was not among them. Each side claimed to have achieved its goals, but neither did.

Israel did not win the freedom of the two soldiers captured by Hezbollah on July 12. Israel also failed to quash Hezbollah militarily, although it did kill a sizable percentage of the group's 2,000 or so armed fighters and it did damage Hezbollah's military infrastructure in southern Lebanon—along with wide swaths of the countryside and thousands of Lebanese homes. The war also had enormous negative consequences inside Israel, starting with the deaths of civilians and the damage to cities and towns caused by Hezbollah's rockets.

Of perhaps greater long-term significance was the impression, both in Israel and in Lebanon, that Hezbollah had "won" the war simply by surviving the onslaught by the most powerful army in the Middle East. Tens of thousands of Israelis spent much of the war in bomb shelters, an embarrassing testament to the government's failure to protect them. In the weeks following the war, second-guessing of Israel's military and political leadership exceeded anything since the October 1973 war, when Israel had been caught unawares by its Arab neighbors. Under intense pressure, Prime Minister Olmert appointed a commission to investigate his government's handling of the war, but he refused to give the panel total independence to conduct its work. The investigation was still pending at year's end.

Yet another casualty in Israel was Olmert's plan to withdraw some Israeli settlements from the West Bank. Olmert had promoted such a plan during his election campaign early in the year, but Hezbollah's rocket attacks made security, not peace with the Palestinians, the preeminent issue for Israelis in the second half of 2006.

Although it remained intact as an organization and said it retained thousands of rockets and other weapons, Hezbollah also failed to achieve the objective it stated at the outset of the war: forcing Israel to release several dozen Lebanese and thousands of Palestinians from prison. Hezbollah also claimed to be fighting to secure the return to Lebanon of a small agricultural area known as the Shebaa Farms, which Israel had controlled for years and was claimed by Lebanon. The area remained in Israel's hands at the end of the war, with little chance of a resolution of the dispute anytime soon.

By provoking Israel's massive retaliation, Hezbollah angered many Lebanese, who wondered what the group's leaders were thinking when they approved the raid into Israel. Hezbollah leader Hassan Nasrallah said he would not have approved the raid had he known how Israel would respond. Even so, Hezbollah and Nasrallah emerged from the war with their overall reputations enhanced in Lebanon and much of the Middle East for having stood up to Israel. Nasrallah certainly pulled out all the stops to reinforce the impression that Hezbollah had won. Speaking to an enormous crowd in Beirut on September 22, he claimed Hezbollah had won a "divine victory" over Israel and would complete it by rebuilding Lebanon—a promise the official government could not yet make on its own.

Arab Support for Hezbollah

One of the most remarkable outcomes of the summer's war in Lebanon was the burst of support throughout the Arab world for Hezbollah, a Shiite militia that previously had been scorned by many Arabs, notably those in countries dominated by Sunni Muslims. In the early days of the war, in fact, spokesmen in Saudi Arabia and several other Arab countries denounced Hezbollah for provoking Israel. That attitude quickly changed, however, as the fighting dragged on and it became clear that Hezbollah was able to survive the enormous Israeli military attack, which came under criticism from much of the world.

By late July even some of the region's most conservative Arab leaders were expressing solidarity with Hezbollah—or at least moving as quickly as possible to distance themselves from the United States, which was seen by Arabs as Israel's patron and protector. Another extraordinary development was the sudden popularity in many Arab lands of Hezbollah's leader, Nasrallah. Images of Nasrallah appeared on television screens, banners, and posters and were featured in large rallies called to demonstrate "solidarity" with Lebanon. This was remarkable because Nasrallah long had been associated with Iran's radical Shiite leadership, making him a figure of contempt for many Sunni Arabs throughout the region. Suddenly, Nasrallah appeared to be a more potent source of solidarity than any Arab leader since Egypt's president Gamal Abdel Nasser, who had moved enormous crowds with his pan-Arab rhetoric but had led Arabs into their greatest defeat at Israel's hands, in June 1967.

In the often zero-sum atmosphere of the Middle East, the sudden explosion of Arab support for Hezbollah also reflected the tumbling stature of the United States in the region. Many moderate Arabs had been appalled by the September 11, 2001, terrorist attacks against the United States by the Islamist group al Qaeda, and some had been encouraged by the Bush administration's subsequent pressure on autocratic regimes in Egypt and elsewhere to move toward democracy. But Washington's apparent siding with Israel in the Lebanon war, coming on top of its inability to bring a successful conclusion to its occupation of Iraq, soured Arab opinion about the United States. Many Arabs were particularly angered by Rice's comment on July 21 that the violence was an aspect of "the birth pangs of a new Middle East." A broad spectrum of Arabs said that remark appeared to approve of the carnage in Lebanon as necessary to achieve U.S. policy in the region—a criticism Rice and the administration rejected.

Antigovernment Protests

In the months after the war, Nasrallah sought to capitalize on the increased public support for Hezbollah by stepping up pressure on the Lebanese government, in which Hezbollah technically was a coalition partner. At the giant rally in Beirut on September 22, Nasrallah demanded that Prime Minister Siniora allow creation of a "national unity" government—in other words, a government subject to veto power by Hezbollah. Nasrallah followed this demand with a daily series of rallies in Beirut starting in November; these rallies turned into a continuous occupation of one of Beirut's central squares by several hundred protesters and was still under way at the end of the year. Hezbollah and allied pro-Syrian parties had mounted similar protests earlier in the year, notably a large demonstration on May 10 denouncing a tax increase and calling on Siniora to resign.

Siniora refused to yield to Nasrallah's demands, saying his government had been legitimately elected in 2005 and denouncing the Hezbollah protests as an attempted coup d'etat. Although he had strong support from the United States, most European countries, and some Arab countries, Siniora appeared to be in a fragile position, and it was unclear at year's end how long his government could survive under siege. A key test for Lebanon's future was expected to be the a requirement that parliament appoint a new president in 2007 to succeed Emile Lahoud, a pro-Syrian Maronite Christian whose reappointment to that post at Syrian insistence in late 2004 had set in motion the train of events leading to the assassination of former prime minister Hariri in February 2005. The chief clamant for the post appeared to be former general Michel Aoun, who had played a major role in Lebanon's civil war and had recently transformed himself from a staunch critic of Syria into an unlikely ally of both Syria and Hezbollah.

While the Hezbollah-inspired protests against the government were under way, Lebanon received another reminder of its violent past. On November 21, gunmen in Beirut assassinated Pierre Gemayel, a member of Siniora's cabinet and a staunch opponent of Syrian influence in Lebanon. The thirty-four-year-old Gemayel was the grandson and namesake of Lebanon's most prominent Maronite Christian leader during the middle part of the twentieth century, and he was the son of Amin Gemayel, who served as president in the 1980s, during the final years of Lebanon's long civil war. A failed assassination attempt against the senior Pierre Gemayel, in April 1975, was considered the triggering event for the civil war, which raged until 1990.

Hariri Bombing Investigation

Lebanon had seen many political assassinations in the turbulent years since its independence from France in 1946, but none caused as much outrage as a massive bombing in February 2005 that killed Hariri, six of his bodyguards, and fourteen bystanders. A wealthy contractor, Hariri had helped rebuild Lebanon during his three different terms as prime minister since the early 1990s, and he was widely seen as the most unifying figure in a country fractured by sectarian differences. Domestic and international revulsion at the bombing forced Syria to withdraw its military from Lebanon after nearly three decades and contributed to the victory of Siniora's coalition in elections held in late May and early June 2005.

In an unusual step, the United Nations appointed an independent commission to probe the Hariri killing. German prosecutor Detlev Mehlis headed that investigation from April 2005 through early January 2006, and he submitted two reports implicating high-level Syrian intelligence and security officials in the killing. After Mehlis withdrew, UN Secretary General Annan appointed a Belgian prosecutor, Serge Brammertz, to head the investigation. Brammertz had been deputy prosecutor of the International Criminal Court, a human rights tribunal the UN had established over vigorous U.S. opposition. *(Criminal court background, Historic Documents of 2003, p. 99)*

In his first report to the UN Security Council, on March 14, Brammertz said Hariri's killers appeared to have been "very professional" in their approach and likely had experience "in this type of terrorist activity." Following this report, the council voted on March 29 in favor of creating an international tribunal to try any suspects in the case. The creation of such a tribunal was contingent on agreement by the Lebanese government. Over staunch opposition by Hezbollah and its allies, Siniora's cabinet approved such a tribunal on November 13. President Lahoud declared that move invalid, but the UN Security Council went ahead on November 23 with the authorization for the tribunal.

A separate report to the council on April 19, by special UN envoy Terje Roed-Larsen, put additional pressure on Syria and its supporters in the Lebanese government. Roed-Larsen quoted Lebanese legislators as saying that Syria had threatened Hariri in late 2004 to allow the extension of Lahoud's term in office. The president's term was to have expired in November 2004, but the parliament allowed Lahoud three more years, reportedly after Syrian officials demanded that Hariri—who was then prime minister—allow a legislative vote on the matter. Hariri relented, then resigned as prime minister, only to be killed in the February 2005 bombing. Syrian president Bashar al-Assad vehemently denied that he, or any of his aides, threatened Hariri or had anything to do with his murder.

> *Following is the text of United Nations Security Council Resolution 1701, adopted on August 11, 2006, imposing a cease-fire in the war between Israel and the Hezbollah militia in Lebanon and authorizing expansion of a peacekeeping force in southern Lebanon known as the United Nations Interim Force in Lebanon.*

████████████ **DOCUMENT** ████████████

"Resolution 1701 (2006)"

The Security Council,

Recalling all its previous resolutions on Lebanon, in particular resolutions 425 (1978), 426 (1978), 520 (1982), 1559 (2004), 1655 (2006) 1680 (2006) and 1697 (2006), as well as the statements of its President on the situation in Lebanon, in particular the statements of 18 June 2000 (S/PRST/2000/21), of 19 October 2004 (S/PRST/2004/36), of 4 May 2005 (S/PRST/2005/17), of 23 January 2006 (S/PRST/2006/3) and of 30 July 2006 (S/PRST/2006/35),

Expressing its utmost concern at the continuing escalation of hostilities in Lebanon and in Israel since Hizbollah's attack on Israel on 12 July 2006, which has already caused hundreds of deaths and injuries on both sides, extensive damage to civilian infrastructure and hundreds of thousands of internally displaced persons,

Emphasizing the need for an end of violence, but at the same time *emphasizing* the need to address urgently the causes that have given rise to the current crisis, including by the unconditional release of the abducted Israeli soldiers,

Mindful of the sensitivity of the issue of prisoners and *encouraging* the efforts aimed at urgently settling the issue of the Lebanese prisoners detained in Israel,

Welcoming the efforts of the Lebanese Prime Minister and the commitment of the Government of Lebanon, in its seven-point plan, to extend its authority over its territory, through its own legitimate armed forces, such that there will be no weapons without the consent of the Government of Lebanon and no authority other than that of the Government of Lebanon, *welcoming also* its commitment to a United Nations force that is supplemented and enhanced in numbers, equipment, mandate and scope of operation, and *bearing in mind* its request in this plan for an immediate withdrawal of the Israeli forces from southern Lebanon,

Determined to act for this withdrawal to happen at the earliest,

Taking due note of the proposals made in the seven-point plan regarding the Shebaa farms area,

Welcoming the unanimous decision by the Government of Lebanon on 7 August 2006 to deploy a Lebanese armed force of 15,000 troops in South Lebanon as the Israeli army withdraws behind the Blue Line and to request the assistance of additional forces from the United Nations Interim Force in Lebanon (UNIFIL) as needed, to facilitate the entry of the Lebanese armed forces into the region and to restate its intention to strengthen the Lebanese armed forces with material as needed to enable it to perform its duties,

Aware of its responsibilities to help secure a permanent ceasefire and a long-term solution to the conflict,

Determining that the situation in Lebanon constitutes a threat to international peace and security,

1. *Calls for* a full cessation of hostilities based upon, in particular, the immediate cessation by Hizbollah of all attacks and the immediate cessation by Israel of all offensive military operations;

2. Upon full cessation of hostilities, *calls upon* the Government of Lebanon and UNIFIL as authorized by paragraph 11 to deploy their forces together throughout the South and *calls upon* the Government of Israel, as that deployment begins, to withdraw all of its forces from southern Lebanon in parallel;

3. *Emphasizes* the importance of the extension of the control of the Government of Lebanon over all Lebanese territory in accordance with the provisions of resolution 1559 (2004) and resolution 1680 (2006), and of the relevant provisions of the Taif Accords, for it to exercise its full sovereignty, so that there will be no weapons without the consent of the Government of Lebanon and no authority other than that of the Government of Lebanon;

4. *Reiterates* its strong support for full respect for the Blue Line;

5. *Also reiterates* its strong support, as recalled in all its previous relevant resolutions, for the territorial integrity, sovereignty and political independence of Lebanon within its internationally recognized borders, as contemplated by the Israeli-Lebanese General Armistice Agreement of 23 March 1949;

6. *Calls on* the international community to take immediate steps to extend its financial and humanitarian assistance to the Lebanese people, including through facilitating the safe return of displaced persons and, under the authority of the Government of Lebanon, reopening airports and harbors, consistent with paragraphs 14 and 15, and *calls on* it also to consider further assistance in the future to contribute to the reconstruction and development of Lebanon;

7. *Affirms* that all parties are responsible for ensuring that no action is taken contrary to paragraph 1 that might adversely affect the search for a long-term solution, humanitarian access to civilian populations, including safe passage for humanitarian convoys, or the voluntary and safe return of displaced persons, and *calls on* all parties to comply with this responsibility and to cooperate with the Security Council;

8. *Calls for* Israel and Lebanon to support a permanent ceasefire and a long-term solution based on the following principles and elements:

> full respect for the Blue Line by both parties;
> security arrangements to prevent the resumption of hostilities, including the establishment between the Blue Line and the Litani river of an area free of any armed personnel, assets and weapons other than those of the Government of Lebanon and of UNIFIL as authorized in paragraph 11, deployed in this area;
> full implementation of the relevant provisions of the Taif Accords, and of resolutions 1559 (2004) and 1680 (2006), that require the disarmament of all armed groups in Lebanon, so that, pursuant to the Lebanese cabinet decision of 27 July 2006, there will be no weapons or authority in Lebanon other than that of the Lebanese State;
> no foreign forces in Lebanon without the consent of its Government;
> no sales or supply of arms and related materiel to Lebanon except as authorized by its Government;
> provision to the United Nations of all remaining maps of landmines in Lebanon in Israel's possession;

9. *Invites* the Secretary-General to support efforts to secure as soon as possible agreements in principle from the Government of Lebanon and the Government of Israel to the principles and elements for a long-term solution as set forth in paragraph 8, and *expresses* its intention to be actively involved;

10. *Requests* the Secretary-General to develop, in liaison with relevant international actors and the concerned parties, proposals to implement the relevant provisions of the Taif Accords, and resolutions 1559 (2004) and 1680 (2006), including disarmament, and for delineation of the international borders of Lebanon, especially in those areas where the border is disputed or uncertain, including by dealing with the Shebaa farms area, and to present to the Security Council those proposals within thirty days;

11. *Decides*, in order to supplement and enhance the force in numbers, equipment, mandate and scope of operations, to authorize an increase in the force strength of UNIFIL to a maximum of 15,000 troops, and that the force shall, in addition to carrying out its mandate under resolutions 425 and 426 (1978):

(a) Monitor the cessation of hostilities;

(b) Accompany and support the Lebanese armed forces as they deploy throughout the South, including along the Blue Line, as Israel withdraws its armed forces from Lebanon as provided in paragraph 2;

(c) Coordinate its activities related to paragraph 11 (b) with the Government of Lebanon and the Government of Israel;

(d) Extend its assistance to help ensure humanitarian access to civilian populations and the voluntary and safe return of displaced persons;

(e) Assist the Lebanese armed forces in taking steps towards the establishment of the area as referred to in paragraph 8;

(f) Assist the Government of Lebanon, at its request, to implement paragraph 14;

12. Acting in support of a request from the Government of Lebanon to deploy an international force to assist it to exercise its authority throughout the territory, *authorizes* UNIFIL to take all necessary action in areas of deployment of its forces and as it deems within its capabilities, to ensure that its area of operations is not utilized for hostile activities of any kind, to resist attempts by forceful means to prevent it from discharging its duties under the mandate of the Security Council, and to protect United Nations personnel, facilities, installations and equipment, ensure the security and freedom of movement of United Nations personnel, humanitarian workers and, without prejudice to the responsibility of the Government of Lebanon, to protect civilians under imminent threat of physical violence;

13. *Requests* the Secretary-General urgently to put in place measures to ensure UNIFIL is able to carry out the functions envisaged in this resolution, *urges* Member States to consider making appropriate contributions to UNIFIL and to respond positively to requests for assistance from the Force, and *expresses* its strong appreciation to those who have contributed to UNIFIL in the past;

14. *Calls upon* the Government of Lebanon to secure its borders and other entry points to prevent the entry in Lebanon without its consent of arms or related materiel and *requests* UNIFIL as authorized in paragraph 11 to assist the Government of Lebanon at its request;

15. *Decides* further that all States shall take the necessary measures to prevent, by their nationals or from their territories or using their flag vessels or aircraft:

(a) The sale or supply to any entity or individual in Lebanon of arms and related materiel of all types, including weapons and ammunition, military vehicles and equipment, paramilitary equipment, and spare parts for the aforementioned, whether or not originating in their territories; and

(b) The provision to any entity or individual in Lebanon of any technical training or assistance related to the provision, manufacture, maintenance or use of the items listed in subparagraph (a) above; except that these prohibitions shall not apply to arms, related material, training or assistance authorized by the Government of Lebanon or by UNIFIL as authorized in paragraph 11;

16. *Decides* to extend the mandate of UNIFIL until 31 August 2007, and *expresses its intention* to consider in a later resolution further enhancements to the mandate and other steps to contribute to the implementation of a permanent ceasefire and a long-term solution;

17. *Requests* the Secretary-General to report to the Council within one week on the implementation of this resolution and subsequently on a regular basis;

18. *Stresses* the importance of, and the need to achieve, a comprehensive, just and lasting peace in the Middle East, based on all its relevant resolutions including its resolutions 242 (1967) of 22 November 1967, 338 (1973) of 22 October 1973 and 1515 (2003) of 19 November 2003;

19. *Decides* to remain actively seized of the matter.

Source: United Nations. Security Council. "Resolution 1701 (2006)." S/RES/1701 (2006), August 11, 2006. www.un.org/Docs/sc/unsc_resolutions06.htm (accessed January 22, 2007).

FDA on Approval of the Plan B Emergency Contraceptive Drug

August 24, 2006

Social conservatives who sought to chip away at abortion rights by restricting the circumstances under which women could legally end their pregnancies lost several battles in 2006. After years of controversy, the U.S. Food and Drug Administration (FDA) approved over-the-counter sales of emergency contraception to women aged eighteen and older. The medication, which many right-to-life advocates said was tantamount to abortion, would continue to be available to younger girls by prescription. Voters in South Dakota overturned that state's strict ban on abortions, and the House and Senate failed to reconcile their differences on legislation that would make it a federal crime to transport minors across state lines for abortions.

While social conservatives lost some short-range fights, they may have won some long-term battles. In January the Senate confirmed Judge Samuel A. Alito Jr. to fill the vacancy on the Supreme Court left by the retirement of Justice Sandra Day O'Connor. Although Alito would not discuss his views on abortion directly at his confirmation hearings, his prior record indicated that he might work to weaken, if not overrule, *Roe v. Wade,* the 1973 case establishing a constitutional right to abortion. Evidence on that score was likely to come quickly—the Supreme Court heard arguments in November on the constitutionality of a federal ban on a medical procedure commonly known as the partial birth abortion. A ruling was expected by the middle of 2007.

FDA Decision on Plan B

A long-standing controversy involving Plan B, an emergency contraceptive pill, came to a sudden and somewhat surprising conclusion in 2006 when the FDA agreed that the medication could be sold without prescription to women age eighteen and older. Women younger than eighteen would still be required to have a doctor's prescription to obtain the drug, and it would be available only at pharmacies and health clinics.

Manufactured by Barr Laboratories, Plan B, also known as the "morning-after" pill, could prevent conception if taken by a woman within seventy-two hours of unprotected sexual intercourse. The medication had been available by prescription since 1999, and in 2003 Barr asked the FDA to approve Plan B for over-the-counter sales because the drug was generally more effective the sooner it was taken. Unless a woman already had a supply on hand, three days could easily pass before she was able to obtain and fill a prescription. Supporters said widespread availability of the drug could prevent as many as 1.5 million unintended pregnancies each year and consequently reduce the number of abortions. Abortion foes argued that easier availability would increase promiscuity, particularly among minors, as well as the incidence of sexually transmitted diseases. They also objected because the pill occasionally prevented a fertilized egg from implanting in the uterus; for those who believed that life began with fertilization, the pill was not considered emergency contraception but a drug that induced abortion.

Overruling two of its own advisory committees, the FDA rejected Barr's request in May 2004. In July Barr amended its application asking that the drug be made available without prescription to women sixteen and older. When the FDA failed to make a decision on the request by the January 2005 deadline, two pro-choice senators, Democrats Hillary Clinton of New York and Patty Murray of Washington, put a hold on the Senate confirmation of Lester M. Crawford as FDA commissioner until the FDA made a decision on Barr's application. After Health and Human Services Secretary Michael O. Levitt promised a decision by September 1, Clinton and Murray lifted their hold, and Crawford was confirmed.

On August 26, Crawford announced that the agency was delaying a decision on Barr's application indefinitely. Clinton and Murray were furious, the assistant FDA commissioner for women's health resigned in protest, and abortion rights activists charged that the FDA was bowing to pressure from the antiabortion lobby and its supporters and putting political considerations ahead of sound medical practice. Those views received some support from the General Accountability Office, which in November reported evidence that the decision to stall on Barr's application was made before the formal scientific review process had been completed. *(Background, Historic Documents of 2005, p. 814)*

Meanwhile, shortly after being confirmed, Crawford abruptly resigned in September 2005. President George W. Bush named Andrew C. von Eschenbach, the head of the National Cancer Institute and a longtime Bush family friend, as acting FDA director, and in March 2006 Bush formally nominated Eschenbach for the post. In what looked like a replay of Crawford's nomination, Clinton and Murray put a block on a vote on Eschenbach's confirmation. "If they don't come to a decision on Plan B, the White House is going to need a Plan C on their nominee," Murray said in March.

The situation appeared to be at stalemate. In May the American College of Obstetricians and Gynecologists formally advised women to get an advance prescription for Plan B so they would have it on hand if they needed it. Then, on July 31, the evening of Eschenbach's Senate confirmation hearing, the FDA announced that it was considering approving Plan B for sale without prescription for women age eighteen and older. Eschenbach faced sharp questioning at his hearing on the timing of the announcement but insisted that the decision was based on "medical ideology," not "political ideology." Nonetheless, Clinton and Murray refused to lift their hold.

On August 8, the FDA and Barr officials announced that they had reached agreement and that Barr would submit another revised application. On August 24, the FDA announced that it had approved over-the-counter sales of Plan B for any woman over age seventeen; buyers would be required to show proof of age. Men could also buy the drug. "This long overdue decision is a victory for women's health and for the American people who have waiting for years for the FDA to act," Clinton and Murray said in a statement. Opponents of the decision threatened political retaliation against the president. "Let there be no mistake about it," the Rev. Thomas J. Euteneuer, president of Human Life International, a pro-life group, said. "Today's decision lies at the feet of President Bush and has created a lasting rift with the Catholic faithful who comprise a large part of his support base."

Even though Clinton and Murray released their hold on Eschenbach's confirmation on August 24, the full Senate did not vote on the nomination until December 7; the vote to confirm was 80–11. National distribution of Plan B for over-the-counter sales began on November 6, and the drug was widely available by the time Eschenbach was confirmed.

South Dakota Abortion Ban Rejected

Voters in South Dakota soundly rejected a comprehensive ban on abortion that had been enacted earlier in the year. The margin in the statewide referendum on November 7 was 56 percent to 44 percent. The law made it a crime for doctors to perform abortions for any reason except to save the life of the mother, and even then doctors were instructed to try to save the life of the fetus as well. No exceptions were made for pregnancies caused by rape or incest. The law's backers intended it as a direct challenge to the Supreme Court's decision in *Roe*, and Planned Parenthood, which ran the only abortion clinic in the state, had said it would challenge the law in court. Meanwhile a broad coalition, called the South Dakota Campaign for Healthy Families, undertook a successful campaign to collect enough signatures to place the issue on the November ballot.

Even some right-to-life advocacy groups were not unhappy to see the ban rejected. The South Dakota law had touched off a testy debate among opponents of abortion, many of whom questioned the timing of a direct challenge to *Roe*. They noted that five sitting members of the Supreme Court had voted to reaffirm a woman's right to an abortion in 1992, the last time the Court had ruled directly on the issue. And they said it was not clear that the Court's two newest members, Alito and Chief Justice John Roberts, were prepared to overturn *Roe;* a direct challenge to *Roe* that did not succeed might serve only to reinforce it as precedent, they said. This wing of the antiabortion movement argued that the surest way of attacking *Roe* was to undermine it by enacting restrictions on the circumstances under which a woman could legally end her pregnancy. *(1992 case, Historic Documents of 1992, p. 589)*

In the only other antiabortion initiatives on state ballots, voters in California and Oregon defeated referendums that would have established parental notification laws for minors seeking abortions.

Partial Birth Abortion

In February the Supreme Court agreed to hear a case challenging one of the more controversial restrictions on abortion—a federal ban on a procedure called dilation and extraction, commonly known as the "partial birth abortion" by its opponents. In 2000 the Court had rejected a Nebraska law banning the late-term procedure. The Court said that the language of the prohibition was unconstitutionally broad and that the law was fatally flawed because it did not contain an exception to protect the health of the mother. The vote was 5–4, with Justice Sandra Day O'Connor casting the deciding ballot. (Stenberg v. Carhart, *Historic Documents of 2000, p. 429*)

In 2003 Congress passed a federal ban on partial birth abortion that was very similar in language to the unconstitutional Nebraska ban. Like the state law, the federal ban made no exception to protect the health of the mother. The law was immediately challenged and so never took effect. *(Federal ban, Historic Documents of 2003, p. 995)*

Court watchers thought the Court might tip its hand on the issue in a case involving a New Hampshire parental notification law that was being challenged because it did not make an exception to notification when a minor needed an abortion in a medical emergency that was not life threatening. On January 18, 2006, however, a unanimous Court ruled that the lower courts had gone too far when they invalidated the entire law. In her last opinion for the Court, O'Connor said the lower courts erred when they chose a "blunt remedy"—nullifying the law in its entirety—rather than a "more finely drawn" remedy that might have addressed just the issue of the medical exception. "We try not to nullify more of a legislature's work than is necessary," O'Connor wrote, returning the case to the lower court for a determination of legislative intent.

Pending at the time of the New Hampshire decision was an appeal by the Bush administration of a federal appeals court ruling declaring the federal partial birth abortion ban to be unconstitutional. In February the Court agreed to review the case of *Gonzalez v. Carhart.* The case came from the Court of Appeals for the Eighth Circuit, which held that the failure to include a mother's health exception invalidated the entire federal law. In June the Supreme Court agreed to expand its review of the federal ban, adding a second case, *Gonzalez v. Planned Parenthood.* In this case the Court of Appeals for the Ninth Circuit had ruled that the language of the federal ban violated due process because it was so vague that it could have the effect of criminalizing a common procedure for ending a pregnancy before the fetus was viable. Planned Parenthood of America had petitioned the Court to add the case because, the organization said, the Ninth Circuit decision was broader and provided "the most complete available record" on the likely effect of the statute. The Court heard arguments in the case on November 8; a decision was expected before the end of the 2006–2007 term.

Parental Consent

Parental consent was at issue in the only abortion legislation considered by Congress in 2006. Aided by the looming midyear congressional elections, social conservatives seemed poised to win another victory in their campaign to restrict abortions in increments, when the Senate on July 25, 2006, handily passed a measure (S 403) making it a federal crime to transport minors across state lines to have abortions in a state that did not have parental consent or notification laws. The House had easily passed a similar measure (HR 748) in 2005. The Senate bill did not include House-passed provisions that would require doctors to notify parents of an out-of-state minor's request for an abortion and would allow parents or guardians of the minor to sue doctors who did not comply. But it did carry provisions to stop fathers or other family members who committed incest from transporting a pregnant minor across state lines for an abortion and to stop fathers who raped their minor daughters from suing adults who helped the girls end the pregnancy.

The Senate measure ran into trouble, however, when Democratic Whip Richard J. Durbin of Illinois used a procedural tactic to block the bill from going to a House-Senate conference. The Senate bill was sent instead to the House, which could either clear it as passed by the Senate or amend it. The House on September 26 chose to amend the bill, adding its earlier provisions on penalizing out-of-state doctors who did not notify parents of a minor's abortion request, before returning the bill to the Senate for final action. Although fourteen Democratic senators had voted for the original Senate measure, eight balked at the addition of the House provisions, and a motion to invoke cloture (cut off debate) failed, 57–42—three votes short of the sixty votes needed for a cloture motion to prevail. The September 29 vote, coming just days before Congress was to recess for the midterm election campaign, effectively killed the measure for the session.

Following is the text of a press release issued August 24, 2006, by the U.S. Food and Drug Administration announcing its approval of over-the-counter sales of Plan B, an emergency contraceptive, to women over age seventeen.

DOCUMENT

"FDA Approves Over-the-Counter Access for Plan B for Women"

The U.S. Food and Drug Administration (FDA) today announced approval of Plan B, a contraceptive drug, as an over-the-counter (OTC) option for women aged 18 and older. Plan B is often referred to as emergency contraception or the "morning after pill." It contains an ingredient used in prescription birth control pills–only in the case of Plan B, each pill contains a higher dose and the product has a different dosing regimen. Like other birth control pills, Plan B has been available to all women as a prescription drug. When used as directed, Plan B effectively and safely prevents pregnancy. Plan B will remain available as a prescription-only product for women age 17 and under.

Duramed, a subsidiary of Barr Pharmaceuticals, will make Plan B available with a rigorous labeling, packaging, education, distribution and monitoring program. In the CARE (Convenient Access, Responsible Education) program Duramed commits to:

- Provide consumers and healthcare professionals with labeling and education about the appropriate use of prescription and OTC Plan B, including an informational toll-free number for questions about Plan B;
- Ensure that distribution of Plan B will only be through licensed drug wholesalers, retail operations with pharmacy services, and clinics with licensed healthcare practitioners, and not through convenience stores or other retail outlets where it could be made available to younger women without a prescription;
- Packaging designed to hold both OTC and prescription Plan B. Plan B will be stocked by pharmacies behind the counter because it cannot be dispensed without a prescription or proof of age; and
- Monitor the effectiveness of the age restriction and the safe distribution of OTC Plan B to consumers 18 and above and prescription Plan B to women under 18.

Today's action concludes an extensive process that included obtaining expert advice from a joint meeting of two FDA advisory committees and providing an opportunity for public comment on issues regarding the scientific and policy questions associated with the application to switch Plan B to OTC use. Duramed's application raised novel issues regarding simultaneously marketing both prescription and non-prescription Plan B for emergency contraception, but for different populations, in a single package.

The agency remains committed to a careful and rigorous scientific process for resolving novel issues in order to fulfill its responsibility to protect the health of all Americans.

Source: U.S. Department of Health and Human Services. Food and Drug Administration. "FDA Approves Over-the-Counter Access for Plan B for Women 18 and Older: Prescription Remains Required for Those 17 and Under." Press release P06-118, August 24, 2006. www.fda.gov/bbs/topics/NEWS/2006/NEW01436.html (accessed December 15, 2006).

Other Historic Documents of Interest

International Astronomical Union on Downgrading Pluto's Status

August 24, 2006

For about seventy years, schoolchildren around the world were taught that the solar system had nine planets. Recent discoveries led a majority of leading astronomers to decide on August 24, 2006, that Pluto—the last planet to be discovered—really did not merit that designation. Instead, the members of the International Astronomical Union voted to reclassify Pluto as a "dwarf planet," as it was too small and did not meet other characteristics of the first-ever technical definition of what it meant to be a planet. This ruling returned the number of planets to eight—the number used before Pluto was discovered in 1930. In order of distance from the Sun, they were Mercury, Venus, Earth, Mars, Saturn, Jupiter, Uranus, and Neptune.

This new accounting of the solar system had little practical effect other than pleasing astronomers who yearned for precision and making millions of textbooks, almanacs, and encyclopedias out of date. The move was not universally embraced, however. Some astronomers were perfectly content to keep calling Pluto a planet, and they said something was lost in the rush to take away its title.

The rebranding of Pluto highlighted another year of important discoveries in space, notably yet more findings by the hardy duo of National Aeronautics and Space Administration (NASA) rovers on Mars—*Opportunity* and *Spirit*—which kept working all through 2006, long past the time when they were supposed to have succumbed to the rigors of the Martian surface.

Pluto's Loss of Status

U.S. astronomer Clyde Tombaugh was given credit for discovering Pluto on February 18, 1930. He found it as a tiny, dim object, well beyond the orbit of what scientists previously had thought was the most distant planet, Neptune. Even with later advances in telescopes and other scientific instruments, including the orbiting Hubble telescope, Pluto remained only a vague object to observers on Earth and thus had received only a fraction of the scientific attention paid to bigger, and closer, planets.

In 1951 a Dutch-American astronomer, Gerard Kuiper, proposed the existence of thousands of small objects circling the sun in the remote distance where Pluto had been found. The first of these objects, which came to be called Kuiper Belt objects, was found in 1992. Since then, more than 1,000 such objects had been discovered—and with those discoveries came the debate about whether Pluto really was a planet or just another large ball of rock and ice in the Kuiper Belt. Most scientists believed the Kuiper Belt objects were the remnants of the massive clouds of gas and dust that formed the solar system about 4.6 billion years ago. One of the first indications that many astronomers were uncomfortable calling Pluto a planet was a decision in 2001 by the Hayden Planetarium, part of the American Museum of Natural History in New York City, to remove Pluto from its planetary gallery.

The debate over Pluto's status became more intense in 2005 when Michael E. Brown, of the California Institute of Technology, discovered an object in the Kuiper Belt that was brighter than and appeared to be slightly larger than Pluto. He called it Zena, after a character in a television series; the official temporary name was 2003 UB313 (the 2003 designation was because the images Brown used had been taken in that year). The Hubble space telescope in 2006 measured 2003 UB313 and found it to be about 1,490 miles in diameter, nearly identical to Pluto in size. Whatever its name—Zena or 2003 UB313—the object was the most distant object yet found in the solar system; at the furthest reach of its elongated orbit, the object was about twice as far from the Sun as Pluto.

By 2006 the International Astronomical Union—the world's leading gathering of astronomers—had created a committee to propose a formal definition of what constituted a planet. It turned out this was something the world had lacked, even if most people were unaware of its absence.

When the astronomers began debating various proposals in mid-August, it appeared at first that Pluto would keep its title. In fact, one proposal added two more planets to the list: 2003 UB313 (or Zena) and Ceres, the largest asteroid ever discovered. After several more meetings, the committee on August 22 settled instead for a new system that downgraded Pluto. Under this system, the large bodies in the solar system were to be put into three classifications: the traditional eight planets (sans Pluto), smaller items to be called "dwarf planets" (including Pluto), and a much larger collection of various "solar system bodies," including asteroids and comets. Not all committee members were happy with this state of affairs, however. News reports said the committee's initial meeting, when a new anti-Pluto definition was proposed, was an angry one, with astronomers passionately arguing for and against Pluto's status.

The final decision came on August 24 when the astronomers voted on a series of resolutions establishing precise definitions for planets and the other nonplanetary bodies. The final definition approved by the astronomers set three criteria for a planet: it must orbit the Sun, it must have enough mass for its own gravity to make it a ball, and it must have cleared away all other objects from the neighborhood of its orbit around the Sun. Pluto and 2003 UB313 met the first two criteria but not the last because both orbited amid hundreds of other objects. The astronomers decided to classify Pluto, 2003 UB313, and Ceres as "dwarf planets." A competing proposal to retain Pluto as one of the nine "classical planets" was rejected.

Michael Brown, the astronomer whose discovery of 2003 UB313 intensified the planetary debate, said he was glad the matter was settled. "Through this whole crazy circus-like procedure, somehow the right answer was stumbled on," he said. "It's been a long time coming. Science is self-correcting eventually, even when strong emotions are involved."

Not everyone was satisfied, however. Alan Stern, of the Southwest Research Institute in Boulder, Colorado, told the *New York Times* that the new definition of planets would appear to disqualify even Earth and Jupiter because neither had totally cleared asteroids from their neighborhoods. "This is so scientifically sloppy and internally inconsistent . . . that it is embarrassing," he said. Stern and other astronomers subsequently drafted a petition, signed by more than three hundred of their colleagues, protesting the new planetary definition that disqualified Pluto. These protesters said they planned a conference in 2007 to discuss the matter further.

Stern had a practical reason for standing by Pluto. He was lead researcher for a spacecraft, called *New Horizons*, that NASA launched on January 19 on a planned nine-year journey to Pluto. Once it arrived in 2015, the craft was to take photographs and scientific readings of Pluto, its large moon Charon, and the two smaller moons that were discovered in 2004. On its journey, *New Horizons* was to pass close by Jupiter—not to do any observations but to use the giant planet's gravity to help propel it onward to Pluto, much like a stone in a slingshot. This maneuver was intended to reduce *New Horizon*'s total travel time by about five years.

The year's final indignity for Pluto came on September 14 when the astronomical union assigned it a number in its catalog of nonplanetary objects in the solar system: 134340. Pluto's "dwarf planet" companion, 2003 UB313, finally got its formal name: Eris, chosen by Brown, its discoverer. Appropriately, this was the name of the Greek goddess of discord. Its catalog number was 136199.

Mars Rovers Still Roving

NASA's two phenomenal rovers continued their work on Mars throughout 2006, long past their original, intended life spans of three months. The rovers took photographs of the Martian surface and used scientific instruments to examine rocks and soil—adding immeasurably to knowledge about the history and geology of the Red Planet, which long had fired human imagination. *Spirit* landed on Mars on January 3, 2004, and *Opportunity* arrived exactly three weeks later. Despite occasional technical problems, the two golf cart size vehicles kept running, and NASA scientists kept scooping up, and celebrating, the data they sent back. *(Background, Historic Documents of 2005, p. 501; Historic Documents of 2004, p. 3)*

Early in 2006 *Spirit* began examining a flat surface in the Gusev Crater that scientists called "Home Plate." This area turned out to consist of layered rocks, a finding that intrigued scientists because the layering of rocks could provide information about how the surface of Mars was formed.

After nearly two years of arduous travel, *Opportunity* in late September reached the rim of Victoria Crater, a 230-foot crater caused by an impact of some kind. Scientists believed the crater held many secrets about the formation of rocks in the Martian surface. An one point on its trip to the crater, *Opportunity*'s wheels got stuck in deep sand; it took technicians about five weeks to work out a scheme for freeing the rover so it could continue on its way. Also in September, NASA extended the mission of the rovers for another year, meaning that scientists and technicians could keep working on the project so long as the vehicles kept running.

Another spacecraft arrived in the neighborhood of Mars in March. *Mars Reconnaissance Orbiter*, a NASA project, on March 10 eased into the early stages of an orbit around Mars, making it the fourth satellite currently conducting scientific surveys. NASA planned to have the orbiter spend two years mapping the planet and searching both for water and for potential landing sites for future missions. After that work was done, the orbiter was to continue as a communications satellite.

The first images from the orbiter were released on October 16. These included detailed pictures of rocks in the Martian ice cap and of a deep valley. One image showed the rover *Opportunity* sitting at the rim of Victoria Crater, casting a shadow on the surface of Mars.

Meanwhile, NASA announced in November that another spacecraft orbiting Mars apparently had succumbed to old age. *Mars Global Surveyor* had orbited Mars since September 1997, about five times as long as its original schedule. Among the *Global Surveyor's* many achievements were photographs of eroded gullies that provided some of the strongest evidence so far that the Martian surface had water. Scientists announced on December 6 that a new examination of pictures taken several years apart by *Global Surveyor* appeared to show that liquid water might still be present on Mars, at least on an occasional basis. The photographs showed that two gullies had experienced erosion by water—possibly flash floods—sometime between 1999 and 2005.

Shuttle Launches

Three space shuttle missions were carried out successfully and without major incident during 2006, apparently confirming that the shuttle program was back on track—at least until its scheduled termination in 2010. The shuttle fleet was grounded for more than two years after *Columbia* exploded during landing in February 2003, killing the five crewmembers aboard. The first flight since then was of the shuttle *Discovery* in July–August 2005. *(Background, Historic Documents of 2005, p. 498)*

Discovery took a crew of seven astronauts and supplies to the International Space Station on a mission that began on July 4 and ended on July 17, 2006. The shuttle *Atlantis* also flew astronauts and supplies to the space station on a mission that began on September 9 and ended on September 21. *Atlantis* delivered materials that allowed astronauts to resume construction of the space station, which had been halted since the *Columbia* accident. The space station was years behind schedule. *Discovery* returned to space on December 9 for a mission that involved extensive electrical work to improve the space station's ability to generate solar power. *Discovery* returned safely on December 26. *(Background, Historic Documents of 2005, p. 498)*

The July 2006 launch of *Discovery* had been opposed by NASA's top safety officer, Bryan O'Connor, a former shuttle commander, and the agency's chief engineer, Christopher Scolese. The two men said they worried about potential damage to the spacecraft if parts of the foam covering its external fuel tank dislodged during the launch; this had been determined to be the cause of the *Columbia* accident. Their concerns were overridden by NASA administrator Michael D. Griffin, and both men went along with the decision, saying there was no significant danger to shuttle crew members who could take refuge in the International Space Station. In the event, only tiny pieces of foam peeled away at liftoff, none of them large enough to cause any damage to the shuttle. The year's other two missions also saw no serious safety problems.

Plans for the Moon

NASA on December 4 unveiled its plans for return trips to the moon, part of a new series of manned expeditions first outlined by President George W. Bush in 2004. The agency's schedule called for the first tests to begin in 2009 of a new lunar spaceship called *Orion,* which was currently under construction by a consortium headed by Lockheed-Martin Corp. A manned test flight of the *Orion* would tentatively take place in 2014; the first flight to the moon by a crew of four astronauts was scheduled for 2020. These flights would be followed by regular visits to the moon, each lasting about one week. *(Bush plan, Historic Documents of 2004, p. 9)*

By 2024 NASA would have established a permanent station on the moon, probably at the south pole. Astronauts, space tourists, and even commercial companies could use the station, which would be powered by sunlight. NASA offered no cost estimates for these plans, but independent experts projected the cost, in current dollars, at several hundred billion dollars. The plan already was coming under criticism from scientists, members of Congress, and others who said it would force NASA to pare back other space research programs. NASA administrator Griffin acknowledged during 2006 that the agency would have to cut spending on space science—long considered one of its "crown jewels"—to pay for the manned missions. An even more ambitious element of Bush's space plan called for manned missions to Mars, but NASA had not yet plotted out the specifics.

Other Space Missions and Findings

Among the other space missions operating and scientific findings issued in 2006 were these:

- NASA's *Stardust* mission returned to Earth on January 15 after a seven-year journey around the inner solar system. Using a tennis racket-size collector, *Stardust* captured the tracks of thousands of particles that scientists believed were residue from the formation of the solar system. NASA scientists said the amount of material collected by *Stardust* far exceeded their expectations. The December 15 issue of the journal *Science* contained seven reports based on findings from *Stardust*. One of the most interesting findings was that a comet, Wild 2, contained material that originated with the birth of the solar system—not just rock and ice picked up on the comet's travels through space.
- The *Deep Impact* space probe, which NASA deliberately plunged into the Tempel 1 comet in July 2005, sent back information showing that a large portion of the comet was covered with layers of ice.
- NASA on October 31 announced plans to send a space shuttle to the orbiting Hubble telescope in May 2008. The mission would replace batteries, gyroscopes, and other equipment to extend the life of the telescope at least to 2013. After the *Columbia* disaster, NASA announced that it was too dangerous to send shuttles to the Hubble telescope. NASA later considered sending a robotic mission to repair Hubble but concluded this was not practical.

Following are excerpts from two statements issued by the International Astronomical Union on August 24, 2006, at the conclusion of meetings in Prague, Czech Republic, that dealt with, among other things, the definition of planets.

DOCUMENT

"Result of the IAU Resolution Votes"

. . . The IAU [International Astronomical Union] members gathered at the 2006 General Assembly agreed that a "planet" is defined as a celestial body that (a) is in orbit around the Sun, (b) has sufficient mass for its self-gravity to overcome rigid body forces so that it assumes a hydrostatic equilibrium (nearly round) shape, and (c) has cleared the neighbourhood around its orbit.

This means that the Solar System consists of eight "planets" Mercury, Venus, Earth, Mars, Jupiter, Saturn, Uranus and Neptune. A new distinct class of objects called "dwarf planets" was also decided. It was agreed that "planets" and "dwarf planets" are two distinct classes of objects. The first members of the "dwarf planet" category are Ceres, Pluto and 2003 UB313 (temporary name). More "dwarf planets" are expected to be announced by the IAU in the coming months and years. Currently a dozen candidate "dwarf planets" are listed on IAU's "dwarf planet" watchlist, which keeps changing as new objects are found and the physics of the existing candidates becomes better known.

The "dwarf planet" Pluto is recognised as an important proto-type of a new class of trans-Neptunian objects. The IAU will set up a process to name these objects.

Results

Resolution 5A: "Definition of Planet" was not counted but was passed with a great majority.

Resolution 5B: "Definition of Classical Planet" had 91 votes in favour, but many more against so there was no count.

Resolution 6A: "Definition of Pluto-class objects" was passed with 237 votes in favour, 157 against and 17 abstentions.

Resolution 6B: "Definition of Plutonian Objects" had 183 votes in favour and 186 votes against.

Below are the planet definition Resolutions that were passed. . . .

The IAU is the international astronomical organisation that brings together distinguished astronomers from all nations of the world. Its mission is to promote and safeguard the science of astronomy in all its aspects through international cooperation. Founded in 1919, the IAU is the world's largest professional body for astronomers. The IAU General Assembly is held every three years and is one of the largest and most diverse meetings on the astronomical community's calendar. . . .

Resolutions

Resolution 5A is the principal definition for the IAU usage of "planet" and related terms.

Resolution 6A creates for IAU usage a new class of objects, for which Pluto is the prototype. The IAU will set up a process to name these objects.

IAU Resolution: Definition of a Planet in the Solar System

Contemporary observations are changing our understanding of planetary systems, and it is important that our nomenclature for objects reflect our current understanding. This applies, in particular, to the designation "planets". The word "planet" originally described "wanderers" that were known only as moving lights in the sky. Recent discoveries lead us to create a new definition, which we can make using currently available scientific information.

Resolution 5A

The IAU therefore resolves that "planets" and other bodies in our Solar System, except satellites, be defined into three distinct categories in the following way:

1. A "planet" [Mercury, Venus, Earth, Mars, Jupiter, Saturn, Uranus, and Neptune] is a celestial body that (a) is in orbit around the Sun, (b) has sufficient mass for its self-gravity to overcome rigid body forces so that it assumes a hydrostatic equilibrium (nearly round) shape, and (c) has cleared the neighbourhood around its orbit.

2. A "dwarf planet" is a celestial body that (a) is in orbit around the Sun, (b) has sufficient mass for its self-gravity to overcome rigid body forces so that it assumes a hydrostatic equilibrium (nearly round) shape [an IAU process will be established to assign borderline objects into either dwarf planet and other categories], (c) has not cleared the neighbourhood around its orbit, and (d) is not a satellite.

3. All other objects [these currently include most of the Solar System asteroids, most Trans-Neptunian Objects (TNOs), comets, and other small bodies except satellites orbiting the Sun] shall be referred to collectively as "Small Solar-System Bodies".

Resolution 6A

The IAU further resolves:

Pluto is a "dwarf planet" by the above definition and is recognized as the prototype of a new category of trans-Neptunian objects.

Source: International Astronomical Union. IAU XXVIth General Assembly. "Result of the IAU Resolution Votes." Prague, Czech Republic. Press release, August 24, 2006. www.astronomy2006.com/press-release-24-8-2006-2.php (accessed February 27, 2007).

■■■ DOCUMENT ■■■

"Questions and Answers 2"

Q: What is the origin of the word "planet"?
A: The word "planet" comes from the Greek word for "wanderer," meaning that planets were originally defined as objects that moved in the night sky with respect to the background of fixed stars.

Q: Why is there a need for a new definition for the word "planet"?
A: Modern science provides much more knowledge than the simple fact that objects orbiting the Sun appear to move with respect to the background of fixed stars. For example, recent new discoveries have been made of objects in the outer regions of our Solar System that have sizes comparable to and larger than Pluto. (Noting that historically Pluto has been recognized as "the ninth planet.") Thus these discoveries have rightfully called into question whether or not they should be considered as new "planets."

Q: How did astronomers reach a consensus for a new definition of "planet"?
A: The world's astronomers, under the auspices of the International Astronomical Union, have had official deliberations on a new definition for the word "planet" for nearly two years. The results of these deliberations were channelled to a Planet Definition Committee and

ultimately proposed to the IAU General Assembly. Continued evolution of the definition allowed a final consensus and vote.

Q: What new terms are used in the official IAU definition?
A: There are three new terms adopted as official definitions by the IAU. The terms are: "planet," "dwarf planet," and "small solar system body."

Q: In plain language, what is the new definition of "planet"?
A: A "planet" is an object in orbit around the Sun that is large enough (massive enough) to have its self-gravity pull itself into a round (or nearly round) shape. In addition a "planet" orbits in a clear path around the Sun—there are no other bodies in its path that it must sweep up as it goes around the Sun.

Q: What is the exact wording of the official IAU proposed definition of "planet"?
A: A "planet" is a celestial body that (a) is in orbit around the Sun, (b) has sufficient mass for its self-gravity to overcome rigid body forces so that it assumes a hydrostatic equilibrium (nearly round) shape, and (c) has cleared the neighbourhood around its orbit.

Q: Does a body have to be perfectly spherical to be called a "planet"?
A: No. For example, the rotation of a body can slightly distort the shape so that it is not perfectly spherical. Earth, for example, has a slightly greater diameter measured at the equator than measured at the poles.

Q: Based on this new definition, how many planets are there in our solar system?
A: There are eight planets in our Solar System: Mercury, Venus, Earth, Mars, Jupiter, Saturn, Uranus, Neptune. "My very educated mother just served us nachos."

Q: Is that all, only eight planets?
A: No. In addition to the eight planets, there are also three known "dwarf planets." Many more "dwarf planets" are likely to be discovered soon.

Q: What is a dwarf planet?
A: A dwarf planet is an object in orbit around the Sun that is large enough (massive enough) to have its own gravity pull itself into a round (or nearly round) shape. Generally, a dwarf planet is smaller than Mercury. A dwarf planet may also orbit in a zone that has many other objects in it. For example, an orbit within the asteroid belt is in a zone with lots of other objects.

Q: How many dwarf planets are there?
A: Currently there are three known dwarf planets: Ceres, Pluto, and 2003 UB313.

Q: What is Ceres?
A: Ceres is (or now we can say it was) the largest asteroid, about 1000 km across, orbiting in the asteroid belt between Mars and Jupiter. Ceres now qualifies as a dwarf planet because it is now known to be large enough (massive enough) to have self-gravity pulling itself into a nearly round shape. . . . Ceres orbits within the asteroid belt and is an example of a case

of an object that does not orbit in a clear path. There are many other asteroids that can cross the orbital path of Ceres.

Q: Didn't Ceres used to be called an asteroid or minor planet?
A: Historically, Ceres was called a "planet" when it was first discovered (in 1801) orbiting in what is known as the asteroid belt between Mars and Jupiter. Because 19th century astronomers could not resolve the size and shape of Ceres, and because numerous other bodies were discovered in the same region, Ceres lost its planetary status. For more than a century, Ceres has been referred to as an asteroid or minor planet.

Q: Why is Pluto now called a dwarf planet?
A: Pluto now falls into the dwarf planet category on account of its size and the fact that it resides within a zone of other objects, known as the Kuiper Belt.

Q: Is Pluto's moon Charon a dwarf planet?
A: For now, Charon is considered just to be Pluto's moon. The idea that Charon might qualify to be called a dwarf planet on its own, may be considered later. (Charon may receive consideration because Pluto and Charon are comparable in size and orbit each other, rather than just being a moon orbiting a planet.)

Q: Jupiter and Saturn, for example, have large spherical satellites in orbit around them. Are these large spherical satellites now to be called dwarf planets?
A: No. All of the large satellites of Jupiter (for example, Europa) and Saturn (for example, Titan) orbit around a common centre of gravity (called the "barycentre") that is deep inside of their massive planet. Regardless of the large size and shapes of these orbiting bodies, the location of the barycentre inside the massive planet is what defines large orbiting bodies such as Europa, Titan, etc. to be "satellites" rather than planets.

Q: What is 2003 UB313?
A: "2003 UB313" is a provisional name given to a large object discovered in 2003 that resides in an orbit around the Sun beyond Neptune.

Q: Is 2003 UB313 a planet?
A: No. It is a dwarf planet.

Q: Why is 2003 UB313 a dwarf planet?
A: Recent Hubble Space Telescope images have resolved the size of 2003 UB313 showing it to be as large as, or larger than Pluto. Any object having this size, and any reasonable estimate of density, is understood to have sufficient mass that its own gravity will pull it into a nearly spherical shape. 2003 UB313 also orbits within the Kuiper Belt—a region that has not been cleared out. Therefore, 2003 UB313 is a dwarf planet. . . .

Q: Will the new dwarf planet 2003 UB313 receive a name? When?
A: Yes. The International Astronomical Union has the official authority to assign names to objects in space. This object has been popularly called "Xena," but this is not an official

name. A decision and announcement of the new name are likely to be made within a few months.

Q: What is an object called that is too small to be a planet or dwarf planet?
A: All objects that orbit the Sun, which are too small (not massive enough) for their own gravity to pull them into a nearly spherical shape are now defined as being "small solar system bodies." This class currently includes most of the solar system asteroids, near-Earth objects (NEOs), Mars and Jupiter Trojan asteroids, most Centaurs, most Trans-Neptunian objects (TNOs), and comets.

Q: What is a "small solar system body"?
A: The term "small solar system body" is a new IAU definition to encompass all objects orbiting the Sun that are too small (not sufficiently massive) to satisfy the definition of planet or dwarf planet.

Q: Is the term "minor planet" still to be used?
A: The term "minor planet" may still be used. But generally the term "small solar system body" will be preferred.

Q: For any newly discovered object, how will a decision be reached on whether or not to officially call it a planet, dwarf planet, or other?
A: The decision on how to classify newly discovered objects will be made by a review committee within the IAU. The review process will be an evaluation, based on the best available data, of whether or not the physical properties of the object satisfy the definitions. It is likely that for many objects, a period of time of several years may be required in order for sufficient data to be gathered.

Q: Are there additional "planet" candidates currently being considered?
A: No. None appear likely in our Solar System. But there are planet discoveries galore around other stars.

Q: Are there additional "dwarf planet" candidates currently being considered?
A: Yes. Some of the largest asteroids may be candidates for "dwarf planet" status and some additional "dwarf planet" candidates beyond Neptune will soon be considered. The total number of dwarf planets to be found in the coming months and years could reach to over 100.

Q: When will additional new dwarf planets likely be announced?
A: Probably within a few months.

Q: How many more new dwarf planets are there likely to be?
A: There may be dozens or perhaps more than 100 waiting to be discovered.

Source: International Astronomical Union. IAU XXVIth General Assembly. "Questions and Answers 2." Prague, Czech Republic. Press release, August 24, 2006. www.astronomy2006.com/press-release-24-8-2006-2-two.php (accessed February 27, 2007).

National Park Service Guidelines for Managing the Parks

August 31, 2006

■■■■ THE DOCUMENT IN CONTEXT ■■■■

A bitter controversy over opening national park lands to greater recreational and commercial use was laid to rest, at least temporarily, with an announcement that the new guidelines for the National Park System would maintain the Department of Interior's traditional emphasis on conservation. "When there is a conflict between conserving resources unimpaired for future generations and the use of those resources, conservation will be predominant," Secretary of the Interior Dirk Kempthorne said on June 19, 2006. The new guidelines, formally published on August 31, overturned earlier drafts of proposed new park management guidelines that would have allowed much greater use of recreational vehicles, such as snowmobiles and all terrain vehicles, which environmentalists said would damage fragile lands and worsen air and noise pollution.

The announcement was Kempthorne's first significant policy statement since taking over the helm of the Department of the Interior in May. A former U.S. senator (1993–1999), Kempthorne resigned as governor of Idaho to take the cabinet position. He replaced Gail Norton, who had announced in March that she was resigning and returning to Colorado, where she had once served as the state's attorney general. During her five-year reign at the Interior Department, Norton had been at the center of several divisive controversies, including an unsuccessful battle to open the Artic National Wildlife Refuge to oil and gas drilling, and a brewing controversy over royalty fees paid by oil companies for the right to drill for oil and gas on public lands. Many environmentalists charged that Norton was more supportive of industry and development interests than conservation of the public lands in the department's trust. Under her tenure the department was also tainted by the corruption scandal involving the lobbyist Jack Abramoff.

Managing the Parks

The National Park Service was created within the Department of the Interior in 1916 with a mission to "conserve unimpaired each park's natural and cultural resources and values for the enjoyment, education, and inspiration of present and future generations." That mission remained essentially the same even as the park system expanded to include historical, urban, and recreational sites as well as more traditional park lands. In 2006 the park system managed nearly 400 parks, battlefields and other historical sites, recreational areas, national monuments, and other preserves covering some 84 million acres of land in the United States and its territories.

The traditional mission came under challenge in 2005 as the park system drafted new management guidelines. Amid heavy lobbying by the American Recreation Coalition and manufacturers of recreational equipment, a draft was produced in August 2005 that would make recreation a core park mission. As written under the direction of Paul Hoffman, a political appointee and then the deputy assistant secretary for fish, wildlife, and parks, the draft would have required that an activity, such as snowmobiling or jet boat skiing, could not be prohibited unless it was shown to "permanently and irreversibly adversely affect a resource or value." Existing guidelines allowed such activities to be banned if they "impaired" natural resources in the park. The draft also would have eased restrictions on livestock grazing and mining and reduced air quality standards.

Less than a month after taking office, Kempthorne threw out the draft and endorsed a version that largely followed the guidelines already in place. Under these guidelines, park supervisors would have to determine not only whether the proposed use would damage the air, water, land, or wildlife but also "the atmosphere of peace and tranquility and natural soundscapes" in the nation's parks.

The new guidelines, released August 31, were widely hailed by current and former park employees as well as environmental and conservation advocacy groups. "Secretary Kempthorne delivered strong and effective policies that protect parks and improve the visitor experience," said Thomas C. Kiernan, president of the National Parks Conservation Association. Bill Wade, a former superintendent at Shenandoah National Park in Virginia, agreed. "This is a victory. Now the emphasis is on preventing and avoiding damage, not mitigating," he told the *Los Angles Times.* "We credit the career professionals of the National Park Service for collectively standing up against the onslaught of Department of Interior political operatives."

Those who had lobbied for more emphasis on recreation were disappointed. "Our concern is we don't want the administration to go back to the Clinton-era policy of putting preservation over recreation," Don Amador of the Blue Ribbon Coalition, a national group representing park users. "They're both important, and motorized access to national parks, whether it's snowmobiling in Yellowstone or riding a sports utility vehicle in the desert Southwest, are important ways for people to use and enjoy their parks. We just want to see a balance."

Snowmobiling in Yellowstone

The new management guidelines did not resolve what had come to be the symbol for the controversy over recreation in the parks—snowmobiling in Yellowstone National Park in Wyoming's northwest corner. The oldest park in the national park system, Yellowstone was noted for its spectacular scenery, buffalo herds, geological features such as the Old Faithful Geyser, and in winter for its snowmobilers. Environmentalists had long complained that the noisy, gasoline-powered machines disturbed the wildlife, damaged the land, polluted the air, and destroyed the natural serenity of the park. In 2000 President Bill Clinton banned snowmobiles in the park. President George W. Bush rescinded the ban upon taking office in 2001, but regulations for their use had not been issued.

In late November 2006 the National Park Service released a draft environmental impact statement that would allow up to 720 snowmobiles a day in the park. Currently about 250 snowmobiles were using the park every day, in part because of confusion over the regulations. Before the ban in 2000, an average of 795 machines used the park daily. The latest proposal drew fire from a number of environmental groups who threatened to try to block it in court if it went into effect.

Park Funding Woes

To commemorate the park system's ninetieth birthday, President Bush and Secretary Kempthorne promised to embark on a ten-year plan to improve the parks. Whether additional funding for the parks would be forthcoming remained to be seen. For years funding for the park service had fallen short of its needs, and individual parks were forced to cut back on visitor and education services and staffing, decrease resource protection operations, close some facilities within the parks, and charge higher fees. About 270 million visitors toured the parks each year, with some popular parks such as the Great Smoky Mountains, Grand Canyon, Yellowstone, Yosemite, and Zion each receiving millions of visitors and others receiving only a few thousand.

Although the park service's operating budget had been increasing, to $1.7 billion in 2006, it was barely keeping pace with inflation. The Coalition of National Park Service Retirees, an organization of more than 500 former park service employees, said in June 2006 that the parks needed at least another $600 million annually to maintain their services. That did not include a maintenance backlog, estimated to range from $4.5 billion to $9.7 billion, according to a report issued by the Congressional Research Service in March 2005. During his 2000 campaign, President Bush pledged to eliminate the backlog of deferred maintenance in the parks, which was then estimated at $4.9 billion. During his first five years in office, just $800 million was added to the park maintenance fund.

In a related development, the National Park Service in May abandoned proposals to allow more advertising in the parks. The park service received about $100 million in corporate and other donations every year, and the proposal would have recognized some of those contributions by allowing some minimal naming rights and signage bearing donors' logos. The park service also rejected a proposal to allow it to accept donations from tobacco and alcohol companies for the first time. Opponents of the proposal, including park service personnel, said the advertising would have overly commercialized the parks.

New Marine Refuge

President Bush announced on June 15 that he was designating a 1,200-mile chain of tiny Hawaiian islands and their surrounding reefs and waters as a national monument. The region, which was nearly as large as California and was home to some 7,000 species of wildlife, would be the largest protected marine refuge in the world. Commercial and sports fishing would be phased out of the area, known as the Northwestern Hawaiian Islands.

Meanwhile, private landowners were increasingly taking steps to conserve habitats and prevent development. According to the Land Trust Alliance, a consortium of local, state, and national conservation groups, the acreage of private land set aside in land conservation trusts rose 54 percent over the past five years, from 24 million acres in 2000 to 37 million acres in 2005. That represented an area larger than New England.

Following are excerpts from "Management Policies 2006," the management guidelines for the National Park Service issued by the U.S. Department of the Interior on August 31, 2006.

DOCUMENT

"Management Policies 2006"

The national park system was created to conserve unimpaired many of the world's most magnificent landscapes, places that enshrine our nation's enduring principles, and places that remind us of the tremendous sacrifices Americans have made on behalf of those principles. They are the most remarkable collection of places in America for recreation and learning. Visitors can immerse themselves in places where events actually happened and enjoy some of the most significant natural and historic places in America. These are places that offer renewal for the body, the spirit and the mind. As required by the 1916 Organic Act, these special places must be managed in a special way—a way that allows them to be enjoyed not just by those who are here today, but also by generations that follow. Enjoyment by present and future generations can be assured only if these special places are passed on to them in an unimpaired condition. And that is the challenge that faces all the employees of the National Park Service. It is a challenge eagerly embraced, but employees must have the tools required to perform the job successfully. The *Management Policies* contained in these pages represent one of the most important tools available. Through their judicious and consistent application, these policies will set a firm foundation for stewardship that will continue to earn the trust and confidence of the American people.

Underlying Principles

The National Park Service adhered to a number of principles in preparing this 2006 edition of *Management Policies*. The key principles were that the policies must:

- comply with current laws, regulations and executive orders;
- prevent impairment of park resources and values;
- ensure that conservation will be predominant when there is a conflict between the protection of resources and their use;
- maintain NPS responsibility for making decisions and for exercising key authorities;
- emphasize consultation and cooperation with local/state/tribal/federal entities;
- support pursuit of the best contemporary business practices and sustainability;
- encourage consistency across the system—"one national park system";
- reflect NPS goals and a commitment to cooperative conservation and civic engagement;
- employ a tone that leaves no room for misunderstanding the National Park Service's commitment to the public's appropriate use and enjoyment, including education and interpretation, of park resources, while preventing unacceptable impacts;
- pass on to future generations natural, cultural, and physical resources that meet desired conditions better than they do today, along with improved opportunities for enjoyment. . . .

8   Use of the Parks

National parks belong to all Americans, and the National Park Service will welcome all Americans to experience their parks. The Service will focus special attention on visitor enjoyment of the parks while recognizing that the NPS mission is to conserve unimpaired each park's natural and cultural resources and values for the enjoyment, education, and inspiration of present and future generations. The Service will also welcome international visitors, in keeping with its commitment to extend the benefits of natural and cultural resource conservation and outdoor recreation throughout the world.

8.1   General

Many different types of uses take place in the hundreds of park units that make up the national park system. Some of those uses are carried out by the National Park Service, but many more are carried out by park visitors, permittees, lessees, and licensees. The 1916 Organic Act, which created the National Park Service, directs the Service to conserve park resources "unimpaired" for the enjoyment of future generations. The 1970 National Park System General Authorities Act, as amended in 1978, prohibits the Service from allowing any activities that would cause derogation of the values and purposes for which the parks have been established (except as directly and specifically provided by Congress). Taken together, these two laws establish for NPS managers (1) a strict mandate to protect park resources and values; (2) a responsibility to actively manage all park uses; and (3) when necessary, an obligation to regulate their amount, kind, time, and place in such a way that future generations can enjoy, learn, and be inspired by park resources and values and appreciate their national significance in as good or better condition than the generation that preceded them. (Throughout these *Management Policies*, the term "impairment" is construed to also encompass "derogation.")

8.1.1   *Appropriate Use*

The concept of appropriate use is especially important with regard to visitor enjoyment because, in accordance with the Organic Act, the fundamental purpose of all parks also includes providing for the enjoyment of park resources and values by present and future generations. . . . Appropriate forms of visitor enjoyment emphasize appropriate recreation consistent with the protection of the park. This includes interpretation of park resources and contemplation and understanding of the purposes for which a park unit's resources are being preserved. Many of these forms of enjoyment support the federal policy of promoting the health and personal fitness of the general public. . . .

Providing opportunities for appropriate public enjoyment is an important part of the Service's mission. Other park uses—unrelated to public enjoyment—may sometimes be allowed as a right or a privilege if they are not otherwise prohibited by law or regulation. In exercising its discretionary authority, the Service will allow only uses that are (1) appropriate to the purpose for which the park was established, and (2) can be sustained without causing unacceptable impacts. Recreational activities and other uses that would impair a park's resources, values, or purposes cannot be allowed. The only exception is when an activity that would cause impairment is directly and specifically mandated by Congress.

The fact that a park use may have an impact does not necessarily mean it will be unacceptable or impair park resources or values for the enjoyment of future generations. Impacts may affect park resources or values and still be within the limits of the discretionary authority conferred by the Organic Act. In these situations, the Service will ensure that the impacts are unavoidable and cannot be further mitigated. Even when they fall far short of impairment, unacceptable impacts can rapidly lead to impairment and must be avoided.

For this reason, the Service will not knowingly authorize a park use that would cause unacceptable impacts.

When a use is mandated by law but causes unacceptable impacts on park resources or values, the Service will take appropriate management actions to avoid or mitigate the adverse effects. When a use is authorized by law but not mandated, and when the use may cause unacceptable impacts on park resources or values, the Service will avoid or mitigate the impacts to the point where there will be no unacceptable impacts; or, if necessary, the Service will deny a proposed activity or eliminate an existing activity.

8.1.2   *Process for Determining Appropriate Uses*
All proposals for park uses will be evaluated for

- consistency with applicable laws, executive orders, regulations, and policies;
- consistency with existing plans for public use and resource management;
- actual and potential effects on park resources and values;
- total costs to the Service; and
- whether the public interest will be served.

Superintendents must continually monitor and examine all park uses to ensure that unanticipated and unacceptable impacts do not occur. Superintendents should also be attentive to existing and emerging technologies that might further reduce or eliminate impacts from existing uses allowed in parks. Unless otherwise mandated by statute, only uses that meet the criteria listed in section 8.2 may be allowed.

Specific park uses will be guided by the following subsections of this chapter, and must comply also with the other chapters of these *Management Policies*. The Service will coordinate with appropriate state authorities regarding activities that are subject to state regulation or to joint federal/state regulation. . . . Some activities may be allowed in parks only after park-specific regulations have been published, which requires extensive analysis and opportunities for civic engagement.

The National Park Service will always consider allowing activities that are appropriate to the parks, although conditions may preclude certain activities or require that limitations be placed on them. In all cases, impacts from park uses must be avoided, minimized, or mitigated through one or more of the following methods:

- visitor education and civic engagement
- temporal, spatial, or numerical limitations on the use
- the application of best available technology
- the application of adaptive management techniques

If, in monitoring a park use, unanticipated impacts become apparent, the superintendent must further manage or constrain the use to minimize the impacts, or discontinue the use if the impacts are unacceptable.

8.2   Visitor Use

Enjoyment of park resources and values by the people of the United States is part of the fundamental purpose of all parks. The Service is committed to providing appropriate, high-quality opportunities for visitors to enjoy the parks, and the Service will maintain within the parks an atmosphere that is open, inviting, and accessible to every segment of

American society. However, many forms of recreation enjoyed by the public do not require a national park setting and are more appropriate to other venues. The Service will therefore

- provide opportunities for forms of enjoyment that are uniquely suited and appropriate to the superlative natural and cultural resources found in the parks;
- defer to local, state, tribal, and other federal agencies; private industry; and nongovernmental organizations to meet the broader spectrum of recreational needs and demands.

To provide for enjoyment of the parks, the National Park Service will encourage visitor activities that

- are appropriate to the purpose for which the park was established; and
- are inspirational, educational, or healthful, and otherwise appropriate to the park environment; and
- will foster an understanding of and appreciation for park resources and values, or will promote enjoyment through a direct association with, interaction with, or relation to park resources; and
- can be sustained without causing unacceptable impacts to park resources or values.

The primary means by which the Service will actively foster and provide activities that meet these criteria will be through its interpretive and educational programs.... The Service will also welcome the efforts of nongovernmental organizations, tour companies, guides, outfitters, and other private sector entities to provide structured activities that meet these criteria. In addition to structured activities, the Service will, to the extent practicable, afford visitors ample opportunity for inspiration, appreciation, and enjoyment through their own personalized experiences—without the formality of program or structure.

The Service may allow other visitor uses that do not meet all the above criteria if they are appropriate to the purpose for which the park was established and they can be sustained without causing unacceptable impacts to park resources or values. For the purposes of these policies, unacceptable impacts are impacts that, individually or cumulatively, would

- be inconsistent with a park's purposes or values, or
- impede the attainment of a park's desired conditions for natural and cultural resources as identified through the park's planning process, or
- create an unsafe or unhealthy environment for visitors or employees, or
- diminish opportunities for current or future generations to enjoy, learn about, or be inspired by park resources or values, or
- unreasonably interfere with
  o park programs or activities, or
  o an appropriate use, or
  o the atmosphere of peace and tranquility, or the natural soundscape maintained in wilderness and natural, historic, or commemorative locations within the park, or
  o NPS concessioner or contractor operations or services.

Management controls and conditions must be established for all park uses to ensure that park resources and values are preserved and protected for the future. If and when a superintendent has a reasonable basis for believing that an ongoing or proposed public use would cause unacceptable impacts to park resources or values, the superintendent must make adjustments to the way the activity is conducted to eliminate the unacceptable impacts. If the adjustments do not succeed in eliminating the unacceptable impacts, the superintendent may (1) temporarily or permanently close a specific area, or (2) place limitations on the use, or (3) prohibit the use. Restrictions placed on recreational uses that have otherwise been found to be appropriate will be limited to the minimum necessary to protect park resources and values and promote visitor safety and enjoyment.

Any closures or restrictions—other than those imposed by law—must be consistent with applicable laws, regulations, and policies, and (except in emergency situations) require a written determination by the superintendent that such measures are needed to

- protect public health and safety;
- prevent unacceptable impacts to park resources or values;
- carry out scientific research;
- minimize visitor use conflicts; or
- otherwise implement management responsibilities.

When practicable, restrictions will be based on the results of study or research, including (when appropriate) research in the social sciences. Any restrictions imposed will be fully explained to visitors and the public. Visitors will be given appropriate information on how to keep adverse impacts to a minimum, and how to enjoy the safe and lawful use of the parks.

8.2.1   *Visitor Carrying Capacity*

Visitor carrying capacity is the type and level of visitor use that can be accommodated while sustaining the desired resource and visitor experience conditions in the park. By identifying and staying within carrying capacities, superintendents can manage park uses that may unacceptably impact the resources and values for which the parks were established. Superintendents will identify visitor carrying capacities for managing public use. Superintendents will also identify ways to monitor for and address unacceptable impacts on park resources and visitor experiences.

When making decisions about carrying capacity, superintendents must use the best available natural and social science and other information, and maintain a comprehensive administrative record relating to their decisions. The decision-making process should be based on desired resource conditions and visitor experiences for the area, quality indicators and standards that define the desired resource conditions and visitor experiences, and other factors that will lead to logical conclusions and the protection of park resources and values. The level of analysis necessary to make decisions about carrying capacities is commensurate with the potential impacts or consequences of the decisions. The greater the potential for significant impacts or consequences on park resources and values or the opportunities to enjoy them, the greater the level of study and analysis and civic engagement needed to support the decisions.

The planning process will determine the desired resource and visitor experience conditions that are the foundation for carrying capacity analysis and decision-making. If the time frame for making decisions is insufficient to allow the application of a carrying capacity planning process, superintendents must make decisions based on the best available science, public input, and other information. In either case, such planning must be accompanied by appropriate environmental impact analysis. . . .

As park use changes over time, superintendents must continue to decide if management actions are needed to keep use at sustainable levels and prevent unacceptable impacts. If indicators and standards have been prescribed for an impact, the acceptable level is the prescribed standard. If indicators and standards do not exist, the superintendent must determine how much impact is acceptable before management intervention is required.

If and when park uses reach a level at which they must be limited or curtailed, the preferred choice will be to continue uses that are encouraged under the criteria listed in section 8.2, and to limit or curtail those that least meet those criteria. The Service will consult with tourism organizations and other affected service providers in seeking ways to provide appropriate types and levels of visitor use while sustaining the desired resource and visitor experience conditions.

8.2.2   *Recreational Activities*

The National Park Service will manage recreational activities according to the criteria listed in sections 8.1 and 8.2. . . . Examples of the broad range of recreational activities that take place in parks include, but are not limited to, boating, camping, bicycling, fishing, hiking, horseback riding and packing, outdoor sports, picnicking, scuba diving, cross-country skiing, caving, mountain and rock climbing, earth caching, and swimming. Many of these activities support the federal policy of promoting the health and personal fitness of the general public. . . . However, not all of these activities will be appropriate or allowable in all parks; that determination must be made on the basis of park-specific planning.

Service-wide regulations addressing aircraft use, off-road bicycling, hang gliding, off-road vehicle use, personal watercraft, and snowmobiling require that special, park-specific regulations be developed before these uses may be allowed in parks. . . .

The Service will monitor new or changing patterns of use or trends in recreational activities and assess their potential impacts on park resources. A new form of recreational activity will not be allowed within a park until a superintendent has made a determination that it will be appropriate and not cause unacceptable impacts. Restrictions placed on recreational uses that have been found to be appropriate will be limited to the minimum necessary to protect park resources and values and promote visitor safety and enjoyment. . . .

Park managers will (1) identify what levels and types of sounds contribute to or hinder visitor enjoyment, and (2) monitor, in and adjacent to parks, noise-generating human activities—including noise caused by mechanical or electronic devices—that adversely affect visitor opportunities to enjoy park soundscapes. Based on this information, the Service will take action to prevent or minimize those noises that adversely affect the visitor experience or that exceed levels that are acceptable to or appropriate for visitor uses of parks.

8.2.2.1   *Management of Recreational Use*

Superintendents will develop and implement visitor use management plans and take action, as appropriate, to ensure that recreational uses and activities in the park are consistent with its authorizing legislation or proclamation and do not cause unacceptable impacts on park resources or values. Depending on local park needs and circumstances, these plans may be prepared (1) as coordinated, activity-specific documents (such as a river use plan, a backcountry use plan, a wilderness management plan, an off-road vehicle use plan, a winter use plan); (2) as action-plan components of a resource management plan or general management plan; or (3) as a single integrated plan that addresses a broad spectrum of recreational activities. Regardless of their format or complexity, visitor use management plans will (1) contain specific, measurable management objectives related to the activity or activities being addressed; (2) be periodically reviewed and updated; and (3) be consistent with the carrying capacity decisions made in the general management plan.

The Service will seek consistency in recreation management policies and procedures on both a Service-wide and interagency basis to the extent practicable. However, because of differences in the enabling legislation and resources of individual parks, and differences in the missions of the Service and other federal agencies, an activity that is entirely appropriate when conducted in one location may be inappropriate when conducted in another. The Service will consider a park's purposes and the effects on park resources and visitors when determining the appropriateness of a specific recreational activity.

Superintendents will consider a wide range of techniques in managing recreational use to avoid adverse impacts on park resources and values or desired visitor experiences. Examples of appropriate techniques include visitor information and education programs, separation of conflicting uses by time or location, "hardening" sites, modifying maintenance practices, and permit and reservation systems. Superintendents may also use their discretionary authority to impose local restrictions, public use limits, and closures and designate areas for a specific use or activity.... Any restriction of appropriate recreational uses will be limited to what is necessary to protect park resources and values, to promote visitor safety and enjoyment, or to meet park management needs. To the extent practicable, public use limits established by the Service will be based on the results of scientific research and other available support data. However, an activity will be restricted or prohibited when, in the judgment of the superintendent, its occurrence, continuation, or expansion would (1) violate the criteria listed in section 8.2, or (2) conflict with the findings of a carrying capacity analysis with no reasonable alternative that would avoid or satisfactorily mitigate the violation or conflict....

8.2.2.5   *Fishing*

Recreational fishing will be allowed in parks when it is authorized or not specifically prohibited by federal law provided that it has been determined to be an appropriate use per section 8.1 of these policies. When fishing is allowed, it will be conducted in accordance with applicable federal laws and treaty rights, and nonconflicting state laws and regulations. The Service will manage fishing activities to achieve management objectives. Before the Service issues regulations or other restrictions, representatives of appropriate tribes and state and federal agencies will be consulted to ensure that all available scientific data are considered in the decision-making process. Any such regulations or other restrictions will be developed with public involvement and in consultation with fish and wildlife management agencies as appropriate, consistent with departmental policy....

Commercial fishing will be allowed only when specifically authorized by federal law or treaty right.

8.2.2.6   *Hunting and Trapping*

Hunting, trapping, or any other methods of harvesting wildlife by the public will be allowed where it is specifically mandated by federal law. Where hunting activity is not mandated but is authorized on a discretionary basis under federal law, it may take place only after the Service has determined that the activity is an appropriate use and can be managed consistent with sound resource management principles....

8.2.2.8   Recreational Pack and Saddle Stock Use

Equine species such as horses, mules, donkeys and burros, and other types of animals (including llamas, alpacas, goats, oxen, dogs and reindeer) may be employed when it is an appropriate use to support backcountry transport of people and materials and will not result in unacceptable impacts....

8.2.3   Use of Motorized Equipment

The variety of motorized equipment—including visitor vehicles, concessioner equipment, and NPS administrative or staff vehicles and equipment—that operates in national parks could adversely impact park resources, including the park's natural soundscape and the flow of natural chemical information and odors that are important to many living organisms. In addition to their natural values, natural sounds (such as waves breaking on the shore, the roar of a river, and the call of a loon), form a valued part of the visitor experience. Conversely, the sounds of motor vehicle traffic, an electric generator, or loud music can greatly diminish the solemnity of a visit to a national memorial, the effectiveness of a park interpretive program, or the ability of a visitor to hear a bird singing its territorial song. Many parks that appear as they did in historical context no longer sound the way they once did.

The Service will strive to preserve or restore the natural quiet and natural sounds associated with the physical and biological resources of parks. To do this, superintendents will carefully evaluate and manage how, when, and where motorized equipment is used by all who operate equipment in the parks, including park staff. Uses and impacts associated with the use of motorized equipment will be addressed in park planning processes. Where such use is necessary and appropriate, the least impacting equipment, vehicles, and transportation systems should be used, consistent with public and employee safety. The natural ambient sound level—that is, the environment of sound that exists in the absence of human-caused noise—is the baseline condition, and the standard against which current conditions in a soundscape will be measured and evaluated....

8.2.3.1   Motorized Off-road Vehicle Use

Off-road motor vehicle use in national park units is governed by Executive Order 11644 (Use of Off-road Vehicles on Public Lands, as amended by Executive Order 11989), which defines off-road vehicles as "any motorized vehicle designed for or capable of cross-country travel on or immediately over land, water, sand, snow, ice, marsh, swampland, or other natural terrain" (except any registered motorboat or any vehicle used for emergency purposes). Unless otherwise provided by statute, any time there is a proposal to allow a motor vehicle meeting this description to be used in a park, the provisions of the executive order must be applied.

... [R]outes and areas may be designated only in national recreation areas, national seashores, national lakeshores, and national preserves, and only by special regulation. In accordance with the executive order, they may be allowed only in locations where there will be no adverse impacts on the area's natural, cultural, scenic, and esthetic values, and in consideration of other existing or proposed recreational uses. The criteria for new uses, appropriate uses, and unacceptable impacts listed in sections 8.1 and 8.2 must also be applied to determine whether off-road vehicle use may be allowed. As required by the executive order and the Organic Act, superintendents must immediately close a designated off-road vehicle route whenever the use is causing or will cause unacceptable impacts on the soil, vegetation, wildlife, wildlife habitat, or cultural and historic resources.

NPS administrative off-road motor vehicle use will be limited to what is necessary to manage the public use of designated off-road vehicle routes and areas; to conduct emergency operations; and to accomplish essential maintenance, construction, and resource protection activities that cannot be accomplished reasonably by other means.

8.2.3.2   *Snowmobiles*
Snowmobile use is a form of off-road vehicle use governed by Executive Order 11644 . . . and in Alaska also by provisions of the Alaska National Interest Lands Conservation Act. . . . Outside Alaska, routes and areas may be designated for snowmobile and oversnow vehicle use only by special regulation after it has first been determined through park planning to be an appropriate use . . . and not otherwise result in unacceptable impacts. Such designations can occur only on routes and water surfaces that are used by motor vehicles or motorboats during other seasons. In Alaska, the Alaska National Interest Lands Conservation Act provides additional authorities and requirements governing snowmobile use. . . .

8.2.3.3   *Personal Watercraft Use*
Personal watercraft use is generally prohibited. . . . However, it may be allowed within a park by special regulation if it has first been determined through park planning to be an appropriate use that will not result in unacceptable impacts. . . .

8.5   Use by American Indians and Other Traditionally Associated Groups

The National Park Service will develop and implement its programs in a manner that reflects knowledge of and respect for the cultures of American Indian tribes or groups with demonstrated ancestral ties to particular resources in parks. Evidence of such ties will be established through systematic archeological or anthropological studies, including ethnographic oral history and ethnohistory studies or a combination of these sources. For purposes of these policies, the term American Indian tribe means any tribe, band, nation, or other organized group or community of Indians, including any Alaska Native Village, which is recognized as eligible for the special programs and services provided by the United States to Indians because of their status as Indians. Other groups of people with traditional associations to park lands or resources include native peoples of the Caribbean; Native Hawaiians and other native Pacific islanders; and state-recognized tribes and other groups who are defined by themselves and known to others as members of a named cultural unit that has historically shared a set of linguistic, kinship, political, or other distinguishing cultural features. . . .

8.6.4   *Rights-of-Way for Utilities and Roads*
8.6.4.1   *General*
A right-of-way is a special park use allowing a utility to pass over, under, or through NPS property. It may be issued only pursuant to specific statutory authority, and generally only if there is no practicable alternative to such use of NPS lands. The criteria listed in section 8.2 must also be met. New roads may not be permitted with a right-of-way permit, but require specific statutory authority. . . .

8.6.4.2 Utilities

Utility rights-of-way over lands administered by the Park Service are governed by statutory authorities.... If not incompatible with the public interest, rights-of-way issued under 16 USC 5 or 79 are discretionary and conditional upon a finding by the Service that the proposed use will not cause unacceptable impacts on park resources, values, or purposes.

8.6.4.3 Telecommunication Sites

Requests to site non-NPS telecommunication antennas and related facilities on NPS lands will be considered in accordance with the Telecommunications Act of 1996 ...which authorizes but does not mandate a presumption that such requests be granted absent unavoidable conflict with the agency mission, or the current or planned use of the property or access to that property....

Superintendents will require the best technology available. For example, consideration should be given first to co-locating new facilities, constructing towers that are camouflaged to blend in with their surroundings, and installing micro-sites. New traditional towers (i.e., monopole or lattice) should be approved only after all other options have been explored. If a traditional tower is necessary, it should not be visible from any significant public vantage point.

As appropriate, superintendents should consider making use of available interpretive media to caution park users of the limited (or nonexistent) cellular service and their personal responsibility to plan accordingly.

When construction of telecommunication facilities on nonpark lands might adversely impact park resources and values, superintendents will actively participate in the applicable planning and regulatory processes and seek to prevent or mitigate the adverse impacts....

8.6.4.4 Roads and Highways and Petroleum-based Pipelines

There are no general NPS statutory authorities for non-NPS roads or for gas pipelines. However, such authorization is sometimes contained in park-specific enabling legislation.... The Service will generally object to proposals for the use of park lands for highway purposes that do not directly benefit a park....

8.6.7 Agricultural Uses

Agricultural uses and activities are authorized in parks in accordance with the direction provided by a park's enabling legislation and general management plan. Agricultural practices and techniques, including the use of pesticides and other biocontrol agents such as genetically modified or engineered organisms, should be specified in an approved resource stewardship strategy, and are subject to review and approval by the NPS integrated pest management (IPM) program manager. These practices and techniques are also subject to the provisions of federal and state laws, [and] NPS regulations and policies.... In general, agricultural activities should be conducted in accordance with accepted best management practices.

8.7 Mineral Exploration and Development

Mineral exploration and development include exploration, extraction, production, storage, and transportation of minerals. Mineral exploration or development may be allowed in parks only when prospective operators demonstrate that they hold rights to valid mining claims, federal mineral leases, or nonfederally owned minerals. If this right is not clearly demonstrated, the National Park Service will inform the prospective operator that, until proof of a property right is documented, the Service will not further consider the proposed activity. Unless otherwise directed by Congress, if the Service determines that the proposed mineral development would impair park resources or values, or that such development is not consistent with park purposes or does not meet approval standards under applicable NPS regulations and cannot be sufficiently modified to meet those standards, the Service will seek to extinguish the associated mineral right through acquisition. In some parks, all or certain types of mineral development are specifically prohibited by law.

All persons who conduct mineral development within parks will do so only in conformance with applicable statutes, regulations, and NPS policies. . . .

Persons may not use or occupy surface lands in a park for purposes of removing minerals outside the park unless provided for in law. General management plans, land protection plans, and other planning documents for parks with mining claims, federal mineral leases, or nonfederally owned mineral interests will address these nonfederal property interests as appropriate. Lands with mineral interests will be zoned according to their anticipated management and use—based on their resource values, park management objectives, and park-specific legislative provisions relating to mineral interests.

8.7.1   Mining Claims

The location of new mining claims pursuant to the General Mining Act of 1872 is prohibited in all park areas. Under the Mining in the Parks Act, the National Park Service may permit mineral development only on existing patented and valid unpatented mining claims in conformance with the park's enabling legislation and the regulations for mining claims. . . .

8.7.2   Federal Mineral Leases

All parks are closed to new federal mineral leasing except for three national recreation areas (Lake Mead, Whiskeytown, and Glen Canyon) where Congress has explicitly authorized federal mineral leasing in each area's enabling legislation. Through park planning documents, the National Park Service has closed portions of these areas to federal mineral leasing because of the presence of sensitive resources. No person may explore for federal minerals in any of these areas except under a lease issued pursuant to regulations . . . or a prospecting permit. . . . Before consenting to a federal mineral lease or subsequent mineral development connected with a lease, the regional director must find, in writing, that leasing and subsequent mineral development will not result in a significant adverse effect on park resources or administration.

Some park areas contain leases that existed at the time the park was created or expanded. These leases are valid existing rights and will continue to exist until they expire under the regulations that govern federal mineral leasing. . . .

8.7.3   Nonfederally Owned Minerals

Nonfederal mineral interests in park units consist of oil and gas interests, rights to mineral interests other than oil and gas (such as private outstanding mineral rights, mineral rights through general land grant patents, homestead patents, or other private mineral rights that did not derive from the General Mining Act). The Park Service governs activities associated with these two categories of nonfederal mineral rights under separate regulatory schemes.

The Park Service may approve operations associated with nonfederal oil and gas interests. . . . If an operator's plan fails to meet the approved standards of these regulations, the Park Service generally has authority to deny the operation and may initiate acquisition. Absent a decision to acquire the property, application of the regulations is not intended to result in a taking of the property interest, but rather to impose reasonable regulation of the activity. . . .

The Service must determine that operations associated with these mineral interests would not adversely impact "public health and safety, environmental or scenic values, natural or cultural resources, scientific research, implementation or management responsibilities, proper allocation and use of facilities, or the avoidance of conflict among visitor use activities. . . . " If the impacts from the operation on the resource cannot be sufficiently mitigated to meet this standard, the Park Service may seek to acquire the mineral interest.

Source: U.S. Department of the Interior. National Park Service. "Management Policies 2006." August 31, 2006. Washington, D.C.: U.S. Government Printing Office. www.nps.gov/policy/MP2006.pdf (accessed January 28, 2007).

UN Security Council Resolution on Darfur Crisis in Sudan

August 31, 2006

■■■■■■■ **THE DOCUMENT IN CONTEXT** ■■■■■■■

The fourth year of a civil war in the Darfur region of western Sudan saw an escalation of international diplomacy and rhetoric but little concrete action to stop the violence that had killed an estimated 200,000 or more people, dislocated more than 2 million others, and been called genocide by the U.S. government. The Sudanese government and one of several rebel groups signed a peace agreement that brought no real peace, and diplomats at the United Nations engaged in prolonged negotiations to provide more support for an African Union peacekeeping mission that lacked the manpower or the mandate to enforce a peace.

While the diplomats debated and negotiators met in round-the-clock sessions, the atrocities continued in Darfur—generally at a lower level than in the past but still terrifying and often deadly for the victims. The fighting became even more complex during 2006 than in the past because latent rivalries between rebel groups broke out into open warfare among them. Civilians were endangered both by armed forces aligned with the government and by rebel groups supposedly fighting the government on their behalf. Both sides raided villages and refugee camps, where they killed or drove off the men and raped the women, and the government's air force continued to bomb those same villages and camps. Fighting also increasingly spread into neighboring Chad, where about 200,000 Darfurians had taken refuge and where that government faced a separate insurgency that it said was supported by the Sudanese regime.

In the United States, a coalition of religious and human rights advocacy groups launched a national campaign to focus attention on Darfur. Their efforts included large rallies in Washington and other cities in late April. These campaigners also pressed states, municipalities, universities, and other institutions to divest themselves of stocks in businesses having ties to the Sudanese government. By year's end at least six states, including California, enacted divestiture legislation. *(Darfur background, Historic Documents of 2005, p. 514)*

Getting the UN into Sudan

In many conflict situations, one of the international community's first responses was to rush in a UN peacekeeping force—in some cases to separate the warring parties, and in others to monitor or even enforce a signed peace agreement. The UN's ability to intervene in the Darfur crisis faced two limitations, however. One was the refusal of the Sudanese government to accept a UN peacekeeping force, which officials in Khartoum said would infringe on the country's sovereignty. A second, related factor was the opposition to such a force by China and Russia, two of the Security Council's five veto-bearing members. China had growing commercial interests in Sudan (notably the development of oilfields there), and Russia often was reluctant to use UN intervention to address human rights abuses in other countries.

Sudan in 2004 agreed to allow a small military force from other African countries, under the banner of the African Union, to monitor a cease-fire in the Darfur conflict. The African force had a mandate that meant it could report cease-fire violations but not do anything about them—a limitation that frustrated the African soldiers and angered the Darfurians, who wanted more protection. This force also was chronically short of troops and equipment, much of which was donated by Western countries. At the beginning of 2006 it had about 7,000 troops to cover an area the size of Texas.

UN Secretary General Kofi Annan long had called for a UN peacekeeping force for Darfur, arguing that such a force would have more credibility and international support than the limited African Union mission. U.S. officials, who generally had been reluctant to support Annan's position, suddenly embraced it in January 2006 and began pushing for action at the UN, saying the situation was more urgent than before.

There were two options for creation of such a UN force. One was to incorporate the African Union mission into a broader, UN-mandated force. Another option was to expand the mandate of the existing peacekeeping force the UN had established to monitor the peace agreement in January 2005 that ended the twenty-year war between the Sudanese government and rebels in the southern part of the country. The UN had created a 10,000-man peacekeeping force, called the United Nations Mission in Sudan (UNMIS), to ensure that both sides kept the peace agreement. While the Khartoum government had accepted that UN force, it refused to consider a similar one for Darfur.

The Security Council took a first step toward action on February 3, approving a U.S. proposal directing Annan to begin planning for a UN force that incorporated the African Union mission. UN officials said they hoped the new force would have as many as 20,000 troops, including the African Union soldiers and policemen. Although the council asked Annan to begin his planning "without delay," officials said it could be up to a year before the expanded force was in place. Ten days later, Annan met with President George W. Bush and asked for U.S. help in getting the new force in place. Bush endorsed the call for more troops, possibly with increased logistical support from the NATO alliance, but refused to consider putting U.S. personnel on the ground in Darfur.

The new push for a UN force quickly ran into resistance from Sudan, which sent diplomats to capitals represented on the Security Council to lobby against it. Despite Sudanese resistance, the African Union on March 10 voted to support, in principle, the transition of its force in Sudan to a UN operation.

In a partial response to widespread calls for direct action against key individuals behind the violence in Darfur, the Security Council on April 25 adopted financial and travel sanctions against a Sudanese general in the region and three militia leaders, two of them rebels and one a leader of progovernment forces called the *Janjaweed*. The four men reportedly were among fifty-one people named by a UN investigating commission in 2005 as being responsible for much of the violence. Conspicuously absent from the list of those sanctioned by the Security Council were senior Sudanese government officials, notably security chief Salah Abdallah Gosh, who reportedly was a key source for the Central Intelligence Agency in the Bush administration's war against al Qaeda and other terrorist groups. China, Qatar, and Russia abstained on adoption of the resolution imposing the sanctions.

A Peace Accord, Sort Of

One point of the Security Council's resolution was to put pressure on the government and rebel groups, which were meeting in Abuja, Nigeria, to negotiate a peace agreement. Those negotiations were scheduled to end on April 30, with or without an agreement, but they proved to be a cliffhanger, featuring the last-minute departure of the Sudanese government's chief negotiator and the last-minute arrival of the U.S. government's point man on Darfur—Deputy Secretary of State Robert B. Zoellick. The deadline was pushed back day by day after Zoellick's arrival. Even President Bush entered the equation by calling Sudan's president, Omar al-Bashir, to request that the government negotiator, Vice President Ali Osman Taha, return to the talks.

The theatrics and high-stakes diplomacy paid off with the signing on May 5 of what was called a "comprehensive" peace settlement of the Darfur conflict. The agreement itself covered all the conventional aspects of such an accord, including the establishment of a "transitional" government for Darfur with the prospect of more autonomy for the region in the future.

The agreement did not have comprehensive support, however, as only Minni Minnawi, head of the largest rebel group, the Sudan Liberation Army, signed it. The leaders of a rival faction of that group and another rebel group, the Justice and Equality Movement, refused to sign. The holdouts said the agreement failed to meet their minimal demands for concessions by the Khartoum government. Zoellick said personality conflicts played a role, noting that leaders of the three rebel factions rarely spoke to one another. Ethnic differences also were important: Minnawi was a leader of the Zaghawa tribe of herdsmen, while his chief rival within the Sudan Liberation Army, Abdul Wahid al-Nur, was from the much larger tribal group called the Fur, most of whose members were settled farmers.

In Darfur, the rival groups jockeyed for position in advance of the peace agreement taking effect, and a high-profile incident illustrated just how violent the region remained. On May 8, Jan Egeland, the UN undersecretary general for humanitarian affairs and emergency relief coordinator, was forced to flee the huge Kalma refugee camp when violence broke out in a dispute over the identity of a translator. A shaken Egeland and other officials escaped unharmed, but the translator was hacked to death and the incident raised new questions about the capability of the African Union peacekeeping force, which supposedly was protecting the camp.

Despite the tenuous nature of the Darfur peace agreement, the African Union endorsed it on May 15 and the UN Security Council followed suit the following day. Both institutions called on the Khartoum government to agree to putting the United Nations in charge of the African Union peacekeeping force in Darfur, and the African leaders also called on the holdout rebels to accept the peace agreement.

More Violence, More Diplomacy

Any illusions that the May 5 peace agreement would end the violence in Darfur were quickly swept aside in subsequent weeks as the rival rebel groups and the Khartoum government stepped up their military operations in a competition for control of territory. On June 5, exactly one month after the peace agreement was signed, a delegation from the UN Security Council arrived in Khartoum on a mission to convince the government to accept a UN peacekeeping force in Darfur. President Bashir agreed to further talks on the idea but two weeks later flatly rejected it. "These are colonial forces and we will not accept colonial forces coming into the country," he said on June 20.

Bashir later put forward a competing plan under which his government would send 10,000 troops to Darfur; UN officials said that plan was unacceptable because government forces were a major source of the violence in the region. Bashir received important support for his position from the Arab League, which offered to finance a somewhat larger African Union force as an alternative to a UN mission. Bashir and his government were members of the Arab minority that long had dominated Sudan; most of the Darfur rebels were black Africans.

Despite Bashir's resistance, the UN staff moved ahead with plans for a peacekeeping force. Annan on August 4 sent the Security Council a detailed report saying that the UN could take over responsibility for peacekeeping in Darfur no earlier than January 2007 and that they would need at least 15,000 troops and possibly as many as 18,600, along with at least 3,300 police officers. The higher end of the range would make the Darfur force the largest UN peacekeeping mission ever, exceeding an operation still under way in the Congo.

In the meantime, fighting continued in Darfur, but most of it was among the rebel factions rather than between the rebels and the government. The combatants were rebels supporting Minnawi (who had signed the May 5 peace accord) and those aligned with the leaders who refused to sign the agreement. The latter groups had formed a new rebel alliance, the National Redemption Front. Fulfilling one condition of the peace accord, Bashir on August 5 named Minnawi as a presidential assistant. In subsequent months, the leaders of other rebel groups claimed that some of Minnawi's fighters were now acting as surrogates for the government—a claim that international observers supported.

Another Security Council Resolution

With Sudan still insisting it would not cooperate with a UN force, the UN Security Council on August 31 went ahead with plans for such a force. The council adopted Resolution 1706, authorizing up to 17,300 troops and 3,300 police officers for a UN force in Darfur that would assume the duties of the African Union force. The resolution was sponsored by Britain and the United States and supported by ten other nations represented on the council; once again, China, Qatar, and Russia abstained.

The key language in the resolution dealt with the question of Khartoum's willingness to accept the new force. To head off a potential veto by China or Russia—both of which adamantly opposed requiring Sudan to accept a UN force—the resolution said the Security Council "invites the consent of" the Khartoum government. That government made clear it would not consent, and diplomats at the UN issued conflicting opinions about whether Khartoum's consent was required, or optional, under the resolution. John R. Bolton, the acting U.S. ambassador to the UN, said speed was necessary in any event: "Every day we delay only adds to the suffering of the Sudanese people and extends the genocide."

Raising the stakes even further, the Sudanese government on September 4 demanded that the African Union reject the UN peacekeeping force (which the African leaders previously had requested) and instead accept funding from the Arab League for its current force in Darfur. Sudan demanded a response in one week and made clear it would not extend the mandate for the African Union's force past the scheduled expiration on September 30. At the same time, the government launched a new air and ground offensive against the rebel groups that had refused to sign the May 5 peace accord. The government's attacks brought renewed warnings from UN and aid officials about dangers faced by displaced civilians. "An already bad situation is worsening by the day," United Nations High Commissioner for Refugees António Guterres said on September 8.

Both sides blinked in the showdown, averting, for the moment, either the forced withdrawal of the African force or the forced entry of UN peacekeepers. During a meeting at UN headquarters on September 20, African Union leaders agreed to extend their force in Darfur through the end of the year, and Bashir agreed to allow the UN to provide additional material and logistical support for the force. This agreement also provided for an additional 1,200 African troops and a stronger mandate allowing the troops to protect civilians—not just observe violence against them. UN officials said this agreement did not eliminate the need for a broader United Nations force in Darfur; instead, it simply defused the immediate controversy over the status of the African peacekeepers.

The volatile nature of relations between the UN and Sudan was illustrated again in late October, when the Khartoum government expelled Jan Pronk, the UN's senior envoy there, declaring him to be an "enemy" of Sudan. A former Dutch cabinet minister, Pronk had been a forceful advocate of international action to save civilians in Darfur. The government's action against Pronk apparently resulted from statements in his personal blog reporting on rebel victories over government forces in two recent battles in Darfur. Pronk flew to New York for "consultations" at UN headquarters, then returned briefly to Khartoum in November and wrapped up his work as head of the UN mission. He was succeeded by Jan Eliasson, a Swedish diplomat.

No sooner had the furor over Pronk's comments died down when another frustrated UN official spoke out. Jan Egeland traveled to Sudan in mid-November for his last visit before stepping down at year's end as head of UN humanitarian operations worldwide. After visiting Darfur, he told the Associated Press "the government and its militias are conducting inexplicable terror against civilians." Egeland said he was particularly disgusted to witness evidence of "the intentional killing of children" by militias cooperating with the government.

One more attempt toward a diplomatic resolution of the dispute about peacekeepers was made in mid-November when Annan supervised negotiations in the Ethiopian capital of Addis Ababa. These talks produced an agreement on November 16 for a "hybrid" or "mixed" UN–African Union peacekeeping force of about 17,000 soldiers and 3,000 police officers. Under this agreement, the UN was to provide beefed-up logistical support for the African peacekeepers, including senior-level military and police advisers and additional troops. After initially agreeing to this plan, the Khartoum government rejected it on December 4. Repeating his past denunciations of UN "interference," Bashir said that "international troops are a colonization of Sudan." A clearly frustrated Annan said the Sudanese government might have to answer "individually and collectively" for failing to protect the people of Darfur.

The Security Council on December 19 endorsed the Addis Ababa agreement and called on all parties to implement it "without delay." Annan then sent a personal envoy to Khartoum asking for formal acceptance of that agreement. In a letter of reply, made public on December 26, Bashir said he agreed to the "hybrid" UN–African force, but he did not answer all of Annan's questions about Sudan's position on the matter. Even so, Annan told the council on December 27 that the letter generally was "positive," and he said the UN should move quickly "as a way of testing the government's willingness to cooperate." The first UN support personnel arrived in Darfur the very next day: thirteen military staff officers and twelve police officers who were shifted from UN offices in Khartoum.

Annan's assignment of these personnel to Darfur was one of his last acts as secretary general; his second five-year term ended on December 31, and he was succeeded by former South Korean foreign minister Ban Ki-moon. At year's end Sudanese officials were raising new objections to the UN–African Union force proposal, suggesting that Khartoum would allow only technical and logistical experts from the UN into Darfur—not actual peacekeeping troops.

Humanitarian Situation

The signing of a peace agreement and the diplomatic negotiations over a peacekeeping force did little to improve the fate of some 4 million people in Darfur who were classified as "at risk" by the United Nations. More than half of these people lived in displaced-person or refugee camps—most in Darfur but about 200,000 across the border in Chad. The rest depended on food aid and other relief supplies because the war had destroyed their crops and animals. UN officials estimated that about 200,000 people had died from the violence or disease and starvation related to it since the war began in 2003. Some independent experts put the death toll at twice that number, or more.

As in previous years, aid agencies repeatedly suspended their operations because of the danger or because the Khartoum government imposed restrictions on their work. The United Nations High Commissioner for Refugees announced on March 9 that the security situation in the western provinces of Darfur had become so precarious that it had to cut back operations there. Officials said about 200,000 people were forced from their homes by fighting in late 2005 and the early months of 2006; these were in addition to some 1.6 million already displaced. The refugee agency cut its planned budget for the year nearly in half because violence had restricted the access of aid workers to much of the region, putting about 500,000 people out of reach of international aid.

Similarly, the World Food Programme said in late April that it was cutting in half the daily rations it supplied for some 3 million people in Darfur—nearly half the region's entire population. The agency blamed the continuing fighting and a shortfall of funding by international donors. "Haven't the people of Darfur suffered enough? We are adding insult to injury," agency head James Morris said as he announced the cutbacks. Morris's actions caught the world's attention, and subsequent increases in donations enabled the agency to cancel some of its ration cuts.

The continuing violence and the government's restrictions led the Norwegian Refugee Council to announce in November that it was ending its aid to nearly 300,000 people. The private agency said it had been forced to suspend operations for about 25 percent of the time since it began helping Darfur refugees in mid-2004 and had reluctantly concluded that working conditions there were "impossible."

Status of Peace in Southern Sudan

The January 2005 peace agreement that ended the war between the Khartoum government and rebels in the southern part of the country generally held through 2006. One major exception was a series of battles in late November between government forces and the former rebels in the Nile River town of Malakah. A UN official said on December 2 that at least 150 people had been killed and more than 400 wounded in the fighting, which reportedly was sparked when a government-backed militia tried to kill a local leader of the Sudan People's Liberation Movement. UN officials also warned that neither the government nor the rebels were fully carrying out other promises under the peace agreement—suggesting the potential for the process to fall apart.

Meanwhile, another low-level insurgency against the central government may have come to an end in late 2006. For several years in eastern Sudan rebels of the Beja ethnic minority known as the Eastern Rebel Front had fought for more autonomy, and more financial support, from Khartoum. On October 14 these rebels signed a peace agreement with the Khartoum government that called for a cease-fire and an increase in government aid for economic development in the region. Eastern Sudan also had its own refugee problem; nearly 100,000 refugees from neighboring Eritrea and Ethiopia were living in a dozen camps there, many of them having been there for several decades. Some had fled into Sudan during the 1977–1993 conflict that led to Eritrea's independence from Ethiopia, while others fled a major war between those countries in the late 1990s. *(Eritrea-Ethiopia war, Historic Documents of 2000, p. 753)*

Following is the text of United Nations Security Council Resolution 1706, adopted on August 31, 2006, authorizing a peacekeeping force to assume the duties of the African Union force in the region.

DOCUMENT

"Resolution 1706 (2006)"

The Security Council,

Recalling its previous resolutions concerning the situation in the Sudan, in particular resolutions 1679 (2006) of 16 May 2006, 1665 (2006) of 29 March 2006, 1663 (2006) of 24 March 2006, 1593 (2005) of 31 March 2005, 1591 (2005) of 29 March 2005, 1590 (2005) of 24 March 2005, 1574 (2004) of 19 November 2004, 1564 (2004) of 18 September 2004 and 1556 (2004) of 30 July 2004 and the statements of its President concerning the Sudan,

Recalling also its previous resolutions 1325 (2000) on women, peace and security, 1502 (2003) on the protection of humanitarian and United Nations personnel, 1612 (2005) on children and armed conflict, and 1674 (2006) on the protection of civilians in armed conflict, which reaffirms inter alia the provisions of paragraphs 138 and 139 of the 2005 United Nations World Summit outcome document, as well as the report of its Mission to the Sudan and Chad from 4 to 10 June 2006,

Reaffirming its strong commitment to the sovereignty, unity, independence, and territorial integrity of the Sudan, which would be unaffected by transition to a United Nations operation in Darfur, and to the cause of peace, *expressing its determination* to work with the Government of National Unity, in full respect of its sovereignty, to assist in tackling the various problems confronting the Sudan and that a United Nations operation in Darfur shall have, to the extent possible, a strong African participation and character,

Welcoming the efforts of the African Union to find a solution to the crisis in Darfur, including through the success of the African Union-led Inter-Sudanese Peace Talks on the Conflict in Darfur in Abuja, Nigeria, in particular the framework agreed between the parties for a resolution of the conflict in Darfur (the Darfur Peace Agreement), *commending* the efforts of the signatories to the Darfur Peace Agreement, *expressing* its belief that the Agreement provides a basis for sustained security in Darfur, *reiterating* its welcome of the statement of 9 May 2006 by the representative of the Sudan at the United Nations Security Council Special Session on Darfur of the Government of National Unity's full commitment to implementing the Agreement, *stressing* the importance of launching, with the African Union, the Darfur-Darfur dialogue and consultation as soon as possible, and *recognizing* that international support for implementation of the Agreement is critically important to its success,

Commending the efforts of the African Union for the successful deployment of the African Union Mission in the Sudan (AMIS), as well as the efforts of Member States and regional and international organizations that have assisted it in its deployment, and AMIS' role in reducing large-scale organized violence in Darfur, *recalling* the decision of the African Union Peace and Security Council of 10 March 2006, and its decision of 27 June 2006 as outlined in paragraph 10 of its Communiqué that the African Union is ready to review the mandate of AMIS in the event that the ongoing consultations between the Government of National Unity and the United Nations conclude on an agreement for a transition to a United Nations peacekeeping operation, *stressing* the need for AMIS to assist implementation of the Darfur Peace Agreement until transition to the United Nations force in Darfur is completed, *welcoming* the decision of the African Union Peace and Security Council of 27 June 2006 on strengthening AMIS' mandate and tasks, including on the protection of civilians, and *considering* that AMIS needs urgent reinforcing,

Reaffirming its concern that the ongoing violence in Darfur might further negatively affect the rest of the Sudan as well as the region, in particular Chad and the Central African Republic, and *stressing* that regional security aspects must be addressed to achieve long lasting peace in Darfur,

Remaining deeply concerned over the recent deterioration of relations between the Sudan and Chad, calling on the Governments of the two countries to abide by their obligations under the Tripoli Agreement of 8 February 2006 and the agreement between the Sudan and Chad signed in N'djamena on 26 July 2006 and to begin implementing the confidence-building measures which they have voluntarily agreed upon, welcoming the recent re-establishment of diplomatic relations between the Sudan and Chad, and calling upon all States in the region to cooperate in ensuring regional stability,

Reiterating its strong condemnation of all violations of human rights and international humanitarian law in Darfur, and *calling upon* the Government of National Unity to take urgent action to tackle gender-based violence in Darfur including action towards implementing its Action Plan to Combat Violence Against Women in Darfur with particular focus on the rescission of Form 8 and access to legal redress,

Expressing its deep concern for the security of humanitarian aid workers and their access to populations in need, including refugees, internally displaced persons and other war-affected populations, and *calling upon* all parties, in particular the Government of National Unity, to ensure, in accordance with relevant provisions of international law, the full, safe and unhindered access of relief personnel to all those in need in Darfur as well as the delivery of humanitarian assistance, in particular to internally displaced persons and refugees,

Taking note of the communiqués of 12 January, 10 March, 15 May and 27 June 2006 of the Peace and Security Council of the African Union regarding transition of AMIS to a United Nations operation,

Taking note of the report of the Secretary-General on Darfur dated 28 July 2006,

Determining that the situation in the Sudan continues to constitute a threat to international peace and security,

1. *Decides*, without prejudice to its existing mandate and operations as provided for in resolution 1590 (2005) and in order to support the early and effective implementation of the Darfur Peace Agreement, that UNMIS' mandate shall be expanded as specified in paragraphs 8, 9 and 12 below, that it shall deploy to Darfur, and therefore invites the consent of the Government of National Unity for this deployment, and *urges* Member States to provide the capability for an expeditious deployment;

2. *Requests* the Secretary-General to arrange the rapid deployment of additional capabilities for UNMIS, in order that it may deploy in Darfur, in accordance with the recommendation contained in his report dated 28 July 2006;

3. *Decides* that UNMIS shall be strengthened by up to 17,300 military personnel and by an appropriate civilian component including up to 3,300 civilian police personnel and up to 16 Formed Police Units, and *expresses its determination* to keep UNMIS' strength and structure under regular review, taking into account the evolution of the situation on the ground and without prejudice to its current operations and mandate as provided for in resolution 1590 (2005);

4. *Expresses* its intention to consider authorizing possible additional temporary reinforcements of the military component of UNMIS, at the request of the Secretary-General, within the limits of the troop levels recommended in paragraph 87 of his report dated 28 July 2006;

5. *Requests* the Secretary-General to consult jointly with the African Union, in close and continuing consultation with the parties to the Darfur Peace Agreement, including the Government of National Unity, on a plan and timetable for transition from AMIS to a United Nations operation in Darfur; *decides* that those elements outlined in paragraphs 40 to 58 of the Secretary-General's report of 28 July 2006 shall begin to be deployed no later than 1 October 2006, that thereafter as part of the process of transition to a United Nations operation additional capabilities shall be deployed as soon as feasible and that UNMIS shall take over from AMIS responsibility for supporting the implementation of the Darfur Peace Agreement upon the expiration of AMIS' mandate but in any event no later than 31 December 2006;

6. *Notes* that the Status of Forces Agreement for UNMIS with the Sudan, as outlined in resolution 1590 (2005), shall apply to UNMIS' operations throughout the Sudan, including in Darfur;

7. *Requests* the Secretary-General to take the necessary steps to strengthen AMIS through the use of existing and additional United Nations resources with a view to transition to a United Nations operation in Darfur; and *authorizes* the Secretary-General during this transition to implement the longer-term support to AMIS outlined in the report of the Secretary-General of 28 July 2006, including provision of air assets, ground mobility package, training, engineering and logistics, mobile communications capacity and broad public information assistance;

8. *Decides* that the mandate of UNMIS in Darfur shall be to support implementation of the Darfur Peace Agreement of 5 May 2006 and the N'djamena Agreement on Humanitarian Cease-fire on the Conflict in Darfur ("the Agreements"), including by performing the following tasks:

(a) To monitor and verify the implementation by the parties of Chapter 3 ("Comprehensive Cease-fire and Final Security Arrangements") of the Darfur Peace Agreement and the N'djamena Agreement on Humanitarian Cease-fire on the Conflict in Darfur;

(b) To observe and monitor movement of armed groups and redeployment of forces in areas of UNMIS deployment by ground and aerial means in accordance with the Agreements;

(c) To investigate violations of the Agreements and to report violations to the Cease-fire Commission; as well as to cooperate and coordinate, together with other International Actors, with the Cease-fire Commission, the Joint Commission, and the Joint Humanitarian Facilitation and Monitoring Unit established pursuant to the Agreements including through provision of technical assistance and logistical support;

(d) To maintain, in particular, a presence in key areas, such as buffer zones established pursuant to the Darfur Peace Agreement, areas inside internally displaced persons camps and demilitarized zones around and inside internally displaced persons camps, in order to promote the re-establishment of confidence, to discourage violence, in particular by deterring use of force;

(e) To monitor transborder activities of armed groups along the Sudanese borders with Chad and the Central African Republic in particular through regular ground and aerial reconnaissance activities;

(f) To assist with development and implementation of a comprehensive and sustainable program for disarmament, demobilization and reintegration of former combatants and women and children associated with combatants, as called for in the Darfur Peace Agreement and in accordance with resolutions 1556 (2004) and 1564 (2004);

(g) To assist the parties, in cooperation with other international actors, in the preparations for and conduct of referendums provided for in the Darfur Peace Agreement;

(h) To assist the parties to the Agreements in promoting understanding of the peace accord and of the role of UNMIS, including by means of an effective public information campaign, targeted at all sectors of society, in coordination with the African Union;

(i) To cooperate closely with the Chairperson of the Darfur-Darfur Dialogue and Consultation (DDDC), provide support and technical assistance to him, and coordinate other United Nations agencies' activities to this effect, as well as to assist the parties to the DDDC in addressing the need for an all-inclusive approach, including the role of women, towards reconciliation and peace building;

(j) To assist the parties to the Darfur Peace Agreement, in coordination with bilateral and multilateral assistance programs, in restructuring the police service in the Sudan, consistent with democratic policing, to develop a police training and evaluation program, and to otherwise assist in the training of civilian police;

(k) To assist the parties to the Darfur Peace Agreement in promoting the rule of law, including an independent judiciary, and the protection of human rights of all people of the Sudan through a comprehensive and coordinated strategy with the aim of combating impunity and contributing to long-term peace and stability and to assist the parties to the Darfur Peace Agreement to develop and consolidate the national legal framework;

(l) To ensure an adequate human rights and gender presence, capacity and expertise within UNMIS to carry out human rights promotion, civilian protection and monitoring activities that include particular attention to the needs of women and children;

9. *Decides* further that the mandate of UNMIS in Darfur shall also include the following:

(a) To facilitate and coordinate in close cooperation with relevant United Nations agencies, within its capabilities and in its areas of deployment, the voluntary return of refugees and internally displaced persons, and humanitarian assistance inter alia by helping to establish the necessary security conditions in Darfur;

(b) To contribute towards international efforts to protect, promote and monitor human rights in Darfur, as well as to coordinate international efforts towards the protection of civilians with particular attention to vulnerable groups including internally displaced persons, returning refugees, and women and children;

(c) To assist the parties to the Agreements, in cooperation with other international partners in the mine action sector, by providing humanitarian demining assistance, technical advice, and coordination, as well as mine awareness programs targeted at all sectors of society;

(d) To assist in addressing regional security issues in close liaison with international efforts to improve the security situation in the neighboring regions along the borders between the Sudan and Chad and between the Sudan and the Central African Republic, including through the establishment of a multidimensional presence consisting of political, humanitarian, military and civilian police liaison officers in key locations in Chad, including in internally displaced persons and refugee camps, and if necessary, in the Central African Republic, and to contribute to the implementation of the Agreement between the Sudan and Chad signed on 26 July 2006;

10. *Calls upon* all Member States to ensure the free, unhindered and expeditious movement to the Sudan of all personnel, as well as equipment, provisions, supplies and other goods, including vehicles and spare parts, which are for the exclusive and official use of UNMIS in Darfur;

11. *Requests* the Secretary-General to keep the Council regularly informed of the progress in implementing the Darfur Peace Agreement, respect for the ceasefire, and the implementation of the mandate of UNMIS in Darfur, and to report to the Council, as appropriate, on the steps taken to implement this resolution and any failure to comply with its demands;

12. Acting under Chapter VII of the Charter of the United Nations:

(a) *Decides* that UNMIS is authorized to use all necessary means, in the areas of deployment of its forces and as it deems within its capabilities:

- to protect United Nations personnel, facilities, installations and equipment, to ensure the security and freedom of movement of United Nations personnel, humanitarian workers, assessment and evaluation commission personnel, to prevent disruption of the implementation of the Darfur Peace Agreement by armed groups, without prejudice to the responsibility of the Government of the Sudan, to protect civilians under threat of physical violence,
- in order to support early and effective implementation of the Darfur Peace Agreement, to prevent attacks and threats against civilians,
- to seize or collect, as appropriate, arms or related material whose presence in Darfur is in violation of the Agreements and the measures imposed by paragraphs 7 and 8 of resolution 1556, and to dispose of such arms and related material as appropriate;

(b) *Requests* that the Secretary-General and the Governments of Chad and the Central African Republic conclude status-of-forces agreements as soon as possible, taking into consideration General Assembly resolution 58/82 on the scope of legal protection under the Convention on the Safety of United Nations and Associated Personnel, and *decides* that pending the conclusion of such an agreement with either country, the model status-of-forces agreement dated 9 October 1990 (A/45/594) shall apply provisionally with respect to UNMIS forces operating in that country;

13. *Requests* the Secretary-General to report to the Council on the protection of civilians in refugee and internally displaced persons camps in Chad and on how to improve the security situation on the Chadian side of the border with Sudan;

14. *Calls upon* the parties to the Darfur Peace Agreement to respect their commitments and implement the Agreement without delay, *urges* those parties that have not signed the Agreement to do so without delay and not to act in any way that would impede implementation of the Agreement, and *reiterates* its intention to take, including in response to a request by the African Union, strong and effective measures, such as an asset freeze or travel ban, against any individual or group that violates or attempts to block the implementation of the Agreement or commits human rights violations;

15. *Decides* to remain seized of the matter.

Source: United Nations. Security Council. "Resolution 1706 (2006)." S/RES/1706 (2006), August 31, 2006. www.un.org/Docs/sc/unsc_resolutions06.htm (accessed February 27, 2007).

Other Historic Documents of Interest

September

President Bush on the Secret Detention of Terrorism Suspects

September 6, 2006

■■■■■■■■■■■■ **THE DOCUMENT IN CONTEXT** ■■■■■■■■■■■■

President George W. Bush announced on September 6 that Khalid Sheikh Mohammad, the alleged mastermind of the 2001 terrorist attacks on New York and Washington, and thirteen other "high-value" terrorism suspects had been brought to the military prison at Guantanamo Bay, Cuba, where they would be tried for crimes against the United States. In making the announcement, Bush acknowledged for the first time that the CIA had detained terrorism suspects in secret prisons overseas where they were interrogated under procedures that many critics said amounted to torture. Bush denied that the suspects had been tortured but refused to divulge any details other than to assert that the interrogations gave the United States "information that has saved innocent lives by helping us stop new attacks—here in the United States and across the world."

Bush's announcement came in conjunction with the administration's push for legislation that would authorize it to try terrorist suspects in special military tribunals that, among other things, would allow the use of evidence coerced during secret interrogations. In June the Supreme Court had ruled that similar tribunals set up by the administration were unconstitutional because they had not been authorized by Congress and because they violated standards of U.S. military justice and the Geneva Conventions governing war crimes. The announcement also came one week before the fifth anniversary of the September 11, 2001, attacks, which killed nearly 3,000 people in the United States and led to ongoing U.S. wars in Afghanistan and Iraq. The Bush announcement was also aimed at Americans who would be voting in the midterm elections in November, reminding them of the Republican administration's tough stance against terrorism and successes in capturing key terrorist figures.

While some countries openly supported the Bush administration's use of the secret prisons, most said the secrecy surrounding the prisons, including Guantanamo, and the allegations of detainee abuses sewed distrust with America's allies, turned many Muslims and others against the United States, and undermined America's claim to hold high moral principles. "I cannot believe that there can be a trade between the effective fight against terrorism and protection of civil liberties," United Nations Secretary General Kofi Annan said September 7. "If as individuals we are asked to give up our freedom, our liberties, our human rights, as protection against terrorism, do we in the end have protection?"

Background

Since late 2002 news organizations had reported that the CIA was holding terrorism suspects at secret locations in other countries and in some cases turning those suspects over to foreign security services known for their use of torture. News reports early in 2005 suggested that as many as 150 suspects had been removed to other countries under this "rendition" program. The administration routinely deflected all questions about the program, disavowed the use of torture, and denied that any government personnel were authorized to use torture. Prisoner abuses, such as those revealed at Abu Ghraib prison in Baghdad, were isolated incidents, the administration maintained. *(Abu Ghraib scandal, Historic Documents of 2004, pp. 207, 336; Historic Documents of 2005, p. 911)*

Questions about the CIA's role in hiding terrorism suspects were renewed in late 2005 after the *Washington Post* reported on November 2 that the CIA had established a "covert prison system" for housing key terrorism suspects, adding that the CIA was holding its "most important al Qaeda captives at a Soviet-era compound in Eastern Europe"; the paper did not name the country. Human Rights Watch, a human rights watchdog organization, subsequently reported that it had circumstantial evidence suggesting that the CIA had secret prisons in Poland and Romania; both countries denied the allegation. *(Background, Historic Documents of 2005, p. 905)*

The *Post* story was the first substantial report suggesting that U.S. terrorism suspects had been housed anywhere in Europe, and it did not allege that these detainees had been tortured. But numerous other media reports suggested they had been, leading to demands from European leaders and the public that the U.S. government clarify its actions. On a trip to several European capitals in December 2005, Secretary of State Condoleezza Rice managed to quell much of the speculation about the use of torture against terrorist suspects. But her assurances that U.S. personnel did not engage in cruel, inhumane, and degrading treatment of prisoners, no matter where they were, did not put to rest several investigations in Europe looking into whether European intelligence agencies had aided the CIA in its rendition program in violation of various human rights treaties and conventions. Those investigations were fueled by numerous reports that airplanes owned by or contracted to the CIA had made dozens of stops at various European airports since 2001 on their way to or from Afghanistan, Pakistan, and various countries in the Middle East.

EU Investigations, Other Reports

A special committee of the European Parliament initiated a formal inquiry on January 20 to find out whether and what individual European governments might have known about the secret prisons. European Union (EU) Commissioner for Justice, Freedom, and Security Franco Frattini warned that any EU nation found to have aided the CIA with abductions, imprisonments, and renditions could lose its EU voting rights. In an interim report released on April 26 the committee said it had evidence that the CIA had operated more than 1,000 flights through European airspace since 2001. The committee admitted that it did not know how many of the flights might have involved illegal transfers of terrorist suspects from one prison to another, but Giovanni Claudio Fava, an Italian legislator who headed the committee, said the "routes for some of these flights seem to be quite suspect. They are rather strange routes for flights to take. It is hard to imagine those stopovers were simply for providing fuel."

A second investigation was conducted by Dick Marty, a Swiss senator, on behalf of the Council of Europe, a human rights agency responsible for enforcing the European Convention on Human Rights. In a report released June 7, Marty said he did not have irrefutable proof, but he said there were "serious indications" that the CIA operated secret prisons in Poland and Romania and that twelve other European countries had participated wittingly or unwittingly in the CIA's detention and transfers of terrorism suspects. "It is now clear," Marty said in his sixty-seven-page report, "that authorities in several European countries actively participated with the CIA in these unlawful activities. Other countries ignored them knowingly, or did not want to know." Marty said seven of these countries—Britain, Bosnia-Herzegovina, Germany, Italy, Macedonia, Sweden, and Turkey—"could be held responsible for violations of the rights of specific individuals" handed over or captured by the CIA in those countries. He named five other countries—Cyprus, Greece, Ireland, Portugal, and Spain—that he said had colluded passively with the CIA. State Department spokesman Sean McCormack dismissed Marty's report as "sort of rehash" and short on "solid facts."

Speculation about whether detainees in these prisons were tortured also continued. On May 19 the UN Committee Against Torture called on the United States to take "immediate measures" to stop torture and abuse of detainees by U.S. personnel "in any territory under its jurisdictions." The committee also called on the United States to close its prison at Guantanamo Bay and stop transferring detainees to countries where they faced the risk of torture. Two months later, on July 28, the UN Human Rights Committee told the U.S. government to "immediately abolish all secret detention," warning that such secret prisons were banned under international law. Meanwhile, Amnesty International released a report on July 23 in which it accused the United States of sending detainees to Jordan where they were tortured by Jordanian security agents.

Supreme Court Decision

According to later news reports, public and private pressure from European capitals had an affect on the debate among high-ranking U.S. officials about the wisdom of continuing to conceal the existence of the secret prisons. But the deciding factor was apparently the Supreme Court's June 29 decision in the case of *Hamdan v. Rumsfeld.* Among other things, that ruling held that suspects detained in the war on terrorism were protected under Common Article 3 of the Geneva Conventions, which prohibited "humiliating and degrading treatment" of prisoners captured during war. The Bush administration had argued that terrorist suspects fell outside the war crimes protections contained in the Geneva Conventions and so were not subject to the same protections.

The Court also struck down as unconstitutional the special military tribunals that the Bush administration had set up to try terrorist suspects at Guantanamo Bay. As a result, the administration had to seek authorization from Congress for the commissions, including the authority for them to consider evidence obtained from detainees by coercion and possibly torture. That forced the administration to confront the issue of the secret prisons directly, and over the course of several meetings top officials and then the president himself reportedly said it was time to reveal their existence. The *Hamdan* decision "forced our hand," White House counselor Dan Bartlett told the *Washington Post.* "We knew there was going to have to be some acknowledgement that they [the terrorist suspects] were in our hands." As the *Post* and other news outlets reported, by that time, several governments had already asked the United States to close the prisons in their countries and others were refusing to cooperate with U.S. intelligence agencies. Secretary of State Rice reportedly also argued that the prisons should be closed on moral as well as policy grounds.

On September 6, President Bush announced from the White House that fourteen high-value terrorist suspects had been transferred to Guantanamo from secret prisons overseas, and he urged Congress to authorize the tribunals struck down by the

Supreme Court so that the fourteen men could be brought to trial. "These are dangerous men with unparalleled knowledge about terrorist networks and their plans for new attacks," Bush said. In addition to Khalid Sheikh Mohammad, the detainees included "the key architects" involved in the suicide bombing of the USS *Cole* in Yemen in October 2000 and the truck bombings of the U.S. embassies in Kenya and Tanzania in 1998. Also taken to Guantanamo was an Indonesian known as Hambali, who was said to be the operational chief of an Islamist extremist group Jemaah Islamiah in Southeast Asia. Hambali was linked to the 2002 bombings of nightclubs in Bali and the 2003 bombing of a Marriott hotel in Jakarta. *(USS* Cole *bombing, Historic Documents of 2001, p. 3; Kenya-Tanzania bombings, Historic Documents of 2002, p. 1014; Hambali arrest, Historic Documents of 2003, p. 1052)*

In acknowledging the existence of the secret prisons, Bush said there were "now no terrorists in the CIA program," but he said the program would continue. "Having a CIA program for questioning terrorists will continue to be crucial to getting lifesaving information," the president said. Bush all but acknowledged that the CIA had used interrogation methods that might be defined as torture. He said that after one of the terrorist suspects "stopped talking," the CIA turned to "an alternative set of procedures" to extract information. Bush would not elaborate other than to say that the tactics were "tough . . . lawful and necessary" and that after they were used, the suspect again began to provide information. According to news reports, U.S. officials confirmed off the record that one tactic used was "waterboarding," a procedure that made a detainee think he was drowning. Bush also asked Congress to protect CIA operatives from lawsuits by terrorist suspects alleging that they had been tortured.

Congress voted to give the president most of what he wanted, but not before objections to his request to redefine U.S. obligations on humane treatment of prisoners under Common Article 3 of the Geneva Conventions by three Republican senators stalled action on the measure for nearly a month. In the end the three senators—John McCain of Arizona, John Warner of Virginia, and Lindsey Graham of South Carolina— persuaded the administration to drop its reinterpretation of those obligations. Instead the administration and the three dissident senators agreed to language that listed nine types of offense—including torture, rape, and hostage-taking—that would be considered grave breaches of Common Article 3 and could be prosecuted in U.S. federal court under the War Crimes Act. The rest of the administration's measure setting up the special military tribunals was passed largely intact. Congress cleared the bill (S 3930—PL 109–366) on September 29, and the president signed it into law on October 17. The first trials of the detainees were expected in mid-2007.

More Details on Prisons Emerge

In the following months, more details began to emerge on the secret CIA prisons and on the cooperation some countries and intelligence services apparently provided. On November 28, the European Parliament's special committee investigating the secret prisons released a draft of its final report. The report detailed the committee's strong suspicions that eleven EU governments had knowledge of secret CIA counterterrorism measures being taken on European soil: Austria, Britain, Cyprus, Germany, Greece, Ireland, Italy, Poland, Portugal, Spain, and Sweden. Although no European country had admitted to allowing the CIA to operate prisons on its territory, the committee said that it had obtained records describing an "informal" meeting of EU and NATO foreign ministers on December 7, 2005, "confirming that member states had knowledge" of the prisons. According to the EU committee, Secretary of State Rice and other U.S. officials attended this meeting. "The decision has been to keep mum and shroud decisions in secrecy," said Fava, the head of the investigation.

The committee also said it had obtained "serious circumstantial evidence" that the CIA housed al Qaeda prisoners at the Polish intelligence training center at Stare Kiejkuty in northeastern Poland. The committee acknowledged it had no firm proof but cited testimony by employees of a nearby airport who said Polish military officials stopped them from going near or conducting passenger checks or customs inspections on several flights. Altogether, the report said, it had records that at least 1,245 CIA-operated flights had land at European airports or passed through European air space since 2001.

Subjects of the investigation firmly denied the committee's findings. Calling the report "hysterical in its hyperbole," John A. Bellinger III, the legal adviser to Rice, told the *Washington Post* that it was wrong for the committee to imply that all CIA flights had "nefarious" intent. "There are numerous, numerous reasons for CIA flights to Europe," he said. "By and large, they are a symbol of cooperation between our countries and the sharing of information, not illegal activity." A spokesman for Poland's minister of special services told the Associated Press that the committee's findings regarding Poland were "not based on any strong proof but only common repeated assumptions, suspicions, and probabilities." The EU committee was expected to issue a final report early in 2007.

Although neither the EU parliament nor the Council of Europe investigations had uncovered direct evidence of secret prisons and extraordinary renditions to third countries, substantial anecdotal evidence buttressed such allegations. One such incident involved Khalid el-Masri, a German national who said he was picked up in Macedonia and flown to a prison in Afghanistan, where he was held for five months in a U.S.-operated prison and then released. Although the U.S. government admitted that it had mistaken Masri for someone else, it had not confirmed that Masri had been seized in Macedonia. In February German prosecutors began an investigation into Masri's allegations that a senior German police official had questioned him in Kabul on three separate occasions. The prosecutors were also investigating whether the German embassy in Skopje, Macedonia, had been told of Masri's abduction and done nothing about it.

With the aid of the American Civil Liberties Union, Masri was also trying to sue former CIA director George Tenet and others in federal U.S. court. In May a U.S. district court dismissed the case after the government invoked the "state secrets" privilege, arguing that proceeding with Masri's suit in open court would endanger national security, a danger the government said outweighed any rights Masri might have. Masri appealed the case, but a decision had not been issued by the end of the year.

Another incident involved Abu Omar (also known as Osama Moustafa Hassan Nasr), a radical Muslim cleric who claimed the CIA snatched him in Milan, Italy, in February 2003 and flew him secretly through Germany to Cairo, where he said he was tortured for months with electric shocks and sexually abused. Omar, an Egyptian national who had been given political asylum in Italy, made his allegations in a letter smuggled out of the prison where he was still in custody at the end of 2006. Prosecutors in Milan opened an investigation that resulted in December 2006 in the indictments of Italy's former intelligence chief and twenty-five CIA operatives for their involvement in the kidnapping. The case, which raised questions about Italy's active cooperation with the CIA in making extraordinary renditions, threatened to cause a major scandal.

A third incident involved Maher Arar, a citizen of Canada and Syria who lived in Ottawa. In September 2002, Arar was arrested in New York and then deported to Syria after Canadian police misidentified him as an Islamic extremist. Arar, who said he was tortured while in a Syrian prison, was freed in 2003. On September 18, 2006, a Canadian commission investigating the incident cleared Arar of any connection to terrorists and said information provided about Arar to U.S. authorities by the Royal Canadian Mounted Police may have played a role in his deportation and detention. (In early January 2007, the Canadian government formally apologized to Arar and paid him $12.5 million in compensation. The United States, however, continued to bar Arar from entering the United States and refused to remove his name from a terrorist watch list.)

Following is the text of remarks made by President George W. Bush at the White House on September 6, 2006, announcing that fourteen high-value terrorism suspects had been transferred from secret prisons operated by the CIA to the military prison at Guantanamo Bay, Cuba, and asking Congress to authorize the establishment of special military commissions to try the detainees.

DOCUMENT

"Remarks on the War on Terror"

Thank you. Thanks for the warm welcome. Welcome to the White House. Mr. Vice President [Dick Cheney], Secretary [of State Condoleezza] Rice, Attorney General [Alberto] Gonzales, Ambassador [to the United Nations John D.] Negroponte, General [Michael] Hayden, Members of the United States Congress, families who lost loved ones in the terrorist attacks on our Nation, and my fellow citizens: Thanks for coming.

On the morning of September the 11th, 2001, our Nation awoke to a nightmare attack. Nineteen men armed with box cutters took control of airplanes and turned them into missiles. They used them to kill nearly 3,000 innocent people. We watched the Twin Towers collapse before our eyes, and it became instantly clear that we'd entered a new world and a dangerous new war.

The attacks of September the 11th horrified our Nation. And amid the grief came new fears and urgent questions: Who had attacked us? What did they want? And what else were they planning? Americans saw the destruction the terrorists had caused in New York and Washington and Pennsylvania, and they wondered if there were other terrorist cells in our midst poised to strike; they wondered if there was a second wave of attacks still to come.

With the Twin Towers and the Pentagon still smoldering, our country on edge, and a stream of intelligence coming in about potential new attacks, my administration faced immediate challenges. We had to respond to the attack on our country. We had to wage an unprecedented war against an enemy unlike any we had fought before. We had to find the terrorists hiding in America and across the world, before they were able to strike our country again. So in the early days and weeks after 9/11, I directed our Government's senior national security officials to do everything in their power, within our laws, to prevent another attack.

Nearly 5 years have passed since these—those initial days of shock and sadness, and we are thankful that the terrorists have not succeeded in launching another attack on our soil. This is not for the lack of desire or determination on the part of the enemy. As the recently foiled plot in London shows, the terrorists are still active, and they're still trying to strike America, and they're still trying to kill our people. One reason the terrorists have not succeeded is because of the hard work of thousands of dedicated men and women in our Government, who have toiled day and night, along with our allies, to stop the enemy from carrying out their plans. And we are grateful for these hard-working citizens of ours. Another reason the terrorists have not succeeded is because our Government has changed its policies and given our military, intelligence, and law enforcement personnel the tools they need to fight this enemy and protect our people and preserve our freedoms.

The terrorists who declared war on America represent no nation; they defend no territory; and they wear no uniform. They do not mass armies on borders or flotillas of warships on the high seas. They operate in the shadows of society. They send small teams of operatives to infiltrate free nations; they live quietly among their victims; they conspire in secret, and then they strike without warning. In this new war, the most important source of information on where the terrorists are hiding and what they are planning is the terrorists themselves.

Captured terrorists have unique knowledge about how terrorist networks operate. They have knowledge of where their operatives are deployed and knowledge about what plots are underway. This intelligence—this is intelligence that cannot be found any other place, and our security depends on getting this kind of information. To win the war on terror, we must be able to detain, question, and, when appropriate, prosecute terrorists captured here in America and on the battlefields around the world.

After the 9/11 attacks, our coalition launched operations across the world to remove terrorist safe havens and capture or kill terrorist operatives and leaders. Working with our allies, we've captured and detained thousands of terrorists and enemy fighters in Afghanistan, in Iraq, and other fronts of this war on terror. These enemy—these are enemy combatants who were waging war on our Nation. We have a right under the laws of war, and we have an obligation to the American people, to detain these enemies and stop them from rejoining the battle.

Most of the enemy combatants we capture are held in Afghanistan or in Iraq, where they're questioned by our military personnel. Many are released after questioning or turned over to local authorities—if we determine that they do not pose a continuing threat and no longer have significant intelligence value. Others remain in American custody near the battlefield to ensure that they don't return to the fight.

In some cases, we determine that individuals we have captured pose a significant threat or may have intelligence that we and our allies need to have to prevent new attacks. Many are Al Qaida operatives or Taliban fighters trying to conceal their identities, and they withhold information that could save American lives. In these cases, it has been necessary to move these individuals to an environment where they can be held secretly, questioned by experts, and, when appropriate, prosecuted for terrorist acts.

Some of these individuals are taken to the United States Naval Base at Guantanamo Bay, Cuba. It's important for Americans and others across the world to understand the kind of people held at Guantanamo. These aren't common criminals or bystanders accidentally swept up on the battlefield. We have in place a rigorous process to ensure those held at Guantanamo Bay belong at Guantanamo. Those held at Guantanamo include suspected bombmakers, terrorist trainers, recruiters and facilitators, and potential suicide bombers. They are in our custody so they cannot murder our people. One detainee held at Guantanamo told a questioner questioning him—he said this: "I'll never forget your face. I will kill you, your brothers, your mother, and your sisters."

In addition to the terrorists held at Guantanamo, a small number of suspected terrorist leaders and operatives captured during the war have been held and questioned outside the United States, in a separate program operated by the Central Intelligence Agency. This group includes individuals believed to be the key architects of the September the 11th attacks and attacks on the USS Cole, an operative involved in the bombings of our Embassies in Kenya and Tanzania, and individuals involved in other attacks that have taken the lives of innocent civilians across the world. These are dangerous men with unparalleled knowledge about terrorist networks and their plans for new attacks. The security of our Nation and the lives of our citizens depend on our ability to learn what these terrorists know.

Many specifics of this program, including where these detainees have been held and the details of their confinement, cannot be divulged. Doing so would provide our enemies with information they could use to take retribution against our allies and harm our country. I can say that questioning the detainees in this program has given us information that has saved innocent lives by helping us stop new attacks—here in the United States and across the world.

Today I'm going to share with you some of the examples provided by our intelligence community of how this program has saved lives, why it remains vital to the security of the United States and our friends and allies, and why it deserves the support of the United States Congress and the American people.

Within months of September the 11th, 2001, we captured a man named Abu Zubaydah. We believe that Zubaydah was a senior terrorist leader and a trusted associate of Usama bin Laden. Our intelligence community believes he had run a terrorist camp in Afghanistan where some of the 9/11 hijackers trained and that he helped smuggle Al Qaida leaders out of Afghanistan after coalition forces arrived to liberate that country. Zubaydah was severely wounded during the firefight that brought him into custody, and he survived only because of the medical care arranged by the CIA.

After he recovered, Zubaydah was defiant and evasive. He declared his hatred of America. During questioning, he at first disclosed what he thought was nominal information—and then stopped all cooperation. Well, in fact, the "nominal" information he gave us turned out to be quite important. For example, Zubaydah disclosed Khalid Sheikh Mohammed—or KSM—was the mastermind behind the 9/11 attacks and used the alias Muktar. This was a vital piece of the puzzle that helped our intelligence community pursue KSM. Zubaydah also provided information that helped stop a terrorist attack being planned for inside the United States, an attack about which we had no previous information. Zubaydah told us that Al Qaida operatives were planning to launch an attack in the U.S. and provided physical descriptions of the operatives and information on their general location. Based on the information he provided, the operatives were detained—one while traveling to the United States.

We knew that Zubaydah had more information that could save innocent lives, but he stopped talking. As his questioning proceeded, it became clear that he had received training on how to resist interrogation. And so the CIA used an alternative set of procedures. These procedures were designed to be safe, to comply with our laws, our Constitution, and our treaty obligations. The Department of Justice reviewed the authorized methods extensively and determined them to be lawful. I cannot describe the specific methods used—I think you understand why—if I did, it would help the terrorists learn how to resist questioning and to keep information from us that we need to prevent new attacks on our country. But I can say the procedures were tough, and they were safe and lawful and necessary.

Zubaydah was questioned using these procedures, and soon he began to provide information on key Al Qaida operatives, including information that helped us find and capture more of those responsible for the attacks on September the 11th. For example, Zubaydah identified one of KSM's accomplices in the 9/11 attacks—a terrorist named Ramzi bin al-Shibh. The information Zubaydah provided helped lead to the capture of bin al-Shibh. And together these two terrorists provided information that helped in the planning and execution of the operation that captured Khalid Sheikh Mohammed.

Once in our custody, KSM was questioned by the CIA using these procedures, and he soon provided information that helped us stop another planned attack on the United States. During questioning, KSM told us about another Al Qaida operative he knew was in CIA custody—a terrorist named Majid Khan. KSM revealed that Khan had been told to deliver $50,000 to individuals working for a suspected terrorist leader named Hambali, the leader of Al Qaida's Southeast Asian affiliate known as JI. CIA officers confronted Khan with this information. Khan confirmed that the money had been delivered to an operative named Zubair and provided both a physical description and contact number for this operative.

Based on that information, Zubair was captured in June of 2003, and he soon provided information that helped lead to the capture of Hambali. After Hambali's arrest, KSM was questioned again. He identified Hambali's brother as the leader of a JI cell and Hambali's conduit for communications with Al Qaida. Hambali's brother was soon captured in Pakistan and in turn led us to a cell of 17 Southeast Asian JI operatives. When confronted with the news that his terror cell had been broken up, Hambali admitted that the operatives were being groomed at KSM's request for attacks inside the United States—probably using airplanes.

During questioning, KSM also provided many details of other plots to kill innocent Americans. For example, he described the design of planned attacks on buildings inside the United States and how operatives were directed to carry them out. He told us the operatives had been instructed to ensure that the explosives went off at a point that was high enough to prevent the people trapped above from escaping out the windows.

KSM also provided vital information on Al Qaida's efforts to obtain biological weapons. During questioning, KSM admitted that he had met three individuals involved in Al Qaida's efforts to produce anthrax, a deadly biological agent—and he identified one of the individuals as a terrorist named Yazid. KSM apparently believed we already had this information, because Yazid had been captured and taken into foreign custody before KSM's arrest. In fact, we did not know about Yazid's role in Al Qaida's anthrax program. Information from

Yazid then helped lead to the capture of his two principal assistants in the anthrax program. Without the information provided by KSM and Yazid, we might not have uncovered this Al Qaida biological weapons program or stopped this Al Qaida cell from developing anthrax for attacks against the United States.

These are some of the plots that have been stopped because of the information of this vital program. Terrorists held in CIA custody have also provided information that helped stop a planned strike on U.S. marines at Camp Lemonier in Djibouti—they were going to use an explosive laden water tanker. They helped stop a planned attack on the U.S. consulate in Karachi using car bombs and motorcycle bombs, and they helped stop a plot to hijack passenger planes and fly them into Heathrow or the Canary Wharf in London.

We're getting vital information necessary to do our jobs, and that's to protect the American people and our allies. Information from the terrorists in this program has helped us to identify individuals that Al Qaida deemed suitable for Western operations, many of whom we had never heard about before. They include terrorists who were set to case targets inside the United States, including financial buildings in major cities on the east coast. Information from terrorists in CIA custody has played a role in the capture or questioning of nearly every senior Al Qaida member or associate detained by the U.S. and its allies since this program began. By providing everything from initial leads to photo identifications to precise locations of where terrorists were hiding, this program has helped us to take potential mass murderers off the streets before they were able to kill.

This program has also played a critical role in helping us understand the enemy we face in this war. Terrorists in this program have painted a picture of Al Qaida's structure and financing and communications and logistics. They identified Al Qaida's travel routes and safe havens and explained how Al Qaida's senior leadership communicates with its operatives in places like Iraq. They provided information that allows us—that has allowed us to make sense of documents and computer records that we have seized in terrorist raids. They've identified voices in recordings of intercepted calls and helped us understand the meaning of potentially critical terrorist communications.

The information we get from these detainees is corroborated by intelligence, and we've received—that we've received from other sources, and together this intelligence has helped us connect the dots and stop attacks before they occur. Information from the terrorists questioned in this program helped unravel plots and terrorist cells in Europe and in other places. It's helped our allies protect their people from deadly enemies. This program has been and remains one of the most vital tools in our war against the terrorists. It is invaluable to America and to our allies. Were it not for this program, our intelligence community believes that Al Qaida and its allies would have succeeded in launching another attack against the American homeland. By giving us information about terrorist plans we could not get anywhere else, this program has saved innocent lives. This program has been subject to multiple legal reviews by the Department of Justice and CIA lawyers; they've determined it complied with our laws. This program has received strict oversight by the CIA's Inspector General. A small number of key leaders from both political parties on Capitol Hill were briefed about this program. All those involved in the questioning of the terrorists are carefully chosen, and they're screened from a pool of experienced CIA officers. Those selected to conduct the most sensitive questioning had to complete more than 250 additional hours of specialized training before they are allowed to have contact with a captured terrorist.

I want to be absolutely clear with our people and the world: The United States does not torture. It's against our laws, and it's against our values. I have not authorized it, and I will not authorize it. Last year, my administration worked with Senator John McCain, and I signed into law the Detainee Treatment Act, which established the legal standard for treatment of detainees wherever they are held. I support this act. And as we implement this law, our Government will continue to use every lawful method to obtain intelligence that can protect innocent people and stop another attack like the one we experienced on September the 11th, 2001.

The CIA program has detained only a limited number of terrorists at any given time, and once we've determined that the terrorists held by the CIA have little or no additional intelligence value, many of them have been returned to their home countries for prosecution or detention by their governments. Others have been accused of terrible crimes against the American people, and we have a duty to bring those responsible for these crimes to justice. So we intend to prosecute these men, as appropriate, for their crimes.

Soon after the war on terror began, I authorized a system of military commissions to try foreign terrorists accused of war crimes. Military commissions have been used by Presidents from George Washington to Franklin Roosevelt to prosecute war criminals, because the rules for trying enemy combatants in a time of conflict must be different from those for trying common criminals or members of our own military. One of the first suspected terrorists to be put on trial by military commission was one of Usama bin Laden's bodyguards—a man named Hamdan. His lawyers challenged the legality of the military commission system. It took more than 2 years for this case to make its way through the courts. The Court of Appeals for the District of Columbia Circuit upheld the military commissions we had designed, but this past June, the Supreme Court overturned that decision. The Supreme Court determined that military commissions are an appropriate venue for trying terrorists but ruled that military commissions needed to be explicitly authorized by the United States Congress.

So today I'm sending Congress legislation to specifically authorize the creation of military commissions to try terrorists for war crimes. My administration has been working with members of both parties in the House and Senate on this legislation. We put forward a bill that ensures these commissions are established in a way that protects our national security and ensures a full and fair trial for those accused. The procedures in the bill I am sending to Congress today reflect the reality that we are a nation at war and that it's essential for us to use all reliable evidence to bring these people to justice.

We're now approaching the 5-year anniversary of the 9/11 attacks, and the families of those murdered that day have waited patiently for justice. Some of the families are with us today. They should have to wait no longer.

So I'm announcing today that Khalid Sheikh Mohammed, Abu Zubaydah, Ramzi bin al-Shibh, and 11 other terrorists in CIA custody have been transferred to the United States Naval Base at Guantanamo Bay. They are being held in the custody of the Department of Defense. As soon as Congress acts to authorize the military commissions I have proposed, the men our intelligence officials believe orchestrated the deaths of nearly 3,000 Americans on September the 11th, 2001, can face justice. We'll also seek to prosecute those believed to be responsible for the attack on the USS Cole and an operative believed to be involved in the bombings of the American Embassies in Kenya and Tanzania. With these prosecutions, we will send a clear message to those who kill Americans: No longer—how long it takes, we will find you, and we will bring you to justice.

These men will be held in a high-security facility at Guantanamo. The International Committee of the Red Cross is being advised of their detention and will have the opportunity to meet with them. Those charged with crimes will be given access to attorneys who will help them prepare their defense, and they will be presumed innocent. While at Guantanamo, they will have access to the same food, clothing, medical care, and opportunities for worship as other detainees. They will be questioned subject to the new U.S. Army Field Manual, which the Department of Defense is issuing today. And they will continue to be treated with the humanity that they denied others.

As we move forward with the prosecutions, we will continue to urge nations across the world to take back their nationals at Guantanamo who will not be prosecuted by our military commissions. America has no interest in being the world's jailer. But one of the reasons we have not been able to close Guantanamo is that many countries have refused to take back their nationals held at the facility. Other countries have not provided adequate assurances that their nationals will not be mistreated or they will not return to the battlefield, as more than a dozen people released from Guantanamo already have. We will continue working to transfer individuals held at Guantanamo and ask other countries to work with us in this process. And we will move toward the day when we can eventually close the detention facility at Guantanamo Bay.

I know Americans have heard conflicting information about Guantanamo. Let me give you some facts. Of the thousands of terrorists captured across the world, only about 770 have ever been sent to Guantanamo. Of these, about 315 have been returned to other countries so far, and about 455 remain in our custody. They are provided the same quality of medical care as the American servicemembers who guard them. The International Committee of the Red Cross has the opportunity to meet privately with all who are held there. The facility has been visited by government officials from more than 30 countries and delegations from international organizations as well. After the Organization for Security and Cooperation in Europe came to visit, one of its delegation members called Guantanamo "a model prison" where people are treated better than in prisons in his own country. Our troops can take great pride in the work they do at Guantanamo Bay, and so can the American people.

As we prosecute suspected terrorist leaders and operatives who have now been transferred to Guantanamo, we'll continue searching for those who have stepped forward to take their places. This Nation is going to stay on the offense to protect the American people. We will continue to bring the world's most dangerous terrorists to justice, and we will continue working to collect the vital intelligence we need to protect our country. The current transfers mean that there are now no terrorists in the CIA program. But as more high-ranking terrorists are captured, the need to obtain intelligence from them will remain critical. And having a CIA program for questioning terrorists will continue to be crucial to getting life-saving information.

Some may ask: Why are you acknowledging this program now? There are two reasons why I'm making these limited disclosures today. First, we have largely completed our questioning of the men, and to start the process for bringing them to trial, we must bring them into the open. Second, the Supreme Court's recent decision has impaired our ability to prosecute terrorists through military commissions and has put in question the future of the CIA program. In its ruling on military commissions, the Court determined that a provision of the Geneva Conventions known as Common Article Three applies to our war with Al Qaida. This article includes provisions that prohibit "outrages upon personal dignity" and "humiliating and degrading treatment." The problem is that these and other provisions of Common Article Three are vague and undefined, and each could be interpreted in different ways by American or foreign judges. And some believe our military and intelligence personnel involved in capturing and questioning terrorists could now be at risk of prosecution under the War Crimes Act, simply for doing their jobs in a thorough and professional way.

This is unacceptable. Our military and intelligence personnel go face to face with the world's most dangerous men every day. They have risked their lives to capture some of the most brutal terrorists on Earth. And they have worked day and night to find out what the terrorists know so we can stop new attacks. America owes our brave men and women some things in return. We owe them their thanks for saving lives and keeping America safe. And we owe them clear rules, so they can continue to do their jobs and protect our people.

So today I'm asking Congress to pass legislation that will clarify the rules for our personnel fighting the war on terror. First, I'm asking Congress to list the specific, recognizable offenses that would be considered crimes under the War Crimes Act so our personnel can know clearly what is prohibited in the handling of terrorist enemies. Second, I'm asking that Congress make explicit that by following the standards of the Detainee Treatment Act, our personnel are fulfilling America's obligations under Common Article Three of the Geneva Conventions. Third, I'm asking that Congress make it clear that captured terrorists cannot use the Geneva Conventions as a basis to sue our personnel in courts—in U.S. courts. The men and women who protect us should not have to fear lawsuits filed by terrorists because they're doing their jobs.

The need for this legislation is urgent. We need to ensure that those questioning terrorists can continue to do everything within the limits of the law to get information that can save American lives. My administration will continue to work with the Congress to get this legislation enacted, but time is of the essence. Congress is in session just for a few more weeks, and passing this legislation ought to be the top priority.

As we work with Congress to pass a good bill, we will also consult with congressional leaders on how to ensure that the CIA program goes forward in a way that follows the law, that meets the national security needs of our country, and protects the brave men and women we ask to obtain information that will save innocent lives. For the sake of our security, Congress needs to act and update our laws to meet the threats of this new era. And I know they will.

We're engaged in a global struggle, and the entire civilized world has a stake in its outcome. America is a nation of law. And as I work with Congress to strengthen and clarify our laws here at home, I will continue to work with members of the international community who have been our partners in this struggle. I've spoken with leaders of foreign governments and worked with them to address their concerns about Guantanamo and our detention policies. I'll continue to work with the international community to construct a common foundation to defend our nations and protect our freedoms.

Free nations have faced new enemies and adjusted to new threats before, and we have prevailed. Like the struggles of the last century, today's war on terror is, above all, a struggle for freedom and liberty. The adversaries are different, but the stakes in this war are the same: We're fighting for our way of life and our ability to live in freedom. We're fighting for the cause of humanity against those who seek to impose the darkness of tyranny and terror upon the entire world. And we're fighting for a peaceful future for our children and our grandchildren.

May God bless you all.

Source: U.S. Executive Office of the President. "Remarks on the War on Terror." September 6, 2006. *Weekly Compilation of Presidential Documents* 42, no. 36 (September 11, 2006): 1569–1575. Washington, D.C.: National Archives and Records Administration. www.gpoaccess.gov/wcomp/v42no36.html (accessed March 25, 2007).

Other Historic Documents of Interest

UN Secretary General Annan on the Situation in Afghanistan

September 11, 2006

███████████ **THE DOCUMENT IN CONTEXT** ███████████

Afghanistan was in danger of tipping back into anarchy in 2006, five years after the United States invaded and ousted the Taliban, the extreme Islamist government that had allowed the al Qaeda terrorist network to base itself in Afghan territory. In subsequent years, the Taliban regrouped, using bases in remote regions of southern Afghanistan and across the border in Pakistan. By 2006 the Taliban and other insurgent groups were able to launch thousands of attacks against the new government of Afghanistan and military units from the United States and other countries that were protecting that government.

These attacks turned much of the southern part of the country into a war zone and endangering the still fragile government. An estimated 4,000 people were killed in the year's fighting, nearly three times as many as during 2005. Most of those killed were antigovernment fighters, but about 1,000 civilians and 105 Western soldiers also died, according to official estimates.

In mid-October, the British commander of foreign troops in Afghanistan said the Taliban had been dealt a serious military blow in the year's heavy fighting; even so, he warned that if the Afghan people did not see major improvements in their lives in the next six months, they would choose "the rotten future offered by the Taliban" rather than the still undelivered promises offered by the government in Kabul and its Western backers. The Afghan government and Western leaders had unveiled, in February, a $10 billion, five-year "compact" to deliver on those promises, but an ambitious timetable of reforms slipped behind schedule almost immediately. Meanwhile, narcotics trafficking soared and led many observers to worry that Afghanistan was becoming a state whose chief success was the production of opium for heroin.

In the midst of the deteriorating security situation, the United States turned military command for Afghanistan over to NATO, giving that cold war era alliance its biggest military operation ever. NATO countries poured several thousand additional troops into Afghanistan in hopes of stemming the violence—a belated recognition that the relatively small-scale foreign presence there since the U.S. invasion in 2001 had been inadequate to prevent the Taliban resurgence. NATO commanders said during 2006 that a substantial foreign military presence would be needed in Afghanistan for three to five years, and the country would require some level of foreign military help for up to fifteen years.

U.S. officials spent much of the year assuring President Hamid Karzai and the Afghan people that the United States intended to provide the necessary help. President George W. Bush, Defense Secretary Donald H. Rumsfeld, and Secretary of

State Condoleezza Rice headed the list of senior officials who visited Afghanistan and pledged that the United States was committed to Afghanistan for the long haul. "People are going to see us here for a long time to come," Richard A. Boucher, the assistant secretary of state for South and Central Asia, said during a visit to Kabul on April 3. In one indication of how worried it had become about the situation in Afghanistan, the Bush administration early in the year cancelled plans to withdraw 3,000 of the approximately 20,000 U.S. troops there. *(Background, Historic Documents of 2005, p. 970)*

Upsurge of Taliban Attacks

After ousting the Taliban from power, the Bush administration rejected the advice of some experts that a large-scale foreign military presence would be needed to stabilize Afghanistan, which had been torn by nearly three decades of war. The Taliban had dispersed, and administration officials said they saw no need for a major peacekeeping operation that would tie down U.S. soldiers for years to come. About 10,000 U.S. army and special operations soldiers were to remain in Afghanistan, almost exclusively for the purpose of attacking the remnants of the al Qaeda terrorist network that were alleged to be in eastern Afghanistan and neighboring Pakistan. A small European-dominated peacekeeping unit, called the International Security Assistance Force (ISAF), was confined primarily in Kabul, the capital, where it served essentially as a bodyguard for the new Western-backed government headed by Hamid Karzai, leader of the Pashtun ethnic group. The NATO alliance took command of the ISAF force in 2003 and a year later ISAF moved out of Kabul for the first time, into the relatively quiet northern provinces of Afghanistan. *(Background, Historic Documents of 2002, p. 15)*

In the meantime, the Taliban regrouped and kept up low-level attacks against the U.S. military and representatives of Karzai's government. These attacks grew stronger and bolder in 2005 and continued all through 2006, forcing the United States and its European allies to acknowledge that the Taliban still posed a mortal danger to efforts to bring stability to Afghanistan.

The Taliban was not the only danger. Several other armed groups also sought, for varying reasons, to oust Karzai's government or at least gain control over their own regions. Among them was Gulbuddin Hekmatyar, who had been one of the prime recipients of U.S. aid during the 1980s when he and other Islamists, known as the Mujahideen, fought the Soviet occupation of Afghanistan. Hekmatyar turned violently against the United States after it ousted the Taliban and sidelined him in favor of the more pro-Western Karzai. Hekmatyar issued a video in May 2006 aligning himself with al Qaeda, which remained a significant presence along the eastern border between Afghanistan and Pakistan; his group was particularly active in eastern Kunar province, adjacent to Pakistan.

The Taliban and other groups used various tactics to weaken the Karzai government, terrorize civilians, and demoralize the foreign forces supporting the government. At night, and even increasingly during the day, insurgent fighters set up ambushes in rural areas and mounted raids on military posts, government offices, and civilian communities. Insurgents also used roadside bombs (which the United States called improvised explosive devices) to prevent civilian and military traffic, and they increasingly used suicide bombs—a tactic that until 2005 had been rare in Afghanistan because many local people considered it contrary to the teachings of Islam. U.S. officials acknowledged in 2006 that Afghan insurgents appeared to be copying the tactics of Sunni Muslim insurgents who were using suicide bombs and roadside bombs to battle the U.S. presence in Iraq.

It had been evident since at least 2005 that Taliban members were attempting to eliminate the country's educated elite, who tended to support the Karzai government. Dozens of moderate Muslim clerics, school teachers, and other educated people were abducted and then killed or were simply assassinated in broad daylight, their deaths serving as warnings to their colleagues. A particularly gruesome example came early in January when gunmen broke into the house of a high school teacher in Qalat, the capital of Zabul province, dragged him outside, and beheaded him. An official at the school where the teacher worked said the Taliban had put up posters denouncing the teaching of girls. These posters reflected another Taliban priority: ending the education of girls. During the year, according to UN figures, the Taliban and other groups burned nearly 200 schools, most of them coeducational; as a result, up to 500,000 children were forced out of school.

The Taliban also stepped up direct attacks on leaders who were associated with Karzai's government or who had supported it. Two such attacks came in mid-March. On March 12, a bomb attack injured but failed to kill Sebghatullah Mojadeddi, a former president of Afghanistan who was serving as head of the Meshrano Jirga, the upper house of parliament. Six days later, insurgents ambushed and killed the former governor of the province of Ghazni, in eastern Afghanistan, who been a strong supporter of Karzai. On September 10 a suicide bomber succeeded in killing a sitting provincial governor, Muhammad Hakim Taniwal, of Paktia province, southeast of Kabul, who also was a close friend of Karzai. Another suicide bomber attacked Taniwal's funeral the next day, killing 5 policemen and 2 children and wounding several dozen others. Local police were another favored target of the Taliban; for example, on February 7 an attack on police headquarters in the conflicted southern city of Kandahar killed 13 people and wounded 11 others, most of them policemen.

Although the Taliban-inspired violence angered many Afghanis, a sizable percentage of the population blamed the Karzai government and its foreign backers for failing to protect them. "Outside of the city, everywhere you can easily find the Taliban," a Kandahar clothing merchant named Haji Din Mohammed told the Associated Press in early May. "The government and coalition forces promised us security and an improved economy, but instead the security is bad. I can't go to my nearby village after 5 p.m."

The lack of security thus became a cycle that endangered long-term stability. Taliban attacks undermined support for the government and blocked work on foreign-funded economic development projects that were considered key to gaining local support for the government. This in turn convinced local people that they had no choice except to support the Taliban or acquiesce in its actions, further damaging the government and emboldening the Taliban. As traces of Karzai's government disappeared from some regions under the weight of Taliban assaults, the Taliban stepped in with its promises to provide the protection the government could not.

Some of the foreign military's tactics also proved counterproductive. Air strikes against suspected Taliban targets occasionally hit civilian areas, in part because Taliban guerrillas often hid in neighborhoods. In the worst such case during 2006, 31 civilians died in late October when NATO planes attacked a village in Kandahar province where Taliban fighters were said to be hiding; an investigation found that most of those killed were nomadic shepherds. Such civilian deaths caused deep anger, not at the Taliban but at the United States and other foreign forces whose bombs and missiles were the immediate sources of death. Similarly, U.S. troops carried out aggressive house-to-house searches, often by kicking down doors, that terrorized entire neighborhoods. Karzai repeatedly asked the United States to be more careful, but military commanders said they often had no choice but to respond aggressively when the Taliban moved into villages.

In a generally pessimistic report to the United Nations Security Council on September 11, Secretary General Kofi Annan appeared to offer little hope that the Taliban could be weaned away from violence. Senior leaders of the Taliban and other insurgent groups, he said, "are widely considered not to be open to reconciliation." An Afghan government program intended to integrate insurgents into the political and social life of the nation had had some success with midlevel Taliban leaders, he said, but not with senior commanders. Instead, Annan said the best hope for long-term progress in Afghanistan was the provision of jobs and basic services that gave the people hope for a better future and thus the incentive to support the democratically elected Karzai government.

The Year's Toll

The year was by far the most violent in Afghanistan since the Taliban was pushed from power. The United Nations mission in Afghanistan counted about 4,000 deaths in 2006, compared to about 1,600 in 2005, which had been the bloodiest year to that point. U.S. and NATO military commanders said about half of those killed in 2006 were fighters for the Taliban and other groups. At least several hundred civilians—possibly as many as 1,000, according to Human Rights Watch—also died, most as the result of Taliban attacks but several dozen from misplaced aerial bombardments by U.S. and NATO forces. Most of the deaths occurred in the eastern and southern provinces, where about half of all Afghans lived.

A total of 105 foreign soldiers died in Afghanistan during the year, including 87 from the United States and 18 from other NATO countries. The number of American deaths dropped from 93 the previous year, largely because NATO troops from Canada and Europe were doing more of the fighting.

All major indicators of violent activity by the Taliban and other insurgent groups rose sharply during 2006. According to the Pentagon, these groups carried out 4,542 violent attacks using assault rifles and other weapons in 2006, nearly three times the 1,558 total for the previous year. Similarly, the Pentagon counted 1,677 roadside bomb attacks in 2006, compared to 737 in 2005.

Suicide bomb attacks rose most sharply of all, from 27 in 2005 to 139 in 2006. Although many of the suicide attacks appeared aimed at foreign troops or Afghan government targets, civilians were among the most frequent victims; at least 200 civilians were killed by suicide bombs during the year, according to UN reports. Starting late in the year many suicide bombs appeared to be aimed expressly at civilians. An example was a November 26 attack on a restaurant in the town of Urgun, near the Pakistan border, that killed 15 people.

NATO Takes Control from the United States

In a momentous step for the Western nations providing security to Afghanistan—and for the people of Afghanistan—the United States gradually turned over to NATO the prime responsibility for security in nearly all the country. The United States remained the largest single source of foreign troops in Afghanistan, and a U.S. general was scheduled to assume command of the NATO force in 2007. But NATO's new role broadened the international stake in Afghanistan's future by transferring some of the responsibility from the United States to its allies. The assignment also became a major gamble for NATO, which had been struggling to define itself, even as it expanded its membership, since the collapse in late 1991 of its original enemy, the Soviet Union. *(NATO background, Historic Documents of 2004, p. 135)*

Since taking command of the ISAF peacekeeping force in 2003, NATO had gradually expanded its presence beyond the original limits of the Kabul area: first to the relatively quiet eight northern provinces in 2004 and then to the four western provinces in 2006. A much bigger step came in February 2006 when Canada assumed command of the ISAF troops in Kandahar, the southern province that was the home territory of the Taliban and that had become the most dangerous part of the country. Just two months later, ISAF and Afghan troops launched a large attack on Taliban concentrations in the region and reportedly killed about 40 Taliban fighters.

One immediate result of the change was that some areas of southern Afghanistan saw the regular presence of foreign troops for the first time since the ouster of the Taliban. NATO stationed about 1,000 troops in long-troubled Helmand province. As could be expected, the increased presence of foreign troops led to a cycle of greater violence. With its larger force in the area, NATO was more aggressive in seeking out insurgents, who in turn launched more attacks.

The new commander of the ISAF, British Lt. Gen. David Richards, also said his troops would strive to be "people friendly." One regular criticism of U.S. troops was that they had an overly aggressive approach to dealing with civilians (for example, by launching air strikes that occasionally killed civilians or by breaking down doors of homes when searching neighborhoods for suspected Taliban fighters). Karzai had complained about U.S. tactics in 2005 but his complaints had been brushed aside. He repeated those complaints on June 22, 2006, saying civilian deaths undermined support for his government. Karzai also said Afghanistan's foreign allies needed to concentrate more effort on improving local government and strengthening the country's army and police services.

The ISAF launched another major operation, called Operation Mountain Thrust, on June 10; it consisted of coordinated assaults by more than 10,000 Afghan and coalition forces on suspected Taliban bases throughout southern Afghanistan. For nearly eight weeks, ending in late July, that operation killed more than 600 suspected Taliban militants, according to ISAF officials.

Another big step came on June 31 when General Richards took command from the United States of all foreign military operations throughout southern Afghanistan, where the bulk of the violence was occurring. On September 2 the NATO-led ISAF launched Operation Medusa, another large-scale anti-Taliban operation. It was the biggest combat operation in Afghanistan since the U.S. invasion in 2001 and it focused on southern Kandahar province. NATO's supreme commander, Gen. James L. Jones, said on September 20 that at least 1,000 and possibly as many as 1,500 Taliban had been killed in the fighting, resulting in what he called a "tactical defeat" for the insurgents. Jones estimated that the Taliban still had about 3,000 to 4,000 "hard-core fighters." This figure was substantially higher than previous U.S. estimates, which put the Taliban fighting force in the low hundreds. Several independent experts on Afghanistan said Jones's figures demonstrated the ease with which Taliban commanders were able to recruit fighters among the population of unemployed, disillusioned young men who were enticed by the prospect of engaging in an Islamic *jihad* against hostile Westerners.

The final step in NATO's assumption of overall responsibility for security in Afghanistan came on October 5 when the alliance took command of ISAF operations in the twelve eastern provinces, where U.S. forces had been concentrated since late 2001. Several of these provinces were along the mountainous border with Pakistan, where remnants of the al Qaeda terrorist network reportedly were based. About 12,000 U.S. soldiers came under NATO command at this point, marking the first time since World War II that such a large number of American troops were commanded by a foreign general.

As part of its takeover of the military effort in Afghanistan, NATO significantly boosted the number of non-U.S. troops there—but also faced significant challenges posed by the reluctance of European countries to have their soldiers put in harms way. The ISAF force had totaled about 10,000 troops as of late 2005, but about 6,000 additional troops were added in the early months of 2006; most of the additional troops (about 4,000) came from Great Britain, with others coming from Canada and the Netherlands. NATO commanders asked in September 2006 for another 2,500 troops but faced resistance because many NATO countries said their militaries already were stretched by commitments to peacekeeping missions in Bosnia, Kosovo, Iraq, Lebanon, and elsewhere. At year's end it appeared that the additional 2,500 troops would be in place by early 2007, in time for the next round of fighting in the spring.

In addition to struggling to get more soldiers into Afghanistan, NATO commanders had to deal with strict limitations (called "caveats") that some troop-contributing countries had put on what their soldiers could do. For example, Germany allowed its 2,800 troops to be stationed only near Kabul, and Turkey allowed its 900 soldiers to help rebuild Kabul, but not to fight. Other countries said their soldiers could not carry out patrols at night, when most Taliban attacks occurred. This meant that the actual number of soldiers available to battle the insurgents was far less than the 31,000 listed on the ISAF's roster at year's end. NATO officials made a big push late in the year to get countries to drop these restrictions. The best they could achieve was an agreement, at the annual NATO summit meeting in Latvia on November 29, that NATO troops would rush to each other's aid in emergencies, regardless of the restrictions placed on their operations.

U.S. soldiers continued to be involved in some of the heaviest fighting in the country. The upsurge in Taliban attacks forced the Bush administration to reverse its earlier plans for a small withdrawal from Afghanistan. The United States had more than 16,000 troops in Afghanistan during the first half of 2005 but boosted that total to about 20,000 in advance of the parliamentary elections scheduled for September 2005. That number was to have been reduced back to around 16,500 by the spring of 2006, but in May Gen. Karl W. Eikenberry, the commander of U.S. forces in Afghanistan, said the U.S. presence instead was being increased to about 23,000. After 12,000 of the U.S. soldiers came under NATO command in October, the rest remained under a U.S. command that had the specific mission of rooting out al Qaeda fighters along the Afghan-Pakistan border.

Afghan Security Forces

A cornerstone of the international plan to stabilize Afghanistan after 2001 had been the assumption that tens of thousands of Afghan soldiers and policemen could be trained quickly so they could provide the bulk of the country's security. In subsequent years the United States and its allies poured more than $1 billion into new security forces for Afghanistan. By 2006, however, the new Afghan army was still acting only in a supporting role and the new police forces were widely considered corrupt and incompetent.

The new army reached half-way to the government's goal of 70,000 trained soldiers. Most of the training was being done by the United States. Afghan units increasingly went out on patrols with U.S. and NATO forces and even participated in some of the year's heaviest fighting against the Taliban in southern provinces. International officials said the new army was not prepared for combat entirely on its own, however, and ISAF commander Richards told a visiting delegation from the UN Security Council in September that only about 14,000 troops were "present and available for duty" out of the nearly 35,000 listed on Afghan army rosters.

Afghanistan's new police forces were an even bigger problem, according to news accounts, official reports, and independent assessments. After the 2001 invasion, Germany and the United States split responsibility for training new Afghan police forces. Germany assumed the role of training the national police, while the United States was responsible for training officers to patrol the borders and highways; most of the U.S. training was done by a private contractor, DynCorp. By 2006 the German effort had come under strong international criticism as inadequate; Germany assigned only about 40 officers to Afghanistan and had trained only 16,000 personnel, most of them in the middle and higher ranks. The United States said it had trained about 40,000 border and highway policemen.

Numerous reports during the year suggested that many of Afghanistan's policemen were corrupt or had been subverted by narcotics traffickers and local warlords. One such report, issued on December 3 by the inspectors general of the U.S. Defense and State departments, said most police recruits were illiterate and underpaid and therefore were willing to accept bribes to secure the release of criminal suspects. Police commanders often skimmed the salaries of their subordinates, the report said, and many were in league with narcotics traffickers or other corrupt government officials. In a November 2 report, the International Crisis Group (a Brussels-based international research group) said the police often were little more than private militias that were "regarded in nearly every district more as a source of insecurity than protection. Instead of gaining the confidence of communities, their often-predatory behavior alienates locals further."

To make up for the lack of trained police, Karzai in August approved creation of "auxiliary police" units totaling about 11,500 policemen, most of them in the southern provinces. Some local officials complained that these police—who were to receive only ten days of training—would turn out to be the private armies of warlords, only with new guns and government uniforms.

Several incidents during the year illustrated the problems involved with creating security forces in an ethnically divided country that had experienced near constant warfare for a generation. Perhaps the most telling incident was a large riot in Kabul on May 29 following a traffic accident caused when the brakes failed on a U.S. army truck. Three Afghan civilians died in the accident, and witnesses said 4 more were killed when frightened American soldiers fired into an angry crowd that gathered at the scene. During an ensuing riot another 20 people were killed and several buildings housing UN and other international agencies were looted or burned.

The violent reaction to the incident illustrated the ambivalence of many Afghans toward the overwhelming presence (especially in the capital) of soldiers, aid workers, and others from Western countries. While many people were grateful for the money and security brought by the Western presence, others were angered by the elements of Western culture that also had been implanted in Kabul, such as luxury hotels, restaurants, shops—all of which stood in stark contrast to the crushing poverty endured by average Afghan citizens.

In response to the riot, Afghan president Karzai appointed a new police chief for Kabul—a man with well-known links to organized crime. Karzai said the man could improve security in the capital, but the president's willingness to put him in such a sensitive position left foreign diplomats and other Afghan political leaders wondering about Karzai's priorities.

UN Disarmament Program

The United Nations in 2006 completed the last phase of a complex program to disarm and reintegrate into society tens of thousands of fighters who had been on the payroll of Afghanistan's official security services before the U.S. invasion in 2001. The initial phases had been completed in mid-2005 with the disarmament and demobilization of some 62,000 fighters. The vast majority of these fighters entered what the UN called the "reintegration" phase, which included various training programs or assistance in returning to (or entering) agricultural life. This phase ended on June 30, with the UN reporting that 55,804 former fighters had been successfully reintegrated into society; of these, nearly 23,000 entered agricultural work and more than 14,000 were given training and other assistance to start their own small businesses. Only about 800 of these former fighters entered the Afghan national army or police forces.

A more difficult challenge for the UN was a follow-up program intended to disband dozens of illegal militias and other armed groups that remained at large, many of them commanded by regional warlords. The UN sent letters to 137 militia commanders and 42 government officials linked to armed groups demanding that they disband their groups and hand over their weapons. As of early September, only about one-third of these men responded, and they handed over only 616 weapons (most of them unserviceable). Secretary General Annan said that handover fell "far short" of the more than 23,000 weapons the UN had estimated were held by these groups. Many of the commanders insisted they needed to keep their armed groups intact because of Taliban attacks and other security problems in the southern part of the country.

Following are excerpts from "The Situation in Afghanistan and Its Implications for Peace and Security," the semiannual report delivered to the United Nations Security Council on September 11, 2006, by Secretary General Kofi Annan.

DOCUMENT

"The Situation in Afghanistan and Its Implications for Peace and Security"

II. Current Security Situation

2. Since my previous report [on March 7, 2006], the most significant development in Afghanistan has been the upsurge in violence, particularly in the south, south-east and east of the country. Security has, once again, become the paramount concern of a majority of Afghans. It is estimated that over 2,000 people, at least one third of them civilians, have lost their lives in the fighting since the start of 2006. This represents a three- to four-fold

increase in the rate of casualties compared to 2005. The number of security incidents involving anti-Government elements has increased from fewer than 300 per month at the end of March 2006 to close to 500 per month subsequently.

3. The growing number of casualties in the south can be attributed both to a rise in anti-Government attacks and to a corresponding increase in offensive military operations being conducted by the Afghan National Army and its international partners.... In the south-east, where major military operations are only just getting under way, insurgent activity has been conducted largely unchecked. Suicide attacks continue to be a highly emotive issue and are widely reported in the international media. The phenomenon is now well established in Afghanistan. The number of suicide attacks already stood in mid-August at 65, against 17 such incidents during all of 2005.

4. While previous reporting periods have been marked by progressive and significant deteriorations in the security situation, the recent upsurge of violence represents a watershed. At no time since the fall of the Taliban in late 2001 has the threat to Afghanistan's transition been so severe. In recognition of the gravity of the situation, President Hamid Karzai convened Afghan security forces, their international counterparts, some representatives from Member States with a significant troop presence in the south and UNAMA to produce a shared assessment of the sources of instability. A high degree of consensus emerged from these consultations regarding the nature of the conflict. In addition to a quantitative spike in their activities, a qualitative shift was detected in the operations and coordination of the insurgent forces' intent on overthrowing the Government through violent means.

5. The insurgency is being conducted mostly by Afghans operating inside Afghanistan's borders. However, its leadership appears to rely on support and sanctuary from outside the country. The insurgency's current centre of gravity falls in and around the provinces of Kandahar, Helmand, Uruzgan and increasingly, Farah. Anti-Government operations nevertheless continue in many parts of the east and south-east and have become an acute concern in Wardak and Logar provinces, close to the capital. The insurgency now covers a broad arc of mostly Pashtun-dominated territory, extending from Kunar province in the east to Farah province in the west; it also increasingly affects the southern fringe of the central highlands, in Ghor and Day Kundi provinces.

6. Five distinct leadership centers of the insurgency can be identified. They appear to act in loose coordination with each other and a number benefit from financial and operational links with drug trafficking networks. They include: the wing of the Hezb-i-Islami party led by Gulbuddin Hekmatyar, in Kunar province and neighboring areas; the Taliban northern command, for Nangarhar and Laghman provinces; networks led by Jalaluddin Haqqani, a former minister in the Taliban regime, mainly for Khost and Paktya provinces; the Wana Shura, for Paktika; and the Taliban southern command, for the provinces of Zabul, Kandahar, Hilmand, and Uruzgan. The Taliban southern command has recently begun to establish parallel civil administrations and courts in its area of operations, although they remain marginal in most districts. Leadership and support structures for the insurgency straddle the southern border of Afghanistan.

7. The leadership centers form the hard core of the insurgency and are widely considered not to be open to reconciliation. The "strengthening peace" program, a national initiative to reintegrate Taliban and other insurgent combatants, has had successes with mid-level Taliban commanders but has not focused on attracting senior commanders.

8. The leadership relies heavily on cross-border fighters, many of whom are Afghans drawn from nearby refugee camps and radical seminaries in Pakistan. The fighters are typically indoctrinated, unemployed young men whose sense of identity has been blurred by years in exile. They are trained and paid to serve as medium level commanders, leading operations inside Afghanistan, and they are able to retreat back to safe havens outside the country.

9. The foot soldiers of the insurgency are Afghans recruited within Afghanistan; they are driven by poverty, poor education and general disenchantment with their place in society. These internal fighters are not ideologically driven, but their ranks have expanded to support the growing upper echelons of the insurgency. They are thought to be ready to disengage from the insurgency if the appropriate incentives, particularly economic, are provided.

10. Dialogue with elders, clerics and other community leaders in areas affected by the insurgency has revealed a consistent set of grievances that, if properly addressed, these leaders believe could significantly weaken support for the insurgency. Government corruption at the provincial and district levels, particularly within the police and the judiciary, has alienated local populations as have unfulfilled expectations of development following the fall of the Taliban regime. Imbalances in the distribution of power between different Pashtun tribes at the provincial level have also contributed to a sense of marginalization felt by entire tribes. Finally, conservative elements of the population—a clear majority in rural areas—often view the Government's social policies as insufficiently protective of, or even harmful to, traditional religious, tribal and cultural norms.

11. The trend towards instability has not been restricted to areas affected by the insurgency. A sense of volatility has also gripped Kabul over the past three months, triggered by the violent riots that broke out in the capital on 29 May following a tragic traffic incident involving the United States-led coalition forces in the northern districts of the city. At least 25 people died on that day, and several properties were looted or burned, including four United Nations guesthouses and several compounds belonging to aid organizations.

12. Factional fighting between former commanders continues to pose a threat to security in some provinces such as Faryab, which was rocked by violent clashes between the Hizb-e-Azadi (Azadi) and National Islamic Movement of Afghanistan (Junbesh) factions. On 30 July, a confrontation between armed groups linked to both parties resulted in the death of four Azadi members and the injury of three others. Fighting continued until 9 August, reportedly killing another Azadi member and three Junbesh members. Serious human rights abuses were also reported, including numerous rapes. . . .

X. Observations

75. Since my last report to the Security Council on Afghanistan, the country has made some impressive strides for which its Government and people are to be congratulated. The new National Assembly has demonstrated independent, reformist and democratic credentials. Provincial councils are now functioning in all 34 of Afghanistan's provinces. The Joint Coordination and Monitoring Board has been established, bringing together senior Afghan officials and their international counterparts to oversee the implementation of the Afghanistan Compact.

76. At the same time, Afghanistan finds itself in the midst of a new crisis. A third of the country is racked by violent insurgency. The situation in the south, south-east and east is unlikely to improve in the near future and the prospect of further deterioration cannot be excluded. While the rest of the country remains relatively secure, Afghans everywhere understand that the insurgency poses a grave threat to the political transition nationwide. If not addressed urgently and comprehensively, the insurgency could jeopardize the considerable achievements of the Bonn process and plunge parts of the country into chaos and uncertainty, with considerable spillover effects across Afghanistan. Although events on the ground have tempered the optimism that surrounded the London Conference earlier this year, they must not lessen our resolve. The Government of Afghanistan, its regional partners and the rest of the international community must stand ready to redouble our collective efforts—including political and financial commitments—to stabilize Afghanistan and support its transition in the face of growing challenges.

77. In the light of the above, the expansion of the International Security Assistance Force to the south of Afghanistan is a particularly welcome and timely development. I recognize the contributions and sacrifices being made by all Member States currently taking part in the Force, and I strongly encourage all nations to continue to support the Force as it expands its command to the rest of the country.

78. Elements of a strategy to tackle the insurgency are emerging from discussions led by the Government and members of the international community involved in the areas of the country affected by the surge in violence. The leadership centers of the insurgency described in the present report must be dealt with through robust military and law enforcement measures wherever they are found in Afghanistan or elsewhere. The nature and scope of dialogue among all actors involved must be enhanced with a particular view to disengaging the bulk of combatants from the leaders of the insurgency. Communities need to be further engaged and empowered to play a greater role in bringing stability to their areas. At the same time, the capacity of the Government to deliver security and other basic services and bring development must be reinforced, not least to address growing frustration at the slow pace of change in the lives of ordinary Afghans.

79. In that regard, the international community and the Government must intensify their efforts to improve and accelerate reform of the Afghan police. The international community should, wherever possible, provide intensified advising, mentoring and training through the provision of additional qualified police personnel deployed with the Afghan National Police in the field and within the frameworks of existing training regimes. The Government and the international community must study current administrative, budgetary and logistical systems in place and take immediate steps to ensure that the men and women of the Afghan National Police receive their salaries and other support in full and in a timely fashion to stem defections and maintain morale and dedication in the rank and file.

80. President Hamid Karzai is to be commended for his handling of the cabinet confirmation process and for the appointment and confirmation of a highly qualified Supreme Court. The prospect of stronger judicial institutions—one of the principal demands expressed by Afghans—has been revived by the arrival of the new judicial leadership. This moment of opportunity should not be lost, and I urge the national and international bodies working on justice reform to redouble their efforts to extend the rule of law in Afghanistan.

81. The program to disband illegal armed groups addresses one of the clearest and most consistently expressed demands of the Afghan people, but compliance to date has been disappointing. The Government and the international community must continue to make the disbandment of illegal armed groups program a priority as it is a prerequisite for meeting other core objectives under the Afghanistan Compact, particularly with respect to security, governance and the rule of law.

82. Corruption and the narcotics industry continue to threaten Afghanistan's transition and must be dealt with as matters of priority by the Government and the international community. I am increasingly concerned that administrative corruption continues to hamper efforts to improve governance and government service delivery at all levels in Afghanistan. Similarly, the growth of the drug trade, which fuels both insurgency and corruption, calls for new strategic direction in current policy. This will need to include more decisive action against traffickers and those who protect them, as well as a more integrated rural development strategy.

83. Further attention is required by all to ensure that international principles are upheld in relation to the protection of civilians in armed conflict during this period of increased insecurity and combat. The Taliban and other anti-Government forces continue to demonstrate an inexcusable disregard for the value of human life. Efforts to combat the insurgency should seek to minimize the potential for civilian casualties. Afghan security forces and their international partners must also be wary of invoking the security situation as a justification to suppress human rights guaranteed by the Constitution and under international treaties to which Afghanistan is party. I remain equally concerned about the human rights situation in areas not directly affected by the current wave of violence. We must not allow the protection of human rights throughout Afghanistan to become another casualty of the current conflict. In that respect, the implementation of the National Action Plan on Peace, Reconciliation and Justice adopted in December 2005 has yet to gain momentum.

84. The challenges facing the country are daunting but the international community as well as local communities must continue to work hand in hand with the Government towards the long-term vision expressed in the Afghanistan Compact. Productive partnership between the Government and international donors resulted in a single development process in the form of the Joint Coordination and Monitoring Board and the interim Afghanistan National Development Strategy framework. This aims to deliver results as much as it aims to build sustainable Afghan institutions. This dual imperative should be enhanced through improved coordination, cooperation and implementation.

85. The ability of the Board to engender high-level collaboration will depend on its ability to move from process and planning to action and oversight. It has yet to become the active custodian of the Compact envisioned during the London Conference that will hold the Afghan Government and its international partners to account. Afghan and international members of the Board will need to work more closely in a spirit of partnership and effectiveness to ensure that the ambitious agenda is achieved to the greatest benefit of the Afghan people.

86. In conclusion, I would like to convey my sincere appreciation to the Security Council and other Member States for their continued support to Afghanistan. I would like to pay tribute to the dedicated efforts of my Special Representative, and to the women and men of the United Nations Assistance Mission in Afghanistan and their partner organizations

who continue to carry out their mission under difficult and increasingly dangerous circumstances. I salute their courage, dedication and commitment.

Source: United Nations. General Assembly/Security Council. "The Situation in Afghanistan and Its Implications for Peace and Security: Report of the Secretary-General." A/61/326-S/2006/727, September 11, 2006.
www.un.org/Docs/sc/sgrep06.htm (accessed December 18, 2006).

Other Historic Documents of Interest

"Compact" on Afghanistan, p. 48   *State of the Union, p. 23*
Security in Iraq, p. 702

FDA on Foodborne Illness and the Safety of Fresh Produce

September 14 and November 15, 2006

Four separate incidents of foodborne illness in the last half of the year that together sickened hundreds of people throughout the United States renewed concerns about food safety, but there was little agreement about how best to prevent such incidents in the future. All four outbreaks involved fresh produce—spinach, tomatoes, and lettuce—and all involved contamination that occurred either during the growing or processing of the produce. That knowledge left farmers, producers, and state and federal officials scrambling to determine the source of the contamination and devising procedures to prevent further outbreaks. "It's fairly clear something needs to change," David W. K. Acheson, a leading food safety expert with the Food and Drug Administration (FDA), said in December. "Having illness and repeated outbreaks, especially the ones we've seen in the last couple of months, is clearly unacceptable to everyone."

Overall, the incidence of foodborne illness in the United States did not appear to be increasing. The federal Centers for Disease Control and Prevention estimated that about 79 million people suffered from food poisoning every year and an estimated 5,000 died. But where contaminated meat and seafood had once been the main culprits, in recent years fresh produce was increasingly associated with outbreaks. The Center for Science in the Public Interest, a consumer advocacy group, said that people were now more likely to get sick from eating contaminated produce than from any other food source. *(Background on meat safety, Historic Documents of 2002, p. 579)*

Fresh produce could be contaminated at any of a number of points in the growing and processing chain. Like meat, contamination in produce came from E. coli, salmonella, and other bacteria that was carried in fecal material. A field of lettuce, for example, could be contaminated by water runoff from nearby livestock operations, by wild animals moving through the field, or even by farm workers who relieved themselves in the field. Washing did not always remove all contamination, especially in leafy greens, and processors typically mixed produce from many different farms and fields before packaging it, a practice that could spread the bacteria. Failure to keep produce properly refrigerated during processing and distribution could also contribute to contamination. Although the bacteria were killed when exposed to the heat of cooking, much produce was consumed raw.

The Outbreaks

The four outbreaks in late 2006 showed signs of most of these mechanisms of contamination. The first incident was an outbreak of E. coli bacteria in late August and early September that ultimately caused three deaths and approximately two hundred illnesses in several states. E. coli caused severe, sometimes bloody diarrhea and strong abdominal cramping, and in a few cases could lead to kidney failure and death. The contamination in this outbreak was fairly quickly traced to fresh, bagged spinach. The FDA on September 14 warned consumers not to eat bagged spinach until further notice. On September 16, the FDA expanded its warning to all fresh spinach, loose or bagged, as well as to any products containing fresh spinach.

The contaminated spinach was traced to Natural Selections Foods, based in San Juan Bautista, California. One of the largest producers of organic foods, Natural Selections packaged and sold its spinach under thirty-one brand names, including Dole, Emeril, and Trader Joe's. The company voluntarily recalled its spinach products. Within a week the FDA had tracked the source of the contamination to spinach farms in three California counties, and by September 29 the agency had narrowed the ban to specific brands packaged on specific dates. The warning for all other spinach was lifted.

Although safety officials were able to determine where the contaminated spinach had come from, they could not identify the specific source of the contamination with certainty. Testing on and around the four suspect farms found the E. coli strain (E. coli 0157:H7) that caused the human illness in a dead wild pig and in creek water near one of the farms, but as of late October inspectors were still not certain of the exact source or sources of the contamination.

A second outbreak of E. coli in late November was traced to Taco Bell restaurants in New York, New Jersey, and eventually Pennsylvania. On December 6, the fast food chain removed green onions from its 5,800 restaurants nationwide, saying they might have been the source of the E. coli contamination. But on December 12 federal officials said their testing found no E. coli in the onions and that the more likely source was contaminated lettuce. Finding the source of that contamination was likely to prove difficult; the lettuce had come from many different farms and had been mixed together and shredded before being distributed to the individual restaurants. Altogether about 400 people in several states were sickened in the outbreak.

In October and November two outbreaks of salmonella, traced to tomatoes, sickened nearly two hundred people in at least nineteen states. Like E. coli, salmonella caused diarrhea and cramping and could be fatal in young children and the elderly. Although salmonella infections were most often caused by eating undercooked meat, poultry, or eggs contaminated with the bacteria, the Center for Science in the Public Interest said eleven salmonella outbreaks had been associated with tomatoes since 1990.

Policy Issues

Virtually everyone involved in growing, producing, and consuming fresh produce agreed on the need for stronger standards, better procedures, and more oversight for bringing fresh produce to market. There was considerably less agreement on what those standards should be and whether they should be voluntary or mandatory. After the spinach outbreak, the FDA "advised" the produce industry in California to develop a plan for minimizing the risk of another outbreak, but the FDA had no authority to impose safety requirements on growers or processors.

Eight major supermarket chains and distributors also demanded that the growers develop a safety program for spinach and leafy greens by December 15. Thomas Nassif, president of Western Growers, an association of about 3,000 farmers in California and Arizona, said his group was working on creating uniform farming standards in California, including formal inspections of farms and stricter rules on testing water and soil for contaminants and worker sanitation, that would be enforced by the state department of agriculture. Those guidelines were still being reviewed at the end of the year.

In December Western Growers joined the United Fresh Produce Association and the Produce Marketing Association in calling for government regulation, if necessary, to ensure that standards were developed and enforced. The groups said such regulation might be the only way to restore consumer confidence, which had sagged badly since the outbreak. In mid-October, United Fresh Produce said sales of bulk and bagged spinach were down 60 percent compared with the previous year, while sales of other packaged salad greens had dropped 10 percent. "At this point, because of the seriousness of the issue, we are open to any and all solutions including regulation at the federal or state level," said a spokesman for United Fresh Produce. "Certain segments of the industry are under the gun to do everything possible."

David Acheson, the chief medical officer at the FDA's Center for Food Safety and Applied Nutrition said the agency would certainly look at possible regulations but warned that it might not have the resources to enforce them. Acheson and others noted that the center's budget had been cut almost in half, from $48 million in 2003 to about $25 million for 2007; the number of FDA food inspectors had also declined by about 300 during the same period. The FDA was responsible for monitoring about 100,000 food processors in the United States, which represented about 80 percent of the food supply. The Department of Agriculture was responsible for ensuring the safety of meat and poultry. "The reality of FDA's situation is they don't have the basic inspectors to inspect the food supply they're in charge of," Carolina Smith DeWaal, of the Center for Science in the Public Interest, told the *Washington Post*. "They just don't have the people . . . to manage this problem at the farm level."

Tommy G. Thompson, secretary of the Department of Health and Human Services from 2001 to 2005, was one of the leaders of a bipartisan group called Coalition for a Stronger FDA that was lobbying Congress to increase the FDA's budget. "You can't do it on the cheap," Thompson told the *New York Times* in December. "You are going to have to put more dollars in the FDA." Another advocate of a bigger budget for the agency was William K. Hubbard, a former FDA associate commissioner who retired in 2005 after thirty years at the agency. "The FDA is in a position that all they can do is send in inspectors after the cow has left the barn," Hubbard said. "They don't have the ability to set standards and enforce standards."

While much of the debate focused on guidelines for growing and processing fresh produce, some Democrats in Congress were proposing to consolidate all responsibility for regulating and monitoring food safety into a single agency, to be known as the Food Safety Administration. Currently those responsibilities were divided among twelve government agencies or subagencies, including the FDA and the Department of Agriculture. The chief proponents of a consolidated agency were Rep. Rosa DeLauro, D-Conn., and Sen. Dick Durbin, D-Ill., who said merging all responsibility in a single agency would be more efficient. They promised to push their legislation when Democrats took control of Congress in 2007.

Mad Cow Disease

Even as the government was ratcheting up its monitoring of leafy greens and other vegetables, it had decided to cut back on testing for mad cow disease. Mike Johanns, secretary of the Department of Agriculture, announced the cutback on July 20, saying the number of cattle found to have the disease was too low to justify the level of testing currently being done. Since December 2003, when mad cow disease was found in a

Canadian-born cow on a Washington farm, only two other cows in the United States had tested positive for the disease. The department said it had tested more than 759,000 cows over an eighteen-month period between 2004 and 2006.

Mad cow disease, or bovine spongiform encephalopathy (BSE), attacked the nervous system of infected cattle, eventually destroying the brain and causing death. Thought to be caused by abnormal protein cells, BSE was not contagious but was transmitted when cattle ate feed containing the ground meat and bone products from infected cattle. Such feed additives had been banned in the United States since 1997. Consumption of certain parts of infected cattle could also cause a rare but incurable wasting disease in humans known as variant Creutzfeldt-Jacob disease. About 150 people had died of the disease since it was first identified in Britain in 1996. Immediately after the Washington cow was found to have BSE in 2003, the Agriculture Department issued new guidelines to prevent certain parts of cattle, including central nervous system tissue, from being used in any products intended for human consumption. *(Background, Historic Documents of 2003, p. 1234)*

In his announcement Johanns said the department would conduct about 100 tests a day for BSE, down from about 1,000 a day. That higher figure represented about 1 percent of the 35 million cattle slaughtered in the United States every year. Noting that the reduction in testing would save millions of dollars, Johanns said "it's time that our surveillance efforts reflect what we now know is a very, very low level of BSE in the United States." A spokesperson for Consumers Union, publisher of *Consumer Reports*, was highly critical of the decision. "We think this is just absurd," Michael K. Hansen told the *New York Times*. "They're playing Russian roulette with public health."

Following are the texts of two documents: first, a news release from the Food and Drug Administration, issued on September 14, 2006, warning consumers of an E. coli outbreak and advising them to avoid bagged spinach; second, excerpts of testimony to the Senate Committee on Health, Education, Labor and Pensions on November 15, 2006, by Robert E. Brackett, director of the FDA's Center for Food Safety and Applied Nutrition, on the steps the agency was taking to enhance the safety of fresh produce.

■■■■■■■■■■■■ DOCUMENT ■■■■■■■■■■■■

"FDA Warning on Foodborne E. Coli O157:H7 Outbreak"

The U.S. Food and Drug Administration (FDA) is issuing an alert to consumers about an outbreak of E. coli O157:H7 in multiple states that may be associated with the consumption of produce. To date, preliminary epidemiological evidence suggests that bagged fresh spinach may be a possible cause of this outbreak.

Based on the current information, FDA advises that consumers not eat bagged fresh spinach at this time. Individuals who believe they may have experienced symptoms of illness after consuming bagged spinach are urged to contact their health care provider.

"Given the severity of this illness and the seriousness of the outbreak, FDA believes that a warning to consumers is needed. We are working closely with the U.S. Centers for Disease Control and Prevention (CDC) and state and local agencies to determine the cause and scope of the problem," said Dr. Robert Brackett, Director of FDA's Center for Food Safety and Applied Nutrition (CFSAN).

E. coli O157:H7 causes diarrhea, often with bloody stools. Although most healthy adults can recover completely within a week, some people can develop a form of kidney failure called Hemolytic Uremic Syndrome (HUS). HUS is most likely to occur in young children and the elderly. The condition can lead to serious kidney damage and even death. To date, 50 cases of illness have been reported to the Centers for Disease Control and Prevention, including 8 cases of HUS and one death.

At this time, the investigation is ongoing and states that have reported illnesses to date include: Connecticut, Idaho, Indiana, Michigan, New Mexico, Oregon, Utah and Wisconsin.

FDA will keep consumers informed of the investigation as more information becomes available.

Source: U.S. Department of Health and Human Services. Food and Drug Administration. "FDA Warning on Serious Foodborne E. coli O157:H7 Outbreak: One Death and Multiple Hospitalizations in Several States." Press release P06–131, September 14, 2006. www.fda.gov/bbs/topics/NEWS/2006/NEW01450.html (accessed December 13, 2006).

▄▄▄▄▄▄▄▄▄▄▄▄▄▄ **DOCUMENT** ▄▄▄▄▄▄▄▄▄▄▄▄▄▄

"Statement of Robert E. Brackett"

Introduction

Good afternoon.... I am Dr. Robert Brackett, Director of the Center for Food Safety and Applied Nutrition (CFSAN) at the Food and Drug Administration (FDA or the Agency), which is part of the Department of Health and Human Services (HHS).... FDA appreciates the opportunity to discuss the recent outbreak of Escherichia coli (E. coli) O157:H7 linked to fresh spinach and the lessons learned from this outbreak.

Ensuring the safety of the food supply continues to be a top priority for FDA and the Administration. In recent years, we have done a great deal to protect the food supply from unintentional contamination and from deliberate contamination. We have made significant progress in both, but will continue to strive to reduce the incidence of foodborne illness to the lowest level possible.

A recent report (April 2006) issued by CDC [Centers for Disease Control and Prevention], in collaboration with FDA and the United States Department of Agriculture (USDA), shows that progress has been made in reducing foodborne infections. This report provided preliminary surveillance data that show important declines in foodborne infections due to common pathogens in 2005 when compared against baseline data for the period 1996 through 1998. The report showed that the incidence of infections caused by Campylobacter, Listeria, Salmonella, Shiga toxin-producing E. coli O157, Shigella, and Yersinia has declined. Campylobacter and Listeria incidence are approaching levels targeted by national health objectives. This report shows that FDA's and USDA's efforts are working, and we are making progress. However, the recent E. coli outbreak shows that further progress is needed, particularly with ready-to-eat produce.

Ready-to-eat fresh vegetables, fruits, and prepared salads have a high potential risk of contamination because they are generally grown in a natural environment (for example, a field or orchard) and are often consumed without cooking or other treatments that could eliminate pathogens if they are present. The number of illnesses associated with fresh produce is a continuing concern of the Agency, and we have worked on a number of initiatives to reduce the presence of pathogens in these foods. . . .

Recent E. Coli O157:H7 Outbreak Linked to Fresh Spinach

On the afternoon of September 13, CDC informed FDA of a multi-state foodborne illness outbreak, that appeared to be ongoing, of E. coli O157:H7 possibly associated with the consumption of fresh spinach. On September 14, CDC notified FDA that the epidemiological data confirmed that fresh spinach was implicated as the source of the illnesses. That day, FDA, CDC, and California and other state officials began holding daily conference calls to share information, coordinate efforts to contain the spread of the outbreak, and investigate the cause.

Also that day, FDA's San Francisco District Office and California Department of Health Services' Food and Drug Branch hosted a conference call with three spinach-processing firms to advise them of the outbreak and to suggest that they consider the possible need to recall spinach products. We informed these firms that FDA would begin on-site investigations of processing facilities that day. FDA, in conjunction with the California Food and Drug Branch, also activated the California Food Emergency Response Team (CalFERT), a joint California and FDA response team to investigate the source of E. coli O157:H7 and determine the extent of possibly contaminated product.

Once CDC notified FDA that they had confirmed that fresh spinach was the source of the outbreak, FDA immediately took action to prevent further illnesses by alerting consumers. On September 14, FDA held a press teleconference and issued a press release alerting consumers about the outbreak, stating that preliminary epidemiological evidence suggested that bagged fresh spinach may be the cause and advising consumers to avoid bagged fresh spinach. Over the course of the next few days, the advisory was expanded to include all fresh spinach to ensure that consumers could adequately avoid eating any tainted product. This revision to the initial advisory became necessary when we learned that bagged spinach was sometimes sold in an un-bagged form at the retail level. This revised advisory remained in effect until September 22, when we were confident that the source of the tainted spinach was restricted to the three implicated counties in California. At that time, we advised consumers that spinach from outside these counties was not implicated in the outbreak and could be consumed.

During the outbreak, on an almost daily basis, FDA held press conferences (that included spokespersons from the State of California), issued press releases, and posted updates on our website to limit the spread of the outbreak by keeping the public informed.

FDA also worked closely with foreign government's food safety officials to provide them up-to-date information regarding the recall.

FDA, the State of California, CDC, and the USDA continue to investigate the cause of the outbreak. The environmental and on-site investigation has included inspections and sample collection in facilities, the environment, and water. In addition, investigators have reviewed and evaluated animal management practices, water use, and the environmental conditions that could have led to contamination of the spinach. The field investigation team has included experts in multiple disciplines from FDA, CDC, USDA, and the State of California.

The joint FDA/State of California field investigation found the same strain of E. coli O157:H7 as was involved in the illness outbreak in samples taken from a stream and from feces of cattle and wild pigs present on ranches implicated in the outbreak. The investigation team also found evidence that wild pigs have been in the spinach fields. We continue to look for more information as to the source and mechanism of contamination.

FDA Initiatives to Enhance Safety of Produce

As I mentioned earlier, FDA continues to be concerned about the number of foodborne illness outbreaks associated with fresh produce. In the past decade, consumption of produce, particularly "ready-to-eat" products, has increased dramatically. These products are usually consumed in their raw state without processing to reduce or eliminate pathogens that may be present. Consequently, the manner in which they are grown, harvested, packed, processed, and distributed is crucial to ensuring that microbial contamination is minimized, thereby reducing the risk of illness to consumers.

FDA has initiated several activities to address safety concerns associated with the production of fresh produce in response to the increase in illnesses associated with consumption of fresh produce. Some of these activities include: developing guidance, conducting outreach to consumers, sampling and analyzing both domestic and imported produce for pathogens, and working with industry to promote the use of good growing, harvesting, packing, transporting, and processing practices. . . . In October 2004, FDA announced its Produce Safety Action Plan to help reduce the incidence of foodborne illness attributed to the consumption of produce. The Action Plan has the following four objectives: 1) preventing contamination of fresh produce with pathogens; 2) minimizing the public health impact when contamination of fresh produce occurs; 3) improving communications with producers, preparers and consumers about fresh produce safety; and 4) facilitating and supporting research relevant to fresh produce. This Plan represents the first time that FDA had developed a comprehensive food safety strategy specific to produce.

Since 2005, as part of the Produce Safety Action Plan, FDA has provided technical assistance to industry in developing guidance for five commodity groups: cantaloupes, lettuce and leafy greens, tomatoes, green onions, and herbs. These commodities account for more than 80% of the foodborne outbreaks associated with produce. Three of the guidance documents (for cantaloupes, tomatoes, and lettuce and leafy greens) have been completed. We have recently made these guidance documents available, and FDA has done outreach and training with the industry to implement the guidance. FDA is still working on the commodity-specific guidance for herbs and green onions. In March of this year, we released draft guidance for the fresh-cut produce industry. . . . We are currently working to finalize this guidance document.

In August 2006, FDA met with Virginia officials to discuss outbreaks associated with tomatoes produced on the eastern shore of Virginia. FDA is working with the Florida Tomato Exchange and the University of Florida's Institute of Food and Agricultural Sciences to arrange a forum to discuss ways to improve the safety of tomatoes. . . . Once our investigation of the recent Salmonella Typhimurium outbreak linked to fresh tomatoes served in restaurants is complete, we will also reexamine the need for additional safety measures to ensure tomato safety.

We also are working in a broader context to address food safety concerns for all leafy greens. In the past two years, FDA twice wrote to industry to express FDA's concerns with continuing illness outbreaks and to express our expectations for industry to enhance the safety of these products. . . . More recently, in August 2006, FDA and the State of California launched the Lettuce Safety Initiative at the "Forum for Discussion of Lettuce Safety," hosted by the Western Institute for Food Safety and Security (WIFSS). This initiative was developed as a response to the recurring outbreaks of E. coli O157:H7 associated with fresh and fresh-cut lettuce and leafy greens, primarily, but not exclusively, from the Salinas Valley area. The multi-year initiative is intended to reduce public health risks by focusing on the product, agents, and areas of greatest concern. The four objectives of the proactive initiative are to: 1) assess current industry approaches and actions to address the issue of improving lettuce safety and, if appropriate, stimulate segments of the industry to further advance efforts in addressing all aspects of improving lettuce safety; 2) alert consumers early and respond rapidly in the event of an outbreak; 3) obtain information for use in developing and/or refining guidance and policy that will minimize future outbreaks; and 4) consider regulatory action, if appropriate.

Through its investigations of farms implicated in previous outbreaks, FDA has identified many possible factors that contribute to the contamination of fresh produce. These factors include the exposure of produce to poor quality water, manure used for fertilizer, workers with poor hygiene, and animals, both domesticated and wild, on the farm. FDA has been working with the State of California and the industry to promote the adoption of measures to prevent contamination of fresh produce.

Next Steps

In view of this recent E. coli O157:H7 outbreak, and after discussions with industry, FDA and the State of California advised the industry to develop a plan to minimize the risk of another outbreak in all leafy greens, including lettuce. Once we have completed our current investigation, FDA will hold a public meeting to address the larger issue of foodborne illness linked to leafy greens. We will also be examining whether improvements in the following four areas could help prevent or contain future outbreaks: 1) strategies to prevent contamination; 2) ways to minimize the health impact after an occurrence; 3) ways to improve communication; and 4) specific research. We also will be holding a series of meetings with industry groups to discuss ways to improve the safety of fresh produce. As part of our evaluation, we will consider whether additional guidance and/or additional regulations are necessary.

As we continue to look for a better path to improving the safety of fresh produce, research will remain a critical element. This element of a critical path to safer foods will need to include research on analytical technologies that enable faster detection of foodborne pathogens and better intervention strategies. Our current research agenda is focused on improving the identification and detection of disease-causing bacteria and toxins in a variety of foods. More rapid and precise testing methods are important to minimizing the spread of foodborne disease once it occurs. We are also studying possible intervention strategies, such as use of thermal treatment and irradiation, which could be applied to fresh produce products to reduce the level of bacteria and viruses that are in or on the product.

In addition, we are working with universities, industry, and state governments to develop both risk-based microbiological research programs and technology transfer programs to ensure that the latest food technology reaches the appropriate end users along the supply chain. We will continue to work with these partners to develop guidance, conduct research, produce educational outreach documents, and to initiate other commodity- or region-specific programs that will enhance the safety of fresh produce....

Source: U.S. Department of Health and Human Services. Food and Drug Administration. "Statement of Robert E. Brackett, Ph.D., Director, Center for Food Safety and Applied Nutrition, Food and Drug Administration, before the Committee on Health, Education, Labor and Pensions, United States Senate." November 15, 2006. www.fda.gov/ola/2006/foodsafety1115.html (accessed December 13, 2006).

Other Historic Documents of Interest

FBI Report on Crime
in the United States

September 18, 2006

■■■■■■■■■■ **THE DOCUMENT IN CONTEXT** ■■■■■■■■■

Although property crimes declined in 2005, murder, robbery, and other violent crime in the United States rose 2.3 percent, according to the Federal Bureau of Investigation. This was the first increase in violent crime since 2001 and the largest increase since 1991. Some of the highest spikes in crime were appearing in medium-size cities and areas in the Midwest, which had largely escaped the worst of the crime wave in the late 1980s and early 1990s. Preliminary FBI data for 2006 showed that violent crime continued to increase, rising 3.7 percent in the first six months of the year compared with the first six months of 2005. Although they acknowledged that the increase was a cause for concern, government officials and others observed that overall violent crime had declined by more than 17 percent since 1996. *(2004 crime data, Historic Documents of 2005, p. 677)*

The number of people in prison or jail also increased in 2005, rising by 2.7 percent, to 2.2 million people, according to the Justice Department's Bureau of Justice Statistics. Overall 7 million people—one of every thirty-two American adults—was behind bars, on probation, or on parole at the end of 2005. Nearly half the prison population growth between 1995 and 2003 was attributable to people sent to federal prison on drug offenses.

Crime Rates

The FBI's *Crime in the United States, 2005,* which was released on September 18, 2006, and was based on police reports from across the country, said there were 1.39 million violent crimes—murder, robbery, rape, and aggravated assault—during the year, up about 30,000 from 2004. The only category that did not increase was rape, which declined 1.2 percent. The number of murders rose 3.4 percent in 2005, to 16,692 people, while the estimated number of robberies increased 3.9 percent. For the first six months of 2006, murders rose 1.4 percent, while robberies shot up 9.7 percent, compared with the first six months of 2005. Aggravated assault also increased 1.8 percent in 2005 and 1.2 percent in the first six months of 2006.

Overall property crimes—burglary, larceny-theft, motor vehicle theft, and arson—declined 1.5 percent in 2005; an estimated 10.2 million property crimes were committed during the year for an estimated total of $16.5 billion in losses (not counting losses from arson). Overall, there were 67,504 arsons reported to the FBI in 2005; the average loss was just under $15,000.

The number of arrests in 2005 increased only 0.2 percent over the number in 2004, but arrests for murder jumped 7.3 percent. Arrests of juveniles (under age eighteen) for murder rose 19.9 percent over 2004, while juvenile arrests for robbery rose 11.4 percent. Although 67.5 of all juveniles arrested in 2005 were white, nearly 50 percent of juveniles arrested for violent crimes were black.

Victimization Report

A look at crime from a different perspective—that of the victims—found that the violent crime rate for 2005 was virtually unchanged from 2004, while a decrease in the rate of theft caused a drop in the overall property crime rate. That meant that rates of both violent crime and property crime were at their lowest levels since 1973, the first year that the Bureau of Justice Statistics conducted its National Crime Victimization Survey. The survey was based on interviews with 134,000 households, and it covered crimes that were never reported to police as well as those that were. Because it was a survey of victims, it did not report on murders. It also included simple assault and personal theft, two categories not covered by the FBI's Uniform Crime Reporting Program.

Although the survey, released on September 10, found that overall violent crime remained stable, it reported worrisome increases in robberies and in crimes committed with guns. According to the survey, gun-related crimes rose from 1.4 for every 1,000 persons in 2004 to 2.0 in 2005. Robberies rose from 2.1 per 1,000 persons to 2.6. The FBI crime report found that guns were used in 45 percent of all robberies. Deputy Attorney General Paul McNulty told the Associated Press that the administration was "concerned about" increased gun violence, but he cautioned that data for a single year could not be considered a trend.

That might not have been terribly reassuring in several of the nation's major cities, including New York, Chicago, and Houston, which reported sharply increased murder rates at the end of the year. Perhaps most disturbing was a trend among young people to shoot people who did not accord them the respect they thought they deserved. "They hurt each other over personal stuff," one crime expert told the *New York Times* early in the year. "It's respect and disrespect, and it's girls." Criminal justice experts, police, and government officials offered several additional explanations for the increase in violent crime, including the rise of criminal gangs in smaller cities and a surge in the number of inmates released from U.S. prisons. Other factors were federal budget cuts for police during the Bush administration and a shift in priorities from policing crime to homeland security and antiterrorism efforts.

Many experts saw the increase in violent crime as a wake-up call to lawmakers and the Bush administration. "We have to worry about not just homeland security but also hometown security," James Alan Fox, a criminal justice professor at Northeastern University, told the *Washington Post* in June. In speech to the International Association of Chiefs of Police on October 16, Attorney General Alberto Gonzales offered no new federal law enforcement funding but said that the Justice Department was studying several cities to determine what might be causing the upsurge in violent crime.

Rates of Incarceration

The Bureau of Justice Statistics released its annual report on incarceration November 30. In addition to the 2.2 million people behind bars at the end of 2005, the report said that more than 4.1 million were on probation and nearly 780,000 were on parole. As in past years, a disproportionate share of the nation's African Americans were imprisoned. Slightly more than 8 percent of all black men in the 25–29 age group were incarcerated, compared with 2.6 percent of Hispanic men and 1.1 percent of white men.

While the number of men in prison or jail was far greater than the number of women, the female population was growing at a rate of 2.6 percent a year, compared with 1.9 percent for males. Marc Mauer, the executive director of the Sentencing Project, a Washington-based advocacy group supporting reform of the criminal justice system, said the statistics on female inmates told only part of the story. "Today's figures fail to capture incarceration's impact on the thousands of children left behind by mothers in prison," Mauer said in a statement. "Misguided policies that create harsher sentences for nonviolent drug offenses are disproportionately responsible for the increasing rates of women in prisons and jails."

A private bipartisan study group, sponsored by the nonprofit Vera Institute of Justice, released the results of a fifteen-month study June 7, concluding that the American prison system was failing its inmates, and the American public was failing the prison system. Despite the nearly $60 billion spent on corrections every year, the study group said, there was far too much violence, far too little medical and mental health care, and far too few of the "productive activities" that "make rehabilitation possible." Americans, the report said, "should be astonished by the size of the prisoner population, troubled by the disproportionate incarceration of African-Americans and Latinos, and saddened by the waste of human potential." Known as the Commission on Safety and Abuse in America's Prisons, the study group was formed to examine U.S. prison conditions in the wake of the Abu Ghraib prison abuse scandal in Iraq. (Abu Ghraib prison scandal, Historic Documents of 2004, p. 207; Study group, Historic Documents of 2005, p. 679)

An estimated 60 percent of all inmates committed another crime after they were released. The study group said that even modest amounts of medical care and attention to inmates could reduce recidivism significantly and said it would ask Congress to make Medicare and Medicaid available to eligible inmates without copayments. Building on reports that one indicator of success upon leaving prison was an inmate's connection to family, the report recommended that the cost of telephone calls for prisoners be lowered, that visiting rooms be expanded to accommodate families, and that families of prisoners be offered counseling. The study group also urged greater public monitoring of the prison system.

Following are highlights from Crime in the United States, 2005, *an annual report of the Federal Bureau of Investigation, issued on September 18, 2006.*

◼◼◼ DOCUMENT ◼◼◼

Crime in the United States, 2005

Violent Crime

...An estimated 1,390,695 violent crimes occurred nationwide in 2005.

During 2005, there were an estimated 469.2 violent crimes per 100,000 inhabitants.

From 2004 to 2005, the estimated volume of violent crime increased 2.3 percent. The 5-year trend indicated that violent crime decreased 3.4 percent. For the 10-year trend (1996 compared with 2005) violent crime declined 17.6 percent.

Aggravated assault accounted for 62.1 percent, robbery accounted for 30.0 percent, forcible rape accounted for 6.8 percent, and murder accounted for 1.2 percent of the violent crimes in 2005. . . .

Murder

. . . An estimated 16,692 persons were murdered nationwide in 2005, an increase of 3.4 percent from the 2004 figure.

Murder comprised 1.2 percent of the overall estimated number of violent crimes in 2005.

There were an estimated 5.6 murders per 100,000 inhabitants. . . .

Forcible Rape

. . . There were an estimated 93,934 forcible rapes reported to law enforcement in 2005, a 1.2 decrease when compared to the 2004 estimate.

When compared to 2001 data, the number of forcible rapes increased an estimated 3.4 percent, but when compared to 1996 data, the number of forcible rape offenses declined 2.4 percent during the 10-year period.

The rate of forcible rapes in 2005 was estimated at 62.5 offenses per 100,000 female inhabitants, a 2.0 percent decrease when compared to the 2004 estimate of 63.8 forcible rapes per 100,000 female inhabitants. . . .

Robbery

. . . Nationwide in 2005, there were an estimated 417,122 robbery offenses.

In terms of robbery trends, robbery had the largest percentage increase, 3.9 percent, in the estimated number of offenses when compared with the 2004 estimate. The estimated number of robbery offenses declined 22.1 percent in a comparison with the data from 10 years earlier (1996 and 2005).

By location type, most robberies (44.1 percent) were committed on streets or highways. Firearms were used in 42.1 percent of reported robberies.

The average dollar value of property stolen per robbery offense was $1,230. By location type, bank robbery had the highest average dollar value taken—$4,169 per offense. . . .

Aggravated Assault

. . . Nationwide, an estimated 862,947 aggravated assaults were reported during 2005.

In looking at 2- and 10-year trends, the estimated number of aggravated assaults in 2005 increased 1.8 percent from the 2004 estimate but declined 16.8 percent from the 1996 estimate.

In 2005, the rate of aggravated assaults in the Nation was estimated at 291.1 offenses per 100,000 inhabitants.

An examination of the 10-year trend data for the rate of aggravated assaults revealed that rate in 2005 declined 25.5 percent when compared with the rate for 1996.

In 2005, 25.0 percent of aggravated assaults for which law enforcement agencies submitted expanded data involved a physical (hands, fists, feet, etc.) confrontation. Twenty-one percent of aggravated assaults involved offenders with a firearm. . . .

Property Crime

. . . An estimated 10.2 million (10,166,159) property crimes were reported nationwide during 2005.

An examination of 2- and 10-year trends shows that the estimated number of property crimes in 2005 decreased 1.5 percent from the 2004 estimate and declined 13.9 percent when compared with estimate for 1996.

During 2005, there were an estimated 3,429.8 property crimes per 100,000 inhabitants.

Two-year and 10-year trends show the rate of property crimes in 2005 decreased by 2.4 percent from data for 2004 and declined 22.9 percent when compared with data for 1996.

Two-thirds of all property crimes in 2005 were larceny-thefts.

Property crimes accounted for an estimated $16.5 billion dollars in losses in 2005. . . .

Burglary

. . . In 2005, law enforcement agencies reported an estimated 2,154,126 burglary offenses—a 0.5-percent increase compared with 2004 data.

An examination of 5- and 10-year trends revealed a 1.8-percent increase in the number of burglaries compared with the 2001 estimate, and a 14.1-percent decline from the 1996 number.

Burglary accounted for 21.2 percent of the estimated number of property crimes committed in 2005.

The average dollar loss per burglary offense in 2005 was $1,725.

Of all burglary offenses in 2005, 65.8 percent were of residential structures.

Most (62.4 percent) of residential burglaries in 2005 for which time of occurrence was known took place during the day, between 6 a.m. and 6 p.m.

Among burglaries of nonresidential structures when time of occurrence was known, 58.0 percent occurred at night. . . .

Larceny-theft

. . . There were an estimated 6.8 million (6,776,807) larceny-theft offenses nationwide during 2005.

An examination of 2- and 10-year trends revealed a 2.3-percent decrease in the estimated number of larceny-thefts compared with the 2004 figure, and a 14.3-percent decline from the 1996 estimate.

Two-thirds of all property crimes in 2005 were larceny-thefts.

During 2005, there were an estimated 2,286.3 larceny-theft offenses per 100,000 inhabitants.

From 2004 to 2005 the rate of larceny-thefts declined 3.2 percent, and from 1996 to 2005, the rate declined 23.3 percent.

The average value for property stolen during the commission of a larceny-theft was $764 per offense. . . .

Motor Vehicle Theft

. . . Nationwide in 2005, there were an estimated 1.2 million motor vehicle thefts, or approximately 416.7 motor vehicles stolen for every 100,000 inhabitants.

The estimated volume and rate of motor vehicle thefts in 2005 decreased 0.2 percent and 1.1 percent, respectively, when compared with data for 2004.

When considering data for 10 years earlier, the estimated volume and rate of motor vehicle thefts in 2005 decreased 11.4 percent and 20.7 percent, respectively, when compared with estimates for 1996.

An estimated 93.3 percent of the Nation's motor vehicle thefts occurred in Metropolitan Statistical Areas in 2005.

Property losses due to motor vehicle theft in 2005 were estimated at $7.6 billion, averaging $6,173 per stolen vehicle.

Among vehicle types, automobiles comprised 73.4 percent of the motor vehicles reported stolen in 2005. . . .

Arson

. . . Nationally, 67,504 arson offenses were reported by 13,868 agencies that submitted arson data in 2005 to the UCR Program. . . . Arsons involving structures (residential, storage, public, etc.) accounted for 43.6 percent of the total number of arson offenses. Mobile property was involved in 29.0 percent of arsons. The rest were arsons of other types of property.

The average value loss per arson offense was $14, 910.

Arsons of industrial and manufacturing structures resulted in the highest average dollar losses (an average of $356,324 per arson).

In 2005, arson offenses declined 2.7 percent when compared to arson data from the previous year.

The rate of arson was 26.9 offenses for every 100,000 inhabitants of the United States in 2005. . . .

Offenses Cleared

. . . Nationwide in 2005, 45.5 percent of violent crimes and 16.3 percent of property crimes were cleared by arrest or exceptional means.

Of the violent crimes of murder and nonnegligent manslaughter, forcible rape, robbery, and aggravated assault, murder had the highest percentage—62.1 percent—of offenses cleared.

Of the property crimes of burglary, larceny-theft, and motor vehicle theft, burglary was the offense least often cleared with 12.7 percent cleared by arrest or exceptional means.

Nationwide in 2005, 42.2 percent of arson offenses cleared by arrest or exceptional means involved juveniles, the highest percentage of all offense clearances involving only juveniles. . . .

Arrests

. . . In 2005, the FBI estimated that 14,094,186 arrests occurred nationwide for all offenses (except traffic violations), of which 603,503 were for violent crimes, and 1,609,327 for property crimes.

Law enforcement officers made more arrests for drug abuse violations in 2005 (an estimated 1.8 million arrests, or 13.1 percent of the total) than for any other offense.

Nationwide, the 2005 rate of arrests was estimated at 4,761.6 arrests per 100,000 inhabitants; for violent crime, the estimate was 204.8 per 100,000; and for property crime, the estimate was 549.1 per 100,000.

Although the number of arrests in 2005 increased only a slight 0.2 percent from the 2004 figure, arrests for murder rose 7.3 percent.

Arrests of juveniles (under 18 years of age) for murder climbed 19.9 percent in 2005 compared with 2004 arrest data; for robbery, arrests of juveniles rose 11.4 percent over the same 2-year period.

In 2005, 76.2 percent of all persons arrested were male, 82.1 percent of persons arrested for violent crime were male, and 68.0 percent of persons arrested for property crime were male.

Among the four categories of race reflected in UCR arrest data, 69.8 percent of all persons arrested were white, 59.0 percent of persons arrested for violent crime were white, and 68.8 percent of persons arrested for property crime were white.

White juveniles comprised 67.5 percent of all juveniles arrested in 2005 and 67.2 percent of juveniles arrested for property crime.

Black juveniles comprised 49.8 percent of all juveniles arrested in 2005 for violent crime. . . .

Police Employees

. . . In 2005, sworn officers accounted for 69.5 percent of all law enforcement personnel.

The rate of full-time law enforcement employees (civilian and sworn) per 1,000 inhabitants in the Nation for 2005 was 3.5; the rate of sworn officers was 2.4 per 1,000. . . . The UCR Program computes these rates by taking the number of employees, dividing by the population of agency's jurisdiction, and multiplying by 1,000.

Female employees accounted for 61.8 percent of all full-time civilian law enforcement employees in 2005.

Males accounted for 88.4 percent of all full-time sworn law enforcement officers in 2005....

_____

Source: U.S. Department of Justice. Federal Bureau of Investigation. *Crime in the United States, 2005.* September 18, 2006. www.fbi.gov/ucr/05cius/index.html (accessed November 15, 2006).

Other Historic Documents of Interest

Conviction of Enron executives, p. 239
Domestic spying, p. 61

Safeguarding personal information,
p. 273

Military Junta Leaders on the Coup in Thailand

September 19 and 20, 2006

█████████ ██ **THE DOCUMENT IN CONTEXT** ██ █████████

Thailand's autocratic but popular prime minister was ousted from power by the country's military in September 2006 following months of political upheaval resulting from protests over his family's tax-free sale of stock in the business empire that had made him one of Asia's wealthiest businessmen. Thaksin Shinawatra had won elections in 2001 and 2005, bringing an unusual degree of political stability to a country that had long been governed either by the military or by unsteady civilian coalitions. His pugnacious governing style won him many enemies, however, apparently including the military and even the country's revered king, Bhumibol Adulyadej, who had been on the throne since 1946 and was the world's longest serving monarch.

The coup marked at least a pause in what had been an impressive march toward democracy in Thailand. The country had been governed by the military for much of the seven decades since it became a constitutional monarchy in 1932. Civilian governments did not last long during those decades, and many were ended by military coups and large-scale popular protests. Thailand had seen relative stability under elected civilian leaders since 1992, however, in part because a military junta that seized power the previous year had proven to be unpopular.

Thaksin was one of the two billionaire businessmen to lose power during 2006. The other, Italian prime minister Silvio Berlusconi, was defeated in an election in April but as of year's end appeared to be angling for another term in office, which if successful would be his third.

Background

A former policeman who went into business for himself in 1987, Thaksin was the most prominent businessman in Thailand, having built a giant media and telecommunications conglomerate from a small computer dealership. Thaksin entered politics in the 1990s, and his rise to power was in large part a response to the 1997 Asian financial crisis, which was triggered by a collapse of the real estate market and currency in Thailand. That crisis severely damaged the then-ruling Democratic Party and created an opening for the new party Thaksin founded in 1999. He called it Thai Rak Thai ("Thais Love Thais"). *(Asian financial crisis, Historic Documents of 1997, p. 832)*

Describing himself as the "CEO prime minister," Thaksin led his party to a first-place finish in parliamentary elections in 2001. He then secured a working majority with the aid of several smaller parties. Once in office, Thaksin's social programs broadened his appeal in the poverty-stricken north; among other things, his government offered a debt moratorium for farmers, cash grants to rural villages for small business loans, and low-cost health care. Thaksin's generally effective response to the December 2004 Indian Ocean tsunami added to his popularity. His party won 376 of the 500 parliamentary seats in February 2005 elections, marking the first time a single party had a true majority. *(Tsunami background, Historic Documents of 2005, p. 990)*

A business deal proved to be Thaksin's undoing. On January 24, 2006, his children and other family members sold a 49.6 percent holding in the large telecommunications corporation Shin Corporation, which was the basis of his fortune, to Temasek Holdings Company, an investment firm owned by the government of Singapore. The $1.9 billion sale generated immediate controversy in Thailand, for two reasons. First, the sale was structured in such a way that Thaksin's family avoided paying any taxes on the proceeds. Second, many Thais were angered that such an important Thai company would fall into the hands of a foreign government.

This dispute was just the latest of a series of allegations that Thaksin had hidden his business interests while serving in government. The government's anticorruption commission in 2001 had indicted Thaksin on charges of hiding business assets, but the constitutional court acquitted him.

These controversies over Thaksin's business were by far the most serious, in political terms, of several matters that had undermined support for him, particularly among the educated elites in Bangkok and among residents in the southern part of the country. Many of the former had been upset by the prime minister's strong-arm style of governing, in particular his use of pressure to stifle criticism of the government by the broadcast news media (most of which was state controlled). Critics also said Thaksin used his appointment powers to strip the judiciary of its independence and to place business colleagues and political cronies in key government positions, including the military and other supposedly independent bodies. In addition, many residents of southern Thailand were angered by the government's uncompromising military campaign against a Muslim insurgency in that region, which flared in 2004 after having been relatively quiet for more than a decade. At least 1,700 people died as a result of the renewed fighting. An ailing economy, damaged by high prices for oil imports, also weakened public support for the government.

In response to rapidly growing public protests over the sale of Shin Corporation, Thaksin dissolved parliament on February 24 and called snap elections for April 2. That move failed to stem the criticism of his family's business dealings, and opposition groups staged large protests in Bangkok from late February until shortly before the April elections. Leading the protests were student groups, labor unions, teachers and other professionals, prodemocracy activists, and a contingent of Buddhist monks.

In the early stages of the protests, military leaders said they would stay out of the dispute. "The military will not interfere in the political conflict," military commander Gen. Rueangrot Mahasaranon said on March 1.

Opposition parties urged a boycott of the elections, however, which meant that the results were far from clear. Thaksin's party won more than 50 percent of the overall vote, but the boycott, coupled with the voiding of ballots by many opposition supporters, meant that dozens of Thaksin's candidates did not meet a legal requirement of winning 20 percent of the eligible votes in their districts. As a result, 40 seats went unfilled, thereby preventing the new parliament from convening because another provision of the constitution required all 500 seats to be filled before parliament could sit.

Catching everyone off-guard, Thaksin announced on April 4 that he would resign; this announcement came after he met with the king, leading to speculation that the monarch had played a role in the decision. "We have no time to quarrel," Thaksin said. "I want to see Thai people unite and forget what has happened." Thaksin handed power over to a caretaker prime minister, but it was widely assumed that he was only biding his time until the political situation calmed down.

Follow-up rounds of elections failed to fill all of the 40 legislative seats that had been left empty, deepening the political crisis. King Bhumibol rejected widespread calls that he intervene, saying in a rare televised speech on April 25 it was up to the courts to resolve what he called "a mess." Even so, the king criticized the results of the election process because many candidates ran unopposed. "Having an election with only one candidate running is impossible," he said. "This is not a democracy."

Apparently responding to the king, Thailand's Constitutional Court on May 8 ruled the April 2 elections invalid, called for new elections in sixty days, and demanded that members of the national election commission resign because they failed to prevent abuses in the voting. The commissioners rebuffed that demand, however, and one week later suggested holding new elections in October. These developments raised serious questions about who, if anyone, actually was running the country. Seeking to fill the void, Thaksin said on May 23 that he was returning to work as prime minister after what he called a seven-week "rest."

Thaksin's return to office generated new rounds of political protest but did not mar an important ceremonial occasion two weeks later: celebrations commemorating King Bhumibol's sixtieth anniversary on the throne. Millions of people—nearly all of them wearing the royal color of yellow—crowded into Bangkok on June 9 hoping to catch a rare glimpse of the king in person. In a brief speech, the seventy-eight-year-old king called for unity but made no overtly political remarks.

The next several months saw continued stalemate. The new elections, scheduled for mid-October, were postponed at least until November, and later cancelled altogether. Thaksin remained in office over the next several months while opposition parties weighed their next steps against a prime minister who was still popular with the country's poor majority and who did not shy from using government agencies and the news media to get his way.

The Military Intervenes

In mid-September an apparently overconfident Thaksin traveled to New York for the annual opening session of the United Nations General Assembly. While he was out of the country, military leaders announced on September 19 that a Council of Administrative Reform had taken power from Thaksin's government and revoked the constitution adopted in 1997. The military's statement was rather meek for such an occasion, offering apologies "for any inconvenience caused" to the public. Thaksin responded by saying he was firing the army commander and declaring a state of emergency; neither declaration had any effect.

The next morning, army commander Sonthi Boonyaratglin, appeared on television, accompanied by the heads of other security forces, and unleashed a torrent of criticism of Thaksin's rule, which he said had "led to severe disunity among the Thai people unprecedented before in Thai society." In particular, the general cited "signs of rampant corruption, malfeasance and nepotism," interference with independent organizations, and actions that "verged upon lèse-majesté " against the king. General Sonthi also said that the military would restore the "democratic governmental system," under the king, "as soon as possible." Sonthi followed this speech with another statement giving a somewhat more detailed list of grievances against Thaksin and saying the coup was in response to "numerous requests." He also said an interim government would be selected within two weeks and a new constitution drafted within one year. The military issued several decrees that appeared aimed at dampening protest, for example by demanding cooperation from the news media "to create unity" and barring political gatherings of more than five people.

For his part, Thaksin immediately flew from New York to London, where he owned an apartment, and appeared to accept the fact that he was now out of power. "I was prime minister when I came" to New York, he said, "and I was jobless on the way back." Thaksin also said he would take a "deserved rest." Thaksin later resigned from his party, saying it was necessary to keep it intact.

For a variety of reasons, the immediate public reaction in Thailand to the coup was muted. The streets of Bangkok and other cities were calm and political leaders across the spectrum generally withheld comment or simply expressed relief that the prolonged political crisis had ended.

Internationally, most leaders expressed customary dismay at the military intervention and demanded a return to democracy. However, there appeared to be few demonstrations of genuine outrage—suggesting that Thaksin's autocratic rule had not endeared him to his fellow democratic leaders. Even so, officials in the United States and other countries said they worried the coup would set back attempts to promote democracy in Asia by reinforcing the impression that it led to instability. In one of the most visible expressions of concern, the United States on September 28 announced it was suspending $24 million in military aid to Thailand to protest the coup. Secretary of State Condoleezza Rice had said the coup leaders needed to "get back on a democratic path very, very quickly."

It was unclear whether the king had endorsed the coup ahead of time, but it quickly became clear that he supported it once it occurred. The military leaders said they had met with the king on the evening of the coup, and soldiers affixed yellow ribbons to their uniforms—apparently aligning the military with the royal color. Any doubt about the king's position was erased on September 22, when an army officer read what he said was a royal decree approving the new government.

An "Interim" Government

Thailand's generals on October 1 installed what they said would be an interim government, headed by retired army commander Syrayud Chulanont as prime minister. This appointment was accompanied by the announcement of a temporary constitution, approved by the king, that gave military leaders (in their new guise as the Council for National Security) the power to appoint key government officials and veto the text of a new permanent constitution.

The appointment of Syrayud was approved by the king and won broad praise, even from a spokesman for Thaksin's party, who called the interim prime minister "someone with knowledge and ability." U.S. ambassador Ralph Boyce was the first foreign diplomat to meet with Syrayud after he took office, and Boyce later told reporters the new prime minister gave assurances of "a speedy return to democratically elected government and protection of civil liberties during the interim."

In a sign that the military did not intend to allow Thaksin to return to power, a new government established a committee to investigate corruption during his time in power. Although some Thais supported this move, others said it resembled Thaksin's use of government power to intimidate or punish his enemies. The new government also signaled that it would take a softer approach to confronting Islamic guerrillas in the south, saying it planned to focus on peace initiatives rather than a military crackdown. That move appeared to have little success, however, as violence, including bombings, appeared to be on the increase. In November the government lifted martial law in most of the country but kept it in place in the south.

All through the last three months of the year the new government appeared to be struggling to gain its footing, with some of its actions provoking the same types of criticism that had been leveled against Thaksin. Perhaps the most serious challenge was a sharp sell-off in local financial markets on December 18 after the central bank imposed controls on speculative investments by foreigners. The withdrawal of foreign capital had set off the 1997 financial crisis, and in 2006 the central bank intervened to stem a surge of capital into the country's bond markets—a surge that put enormous pressure on Thailand's currency, the *baht*. Financial markets dropped precipitously after the bank acted, however, leading the bank to reverse its policy a day later. These moves damaged international confidence in Thailand's economy and in its new government.

Following are the texts of three statements by the military rulers of Thailand, calling themselves the Council for Democratic Reform, after their coup removing Prime Minister Thaksin Shinawatra on September 19, 2006.

DOCUMENT

"Situation under Control Announcement"

At 23.00 hours on 19 September B.E. 2549 (2006), the TV Pool of Thailand broadcasted an announcement from the Council for Democratic Reform as follows:

"At the moment, the Council for Democratic Reform, which is composed of the Commanders-in-Chief of the armed forces and the Commissioner-General of the Royal Thai Police, has successfully taken control over Bangkok and its vicinity without meeting any resistance. So as to maintain peace and order in the nation, the Council seeks the cooperation of the public to remain calm and offers its apologies for any inconvenience caused."

Source: Kingdom of Thailand. Ministry of Foreign Affairs. "Statement by the Council for Democratic Reform: Situation under Control Announcement." September 19, 2006. Unofficial translation. www.mfa.go.th/internet/document/2827.pdf (accessed January 14, 2007).

DOCUMENT

"Statement by General Sonthi Boonyaratglin"

At approximately 09.00 hours on 20 September B.E. 2549 (2006), General Sonthi Boonyaratglin, Commander-in-Chief of the Royal Thai Army, in his capacity as Leader of the

Council for Democratic Reform, made the following televised address, in the presence of General Ruengroj Mahasaranond, Supreme Commander of the Royal Thai Armed Forces, Air Chief Marshal Chalit Pookphasuk, Commander-in-Chief of the Royal Thai Air Force, Admiral Satirapan Keyanon, Commander-in-Chief of the Royal Thai Navy, and Police General Kovit Wattana, Royal Thai Police Commissioner-General:

"Fellow Thai citizens, pursuant to the seizure of control of Thailand's administration by the Council for Democratic Reform—resulting in the abrogation of the Constitution of the Kingdom of Thailand B.E. 2540 (1997) and the abolition of the Senate, the House of Parliament, the Council of Ministers and the Constitutional Court—the Council, comprising the Supreme Commander, the Commanders-in-Chief of the Thai Armed Forces, and the Commissioner-General of the Royal Thai Police, concurred that the administration of caretaker government has led to severe disunity among the Thai people unprecedented before in Thai society, that there were signs of rampant corruption, malfeasance and nepotism, that independent organizations had been interfered with, crippling their ability to perform their duties properly or to effectively resolve important problems faced by the nation, which if left unaddressed, would adversely affect the nation's security and overall economy situation. In addition, some political activities undertaken verged upon lèse-majesté against His Majesty the King who is highly respected and revered by the Thai people.

The Council was therefore found it necessary to seize control of Thailand's administration so as to quickly resolve the country's situation and restore normalcy. The Council wishes to reaffirm that it does not intend to administer the country itself and will restore the democratic governmental system with a monarch as head of state to the Thai people as soon as possible. In addition, the Council will maintain peace and order within the Kingdom as well as extend the highest reverence to the monarchy, which is deeply beloved by all the Thai people. The Council therefore requests cooperation from all fellow citizens to remain calm and to support this undertaking so that it achieves its well-intentioned objectives."

Source: Kingdom of Thailand. Ministry of Foreign Affairs. "Statement by the Council for Democratic Reform by General Sonthi Boonyaratglin." September 20, 2006. Unofficial translation. www.mfa.go.th/internet/document/2832.pdf (accessed January 14, 2007).

DOCUMENT

"Briefing by Sonthi Boonyaratglin to the Diplomatic Corps"

The Council undertook this important mission for the following reasons:

- Lack of political confidence in Thailand and impasse of political differences
- Severe increase of disunity among the Thai people
- Rampant corruption, malfeasance and widespread nepotism
- Inability to proceed with the reform process as intended by the Constitution
- Interference of national independent agencies, crippling their ability to function properly and to effectively solve the nation's problems

- Certain substantive democratic elements in the Constitution have been undermined
- The existence of social injustice
- Evidence of words and actions which have shaken and been proven to be against the very foundation of Thailand's democracy with HM the King as Head of State.

Given these reasons, all members of the Council including myself, have received numerous requests to undertake this mission in order to restore peace, security and justice to the country.

The Council undertook this mission to end the political impasse, uncertainty and lack of political confidence, which have protracted for so long.

I would like to reaffirm that Thailand will adhere to the UN Charter and remain committed to international treaties and agreements, under the basis of equality of states. The existing relationship between the Kingdom of Thailand and other countries shall be fostered and enhanced.

The Council has, so far, received cooperation from all sectors of Thai society, without any resistance. More importantly, the Council members and I have been graciously granted a Royal Audience to report on our action and the situation to Their Majesties the King and Queen last night.

The Council will ensure that a *provisional constitution* will be announced *within two weeks* so that a government under a civilian Prime Minister can be set up at once to run the country. There will be a legislative body responsible for legislation and the drafting of the new constitution, which will lead to early general elections.

All actions and activities, from this point on, will be strictly in compliance and conformity with the legal norms and laws.

The Council for Democratic Reform under the Constitutional Monarchy

Pointers: Questions and Answers

1. The legitimacy of the Council and the coup d'etat?

Due to political tensions and the division in society which has roused our democratic system with the King as the head of state, the Council found it necessary to resolve the situation. This will be implemented in the shortest period of time to end the confusion, resolve uncertainty and end the political crisis. The Council has no intention to become the administrator of the country.

2. Why was the constitution abrogated?

The constitution could not resolve the problems that arose in our society and the democratic process was not carried out according to the constitution's objective. Moreover, there were proposals to amend various points. The temporary constitution that will be created will pave the way for the drafting of a permanent constitution that is truly democratic.

3. Elimination of press freedom, blockage of television broadcasts by international news agencies?

Control of media outlets at the start of the task was necessary and a temporary measure. The Council recognizes that freedom of the press is an important part of a democracy and is uncomfortable with the fact that our task was carried out in a way that appeared to control the freedom of the press.

4. Will you allow former Prime Minister Thaksin and his family return to Thailand?
That shouldn't be a problem. All Thai people can live in Thailand.

5. Will former Prime Minister Thaksin face prosecution?
Everything will be carried out under the rule of law.

Source: Kingdom of Thailand. Ministry of Foreign Affairs. "Briefing by General Sonthi Boonyaratglin, Head of the Council for Democratic Reform under Constitutional Monarchy, to the Diplomatic Corps." September 20, 2006. Unofficial translation. www.mfa.go.th/internet/document/2821.pdf (accessed January 14, 2007).

Chavez on Relations between Latin America and the United States

September 20, 2005

■■■■■■■■■■■■■■ **THE DOCUMENT IN CONTEXT** ■■■■■■■■■■■■■■

The leftward shift in Latin American politics, which had been under way for several years, continued during 2006 with the election of a new far-left leader in Ecuador and the reelection or return to office of left-leaning presidents in several other countries. These leaders varied widely in their political philosophies, however, and one of the few common characteristics appeared to be a coolness—in a few cases outright hostility—toward the United States and the free-market economic policies Washington long had prescribed for the region.

The man who portrayed himself as the leader of the region's swing to the left—President Hugo Chavez of Venezuela—cruised to an easy reelection win in December and began talking about serving in office indefinitely. The successful leftist candidate in 2006 who most resembled Chavez was Rafael Correa of Ecuador.

Also winning reelection, despite scandals that had rocked his political party, was President Luiz Inacio Lula da Silva (known universally as Lula), who in 2002 had become Brazil's first left-of-center president.

Two leftist leaders from the 1980s returned to office as a result of elections in 2006, but both claimed to have moderated their views. Daniel Ortega, who headed the Sandinista regime in Nicaragua until its political defeat in 1990, won election as president on November 5. In Peru, Alan Garcia, whose one term as president of Peru in the late 1980s was generally considered a failure, won election for another term on June 4.

The most important conservatives to win presidential elections in Latin America during the year were Felipe Calderón, who won a hotly contested election in Mexico, and Alvaro Uribe, who easily won reelection in Colombia.

From a satellite in space, it might have appeared that in most of the dozen elections held in Latin America and the Caribbean between November 2005 and December 2006 the region had been swept by what some commentators called a "pink tide." But a closer inspection of each country showed marked differences in the elected leaders, why they succeeded, and what their agendas were. Rebutting widespread commentary that the region appeared to be following Chavez's lead, one analyst said: "There is no Chavismo across Latin America." Adrian Bonilla, a political analyst at the Latin American Faculty of Social Sciences in Quito, Ecuador, told the *Christian Science Monitor* in December that "what we have is a lot of new governments with different ideological trends. You don't have a continental leader." *(Background, Historic Documents of 2005, p. 765)*

Chavez and Venezuela

For much of 2006 Venezuela's Chavez was exactly where he liked to be: at the center of attention in Latin America. With an oversized ego and unlimited ambition, Chavez worked hard to position himself as the Latin leader most able to represent the region's poor and to stand up to the United States—a country he called the "empire," among other things.

In a region famous for its tumultuous politics, Chavez for fifteen years had made Venezuelan politics as turbulent as possible. As an army colonel, he led an unsuccessful coup in 1992, then turned to politics and won election as president in 1998. After forcing through a revision of the constitution that boosted the powers of the presidency and diminished the role of parliament, Chavez won another election in 2000 giving him a six-year term. Chavez survived two attempts to oust him: a bungled coup in 2002 and then an oft-delayed recall referendum in 2004. His party won total control of the parliament after all opposition parties boycotted elections in December 2005. The new constitution set a limit of two terms for the president, but Chavez said repeatedly in 2006 that he might seek to remove that limit and serve for another twenty-five years.

In gearing up for another presidential election in December 2006, Chavez sought to portray himself as the one Latin leader who was able and willing to prevent the United States from continuing to dominate the region. He began warning in February that the United States was planning to oust him in a military invasion, and he ordered the military on alert to repel the expected invasion. Chavez also stepped up his rhetorical attacks, calling U.S. president George W. Bush at various times a "madman," a "drunkard," and a "donkey."

Beyond the rhetoric, Chavez sought to align himself—and Venezuela—with other countries that were in disfavor with Washington. Cuba topped his list of allies, but others included Iran, which in recent years had become a major investor in Venezuela, and Syria, which Chavez visited at the end of August.

The high—or low—point of Chavez's attacks on the United States, and on Bush personally, came in his September 20 speech to the annual opening session of the United Nations General Assembly. Speaking just one day after Bush, Chavez devoted nearly all his remarks to criticisms of the United States and the United Nations, which he said was under the sway of Washington. "The Devil came here yesterday," he told the delegates. "Yesterday, the Devil was here in this very place. This rostrum still smells like sulfur." To emphasize the point, Chavez made the sign of the cross and placed his hands together, as if in prayer. "Yesterday, ladies and gentlemen, from this podium, the president of the United States, whom I refer to as the devil, came here talking as if he owned the world. It would take a psychiatrist to analyze the speech he delivered yesterday."

These remarks brought chuckles and some applause from the audience, but did not please U.S. delegates. John R. Bolton, the U.S. ambassador, called the speech "insulting," and Secretary of State Condoleezza Rice said Chavez's attacks were "not becoming for a head of state." Apparently pleased by the attention he had gained for himself, Chavez renewed his personal attacks on Bush the next day. Speaking at a church in Harlem, Chavez called Bush an "alcoholic" who was "very dangerous because he has lots of power."

Chavez's rhetoric fell on many sympathetic ears in Latin America, where about 40 percent of the population lived on less than $2 a day. In recent years there had been increasing resistance in the region to the free-market, open-trading economic reforms that the United States had advocated and that many countries had adopted in the 1980s and early 1990s. By the late 1990s these policies had produced sustained economic growth in only a few countries (notably Chile) and had done little to narrow the enormous gap between the rich and everyone else.

Despite his flamboyant manners and rhetoric, Chavez might have received little attention internationally had it not been for the fact that Venezuela was a significant producer of oil. The country's proven oil reserves were the fifth largest in the world, and Venezuela was the single largest source of oil imports for the United States. The sudden rise in world oil prices since 2003 had poured tens of billions of dollars into Venezuela's coffers—and had given Chavez enormous political leverage that the leader of an under-developed country of 26 million people normally would not have.

Chavez promised to use Venezuela's oil wealth to provide jobs, housing, medical care, and other services for the poor, but his promises far outstripped the actual results. In 2005, for example, the government built only 25 percent of the 120,000 homes Chavez had promised, unemployment remained high (at nearly 10 percent, according to official statistics), and the country's hospitals were unable to cope with demand—even with the help of thousands of doctors imported from Cuba. Under Chavez, the government also was slow to invest in the country's basic infrastructure. A notable example came in January when the government was forced to close the only highway linking Caracas, the capital, and the country's main airport because a vital bridge was in danger of collapsing. Despite his frequent failures to follow through on promises, Chavez remained a beloved figure among the country's poor, and he cultivated personal loyalty through rhetoric embracing the poor and such touches as liberally distributing posters that portrayed him in heroic fashion.

Chavez spent billions of dollars in oil profits promoting his message overseas, including in the United States. For several years the state-owned oil company, Petroleos de Venezuela, had provided subsidized home heating oil to poor families in the U.S. northeastern states. Venezuela also purchased $2.5 billion in debt from Argentina so that country could pay off the International Monetary Fund, subsidized oil shipments to Cuba and other countries in the Caribbean, and even provided aid to several countries in Africa.

Chavez predicted during the year that he would win at least 10 million votes in the presidential election, a result that would have given him nearly unanimous approval of the 11 million or so voters expected to go to the polls on December 3. Chavez's margin of victory fell well short of that goal, however, because opposition groups—which in the past had been sharply divided—managed to agree on a strong consensus candidate. Manuel Rosales, the governor of Zulia state, mounted a vigorous campaign and accused Chavez of intending to turn Venezuela into a dictatorship. In the end, Chavez won by a margin of 61 percent to 38 percent, which meant he received just under 7 million votes. In a victory speech on election night, Chavez told cheering supporters—all of them wearing red, his official color: "Long live socialist revolution. Destiny has been written. No one should fear socialism. Socialism is human. Socialism is love."

UN Security Council Seat

The choice of a Latin American representative for the UN Security Council developed into an international political struggle between Venezuela and the United States and ended as a victory for neither one. Chavez announced in July that Venezuela would seek one of the ten Security Council seats that were to become open for two-year terms in January 2007. The Bush administration adamantly opposed Venezuela obtaining a seat, saying its presence on the council would be disruptive, and backed Guatemala instead.

The General Assembly, which chose the ten nonpermanent Security Council members, began voting on October 16 but quickly became deadlocked. The assembly held nearly four dozen ballots over a two-week period, but neither Guatemala nor Venezuela came close to the required two-thirds majority in the 192-member assembly. Finally, Ecuador's ambassador to the UN mediated between the two countries and won a compromise, on November 1, under which both Guatemala and Venezuela withdrew in favor of Panama.

Other Elections in Latin America

The year's political developments included elections in the following countries:

Bolivia. After Chavez, probably the most radical of the recent crop of leftist leaders in Latin America was Evo Morales, who won election as president of Bolivia in December 2005 and took office on January 22. Morales was the first full-blooded Indian to win the presidency in the country, where the majority of people were of Indian descent. He had risen to prominence as leader of the nation's coca farmers, whose crop was used to produce cocaine.

Morales on April 29 signed a trade agreement with Cuba and Venezuela—called the Bolivarian Alternative for the Americas—and rejected participation in free-trade deals with the United States. Two days later, on May 1, Morales followed through on a campaign promise and ordered the nationalization of the natural gas industry. This step brought him into conflict with Lula of Brazil, whose state-owned Petrobras SA firm was the biggest investor in Bolivia's energy sector. The nationalization process proved more difficult than Morales apparently envisioned, however, and it was not until December 2 that he was able to sign contracts formally assuming government control of the foreign-held stakes in Bolivian energy companies.

Emulating Chavez, Morales also began the process of rewriting Bolivia's constitution. The goal, he said, was to give more political power to Indians. Voters on July 2 selected a national assembly to write a new constitution and gave a narrow majority of seats to allies of Morales. The assembly began work in August but quickly became bogged down in strife over opposition charges that Morales was maneuvering to expand his own power at the expense of four eastern provinces, which held most of Bolivia's natural gas reserves. Opposition groups mounted public protests in November and December after Morales attempted to force through constitutional changes with a simple majority of the assembly, rather than a two-thirds majority, as had been planned. Debate over the constitution was still under way at year's end.

The United States had spent millions of dollars on antinarcotics programs in Bolivia since the 1980s, and the election of Morales raised questions about the future of those programs. Once he took office, Morales allowed the existing antinarcotics programs to continue but promoted the legal use of coca leaf in medicines, tea, and other nonnarcotic consumer products.

Brazil. For much of 2005, it had appeared that Lula of Brazil was destined to be a one-term president. A corruption scandal, involving payoffs to legislators from his Workers Party, coupled with disappointment among supporters about Lula's inability to carry out many of his campaign promises to the poor, had seemed to doom his reelection chances. But Lula initiated new social programs and embarked on a series of trips around the country that, by February 2006, put him back in the lead over the chief opposition candidates. Moreover, the corruption scandals forced some of Lula's closest associates from office but never directly reached him. *(Background, Historic Documents of 2002, p. 774)*

Lula had hoped to avoid a runoff by winning an absolute majority in the first round of voting on October 1 but fell just short, winning 48.6 percent of the vote. Lula won a landslide victory in the second round, defeating Geraldo Alckmin, the popular former governor of São Paulo state, despite yet another scandal just before the voting. This scandal involved an apparent effort by some of Lula's closest supporters to buy negative information about opposition figures. Lula won 61 percent of the vote, giving him one of the most sweeping victories in Brazil's history. Even so, the corruption scandals that had marred his first term were likely to dog him at least through the early years of his second term, and his Workers Party had lost its once-dominant position in the Congress.

Colombia. The Latin American country that most clearly bucked the region's leftward trend was Colombia, where President Uribe had won widespread popularity with his firm stance against the leftist guerrilla movements that had plagued the country for decades. Political parties allied with Uribe won about 60 percent of the seats in both chambers of Congress in elections on March 12, and Uribe himself coasted to an easy victory in the May 28 presidential election, winning 62 percent of the vote.

Despite these convincing political victories, Uribe's government was shaken late in the year by an emerging scandal over allegations that powerful members of Congress and local politicians, all aligned with Uribe, had collaborated with right-wing paramilitary armies. Uribe had overseen a process in which some 30,000 fighters from major paramilitary groups had demobilized, but the new allegations raised questions about how committed his government was to dismantling these groups. Major landowners had supported the paramilitaries in the 1960s and 1970s as a means of battling leftist guerrillas, but the paramilitaries later developed into lawless bands that engaged in narcotics trafficking. One of the most feared paramilitary leaders, Salvatore Mancuso, testified in a closed-door court session on December 19; having accepted a government amnesty program, he was the first such leader to submit himself to the government's justice system. At several points during the year it appeared that Uribe's government might enter negotiations with the largest leftist guerrilla group, the Revolutionary Armed Forces of Colombia; however, the talks had not come to pass as of year's end.

Costa Rica. One of Central America's best-known statesmen, Oscar Arias, returned to the presidency after an absence of sixteen years—but only after narrowly winning a hotly contested election. As president in the mid-1980s, Arias had won the 1987 Nobel Peace Prize for his work to mediate civil wars in El Salvador and Nicaragua. Arias decided to return to politics and had been expected to win in a landslide, but his candidacy was caught in a backlash of opposition to a free-trade agreement between Central American countries (including Costa Rica) and the United States. Arias's support for that treaty became controversial after the U.S. ambassador, Mark Langdale, made comments that were seen as threatening Costa Rica if it did not ratify the treaty. On March 7, more than a month after the presidential election, Arias was declared the winner, with a margin of little more than 18,000 votes of the 1.6 million cast.

Ecuador. Joining Chavez and Morales on the far left of the Latin political spectrum was Rafael Correa of Ecuador. A U.S.-educated economist, Correa rattled financial markets during the campaign season with a pledge to reduce the country's payments on foreign debt. Correa also endorsed Chavez's personal attacks on Bush, but with a twist. A week after Chavez called Bush the devil at the UN, Correa said that statement was "offending the devil" because the devil, unlike Bush, was intelligent. "I believe Bush is a tremendously dimwitted president who has done great damage to his country and to the world," Correa said. Correa had been expected to win the first round of voting on October 15 but instead finished second to Ecuador's richest man, banana tycoon Alvaro Noboa, who passed out money to voters at campaign rallies. Correa won the runoff election on November 26, however, largely on the basis of votes from impoverished Indians who demanded a greater share of the profits from oil production.

Nicaragua. Of all the major Latin political candidates in 2006, none had a longer history—and none, not even Chavez, had been so despised in Washington—as Daniel Ortega, who headed the leftist Sandinista government in Nicaragua from 1979 until his defeat in elections in 1990. President Ronald Reagan (1981–1989) had tried to oust Ortega and his fellow Sandinistas from power, primarily by backing a right-wing guerrilla group called the contras in the mid-1980s. That attempt failed, but under international pressure Ortega allowed free elections, which he lost to Violeta Barrios de Chamorro, the widow of a revered political leader. *(Background, Historic Documents of 1990, p. 259)*

Ortega tried three times for a comeback in subsequent years but could not gain traction against a succession of conservative political leaders—until 2006. Ortega returned to the political arena, claiming to have moderated his views and concentrating on a "peace and love" platform more reminiscent of the late 1960s than the radical Sandinista platform of the 1970s. Ortega also had a major tactical advantage; he was the best-known of the five candidates on the November 5 ballot, and he needed only 35 percent of the vote to win. Ortega barely edged past that mark, getting 38 percent of the vote.

Peru. Voters in Peru rebuffed one of the most far-left presidential candidates any-where in Latin America but gave his new political movement, the Nationalist Party, control of the parliament. The central figure in Peru's 2006 election was Ollanta Hu-mala, a retired army lieutenant colonel who ran on a nationalist and socialist platform and—like Correa in Ecuador—explicitly modeled himself after Venezuela's Chavez. Humala and Chavez had many things in common, including their past attempts to oust elected leaders in coups; in Humala's case, it was a failed coup in 2000 against President Alberto Fujimori. *(Background, Historic Documents of 2000, p. 923)*

Humala finished first in the initial round of voting on April 9 and was widely expected to win the runoff on June 4. Former president Alan Garcia pulled out a surprising win, however, boosted in part by a voter backlash when Chavez openly endorsed Humala and called Garcia "an irresponsible demagogue and thief." Polls showed that the vast majority of Peruvians resented Chavez's interference, which also was denounced by outgoing president Alejandro Toledo.

Garcia remained controversial in Peru. His one term as president from 1985 to 1990 was marred by hyperinflation, corruption scandals, and human rights abuses in a war between the army and leftist guerrillas. Garcia returned to politics in 2006 with a new platform that was sharply different from the leftist program that propelled him into office the first time; he portrayed himself as the more responsible candidate and said he had learned from the failures of his first term in office.

Following are excerpts from a speech by Hugo Chavez, the president of Venezuela, to the United Nations General Assembly on September 20, 2006.

DOCUMENT

"Statement by Hugo Chavez Frias, at the 61st UN General Assembly"

Madam President, Excellencies, Heads of State and Government, and high ranking representatives of governments from across the world. A very good day to you all.

First of all, with much respect, I would like to invite all of those who have not had a chance to read this book, to do it. "Hegemony or Survival: America's Quest for Global Dominance," is one of the most recent works of Noam Chomsky, one of the most famous intellectuals of America and the world. An excellent piece to help us understand not only what has happened in the world during the 20th century, but what is happening today, and the greatest threat looming over our Planet: the hegemonic pretension of the U.S. imperialism that puts at risk the very survival of humankind itself. We continue to warn the world of this danger, and call on the people of the United States and worldwide to halt this threat, which is like the sword of Damocles.

I was thinking of reading a chapter of this book, but in order to respect the time limit, I rather leave it merely as a recommendation. This is an easy-to-read book, a good reading, and surely you are familiar with it, Madam President. I am certain it has been published in English, German, Russian, and Arabic. I believe that the first to read this book should be our brothers and sisters of the United States, because the main threat is on their homeland. The devil is here. The devil; the devil himself is in their homes.

The Devil came here yesterday. Yesterday, the Devil was here in this very place. This rostrum still smells like sulfur. Yesterday, ladies and gentlemen, from this podium, the President of the United States, whom I refer to as the Devil, came here talking as if he owned the world. It would take a psychiatrist to analyze the speech he delivered yesterday.

As the spokesperson for imperialism, he came to give us his recipes for maintaining the current scheme of domination, exploitation and pillage over the peoples of the world. His speech perfectly fit an Alfred Hitchcock movie, and I could even dare to suggest a title: "The Devil's Recipe." That is to say, the U.S. imperialism, as stated by Chomsky in a very clear, evident and profound manner, is making desperate efforts to consolidate its hegemonic system of domination. We cannot allow this to happen. We cannot allow a world dictatorship to be installed or consolidated.

The statement by the tyrannical president of the world was full of cynicism and hypocrisy. Basically, it is with imperial hypocrisy that he attempts to control everything. They want to impose upon us the democratic model they devised, the false democracy of elites. And, moreover, a very original democratic model, imposed with explosions, bombings, invasions and bullets. What a democracy! In light of this, Aristotle's and those theories made by the first Greek thinkers who spoke about democracy shall be reviewed, so as to analyze what kind of democracy that is, one which imposes itself through marines, invasions, aggressions and bombs.

Yesterday, the United States' President said in this same Hall the following, I quote: "Wherever you look at, you hear extremists telling you that violence, terror and torture can help you escape from misery and recover your dignity." Wherever he looks he sees extremists. I am sure he sees you, my brother, with your skin color, and he thinks you are an extremist. With his color, the Honorable president of Bolivia, Evo Morales, who came here yesterday, is also an extremist. Imperialists see extremists everywhere. No, we are not extremists, what happens is that the world is waking up, and people are rising up everywhere. I have the feeling, Mister Imperialist Dictator, that you are going to live as if in a nightmare the rest of your days, because no matter where you look at, we will be rising up against the U.S. imperialism. They call us extremists, since we demand total freedom in the world, equality among the peoples, and respect for sovereignty of nations. We are rising up against the Empire, against its model of domination.

Then, the President continued to say, "Today I want to talk directly to the populations in the Middle East. My country desires peace." It is true that people of the United States want peace; if you walk the streets of the Bronx, or through the streets of New York, Washington, San Diego, California, San Antonio, San Francisco, any city, and you ask people on the streets; definitely all of them want peace. The difference lies on the fact that their government, the United States' Government, does not want peace; it seeks to impose its model of exploitation, plundering and its hegemony upon us under threat of war. That is the difference. People want peace, and then we wonder what is happening in Iraq? And what happened in Lebanon and Palestine? What has happened over 100 years in Latin America and the world; and most recently the threats against Venezuela, and new threats against Iran?

He addressed the people of Lebanon. "Many of you"—he said—"have seen your homes and communities trapped in the middle of crossfire." What cynicism! What capacity to blatantly lie before the world! Do you consider the bombs in Beirut, launched with such millimetric precision, as crossfire? I believe that the President is referring to those western movies in which cowboys dueled and someone ends up caught in the middle.

Imperialist fire! Fascist fire! Murderous Fire! Genocidal fire against the innocent people of Palestine and Lebanon by the Empire and Israel. That is the truth. Now, they say that "they are suffering" because they see their houses destroyed.

The President of the United States addressed the peoples of Afghanistan, the people of Lebanon and to the people of Iran. Well, one has to wonder, when listening to the U.S. President speak to those people: if those people could talk to him, what would they say?

I am going to answer on behalf of the peoples because I know their soul well, the soul of the peoples of the South, the downtrodden peoples would say: Yankee imperialist, go home! That would be the shout springing up everywhere, if the peoples of the world could speak in unison to the United States' Empire.

Therefore, Madam President, colleagues, and friends, last year we came to this same Hall, as every year over the last eight, and we said something that has been completely confirmed today. I believe that almost no one in this room would dare to stand up and defend the United Nations system, let us admit this with honesty: the United Nations system that emerged after World War II has collapsed, shattered, it does not work anymore.

Of course, the UN is good for coming here once a year to deliver speeches; that is what it is good for. And also to draft very long documents, make good reflections and listen to good speeches like Evo's yesterday, and Lula's. Definitely, to that end it does work; and for many other speeches, as the one we just listened from the President of Sri Lanka and from Madam President of Chile. But, this Assembly has been turned into a deliberative body, with no power to exert the slightest impact on the terrible reality the world is experiencing. That is why we propose once again, today the 20th of September to join our efforts to rebuild the United Nations. Madam President, last year we presented four modest proposals that we consider cannot be postponed; they must be taken into consideration and discussed by the Heads of State and Government, our Ambassadors and representatives.

First, the expansion of the Security Council—as it was also said by President Lula yesterday, in this same place—both in its permanent and non permanent membership categories, envisaging the entry of new developed and developing countries, which is the Third World, as new permanent members.

Secondly, achieve the implementation of effective methods of addressing and resolving world conflicts, transparent methods of debate and decision making.

Thirdly, we consider fundamental the immediate suppression of anti-democratic veto mechanism, the veto power on decisions of the Security Council. This is a common clamor. A recent example is the immoral veto of the U.S. Government, which openly allowed Israel forces to destroy Lebanon just before our eyes, by blocking a solution in the UN Security Council.

And finally, as we have previously said, the role and functions of the United Nations Secretary General needs to be strengthened. The UN Secretary General addressed yesterday practically a farewell speech, and he recognized that throughout these ten years the world has become complicated and that the serious problems of the world such as hunger, misery, violence, Human Rights violation has worsened, as a consequence of the terrible collapse in the UN system and the U.S. imperialist pretension.

On the other hand, Madam President, Venezuela has decided several years ago, to wage this battle within the United Nations with our voice and our modest statements. We are an independent voice, representing dignity and the pursuit of peace as well as the reform of the international system to denounce persecution and hegemonic aggressions against the peoples of the Planet. That is why Venezuela, Bolivar's native country, has nominated itself for one of the seats as non Permanent Member on the Security Council. God knows why the US government has started an open and immoral aggression in the whole world to hinder Venezuela from being freely elected to obtain a seat on the Security Council.

They fear the truth. The Empire is afraid of the truth and of independent voices, accusing us of being extremists. They are the extremists!

I wish to thank all countries that have announced their support to Venezuela, even though the vote is secret and it is not necessary for anyone to reveal their vote. But, I think that the open aggression of the U.S. Empire has reinforced the support of many countries, which morally strengthened Venezuela, our people and our Government.

For instance, MERCOSUR [the Southern Cone Common Market], our brothers of MERCOSUR, as a block, have announced its support to Venezuela. Venezuela is now a full member of MERCOSUR along with Brazil, Argentina, Uruguay, and Paraguay. Other Latin America countries such as Bolivia and all the CARICOM [Caribbean Community] nations have pledged their support to Venezuela. Likewise, the entire League of Arab States has announced its support to the candidature of Venezuela. I would very much like to thank the Arab world, our brothers of Arabia and of the Caribbean. Nearly, the African Union countries have announced its support to Venezuela, as well as other countries as Russia, China and many others across the globe. On behalf of Venezuela, of our people and of the truth, I thank you all deeply, because Venezuela upon occupying a seat on the Security Council will not only bring to it the voice of Venezuela, but also the voice of the Third World, the voice of the peoples of the Planet. There we will be defending dignity and truth.

Despite all this, Madam President, I believe that there are many reasons to be optimistic. Hopelessly optimistic, as a poet may say, because beyond the threats, bombs, wars, aggressions, preventive war, destruction of entire peoples, one can see that a new era is dawning, as Silvio Rodriguez says in his song: "this era is giving birth to a heart." Streams, alternative thoughts and movements, youths with different ideas are arising. In barely a decade, it has been demonstrated that the theory of the End of History was totally false, as totally false were also the theory of the founding of the American Empire, the American peace, the establishment of the capitalist and neo-liberal model that generates misery and poverty. This theory is totally false, and it has fallen down. Now it is time to define the future of the world. There is a new dawning on this Planet that can be seen everywhere: in Latin America, Asia, Africa, Europe, and Oceania. I would like to highlight this vision of optimism to strengthen our conscience and our willingness to fight in favor of the world's salvation and for the construction of a new, a better world.

Venezuela has joined this struggle and for this reason, we are threatened. The U.S. has already planned, financed and led a coup in Venezuela. And the U.S. continues to support coup plotter movements in our country. The U.S. continues to support terrorism. President Michel Bachelet mentioned days ago, pardon me, minutes ago, the horrible murder of Orlando Letelier, former Chilean Foreign Minister. I would only add the following: the offenders are not in prison. And those responsible for that deed, in which a U.S. citizen was also killed, are American, CIA agents; CIA terrorists.

In addition, in a few days it will be the 30th anniversary of that murder and of the terrorist attack when a Cubana de Aviacion airplane was blasted and 73 innocent people died. And where is the worst terrorist of this continent, the one who admitted being the intellectual author of the Cuban airplane blasting? He was convicted in Venezuela for years and he escaped with the complicity of CIA officials and the Venezuelan government of that time. Now, he is living here in the US, protected by the US government. He confessed and was imprisoned. Evidently, the U.S. government has double standards and protects terrorism.

I am making these statements to demonstrate that Venezuela is committed to the fight against terrorism, against violence and joins with all the peoples who are engaged in the fight for peace and for an equal world. . . . I believe the United Nations must be located in another country, in some city of the South. We have proposed this from Venezuela. You all know that my medical personnel had to remain inside the airplane as well as my Chief of Security. They both were denied to enter the United Nations. This is another abuse and an outrage, Madam President that we request to be registered as a personal abuse by the Devil, it smells like sulfur, but God is with us.

A warm embrace and God bless us all. Thank you.

Source: Bolivarian Republic of Venezuela. [United Nations] Mission of the Bolivarian Republic of Venezuela. "Statement by H. E. Hugo Chavez Frias, President of the Bolivarian Republic of Venezuela, at the 61st United Nations General Assembly." New York, September 20, 2006. Unofficial translation. www.venezuelaonu.gob. ve/venezuela-e.pdf (accessed March 27, 2007).

Other Historic Documents of Interest

U.S. National Intelligence Estimate on Foreign Terrorism

September 26, 2006

■■■■■■■ **THE DOCUMENT IN CONTEXT** ■■■■■■■

Terrorism by radical Islamists was growing in strength and posing a broader problem in the world—rather than contracting—according to a U.S. intelligence assessment, portions of which were made public in late September. The joint assessment by all of the government's intelligence agencies also said the war in Iraq had become a *cause célèbre* for Islamists wanting to carry out a jihad, or holy war, against the United States and other Western interests.

Iraq continued to be the world's epicenter of terrorism during 2006, with suicide bombings, roadside bombings, and sectarian attacks occurring almost on a daily basis. Similar incidents of terrorism also were becoming more common in Afghanistan, where suicide bombings had been virtually unknown until 2005. Terrorist attacks were carried out in several other countries during 2006—notably in Egypt and India—but authorities in Britain and Canada claimed to have broken up networks planning major attacks there.

Intelligence Estimate on Terrorism

The sixteen U.S. intelligence agencies periodically prepared joint assessments, called National Intelligence Estimates (NIEs), on important topics. The documents were highly classified and rarely made it into the news. When they did become news, however, it usually was in a big way. Such was the case in 2003 when the Bush administration released a declassified version of an estimate concluding that Iraq's government had built a large arsenal of biological and chemical weapons and was attempting to develop nuclear weapons. That assessment, which the administration had used in its 2002 campaign to convince Congress to endorse a war against Iraq, brushed aside dissenting views from some intelligence officials—and it later turned out to be entirely wrong. *(Background, Historic Documents of 2004, p. 711)*

The intelligence agencies reportedly had not completed a full-scale National Intelligence Estimate on international terrorism since the run-up to the U.S. invasion of Iraq in 2003; as part of that estimate, the CIA warned that Islamic extremists likely would use the invasion to foment anti-U.S. sentiments in the Muslim world. A new estimate on terrorism finally was completed in April 2006 but remained secret until a *New York Times* report about it on September 24. Quoting officials and terrorism experts who were familiar with the intelligence estimate—but not the text of the report itself—the *Times* report said the U.S. occupation of Iraq "has helped spawned a new generation of Islamic radicalism."

The *Times* report created a firestorm of controversy just six weeks before the congressional midterm elections. Democrats who opposed the Iraq War said the report proved their point that the U.S. invasion of Iraq had been a distraction from the broader battle against terrorism and had, in fact, made that battle more difficult. "The reality is that the war in Iraq has inflamed Islamic extremism and hatred toward the United States," John D. Rockefeller IV, the ranking Democrat on the Senate Intelligence Committee said. "It has given the terrorists a centralized place to attack and kill Americans, and it has created a training ground for the next generation of terrorists." Republicans, by contrast, insisted the intelligence estimate put U.S. antiterrorism efforts in a more positive light. "The NIE says that the U.S.-led counterterrorism efforts have not only severely damaged al Qaeda and disrupted its terrorist operations, but that U.S. success in Iraq is the key to ensuring that this terrorist threat does not grow," House Majority Leader John A. Boehner said.

After a full day of partisan sparring over the matter, the White House on September 26 ordered the release of an abridged, unclassified version of the estimate's summary, called "Key Judgments." This summary did not include any of the detailed analysis and factual reporting that underpinned the overall conclusions, nor did it disclose any competing views within the intelligence community.

The headline news from the summary was contained in three sentences: "We assess that the Iraqi jihad [the anti-U.S. insurgency in Iraq] is shaping a new generation of terrorist leaders and operatives; perceived jihadist success there would inspire more fighters to continue their struggle elsewhere. The Iraq conflict has become a 'cause célèbre' for jihadists, breeding a deep resentment of U.S. involvement in the Muslim world and cultivating supporters for the global jihadist movement. Should jihadists leaving Iraq perceive themselves, or be perceived, to have failed, we judge fewer fighters will be inspired to carry on the fight."

These sentences contained nothing that countless experts on terrorism and the Middle East had not said repeatedly over the previous three years. Even so, the conclusion was startling given its source: U.S. intelligence officials who had the responsibility to give such conclusions, in confidence, to President George W. Bush and his chief aides. The assessment also called into question Bush's repeated statements that Iraq was the "central front" in what he called the "global war on terror."

Announcing release of the summary at a news conference, Bush sought to shore up his position on the matter. "You know, to suggest that if we weren't in Iraq, we would see a rosier scenario, with fewer extremists joining the radical movement, requires us to ignore twenty years of experience," he said.

Other Issues in the Terrorism Assessment

The role of the Iraq War in encouraging terrorism grabbed the headlines, but other elements of the estimate were equally important—and, in general, no more encouraging. This was especially true of the central assessments that the al Qaeda terrorist network was the single "greatest threat" to U.S. domestic and international interests and that Islamist terrorism was spreading despite the U.S. war against it.

The status of al Qaeda was of particular interest in 2006, especially in the period around the fifth anniversary of the September 11 attacks that destroyed the World Trade Center towers in New York City and damaged the Pentagon outside Washington. *(Background, Historic Documents of 2001, p. 614)*

The administration in June 2006 had scored what at the time was seen as a major victory against al Qaeda: the killing of Abu Musab al-Zarqawi, a Jordanian terrorist who had been in Iraq for several years and headed what he called al Qaeda in Mesopotamia. Zarqawi claimed responsibility for some of the deadliest attacks against U.S. and other international targets in Iraq, and he had boasted of starting a sectarian war, between Shiite and Sunni Muslims, as part of a jihad against the West. The killing of Zarqawi dampened violence in Iraq only momentarily, however, and within a few weeks his group and other Sunni insurgents were back in business.

More broadly, it appeared by late 2006 that the international al Qaeda organization, headed by Osama bin Laden and his deputy, Ayman al-Zawahiri, had rebuilt much of its infrastructure and network that had been destroyed during the U.S. invasion of Afghanistan in October 2001. The base of al Qaeda operations had been moved from Afghanistan into the mountainous and lawless region of North Wajiristan, which was part of the Northwest Frontier province of Pakistan—just across the border from east-central Afghanistan. This was the same region where bin Laden, Zawahiri, and other al Qaeda leaders were said to have fled after the 2001 invasion of Afghanistan. The Pakistani government traditionally had little control over this region. Pakistan's president, Pervez Musharraf, surrendered much of the control his government did have in September 2006, when he signed an agreement with local leaders there; the agreement effectively withdrew government forces in exchange for a promise by the leaders to prevent cross-border attacks into Afghanistan.

Al Qaeda appeared to step up its public relations campaign during the year, issuing more than twenty audio and videotapes addressed to various audiences. Among these were the first tapes from bin Laden since early 2005. On January 19, for example, Arab networks aired an audiotape in which bin Laden offered a "long-term truce" if the United States withdrew its forces from Iraq and Afghanistan.

On the broader issue of Islamist-based terrorism globally, the National Intelligence Estimate generally offered dour assessments, saying that this type of terrorism was "spreading" rather than contracting. Specifically, the assessment said the number of terrorists was "increasing in both number and geographic dispersion"—meaning that they posed a broader threat around the world than just in the Middle East or even in the United States.

The "jihadist movement" was fueled by four factors, the assessment said, including the war in Iraq; various grievances in the Muslim world, such as corruption, injustice, and fear of Western domination; the slow pace of economic, political, and social reforms in Muslim countries; and "pervasive anti-U.S. sentiment among most Muslims." The assessment said several factors could "begin to slow the spread" of the jihadist movement, but it added that this would take many years and require "coordinated multilateral efforts that go well beyond operations to capture or kill terrorist leaders."

No Iraq Link to al Qaeda

Another report in 2006 briefly revived an old controversy over the Bush administration's past statements implying a link between al Qaeda and the Iraqi government under Saddam Hussein. Starting in late 2001 and continuing until well after the 2003 invasion of Iraq, Bush, Vice President Dick Cheney, and other senior officials made statements that, in most cases, indirectly suggested that Saddam's government somehow was cooperating with, or possibly even aiding, al Qaeda and other Middle Eastern terrorists. Cheney was the most explicit on this matter, frequently noting reports of a meeting between senior Iraqi officials and Zarqawi, who had spent time in Iraq before the U.S. invasion. These statements by administration officials contributed to a widespread belief among Americans, as shown in numerous opinion polls, that Iraq had some role in the September 11 terrorist attacks.

On September 8, 2006, the Senate Intelligence Committee released a long-delayed report concluding that there was no evidence that Saddam's government had any links with al Qaeda in general or Zarqawi in particular. The 400-page report quoted transcripts of interrogations of Saddam and some of his top aides—all of them captured after the U.S. invasion—in which they scorned al Qaeda and denied having supported it in any way.

Other Terrorism Matters

Among other developments during 2006 related to international terrorism were the following:

- A jury in London on February 7 convicted Abu Hamza al-Masri on charges of soliciting murder and racial hatred. The Egyptian-born Masri was the most prominent among a number of Muslim clerics in Britain who had preached sermons calling on followers to kill non-Muslims. Among those who had attended services at his Finsbury Park mosque in north London were Zacarias Moussaoui, who in May was imprisoned in the United States in connection with the September 11 attacks; and Richard Reid, who tried to ignite a bomb in one of his shoes while traveling on an airplane from London to the United States in late 2001. Masri was arrested in May 2004 after U.S. authorities sought his extradition on terrorism-related charges.
- Two suicide bombers, reportedly affiliated with al Qaeda, failed in a February 24 attempt to bomb the world's biggest oil processing plant, at Abqaiq in eastern Saudi Arabia. Police foiled the attack, and both bombers were killed. Four days later, Saudi authorities said the al Qaeda leader in Saudi Arabia, Fahd Faraaj al-Juwair, and two of his associates who had been involved in the attack on the Abqaiq plant, were killed in a shootout.
- Intelligence authorities in Spain said on March 9 that two years of investigation into the 2004 bombings of the Madrid train system, which killed 191 people, had found no evidence of a direct al Qaeda role. The officials told reporters that the bombers, who struck on March 11, 2004, may have been encouraged by public statements of al Qaeda leader bin Laden but had not been in direct contact with al Qaeda or any other international terrorist organization. A judge on April 11 indicted twenty-nine people on charges related to the Madrid bombings; trials were expected to begin early in 2007. *(Background, Historic Documents of 2004, p. 105)*
- The Basque separatist group in Spain, known as ETA, on March 22 declared what it called a "permanent cease-fire" in its decades-long fight against the government. ETA had killed more than 800 people—most of them policemen, judges, and other government officials— in its campaign to win independence for the Basque region that straddles the border between northern Spain and southern France. The group said in a statement it would turn to "the democratic process" to achieve its aims.
- On April 24 three bombs killed 21 people and wounded more than 100 in the Egyptian resort town of Dahab on the Gulf of Aqaba. Egyptian resorts had become frequent targets of terrorist attacks in recent years, apparently as a means of putting pressure on the government of President Hosni Mubarak; tourism was one of Egypt's most important industries. Most victims of previous bombings were tourists from Israel or Western countries, but most of those killed in this bombing were Egyptians on holiday.
- Reports released by British authorities on May 11 said the four men who had bombed buses and subway trains in London in July 2005 had acted together but without evident support from an outside group. The bombings had killed 52 people. The reports also said

that there appeared to be no connection between those four bombers and another group of men who tried, and failed, to carry out similar bombings two weeks later. *(Background, Historic Documents of 2005, p. 393)*

- Police in Ontario, Canada, on June 2–3 arrested and charged twelve adult men and five teenagers with planning bomb attacks in southern Ontario. Authorities said this was the largest terrorism plot in Canada's history. The suspects reportedly had attempted to purchase three tons of ammonium nitrate fertilizer, which can be used to make powerful bombs when mixed with fuel oil.
- A series of bombings on seven commuter trains in Mumbai (formerly Bombay), India, on July 10 killed 185 people and wounded several hundred others. Indian authorities immediately blamed the attacks on the Kashmiri separatist group, Lashkare-Toiba, which denied responsibility. Later, on September 30, Mumbai's police chief said the bombings had been arranged by Pakistan's military intelligence service—a charge the Pakistani government denied. Police on November 30 charged thirty people in connection with the bombings, which they said were masterminded by a Pakistani man, Azam Cheema.
- British authorities said on August 10 that they had disrupted a complex plot to blow up ten airplanes headed to the United States using liquid explosives. Twenty-three British-born Muslims, most of them with family ties to Pakistan, were arrested; eleven later were charged with terrorism-related crimes and several others were charged with lesser offenses. The disruption of this plot led authorities in Europe, the United States, and much of the rest of the world to ban passengers from carrying any liquids on board airplanes; most of these prohibitions later were modified to allow for small quantities of baby milk or medicines. British and U.S. officials later said the plotters had been monitored for several months and had recently stepped up their planning, at which point the arrests were made.
- In a rare public speech, the head of British's domestic intelligence service, MI-5, said the agency was monitoring about thirty terrorist conspiracies in Britain, involving about 1,600 individuals in 200 different cells. Dame Eliza Manningham-Buller, the agency head, told a group of academics: "More and more people are moving from passive sympathy towards active terrorism through being radicalized or indoctrinated by friends, families, in organized training events here and overseas, by images on television, through chat rooms and Web sites on the Internet."

Following is the text of "Trends in Global Terrorism: Implications for the United States," the declassified key judgments of the National Intelligence Estimate released on September 26, 2006, by the Office of the Director of National Intelligence. The full estimate (which was not made public) was dated April 2006.

DOCUMENT

"Trends in Global Terrorism: Implications for the United States"

Key Judgments

United States-led counterterrorism efforts have seriously damaged the leadership of al Qaeda and disrupted its operations; however, we judge that al Qaeda will continue to pose the greatest threat to the Homeland and US interests abroad by a single terrorist organization. We also assess that the global jihadist movement—which includes al Qaeda, affiliated and independent terrorist groups, and emerging networks and cells—is spreading and adapting to counterterrorism efforts.

- Although we cannot measure the extent of the spread with precision, a large body of all-source reporting indicates that activists identifying themselves as jihadists, although a small percentage of Muslims, are increasing in both number and geographic dispersion.
- If this trend continues, threats to US interests at home and abroad will become more diverse, leading to increasing attacks worldwide.
- Greater pluralism and more responsive political systems in Muslim majority nations would alleviate some of the grievances jihadists exploit. Over time, such progress, together with sustained, multifaceted programs targeting the vulnerabilities of the jihadist movement and continued pressure on al Qaeda, could erode support for the jihadists.

We assess that the global jihadist movement is decentralized, lacks a coherent global strategy, and is becoming more diffuse. New jihadist networks and cells, with anti-American agendas, are increasingly likely to emerge. The confluence of shared purpose and dispersed actors will make it harder to find and undermine jihadist groups.

- We assess that the operational threat from self-radicalized cells will grow in importance to US counterterrorism efforts, particularly abroad but also in the Homeland.
- The jihadists regard Europe as an important venue for attacking Western interests. Extremist networks inside the extensive Muslim diasporas in Europe facilitate recruitment and staging for urban attacks, as illustrated by the 2004 Madrid and 2005 London bombings.

We assess that the Iraq jihad is shaping a new generation of terrorist leaders and operatives; perceived jihadist success there would inspire more fighters to continue the struggle elsewhere.

- The Iraq conflict has become the ìcause celebreî for jihadists, breeding a deep resentment of US involvement in the Muslim world and cultivating supporters for the global jihadist movement. Should jihadists leaving Iraq perceive themselves, and be perceived, to have failed, we judge fewer fighters will be inspired to carry on the fight.

We assess that the underlying factors fueling the spread of the movement outweigh its vulnerabilities and are likely to do so for the duration of the timeframe of this Estimate.

- Four underlying factors are fueling the spread of the jihadist movement: (1) Entrenched grievances, such as corruption, injustice, and fear of Western domination, leading to anger, humiliation, and a sense of powerlessness; (2) the Iraq "jihad"; (3) the slow pace of real and sustained economic, social, and political reforms in many Muslim majority nations; and (4) pervasive anti-US sentiment among most Muslims—all of which jihadists exploit.

Concomitant vulnerabilities in the jihadist movement have emerged that, if fully exposed and exploited, could begin to slow the spread of the movement. They include dependence on the continuation of Muslim-related conflicts, the limited appeal of the jihadists' radical ideology, the emergence of respected voices of moderation, and criticism of the violent tactics employed against mostly Muslim citizens.

- The jihadists' greatest vulnerability is that their ultimate political solution—an ultra-conservative interpretation of Shari 'a-based governance spanning the Muslim world—is unpopular with the vast majority of Muslims. Exposing the religious and political straitjacket that is implied by the jihadists' propaganda would help to divide them from the audiences they seek to persuade.

- Recent condemnations of violence and extremist religious interpretations by a few notable Muslim clerics signal a trend that could facilitate the growth of a constructive alternative to jihadist ideology: peaceful political activism. This also could lead to the consistent and dynamic participation of broader Muslim communities in rejecting violence, reducing the ability of radicals to capitalize on passive community support. In this way, the Muslim mainstream emerges as the most powerful weapon in the war on terror.
- Countering the spread of the jihadist movement will require coordinated multilateral efforts that go well beyond operations to capture or kill terrorist leaders.

If democratic reform efforts in Muslim majority nations progress over the next five years, political participation probably would drive a wedge between intransigent extremists and groups willing to use the political process to achieve their local objectives. Nonetheless, attendant reforms and potentially destabilizing transitions will create new opportunities for jihadists to exploit. Al Qaeda, now merged with Abu Musab al-Zarqawi's network, is exploiting the situation in Iraq to attract new recruits and donors and to maintain its leadership role.

- The loss of key leaders, particularly Osama Bin Laden, Ayman al-Zawahiri, and al-Zarqawi, in rapid succession, probably would cause the group to fracture into smaller groups. Although like-minded individuals would endeavor to carry on the mission, the loss of these key leaders would exacerbate strains and disagreements. We assess that the resulting splinter groups would, at least for a time, pose a less serious threat to US interests than does al Qaeda.
- Should al-Zarqawi continue to evade capture and scale back attacks against Muslims, we assess he could broaden his popular appeal and present a global threat.
- The increased role of Iraqis in managing the operations of al Qaeda in Iraq might lead veteran foreign jihadists to focus their efforts on external operations.

Other affiliated Sunni extremist organizations, such as Jemaah Islamiya, Ansar al-Sunnah, and several North African groups, unless countered, are likely to expand their reach and become more capable of multiple and/or mass-casualty attacks outside their traditional areas of operation.

- We assess that such groups pose less of a danger to the Homeland than does al- Qaeda but will pose varying degrees of threat to our allies and to US interests abroad. The focus of their attacks is likely to ebb and flow between local regime targets and regional or global ones.

We judge that most jihadist groups—both well-known and newly formed—will use improvised explosive devices and suicide attacks focused primarily on soft targets to implement their asymmetric warfare strategy, and that they will attempt to conduct sustained terrorist attacks in urban environments. Fighters with experience in Iraq are a potential source of leadership for jihadists pursuing these tactics.

- CBRN [chemical, biological, radiological, and nuclear weapons] capabilities will continue to be sought by jihadist groups.

While Iran, and to a lesser extent Syria, remain the most active state sponsors of terrorism, many other states will be unable to prevent territory or resources from being exploited by terrorists. Anti-US and anti-globalization sentiment is on the rise and fueling other radical ideologies. This could prompt some leftist, nationalist, or separatist groups to adopt terrorist methods to attack US interests. The radicalization process is occurring more quickly, more widely, and more anonymously in the Internet age, raising the likelihood of surprise attacks by unknown groups whose members and supporters may be difficult to pinpoint.

- We judge that groups of all stripes will increasingly use the Internet to communicate, propagandize, recruit, train, and obtain logistical and financial support.

Source: U.S. Office of the Director of National Intelligence. "Declassified Key Judgments of the National Intelligence Estimate 'Trends in Global Terrorism: Implications for the United States' dated April 2006." September 26, 2006. www.odni.gov/press_releases/Declassified_NIE_Key_Judgments.pdf (accessed March 20, 2007).

Other Historic Documents of Interest

Japanese Prime Minister Abe
on His Inauguration

September 29, 2006

■■■■ ■ THE DOCUMENT IN CONTEXT ■■■■■

Junichiro Koizumi—Japan's most charismatic, successful, and atypical prime minister in many years—stepped aside in September 2006 after five years in power. He was succeeded by Shinzo Abe, who was a much more typical representative of Japan's political elite but also the country's first prime minister born after World War II.

Koizumi helped guide Japan to a tenuous economic recovery after more than a decade of stagnation that had sapped the country's confidence, particularly in the face of the rapid rise to power, regionally and even globally, of its old rival, China. Japan's economic revival was spurred, in part, by numerous policy changes, including tax cuts and deregulation, that Koizumi had advocated in the name of "reform." Even so, the result was a Japan that was more polarized economically than in several generations, with higher unemployment and income disparities. Other aspects of Koizumi's reforms were still in the planning stages when he left his post, and still others had died as a result of political resistance. *(Background, Historic Documents of 2001, p. 304)*

A Somewhat Smooth Political Transition

Except for a brief period in 1993, Japan had been ruled since World War II by various factions of the Liberal Democratic Party. Despite its name, the party was neither liberal nor very democratic. In recent decades it represented business elites, government officials, and other conservative elements of society, and its leaders traditionally were chosen not by democratic consensus but through an arcane process of selection by the heads of various party fiefdoms. Koizumi's unorthodox rise to power in 2001— over the opposition of key party leaders—had appeared to break the "old boy" system of party rule, but elements of the system remained in place as the party chose his successor in 2006.

Koizumi had signaled in 2005 that he would step down in September 2006 after completing slightly more than five years in office, a tenure about twice as lengthy as most of his recent predecessors. The Liberal Democratic Party strengthened its grip on power in the September 2005 elections, which gave it (along with its coalition partner, the New Komeito Party), two-thirds of the seats in the lower house, the Diet. The main opposition party, the Democratic Party of Japan, took another tumble in March 2006, when the entire party leadership was forced to resign because of a fake e-mail a party leader had sent attempting to capitalize on a financial scandal affecting the Liberal Democrats.

The scandal involved an Internet firm named the Livedoor Company. Prosecutors raided the company offices in January as part of an investigation into possible violation of security laws, including falsification of financial statements. That move caused a general sell-off in the Tokyo Stock Exchange and deeply embarrassed Koizumi's party, which had urged Livedoor's flamboyant president, Takafumi Horie, to run for a parliamentary seat in the 2005 elections—a bid that he lost. The party's embarrassment deepened on February 13, when Horie was charged with breaking security laws; his trial on those charges was still under way at year's end.

In the final months leading up to the Liberal Democratic Party's selection of a successor to Koizumi, one of the most prominent issues was an old one: the wisdom of Koizumi's annual visits to the Yasukuni Shrine, a memorial in Tokyo where fourteen Japanese war criminals from World War II were buried (along with some 2 million other war dead) in a setting that glorified the country's imperial past. Koizumi said he prayed for peace on his visits to the shrine, which came on the August 15 anniversary date of Japan's surrender. However, each visit generated extreme anger in China and South Korea, both of which had suffered grievously under Japanese occupation before and during World War II.

Abe, who worked for Koizumi in the cabinet, supported the visits, while his main opponent, Yasuo Fukuda, opposed the visits and emphasized the importance for Japan of improving relations with China and other countries in East Asia. Abe also stirred controversy in April when he told Japanese reporters that "China and Japan have nothing in common." That remark sparked predictable protests in China and raised concerns that Japan's new leader might be even more confrontational toward China than Koizumi had been.

Polls taken early in the year showed Fukuda gaining popular support because of his position on the shrine visits and their regional impact. Abe and Fukuda also appeared to differ on an approach to North Korea, which claimed to have built nuclear weapons and in July conducted tests of medium-range missiles. Abe took a hard line, endorsing the idea of a preemptive military strike against North Korea (presumably to be carried out by the United States), while Fukuda emphasized negotiation as the only way to convince North Korea to surrender its weapons.

Under Japanese rules, the leader of the party with the most seats in parliament automatically became prime minister, and so the race to succeed Koizumi really was for the leadership of the Liberal Democratic Party. Until Koizumi upended tradition in 2001, the party leader had been chosen by leaders of the various factions, who presented a single name to the more than 1 million party members for ratification.

Fukuda's campaign to succeed Koizumi faltered midyear, and he bowed out of the race in late July, leaving Abe with a commanding lead, both in public opinion polls and among party leaders. His only challengers were the sitting finance minister and foreign minister, neither of whom had broad support. A brief version of an election campaign began on September 9, when the three candidates held a policy debate at party headquarters, and ended with voting by the more than 1 million party members on September 20. Abe won overwhelmingly, and parliament ratified his selection as prime minister on September 26.

Although at age fifty-one he was young by the standards of recent Japanese leaders, Abe was a familiar presence in politics because of his family. His grandfather, Nobusuke Kishi, was prime minister in the late 1950s; his father, Shintaro Abe, had been foreign minister in the 1980s but failed to achieve his dream of being prime minister when he fell ill with cancer; and Abe's great uncle, Eisuke Sato, held the modern record of service as prime minister, from 1964 to 1972.

The brief election campaign had failed to answer many questions about Abe's views on key issues facing Japan, so the new prime minister's first chance to explain his planned policies came with his opening speech to parliament on September 29. Abe devoted a significant portion of his speech to foreign policy, which was striking in itself because Japan since World War II generally had shied away from controversies overseas. In language that many observers considered exceptionally nationalistic in tone, Abe painted a picture of Japan as an assertive, positive force in world affairs. "I believe it's entirely possible to create a country brimming with attractiveness and vigor, while maintaining the noble virtues of the Japanese people," he said. "I aim for a country that is trusted, revered, and loved by the world and asserts its leadership." This last phrase was bound to raise concerns elsewhere in Asia, where memories of Japan's exercise of regional leadership, prior to World War II, were still raw. Even so, Abe said he hoped for "relationships of trust" with China and South Korea, placing emphasis on communicating with them "candidly and in a forward-looking way."

Abe also said he intended to follow through on one of the few specific pledges during his campaign: revising the Japanese constitution, which had been written by U.S. occupation authorities following World War II. He offered no specifics, except to say he would consult with leaders of the ruling and opposition parties to develop a "clear sense of direction" on any changes. One change widely discussed in Japan was the possible revision of article nine of the constitution, which limited Japan's military to a self-defense role and prohibited involvement in international conflicts. Abe had suggested that article could be amended to give Japan broader leeway to participate in United Nations peacekeeping forces.

Following through on his rhetorical calls for regional dialogue, Abe on October 8 traveled to Beijing for meetings with President Hu Jintao and Prime Minister Wen Jiabao—the first summit sessions between China and Japan in five years. The Chinese greeted Abe warmly, but the day's sessions were overshadowed by a threat by North Korea to conduct its first test of a nuclear weapon. Abe flew to South Korea the next day, October 9, for meetings with President Roh Moo-hyun. Shortly after these meetings North Korea said it had tested a bomb. Although it had been widely assumed for years that North Korea had developed nuclear weapons, this was the first claimed test of such a weapon, and it was a step that heightened regional tensions.

Abe's government quickly imposed unilateral trade sanctions against North Korea. This was an unusual move for Japan, which in the past usually waited for the United States and other countries to take such steps. Because trade between Japan and North Korea was limited, the sanctions had little economic impact and generally were seen primarily as a political statement.

The sense of crisis caused by the North Korean weapons test boosted prospects for several nationalist measures Abe had promoted during his campaign and the early days of his term in office. On December 15, parliament approved landmark measures upgrading the status of the country's Defense Agency to a full cabinet ministry for the first time since World War II and requiring schools to promote patriotism. The government said the latter measure was intended to spur national pride, but critics said it was likely to result in the wider use of textbooks that played down Japanese atrocities during World War II.

The Economy: More Ups and Downs

Koizumi entered office in April 2001 at one of the low points in Japan's long economic slide, and he promised a sweeping series of structural changes in government policy that, he said, would revive the economy and put Japan back on the road to long-term growth. Many of Koizumi's promised changes, which he called reforms, were intended to ease government control of the economy. Although it was, in principle, a capitalist society, Japan since World War II had developed a complex system under which government spending played a much more important role than in the United States. Among other things, the government poured billions of dollars into roads, harbors, and other infrastructure projects that had little practical utility other than subsidizing corporations and providing jobs.

Koizumi's most important reform, by far, also was one of the most controversial actions of his entire time in office: the partial privatization of Japan Post, a giant savings institution associated with the national post office. When Koizumi's plan to sell off much of the postal-savings system was blocked by parliament in August 2005, he called new elections and characterized the voting as a referendum on his plan. The result was an overwhelming victory for Koizumi, and a consequent defeat for those in his party who defended the old ways of conducting government business. During his tenure Koizumi also lowered taxes on high incomes and capital gains—taxes that previous governments had kept high as a means of redistributing wealth in Japanese society. However, numerous other economic measures advocated by Koizumi, such as tightening lending standards for banks, languished in parliament.

An economic recovery began in 2002, but showed signs of slowing in 2004, notably in the second quarter when the gross domestic product shrank for the first time in two years, before entering positive territory again through the first half of 2006. Another slowdown came in the third quarter of 2006, when government figures showed the economy grew by only 0.8 percent, less than half the consensus estimate.

Following are excerpts from the inaugural "policy speech" on September 29, 2006, by Prime Minister Shinzo Abe to the 166th session of the Japanese Diet (parliament).

DOCUMENT

"Policy Speech by Prime Minister to the 165th Session of the Diet"

(Introduction)

I have just been appointed to the office of Prime Minister. As the first Japanese Prime Minister born in the postwar years, and at a time when Japan has come through a severe period and stands at the start of its development in the new century, I am bracing myself to shoulder the heavy responsibilities of directing the national government. I accept the expectations of the many people of Japan squarely and seriously, and I will stake my life on carrying out my duties.

In conducting the affairs of State, I will first clarify my own political stance to the people of Japan and to the members of the Diet. I have no intention of conducting governance for the benefit of specific organizations or individuals; instead I will conduct governance on behalf of the entire people—the ordinary people who live by the sweat of their brows, love their families, wish to improve their own communities and hometowns, and who want to believe in the future of Japan. I promise to make a total commitment to governance that allows everyone to take part, that opens up a new era, and that is aimed at building a society open to everyone and giving each individual a chance to take on challenges.

Thanks to the synergetic effects of the structural reforms covering the entire fabric of Japan's economy and society and of the efforts of the people, the results of the reforms have begun to manifest themselves, and the country is leaving a long tunnel of stagnation, and is in the process of emerging from deflation. Bright prospects are opening before us.

On the other hand, at the very time when population decline is becoming a reality, we are being confronted with several important problems that need to be resolved in the interests of Japan's future development. For example, we face the challenges of the imbalance between urban and rural areas, the concern over the stratification of society into winners and losers, and the continuing severe financial situation. There have been painful incidents fueled by the loss of family values and the mutual support of communities. Scandals have been occurring frequently due to companies that pay little heed to the rules. Furthermore, new threats to international peace and security have arisen such as the missile launches by North Korea (Democratic People's Republic of Korea) and terrorist attacks throughout the world.

Against this background, I consider it my mission as the leader of the country to clearly point out to the nation with courage the direction in which Japan should be moving. The vision I am aiming for is that of "a beautiful country, Japan"—a country filled with vitality, opportunity, and compassion, which cherishes a spirit of self-discipline, and is open to the world. I visualize this beautiful country as follows:

Firstly, "a beautiful country, Japan" is a country that values culture, tradition, history, and nature.

Secondly, "a beautiful country, Japan" is a country underpinned by free society, respects discipline, and has dignity.

Thirdly, "a beautiful country, Japan" is a country that continues to possess the vitality to grow toward the future.

And fourthly, "a beautiful country, Japan" is a country that is trusted, respected, and loved in the world, and which demonstrates leadership.

In order to realize my vision of a beautiful country, I have formed a "Cabinet for the creation of a beautiful country" based on the stable foundation of the coalition government of the Liberal Democratic Party (LDP) and the New Komeito Party. I will strengthen the fundamental functions of the Prime Minister's Office and establish political leadership, so as to enable decision-making which responds quickly and accurately to the changing times in a globalizing world. As part of such efforts, I will eliminate the personnel structure whereby Prime Minister's staff are seconded and rotated by various ministries, and swiftly construct a framework in which the Prime Minister himself selects his staff even from the private sector. With my conviction that a bright future is open before us, I am determined undauntedly to keep the torch of reform burning.

(Constructing an Open Economy Full of Vitality)

It goes without saying that sustained and stable economic growth is indispensable for Japan to prosper as a beautiful country in the 21st century. Economic growth is possible, even when faced with a declining population. I will channel in new vitality to the Japanese economy through the power of innovation and openness.

Aiming at the creation of innovation that contributes to growth, I will compile and put into effect a long-term strategic guideline, "Innovation 25," which will have a range of prospects up to 2025 in medicine, engineering, information technology, and a variety of other fields. By making full use of a world-leading high-speed Internet infrastructure, my goal is to substantially improve productivity by, for example, doubling the number of teleworkers who work from home.

In order for Japan to draw on the growth and vitality of Asia and the world, I will strengthen efforts to conclude Economic Partnership Agreements (EPAs) and will also work towards the resumption of the WTO Doha Round negotiations. I will aim for the early achievement of the plan to double, by 2010, investment from abroad by the GDP ratio, which will also contribute to the vitalization of the local regions. I will develop a Japanese Cultural Industry Strategy, which will reinforce Japan's international competitiveness and capability to dispatch information to the world in the field of contents, including animation and music, as well as food culture, and traditional culture. I will expand the number of major international conferences held in Japan by at least 50 percent within five years, with the aim of making Japan the largest international conference host nation in Asia. Furthermore, I will proceed rapidly to strengthen the functions of international airports in Japan, including efforts to enhance their usability. All in all, I will promote the Asian Gateway Vision, which will make Japan a conduit between Asia and the rest of the world in terms of the flows of people, goods, money, culture, and information.

The kind of society that Japan should aim at is a society in which the efforts of people are rewarded, a society in which there is no stratification into winners and losers, and a society in which ways of working, learning, and living are diverse and multi-tracked- in other words, a society of opportunity where everyone has a chance to challenge again. If there are people who sense they are facing inequality, it is the role of politics to shed light on them. I will promote comprehensive "Challenge Again Assistance Measures" as an important task of my Cabinet.

I will re-examine the current system of employing new graduates en masse, expand the application of social insurance coverage to part-time workers, and strive to lower the barriers preventing people from re-starting employment. For example, I will establish a system that allows people to experience the workplace in order to re-start work, and I will promote the re-employment of experienced workers such as baby boomers. I will also promote the employment of women and elderly people, "NEETs" (people Not in Employment, Education or Training), and "freeters" (job-hopping part-timers), and target a reduction in the number of freeters to 80 percent of the peak level by 2010. I will support fundraising by challenge-again entrepreneurs, and I will promote financing that is not overdependent on personal guarantees. In order to assist such endeavors by the private sector and local governments in support of diverse challenge-again measures, I will establish new Prime Ministerial awards.

A nation will not be vitalized unless its regions are vitalized. With this in mind, I will proceed with the decentralization of power from central government to local governments including the development of a system that will prove essential if highly motivated regions are to develop their own measures freely and be reborn as attractive regions. With the aim of realizing regions with an abundance of knowledge and ingenuity, support will be provided.

I will initiate a "Helping Striving Regions to Help Themselves Program," under which assistance in the form of local allocation taxes will be newly provided to local governments that develop original regional projects, work proactively to identify local products and turn them into brands, tackle the declining birthrate, or attract overseas enterprises.

The vitality of the 4.3 million small and medium enterprises throughout the country is essential to maintain an energetic economy. By making use of the know-how and motivation of these enterprises, I will promote the development and sales of new products and new services that make use of local resources.

As industries that support the local regions, agriculture, forestry, and the fisheries have significant potential as strategic industries suitable for the new century. In order to break the stereotype that Japanese agriculture, forestry, and fishery products including foodstuffs are exclusively for domestic use, I aim to raise the scale of exports of delicious and safe Japanese products to one trillion yen by 2013. Also, I will build a mechanism for the promotion of employment with the aim of realizing two successful careers in one lifetime.

I will seek to establish a new partnership between the public and private sectors by giving support to the providers of public services such as non-profit organizations (NPOs).

(Resolute Implementation of Fiscal Consolidation and Administrative Reform)

Japan is facing an extremely severe fiscal situation. If the population decline continues, and the decrease in the birthrate and the aging of society accelerate, it is clear that an even heavier burden will be placed on future generations. I will unflinchingly work on the integral reform of expenditure and revenue. Under the principle that there can be no fiscal consolidation without growth, a thorough reduction in expenditure and zero-based review will continue, while maintaining economic growth and placing top priority on minimizing the financial burden on taxpayers. I will utilize the Council on Economic and Fiscal Policy (CEFP) in this endeavor.

In order to reduce the GDP ratio of government debt in a stable manner by the mid 2010s, I will systematically carry out expenditure reform during the next five years. Firstly, I will definitely achieve a surplus in the primary balance of the central and local governments in FY2011. I will take first steady steps in budget formulation for the next fiscal year to reach this goal by holding down the issuance of new government bonds to below the level of the current fiscal year of 29.973 trillion yen. This will be achieved by prioritizing budget allocations to areas that contribute to growth, by thoroughly improving efficiency, and by achieving a well-modulated distribution of outlays.

We cannot ask the people to bear an increased burden while doing nothing to cut waste and inefficiency by central and local governments. I will organize a simple yet efficient lean government by steadily promoting fundamental administrative reform. . . .

(Shift to Proactive Diplomacy)

The missiles launched by North Korea this July once again underscored the fact that Japan is faced with a major security issue. In response to the missile launches, Japan took the initiative and proposed a draft resolution to the United Nations Security Council that would impose sanctions on North Korea which, under close coordination with the United States, was adopted unanimously. The times demanded that Japan shift to proactive diplomacy based on new thinking. I will demonstrate the "Japan-U.S. Alliance for Asia and the World" even further, and to promote diplomacy that will actively contribute to stalwart solidarity in Asia.

In order to enable swift decisions under strong political leadership on national security and diplomatic strategies, the headquarters function of the Prime Minister's Office will be reorganized and strengthened, and intelligence gathering functions will also be enhanced.

Regarding the Japan-U.S. alliance, I will put in place a framework that ensures constant communication between the Prime Minister's Office and the White House in order to further consolidate the trust, which forms the bedrock of the alliance. The realignment of U.S. Forces in Japan reduces the burdens on local communities while maintaining the deterrence. Every effort will be made to make its steady progress by listening to the voices from the heart of local communities including Okinawa, and working strenuously on revitalizing those communities.

China (People's Republic of China) and South Korea (Republic of Korea) are important neighboring countries. Japan-China and Japan-South Korea relations are now unprecedentedly close in economic and so many other areas. I believe that strengthening bonds of trust with both countries is extremely important for the Asian region and the entire international community, and it is essential to make mutual efforts so that we can have future-oriented, frank discussions with each other.

There can be no normalization of relations between Japan and North Korea unless the abduction issue is resolved. In order to advance comprehensive measures concerning the abduction issue, I have decided to establish the "Headquarters on the Abduction Issue" chaired by myself, and to assign a secretariat solely dedicated to this Headquarters. Under the policy of dialogue and pressure, I will continue to strongly demand the return of all abductees assuming that they are all still alive. Regarding nuclear and missile issues, I will strive to seek resolution through the Six-Party Talks, while ensuring close coordination between Japan and the United States.

Russia is also an important neighboring country. The development of Japan-Russia relations has vast potential to bring benefits to both countries, and for this reason as well, I will persistently work toward the resolution of the territorial issue.

I will further promote cooperation with the Association of Southeast Asian Nations (ASEAN), and as a democratic nation in Asia, I will engage in strategic dialogues at the leader's level with countries that share fundamental values such as Australia and India, with a view to widening the circle of free societies in Asia as well as in the world.

It is a historic achievement that the Ground Self-Defense Force (GSDF) has completed its humanitarian and reconstruction assistance activities in Iraq without a single casualty. I am proud from my heart of the SDF personnel who toiled with sweat in harsh environment. Japan will continue to assist the reconstruction of Iraq through air lift support by the Air Self-Defense Force (ASDF) and official development assistance (ODA) in coordination with non-governmental organizations (NGOs).

I will make every effort to prevent and eliminate terrorism and international organized crime in cooperation with the international community, including by extending the expiration date of the Anti-Terrorism Special Measures Law.

In light of the changes in the international situation such as the proliferation of weapons of mass destruction (WMDs) and missiles, and the fight against terrorism, as well as the advancements in military technologies, and the rising expectations toward Japan's international contribution, we will thoroughly study individual, specific cases to identify what kind of case falls under the exercise of the right of collective self-defense which is forbidden under the Constitution, so that the Japan-U.S. alliance functions more effectively and peace is maintained.

Japan will provide ODA strategically with the Overseas Economic Cooperation Council headed by myself playing the central role.

As the prices of oil and other resources have been continuing to soar, we will make efforts to ensure the stable provision of energy resources.

It has been 50 years since Japan joined the United Nations. I believe that Japan must take on its full responsibilities through gaining permanent membership in the Security Council. In order to transform the U.N., which was established shortly after WWII, into one that is suitable for the 21st century, Japan will continue its efforts toward U.N. reform including its pursuit of permanent membership in the Security Council.

(Conclusion)

I attach utmost importance to dialogue with the people of Japan. In addition to enhancing the E-mail Magazine and Town Meetings, I will begin "Live Talk Kantei," to talk to the people directly through government internet TV in order to be fully accountable to the people.

It is also important to appeal to the world the charms of "a beautiful country, Japan." In the past, "Made in Japan" was synonymous with poor quality. The late Akio Morita strove to rectify this image, unabashedly emphasizing in the U.S. the high quality of Japanese products, and winning the recognition in the world as a high-quality brand. It is quintessential for Japan to present its new "country identity" for the future to the world, that is, our country's ideals, the direction in which we should aspire, and the way in which we convey our Japanese-ness to the world. I will gather wisdom from across Japan to implement a strategy for overseas public relations.

The country's ideals and vision are embodied in the constitution. The present Constitution of Japan was formulated nearly 60 years ago when Japan was under military occupation. Active discussions have been ongoing regarding the formulation of a constitution that befits a new era. I hope that discussions within and among the ruling and opposition parties will be further deepened, and there will emerge clear sense of direction. As the first step, I hope for an early enactment of a bill on the procedures for amending the Constitution.

Our country Japan possesses beautiful nature, long history, culture and traditions, which we could be proud of in the world. With this tacit pride in our hearts, the time has now come to take a step forward toward a new nation building.

Once, when Albert Einstein visited Japan, he said, "It is my sincere wish that the Japanese people keep intact and never forget those traits which you have intrinsically possessed: humbleness and simplicity essential to an individual, pure and calm Japanese heart." I believe it is fully possible to build a 21st century Japan, which retains the Japanese virtues which Einstein admired, and filled with charm and vitality. I believe that the Japanese people have the ability to realize this.

I hope that all the people of Japan who want to challenge together in this new nation building will take part. It is the responsibility of politics to ensure an environment in which anybody can participate regardless of age, gender, or disability. Together with the hardened generation born before and during the war, and the young people who are eager to contribute to the people and the country, I will put all my body and soul in leading the challenge to create "a beautiful country, Japan," a country admired and respected by people in the world, a country our children's generation can have self-confidence and pride in.

I ask from my heart for the understanding and cooperation of the people of Japan and the members of the Diet.

Source: Japan. Prime Minister of Japan and His Cabinet. "Policy Speech by Prime Minister Shinzo Abe to the 165th Session of the Diet." September 29, 2006. Provisional translation. www.kantei.go.jp/foreign/abespeech/2006/09/29speech_e.html (accessed December 8, 2006).

Other Historic Documents of Interest

International attitudes toward the United States, p. 286
North Korean nuclear weapons issue, p. 606

Outlook for the U.S. economy, p. 151
State of the Union, p. 23

October

House Speaker Hastert on Foley Resignation

October 5, 2006

Republican representative Mark Foley of Florida abruptly resigned his U.S. House seat on September 29, 2006, amid allegations that he had made inappropriate advances to teenage male House pages. Attention immediately focused on whether and how long the House leadership had known about Foley's misconduct and whether they could have or should have done more to protect the pages, who generally are high school juniors who live on Capitol Hill for a year and run errands for lawmakers. Democrats and even a handful of Republicans called on House Speaker J. Dennis Hastert, R-Ill., to resign. But Hastert refused, maintaining that he did not know anything about Foley's misconduct until the day he resigned.

Foley's resignation and the resulting fallout could not have come at a worse time for Republicans. In the previous twelve months, three Republican House members, including former majority leader Tom DeLay of Texas, had resigned under an ethics cloud, and allegations of financial wrongdoing and misconduct continued to swirl around several specific legislators, most of them Republican. Those allegations, and the failure of the Republican leadership to strengthen House and Senate rules of conduct and ethics, had given Democrats a powerful campaign tool to use in the November 7 midterm elections. The Foley incident, coming just five weeks before the elections, allowed Democrats to reinforce the message.

In December an inquiry by the House ethics committee cleared Hastert and other lawmakers of violating any House rules in the matter but chastised them for ignoring early signals that Foley might be menacing young boys. By that time, however, the damage had been done. Democrats took Foley's seat in the election along with twenty-nine others held by Republicans, giving them control of the House in the next Congress. As a result of those losses, Hastert announced he would not seek a leadership job in the Republican minority and would instead join the rest of the GOP rank and file.

Foley's Resignation

Foley was a well-liked, affable, six-term legislator from Florida who served as a top deputy in the House Republican whip operation. He resigned his seat, and withdrew from the election, on September 29 after news organizations disclosed his sexually explicit e-mail exchanges with teenagers and young men who had served as House pages. ABCNews.com broke the story about the e-mails on September 28. The Web site reported that a former sixteen-year-old page became uncomfortable with some messages allegedly sent by Foley, which included inquiries about the youth's well being, what he wanted for his birthday, and a request that he send Foley a picture of himself. In an excerpt of a separate e-mail published on the Web site, the youth wrote, "Maybe it is just me being paranoid, but seriously. This freaked me out." The former page later called the e-mails from Foley "sick sick sick sick sick."

On September 29, ABCNews.com published additional, sexually explicit, instant message transcripts described as being between Foley and former pages. Foley resigned that afternoon. "I am deeply sorry and I apologize for letting down my family and the people of Florida I have had the privilege to represent," he said in a statement. In the following days, attorney David Roth announced that Foley was entering a treatment facility for alcoholism and that a member of the clergy had sexually abused him as a youth. Roth acknowledged that Foley was gay and said that he had written many of the explicit e-mails when he had been drinking. But the attorney denied that Foley had ever had sexual contact with a minor.

Leadership Crisis

Almost as soon as Foley resigned, reports began to circulate that a handful of Republican legislators and staff members, including some in Hastert's office, had known about Foley's contacts with former pages long before he resigned but had taken no action against Foley. Hastert himself contributed to the confusion and contradictory stories swirling around Capitol Hill and the media when, immediately after Foley resigned, he stated that he had only just learned about Foley's problem that day. After other legislators came forward to say they had previously discussed the matter with Hastert's office and with Hastert himself, the Speaker revised his position, saying on September 30 that he did "not explicitly recall" any conversation about the matter.

Meanwhile, Democrats immediately assailed the Republican leadership for not dealing with Foley's misconduct much sooner. Democrats also suggested the Republicans had failed to act because they did not want another scandal to erupt right before the election. Senate Minority Leader Harry Reid called for a criminal probe. "The allegations against Congressman Foley are repugnant," Reid said, "but equally as bad is the possibility that Republican leaders in the House of Representatives knew there was a problem and ignored it to preserve a congressional seat this year."

The Republican leadership also had to fend off attacks from its own conservative wing. Paul M. Weyrich, a conservative activist, reported on a conference call held among about six dozen leaders of socially conservative groups on October 2. "They are outraged by how Hastert handled this," Weyrich told the *Washington Post.* Some Republicans worried openly that evangelical Christians, who formed the party's voting core, would protest by not going to the polls on November 7. Several conservative leaders, including Weyrich, called on Hastert to resign, and many Republicans in tight election races tried to put distance not only between themselves and Foley but also between themselves and the GOP leadership, notably Hastert.

By October 3, however, Republican House leaders were actively defending Hastert. President George W. Bush also weighed in for the first time October 3, saying he was "dismayed and shocked" to learn of Foley's "unacceptable behavior" and praising Hastert's integrity. "I know Denny Hastert, I meet with him a lot....He is a father, teacher, coach, who cares about the children of this country. I know that he wants all the facts to come out, and I know that he wants to ensure that all the children up on Capitol Hill are protected."

For his part, Hastert turned to conservative talk radio to say he had no intention of resigning and that calls for his ouster were clearly tied to the elections. Hastert also continued to defend his handling of the situation. At an October 5 news conference at his Batavia, Illinois, congressional office, Hastert took full responsibility for missed opportunities for stopping Foley sooner. "I'm deeply sorry that this has happened," he said. "And the bottom line is that we're taking responsibility, because, ultimately, as someone has said in Washington before, the buck stops here."

But the Speaker continued to maintain that members of his staff only knew about the e-mail message to the sixteen-year-old and not about the sexually explicit messages. "When the Congress found out about the explicit messages, Republicans dealt with it immediately and the culprit was gone," he said at the Batavia news conference.

Hours after Foley resigned, the House unanimously passed a resolution calling on its ethics committee, formally known as the Committee on Standards of Official Conduct, to undertake an investigation. On October 1 Hastert asked U.S. Attorney General Alberto Gonzalez and Florida governor Jeb Bush to begin investigations of the Foley matter. Hastert also said he would take steps to ensure the safety of the students in the page program. He planned to strengthen the adult supervision of the program and set up a toll-free number to the House clerk's office for current and former pages and their parents to report misconduct.

Ethics Committee Exoneration

On December 8, the House ethics subcommittee released an eighty-nine page report taking Hastert, other lawmakers, and congressional aides to task for not doing more to protect pages from Foley's apparently homosexual advances. However, the panel said none of the legislators or aides had violated any laws or House rules, and it recommended that no further action be taken in the case.

The panel said Hastert and others had "failed to exercise appropriate diligence and oversight" of Foley's contact with pages. "Rather than addressing the issues fully, some . . . did far too little, while attempting to pass the responsibility for acting to others. Some relied on unreasonably fine distinctions regarding their defined responsibilities. Almost no one followed up adequately on the limited actions they did take," the subcommittee said.

In a statement released by his office, Hastert said he was "glad the committee made clear that there was no violation of any House rules by any member or staff." He also noted that the inquiry "uncovered no evidence" indicating that any lawmaker or House officials knew about any explicit instant messages that Foley had been sending former pages—although the committee did find that Hastert's chief of staff knew as early as 2002 or 2003 about possibly inappropriate behavior by Foley and that "concerns" about Foley had been raised soon after he entered Congress in 1995. Howard Berman, the ranking Democrat on the ethics committee and on the subcommittee inquiring into the scandal, defended the panel's conclusions as "the right report on this subject." He said its "most important contribution" was to "tell the story of what happened."

Following is the text of a news conference held by Speaker of the House J. Dennis Hastert, R-Ill., at his congressional office in Batavia, Illinois, on October 5, 2006, where he discussed his handling of the scandal involving the resignation of Rep. Mark Foley, R-Fla.

█████ **DOCUMENT** █████

"House Speaker Hastert Holds News Conference, Batavia, Ill."

Well, thank you very much for everybody showing up today.

I'm sorry—you know, when you talk about the page issue and what's happened in the Congress, I'm deeply sorry that this has happened. And the bottom line is that we're taking responsibility, because ultimately, as someone has said in Washington before: The buck stops here.

For something like this to occur, our system obviously isn't designed for the electronic age of instant messages.

When the Congress found out about the explicit messages, Republicans dealt with it immediately and the culprit was gone. We are now trying to correct the problem. We've asked the Ethics Committee to look into this matter and we asked for criminal investigations to be opened by the Justice Department, the FBI, and the State of Florida.

We have a toll-free number where people can confidently call. And we've reached out to experts around the country to put a system in place to make sure this never happens again. The tip number is 1–866–384–0481.

We will do everything possible to make the program safe for the kids while they're in our care in Washington, D.C. And we will make sure that we can be a resource for their parents once they return home.

We are looking for a person of high caliber to advise us on the page program. I reached out to the Democrat leader and shared with her some of the ideas and we hope to resolve this soon.

Final point: Our children need to be protected. And we're going to do everything we can to protect them.

I'll take some questions.

Question: In the [*Chicago*] *Tribune* the report is saying that the people who want to see this thing blow up are ABC News and a lot of Democratic operatives, people funded by George Soros. Are you maintaining, Mr. Speaker, that this story was fueled by political opponents?

Hastert: No. On that point, I only know what I've seen in the press and what I've heard. There's no ultimate, real source of information, but that's what I've read. And that's what I've heard in the press.

And so the fact is: We've turned this whole thing over to the FBI for us to try to find out what happened. And that's what we want to do. And any member of Congress that is involved in this, or any staffer, needs to comply. And the results will be there.

Question: Mr. Speaker, will you set the record straight on a couple of things? Tell us once again, if you will, when you learned that there was more than a minor problem, that this was truly something that had a predatory feel to it? And secondly, after you've answered that question, if you really did only learn a week or so ago, were you not let down by staff members who seem to have known much more and if heads ought to role, shouldn't some of them come from your own staff if not you personally?

Hastert: I, first of all, learned of this last Friday, when we were about to leave Congress for the break, to go out and campaign. And that's the first time that I heard of the explicit language.

When it happened, Republicans acted. And the guy's gone. But the fact is that I don't know who knew what, when. We know that there are reports of people that knew it and, kind of fed it out or leaked it to the press.

You know, that's why we've asked for an investigation. So let me just say—that's why we've asked for an investigation: to find who that is. If it's members of my staff or they didn't do the job, we will act appropriately. If it's somebody else's staff, they ought to act appropriately as well.

Question: Nobody's admitted it to you? No one in your own staff has acknowledged knowing the seriousness of the problem, one, two, or three years ago and, certainly, no one told you about it?

Hastert: No.

Question: And, if they didn't, were they derelict?

Hastert: I didn't hear the rest of your question.

Question: Were they derelict, Mr. Speaker, if they didn't let you know what was going on?

Hastert: Well, my staff has been—if somebody didn't let us know, then there's a problem. And I think the investigation will find that out.

Question: How were the e-mails characterized? How were they characterized? Were they just "overly friendly?" And not only as the speaker, but as a former teacher, coach, did that not ring any alarms to you?

Hastert: We were advised—in our office and then to the clerk's office and then to the chairman of the page board, that there was a Katrina message, period. We knew of no other e-mails—we—in that system. There were no other e-mails other than that one that I know of. And we didn't even have the e-mail because the parents didn't want to give the e-mail out. They said, "Stop it."

The guy that I asked to do that job a long time ago was John Shimkus. John Shimkus is an Army ranger. He's a tough guy. He goes right to the point when there's a problem. He confronted the member. And the member said that he would stop doing that; asked if there was any other messages, he said no. And he said, "Don't do it again." You know, that's what we did. The parents were happy.

Could we have done it better? Could the page board have handled it better? In retrospect, probably, yes. But at that time, what we knew and what we acted upon was what we had.

Question: Mr. Speaker, Kirk Fordham said that he passed this information along to Scott Palmer as early as 2002, four years ago.

Hastert: You know, it's interesting: Kirk Fordham also said just about three or four days ago that he worked for this guy for 10 years and he never did anything wrong. So there's a little bit of difference in the testimony or what he said.

Question: Mr. Speaker, over the last several days I'm sure you've been considering your own future and the impact of all of this upon the upcoming election. Why have you decided to remain, if that's what you have decided, and will there be any other changes among the Republican leadership?

Hastert: I'm going to run, and presumably win, in this election. And when we do, I expect to run for leader—for speaker. And, you know, I think everybody else will too. But our members ultimately make that decision.

Question: Mr. Speaker, there are reports that you've told some conservative groups that if you view that your staying as speaker hurts the party, that you would step down. Could you tell us what—

Hastert: Well, ultimately, any time that a person has to, as a leader, be on the hot seat and he is a detriment to the party, you know, there ought to be a change. I became speaker in a situation like that.

I don't think that's the case. I said I haven't done anything wrong, obviously. And we need to come back. What we need to do is start talking about the issues.

We have a great economy. It's because of Republican tax cuts and Republican handling of the economy, of holding the line on spending.

We have addressed the war on terror. We've done that continually over the last five years, and today we have a pretty safe America.

And, you know, a lot of people wanted us to address the issue about the border, and we did exactly that. And, you know, last Friday, we culminated in appropriations that did fix the border.

So, you know, we have a good story to tell.

Our friends on the other side of the aisle really don't have a story to tell. And maybe they're resolving to another way to—to—another political tactic.

Thank you very much.

Source: CQ.com. CQ Transcriptions. "House Speaker Hastert Holds News Conference, Batavia, Ill." October 5, 2006 (accessed March 8, 2007).

Other Historic Documents of Interest

DeLay resignation from Congress,
   p. 264

Ethics scandals, p. 103
Midterm elections, p. 645

Census Bureau on
U.S. Population Growth

October 12, 2006

■■■■■■■■■■■ **THE DOCUMENT IN CONTEXT** ■■■■■■■■

Fueled by a strong birth rate, rising life expectancy, and immigration, the U.S. population surpassed 300 million in 2006, reaching an estimated 300,888,812 people as of January 1, 2007, according to the U.S. Census Bureau. The country reached the 200 million mark in 1967 and was expected to reach 400 million in 2043 if current demographic trends continued. The United States remained the third largest country in the world, behind China (with 1.3 billion people) and India (1.1 billion), and it was the only developed country to be steadily gaining population. Japan and Russia were losing population, as were some European countries, such as Italy; in many European countries the birthrate was stagnant. Currently at 6.5 billion, the world's population was expected to top 9 billion by 2050.

In a news release dated October 12, 2006, the Census Bureau said the 300 million mark would officially be reached at 7:46 a.m. Eastern Daylight Time on October 17, but many demographers thought that the milestone had probably quietly come and gone weeks or even months earlier. It could not be determined who the 300 millionth person was—a newborn baby or an immigrant coming into the United States, either legally or illegally. The fact that the official benchmark arrived just three weeks before the midterm election in which immigration and border security were major campaign issues may have helped explain why there was relatively little fanfare in Washington marking the event. In a statement released late in the day on October 17, President George W. Bush said the continued population growth was "a testament to our country's dynamism. So long as we insist on high standards in education, place our trust in the talents and ingenuity of ordinary Americans, and protect our freedoms, we will remain the land of opportunity for generations to come." In comparison, when the population reached 200 million in 1967, President Lyndon B. Johnson held a news conference at the Commerce Department to commemorate the event, using the occasion to talk about the achievements of the past and the challenges ahead.

Almost everyone agreed that America's growing population and demographic shifts would present challenges that affected virtually every aspect of American life. But the severity of each of those challenges—including issues of race and ethnicity, providing for an aging population, and degradation of the environment—as well as the country's capacity for dealing with them was a matter of great debate.

Birth, Death, and Immigration Rates

The United States population grew by about 2.8 million people in 2006. About 40 percent of that increase was attributable to immigration. The remaining growth was attributable to the increase from births minus the loss from deaths. In 2006 the Census Bureau's "population clock" estimated a birth every seven seconds, a death every thirteen seconds, and a new immigrant every thirty-one seconds, amounting to one new U.S. resident every eleven seconds. For 2007 the clock predicted a slight slowing, to one new resident every fifteen seconds.

Immigrants comprised 12 percent of the U.S. population in 2006; an estimated 11 million to 12 million of these immigrants were illegal (many demographers believed the accurate number was higher). The share of immigrants was more than double the 5 percent share in 1967 but was still a smaller proportion than in 1915, when foreign-born residents composed 15 percent of the population. Then the leading country of origin was Germany; in 1967 it was Italy, and in 2006 it was Mexico. About 55 percent of the population growth since 1967 was attributable to immigrants and their children and grandchildren, according to the Pew Hispanic Center, a nonpartisan research organization. Had all immigration been stopped in 1967, the population would have grown by only about 45 million, to 245 million in 2006. Moreover, the center noted, a much greater proportion of the immigrants since 1967 were Hispanic and Asian, rather than white and black, leading to even broader racial and ethnic diversity in the United States than it had historically enjoyed.

The Census Bureau reported that while California, Florida, New York, and Texas continued to have the largest concentrations of immigrants, immigrant populations were growing in almost every state and many large cities as newcomers to the country moved away from their traditional points of entry in search of better jobs and more affordable homes. South Carolina's immigrant population grew by 47 percent between 2000 and 2005, the most of any state.

Race and Ethnicity

According to the U.S. Census Bureau, Hispanics, African Americans, Asians, and other racial minorities accounted for about one of every three Americans in 2006. The largest minority group, at about 43 million, was Hispanics, who could be of any race. Non-Hispanic blacks made up the second largest group, at about 40 million. There were about 14.5 million Asians, 4.5 million American Indians and Alaska natives, and just under 1 million native Hawaiians and other Pacific islanders. Non-Hispanic whites totaled about 200 million. *(Background on Hispanic population, Historic Documents of 2003, p. 349)*

Based on current trends, by 2043 about 24 percent of the nation's residents would be Hispanic, about 15 percent non-Hispanic black, and about 8 percent Asian. Non-Hispanic whites would make up only a bare majority of the population. Whites were already a minority in four states—California, Hawaii, New Mexico, and Texas—as well as in the District of Columbia and were on their way to becoming a minority in Georgia, Maryland, and Nevada. The proportion of whites in the total population grew in only two states between 2000 and 2005—Hawaii, where they were a minority, and West Virginia. Demographers also expected whites to become a minority in at least thirty-five of the nation's fifty largest cities by mid-century.

An even bigger change was likely to be the blurring of racial lines. More than 7 million Americans reported in the 2000 census that they were multiracial. William H. Frey, a demographer at the Brookings Institution in Washington, D.C., predicted that by 2050 as much as 30 percent of the population would be multiracial. "The fact that today we see young people intermarrying more, interracial dating much more common—all of that I think portends that we're going to become much more ecumenical in the way we look at things than we were in the past," Frey told the *Christian Science Monitor.* "I think we'll have much more tolerance for people of other backgrounds, cultures, and languages, points of view, and religious and belief systems." Carl Haub, a senior demographer for the Population Reference Bureau, agreed. "The baby who's born this year, as they grow up, they may not know what we mean by diversity. And somewhere along mid-century the word majority will disappear," Haub told the *New York Times.*

An Aging Population

Another significant change was the aging of the American population. Thanks to medical advances, improvements in diet and health care, and higher standards of living, life expectancy rose from 70.5 years in 1967 to 77.8 years in 2006 and was expected to reach 85 or even 90 years by mid-century. Currently, nearly 37 million people, or about 12 percent of U.S. residents, were age 65 or older in 2006 and 5 million of those were 85 or older. Those numbers were projected to go even higher as the massive baby boom generation (those born between 1946 and 1964) began to reach senior status, starting in 2011. Projections suggested that by mid-century 20 percent of the population would be 65 or older. Meanwhile, the share of the population of working age was declining.

The age shift was also marked by a racial shift, with whites being proportionately older and minorities being younger overall. The median age for whites was 40.3 years, compared with 27.2 for Hispanics, 30.0 for blacks, and 33.2 for Asians. The age shift in the population was expected to create substantial stress as the huge number of aging citizens made unprecedented demands on the nation's health care and pension systems.

Dangers of Overpopulation

Some individuals and groups opposed to immigration and population growth used the milestone to highlight their concerns. They pointed to suburban sprawl, traffic congestion, overcrowded schools and hospitals, and a continuing loss of open land to development as evidence that population growth in general and immigration in particular were contributing to a decline in the quality of American life. Others saw advantages to continued immigration, ranging from the cultural richness offered by people of different nationalities to the vitality of the workforce that would help keep the United States competitive in a global economy. Without steady inflows of younger workers, some demographers noted, the United States would look much more like Japan and many parts of Europe, where societies were aging even more quickly than in the United States, putting intense pressure on economies struggling to grow.

Many environmentalists raised concerns about the impact of a growing population on the environment, citing rising demands for water and energy resources, as more and more people moved into water-scarce areas of the country and commuted longer distances. Between 1967 and 2006 the number of households doubled, the number of motor vehicles more than doubled, and the number of miles driven nearly tripled. Even the amount of trash generated rose dramatically, from a little more than three pounds for every American to five pounds per person. "The natural resource base that is required to support each person keeps rising," Michael Replogle, the transportation director for Environmental Defense, told the Associated Press. "We're heating and cooling more space, and the housing units are more spread out than ever before." Greater energy consumption, particularly of fossil fuels, would also contribute to global warming, which in turn was expected to make some of the most heavily populated areas of the United States extremely vulnerable to flooding, while temperature changes could affect food production.

Some futurists projected that technology and economics would force Americans to develop new, more efficient habits of consumption. "I feel very hopeful that the evolution to the solar age could happen much quicker than we might have expected because it's being driven by so many stress points, from global warming to water shortages to desertification," futurist Hazel Henderson told the *Christian Science Monitor* in October. "Cars will be getting 100 m.p.g. if they're still using gasoline instead of fuel cells. . . . Cities and towns will get more and more compact as these sprawling suburbs end up being too costly and inefficient." Others saw dangers in such thinking. "We have sort of a cornucopia fantasy. People say, 'Not to worry. Technology will solve the problem,'" said Russell Hopfenberg, a consulting faculty member at Duke University. "Don't get lulled into complacency," he warned.

Social Trends

While not directly related to population growth, several social trends were likely to have an impact on how society dealt with its effects. According to an analysis by the *New York Times* of the Census Bureau's American Community Survey, married couples made up just under 50 percent of all American households in 2005, down about three percentage points from 2000. Most of the rest were made up of single households or groups of singles. Slightly more than 5 percent of households were made up of unmarried opposite-sex couples, and less than 1 percent (about 776,000) households were made up of gay or lesbian couples. The trend away from marriage was reflected primarily in younger households—those where the householder was under 35.

Other data from the Census Bureau appeared to confirm the *Times* findings, showing that both men and women were waiting longer to marry. The median age of marriage for men was 27.1 years in 2005; for women, it was 25.8 years. By the time they reached their early thirties, however, 72 percent of all Americans had been married, and 96 percent of all men and women age 65 and older had been married at some point in their lives. At the same time, more women were giving birth to babies out-of-wedlock. In 2005, 37 percent of all births were to unmarried women, the highest level ever recorded. The biggest increase was among unmarried women in their twenties. Teenage pregnancies, which had been steadily declining, dropped to their lowest levels ever.

Whether never married, divorced, or widowed, with children or without, the growing proportion of Americans who remained single represented a trend that "changes the social weight of marriage in the economy, in the work force, in sales of homes and rentals, and who manufacturers advertise to," Stephanie Coontz of the Council on Contemporary Families told the *Times*. "It certainly challenges the way we set up our work policies," she said, adding that "we have an anachronistic view as to what extent you can use marriage to organize the distribution and redistribution of benefits."

Following is the text of a press release issued October 12, 2006, by the U.S. Census Bureau announcing that the U.S. population was expected to reach 300 million on October 17, 2006.

DOCUMENT

"Nation's Population to Reach 300 Million on Oct. 17"

The U.S. Census Bureau today reported that the nation's population will reach the historic milestone of 300 million on Oct. 17 at about 7:46 a.m. (EDT). This comes almost 39 years after the 200 million mark was reached on Nov. 20, 1967.

The estimate is based on the expectation that the United States will register one birth every seven seconds and one death every 13 seconds between now and Oct. 17, while net international migration is expected to add one person every 31 seconds. The result is an increase in the total population of one person every 11 seconds.

Source: U.S. Department of Commerce. Census Bureau. Public Information Office. "Nation's Population to Reach 300 Million on Oct. 17." Press release CB06-156, October 12, 2006. www.census.gov/Press-Release/ www/releases/archives/population/007616.html (accessed January 22, 2007).

Other Historic Documents of Interest

UN Security Council on Nuclear Weapons Tests by North Korea

October 14, 2006

North Korea in October conducted a low-level nuclear explosion, thus confirming its claim that it had developed nuclear weapons. The explosion came a little more than a year after North Korea signed an agreement with four of its neighbors and the United States promising to give up its nuclear weapons—an agreement that had been on hold ever since.

As with all of its previous actions on the nuclear issue, North Korea's bomb test clearly was intended to get the world's attention. It succeeded, but probably not in the way Pyongyang had hoped. The test so angered China, which had been North Korea's chief benefactor and protector, that Beijing quickly supported a drive at the United Nations by Japan and the United States to impose economic sanctions against North Korea. The sanctions were tougher punishment of its neighbor than anything China had been willing to support in the past. At year's end it was unclear whether the sanctions would force North Korea back to the bargaining table or would drive it to even more extreme behavior. *(Background, Historic Documents of 2005, p. 604)*

North Korea was one of two countries under international pressure to halt work toward nuclear weapons. The other was Iran, which reportedly was still several years from building an actual weapon but moving quickly toward that goal. The United States and its European allies had engaged for two years in unsuccessful negotiations to persuade Iran to drop its weapons program. It was widely assumed that North Korea's nuclear test might further embolden Iran to resist the international pressure.

Stalled Negotiations

It had been clear for years that North Korea was attempting to build nuclear weapons, and a 1994 agreement with the United States temporarily derailed one weapons program based on the extraction of plutonium from a reactor near the city of Yongbyon, north of the capital. The Bush administration in 2002 accused North Korea of violating that agreement by developing a weapons program using a different fuel—highly enriched uranium. North Korea responded by withdrawing from the 1994 agreement and ousting inspectors from the International Atomic Energy Agency, which had been monitoring the Yongbyon reactor.

The first in a series of Six-Party Talks between North Korea and five countries that had an interest in preventing it from getting nuclear weapons—China, Japan, Russia, South Korea, and the United States—convened in China in 2003. These negotiations took place intermittently for two years until a dramatic breakthrough on September 19,

2005, when North Korea signed an agreement promising to end its weapons program in exchange for aid. Unresolved issues were tabled for subsequent meetings, and after another round of negotiations in November 2005 the Six-Party Talks were put on the back burner when North Korea said it would boycott any future meetings. Pyongyang objected bitterly to U.S. sanctions against a bank in Macao that gave Pyongyang access to the international financial system. The Bush administration said it imposed the sanctions because North Korea had used the bank to launder the proceeds from narcotics trafficking and counterfeiting of U.S. currency. North Korea twice invited a senior U.S. envoy, Christopher R. Hill, to Pyongyang for direct negotiations, but the Bush administration rebuffed the invitation and said negotiations could take place only in the context of the Six-Party Talks.

With the nuclear talks on hold, Pyongyang and Washington exchanged heated rhetoric throughout the first months of 2006, with each side accusing the other of bad faith. The war of words escalated in mid-June when the Bush administration warned that North Korea was preparing to test a long-range missile, the Taepodong-2, which had been under development for many years. The missile had the potential to reach Alaska and possibly parts of the western United States, but it was widely assumed that North Korea had not yet built a nuclear bomb that could be carried on such a missile. North Korea frequently tested short-range missiles but had not tested such a long-range missile since 1998. Under pressure from the Clinton administration, North Korea in 1999 had declared a moratorium on further tests.

China, Japan, South Korea, and other countries warned North Korea against testing the Taepodong-2 missile, and prominent officials from the former Clinton administration even suggested that the United States destroy the missile on its launching pad. Pyongyang ignored the warnings and fired seven missiles on July 4. One of the missiles was a Taepodong-2, according to U.S. officials, but it failed during its first phase, less than one minute after launch. Weapons experts noted that even a failed test could provide useful information for North Korea. The United States monitored the test with its Aegis missile-tracking system aboard naval ships in the Sea of Japan.

The Bush administration in 2001 began building an ambitious and expensive missile defense system, largely because of the potential threat of North Korean missiles; by 2006, however, that system was still incomplete and most of its tests had been failures. Bush said on July 7 that the United States would have had "a reasonable chance" of shooting down the North Korean missile had it remained airborne, but most independent experts disputed that assertion. *(Missile defense background, Historic Documents of 2004, p. 176)*

The White House condemned the North Korean missile test as "provocative behavior," and officials in the United States and Japan immediately began talking about imposing tough international sanctions to punish Pyongyang. China and Russia were not yet ready for such a step, however, and each had veto power in the United Nations Security Council. South Korea, which long had pushed for international engagement with the north, also took a softer line on the missile test. While obviously concerned about the possibility of North Korea having both nuclear weapons and long-range missiles, China and South Korea were worried even more that international pressure could force the collapse of Kim Jong Il's regime, resulting in chaos and a surge of refugees across their borders.

The Security Council on July 15 took a limited step, unanimously adopting Resolution 1695, which condemned North Korea's missile test and called on other countries to block the export to North Korea of money or supplies that could be used for missiles or nuclear weapons. The resolution also called on North Korea to return immediately to the Six-Party Talks. Although the Security Council often had discussed North Korea's nuclear weapons ambitions, this was the council's first resolution on the matter since 1993.

North Korea's Test

Any expectation that the international condemnation of North Korea's missile test would prevent Pyongyang from taking further provocative steps proved wrong. On October 3, North Korea announced that it planned to conduct "a nuclear test" in the future, without giving a date. There had been reports since May 2005 that North Korea was preparing to test a nuclear weapon for the first time—a step experts said was necessary before any country could know whether its work toward a bomb actually was successful. A U.S. intelligence estimate early in 2006 reportedly suggested that North Korea had accumulated enough fuel for about a half-dozen bombs; previous estimates by U.S. officials and independent experts had said North Korea might have built anywhere from two to a dozen bombs.

Once again, China, South Korea, and other countries warned North Korea not to follow through on its threats, and the UN Security Council on October 6 issued a statement expressing "deep concern" about the proposed test. The warnings did no good. On the morning of October 9, North Korea announced that it had "successfully conducted an underground nuclear test." In rhetoric typical of such statements, it added that the test came "at a stirring time when all the people of the country are making a great leap forward in the building of a great, prosperous, powerful socialist nation."

Based on seismographic measurements of the impact of the test, U.S. weapons experts said the North Korean bomb appeared to be a very small one, possibly with the destructive power of only about one kiloton—a fraction of the U.S. nuclear bombs that destroyed the Japanese cities of Hiroshima and Nagasaki in 1945. Some experts also suggested the test was, at best, a partial success.

Regardless of whether it was a technical failure or success, the North Korean nuclear test had an enormous political impact. Condemnations poured in from capitals all over the world. The most important came from China, Russia, and South Korea—all of which, at various stages, resisted the Bush administration's hard-line approach to Pyongyang. Suddenly, with North Korea having twice in three months defied international calls for restraint, these three countries now had little choice but to take a tougher position. In an exceptionally angry statement, China said the test was "flagrant and brazen," and Beijing for the first time said it would support "punitive actions" in response. Russian president Vladimir Putin said in a televised meeting with his cabinet that the test had inflicted "huge damage" on the decades-long effort to halt the spread of nuclear weapons. South Korean president Roh Moo-Huyn called the test "a grave threat to peace, not only in the Korean peninsula but in the region." U.S. president George W. Bush used similar language, adding a warning to North Korea that any attempt by it to export nuclear technology to other countries or terrorist groups "would be considered a grave threat to the United States" and North Korea would be held "fully accountable." U.S. officials and weapons experts in the past had accused North Korea of selling missile systems and components to Iran, Libya, Syria, and several other countries.

Security Council Resolution

The UN Security Council often spent weeks, or even months, debating how to respond to important world events. The debate over a response to North Korea's nuclear test was extraordinarily short, lasting less than five days while China, Russia, and the United States negotiated just how strong to make the language. The final version, adopted unanimously on October 14 as Resolution 1718, strongly condemned the test and imposed a range of sanctions intended to curtail North Korea's trade in weapons and to prevent Kim Jong-Il and other senior officials from getting access to luxury goods. U.S. officials had accused the North Korean leader and his senior colleagues of importing large quantities of fine liquors and expensive automobiles while the vast majority of their countrymen lived in extreme poverty.

The key compromise in negotiations on the resolution involved a proposal by Japan and the United States requiring countries trading with North Korea to inspect all cargo headed to or coming from that country. At China's insistence, the final resolution simply called on countries to inspect shipments to or from North Korea—something China said it would not do. Japan, which had been one of North Korea's most important trading partners, already had imposed a series of economic sanctions against that country in response to the nuclear test.

Bush administration officials portrayed North Korea's test, and the Security Council response, in historic terms. John Bolton, the U.S. ambassador to the United Nations, said that the test "unquestionably poses one of the gravest threats to international peace and security that this council has ever had to confront." Bolton described the council's resolution as "clear, firm, and punitive action." North Korea condemned the resolution, with its UN ambassador, Pak Gil Yon, saying the Security Council had acted in "gangster-like" fashion.

In the weeks after the Security Council acted, all of North Korea's neighbors announced plans to curtail trade with that country, including South Korea, which in the past had been reluctant to abandon its policy of improving relations with the north. However, reporters who visited key border crossings between China and North Korea reported that trade continued as before, with no sign that Chinese officials had ordered inspections of goods passing across the border.

The UN sanctions appeared to have a political impact on North Korea, however. On October 31, the Pyongyang government announced that it was willing to return to the Six-Party Talks for the first time in nearly a year. This move resulted from secret meetings in Beijing between Hill, the senior U.S. envoy, and his North Korean counterpart, Kim Kye-Gwan; such meetings were the kind of direct contacts the Bush administration had long said it would not accept with North Korea. The two envoys met in Beijing again in late November. During those sessions, U.S. officials said, Hill offered a package of economic aid and energy assistance to North Korea in exchange for its renunciation of nuclear weapons. Once again, this step ran counter to what had been a strict Bush administration policy of opposing what some officials called "concessions" to North Korea.

The Six-Party Talks resumed in Beijing on December 18 and lasted five days, but no apparent breakthroughs were made despite at least one new direct meeting between Hill and the North Koreans. Hill told reporters on December 22 that this series of talks faltered on North Korea's demand that the United States take the first step toward any agreement by lifting its financial sanctions against that country. Of North Korea's penchant for raising problems during the negotiations, he said, "one day it's financial issues, another day it's something they want but know they can't have, another day it's something we said about them that hurt their feelings. What they need to do is to get serious about the issue that made them such a problem . . . their nuclear activities."

UN Aid to North Korea Ended

The UN's World Food Programme said on January 6 that it had ended all its programs that had provided food for about one-third of North Korea's 22 million people. The North Korean government had demanded the end to such aid programs, saying the country had a bumper crop in the 2005 fall harvest and now needed aid for economic development rather than humanitarian emergencies. A severe famine in the mid-1990s caused widespread hardship in the country and led to the UN aid program, one of the largest in the world. Despite the political disagreements between Washington and Pyongyang, the United States was one of the largest donors of food to North Korea. U.S. aid was ended in late 2005, however, after North Korea imposed restrictions on the UN's monitoring system intended to ensure the food went to needy civilians, not to the military.

North Korea suffered another significant natural disaster in mid-July—at about the same time as the controversy over its missile tests—when large-scale floods inundated several hundred thousand acres of farmland and destroyed hundreds of bridges and roads. North Korea at first rejected offers of aid from South Korea but in mid-August accepted more than $70 million in food and other relief supplies from the South Korean Red Cross. Another South Korean charity, Good Friends, said it had received information that more than 57,000 people had been killed in the floods and more than 2 million had been left homeless. North Korea, which typically played down the extent of disasters, had said only that "hundreds" had been killed.

Following is the text of United Nations Security Council Resolution 1718, adopted unanimously on October 14, 2006, imposing sanctions against North Korea in response to its testing of a nuclear weapon on October 9.

DOCUMENT

"Resolution 1718 (2006)"

The Security Council,

Recalling its previous relevant resolutions, including resolution 825 (1993), resolution 1540 (2004) and, in particular, resolution 1695 (2006), as well as the statement of its President of 6 October 2006 (S/PRST/2006/41),

Reaffirming that proliferation of nuclear, chemical and biological weapons, as well as their means of delivery, constitutes a threat to international peace and security,

Expressing the gravest concern at the claim by the Democratic People's Republic of Korea (DPRK) that it has conducted a test of a nuclear weapon on 9 October 2006, and at the challenge such a test constitutes to the Treaty on the Non-Proliferation of Nuclear Weapons and to international efforts aimed at strengthening the global regime of non-proliferation of nuclear weapons, and the danger it poses to peace and stability in the region and beyond,

Expressing its firm conviction that the international regime on the non-proliferation of nuclear weapons should be maintained and recalling that the DPRK cannot have the status of a nuclear-weapon state in accordance with the Treaty on the Non-Proliferation of Nuclear Weapons,

Deploring the DPRK's announcement of withdrawal from the Treaty on the Non-Proliferation of Nuclear Weapons and its pursuit of nuclear weapons,

Deploring further that the DPRK has refused to return to the Six-Party talks without precondition,

Endorsing the Joint Statement issued on 19 September 2005 by China, the DPRK, Japan, the Republic of Korea, the Russian Federation and the United States,

Underlining the importance that the DPRK respond to other security and humanitarian concerns of the international community,

Expressing profound concern that the test claimed by the DPRK has generated increased tension in the region and beyond, and *determining* therefore that there is a clear threat to international peace and security,

Acting under Chapter VII of the Charter of the United Nations, and taking measures under its Article 41,

1. *Condemns* the nuclear test proclaimed by the DPRK on 9 October 2006 in flagrant disregard of its relevant resolutions, in particular resolution 1695 (2006), as well as of the statement of its President of 6 October 2006 (S/PRST/2006/41), including that such a test would bring universal condemnation of the international community and would represent a clear threat to international peace and security;

2. *Demands* that the DPRK not conduct any further nuclear test or launch of a ballistic missile;

3. *Demands* that the DPRK immediately retract its announcement of withdrawal from the Treaty on the Non-Proliferation of Nuclear Weapons;

4. *Demands* further that the DPRK return to the Treaty on the Non-Proliferation of Nuclear Weapons and International Atomic Energy Agency (IAEA) safeguards, and *underlines* the need for all States Parties to the Treaty on the Non-Proliferation of Nuclear Weapons to continue to comply with their Treaty obligations;

5. *Decides* that the DPRK shall suspend all activities related to its ballistic missile program and in this context re-establish its pre-existing commitments to a moratorium on missile launching;

6. *Decides* that the DPRK shall abandon all nuclear weapons and existing nuclear programs in a complete, verifiable and irreversible manner, shall act strictly in accordance with the obligations applicable to parties under the Treaty on the Non-Proliferation of Nuclear Weapons and the terms and conditions of its International Atomic Energy Agency (IAEA) Safeguards Agreement (IAEA INFCIRC/403) and shall provide the IAEA transparency measures extending beyond these requirements, including such access to individuals, documentation, equipments and facilities as may be required and deemed necessary by the IAEA;

7. *Decides* also that the DPRK shall abandon all other existing weapons of mass destruction and ballistic missile program in a complete, verifiable and irreversible manner;

8. *Decides* that:

(a) All Member States shall prevent the direct or indirect supply, sale or transfer to the DPRK, through their territories or by their nationals, or using their flag vessels or aircraft, and whether or not originating in their territories, of:

(i) Any battle tanks, armored combat vehicles, large calibre artillery systems, combat aircraft, attack helicopters, warships, missiles or missile systems as defined for the purpose of the United Nations Register on Conventional Arms, or related materiel including spare parts, or items as determined by the Security Council or the Committee established by paragraph 12 below (the Committee);

(ii) All items, materials, equipment, goods and technology as set out in the lists in documents S/2006/814 and S/2006/815, unless within 14 days of adoption of this resolution the Committee has amended or completed their provisions also taking into account the list in document S/2006/816, as well as other items, materials, equipment, goods and technology, determined by the Security Council or the Committee, which could contribute to DPRK's nuclear-related, ballistic missile-related or other weapons of mass destruction related programs;

(iii) Luxury goods;

(b) The DPRK shall cease the export of all items covered in subparagraphs (a) (i) and (a) (ii) above and that all Member States shall prohibit the procurement of such items from the DPRK by their nationals, or using their flagged vessels or aircraft, and whether or not originating in the territory of the DPRK;

(c) All Member States shall prevent any transfers to the DPRK by their nationals or from their territories, or from the DPRK by its nationals or from its territory, of technical training, advice, services or assistance related to the provision, manufacture, maintenance or use of the items in subparagraphs (a) (i) and (a) (ii) above;

(d) All Member States shall, in accordance with their respective legal processes, freeze immediately the funds, other financial assets and economic resources which are on their territories at the date of the adoption of this resolution or at any time thereafter, that are owned or controlled, directly or indirectly, by the persons or entities designated by the Committee or by the Security Council as being engaged in or providing support for, including through other illicit means, DPRK's nuclear-related, other weapons of mass destruction-related and ballistic missile related programs, or by persons or entities acting on their behalf or at their direction, and ensure that any funds, financial assets or economic resources are prevented from being made available by their nationals or by any persons or entities within their territories, to or for the benefit of such persons or entities;

(e) All Member States shall take the necessary steps to prevent the entry into or transit through their territories of the persons designated by the Committee or by the Security Council as being responsible for, including through supporting or promoting, DPRK policies in relation to the DPRK's nuclear-related, ballistic missile-related and other weapons of mass destruction-related programs, together with their family members, provided that nothing in this paragraph shall oblige a state to refuse its own nationals entry into its territory;

(f) In order to ensure compliance with the requirements of this paragraph, and thereby preventing illicit trafficking in nuclear, chemical or biological weapons, their means of delivery and related materials, all Member States are called upon to take, in accordance with their national authorities and legislation, and consistent with international law, cooperative action including through inspection of cargo to and from the DPRK, as necessary;

9. *Decides* that the provisions of paragraph 8 (d) above do not apply to financial or other assets or resources that have been determined by relevant States:

(a) To be necessary for basic expenses, including payment for foodstuffs, rent or mortgage, medicines and medical treatment, taxes, insurance premiums, and public utility charges, or exclusively for payment of reasonable professional fees and reimbursement of incurred expenses associated with the provision of legal services, or fees or service charges, in accordance with national laws, for routine holding or maintenance of frozen funds, other financial assets and economic resources, after notification by the relevant States to the Committee of the intention to authorize, where appropriate, access to such funds, other financial assets and economic resources and in the absence of a negative decision by the Committee within five working days of such notification;

(b) To be necessary for extraordinary expenses, provided that such determination has been notified by the relevant States to the Committee and has been approved by the Committee; or

(c) To be subject of a judicial, administrative or arbitral lien or judgment, in which case the funds, other financial assets and economic resources may be used to satisfy that lien or judgment provided that the lien or judgment was entered prior to the date of the present resolution, is not for the benefit of a person referred to in paragraph 8 (d) above or an individual or entity identified by the Security Council or the Committee, and has been notified by the relevant States to the Committee;

10. *Decides* that the measures imposed by paragraph 8 (e) above shall not apply where the Committee determines on a case-by-case basis that such travel is justified on the grounds of humanitarian need, including religious obligations, or where the Committee concludes that an exemption would otherwise further the objectives of the present resolution;

11. *Calls upon* all Member States to report to the Security Council within thirty days of the adoption of this resolution on the steps they have taken with a view to implementing effectively the provisions of paragraph 8 above;

12. *Decides* to establish, in accordance with rule 28 of its provisional rules of procedure, a Committee of the Security Council consisting of all the members of the Council, to undertake the following tasks:

(a) To seek from all States, in particular those producing or possessing the items, materials, equipment, goods and technology referred to in paragraph 8 (a) above, information regarding the actions taken by them to implement effectively the measures imposed by paragraph 8 above of this resolution and whatever further information it may consider useful in this regard;

(b) To examine and take appropriate action on information regarding alleged violations of measures imposed by paragraph 8 of this resolution;

(c) To consider and decide upon requests for exemptions set out in paragraphs 9 and 10 above;

(d) To determine additional items, materials, equipment, goods and technology to be specified for the purpose of paragraphs 8 (a) (i) and 8 (a) (ii) above;

(e) To designate additional individuals and entities subject to the measures imposed by paragraphs 8 (d) and 8 (e) above;

(f) To promulgate guidelines as may be necessary to facilitate the implementation of the measures imposed by this resolution;

(g) To report at least every 90 days to the Security Council on its work, with its observations and recommendations, in particular on ways to strengthen the effectiveness of the measures imposed by paragraph 8 above;

13. *Welcomes and encourages further* the efforts by all States concerned to intensify their diplomatic efforts, to refrain from any actions that might aggravate tension and to facilitate the early resumption of the Six-Party Talks, with a view to the expeditious implementation of the Joint Statement issued on 19 September 2005 by China, the DPRK, Japan, the Republic of Korea, the Russian Federation and the United States, to achieve the verifiable denuclearization of the Korean Peninsula and to maintain peace and stability on the Korean Peninsula and in north-east Asia;

14. *Calls upon* the DPRK to return immediately to the Six-Party Talks without pre-condition and to work towards the expeditious implementation of the Joint Statement issued on 19 September 2005 by China, the DPRK, Japan, the Republic of Korea, the Russian Federation and the United States;

15. *Affirms* that it shall keep DPRK's actions under continuous review and that it shall be prepared to review the appropriateness of the measures contained in paragraph 8 above, including the strengthening, modification, suspension or lifting of the measures, as may be needed at that time in light of the DPRK's compliance with the provisions of the resolution;

16. *Underlines* that further decisions will be required, should additional measures be necessary;

17. *Decides* to remain actively seized of the matter.

Source: United Nations. Security Council. "Resolution 1718 (2006)." S/RES/1718 (2006), October 14, 2006. www.un.org/Docs/sc/unsc_resolutions06.htm (accessed January 8, 2007).

British Treasury Report on the Economics of Climate Change

October 30, 2006

■■■■■■■■ **THE DOCUMENT IN CONTEXT** ■■■■■■■■

The international debate about climate change, and what to do about it, reached a new level in 2006 with the first-ever significant study purporting to show an enormous economic cost in failing to curb emissions of the gases that scientists said caused global warming. A study by British economist Nicholas Stern suggested that the world faced a huge financial setback by the middle of the twenty-first century unless it acted soon. Stern's study, which was sponsored by the British government but challenged by some economists, sought to refute the Bush administration's argument that strong action to curb emissions of so-called greenhouse gases would cause immediate economic damage and was not worth the cost.

This new debate on economic issues came as yet more scientific studies showed continuing damage to the world's environment as a result of climate change—from the melting of permafrost in Siberia to the deterioration of the massive ice cap on Greenland. The Bush administration implicitly acknowledged one of these consequences at year's end when it started the process of listing the polar bear as an endangered species. Polar bear populations were declining not because of hunting or other factors but because the Arctic ice necessary to their survival was disappearing rapidly.

While the official reports had some impact in academic circles, among nongovernmental organizations, and even among policymakers, nothing written or said about climate change had anywhere near the public impact in the United States as a book-movie combination by former vice president and failed presidential candidate Al Gore. Called *An Inconvenient Truth,* the book and accompanying documentary movie put complex scientific studies into an easily understandable format and made a dramatic case for Gore's argument that mankind had little time left to battle the long-term consequences of climate change. The book rose to bestseller lists in the United States and many other countries, and the movie drew large and responsive audiences. *(Climate change background, Historic Documents of 2005, p. 919)*

Stern Report

The potential economic consequences of climate change, and of measures to deal with it, long had been one of the great unknowns in international debates about the issue. By far the most comprehensive and credible effort so far to answer the economic questions of climate change came in a study released on October 30, 2006, by the British government. The study was written by Stern, a former chief economist for the World Bank who had since taken a post as chief economist for Britain.

In his 700-page report, Stern used the most recent scientific findings by United Nations panels and other experts to extrapolate the consequences of climate changes for the world's economy. He found that if climate change continued at the current rate, and little or nothing was done to control the man-made causes of it, the global domestic economy likely would suffer the equivalent of losing at least 5 percent, and possibly as much as 20 percent, of total gross domestic product (GDP) each year "now and forever." Stern said this economic damage would be on the scale of the Great Depression of the 1930s or either of the World Wars in the twentieth century.

Despite this doom-and-gloom warning, Stern said the world could mitigate the effects of climate change by changing consumption patterns and investing in technology that would substantially reduce emissions of carbon dioxide (CO_2), methane, and other gases. If the world invested about 1 percent of its GDP into curbing greenhouse gas emissions, he said, the long-term savings would be worth the investment. Examples of action included taxation and regulation to reduce the use of fossil fuels (primarily coal, oil, and natural gas) that caused greenhouse gas emissions, financial incentives for alternative energy sources, and investments in new technologies such as "carbon sequestration" that would pump liquefied carbon dioxide beneath the oceans to prevent its escaping into the atmosphere. Over the long term, Stern said, these steps would lead to economic growth rather than depression. "We can grow and be green," he said.

British prime minister Tony Blair embraced the Stern report, saying it pointed to the need for immediate action, not more talk. "Unless we act now, not some time distant but now, these consequences, disastrous as they are, will be irreversible," he said. "So there is nothing more serious, more urgent or more demanding of leadership, here of course but most importantly, in the global community." Blair had been pressing President George W. Bush for a stronger commitment to address climate change issues but had met with little success.

Stern's report set off a furious debate among economists and policymakers worldwide, some focusing on the details of the economic analysis and others on the policy prescriptions he outlined. Among the economists who challenged many of Stern's underlying assumptions was William D. Nordhaus of Yale University, who said Stern's models gave too much weight to the potential consequences of climate change on future generations and failed to acknowledge the price to be paid by current generations from restrictions on energy consumption.

Criticism of Stern's proposed policies spanned the range from those who said they were too drastic to those who said they were too modest. While embracing Stern's economic analysis, some environmental groups said his proposed steps were too little, too late to be effective in curbing the extent of climate change. Even so, environmental groups were pleased with his argument showing the potential economic costs of climate change.

The Endangered Polar Bears

Complex economic and scientific theories about climate change might not have caught the public imagination but the fate of one of the world's most popular wild animal species—the polar bear—clearly did. For years, scientific reports had shown the rapid shrinking of sea ice in the Arctic Ocean; according to a study by the United Nations

Environment Program, the extent of summer sea ice in the Arctic had shrunk by more than 25 percent over the past half-century. Polar bears depended on sea ice to reach their primary food source, seals, and to travel long distances; several studies showed that the total population of polar bears had declined by 20–30 percent over the past several decades. Environmental groups used movies and photographs of distressed polar bears to illustrate, graphically, the effect of climate change in ways that data sets could not.

In 2005 several environmental groups filed suit against the U.S. Department of the Interior demanding that the government list polar bears as an endangered species under the Endangered Species Act. The suit argued that the long-term survival of polar bears as a species was threatened by the diminishing Arctic sea ice, which in turn was caused by climate change.

Facing a December 27, 2006, deadline for responding to that suit, the Interior Department gave in and announced it was proposing to designate the polar bear as an endangered species. The actual designation would take place in about one year, after the standard three-month public comment period and additional studies were conducted.

Secretary of the Interior Dirk Kempthorne insisted that the proposed action to protect polar bears was not directly related to climate change, a matter he said was outside the jurisdiction of his department or even the Endangered Species Act. Environmental activists, however, said the administration would have to deal with the climate change question when it proposed specific actions to protect the polar bear—as it was required to do by the Endangered Species Act.

California Acts

In the face of the Bush administration's long reluctance to accept scientific findings on climate change—and its refusal to embrace environmental restrictions that it said would curb economic growth—some states, municipalities, and even businesses began adopting their own modest steps to curtail greenhouse gas emissions. These had ranged from laws banning the idling of motor vehicles to incentive programs for reducing the CO_2 emissions of power plants.

Perhaps the strongest indication yet of the political power of the climate change debate came in California where, a little more than three months before the November elections, the Republican governor and Democratic-run legislature on August 30 agreed on what could become the nation's strictest controls on CO_2 emissions. The plan called for a 25 percent cut in CO_2 emissions by 2020, with controls placed on emissions by large industrial polluters starting in 2012.

Many Republicans and business leaders opposed the plan, which Gov. Arnold Schwarzenegger signed into law on September 27. "We simply must do everything in our power to slow down global warming before it is too late," he said. The limits would not be imposed for several years, and the legislation did not mandate specific steps for reaching them. Even so, environmental advocates hailed the measure as a significant step showing that politicians could respond to voters' concerns about climate change.

Schwarzenegger followed this legislation with an executive order on October 17 that aligned California with a plan by seven northeastern states to curb carbon dioxide emissions at power plants starting in 2009. Called the Northeast Regional Greenhouse Gas Institutive, the plan established a "cap and trade" system under which power plants could buy or sell credits to reach established limits of CO_2 emissions. Connecticut, Delaware, Maine, New Hampshire, New Jersey, New York, and Vermont were part of this system. Schwarzenegger's order enabled California power plants to participate in it, potentially helping them meet the requirements of the state's new climate change law. Schwarzenegger easily won reelection in November.

Climate change also reached the U.S. Supreme Court for the first time ever on November 29. Justices heard arguments in a case brought by ten states against the Environmental Protection Agency because of its refusal to regulate carbon dioxide pollution. Filing the suit were California, Connecticut, Maine, Massachusetts, New Mexico, New York, Oregon, Rhode Island, Vermont, and Wisconsin, along with the cities of Baltimore, New York City, and Washington, D.C., and several major environmental groups. Most observers said the justices appeared to be split on the matter, with the deciding vote likely to be cast by Justice Anthony Kennedy when the Court ruled in 2007.

Other Reports and Findings

Once again, scientists continued to flood technical publications with research reports on climate change, most of which documented what appeared to be an accelerating rate of change. Among the reports:

- Several reports said the glaciers and ice sheets in Greenland and the Antarctic were melting faster than previously believed. On February 16, two U.S. scientists published findings in the journal *Science* citing satellite imagery showing that Greenland's glaciers were melting twice as fast as earlier projections had shown. Two weeks later, other studies by U.S. scientists, also based on satellite surveys, suggested that the giant ice sheets covering Antarctica were losing ice faster than could be replaced by snowfall. Fresh water melting from glaciers and ice sheets on Greenland and Antarctica flowed into the sea, contributing to a rise in ocean levels.
- The U.S. National Oceanic and Atmospheric Administration (NOAA) on March 14 issued preliminary findings saying that the concentration of CO_2 in the atmosphere had reached a record level: 381 parts per million (ppm) in 2005, an increase of 2.6 ppm over the previous year. The new figure was more than 30 percent higher than the preindustrial level of the late eighteenth century, NOAA scientists said. In a separate report, the United Nations' World Meteorological Organization put the CO_2 figure for 2005 at 379.1 ppm, slightly less than the NOAA figure.
- The continued rise in water temperatures in tropical areas—notably in the Caribbean and in the Indian and Pacific oceans—was killing large amounts of coral, which in turn was necessary for the survival of many fish species. Reports by NOAA and other organizations said very high percentages of many types of coral suffered from "bleaching"—the loss of the algae that was food for coral. Coral that was bleached for more than a week or so usually died. In St. Croix, in the U.S. Virgin Islands, for example, at least 60 percent, and in some cases more than 90 percent, of various types of coral were bleached, NOAA said in February.
- The year saw a flurry of scientific studies on the politically charged question of whether global climate change had caused, or at least contributed to, the record-setting number of hurricanes in the Atlantic Ocean during 2005. The devastation of parts of the U.S. Gulf coast by hurricanes Katrina and Rita had heightened interest in the question, which had been debated by scientists for several years. A variety of studies published in scientific journals offered evidence for both sides of the question. Most scientists agreed only that more research was needed.

- The melting of permafrost in Siberia and other areas in high latitudes might be releasing enormous quantities of methane gas, which was a much more powerful greenhouse gas than carbon dioxide, according to at least two studies published in scientific journals during the year. One of the studies, published on September 6 in the journal *Nature*, used new measurement techniques to show that methane was escaping from melting permafrost about five times faster than previously thought. Scientists said they worried about a cycle in which higher global temperatures caused permafrost melting, thus releasing more methane, which heightened the greenhouse effect, thereby causing more global warming.
- New evidence of China's impact on climate change came on November 7 when the International Energy Agency said China would surpass the United States in 2009 as the world's major emitter of carbon dioxide. That date was about 10 years earlier than most previous forecasts. Most of China's CO_2 emissionscame from burning coal in power plants. China, India, and other developing countries were exempt from a controversial international treaty, the Kyoto Protocol on Climate Change, which required developed nations to curb their greenhouse gas emissions. That treaty went into effect in 2005, without support from the United States. Much of the U.S. opposition to the treaty was based on the exemption of China and India, two of the world's fastest growing economies, each with more than 1 billion people.

Another Warm Year

The year 2006 joined the ranks of the ten warmest years on record but failed to crack the all-time record set in 2005. Early in 2006 meteorologists confirmed that 2005 barely edged out 1998 as the warmest year globally since instrumental temperature readings began in the 1860s.

At the end of 2006 the World Meteorological Organization reported preliminary figures showing the year was the sixth warmest on record, with global mean temperatures estimated at 0.75 degrees Fahrenheit (0.42°C.) above the long-term average of 1961–1990. Another report from the U.S. National Climate Data Center said 2006 appeared to be the fifth warmest year ever globally; this report said the global average was 0.97 degrees Fahrenheit (0.54°C.) above the long-term average. The latter report said 2006 was the warmest ever for the lower forty-eight states of the United States, with seven of the twelve months running well above average. The summer of 2006 was particularly hot in the northern hemisphere; much of Western Europe experienced the highest ever temperatures in mid-July. The same period saw exceptionally high temperatures in the western United States, with California reporting 140 deaths due to the extreme heat. By contrast, New Delhi saw frost for the first time in seventy years (on January 9) and Russia's winter was one of the coldest since the late 1970s.

All world meteorological agencies had reported a sharp rise in temperatures since 1976; over that period the average global temperature had risen about one-third of a degree Fahrenheit a decade, for total increase of about 1 degree Fahrenheit. One study, published on September 25 by several scientists, including James E. Hansen of NASA's Goddard Institute for Space Studies, cited evidence that global temperatures were the highest since the last ice age of about 12,000 years ago. "The evidence implies that we are getting close to dangerous levels of human-made pollution," Hansen said. The study was published in the *Proceedings of the National Academy of Sciences*.

Following are two documents: first, the text of the summary of conclusions from the "Stern Review on the Economics of Climate Change," released on October 30, 2006, by the British Treasury; second, the text of a statement the same day by Prime Minister Tony Blair at the news conference where the report was made public.

■■■■■■■■■■■■■ **DOCUMENT** ■■■■■■■■■■■■■

"Stern Review on the Economics of Climate Change"

Summary of Conclusions

There is still time to avoid the worst impacts of climate change, if we take strong action now.

The scientific evidence is now overwhelming: climate change is a serious global threat, and it demands an urgent global response.

This Review has assessed a wide range of evidence on the impacts of climate change and on the economic costs, and has used a number of different techniques to assess costs and risks. From all of these perspectives, the evidence gathered by the Review leads to a simple conclusion: the benefits of strong and early action far outweigh the economic costs of not acting.

Climate change will affect the basic elements of life for people around the world—access to water, food production, health, and the environment. Hundreds of millions of people could suffer hunger, water shortages and coastal flooding as the world warms.

Using the results from formal economic models, the Review estimates that if we don't act, the overall costs and risks of climate change will be equivalent to losing at least 5% of global GDP each year, now and forever. If a wider range of risks and impacts is taken into account, the estimates of damage could rise to 20% of GDP or more.

In contrast, the costs of action—reducing greenhouse gas emissions to avoid the worst impacts of climate change—can be limited to around 1% of global GDP each year.

The investment that takes place in the next 10–20 years will have a profound effect on the climate in the second half of this century and in the next. Our actions now and over the coming decades could create risks of major disruption to economic and social activity, on a scale similar to those associated with the great wars and the economic depression of the first half of the 20th century. And it will be difficult or impossible to reverse these changes.

So prompt and strong action is clearly warranted. Because climate change is a global problem, the response to it must be international. It must be based on a shared vision of long-term goals and agreement on frameworks that will accelerate action over the next decade, and it must build on mutually reinforcing approaches at national, regional and international level.

Climate change could have very serious impacts on growth and development.

If no action is taken to reduce emissions, the concentration of greenhouse gases in the atmosphere could reach double its pre-industrial level as early as 2035, virtually committing us to a global average temperature rise of over 2°C. In the longer term, there would be more than a 50% chance that the temperature rise would exceed 5°C. This rise would be very dangerous indeed; it is equivalent to the change in average temperatures from the last ice age to today. Such a radical change in the physical geography of the world must lead to major changes in the human geography—where people live and how they live their lives.

Even at more moderate levels of warming, all the evidence—from detailed studies of regional and sectoral impacts of changing weather patterns through to economic models of the global effects—shows that climate change will have serious impacts on world output, on human life and on the environment.

All countries will be affected. The most vulnerable—the poorest countries and populations—will suffer earliest and most, even though they have contributed least to the causes of climate change. The costs of extreme weather, including floods, droughts and storms, are already rising, including for rich countries.

Adaptation to climate change—that is, taking steps to build resilience and minimize costs—is essential. It is no longer possible to prevent the climate change that will take place over the next two to three decades, but it is still possible to protect our societies and economies from its impacts to some extent—for example, by providing better information, improved planning and more climate-resilient crops and infrastructure. Adaptation will cost tens of billions of dollars a year in developing countries alone, and will put still further pressure on already scarce resources. Adaptation efforts, particularly in developing countries, should be accelerated.

The costs of stabilising the climate are significant but manageable; delay would be dangerous and much more costly.

The risks of the worst impacts of climate change can be substantially reduced if greenhouse gas levels in the atmosphere can be stabilised between 450 and 550ppm CO_2 equivalent (CO_2e). The current level is 430ppm CO_2e today, and it is rising at more than 2ppm each year. Stabilisation in this range would require emissions to be at least 25% below current levels by 2050, and perhaps much more.

Ultimately, stabilisation—at whatever level—requires that annual emissions be brought down to more than 80% below current levels.

This is a major challenge, but sustained long-term action can achieve it at costs that are low in comparison to the risks of inaction. Central estimates of the annual costs of achieving stabilisation between 500 and 550ppm CO_2e are around 1% of global GDP, if we start to take strong action now.

Costs could be even lower than that if there are major gains in efficiency, or if the strong co-benefits, for example from reduced air pollution, are measured. Costs will be higher if innovation in low-carbon technologies is slower than expected, or if policy-makers fail to make the most of economic instruments that allow emissions to be reduced whenever, wherever and however it is cheapest to do so.

It would already be very difficult and costly to aim to stabilise at 450ppm CO_2e. If we delay, the opportunity to stabilise at 500–550ppm CO_2e may slip away.

Action on climate change is required across all countries, and it need not cap the aspirations for growth of rich or poor countries.

The costs of taking action are not evenly distributed across sectors or around the world. Even if the rich world takes on responsibility for absolute cuts in emissions of 60–80% by 2050, developing countries must take significant action too. But developing countries should not be required to bear the full costs of this action alone, and they will not have to. Carbon markets in rich countries are already beginning to deliver flows of finance to support low-carbon development, including through the Clean Development

Mechanism. A transformation of these flows is now required to support action on the scale required.

Action on climate change will also create significant business opportunities, as new markets are created in low-carbon energy technologies and other low-carbon goods and services. These markets could grow to be worth hundreds of billions of dollars each year, and employment in these sectors will expand accordingly.

The world does not need to choose between averting climate change and promoting growth and development. Changes in energy technologies and in the structure of economies have created opportunities to decouple growth from greenhouse gas emissions. Indeed, ignoring climate change will eventually damage economic growth.

Tackling climate change is the pro-growth strategy for the longer term, and it can be done in a way that does not cap the aspirations for growth of rich or poor countries.

A range of options exists to cut emissions; strong, deliberate policy action is required to motivate their take-up.

Emissions can be cut through increased energy efficiency, changes in demand, and through adoption of clean power, heat and transport technologies. The power sector around the world would need to be at least 60% decarbonized by 2050 for atmospheric concentrations to stabilise at or below 550ppm CO_2e, and deep emissions cuts will also be required in the transport sector.

Even with very strong expansion of the use of renewable energy and other low carbon energy sources, fossil fuels could still make up over half of global energy supply in 2050. Coal will continue to be important in the energy mix around the world, including in fast-growing economies. Extensive carbon capture and storage will be necessary to allow the continued use of fossil fuels without damage to the atmosphere.

Cuts in non-energy emissions, such as those resulting from deforestation and from agricultural and industrial processes, are also essential.

With strong, deliberate policy choices, it is possible to reduce emissions in both developed and developing economies on the scale necessary for stabilisation in the required range while continuing to grow.

Climate change is the greatest market failure the world has ever seen, and it interacts with other market imperfections. Three elements of policy are required for an effective global response. The first is the pricing of carbon, implemented through tax, trading or regulation. The second is policy to support innovation and the deployment of low-carbon technologies. And the third is action to remove barriers to energy efficiency, and to inform, educate and persuade individuals about what they can do to respond to climate change.

Climate change demands an international response, based on a shared understanding of long-term goals and agreement on frameworks for action.

Many countries and regions are taking action already: the EU, California and China are among those with the most ambitious policies that will reduce greenhouse gas emissions. The UN Framework Convention on Climate Change and the Kyoto Protocol provide a basis for international co-operation, along with a range of partnerships and other approaches. But more ambitious action is now required around the world.

Countries facing diverse circumstances will use different approaches to make their contribution to tackling climate change. But action by individual countries is not enough.

Each country, however large, is just a part of the problem. It is essential to create a shared international vision of long-term goals, and to build the international frameworks that will help each country to play its part in meeting these common goals.

Key elements of future international frameworks should include:

- *Emissions trading:* Expanding and linking the growing number of emissions trading schemes around the world is a powerful way to promote cost-effective reductions in emissions and to bring forward action in developing countries: strong targets in rich countries could drive flows amounting to tens of billions of dollars each year to support the transition to low-carbon development paths.
- *Technology cooperation:* Informal co-ordination as well as formal agreements can boost the effectiveness of investments in innovation around the world. Globally, support for energy R&D should at least double, and support for the deployment of new low-carbon technologies should increase up to five-fold. International cooperation on product standards is a powerful way to boost energy efficiency.
- *Action to reduce deforestation:* The loss of natural forests around the world contributes more to global emissions each year than the transport sector. Curbing deforestation is a highly cost-effective way to reduce emissions; large-scale international pilot programs to explore the best ways to do this could get underway very quickly.
- *Adaptation:* The poorest countries are most vulnerable to climate change. It is essential that climate change be fully integrated into development policy, and that rich countries honor their pledges to increase support through overseas development assistance. International funding should also support improved regional information on climate change impacts, and research into new crop varieties that will be more resilient to drought and flood.

Source: United Kingdom. HM Treasury. "Stern Review on the Economics of Climate Change." Summary of Conclusions. October 30, 2006. www.hm-treasury.gov.uk/media/999/76/CLOSED_SHORT_executive_summary.pdf (accessed March 13, 2007).

■■■■■■■■ **DOCUMENT** ■■■■■■■■

"PM's Comments on the Launch of the Stern Review"

This is the most important report on the future published by the Government in our time in office.

Some will always make a case for doubt in an issue such as this, partly because its implications are so frightening. But what is not in doubt is that the scientific evidence of global warming caused by greenhouse gas emissions is now overwhelming. It is not in doubt that if the science is right, the consequences for our planet are literally disastrous. And this disaster is not set to happen in some science fiction future, many years ahead, but in our lifetime.

What is more, unless we act now, not some time distant but now, these consequences, disastrous as they are, will be irreversible. So there is nothing more serious, more urgent or more demanding of leadership, here of course but most importantly, in the global community.

Britain is more than playing its part. But it is 2% of worldwide emissions. Close down all, all of Britain's emissions and in less than two years just the growth in China's emissions would wipe out the difference. So this issue is the definition of global interdependence. We have to act together. This is an international challenge. Only an international solution will meet it.

It's why we put so much effort in getting agreement on Kyoto. It's why I put it top of our G8 [Group of Eight industrialized countries] and EU [European Union] agenda. That is why the G8 + 5 [the Group of Eight countries plus five major developing countries] dialogue began last year at Gleneagles is utterly critical. It involves all the leading players responsible for 70% of emissions. It is the key to getting a binding framework of action after the Kyoto Protocol expires in 2012.

This report will be seen as a landmark in the struggle against climate change.

It offers a stark warning but also hope over climate change.

It also gives us the clearest evidence yet that bold and decisive action can still prevent it.

But without radical international measures to reduce carbon emissions within the next 10 to 15 years, there is compelling evidence to suggest we might lose the chance to control temperature rises.

Failure to act will make an increase of between 2 and 5 degrees in average temperatures almost inevitable.

The consequences are stark, for our planet and for the people who live on it, threatening the basic elements of life—access to water, food production, health and our environment.

A rise of between two and three degrees means

- Disappearing glaciers will significantly reduce water supply to over a billion people.
- Rising sea levels could lead to 200 million people being displaced
- Declining crops yields will lead to famine and death particularly in Africa.
- Diseases like Malaria will spread.
- As many as 40% of species could face extinction

And while we will all suffer, poor countries will be hurt most.

But what the Stern Review shows is how the economic benefits of strong early action easily outweighs any costs.

It proves tackling climate change is the pro growth strategy.

Stern shows that if we fail to act, the cost of tackling the disruption to people and economies would cost at least five per cent—and possible as much as 20%—of the world's output. In contrast, the cost of action to halt and reverse climate change would cost just 1%.

Or put another way for every £1 we invest now, we can save at least £5 and possibly much more.

And it shows how this can be done without capping the aspirations of rich or poor countries.

In the UK, we have already exposed the false choice between growth and the environment.

Our economy has grown by 25% since 1997 while cutting our emissions by 7%.

We have increased jobs in cutting edge green industries from 170,000 in 2001 to over 400,000 today.

The review sets out a framework for international action that is both ambitious and realistic—one that creates certainty and a carbon price.

This framework includes:

- A goal to stabilise concentrations of emissions in the atmosphere.
- A range of policy tools, including a global cap and trade scheme, regulation and tax which can be used by countries to help create a carbon price and encourage investment in the low-carbon technologies that we already have.
- Accelerating technological innovation through R and D and demonstration projects and allowing new technologies to come to market.
- Stronger measures to help poor countries adapt

So it offers us hope and the way forward.

But we can't wait the 5 years it took to negotiate Kyoto. We simply don't have the luxury of time.

We need to accelerate the international discussions on a future framework for after 2012.

During the coming year, we must take major steps to agreeing the elements of this future framework. The German G8 in 2007 will be vital. This report will form the essential context for such discussion.

And in Europe we must go further too. We should extend the EU Emissions Trading Scheme beyond 2012 and bring aviation into the heart of it.

We should find ways to join this EU trading scheme up with others around the world including the one I helped launch with Governor [Arnold] Schwarzenegger and his Democrat colleagues in California a few weeks ago.

We must agree new EU energy efficiency standards and launch a new initiative to make all new coal power stations carbon neutral.

And at home we must do more too. Already we are on track to achieve double our Kyoto target, a record no other country in the world can match. But we must go further.

We must implement the energy review to get on trajectory to our 2050 target.

We must develop new measures to encourage individuals to take action.

We are looking at carbon budgets and a climate change bill. I accept we should be bolder at home—it gives us international influence—but let's be honest, it is only international action that will really address the problem on the scale needed.

[Chancellor of the Exchequer] Gordon [Brown] will set in more detail the governments response to the Stern review but it is clear we must be bolder at home, in Europe and internationally.

The Stern Review has done a crucial job. And I thank Nick and his team for all their hard work.

It has demolished the last remaining argument for inaction in the face of climate change.

We know it is happening. We know the consequences for the planet.

We now know urgent action will prevent catastrophe and investment in preventing it, will pay us back many times over.

We will not be able to explain ourselves to future generations if we fail.

Source: United Kingdom. 10 Downing Street Website. "PM's Comments on the Launch of the Stern Review." October 30, 2006. www.pm.gov.uk/output/Page10300.asp (accessed March 13, 2007).

Other Historic Documents of Interest

Census Bureau on population growth, p. 601

Food safety, p. 538

Katrina recovery, p. 73

Mine safety regulations, p. 317

Supreme Court on wetlands regulation, p. 323

November

Chinese President Hu on Relations between China and Africa

November 4, 2006

■■■■■ **THE DOCUMENT IN CONTEXT** ■■■■■

The complexities of China's rapid march to superpower status compelled that country's leaders to take some controversial actions in 2006. At home, that meant suppressing dissent against the Communist Party's rigid political system, even while trying to assure the more than 800 million poor people in the rural provinces that Beijing was trying to improve their living conditions. Overseas, the Chinese government stepped up efforts to ensure long-term supplies of oil and other basic commodities. The leadership placed a particular premium on economic relations with Africa, the world's poorest continent but also a principle source of minerals needed to fuel Chinese factories.

China's economic expansion continued at the torrid pace set nearly two decades earlier, when the communist government made the strategic decision to embrace some elements of capitalism. The economy grew by just under 10 percent in 2005 and soared by another 10.5 percent in 2006, cementing China's place as the world's fourth-largest economy, behind the United States, Japan, and Germany. Most economists expected China's growth rate to slow marginally during the rest of the decade—but their economy had defied similar predictions in previous years and kept on booming. *(Background on China's rise, Historic Documents of 2005, p. 612)*

China's Outreach to Developing Countries

China increasingly was becoming the dominant economic player in much of the developing world, taking the place of the United States and, before it, the European countries with their empires. In its dealings with Africa, elsewhere in Asia, and in Latin America, China sought secure supplies of basic commodities for its economy: oil, copper, diamonds, iron ore, timber, and a host of other products that either were unavailable in China or that had been depleted there. In turn, China sold cheap consumer goods to developing countries, just as it was doing in the United States and other wealthy countries.

This trade boosted the economies of the developing world. China's trade with sub-Saharan Africa, for example, zoomed from less than $11 billion in 2000 to more than $40 billion in 2005, playing a major role in the near doubling of the continent's annual economic growth rate during the same period. Unlike the United States and its European allies, China did not accompany its trade with lectures on democracy, human rights, and economic reforms. China saw its transactions in purely economic terms and had no qualms about doing business with dictators and governments with atrocious human rights records.

For many developing countries, however, Chinese economic influence had some of the same downsides as the interventions of Western powers in previous decades. China extracted basic commodities at the lowest possible price, bought very little in the way of finished goods from these countries, made few investments to stimulate local production, and in turn saw the developing world as a vast market for exports of inexpensive Chinese products and services—effectively shutting out competition by local producers. In the 1990s, for example, many African countries saw a bright future in producing textiles for the world market, but by 2006 the continent had lost tens of thousands of jobs to stiff Chinese competition.

During 2006 China appeared to be making a particular effort to boost its economic ties with sub-Saharan Africa, which was a significant source of some of the world's most important minerals and other commodities, notably oil. President Hu Jintao visited Kenya, Morocco, and Nigeria in April, and Prime Minister Wen Jiabao led a trade delegation to seven countries in Africa in mid-June.

Early in November, China hosted what it called the Forum on China-Africa Cooperation, a series of meetings that brought senior leaders of all but five African countries to Beijing; absent were the countries that had official diplomatic relations with Taiwan, the island that Beijing claimed as part of China. In a keynote speech to the forum, on November 4, Hu offered a list of promises for aid to and business with Africa, including $5 billion in preferential loans and credits, a $5 billion fund to encourage investment in Africa by Chinese companies, and the cancellation of an unspecified amount of debt owed China by African countries. "China will remain a close friend, reliable partner, and a good brother of Africa," Hu told the leaders. The speech included none of the calls for democracy, human rights, and combating corruption that were standard in similar speeches by Western leaders. In another speech to delegates, Prime Minister Wen reminded the African leaders that China's assistance "has no strings attached"— a clear reference to conditions that the United States and most European countries placed on their aid.

Even while it was stepping up its presence in Africa, China's dealings there came under increasing scrutiny. In Africa, trade union officials and business executives praised China's trade but called for longer-term investments that would help African countries move past their near total reliance on extractive industries for economic growth. Human rights groups in Western countries, and some of Africa's intellectual leaders, also said China was supporting and even protecting some of the continent's most autocratic regimes, notably the Sudanese government, which was resisting international pressure to halt the killing of minorities in the Darfur region, and Zimbabwe's corrupt president, Robert Mugabe. Hu rejected such criticism, saying during his Africa visit in April that his country followed "the principle of noninterference in others' internal affairs."

China also was expanding its economic ties with the rest of Asia and with Latin America, in nearly all cases by emphasizing imports of commodities. China's trade contacts with Latin America had reached the point that the U.S. State Department in March called for a series of "conversations" between Bejing and Washington on the matter. Officials in Washington had watched nervously in recent years as China extended its economic reach into a part of the world the United States considered its backyard. China in recent years had signed contracts to buy large quantities of oil from Venezuela, soybeans and other agricultural commodities from Argentina and Brazil, and copper from Chile. China's dealings with Venezuela, and its prickly anti-U.S. leader Hugo Chavez, were of particular concern to the Bush administration. Despite the frosty diplomatic relations, Venezuela remained an important source of oil for the

United States; losing some of that oil to China could cause a serious disruption in the U.S. energy market.

U.S.-China Relations

President Hu in April made his first official visit to Washington since assuming power in 2003–2004. The generally cordial visit was remarkable primarily for two embarrassing White House gaffes at an opening ceremony on the south lawn of the presidential mansion on April 20. An announcer mistakenly identified Hu as representing the Republic of China (the official title for Taiwan's government) rather than the People's Republic of China. Also, a member of Falun Gong, a religious sect banned in China, used a temporary news media accreditation to gain entry to the ceremony, where she interrupted Hu's speech with shouts in Chinese and English.

Hu and Bush reportedly discussed, but reached no consensus on, more substantive issues that divided the two countries. Chief among these, at least from Washington's perspective, was a claim that China artificially depressed the value of its currency, the yuan, thereby making its exports more attractive on world market and raising a financial hurdle for Chinese imports of goods and services from the United States. Under consistent U.S. pressure, China in 2005 took limited steps that, by mid-2006, had raised the value of the yuan by about 3 percent. In a May 10 report to Congress, the Bush administration said it was "extremely dissatisfied" with China's response so far on the yuan. Even so, the administration said it would not take the formal step of declaring that China was deliberately manipulating its currency—a step that would have heightened calls in Congress for punitive sanctions against China.

Fueled in part by the undervalued yuan, China's trade surplus with the United States continued on its upward trajectory, reaching record levels in both 2005 ($202 billion) and 2006 (an estimated $232 billion). China had a trade deficit with most other countries, generally because its imports of basic commodities from them exceeded its exports to them of finished goods.

In an apparent move to blunt U.S. criticism of Chinese economic policies, Beijing in March sent a delegation of nearly 200 business leaders to the United States on what was frankly labeled a "buying mission." The Chinese signed more than $16 billion worth of contracts for U.S.-made aircraft, computer software, and agricultural goods. All the contracts had been in process for months, but the high-profile mission clearly was intended to show skeptical Americans that trade with China was a two-way street. President Hu also had dinner with Microsoft Corporation chairman Bill Gates in April on his way to visit President George W. Bush in Washington, D.C.

Another matter that continued to roil relations between Beijing and Washington was the contention of some Bush administration officials that China's military expansion was unwarranted. In the weeks before Hu's visit to the White House, senior U.S. officials raised questions about China's military buildup, saying the country's spending on manpower and weapons was much greater than Beijing had acknowledged. Secretary of Defense Donald H. Rumsfeld had raised similar concerns in 2005 and questioned why China, with no known enemies and no overseas bases, was spending so much on its military.

Dissent Continues at Home

China's rapid expansion benefited the country's economy as a whole and lifted millions of people out of poverty, but as of 2006 about 800 million of the 1.3 billion Chinese lived in impoverished rural areas that had seen little direct benefit from industrialization. About 25 percent of the rural population, 200 million, still lived in what the World Bank defined as "extreme poverty," with a per capita income of less than $1 a day.

The government's inability to manage development in a way that was seen as equitable—coupled with the country's top-down decision-making process—led almost inevitably to protests at the local level. Most protests involved small-scale street demonstrations, but an unknown number escalated to violent confrontations in which citizens attacked symbols of authority (such as government offices or police stations) and the police used force to suppress the protests. A senior police official in Beijing revealed that the country had experienced about 74,000 "public order disturbances" in 2004 and 87,000 in 2005—an increase of about 17 percent; a comparable figure for 2006 had not been announced as of year's end.

An unknown but apparently large proportion of the protests were against the government's seizure of rural land for development projects, such as factories. Nearly all Chinese farmers were tenants who rented land from the government; when the government seized the land for its own use, the farmers generally were left without sources of income and were not even compensated for their losses. In addition to land seizures, protesters complained about arbitrary taxes, nonpayment of wages, pervasive corruption (which at the local level meant having to pay bribes for government services), and general social conditions in rural areas, which lagged well behind those in the cities.

Top officials said they were aware of the problems in rural areas and were determined to correct them. In a speech given in late December 2005 but not published until January 20, Prime Minister Wen criticized what he called unlawful land seizures, without adequate compensation, by local authorities. "We absolutely can't commit an historic error over land problems," he said. On January 29, Hu and Wen spent the Chinese New Year with farmers and other local citizens in rural areas—Hu in northwestern Yanan province and Wen in the eastern Shandong province. Their visits were featured prominently on state television in a clear effort to demonstrate the national government's concern about the rural poor.

In keeping with its long history of issuing national plans, the government announced several plans during 2006 to address some of the specific problems that led to protests. On February 15 the government unveiled a broad plan to clean up the most heavily polluted regions by 2010. The plan required regional governments to set environmental targets and for the first time said local officials would be judged on their performance in environmental matters, not just their success in promoting economic development. Reports said this plan was largely a response to a major spill of toxic chemicals the previous November into the Songhau River in northeast China—a spill that temporarily deprived millions of people of fresh water. Another plan, announced on February 21 and approved by the National People's Congress three weeks later—called for increased spending on schools, health care, and aid to farmers in rural areas. The official Xinhua news service said the plan "makes it clear that China is tilting its fiscal investment to agriculture and farmers, and shifting the focus of infrastructure construction from cities to countryside."

Chinese leaders also wanted to be seen as fighting corruption. On February 14 the government announced that the Communist Party had disciplined more than 115,000 party members for corruption and similar violations in 2005; the cases of more than

15,000 of those members had been turned over to the courts for prosecution. In September leaders in Shanghai and several other regions were arrested or removed from their posts, among them the Shanghai party chief who served on the country's top ruling council, the Politburo Standing Committee. News reports noted that many of the senior officials targeted in this crackdown were aligned with party factions at odds with the current leadership—suggesting that fighting corruption might not have been the only motivation.

Suppressing Political Dissent

Despite their frequent claims that they were taking seriously the protests of rural farmers and workers, China's leaders remained unwilling to tolerate any kind of political dissent that, in their view, endangered the Communist Party's grip on power. A key component of stifling dissent was the government's control of information, which remained unimpaired even in the age of increased information flow via the Internet.

The Chinese government continued its relentless attacks on dissidents and others who were perceived as threatening the government's control of information. Among those who were jailed on various charges were Gao Zhisheng, a lawyer who had represented several people who claimed to have been victimized by government agencies and who himself was charged in October with subversion; Hu Jia, who had launched a one-man human rights campaign to aid other dissidents; and Zhao Yan, a researcher in the Beijing bureau of the *New York Times* who was jailed on a fraud charge but whose principal crime apparently was giving the newspaper information about the resignation of former president Jiang Zemin from his sole remaining government post in 2004. The government in January closed down a feisty weekly newspaper, *Bing Dian* ("Freezing Point"), that had exposed wrongdoing in high places. The newspaper was allowed to reopen in March but without the editor and investigative reporter who had stirred the ire of government and party officials.

The government's attempts to manage the news generated controversy internationally but not at home, where virtually none of it was reported. By far the most controversial step was the government's insistence that the major U.S.-based Internet service companies, including Google, Microsoft, and Yahoo, eliminate Web sites not approved by the government from Internet searches done in China. The companies complied, arguing that this was the cost of doing business in China.

In September the government announced that the Associated Press, Reuters, and other international wire services were prohibited from circulating reports inside China that would disrupt the country's "economic and social order or undermine China's social stability." These regulations gave the government's official news agency, Xinhua, control over the domestic distribution of all news, even by foreign news outlets.

Following are excerpts from a speech by Chinese president Hu Jintao, on November 4, 2006, at the opening ceremony of the Beijing Summit of the Forum on China-Africa Cooperation, attended by senior officials from China and several dozen heads of state from African countries.

DOCUMENT

"Address at the Opening of the Summit on China-Africa Cooperation"

Our meeting today will go down in history. We, leaders of China and African countries, in a common pursuit of friendship, peace, cooperation and development, are gathered in Beijing today to renew friendship, discuss ways of growing China-Africa relations and promote unity and cooperation among developing countries. On behalf of the Chinese Government and people and in my own name, I wish to extend a very warm welcome to you and deep appreciation to you for attending the Summit. I also want to extend, through the African leaders present today, the cordial greetings and best wishes of the Chinese people to the brotherly African people.

The Forum on China-Africa Cooperation was jointly set up by China and Africa in October 2000, a major initiative taken to promote traditional China-Africa friendship and cooperation. In the six years since then, two ministerial conferences have been held, first in Beijing and then in Addis Ababa. Today, the Forum serves as an important platform and effective mechanism for conducting collective dialogue, exchanging experience in governance and enhancing mutual trust and cooperation in practical terms between China and African countries.

Dear colleagues and friends,

This year marks the 50th anniversary of the inauguration of diplomatic ties between New China and African countries. Though vast oceans keep China and Africa far apart, the friendship between our peoples has a long history and, having been tested by times, is strong and vigorous. In the long course of history, the Chinese and African peoples, with an unyielding and tenacious spirit, created splendid and distinctive ancient civilizations. In the modern era, our peoples launched unremitting and heroic struggle against subjugation, and have written a glorious chapter in the course of pursuing freedom and liberation, upholding human dignity, and striving for economic development and national rejuvenation. The progress and development of China and Africa are a major contribution to the advancement of human civilization.

During the past five decades, the Chinese and African peoples have forged close unity, and our friendship has flourished. China-Africa exchanges and cooperation have grown in all fields and yielded fruitful results. In international affairs, China and Africa enjoy trust and cooperate closely to uphold the legitimate rights and interests of the developing world.

In all these years, China has firmly supported Africa in winning liberation and pursuing development. China has trained technical personnel and other professionals in various fields for Africa. It has built the Tanzara Railway and other infrastructural projects and sent medical teams and peacekeepers to Africa. All this testifies to the friendship cherished by the Chinese people towards the African people. We in China will not forget Africa's full support for restoring the lawful rights of the People's Republic of China in the United Nations. Nor will we forget the sincere and ardent wish of African countries and people for China to realize complete and peaceful reunification and achieve the goal of building a modern nation.

Today, China-Africa friendship is deeply rooted in the hearts of our two peoples, and our friendship has endured the test of time and changes in the world. This is because we have never strayed from the principle of enhancing friendship, treating each other as equals, extending mutual support and promoting common development in building our ties.

- Friendship provides a solid foundation for reinforcing China-Africa friendly ties. We both value our traditional friendship and are committed to enhancing it.
- Treating each other as equals is crucial for ensuring mutual trust. We both respect the development path independently embarked upon by the other side. We both are serious in addressing each other's concerns and are eager to benefit from each other's practice in development.
- Mutual support is the driving force behind the ever growing China-Africa cooperation. We both wish to see progress in the development endeavor of the other side and sincerely support such endeavor. And we are engaged in comprehensive cooperation.
- Common development is the shared aspiration of the Chinese and African peoples. We are committed to pursuing mutually beneficial cooperation to bring the benefits of development to our peoples.

Dear colleagues and friends,

The world today is undergoing profound and complex changes. But peace, development and cooperation remain the calling of the times. There is a growing trend towards multipolarity and economic globalization. Science and technology are making daily advance, regional cooperation is deepening and there is increasing interdependence among nations. All this has created rare development opportunities for the international community. On the other hand, imbalance in global development, widening gap between North and South, the combination of traditional and non-traditional security threats as well as increasing factors of instability and uncertainty standing in the way of peace and development all pose a daunting challenge to developing countries in their pursuit of sustainable development.

China is the largest developing country, and Africa is home to the largest number of developing countries. Our combined population accounts for over a third of the world total. Without peace and development in China and Africa, there will be no global peace and development.

In this new era, China and Africa share increasing common interests and have a growing mutual need. The forging of a new type of China-Africa strategic partnership is determined by the dynamics of China-Africa cooperation, and it represents our wish to promote global peace and development. Building strong ties between China and Africa will not only promote development of each side, but also help cement unity and cooperation among developing countries and contribute to establishing a just and equitable new international political and economic order. To enhance this new type of strategic partnership, China will strengthen cooperation with Africa in the following fields:

First, deepen political relation of equality and mutual trust. We will maintain high-level contacts and mutual visits, establish a regular high-level political dialogue mechanism and conduct strategic dialogue to enhance mutual political trust and traditional friendship and achieve common progress through unity.

Second, broaden win-win economic cooperation. We will give full play to our respective strength, enhance economic and trade ties, broaden areas of cooperation, support cooperation between our business communities, upgrade cooperation in human resources development and explore new ways of cooperation so that both sides will share the benefits of development.

Third, expand exchange for cultural enrichment. We will strengthen cultural and people-to-people exchanges to increase mutual understanding and friendship between our two peoples and particularly between the younger generation. We will enhance exchanges and cooperation in education, science and technology, culture, public health, sports and tourism to provide intellectual motivation and cultural support for China-Africa cooperation.

Fourth, promote balanced and harmonious global development. We will enhance South-South cooperation and promote North-South dialogue. We urge developed countries to honor their promises on market access, aid and debt relief. We should strive to meet the Millennium Development Goals and steer economic globalization in the direction of creating prosperity for all.

Fifth, strengthen cooperation and mutual support in international affairs. We are committed to upholding the purposes and principles of the UN Charter, respecting diversity of the world and promoting democracy in international relations. We call for enhancing international security cooperation based on mutual trust and benefit and addressing each other's concerns through consultation and coordination so that we can jointly respond to threats and challenges to global security.

Dear colleagues and friends,

China values its friendship with Africa. To strengthen unity and cooperation with Africa is a key principle guiding China's foreign policy. China will continue to support Africa in implementing the New Partnership for Africa's Development and in its effort to strengthen itself through unity, achieve peace and stability and economic revitalization in the region and raise its international standing.

To forge a new type of China-Africa strategic partnership and strengthen our cooperation in more areas and at a higher level, the Chinese Government will take the following eight steps:

1. Double its 2006 assistance to Africa by 2009.
2. Provide US$3 billion of preferential loans and US$2 billion of preferential buyer's credits to Africa in the next three years.
3. Set up a China-Africa development fund which will reach US$5 billion to encourage Chinese companies to invest in Africa and provide support to them.
4. Build a conference centre for the African Union to support African countries in their efforts to strengthen themselves through unity and support the process of African integration.
5. Cancel debt in the form of all the interest-free government loans that matured at the end of 2005 owed by the heavily indebted poor countries and the least developed countries in Africa that have diplomatic relations with China.
6. Further open up China's market to Africa by increasing from 190 to over 440 the number of export items to China receiving zero-tariff treatment from the least developed countries in Africa having diplomatic ties with China.
7. Establish three to five trade and economic cooperation zones in Africa in the next three years.

8. Over the next three years, train 15,000 African professionals; send 100 senior agricultural experts to Africa; set up 10 special agricultural technology demonstration centers in Africa; build 30 hospitals in Africa and provide RMB 300 million of grant for providing artemisinin and building 30 malaria prevention and treatment centers to fight malaria in Africa; dispatch 300 youth volunteers to Africa; build 100 rural schools in Africa; and increase the number of Chinese government scholarships to African students from the current 2000 per year to 4000 per year by 2009.

Dear colleagues and friends,

Both China and Africa are cradles of human civilization and lands of great promise. Common destiny and common goals have brought us together. China will remain a close friend, reliable partner and good brother of Africa.

Let's join hands and endeavor to promote development in both China and Africa, improve the well-being of our peoples and build a harmonious world of enduring peace and common prosperity!

Thank you.

Source: People's Republic of China. Ministry of Foreign Affairs. "Address by Hu Jintao President of the People's Republic of China at the Opening Ceremony of the Beijing Summit of the Forum on China-Africa Co-operation." Beijing, November 4, 2006. www.fmprc.gov.cn/eng/wjdt/zyjh/t278762.htm (accessed December 4, 2006).

Other Historic Documents of Interest

President Bush on the Trial and Execution of Saddam Hussein

November 5 and December 29, 2006

Saddam Hussein, who had ruled Iraq with an iron hand for nearly a quarter century and had been responsible for the deaths of hundreds of thousands of people, in his own country and elsewhere in the region, was executed by hanging on December 30, 2006. An Iraqi court, established by the new government after the United States ousted Saddam from power in 2003, had found the former leader guilty of ordering the deaths of 148 boys and men in 1982. The execution brought a halt to a separate prosecution of Saddam on the much more serious charge of ordering the murder of tens of thousands of Iraqi Kurds in the late 1980s.

Saddam's execution brought joy to those who had been victims of his long dictatorship, notably the Kurds and Shiites, who were now in charge in Iraq. But the new government's rush to execute Saddam before year's end—and at the advent of an important Muslim holy festival—was widely condemned elsewhere, especially in the Middle East. A videotape showing Saddam being taunted by guards as he stood ready to be hanged generated a sudden wave of sympathy for a man who, in power, had not shown compassion for those who suffered at his hand.

The Trial of Saddam

After he was ousted from power by the U.S. invasion of Iraq in March 2003, Saddam spent nearly eight months in hiding. The U.S. army captured him the following December, and the new Iraqi government announced plans to put him on trial on numerous charges stemming from his brutal suppression of Kurds, Shiites, and anyone else in Iraq who opposed his regime. Saddam was a Sunni, the Muslim sect that was a minority in Iraq but long had held power there.

The first trial of Saddam started on October 19, 2005. Saddam and seven codefendants were charged with responsibility for the killings in 1982 of 148 men and boys in the Shiite town of Dujail, about thirty-five miles north of Baghdad, following a failed assassination attempt against Saddam. *(Background, Historic Documents of 2005, p. 949; capture of Saddam, Historic Documents of 2003, p. 1189)*

The trial continued until early December 2005, then recessed for a month, during the holding of Iraq's parliamentary elections. Early in January 2006, the judge, Rizgar Muhammad Amin, submitted his resignation, saying he could no longer put up with criticism from government officials that he had not been tough enough with Saddam. After a period of confusion, a tribunal of senior judges on January 23 appointed a new judge, Raouf Abdel-Rahman, a Kurd.

The trial resumed on January 29, and Judge Abdel-Rahman took a much tougher stance than had his predecessor, saying that he would not allow Saddam and his fellow defendants to continue disrupting the proceedings with long-winded speeches. When one of the co-defendants refused to quiet down, the judge had him removed from the courtroom, kicking and screaming. One defense lawyer also was removed when he began screaming. After the judge ordered the removal of Saddam and two other defendants, the remaining defense lawyers walked out in protest. The defendants missed several sessions over the next two weeks but were ordered back into court on February 13, after which Saddam announced that he was going on a hunger strike. The lawyers continued to boycott the trial, forcing the judge to appoint new lawyers to represent the defendants.

It took a few weeks, but the judge's tough stance helped settle down the atmosphere in the courtroom. A key turning point came on February 28, when the prosecutors presented what they said was Saddam's signature on papers ordering the execution of the boys and men in Dujail. The next day, Saddam told the court that he had ordered trials for some residents of the town because of the attempted assassination of him there, but he denied having ordered the killing of innocent people. "Saddam Hussein is telling you that he's responsible" for some actions following the assassination attempt, he told the court. "Do you think I'm going to deny responsibility or rely on others?"

Although he had given many speeches from the defendants' box, Saddam had not formally testified in the trial until March 15, when he took the stand and made a lengthy speech denouncing the U.S. occupation of Iraq and calling on his former subjects to stop killing each other. Under cross-examination by the prosecution on April 5, Saddam acknowledged for the first time that he had signed orders for the Dujail executions. Saddam said he had reviewed the orders only briefly before signing them because he did not have the time to read them carefully.

Another major step came on May 15 when the judge formally charged Saddam and the other defendants with the crimes the prosecutors had lodged against them. This was in keeping with an Iraqi procedure under which the indictment followed the prosecution's presentation of the evidence. Saddam refused to acknowledge the charges or to plead guilty or not guilty, so the judge entered a not guilty plea on his behalf.

On June 19, the chief prosecutor in the case, Jaafer al-Moussawi, urged the court to impose the death sentence against Saddam and his three chief codefendants: Saddam's half-brother, Barzan Ibrahim al-Tikriti, who had headed the secret police; Taha Yassin Ramadan, who had been Saddam's vice president; and Awad al-Bandar, who had headed the court that approved the death sentences for the boys and men of Dujail. Moussawi urged the acquittal of one other defendant and minimal sentences for three others—all four of whom were men from Dujail accused of collaborating in the executions. Upon hearing the request for the death sentence against him, Saddam called out, sarcastically: "Well done."

Saddam and his three main codefendants again went on a hunger strike in mid-July after a defense lawyer was kidnapped and killed. The lawyer was the third member of the defense team to be killed since the trial began, leading the defendants and the lawyers to demand better protection.

The trial adjourned on July 27 after a final round of closing arguments by the defendants and their lawyers. Throughout the trial Saddam had predicted that he would be condemned to death, and on November 5 he learned that he had been correct. As Judge Abdel-Rahman read an order calling for Saddam to be executed by hanging, the former Iraqi leader shouted in defiance: "Long live the people! Long live the Arab nation! Down with the spies! God is great!" Two codefendants, Ibrahim and al-Bandar, also were sentenced to death. Ramadan was sentenced to life in prison, the three Dujail officials of Saddam's Ba'ath Party were sentenced to prison terms, and a fourth local man was acquitted and ordered released from custody.

The death sentence for Saddam prompted celebrations across much of Iraq, particularly in the Shiite-majority regions. "I think he got his punishment," a Shiite shop owner in Baghdad told a reporter from the New York Times. "There was no Iraqi house that didn't have damage because of Saddam Hussein." As could be expected, the mood was substantially different in Sunni regions. Demonstrators marched through the streets of several Sunni cities and neighborhoods, many displaying photographs of Saddam in heroic poses and denouncing the new government and the American occupation of Iraq.

Prime Minister Nouri al-Maliki gave a nationally televised address saying executing Saddam "is not worth the blood he spilled" but nevertheless was justified because "it may bring some comfort to the families of the martyrs." President George W. Bush, traveling at the time in Waco, Texas, called the verdict against Saddam "a major achievement for Iraq's young democracy and its constitutional government."

Internationally, the proclamation of the death sentence brought mixed reactions concerning the conduct of the trial. A United Nations expert on legal matters, Leandro Despouy, issued a statement arguing that the trial failed to meet international legal standards and was of "doubtful legitimacy and credibility" because it was carried out under procedures created by the former U.S. occupation authority; among other things, Saddam had been charged retroactively with crimes that had not been on the books when he was in power. Despouy also expressed concern that the execution of Saddam would "deepen the armed violence and the political and religious polarization in Iraq, bringing with it the almost certain risk that the crisis will spread to the entire region." Other experts acknowledged that elements of the trial were unfair and inconsistent with international standards but said the end result was a legitimate one. The verdict "certainly is consistent with the evidence presented," Jonathan Drimmer, a professor of war crimes law at the Georgetown University Law Center in Washington, D.C., told the New York Times.

Other Cases against Saddam

While the Dujail trial was under way, Saddam on April 4 was charged with genocide in connection with his government's mass killing of Iraqi Kurds in 1988, at the close of the long Iran-Iraq War. An investigating judge said Saddam was responsible for the deaths of at least 50,000 Kurds in what was called the Anfal (or "spoils of war") campaign. Kurdish and international human rights groups had said at least 150,000 Kurds had died as the result of various attacks by Saddam's government over the years.

A trial on the Anfal charges got under way on August 20 with Kurds describing poison gas attacks that had killed thousands of people. The judge in this trial was removed on September 19 after he told Saddam he was "not a dictator" when in office. On December 18, the chief prosecutor in the case presented letters and other evidence directly linking Saddam to poison gas attacks and other killings of Kurds. In response, Saddam said he accepted responsibility, but he denied having ordered the killing of women and children. This trial was still under way when Saddam was executed. Saddam never faced formal charges in the other large-scale atrocity of his presidency: the brutal suppression in 1991 of an uprising among Shiites following the Persian Gulf War.

The Execution and Aftermath

Under Iraqi law, the death penalty sentences against Saddam and two of his codefendants in the Dujail case were submitted automatically to an appellate court. The appellate court upheld the sentences on December 26—a ruling that required the execution to take place within thirty days. The matter then fell into the hands of Prime Minister Maliki and his colleagues in the government, many of whom appeared anxious to carry out the execution as quickly as possible.

While top government officials were debating their course of action, the Web site of Saddam's former Ba'ath Party on December 27 posted a copy of what was described as a letter from Saddam to the Iraqi people, written after the November 5 death sentence was handed down. Remarkably muted in tone, the letter called on Iraqis "not to hate because hate does not leave a space for a person to be fair and it makes you blind and closes all doors of thinking and keeps [one] away from balanced thinking and making the right choice." In an apparent reference to the United States, the letter also said Iraqis should not hate "the peoples of the other countries that attacked us" and should "differentiate between the decision-makers and peoples."

The end for Saddam came quickly, but not without one last round of the circus-like atmosphere that often had prevailed throughout his trial. This time, however, the outburst was caused not by Saddam but by some of those guarding him.

Early in the morning of December 30, the U.S. military—which had housed Saddam since his capture three years earlier—turned the former Iraqi leader over to the Iraqi government. At about 6 a.m. on that Saturday, Saddam was led by guards from the Iraqi national police into a cramped room at a U.S. military base located at the headquarters in central Baghdad of Saddam's former military intelligence service. Two videotapes were made of the execution scene: an official tape, without sound, that stopped just short of the actual hanging, and an unauthorized tape, made on a cell phone camera by someone in the audience, that included sound.

The cell phone tape, later shown repeatedly on Arabic television channels and Internet sites, showed Saddam calling out "Long live the nation!" as the death penalty verdict was read again to him. Then, witnesses and guards in the execution chamber chanted the traditional Muslim prayer: "Prayers be upon Mohammed and his holy family." At that point, two guards shouted: "Supporting his son, Moqtada, Moqtada, Moqtada." This was a reference to Moqtada al-Sadr, a junior cleric who headed a Shiite militia and was the son of a revered cleric who had been killed by Saddam's government in 1999. This sparked a series of angry exchanges between Saddam and the guards, ending with mutual curses.

Saddam was then led up the gallows, where he refused the offer of a hood. After one last prayer and a curse—"Down with the traitors, the Americans, the spies, and the Persians" (a reference to Iran)—the trapdoor opened and Saddam, age sixty-nine and with a look of grim determination on his face, fell to his death. He was buried the next day, in a plain wooden coffin, in his home town of Awja, north of Baghdad on the banks of the Tigris River. Just a few miles away, Saddam had been captured three years earlier by U.S. soldiers, who found him hiding in a hole in the ground.

The execution of Saddam Hussein was cheered by many of those Iraqis whom he had tormented for decades—notably the Kurds and the Shiites—and by many in

Iran, which had fought a long and bloody war with Saddam's Iraq during the 1980s. Some Kurds, however, expressed bitter disappointment that the trial of Saddam on the charges of killing Kurds was left incomplete. There were a few immediate protests in Sunni areas, but the sudden upsurge in violence that U.S. and Iraqi officials had expected did not occur. In a statement issued by the White House late on December 29 (Washington time) after the execution was confirmed, Bush said the trial and execution of Saddam was "the kind of justice he denied the victims of his brutal regime."

In much of the world, the videotape showing the undignified verbal attack on Saddam moments before his execution was seen as a symbol of incompetence by the new Iraqi government in its rush to dispatch the former dictator. This was particularly true in other Arab countries, where many people portrayed Saddam as an Arab hero. "Suddenly, we forgot that he was a dictator and that he killed thousands of people," Roula Haddad, a young Lebanese Christian in Beirut told the *New York Times.* "All our hatred for him suddenly turned into sympathy, sympathy with someone who was treated unjustly by an occupation force and its collaborators." Egyptian president Hosni Mubarak, who had long been at odds with Saddam, said the execution had turned his former nemesis into a martyr. U.S. military officials appeared to be embarrassed by the event, but they said all decisions about Saddam's execution were made by Iraqis.

As the days passed, Iraqi Sunnis became increasingly angry at the treatment of Saddam, many of them noting that the hanging took place at the beginning of one of the most important religious holidays of the year, the festival known as Eid al-Adha. Facing rising protests, the Iraqi government on January 3, 2007, arrested two of the guards and one of the officials who had supervised the hanging of Saddam.

On January 15, the government executed Saddam's two codefendants in the Dujail case: his half-brother Ibrahim (the former secret police chief) and al-Bandar (the former judge). These executions also sparked widespread anger after it became known that Ibrahim's head was severed from his body when he was hung. People in his hometown of Ouja accused the government of deliberately decapitating Ibrahim and refused to accept the official explanation that the beheading was inadvertent.

> *Following are the texts of two statements by President George W. Bush: first, a statement on November 5, 2006, concerning the death penalty verdict issued earlier that day against former Iraqi leader Saddam Hussein; second, a statement issued on December 29, 2006, after the execution of Saddam (the execution took place early on December 30, Iraq time).*

■■■■■■■■■■■■■■ DOCUMENT ■■■■■■■■■■■■■■

"Remarks on Departure from Waco, Texas: Hussein Trial Verdict"

Today Saddam Hussein was convicted and sentenced to death by the Iraqi High Tribunal for the massacres committed by his regime in the town of Dujail. Saddam Hussein's trial is a milestone in the Iraqi people's efforts to replace the rule of a tyrant with the rule of law. It's a major achievement for Iraq's young democracy and its constitutional government.

During Saddam Hussein's trial, the court received evidence from 130 witnesses. The man who once struck fear in the hearts of Iraqis had to listen to free Iraqis recount the acts of torture and murder that he ordered against their families and against them. Today the victims of this regime have received a measure of the justice which many thought would never come.

Saddam Hussein will have an automatic right to appeal his sentence; he will continue to receive the due process and the legal rights that he denied to the Iraqi people. Iraq has a lot of work ahead as it builds its society that delivers equal justice and protects all its citizens. Yet history will record today's judgment as an important achievement on the path to a free and just and unified society.

The United States is proud to stand with the Iraqi people. We will continue to support Iraq's unity Government as it works to bring peace to its great country. We appreciate the determination and bravery of the Iraqi security forces, who are stepping forward to defend their free nation. And we give our thanks to the men and women of America's Armed Forces, who have sacrificed so much for the cause of freedom in Iraq—and they've sacrificed for the security of the United States. Without their courage and skill, today's verdict would not have happened. On behalf of the American people, I thank every American who wears the uniform, I thank their families, and I thank them for their service and their sacrifice.

Thank you very much.

Source: U.S. Executive Office of the President. "Remarks on Departure from Waco, Texas: Former Iraqi President Hussein Trial Verdict." November 5, 2006. *Weekly Compilation of Presidential Documents* 42, no. 45 (November 13, 2006): 1992–1993. Washington, D.C.: National Archives and Records Administration. www.gpoaccess.gov/wcomp/v42no45.html (accessed March 28, 2007).

■■■■■■■■■■ **DOCUMENT** ■■■■■■■■■■

"Statement on the Death of Former President Saddam Hussein of Iraq"

Today Saddam Hussein was executed after receiving a fair trial—the kind of justice he denied the victims of his brutal regime.

Fair trials were unimaginable under Saddam Hussein's tyrannical rule. It is a testament to the Iraqi people's resolve to move forward after decades of oppression that, despite his terrible crimes against his own people, Saddam Hussein received a fair trial. This would not have been possible without the Iraqi people's determination to create a society governed by the rule of law.

Saddam Hussein's execution comes at the end of a difficult year for the Iraqi people and for our troops. Bringing Saddam Hussein to justice will not end the violence in Iraq, but it is an important milestone on Iraq's course to becoming a democracy that can govern, sustain, and defend itself and be an ally in the war on terror.

We are reminded today of how far the Iraqi people have come since the end of Saddam Hussein's rule and that the progress they have made would not have been possible without the continued service and sacrifice of our men and women in uniform.

Many difficult choices and further sacrifices lie ahead. Yet the safety and security of the American people require that we not relent in ensuring that Iraq's young democracy continues to progress.

Source: U.S. Executive Office of the President. "Statement on the Death of Former President Saddam Hussein of Iraq." December 29, 2006. *Weekly Compilation of Presidential Documents* 43, no. 1 (January 8, 2007): 113. Washington, D.C.: National Archives and Records Administration. www.gpoaccess.gov/wcomp/v43no1.html (accessed March 28, 2007).

Other Historic Documents of Interest

Iraq reconstruction, p. 161
Iraq's new government,
*   p. 171*

Rumsfeld resignation, p. 645
Security in Iraq, p. 702
U.S. policy on Iraq, p. 725

President Bush and Minority Leader Pelosi on Midterm Election Results

November 8, 2006

■■■■■■■■■ **THE DOCUMENT IN CONTEXT** ■■■■■■■■■

In what most analysts viewed as a sharp repudiation of President George W. Bush's policies in Iraq, the American voters turned control of both chambers of Congress over to the Democrats in the November 7 elections. In a stunning victory, House Democrats won a thirty-seat edge over Republicans, who had controlled that chamber since 1995. In the Senate, Democrats just barely eked out a majority, which included two senators who ran and won as independents. "The American people have sent a resounding and unmistakable message of change and new direction for America," said Rep. Rahm Emanuel of Illinois, who as chairman of the Democratic Congressional Campaign Committee was the chief architect of the Democrats' takeover of the House.

At a news conference on November 8, President Bush acknowledged that he was "disappointed" with the results and admitted that he shared "a large part of the responsibility" for his party's losses. Noting voters' "displeasure with the lack of progress being made" in Iraq, Bush announced that Secretary of Defense Donald H. Rumsfeld was resigning. Rumsfeld's tenure had grown increasingly controversial as the secretary refused to acknowledge publicly that the war in Iraq was not going well.

The Democratic victory had implications for the last two year's of Bush's presidency, with Democrats likely to push their own agenda on the war in Iraq and other issues and to exercise oversight of executive branch actions that had largely been left unexamined by the Republican-led Congress. While leaders in both parties pledged cooperation and comity, it seemed inevitable that over the next two years the Democratic Congress and the Republican president would clash on many issues in addition to the Iraq War. With Democrats themselves not always in agreement and with the Senate nearly evenly divided between the two parties, the opportunities for gridlock seemed abundant.

The election also had implications for the 2008 presidential election, the first presidential election since 1928 in which neither the sitting president nor vice president was a candidate. Analyses of the election returns showed that Democrats had made significant gains in several categories of voters that they had been losing to the Republicans in recent elections, including women, whites, Latinos, Catholics, and independent voters. Whether Democrats could hold on to these voters over the next two years remained to be seen.

The Campaign

Midterm elections were usually about local politics. Turnover was typically low, and most incumbents seeking reelection, especially in the House, could count on winning.

But the war in Iraq and a series of corruption scandals involving Republican legislators allowed Democrats to "nationalize" the 2006 election to an unusual extent. Support for the Iraq War, and for the way the president was conducting it, had been declining ever since Bush won election in 2004. By the beginning of 2006, sectarian violence appeared to have taken hold in Iraq, and the country seemed to be heading into a bloody civil war. The daily news and television reports on the violence contradicted the optimistic reports coming from the White House and Pentagon, leading many voters to conclude that Bush had gotten the United States into a no-win situation in Iraq. Opinion polls throughout the year showed a majority of Americans viewing the March 2003 invasion as a mistake and supporting a timetable for withdrawing American troops from combat. Support for Bush's handling of his job as president dipped well below 40 percent for most of the year. Support for his Iraq policy slid to around 30 percent.

Meanwhile, several Republican legislators were dogged by ethics scandals. The most prominent was Rep. Tom DeLay of Texas, who was forced to step down as House majority leader in September 2005 after being indicted in Texas on money laundering charges involving campaign contributions. DeLay also had close ties to Republican lobbyist Jack Abramoff, who was convicted of federal corruption charges in January 2006. In June 2006, DeLay resigned from Congress altogether, apparently because he was in danger of losing his reelection bid and because he did not want to be blamed if the GOP lost control of the House in November. Two other Republican representatives resigned from Congress before the election after pleading guilty to bribery and other charges—Randy "Duke" Cunningham of California in December 2005, and Bob Ney of Ohio on November 3, 2006, just four days before the election. Continuing investigations in the Abramoff case and in the scandal involving Cunningham also threatened several other Republican legislators, all of which allowed Democrats to paint the Republicans as the party of corruption.

Democrats, political pundits, and many voters also said the Republican Party had lost its direction in order to maintain itself in power. Republicans who had once called for smaller government, these critics said, had adopted the prescription drug entitlement—the largest expansion of Medicare in its history—and they abandoned fiscal responsibility to spend millions on pork barrel projects. Some of these charges were reflected in public opinion polls showing broad dissatisfaction with Congress. By mid-May, polls were showing that respondents thought Democrats would do a better job than Republicans in dealing with the war, gasoline prices, and immigration among other issues, and more than half said they wanted to see Democrats take control of Congress in the November elections.

Focusing public attention on the war, the unpopular president, and GOP scandals in Washington, Democratic candidates pounded home the message that it was time for a change. They also offered an agenda of legislative priorities that a majority of voters said they supported, including a hike in the minimum wage, implementation of several homeland security measures, and a reinstatement of congressional mechanisms to control the federal budget deficit. Democrats also tried to avoid taking positions that could be labeled "liberal," seeking instead to appeal to the broad swath of independent voters in the middle of political spectrum.

Although Bush and other top Republicans vowed to "stay the course" in Iraq and accused the Democrats of a "cut and run" policy, many Republican candidates tried to distance themselves from the president and keep their individual campaigns focused on local issues. An effort by the GOP in Congress to rev up support among social conservatives by advancing an "American Values Agenda" fell flat, when the leadership could not muster enough Republican support to enact measures dealing with a host of ideological issues such as abortion, gay marriage, gun rights, flag burning, and the Pledge of Allegiance.

By late summer, with Republican control of Congress now more clearly in jeopardy, Bush tried to divert the political conversation away from the war in Iraq and toward the war on terror—the one issue on which a large proportion of voters still found him persuasive. In early September he announced that fourteen "high-value" terror suspects, including the man said to be the architect of the September 11, 2001, attacks, had been transferred to a military prison in Guantanamo Bay, Cuba, where they would stand trial, starting in mid-2007. The announcement, coming just days before the fifth anniversary of the September 11 attacks, gave the president an opportunity to remind voters of the measures the administration had taken to protect the homeland from future terrorist attacks. But that message was undercut in late September, when portions of a National Intelligence Estimate were made public saying that the war in Iraq was promoting the terrorism it was intended to fight. That report, a joint assessment by the nation's intelligence agencies, brought the war back to the front of public consciousness, as did the release of a new book by *Washington Post* writer Bob Woodward, which recounted many allegations of missteps and miscalculations by the administration in its conduct of the war. One week before the election a *New York Times*/CBS News poll found that only 29 percent of those surveyed approved of the way Bush was managing the war in Iraq. Nearly 70 percent said he did not have a plan to end the war, and 80 percent said the president's pre-election offensive to drum up support for the war amounted to a change in language rather than a change in policy.

The final blow for Republicans, however, may have been the abrupt resignation of GOP representative Mark Foley of Florida on September 29. The revelation that Foley, a deputy whip, had made homosexual advances in e-mails to House pages was particularly embarrassing to a party that had used opposition to same-sex marriage to turn out voters in the past three elections. The resignation also tarnished House Speaker J. Dennis Hastert and others in the House GOP leadership who were accused of knowing about Foley's actions but failing to do anything about them. Although Hastert was cleared in December of violating any House rules, questions about his role kept the Foley incident on the front pages through Election Day and further intensified anti-incumbent, anti-Republican sentiment.

Election Results

When all the results were in, the 2006 midterm elections gave control of both chambers of Congress to the Democrats for the first time since 1994—although control was a word that might best be used with caution. In the Senate, Democrats and Republicans each had forty-nine slots; the Democrats' majority came from two independents who caucused with them, Bernie Sanders of Vermont and Joseph I. Lieberman, a Connecticut Democrat who ran as an independent in support of the Iraq War after he was defeated in the primary by an antiwar Democrat.

The party gained thirty seats in the House, fifteen more than needed to wrest control from the GOP. But many of those seats were won by centrist, even conservative Democrats who were likely to add to the party's traditional difficulties in speaking with a single voice. Democrats won seats across the nation, particularly in the Northeast and the Ohio River Valley, as well as in reliable Republican states such as Kansas. Democrats won both House seats in New Hampshire for the first time since 1912, unseated two GOP incumbents in New York, and ousted four in Pennsylvania. On the

West Coast, Democrats cheered the defeat of Richard W. Pombo of California, the controversial chairman of the House Resources Committee. In Minnesota, Democrat Keith Ellison, who converted to Islam when he was a college student, became the first Muslim ever elected to Congress and the first African American to represent Minnesota in the House. Democrats also took eight seats where the Republican had been tainted by corruption or scandal, including the seats once held by DeLay, Ney, and Foley.

Republican moderates bore a disproportionate share of the party's losses. Even though many of them frequently were at odds with the Bush administration, they tended to represent districts that normally were politically competitive or even leaned Democratic; in a year that favored the Democrats, the GOP moderates came up short. The most prominent GOP moderate to lose his House seat was Jim Leach, a thirty-year veteran from Iowa who had voted against the war in Iraq.

Thomas M. Reynolds of New York, chairman of the National Republican Congressional Committee, nearly lost his seat in a backlash over the Foley incident. He said many of the Republicans who lost had failed to recognize the strength of the voter dissatisfaction with the president and the party. "Unprepared members were swallowed up by the sour national environment," he said the days after the election.

In the Senate, Democrats barely eked out a majority, but that was considered a landslide victory given the odds they faced going into the election. To win control, they had to defend all fifteen of their incumbents, including four who appeared very vulnerable; hold on to three open Democratic seats; and defeat six of the fourteen Republicans running for reelection. The final results in two critical races were not known for two days after the first election results came in, but razor-thin Democratic victories in Montana and Virginia gave the Democrats and Republicans each forty-nine seats, with Sanders and Lieberman, the two independents, caucusing with the Democrats. That gave the party a one-vote margin, perhaps not enough to carry the day on crucial votes, but just enough to organize the Senate and set its agenda.

(The precariousness of the Democrats' control of the Senate was made even clearer on December 13 when Democrat Tim Johnson of South Dakota underwent emergency brain surgery to treat a life-threatening condition known as arteriovenous malformation. Johnson survived the operation but was expected to undergo a long period of recuperation. At year's end it was unclear whether or when he would return to his Senate duties.)

The Democrats' campaign strategy of nationalizing the issues and asking voters to choose between a change in direction or more of the same helped them win four crucial states—Missouri, Ohio, Pennsylvania, and Rhode Island. In Virginia, former navy secretary Jim Webb also benefited from a gaffe by the Republican incumbent. George Allen, who had been considered a potential GOP presidential candidate in 2008, suffered after he made comments that some construed as racially insensitive. In Montana the president of the state senate, Jon Tester, won a narrow victory over incumbent Republican Conrad Burns, who had been stained by his ties to convicted lobbyist Jack Abramoff, as well as Burns's own proclivity for inopportune comments.

Republicans held on to two other Senate seats, in Arizona and Tennessee, that had been considered vulnerable, while Democrats fended off a serious threat to New Jersey incumbent Robert Menendez and held onto three open seats that had been occupied by Democrats. Another ten Democrats and seven Republicans all won reelection with relative ease. Democrats also had a good shot at expanding their majority in 2008, when the GOP would have to defend twenty-one Republican Senate seats, compared with the Democrats' dozen.

Democrats also ran well in gubernatorial races, picking up six seats formerly held by Republicans. When all the ballots were counted, Democrats held the governorship in twenty-eight states—their first gubernatorial majority since 1994. The elections broadened the Democratic base in the states and, potentially, the party's regional influence. Only one incumbent was defeated; Maryland Republican governor Robert L. Ehrlich Jr. lost to Baltimore mayor Martin O'Malley. Among the newly elected governors were Democrat Eliot Spitzer of New York, the former state attorney general who was active in suing polluters and moving against abuses in Wall Street brokerage houses and insurance companies, and Democrat Deval Patrick of Massachusetts, who became the second African American ever elected governor (the first was L. Douglas Wilder of Virginia in 1989). Democrats also increased their representation in state legislatures, particularly in the Midwest. After the 2004 elections, the two parties were virtually tied in control of state legislatures. In 2007 Democrats would have a majority in both houses in twenty-two states, compared with the GOP's fifteen. Twelve states were split and one, Nebraska, had a nonpartisan, unicameral legislature.

New Leadership, New Priorities

The new Speaker of the House was slated to be Nancy Pelosi of California, the current Democratic leader. Pelosi would be the first woman to hold that office, the highest ranking elective position ever held by a woman in the United States. Speaking at a news conference on November 8, Pelosi said the new Democratic majority had "heard the voices of the American people" and pledged that her party would govern with civility, bipartisanship, integrity, and fiscal responsibility. On the Republican side, Hastert said he would not seek a leadership post in the new Congress. In his place the GOP caucus elected John A. Boehner of Ohio.

In the Senate, Harry Reid of Nevada would remain the Democratic leader. Republicans elevated Mitch McConnell of Kentucky to be minority leader in the new Congress, succeeding Bill Frist of Tennessee, who did not stand for reelection and retired from Congress at the end of the year. Moving into McConnell's place as Republican whip was Trent Lott of Mississippi. Lott had been forced to resign as Republican leader in 2002 after making a racially insensitive remark at a one hundredth birthday party for Sen. Strom Thurmond, R-S.C., who had been an active segregationist at an early stage of his long life. *(Lott remarks, Historic Documents of 2002, p. 969)*

Under Pelosi's guidance, House Democrats pledged to pass nine initiatives in the first hundred hours of the 110th Congress. Among these items were a hike in the minimum wage, authority for the government to negotiate lower drug prices for seniors, expanded federal funding for stem call research, a cut in the interest rates on student loans, tougher ethics rules, and a rollback of subsidies for big oil producers. Whether House Democrats could meet this schedule, and whether Senate Democrats could win enough Republican support to enact these measures, remained to be seen.

But it was clear that the war in Iraq was going to be at the top of the congressional agenda when the new Congress convened in 2007. "We know that 'stay the course' is not working, has not made our country safer, it has not honored our commitment to our troops, and it has not brought stability to the region," Pelosi said in her November 8 news conference. "We must not continue on this catastrophic path." But by the end of the year, Bush had signaled that he was likely to stick to his current policy and that, rather than begin to withdraw troops as the voters had indicated they wanted, he was considering sending another 20,000 troops to bolster the U.S. forces already fighting in Iraq.

*Following are excerpts from two statements concerning the Democratic takeover
of the House and Senate following the November 7, 2006, midterm elections: first,
from a news conference given by President George W. Bush at the White House
on November 8; second, from a news conference given by House Minority Leader
Nancy Pelosi, D-Calif., on November 8 at the Capitol.*

▮ DOCUMENT ▮

"The President's News Conference"

The President: Thank you. Say, why all the glum faces?

Yesterday the people went to the polls, and they cast their vote for a new direction in the House of Representatives. And while the ballots are still being counted in the Senate, it is clear the Democrat Party had a good night last night, and I congratulate them on their victories.

This morning I spoke with Republican and Democrat leadership in the House and Senate. I spoke with Republican leaders, Senator [Bill] Frist and Senator [Mitch] McConnell and Speaker [Dennis] Hastert and John Boehner and Roy Blunt. I thanked them for their hard-fought contests. I appreciated the efforts they put in for our candidates.

I'm obviously disappointed with the outcome of the election, and as the head of the Republican Party, I share a large part of the responsibility. I told my party's leaders that it is now our duty to put the elections behind us and work together with the Democrats and independents on the great issues facing this country.

This morning I also spoke with the Democrats. I spoke with Senators [Harry] Reid and [Richard] Durbin. I congratulated them on running a strong campaign in the Senate, and I told them that, regardless of the final outcome, we can work together over the next 2 years. I also congratulated Congresswoman [Nancy] Pelosi and Congressman [Steny] Hoyer. They ran a disciplined campaign. Their candidates were well-organized and did a superb job of turning out their vote.

I told Congresswoman Pelosi that I look forward to working with her and her colleagues to find common ground in the next 2 years. As the majority party in the House of Representatives, they recognize that in their new role, they now have greater responsibilities. And in my first act of bipartisan outreach since the election, I shared with her the names of some Republican interior decorators who can help her pick out the new drapes in her new offices.

I believe that the leaders of both political parties must try to work through our differences. And I believe we will be able to work through differences. I've reassured the House and Senate leaders that I intend to work with the new Congress in a bipartisan way to address issues confronting this country. I invited them to come to the White House in the coming days to discuss the important work remaining this year and to begin conversations about the agenda for next year.

The message yesterday was clear: The American people want their leaders in Washington to set aside partisan differences, conduct ourselves in an ethical manner, and work together to address the challenges facing our Nation.

We live in historic times. The challenges and opportunities are plain for all to see: Will this country continue to strengthen our economy today and over the long run? Will we provide a first-class education for our children? And will we be prepared for the global challenges of the 21st century? Will we build upon the recent progress we've made in addressing our energy dependence by aggressively pursuing new technologies to break our addiction to foreign sources of energy? And most importantly, will this generation of leaders meet our obligation to protect the American people?

I know there's a lot of speculation on what the election means for the battle we're waging in Iraq. I recognize that many Americans voted last night to register their displeasure with the lack of progress being made there. Yet I also believe most Americans and leaders here in Washington from both political parties understand we cannot accept defeat.

In the coming days and weeks, I and members of my national security team will meet with the members of both parties to brief them on latest developments and listen to their views about the way forward. We'll also provide briefings to the new Members of Congress so they can be fully informed as they prepare for their new responsibilities.

As we work with the new leaders in Congress, I'm also looking forward to hearing the views of the bipartisan Iraq Study Group, cochaired by Secretary James Baker and Congressman Lee Hamilton. This group is assessing the situation in Iraq and are expected to provide—and the group is expected to provide recommendations on a way forward. And I'm going to meet with them, I think, early next week.

The election has changed many things in Washington, but it has not changed my fundamental responsibility, and that is to protect the American people from attack. As the Commander in Chief, I take these responsibilities seriously. And so does the man who served this nation honorably for almost 6 years as our Secretary of Defense, Donald Rumsfeld. Now, after a series of thoughtful conversations, Secretary Rumsfeld and I agreed that the timing is right for new leadership at the Pentagon.

Our military has experienced an enormous amount of change and reform during the last 5 years while fighting the war on terror, one of the most consequential wars in our Nation's history. Don Rumsfeld has been a superb leader during a time of change. Yet he also appreciates the value of bringing in a fresh perspective during a critical period in this war. Don Rumsfeld is a patriot who served our country with honor and distinction. He's a trusted adviser and a friend, and I'm deeply grateful to his service to our country.

I've asked Bob Gates to serve as the Secretary of Defense. Bob is a former Director of the CIA and current president of Texas A&M University. If confirmed by the Senate, Bob will bring more than 25 years of national security experience and a stellar reputation as an effective leader with sound judgment. He's served six Presidents from both political parties and rose from an entry-level employee in the CIA to become the Director of Central Intelligence. During his service at the CIA and at the National Security Council, Bob Gates gained firsthand knowledge that will help him meet the challenges and opportunities our country faces during the next 2 years. He is serving as a member of the Baker-Hamilton Commission. He's a steady, solid leader who can help make the necessary adjustments in our approach to meet our current challenges.

I will have more to say about Secretary Rumsfeld and Bob Gates later today here at the White House.

Amid this time of change, I have a message for those on the frontlines. To our enemies: Do not be joyful; do not confuse the workings of our democracy with a lack of will. Our

Nation is committed to bringing you to justice. Liberty and democracy are the source of America's strength, and liberty and democracy will lift up the hopes and desires of those you are trying to destroy.

To the people of Iraq: Do not be fearful. As you take the difficult steps toward democracy and peace, America is going to stand with you. We know you want a better way of life, and now is the time to seize it.

To our brave men and women in uniform: Don't be doubtful. America will always support you. Our Nation is blessed to have men and women who volunteer to serve and are willing to risk their own lives for the safety of our fellow citizens.

When I first came to Washington nearly 6 years ago, I was hopeful I could help change the tone here in the Capital. As Governor of Texas, I had successfully worked with both Democrats and Republicans to find commonsense solutions to the problems facing our State. While we made some progress on changing the tone, I'm disappointed we haven't made more. I'm confident that we can work together. I'm confident we can overcome the temptation to divide this country between red and blue. The issues before us are bigger than that, and we are bigger than that. By putting this election and partisanship behind us, we can launch a new era of cooperation and make these next 2 years productive ones for the American people.

I appreciate your interest. Now, I'll answer some questions.

U.S. Armed Forces in Iraq

Question: Thank you, Mr. President. Does the departure of Don Rumsfeld signal a new direction in Iraq? A solid majority of Americans said yesterday that they wanted some American troops, if not all, withdrawn from Iraq. Did you hear that call, and will you heed it?

President: I'd like our troops to come home too, but I want them to come home with victory, and that is a country that can govern itself, sustain itself, and defend itself. And I can understand Americans saying, "Come home." But I don't know if they said come home and leave behind an Iraq that could end up being a safe haven for Al Qaida. I don't believe they said that. And so, I'm committed to victory. I'm committed to helping this country so that we can come home.

Now, the first part about . . . a new direction. Well, there's certainly going to be new leadership at the Pentagon. And as I mentioned in my comments, that Secretary Rumsfeld and I agree that sometimes it's necessary to have a fresh perspective, and Bob Gates will bring a fresh perspective. He'll also bring great managerial experience.

And he is—I had a good talk with him on Sunday in Crawford. I hadn't—it took me a while to be able to sit down and visit with him, and I did, and I found him to be of like mind. He understands we're in a global war against these terrorists. He understands that defeat is not an option in Iraq. And I believe it's important that there be a fresh perspective, and so does Secretary Rumsfeld.

Resignation of Secretary of Defense Rumsfeld

Question: Thank you, Mr. President. Last week you told us that Secretary Rumsfeld will be staying on. Why is the timing right now for this, and how much does it have to do with the election results?

President: Right. No, you [Steve Holland, Reuters] and [Terrence] Hunt [Associated Press], and Keil [Richard Keil, Bloomberg News] came in the Oval Office, and Hunt asked me the question one week before the campaign, and basically it was, "Are you going to do something about Rumsfeld and the Vice President?" And my answer was, they're going to stay on. And the reason why is, I didn't want to inject a major decision about this war in the final days of a campaign. And so the only way to answer that question and to get you on to another question was to give you that answer.

The truth of the matter is, as well—I mean, that's one reason I gave the answer, but the other reason why is, I hadn't had a chance to visit with Bob Gates yet, and I hadn't had my final conversation with Don Rumsfeld yet at that point.

I had been talking with Don Rumsfeld over a period of time about fresh perspective. He likes to call it fresh eyes. He himself understands that Iraq is not working well enough, fast enough. And he and I are constantly assessing. And I'm assessing, as well, all the time, by myself about, do we have the right people in the right place or do we—got the right strategy? As you know, we're constantly changing tactics, and that requires constant assessment.

And so he and I both agreed in our meeting yesterday that it was appropriate that I accept his resignation. And so the decision was made—actually, I thought we were going to do fine yesterday. Shows what I know. But I thought we were going to be fine in the election. My point to you is, is that, win or lose, Bob Gates was going to become the nominee.

Bipartisan Cooperation in Congress

Question: Thank you, Mr. President. You said you're interested in changing the tone and committed to changing the tone in Washington. Just a few days before this election, in Texas, you said that Democrats, "No matter how they put it, their approach to Iraq comes down to terrorists win; America loses." What has changed today, number one? Number two, is this administration prepared to deal with the level of oversight and investigation that is possibly going to come from one chamber or two in Congress?

President: What's changed today is the election is over, and the Democrats won. And now we're going to work together for 2 years to accomplish big objectives for the country. And secondly, the Democrats are going to have to make up their mind about how they're going to conduct their affairs. And I haven't had a chance to talk with the leadership yet about these issues, but we'll begin consultations with the Democrat leadership starting Thursday and Friday.

Implications of 2006 Elections/War on Terror

Question: Mr. President, thank you. You acknowledged that this is a message election on the war in Iraq. And so the American public today, having voted, will want to know what you mean in terms of "course correction on Iraq." And particularly in light of this fact, that last week the Vice President pointed out that you and he aren't running for anything anymore, and that it's full speed ahead on Iraq. So which is it? Are you listening to the voters, or are you listening to the Vice President? And what does that mean?

President: I believe Iraq had a lot to do with the election, but I believe there was other factors as well. People want their Congress—Congressmen to be honest and ethical. So in some races, that was the primary factor. There were different factors that determined the outcome of different races, but no question, Iraq was on people's minds. And as you have just learned, I am making a change at the Secretary of Defense to bring a fresh perspective as to how to achieve something I think most Americans want, which is a victory.

We will work with Members of Congress; we will work with the Baker-Hamilton Commission. My point is, is that while we have been adjusting, we will continue to adjust to achieve the objective. And I believe that's what the American people want.

Somehow it seeped in their conscious that my attitude was just simply, stay the course. "Stay the course" means, let's get the job done, but it doesn't mean staying stuck on a strategy or tactics that may not be working. So perhaps I need to do a better job of explaining that we're constantly adjusting. And so there's fresh perspective—so what the American people hear today is we're constantly looking for fresh perspective.

But what's also important for the American people to understand is that if we were to leave before the job is done, the country becomes more at risk. That's what the Vice President was saying—he said, "If the job is not complete, Al Qaida will have safe haven from which to launch attacks." These radicals and extremists have made it clear they want to topple moderate governments to spread their ideology. They believe that it's just a matter of time before we leave so they can implement their strategies. We're just not going to let them do that. We're going to help this Government become a government that can defend, govern, and sustain itself, and an ally in the war on terror. . . .

Robert M. Gates

Question: Mr. President, thank you. Can I just start by asking you to clarify, sir, if, in your meeting with Steve and Terry and Dick, did you know at that point—

President: I did not.

Question:—you would be making a change on Secretary Rumsfeld?

President: No, I did not. And the reason I didn't know is because I hadn't visited with his replacement—potential replacement.

Question: But you knew he would be leaving, just not who would replace him?

President: No, I didn't know that at the time.

Question: Okay. May I ask you about Nancy Pelosi—

President: The other thing I did know, as well, is that that kind of question, a wise question by a seasoned reporter, is the kind of thing that causes one to either inject major military decisions at the end of a campaign, or not. And I have made the decision that I wasn't going to be talking about hypothetical troop levels or changes in command structure coming down the stretch.

And I'll tell you why I made that decision. I made that decision because I think it sends a bad signal to our troops if they think the Commander in Chief is constantly adjusting tactics and decisions based upon politics. And I think it's important in a time of war that, to the extent possible, we leave politics out of the major decisions being made. And it was the right decision to make, by the way.

And secondly, I hadn't visited with Bob Gates. I told you I visited with him last Sunday in Crawford. You can't replace somebody until you know you got somebody to replace him with. And finally, I hadn't had my last conversation with Secretary Rumsfeld, which I had yesterday.

Rep. Nancy Pelosi

Question: Mr. President, I'd like to ask you: Nancy Pelosi has been quite clear about her agenda for the first 100 hours. She mentions things like raising minimum wage, cutting interest rates on student loans, broadening stem cell research, and rolling back tax cuts. Which of those can you support, sir?

President: I knew you'd probably try to get me to start negotiating with myself. I haven't even visited with Congresswoman Pelosi yet. She's coming to the Oval Office later this week; I'm going to sit down and talk with her. I believe on a lot of issues we can find common ground, and there's a significant difference between common ground and abandoning principle. She's not going to abandon her principles, and I'm not going to abandon mine. But I do believe we have an opportunity to find some common ground to move forward on.

In that very same interview you quoted, one of these three characters asked me about minimum wage. I said, there's an area where I believe we can make some—find common ground. And as we do, I'll be, of course, making sure that our small businesses are—there's compensation for the small businesses in the bill. . . .

Vice President Dick Cheney

Question: Thank you, Mr. President. . . . Vice President Cheney, of course, has made—takes many of the same positions that Secretary Rumsfeld did on the war. Does he still have your complete confidence?

President: Yes, he does.

Question: Do you expect him to stay—

President: The campaign is over. Yes, he does.

Question: And he'll be here for the remainder of your term?

President: Yes, he will. Thank you.

Bipartisan Cooperation in Congress

Question: Thank you, Mr. President. With all due respect, Nancy Pelosi has called you incompetent, a liar, the emperor with no clothes, and as recently as yesterday, dangerous. How will you work with someone who has such little respect for your leadership and who is third in line to the Presidency?

President: I've been around politics a long time; I understand when campaigns end, and I know when governing begins. And I am going to work with people of both parties.

Look, people say unfortunate things at times. But if you hold grudges in this line of work, you're never going to get anything done. And my intention is to get some things done. And as I said, I'm going to start visiting with her on Friday, with the idea of coming together.

Look, this was a close election. If you look at race by race, it was close. The cumulative effect, however, was not too close—it was a thumping. But nevertheless, the people expect us to work together. That's what they expect. And as I said in my opening comments, there comes responsibility with victory. And that's what Nancy Pelosi told me this morning. She said in the phone call she wants to work together. And so do I. And so that's how you deal with it.

This isn't—this isn't my first rodeo. In other words, I haven't—this is not the first time I've been in a campaign where people have expressed themselves, and in different kinds of ways. But I have learned that if you focus on the big picture, which, in this case, is our Nation and issues we need to work together on, you can get stuff done. For example, the No Child Left Behind Act is going to come up for reauthorization. There's an area where we must work together for the sake of our children and for the sake of a competitive America. And I believe we can get a lot done. And I know it's the spirit of the new leadership to try to get a lot done, and I look forward to talking to them about it.

Implications of 2006 Elections

Question: Thank you, Mr. President. You just described the election results as a "thumping."

President: ... Let's make sure we get it—the facts. I said that the elections were close; the cumulative effect—

Question: Is a thumping.

President:—thumping. ...

Question: But the results are being interpreted as a repudiation of your leadership style in some quarters. I wonder what your reaction is to that. And do you—should we expect a very different White House? Should we expect a very different leadership style from you in these last 2 years, given that you have a whole new set of partners?

President: You know, I really haven't—I'm still going to try to speak plainly about what I think are the important priorities of the country, and winning this war on terror is, by far, the most important priority. And making sure this economy continues to grow is an important priority. And making sure our children have a good education is an important priority.

Obviously, there's a shift in the Congress and, therefore, in order to get legislation passed, we've got to work with the Democrats. They're the ones who will control the committees; they're the ones who will decide how the bills flow. And so you'll see a lot of meetings with Democrats and a lot of discussion with Democrats.

And in terms of the election, no question Iraq had something to do with it. And it's tough in a time of war when people see carnage on their television screens. The amazing thing about this election, and what surprised me somewhat—which goes to show I should not try punditry—is that this economy is strong. And a lot of times, off years are decided by the economy. And yet, obviously there was a different feel out there for the electorate. The economy—the good news in the economy was overwhelmed by the toughness of this fight and toughness of the war.

And so, Jim, look, I understand people don't agree—didn't agree with some of my decisions. I'm going to continue making decisions based upon what I think is right for the country. I've never been one to try to fashion the principles I believe or the decisions I make based upon trying to—kind of short-term popularity. I do understand where the people—the heart of the people. I understand they're frustrated. I am too, as I said the other day. I wish this had gone faster. So does Secretary Rumsfeld. But the reality is, is that it's a tough fight, and we're going to win the fight. And I truly believe the only way we won't win is if we leave before the job is done. . . .

Immigration Reform

Question: Thank you, Mr. President. On immigration, many Democrats had more positive things to say about your comprehensive proposal than many Republicans did. Do you think a Democratic Congress gives you a better shot at comprehensive immigration reform?

President: You know, I should have brought this up. I do. I think we have a good chance. And thank you. It's an important issue, and I hope we can get something done on it. I meant to put that in my list of things that we need to get done.

I would hope Republicans have recognized that we've taken very strong security measures to address one aspect of comprehensive immigration reform. And I was talking to Secretary [Michael] Chertoff today; he thinks that these measures we're taking are beginning to have measurable effects and that catch-and-release has virtually been ended over the last couple of months. And that's positive.

And that's what some Members were concerned about prior to advancing a comprehensive bill. In other words, they said, "Show me progress on the border, and then we'll be interested in talking about other aspects." Well, there's progress being made on the border in terms of security, and I would hope we can get something done. It's a vital issue. It's an issue that—there's an issue where I believe we can find some common ground with the Democrats.

Question: What are the odds for a guest-worker provision?

President: Well, that's got to be an integral part of a comprehensive plan. When you're talking comprehensive immigration reform, one part of it is a guest-worker program, where people can come on a temporary basis to do jobs Americans are not doing. I've always felt like that would be an important aspect of securing the border. In other words, if somebody is not trying to sneak in in the first place, it makes—decreases the work load on our Border Patrol and lets the Border Patrol focus on drugs and guns and terrorists. But that's a—I appreciate you bringing that up. I should have remembered it.

Listen, thank you all very much for your time. I appreciate your interest.

Source: U.S. Executive Office of the President. "The President's News Conference." November 8, 2006. *Weekly Compilation of Presidential Documents* 42, no. 45 (November 13, 2006): 2023–2033. Washington, D.C.: National Archives and Records Administration. www.gpoaccess.gov/wcomp/v42no45.html (accessed December 21, 2006).

■ DOCUMENT ■

"Pelosi Holds News Conference on Legislative Agenda"

Rep. Nancy Pelosi: Good afternoon....

You were there. You saw the children. Weren't they wonderful? Could I ever exaggerate how exhilarating it was to be welcomed to the Capitol by these wonderful, beautiful little children who were so proud of themselves and how they hoped that we would understand that they are the future, that they would be somebody, and that was our responsibility to help them be so?

And as I said, it was part of our campaign all along that this election is about the future, about the responsibility one generation has to the next to make the future better.

So I thought it was heaven-sent, really; just a perfect, perfect way to start a new day after the election.

That was this morning.

Yesterday, the beauty and the genius of our democracy—the American people—spoke with their vote.

And they spoke for change and they spoke in support of a new direction for all Americans.

Supporting a great array of magnificent, talented Democratic candidates, they chose a Democratic majority to address the concerns of America's working families and, of course, to address the concern that the American people have about the war in Iraq.

This new Democratic majority has heard the voices of the American people. They spoke out for a new direction to bring integrity—integrity—back to Washington. And we will make this the most honest, ethical and open Congress in history.

The American people spoke out for a return to civility in the capitol in Washington and how Congress conducts its work.

And Democrats pledge stability and bipartisanship in the conduct of the work here.

And we pledge partnerships with the Republicans in Congress and with the president, and not partisanship.

And they talked about the new direction in terms of the fairness of our economy in our country. And Democrats are working for an economy that enables all Americans to participate in the economic success of our country.

But nowhere was the call for a new direction more clear from the American people than in the war in Iraq.

This is something that we must work together with the president. We know that "stay the course" is not working, has not made our country safer, it has not honored our commitment to our troops, and it has not brought stability to the region. We must not continue on this catastrophic path.

And so, hopefully, we can work with the president for a new direction, one that solves the problem in Iraq.

So with integrity, with civility, with bipartisanship that goes with that, with fiscal responsibility so that we're not heaping mountains of debt on those young children that were at the foot of the steps of the Capitol this morning, we intend to go forward wit our Six for '06 that we talked about in the campaign: to make America safer, to make our economy fair, to make college more affordable, to make health care more accessible and better by promoting stem cell research, to move toward energy independence, to guarantee a dignified retirement—to do this, again, in a fiscally sound way with civility, integrity and bipartisanship.

That is where we are going with this. The American people, with their votes yesterday, placed their trust in the Democrats. We will honor that trust. We will not disappoint.

Question: To the extent—you mentioned that Iraq was the biggest issue . . . what can you do as the leader of the House of Representatives and what will you do specifically [about] policy on Iraq?

Rep. Pelosi: It's not about the Democrats in Congress forcing the president's hand. The American people have spoken.

It's important for us to work in a bipartisan way with the president, again, to solve the problem, not to stay the course. That's not working. That's clear.

And if there's anything clear in the election results was that the more the president campaigned on the war, the fewer votes the Republicans who supported that got. And that took its toll on the Republicans.

So the campaign is over, as I said. Democrats are ready to lead. We're prepared to govern. But that means in a bipartisan way in a system that is self-evident.

The president is the president of the United States. I hope that he will listen to the voices of the people and, again, putting aside partisanship and looking to a partnership to end this war.

We've written to him in the past on this subject. Senator Harry Reid and I, the leader in the Senate, and the leadership of the committees of jurisdiction on this subject, and said that we want to work together in a bipartisan way to send a clear message to the Iraqi government and people that they must disarm the militias; they must amend their constitution; they must engage in regional diplomacy to bring more stability and reconstruction to Iraq; and that we must begin the responsible redeployment of our troops outside of Iraq.

We've said that over and over again.

Question: You have called for the redeployment to begin by the end of the year.

Rep. Pelosi: That's right. That's what we have. And we look forward to having a conversation with the president. And I hope that, as respectful as we are of the results of the election, I'm certain the president will be, too.

In fact, I spoke with the president this morning. And he said he looked—we didn't talk about Iraq, but we both expressed our wish to work in a bipartisan way for the benefit of the American people.

And I think that nowhere is that more necessary than ending the problem in Iraq.

Question: The expectations, at this point, do seem to be rather high . . . that because there is a new House of Representatives that the policy in Iraq will change.

How you manage expectations, given the reality of the fact that it is the president who dictates foreign policy, especially when it comes to war policy?

Rep. Pelosi: Well, I think that there has to be a signal of a change of direction on the part of the president.

The one good place he could start is a place where not only the Democrats and large numbers of the American people, but the voices of the military have spoken out, and that is to change the civilian leadership at the Pentagon. That would signal an openness to new, fresh ideas on the subject.

But, again, that's not something we're going to resolve in this conversation here. That's a conversation that will—time will be better spent in conversation with the president. . . .

. . . I think that we should have as much discussion as possible—as I think I've said now—in a bipartisan way on the war in Iraq.

This is not the way you go to war—in a partisan way—it really isn't. And so maybe a way to solve the problem is to do so in a bipartisan way.

And then in terms of the outcome of the election—we [won't] know, maybe, for a couple of weeks what is going to happen on the Senate side.

But whatever the outcome, in terms of the final two elections to be resolved, the numbers picked up by the Senate bode very well for having more success for our Six for '06. . . .

Maybe I should just say it again for those of you who weren't following us on the campaign trail: Our Six for '06 is to make America safer by . . . enacting 9/11 Commission recommendations; make the economy fair by raising the minimum wage and repealing incentives to companies to send jobs overseas; to make college more affordable by cutting in half the interest rates on student loans and making some tuition tax deductible; by making, as I mentioned earlier, improving health care in America by advancing stem-cell research and by enabling the secretary to negotiate for lower prices for prescriptions drugs; moving toward energy independence, by repealing the subsidies to big oil and using the money for a search into alternative energy resources and every day that we are to work for preserving Social Security.

The first five, we'll do in the first 100 hours. Number six, preserving Social Security, we'll do every day that we are here.

Question: Now that the election is over and there are going to be leadership races in the Democratic caucus, are you going to endorse people publicly or privately?

Rep. Pelosi: I haven't even gotten to that. We haven't even finished counting the votes from last night's election.

Question: . . . Can you, sort of, present how you are going to engage the White House? And will you unleash your lieutenants to do any of those things?

Rep. Pelosi: Thank you for that question.

My friend. What I said is . . . Democrats are not about getting even. Democrats are about helping the American people to get ahead. And that's what our agenda is about.

And while some people are excited about prospects that they have, in terms of their priorities, they are not our priorities.

I have said and I say again that impeachment is off the table. This election was about the future . . . not about the Republicans.

And so we will go forward with an agenda on issues that are relevant to the lives of the American people, addressing their priorities. That's how we use our time. And we will again strive to work in a bipartisan fashion.

And don't just take it from what I say here. We have put it in writing in our civility-integrity package and our fiscal discipline package on how we will proceed.

So while the Republicans like to describe me as the person they feared most, I take great pride in representing the city of San Francisco and the Congress of the United States. I understand my role as leader of the Democrats, but even more important than that, I very, very, very much respect that I will be the Speaker of the House, not of the Democrats.

Source: CQ Transcriptions. "House Minority Leader Pelosi Holds News Conference on Legislative Agenda." November 8, 2006 (accessed December 20, 2006).

Other Historic Documents of Interest

President Bush on Replacing the Secretary of Defense

November 8, 2006

One day after his party suffered a stunning defeat in midterm congressional elections, President George W. Bush on November 8, 2006, fired his secretary of defense, Donald H. Rumsfeld, who had been a lightening rod for criticism of U.S. policy in Iraq. Bush replaced Rumsfeld with Robert M. Gates, who had served as director of the Central Intelligence Agency under the president's father, President George H. W. Bush.

Rumsfeld had become one of the most controversial cabinet officers in recent decades because of his management of the war in Iraq and his staunch refusal to acknowledge publicly that the war was not going well. He headed the Pentagon for nearly six turbulent years, falling just short of the record for tenure in that post held by Robert S. McNamara, whose management of the Vietnam War during the 1960s was equally controversial.

Gates took office on December 18, shortly after he was confirmed by the Senate. Although he had been a controversial figure at one point in his career, Gates generally was seen as much less combative than Rumsfeld. At year's end it was clear Gates would need every ounce of political support he could muster to carry out the next phase of Bush's policy in Iraq, which reportedly was to involve a short-term "surge" of some 20,000 troops, in addition to the 140,000 troops already there. *(Background, Historic Documents of 2005, p. 832)*

Rumsfeld at the Pentagon

In the course of a little more than three decades, Rumsfeld served twice as defense secretary, the first time as the youngest person ever to hold that post and the second time as the oldest. President Gerald R. Ford (1974–1976) put him in the Pentagon job in 1975, when Rumsfeld was just forty-three years old. After Ford was defeated in the 1976 elections, Rumsfeld left public life and went to work as a corporate executive. He did not stay entirely out of the public eye, however; in 1998 he chaired a group of hawkish defense experts who called for a major push to develop a system to protect the United States against a ballistic missile attack. *(Background, Historic Documents of 1998, p. 481)*

In December 2000, after George W. Bush was declared the winner of the disputed 2000 presidential elections, Bush appointed Rumsfeld as defense secretary. Rumsfeld thus joined his colleague and friend from the Ford White House, Dick Cheney, who was Bush's vice president. When he took office the following January, Rumsfeld, at age sixty-nine, was the oldest-ever defense secretary. *(2000 elections, Historic Documents of 2000, p. 906)*

Rumsfeld entered office with two chief priorities: building the missile defense system he had advocated three years earlier and "transforming" the military. Both were ambitious tasks, but the latter one was the challenge that truly excited the new Pentagon chief. Rumsfeld argued that the U.S. military was still trained and equipped to fight the Soviet Union in the era of the cold war, which had ended almost a decade earlier with the collapse of the Soviet Union in December 1991. The military needed to become more fleet and agile, he said, able to tackle new challenges, including the acquisition of nuclear weapons and long-range ballistic missiles by such countries as Iran and North Korea. *(Missile defense background, Historic Documents of 2004, p. 176)*

This posture brought Rumsfeld into direct conflict with some of the armed services, which resisted rapid change, and major defense contractors, who feared the loss of their long-term contracts to build ships, planes, and other expensive weapons systems. Partly because of that opposition, the changes Rumsfeld was able to implement during his tenure ended up being much less dramatic than his initial rhetoric had suggested. In February 2006, the Pentagon published its latest overarching strategy document, known as the Quadrennial Defense Review, which revealed that most of Rumsfeld's grand plans for transforming the military had come to naught. Nearly all of the military's cold war weapons systems, and plans for similar ones, had survived. The military that Rumsfeld left to Gates at the end of 2006 was similar to the one Rumsfeld had inherited in January 2001—except that it had been worn down by nearly five grinding years of war in Iraq.

Rumsfeld and Iraq

The September 11, 2001, terrorist attacks against the United States brought a quick change in the Bush administration's military priorities, but it also energized what had been a behind-the-scenes campaign by so-called neoconservatives inside and outside the administration for a more aggressive posture toward Iraq. Nine days after the attacks, Bush went before Congress to declare a "global war on terror," a war he said would be carried out both by conventional military means and by other measures, such as law enforcement and intelligence gathering. *(Terrorist attacks, Historic Documents of 2001, p. 637)*

The first battle in Bush's antiterrorism war took place in Afghanistan, which had been the home base of the al Qaeda terrorist network that Bush accused of sponsoring the September 11 attacks. The U.S. military, with help from Britain and other countries plus local Afghan groups opposed to the government there, quickly drove the Afghan government from power and dispersed hundreds of al Qaeda fighters. The Afghan operation illustrated much of what Rumsfeld had in mind for his transformed military; it relied heavily on small teams of special forces troops operating in secret, and the United States withdrew the bulk of its forces soon after the Taliban leaders of Afghanistan fled from Kabul. *(Background, Historic Documents of 2001, p. 686)*

However, the rapid U.S. pullout from Afghanistan proved controversial almost immediately. The country was left in chaos and the major sources of "security" for most areas outside Kabul were militias loyal to numerous warlords, most of whom had allied themselves with the United States only as a matter of convenience. Also, the man who the United States most wanted to capture—al Qaeda leader Osama bin Laden—managed to escape and was presumed to be hiding in the rugged mountainous area alongside the Afghan-Pakistan border. By 2006 Afghanistan once again was becoming a violent place, particularly in the southern provinces, where the Taliban appeared to be making a comeback.

The invasion of Afghanistan proved to be a dress rehearsal for a much bigger and more complex operation: the invasion of Iraq in March 2003. The two countries had roughly comparable populations of about 25 million each, but Iraq had a long-entrenched dictatorship with a battle-tested army. Moreover, Bush administration officials believed Iraq possessed large quantities of biological and chemical weapons and might use them against the invading armies.

It was little known at the time, but as plans for the Iraq invasion were being laid in 2002 and early 2003, Rumsfeld and his chief aides successfully fought bureaucratic battles with the State Department to retain control of U.S. policy toward Iraq after the invasion. The Pentagon brusquely rebuffed State Department experts who wanted to develop detailed plans for how Iraq would be managed once its leader, Saddam Hussein, was pushed from power. Subsequent reports by investigative journalists and disgruntled generals showed that Rumsfeld actively discouraged serious planning for the postinvasion phase; instead, he turned that task over to a retired army lieutenant general, Jay Garner, who was given little staff or time to prepare for running the country.

The initial phase of the war in Iraq went nearly as well as Rumsfeld and his generals had planned. The Iraqi army collapsed, and did not use its supposedly vast arsenal of biological and chemical weapons—none of which turned out to exist. Saddam lost his grip on Baghdad in just three weeks and went into hiding. *(Historic Documents of 2003, pp. 146, 874)*

From that point onward, virtually nothing in Iraq went according to plan; more accurately, just about every aspect of U.S. policy failed, in large part because the United States had no realistic postwar plans for Iraq. The Bush administration replaced Garner after he had been on the ground for just a few days. The replacement was a former ambassador, L. Paul Bremer III, who reported to the Pentagon, not the State Department, and was given full power to run Iraq as he saw fit. Bremer's first major moves were fateful ones: he disbanded the Iraqi army, thus angering a quarter-million men with guns, and he fired all government officials who had been members of Saddam's Ba'ath Party. The latter step eliminated not only the former dictator's close allies but also anyone with the expertise to run oil refineries, electrical generating facilities, health departments, schools, and other vital services.

Most independent observers later agreed that all these early actions in Iraq by Pentagon officials were at least partly responsible for spawning what the United States called an "insurgency" against the U.S. occupation. By 2006 that insurgency, led primarily by angry Sunni Muslims, had metastasized into a bloody cycle of sectarian violence that killed an estimated 34,000 Iraqis during the year and kept killing U.S. soldiers and marines at the rate of more than 800 a year.

During all this, Rumsfeld insisted the United States was doing the right thing and the Pentagon had made few, if any, mistakes. Rumsfeld acknowledged only one major blunder on the military's part: allowing a situation, at the Abu Ghraib prison near Baghdad, in which military police personnel from an army reserve unit abused Iraqi detainees. Early in 2004, when photographs of the abuse were shown worldwide and sparked outrage in the Muslim world, Rumsfeld offered to resign—an offer Bush refused to accept. *(Abu Ghraib, Historic Documents of 2004, p. 207)*

Rumsfeld was equally defensive when critics, both inside and outside the military, said the long-term deployments in Iraq were causing serious stresses that, over time, would damage the services, particularly, the U.S. Army, Marine Corps, and the National Guard and Reserves. By 2005 military recruiters were having difficulty meeting their targets, and the army resorted to lowering its standards for recruits and providing enlistment "bonuses" simply to get bodies in the door.

In January 2006, two studies by respected military experts drew new attention to the stresses on the military—and brought a tart response from Rumsfeld. One study, conducted by former secretary of defense William J. Perry and commissioned by congressional Democrats, faulted the Pentagon's planning of the Iraq War and said the U.S. Army and Marine Corps were under "enormous strain" because they lacked enough troops and equipment for their work in Iraq. The other study, by counterinsurgency expert Andrew F. Krepinevich, quoted army leaders as worrying about the impact of long deployments in Iraq on recruitment and retention of soldiers. Rumsfeld angrily rejected both studies. "The force is not broken" he told reporters on January 25. "I just can't imagine someone looking at the United States armed forces today and suggesting that they're close to breaking. That's just not the case."

Retired Generals Speak Out

The trickle of criticism from Perry, Krepinevich, and other experts soon turned into an extraordinary flood of condemnation of Rumsfeld and his methods by senior retired military officers. Starting around the time of the third anniversary of the beginning of the Iraq War, in mid-March 2006, retired generals issued detailed critiques of how the Pentagon was managing the war, and some of them called for Rumsfeld to resign. The criticisms were highly unusual because so many former generals were speaking out, and many of them appeared to be acting from deep frustration. In addition to public appearances in the news media and before congressional committees, some of the critics had been key sources for a series of books during 2005 and 2006 that detailed the Bush administration's failures in Iraq.

Two of the first retired generals to speak out were among those with detailed knowledge of the Middle East and the war in Iraq. They were Army Maj. Gen. Paul D. Eaton, who was in charge of training a new Iraqi army from 2003 to 2004, and Marine Gen. Anthony C. Zinni, who headed the U.S. Central Command (covering the Middle East) from 1997 to 2000 and had briefly served as Bush's special envoy in the Israeli-Palestinian dispute. Zinni's criticism of Rumsfeld was particularly harsh; he said the secretary valued loyalty above "honesty and performance and competence."

By mid-April another dozen or so retired generals and senior officers, some of whom had served in Iraq or held other positions during Rumsfeld's tenure, had stepped forward with criticisms that ranged from the lack of planning for the war to the secretary's refusal to listen to contrary advice. Some called on Rumsfeld to resign, while others simply offered negative comments on his policies.

Rumsfeld dismissed the criticism as routine, saying military officers throughout history had groused about their civilian superiors. "It's historic, it's always been the case, and I see nothing really very new or surprising about it," he told reporters. Most historians, however, said the depth and extent of the criticism was highly unusual and reflected frustrations dating to the Vietnam War, when many officers believed their military advice was ignored by civilian leaders for political reasons.

As could be expected, Rumsfeld received support from top military officers currently serving under him. Marine Gen. Peter Pace, the chairman of the Joint Chiefs of Staff, said officers had never been prevented from offering their views about the Iraq War before it was launched and in the years since then. "We had then and have now every opportunity to speak our minds, and if we do not, shame on us," he said. Although the criticism continued, Bush made clear on April 14 that he was not listening—at least not yet. "Early today I spoke with Don Rumsfeld about ongoing military operations in the global war on terror," he told reporters. "I reiterated my strong support of his leadership during this historic and challenging time for our nation." Rumsfeld also defended himself again, saying he was not bothered by criticism from a handful of generals among the "thousands and thousands" of current and retired flag-grade officers. Rumsfeld suggested that the criticism stemmed not from problems in Iraq but from the institutional resistance of some in the officer corps to his plans for transforming the military.

Rumsfeld as Political Target

The criticism from generals offered political cover for many Democrats and a few Republicans to join in the calls for Rumsfeld to resign. Among the most prominent voices were Sen. Hillary Rodham Clinton, D-N.Y., who at the time was her party's leading presidential candidate for 2008, and Sen. Joe Lieberman, the conservative Connecticut Democrat who often had been a key congressional ally of the Bush administration. Lieberman spoke out on August 20, two weeks after he lost the Democratic nomination for another Senate term to a fierce Iraq War critic; he ran instead as an independent in the general election—a race he easily won. Numerous Republicans in tight races also spoke out against Rumsfeld, some saying he should resign or be fired by the president. "It's probably the only thing in my life I've ever agreed with Hillary Clinton about," Rep. Jo Ann Davis, R-Va., said in early September. "He's probably a nice guy, but I don't think he's a great secretary of defense."

The November midterm elections turned into the equivalent of a national referendum on the Iraq War, with Rumsfeld often featured by Democrats as the chief architect of what they called the failures of that war. The election results, with Democrats capturing a solid majority of the House of Representatives and a one-seat majority in the Senate, were therefore seen by members of both parties as a popular expression of dissatisfaction with the war—and with Rumsfeld.

Even so, it came as a surprise when on November 8, the day after the election, a chastened Bush appeared before reporters at the White House to announce that Rumsfeld had resigned and would be replaced by former CIA director Gates. Bush offered nothing but praise for Rumsfeld, saying, "America is safer and the world is more secure because of the service and the leadership of Donald Rumsfeld." He noted that the defense secretary had planned and carried out the Iraq War "on my orders," an apparent attempt to accept some of the responsibility for what had gone wrong, but without directly acknowledging that anything had, in fact, gone wrong in Iraq. Bush also lavished praise on Gates, calling him "one of our nation's most accomplished public servants."

White House officials told reporters that discussions about replacing Rumsfeld had been under way for weeks, and that the president and his defense secretary had held several personal discussions on the course of the war and other matters. Gates and Bush met secretly two days before the election at the president's ranch in Crawford, Texas, but it was unclear whether he was offered the Pentagon job at that time. Aides said Bush informed Rumsfeld of the impending change after he returned to Washington on Election Day.

With Rumsfeld's departure, all of the senior Pentagon officials who had been responsible for planning the Iraq War and executing the early stages of it had moved on. Chief among the others were Paul Wolfowitz, who had been deputy secretary of defense and had since left to become president of the World Bank, and Douglas J. Feith, the undersecretary of defense for policy, who became a consultant.

Gates spent most of his career at the CIA, which he joined as a junior analyst in 1966. He rose steadily through the ranks, became a specialist on the Soviet Union, and served twice on the National Security Council staff at the White House. President Ronald Reagan (1981–1989) chose Gates to head the CIA in 1987, but Gates withdrew because of charges by some senators that he had not been forthcoming in testimony about the Iran-contra scandal.

President George H. W. Bush (1989–1993) nominated Gates for the same post in 1991, and again there was opposition, this time because of charges that he had slanted intelligence reporting on the Soviet Union to support administration positions. Gates was confirmed on a 61–31 vote, and he remained in the post until after Bush was defeated for reelection the following year. He went into business then joined Texas A&M University as dean of the school of government, which was named after the senior President Bush. Gates became president of the university in 2002; he later described that post as the best job he ever held. Gates was serving as a member of the bipartisan Iraq Study Group, which was preparing Iraq policy options for the president and Congress, when Bush named him to the Pentagon post. Gates stepped aside and was replaced by former secretary of state Lawrence S. Eagleburger. *(Gates CIA nomination, Historic Documents of 2001, p. 651)*

The Senate acted quickly on the Gates nomination. The Armed Services Committee, still under Republican leadership, held a remarkably congenial confirmation hearing on December 5; Gates spoke openly of the problems facing the United States in Iraq but declined to give detailed prescriptions, saying he needed to examine the situation more closely. The full Senate approved the nomination the next day on a vote of 95–2; the two "no" votes came from conservative Republicans Jim Bunning of Kentucky and Rick Santorum of Pennsylvania, the latter having been defeated for reelection. Several Democrats who had voted against Gates's confirmation at CIA director fifteen years earlier voted "yes" this time.

Bush, Cheney, and other senior administration officials attended an outdoor ceremony at the Pentagon on December 15 to mark Rumsfeld's last day in office. Rumsfeld had served in office just ten days shy of the record tenure for the job, held by McNamara. Gates took office on December 18 and immediately set about developing new policy proposals for Iraq, which Bush was expected to announce early in January 2007.

Calling for a "Major Adjustment" in Iraq

Rumsfeld was serving his last days in office when, on December 2, the *New York Times* published the text of a memorandum he had written to the president proposing a "major adjustment" of Iraq policy because the current policy "is not working well enough or fast enough." The memo was dated November 6—one day before the congressional elections and two days before Bush announced Rumsfeld's replacement. In its report, the *Times* said it was unclear what, if any, connection there was between the memo and the timing of Rumsfeld's departure.

In the memo, Rumsfeld said the time had come for "a major adjustment" in Iraq policy. The memo then laid out a series of "illustrative options," some of which were listed as "above the line" (acceptable) and others of which were "below the line" (or "less attractive"). Among the former were several ideas that were to be offered a week later by the Iraq Study Group, including significantly increasing the training of Iraqi security forces and laying out "benchmarks" for progress by the Iraqi government.

The less attractive options included the one with which Rumsfeld was most identified in the public mind: "continue on the current path."

Following is the text of the announcement at the White House by President George W. Bush on November 8, 2006, that he was nominating Robert M. Gates to succeed Donald H. Rumsfeld as secretary of defense, along with statements by Gates and Rumsfeld.

DOCUMENT

"President Bush Nominates Robert Gates to Be Secretary of Defense"

President Bush: Good afternoon, and welcome to the White House. Earlier today I announced my intent to nominate Robert Gates to be the next Secretary of Defense. And now I'm pleased to introduce him to the American people. I also am looking forward to paying tribute to the man he will succeed.

America remains a nation at war. We face brutal enemies who despise our freedom and want to destroy our way of life. These enemies attacked our country on September the 11th, 2001; they fight us in Afghanistan and Iraq, and they remain determined to attack our country again. Against such enemies, there's only one way to protect the American people: We must stay on the offense and bring our enemies to justice before they hurt us again.

In this time of war, the President relies on the Secretary of Defense to provide military advice and direct our nation's Armed Forces as they engage our enemies across the world. The Secretary of Defense must be a man of vision who can see threats still over the horizon, and prepare our nation to meet them. Bob Gates is the right man to meet both of these critical challenges.

Bob is one of our nation's most accomplished public servants. He joined the CIA in 1966, and has nearly 27 years of national security experience, serving six Presidents of both political parties. He spent nearly nine years serving on the National Security Council staff. And at the CIA, he rose from an entry-level employee to become the Director of the Central Intelligence. And his experience has prepared him well for this new assignment.

Bob understands the challenges we face in Afghanistan. As President [Ronald] Reagan's Deputy Director of Central Intelligence, he helped lead America's efforts to drive Soviet forces from Afghanistan. Success in these efforts weakened the Soviet regime and helped hasten freedom's victory in the Cold War.

Bob understands the challenges facing our nation in Iraq. He served as Deputy National Security Advisor to the first President Bush during Operation Desert Storm as American troops repelled Iraqi aggression and drove Saddam Hussein's forces from Kuwait. More recently, he served as a member of the Iraq Study Group, a distinguished independent panel of Republicans and Democrats led by former Secretary of State Jim

Baker and former Congressman Lee Hamilton. As part of this commission, he has traveled to Iraq and met with the country's leaders and our military commanders on the ground. He'll provide the department with a fresh perspective and new ideas on how America can achieve our goals in Iraq.

Bob understands how to lead large, complex institutions and transform them to meet new challenges. As Director of Central Intelligence, following the collapse of the Soviet Union, he was responsible for leading all the foreign intelligence agencies of the United States. And he's brought that same leadership and abilities as his work as President of our nation's sixth largest university, Texas A&M. When the A&M board of regents interviewed him for the job, he described himself as an agent of change. As president, he delivered on that promise, initiating wide-ranging reforms to almost every aspect of campus life. He'll bring that same transformational spirit to his work in the Department of Defense.

Bob Gates is a patriot whose love for country was nurtured in the Kansas community where he was raised. He's worn our nation's uniform. He's a strategic thinker who was educated at three of America's finest universities, receiving his bachelor's degree from William & Mary, a master's degree in history from Indiana University, and a doctorate in Russian and Soviet history from Georgetown.

He's a leader in the business community who served on the boards of several major corporations. He's a man of integrity, candor and sound judgment. He knows that the challenge of protecting our country is larger than any political party, and he has a record of working with leaders of both sides of the aisle to strengthen our national security. He has my confidence and my trust, and he will be an outstanding Secretary of Defense.

Bob follows in the footsteps of one of America's most skilled and capable national security leaders, Donald Rumsfeld. Don is the longest-serving member of my Cabinet, and next month he will reach another milestone when he becomes the longest-serving Secretary of Defense in the history of our nation. I appreciate his willingness to continue serving until his successor is in place, because in a time of war, our nation cannot be without a strong and steady hand leading our Department of Defense.

Don has served in times of great consequence for our nation. Few will forget the image of Don Rumsfeld as he helped rescue workers carry the victims from the rubble of the Pentagon on September the 11th, 2001. In the weeks that followed, he directed the effort to plan our nation's military response to an unprecedented attack on our soil. Under his leadership, U.S. and coalition forces launched one of the most innovative military campaigns in the history of modern warfare, driving the Taliban and its al Qaeda allies from power in a matter of weeks.

In 2003, on my orders, he led the planning and execution of another historic military campaign, Operation Iraqi Freedom, that drove Saddam Hussein from power and helped the Iraqi people establish a constitutional democracy in the heart of the Middle East. History will record that on Don Rumsfeld's watch, the men and women of our military overthrew two terrorist regimes, liberated some 50 million people, brought justice to the terrorist Zarqawi and scores of senior al Qaeda operatives, and helped stop new terrorist attacks on our people.

America is safer and the world is more secure because of the service and the leadership of Donald Rumsfeld. As he led the Pentagon in an unprecedented war, Don never took his eye off another vital responsibility, preparing America for the threats that await us as this new century unfolds. He developed a new defense strategy. He established a new

Northern Command to protect the homeland, a new Joint Forces Command to focus on transformation, a new Strategic Command to defend against long-range attack, and transformed the U.S. Special Operations Command for the war on terror.

He led our efforts to create a new NATO Response Force that allows NATO to deploy rapidly anywhere in the world. He undertook the most sweeping transformation of America's global force posture since the end of World War II. He revitalized America's efforts to develop and deploy ballistic missile defenses, and led a comprehensive review of America's nuclear forces that has allowed us to undertake dramatic reductions in offensive nuclear weapons.

Don's work in these areas did not often make the headlines. But the reforms that he has set in motion are historic, and they will enhance the security of the American people for decades to come.

Over the past six years, I've relied on Don Rumsfeld's advice and counsel. I've come to know his character and his integrity. As the Secretary of Defense, he has been dedicated to his mission, loyal to his President, and devoted to the courageous men and women of our Armed Forces.

Don once famously said, "There are known knowns; there are known unknowns; and there are unknown unknowns." Well, Mr. Secretary, here is a known known: Your service has made America stronger, and made America a safer nation. You will be missed, and I wish you and Joyce all the best in the years to come.

Don Rumsfeld is a tough act to follow. That's why I picked a man of Bob Gates's caliber to succeed him. When confirmed by the Senate, Bob will bring talent, energy and innovation to the Department of Defense. He'll work every day to keep the American people safe and to make our nation more secure. And he'll do a superb job as America's next Secretary of Defense.

Bob, I appreciate you agreeing to serve our nation again, and congratulations.

Robert Gates: Thank you, sir. Mr. President, thank you for this high honor and for your confidence. And let me add my thanks to Secretary Rumsfeld for his service.

I entered public service 40 years ago last August. President Bush will be the seventh President I have served. I had not anticipated returning to government service, and have never enjoyed any position more than being president of Texas A&M University. However, the United States is at war, in Iraq and Afghanistan. We're fighting against terrorism worldwide. And we face other serious challenges to peace and our security. I believe the outcome of these conflicts will shape our world for decades to come. Because our long-term strategic interests and our national and homeland security are at risk, because so many of America's sons and daughters in our Armed Forces are in harm's way, I did not hesitate when the President asked me to return to duty.

If confirmed by the Senate, I will serve with all my heart, and with gratitude to the President for giving me the opportunity to do so.

Secretary Rumsfeld: Bob Gates, my congratulations to you on this nomination. My very best wishes. Look forward to working with you in the transition.

Mr. President, thank you for your kind words, and the wholly unexpected opportunity you provided me to serve in the Department of Defense again these past years—six years. It's been quite a time. It recalls to mind the statement by Winston Churchill, something to the effect that "I have benefited greatly from criticism, and at no time have I suffered a lack thereof."

The great respect that I have for your leadership, Mr. President, in this little understood, unfamiliar war, the first war of the 21st century—it is not well-known, it was not well-understood, it is complex for people to comprehend. And I know, with certainty, that over time the contributions you've made will be recorded by history.

I must say that it's been the highest honor of my life to serve with the talented men and women of the Department of Defense, the amazing men and women—young men and women in uniform. It's a privilege. And their patriotism, their professionalism, their dedication is truly an inspiration. They have my respect; they will remain in my prayers always.

Thank you.

Source: U.S. Executive Office of the President. Office of the Press Secretary. "President Bush Nominates Dr. Robert M. Gates to Be Secretary of Defense." Press release. November 8, 2006. www.whitehouse.gov/news/releases/2006/11/20061108-4.html (accessed January 4, 2007).

Governor Vilsack and Senator Bayh on Presidential Campaign Decisions

November 9 and December 15, 2006

■■■■■■■ **THE DOCUMENT IN CONTEXT** ■■■■■■■

No sooner had the states put away their voting machines after the November 7, 2006, midterm elections than contenders began announcing their intentions for the 2008 presidential race. On November 9 Democrat Tom Vilsack, who was stepping down as Iowa's governor after two terms, became the first candidate of either party to formally announce that he was seeking the presidential nomination. On December 15, Democratic senator Evan Bayh of Indiana, who had all but thrown his hat in the ring only two weeks earlier, announced that he had decided against making the run. In the meanwhile, several candidates from both parties had taken formal steps to seek the presidency, and several more were expected to announce their intentions early in 2007.

There were a number of reasons for the unusually early start to the formal presidential campaign—and the unusually large number of contenders. The overarching incentive was thought to be the fact that, for the first time since 1928, neither the sitting president nor vice president would be a candidate. George W. Bush was serving his second and last term as president, and Vice President Dick Cheney had made it clear from the outset that he was not going to run. That left the field wide open.

Given the large number of potential contenders, fundraising became a major issue. Campaign finance experts expected the 2008 presidential race to be the most expensive ever, with some saying the two nominees might spend upward of $500 million apiece on their campaigns. Others suggested that to stay in the race a candidate would need to raise at least $30 million in 2007 and more realistically as much as $50 million or more. Candidates needed an early start to line up potential contributors. Those waiting too long to enter the race might find that major contributors were already supporting other candidates. The finite number of experienced campaign managers, fundraisers, field organizers, strategists, and other political consultants available to run a viable campaign provided additional incentive to get into the race as early as possible.

Yet another inducement for an early start was the likelihood that several large states would move their primaries to the start of the campaign season, most likely one week after the New Hampshire primary. Among those considering such a move were the populous states of California, Florida, Illinois, and New Jersey. Candidates wishing to be competitive in those states would need well-established campaign organizations and plenty of funds to buy advertising.

The extraordinarily early start to the 2008 presidential campaign ran the risk of exhausting both the voters and the candidates well before the election. At least one candidate had already cited the personal and family stress of a long and grueling campaign as a reason for deciding not to run. Democrat Mark Warner, a former governor of Virginia, was touted by many Democrats as a political moderate who could appeal to centrist voters of both parties. In a surprise announcement on October 12, Warner said he would not run because he did not want to put his "real life" on hold for the next two years.

The Democrats

The frontrunner for the Democratic presidential nomination was New York senator Hillary Rodham Clinton. Although she had not formally announced by the end of the year, Clinton had been leading all other Democrats in the polls for months. Clinton was a well-respected senator who easily won reelection in 2006; she had a proven ability to raise campaign funds as well as the support of many in the Democratic establishment who had worked with her husband, Bill Clinton, during his eight years in the White House. She also may have had greater name recognition than any other candidate likely to run. But many Democrats worried that Clinton was too polarizing a figure and that she could not win enough support from the political center to win the presidency.

The only other Democrat who came close to Clinton in the opinion polls was Barack Obama, the African American senator from Illinois whose keynote speech at the 2004 Democratic Convention caught the attention of viewers across the nation. Obama's announcement in late October that he was considering a run was followed up by a visit to New Hampshire in early December, where he seemed to be surprised by the large number of voters who came out to meet him. Obama had a charismatic personality and positive message that called for moving beyond the "slash-and-burn, highly ideological politics" of the past decade. Against those pluses was his relative lack of experience—he had served eight years as an Illinois state senator before being elected to the U.S. Senate in 2004. And, despite writing two memoirs that both reached and stayed on the bestseller lists, Obama had never ever been subjected to the scrutiny of every aspect of his political and personal life that modern presidential candidates had to endure. *(2004 Democratic Convention, Historic Documents of 2004, p. 483)*

Obama's hints that he might enter the race apparently affected the timing of Vilsack's announcement. Aides to the popular retiring governor said a main reason for his early announcement was to gain some visibility in the national media before attention to the heavyweights closed him out. Obama also apparently played a role in Bayh's decision to get out of the race. The former governor of Indiana and the son of former senator Birch Bayh, Bayh said on December 3 that he would form a formal exploratory committee within a few days and make a final decision over the holidays. But, on December 15, he announced that he would not run. Bayh's decision came after a trip to New Hampshire on December 10, which was eclipsed by the attention showered on Obama, who happened to be visiting the state on the same day. Bayh's announcement came as somewhat of a surprise. The moderate Democrat had amassed about $10 million and been planning for the race since winning reelection to the Senate in 2004. Another senator who explored the possibility of running but decided against it was Russell Feingold of Wisconsin.

John Edwards, the losing vice presidential candidate in 2004 and a one-term senator from North Carolina, formally announced his candidacy on December 28. Edwards made his announcement in New Orleans, where he was helping to clear debris from a house devastated by Hurricane Katrina in August 2005. Edwards pledged that his campaign would be "a grassroots, ground-up campaign, where we ask people to take action" and "change this country." Edwards's running mate in 2004, Massachusetts senator John F. Kerry, was also contemplating entering the 2008 race, although he might have had second thoughts when an unfortunate remark he made about the volunteer army just before the midterm election created such a backlash that he was forced to stop campaigning for Democratic candidates. *(2004 presidential elections results, Historic Documents of 2004, p. 773)*

At least two other candidates from 2004 were also contemplating running in 2008. Rep. Dennis Kucinich, former mayor of Cleveland, said he was planning to enter the race because the Democrats were not working hard enough to end the war in Iraq, including ending funding for it. Wesley Clark acknowledged in late November that he was considering another run. The retired general and former NATO commander joined the 2004 race in September 2003 and dropped out in February 2004 after winning only one of fourteen primaries and caucuses that he contested. Clark said his late entry into the race doomed his chances and he vowed not to make that mistake again in 2008.

As the year ended, a raft of other Democrats were also deciding whether to enter the race. Among them were Sen. Joseph R. Biden Jr. of Delaware, Sen. Christopher J. Dodd of Connecticut, and Gov. Bill Richardson of New Mexico. Dodd said he was not discouraged by the early support for Clinton and Obama. "This is only 2006," he said in mid-December.

The Republicans

On the Republican side, the early frontrunners were Sen. John McCain of Arizona and former New York City mayor Rudolph F. Giuliani, who leaped to national recognition with his calm but firm handling of the chaos that engulfed the city on September 11, 2001. Mitt Romney, who stepped down as governor of Massachusetts early in 2007, was also in contention.

McCain, who formally set up his exploratory committee on November 17, was a former navy pilot who served four years in the U.S. House before being elected to the Senate in 1986. McCain made an unsuccessful run for the presidency in 2000 against Bush and differed with the president on several key issues, including the president's policies on interrogations of war prisoners. But McCain was a staunch supporter of the Iraq War, arguing that more U.S. troops should be put into the battle. If elected, McCain would be seventy-two when he entered the White House in January 2009, making him the oldest president elected to a first term in U.S. history. McCain also had some health issues, including cancerous skin lesions and residual problems stemming from his years as a Vietnam prisoner of war. In recent speeches, McCain had been working hard to repair his relations with the conservative religious wing of the party that had formed the core of Bush's support; during his 2000 campaign, McCain had accused leaders such as the Rev. Jerry Falwell of being intolerant.

Although early polls gave Giuliani a slight edge over McCain, many political pundits thought Giuliani's political views were too liberal for him to win the Republican nomination. Giuliani filed papers on November 20 and named the political director of the Republican National Committee to head his exploratory committee. Giuliani's support of abortion, gun control, and immigrant rights put him at odds with social conservatives, but his early campaign messages emphasized fighting crime, cutting taxes, and restoring fiscal responsibility, all issues that resonated with other elements of the GOP. Giuliani was also a strong supporter of both the war in Iraq and the president's war on terror.

Romney, who had not filed formal papers by the end of the year, was more conservative than either McCain or Giuliani on social issues. But he had shifted his positions on gay marriage and abortion since mounting an unsuccessful campaign against Sen. Edward M. Kennedy of Massachusetts in 1994, and many in the party questioned his sincerity. Romney's Mormon religion was also considered a potential obstacle.

Several Republican long-shots had either already entered the race or were poised to do so as 2006 ended. Among those who had set up formal exploratory committees were Sen. Sam Brownback of Kansas, well-known for his outspoken opposition to abortion, gay marriage, and embryonic stem cell research; James S. Gilmore III, former Virginia governor and former chairman of the Republican National Committee, who said he was running because no other "committed conservative" was in the race; and Rep. Duncan Hunter of California. Other potential candidates included former House speaker Newt Gingrich of Georgia; George E. Pataki, who was stepping down as governor of New York after twelve years in office; Arkansas governor Mike Huckabee; Tommy Thompson, a former governor of Wisconsin; and Rep. Tom Tancredo of Colorado, who was secretary of health and human services during Bush's first term and whose anti-immigration position appealed to some voters in the Southwest.

Senate Majority Leader Bill Frist, whose departure from the Senate after two terms was widely seen as a prelude to his presidential candidacy, said on November 29 that he would not run. Frist had leapfrogged over more senior senators to become the Republican leader in 2002 after Trent Lott was forced to resign after making a remark that appeared to endorse segregationist policies. But by most accounts Frist had not been a forceful or effective leader in the Senate, and he took high-profile positions that cost him support among both conservatives and moderates. In July 2005, conservatives were dismayed when he switched his position to support lifting federal restrictions on funding human embryonic stem cell research. Earlier in that year many moderates were appalled when Frist, a heart transplant surgeon, reviewed videotapes of Terri Schiavo and said that he believed she was not suffering from irreversible brain damage. Schiavo was at the center of a right-to-die dispute that embroiled Congress in what much of the public thought was a family matter. Tests conducted after Schiavo died confirmed that she had irreversible brain damage. *(Lott resignation, Historic Documents of 2002, p. 969; Schiavo affair, Historic Documents of 2005, p. 154)*

Another potential contender, Virginia senator George Allen, effectively removed himself from the race in August by making what many considered to be racially insensitive comments, a tape of which flooded the airwaves for several days. Allen was a popular one-term governor before being elected to the Senate in 2000, and he had been expected to breeze to reelection to the Senate in 2006. But on November 7 he lost his reelection bid and any hope of winning the GOP presidential nomination.

Following are the texts of two press releases: first, issued on November 9, 2006, announced that Tom Vilsack, the departing governor of Iowa, was filing official papers declaring his presidential candidacy in 2008; second, issued on December 15, announced that Sen. Evan Bayh, D-Ind., had decided not to run for president in 2008.

DOCUMENT

"Tom Vilsack Files Official Papers to Declare Presidential Candidacy"

Iowa Governor Tom Vilsack today took the first formal step toward running for President of the United States by filing documents with the Federal Election Commission to establish his presidential campaign committee, Tom Vilsack for President.

Tom Vilsack for President, will be headquartered in Des Moines, IA and will be publicly launched with a multi-state campaign kick-off tour scheduled to begin in Mt. Pleasant, Iowa on November 30 and include announcement events in New Hampshire, Pennsylvania, Nevada and South Carolina.

Tom Vilsack is the longest serving Democratic governor in the United States. As Chair of the Democratic Leadership Council and former Chair of the Democratic Governors Association, he is a recognized national leader on education, healthcare, economic development and renewable energy. Tom Vilsack was the first Democratic governor elected in Iowa since 1968. In 1998, he promised to serve only two terms—a pledge that he kept in 2006 despite healthy job approval ratings in his home state.

"Americans sent a clear message on Tuesday. They want leaders who will take this country in a new direction." said Vilsack, Iowa's two-term Governor. "They want leaders who share their values, understand their needs, and respect their intelligence. That's what I've done as Governor of Iowa, and that's what I intend to do as President."

"I couldn't be more honored that my wife, Christie, and our sons, Doug and Jess, are committed to joining my effort to offer the people of America and the Democratic Party my vision for the future of our country as a candidate for President," he said. Over the next several weeks, they and the rest of my team will put together the building blocks needed to run a successful national presidential campaign. I invite all Americans to join with us in working for America's future."

Official announcement activities are scheduled to begin in Vilsack's hometown of Mt. Pleasant, IA on November 30 and will be followed by events in New Hampshire, Pittsburgh, PA, Nevada and South Carolina.

A "Gala Celebration of American Community" is schedule in Des Moines on December 2 as the inaugural fundraising event for the campaign. . . .

More information about the campaign and how to become involved is available on the campaign's new website: http://www.tomvilsack08.com.

Source: Tom Vilsack President 2008. "Tom Vilsack Files Official Papers to Declare Presidential Candidacy." Press release, November 9, 2006. www.tomvilsack08.com/press/releases/tom_vilsack_files_official_papers_to_declare_presidential_candidacy (accessed December 21, 2006).

DOCUMENT

"Statement from Senator Bayh on His Decision Not to Run in 2008"

During my two terms as Governor and now in the United States Senate, it has always been more about the people I was able to help than the job I held. As you know I have been exploring helping the people of my state and our country in a different capacity. After talking with family and friends over the past several days, I have decided that this is not the year for me to run for President and I will not be a candidate for the presidency in 2008. It wasn't an easy decision but it was the right one for my family, my friends and my state. I have always prided myself on putting my public responsibilities ahead of my own ambitions.

The odds were always going to be very long for a relatively unknown candidate like myself, a little bit like David and Goliath. And whether there were too many Goliaths or whether I'm just not the right David, the fact remains that at the end of the day, I concluded that due to circumstances beyond our control the odds were longer than I felt I could responsibly pursue. This path—and these long odds—would have required me to be essentially absent from the Senate for the next year instead of working to help the people of my state and the nation.

I am immensely grateful for the support of my family and friends and the thousands of people around the country who helped me with their time and their resources. There may be no campaign in the near future, but there is much work to be done. When the Senate returns, I will focus on the issues that matter to the people of my state and are critical to the future of the nation including reducing our dependence on foreign oil, creating opportunity for middle class families, and implementing a national security strategy that is both tough and smart.

Source: All America PAC. "Statement from Senator Bayh on His Decision Not to Run in 2008." Press release, December 15, 2006. http://blog.4president.org/2008/evan_bayh/index.html (accessed December 17, 2006).

Peace Agreement between Nepalese Government and Maoist Rebels

November 21, 2006

A ten-year civil war in Nepal that had killed more than 12,000 people came to an apparent end during 2006, largely as the result of nearly three weeks of street protests in April against the country's autocratic king. The war had pitted one of the world's last significant Maoist insurgencies against the world's only Hindu monarchy.

A peace agreement signed on November 21 between the government and the Maoist rebels officially ended the war and was to lead to new elections in the first half of 2007. Nepal was one of the poorest countries in the world, best known for the Himalaya Mountains it shared with its neighbors. It had been governed by a monarchy since 1768, although a new constitution in 1990 ushered in a brief era of multiparty democracy.

Background

Maoist rebels, calling themselves the People's Liberation Army, launched their war in February 1996, saying they wanted to establish a communist government modeled after that of China. The rebels were led by a former schoolteacher, Pushpa Kamal Dahal, who called himself Prachanda ("the fierce one").

A classic guerilla war between the rebels and the government continued at a low level for five years, but the conflict intensified in June 2001, when Crown Prince Diprendra—reportedly in an alcohol- and drug-induced rage—went on a rampage and killed both his parents, King Birendra and Queen Aishwarya, and seven other family members before killing himself. Gyanendra, the younger brother of the king, then assumed the throne. After a cease-fire and negotiations between the government and rebels led nowhere, the Maoists intensified their attacks and Gyanendra dismissed the parliament in 2002. By that time the rebels, who claimed to have more than 10,000 fighters, had gained at least some degree of control over most of the rural areas of Nepal.

The most recent cycle of events began on February 1, 2005, when King Gyanendra ousted a prime minister he had appointed just seven months earlier, assumed absolute power for himself, imposed a state of emergency, suspended all civil liberties, and arrested several hundred political leaders and other opposition figures. The king said he would restore democracy within three years. Although decidedly undemocratic, the king's move won broad support at the time, largely because Nepal's political leaders were widely viewed as corrupt, indecisive, and more devoted to bickering than to governing.

In May 2005, Nepal's major political parties formed a Seven-Party Alliance. This move eventually produced a unilateral cease-fire by the Maoists and an agreement between the Maoists and the alliance for joint political action to force the king to allow "total democracy" immediately. This agreement put new pressure on Gyanendra by uniting parties that previously had been bitterly opposed and by depriving him of support from the country's leading political figures.

Another Crackdown, Then Protests

It was clear from the start that 2006 would be a tumultuous year for Nepal. On January 2, the Maoists abandoned their cease-fire and began attacking government outposts, particularly in rural regions. The government launched another crackdown on January 19, this one involving the arrests of nearly 100 political activists—including a former prime minister—just before a planned opposition rally in Katmandu. Several dozen people were injured in demonstrations two days later, and on the same day Maoist rebels launched a major attack on an army post, resulting in the deaths of six army personnel and seventeen rebels. On the February 1 anniversary of his seizing absolute power, Gyanendra claimed success in weakening the rebels, and he promised national elections within fifteen months.

The government on February 8 held municipal elections, which were boycotted by the Seven-Party Alliance and other parties despite being the first in the country in nearly seven years. With few exceptions, all the candidates represented progovernment parties, and many of them spent the campaign period living under government protection. To encourage participation, the government offered life insurance policies for candidates. Even so, the vast majority of voters stayed away from the polls, and opposition leaders insisted the low turnout had given them an important victory against the king. Gyanendra suffered another setback ten days later when the Supreme Court, which had managed to maintain a large degree of independence, ordered the release of dozens of jailed opposition figures and abolished a royal commission Gyanendra had established to combat corruption; opposition leaders had said the commission really was a tool for the king to assert his authority.

Stepping up pressure on the king, opposition leaders called a general strike for early April, which won the endorsement of the Marxist rebels. The government began arresting dozens of opposition leaders in advance of the April 6 start of the strike, then imposed curfews. The crackdown failed to prevent large turnouts at demonstrations around the country that snowballed as the days went on; originally scheduled to last just four days, the strike continued despite harsh repression by the police and a vague call by the king on April 14 for a "dialogue" and new elections within a year. In subsequent days, tens of thousands of people gathered for demonstrations in Katmandu and other cities, even as the general strike caused severe shortages of food and fuel in many areas.

On April 20 multiple demonstrations in the capital attracted an estimated 100,000 people despite a curfew. Most of the day's demonstrations were peaceful, but police fired on the crowd in one neighborhood, killing three people and wounding dozens of others. Many of the demonstrators were young men and women who bitterly denounced the king; some even chanted "death to the king" and similar slogans. That same day also brought the first known direct intervention by India, Nepal's giant neighbor to the south. An Indian envoy, who was distantly related to Gyanendra, met with the king and later said he expected an announcement from the palace that would "help considerably defuse the situation."

That announcement came the next day, April 21, when the king appeared briefly on state-run television and announced that he would appoint a prime minister named by the Seven-Party Alliance. "Executive power of the kingdom of Nepal, which was in our safekeeping, shall, from this day, be returned to the people," he said.

The king's offer brought praise from two of Nepal's important international backers—India and the United States. By that point, however, the offer was too little, too late for the thousands of predominantly youthful protesters, who were now enraged not just at the king but also at the foreign powers that, they said, were backing him. Opposition leaders were more cautious but said the king's statement was too vague and fell short of the popular demand for full democracy, including a restoration of parliament and a referendum to decide on the status of the monarchy.

The street protests continued for three more days, with renewed energy stemming from anger both at the king's belated concessions and continued repression by police. The culmination came late on the evening of April 24 when King Gyanendra appeared on state-run television with concessions to what he called "the ongoing people's movement." The king said he was recalling the parliament he had dissolved four years earlier and turning over to the Seven-Party Alliance the governing power he had seized nearly fifteen months earlier. He did not, however, call for a referendum on a new constitution or renounce his position as monarch. "We are confident the nation will forge ahead towards sustainable peace, progress, full-fledged democracy, and national unity," he said.

This time, the king's concessions met the bottom-line demands of the protesters, most of whom quickly dispersed. "Long live democracy," chanted protesters in one neighborhood of the capital. Shops that had been closed for more than two weeks opened the next day, and security forces returned to their barracks.

Seventeen people died as a result of shootings and beatings by the security forces during the demonstrations, according to news reports. Even so, the largely peaceful demonstrations had accomplished in a few weeks much of what the Maoist insurgents had been striving for in a decade-long war that cost thousands of lives.

A New Government Moves toward Peace

By conceding to protesters' demands, the king suddenly placed full responsibility for Nepal in the hands of an alliance of parties that had little in common other than their opposition to the king's autocratic moves in recent years. Some of these parties and their leaders had themselves been the targets of public complaints about corruption and disregard for the welfare of Nepal's poor majority. The alliance also had to face the difficult task of dealing with the Maoist insurgents, who for tactical reasons had supported the protests against the king and initially wanted to kept them going even after the king backed down. Maoist leader Prachanda called the king's speech "a new ploy to break the Nepali people and save his autocratic monarchy," and his group said the alliance's acceptance of the king's concessions was "a historic blunder." The rebels quickly backed down, however, saying a few days later that they would observe a three-month truce.

The alliance on April 25 named Girija Prasad Koirala, the country's most respected politician, as its prime minister. He had previously served as head of the largest political party, the Nepali Congress Party; had been jailed during the 1960s for advocating democracy; and had served three terms as prime minister during the 1990s. Koirala had been one of many senior political figures placed under house arrest during the king's crackdown in January.

The lower house of parliament on April 28 held its first session in nearly four years; it was a brief meeting and took place without the eighty-four-year-old Koirala, who was ill. Koirala finally took office as prime minister on April 30. He formally invited the Maoists to enter into negotiations, and the parliament unanimously endorsed his proposal for elections for a constituent assembly that would draft a new constitution—thus meeting one of the Maoists' chief demands. Another important step came on May 3, when the government declared an indefinite cease-fire, offered peace talks with the rebels, and withdrew the official designation of the Maoists as terrorists. The Maoists accepted the offer of talks the next day. Even so, key differences already were emerging, both within the Seven-Party Alliance and between the alliance and the Maoists. Some of the differences concerned the timing of elections and the drafting of a new constitution, but others dealt with such basic matters as the status of the monarchy, which some political leaders wanted to preserve in a limited form and others, including the rebels, wanted to abolish entirely.

The parliament took an intermediate step on the monarchy question on May 18, approving a proposal by Prime Minister Koirala to put the army under the control of the government, rather than the king. The proposal also declared Nepal to be a secular nation and said the people were sovereign, not the king, so the government would no longer be called "His Majesty's Government." Parliament later stripped the king of his legal immunity and his right to veto laws, effectively eliminating his once-total political power.

The first major political agreement between the government and the Maoists came on June 16 when rebel leader Prachanda appeared publicly in Katmandu for the first time in ten years. He and leaders of the Seven-Party Alliance signed an eight-point agreement under which parliament would be dissolved, the rebels would join an interim government while a new constitution was being written, and all parties would ask the United Nations to supervise the weapons of both the rebels and the army.

Both sides hailed this agreement as historic, but important details were left unresolved, and some political leaders aligned with the government were angered by the concessions to the Maoists. Talks between the government and the rebels over implementing the details of their June 16 agreement dragged on for nearly five months, largely because of disputes over the status of the rebel fighters and Prachanda's demand that the monarchy be scrapped as part of any constitution. The two sides reached an important agreement on October 10 for the holding of elections for a constituent assembly by May 2007, and on November 8 they finally resolved most outstanding questions, including how the United Nations would supervise rebel fighters and their weapons.

On November 21, Koirala and Prachanda signed what was called a Comprehensive Peace Agreement, incorporating the results of the months of bargaining. Its basic elements ended the war, called for the rebels to join an interim government, and required elections in 2007 for the assembly that would write a new constitution, thereby determining the fate of the monarchy and other key questions.

"It is the beginning of a new beginning," Prachanda said after signing the accord at the convention center in Katmandu. In an apparent attempt to reinforce his own dramatic change of rhetoric, Prachanda insisted he and his group were determined to abide by the results of elections. "We are not dogmatic communists and we are prepared to change and debate our beliefs with anybody," he said. Koirala said the agreement offered a message for those involved in other conflicts around the world, "that no conflict can be resolved by guns. It can be done by dialogue." In the capital, many people lit candles in celebration. Diplomats and political analysts expressed hope that the peace accord actually would end the war, but they noted that the agreement was a fragile one that depended on the rebels adhering to their promise to lay down their weapons.

One week later, on November 28, the government and rebels signed a follow-up agreement under which the United Nations would supervise both the rebel fighters and the Nepalese army until the elections in 2007. The rebels were to gather in seven camps (called cantons) and hand over their weapons to storage monitored by the UN; army units were to return to their barracks. The UN Security Council approved this agreement on December 1 and sent a delegation of experts to Nepal to work out the details of implementing it.

Despite the optimistic talk at the peace-signing ceremony, disagreements continued to plague Nepal through the end of the year. News reports said the rebels were continuing to recruit fighters and that many teenage rebels insisted they would refuse to hand over their weapons and enter the UN camps. UN officials also said they could not meet the ambitious timetable laid out in the peace agreement, under which the camps were to have been built within just a few days.

The government and rebels on December 16 finally approved the outlines of an interim constitution, which would enable several dozen rebel leaders to enter the parliament and help form a new interim government. However, a dispute over the government's appointment of ambassadors contributed to yet another delay that prevented the new government from taking office by the end of the year.

Following are excerpts from the unofficial translation of the "Comprehensive Peace Agreement between the Government of Nepal and the Communist Party of Nepal (Maoist)," signed in Katmandu on November 21, 2006, by Prime Minister Girija Prasad Koirala and Prachanda, chairman of the Communist Party of Nepal (Maoist).

DOCUMENT

"Comprehensive Peace Agreement"

Preamble

Respecting the popular mandate in favour of democracy, peace and progress expressed through repeated historic struggles and people's movements from the pre-1951 era to date;

Reaffirming total commitment to the 12-point understanding and the 8-point agreement concluded between the Seven Political Parties and the CPN (Maoist) and the 25-point codes of conduct agreed between the Government of Nepal and the CPN (Maoist), all agreements, understandings, codes of conduct concluded between the Government of Nepal and the CPN (Maoist) as well as the decisions of the Summit Meeting of the Seven-Party Alliance and the CPN (Maoist) adopted on November 8, 2006 and letters of similar spirit sent to the United Nations by the Government of Nepal and the Maoists;

Pledging for forward-looking restructuring of the state by resolving the prevailing problems related to class, ethnicity, regional and gender differences;

Reiterating commitments to competitive multiparty democratic system, civil liberties, fundamental rights, human rights, complete press freedom and all other democratic norms and values including the concept of rule of law;

Remaining committed to the Universal Declaration of Human Rights 1948, international humanitarian laws and the fundamental principles and basic principles and norms related to human rights;

Guaranteeing the fundamental right of the Nepali people to participate in a free and fair Constituent Assembly election in an environment free from fear;

Keeping democracy, peace, prosperity, forward looking economic and social transformation as well as independence, integrity, sovereignty and dignity of the country at the centre;

Expressing confidence to implement the commitment of holding the election to the Constituent Assembly in a free and fair manner within June 15, 2007;

Declaring the beginning of a new chapter of peaceful collaboration by ending the armed conflict plaguing the country since 1996 on the basis of political consensus reached between the two parties to ensure the sovereignty of the Nepali people, forward looking political resolution, democratic restructuring of the state and economic-social and cultural transformation through the Constituent Assembly;

The Government of Nepal and CPN (Maoist) hereby conclude this Comprehensive Peace Agreement with commitments to convert the present ceasefire into lasting peace. . . .

[Sections 1 and 2 omitted.]

3. Political—Economic—Social Transformation and Conflict Management

Both the parties are in agreement to pursue the following policy and program for political-economic and social transformation and to affirmatively resolve existing conflict in the country:

3.1. To ensure forward moving political, economic and social transformation on the basis of decisions made in summit meeting between Seven Political Parties and CPN (Maoist) held on November 8, 2006.

3.2. To constitute Interim Legislature—Parliament as per the Interim Constitution, to have the elections to Constituent Assembly held by the Interim Government in a free and fair manner within June 15, 2006 and to practically guarantee sovereignty inherent in the Nepali people.

3.3. No state powers shall remain with the king. The properties owned by the late King Birendra, the late Queen Aishwarya and their family members shall be brought under the control of the Government of Nepal and used in the interest of the nation through a trust. All properties (such as palaces at various places, forests and National Parks, heritages of historical and archaeological significance etc.) acquired by King Gyanendra in his monarchical capacity shall be nationalised. The issue of whether to continue or scrap the institution of monarchy shall be decided by a simple majority of the Constituent Assembly in its first meeting.

3.4. To pursue a political system that fully complies with the universally accepted fundamental human rights, competitive multiparty democratic system, sovereignty inherent in the people and the supremacy of the people, constitutional check and balance, rule of law, social justice and equality, independent judiciary, periodic elections, monitoring by civil society, complete press freedom, people's right to information, transparency and accountability in the activities of political parties, people's participation and the concepts of impartial, competent, and fair administration.

3.5. In order to end discriminations based on class, ethnicity, language, gender, culture, religion and region and to address the problems of women, Dalit, indigenous people, ethnic minorities (Janajatis), Terai communities (Madheshis), oppressed, neglected and minority communities and the backward areas by deconstructing the current centralised and unitary structure, the state shall be restructured in an inclusive, democratic and forward looking manner.

3.6. A common minimum program for socio-economic transformation in order to end all forms of feudalism shall be prepared and implemented on the basis of mutual understanding.

3.7. Policies shall be formulated to implement a scientific land reform program by doing away with the feudal land ownership practice.

3.8. Policies to protect and promote national industries and resources shall be followed.

3.9. Policies shall be undertaken to establish the rights of all the citizens to education, health, shelter, employment and food security.

3.10. Policies shall be pursued to provide land and socio-economic security to backward communities like the landless squatters, bonded labourers, tillers, bonded domestics, bonded cattle-tenders and such other groups.

3.11. Policies shall be adopted to take strict actions against those who, occupying governmental positions of benefit, have amassed huge properties through corruption.

3.12. A common development concept shall be adopted for the socio-economic transformation of the country and for making the country advanced and economically prosperous in a just manner within a short span of time.

3.13. Policies shall be followed for ensuring the professional rights of workers and increasing investment for the promotion of industries, trade, export etc. in order to significantly enhance employment and income generating opportunities.

4. Management of Army and Arms

The following shall be done in order for holding the election to the Constituent Assembly in a peaceful and fair environment free from fear and for the democratisation and restructuring of the Army in line with the spirit of the 12-point understanding, 8-point agreement, 25-point code of conduct, the 5-point letters sent to the United Nations and the decisions of the Summit Meeting of the Seven-Party Alliance and the CPN (Maoist) reached on November 8, 2006:

Relating to the Maoist Army

4.1. As per the commitments expressed in the letters sent to the United Nations by the Government of Nepal and the Maoists on August 9, 2006, the combatants of the Maoist army shall be confined to the following temporary cantonments. The United Nations shall verify and monitor them.

The main cantonments shall be located in the following places: 1. Kailali, 2. Surkhet, 3. Rolpa, 4. Palpa, 5. Kabhre, 6. Sindhuli, 7. Ilam.

There shall be three smaller camps located in the periphery of each of these main cantonments.

4.2. All the arms and ammunitions shall be securely stored within the cantonments except those needed for providing security to the cantonments after the Maoist combatants are sent to the cantonments. The arms and ammunitions shall be locked with a single padlock and the side concerned shall keep the key to it. For the UN to monitor it, a device with siren as well as recording facility shall be installed during the process of padlocking. The UN shall make necessary inspections of the stored arms in the presence of the party concerned. Technical details in this regard including camera monitoring shall be as per the agreement among the United Nations, the CPN (Maoist) and the Government of Nepal.

4.3. Once the Maoist combatants are confined to the cantonments, the Government of Nepal shall take care of their ration as well as other arrangements necessary.

4.4. The Interim Cabinet shall constitute a Special Committee to carry out monitoring, adjustment and rehabilitation of the Maoist combatants.

4.5. Security arrangements for the Maoist leaders shall be made with the consent of the Government of Nepal.

Relating to the Nepali Army

4.6. The Nepali Army shall be confined to the barracks as per the commitments made in the letters sent to the United Nations. Non-use of its arms for or against either side shall be guaranteed. Like number of arms as those stored by the Maoist Army shall be safely stored also by the Nepali Army. These arms shall be locked with a single padlock and the party concerned shall keep the key to it. For the UN to monitor it, a device with siren as well as recording facility shall be installed during the process of padlocking. The UN shall make necessary inspections of the stored arms in the presence of the party concerned. Technical details in this regard including camera monitoring shall be as per the agreement among the United Nations, the Government of Nepal and the CPN (Maoist).

4.7. The Council of Ministers shall control, mobilise and manage the Nepali Army in accordance with the new Military Act. The Interim Council of Ministers shall prepare and implement the detailed action plan for the democratisation of the Nepali Army on the basis of political consensus and the suggestions of the committee concerned of the Interim Legislature. This includes, among other things, right-sizing, democratic restructuring reflecting the national and inclusive character and imparting training to the Nepali Army on the values of democracy and human rights.

4.8. Such functions as border security and security of the conservation areas, National Parks, banks, airports, powerhouses, telephone towers, central secretariat and the distinguished personalities hitherto being carried out by the Nepali Army shall continue.

5. Cease-Fire

5.1. Ending of military action and mobilisation of armed personnel:

5.1.1. Both sides express commitments to refrain from carrying out following activities:

(a) Direct or indirect use of any type of weapon or acts of attack against each other.
(b) Searching or confiscating weapons belonging to the other side with or without weapons at the place where the arms have been stored as per the understanding reached between both sides.
(c) Acts rendering harm to or mental pressure on any individuals.
(d) Acts of setting up ambush targeting each other.
(e) Acts of murder and violence.
(f) Acts of kidnappings/detentions/imprisonments/disappearances.
(g) Acts rendering loss to public/private/governmental or military properties.
(h) Arial attacks or bombings.
(i) Mining and sabotage.
(j) Spying military activities of each other.

5.1.2. Neither side shall recruit additional troops, transport arms, ammunitions and explosives and conduct military activities against each other. However, the Interim Government may deploy the security forces for patrolling, searching and confiscating for the prevention of illegal trafficking of the arms and explosive materials and parts and/or raw materials thereof at the international borders or customs points.

5.1.3. No individual or group shall carry any illegal arms, ammunitions and explosives while travelling.

5.1.4. Both sides shall assist each other by providing information as regards the location sketches and storage of ambushes and landmines used during the war time within 30 days and by defusing and destroying them within 60 days.

5.1.5. Armies of neither side shall be present with arms and in combat fatigue in any civil assembly, political meetings and public programmes.

5.1.6. The Nepal Police and the Armed Police Force shall continue the task of maintaining lawful arrangements and peace and order as well as that of criminal investigation in line with the norms and spirit of the people's movement and the peace accord and as per the prevailing laws.

5.1.7. Both sides shall issue circulars to their respective armed bodies or personnel imposing restrictions on using the term 'enemy' while addressing or making any other dealings with the armed personnel of the other side.

5.1.8. Both sides agree to keep records and return immediately the government, public and private buildings, land and other property seized, locked up or forbidden for use during the armed conflict.

5.2 Measures for the Normalization of Situation:

5.2.1. Forced and unlawful collection of donations in cash or kind and illegal collection of tax shall not be allowed.

5.2.2. Both sides agree to make public the status of the people under their respective custodies and release them within 15 days.

5.2.3. Both sides agree to make public within 60 days of the signing of the agreement the correct and full names and addresses of the people who 'disappeared' or were killed during the conflict and convey such details to the family members.

5.2.4. Both sides agree to constitute a National Peace and Rehabilitation Commission and carry out works through it for the normalization of the difficult situation that arose as a result of the armed conflict, maintain peace in the society and run relief and rehabilitation activities for the victims of conflict and those displaced.

5.2.5. Both sides agree to set up with mutual consent a High-level Truth and Reconciliation Commission in order to probe into those involved in serious violation of human rights and crime against humanity in course of the armed conflict for creating an atmosphere for reconciliation in the society.

5.2.6. Both sides pledge to abandon all types of wars, attacks, counter-attacks, violence and counter-violence in the country with a commitment to ensure democracy, peace and forward-looking transformation of the Nepali society. The two sides also agree to cooperate with each other for bringing about peace and maintaining law and order.

5.2.7. Both sides guarantee to withdraw political accusations, claims, complaints and cases under-consideration against various individuals and to instantly make public the status of those detained and release them immediately.

5.2.8. Both sides express commitment to allow without any political prejudice the people displaced during the armed conflict to return voluntarily to their respective places of ancestral or former residence, to reconstruct the infrastructure destroyed as a result of the conflict and to honourably rehabilitate and reintegrate the displaced people into the society.

5.2.9. Both sides agree to take individual and collective responsibility for resolving any problem arising in the aforementioned context on the basis of mutual agreement including with the support of all political parties, civil society and local organizations, and for creating an atmosphere conducive to the normalization of mutual relations and reconciliation.

5.2.10. Both sides express commitment not to discriminate against or exert any kind of pressure on any member of a family on the basis involvement with one or the other side.

5.2.11. Both sides agree not to raise any obstacle and not to allow the creation of any kind of obstruction to the employees of the Government of Nepal and other Public Bodies in the freedom of movement throughout the country, in the discharge of their duties and in carrying out their functions thus facilitating them in their work.

5.2.12. Both sides agree to allow unrestricted lawful movement throughout the State of Nepal to the personnel of the United Nations, International Donor Community, Diplomatic Missions based in Nepal, National and International Non-Governmental Organizations, Press Community, Human Rights Activists, Election Observers and foreign tourists.

5.2.13. Both sides are committed to organizing publicity programs in a decent and respectable manner.

6. End of Conflict

6.1. On the basis of the historic decisions reached between the Seven Political Parties and the CPN (Maoist) on November 8, 2006, we hereby declare that the armed conflict ongoing in the country since 1996 has been brought to an end and that the current cease-fire between the Government and the Maoists has been made permanent.

6.2. The decisions of the meeting of the summit leaders of the Seven Political Parties and the CPN (Maoist) held on November 8, 2006 shall be the main policy foundation for long-term peace.

6.3. Following the confinement of the Nepali Army to the barracks and the combatants of the Maoist Army to the temporary cantonments, possession and display of arms and intimidation as well as use of violence and arms in any manner contravening the existing understandings and agreements and prevailing laws shall be punishable under law.

6.4. Armies of both the sides shall not be allowed to campaign or work for or against any side. However, they shall not be deprived of their voting right.

7. Compliance to Human Rights, Fundamental Rights and Humanitarian Laws

While remaining committed to the Universal Declaration of Human Rights, 1948, the International Humanitarian Laws and the fundamental principles and values of human rights, both the sides agree as follows:

7.1. **Human Rights:**

7.1.1. Both sides reiterate their commitment to the respect and protection of human rights and the international humanitarian laws and agree that no individual shall be discriminated on the basis of colour, gender, language, religion, age, race, nationality or social origin, property, disability, birth and other status and thought or belief.

7.1.2. Both sides agree to create an atmosphere where the Nepali people can enjoy their civil, political, economic, social and cultural rights and are committed to ensuring that such rights are not violated under any circumstances in the future.

7.1.3. Both sides express their commitment that impartial investigation shall be carried out and lawful action would be taken against individuals responsible for obstructions in the exercise of the rights contained in the agreement and guarantee not to encourage impunity. Apart from this, they shall also guarantee the right to relief of the families of victims of conflict, torture and disappearance.

7.1.4. Both sides shall refrain from inflicting torture, kidnapping and coercing the ordinary people to any work, and shall take necessary actions to discourage such acts.

7.1.5. Both sides shall respect the social, cultural and religious sensitivities, and the protection of religious sites and beliefs of any individual based on the values and norms of secularism,

7.2. **Right to Life:**

7.2.1. Both sides respect and protect the fundamental right to life of any individual. No individual shall be deprived of this fundamental right and no law that provides capital punishment shall be enacted.

7.3. **Right to Individual Dignity, Freedom and Movement:**

7.3.1. Both sides respect and protect the right to individual dignity. In this connection, no person including those deprived of the enjoyment of freedom under law shall be subjected to torture or any other cruel, inhuman or degrading behaviour or punishment. The citizen's lawful right to privacy shall be respected.

7.3.2. Both sides shall fully respect the individual's right to freedom and security, shall not keep anyone under arbitrary or illegal detention, and shall not kidnap or hold anybody captive in a like manner. Both sides agree to make public the status of every individual disappeared and held captive and provide such information to their family members, legal counsel, and any other authorized persons.

7.3.3. Both sides shall respect and protect the citizens' right to freedom of movement and the right to choose the location of one's residence in a manner acceptable under prevailing laws, and express their commitments to respect the right of individuals and families displaced during the conflict to return to their original places of residence or to settle in any other places of their choice.

7.4. **Civil and Political Rights:**

7.4.1. Both sides are committed to respect individual freedom of speech, expression, association and peaceful assembly and right against exploitation.

7.4.2. Both sides respect the right of every citizen to participate directly or through one's nominated representative in issues of public concern, to vote, to be elected to public office and to enjoy equal opportunities for public employment.

7.4.3. Both sides are committed to respect the individual right to be informed.

7.5. **Economic and Social Rights:**

7.5.1. Both sides are committed to respect and protect the individual's right to livelihood through employment of their choice or acceptance.

7.5.2. Both sides are committed to respect and guarantee the right to food security of all the people. They assure that there shall be no interference in the use, transportation and distribution of food items, food products and food grains.

7.5.3. Both sides accept the fact that the citizens' right to health should be respected and protected. Both sides shall not obstruct the supply of medicines and health related assistance and campaigns, and express commitment to provide medical treatment to those injured in course of the conflict and to work for their rehabilitation.

7.5.4. With the realization of the fact that the right to education to all should be guaranteed and respected, both sides are committed to maintaining a congenial academic environment in educational institutions. Both sides agree to guarantee that the right to education shall not be violated. They agree to immediately put an end to such activities as capturing educational institutions and using them, abducting teachers and students, holding them captives, causing them to disappear, and not to set up army barracks in a way that would adversely impact schools and hospitals.

7.5.5. Both sides agree that the private property of any individual shall not be seized or usurped unlawfully.

7.5.6. Both sides believe in the fact that industrial production should continue, the right to collective bargaining and social security in the industrial establishments should be respected and the establishment and workers should be encouraged to seek peaceful settlement of any disputes between them without disturbing the industrial climate of the country, and respect the standards of work as determined by the International Labour Organization.

7.6. **Rights of Women and Children:**

7.6.1. Both sides fully agree to special protection of the rights of women and children, to immediately stop all types of violence against women and children, including child labour as well as sexual exploitation and abuse, and not to conscript or use children who are aged 18 or below in the armed force. Children thus affected shall be rescued immediately and appropriate assistance as may be needed shall be provided for their rehabilitation.

7.7 **Right to Individual Liberty:**

7.7.1. Both sides agree to enforce and cause to be enforced the freedom of thought and opinion, freedom of expression and publication, freedom of peaceful assembly without arms, freedom of movement, freedom of choice of profession or occupation, freedom of acquisition, ownership and disposal of property, freedom to participate in peaceful political activities, the right to equality before law and a just legal system.

8. Differences Settlement and Implementation Mechanism

8.1. Both sides agree to take individual as well as collective responsibility for not repeating the mistakes committed in the past and making correction gradually in the future.

8.2. The National Peace and Rehabilitation Commission may set up necessary mechanisms for the success of the peace campaign. The constitution and working procedure of the Commission shall be as determined by the Interim Council of Ministers.

8.3. Both sides are committed to settle all kinds of issues and mutual differences, current or that may arise in future, through mutual talks, understanding, consensus and dialogue.

8.4. Both sides express their commitments that the Interim Council of Ministers may constitute and determine the working procedures of the National Peace and Rehabilitation Commission, the Truth and Reconciliation Commission, the High-Level State Restructuring Recommendation Commission and other mechanisms as may be necessary for the implementation of this Agreement, the Interim Constitution and all the decisions, agreements and understandings reached between the Seven Parties or the Government of Nepal and the CPN (Maoist).

9. Implementation and Monitoring

Both sides agree to make the following arrangements for the implementation of the understandings contained in this agreement and for their follow-up:

9.1. Both sides agree to give continuity to the task of monitoring of the human rights provisions mentioned in this agreement by the United Nations Office of the High Commissioner for Human Rights, Nepal.

9.2. Both sides agree to the monitoring of the management of arms and the armies by the United Nations Mission in Nepal as per the provisions of the five-point letters sent earlier to the UN and those of the present agreement and agree to facilitate the process.

9.3. Both sides agree to have the United Nations observe the election to the Constituent Assembly.

9.4. The National Human Rights Commission shall also carry out responsibilities related to the monitoring of human rights as mentioned in this agreement together with the responsibility assigned to it as per the laws. While carrying out its functions, the Commission may liaison with and seek assistance from national as well as international human rights related organizations.

9.5. Both sides agree to receive the reports submitted by the above-mentioned bodies, to provide requisite information to them, and to implement their suggestions and recommendations on the basis of discussions and consensus.

10. Miscellaneous

10.1. Pursuant to the essence of the decisions of November 8 and the spirit of the peace agreement, both sides agree not to run any structure, including those parallel to the government, in any areas of government or state apparatus.

10.2. Both sides agree to sign additional supplementary agreements as may be necessary for the implementation of the present agreement.

10.3. This agreement may be amended any time with the consent of both sides. In case an amendment is desired, both sides agree to provide a notice in writing to the other side. Pursuant to such a notice, amendments may be made to the agreement with the consent of both sides. The provisions to be covered by such an amendment shall not be inferior to universally accepted norms of international human rights, standards of international humanitarian laws and the core spirit of the establishment of peace.

10.4. If any dispute arises in the interpretation of this agreement, a joint mechanism comprising both sides shall make the interpretation as per the spirit of the preamble and the documents annexed to this agreement, and such interpretation shall be final.

10.5. The concept and existence of the 'two sides' as mentioned in this agreement shall automatically come to an end after the constitution of the Interim Legislature-Parliament. Thereafter, all the responsibility of implementing the obligations mentioned in this agreement shall be as per the arrangements made by the Interim Council of Ministers. It shall be the duty and responsibility of all political parties to extend cooperation in the compliance and implementation of the agreement.

10.6. At a time when the entire country is focused on the principal campaign of the election to the Constituent Assembly, we sincerely request to all to have their problems and demands resolved through talks and dialogue and to contribute to the election of the Constituent Assembly and to the maintenance of law and order.

10.7. We sincerely appeal to the civil society, the professional groups, the class organizations, the media, the intellectuals and the entire Nepali people to actively participate and make successful the historic campaign of building a new democratic Nepal and establishing lasting peace through the election of the Constituent Assembly thus ending the armed conflict.

10.8. We sincerely request the international community including all friendly countries and the United Nations to extend support to Nepal in the campaign of establishing a full-fledged democracy and lasting peace.

Having realized the responsibility towards the future of the country and the people, and remaining fully committed to this Comprehensive Peace Agreement, we, on behalf of the Government of Nepal and the Communist Party of Nepal (Maoist), hereby sign this comprehensive peace agreement and make it public.

Prachanda   Girija Prasad Koirala
Chairman   Prime Minister
Communist Party of Nepal (Maoist)   Government of Nepal

Signed on November 21, 2006

Source: Government of Nepal. Ministry of Foreign Affairs. "Unofficial Translation of the Comprehensive Peace Agreement Concluded Between the Government of Nepal and the Communist Party of Nepal (Maoist)." November 21, 2006. www.mofa.gov.np/November 21.doc (accessed December 19, 2006).

Other Historic Documents of Interest

U.S.-India agreement on nuclear trade,   *Violence in Sri Lanka, p. 249*
*   p. 93*

December

2006 HISTORIC DOCUMENTS

Calderón on His Inauguration as President of Mexico

December 1, 2006

Just six years after it had its first truly competitive election in decades, Mexico in 2006 had one of the most bizarre elections imaginable, with the losing candidate refusing to concede defeat, sending his supporters into the streets, and even declaring himself president and appointing his own cabinet. In the end, this behavior by leftist candidate Andrés Manuel López Obrador cost him much of his public support and generated sympathetic backing for the election winner, Felipe Calderón of the conservative National Action Party. Even so, the outcome raised new doubts about whether Mexico was any closer to the stable democracy that many Mexicans craved after so recently throwing off one-party rule.

Calderón took office, as scheduled, on December 1, nearly five months after the July 2 election, and after much of the furor over López Obrador's protests had died down. In a speech to the nation just before taking the oath of office, Calderón appealed to Mexicans to "put an end to our disagreements today and begin a new stage in which the only aim is to place national interest above our differences."

Calderón was only the second president of Mexico since 1920 who did not represent the Institutional Revolutionary Party (PRI), which had dominated the country for seven decades through what many people called a dictatorship in democratic disguise. The PRI's long rule was ended in 2000 when Vicente Fox, a businessman representing the conservative National Action Party (PAN), won election as president by capitalizing on popular disaffection with the status quo. Calderón also represented the PAN, and he had to overcome widespread dissatisfaction with Fox's inability to carry out the changes he promised. *(Fox election, Historic Document of 2000, p. 963)*

Election

From the outset, the year's election campaign revolved around López Obrador. This was in part because he long was considered the front-runner, but even more because he was such a polarizing figure. His supporters, primarily Mexico's impoverished majority, adored him as a populist who insisted he would bring them the jobs and social services others had promised for decades but had never delivered. His detractors portrayed him as a dangerous, messianic zealot who did not understand his own limitations. López Obrador had support to lose when the campaign started, and during the campaign he lost just enough of it to shift the election to Calderón.

A native of Tabasco state and the son of working-class parents, López Obrador was elected mayor of Mexico City in 2000 but stepped down in 2005 to run for president. As mayor he reformed the huge bureaucracy and took steps to ease the city's notorious traffic congestion, but crime also soared during his time in office. López Obrador was a skilled orator and indefatigable campaigner who generated enthusiasm among his supporters with leftist rhetoric against the rich and with promises—which he called "commitments"—to make life better for the half of Mexico's population that lived in poverty.

López Obrador's party, the Party of the Democratic Revolution (PRD), was Mexico's newest major party, founded in 1989 by Cuauthémoc Cárdenas, the son of one of the PRI's most successful presidents, Lázaro Cárdenas, who served in the 1930s. The younger Cárdenas formed the PRD a year after he lost the presidential election—or, according to most accounts, the election was stolen from him by the PRI. In the 1990s the PRD won numerous state and local posts, and Cárdenas served one term as mayor of Mexico City before losing the 2000 presidential election to Fox. Cárdenas kept his distance from López Obrador during the campaign, leading many observers to believe he did not entirely trust his party's current presidential candidate.

Felipe Calderón was the son of one of the founders of the conservative, probusiness National Action Party and was a skilled politician at age forty-three. He led the party's congressional delegation for Fox's first three years in office and then served in the cabinet as energy secretary, but he was not Fox's first choice as successor.

Technically, the 2006 race was a three-man affair, but for the first time the third-ranking party was the PRI—a symbol of how far it had fallen since its defeat by Fox in 2000. Representing the PRI was Roberto Madrazo, the party president who in 1994 had defeated López Obrador in a race for the governorship of their native Tabasco state. Madrazo had strong support from party leaders but, rightly or wrongly, was seen by many Mexicans as a typically corrupt party boss of the past, and he had little charisma on the stump.

The three major candidates kicked off the campaign on January 19, with López Obrador at least ten points in the lead, followed by Calderón and Madrazo, according to most opinion polls. The charismatic López Obrador tailored his appeal to the poor, saying in his opening speech that he would listen to everyone, "but the poor and the forgotten of Mexico will get preferential treatment."

At first, López Obrador surged ahead of his two rivals with a populist campaign calling for change and portraying Calderón and Madrazo as representing the failures of Mexico's past. López Obrador committed a major blunder in February by denouncing Fox for what he said was meddling in the campaign. López Obrador told the president to "shut up"—offending millions of Mexicans who respected the presidency even if they disagreed with the man holding the office. López Obrador also refused to take part in the first of two candidate debates, allowing his opponents to appear as the responsible candidates.

By late May, Calderón had caught up or even surpassed López Obrador, according to some polls, using a hard-nosed series of radio and television advertisements attacking him as an irresponsible leftist whose policies would throw Mexico into bankruptcy. Some of Calderón's ads compared López Obrador to Venezuela's outspoken leftist president Hugo Chavez and directly charged that López Obrador would be a "danger to Mexico." Calderón withdrew those ads after López Obrador protested, but the message had been delivered. Calderón also relentlessly pushed a simple, one-word campaign theme: jobs. "My job is to make sure you have a job," became his slogan. To back it up, he promised to lure foreign investment to Mexico, something Fox also had promised but had been unable to deliver in any quantity.

On June 30, just two days before the elections, Mexicans got a reminder of the country's violent past when a court issued an arrest warrant for former president Luis Echeverría. Echeverría was charged with ordering the killing of student protesters in Mexico City's Tlateloco Square just before the opening of the summer Olympic Games in 1968. Echeverría was interior minister at the time of the killings, which were a foretaste of what Mexicans called the "dirty war" against leftists from the late 1960s through the early 1980s. Echeverría was president from 1970 to 1976. Charges against him were dismissed by one court, on the grounds that the statute of limitations had expired, but were reinstated on November 29 by an appeals court.

A years-long government-commissioned investigation into the dirty war was completed early in 2006, but a detailed report on its findings was withheld until late November, just before Fox left office. The report confirmed past allegations that the government had murdered more than 700 people in its long campaign against student protesters and leftists. The report included documentation showing that the dirty war was official government policy, not a rogue operation by renegade military officers, as some officials had claimed.

Obrador's Continuing Campaign

After the polls closed on Election Day, July 2, election officials said the race was too close to call. Even so, both López Obrador and Calderón declared victory, with the former insisting he had won by at least a half-million votes even before all the votes had been counted. Fox went on national television pleading with all sides, including voters, to respect whatever results were published by the Federal Electoral Institute.

The uncertainty continued for three days as the vote count showed Calderón holding a very slim lead over López Obrador and some 3 million votes were found to be illegible or had not been delivered on time to the federal authorities. Finally, on July 6, election authorities announced that Calderón had won by a margin of 243,000 votes over López Obrador, out of a total of 41 million votes cast. Madrazo was a distant third.

Calderón again declared victory and promised to govern on behalf of all Mexicans. So did López Obrador, who again insisted he had won, demanded a recount, and called for massive street demonstrations nationwide to pressure the government. On Saturday, July 8, supporters of López Obrador staged what turned out to be the first of many mass protests on his behalf. The protest in Mexico City drew an estimated 280,000 people, and López Obrador gave an impassioned speech pledging to defeat the "powerful interests" who, he said, were determined to defeat the poor.

This was the third time López Obrador had turned to street demonstrations as a means of bolstering his position. In 1994, after losing the governorship of Tabasco state to Madrazo in a campaign rife with charges of fraud, López Obrador mounted street protests and said the election had been stolen from him, but to no avail. In 2005 federal authorities ruled that he could not run for president because he had violated a court order in his position as mayor of Mexico City. Again, Obrador sent his supporters into the streets for a series of protests that led to his reinstatement as a candidate.

López Obrador kept up the pressure in 2006 with a demand for a full recount and a threat of unspecified civil disobedience by his supporters if this did not happen. On July 30 López Obrador's supporters held another huge rally in Mexico City and set up camps in the center of the capital, saying they would remain until an electoral court ordered a recount. López Obrador also launched a harsh rhetorical attack against his political opponents, calling electoral officials "criminals" and accusing President Fox of being a "traitor to democracy."

More than a month after the election, Mexico's electoral court on August 5 rejected López Obrador's call for a full recount but ordered a recount of votes in about 12,000 polling places, about 9 percent of the total. López Obrador's supporters—many of them still camped in the capital's public squares and streets—angrily denounced the decision, and the candidate himself said he would continue his fight. On August 29, the election judges said the recount had found irregularities—but no signs of fraud—in dozens of polling places; even so, the underlying results remained the same. López Obrador again cried foul, saying the judges were carrying out "a coup d'etat." Members of Congress from López Obrador's party, the PRD, took the protest to a new level on September 1, seizing control of the lower house of Congress (the Chamber of Deputies) and preventing Fox from delivering his final State of the Nation address. The incident deeply embarrassed Fox but also illustrated the lengths to which López Obrador and his supporters would go.

The electoral judges on September 5 finally declared Calderón the winner of the election, rejecting a legal challenge López Obrador had raised because of the negative attacks waged by Calderón's supporters during the campaign. The electoral court said Calderón had won by a margin of 233,831 votes—about one-half of a percent. Once again, López Obrador denounced the electoral judges as "traitors" and said he would refuse to accept their judgment, or a Calderón presidency.

His demand for a vote-by-vote recount having failed, López Obrador on September 8 announced a new strategy: he said he would set up his own government, one that would focus on the needs of the poor. The candidate's supporters ended their street protests in the capital on September 15, nearly seven weeks after they started, but two days later several hundred thousand supporters held another mass rally and, by a show of hands, "elected" López Obrador as their president.

López Obrador staged an "inauguration" ceremony in Mexico City on November 20, during which he took the oath of office as president and was draped with a version of the ceremonial red, green, and white sash signifying the presidential office. He also appointed his own cabinet, which he said would enact the help-the-poor policies he had advocated, with money donated by supporters.

López Obrador said he would try to prevent Calderón from taking office, and one element of his effort became clear on November 28 when representatives of his party engaged in a fistfight in the Chamber of Deputies with representatives from Calderón's party. This event occurred shortly after Calderón named the members of his cabinet. His appointments were top-heavy with security officials, in keeping with his postelection pledge to focus on fighting organized crime. The most controversial appointment was that of Francisco Ramírez Acuña as interior minister, in charge of domestic security services; as governor of Jalisco state in 2004, Acuña had harshly suppressed leftist protesters.

Calderón officially took office during a private ceremony at the president's official residence at the stroke of midnight on December 1. In this televised ceremony, Calderón gave a short speech urging Mexicans to set aside their disagreements and calling for legislators to allow the public swearing-in ceremony later in the day. That public ceremony did not present an auspicious beginning for the new president's six-year term. After yet another fistfight in Congress, Calderón appeared briefly in the Chamber of Deputies, took the oath of office while leftist lawmakers protested, accepted the presidential sash from Fox, and left the chamber. On the streets of Mexico

City, thousands of López Obrador's supporters gathered again in protest and heard their candidate insist that a "neofascist oligarchy" had stolen the election from him.

By inauguration day, opinion polls showed that a very passionate minority still supported López Obrador and his claim to be the legitimate electoral victor—but a large majority of Mexicans had tired of the protests and López Obrador's heated rhetoric. Calderón also moved quickly to undercut his opponent's popular base. In his first days in office, he imposed a 10 percent cut on his own salary, and those of other senior officials, and pledged the money would be spent on social programs.

Calderón also signaled a tough law-and-order approach against leftist protesters who had created chaos in the southern tourist destination of Oaxaca. Accusing the local governor of corruption, protesters had tied the city in knots for five months, leading to violence in which at least a dozen people were killed; most reports linked the violence to gunmen aligned with the governor, Ulises Ruiz Ortiz. Calderón ordered the arrest of the protest leader but took no action against the controversial governor. On December 11 Calderón also sent about 4,000 troops into his home state of Michoacan as part of a crackdown on narcotics smuggling. That crackdown quickly resulted in the arrest of one of Mexico's chief drug lords, Alfonso Barajas, also known as "Ugly Poncho."

Fox's Legacy

Fox's convincing electoral victory in 2000 fostered widespread hopes in Mexico, even among some PRI supporters, that change was about to happen. Regardless of their views on specific policies, many Mexicans across the political spectrum realized that the PRI's long period in power had been stultifying and that it was time for fresh ideas and new leadership.

As a former business executive and as the representative of a staunchly probusiness party, Fox emphasized free market solutions for most of Mexico's problems and a more businesslike approach to government. He also offered proposals to help the poor, notably low-cost mortgages that helped several million people buy their own homes. His tenure did not spawn the job creation he had promised as a candidate, however; as a result, illegal emigration across the border to the United States soared.

Fox faced a huge institutional hurdle as president, one that Calderón also would face, as the PAN had only a minority of seats in the Congress, and legislators from the two opposition parties (the PRI and the PRD) often banded together to block Fox's key proposals on taxes and other matters. Moreover, Fox's own party was internally divided, and its representatives did not always support the president.

Some critics also said Fox did not put in place the sophisticated style of corporate governance he had seemed to promise in his campaign. Few of his high-level appointments were of individuals with distinguished records. Moreover, Fox was unable to capitalize on what he claimed to be a close relationship with U.S. president George W. Bush, who took office just two months after Fox did. The two leaders appeared to be working in tandem on immigration issues early in 2001, but then the September 11, 2001, terrorist attacks against the United States diverted Bush's attention and, ultimately, hardened public attitudes in the United States against immigration. Fox was particularly embarrassed in 2006 when the U.S. Congress passed legislation, which Bush signed, to erect a 700-mile fence along the border to keep out illegal Mexican immigrants. *(Background, Historic Documents of 2001, p. 764)*

In six years Fox failed to carry out many of the specific promises he had made, most important his pledges to reduce crime and narcotics trafficking and to improve living standards for the poor. His most significant accomplishment, according to many observers, was to maintain his own personal incorruptibility; by most accounts he left office no richer than when he entered it, in contrast to many of his predecessors. Fox also encouraged open political discourse and freedom of the press, also in contrast to most PRI leaders of the past.

Following is the text of a speech by Felipe Calderón, on December 1, 2006, after he officially took the office of president of Mexico.

DOCUMENT

"First Message to the Nation by F. Calderon as President of Mexico"

Mexican men and women:

Good evening. Later on, I shall appear in Congress to be sworn in, in accordance with Article 87 of the Constitution. I call for respect for the investiture of Congress, the need to strengthen Mexico's institutional life and for patriotism on the part of legislators, to ensure that everything is carried out with full respect for the Constitution.

Although I am not unaware of the political moment we are experiencing, I am convinced that today we should put an end to our disagreements today and begin a new stage in which the only aim is to place national interest above our differences. I hope that the swearing-in ceremony will comply with the law and ensure respect for all the Mexicans whose vote has marked the start of this new stage beginning today. I am assuming the Presidency of Mexico and through the latter, the legitimate mandate of serving you over the next six years and acting as Head of State and Head of Government.

I am aware of the complexity of circumstances in which I am receiving the government of Mexico, which is why, a few minutes ago, I ordered my government to receive the secretariats from the outgoing government, whose permanent functioning and performance of the most urgent tasks is essential in ensuring the continuation of government's actions. I was given the national flag from President Vicente Fox as a symbol of the responsibility transmitted to continue working for each and every one of you. As a Mexican, I would like to express my sincerest gratitude to Vicente Fox, who has completed his mandate with loyalty, honesty and work for the good of Mexico.

I accept the commitment of being the president of all Mexicans, regardless of their political preferences, the religion they profess, their ethnic origin, income level, social position, or the place where they live in our beloved country. Today marks the end of one long journey and the start of another. I invite all Mexicans to write a new chapter in national history. I believe in a successful, strong, self-confident Mexico that is proud of its natural wealth and history, its culture, identity and above all, one that is strengthened by the invincible nature of its people. I believe in a Mexico that is capable of overcoming adversity and achieving a different, better future for all. Within my government, I will be the first to use actions to show that this different Mexico is possible.

That is why I invite you to construct a different, better, successful Mexico. I would like to thank you for your attention and look forward to seeing you soon.

———————————

Source: Mexico. Presidency of the Republic. "First Message to the Nation by Felipe Calderon as President of Mexico." December 1, 2006. www.presidencia.gob.mx/en/press/speeches/?contenido=28453 (accessed February 8, 2007).

Other Historic Documents of Interest

Border security problems,
  p. 118
Immigration reform, p. 230

Relations between Latin America and
  U.S., p. 563
State of the Union, p. 23

UN Secretary General Annan on the Situation in Iraq

December 5, 2006

■■■■■ THE DOCUMENT IN CONTEXT ■■■■■

Sectarian violence emerged during 2006 as the greatest threat to Iraq's future, and it made the year the deadliest since the United States invaded in 2003. Violence between Iraq's Shiite Muslim majority and its Sunni Muslim minority was responsible for most of the thousands of civilian deaths reported in Iraq during 2006, according to the United Nations and other official sources. The scale of the violence was so great, and the new Iraqi government's inability or unwillingness to control it was so evident, that many Iraqis believed their country had fallen into a civil war. The administration of President George W. Bush refused to use that term, apparently fearing the negative impact on already dwindling public support for the large-scale U.S. military presence in Iraq.

At year's end, the United Nations Mission in Iraq estimated that 34,452 civilians had been killed in Iraq during the year, and another 36,685 were injured. That estimate, based on reports from Iraqi agencies, was substantially higher than year-end estimates by Iraq's Health Ministry (nearly 23,000 deaths) and Defense Ministry (13,896), both of which included policemen and soldiers as well as civilians. It was unclear why the three estimates were so different. Overall, according to various estimates, at least 50,000 Iraqis—and possibly 500,000 or more, according to one U.S. academic study—had been killed in violence since the U.S. invasion in 2003.

In a report to the United Nations Security Council on December 5, Secretary General Kofi Annan noted the high casualty estimates but said the real issue for Iraq "is the predicament of the Iraqi people. The deteriorating security situation has continued to adversely impact on the human rights, humanitarian situations and overall living standards," he said.

The human toll went well beyond deaths and injuries. Hundreds of thousands of Iraqis fled their homes because of the violence, some to other parts of the country and others to neighboring countries in the Middle East and overseas. The United Nations estimated that somewhere between 10 percent and 14 percent of Iraq's 26 million people were displaced from their homes at year's end.

Although appalled by the violence against Iraqis, Americans tended to pay closer attention to U.S. casualties, which continued on the same upward path as Iraqi casualties, though in much smaller numbers. On December 31, the total number of American service personnel killed in Iraq since the March 2003 invasion reached 3,001; of these, 821—or 27 percent—-occurred in 2006. *(Background on the violence, Historic Documents of 2005, p. 659)*

The Rise of Sectarian Violence

By 2006 there appeared to be three main sources of violence in Iraq. First, Sunni insurgents and radical Sunni Islamists such as al Qaeda targeted both foreign armies and Shiite civilians. Second, Shiite militias (the largest of which were aligned with political parties taking part in the government), primarily attacked Sunni civilians and each other but occasionally attacked U.S. and other foreign troops. Finally, criminal gangs sought financial gain by terrorizing civilians and even the foreign armies.

Americans and many other Westerners tended to view the violence in Iraq as senseless mayhem perpetrated by radicals. In fact, according to most independent observers in Iraq, the vast majority of violent acts were carried out by well-organized groups with specific grievances against the United States and other foreigners, against other ethnic groups or rival tribes, against the new Iraqi governments, or even against a combination of those.

During the first two years after the U.S. invasion in 2003, most of the violence in Iraq appeared to be fomented by Sunnis, including loyalists to Saddam Hussein's ousted regime and radical Islamists. Some of the latter were loyal to the al Qaeda terrorist network, the local branch of which called itself "al Qaeda in Mesopotamia," using the ancient name for the region surrounding the confluence of the Tigris and Euphrates rivers. A small number of those affiliated with al Qaeda were Arabs from other countries—lured to Iraq by the opportunity to strike against the United States.

Conflict between Iraqi Shiites and Sunnis became more prevalent starting in 2005, when the country went through the process of conducting three elections, all of which were dominated by the majority Shiites. Sunnis were angered not only by their loss of power since the ousting of Saddam but also by the realization that they almost certainly would never regain that power; some Sunnis also refused to believe they were a minority population. Most Sunnis boycotted the first two elections in 2005 but participated in the third election, which installed the "permanent" new government and therefore represented their last chance of having a significant voice in Iraq's future.

Determined to hold on to their first-ever grasp of power, Shiites retaliated against Sunni violence—setting off a cycle of attack and counterattack that became the dominant feature of Iraqi society in 2006. The largest Shiite militias were the Jaysh al-Mahdi, or Mahdi Army, which was under the general direction (but not total control) of a junior cleric, Moqtada al-Sadr, who was violently opposed to the U.S. presence in Iraq; and the Badr Organization, the armed wing of the Iranian-backed political party called the Supreme Council for the Islamic Revolution in Iraq. U.S. officials said each militia counted tens of thousands of armed fighters, some of whom were intensely loyal to the top leaders but others of whom followed local leaders with their own agendas.

By 2006 two types of violence had emerged as the main killers in Iraq. One was bombings, which often killed large groups of people and usually were directed at the U.S. military or at Iraqi security forces. Car bombs and makeshift bombs called "improvised explosive devices" by the U.S. military were most common; suicide bombs also were becoming a frequent tactic. Most of the bombings appeared to be carried out by Sunni insurgents. The deadliest spate of bombings was on November 23, when five car bombs and a mortar shell exploded in crowded areas of Sadr City, a huge Shiite slum in Baghdad; more than 200 people were killed in the bombing and subsequent attacks.

A second type of violence, practiced primarily by Shiites, was the kidnapping and subsequent murder of individuals, or even groups of people, by sectarian militias or criminal gangs. Often, the kidnappers demanded ransom, but they rarely turned over the victims even when family members paid thousands of dollars. In other cases, the apparent goal of the kidnappers was eliminating members of opposing sects from a neighborhood. These gangland-type kidnappings soared during 2006. In Baghdad, two or three dozen men were kidnapped each day and their mutilated bodies were often found dumped into ditches or stuffed into garbage bins—or simply left to rot on streets. The vast majority of these victims were Sunnis, many of whom lived in Shiite-majority neighborhoods, suggesting that they were killed by Shiite militias to "cleanse" the neighborhoods of Sunni residents. As a result, Baghdad became increasingly seg-regated along sectarian lines, with most Sunnis living to the west of the Tigris River and most Shiites living to the east; a rapidly diminishing number of people lived in mixed neighborhoods. Shiites also had gained political control of the city; only one of Baghdad's fifty-one provincial council members was a Sunni, as of late 2006.

In its latest quarterly report on "security and stability" in Iraq, made public on December 18, the Pentagon said the average weekly number of violent attacks in Iraq rose from just under 600 during late 2005 and early 2006 to nearly 1,000 in the third quarter of 2006. About two-thirds of the attacks were against U.S. and other (primarily British) foreign troops, with the rest about evenly divided between attacks against Iraqi civilians and members of Iraqi security forces. Iraqi civilians represented the vast majority of casualties, however—a trend that had taken hold in late 2005 with the rise of sectarian violence.

Samarra Mosque Bombing

The bombing of a famed Shiite shrine was a driving factor in the year's escalation of sectarian violence. The bombing came on the morning of February 22, when gunmen dressed as policemen took control of the golden-domed Askariya mosque in Samarra, about sixty miles north of Baghdad, then set off explosives that collapsed the famed dome into rubble and destroyed most of the rest of the mosque. The mosque was the burial site of two of the most important leaders in ancient Shiite history and, as such, was revered by Shiites the world over.

Enraged Shiites retaliated by attacking Sunni mosques around Iraq, and for more than a week members of the two sects engaged in an orgy of violence that killed hun-dreds of people. Iraq's leaders called for calm, but for a time it appeared that the country finally had entered into the full-scale civil war that long had loomed on the horizon.

Both sides found in the violence new grievances against the United States. Sunnis stepped up their criticism that the U.S. military failed to protect them against Shiite militias, while Shiites bridled at the restraints Washington tried to impose on their retaliations against the Sunnis. "Everything that is going on between the Sunnis and Shiites, the troublemaker in the middle is America," was the assessment offered to the New York Times by Abdul-Qader Ali, a clothing merchant in the Sunni town of Adhamiya. Such views were expressed not just by angry men on the street but also by some Iraqi leaders who faulted the United States for siding with the "wrong" sect. Shiite leaders laid particular blame on U.S. ambassador Zalmay Khalilzad, who was suspect in their eyes because he was a Sunni Muslim born in Afghanistan.

In an attempt to prevent another upsurge of violence after Friday prayers on Febru-ary 24, the Iraqi government imposed a daytime curfew on Baghdad and three other provinces, one of the first such crackdowns since the U.S. invasion. That move had some temporary calming effect, but it did not prevent Shiite militias from patrolling the streets alongside the official police, occupying dozens of mosques, and kidnapping dozens or even hundreds of Sunnis from their homes—one of many indications during the year that the militias could act virtually with impunity. One week later, on March 3, the government imposed a ban on vehicle traffic in Baghdad, another measure that stemmed violence temporarily but could not be a permanent solution because of its stifling impact on daily life in the city.

Six weeks after the Samarra bombing, on April 7, three suicide bombers attacked a Shiite mosque in Baghdad during Friday prayers, killing 85 people and wounding another 140. The Baratha mosque in northern Baghdad was an important gathering place for supporters of a major Shiite political party, the Supreme Council for the Islamic Revolution in Iraq.

Some Regions More Violent Than Others

Many news media reports—in Iraq, elsewhere in Middle East, and internationally—created the impression that all of Iraq was engulfed in unending violence. It certainly was true that much of Iraq was violent and that residents of major cities could not be certain of their safety. Even so, some parts of Iraq generally were peaceful during 2006. The three Kurdish-majority provinces in northern Iraq, collectively called Kurdistan by their inhabitants, had experienced very little violence since the U.S. invasion in 2003 and had prospered economically because they became the center of much of Iraq's trade with neighboring countries. Similarly, some of the Shiite-majority areas in southern Iraq were relatively peaceful.

The international impression of Iraq as a lawless society was close to the mark in much of the five central and western provinces: Anbar, Baghdad, Diyalah, Ninewa, and Salahuddin. Particularly in Baghdad, residents had a good chance of witnessing—or personally experiencing—violent acts on any given day. Of the 34,452 civilians killed in Iraq during 2006, according to UN figures, more than two-thirds were residents of the capital. Baghdad's share of the carnage was particularly high in the late months of the year; during November and December, for example, just under three-fourths of all violent deaths occurred in the capital city.

Outside of Baghdad, the most dangerous part of Iraq was the Sunni-majority province of Anbar, immediately to the west of the capital. In the south, the predominantly Shiite city of Basra had been relatively quiet until 2006, when it experienced increasing turmoil as rival Shiite militias battled for dominance and criminal gangs roamed the streets. Similarly, violence became more common during 2006 in Kirkuk and Mosul, Iraq's two largest northern cities. Kirkuk was a particular flashpoint because Kurds and Sunni Arabs each claimed the historical right to control of the city, which was the center of Iraq's northern oil industry. While political leaders discussed how to deal with those conflicting claims, extremists on both sides took matters into their own hands. Car bombs, suicide bombs, kidnappings, and other forms of violence became more common in Kirkuk during the year. In response, the government stepped up patrols of the city and even dug a ten-mile trench around the southern and western neighborhoods (dominated by Sunnis) in hopes of keeping out car bombs.

Involvement of the Army and Police

In a normal situation, people besieged by the type of violence afflicting Iraqis would turn for help and protection to the police or possibly the army. But in the Iraq of 2006, security forces—or men disguised as policemen or soldiers—often caused or condoned the violence. In a typical case, a white pickup truck bearing police insignia and loaded with uniformed men would pull into a neighborhood late at night, and then the men would burst into homes and drag away many of the male occupants, who were never seen again, except possibly when their mutilated bodies were found miles away. This scenario was repeated daily in Baghdad and occasionally in other cities. By midyear many Iraqis, especially Sunnis, would flee whenever the police arrived.

The apparent participation by the police in violence against civilians arose from two factors, both related primarily to the Shiite militias loyal to major political parties in the government. First, the militias infiltrated both local and national policeunits. Theactual extent of infiltration was difficult to determine, but reports by journalists and other independent observers suggested that the militias had placed thousands of their fighters into police forces, where they used their official status to attack Sunnis and other perceived enemies of the militias. A second factor was more prosaic: police uniforms were easy to copy or steal in Iraq, and so criminal gangs and other armed groups routinely used them as disguises. In some cases members of Shiite militias barely attempted to disguise themselves as police officers, often simply pinning badges to their militia uniforms. The government ordered 25,000 new police uniforms that were supposed to be difficult, if not impossible, to copy, but only one in five police officers working for the Interior Ministry were to get them.

The Iraqi government appeared to do little to control police violence until late in the year, when U.S. officials stepped up pressure for action. On October 4 the Interior Ministry announced that it had suspended a brigade of 700 policemen in Baghdad because of suspected links to death squads. Just three days earlier the brigade had failed to respond when gunmen kidnapped two dozen workers from a meat-processing factory. The bodies of seven workers were later found several miles away, and local reports said some of the police officers had participated in the killings. U.S. military officers reportedly had pushed for action against the police brigade.

On the flip side, Iraq's policemen were among the most frequent targets of violence—in many cases being killed by the dozens when car bombs or suicide bombs were exploded at police stations or recruiting areas. The Interior Ministry reported on December 24 that some 12,000 police officers had been killed since 2003, a figure that worked out to a daily average of about 10 policemen. Numerous attacks against the police resulted in multiple single-day fatalities during 2006; one example was a coordinated attack by two suicide bombings against an Interior Ministry compound in Baghdad on January 9, killing 18 police officers and wounding 25 others.

Killing of Zarqawi

For an all-too-brief period in early June, U.S. officials believed they might have broken the back of one of the chief sources of violence in Iraq: the al Qaeda in Mesopotamia network led by a Jordanian terrorist, Abu Musab al-Zarqawi. Acting on information from an informant, the U.S. military tracked Zarqawi to a house in the city of Baquba, and on June 7 U.S. Air Force F-16s dropped two 500-pound bombs on the house, killing Zarqawi and five associates. President Bush praised the assassination, saying, "This violent man will never murder again."

Zarqawi had emerged in 2004 as a leader of the Iraqi branch of the Sunni terrorist organization that was dedicated, in large part, to expelling the United States from the Middle East. Zarqawi also advocated the killing of Shiites, saying in a letter captured by the U.S. military in 2004 that a "sectarian war" in Iraq would attract Sunnis from elsewhere in the Middle East to Iraq, where they could help achieve a Sunni victory. Zarqawi's group—or others claiming to be part of it—carried out numerous spectacular attacks, including the February 22 bombing of the Shiite shrine in Samarra that set off the most recent wave of sectarian violence.

Any hopes that Zarqawi's death would lead to a reduction of violence were quickly dashed, however. The al Qaeda network quickly named a new leader, Abu Ayub al-Masri (whose name meant "the Egyptian," indicating his nationality), and it and other armed groups maintained, and even increased, the pace of killing through the rest of the year.

Attempting to Stabilize Baghdad

By 2006 it was clearer than ever before that the fate of Iraq, at least for the time being, would be determined by the fate of Baghdad. About one-fourth of all Iraqis lived in or near the capital, but more than two-thirds of all violent deaths in the country were occurring there.

The U.S. military and the Iraqi government made two extended drives to curb the violence in the capital. The first came in mid-June, after the U.S. military stepped up its presence in the city and the Iraqi army established additional checkpoints and carried out several raids against Sadr's Mahdi Army. If the point was to reduce the killing, the security drive failed: the Baghdad morgue collected 1,554 bodies in June (a 20 percent increase over May) and 1,855 in July (a 20 percent increase over June).

A second united campaign, called "Operation Together Forward II," got under way on August 7. In that campaign, the number of U.S. troops in Baghdad was nearly doubled from 7,200 to about 14,200, and Iraq was supposed to send six additional battalions of soldiers, or about 5,000 troops. Only two additional Iraqi battalions showed up. The campaign had some initial success in reducing the number of killings, but violence soared again in the capital from September through December. According to government figures, an average of about 2,500 civilians were killed in Baghdad during each of those four months—a level about 50 percent higher than the monthly average for the first six months of the year. During November and December, according to the UN, killings in Baghdad accounted for almost three-fourths of the 6,376 violent civilian deaths in Iraq.

Refugees and the Displaced

The violence had a broad impact in Iraq beyond the deaths and injuries of thousands of people. Many of the thousands of people wounded in the violence required medical care, something that was available only to the relatively well-to-do or to those lucky enough to get aid from U.S. and other foreign forces. Moreover, the majority of dead and wounded were men, who tended to be the sole breadwinners in Iraqi families. Thousands of families thus were left with no sources of income, and with no prospect of help from a government unable to provide even the most basic social services.

Many Iraqis—by UN estimates more than 10 percent of the country's entire population of some 26 million—responded by fleeing their homes, many of them almost certainly never to return. By late 2006, according to the United Nations High Commissioner for Refugees (UNHCR), about 1.6 million Iraqis had fled the country since the U.S. invasion in 2003. Most of the refugees went to neighboring Jordan and Syria, but tens of thousands fled to Europe and other distant lands. At least during the first half of the year, an average of 2,000 Iraqis fled each day to Syria and 1,000 fled to Jordan, the UNHCR said. By the end of 2006 UNHCR provided aid (food, shelter, medicine, and other necessities) to 200,000 Iraqi refugees in other countries. Among the refugees were many of Iraq's small base of the educated elite: doctors, lawyers, judges, teachers, business owners, government officials, journalists, and other professionals, some of whom had been threatened simply because they were educated.

Another 1.7 million or so Iraqis had fled their homes but remained in Iraq, according to UN figures. In UN terminology, these were "internally displaced persons." The UN estimated that nearly one-third of that total—about 500,000 people—left their homes in 2006 because of the upsurge of violence following the February 22 bombing of the Samarra mosque. Under international law, Iraq's government was responsible for caring for the internally displaced, but the ongoing violence and the general disorganization of the government in Baghdad made that task all but impossible in most cases.

Kidnapping Foreigners

Along with thousands of Iraqis, several hundred foreigners were kidnapped in Iraq in the years after the U.S. invasion. Most of the kidnapped Iraqis were never seen again, but the majority of foreigners were released unharmed after the kidnappers received international attention for their grievances or, in a few cases, were paid ransoms. Journalists, foreign aid workers, and civilian contractors were the most frequent kidnap victims because of their high visibility, both in Iraq and internationally.

One of the most prominent cases during 2006 was the kidnapping in Baghdad on January 7 of Jill Carroll, an American reporter who wrote for the *Christian Science Monitor* and other publications. Her abductors issued videos demanding the release of all female detainees in Iraq and showing footage of a tearful Carroll pleading for her life. Carroll was released unharmed on March 30.

A dozen or more others holding U.S. citizenship—some of them reportedly Iraqi-Americans—also had been kidnapped and remained in the hands of their abductors through much of 2006. Another thirty or so foreigners from Europe or elsewhere in the Middle East also were held by kidnappers, according to the U.S. embassy.

Following are excerpts from a quarterly report on the situation in Iraq submitted to the United Nations Security Council on December 5, 2006, by Secretary General Kofi Annan.

DOCUMENT

"Report of the Secretary-General Pursuant to Resolution 1546 (2004)"

[Parts I through III–C omitted.]

D. Reconstruction, Development and Humanitarian Assistance

32. UNAMI [United Nations Assistance Mission for Iraq] and United Nations agencies, programs and funds continued to support the Government of Iraq by working to strengthen

ministerial capacities, to provide and coordinate access to basic services and to restore public infrastructure. During the period under review, the primary focus was on providing substantive support to the Government in preparation for the International Compact with Iraq.

33. The implications of the content and direction of the Compact have influenced the strategic planning of the United Nations role in Iraq. The United Nations country team has recalibrated its focus and programming to complement the Compact. In this regard, a two-pronged assistance strategy is being employed whereby the United Nations will continue to focus on providing assistance for the delivery of essential social services, while providing targeted institutional and operational capacity-building support to the Government of Iraq.

34. UNAMI continued to emphasize the need for Iraqi leadership of humanitarian development initiatives as an essential means to promote national stability. To this end, the consultancy services of a contingency planning adviser from the Office for the Coordination of Humanitarian Affairs, as well as a civil society legal adviser provided through the United Nations Office for Project Services, have been secured and made available to the relevant government institutions, including the Office of the Prime Minister and the Ministry of Civil Society Affairs.

35. Sectarian violence and ongoing military operations continue to adversely affect large numbers of Iraqi civilians in many areas of the country. The number of displaced Iraqis continues to increase, either because of threats or acts of aggression by various elements. According to the Office of the United Nations High Commissioner for Refugees (UNHCR), the International Organization for Migration and Government sources at the time of the publication of the present report, the number of displaced persons since the Samarra attack on 22 February 2006 exceeds 450,000, including approximately 27,000 individuals displaced in Al-Anbar Governorate alone, as a result of recent military operations. That total added to displacements previous to the Samarra events brings the total number of displaced persons in Iraq to over 1.6 million people. With the approaching winter, there are increasing concerns about the well-being and basic rights of the displaced, especially women, children, the disabled and the elderly.

36. UNHCR estimates that an additional 1.6 million people have become refugees outside the country since 2003, of which between 500,000 and 700,000 are currently in Jordan; approximately 600,000 are in Syria, and about 100,000 are in Saudi Arabia and Kuwait. A total of 436,000 Iraqis have moved to Europe, the Americas, Africa and Asia. Every day approximately 2,000 Iraqis flee the country to the Syrian Arab Republic and 1,000 to Jordan. The United Nations agencies and their partners continue to provide food, shelter and non-food items to as many displaced Iraqis as resources permit. However, the resources available are not sufficient to adequately address the growing humanitarian crisis faced by Iraqis displaced within and outside of the country.

37. In order to address the overall human security situation in Iraq, my Emergency Relief Coordinator convened a series of meetings with donors to raise awareness and promote an integrated approach that would address the immediate and long-term needs of Iraqi civilians. In this regard, I encourage the international community to identify additional means for supporting United Nations agencies in their work with displaced Iraqis. In all instances, the United Nations will continue to actively assist all displaced persons and affected host communities and prepare for all likely scenarios by developing contingency plans.

E. Human Rights Activities

38. Although the Government of Iraq has resolved to promote the protection of human rights and the rule of law, human rights violations continue to rise. Abuses continue to be committed by terrorists, insurgents, militias and criminal armed groups. The excessive use of force by the multinational force and the Iraqi security forces in responding to these elements is also a matter of concern. Ongoing military operations also continue to challenge the principles of international humanitarian law as civilian casualties mount and access to public services by the affected populations is limited or obstructed. The sectarian carnage has resulted in a vicious cycle of violence fuelled by revenge killings. The end result is an environment of lawlessness and insecurity.

39. I remain particularly concerned by the abhorrent bombings and other attacks inflicting death and injury on civilians, as well as the kidnappings and murder of scores of people by death squads, allegedly operating in collusion with law enforcement agencies. According to the Ministry of Health, the number of civilians violently killed in the country was 3,345 in September and 3,709 in October, compared to 3,590 in July and 3,009 in August. The number of wounded reached 3,481 in September and 3,944 in October. In Baghdad alone the total number of civilians violently killed in September and October was 4,984.

40. Estimates by apparently reputable sources of the number of Iraqis killed over the past three and a half years are truly shocking and indicate the possibility of a humanitarian and human rights catastrophe in Iraq. Previous reporting by the Iraqi Body Count estimated that approximately 50,000 civilians have been killed since March 2003. However, recent estimates put the human toll of the conflict much higher than previously thought. On 9 November 2006, the Minister of Health of Iraq estimated that 150,000 civilians had been killed, while a study by the Johns Hopkins University Bloomberg School of Public Health published in the October 2006 issue of *The Lancet* estimated that 601,027 excess violent deaths have occurred in Iraq since March 2003. While questions on the methodology contained in the Johns Hopkins study have been raised by, inter alia, the Iraq Body Count, it nonetheless represents a serious attempt to quantify the loss of life in Iraq during this period.

41. The UNAMI Human Rights Office continues to work closely with Iraqi institutions, including the Higher Judicial Council, the Ministry of Human Rights and the Ministry of Justice, among others, to strengthen the rule of law and create a strong and effective national human rights protection system. A draft law on the establishment of a national human rights commission, prepared by the Human Rights Committee of the Council of Representatives during the previous period, has yet to be approved. Thirty leading parliamentarians who participated in a workshop, jointly organized by the Office of the High Commissioner for Human Rights and UNAMI in Amman on 17 and 18 October 2006, stressed the urgency for the Council of Representatives to enact this law to establish this important independent commission.

42. On 5 November 2006, the Iraqi Higher Criminal Tribunal sentenced former President Saddam Hussein and two other co-defendants to death for their role in the 1984 execution of 148 people convicted of involvement in the attempted assassination of the former President in Dujail. On the same day, the United Nations High Commissioner for Human Rights, Louise Arbour, issued a statement urging the Iraqi authorities to ensure

that the right of appeal of persons convicted and sentenced by the Tribunal would be fully respected. The High Commissioner also expressed the hope that the Government would observe a moratorium on executions.

43. I am also concerned about the targeting of various professional and minority groups inside Iraq. An increasing number of journalists and media workers are apparently targeted specifically because of their work, putting the right to freedom of expression under threat. Minorities continue to be targeted, and attacks against Christians have intensified since September. Members of the Sabean-Mandean community and other minority groups report continuous suffering at the hands of extremists. In addition, the situation of women has deteriorated further and an increasing number were recorded to be either victims of religious extremists or of "honor killings". The targeting of academics, including teachers and professors, as well as students, is seriously disrupting the education system, and has forced some to leave the country.

44. Significant progress in defending human rights will be difficult unless the professionalism and discipline of the country's law enforcement agencies are enhanced. The lack of proper training, standing orders and internal accountability systems continue to undermine respect for human rights and have consequentially eroded public confidence in Iraqi security forces. Perpetrators of criminal activities remain unpunished due to the shortage and intimidation of judges, prosecutors and court officials. Additionally, living conditions in prisons do not meet minimum international standards, and, although there have been some reports of improvement regarding the treatment of prisoners, the UNAMI Human Rights Office continues to receive reports of torture and other inhuman and degrading treatment of detainees, especially among juveniles. I am also concerned about reports of police and militias colluding to abduct people to extract bribes from their families. I welcome the decision of the Ministry of Interior to intensify the screening of police officers and commence more stringent vetting measures, including the suspension of police officers involved in abductions, the mistreatment of detainees and assassinations.

45. According to the Ministry of Human Rights, the total number of detainees for the entire country was 29,256 (13,571 of whom are in multinational force detention facilities) at the end of October, a slight decrease from the 30,104 detainees reported in September. In spite of ongoing efforts to release detainees and bring them under the jurisdiction of the Ministry of Justice, I remain troubled by the continued detention of thousands of Iraqis, which, in the absence of speedy judicial oversight, amounts to de facto arbitrary detention.

46. More than one year after the discovery of a secret detention facility in Al-Jadiriya, I would like to reiterate the call made by the United Nations High Commissioner for Human Rights and my Special Representative for the immediate release of the report on the Government investigation of this case. That issue notwithstanding, I take note of the action recently announced by the Minister of Interior with respect to human rights violations committed by officials of the Ministry at the detention centre known as Site 4. Prosecution of those responsible is necessary in order to combat the prevailing impunity and will act as a deterrent against further violations.

47. Vibrant and independent non-governmental organizations are critical components of a democracy based on the rule of law and respect for human rights. However, the activities and freedoms of civil society organizations operating in Iraq could be curtailed

if a law recently drafted by the Iraq Ministry of Civil Society Affairs is passed by the Council of Representatives. Therefore, I am hopeful that the legislation being considered will ultimately conform to international standards and best practices.

48. On 6 September 2006, 27 individuals, including one woman, were executed in Baghdad for murder, kidnapping and terrorism-related charges. Officially, since the reinstatement of the death penalty in 2004, more than 150 individuals have received death sentences, 51 of whom have already been executed. My Special Representative expressed his concern over these death sentences to the Iraqi presidency and called for moratorium. I urge the Government of Iraq to abolish capital punishment and implement a moratorium on death sentences.

49. Discussions on the future of the de-Baathification process in Iraq continued during the reporting period. It is important that this process embrace the principle of individual responsibility as opposed to collective punishment. At the same time, a comprehensive general amnesty currently being considered as part of the Prime Minister's National Reconciliation Plan is a possible means to promote peace and reconciliation. Draft legislation has yet to be circulated, although it is expected that amnesty in Iraq will primarily benefit individuals currently in detention, mostly those who have neither been charged nor convicted, as well as individual members of the insurgency, militias and other armed groups who renounce violence and, consistent with international standards, have not been responsible for war crimes, crimes against humanity or genocide. While recognizing the need for amnesty, I firmly believe this should not prejudice the victims' rights to truth and reparations. . . .

[Part IV omitted.]

V. Security and Operational Issues

A. Assessment of the Security Situation

53. The level of violence in Iraq remains elevated, with casualty levels among civilians at their highest since March 2006. The violence is characterized by a conflict that is increasingly sectarian in nature, a continuing insurgency, and violence by extremist groups, some affiliated with Al-Qaeda in Iraq. Intracommunal violence is also on the rise, with clashes reported between some Sunni tribes and among Shia groups in the south of Iraq.

54. Baghdad remains the focus of armed activity and of efforts by the Government of Iraq and the multinational force to reduce the violence. By the end of October, violent incidents in the city had increased 22 per cent over the previous month. That trend was consistent with the spike in violence experienced during the holy month of Ramadan in the previous two years.

55. In areas near Baghdad, the insurgency remains potent, and since September there has been a marked increase in a number of significant attacks against Iraqi security forces, as well as the multinational forces. In particular, the international zone remains a target for armed groups from across the spectrum. The primary means of attack is indirect fire from the surrounding areas. During October there was a direct rocket strike on a concrete car shelter in the UNAMI compound. The incident occurred in the late evening and there were no casualties. Checkpoints leading into the international zone also remain subject to sporadic attacks.

56. During the period under review, the situation in north-western and north central parts of Iraq, such as the Governorates of Ta'mim, Mosul and Diyala, was increasingly volatile. In the west, Al-Anbar Governorate continues to witness heavy fighting involving tribal, Al-Qaeda and armed groups. The situation in southern governorates remained tense. From 19 to 21 October 2006, the predominantly Shiite town of Ammara was witness to violent clashes between rival militias seeking to establish control over the city. Incident rates are rising in the Governorates of Qadissiya, Maysan, Wassit, Karbala and Babil. In northern Iraq, the security situation varies in intensity and character. In the far north, violence is mostly concentrated in Mosul, with Erbil remaining relatively peaceful.

57. Basra has witnessed a high number of incidents since August and appears to be in turmoil. The fragile political balance in the Governorate Council is challenged on the street by a nexus of informal groups associated with smuggling and criminal activities. The Basra Palace compound and other multinational force centers are the primary targets. Indirect fire is a constant threat and a frequent occurrence. United Nations staff presence in Basra continues to be maintained at an absolute minimum, with accommodation in hardened facilities.

58. United Nations international staff in the international zone continue to be exposed to a medium level of risk. Staff numbers are continuously reviewed and monitored to ensure that they are kept at acceptable levels. Nevertheless, the risk to national staff remains very high due to the rampant violence afflicting Baghdad. They are at risk of abduction, serious physical injury and death, particularly as they enter and exit the international zone.

59. The deteriorating security situation in Iraq has put severe constraints on the ability of the Organization to carry out its activities. UNAMI continues to work to adjust its operating procedures to respond to these changing conditions and to promote effective Mission operations that are compatible with the security environment. Although there appears to be greater Iraqi and international support for a more active United Nations role, should there be a further deterioration of the security situation, the viability of maintaining a significant United Nations presence in Iraq might be called into question. There can be no tolerance for exposing United Nations personnel to unacceptable risk. . . .

Observations

66. In my last report, I stated that Iraq was at an important crossroads and that the Iraqi people and their leaders faced a fundamental choice between taking the high road to negotiation and compromise or descending further into fratricidal sectarian conflict. Three months onwards, the situation in Iraq has further deteriorated in many parts of the country with a significant rise in sectarian violence, insurgent and terrorist attacks, and criminal activities. The growing militia activities have led to further destabilization. Across many parts of the country, an increasing number of Iraqis have been affected by growing violence and insecurity. High levels of civilian casualties and displacement on a daily basis are breeding an increasing sense of insecurity and deep pessimism among Iraqis. The prospects of all-out civil war and even a regional conflict have become much more real. Therefore, the challenge is not only to contain and defuse the current violence, but also to prevent its escalation.

67. Although the figures on civilian casualties since March 2003 vary between 50,000 and more than 600,000, depending on the sources, the real issue is the predicament of the Iraqi people. The deteriorating security situation has continued to adversely impact on

the human rights, humanitarian situations and overall living standards. The large number of casualties is having a much wider social impact than immediate death or injury. Fatal incidents invariably produce widows, orphans and female-headed households who must bear the burden of lost breadwinners and broken families. This is becoming a permanent disabling factor for human development and greatly adds to the burden of reliable access to proper health care, social services, education, employment and economic opportunities, which remain largely absent in Iraq today.

68. While I note the efforts of the Government of Iraq to improve security and promote national reconciliation, it must undertake an urgent review of strategies, policies and measures, with the aim of implementing a consensus-based action plan to halt and reverse current political and security trends in the country, which needs to be supported by a much broader and inclusive regional and international effort. In this effort, the Government faces three overarching challenges.

69. First, it needs to develop a fully inclusive political process that is focused on bringing all disenfranchised and marginalized communities into the political mainstream. While this will require hard political choices, the Government must ensure equitable access to political power, the institutions of the State and its natural resources by all Iraqi communities. This will require, inter alia, an approach to resource-sharing that is guided by the broader national interest rather than the interests of particular constituencies. Only when all Iraqi constituencies have a real stake in the future of the country will Iraq be on a path towards greater stability and prosperity.

70. Secondly, the Government must establish a monopoly over the use of force through the instruments of security and law enforcement within the framework of the rule of law. This will require addressing the terrorist, insurgency, sectarian and criminal violence, and will have to include dealing with the problem of militias inside the communities of Iraq, as well as the removal of militia elements from all ministries and the Iraqi security forces.

71. Thirdly, there is a need to cultivate a regional environment that is supportive of Iraq's transition. The Government has a special responsibility to normalize its relations with its neighbors, which in turn requires the neighbors to work towards fostering greater stability and security in Iraq.

72. To meet these challenges, the Government must now be fully empowered to deliver concrete results on all fronts—security, political, economic and human rights. The limited impact of existing policies has demonstrated that there is an urgent need for new approaches at the national, regional and international levels.

73. At the national level, the constitutional review process that has just begun and is supported by the United Nations offers a real opportunity for all Iraqi communities to reach a broad consensus on the fundamental issues that continue to divide them. I therefore once again urge Iraqi leaders and key international actors to demonstrate their commitment and make this review a top priority. Other important initiatives, such as key pieces of new legislation, including the law on the formation of regions and the hydrocarbon law, should satisfy the legitimate interests of all Iraqi communities, and thereby provide a firm basis for national reconciliation. In addition, there is a particular need to promote confidence-building measures between communities in potential flashpoint areas, such as Kirkuk. The United Nations stands ready to assist in this effort. Increased efforts are also needed to review the de-Baathification process and to pass an amnesty law without prejudice to the victims' rights to truth and reparation.

74. At the regional level, there is an increasing realization that a worsening conflict in Iraq would have implications not only for cross-border security, but that it could also aggravate a range of underlying tensions in neighboring countries. I have for some time now been urging Iraq's neighbors to contribute in a tangible manner to the stabilization of Iraq, which would also be beneficial to their own security. I welcome the ongoing dialogue between Iraq and its neighbors through periodic meetings of regional Foreign Ministers and Interior Ministers, in which my Special Representative regularly participates. However, in the light of the deteriorating situation in Iraq and its potentially grave regional implications, it may be necessary to consider more creative ways for fostering regional dialogue and understanding, which could result in concrete confidence-building measures between Iraq and its neighbors. This process could be broadened to include the permanent members of the Security Council. The United Nations is prepared to explore the possibilities of such a process in consultation with all concerned.

75. At the international level, the International Compact with Iraq, supported by the United Nations and the international community, provides an important framework for mobilizing national, regional and international actors in support of Iraq's transition. However, the Compact can only become a genuine partnership if it is based on a consensus on the way forward shared by all the major stakeholders inside Iraq. Its success will ultimately depend on the ability of the Government of Iraq and the international community to deliver on their mutual commitments. Achieving tangible progress during the first six months of its implementation will therefore be critical.

76. There is an urgent need to promote convergence at the national, regional and international levels to stabilize the situation in Iraq. In this regard, as I have publicly stated recently, beyond the measures mentioned above, it may be worthwhile to consider a larger framework for fostering dialogue and understanding at all three levels. Drawing on the positive experiences of the United Nations in other parts of the world, such as the Bonn peace accords for Afghanistan, it may be worthwhile to consider an arrangement that could bring Iraqi political parties together, possibly outside Iraq, with the United Nations playing a facilitating role. This would also require the active engagement of regional countries and the international community. The recent positive experience of the International Compact with Iraq in which national, regional and international actors have been engaged, demonstrates that the political will for such a process can be effectively mobilized.

77. During the 10 years of my tenure as Secretary-General, Iraq has been one of the biggest challenges for the Organization. Certainly one of the darkest moments in my career was the bombing of the United Nations compound on 19 August 2003, in which the United Nations lost 22 friends and colleagues, including the head of the mission, Sergio Vieira de Mello. This tragedy serves as a constant reminder of both the importance of remaining vigilant with respect to staff security, and the need for the United Nations to continue its work in Iraq. Despite the loss of United Nations staff, and bearing in mind the limits of what the United Nations can do under the prevailing circumstances, the Organization has remained steadfast in its support for the people of Iraq who have suffered so much.

78. Based on its mandate under resolution 1546 (2004), the United Nations has been implementing its tasks "as circumstances permit", while continuously assessing the extent to which the Organization is able to implement these tasks in the light of the very challenging security environment and its limited capacity. This assessment has enabled the United Nations to maximize its impact and prioritize its tasks with a focus on its

core political, electoral and constitutional activities under paragraph 7 (a) of its mandate under resolution 1546 (2004). Due to the security situation, activities in the areas of reconstruction, development, human rights and the rule of law under paragraph 7 (b) of its mandate have remained limited and have continued to be carried out mainly from outside Iraq. However, I am pleased that over the past six months, the United Nations has been able to play a lead role in the development of the International Compact, which provides a tangible long-term framework for the reconstruction and development of the country.

79. I would like to reiterate my appreciation to Member States, from both within and outside the multinational force, that have supported the United Nations in Iraq by providing military advisers and guard forces, as well as movement and aviation support. Despite efforts to increase our own security and logistical support, the United Nations will remain dependent on the support of the multinational force for the foreseeable future, owing to the complex security situation. In addition, if there is a further deterioration of the security situation, maintaining a United Nations presence in Iraq might be called into question.

80. I also wish to take this opportunity to thank my Special Representative for Iraq, Ashraf Jehangir Qazi, for his outstanding leadership and the Mission's national and international staff, as well as the personnel of United Nations agencies, programs and funds, for their dedicated work in fulfilling their mandated tasks under extremely difficult conditions.

Source: United Nations. Security Council. "Report of the Secretary-General Pursuant to Paragraph 30 of Resolution 1546 (2004)." S/2006/945, December 5, 2006. www.un.org/Docs/sc/sgrep06.htm (accessed January 7, 2007).

Other Historic Documents of Interest

UN Security Council Resolution on Peacekeeping in Somalia

December 6, 2006

Somalia, which in the past fifteen years had seen far more than its share of warfare and political turmoil, experienced an extraordinary year of both those things in 2006. Early in the year, a weak "transitional" government finally seemed to be getting its act together after two years of infighting, but in midyear most of Somalia came under the control of a group of Islamists. Although the Islamists at first brought a measure of stability, they were opposed by the United States and, more important, Somalia's powerful neighbor, Ethiopia. The Ethiopian army invaded Somalia in October and by late December had driven the new Islamist government out of power and out of Somalia. At year's end, much of the country was under Ethiopian protection, and the transitional government was given another chance to assert itself.

Somalia had been without a truly functioning national government since 1991, when local warlords ousted longtime dictator Mohamed Siad Bare. The United States and several allies intervened militarily at the end of 1992 with the stated mission of allowing aid agencies to care for the victims of civil strife and drought. That mission was frustrated by warlords determined to hold on to power, however, and it came to an ignominious end in March 1994 when the United States withdrew just six months after eighteen of its soldiers were killed.

In subsequent years numerous warlords divided Somalia into personal fiefdoms—in fact, the northern half of the country had been split off since 1991 into de facto separate countries called Puntland and Somaliland. Leaders of regional governments—using an institution called the Intergovernmental Authority on Development—in August 2004 created what they called a "transitional" government for Somalia; by some counts, it was the fourteenth attempt to create a national government since 1991.

The president of this new government was Abdullahi Yusuf Ahmed, a warlord who had strong support from Ethiopia. That government was split into factions, however, and carried little real authority. One faction was headed by Yusuf, who operated from the town of Jowhar, just north of the capital, Mogadishu. The other was led by parliament speaker Sharif Hassan Sheikh Adan, who was based in Mogadishu. In the meantime, rival warlords continued to run most of the country. The United Nations had imposed an arms embargo on Somalia, but that failed to prevent the country from becoming one of the most heavily armed places on Earth.

Early in the Year

The beginning of the year saw an unusual move toward harmony. On January 5, Yusuf and Sharif signed an agreement in Yemen promising to resolve their differences. The two leaders, joined by Prime Minister Ali Mohamed Gedi, held other meetings later in January, leading to a meeting of parliament in the town of Baidoa, northwest of Mogadishu, on February 26; it was the first-ever session inside Somalia of the parliament that had been appointed by local leaders in 2004.

This move toward political reconciliation was accompanied by a rise in fighting among various militias starting in late February; much of the fighting took place in and around Mogadishu. Some militias, calling themselves the Alliance for the Restoration of Peace and Counterterrorism (ARPC), were aligned with warlords and business leaders represented in the government. Other militias represented a recent phenomenon in Somalia: Islamic courts that sought to use Muslim law, known as *Shariah*, to bring justice, and some stability, to an otherwise lawless society. These militias had banned together under the title Islamic Courts Union (ICU), which controlled much of the capital.

The U.S. government charged that some leaders of the ICU were linked to the al Qaeda terrorist network. U.S. officials also said the ICU harbored several al Qaeda members who had carried out two major terrorist attacks in East Africa in recent years: the 1998 bombing of U.S. embassies in Kenya and Tanzania, and the 2002 bombing of a Kenyan hotel that catered primarily to Israelis. *(Embassy bombings, Historic Documents of 1998, p. 555; hotel bombing, Historic Documents of 2002, p. 1014)*

Somalia was awash in rumors that the CIA was supporting the ARPC, at least financially; these rumors appeared to be validated by the group's truckloads of new guns and the stacks of dollar bills handed out to its fighters. Bush administration officials acknowledged talking to the alliance leaders but refused to comment on the reports of U.S. aid to them. Some Somalis said U.S. aid to the ARPC was counterproductive because it undermined local support for them. This view reportedly was seconded by some Americans diplomats in Kenya, one of whom filed a dissent through standard channels and was reassigned to another embassy, at his request.

Rise of the Islamic Courts

Fighting in Mogadishu between the rival militias escalated sharply in May, with artillery battles forcing hundreds of people from their homes and killing at least 300 people, most of them civilians. On June 5 the Islamic militias declared victory, saying they had gained total control of the capital. In a public letter, leaders of the Islamic Courts denied having links to al Qaeda and other terrorist groups and said they wanted a "friendly relationship with the international community."

In the following weeks, the Islamic Courts militias consolidated their hold on much of the rest of Somalia, notably by seizing the town of Jowhar. On July 22, the transitional government—still based in Baidoa—signed a cease-fire and "mutual recognition" agreement with the Islamic Courts. This accord, mediated by the Arab League, appeared to be an attempt by both parties to stabilize the situation.

The rise to power in Mogadishu of the Islamic Courts prompted a debate in international circles, particularly in Washington, where the Bush administration's support for the alliance warlords was coming under question. Some Western experts saw the Islamic Courts takeover as a potentially positive development, arguing that Somalia's Islamists were not as extreme as the al Qaeda terrorist network and might provide

Somalia with the stability it had long lacked. These observers pointed in particular to the Islamic Courts's nominal leader, Sheikh Sharif Ahmed, a former geography teacher who was believed to be among the moderates.

Administration officials did not accept this view and argued that some Islamic Courts leaders were linked to al Qaeda. The most important of these leaders was Sheikh Hassan Dahir Aweys, who on June 24 emerged as the apparent head of the new government, now formally calling itself the Conservative Council of Islamic Courts. A former Somalia army colonel, Aweys had been a leader in the 1990s of an Islamist group, al-Itihaad al-Islamiya, listed by the United States as a terrorist organization. Aweys told journalists in 2006 that the group no longer existed, and he insisted he had no past or current ties to al Qaeda. Aweys's rise to leadership in late June appeared to result from a power struggle within the Islamic Courts, one that led to the marginalization of Ahmed and other more moderate leaders.

The new leaders were popular within Somalia, at least initially, because they brought peace and security and, most important, they ousted the alliance warlords who had preyed on the civilian population. Even so, residents of Mogadishu expressed concern that the new leaders would try to impose hard-line Islamist rule, much as the Taliban regime had done in Afghanistan before it was ousted by the United States in 2001. By mid-August the Islamic Courts had consolidated its control over much of southern Somalia, except for the town of Baidoa, the only place where Yusuf's transitional government had any authority.

Fall of the Islamic Courts

The outside power that, arguably, was least happy about the rise to power of the Islamic Courts—and most willing to do something about it—was the government of Ethiopia. Islamic Courts leader Aweys had battled in the early 1990s with the Addis Ababa government headed by Prime Minister Meles Zenawi, who in turn was fearful of a challenge from Islamist groups in his country and elsewhere in the Horn of Africa. Most Ethiopians were Christians, but Islamist groups had become increasingly active there in recent years. Zenawi in 2005 had accused al-Itihaad (the group Aweys had headed but said no longer existed) of carrying out several bombings in Addis Ababa. Another factor was Eritrea, which had fought a fierce border war with Ethiopia from 1998 to 2000. According to UN officials, Eritrea had been a major source of weapons for Aweys's group. *(Eritrea-Ethiopia war, Historic Documents of 2000, p. 755)*

By late June there were numerous reports that Ethiopia had sent its army across the border into Somalia. Zenawi denied these reports, at first saying his army merely was stationed along the border "to prevent any threat to our security that might emanate from the resurgent Jihadists in Mogadishu." By mid-July the presence of Ethiopian troops in Somalia was more obvious, but Zenawi said he had sent only "trainers" to help President Yusuf's transitional government.

The peace brought on by the Islamic Courts's victory proved to be short-lived. New clashes between Islamic Courts militias and the last warlord still active in Mogadishu killed more than 100 people in mid-July. The truce between the Islamic Courts and the transitional government also was strained, apparently the result of the rise to power of Aweys and fellow hard-liners. By July 19 Islamic Courts militias were deployed outside the Yusuf government's headquarters in Baidoa, and Ethiopian troops reportedly were rushed into the city to defend it.

Diplomatic efforts to stabilize the situation continued all through August and into September. These efforts included a plan by regional countries to send 3,500 peace-keepers into Somalia to support Yusuf's transitional government—a plan that was opposed by the Islamic Courts and hampered by intense discord within Yusuf's government. Two events in September sent the situation spinning out of control. The first was Somalia's first-ever suicide bombing, on September 18, targeting Yusuf. He survived a large car bomb, but twelve others, including his brother, were killed in the bombing and an ensuing gun battle. A week later, the Islamic Courts militias gained control of the important port town of Kismayo near the border with Kenya, further endangering Yusuf's government.

Reportedly in response to the latter development, Ethiopia stepped up its military presence in Baidoa and other parts of Somalia, while Eritrea appeared to be coming to the aid of the Islamic Courts. On October 25 Zenawi said Ethiopia was "technically" at war with the Islamic Courts, which he said were "spoiling for a fight."

Also late in October, excerpts from a confidential UN report were leaked to the news media. Warning that "an all-out war is possible," the report cited evidence that 6,000 to 8,000 troops from Ethiopia and some 2,000 from Eritrea were in Somalia. This report said each of the competing forces in Somalia had important outsider backers. The transitional government, it said, was backed by Ethiopia, Uganda, and Yemen, while the Islamic Courts was receiving aid from Djibouti, Egypt, Eritrea, Iran, Libya, Saudi Arabia, and Syria. Officially made public on November 14, the UN report included detailed information about weapons shipments into Somalia despite an arms embargo imposed by the Security Council in 1992. Citing these findings, the Security Council reaffirmed the embargo on November 29 and called on all countries in the region to abide by it.

The council's action preceded—and had no apparent dampening effect on—a sudden escalation of violence. On November 30 three suicide bombers, one of them a woman, set off bombs outside Baidoa, killing two policemen as well as the bombers and their accomplices. On the same day, the Ethiopian parliament authorized military action against any attack—a clear reference to the Islamic Courts, which Zenawi accused of collaborating with Eritrea against Ethiopia.

Responding to these events and a general increase in tensions, the Security Council acted again on December 6—this time modifying the arms embargo it had just reaffirmed a week earlier. In Resolution 1725, adopted unanimously, the council authorized African nations to create a "protection and training mission" to support President Yusuf's transitional government in Baidoa. The resolution also waived the arms embargo for the purpose of equipping that military mission. John Bolton, the acting U.S. ambassador to the UN, said the African force would help establish conditions for a "credible dialogue" between Yusuf's government and the Islamic Courts.

The Islamic Courts announced on December 7 that it would oppose what it called "invading forces" authorized by the UN, as well as the "aggression" from Ethiopia. After several more rounds of clashes, the Islamic Courts on December 12 set a seven-day deadline for Ethiopia to withdraw its military units, which were the only serious protection Yusuf's government in Baidoa had.

When that deadline expired on December 19, the Islamic Courts attacked government positions outside Baidoa. This turned out to be the prelude to the main event: a full-scale invasion of Somalia by Ethiopia on December 24. Ground forces crossed the border en masse and pushed toward Baidoa, while Ethiopian jets bombed Islamic Courts military targets. In a televised speech to his nation, Ethiopian prime minister Zenawi said he was "forced to enter into war" to protect his country. "We are not trying to set up a government for Somalia, nor we do have an intention to meddle into Somalia's internal affairs," he said.

It may not have been meddling, but Ethiopia was deeply involved in Somalia's affairs. Fighter jets attacked the Mogadishu airport and a nearby military base the next day, and the army headed straight for the capital, first capturing the strategic towns of Burhakaba (on December 26) and Jowhar (on December 27). In Washington, the Bush administration signaled its support for the invasion, calling it a response to "aggression" by the Islamic Courts.

The extraordinary aspect of this invasion was how quickly the Islamic Courts forces collapsed in the face of the Ethiopian assault. Although the Islamic Courts had built broad public support by bringing nearly six months of calm to one of the most violent places on Earth, they lacked the military muscle to repel Ethiopia's army, which was one of the most powerful and battle-tested in Africa. By December 28 the Islamic Courts fighters had fled Mogadishu and headed down the coast to Kismayo. Hours later, the Ethiopians, along with the forces supporting Yusuf's government, moved into Mogadishu and celebrated their victory in traditional style, by firing endless rounds of ammunition into the air. Almost spontaneously, clan leaders and warlords reverted to the activities that had made them so unpopular in the past, and Mogadishu so dangerous: setting up armed checkpoints outside their neighborhoods and charging fees for outsiders to enter.

Members of the transitional government, led by Prime Minister Gedi, arrived in Mogadishu on December 29, courtesy of an Ethiopian armored convoy. Gedi was cheered by people on some streets, but protesters in other sections threw stones at the Ethiopians and burned tires in the streets. Gedi said he was determined to end the clan divisions and feuds among warlords that had prevailed before the Islamic Courts seized control. In the meantime, he said, the Ethiopian army "will stay until we agree to send them back to their country, and this depends on the stability of Somalia."

Under continued pressure from the Ethiopian army, the last units of the Islamic Courts—an estimated 500 to 1,000 fighters—fled from Kismayo on December 31, some apparently headed into Kenya and others into the mangrove swamps along the border. Local elders in Kismayo had asked the Islamic Courts members to leave, arguing that the Ethiopians would destroy the city unless they did so. It was a sudden end to what, just six months earlier, had appeared to be the world's first new Islamist state since the Taliban took control of Afghanistan in 1995. As the year ended, diplomats once again were debating how, and when, to send in the international peacekeeping force that had been authorized by the Security Council on December 6, so the Ethiopians could withdraw without chaos following in their wake.

Humanitarian Situation

The year's violence did nothing to help the 2 million or more Somalians who depended on foreign relief supplies because of a long-term drought and the years of instability. Before 2006 Ethiopia had suffered three consecutive years of poor rainfall, thus putting at risk about 1.7 million people whose crops no longer gave them adequate food supplies. Another 400,000 Somalians were internally displaced; they had been driven from their homes by fighting or instability and forced to live in camps or on their own without adequate resources to sustain themselves.

The end of the year brought two humanitarian emergencies: the manmade upheaval caused by the fighting (which displaced an estimated 70,000 people), and a natural disaster at the opposite end of the scale from the drought of previous years. Heavy rains in November caused large-scale flooding in much of southern Somalia, forcing more than 450,000 people from their homes, according to UN estimates. UN agencies were seeking more than $230 million for emergency aid to Somalia during 2007, but by the end of 2006 had received only 2 percent of that amount.

Following is the text of United Nations Security Council Resolution 1725, adopted on December 6, 2006, authorizing the formation of a peacekeeping operation in Somalia.

▬▬▬▬▬▬ DOCUMENT ▬▬▬▬▬▬

"Resolution 1725 (2006)"

The Security Council,

Recalling its previous resolutions concerning the situation in Somalia, in particular resolution 733 (1992) of 23 January 1992, resolution 1356 (2001) of 19 June 2001, resolution 1425 (2002) of 22 January 2002, and the statements of its President, in particular that of 13 July 2006 (S/PRST/2006/31),

Reaffirming its respect for the sovereignty, territorial integrity, political independence, and unity of Somalia,

Reiterating its commitment to a comprehensive and lasting settlement of the situation in Somalia through the Transitional Federal Charter, and stressing the importance of broad-based and representative institutions and of an inclusive political process, as envisaged in the Transitional Federal Charter,

Reiterating its insistence that all Member States, in particular those in the region, should refrain from any action in contravention of the arms embargo and related measures, and should take all actions necessary to prevent such contraventions,

Emphasizing its willingness to engage with all parties in Somalia who are committed to achieving a political settlement through peaceful and inclusive dialogue, including the Union of Islamic Courts,

Underlining the importance for stability in Somalia of broad-based and representative institutions and of an inclusive political process, *commending* the crucial efforts of the League of Arab States and the Intergovernmental Authority on Development (IGAD) to promote and encourage political dialogue between the Transitional Federal Institutions and the Union of Islamic Courts, *expressing* its full support for these initiatives, and *affirming* its readiness to assist as appropriate an inclusive political process in Somalia,

Urging both the Transitional Federal Institutions and the Union of Islamic Courts to unite behind and continue a process of dialogue, recommit to the principles of the 22

June 2006 Khartoum Declaration and the agreements made at the 2–4 September 2006 Khartoum meeting, and establish a stable security situation inside Somalia,

Calling upon the Union of Islamic Courts to cease any further military expansion and reject those with an extremist agenda or links to international terrorism,

Deploring the bombing in Baidoa on 30 November 2006 and *expressing* the Security Council's concern regarding the continued violence inside Somalia,

Welcoming the agreement reached between the Union of Islamic Courts and the Secretariat of the Intergovernmental Authority on Development dated 2 December 2006, and *encouraging* IGAD to continue discussions with the Transitional Federal Institutions,

Calls upon all parties inside Somalia and all other States to refrain from action that could provoke or perpetuate violence and violations of human rights, contribute to unnecessary tension and mistrust, endanger the ceasefire and political process, or further damage the humanitarian situation,

Taking note of the note verbale dated 16 October 2006 from the Permanent Mission of Kenya to the United Nations to the President of the Security Council transmitting the text of the Deployment Plan for a Peacekeeping Mission of IGAD in Somalia (IGASOM),

Determining that the situation in Somalia continues to constitute a threat to international peace and security in the region,

Acting under Chapter VII of the Charter of the United Nations,

1. *Reiterates* that the Transitional Federal Charter and Institutions offer the only route to achieving peace and stability in Somalia, *emphasizes* the need for continued credible dialogue between the Transitional Federal Institutions and the Union of Islamic Courts, and *affirms* therefore that the following provisions of the present resolution, based on the decisions of IGAD and the Peace and Security Council of the African Union, aim solely at supporting peace and stability in Somalia through an inclusive political process and creating the conditions for the withdrawal of all foreign forces from Somalia;

2. *Urges* the Transitional Federal Institutions and the Union of Islamic Courts to fulfil commitments they have made, resume without delay peace talks on the basis of the agreements reached in Khartoum, and adhere to agreements reached in their dialogue, and *states* its intention to consider taking measures against those that seek to prevent or block a peaceful dialogue process, overthrow the Transitional Federal Institutions by force, or take action that further threatens regional stability;

3. *Decides* to authorize IGAD and Member States of the African Union to establish a protection and training mission in Somalia, to be reviewed after an initial period of six months by the Security Council with a briefing by IGAD, with the following mandate drawing on the relevant elements of the mandate and concept of operations specified in the Deployment Plan for IGASOM:

  a. To monitor progress by the Transitional Federal Institutions and the Union of Islamic Courts in implementing agreements reached in their dialogue;
  b. To ensure free movement and safe passage of all those involved with the dialogue process;
  c. To maintain and monitor security in Baidoa;
  d. To protect members of the Transitional Federal Institutions and Government as well as their key infrastructure;

e. To train the Transitional Federal Institutions' security forces to enable them to provide their own security and to help facilitate the re-establishment of national security forces of Somalia;

4. *Endorses* the specification in the IGAD Deployment Plan that those States that border Somalia would not deploy troops to Somalia;

5. *Decides* that the measures imposed by paragraph 5 of resolution 733 (1992) and further elaborated in paragraphs 1 and 2 of resolution 1425 (2002) shall not apply to supplies of weapons and military equipment and technical training and assistance intended solely for the support of or use by the force referred to in paragraph 3 above;

6. *Encourages* Member States to provide financial resources for IGASOM;

7. *Requests* the Secretary-General, in consultation with the Commission of the African Union and the secretariat of IGAD, to report to the Security Council on the implementation of the mandate of IGASOM within thirty (30) days, and every sixty (60) days thereafter;

8. *Emphasizes* the continued contribution made to Somalia's peace and security by the arms embargo, *demands* that all Member States, in particular those of the region, fully comply with it, and *reiterates* its intention to consider urgently ways to strengthen its effectiveness, including through targeted measures in support of the arms embargo;

9. *Decides* to remain actively seized of the matter.

Source: United Nations. Security Council. "Resolution 1725 (2006)." S/RES/1725 (2006), December 6, 2006. www.un.org/Docs/sc/unsc_resolutions06.htm (accessed February 26, 2007).

Other Historic Documents of Interest

Iraq Study Group Report
on U.S. Policy in Iraq

December 6, 2006

Domestic support in the United States for involvement in Iraq plummeted in 2006, leading to a larger than expected Democratic victory in midterm congressional elections and forcing President George W. Bush to replace the chief architect of his Iraq policy, Secretary of Defense Donald H. Rumsfeld. Late in the year, a blue-ribbon panel of Washington insiders—the Iraq Study Group—offered a slightly different alternative policy, but the president appeared inclined to reject that advice and continue with his current policy and possibly more of it. Bush was expected to announce early in 2007 that he would send another 20,000 U.S. troops to Iraq on a temporary mission to bolster the force of about 140,000 soldiers and marines already there.

Bush in March 2003 had launched a large-scale invasion of Iraq to oust the country's long-time dictatorial leader, Saddam Hussein. The invasion was successful and Saddam was overthrown with ease, but U.S. plans to turn Iraq into a peaceful democracy and withdraw troops quickly soon proved to be fanciful. Violent resistance to the U.S. occupation seemed to grow by the day. The three elections held in 2005 gave Iraq a government with democratic legitimacy but one that lacked the strength or fortitude to govern effectively. Sectarian violence, pitting Shiite and Sunni Muslims against each other, took hold in 2006 and made the year the bloodiest one in Iraq since the U.S. invasion.

News coverage of the violence in Iraq often contradicted the optimistic reports coming from the White House and Pentagon. As the war dragged on, Americans increasingly concluded that the president had gotten the United States into a no-win situation in Iraq. Opinion polls throughout the year showed that a majority of Americans regarded the invasion of Iraq as a mistake and supported a timetable for withdrawing U.S. troops. Approval ratings for Bush's handling of his job as president dipped well below 40 percent for most of the year, the lowest of his presidency. Approval of his Iraq policy slid to around 30 percent. As the November elections approached, many Republicans in Congress began distancing themselves from Bush's Iraq policies. That political move came too late for the party generally, as the Democrats won control of both chambers in an election dominated by voter dissatisfaction with Bush's handling of Iraq. *(Background to U.S. policy in Iraq, Historic Documents of 2005, p. 832)*

The Iraq Study Group

As the domestic political debate over Iraq grew in intensity in late 2005, Rep. Frank R. Wolf, R-Va., steered legislation through Congress providing funds for an independent assessment of U.S. policy. At Wolf's request, the United States Institute of Peace (a federally funded think tank) and three other policy institutions created the Iraq Study Group as a bipartisan commission.

Wolf and other members of Congress selected as cochairmen two of Washington's most experienced and respected foreign policy hands: James A. Baker III, who had been a White House chief of staff under President Ronald Reagan (1981–1989) and secretary of state under President George H.W. Bush (1989–1993); and former representative Lee H. Hamilton, D-Ind., who had chaired the foreign affairs and intelligence committees as well as the House Foreign Affairs Subcommittee on Europe and the Middle East. More recently, Hamilton had cochaired the commission that examined the government's handling of the September 11, 2001, terrorist attacks against the United States. *(September 11 commission, Historic Documents of 2004, p. 450)*

Baker and Hamilton then appointed eight other commission members: former CIA director Robert Gates, prominent lawyer Vernon E. Jordan Jr., former attorney general Edwin Meese III, former Supreme Court justice Sandra Day O'Connor, former House member and White House chief of staff Leon E. Panetta, former secretary of defense William J. Perry, former senator and Virginia governor Charles S. Robb, and former senator Alan K. Simpson. Gates later resigned after Bush chose him to replace Rumsfeld at the Pentagon; he was replaced by former secretary of state Lawrence S. Eagleburger. Overall, the panel was evenly divided, with five Democrats and five Republicans.

The choice of Baker as cochair of the panel generally was seen as a guarantee that its recommendations would receive serious consideration at the White House. Because he had been a confidante of Bush's father for decades, and had led the legal battle to secure the junior Bush's election in 2000, Baker had more political credibility than leaders of most such high-level commissions. *(Contested election, Historic Documents of 2000, p. 999)*

The Iraq Study Group appointed five "working groups" consisting of respected U.S. experts on the Middle East, diplomacy, and military matters; the commission itself held nine full meetings between mid-March and late November. As the panel was working, expectations were high in Washington that it would produce a set of policy recommendations that could gain broad acceptance from both Democrats and Republicans. After Baker and Hamilton said their group would not report its findings until after the November 7 elections, congressional candidates of both parties deflected voters' questions about Iraq policy by saying they were waiting to see the study group's recommendations. The study group's deliberations did not keep Iraq entirely out of politics, however. In June both chambers of Congress rejected plans to withdraw from Iraq quickly: the House on June 16 by a 256–153 vote and the Senate on June 22 by a 86–13 vote. More important, Democrats went on the offensive during the campaign with speeches and advertisements denouncing Bush's "failed" policies in Iraq, while most Republicans tried to avoid the subject. Voters clearly were focused on Iraq, and in the midterm elections many Republicans paid the price for Bush's Iraq policies.

From the outset, Baker and Hamilton insisted they were considering all realistic policy options. Even so, they made it clear that two options were off the table: Baker characterized them as "stay the course," a phrase Bush had used until September to describe his determination to continue his current policy, and "cut and run," a politically charged term Bush and Vice President Dick Cheney often used to denigrate calls by some Democrats for setting a timetable to withdraw from Iraq.

The Iraq Study Group made its report public on December 6, one month after the upheaval of the midterm elections and one month before the new Democratic-led Congress was to take office. Some of the panel's key recommendations had been signaled days or even weeks ahead of time in news media reports, but the breadth of its seventy-nine recommendations and the harshness of its language on the results of Bush's policies in Iraq went well beyond what most Washington insiders had expected.

Most news accounts of the study group's report focused on the opening sentence of its executive summary: "The situation in Iraq is grave and deteriorating." This assessment was much more blunt than anything the Bush administration had been willing to offer, and it set the tone for the subsequent recommendations, which the panel quickly said would not guarantee success in Iraq but might improve the chances of it.

At the center of attention was the one recommendation that was most at odds with Bush's current policy: the increased use of diplomacy in the Middle East in hopes of gaining greater regional support for U.S. policy in Iraq and elsewhere. In particular, the panel called for a regional conference in which the United States would conduct negotiations with Iran and Syria, the two neighbors of Iraq who had been accused by the Bush administration of supporting anti-U.S. forces in Iraq. Baker and Hamilton said they were under no illusions that Iran and Syria would be disposed to help the United States out of its predicament in Iraq, but they said neither country was interested in seeing Iraq collapse. Moreover, Baker and Hamilton, along with their colleagues on the commission, suggested that the Bush administration had crippled its own Iraq policy by refusing to engage in diplomacy with Iraq's neighbors. "It is our view that, in diplomacy, a nation can and should engage its adversaries and enemies to try to resolve conflicts and differences consistent with its own interests," the panel said.

The panel also placed U.S. failures in Iraq in a broader context, saying the administration's reluctance to push hard for peace agreements between Israel and Syria and Israel and the Palestinians had undermined the U.S. standing generally in the region. In a clear, if indirect, criticism of Bush's practice of aligning U.S. policy with that of Israel in nearly all cases, the panel said: "The United States does its ally Israel no favors in avoiding direct involvement to solve the Arab-Israeli conflict."

Other recommendations by the Iraq Study Group called for more subtle changes in U.S. policy—and therefore received less attention in most media reports. In total, however, those recommendations proposed a fundamental shift toward more aggressive pressure by Washington on the Iraq government to follow through on the promises it had made. Most important, the panel laid out a series of "milestones," complete with target dates through the end of 2007, for Iraq to complete work on key governance, national reconciliation, and security matters. For example, the panel said the Bush administration should push the Iraqi parliament to complete work on long-stalled legislation governing such matters as control of the country's oil resources and disbanding sectarian militias. U.S. ambassador Zalmay Khalilzad had laid out some of the same milestones in 2006 but had been rebuffed by Prime Minister Nouri al-Maliki, who insisted Iraq had the sovereign right to set its own timetables.

The study group's dozens of other recommendations dealt with the full range of U.S. policy toward Iraq, as well as the administration's policymaking process, which panelists clearly viewed as deeply flawed. Among other things, the panel faulted the administration for failing to improve intelligence gathering about the Middle East and for structuring its budgeting process for the Iraq War in such a way that Congress did not have a complete picture of how much was being spent at any given time.

In the days after the report was made public, Baker, Hamilton, and other study group members explained and defended the report in congressional hearings and to the broader public through the news media. One consistent message was that the report recommended a comprehensive strategy, components of which were mutually reinforcing. Baker warned the administration and Congress against treating the report's recommendations "like a fruit salad, saying, 'I like this, but I don't like that.' "

Reaction to the Report

President Bush met with the Iraq Study Group panel members on the morning their report was released and said it offered "some really very interesting proposals"—but he refused to endorse any of them automatically. The White House also sought to play down the report's tough criticisms not only of Bush's general policies but also of the administration's implementation of those policies. "You're asking if that [report] is a repudiation of policy," White House spokesman Tony Snow said to reporters. "No, it's an acknowledgement of reality." The next day, December 7, Bush met at the White House with British prime minister Tony Blair—his chief international ally on Iraq—and suggested to reporters that he did not accept many of the report's findings or recommendations. Days later, White House officials told reporters that many of the Baker-Hamilton recommendations were "impractical" and that the president was looking for alternative approaches.

Perhaps the most interesting response to the report on Capitol Hill was what did *not* happen. As a general rule, members did not embrace it wholeheartedly, as many had seemed to suggest they would just a few weeks earlier when they were facing the voters before the election. Instead, members of both parties did exactly what Baker had asked them not to do: they focused on the pieces they liked or did not like—most notably the report's opposition to a major increase in U.S. troop levels in Iraq and its call for regional diplomacy, including negotiations with Iran and Syria. Republicans and Democrats were in near unanimous agreement with the report's assessment that the United States should not, and could not, boost the U.S. presence in Iraq by anything like 100,000 to 200,000 troops; such increases had been advocated by some military experts. Some Democrats were not pleased by the report's caveat that pulling most U.S. combat troops out of Iraq by 2008 should depend on the security situation there. That condition was "a loophole big enough to drive many divisions through," Rep. Rush D. Holt, D-N.J., said. Some also said many elements of the report were out of date because the situation in Iraq had deteriorated significantly during the months it was being written.

Other critics said Baker and Hamilton had pushed too hard for consensus among all study group members and as a result produced a report that failed to recommend dramatic policy changes. This assessment came both from harsh critics of Bush's policies, who had wanted the panel to call for a rapid withdrawal of U.S. forces, as well as from those who advocated a major escalation of the U.S. presence to stop the violence. Panel members responded to such criticism by saying they had deliberately set out to develop a consensus policy that could unite Americans, who had become bitterly divided about the war and the president's policies. "The country cannot be at war and be as divided as we are today. You've got to unify this country," said panel member Leon Panetta, a former member of Congress who served as White House chief of staff under President Bill Clinton.

Much of the reaction focused on the study group's call for U.S. negotiations with all of Iraq's neighbors, including Iran and Syria—both of which were on the Bush administration's do-not-call list. The United States did not even have diplomatic relations with Iran, and the Bush administration had withdrawn the U.S. ambassador from Damascus in 2003. Most Democrats said engaging diplomatically with both countries was worth trying, but some Republicans denounced the idea. "I don't believe that a peace conference with people who are dedicated to your extinction has much short-term gain," Sen. John McCain, R-Ariz., told Baker and Hamilton at an Armed Services Committee hearing on December 7.

Some commentary on the study group report focused on the near impossibility of some of its key recommendations ever being implemented, in particular the numerous calls for the Iraqi government to take steps to promote "national reconciliation." Many of the report's suggestions for Iraqi government policy—for example, dismantling sectarian militias and following through on a pledge to rewrite key parts of the constitution—had long been recommended by U.S. ambassador Khalilzad but resulted in no action. In a detailed critique of the report, the International Crisis Group—an international foreign policy advocacy group based in Brussels, Belgium—said many recommendations were based on the flawed assumption that Iraq's government could or would act to curb the violence and reconcile the country's competing factions. "The government is not a partner in an effort to stem the violence, nor will its strengthening contribute to Iraq's stability," the December 19 report by the crisis group said.

Several prominent foreign policy analysts said the Baker-Hamilton group appeared to be setting the stage for an eventual U.S. withdrawal from Iraq on the basis of the Baghdad government's likely failure to adopt the changes that Americans believed were necessary. "It's the beginning of an effort to shape or control what will be competing narratives on why Iraq was lost, if in fact it turns out to be lost," commented Richard N. Haas, the president of the Council on Foreign Relations who had served as a senior State Department official during Bush's first term.

For their part, Iraqi government officials reacted warily to the Baker-Hamilton report. Jalal Talabani, a Kurdish leader who served as Iraq's figurehead president, complained on December 10 that the report contained "some very dangerous articles which undermine the sovereignty of Iraq and the constitution."

Sending More Troops?

The question of whether the United States had enough troops in Iraq had been at the main topic of debate about Iraq policy since before the March 2003 invasion that toppled Saddam Hussein. In February 2003, Gen. Eric K. Shinseki, then-army chief of staff, told a congressional panel that "several hundred thousand" U.S. troops would be needed to stabilize Iraq, in part because of the possibility of sectarian conflict. That comment ran directly counter to the Pentagon's plans at the time for an invasion force of about 140,000 troops, the vast majority of whom were to be withdrawn from Iraq by the end of 2003. Shinseki's comment reportedly angered top Pentagon officials and led directly to his early retirement.

During the early stages of the war in 2003 and the subsequent occupation, several U.S. generals were quoted, directly and indirectly, in news reports as calling for more troops than they had been given. And on January 8, 2006, L. Paul Bremer III, the man who ran the U.S. occupation authority in Iraq from May 2003 until June 2004, told NBC News that he had informed Defense Secretary Rumsfeld in May 2004 that some 500,000 troops were needed there—more than three times the number stationed in Iraq at the time. A Pentagon spokesman said Bremer's advice had been rejected because U.S. generals said they had enough troops.

As the violence escalated in Iraq during 2006, political leaders, retired military officers, policy analysts, and other opinion makers in the United States engaged in a vigorous debate about the level of U.S. military presence in Iraq, which had ranged from 130,000 to 140,000 troops ever since 2003. Some voices called for a significant increase in U.S. troop levels; among them were several retired generals, analysts at conservative think tanks, and a very few political leaders, notably Senator McCain, who was considered a leading presidential contender for the 2008 elections.

Other voices, including some Democratic leaders in Congress, another group of retired generals, and analysts at centrist or liberal think tanks, called for withdrawing U.S. troops sooner rather than later. These proposals came with varying degrees of intensity. Some proponents said the withdrawal should begin immediately, while others argued for establishing a timetable under which U.S. troops would leave Iraq as the government there met certain benchmarks. The idea that the United States had accomplished all it could in Iraq and should pull out had gained considerable political heft in November 2005 when it was embraced by Rep. John P. Murtha, D-Pa., who was widely respected on Capitol Hill for his military expertise. Murtha said his view was influenced by retired and active-duty military officers who were angered by President Bush's handling of the war.

Until very late in 2006, Bush and his aides rejected both lines of advice, saying U.S. generals in Iraq were satisfied with the existing troop levels. In the early months of the year, the president had taken a combative posture, suggesting to audiences that critics were undermining American troops in Iraq and insisting he would stay the course. "We have a responsibility to our men and women in uniform, who deserve to know that once our politicians vote to send them into harm's way, our support will be with them in good days and in bad days," he told a meeting of the Veterans of Foreign Wars in Washington on January 10. "And we will settle for nothing less than complete victory."

As was the case in previous years since the U.S. invasion, much of the domestic debate about U.S. force levels concerned the impact of the Iraq deployment on the U.S. Army and the Marine Corps—the two services that were bearing nearly all the burden. With solders and marines facing repeated deployments to Iraq, and tens of thousands of reserve and National Guard troops also serving there, the services were under a degree of stress not seen since the Vietnam War. Rumsfeld and other top officials acknowledged the strain on the military but insisted they were taking steps to prevent the problem from becoming unbearable.

In its report, the Iraq Study Group took a middle position, arguing against an increase in the number of U.S. troops in Iraq but calling for changes in mission. The panel said it considered proposals to increase the number of troops by 100,000 to 200,000, but they rejected the idea for two reasons. First, the United States simply did not have that many additional troops for "a sustained deployment" in Iraq, it said. Second, "adding more American troops could conceivably worsen those aspects of the security problem that are fed by the view that the U.S. presence is intended to be a long-term 'occupation.'"

As an alternative to a large-scale military escalation, the panel proposed a rapid increase in the number of U.S. troops assigned to serve alongside, and thereby train, Iraqi soldiers. The panel also argued against an "open-ended commitment" of U.S. forces to Iraq, saying that would reduce the incentive for Iraq's government to make the political compromises necessary to end the violence.

Despite its skepticism about a military solution, the panel added an important qualification, saying it could support "a short-term redeployment or surge of American combat forces to stabilize Baghdad, or to speed up the training and equipping mission, if the U.S. commander in Iraq determines that such steps would be effective." The study group did not include this idea in its list of recommendations, however.

The Bush administration officials immediately seized upon that sentence to support a policy shift the White House was developing at year's end. Robert Gates, the new defense secretary, began sounding out top military officials about the prospects for a short-term "surge" of troops, and Bush on December 11 met with several military experts who were recommending such a step. In a year-end news conference on December 20, Bush insisted that "victory in Iraq is still achievable." The violence there was "troubling" to the American people, he said, "but I don't believe most Americans want us just to get out now." By year's end it appeared all but certain that Bush would announce a phased increase of approximately 20,000 U.S. troops in Iraq during the first half of 2007, with the stated goal of bringing the violence in Baghdad under control.

The administration's new talk of expanding, rather than decreasing, the U.S. military commitment to Iraq set off alarm bells on Capitol Hill. Among those expressing deep skepticism about Bush's apparent plans was Rep. Ike Skelton, a conservative Democrat from Missouri who was in line to become chairman of the House Armed Service Committee in the new, 110th Congress. "Everything I've heard and everything I know to be true lead me to believe that this [possible troop] increase at best won't change a thing, and at worst could exacerbate the situation even further," he told the *New York Times*.

Training and Equipping Iraqi Security Forces

Several of the core recommendations of the Baker-Hamilton report dealt with a central feature of the Bush administration policy toward Iraq: the rapid buildup and training of Iraqi security forces so the United States could withdraw its military sooner rather than later. The Pentagon had spent billions of dollars attempting to create new Iraqi government security forces to replace those that Washington had ordered disbanded shortly after the ouster of Iraqi leader Saddam Hussein in April 2003. In its regular quarterly reports to Congress, the Pentagon cited impressive figures showing the success of that effort; the latest such report, released on December 19, said Iraq's security forces totaled 322,600 men, which was an increase of 45,000 over the previous report in August.

The Iraq Study Group and many other observers, however, said such numbers disguised serious problems that made the Iraqi army and police incapable, at the moment, of solving the country's security problems. Many army units were established along sectarian lines, with soldiers having signed up to serve only in their home regions. Moreover, the study group said, a liberal leave policy and a lack of discipline meant that many units routinely lacked about one-half their personnel. Iraq's numerous police forces were "substantially worse" than the army, the study group said, because of sectarian divisions, corruption, infiltration by Shiite militia members, and lack of equipment.

To speed up improvements in the Iraqi forces, the study group recommended a rapid expansion of the number of U.S. troops assigned to—or "imbedded," in the military's terms—Iraqi army and police units. The U.S. troops would provide advice and on-the-job training to the Iraqis. While saying military commanders should determine the exact numbers, the report suggested placing 10,000 to 20,000 U.S. troops within Iraqi units, compared to what it said was a current level of 3,000 to 4,000.

A specific goal of U.S. policy was giving the Iraqi military total responsibility for security within entire provinces, thus freeing up American troops to concentrate on the most violence-prone areas. Three of Iraq's eighteen provinces came under the overall control of Iraqi security forces during the year, all of them predominantly Shiite areas in the southern part of the country: Muthana, which British forces handed over to Iraqis in July; Dhi Qar, which the Italian military handed over in September; and Najaf, which was handed over on December 20. The provincial capital of Najaf (which had the same name) saw intense fighting at two points in 2004 when the U.S. military tried to contain the Mahdi army militia loyal to Shiite cleric Moqtada al-Sadr; the city had been relatively quiet since then. In addition, Kurdish political parties and their militia, known as the "pesh merga," effectively controlled the three Kurdish-majority provinces of northern Iraq (which Kurds called "Kurdistan").

A Dwindling Coalition

The United States was by far the largest contributor to what was formally called the Multinational Force in Iraq (MNF-I, in Pentagon terminology) but was better known as "the coalition." Even as debate was under way in the United States about U.S. force levels in Iraq, Washington's allies in the coalition were beginning to withdraw.

The Italian defense minister announced on July 19 that his country would withdraw its 3,000 troops from Iraq by the end of 2006. This announcement was intended to take domestic political pressure off the center-right government of Prime Minister Silvio Berlusconi, who was trailing in the polls prior to parliamentary elections in April. Berlusconi was defeated by a center-left coalition headed by Romano Prodi, who carried out the withdrawal.

Another symbolically important withdrawal from Iraq was that of Japan, which had sent 600 troops to Iraq for noncombat missions—its largest military deployment anywhere in the world since its defeat in World War II. Although Japanese troops engaged in humanitarian tasks, such as purifying water, the Iraq deployment was increasingly unpopular at home, in part because of fears it made Japan a potential target for terrorism.

Even Britain, which had been the most steadfast U.S. ally in Iraq, began a gradual withdrawal from the coalition in 2006. Defense secretary John Reid said on March 13 that Britain would reduce its troop strength in Iraq to about 7,000 by May, a cut of about 10 percent. British prime minister Tony Blair had sent about 12,000 marines and other troops to participate in the 2003 invasion. Afterwards, Britain had primary responsibility for security in the southern city of Basra and is environs, and the British contingent gradually dwindled to fewer than 8,000 at the start of 2006. The announced cutback to about 7,000 troops appeared to be a response by Blair's government to the increasing unpopularity of the Iraq mission at home.

U.S. Deaths in Iraq

The policy debate in Washington took place in the context of a steady climb in U.S. casualties in Iraq. Few days went by without U.S. soldiers or marines being killed or wounded while on patrol in Baghdad or other cities. While the number of U.S.casualties paled when compared with Iraqi deaths, the American people were increasingly distressed by the regular appearance in newspapers and on television screens of photographs and stories about dead American servicemen and women.

The total number of U.S. service personnel killed in Iraq reached 3,001 on the last day of 2006. According to news accounts, 486 U.S. service personnel died in Iraq in 2003, 848 in 2004, 846 in 2005, and 821 in 2006. Of the total, 2,422 deaths were caused by "hostile" means (such as shootings or bombings) and the remaining 579 were due to "nonhostile" causes, such as accidents and illness. The Pentagon also said more than 22,000 service personnel had been wounded in hostile action. Of these, about 10,000 returned to duty within seventy-two hours (suggesting that their wounds were relatively minor); the Pentagon offered no data on how many personnel were wounded so severely that they were forced out of service.

More Reports of U.S. Abuses

Ever since early 2004 the U.S. occupation of Iraq had been troubled by reports of the abuse of Iraqis by American soldiers. By far the most damaging incident was the discovery that an army reserve military police unit at the notorious Abu Ghraib prison outside Baghdad had repeatedly abused Iraqi prisoners. Photographs of naked Iraqi men forced to pile on top of one another, being threatened by snarling dogs, and subjected to numerous other humiliations were circulated around the world and caused immense damage to the reputation of the United States, particularly in the Arab world. *(Abu Ghraib scandal, Historic Documents of 2004, p. 207)*

During 2006 the U.S. military uncovered several new incidents in which a small number of American service personnel appeared to demonstrate reckless disregard for the lives of Iraqi civilians—the very people they were supposed to be protecting. The most prominent incident that came to light during the year was the alleged slaughter on November 19, 2005, of twenty-four civilians by U.S. Marines in the town of Haditha, in Anbar province west of Baghdad. The incident came to public attention in March 2006, after a *Time* magazine reporter asked the military about it. After a lengthy investigation, the Marine Corps on December 22 charged four marines with multiple counts of murder. Four officers (a lieutenant colonel, two captains, and a lieutenant) also were charged with dereliction of duty for their alleged failure to report the killings to superior officers. Trials of the defendants were expected to take place in 2007.

Another case that generated wide attention during the year involved an incident that took place on March 12 in the village of Mahmoudiya, about twenty miles south of Baghdad. In that case, three enlisted members of the 101st Airborne Division were charged with raping and then murdering a fourteen-year-old girl and then killing her parents and her seven-year-old sister. One of the soldiers pleaded guilty to rape and murder charges during a November 15 military court hearing at Fort Campbell, Kentucky; he was sentenced to ninety years in prison. Charges against the other three soldiers were still pending at year's end, as were dereliction-of-duty charges against a fifth soldier for failing to report the crimes.

> *Following is the text of the recommendations section, "The Way Forward—A New Approach," from the report made public on December 6, 2006, by the Iraq Study Group, a commission cochaired by former secretary of state James A. Baker III and former House member Lee H. Hamilton.*

■■■■■■■ **DOCUMENT** ■■■■■■■

"The Iraq Study Group Report"

[Part I, Assessment, omitted.]

II. The Way Forward—A New Approach

Progress in Iraq is still possible if new approaches are taken promptly by Iraq, the United States, and other countries that have a stake in the Middle East.

To attain the goals we have outlined, changes in course must be made both outside and inside Iraq. Our report offers a comprehensive strategy to build regional and international support for stability in Iraq, as it encourages the Iraqi people to assume control of their own destiny. It offers a responsible transition.

Externally, the United States should immediately begin to employ all elements of American power to construct a regional mechanism that can support, rather than retard, progress in Iraq. Internally, the Iraqi government must take the steps required to achieve national reconciliation, reduce violence, and improve the daily lives of Iraqis. Efforts to implement these external and internal strategies must begin now and must be undertaken in concert with one another.

This responsible transition can allow for a reduction in the U.S. presence in Iraq over time.

A. The External Approach: Building an International Consensus

The United States must build a new international consensus for stability in Iraq and the region.

In order to foster such consensus, the United States should embark on a robust diplomatic effort to establish an international support structure intended to stabilize Iraq and ease tensions in other countries in the region. This support structure should include every country that has an interest in averting a chaotic Iraq, including all of Iraq's neighbors—Iran and Syria among them. Despite the well-known differences between many of these countries, they all share an interest in avoiding the horrific consequences that would flow from a chaotic Iraq, particularly a humanitarian catastrophe and regional destabilization.

A reinvigorated diplomatic effort is required because it is clear that the Iraqi government cannot succeed in governing, defending, and sustaining itself by relying on U.S. military and economic support alone. Nor can the Iraqi government succeed by relying only on U.S. military support in conjunction with Iraqi military and police capabilities. Some states have been withholding commitments they could make to support Iraq's stabilization and reconstruction. Some states have been actively undermining stability in Iraq. To achieve a political solution within Iraq, a broader international support structure is needed.

1. The New Diplomatic Offensive

Iraq cannot be addressed effectively in isolation from other major regional issues, interests, and unresolved conflicts. To put it simply, all key issues in the Middle East—the

Arab-Israeli conflict, Iraq, Iran, the need for political and economic reforms, and extremism and terrorism—are inextricably linked. In addition to supporting stability in Iraq, a comprehensive diplomatic offensive—the New Diplomatic Offensive—should address these key regional issues. By doing so, it would help marginalize extremists and terrorists, promote U.S. values and interests, and improve America's global image.

Under the diplomatic offensive, we propose regional and international initiatives and steps to assist the Iraqi government in achieving certain security, political, and economic milestones. Achieving these milestones will require at least the acquiescence of Iraq's neighbors, and their active and timely cooperation would be highly desirable.

The diplomatic offensive would extend beyond the primarily economic "Compact for Iraq" by also emphasizing political, diplomatic, and security issues. At the same time, it would be coordinated with the goals of the Compact for Iraq. The diplomatic offensive would also be broader and more far-reaching than the "Gulf Plus Two" efforts currently being conducted, and those efforts should be folded into and become part of the diplomatic offensive.

States included within the diplomatic offensive can play a major role in reinforcing national reconciliation efforts between Iraqi Sunnis and Shia. Such reinforcement would contribute substantially to legitimizing of the political process in Iraq. Iraq's leaders may not be able to come together unless they receive the necessary signals and support from abroad. This backing will not materialize of its own accord, and must be encouraged urgently by the United States.

In order to advance a comprehensive diplomatic solution, the Study Group recommends as follows:

RECOMMENDATION 1: The United States, working with the Iraqi government, should launch the comprehensive New Diplomatic Offensive to deal with the problems of Iraq and of the region. This new diplomatic offensive should be launched before December 31, 2006.

RECOMMENDATION 2: The goals of the diplomatic offensive as it relates to regional players should be to:

(i)   *Support the unity and territorial integrity of Iraq.*

(ii) *Stop destabilizing interventions and actions by Iraq's neighbors.*

(iii) *Secure Iraq's borders, including the use of joint patrols with neighboring countries.*

(iv) *Prevent the expansion of the instability and conflict beyond Iraq's borders.*

(v)   *Promote economic assistance, commerce, trade, political support, and, if possible, military assistance for the Iraqi government from non-neighboring Muslim nations.*

(vi) *Energize countries to support national political reconciliation in Iraq.*

(vii) *Validate Iraq's legitimacy by resuming diplomatic relations, where appropriate, and reestablishing embassies in Baghdad.*

(viii) *Assist Iraq in establishing active working embassies in key capitals in the region (for example, in Riyadh, Saudi Arabia).*

(ix) *Help Iraq reach a mutually acceptable agreement on Kirkuk.*

(x)   *Assist the Iraqi government in achieving certain security, political, and economic milestones, including better performance on issues such as national reconciliation, equitable distribution of oil revenues, and the dismantling of militias.*

RECOMMENDATION 3: As a complement to the diplomatic offensive, and in addition to the Support Group discussed below, the United States and the Iraqi government should support the holding of a conference or meeting in Baghdad of the Organization of the Islamic Conference or the Arab League both to assist the Iraqi government in promoting national reconciliation in Iraq and to reestablish their diplomatic presence in Iraq.

2. The Iraq International Support Group

This new diplomatic offensive cannot be successful unless it includes the active participation of those countries that have a critical stake in preventing Iraq from falling into chaos. To encourage their participation, the United States should immediately seek the creation of the Iraq International Support Group. The Support Group should also include all countries that border Iraq as well as other key countries in the region and the world.

The Support Group would not seek to impose obligations or undertakings on the government of Iraq. Instead, the Support Group would assist Iraq in ways the government of Iraq would desire, attempting to strengthen Iraq's sovereignty—not diminish it.

It is clear to Iraq Study Group members that all of Iraq's neighbors are anxious about the situation in Iraq. They favor a unified Iraq that is strong enough to maintain its territorial integrity, but not so powerful as to threaten its neighbors. None favors the breakup of the Iraqi state. Each country in the region views the situation in Iraq through the filter of its particular set of interests. For example:

- Turkey opposes an independent or even highly autonomous Kurdistan because of its own national security considerations.
- Iran backs Shia claims and supports various Shia militias in Iraq, but it also supports other groups in order to enhance its influence and hedge its bets on possible outcomes.
- Syria, despite facilitating support for Iraqi insurgent groups, would be threatened by the impact that the breakup of Iraq would have on its own multiethnic and multiconfessional society.
- Kuwait wants to ensure that it will not once again be the victim of Iraqi irredentism and aggression.
- Saudi Arabia and Jordan share Sunni concerns over Shia ascendancy in Iraq and the region as a whole.
- The other Arab Gulf states also recognize the benefits of an outcome in Iraq that does not destabilize the region and exacerbate Shia-Sunni tensions.
- None of Iraq's neighbors—especially major countries such as Egypt, Saudi Arabia, and Israel—see it in their interest for the situation in Iraq to lead to aggrandized regional influence by Iran. Indeed, they may take active steps to limit Iran's influence, steps that could lead to an intraregional conflict.

Left to their own devices, these governments will tend to reinforce ethnic, sectarian, and political divisions within Iraqi society. But if the Support Group takes a systematic and active approach toward considering the concerns of each country, we believe that each can be encouraged to play a positive role in Iraq and the region.

Saudi Arabia. Saudi Arabia's agreement not to intervene with assistance to Sunni Arab Iraqis could be an essential quid pro quo for similar forbearance on the part of other neighbors, especially Iran. The Saudis could use their Islamic credentials to help reconcile differences between Iraqi factions and build broader support in the Islamic world for a stabilization agreement, as their recent hosting of a meeting of Islamic religious leaders in

Mecca suggests. If the government in Baghdad pursues a path of national reconciliation with the Sunnis, the Saudis could help Iraq confront and eliminate al Qaeda in Iraq. They could also cancel the Iraqi debt owed them. In addition, the Saudis might be helpful in persuading the Syrians to cooperate.

Turkey. As a major Sunni Muslim country on Iraq's borders, Turkey can be a partner in supporting the national reconciliation process in Iraq. Such efforts can be particularly helpful given Turkey's interest in Kurdistan remaining an integral part of a unified Iraq and its interest in preventing a safe haven for Kurdish terrorists (the PKK).

Egypt. Because of its important role in the Arab world, Egypt should be encouraged to foster the national reconciliation process in Iraq with a focus on getting the Sunnis to participate. At the same time, Egypt has the means, and indeed has offered, to train groups of Iraqi military and security forces in Egypt on a rotational basis.

Jordan. Jordan, like Egypt, can help in the national reconciliation process in Iraq with the Sunnis. It too has the professional capability to train and equip Iraqi military and security forces.

RECOMMENDATION 4: As an instrument of the New Diplomatic Offensive, an Iraq International Support Group should be organized immediately following the launch of the New Diplomatic Offensive.

RECOMMENDATION 5: The Support Group should consist of Iraq and all the states bordering Iraq, including Iran and Syria; the key regional states, including Egypt and the Gulf States; the five permanent members of the United Nations Security Council; the European Union; and, of course, Iraq itself. Other countries—for instance, Germany, Japan and South Korea—that might be willing to contribute to resolving political, diplomatic, and security problems affecting Iraq could also become members.

RECOMMENDATION 6: The New Diplomatic Offensive and the work of the Support Group should be carried out with urgency, and should be conducted by and organized at the level of foreign minister or above. The Secretary of State, if not the President, should lead the U.S. effort. That effort should be both bilateral and multilateral, as circumstances require.

RECOMMENDATION 7: The Support Group should call on the participation of the office of the United Nations Secretary-General in its work. The United Nations Secretary-General should designate a Special Envoy as his representative.

RECOMMENDATION 8: The Support Group, as part of the New Diplomatic Offensive, should develop specific approaches to neighboring countries that take into account the interests, perspectives, and potential contributions as suggested above.

3. Dealing with Iran and Syria

Dealing with Iran and Syria is controversial. Nevertheless, it is our view that in diplomacy, a nation can and should engage its adversaries and enemies to try to resolve conflicts and differences consistent with its own interests. Accordingly, the Support Group should actively engage Iran and Syria in its diplomatic dialogue, without preconditions.

The Study Group recognizes that U.S. relationships with Iran and Syria involve difficult issues that must be resolved. Diplomatic talks should be extensive and substantive, and they will require a balancing of interests. The United States has diplomatic, economic, and military disincentives available in approaches to both Iran and Syria. However, the United States should also consider incentives to try to engage them constructively, much as it did successfully with Libya.

Some of the possible incentives to Iran, Syria, or both include:

(i)   An Iraq that does not disintegrate and destabilize its neighbors and the region.
(ii) The continuing role of the United States in preventing the Taliban from destabilizing Afghanistan.
(iii) Accession to international organizations, including the World Trade Organization.
(iv) Prospects for enhanced diplomatic relations with the United States.
(v)   The prospect of a U.S. policy that emphasizes political and economic reforms instead of (as Iran now perceives it) advocating regime change.
(vi) Prospects for a real, complete, and secure peace to be negotiated between Israel and Syria, with U.S. involvement as part of a broader initiative on Arab-Israeli peace as outlined below.

RECOMMENDATION 9: *Under the aegis of the New Diplomatic Offensive and the Support Group, the United States should engage directly with Iran and Syria in order to try to obtain their commitment to constructive policies toward Iraq and other regional issues. In engaging Syria and Iran, the United States should consider incentives, as well as disincentives, in seeking constructive results.*

Iran. Engaging Iran is problematic, especially given the state of the U.S.-Iranian relationship. Yet the United States and Iran cooperated in Afghanistan, and both sides should explore whether this model can be replicated in the case of Iraq.

Although Iran sees it in its interest to have the United States bogged down in Iraq, Iran's interests would not be served by a failure of U.S. policy in Iraq that led to chaos and the territorial disintegration of the Iraqi state. Iran's population is slightly more than 50 percent Persian, but it has a large Azeri minority (24 percent of the population) as well as Kurdish and Arab minorities. Worst-case scenarios in Iraq could inflame sectarian tensions within Iran, with serious consequences for Iranian national security interests.

Our limited contacts with Iran's government lead us to believe that its leaders are likely to say they will not participate in diplomatic efforts to support stability in Iraq. They attribute this reluctance to their belief that the United States seeks regime change in Iran.

Nevertheless, as one of Iraq's neighbors Iran should be asked to assume its responsibility to participate in the Support Group. An Iranian refusal to do so would demonstrate to Iraq and the rest of the world Iran's rejectionist attitude and approach, which could lead to its isolation. Further, Iran's refusal to cooperate on this matter would diminish its prospects of engaging with the United States in the broader dialogue it seeks.

RECOMMENDATION 10: The issue of Iran's nuclear programs should continue to be dealt with by the United Nations Security Council and its five permanent members (i.e., the United States, United Kingdom, France, Russia, and China) plus Germany.

RECOMMENDATION 11: Diplomatic efforts within the Support Group should seek to persuade Iran that it should take specific steps to improve the situation in Iraq.

Among steps Iran could usefully take are the following:

- Iran should stem the flow of equipment, technology, and training to any group resorting to violence in Iraq.
- Iran should make clear its support for the territorial integrity of Iraq as a unified state, as well as its respect for the sovereignty of Iraq and its government.
- Iran can use its influence, especially over Shia groups in Iraq, to encourage national reconciliation.
- Iran can also, in the right circumstances, help in the economic reconstruction of Iraq.

Syria. Although the U.S.-Syrian relationship is at a low point, both countries have important interests in the region that could be enhanced if they were able to establish some common ground on how to move forward. This approach worked effectively in the early 1990s. In this context, Syria's national interests in the Arab-Israeli dispute are important and can be brought into play.

Syria can make a major contribution to Iraq's stability in several ways. Accordingly, the Study Group recommends the following:

RECOMMENDATION 12: The United States and the Support Group should encourage and persuade Syria of the merit of such contributions as the following:

- *Syria can control its border with Iraq to the maximum extent possible and work together with Iraqis on joint patrols on the border. Doing so will help stem the flow of funding, insurgents, and terrorists in and out of Iraq.*
- *Syria can establish hotlines to exchange information with the Iraqis.*
- *Syria can increase its political and economic cooperation with Iraq.*

4. The Wider Regional Context

The United States will not be able to achieve its goals in the Middle East unless the United States deals directly with the Arab-Israeli conflict.

There must be a renewed and sustained commitment by the United States to a comprehensive Arab-Israeli peace on all fronts: Lebanon, Syria, and President Bush's June 2002 commitment to a two-state solution for Israel and Palestine. This commitment must include direct talks with, by, and between Israel, Lebanon, Palestinians (those who accept Israel's right to exist), and particularly Syria—which is the principal transit point for shipments of weapons to Hezbollah, and which supports radical Palestinian groups.

The United States does its ally Israel no favors in avoiding direct involvement to solve the Arab-Israeli conflict. For several reasons, we should act boldly:

- There is no military solution to this conflict.
- The vast majority of the Israeli body politic is tired of being a nation perpetually at war.

- No American administration—Democratic or Republican—will ever abandon Israel.
- Political engagement and dialogue are essential in the Arab-Israeli dispute because it is an axiom that when the political process breaks down there will be violence on the ground.
- The only basis on which peace can be achieved is that set forth in UN Security Council Resolutions 242 and 338 and in the principle of "land for peace."
- The only lasting and secure peace will be a negotiated peace such as Israel has achieved with Egypt and Jordan.

This effort would strongly support moderate Arab governments in the region, especially the democratically elected government of Lebanon, and the Palestinian Authority under President Mahmoud Abbas.

RECOMMENDATION 13: There must be a renewed and sustained commitment by the United States to a comprehensive Arab-Israeli peace on all fronts: Lebanon and Syria, and President Bush's June 2002 commitment to a two-state solution for Israel and Palestine.

RECOMMENDATION 14: This effort should include—as soon as possible—the unconditional calling and holding of meetings, under the auspices of the United States or the Quartet (i.e., the United States, Russia, European Union, and the United Nations), between Israel and Lebanon and Syria on the one hand, and Israel and Palestinians (who acknowledge Israel's right to exist) on the other. The purpose of these meetings would be to negotiate peace as was done at the Madrid Conference in 1991, and on two separate tracks—one Syrian/Lebanese, and the other Palestinian.

RECOMMENDATION 15: Concerning Syria, some elements of that negotiated peace should be:

- *Syria's full adherence to UN Security Council Resolution 1701 of August 2006, which provides the framework for Lebanon to regain sovereign control over its territory.*
- *Syria's full cooperation with all investigations into political assassinations in Lebanon, especially those of Rafik Hariri and Pierre Gemayel.*
- *A verifiable cessation of Syrian aid to Hezbollah and the use of Syrian territory for transshipment of Iranian weapons and aid to Hezbollah. (This step would do much to solve Israel's problem with Hezbollah.)*
- *Syria's use of its influence with Hamas and Hezbollah for the release of the captured Israeli Defense Force soldiers.*
- *A verifiable cessation of Syrian efforts to undermine the democratically elected government of Lebanon.*
- *A verifiable cessation of arms shipments from or transiting through Syria for Hamas and other radical Palestinian groups.*
- *A Syrian commitment to help obtain from Hamas an acknowledgment of Israel's right to exist.*
- *Greater Syrian efforts to seal its border with Iraq.*

RECOMMENDATION 16: In exchange for these actions and in the context of a full and secure peace agreement, the Israelis should return the Golan Heights, with a U.S. security guarantee for Israel that could include an international force on the border, including U.S. troops if requested by both parties.

RECOMMENDATION 17: Concerning the Palestinian issue, elements of that negotiated peace should include:

- *Adherence to UN Security Council Resolutions 242 and 338 and to the principle of land for peace, which are the only bases for achieving peace.*
- *Strong support for Palestinian President Mahmoud Abbas and the Palestinian Authority to take the lead in preparing the way for negotiations with Israel.*
- *A major effort to move from the current hostilities by consolidating the cease-fire reached between the Palestinians and the Israelis in November 2006.*
- *Support for a Palestinian national unity government.*
- *Sustainable negotiations leading to a final peace settlement along the lines of President Bush's two-state solution, which would address the key final status issues of borders, settlements, Jerusalem, the right of return, and the end of conflict.*

Afghanistan. At the same time, we must not lose sight of the importance of the situation inside Afghanistan and the renewed threat posed by the Taliban. Afghanistan's borders are porous. If the Taliban were to control more of Afghanistan, it could provide al Qaeda the political space to conduct terrorist operations. This development would destabilize the region and have national security implications for the United States and other countries around the world. Also, the significant increase in poppy production in Afghanistan fuels the illegal drug trade and narco-terrorism.

The huge focus of U.S. political, military, and economic support on Iraq has necessarily diverted attention from Afghanistan. As the United States develops its approach toward Iraq and the Middle East, it must also give priority to the situation in Afghanistan. Doing so may require increased political, security, and military measures.

RECOMMENDATION 18: It is critical for the United States to provide additional political, economic, and military support for Afghanistan, including resources that might become available as combat forces are moved from Iraq.

B. The Internal Approach: Helping Iraqis Help Themselves

The New Diplomatic Offensive will provide the proper external environment and support for the difficult internal steps that the Iraqi government must take to promote national reconciliation, establish security, and make progress on governance.

The most important issues facing Iraq's future are now the responsibility of Iraq's elected leaders. Because of the security and assistance it provides, the United States has a significant role to play. Yet only the government and people of Iraq can make and sustain certain decisions critical to Iraq's future.

1. Performance on Milestones

The United States should work closely with Iraq's leaders to support the achievement of specific objectives—or milestones—on national reconciliation, security, and governance. Miracles cannot be expected, but the people of Iraq have the right to expect action and progress. The Iraqi government needs to show its own citizens—and the citizens of the United States and other countries—that it deserves continued support.

The U.S. government must make clear that it expects action by the Iraqi government to make substantial progress toward these milestones. Such a message can be sent only at the level of our national leaders, and only in person, during direct consultation.

As President Bush's meeting with Prime Minister Maliki in Amman, Jordan demonstrates, it is important for the President to remain in close and frequent contact with the Iraqi leadership. There is no substitute for sustained dialogue at the highest levels of government.

During these high-level exchanges, the United States should lay out an agenda for continued support to help Iraq achieve milestones, as well as underscoring the consequences if Iraq does not act. It should be unambiguous that continued U.S. political, military, and economic support for Iraq depends on the Iraqi government's demonstrating political will and making substantial progress toward the achievement of milestones on national reconciliation, security, and governance. The transfer of command and control over Iraqi security forces units from the United States to Iraq should be influenced by Iraq's performance on milestones.

The United States should also signal that it is seeking broad international support for Iraq on behalf of achieving these milestones. The United States can begin to shape a positive climate for its diplomatic efforts, internationally and within Iraq, through public statements by President Bush that reject the notion that the United States seeks to control Iraq's oil, or seeks permanent military bases within Iraq. However, the United States could consider a request from Iraq for temporary bases.

RECOMMENDATION 19: The President and the leadership of his national security team should remain in close and frequent contact with the Iraqi leadership. These contacts must convey a clear message: there must be action by the Iraqi government to make substantial progress toward the achievement of milestones. In public diplomacy, the President should convey as much detail as possible about the substance of these exchanges in order to keep the American people, the Iraqi people, and the countries in the region well informed.

RECOMMENDATION 20: If the Iraqi government demonstrates political will and makes substantial progress toward the achievement of milestones on national reconciliation, security, and governance, the United States should make clear its willingness to continue training, assistance, and support for Iraq's security forces, and to continue political, military, and economic support for the Iraqi government. As Iraq becomes more capable of governing, defending, and sustaining itself, the U.S. military and civilian presence in Iraq can be reduced.

RECOMMENDATION 21: If the Iraqi government does not make substantial progress toward the achievement of milestones on national reconciliation, security, and governance, the United States should reduce its political, military, or economic support for the Iraqi government.

RECOMMENDATION 22: The President should state that the United States does not seek permanent military bases in Iraq. If the Iraqi government were to request a temporary base or bases, then the U.S. government could consider that request as it would in the case of any other government.

RECOMMENDATION 23: The President should restate that the United States does not seek to control Iraq's oil.

Milestones for Iraq

The government of Iraq understands that dramatic steps are necessary to avert a downward spiral and make progress. Prime Minister Maliki has worked closely in consultation with the United States and has put forward the following milestones in the key areas of national reconciliation, security and governance:

NATIONAL RECONCILIATION

By the end of 2006–early 2007:

- Approval of the Provincial Election Law and setting an election date
- Approval of the Petroleum Law
- Approval of the De-Baathification Law
- Approval of the Militia Law

By March 2007:

- A referendum on constitutional amendments (if it is necessary)

By May 2007:

- Completion of Militia Law implementation
- Approval of amnesty agreement
- Completion of reconciliation efforts

By June 2007:

- Provincial elections

SECURITY (pending joint U.S.-Iraqi review)

By the end of 2006:

- Iraqi increase of 2007 security spending over 2006 levels

By April 2007:

- Iraqi control of the Army

By September 2007:

- Iraqi control of provinces

By December 2007:

- Iraqi security self-reliance (with U.S. support)

GOVERNANCE

By the end of 2006:

- The Central Bank of Iraq will raise interest rates to 20 percent and appreciate the Iraqi dinar by 10 percent to combat accelerating inflation.
- Iraq will continue increasing domestic prices for refined petroleum products and sell imported fuel at market prices.

RECOMMENDATION 24: The contemplated completion dates of the end of 2006 or early 2007 for some milestones may not be realistic. These should be completed by the first quarter of 2007.

RECOMMENDATION 25: These milestones are a good start. The United States should consult closely with the Iraqi government and develop additional milestones in three areas: national reconciliation, security, and improving government services affecting the daily lives of Iraqis. As with the current milestones, these additional milestones should be tied to calendar dates to the fullest extent possible.

2. National Reconciliation

National reconciliation is essential to reduce further violence and maintain the unity of Iraq. U.S. forces can help provide stability for a time to enable Iraqi leaders to negotiate political solutions, but they cannot stop the violence—or even contain it—if there is no underlying political agreement among Iraqis about the future of their country.

The Iraqi government must send a clear signal to Sunnis that there is a place for them in national life. The government needs to act now, to give a signal of hope. Unless Sunnis believe they can get a fair deal in Iraq through the political process, there is no prospect that the insurgency will end. To strike this fair deal, the Iraqi government and the Iraqi people must address several issues that are critical to the success of national reconciliation and thus to the future of Iraq.

Steps for Iraq to Take on Behalf of National Reconciliation

RECOMMENDATION 26: Constitution review. Review of the constitution is essential to national reconciliation and should be pursued on an urgent basis. The United Nations has expertise in this field, and should play a role in this process.

RECOMMENDATION 27: De-Baathification. Political reconciliation requires the reintegration of Baathists and Arab nationalists into national life, with the leading figures of Saddam Hussein's regime excluded. The United States should encourage the return of qualified Iraqi professionals—Sunni or Shia, nationalist or ex-Baathist, Kurd or Turkmen or Christian or Arab—into the government.

RECOMMENDATION 28: Oil revenue sharing. Oil revenues should accrue to the central government and be shared on the basis of population. No formula that gives control over revenues from future fields to the regions or gives control of oil fields to the regions is compatible with national reconciliation.

RECOMMENDATION 29: Provincial elections. Provincial elections should be held at the earliest possible date. Under the constitution, new provincial elections should have been held already. They are necessary to restore representative government.

RECOMMENDATION 30: Kirkuk. Given the very dangerous situation in Kirkuk, international arbitration is necessary to avert communal violence. Kirkuk's mix of Kurdish, Arab, and Turkmen populations could make it a powder keg. A referendum on the future of Kirkuk (as required by the Iraqi Constitution before the end of 2007) would be explosive and should be delayed. This issue should be placed on the agenda of the International Iraq Support Group as part of the New Diplomatic Offensive.

RECOMMENDATION 31: Amnesty. Amnesty proposals must be far-reaching. Any successful effort at national reconciliation must involve those in the government finding ways and means to reconcile with former bitter enemies.

RECOMMENDATION 32: Minorities. The rights of women and the rights of all minority communities in Iraq, including Turkmen, Chaldeans, Assyrians, Yazidis, Sabeans, and Armenians, must be protected.

RECOMMENDATION 33: Civil society. The Iraqi government should stop using the process of registering nongovernmental organizations as a tool for politicizing or stopping their activities. Registration should be solely an administrative act, not an occasion for government censorship and interference.

Steps for the United States to Take on Behalf of National Reconciliation
The United States can take several steps to assist in Iraq's reconciliation process.

The presence of U.S. forces in Iraq is a key topic of interest in a national reconciliation dialogue. The point is not for the United States to set timetables or deadlines for withdrawal, an approach that we oppose. The point is for the United States and Iraq to make clear their shared interest in the orderly departure of U.S. forces as Iraqi forces take on the security mission. A successful national reconciliation dialogue will advance that departure date.

RECOMMENDATION 34: The question of the future U.S. force presence must be on the table for discussion as the national reconciliation dialogue takes place. Its inclusion will increase the likelihood of participation by insurgents and militia leaders, and thereby increase the possibilities for success.

Violence cannot end unless dialogue begins, and the dialogue must involve those who wield power, not simply those who hold political office. The United States must try to talk directly to Grand Ayatollah Sistani and must consider appointing a high-level American Shia Muslim to serve as an emissary to him. The United States must also try to talk directly to Moqtada al-Sadr, to militia leaders, and to insurgent leaders. The United Nations can help facilitate contacts.

RECOMMENDATION 35: The United States must make active efforts to engage all parties in Iraq, with the exception of al Qaeda. The United States must find a way to talk to Grand Ayatollah Sistani, Moqtada al-Sadr, and militia and insurgent leaders.

The very focus on sectarian identity that endangers Iraq also presents opportunities to seek broader support for a national reconciliation dialogue. Working with Iraqi leaders, the international community and religious leaders can play an important role in fostering dialogue and reconciliation across the sectarian divide. The United States should actively encourage the constructive participation of all who can take part in advancing national reconciliation within Iraq.

RECOMMENDATION 36: The United States should encourage dialogue between sectarian communities, as outlined in the New Diplomatic Offensive above. It should press religious leaders inside and outside Iraq to speak out on behalf of peace and reconciliation.

Finally, amnesty proposals from the Iraqi government are an important incentive in reconciliation talks and they need to be generous. Amnesty proposals to once-bitter enemies will be difficult for the United States to accept, just as they will be difficult for the Iraqis to make. Yet amnesty is an issue to be grappled with by the Iraqis, not by Americans. Despite being politically unpopular—in the United States as well as in Iraq—amnesty is essential if progress is to take place. Iraqi leaders need to be certain that they have U.S. support as they move forward with this critical element of national reconciliation.

RECOMMENDATION 37: Iraqi amnesty proposals must not be undercut in Washington by either the executive or the legislative branch.

Militias and National Reconciliation

The use of force by the government of Iraq is appropriate and necessary to stop militias that act as death squads or use violence against institutions of the state. However, solving the problem of militias requires national reconciliation.

Dealing with Iraq's militias will require long-term attention, and substantial funding will be needed to disarm, demobilize, and reintegrate militia members into civilian society. Around the world, this process of transitioning members of irregular military forces from civil conflict to new lives once a peace settlement takes hold is familiar. The disarmament, demobilization, and reintegration of militias depends on national reconciliation and on confidence-building measures among the parties to that reconciliation.

Both the United Nations and expert and experienced nongovernmental organizations, especially the International Organization for Migration, must be on the ground with appropriate personnel months before any program to disarm, demobilize, and reintegrate militia members begins. Because the United States is a party to the conflict, the U.S. military should not be involved in implementing such a program. Yet U.S. financial and technical support is crucial.

RECOMMENDATION 38: The United States should support the presence of neutral international experts as advisors to the Iraqi government on the processes of disarmament, demobilization, and reintegration.

RECOMMENDATION 39: The United States should provide financial and technical support and establish a single office in Iraq to coordinate assistance to the Iraqi government and its expert advisors to aid a program to disarm, demobilize, and reintegrate militia members.

3. Security and Military Forces
A Military Strategy for Iraq
There is no action the American military can take that, by itself, can bring about success in Iraq. But there are actions that the U.S. and Iraqi governments, working together, can and

should take to increase the probability of avoiding disaster there, and increase the chance of success.

The Iraqi government should accelerate the urgently needed national reconciliation program to which it has already committed. And it should accelerate assuming responsibility for Iraqi security by increasing the number and quality of Iraqi Army brigades. As the Iraqi Army increases in size and capability, the Iraqi government should be able to take real responsibility for governance.

While this process is under way, and to facilitate it, the United States should significantly increase the number of U.S. military personnel, including combat troops, imbedded in and supporting Iraqi Army units. As these actions proceed, we could begin to move combat forces out of Iraq. The primary mission of U.S. forces in Iraq should evolve to one of supporting the Iraqi army, which would take over primary responsibility for combat operations. We should continue to maintain support forces, rapid-reaction forces, special operations forces, intelligence units, search-and-rescue units, and force protection units.

While the size and composition of the Iraqi Army is ultimately a matter for the Iraqi government to determine, we should be firm on the urgent near-term need for significant additional trained Army brigades, since this is the key to Iraqis taking over full responsibility for their own security, which they want to do and which we need them to do. It is clear that they will still need security assistance from the United States for some time to come as they work to achieve political and security changes.

One of the most important elements of our support would be the imbedding of substantially more U.S. military personnel in all Iraqi Army battalions and brigades, as well as within Iraqi companies. U.S. personnel would provide advice, combat assistance, and staff assistance. The training of Iraqi units by the United States has improved and should continue for the coming year. In addition to this training, Iraqi combat units need supervised on-the-job training as they move to field operations. This on-the-job training could be best done by imbedding more U.S. military personnel in Iraqi deployed units. The number of imbedded personnel would be based on the recommendation of our military commanders in Iraq, but it should be large enough to accelerate the development of a real combat capability in Iraqi Army units. Such a mission could involve 10,000 to 20,000 American troops instead of the 3,000 to 4,000 now in this role. This increase in imbedded troops could be carried out without an aggregate increase over time in the total number of troops in Iraq by making a corresponding decrease in troops assigned to U.S. combat brigades.

Another mission of the U.S. military would be to assist Iraqi deployed brigades with intelligence, transportation, air support, and logistics support, as well as providing some key equipment.

A vital mission of the U.S. military would be to maintain rapid-reaction teams and special operations teams. These teams would be available to undertake strike missions against al Qaeda in Iraq when the opportunity arises, as well as for other missions considered vital by the U.S. commander in Iraq.

The performance of the Iraqi Army could also be significantly improved if it had improved equipment. One source could be equipment left behind by departing U.S. units. The quickest and most effective way for the Iraqi Army to get the bulk of their equipment would be through our Foreign Military Sales program, which they have already begun to use.

While these efforts are building up, and as additional Iraqi brigades are being deployed, U.S. combat brigades could begin to move out of Iraq. By the first quarter of 2008, subject to unexpected developments in the security situation on the ground, all combat brigades not necessary for force protection could be out of Iraq. At that time, U.S. combat forces in Iraq could be deployed only in units embedded with Iraqi forces, in rapid-reaction and special operations teams, and in training, equipping, advising, force protection, and search and rescue. Intelligence and support efforts would continue. Even after the United States has moved all combat brigades out of Iraq, we would maintain a considerable military presence in the region, with our still significant force in Iraq and with our powerful air, ground, and naval deployments in Kuwait, Bahrain, and Qatar, as well as an increased presence in Afghanistan. These forces would be sufficiently robust to permit the United States, working with the Iraqi government, to accomplish four missions:

- Provide political reassurance to the Iraqi government in order to avoid its collapse and the disintegration of the country.
- Fight al Qaeda and other terrorist organizations in Iraq using special operations teams.
- Train, equip, and support the Iraqi security forces.
- Deter even more destructive interference in Iraq by Syria and Iran.

Because of the importance of Iraq to our regional security goals and to our ongoing fight against al Qaeda, we considered proposals to make a substantial increase (100,000 to 200,000) in the number of U.S. troops in Iraq. We rejected this course because we do not believe that the needed levels are available for a sustained deployment. Further, adding more American troops could conceivably worsen those aspects of the security problem that are fed by the view that the U.S. presence is intended to be a long-term "occupation." We could, however, support a short-term redeployment or surge of American combat forces to stabilize Baghdad, or to speed up the training and equipping mission, if the U.S. commander in Iraq determines that such steps would be effective.

We also rejected the immediate withdrawal of our troops, because we believe that so much is at stake.

We believe that our recommended actions will give the Iraqi Army the support it needs to have a reasonable chance to take responsibility for Iraq's security. Given the ongoing deterioration in the security situation, it is urgent to move as quickly as possible to have that security role taken over by Iraqi security forces.

The United States should not make an open-ended commitment to keep large numbers of American troops deployed in Iraq for three compelling reasons.

First, and most importantly, the United States faces other security dangers in the world, and a continuing Iraqi commitment of American ground forces at present levels will leave no reserve available to meet other contingencies. On September 7, 2006, General James Jones, our NATO commander, called for more troops in Afghanistan, where U.S. and NATO forces are fighting a resurgence of al Qaeda and Taliban forces. The United States should respond positively to that request, and be prepared for other security contingencies, including those in Iran and North Korea.

Second, the long-term commitment of American ground forces to Iraq at current levels is adversely affecting Army readiness, with less than a third of the Army units currently at high readiness levels. The Army is unlikely to be able to meet the next rotation of troops in Iraq without undesirable changes in its deployment practices. The Army is now considering breaking its compact with the National Guard and Reserves that limits the number of years that these citizen-soldiers can be deployed. Behind this short-term strain is the longer-term risk that the ground forces will be impaired in ways that will take years to reverse.

And finally, an open-ended commitment of American forces would not provide the Iraqi government the incentive it needs to take the political actions that give Iraq the best chance of quelling sectarian violence. In the absence of such an incentive, the Iraqi government might continue to delay taking those difficult actions.

While it is clear that the presence of U.S. troops in Iraq is moderating the violence, there is little evidence that the long-term deployment of U.S. troops by itself has led or will lead to fundamental improvements in the security situation. It is important to recognize that there are no risk-free alternatives available to the United States at this time. Reducing our combat troop commitments in Iraq, whenever that occurs, undeniably creates risks, but leaving those forces tied down in Iraq indefinitely creates its own set of security risks.

RECOMMENDATION 40: The United States should not make an open-ended commitment to keep large numbers of American troops deployed in Iraq.

RECOMMENDATION 41: The United States must make it clear to the Iraqi government that the United States could carry out its plans, including planned redeployments, even if Iraq does not implement its planned changes. America's other security needs and the future of our military cannot be made hostage to the actions or inactions of the Iraqi government.

RECOMMENDATION 42: We should seek to complete the training and equipping mission by the first quarter of 2008, as stated by General George Casey on October 24, 2006.

RECOMMENDATION 43: Military priorities in Iraq must change, with the highest priority given to the training, equipping, advising, and support mission and to counterterrorism operations.

RECOMMENDATION 44: The most highly qualified U.S. officers and military personnel should be assigned to the imbedded teams, and American teams should be present with Iraqi units down to the company level. The U.S. military should establish suitable career-enhancing incentives for these officers and personnel.

RECOMMENDATION 45: The United States should support more and better equipment for the Iraqi Army by encouraging the Iraqi government to accelerate its Foreign Military Sales requests and, as American combat brigades move out of Iraq, by leaving behind some American equipment for Iraqi forces.

Restoring the U.S. Military
We recognize that there are other results of the war in Iraq that have great consequence for our nation. One consequence has been the stress and uncertainty imposed on our military—the most professional and proficient military in history. The United States will need its military to protect U.S. security regardless of what happens in Iraq. We therefore considered how to limit the adverse consequences of the strain imposed on our military by the Iraq war.

U.S. military forces, especially our ground forces, have been stretched nearly to the breaking point by the repeated deployments in Iraq, with attendant casualties (almost 3,000 dead and more than 21,000 wounded), greater difficulty in recruiting, and accelerated wear on equipment.

Additionally, the defense budget as a whole is in danger of disarray, as supplemental funding winds down and reset costs become clear. It will be a major challenge to meet ongoing requirements for other current and future security threats that need to be accommodated together with spending for operations and maintenance, reset, personnel, and benefits for active duty and retired personnel. Restoring the capability of our military forces should be a high priority for the United States at this time.

The U.S. military has a long tradition of strong partnership between the civilian leadership of the Department of Defense and the uniformed services. Both have long benefited from a relationship in which the civilian leadership exercises control with the advantage of fully candid professional advice, and the military serves loyally with the understanding that its advice has been heard and valued. That tradition has frayed, and civil-military relations need to be repaired.

RECOMMENDATION 46: The new Secretary of Defense should make every effort to build healthy civil-military relations, by creating an environment in which the senior military feel free to offer independent advice not only to the civilian leadership in the Pentagon but also to the President and the National Security Council, as envisioned in the Goldwater-Nichols legislation.

RECOMMENDATION 47: As redeployment proceeds, the Pentagon leadership should emphasize training and education programs for the forces that have returned to the continental United States in order to "reset" the force and restore the U.S. military to a high level of readiness for global contingencies.

RECOMMENDATION 48: As equipment returns to the United States, Congress should appropriate sufficient funds to restore the equipment to full functionality over the next five years.

RECOMMENDATION 49: The administration, in full consultation with the relevant committees of Congress, should assess the full future budgetary impact of the war in Iraq and its potential impact on the future readiness of the force, the ability to recruit and retain high-quality personnel, needed investments in procurement and in research and development, and the budgets of other U.S. government agencies involved in the stability and reconstruction effort.

4. Police and Criminal Justice

The problems in the Iraqi police and criminal justice system are profound.

The ethos and training of Iraqi police forces must support the mission to "protect and serve" all Iraqis. Today, far too many Iraqi police do not embrace that mission, in part because of problems in how reforms were organized and implemented by the Iraqi and U.S. governments.

Recommended Iraqi Actions

Within Iraq, the failure of the police to restore order and prevent militia infiltration is due, in part, to the poor organization of Iraq's component police forces: the Iraqi National Police, the Iraqi Border Police, and the Iraqi Police Service.

The Iraqi National Police pursue a mission that is more military than domestic in nature—involving commando-style operations—and is thus ill-suited to the Ministry of the Interior. The more natural home for the National Police is within the Ministry of Defense, which should be the authority for counterinsurgency operations and heavily armed forces. Though depriving the Ministry of the Interior of operational forces, this move will place the Iraqi National Police under better and more rigorous Iraqi and U.S. supervision and will enable these units to better perform their counterinsurgency mission.

RECOMMENDATION 50: The entire Iraqi National Police should be transferred to the Ministry of Defense, where the police commando units will become part of the new Iraqi Army.

Similarly, the Iraqi Border Police are charged with a role that bears little resemblance to ordinary policing, especially in light of the current flow of foreign fighters, insurgents, and weaponry across Iraq's borders and the need for joint patrols of the border with foreign militaries. Thus the natural home for the Border Police is within the Ministry of Defense, which should be the authority for controlling Iraq's borders.

RECOMMENDATION 51: The entire Iraqi Border Police should be transferred to the Ministry of Defense, which would have total responsibility for border control and external security.

The Iraqi Police Service, which operates in the provinces and provides local policing, needs to become a true police force. It needs legal authority, training, and equipment to control crime and protect Iraqi citizens. Accomplishing those goals will not be easy, and the presence of American advisors will be required to help the Iraqis determine a new role for the police.

RECOMMENDATION 52: The Iraqi Police Service should be given greater responsibility to conduct criminal investigations and should expand its cooperation with other elements in the Iraqi judicial system in order to better control crime and protect Iraqi civilians.

In order to more effectively administer the Iraqi Police Service, the Ministry of the Interior needs to undertake substantial reforms to purge bad elements and highlight best practices. Once the ministry begins to function effectively, it can exert a positive influence over the provinces and take back some of the authority that was lost to local governments through decentralization. To reduce corruption and militia infiltration, the Ministry of the Interior should take authority from the local governments for the handling of policing funds. Doing so will improve accountability and organizational discipline, limit the authority of provincial police officials, and identify police officers with the central government.

RECOMMENDATION 53: The Iraqi Ministry of the Interior should undergo a process of organizational transformation, including efforts to expand the capability and reach of the current major crime unit (or Criminal Investigation Division) and to exert more authority over local police forces. The sole authority to pay police salaries and disburse financial support to local police should be transferred to the Ministry of the Interior.

Finally, there is no alternative to bringing the Facilities Protection Service under the control of the Iraqi Ministry of the Interior. Simply disbanding these units is not an option, as the members will take their weapons and become full-time militiamen or insurgents. All should be brought under the authority of a reformed Ministry of the Interior. They will need to be vetted, retrained, and closely supervised. Those who are no longer part of the Facilities Protection Service need to participate in a disarmament, demobilization, and reintegration program (outlined above).

RECOMMENDATION 54: The Iraqi Ministry of the Interior should proceed with current efforts to identify, register, and control the Facilities Protection Service.

U.S. Actions

The Iraqi criminal justice system is weak, and the U.S. training mission has been hindered by a lack of clarity and capacity. It has not always been clear who is in charge of the police training mission, and the U.S. military lacks expertise in certain areas pertaining to police and the rule of law. The United States has been more successful in training the Iraqi Army than it has the police. The U.S. Department of Justice has the expertise and capacity to carry out the police training mission. The U.S. Department of Defense is already bearing too much of the burden in Iraq. Meanwhile, the pool of expertise in the United States on policing and the rule of law has been underutilized.

The United States should adjust its training mission in Iraq to match the recommended changes in the Iraqi government—the movement of the National and Border Police to the Ministry of Defense and the new emphasis on the Iraqi Police Service within the Ministry of the Interior. To reflect the reorganization, the Department of Defense would continue to train the Iraqi National and Border Police, and the Department of Justice would become responsible for training the Iraqi Police Service.

RECOMMENDATION 55: The U.S. Department of Defense should continue its mission to train the Iraqi National Police and the Iraqi Border Police, which should be placed within the Iraqi Ministry of Defense.

RECOMMENDATION 56: The U.S. Department of Justice should direct the training mission of the police forces remaining under the Ministry of the Interior.

RECOMMENDATION 57: Just as U.S. military training teams are imbedded within Iraqi Army units, the current practice of imbedding U.S. police trainers should be expanded and the numbers of civilian training officers increased so that teams can cover all levels of the Iraqi Police Service, including local police stations. These trainers should be obtained from among experienced civilian police executives and supervisors from around the world. These officers would replace the military police personnel currently assigned to training teams.

The Federal Bureau of Investigation has provided personnel to train the Criminal Investigation Division in the Ministry of the Interior, which handles major crimes. The FBI has also fielded a large team within Iraq for counterterrorism activities.

Building on this experience, the training programs should be expanded and should include the development of forensic investigation training and facilities that could apply scientific and technical investigative methods to counterterrorism as well as to ordinary criminal activity.

RECOMMENDATION 58: The FBI should expand its investigative and forensic training and facilities within Iraq, to include coverage of terrorism as well as criminal activity.

One of the major deficiencies of the Iraqi Police Service is its lack of equipment, particularly in the area of communications and motor transport.

RECOMMENDATION 59: The Iraqi government should provide funds to expand and upgrade communications equipment and motor vehicles for the Iraqi Police Service.

The Department of Justice is also better suited than the Department of Defense to carry out the mission of reforming Iraq's Ministry of the Interior and Iraq's judicial system. Iraq needs more than training for cops on the beat: it needs courts, trained prosecutors and investigators, and the ability to protect Iraqi judicial officials.

RECOMMENDATION 60: The U.S. Department of Justice should lead the work of organizational transformation in the Ministry of the Interior. This approach must involve Iraqi officials, starting at senior levels and moving down, to create a strategic plan and work out standard administrative procedures, codes of conduct, and operational measures that Iraqis will accept and use. These plans must be drawn up in partnership.

RECOMMENDATION 61: Programs led by the U.S. Department of Justice to establish courts; to train judges, prosecutors, and investigators; and to create institutions and practices to fight corruption must be strongly supported and funded. New and refurbished courthouses with improved physical security, secure housing for judges and judicial staff, witness protection facilities, and a new Iraqi Marshals Service are essential parts of a secure and functioning system of justice.

5. The Oil Sector

Since the success of the oil sector is critical to the success of the Iraqi economy, the United States must do what it can to help Iraq maximize its capability.

Iraq, a country with promising oil potential, could restore oil production from existing fields to 3.0 to 3.5 million barrels a day over a three- to five-year period, depending on evolving conditions in key reservoirs. Even if Iraq were at peace tomorrow, oil production would decline unless current problems in the oil sector were addressed.

Short Term

RECOMMENDATION 62:

- *As soon as possible, the U.S. government should provide technical assistance to the Iraqi government to prepare a draft oil law that defines the rights of regional and local governments and creates a fiscal and legal framework for investment. Legal clarity is essential to attract investment.*
- *The U.S. government should encourage the Iraqi government to accelerate contracting for the comprehensive well work-over in the southern fields needed to increase production, but the United States should no longer fund such infrastructure projects.*
- *The U.S. military should work with the Iraqi military and with private security forces to protect oil infrastructure and contractors. Protective measures could include a program to improve pipeline security by paying local tribes solely on the basis of throughput (rather than fixed amounts).*
- *Metering should be implemented at both ends of the supply line. This step would immediately improve accountability in the oil sector.*
- *In conjunction with the International Monetary Fund, the U.S. government should press Iraq to continue reducing subsidies in the energy sector, instead of providing grant assistance. Until Iraqis pay market prices for oil products, drastic fuel shortages will remain.*

Long Term

Expanding oil production in Iraq over the long term will require creating corporate structures, establishing management systems, and installing competent managers to plan and oversee an ambitious list of major oil-field investment projects.

To improve oil-sector performance, the Study Group puts forward the following recommendations.

RECOMMENDATION 63:

- *The United States should encourage investment in Iraq's oil sector by the international community and by international energy companies.*
- *The United States should assist Iraqi leaders to reorganize the national oil industry as a commercial enterprise, in order to enhance efficiency, transparency, and accountability.*
- *To combat corruption, the U.S. government should urge the Iraqi government to post all oil contracts, volumes, and prices on the Web so that Iraqis and outside observers scan track exports and export revenues.*
- *The United States should support the World Bank's efforts to ensure that best practices are used in contracting. This support involves providing Iraqi officials with contracting templates and training them in contracting, auditing, and reviewing audits.*
- *The United States should provide technical assistance to the Ministry of Oil for enhancing maintenance, improving the payments process, managing cash flows, contracting and auditing, and updating professional training programs for management and technical personnel.*

6. U.S. Economic and Reconstruction Assistance

Building the capacity of the Iraqi government should be at the heart of U.S. reconstruction efforts, and capacity building demands additional U.S. resources.

Progress in providing essential government services is necessary to sustain any progress on the political or security front. The period of large U.S.-funded reconstruction projects is over, yet the Iraqi government is still in great need of technical assistance and advice to build the capacity of its institutions. The Iraqi government needs help with all aspects of its operations, including improved procedures, greater delegation of authority, and better internal controls. The strong emphasis on building capable central ministries must be accompanied by efforts to develop functioning, effective provincial government institutions with local citizen participation.

Job creation is also essential. There is no substitute for private-sector job generation, but the Commander's Emergency Response Program is a necessary transitional mechanism until security and the economic climate improve. It provides immediate economic assistance for trash pickup, water, sewers, and electricity in conjunction with clear, hold, and build operations, and it should be funded generously. A total of $753 million was appropriated for this program in FY 2006.

RECOMMENDATION 64: U.S. economic assistance should be increased to a level of $5 billion per year rather than being permitted to decline. The President needs to ask for the necessary resources and must work hard to win the support of Congress. Capacity building and job creation, including reliance on the Commander's Emergency Response Program, should be U.S. priorities. Economic assistance should be provided on a nonsectarian basis.

The New Diplomatic Offensive can help draw in more international partners to assist with the reconstruction mission. The United Nations, the World Bank, the European Union, the Organization for Economic Cooperation and Development, and some Arab League members need to become hands-on participants in Iraq's reconstruction.

RECOMMENDATION 65: An essential part of reconstruction efforts in Iraq should be greater involvement by and with international partners, who should do more than just contribute money. They should also actively participate in the design and construction of projects.

The number of refugees and internally displaced persons within Iraq is increasing dramatically. If this situation is not addressed, Iraq and the region could be further destabilized, and the humanitarian suffering could be severe. Funding for international relief efforts is insufficient, and should be increased.

RECOMMENDATION 66: The United States should take the lead in funding assistance requests from the United Nations High Commissioner for Refugees, and other humanitarian agencies.

Coordination of Economic and Reconstruction Assistance

A lack of coordination by senior management in Washington still hampers U.S. contributions to Iraq's reconstruction.

Focus, priority setting, and skillful implementation are in short supply. No single official is assigned responsibility or held accountable for the overall reconstruction effort. Representatives of key foreign partners involved in reconstruction have also spoken to us directly and specifically about the need for a point of contact that can coordinate their efforts with the U.S. government.

A failure to improve coordination will result in agencies continuing to follow conflicting strategies, wasting taxpayer dollars on duplicative and uncoordinated efforts. This waste will further undermine public confidence in U.S. policy in Iraq.

A Senior Advisor for Economic Reconstruction in Iraq is required. He or she should report to the President, be given a staff and funding, and chair a National Security Council interagency group consisting of senior principals at the undersecretary level from all relevant U.S. government departments and agencies. The Senior Advisor's responsibility must be to bring unity of effort to the policy, budget, and implementation of economic reconstruction programs in Iraq. The Senior Advisor must act as the principal point of contact with U.S. partners in the overall reconstruction effort.

He or she must have close and constant interaction with senior U.S. officials and military commanders in Iraq, especially the Director of the Iraq Reconstruction and Management Office, so that the realities on the ground are brought directly and fully into the policy-making process. In order to maximize the effectiveness of assistance, all involved must be on the same page at all times.

RECOMMENDATION 67: The President should create a Senior Advisor for Economic Reconstruction in Iraq.

Improving the Effectiveness of Assistance Programs
Congress should work with the administration to improve its ability to implement assistance programs in Iraq quickly, flexibly, and effectively.

As opportunities arise, the Chief of Mission in Iraq should have the authority to fund quick-disbursing projects to promote national reconciliation, as well as to rescind funding from programs and projects in which the government of Iraq is not demonstrating effective partnership. These are important tools to improve performance and accountability—as is the work of the Special Inspector General for Iraq Reconstruction.

RECOMMENDATION 68: The Chief of Mission in Iraq should have the authority to spend significant funds through a program structured along the lines of the Commander's Emergency Response Program, and should have the authority to rescind funding from programs and projects in which the government of Iraq is not demonstrating effective partnership.

RECOMMENDATION 69: The authority of the Special Inspector General for Iraq Reconstruction should be renewed for the duration of assistance programs in Iraq.

U.S. security assistance programs in Iraq are slowed considerably by the differing requirements of State and Defense Department programs and of their respective congressional oversight committees. Since Iraqi forces must be trained and equipped, streamlining the provision of training and equipment to Iraq is critical. Security assistance should be delivered promptly, within weeks of a decision to provide it.

RECOMMENDATION 70: A more flexible security assistance program for Iraq, breaking down the barriers to effective interagency cooperation, should be authorized and implemented.

The United States also needs to break down barriers that discourage U.S. partnerships with international donors and Iraqi participants to promote reconstruction. The ability of the United States to form such partnerships will encourage greater international participation in Iraq.

RECOMMENDATION 71: Authority to merge U.S. funds with those from international donors and Iraqi participants on behalf of assistance projects should be provided.

7. Budget Preparation, Presentation, and Review

The public interest is not well served by the government's preparation, presentation, and review of the budget for the war in Iraq.

First, most of the costs of the war show up not in the normal budget request but in requests for emergency supplemental appropriations. This means that funding requests are drawn up outside the normal budget process, are not offset by budgetary reductions elsewhere, and move quickly to the White House with minimal scrutiny. Bypassing the normal review erodes budget discipline and accountability.

Second, the executive branch presents budget requests in a confusing manner, making it difficult for both the general public and members of Congress to understand the request or to differentiate it from counterterrorism operations around the world or operations in Afghanistan. Detailed analyses by budget experts are needed to answer what should be a simple question: "How much money is the President requesting for the war in Iraq?"

Finally, circumvention of the budget process by the executive branch erodes oversight and review by Congress. The authorizing committees (including the House and Senate Armed Services committees) spend the better part of a year reviewing the President's annual budget request. When the President submits an emergency supplemental request, the authorizing committees are bypassed. The request goes directly to the appropriations committees, and they are pressured by the need to act quickly so that troops in the field do not run out of funds. The result is a spending bill that passes Congress with perfunctory review. Even worse, the must-pass appropriations bill becomes loaded with special spending projects that would not survive the normal review process.

RECOMMENDATION 72: Costs for the war in Iraq should be included in the President's annual budget request, starting in FY 2008: the war is in its fourth year, and the normal budget process should not be circumvented. Funding requests for the war in Iraq should be presented clearly to Congress and the American people. Congress must carry out its constitutional responsibility to review budget requests for the war in Iraq carefully and to conduct oversight.

8. U.S. Personnel

The United States can take several steps to ensure that it has personnel with the right skills serving in Iraq.

All of our efforts in Iraq, military and civilian, are handicapped by Americans' lack of language and cultural understanding. Our embassy of 1,000 has 33 Arabic speakers, just six of whom are at the level of fluency. In a conflict that demands effective and efficient communication with Iraqis, we are often at a disadvantage. There are still far too few Arab language–proficient military and civilian officers in Iraq, to the detriment of the U.S. mission.

Civilian agencies also have little experience with complex overseas interventions to restore and maintain order—stability operations—outside of the normal embassy setting. The nature of the mission in Iraq is unfamiliar and dangerous, and the United States has had great difficulty filling civilian assignments in Iraq with sufficient numbers of properly trained personnel at the appropriate rank.

RECOMMENDATION 73: The Secretary of State, the Secretary of Defense, and the Director of National Intelligence should accord the highest possible priority to professional language proficiency and cultural training, in general and specifically for U.S. officers and personnel about to be assigned to Iraq.

RECOMMENDATION 74: In the short term, if not enough civilians volunteer to fill key positions in Iraq, civilian agencies must fill those positions with directed assignments. Steps should be taken to mitigate familial or financial hardships posed by directed assignments, including tax exclusions similar to those authorized for U.S. military personnel serving in Iraq.

RECOMMENDATION 75: For the longer term, the United States government needs to improve how its constituent agencies—Defense, State, Agency for International Development, Treasury, Justice, the intelligence community, and others—respond to a complex stability operation like that represented by this decade's Iraq and Afghanistan wars and the previous decade's operations in the Balkans. They need to train for, and conduct, joint operations across agency boundaries, following the Goldwater-Nichols model that has proved so successful in the U.S. armed services.

RECOMMENDATION 76: The State Department should train personnel to carry out civilian tasks associated with a complex stability operation outside of the traditional embassy setting. It should establish a Foreign Service Reserve Corps with personnel and expertise to provide surge capacity for such an operation. Other key civilian agencies, including Treasury, Justice, and Agriculture, need to create similar technical assistance capabilities.

9. Intelligence

While the United States has been able to acquire good and sometimes superb tactical intelligence on al Qaeda in Iraq, our government still does not understand very well either the insurgency in Iraq or the role of the militias.

A senior commander told us that human intelligence in Iraq has improved from 10 percent to 30 percent. Clearly, U.S. intelligence agencies can and must do better. As mentioned above, an essential part of better intelligence must be improved language and cultural skills. As an intelligence analyst told us, "We rely too much on others to bring information to us, and too often don't understand what is reported back because we do not understand the context of what we are told."

The Defense Department and the intelligence community have not invested sufficient people and resources to understand the political and military threat to American men and women in the armed forces. Congress has appropriated almost $2 billion this year for countermeasures to protect our troops in Iraq against improvised explosive devices, but the administration has not put forward a request to invest comparable resources in trying to understand the people who fabricate, plant, and explode those devices.

We were told that there are fewer than 10 analysts on the job at the Defense Intelligence Agency who have more than two years' experience in analyzing the insurgency. Capable analysts are rotated to new assignments, and on-the-job training begins anew. Agencies must have a better personnel system to keep analytic expertise focused on the insurgency. They are not doing enough to map the insurgency, dissect it, and understand it on a national and provincial level. The analytic community's knowledge of the organization, leadership, financing, and operations of militias, as well as their relationship to government security forces, also falls far short of what policy makers need to know.

In addition, there is significant underreporting of the violence in Iraq. The standard for recording attacks acts as a filter to keep events out of reports and databases. A murder of an Iraqi is not necessarily counted as an attack. If we cannot determine the source of a sectarian attack, that assault does not make it into the database. A roadside bomb or a rocket or mortar attack that doesn't hurt U.S. personnel doesn't count. For example, on one day in July 2006 there were 93 attacks or significant acts of violence reported. Yet a careful review of the reports for that single day brought to light 1,100 acts of violence. Good policy is difficult to make when information is systematically collected in a way that minimizes its discrepancy with policy goals.

RECOMMENDATION 77: The Director of National Intelligence and the Secretary of Defense should devote significantly greater analytic resources to the task of understanding the threats and sources of violence in Iraq.

RECOMMENDATION 78: The Director of National Intelligence and the Secretary of Defense should also institute immediate changes in the collection of data about violence and the sources of violence in Iraq to provide a more accurate picture of events on the ground.

Recommended Iraqi Actions

The Iraqi government must improve its intelligence capability, initially to work with the United States, and ultimately to take full responsibility for this intelligence function.

To facilitate enhanced Iraqi intelligence capabilities, the CIA should increase its personnel in Iraq to train Iraqi intelligence personnel. The CIA should also develop, with Iraqi officials, a counterterrorism intelligence center for the all-source fusion of information on the various sources of terrorism within Iraq. This center would analyze data concerning the individuals, organizations, networks, and support groups involved in terrorism within Iraq. It would also facilitate intelligence-led police and military actions against them.

RECOMMENDATION 79: The CIA should provide additional personnel in Iraq to develop and train an effective intelligence service and to build a counterterrorism intelligence center that will facilitate intelligence-led counterterrorism efforts.

Source: U.S. United States Institute of Peace. Iraq Study Group. "The Iraq Study Group Report." December 6, 2006. http://purl.access.gpo.gov/GPO/LPS76748 (accessed January 8, 2007).

Other Historic Documents of Interest

Execution of Saddam Hussein, p. 638   *Midterm elections, p. 645*
Iraq reconstruction, p. 161   *Rumsfeld resignation, p. 662*
Iraq's new government, p. 171   *Security in Iraq, p. 702*

UN Secretary General Annan on Protecting Human Rights

December 8, 2006

■■■■■■■■■■■■■ **THE DOCUMENT IN CONTEXT** ■■■■■■■■

Kofi Annan stepped down as secretary general of the United Nations at the end of 2006, having served for ten of the most tumultuous years in the world body's six-decade history. An outspoken advocate of human rights and of the UN's potential to wage peace, Annan was succeeded by South Korea's foreign minister, Ban Ki-moon, who appeared to be a much more reticent figure and who said his chief priority would be implementing the UN management reforms Annan had proposed but had been unable to put in place. Ban took office as the UN's eighth secretary general on January 1, 2007.

Annan spent much of 2006 pushing for the sweeping series of reforms he had outlined in March 2005. Some were management reforms to streamline the UN's bulky, and often dysfunctional, bureaucracy; others were budgetary changes to satisfy the United States and other major funders; and others were fundamental changes in some of the UN's chief bodies, notably the discredited Human Rights Commission and the most powerful body of all, the Security Council. Many of Annan's budget and management reforms were blocked by member nations interested in maintaining the status quo. The United Nations did abolish the Human Rights Commission and replaced it with a new Human Rights Council, but at year's end even Annan acknowledged that this council was not living up to his expectations.

To virtually no one's surprise, the UN took no real action to revise the makeup of the Security Council, the agency that held much of the world body's political clout. Annan in 2005 proposed two different plans for expanding the fifteen-member council to better reflect the state of world affairs sixty years after the UN was founded. Both plans, and others put forward by some member nations, were blocked by nations with vested interests in keeping the system unchanged. Among these were the United States, which opposed expanding the council, and various countries that wanted to keep rivals from getting seats on the council.

The man who, more than anyone else, represented the Bush administration's demands for changes at the UN lost his job at year's end because of U.S. domestic politics. John R. Bolton, nominated by President George W. Bush in 2005 as U.S. ambassador to the UN, had been blocked from confirmation in the Senate because of his obvious hostility to the UN; he had served anyway, since August 2005, under a loophole. Bush sought again in 2006 to appoint Bolton to the post, but critics in the Senate made it clear they would block Bolton once more. After the November 7 elections gave Democrats control of Congress, Bush relented and said he would appoint someone else. *(United Nations Background, Historic Documents of 2005, p. 228)*

Annan's Parting Messages

In the early years of his tenure, which started in 1997, Annan had rapidly become one of the world's most recognizable and respected figures. His eloquence on behalf of the downtrodden, his diplomatic skills in getting enemies to talk to each other, and his easy manner endeared him to a broad range of people, including even the UN's harshest critics. Annan carried out important budget changes that long had been demanded by conservatives in the U.S. Congress, he articulated an international obligation to protect human rights even if that meant violating national sovereignty, and he pushed the UN to intervene more vigorously to end civil wars, notably in his home continent of Africa.

Annan's generally good relations with the UN's most powerful member, the United States, began to sour in the run-up to the U.S. invasion of Iraq in March 2003. Much to the Bush administration's annoyance, Annan opposed the invasion and warned it could have catastrophic consequences for the Middle East and the United States.

Eventually the war also had unexpected catastrophic consequences for the UN and for Annan's reputation. Once in Iraq, the United States discovered evidence that the UN had mismanaged the so-called oil-for-food program under which Iraq was allowed to sell some of its oil internationally, despite a UN embargo, if the money was used to buy food and other humanitarian supplies for the Iraqi people. These revelations deeply embarrassed Annan and touched him directly in 2004 when it emerged that his son, Kojo, had worked for a private contractor involved in the oil-for-food program. That same year also saw an upsurge of allegations that soldiers in UN peace-keeping forces had used their positions to demand sexual favors from local women and girls; Annan moved quickly to deal with this problem but new allegations kept arising, and thus kept casting a shadow on the UN's reputation. Annan called 2004 his *annis horribilus*—horrible year.

Toward the end of his last year in office, Annan returned again to the bully pulpit he had used so effectively in the past to argue on behalf of the causes most important to him: human rights and the United Nations, where he had spent his entire working career. On December 8, the annual Human Rights Day, Annan gave a speech in New York arguing that protecting human rights was at the core of everything the UN should be doing. Annan took particular pride in noting that in September 2005 leaders at the annual UN summit had adopted the "Responsibility to Protect" principle he had first advocated in 2001: the world had a responsibility to protect human rights even when the abuser was a sovereign government acting against its own people. Annan called this a "momentous doctrine" because it countered established theory—still embraced by many world leaders—that governments had a sovereign right to act as they saw fit within their own borders. Annan said world leaders were refusing to respect this new principle, however, citing the ongoing abuses in the Darfur region of western Sudan, where the UN estimated that at least 200,000 people had died at the hands of government forces and various militias. "How can an international community which claims to uphold human rights allow this horror to continue?" he asked.

On December 11, Annan traveled to Independence, Missouri—the hometown of Harry S. Truman, the U.S. president in the UN's early years—to talk about another theme close to his heart: the central role of the United States in the United Nations. In a speech reflecting his frustrations in dealing with the Bush administration, Annan called on the United States to exercise restraint, and to work through the United Nations, even when it believed its own interests were threatened. "More than ever, today Americans, like the rest of humanity, need a functioning global system through which the world's peoples can face global challenges together," he said. "And in order to function, the system still cries out for far-sighted American leadership, in the Truman tradition." Annan did not say so explicitly, but it was clear from his words that he believed the current U.S. leadership did not fit that description.

Earlier in the year, Annan had been forced to intervene in a sniping match between his chief aide, Deputy Secretary General Mark Malloch Brown, and Bolton, the U.S. ambassador. Brown, a Briton who had worked for the UN for many years, gave a speech on June 6 sharply critical of the United States for what he said was its refusal to support and work through the United Nations. Reciting a litany of complaints about the Bush administration—notably its unwillingness to stop "UN-bashing"—Brown concluded that the two sides were stuck in an "unhappy marriage." Brown's forthright, if undiplomatic, remarks won him applause from many diplomats at the UN but enraged Bolton, long one of Washington's most outspoken critics of the world body. Bolton telephoned Annan and demanded that he "personally and publicly" repudiate Brown's speech. Annan refused and said he agreed with the thrust of his aide's comments.

Human Rights Council

For years, critics in the United States and some other countries had cited the UN's Human Rights Commission as exemplifying all of the world body's institutional problems. The fifty-three-member commission sat for just six weeks each year, and its membership often included countries with some of the world's worst human rights records; among current members were Cuba, Sudan, and Zimbabwe, each of which regularly violated much of the UN's Universal Declaration of Human Rights. Annan in 2005 proposed creating a full-time Human Rights Council with an expanded mandate to investigate abuses and recommend steps to correct those abuses.

Diplomats spent months debating the details of Annan's proposal and finally agreed in late February 2006 on a new Human Rights Council, with forty-seven members and a meeting schedule totaling ten weeks annually. A complex selection process also was intended to make it somewhat more difficult than in the past for nations with poor human rights records to be elected to the council; even then, their records would be subject to review at least once during a three-year term. Annan said he was disappointed the proposal fell short of his original plan for a strong council. Bolton was scathing in his comments, saying "the strongest argument in favor of this draft is that it is not as bad as it could be."

The General Assembly approved the plan for the new council on March 15 by an overwhelming 170–4 vote, with three abstentions. Israel, the Marshall Islands, and Palau joined the United States in voting no, while Belarus, Iran, and Venezuela abstained.

The old Human Rights Commission held its final session on March 27. The next step was selection of members for the new Human Rights Council. That took place on May 9, with the biggest news being that the United States decided not to seek a seat.

The new council began its work on June 19 and heard an appeal from Annan to avoid "political point-scoring or petty maneuver" in its deliberations. "Think always of those whose rights are denied," he said.

The new council devoted its first sessions to organizational matters, but turned to substance for its second session in September and early October. Just like its predecessor, however, the council found itself sharply divided along political lines and failed in that session to act on any of the four dozen resolutions presented to it on human rights abuses. Perhaps the most glaring failure involved the Darfur region of Sudan. The council finally acted on Darfur on November 28, rejecting a resolution to condemn human rights abuses by the government and its allies and instead adopting a resolution calling on all sides to end abuse. In his December 8 speech on human rights, a clearly frustrated Annan said he had been disappointed by the new council, which he said "so far has clearly not justified all the hopes that so many of us placed in it." Possibly in response to this and other criticisms, the council voted on December 13 to send a team of investigators to Darfur.

Management Changes

Early in his tenure Annan had focused on streamlining the UN's cumbersome bureaucracy and had been able to implement numerous reforms, some of them practically demanded by the U.S. Congress as a condition of continued funding. Even so, the UN remained an unwieldy organization, as demonstrated by the high-profile scandal in 2004–2005 over its haphazard management of the Iraqi oil-for-food program. *(Background, Historic Documents of 2004, p. 891)*

On March 7, Annan proposed a new set of changes to streamline the UN bureaucracy and make the job of managing it easier. Paraphrasing a quote from one of the investigations into the oil-for-food scandal, Annan told the General Assembly: "In short, I am expected to be the world's chief diplomat and at the same time to run a large and complex organization, as it were, in my spare time. This will hardly be less true for my successors." Annan's proposals included a major revamping of the UN's peacekeeping office (which he had once headed), an upgraded information and communications system, better pay and benefits for field staff, buyouts for about 1,000 headquarters employees, and moving some administrative services from the UN's main offices in New York City and Geneva to lower-cost locations. Annan put a $510 million price tag on his proposals.

Annan's proposals won general praise from the United States and other major donors to the UN, but UN employees were not impressed. On March 9, the UN's Staff Union overwhelmingly voted to express "no confidence" in him and his senior managers.

The proposals also encountered resistance from many of those who had an actual vote in the matter: UN member nations. A group of developing nations, known as the Group of 77, opposed the plan, notably parts that shifted some budgeting and personnel responsibilities from the General Assembly—dominated by developing countries—to the secretary general. In a rare outright defeat for a secretary general, these nations succeeded in blocking the heart of Annan's plan on April 29 when it was considered by the General Assembly's key administrative and budget committee. The full General Assembly affirmed the committee's stand on May 8. The 121–50 vote against moving ahead with Annan's plan was one of the clearest demonstrations in years of the voting sway of developing nations in the General Assembly.

Hanging over this debate about management reform was a direct threat by the United States to cut off its funding for the UN unless key reforms were in place by the end of June. As part of the UN's budget for the year, the Bush administration had negotiated a provision giving the UN money only for the first six months of the year. A debate on UN spending went down to the wire, with the General Assembly acting on June 30 to extend the budget for the rest of the year—over U.S. opposition. Diplomats from several developing nations said the U.S. tactic of demanding changes, and threatening to withhold financial support for the UN if its demands were not met, had backfired.

Another key reform was blocked in 2006, this one having to do with the UN's landmark building on the east side of Manhattan. After nearly sixty years, the famed UN headquarters was overcrowded and described by its occupants, when they were being diplomatic, as dilapidated. Annan and his aides put together a $1.6 billion refurbishment plan, which was to be carried out by Louis Frederick Reuter IV, a well-known manager of large building projects. The United States objected to key parts of the plan, however, leading Reuter to resign in frustration on May 4.

A New, Low-Key Secretary General

The process of selecting a new secretary general was a complex and secretive one that involved regional alliances, personalities, and power politics—in short, all the factors that made decision making at the UN difficult and sometimes impossible. Only three factors seemed to be generally agreed upon: the secretary general would not be a native of one of the five permanent member nations of the Security Council, potential candidates could lobby for the job but were supposed to be discreet about it, and he or she would be selected from one of the world's regions according to a rotating schedule. Annan, a Ghanaian by birth, had represented Africa even though he had worked for the UN and lived in the United States for nearly all his adult life. The next region on the list was Asia. The only other secretary general from that region had been U Thant (from Myanmar, then known as Burma), who served two terms ending in 1971. The United States and Britain argued that this regional rotation should be abandoned, but most other countries wanted to stick with it, including two of the other permanent Security Council members: China and Russia.

Early in the year a host of prominent diplomats and other international figures emerged as potential candidates, many of them from outside Asia. Some of the potential candidates announced discreetly that they were available for the job, while others pretended they were not interested—even while acknowledging they could be persuaded to take it. One candidate who was thought to be a strong contender—Thailand's foreign minister Surakiart Sathirathai—quickly faded in September after the government he served was ousted in a military coup.

In theory, the General Assembly and the Security Council had a coequal role in selecting the secretary general. In fact, however, the process gave the Security Council more weight because it chose a candidate whose name was presented to the General Assembly for an up-or-down vote.

Starting in the summer the Security Council took several informal votes, called straw polls, to narrow down the list of candidates. South Korea's Ban Ki-moon emerged as the leading contender in these polls, and he retained his lead all through the process—in part because he had active support from the United States and in part because he had no vociferous opposition. A quiet diplomat, Ban had made few enemies in his career, and his views on major international issues were not widely known. In his low-key campaign for the job, he focused on the need for management reform—the very issue that was a high priority for the United States. The Security Council formally nominated Ban on October 9, in a consensus vote. This action took place just as the Security Council was reacting to North Korea's test earlier that day of a small nuclear weapon. Speaking to a news conference in Seoul, Ban said: "This should be a moment of joy, but instead I stand here with a very heavy heart" because of the North Korean action. The General Assembly ratified Ban's appointment to a five-year term by acclamation on October 13.

Following is the text of a speech by United Nations Secretary General Kofi Annan in New York City on December 8, 2006, calling for protecting human rights to be at the center of the UN's work.

DOCUMENT

"Urging End to Impunity, Annan Sets Forth Ideas to Protect Human Rights"

My dear friends,

Thank you all for being here. I could not ask for better company, on the last International Human Rights Day of my time in office, than this group of courageous human rights leaders from around the world.

I don't need to tell you, of all people, that the United Nations has a special stake, and a special responsibility, in promoting respect for human rights worldwide. But equally— and less happily—I don't need to tell you that the UN has often failed to live up to that responsibility. I know that ten years ago many of you were close to giving up on any hope that an organization of governments, many of which are themselves gross violators of human rights, could ever function as an effective human rights defender.

One of my priorities as Secretary-General has been to try and restore that hope, by making human rights central to all the UN's work. But I'm not sure how far I have succeeded, or how much nearer we are to bringing the reality of the UN in line with my vision of human rights as its "third pillar", on a par with development and peace and security.

Development, security and human rights go hand in hand; no one of them can advance very far without the other two. Indeed, anyone who speaks forcefully for human rights but does nothing about security and development—including the desperate need to fight extreme poverty—undermines both his credibility and his cause. Poverty in particular remains both a source and consequence of rights violations. Yet if we are serious about human deprivation, we must also demonstrate that we are serious about human dignity, and vice versa.

Are you any more confident today than you were ten years ago that an intergovernmental organization can really do this job? I fear the answer may be No, and that the first steps of the Human Rights Council, which we all fought so hard to establish, may not have given you much encouragement. So this morning I suggest that we try and think through, together, what is really needed.

First, we must give real meaning to the principle of "Responsibility to Protect."

As you know, last year's World Summit formally endorsed that momentous doctrine—which means, in essence, that respect for national sovereignty can no longer be used as an excuse for inaction in the face of genocide, war crimes, ethnic cleansing and crimes against humanity. Yet one year later, to judge by what is happening in Darfur, our performance has not improved much since the disasters of Bosnia and Rwanda. Sixty years after the liberation of the Nazi death camps, and 30 years after the Cambodian killing fields, the promise of "never again" is ringing hollow.

The tragedy of Darfur has raged for over three years now, and still reports pour in of villages being destroyed by the hundred, and of the brutal treatment of civilians spreading into neighboring countries. How can an international community which claims to uphold human rights allow this horror to continue?

There is more than enough blame to go around. It can be shared among those who value abstract notions of sovereignty more than the lives of real families, those whose reflex of solidarity puts them on the side of governments and not of peoples, and those who fear that action to stop the slaughter would jeopardize their commercial interests.

The truth is, none of these arguments amount even to excuses, let alone justifications, for the shameful passivity of most governments. We have still not summoned up the collective sense of urgency that this issue requires.

Some governments have tried to win support in the global South by caricaturing responsibility to protect, as a conspiracy by imperialist powers to take back the hard-won national sovereignty of formerly colonized peoples. This is utterly false.

We must do better. We must develop the responsibility to protect into a powerful international norm that is not only quoted but put into practice, whenever and wherever it is needed.

Above all we must not wait to take action until genocide is actually happening, by which time it is often too late to do anything effective about it. Two years ago I announced an action plan for the prevention of genocide, and appointed a Special Adviser to help me implement it. While his work has been extremely valuable, much more needs to be done. I hope my successor will take up this banner, and that member states will support him.

Second, we must put an end to impunity.

We have made progress in holding people accountable for the world's worst crimes. The establishment of the International Criminal Court, the work of the UN tribunals for Yugoslavia and Rwanda, the hybrid ones in Sierra Leone and Cambodia, and the various Commissions of Experts and Inquiry, have proclaimed the will of the international community that such crimes should no longer go unpunished.

And yet they still do. [Ratko] Mladic and [Radovan] Karadzic [Bosnian Serb leaders during the Bosnian war], and the leaders of the Lord's Resistance Army [a guerrilla group in Uganda]—to name but a few—are still at large. Unless these indicted war criminals are brought to court, others tempted to emulate them will not be deterred.

Some say that justice must sometimes be sacrificed in the interests of peace. I question that. We have seen in Sierra Leone and in the Balkans that, on the contrary, justice is a fundamental component of peace. Indeed, justice has often bolstered lasting peace, by de-legitimizing and driving underground those individuals who pose the gravest threat to it. That is why there should never be amnesty for genocide, crimes against humanity and massive violations of human rights. That would only encourage today's mass murderers—and tomorrow's would-be mass murderers—to continue their vicious work.

Third, we need an anti-terrorism strategy that does not merely pay lip-service to the defense of human rights, but is built on it.

All states agreed last year that "terrorism in all its forms and manifestations, committed by whomever, wherever and for whatever purposes" is "one of the most serious threats to international peace and security." They were right. Terrorism in itself is an assault on the most basic human rights, starting with the right to life.

But states cannot fulfil that obligation by themselves violating human rights in the process. To do so means abandoning the moral high ground and playing into the hands of the terrorists. That is why secret prisons have no place in our struggle against terrorism, and why all places where terrorism suspects are detained must be accessible to the International Committee of the Red Cross. Leading promoters of human rights undermine their own influence when they fail to live up to these principles.

We must fight terrorism in conformity with international law, those parts of it that prohibit torture and inhumane treatment, and those that give anyone detained against his or her will the right to due process and the judgment of a court. Once we adopt a policy of making exceptions to these rules or excusing breaches of them, no matter how narrow, we are on a slippery slope. The line cannot be held half way down. We must defend it at the top.

Fourth, let's not content ourselves with grand statements of principle. We must work to make human rights a reality in each country.

Of course, protecting and promoting human rights is first and foremost a national responsibility. Every member state of the UN can draw on its own history to develop its own ways of upholding universal rights. But many states need help in doing this, and the UN system has a vital role to play.

Over the past decade, the UN has rapidly expanded its operational capacity for peace-keeping, and for development and humanitarian aid. Our capacity to protect and promote human rights now needs to catch up.

World leaders recognized this at last year's Summit. They agreed to double the budget of the Office of the High Commissioner for Human Rights over the next five years, and as a result the Office is now rapidly expanding. It is helping states build their capacity, giving them technical assistance where necessary, and bringing urgent situations to the attention of the international community. In some countries, such as Colombia and Nepal, its monitoring missions are making a very important contribution to the resolution of conflict.

But the Office's capacity is still far short of the needs it has to meet. I hope the quality of its work will persuade member states to authorize further increases in the years ahead.

Meanwhile, we must realize the promise of the Human Rights Council, which so far has clearly not justified all the hopes that so many of us placed in it.

Of course it's encouraging that the Council has now decided to hold a special session on Darfur next week. I hope against hope that it will find an effective way to deal with this burning issue.

But I am worried by its disproportionate focus on violations by Israel. Not that Israel should be given a free pass. Absolutely not. But the Council should give the same attention to grave violations committed by other states as well.

And I am also worried by the efforts of some Council members to weaken or abolish the system of Special Procedures—the independent mechanisms for reporting on violations of particular kinds, or in specific countries.

The Special Procedures are the crown jewel of the system. They, together with the High Commissioner and her staff, provide the independent expertise and judgment which is essential to effective human rights protection. They must not be politicized, or subjected to governmental control.

Instead, the Council's agenda should be broadened to reflect the actual abuses that occur in every part of the world. That means that the periodic review of all countries' human rights performance, which the Council will establish in the course of next year, must go beyond the work that the treaty bodies are already doing.

But of course the universal review cannot be a substitute for addressing country-specific situations. Many countries will continue to need technical assistance, or in-country monitoring mechanisms, or both, and some will continue to merit condemnation. Human rights abuses do not occur on paper. They are committed by real people, against real victims, in specific countries.

The world needs an intergovernmental body that deals with human rights. And it needs an intergovernmental body that works. That can only be achieved by a broader leadership. All states that truly believe in human rights, in every part of the world, must work together to transcend narrow interests and make the Human Rights Council live up to its promise. It is a historic opportunity—and history will not be kind if we let it pass.

The truth is, it's not enough just to have the right principles and say what we think should happen. We also have to ask who is going to make it happen. **Who can we look to for support? Who is going to insist that these principles are acted on?**

First, I look to Africa to take the lead.

Africa 's many conflicts are, almost invariably, accompanied by massive human rights violations. Unless Africa wholeheartedly embraces the inviolability of human rights, its struggle for security and development will not succeed.

As I said when I first addressed African heads of state, at Harare in 1997, to treat human rights as an imposition by the industrialized West, or a luxury of the rich countries for which Africa is not ready, demeans the yearning for human dignity that resides in every African heart. Human rights are, by definition, also African rights. It should be every African government's first priority to ensure that Africans can enjoy them.

South African heroes, like Nelson Mandela and Desmond Tutu, have shown the way. The African Union led the way among international organizations on the responsibility to protect, by proclaiming in its Constitutive Act "the right of the Union to intervene in a Member State . . . in respect of grave circumstances, namely war crimes, genocide and crimes against humanity." It has also tried harder than anyone else to act on that doctrine in Darfur, and to bring the former Chadian dictator Hissène Habré to justice.

This is encouraging, but much more needs to be done. In practice, many African governments are still resisting the responsibility to protect. Many, even among the most democratic, are still reluctant to play their role in the Human Rights Council by speaking out impartially against all abuses. They can, and must, do more.

Secondly, I look to the growing power of women—which means we must give priority to women's rights.

The "equal rights of men and women", promised by the UN Charter 61 years ago, are still far from being a reality. The UN can and must play a greater role in empowering women, and to do so, will require a strengthening of the UN's gender architecture. I strongly encourage member states to make this a real priority.

And thirdly, I look to civil society—which means you!

We need dedicated individuals and dynamic human rights defenders to hold governments to account. States' performance must be judged against their commitments, and they must be accountable both to their own people and to their peers in the international community. Thank God, then, for the growth in human rights NGOs we have witnessed in the last decade. There are now an estimated 26,000 of them worldwide, specializing in issues from trafficking to torture, from HIV/AIDS to the rights of children and migrants.

This community is the UN and its Member States' essential partner in the struggle for human rights. Without the information you collect, the treaty bodies would be helpless. Without the spotlight you shine, abuses would go unnoticed. In return, we must do everything to protect you from harassment, intimidation and reprisal, so you can carry on your vital work.

Dear friends,

Throughout my time in office my biggest concern has been to make the UN an organization that serves people, and treats them as people—that is, individual human beings, not abstractions or mere components of a state.

Of course I know that individuals don't exist in a vacuum. Man is a political and social animal, and individual men and women define their identity by their membership of groups. That's why human rights must always include rights to collective self-expression, which are especially important for minorities.

But no one's identity can be reduced to membership of a single group, be it ethnic, national, religious, or whatever. Each one of us is defined by a unique combination of characteristics that make up our personality. And it is that individual person whose rights must be preserved and respected.

The task of ensuring that that happens lies at the very heart of the UN's mission. And of all our tasks it is the one which can least safely be left in the hands of governments, or of a purely intergovernmental organization. In this task more than any other, the UN needs free spirits like yours to fill the leadership vacuum and hold world leaders and the United Nations to account.

So it's no mere figure of speech, dear friends, when I say that I leave the future of the UN's human rights work in your hands.

Thank you very much.

Source: United Nations. "Urging End to Impunity, Annan Sets Forth Ideas to Bolster UN Efforts to Protect Human Rights." December 8, 2006. www.un.org/News/ossg/sg/stories/statments_full.asp?statID=39 (accessed February 1, 2007).

Other Historic Documents of Interest

Microcredit Pioneer Yunus on Accepting the Nobel Peace Prize

December 10, 2006

■■■■■■■ THE DOCUMENT IN CONTEXT ■■■■■■■

The Nobel Peace Prize for 2006 was awarded to Muhammad Yunus, a Bangladeshi economist, and to the Grameen Bank he founded to make credit available to the very poor who did not qualify for traditional loans. Their work, the Norwegian Nobel Committee said, showed that "even the poorest of the poor can work to bring about their own development." Yunus, often referred to as "the banker to the poor," was an early pioneer of the belief that even very small loans could allow the poorest people to start and operate small businesses and help them leave poverty—and that the loans would be repaid. In little more than three decades, his microcredit system and other similar systems had become a popular antipoverty tool, making small loans to more than 100 million people, the vast majority of them women, in more than 130 countries.

In announcing the award on October 13, the Nobel committee contended that the link between peace and microcredit was more tangible than some might think. "Lasting peace cannot be achieved unless large population groups find ways in which to break out of poverty. Microcredit is one such means," the committee said. The committee also acknowledged that it wanted to showcase a positive influence from the Muslim world and try to narrow the gap between the West and Islam. The majority of Bangladeshis, like Yunus, were Muslim.

With the award, Yunus and the Grameen Bank became the latest in a series of people and organizations awarded the Nobel Peace Prize for work not directly related to conflict resolution. Other recent winners in this category included Wangiri Maathai of Kenya, recognized for her contributions to sustainable development; Shirin Ebadi, an advocate of human rights and political reform in Iran; and Médécins sans Frontières (Doctors without Borders), which provided emergency medical care to people affected by conflict and natural disaster. *(Ebadi award, Historic Documents of 2003, p. 1129; Maathai award, Historic Documents of 2004, p. 929)*

Beginning with One Village

The son of a prosperous goldsmith, Muhammad Yunus received a Ph.D. in economics in 1969 from Vanderbilt University in Nashville, Tennessee, where he was a Fulbright scholar, and soon returned home to join the economics faculty at Chittagong University, in eastern Bangladesh. As Yunus himself told the story, the Grameen Bank grew out of a visit he made in 1974 to the village of Jobra near the university. The country was experiencing a devastating famine, and Yunus said he found it "difficult to teach elegant theories of economics" in the classroom against such a backdrop. In the village he met a poor woman who wove bamboo stools. Because no traditional bank would lend her money to buy materials, she was forced to turn to a money lender who charged extortionate rates of interest that ate up nearly all her small profits, making the woman little more than "slave labor," in Yunus's view. Yunus did a little more legwork and found that forty-two women in the village had borrowed a total of $27 from local money lenders. He paid off the loans, and to his surprise found that the women paid him back on time. "Their poverty was not a personal problem due to laziness or lack of intelligence, but a structural one: lack of capital," Yunus said in a 1996 interview with a British newspaper. Yunus then began going to other villages and lending small amounts of money, mostly to poor women, with no collateral. Virtually every loan was repaid in full and on time.

In 1983 Yunus founded the Grameen Bank (rural or village bank, in Bengali) to make loans and take deposits from poor villagers who were not considered credit-worthy by regular banks and had no access to traditional credit. Social pressure, not tangible collateral, was used to guarantee the loans. Borrowers formed small groups to guarantee each other's loans, and none of them could receive another loan unless all of them were current on their payments. Most of the borrowers were women; the bank quickly learned that women had a better loan repayment record than men and tended to use the loans for the benefit of their families. As of October 2006, the bank, which was owned primarily by its borrowers, had 2,200 branches scattered across Bangladesh. It had loaned an estimated $5.7 billion to 6.6 million people since its founding, and it claimed a 98 percent rate of repayment. A typical loan was about $200; the bank charged competitive interest rates. Since 1995 the bank had made all its loans from the money it received in deposits and no longer required donor funding to remain viable.

As the bank grew, it expanded the types of loans it made. Some 640,000 housing units were constructed with Grameen Bank loans, and 7,000 student loans were made each year. The bank also awarded about 30,000 scholarships every year to children of the bank's borrowers. Since 2003 the Grameen Bank had been making interest-free loans to thousands of beggars in Bangladesh, each of whom received about $12 to buy candy, toys, and other items that they sold to supplement their begging. At the Nobel awards ceremony, Yunus proudly reported that the loans had enabled many of the beggars to stop begging for a living.

The microcredit idea caught on quickly in countries around the world, including the United States. One of the earliest to recognize the idea's potential was Bill Clinton, then governor of Arkansas. In 1985 he invited Yunus to help set up a microcredit program for low-income people in the state. Two decades later, as many as 400 organizations were providing some form of microfinance in the United States to help low-income people start or expand a small business. Worldwide more than 3,000 organizations had been set up to channel small loans to the poor. Many international aid agencies and philanthropic foundations were also involved in microcredit projects. Moreover, some of the world's biggest banks and investment funds were beginning to invest in microfinance programs, seeing them as a potential new area of profit as well as a means of contributing to society. Among these organizations were Citibank and TIAA-CREF, the teachers' pension plan, which each were investing $100 million in microcredit operations around the world. Yunus himself was wary of microcredit operations being considered a possible source of profits. "Maybe banks can make a profit from it," he told the *Christian Science Monitor* in October. "But this is what loan sharks do."

Yunus preferred that profits from microcredit operations be ploughed back into the operation or into what he called "social businesses." One example was Grameen Phone, a joint venture between Grameen Bank and Telenor ASA, the Norwegian state-controlled telecommunication company. The idea was for "telephone ladies" to borrow enough to buy mobile phones that they would then rent out. Since 1997 the program had grown to 10 million subscribers. The Grameen Bank had also entered a joint venture with the French company Danone to set up a yogurt factory that would produce inexpensive, fortified yogurt for malnourished children in the country. Yunus said his half share of the $l.4 million in prize money would be used for this business.

Yunus and the Grameen Bank were not without their detractors. Some said the bank had a high repayment rate because it reported a loan as overdue only after a client had missed ten or more payments. At one point in the early 2000s, nearly one-fifth of the bank's loans were overdue, a situation that was remedied. In the early days some Muslims also criticized the bank for encouraging women to defy traditional social customs by becoming their families' primary wage earners and by interacting with men outside their immediate family. Those misgivings gradually gave way as the women's families began to benefit from their participation and the poverty rate in Bangladesh began to decline. "This is a significant change empowering women," the director of a think tank in Dhaka said of the Grameen Bank. "I think Grameen is powering a social revolution in our country."

Accepting the Award

Yunus hailed the October 13 announcement of the peace prize as "fantastic news for all of us, for Grameen Bank, Bangladesh, and all the poor countries and all the poor people around the world." Many Bangladeshis said the recognition represented by the Nobel Peace Prize was the best thing to happen to their country since it won independence from Pakistan in 1971. The country could have been described "as closed because of happiness," Ole Danbolt Mjoes, head of the Nobel committee, said at the awards ceremony in Oslo on December 10.

Yunus used that occasion both to celebrate and to underline his belief that poverty was not only a threat to peace but also a root cause of terrorism. Noting that in 2000 the United Nations pledged to cut world poverty in half by 2015, Yunus lamented the fact that the terrorist attacks on the United States in 2001 had shifted the attention of world leaders from fighting a war on poverty to fighting a war on terror. "[P]utting resources into improving the lives of the poor people is a better strategy than spending it on guns," he said. Peace, he continued "should be understood in a human way, in a broad, social, political, and economic way." So, too, he said, should capitalism, the free market, and globalization, all with their emphasis on maximizing profits. The "rule of 'strongest takes it all' must be replaced by rules that ensure that the poorest have a place and a piece of the action," he said.

Following is the text of the address on December 10, 2006, in Oslo, Norway, by Muhammad Yunus, accepting the 2006 Nobel Peace Prize for his pioneering work in developing programs to lend money to the poor.

DOCUMENT

"The Nobel Lecture by Nobel Peace Prize Laureate 2006, M. Yunus"

Your Majesties, Your Royal Highnesses, Honorable Members of the Norwegian Nobel Committee, Excellencies, Ladies and Gentlemen,

Grameen Bank and I are deeply honoured to receive this most prestigious of awards. We are thrilled and overwhelmed by this honour. Since the Nobel Peace Prize was announced, I have received endless messages from around the world, but what moves me most are the calls I get almost daily, from the borrowers of Grameen Bank in remote Bangladeshi villages, who just want to say how proud they are to have received this recognition.

Nine elected representatives of the 7 million borrowers-cum-owners of Grameen Bank have accompanied me all the way to Oslo to receive the prize. I express thanks on their behalf to the Norwegian Nobel Committee for choosing Grameen Bank for this year's Nobel Peace Prize. By giving their institution the most prestigious prize in the world, you give them unparalleled honour. Thanks to your prize, nine proud women from the villages of Bangladesh are at the ceremony today as Nobel laureates, giving an altogether new meaning to the Nobel Peace Prize.

All borrowers of Grameen Bank are celebrating this day as the greatest day of their lives. They are gathering around the nearest television set in their villages all over Bangladesh, along with other villagers, to watch the proceedings of this ceremony.

This years' prize gives highest honour and dignity to the hundreds of millions of women all around the world who struggle every day to make a living and bring hope for a better life for their children. This is a historic moment for them.

Poverty Is a Threat to Peace

Ladies and Gentlemen:

By giving us this prize, the Norwegian Nobel Committee has given important support to the proposition that peace is inextricably linked to poverty. Poverty is a threat to peace.

World's income distribution gives a very telling story. Ninety four percent of the world income goes to 40 percent of the population while sixty percent of people live on only 6 per cent of world income. Half of the world population lives on two dollars a day. Over one billion people live on less than a dollar a day. This is no formula for peace.

The new millennium began with a great global dream. World leaders gathered at the United Nations in 2000 and adopted, among others, a historic goal to reduce poverty by half by 2015. Never in human history had such a bold goal been adopted by the entire world in one voice, one that specified time and size. But then came September 11 and the Iraq war, and suddenly the world became derailed from the pursuit of this dream, with the attention of world leaders shifting from the war on poverty to the war on terrorism. Till now over $530 billion has been spent on the war in Iraq by the USA alone.

I believe terrorism cannot be won over by military action. Terrorism must be condemned in the strongest language. We must stand solidly against it, and find all the means to end it. We must address the root causes of terrorism to end it for all time to come. I believe that putting resources into improving the lives of the poor people is a better strategy than spending it on guns.

Poverty Is Denial of All Human Rights

Peace should be understood in a human way in a broad social, political and economic way. Peace is threatened by unjust economic, social and political order, absence of democracy, environmental degradation and absence of human rights.

Poverty is the absence of all human rights. The frustrations, hostility and anger generated by abject poverty cannot sustain peace in any society. For building stable peace we must find ways to provide opportunities for people to live decent lives.

The creation of opportunities for the majority of people—the poor—is at the heart of the work that we have dedicated ourselves to during the past 30 years.

Grameen Bank

I became involved in the poverty issue not as a policymaker or a researcher. I became involved because poverty was all around me, and I could not turn away from it. In 1974, I found it difficult to teach elegant theories of economics in the university classroom, in the backdrop of a terrible famine in Bangladesh. Suddenly, I felt the emptiness of those theories in the face of crushing hunger and poverty. I wanted to do something immediate to help people around me, even if it was just one human being, to get through another day with a little more ease. That brought me face to face with poor people's struggle to find the tiniest amounts of money to support their efforts to eke out a living. I was shocked to discover a woman in the village, borrowing less than a dollar from the money-lender, on the condition that he would have the exclusive right to buy all she produces at the price he decides. This, to me, was a way of recruiting slave labor.

I decided to make a list of the victims of this money-lending "business" in the village next door to our campus. When my list was done, it had the names of 42 victims who borrowed a total amount of US $27. I offered US $27 from my own pocket to get these victims out of the clutches of those money-lenders. The excitement that was created among the people by this small action got me further involved in it. If I could make so many people so happy with such a tiny amount of money, why not do more of it?

That is what I have been trying to do ever since. The first thing I did was to try to persuade the bank located in the campus to lend money to the poor. But that did not work. The bank said that the poor were not creditworthy. After all my efforts, over several months, failed I offered to become a guarantor for the loans to the poor. I was stunned by the result. The poor paid back their loans, on time, every time! But still I kept confronting difficulties in expanding the program through the existing banks. That was when I decided to create a separate bank for the poor, and in 1983, I finally succeeded in doing that. I named it Grameen Bank or Village bank.

Today, Grameen Bank gives loans to nearly 7.0 million poor people, 97 per cent of whom are women, in 73,000 villages in Bangladesh. Grameen Bank gives collateral-free income generating, housing, student and micro-enterprise loans to the poor families and offers a host of attractive savings, pension funds and insurance products for its members. Since it introduced them in 1984, housing loans have been used to construct 640,000 houses. The legal ownership of these houses belongs to the women themselves. We focused on women because we found giving loans to women always brought more benefits to the family.

In a cumulative way the bank has given out loans totaling about US $6.0 billion. The repayment rate is 99%. Grameen Bank routinely makes profit. Financially, it is self-reliant and has not taken donor money since 1995. Deposits and own resources of Grameen Bank today amount to 143 per cent of all outstanding loans. According to Grameen Bank's internal survey, 58 per cent of our borrowers have crossed the poverty line.

Grameen Bank was born as a tiny homegrown project run with the help of several of my students, all local girls and boys. Three of these students are still with me in Grameen Bank, after all these years, as its topmost executives. They are here today to receive this honour you give us.

This idea, which began in Jobra, a small village in Bangladesh, has spread around the world and there are now Grameen type programs in almost every country.

Second Generation

It is 30 years now since we began. We keep looking at the children of our borrowers to see what has been the impact of our work on their lives. The women who are our borrowers always gave topmost priority to the children. One of the Sixteen Decisions developed and followed by them was to send children to school. Grameen Bank encouraged them, and before long all the children were going to school. Many of these children made it to the top of their class. We wanted to celebrate that, so we introduced scholarships for talented students. Grameen Bank now gives 30,000 scholarships every year.

Many of the children went on to higher education to become doctors, engineers, college teachers and other professionals. We introduced student loans to make it easy for Grameen students to complete higher education. Now some of them have PhD's. There are 13,000 students on student loans. Over 7,000 students are now added to this number annually.

We are creating a completely new generation that will be well equipped to take their families way out of the reach of poverty. We want to make a break in the historical continuation of poverty.

Beggars Can Turn to Business

In Bangladesh 80 percent of the poor families have already been reached with microcredit. We are hoping that by 2010, 100 per cent of the poor families will be reached.

Three years ago we started an exclusive programme focusing on the beggars. None of Grameen Bank's rules apply to them. Loans are interest-free; they can pay whatever amount they wish, whenever they wish. We gave them the idea to carry small merchandise such as snacks, toys or household items, when they went from house to house for begging. The idea worked. There are now 85,000 beggars in the program. About 5,000 of them have already stopped begging completely. Typical loan to a beggar is $12.

We encourage and support every conceivable intervention to help the poor fight out of poverty. We always advocate microcredit in addition to all other interventions, arguing that microcredit makes those interventions work better.

Information Technology for the Poor

Information and communication technology (ICT) is quickly changing the world, creating distanceless, borderless world of instantaneous communications. Increasingly, it is becoming less and less costly. I saw an opportunity for the poor people to change their lives if this technology could be brought to them to meet their needs.

As a first step to bring ICT to the poor we created a mobile phone company, Grameen Phone. We gave loans from Grameen Bank to the poor women to buy mobile phones to sell phone services in the villages. We saw the synergy between microcredit and ICT.

The phone business was a success and became a coveted enterprise for Grameen borrowers. Telephone-ladies quickly learned and innovated the ropes of the telephone business, and it has become the quickest way to get out of poverty and to earn social respectability. Today there are nearly 300,000 telephone ladies providing telephone service in all the villages of Bangladesh. Grameen Phone has more than 10 million subscribers, and is the largest mobile phone company in the country. Although the number of telephone-ladies is only a small fraction of the total number of subscribers, they generate 19 per cent of the revenue of the company. Out of the nine board members who are attending this grand ceremony today 4 are telephone-ladies.

Grameen Phone is a joint-venture company owned by Telenor of Norway and Grameen Telecom of Bangladesh. Telenor owns 62 per cent share of the company, Grameen Telecom owns 38 per cent. Our vision was to ultimately convert this company into a social business by giving majority ownership to the poor women of Grameen Bank. We are working towards that goal. Someday Grameen Phone will become another example of a big enterprise owned by the poor.

Free Market Economy

Capitalism centers on the free market. It is claimed that the freer the market, the better is the result of capitalism in solving the questions of what, how, and for whom. It is also claimed that the individual search for personal gains brings collective optimal result.

I am in favor of strengthening the freedom of the market. At the same time, I am very unhappy about the conceptual restrictions imposed on the players in the market. This originates from the assumption that entrepreneurs are one-dimensional human beings, who are dedicated to one mission in their business lives to maximize profit. This interpretation of capitalism insulates the entrepreneurs from all political, emotional, social, spiritual, environmental dimensions of their lives. This was done perhaps as a reasonable simplification, but it stripped away the very essentials of human life.

Human beings are a wonderful creation embodied with limitless human qualities and capabilities. Our theoretical constructs should make room for the blossoming of those qualities, not assume them away.

Many of the world's problems exist because of this restriction on the players of free-market. The world has not resolved the problem of crushing poverty that half of its population suffers. Healthcare remains out of the reach of the majority of the world population. The country with the richest and freest market fails to provide healthcare for one-fifth of its population.

We have remained so impressed by the success of the free-market that we never dared to express any doubt about our basic assumption. To make it worse, we worked extra hard to transform ourselves, as closely as possible, into the one-dimensional human beings as conceptualized in the theory, to allow smooth functioning of free market mechanism.

By defining "entrepreneur" in a broader way we can change the character of capitalism radically, and solve many of the unresolved social and economic problems within the scope of the free market. Let us suppose an entrepreneur, instead of having a single source of motivation (such as, maximizing profit), now has two sources of motivation, which are mutually exclusive, but equally compelling a) maximization of profit and b) doing good to people and the world.

Each type of motivation will lead to a separate kind of business. Let us call the first type of business a profit-maximizing business, and the second type of business as social business.

Social business will be a new kind of business introduced in the market place with the objective of making a difference in the world. Investors in the social business could get back their investment, but will not take any dividend from the company. Profit would be ploughed back into the company to expand its outreach and improve the quality of its product or service. A social business will be a non-loss, non-dividend company.

Once social business is recognized in law, many existing companies will come forward to create social businesses in addition to their foundation activities. Many activists from the non-profit sector will also find this an attractive option. Unlike the non-profit sector where one needs to collect donations to keep activities going, a social business will be self-sustaining and create surplus for expansion since it is a non-loss enterprise. Social business will go into a new type of capital market of its own, to raise capital.

Young people all around the world, particularly in rich countries, will find the concept of social business very appealing since it will give them a challenge to make a difference by using their creative talent. Many young people today feel frustrated because they cannot see any worthy challenge, which excites them, within the present capitalist world. Socialism gave them a dream to fight for. Young people dream about creating a perfect world of their own.

Almost all social and economic problems of the world will be addressed through social businesses. The challenge is to innovate business models and apply them to produce desired social results cost-effectively and efficiently. Healthcare for the poor, financial services for the poor, information technology for the poor, education and training for the poor, marketing for the poor, renewable energy—these are all exciting areas for social businesses.

Social business is important because it addresses very vital concerns of mankind. It can change the lives of the bottom 60 per cent of world population and help them to get out of poverty.

Grameen's Social Business

Even profit maximizing companies can be designed as social businesses by giving full or majority ownership to the poor. This constitutes a second type of social business. Grameen Bank falls under this category of social business.

The poor could get the shares of these companies as gifts by donors, or they could buy the shares with their own money. The borrowers with their own money buy Grameen Bank shares, which cannot be transferred to non-borrowers. A committed professional team does the day-to-day running of the bank.

Bilateral and multi-lateral donors could easily create this type of social business. When a donor gives a loan or a grant to build a bridge in the recipient country, it could create a "bridge company" owned by the local poor. A committed management company could be given the responsibility of running the company. Profit of the company will go to the local poor as dividend, and towards building more bridges. Many infrastructure projects, like roads, highways, airports, seaports, utility companies could all be built in this manner.

Grameen has created two social businesses of the first type. One is a yogurt factory, to produce fortified yogurt to bring nutrition to malnourished children, in a joint venture with Danone. It will continue to expand until all malnourished children of Bangladesh are reached with this yogurt. Another is a chain of eye-care hospitals. Each hospital will undertake 10,000 cataract surgeries per year at differentiated prices to the rich and the poor.

Social Stock Market

To connect investors with social businesses, we need to create social stock market where only the shares of social businesses will be traded. An investor will come to this stock-exchange with a clear intention of finding a social business, which has a mission of his liking. Anyone who wants to make money will go to the existing stock-market.

To enable a social stock-exchange to perform properly, we will need to create rating agencies, standardization of terminology, definitions, impact measurement tools, reporting formats, and new financial publications, such as, The Social Wall Street Journal. Business schools will offer courses and business management degrees on social businesses to train young managers how to manage social business enterprises in the most efficient manner, and, most of all, to inspire them to become social business entrepreneurs themselves.

Role of Social Businesses in Globalization

I support globalization and believe it can bring more benefits to the poor than its alternative. But it must be the right kind of globalization. To me, globalization is like a hundred-lane highway criss-crossing the world. If it is a free-for-all highway, its lanes will be taken over by the giant trucks from powerful economies. Bangladeshi rickshaw will be thrown off the highway. In order to have a win-win globalization we must have traffic rules, traffic police, and traffic authority for this global highway. Rule of "strongest takes it all" must be replaced by rules that ensure that the poorest have a place and piece of the action, without being elbowed out by the strong. Globalization must not become financial imperialism.

Powerful multi-national social businesses can be created to retain the benefit of globalization for the poor people and poor countries. Social businesses will either bring ownership to the poor people, or keep the profit within the poor countries, since taking dividends will not be their objective. Direct foreign investment by foreign social businesses will be exciting news for recipient countries. Building strong economies in the poor countries by protecting their national interest from plundering companies will be a major area of interest for the social businesses.

We Create What We Want

We get what we want, or what we don't refuse. We accept the fact that we will always have poor people around us, and that poverty is part of human destiny. This is precisely why we continue to have poor people around us. If we firmly believe that poverty is unacceptable to us, and that it should not belong to a civilized society, we would have built appropriate institutions and policies to create a poverty-free world.

We wanted to go to the moon, so we went there. We achieve what we want to achieve. If we are not achieving something, it is because we have not put our minds to it. We create what we want.

What we want and how we get to it depends on our mindsets. It is extremely difficult to change mindsets once they are formed. We create the world in accordance with our mindset. We need to invent ways to change our perspective continually and reconfigure our mindset quickly as new knowledge emerges. We can reconfigure our world if we can reconfigure our mindset.

We Can Put Poverty in the Museums

I believe that we can create a poverty-free world because poverty is not created by poor people. It has been created and sustained by the economic and social system that we have designed for ourselves; the institutions and concepts that make up that system; the policies that we pursue.

Poverty is created because we built our theoretical framework on assumptions which under-estimates human capacity, by designing concepts, which are too narrow (such as concept of business, credit-worthiness, entrepreneurship, employment) or developing institutions, which remain half-done (such as financial institutions, where poor are left out). Poverty is caused by the failure at the conceptual level, rather than any lack of capability on the part of people.

I firmly believe that we can create a poverty-free world if we collectively believe in it. In a poverty-free world, the only place you would be able to see poverty is in the poverty museums. When school children take a tour of the poverty museums, they would be horrified to see the misery and indignity that some human beings had to go through. They would blame their forefathers for tolerating this inhuman condition, which existed for so long, for so many people. A human being is born into this world fully equipped not only to take care of him or herself, but also to contribute to enlarging the well being of the world as a whole. Some get the chance to explore their potential to some degree, but many others never get any opportunity, during their lifetime, to unwrap the wonderful gift they were born with. They die unexplored and the world remains deprived of their creativity, and their contribution.

Grameen has given me an unshakeable faith in the creativity of human beings. This has led me to believe that human beings are not born to suffer the misery of hunger and poverty.

To me poor people are like bonsai trees. When you plant the best seed of the tallest tree in a flower-pot, you get a replica of the tallest tree, only inches tall. There is nothing wrong with the seed you planted, only the soil-base that is too inadequate. Poor people are bonsai people. There is nothing wrong in their seeds. Simply, society never gave them the base to grow on. All it needs to get the poor people out of poverty for us to create an enabling environment for them. Once the poor can unleash their energy and creativity, poverty will disappear very quickly.

Let us join hands to give every human being a fair chance to unleash their energy and creativity.

Ladies and Gentlemen,

Let me conclude by expressing my deep gratitude to the Norwegian Nobel Committee for recognizing that poor people, and especially poor women, have both the potential and the right to live a decent life, and that microcredit helps to unleash that potential.

I believe this honor that you give us will inspire many more bold initiatives around the world to make a historical breakthrough in ending global poverty.

Thank you very much.

Source: Nobel Foundation. "The Nobel Lecture Given by the Nobel Peace Prize Laureate 2006, Muhammad Yunus." December 10, 2006. Oslo, Norway. nobelpeaceprize.org/eng_lect_2006b.html (accessed December 19, 2006).

UN Security Council on Sanctions against Iran

December 23, 2006

Nearly four years after Iran was found to be conducting secret research apparently aimed at developing nuclear weapons, the United Nations Security Council in December 2006 adopted financial and trade sanctions to force Iran to stop its weapons program. The imposition of sanctions came after numerous diplomatic efforts had failed to achieve that goal. The diplomacy was led by European nations and had reluctant support from the administration of U.S. president George W. Bush, who repeatedly suggested he was considering military action as a final resort to prevent Iran from obtaining nuclear weapons.

At year's end most Western experts said they believed Iran was still several years away from being able to produce a militarily useful nuclear bomb. According to information gleaned from Iran's nuclear facilities by the International Atomic Energy Agency (IAEA), Iran was in the early stages of mastering the techniques of enriching uranium, one of the essential fuels for nuclear power reactors and for nuclear weapons. The UN sanctions imposed in December were intended to slow Iran's progress by tightening existing prohibitions on its purchase of the necessary materials and technology. *(Background, Historic Documents of 2005, p. 589)*

The year's developments on this weapons issue took place against a backdrop of growing confidence among Iranian leaders about the country's role in the Middle East. By 2006 it was clear that Iran would have some bearing on the outcome of the U.S. enterprise in Iraq, and Iran was gaining influence elsewhere in the region in large part through its support for Shiite extremist movements, notably the Hezbollah militia in Lebanon.

Iran was one of two countries that found itself caught up in nuclear controversy. North Korea, which had a much more advanced weapons program, tested a small nuclear bomb in October. The Security Council quickly adopted a resolution imposing trade sanctions against that country. By contrast, India, which had incurred the world's wrath when it tested a nuclear bomb in 1974, was given a large measure of legitimacy as a nuclear power in 2006 when the U.S. Congress approved a plan by President Bush to sell it nuclear supplies and possibly even entire power plants.

Iran Moves Forward, Step by Step

International attempts to thwart Iran's nuclear ambitions had involved a complex process in which Western diplomats sought through diplomacy and pressure to impose restrictions on Iranian behavior. Iran staunchly resisted the restrictions but stopped its nuclear work in late 2004 only to resume it later. The Bush administration periodically threatened economic sanctions or possibly military action against Iran even while gradually moving to accept the diplomatic approach favored by Europeans. Meanwhile, China and Russia generally disapproved of what the other parties—particularly Iran and the United States—were doing.

The basic issue was Iran's contention that it had a sovereign right to develop its nuclear program as it saw fit, in this case to enrich uranium, which was the basic fuel for nuclear reactors; uranium enriched to a very high level also was a fuel for nuclear weapons. Iranian leaders repeatedly insisted they were not developing weapons—a denial that officials in the United States and Europe refused to believe. Because Iran was a party to the 1970 Nuclear Nonproliferation Treaty, it had agreed to international inspections of its nuclear industry but for years had hidden key components of its nuclear work from the UN's inspection agency, the IAEA.

After Iran's violations were uncovered early in 2003, all subsequent diplomacy was based on getting Iran to stop any work that could lead to weapons production and to ensure that all its nuclear installations were subject to unrestricted IAEA inspections. Diplomats from the European Union (EU), led by Britain, France, and Germany, had negotiated with Iran since 2003 and had offered various incentives for it to stop its nuclear research, including technical aid for Iran's civilian nuclear power industry. Russia offered to conduct uranium enrichment on Iran's behalf, thus allowing Iran to have the fuel it said it needed but not the technology it could use to develop weapons.

From the start of 2006, Iran made it clear that it did not intend to give into international pressure. On January 10, Iran announced that it had removed IAEA inspection seals at three facilities where uranium enrichment work had been suspended since late 2004 as a result of previous negotiations. Iran had already restarted uranium conversion work at a fourth facility, in Isfahan, the previous August. This latest action brought angry reactions, including even from Russia, which had substantial trade dealings with Iran and was building a civilian nuclear power plant there in Bushehr under a $800 million contract. European officials said two days later they were giving up on negotiations with Iran and would push for a condemnation of Tehran's action by the board of the IAEA at an emergency meeting in February; such a step would send the issue to the UN Security Council for possible punishment, including sanctions.

In the first of several diplomatic compromises during the year, the European nations, China, Russia, and the United States agreed on January 31 that the IAEA should report Iran's actions to the Security Council. The IAEA board followed suit on February 4, for the first time saying that Iran's "many failures and breaches of its obligations to comply" with the Nonproliferation Treaty warranted a review by the Security Council. Even so, the board withheld sending a formal report to the Security Council for one month, thus giving Iran time to back down. China and Russia supported this step, marking a significant break from their past reluctance to take any action seen as punishing Tehran. Iran promptly announced that it had resumed uranium enrichment. Many Western experts expressed skepticism that Iran really was doing any serious enrichment, but the announcement represented another escalation in the diplomatic tug of war.

Another round of diplomacy made no headway, especially after Iran again rejected Russia's offer to enrich uranium on its behalf. The IAEA board again voted, on March 9, to refer Iran to the UN Security Council. The council officially took up the Iran issue, for the first time ever, on March 29. In a compromise that reflected continued unwillingness at that point by China and Russia to punish Iran, the council adopted, by consensus but without a formal vote, a statement demanding that Iran end its uranium enrichment work immediately. The council asked for another report on the matter from the IAEA in thirty days—in effect setting an April 28 deadline for Iran to stop its nuclear work.

Iran denounced the Security Council statement and said it would press ahead with its nuclear activities. An even more defiant note came two days later with the test-firing of a missile that, the Iranian military said, could carry multiple warheads and evade radar.

In what appeared to be a public relations move to demonstrate that the nuclear question was answered, Iranian president Mahmoud Ahmadinejad headlined a televised celebration on April 11, during which he said: "Iran has joined the nuclear nations of the world." Ahmadinejad was careful to say that Iran had achieved "the desired enrichment [of uranium] for nuclear power plants"—not nuclear weapons. Even so, the event appeared calculated to assure Iranians, and the rest of the world, that efforts to block Iran's nuclear ambitions already had failed.

As expected, the IAEA reported on April 28 that Iran had failed to comply with the UN Security Council's demand that it halt its uranium enrichment programs and had, instead, accelerated that work. The report also said Iran had acted in numerous ways to hamper the IAEA's work of monitoring the nuclear installations.

Once again, diplomats began drafting new proposals in the hope that the major powers could agree on a unified approach for the Security Council. And, once again, China and Russia—each of which had veto power in the council—were reluctant to take strong action that might punish Iran. At this point, Ahmadinejad sent President Bush a letter asking for a "dialogue." This was the first direct contact with the United States by an Iranian leader in years, but the Bush administration dismissed it as a public relations stunt.

Conditional Offers

After a reportedly extensive high-level debate within his administration, President Bush in late May agreed to reverse long-standing U.S. policy against direct involvement in negotiations with Iran. Secretary of State Condoleezza Rice announced on May 31 that the United States had agreed to join the European nations in their negotiations—but only after Iran had resumed its suspension of uranium enrichment. Rice met in Vienna the next day, June 1, with her counterparts from China, the three lead European allies, and Russia. The six countries on June 1 agreed to a package of incentives that were not announced at the time but reportedly included European aid for the construction in Iran of light-water nuclear reactors (a type that did not produce nuclear fuel useful for weapons), a guaranteed five-year supply of fuel for nuclear power plants, and spare parts for Iranian commercial aircraft.

These incentives would be offered if Iran suspended its uranium enrichment activities at least temporarily while negotiations continued on the underlying issues. British foreign secretary Margaret Beckett said the proposals "offer Iran the chance to reach a negotiated agreement based on cooperation." The diplomats said Iran would face "costs" if it rejected the offer, but they refused to say specifically what those costs might be; this was in deference to Chinese and Russian objections to talk of sanctions. The package of incentives was similar to one the Europeans had offered Iran in August 2005, but this new offer was substantially different in that China, Russia, and the United States had joined in it.

Javier Solana, the foreign policy representative of the European Union, formally presented the offer to Iran on June 6. The Iranian officials took their time in responding; in fact, they told Solana and others that a response would not come before mid-August. That proposed delay gave the United States the opening it had sought to convince China, Russia, and the three European allies to step up the pressure. Meeting in Paris on July 12, diplomats from the six countries agreed to return to the UN Security Council for "adoption of measures" that would penalize Iran. Even this threat brought no definitive response from Tehran. On July 31 the Security Council adopted Resolution 1696, which demanded that Iran suspend its uranium enrichment work by August 31 or face the possibility of sanctions. The vote was 14–1, with the sole no vote coming from Qatar. This was the first time China and Russia had supported a resolution with an explicit threat of sanctions against Iran. The Iranian ambassador, Javad Zarif, called the resolution "unwarranted and void of any legal basis or practical utility," and the next day Ahmadinejad defiantly said Iran "considers the peaceful uses of nuclear fuel production technology its right."

Adoption of the UN resolution took place in the midst of the war that broke out mid-July pitting Israel against the forces of Hezbollah, the Iranian-backed Shiite militia in Lebanon. By the end of hostilities in mid-August, more than 1,200 people were killed, most of them in Lebanon. While this conflict ended in what most observes called a "draw," Hezbollah was widely perceived in the region as the psychological victor, thereby adding to the stature of Iran, which reportedly supplied nearly all the group's weapons.

Iranian Defiance

Any hope that Iran would back down in the face of the UN action turned out to be in vain. On August 21, IAEA officials said Iran had refused, for the first time in three years, to allow inspectors into an underground uranium enrichment facility at Natanz, south of Tehran. The next day, the Iranian government finally responded to the offer it had been given more than six weeks earlier. In a twenty-one-page document, Iran said it would engage in "serious talks" on the nuclear issue but would not suspend its uranium enrichment. Western diplomats said Iran was stalling in hopes that China and Russia would block any definitive move toward meaningful sanctions.

On August 29, just two days before the UN's deadline for Iran to suspend its nuclear work, Ahmadinejad held a lengthy news conference in Tehran, during which he challenged President Bush to a televised debate. A White House official dismissed the idea as a "diversion" from the nuclear issue. Speaking to an American Legion convention in Salt Lake City two days later, Bush denounced what he called "defiance and delay" by Iran. "There must be consequences and we must not allow Iran to develop a nuclear weapon," he said.

Also on August 31, the IAEA issued a report saying its inspectors had found small quantities of highly enriched uranium at Iranian facilities, and it dismissed Iran's claims that the material had come from Pakistan.

Back to the UN

Iran's refusal to meet the Security Council's August 31 deadline put the matter back in the hands of China, the European countries, Russia, and the United States—the parties that had crafted the negotiating offer to Iran. This time, because the Security Council had warned of possible sanctions, the stakes were higher, and so the diplomacy was more difficult. At the outset, European and Russian officials said they were not yet ready to impose the sanctions the Security Council had threatened at the end of July. Meeting at the UN on September 20, Rice and her counterparts from the five other countries agreed to give Iran two more weeks to agree to suspend its nuclear work; in essence, this represented the fourth deadline Iran had been given during the year.

As this latest deadline approached, EU negotiator Solana told the European Parliament on October 4 that the talks with Iran were near an end. "Dialogue could not last forever," he said. Solana's warning was coupled with a statement on October 23 from IAEA director Mohammed ElBaradei that Iran had not met the latest deadline and instead had built a second line of centrifuges for enriching uranium at its plant in Natanz. This line was far too small to allow industrial-scale production, but experts said it would help Iran perfect the difficult processes necessary for making fuel for weapons.

In what was widely seen as another show of defiance, Iran on November 2 test-fired several medium-range missiles capable of delivering small warheads throughout much of the Middle East, including all of Israel, the Persian Gulf, and much of Turkey. Iran had tested one of the missile types, known as the Shahad-3, in previous years, but the timing of this test appeared to be linked to the nuclear weapons controversy.

It became clear early in November that the unity behind the earlier Security Council ultimatum to Iran had papered over continuing disagreements over how to deal with Iran. Ambassadors from the six key nations met at the United Nations on November 7 and failed to agree on a follow-up resolution. The United States once again was pushing for tough sanctions, China and Russia were resisting any punitive sanctions, and the European nations found themselves in the middle.

This round of diplomacy finally came to an end on December 23 when the Security Council unanimously adopted its second resolution of the year on Iran. Resolution 1737 required Iran to suspend work on its uranium enrichment program "without delay" and to resume its full cooperation with IAEA inspections. The resolution for the first time imposed sanctions against Iran by prohibiting exports to Iran of materials and technology used for nuclear weapons and ballistic missile programs; it also ordered an international freeze on the assets of ten Iranian government agencies and companies as well as twelve officials and businessmen involved in the nuclear and missile programs. At Russia's insistence, the resolution did not include a U.S. proposal for a ban on international travel by those officials and businessmen. The resolution also did not affect elements of Iran's nuclear industry that had not come under question, notably the power plant in Bushehr that was being built by Russia.

Although the resolution was substantially weaker than previous versions the Bush administration had advocated, administration officials praised it as a tough step that would damage Iran's ability to build nuclear weapons. Nicholas Burns, the undersecretary of state for political affairs, said the resolution would help U.S. efforts to convince other countries, and international financial institutions, to use financial leverage on Iran. The following day, Ahmadinejad said the resolution would have no effect on his country. "The nuclear technology is our right, and no one can take it away from us," he said in comments aimed at the United States and its allies. "You will soon regret this superficial action."

Iran's parliament on December 27 adopted the final version of a bill that appeared aimed at further limiting cooperation with the IAEA. The bill called on the government to "revise its cooperation" with the UN agency; that provision was not defined but it clearly was meant to reduce the freedom of IAEA inspectors. The parliament did not act on a more drastic proposal by some members to withdraw Iran's approval of the Nuclear Nonproliferation Treaty, a step that North Korea had taken early in 2003 and, if duplicated by Tehran, would have meant the end of Iran's cooperation with the IAEA and the expulsion of that agency's inspectors.

Following is the text of United Nations Security Council Resolution 1737, adopted unanimously on December 23, 2006, calling on Iran to suspend its uranium enrichment programs and imposing financial and trade sanctions against companies and individuals involved in that enrichment work.

DOCUMENT

"Resolution 1737 (2006)"

The Security Council,

Recalling the Statement of its President, of 29 March 2006, and its resolution 1696 (2006) of 31 July 2006,

Reaffirming its commitment to the Treaty on the Non-Proliferation of Nuclear Weapons, and recalling the right of States Party, in conformity with Articles I and II of that Treaty, to develop research, production and use of nuclear energy for peaceful purposes without discrimination,

Reiterating its serious concern over the many reports of the IAEA Director General and resolutions of the IAEA [International Atomic Energy Agency] Board of Governors related to Iran's nuclear program, reported to it by the IAEA Director General, including IAEA Board resolution,

Reiterating its serious concern that the IAEA Director General's report of 27 February 2006 lists a number of outstanding issues and concerns on Iran's nuclear program, including topics which could have a military nuclear dimension, and that the IAEA is unable to conclude that there are no undeclared nuclear materials or activities in Iran,

Reiterating its serious concern over the IAEA Director General's report of 28 April 2006 and its findings, including that, after more than three years of Agency efforts to seek clarity about all aspects of Iran's nuclear program, the existing gaps in knowledge continue to be a matter of concern, and that the IAEA is unable to make progress in its efforts to provide assurances about the absence of undeclared nuclear material and activities in Iran,

Noting with serious concern that, as confirmed by the IAEA Director General's reports of 8 June 2006, 31 August 2006, and 14 November 2006, Iran has not established full and sustained suspension of all enrichment-related and reprocessing activities as set out in resolution 1696 (2006), nor resumed its cooperation with the IAEA under the Additional Protocol, nor taken the other steps required of it by the IAEA Board of Governors, nor complied with the provisions of Security Council resolution 1696 (2006) and which are essential to build confidence, and *deploring* Iran's refusal to take these steps,

Emphasizing the importance of political and diplomatic efforts to find a negotiated solution guaranteeing that Iran's nuclear program is exclusively for peaceful purposes, and *noting* that such a solution would benefit nuclear nonproliferation elsewhere, and *welcoming* the continuing commitment of China, France, Germany, the Russian Federation, the United Kingdom and the United States, with the support of the European Union's High Representative to seek a negotiated solution,

Determined to give effect to its decisions by adopting appropriate measures to persuade Iran to comply with resolution 1696 (2006) and with the requirements of the IAEA, and also to constrain Iran's development of sensitive technologies in support of its nuclear and missile programs, until such time as the Security Council determines that the objectives of this resolution have been met,

Concerned by the proliferation risks presented by the Iranian nuclear program and, in this context, by Iran's continuing failure to meet the requirements of the IAEA Board of Governors and to comply with the provisions of Security Council resolution 1696 (2006), *mindful* of its primary responsibility under the Charter of the United Nations for the maintenance of international peace and security,

Acting under Article 41 of Chapter VII of the Charter of the United Nations,

1. *Affirms* that Iran shall without further delay take the steps required by the IAEA Board of Governors in its resolution, which are essential to build confidence in the exclusively peaceful purpose of its nuclear program and to resolve outstanding questions;

2. *Decides*, in this context, that Iran shall without further delay suspend the following proliferation sensitive nuclear activities:

(a) all enrichment-related and reprocessing activities, including research and development, to be verified by the IAEA; and

(b) work on all heavy water-related projects, including the construction of a research reactor moderated by heavy water, also to be verified by the IAEA;

3. *Decides* that all States shall take the necessary measures to prevent the supply, sale or transfer directly or indirectly from their territories, or by their nationals or using their flag vessels or aircraft to, or for the use in or benefit of, Iran, and whether or not originating in their territories, of all items, materials, equipment, goods and technology which could contribute to Iran's enrichment-related, reprocessing or heavy water-related activities, or to the development of nuclear weapon delivery systems, namely:

(a) those set out in sections B.2, B.3, B.4, B.5, B.6 and B.7 of INFCIRC/254/Rev.8/Part 1 in document S/2006/814;

(b) those set out in sections A.1 and B.1 of INFCIRC/254/Rev.8/Part 1 in document S/2006/814, except the supply, sale or transfer of:

(i) equipment covered by B.1 when such equipment is for light water reactors;

(ii) low-enriched uranium covered by A.1.2 when it is incorporated in assembled nuclear fuel elements for such reactors;

(c) those set out in document S/2006/815, except the supply, sale or transfer of items covered by 19.A.3 of Category II;

(d) any additional items, materials, equipment, goods and technology, determined as necessary by the Security Council or the Committee established by paragraph 18 below (herein "the Committee"), which could contribute to enrichment-related, or reprocessing, or heavy water-related activities, or to the development of nuclear weapon delivery systems;

4. *Decides* that all States shall take the necessary measures to prevent the supply, sale or transfer directly or indirectly from their territories, or by their nationals or using their flag

vessels or aircraft to, or for the use in or benefit of, Iran, and whether or not originating in their territories, of the following items, materials, equipment, goods and technology:

(a) those set out in INFCIRC/254/Rev.7/Part2 of document S/2006/814 if the State determines that they would contribute to enrichment-related, reprocessing or heavy water-related activities;

(b) any other items not listed in documents S/2006/814 or S/2006/815 if the State determines that they would contribute to enrichment-related, reprocessing or heavy water-related activities, or to the development of nuclear weapon delivery systems;

(c) any further items if the State determines that they would contribute to the pursuit of activities related to other topics about which the IAEA has expressed concerns or identified as outstanding;

5. *Decides* that, for the supply, sale or transfer of all items, materials, equipment, goods and technology covered by documents S/2006/814 and S/2006/815 the export of which to Iran is not prohibited by subparagraphs 3 (b), 3 (c) or 4 (a) above, States shall ensure that:

(a) the requirements, as appropriate, of the Guidelines as set out in documents S/2006/814 and S/2006/985 have been met; and

(b) they have obtained and are in a position to exercise effectively a right to verify the end-use and end-use location of any supplied item; and

(c) they notify the Committee within ten days of the supply, sale or transfer; and

(d) in the case of items, materials, equipment, goods and technology contained in document S/2006/814, they also notify the IAEA within ten days of the supply, sale or transfer;

6. *Decides* that all States shall also take the necessary measures to prevent the provision to Iran of any technical assistance or training, financial assistance, investment, brokering or other services, and the transfer of financial resources or services, related to the supply, sale, transfer, manufacture or use of the prohibited items, materials, equipment, goods and technology specified in paragraphs 3 and 4 above;

7. *Decides* that Iran shall not export any of the items in documents S/2006/814 and S/2006/815 and that all Member States shall prohibit the procurement of such items from Iran by their nationals, or using their flag vessels or aircraft, and whether or not originating in the territory of Iran;

8. *Decides* that Iran shall provide such access and cooperation as the IAEA requests to be able to verify the suspension outlined in paragraph 2 and to resolve all outstanding issues, as identified in IAEA reports, and *calls upon* Iran to ratify promptly the Additional Protocol;

9. *Decides* that the measures imposed by paragraphs 3, 4 and 6 above shall not apply where the Committee determines in advance and on a case-by-case basis that such supply, sale, transfer or provision of such items or assistance would clearly not contribute to the development of Iran's technologies in support of its proliferation sensitive nuclear activities and of development of nuclear weapon delivery systems, including where such items or assistance are for food, agricultural, medical or other humanitarian purposes, provided that:

(a) contracts for delivery of such items or assistance include appropriate end-user guarantees; and

(b) Iran has committed not to use such items in proliferation sensitive nuclear activities or for development of nuclear weapon delivery systems;

10. *Calls upon* all States to exercise vigilance regarding the entry into or transit through their territories of individuals who are engaged in, directly associated with or providing support for Iran's proliferation sensitive nuclear activities or for the development of nuclear weapon delivery systems, and *decides* in this regard that all States shall notify the Committee of the entry into or transit through their territories of the persons designated in the Annex to this resolution (herein "the Annex"), as well as of additional persons designated by the Security Council or the Committee as being engaged in, directly associated with or providing support for Iran's proliferation sensitive nuclear activities and for the development of nuclear weapon delivery systems, including through the involvement in procurement of the prohibited items, goods, equipment, materials and technology specified by and under the measures in paragraphs 3 and 4 above, except where such travel is for activities directly related to the items in subparagraphs 3 (b) (i) and (ii) above;

11. *Underlines* that nothing in the above paragraph requires a State to refuse its own nationals entry into its territory, and that all States shall, in the implementation of the above paragraph, take into account humanitarian considerations as well as the necessity to meet the objectives of this resolution, including where Article XV of the IAEA Statute is engaged;

12. *Decides* that all States shall freeze the funds, other financial assets and economic resources which are on their territories at the date of adoption of this resolution or at any time thereafter, that are owned or controlled by the persons or entities designated in the Annex, as well as those of additional persons or entities designated by the Security Council or by the Committee as being engaged in, directly associated with or providing support for Iran's proliferation sensitive nuclear activities or the development of nuclear weapon delivery systems, or by persons or entities acting on their behalf or at their direction, or by entities owned or controlled by them, including through illicit means, and that the measures in this paragraph shall cease to apply in respect of such persons or entities if, and at such time as, the Security Council or the Committee removes them from the Annex, and *decides further* that all States shall ensure that any funds, financial assets or economic resources are prevented from being made available by their nationals or by any persons or entities within their territories, to or for the benefit of these persons and entities;

13. *Decides* that the measures imposed by paragraph 12 above do not apply to funds, other financial assets or economic resources that have been determined by relevant States:

(a) to be necessary for basic expenses, including payment for foodstuffs, rent or mortgage, medicines and medical treatment, taxes, insurance premiums, and public utility charges or exclusively for payment of reasonable professional fees and reimbursement of incurred expenses associated with the provision of legal services, or fees or service charges, in accordance with national laws, for routine holding or maintenance of frozen funds, other financial assets and economic resources, after notification by the relevant States to the Committee of the intention to authorize, where appropriate, access to such funds, other financial assets or economic resources and in the absence of a negative decision by the Committee within five working days of such notification;

(b) to be necessary for extraordinary expenses, provided that such determination has been notified by the relevant States to the Committee and has been approved by the Committee;

(c) to be the subject of a judicial, administrative or arbitral lien or judgment, in which case the funds, other financial assets and economic resources may be used to satisfy that lien or judgment provided that the lien or judgment was entered into prior to the date of the present resolution, is not for the benefit of a person or entity designated pursuant to paragraphs 10 and 12 above, and has been notified by the relevant States to the Committee;

(d) to be necessary for activities directly related to the items specified in sub-paragraphs 3 (b) (i) and (ii) and have been notified by the relevant States to the Committee;

14. *Decides* that States may permit the addition to the accounts frozen pursuant to the provisions of paragraph 12 above of interests or other earnings due on those accounts or payments due under contracts, agreements or obligations that arose prior to the date on which those accounts became subject to the provisions of this resolution, provided that any such interest, other earnings and payments continue to be subject to these provisions and are frozen;

15. *Decides* that the measures in paragraph 12 above shall not prevent a designated person or entity from making payment due under a contract entered into prior to the listing of such a person or entity, provided that the relevant States have determined that:

(a) the contract is not related to any of the prohibited items, materials, equipment, goods, technologies, assistance, training, financial assistance, investment, brokering or services referred to in paragraphs 3, 4 and 6 above;

(b) the payment is not directly or indirectly received by a person or entity designated pursuant to paragraph 12 above;

and after notification by the relevant States to the Committee of the intention to make or receive such payments or to authorize, where appropriate, the unfreezing of funds, other financial assets or economic resources for this purpose, ten working days prior to such authorization;

16. *Decides* that technical cooperation provided to Iran by the IAEA or under its auspices shall only be for food, agricultural, medical, safety or other humanitarian purposes, or where it is necessary for projects directly related to the items specified in sub-paragraphs 3 (b) (i) and (ii) above, but that no such technical cooperation shall be provided that relates to the proliferation sensitive nuclear activities set out in paragraph 2 above;

17. *Calls upon* all States to exercise vigilance and prevent specialized teaching or training of Iranian nationals, within their territories or by their nationals, of disciplines which would contribute to Iran's proliferation sensitive nuclear activities and development of nuclear weapon delivery systems;

18. *Decides* to establish, in accordance with rule 28 of its provisional rules of procedure, a Committee of the Security Council consisting of all the members of the Council, to undertake the following tasks:

(a) to seek from all States, in particular those in the region and those producing the items, materials, equipment, goods and technology referred to in paragraphs 3 and 4 above, information regarding the actions taken by them to implement effectively the measures imposed by paragraphs 3, 4, 5, 6, 7, 8, 10 and 12 of this resolution and whatever further information it may consider useful in this regard;

(b) to seek from the secretariat of the IAEA information regarding the actions taken by the IAEA to implement effectively the measures imposed by paragraph 16 of this resolution and whatever further information it may consider useful in this regard;

(c) to examine and take appropriate action on information regarding alleged violations of measures imposed by paragraphs 3, 4, 5, 6, 7, 8, 10 and 12 of this resolution;

(d) to consider and decide upon requests for exemptions set out in paragraphs 9, 13 and 15 above;

(e) to determine as may be necessary additional items, materials, equipment, goods and technology to be specified for the purpose of paragraph 3 above;

(f) to designate as may be necessary additional individuals and entities subject to the measures imposed by paragraphs 10 and 12 above;

(g) to promulgate guidelines as may be necessary to facilitate the implementation of the measures imposed by this resolution and include in such guidelines a requirement on States to provide information where possible as to why any individuals and/or entities meet the criteria set out in paragraphs 10 and 12 and any relevant identifying information;

(h) to report at least every 90 days to the Security Council on its work and on the implementation of this resolution, with its observations and recommendations, in particular on ways to strengthen the effectiveness of the measures imposed by paragraphs 3, 4, 5, 6, 7, 8, 10 and 12 above;

19. *Decides* that all States shall report to the Committee within 60 days of the adoption of this resolution on the steps they have taken with a view to implementing effectively paragraphs 3, 4, 5, 6, 7, 8, 10, 12 and 17 above;

20. *Expresses* the conviction that the suspension set out in paragraph 2 above as well as full, verified Iranian compliance with the requirements set out by the IAEA Board of Governors, would contribute to a diplomatic, negotiated solution that guarantees Iran's nuclear program is for exclusively peaceful purposes, *underlines* the willingness of the international community to work positively for such a solution, *encourages* Iran, in conforming to the above provisions, to re-engage with the international community and with the IAEA, and *stresses* that such engagement will be beneficial to Iran;

21. *Welcomes* the commitment of China, France, Germany, the Russian Federation, the United Kingdom and the United States, with the support of the European Union's High Representative, to a negotiated solution to this issue and encourages Iran to engage with their June 2006 proposals (S/2006/521), which were endorsed by the Security Council in resolution 1696 (2006), for a long-term comprehensive agreement which would allow for the development of relations and cooperation with Iran based on mutual respect and the establishment of international confidence in the exclusively peaceful nature of Iran's nuclear program;

22. *Reiterates* its determination to reinforce the authority of the IAEA, strongly supports the role of the IAEA Board of Governors, *commends* and *encourages* the Director General of the IAEA and its secretariat for their ongoing professional and impartial efforts to resolve all remaining outstanding issues in Iran within the framework of the IAEA, *underlines* the necessity of the IAEA continuing its work to clarify all outstanding issues relating to Iran's nuclear program;

23. *Requests* within 60 days a report from the Director General of the IAEA on whether Iran has established full and sustained suspension of all activities mentioned in this resolution, as well as on the process of Iranian compliance with all the steps required by the IAEA Board and with the other provisions of this resolution, to the IAEA Board of Governors and in parallel to the Security Council for its consideration;

24. *Affirms* that it shall review Iran's actions in the light of the report referred to in paragraph 23 above, to be submitted within 60 days, and:

(a) that it shall suspend the implementation of measures if and for so long as Iran suspends all enrichment-related and reprocessing activities, including research and development, as verified by the IAEA, to allow for negotiations;

(b) that it shall terminate the measures specified in paragraphs 3, 4, 5, 6, 7, 10 and 12 of this resolution as soon as it determines that Iran has fully complied with its obligations under the relevant resolutions of the Security Council and met the requirements of the IAEA Board of Governors, as confirmed by the IAEA Board;

(c) that it shall, in the event that the report in paragraph 23 above shows that Iran has not complied with this resolution, adopt further appropriate measures under Article 41 of Chapter VII of the Charter of the United Nations to persuade Iran to comply with this resolution and the requirements of the IAEA, and underlines that further decisions will be required should such additional measures be necessary;

25. *Decides* to remain seized of the matter.

Annex

A. Entities involved in the nuclear program

1. Atomic Energy Organization of Iran [AEOI]
2. Mesbah Energy Company (provider for A40 research reactor—Arak)
3. Kala-Electric (aka Kalaye Electric) (provider for PFEP [Pilot Fuel Enrichment Plant]—Natanz)
4. Pars Trash Company (involved in centrifuge program, identified in IAEA reports)
5. Farayand Technique (involved in centrifuge program, identified in IAEA reports)
6. Defense Industries Organization (overarching MODAFL [Ministry of Defense and Armed Forces Logistics]-controlled entity, some of whose subordinates have been involved in the centrifuge program making components, and in the missile program)
7. 7th of Tir (subordinate of DIO [Defense Intelligence Office], widely recognized as being directly involved in the nuclear program)

B. Entities involved in the ballistic missile program

1. Shahid Hemmat Industrial Group (SHIG) (subordinate entity of AIO [Aerospace Industries Organization])
2. Shahid Bagheri Industrial Group (SBIG) (subordinate entity of AIO)
3. Fajr Industrial Group (formerly Instrumentation Factory Plant, subordinate entity of AIO)

C. Persons involved in the nuclear program

1. Mohammad Qannadi, AEOI Vice President for Research & Development
2. Behman Asgarpour, Operational Manager (Arak)
3. Dawood Agha-Jani, Head of the PFEP (Natanz)
4. Ehsan Monajemi, Construction Project Manager, Natanz
5. Jafar Mohammadi, Technical Adviser to the AEOI (in charge of managing the production of valves for centrifuges)
6. Ali Hajinia Leilabadi, Director General of Mesbah Energy Company
7. Lt Gen Mohammad Mehdi Nejad Nouri, Rector of Malek Ashtar University of Defense Technology (chemistry dept, affiliated to MODALF, has conducted experiments on beryllium)

D. Persons involved in the ballistic missile program

1. Gen Hosein Salimi, Commander of the Air Force, IRGC [Islamic Republic Guard Corps] (Pasdaran)
2. Ahmad Vahid Dastjerdi, Head of the AIO
3. Reza-Gholi Esmaeli, Head of Trade & International Affairs Dept, AIO
4. Bahmanyar Morteza Bahmanyar, Head of Finance & Budget Dept, AIO

E. Persons involved in both the nuclear and ballistic missile programs

1. Maj Gen Yahya Rahim Safavi, Commander, IRGC (Pasdaran)

Source: United Nations. Security Council. "Resolution 1737 (2006)." S/RES/1737 (2006), December 23, 2006 (released December 27, 2006). www.un.org/Docs/sc/unsc_resolutions06.htm (accessed January 10, 2007).

Other Historic Documents of Interest

Execution of Saddam Hussein, p. 638
Iranian president's comments to the
  United States, p. 212
North Korean nuclear weapons issue,
  p. 606

U.S.-India agreement on nuclear trade,
  p. 93
U.S. policy on Iraq, p. 725
War between Israel and Hezbollah,
  p. 454

Credits

Cumulative Index,
2002–2006

*The years in **boldface** type in the entries indicate which volume is being cited.*

Defense Science Board, U.S. Strategic Communication
Task Force, **2004** 626–638
Defense spending
and budget deficit, **2004** 236
Bush defense budget proposals, **2002** 35–36, 42
comptroller general report on, **2005** 131–132
decline in military spending, **2005** 139
Reagan defense buildup, **2002** 35
Deficit, budget. *See* Budget deficit
DeHaven, Ron, mad cow disease, testing for, **2003** 1238
Del Ponte, Carla
UN war crimes tribunal for Kosovo war, **2003** 1072;
2004 952; **2005** 854; **2006** 366
UN war crimes tribunal for Rwanda, **2003** 99–101,
1072–1073
Delahunt, William D. (D-Mass.)
on Castro's transfer of power to Raul Castro, **2006**
441
Cuban Working Group, **2002** 235
Delahunty, Robert J., Afghanistan detainees,
prisoner-of-war status and Geneva Conventions,
2004 336
Delainey, David W., Enron Corp. collapse, **2003** 337
Delaware, smoking prevention program, **2004** 282
DeLay, Tom (R-Texas)
on "activist" judges, **2005** 364
assault weapons ban, **2004** 764
bribery and money laundering
indictment, **2005** 631–643; **2006** 25, 103
investigations, **2004** 577, 580–581; **2005** 78
eminent domain, **2005** 364
House majority leader, **2005** 632
final speech to congress, **2006** 268–272
resignation, **2005** 78; **2006** 25, 103, 264–272, 595
midterm elections, **2002** 820
NASA moon-Mars missions supporter, **2004** 11
prescription drug benefits for seniors ad campaign,
2004 577
Schiavo end-of-life care case, **2005** 157, 158, 364–365
stem cell research opponent, **2005** 319
Ten Commandments displays, **2005** 379
Dellinger, Walter E., III, presidential signing statements,
2006 451
Deloitte & Touche, federal oversight, **2004** 423
Delphi (auto parts supplier), bankruptcy, **2005** 200, 486
Dembo, Antonio, death of, **2002** 153
Democracy and Rule of Law Project, **2005** 44
Democratic Forces for the Liberation of Rwanda
(FDLR), **2004** 506
Democratic Party
See also Congress, Democratic control of
convention, Boston (2004)
Kerry nomination acceptance speech, **2004**
483–484, 485–493
speeches, **2004** 483–484
Iraq stabilization plan, **2005** 81, 93
primary campaign, **2004** 479–480

State of the Union address
Daschle's response, **2004** 32–34
Gephardt's response, **2002** 38, 46–48
Kaine's response, **2006** 35–38
Locke's response, **2003** 23–24, 36–39
Pelosi's response, **2004** 21–22, 30–32
vision/agenda for the future lacking, **2005** 81
Democratic Republic of the Congo. *See* Congo, Republic
of
Democratization
Bush promoting democracy in Arab lands, **2004**
628–629; **2005** 42–43, 164, 582
"third wave" of, **2005** 22
UN promoting democracy in Arab lands, **2005**
269–289
Dempsey, Mary, Internet pornography filters, **2003**
390
Deng Xiaoping, Chinese leadership, **2002** 851; **2003**
1174
Denmark, support for Iraq, **2003** 42, 49–51
Dennis, Michael J., **2002** 224
Dental diseases, smoking linked to, surgeon general's
report on, **2004** 293
Deoxyribonucleic acid. *See* DNA
Depression
antidepressant drugs and suicide in children, **2004**
640, 746–752; **2006** 129
screening for, federal task force on, **2002** 265–274
Dervis, Kemal, Turkish economics minister resignation,
2002 907
Desai, Nitin, on aging world population, **2002** 193
DeSutter, Paula A., Libya nuclear weapons program
dismantled, **2004** 171
Detainee Treatment Act (DTA, 2005), **2006** 380, 450
Devaney, Earl E., oil and gas industry regulation, **2006**
143
Developing countries
agricultural subsidies, opposition to, **2003** 8, 14,
743
China-African trade relations, **2006** 629–631
"Singapore issues" trade negotiations, **2003** 743–744
WTO Doha Development Agenda, **2003** 742, 746,
766
DeWine, Mike (R-Ohio)
intelligence gathering failures, **2002** 995
NSA warrantless domestic surveillance program, **2006**
63–64
Dhaliwal, Herb, massive power blackout investigation,
2003 1015
DHS. *See* Homeland Security Department
Di Rita, Larry, strategic communications report, **2004**
627–628
Diamond smuggling, "conflict diamonds," **2002** 252
Diarra, Seydou, Ivory Coast prime minister
appointment, **2003** 239; **2004** 820
Dickerson, Vivian, "morning-after" pill controversy,
2003 999